D0187876

Collins
gem

Collins
French
Dictionary

HarperCollins Publishers
Westerhill Road
Bishopbriggs
Glasgow
G64 2QT
Great Britain

Ninth edition/Neuvième édition
2006

Reprint 10 9 8 7 6

ISBN 978-0-00-722397-8

Collins Gem® is a registered
trademark of HarperCollins
Publishers Limited

www.collinslanguage.com

A catalogue record for this book is
available from the British Library

HarperCollins Publishers,
10 East 53rd Street,
New York, NY 10022

COLLINS GEM FRENCH DICTIONARY.
Eighth US Edition 2005

ISBN 978-0-00-712622-4

www.harpercollins.com

Typeset by/Photocomposition
Thomas Callan

Printed in Italy by/Imprimé en
Italie par LEGO Spa, Lavis (Trento),
ITALY.

TABLE DES MATIÈRES   CONTENTS

LES MARQUES DÉPOSÉES
Les termes qui constituent à notre connaissance une marque déposée ont été désignés comme tels. La présence ou l'absence de cette désignation ne peut toutefois être considérée comme ayant valeur juridique.

NOTE ON TRADEMARKS
Words which we have reason to believe constitute trademarks have been designated as such. However, neither the presence nor the absence of such designation should be regarded as affecting the legal status of any trademark.

Acknowledgements
We would like to thank those
authors and publishers who
kindly gave permission for
copyright material to be used in
the Collins Word Web. We would
also like to thank Times
Newspapers Ltd for providing
valuable data.

MANAGING EDITOR/CHEF DE
PROJET
Michela Clari

CONTRIBUTORS/RÉDACTION
Jean-François Allain
Gaëlle Amiot-Cadey
Cécile Aubinière-Robb
Sabine Citron
Wendy Lee
Catherine Love
Rose Rociola

COORDINATION/COORDINATION
Joyce Littlejohn

SERIES EDITOR/
COLLECTION DIRIGÉE PAR
Lorna Knight

Based on the first edition of the
Collins Gem French Dictionary
under the direction of Pierre-Henri
Cousin

Nous sommes très heureux que vous ayez choisi ce dictionnaire et espérons que vous aimerez l'utiliser et que vous en tirerez profit au lycée, à la maison, en vacances ou au travail.

Cette introduction a pour but de vous donner quelques conseils sur la façon d'utiliser au mieux votre dictionnaire, en vous référant non seulement à son importante nomenclature mais aussi aux informations contenues dans chaque entrée. Ceci vous aidera à lire et à comprendre, mais aussi à communiquer et à vous exprimer en anglais contemporain.

Au début du dictionnaire, vous trouverez la liste des abréviations utilisées dans le texte et celle de la transcription des sons par des symboles phonétiques. Vous y trouverez également la liste des verbes irréguliers en anglais, suivis d'une section finale sur les nombres et sur les expressions de temps.

COMMENT UTILISER VOTRE DICTIONNAIRE
Ce dictionnaire offre une richesse d'informations et utilise diverses formes et tailles de caractères, symboles, abréviations, parenthèses et crochets. Les conventions et symboles utilisés sont expliqués dans les sections qui suivent.

ENTRÉES
Les mots que vous cherchez dans le dictionnaire - les entrées - sont classés par ordre alphabétique. Ils sont imprimés en couleur pour pouvoir être repérés rapidement. Les entrées figurant en haut de page indiquent le premier (sur la page

de gauche) et le dernier mot (sur la page de droite) des deux pages en question.

Des informations sur l'usage ou sur la forme de certaines entrées sont données entre parenthèses, après la transcription phonétique. Ces indications apparaissent sous forme abrégée et en italiques (par ex. *(fam)*, *(Comm)*).

Pour plus de facilité, les mots de la même famille sont regroupés sous la même entrée (**ronger, rongeur; accept, acceptance**) et apparaissent également en couleur.

Les expressions courantes dans lesquelles apparaît l'entrée sont indiquées par des caractères romains gras différents (par exemple **retard** : [...] **avoir du ~**).

TRANSCRIPTION PHONÉTIQUE
La transcription phonétique de chaque entrée (indiquant sa prononciation) est indiquée entre crochets immédiatement après l'entrée (par ex. **fumer** [fyme]; **knee** [niː]). La liste des symboles phonétiques figure page xiii.

TRADUCTIONS
Les traductions des entrées apparaissent en caractères ordinaires ; lorsque plusieurs sens ou usages coexistent, ces traductions sont séparées par un point-virgule. Vous trouverez des synonymes de l'entrée en italiques entre parenthèses avant les traductions (par ex. **poser** *(installer : moquette, carrelage)*) ou des mots qui fournissent le contexte dans lequel l'entrée est susceptible d'être utilisée (par ex. **poser** *(question)*).

Une importance particulière est accordée à certains mots français et anglais qui sont considérés comme des « mots-clés » dans chacune des langues. Cela peut être dû à leur utilisation très fréquente ou au fait qu'ils ont divers types d'usage (par ex. vouloir, plus; get, that). L'utilisation de triangles et de chiffres aide à distinguer différentes catégories grammaticales et différents sens. D'autres renseignements utiles apparaissent en italiques et entre parenthèses dans la langue de l'utilisateur.

DONNÉES GRAMMATICALES

Les catégories grammaticales sont données sous forme abrégée et en italiques après la transcription phonétique (par ex. vt, adv, conj). Les genres des noms français sont indiqués de la manière suivante : nm pour un nom masculin et nf pour un nom féminin. Le féminin et le pluriel irréguliers de certains noms sont également indiqués (par ex. directeur, -trice ; cheval, -aux).

Le masculin et le féminin des adjectifs sont indiqués lorsque ces deux formes sont différentes (par ex. noir, e). Lorsque l'adjectif a un féminin ou un pluriel irrégulier, ces formes sont clairement indiquées (par ex. net, nette). Les pluriels irréguliers des noms, et les formes irrégulières des verbes anglais sont indiqués entre parenthèses, avant la catégorie grammaticale (par ex. man [...] (pl men) n ; give (pt **gave**; pp ~n) vt).

We are delighted that you have decided to buy this dictionary and hope you will enjoy and benefit from using it at school, at home, on holiday or at work.

This introduction gives you a few tips on how to get the most out of your dictionary – not simply from its comprehensive wordlist but also from the information provided in each entry. This will help you to read and understand modern French, as well as communicate and express yourself in the language. This dictionary begins by listing the abbreviations used in the text and illustrating the sounds shown by the phonetic symbols. You will also find French verb tables, followed by a final section on numbers and time expressions.

USING YOUR DICTIONARY

A wealth of information is presented in the dictionary, using various typefaces, sizes of type, symbols, abbreviations and brackets. The various conventions and symbols used are explained in the following sections.

HEADWORDS

The words you look up in a dictionary – 'headwords' – are listed alphabetically. They are printed in colour for rapid identification. The headwords appearing at the top of each page indicate the first (if it appears on a left-hand page) and last word (if it appears on a right-hand page) dealt with on the page in question.

Information about the usage or form of certain headwords is given in brackets after the phonetic spelling. This usually appears in abbreviated form and in italics (e.g. (fam), (Comm)).

Where appropriate, words related to headwords are grouped in the same entry (ronger, rongeur; accept, acceptance) and are also in colour. Common expressions in which the headword appears are shown in a bold roman type (e.g. retard: [...] **avoir du ~**).

PHONETIC SPELLINGS

The phonetic spelling of each headword (indicating its pronunciation) is given in square brackets immediately after the headword (e.g. fumer [fyme]; knee [ni:]). A list of these symbols is given on page xiii.

TRANSLATIONS

Headword translations are given in ordinary type and, where more than one meaning or usage exists, these are separated by a semi-colon. You will often find other words in italics in brackets before the translations. These offer suggested contexts in which the headword might appear (e.g. rough (*voice*), [...] (*weather*)) or provide synonyms (e.g. rough (*violent*)). The gender of the translation also appears in italics immediately following the key element of the translation.

KEY WORDS

Special status is given to certain French and English words which are considered as 'key' words in each language. They may, for example, occur very frequently or have several types of usage (e.g. **vouloir, plus; get, that**). A combination of triangles and numbers helps you to distinguish different parts of speech and different meanings. Further helpful information is provided in brackets and italics.

Parts of speech are given in abbreviated form in italics after the phonetic spellings of headwords (e.g. *vt, adv, conj*). Genders of French nouns are indicated as follows: *nm* for a masculine and *nf* for a feminine noun. Feminine and irregular plural forms of nouns are also shown (directeur, -trice; cheval, -aux).

Adjectives are given in both masculine and feminine forms where these forms are different (e.g. noir, e). Clear information is provided where adjectives have an irregular feminine or plural form (e.g. net, nette).

ABRÉVIATIONS

abréviation	ab(b)r	abbreviation
adjectif, locution adjective	adj	adjective, adjectival phrase
administration	Admin	administration
adverbe, locution adverbiale	adv	adverb, adverbial phrase
agriculture	Agr	agriculture
anatomie	Anat	anatomy
architecture	Archit	architecture
article défini	art déf	definite article
article indéfini	art indéf	indefinite article
automobile	Aut(o)	the motor car and motoring
aviation, voyages aériens	Aviat	flying, air travel
biologie	Bio(l)	biology
botanique	Bot	botany
anglais britannique	BRIT	British English
chimie	Chem	chemistry
commerce, finance, banque	Comm	commerce, finance, banking
informatique	Comput	computing
conjonction	conj	conjunction
construction	Constr	building
nom utilisé comme adjectif	cpd	compound element
cuisine	Culin	cookery
article défini	def art	definite article
déterminant: article; adjectif	dét	determiner: article,
démonstratif ou indéfini *etc*		demonstrative *etc*
économie	Écon, Econ	economics
électricité, électronique	Élec, Elec	electricity, electronics
en particulier	esp	especially
exclamation, interjection	excl	exclamation, interjection
féminin	f	feminine
langue familière	fam(!)	colloquial usage
(! emploi vulgaire)		(! particularly offensive)
emploi figuré	fig	figurative use
(verbe anglais) dont la	fus	(phrasal verb) where the
particule est inséparable		particle is inseparable
généralement	gén, gen	generally
géographie, géologie	Géo, Geo	geography, geology
géométrie	Géom, Geom	geometry
langue familière	inf(!)	colloquial usage
(! emploi vulgaire)		(! particularly offensive)
infinitif	infin	infinitive
informatique	Inform	computing
invariable	inv	invariable
irrégulier	irreg	irregular
domaine juridique	Jur	law

grammaire, linguistique	Ling	grammar, linguistics
masculin	m	masculine
mathématiques, algèbre	Math	mathematics, calculus
médecine	Méd, Med	medical term, medicine
masculin ou féminin	m/f	masculine or feminine
domaine militaire, armée	Mil	military matters
musique	Mus	music
nom	n	noun
navigation, nautisme	Navig, Naut	sailing, navigation
nom ou adjectif numéral	num	numeral noun or adjective
	o.s.	oneself
péjoratif	péj, pej	derogatory, pejorative
photographie	Phot(o)	photography
physiologie	Physiol	physiology
pluriel	pl	plural
politique	Pol	politics
participe passé	pp	past participle
préposition	prép, prep	preposition
pronom	pron	pronoun
psychologie, psychiatrie	Psych	psychology, psychiatry
temps du passé	pt	past tense
quelque chose	qch	
quelqu'un	qn	
religion, domaine ecclésiastique	Rel	religion
	sb	somebody
enseignement, système scolaire et universitaire	Scol	schooling, schools and universities
singulier	sg	singular
	sth	something
subjonctif	sub	subjunctive
sujet (grammatical)	su(bj)	(grammatical) subject
superlatif	superl	superlative
techniques, technologie	Tech	technical term, technology
télécommunications	Tél, Tel	telecommunications
télévision	TV	television
typographie	Typ(o)	typography, printing
anglais des USA	US	American English
verbe (auxiliaire)	vb (aux)	(auxiliary) verb
verbe intransitif	vi	intransitive verb
verbe transitif	vt	transitive verb
zoologie	Zool	zoology
marque déposée	®	registered trademark
indique une équivalence culturelle	≈	introduces a cultural equivalent

TRANCRIPTION PHONÉTIQUE

CONSONNES		CONSONANTS
NB. p, b, t, d, k, g sont suivis d'une aspiration en anglais.		NB. p, b, t, d, k, g are not aspirated in French.
poupée	p	puppy
bombe	b	baby
tente thermal	t	tent
dinde	d	daddy
coq qui képi	k	cork kiss chord
gage bague	g	gag guess
sale ce nation	s	so rice kiss
zéro rose	z	cousin buzz
tache chat	ʃ	sheep sugar
gilet juge	ʒ	pleasure beige
	tʃ	church
	dʒ	judge general
fer phare	f	farm raffle
verveine	v	very revel
	θ	thin maths
	ð	that other
lent salle	l	little ball
rare rentrer	ʀ	
	r	rat rare
maman femme	m	mummy comb
non bonne	n	no ran
agneau vigne	ɲ	
	ŋ	singing bank
	h	hat rehearse
yeux paille pied	j	yet
nouer oui	w	wall wail
huile lui	ɥ	
	x	loch

DIVERS		MISCELLANEOUS
pour l'anglais: le r final se prononce en liaison devant une voyelle	ʳ	in English transcription: final r can be pronounced before a vowel
pour l'anglais: précède la syllabe accentuée		in French wordlist: no liaison before aspirate h

En règle générale, la prononciation est donnée entre crochets après chaque entrée. Toutefois, du côté anglais-français et dans le cas des expressions composées de deux ou plusieurs mots non réunis par un trait d'union et faisant l'objet d'une entrée séparée, la prononciation doit être cherchée sous chacun des mots constitutifs de l'expression en question.

PHONETIC TRANSCRIPTION

VOYELLES

NB. La mise en équivalence de certains sons n'indique qu'une ressemblance approximative.

VOWELS

NB. The pairing of some vowel sounds only indicates approximate equivalence.

ici vie lyrique	i i:	heel bead
	ɪ	hit pity
jouer été	e	
lait jouet merci	ɛ	set tent
plat amour	a æ	bat apple
bas pâte	ɑ ɑ:	after car calm
	ʌ	fun cousin
le premier	ə	over above
beurre peur	œ	
peu deux	ø ə:	urgent fern work
or homme	ɔ	wash pot
mot eau gauche	o ɔ:	born cork
genou roue	u	full hook
	u:	boom shoe
rue urne	y	

DIPHTONGUES

DIPHTHONGS

	ɪə	beer tier
	ɛə	tear fair there
	eɪ	date plaice day
	aɪ	life buy cry
	au	owl foul now
	əu	low no
	ɔɪ	boil boy oily
	uə	poor tour

NASALES

NASAL VOWELS

matin plein	ɛ̃
brun	œ̃
sang an dans	ɑ̃
non pont	ɔ̃

In general, we give the pronunciation of each entry in square brackets after the word in question. However, on the English-French side, where the entry is composed of two or more unhyphenated words, each of which is given elsewhere in this dictionary, you will find the pronunciation of each word in its alphabetical position.

FRENCH VERB TABLES

1 Present participle 2 Past participle 3 Present 4 Imperfect 5 Future
6 Conditional 7 Present subjunctive

acquérir 1 acquérant 2 acquis
3 acquiers, acquérons,
acquièrent 4 acquérais
5 acquerrai 7 acquière

ALLER 1 allant 2 allé 3 vais, vas, va,
allons, allez, vont 4 allais 5 irai
6 irais 7 aille

asseoir 1 asseyant 2 assis 3 assieds,
asseyons, asseyez, asseyent
4 asseyais 5 assiérai 7 asseye

atteindre 1 atteignant 2 atteint
3 atteins, atteignons
4 atteignais 7 atteigne

AVOIR 1 ayant 2 eu 3 ai, as, a,
avons, avez, ont 4 avais 5 aurai
6 aurais 7 aie, aies, ait, ayons,
ayez, aient

battre 1 battant 2 battu 3 bats, bat,
battons 4 battais 7 batte

boire 1 buvant 2 bu 3 bois, buvons,
boivent 4 buvais 7 boive

bouillir 1 bouillant 2 bouilli 3 bous,
bouillons 4 bouillais 7 bouille

conclure 1 concluant 2 conclu
3 conclus, concluons
4 concluais 7 conclue

conduire 1 conduisant 2 conduit
3 conduis, conduisons
4 conduisais 7 conduise

connaître 1 connaissant 2 connu
3 connais, connaît, connaissons
4 connaissais 7 connaisse

coudre 1 cousant 2 cousu 3 couds,
cousons, cousez, cousent
4 cousais 7 couse

courir 1 courant 2 couru 3 cours,
courons 4 courais 5 courrai
7 coure

couvrir 1 couvrant 2 couvert
3 couvre, couvrons 4 couvrais
7 couvre

craindre 1 craignant 2 craint
3 crains, craignons 4 craignais
7 craigne

croire 1 croyant 2 cru 3 crois,
croyons, croient 4 croyais
7 croie

croître 1 croissant 2 crû, crue, crus,
crues 3 croîs, croissons
4 croissais 7 croisse

cueillir 1 cueillant 2 cueilli
3 cueille, cueillons 4 cueillais
5 cueillerai 7 cueille

devoir 1 devant 2 dû, due, dus,
dues 3 dois, devons, doivent
4 devais 5 devrai 7 doive

dire 1 disant 2 dit 3 dis, disons,
dites, disent 4 disais 7 dise

dormir 1 dormant 2 dormi 3 dors,
dormons 4 dormais 7 dorme

écrire 1 écrivant 2 écrit 3 écris,
écrivons, écrivais 7 écrive

ÊTRE 1 étant 2 été 3 suis, es, est,
sommes, êtes, sont 4 étais
5 serai 6 serais 7 sois, sois, soit,
soyons, soyez, soient

FAIRE 1 faisant 2 fait 3 fais, fais,
fait, faisons, faites, font
4 faisais 5 ferai 6 ferais 7 fasse

falloir 2 fallu 3 faut 4 fallait
5 faudra 7 faille

FINIR 1 finissant 2 fini 3 finis,
finis, finit, finissons, finissez,
finissent 4 finissais 5 finirai
6 finirais 7 finisse

fuir 1 fuyant 2 fui 3 fuis, fuyons,
fuient 4 fuyais 7 fuie

joindre 1 joignant 2 joint 3 joins,
joignons 4 joignais 7 joigne

lire 1 lisant 2 lu 3 lis, lisons 4 lisais
7 lise

luire 1 luisant 2 lui 3 luis, luisons

xv

maudire 1 maudissant 2 maudit
3 maudis, maudissons
4 maudissait 7 maudisse

mentir 1 mentant 2 menti 3 mens,
mentons 4 mentais 7 mente

mettre 1 mettant 2 mis 3 mets,
mettons 4 mettais 7 mette

mourir 1 mourant 2 mort 3 meurs,
mourons, meurent 4 mourais
5 mourrai 7 meure

naître 1 naissant 2 né 3 nais, naît,
naissons 4 naissais 7 naisse

offrir 1 offrant 2 offert 3 offre,
offrons 4 offrais 7 offre

PARLER 1 parlant 2 parlé 3 parle,
parles, parle, parlons, parlez,
parlent 4 parlais, parlais,
parlait, parlions, parliez,
parlaient 5 parlerai, parleras,
parlera, parlerons, parlerez,
parleront 6 parlerais, parlerais,
parlerait, parlerions, parleriez,
parleraient 7 parle, parles,
parle, parlions, parliez, parlent
impératif parle! parlons! parlez!

partir 1 partant 2 parti 3 pars,
partons 4 partais 7 parte

plaire 1 plaisant 2 plu 3 plais, plaît,
plaisons 4 plaisais 7 plaise

pleuvoir 1 pleuvant 2 plu 3 pleut,
pleuvent 4 pleuvait 5 pleuvra
7 pleuve

pourvoir 1 pourvoyant 2 pourvu
3 pourvois, pourvoyons,
pourvoient 4 pourvoyais
7 pourvoie

pouvoir 1 pouvant 2 pu 3 peux,
peut, pouvons, peuvent 4
pouvais 5 pourrai 7 puisse

prendre 1 prenant 2 pris 3 prends,
prenons, prennent 4 prenais
7 prenne

prévoir like voir 5 prévoirai

RECEVOIR 1 recevant 2 reçu
3 reçois, reçois, reçoit, recevons,
recevez, reçoivent 4 recevais

5 recevrai 6 recevrais 7 reçoive

RENDRE 1 rendant 2 rendu
3 rends, rends, rend, rendons,
rendez, rendent 4 rendais
5 rendrai 6 rendrais 7 rende

résoudre 1 résolvant 2 résolu
3 résous, résout, résolvons
4 résolvais 7 résolve

rire 1 riant 2 ri 3 ris, rions 4 riais
7 rie

savoir 1 sachant 2 su 3 sais,
savons, savent 4 savais 5 saurai
7 sache *impératif* sache! sachons!
sachez!

servir 1 servant 2 servi 3 sers,
servons 4 servais 7 serve

sortir 1 sortant 2 sorti 3 sors,
sortons 4 sortais 7 sorte

souffrir 1 souffrant 2 souffert
3 souffre, souffrons 4 souffrais
7 souffre

suffire 1 suffisant 2 suffi 3 suffis,
suffisons 4 suffisais 7 suffise

suivre 1 suivant 2 suivi 3 suis,
suivons 4 suivais 7 suive

taire 1 taisant 2 tu 3 tais, taisons
4 taisais 7 taise

tenir 1 tenant 2 tenu 3 tiens,
tenons, tiennent 4 tenais
5 tiendrai 7 tienne

vaincre 1 vainquant 2 vaincu
3 vaincs, vainc, vainquons
4 vainquais 7 vainque

valoir 1 valant 2 valu 3 vaux, vaut,
valons 4 valais 5 vaudrai 7 vaille

venir 1 venant 2 venu 3 viens,
venons, viennent 4 venais
5 viendrai 7 vienne

vivre 1 vivant 2 vécu 3 vis, vivons
4 vivais 7 vive

voir 1 voyant 2 vu 3 vois, voyons,
voient 4 voyais 5 verrai 7 voie

vouloir 1 voulant 2 voulu 3 veux,
veut, voulons, veulent 4 voulais
5 voudrai 7 veuille; *impératif*
veuillez!

VERBES IRRÉGULIERS ANGLAIS

PRÉSENT	PASSÉ	PARTICIPE	PRÉSENT	PASSÉ	PARTICIPE
arise	arose	arisen	fight	fought	fought
awake	awoke	awoken	find	found	found
be	was, were	been	flee	fled	fled
(am, is,			fling	flung	flung
are; being)			fly	flew	flown
bear	bore	born(e)	forbid	forbad(e)	forbidden
beat	beat	beaten	forecast	forecast	forecast
become	became	become	forget	forgot	forgotten
begin	began	begun	forgive	forgave	forgiven
bend	bent	bent	forsake	forsook	forsaken
bet	bet,	bet,	freeze	froze	frozen
	betted	betted	get	got	got,
bid (at auction,	bid	bid			(us) gotten
cards)			give	gave	given
bid (say)	bade	bidden	go (goes)	went	gone
bind	bound	bound	grind	ground	ground
bite	bit	bitten	grow	grew	grown
bleed	bled	bled	hang	hung	hung
blow	blew	blown	hang (execute)	hanged	hanged
break	broke	broken	have	had	had
breed	bred	bred	hear	heard	heard
bring	brought	brought	hide	hid	hidden
build	built	built	hit	hit	hit
burn	burnt,	burnt,	hold	held	held
	burned	burned	hurt	hurt	hurt
burst	burst	burst	keep	kept	kept
buy	bought	bought	kneel	knelt,	knelt,
can	could	(been able)		kneeled	kneeled
cast	cast	cast	know	knew	known
catch	caught	caught	lay	laid	laid
choose	chose	chosen	lead	led	led
cling	clung	clung	lean	leant,	leant,
come	came	come		leaned	leaned
cost	cost	cost	leap	leapt,	leapt,
cost (work	costed	costed		leaped	leaped
out price of)			learn	learnt,	learnt,
creep	crept	crept		learned	learned
cut	cut	cut	leave	left	left
deal	dealt	dealt	lend	lent	lent
dig	dug	dug	let	let	let
do (does)	did	done	lie (lying)	lay	lain
draw	drew	drawn	light	lit,	lit,
dream	dreamed,	dreamed,		lighted	lighted
	dreamt	dreamt	lose	lost	lost
drink	drank	drunk	make	made	made
drive	drove	driven	may	might	–
dwell	dwelt	dwelt	mean	meant	meant
eat	ate	eaten	meet	met	met
fall	fell	fallen	mistake	mistook	mistaken
feed	fed	fed	mow	mowed	mown,
feel	felt	felt			mowed

xvii

PRÉSENT	PASSÉ	PARTICIPE	PRÉSENT	PASSÉ	PARTICIPE
must	(had to)	(had to)	spend	spent	spent
pay	paid	paid	spill	spilt, spilled	spilt, spilled
put	put	put	spin	spun	spun
quit	quit, quitted	quit, quitted	spit	spat	spat
read	read	read	spoil	spoiled, spoilt	spoiled, spoilt
rid	rid	rid	spread	spread	spread
ride	rode	ridden	spring	sprang	sprung
ring	rang	rung	stand	stood	stood
rise	rose	risen	steal	stole	stolen
run	ran	run	stick	stuck	stuck
saw	sawed	sawed, sawn	sting	stung	stung
say	said	said	stink	stank	stunk
see	saw	seen	stride	strode	stridden
seek	sought	sought	strike	struck	struck
sell	sold	sold	strive	strove	striven
send	sent	sent	swear	swore	sworn
set	set	set	sweep	swept	swept
sew	sewed	sewn	swell	swelled	swollen, swelled
shake	shook	shaken	swim	swam	swum
shear	sheared	shorn, sheared	swing	swung	swung
shed	shed	shed	take	took	taken
shine	shone	shone	teach	taught	taught
shoot	shot	shot	tear	tore	torn
show	showed	shown	tell	told	told
shrink	shrank	shrunk	think	thought	thought
shut	shut	shut	throw	threw	thrown
sing	sang	sung	thrust	thrust	thrust
sink	sank	sunk	tread	trod	trodden
sit	sat	sat	wake	woke, waked	woken, waked
slay	slew	slain			
sleep	slept	slept	wear	wore	worn
slide	slid	slid	weave	wove	woven
sling	slung	slung	weave (wind)	weaved	weaved
slit	slit	slit	wed	wedded, wed	wedded, wed
smell	smelt, smelled	smelt, smelled	weep	wept	wept
			win	won	won
sow	sowed	sown, sowed	wind	wound	wound
speak	spoke	spoken	wring	wrung	wrung
speed	sped, speeded	sped, speeded	write	wrote	written
spell	spelt, spelled	spelt, spelled			

LES NOMBRES

un (une)	1	one
deux	2	two
trois	3	three
quatre	4	four
cinq	5	five
six	6	six
sept	7	seven
huit	8	eight
neuf	9	nine
dix	10	ten
onze	11	eleven
douze	12	twelve
treize	13	thirteen
quatorze	14	fourteen
quinze	15	fifteen
seize	16	sixteen
dix-sept	17	seventeen
dix-huit	18	eighteen
dix-neuf	19	nineteen
vingt	20	twenty
vingt et un (une)	21	twenty-one
vingt-deux	22	twenty-two
trente	30	thirty
quarante	40	forty
cinquante	50	fifty
soixante	60	sixty
soixante-dix	70	seventy
soixante-et-onze	71	seventy-one
soixante-douze	72	seventy
quatre-vingts	80	eighty
quatre-vingt-un (-une)	81	eighty-one
quatre-vingt-dix	90	ninety
cent	100	a hundred, one hundred
cent un (une)	101	a hundred and one
deux cents	200	two hundred
deux cent un (une)	201	two hundred and one
quatre cents	400	four hundred
mille	1000	a thousand
cinq mille	5000	five thousand
un million	1000000	a million

LES NOMBRES

premier (première), 1er (1ère)
deuxième, 2e or 2ème
troisième, 3e or 3ème
quatrième, 4e or 4ème
cinquième, 5e or 5ème
sixième, 6e or 6ème
septième
huitième
neuvième
dixième
onzième
douzième
treizième
quatorzième
quinzième
seizième
dix-septième
dix-huitième
dix-neuvième
vingtième
vingt-et-unième
vingt-deuxième
trentième
centième
cent-unième
millième

LES FRACTIONS ETC

un demi
un tiers
un quart
un cinquième
zéro virgule cinq, 0,5
trois virgule quatre, 3,4
dix pour cent
cent pour cent

EXEMPLES

elle habite au septième (étage)
il habite au sept
au chapitre/à la page sept
il est arrivé (le) septième

NUMBERS

first, 1st
second, 2nd
third, 3rd
fourth, 4th
fifth, 5th
sixth, 6th
seventh
eighth
ninth
tenth
eleventh
twelfth
thirteenth
fourteenth
fifteenth
sixteenth
seventeenth
eighteenth
nineteenth
twentieth
twenty-first
twenty-second
thirtieth
hundredth
hundred-and-first
thousandth

FRACTIONS ETC

a half
a third
a quarter
a fifth
(nought) point five, 0.5
three point four, 3.4
ten per cent
a hundred per cent

EXAMPLES

she lives on the 7th floor
he lives at number 7
chapter/page 7
he came in 7th

L'HEURE

THE TIME

quelle heure est-il?

what time is it?

il est ...

it's ou it is ...

minuit	midnight, twelve p.m.
une heure (du matin)	one o'clock (in the morning), one (a.m.)
une heure cinq	five past one
une heure dix	ten past one
une heure et quart	a quarter past one, one fifteen
une heure vingt-cinq	twenty-five past one, one twenty-five
une heure et demie, une heure trente	half-past one, one thirty
deux heures moins vingt-cinq, une heure trente-cinq	twenty-five to two, one thirty-five
deux heures moins vingt, une heure quarante	twenty to two, one forty
deux heures moins le quart, une heure quarante-cinq	a quarter to two, one forty-five
deux heures moins dix, une heure cinquante	ten to two, one fifty
midi	twelve o'clock, midday, noon
deux heures (de l'après-midi), quatorze heures	two o'clock (in the afternoon), two (p.m.)
sept heures (du soir), dix-sept heures	seven o'clock (in the evening), seven (p.m.)

à quelle heure?

(at) what time?

à minuit	at midnight
à sept heures	at seven o'clock
dans vingt minutes	in twenty minutes
il y a un quart d'heure	fifteen minutes ago

a [a] *vb voir* **avoir**

🔵 **MOT-CLÉ**

à [a] (*à + le* = **au**, *à + les* = **aux**) *prép*
1 (*endroit, situation*) at, in; **être à Paris/
au Portugal** to be in Paris/Portugal;
être à la maison/à l'école to be at
home/at school; **à la campagne** in the
country; **c'est à 10 km/à 20 minutes
(d'ici)** it's 10 km/20 minutes away
2 (*direction*) to; **aller à Paris/au
Portugal** to go to Paris/Portugal; **aller
à la maison/à l'école** to go home/to
school; **à la campagne** to the country
3 (*temps*): **à 3 heures/minuit** at 3
o'clock/midnight; **au printemps/
mois de juin** in the spring/the month
of June; **à Noël/Pâques** at Christmas/
Easter; **à demain/lundi** see you
tomorrow/on Monday!
4 (*attribution, appartenance*) to; **le livre
est à Paul/à lui/à nous** this book is
Paul's/his/ours; **un ami à moi** a

friend of mine; **donner qch à qn** to
give sth to sb
5 (*moyen*) with; **se chauffer au gaz** to
have gas heating; **à bicyclette** on a *ou*
by bicycle; **à pied** on foot; **à la main/
machine** by hand/machine
6 (*provenance*) from; **boire à la
bouteille** to drink from the bottle
7 (*caractérisation, manière*): **l'homme
aux yeux bleus** the man with the blue
eyes; **à leur grande surprise** much
to their surprise; **à ce qu'il prétend**
according to him, from what he says;
à la russe the Russian way; **à nous
deux nous n'avons pas su le faire**
we couldn't do it, even between the
two of us
8 (*but, destination*): **tasse à café** coffee
cup; **maison à vendre** house for sale;
je n'ai rien à lire I don't have anything
to read; **à bien réfléchir** ... thinking
about it ..., on reflection ...
9 (*rapport, évaluation, distribution*): **100
km/unités à l'heure** 100 km/units per
ou an hour; **payé au mois/à l'heure**
paid monthly/by the hour; **cinq à six**
five to six; **ils sont arrivés à quatre**
four of them arrived

abaisser [abese] *vt* to lower, bring
down; (*manette*) to pull down;
s'abaisser *vi* to go down; (*fig*) to
demean o.s.
abandon [abɑ̃dɔ̃] *nm* abandoning;
giving up; withdrawal; **être à l'~** to
be in a state of neglect; **laisser à l'~**
to abandon
abandonner [abɑ̃dɔne] *vt* (*personne*)
to abandon; (*projet, activité*) to
abandon, give up; (*Sport*) to retire *ou*
withdraw from; (*céder*) to surrender; **s'~**
(*paresse, plaisirs*) to give o.s. up to
abat-jour [abaʒuʀ] *nm inv* lampshade
abats [aba] *nmpl* (*de bœuf, porc*) offal *sg*;
(*de volaille*) giblets
abattement [abatmɑ̃] *nm*:
abattement fiscal = tax allowance
abattoir [abatwaʀ] *nm*

slaughterhouse

abattre [abatʀ] vt (arbre) to cut down, fell; (mur, maison) to pull down; (avion, personne) to shoot down; (animal) to shoot, kill; (fig) to wear out, tire out; to demoralize; **s'abattre** vi to crash down; **ne pas se laisser ~** to keep one's spirits up, not to let things get one down; **s'~ sur** to beat down on; (fig) to rain down on; **~ du travail ou de la besogne** to get through a lot of work

abbaye [abei] nf abbey

abbé [abe] nm priest; (d'une abbaye) abbot

abcès [apsɛ] nm abscess

abdiquer [abdike] vi to abdicate

abdominaux [abdɔmino] nmpl: **faire des ~** to do sit-ups

abeille [abɛj] nf bee

aberrant, e [abeʀɑ̃, ɑ̃t] adj absurd

aberration [abeʀasjɔ̃] nf aberration

abîme [abim] nm abyss, gulf

abîmer [abime] vt to spoil, damage; **s'abîmer** vi to get spoilt ou damaged

aboiement [abwamɑ̃] nm bark, barking

abolir [abɔliʀ] vt to abolish

abominable [abɔminabl] adj abominable

abondance [abɔ̃dɑ̃s] nf abundance

abondant, e [abɔ̃dɑ̃, ɑ̃t] adj plentiful, abundant, copious; **abonder** vi to abound, be plentiful; **abonder dans le sens de qn** to concur with sb

abonné, e [abɔne] nm/f subscriber; season ticket holder

abonnement [abɔnmɑ̃] nm subscription; (transports, concerts) season ticket

abonner [abɔne] vt: **s'~ à** to subscribe to, take out a subscription to

abord [abɔʀ] nm: **au premier ~** at first sight, initially; **abords** nmpl (environs) surroundings; **d'~** first

abordable [abɔʀdabl] adj (prix) reasonable; (personne) approachable

aborder [abɔʀde] vi to land ▷ vt (sujet, difficulté) to tackle; (personne) to

approach; (rivage etc) to reach

aboutir [abutiʀ] vi (négociations etc) to succeed; **~ à** to end up at; **n'~ à rien** to come to nothing

aboyer [abwaje] vi to bark

abréger [abʀeʒe] vt to shorten

abreuver [abʀœve]: **s'abreuver** vi to drink; **abreuvoir** nm watering place

abréviation [abʀevjasjɔ̃] nf abbreviation

abri [abʀi] nm shelter; **être à l'~** to be under cover; **se mettre à l'~** to shelter; **à l'~ de** (vent, soleil) sheltered from; (danger) safe from

abricot [abʀiko] nm apricot

abriter [abʀite] vt to shelter; **s'abriter** vt to shelter, take cover

abrupt, e [abʀypt] adj sheer, steep; (ton) abrupt

abruti, e [abʀyti] adj stunned, dazed ▷ nm/f (fam) idiot, moron; **~ de travail** overworked

absence [apsɑ̃s] nf absence; (Méd) blackout; **avoir des ~s** to have mental blanks

absent, e [apsɑ̃, ɑ̃t] adj absent ▷ nm/f absentee; **absenter: s'absenter** vi to take time off work; (sortir) to leave, go out

absolu, e [apsɔly] adj absolute; **absolument** adv absolutely

absorbant, e [apsɔʀbɑ̃, ɑ̃t] adj absorbent

absorber [apsɔʀbe] vt to absorb; (gén Méd: manger, boire) to take

abstenir [apstəniʀ] vb: **s'~ de qch/de faire** to refrain from sth/from doing

abstrait, e [apstʀɛ, ɛt] adj abstract

absurde [apsyʀd] adj absurd

abus [aby] nm abuse; **~ de confiance** breach of trust; **il y a de l'~!** (fam) that's a bit much!; **abuser** vi to go too far, overstep the mark; **abuser de** (duper) to take advantage of; **s'abuser** vi (se méprendre) to be mistaken; **abusif, -ive** adj excessive; (punition) excessive

académie [akademi] nf academy; (Scol: circonscription) ≈ regional education authority

● **ACADÉMIE FRANÇAISE**

The **Académie française** was founded by Cardinal Richelieu in 1635, during the reign of Louis XIII. It is made up of forty elected scholars and writers who are known as 'les Quarante' or 'les Immortels'. One of the **Académie**'s functions is to keep an eye on the development of the French language, and its recommendations are frequently the subject of lively public debate. It has produced several editions of its famous dictionary and also awards various literary prizes.

acajou [akaʒu] nm mahogany

acariâtre [akaʀjɑtʀ] adj cantankerous

accablant, e [akablɑ̃, ɑ̃t] adj (chaleur) oppressive; (témoignage, preuve) overwhelming

accabler [akable] vt to overwhelm, overcome; **~ qn d'injures** to heap or shower abuse on sb; **~ qn de travail** to overwork sb

accalmie [akalmi] nf lull

accaparer [akapaʀe] vt to monopolize; (suj: travail etc) to take up (all) the time ou attention of

accéder [aksede]: **~ à** vt (lieu) to reach; (accorder: requête) to grant, accede to

accélérateur [akseleʀatœʀ] nm accelerator

accélérer [akseleʀe] vt to speed up ▷ vi to accelerate

accent [aksɑ̃] nm accent; (Phonétique, fig) stress; **mettre l'~ sur** (fig) to stress; **~ aigu/grave/circonflexe** acute/ grave/circumflex accent; **accentuer** vt (Ling) to accent; (fig) to accentuate, emphasize; **s'accentuer** vi to become more marked ou pronounced

acceptation [akseptasjɔ̃] nf acceptance

accepter [aksepte] vt to accept; **~ de**

faire to agree to do; **acceptez-vous les cartes de crédit?** do you take credit cards?

accès [aksɛ] nm access; (Méd: de toux) fit; (: de fièvre) bout; **d'~ facile** easily accessible; **facile d'~** easy to get to; **accès de colère** fit of anger; **accessible** adj accessible; (livre, sujet): **accessible à qn** within the reach of sb

accessoire [akseswaʀ] adj secondary; incidental ▷ nm accessory; (Théâtre) prop

accident [aksidɑ̃] nm accident; **par ~** by chance; **j'ai eu un ~** I've had an accident; **accident de la route** road accident; **accidenté, e** adj damaged; injured; (relief, terrain) uneven; hilly; **accidentel, le** adj accidental

acclamer [aklame] vt to cheer, acclaim

acclimater [aklimate]: **s'acclimater** vi (personne) to adapt (o.s.)

accolade [akɔlad] nf (amicale) embrace; (signe) brace

accommoder [akɔmɔde] vt (Culin) to prepare; **s'accommoder de** vt to put up with; (se contenter de) to make do with

accompagnateur, -trice [akɔ̃paɲatœʀ, tʀis] nm/f (Mus) accompanist; (de voyage: guide) guide; (de voyage organisé) courier

accompagner [akɔ̃paɲe] vt to accompany, be ou go ou come with; (Mus) to accompany

accompli, e [akɔ̃pli] adj accomplished; voir aussi **fait**

accomplir [akɔ̃pliʀ] vt (tâche, projet) to carry out; (souhait) to fulfil; **s'accomplir** vi to be fulfilled

accord [akɔʀ] nm agreement; (entre des styles, tons etc) harmony; (Mus) chord; **d'~!** OK!; **se mettre d'~** to come to an agreement; **être d'~ (pour faire qch)** to agree (to do sth)

accordéon [akɔʀdeɔ̃] nm (Mus) accordion

accorder [akɔʀde] vt (faveur, délai) to

grant; *(harmoniser)* to match; *(Mus)* to tune; *(valeur, importance)* attach

accoster [akɔste] vt *(Navig)* to draw alongside ▷ vi to berth

accouchement [akuʃmɑ̃] nm delivery, (child)birth; labour

accoucher [akuʃe] vi to give birth, have a baby; ~ **d'un garçon** to give birth to a boy

accouder [akude] vi: **s'accouder** vi: **s'~ à/contre/sur** to rest one's elbows on/ against/on; **accoudoir** nm armrest

accoupler [akuple] vt to couple; *(pour la reproduction)* to mate; **s'accoupler** vt to mate

accourir [akuʀiʀ] vi to rush ou run up

accoutumance [akutymɑ̃s] nf *(gén)* adaptation; *(Méd)* addiction

accoutumé, e [akutyme] adj *(habituel)* customary, usual

accoutumer [akutyme] vt: **s'~ à** to get accustomed ou used to

accroc [akʀo] nm *(déchirure)* tear; *(fig)* hitch, snag

accrochage [akʀɔʃaʒ] nm *(Auto)* collision; *(dispute)* clash, brush

accrocher [akʀɔʃe] vt *(fig)* to catch, attract; **s'accrocher** *(se disputer)* to have a clash ou brush; ~ **qch à** *(suspendre)* to hang sth (up) on; *(attacher: remorque)* to hitch sth (up) to; ~ **qch (à)** *(déchirer)* to catch sth (on); **il a accroché ma voiture** he bumped into my car; **s'~ à** *(rester pris à)* to catch on; *(agripper, fig)* to hang on ou cling to

accroissement [akʀwasmɑ̃] nm increase

accroître [akʀwatʀ]: **s'accroître** vi to increase

accroupir [akʀupiʀ]: **s'accroupir** vi to squat, crouch (down)

accru, e [akʀy] pp de **accroître**

accueil [akœj] nm welcome; **comité d'~** reception committee; **accueillir** vt to welcome; *(aller chercher)* to meet, collect

accumuler [akymyle] vt to accumulate, amass; **s'accumuler** vi to accumulate; to pile up

accusation [akyzasjɔ̃] nf *(gén)* accusation; *(Jur)* charge; *(partie)*: **l'~** the prosecution

accusé, e [akyze] nm/f accused; defendant; **accusé de réception** acknowledgement of receipt

accuser [akyze] vt to accuse; *(fig)* to emphasize, bring out; to show; ~ **qn de** to accuse sb of; *(Jur)* to charge sb with; ~ **réception de** to acknowledge receipt of

acéré, e [aseʀe] adj sharp

acharné, e [aʃaʀne] adj *(efforts)* relentless; *(lutte, adversaire)* fierce, bitter

acharner [aʃaʀne] vb: **s'~ contre** to set o.s. against; *(suj: malchance)* to dog; **s'~ à faire** to try doggedly to do; *(persister)* to persist in doing; **s'~ sur qn** to hound sb

achat [aʃa] nm purchase; **faire des ~s** to do some shopping; **faire l'~ de qch** to purchase sth

acheter [aʃ(ə)te] vt to buy, purchase; *(soudoyer)* to buy; ~ **qch à** *(marchand)* to buy ou purchase sth from; *(ami etc: offrir)* to buy sth for; **où est-ce que je peux ~ des cartes postales?** where can I buy (some) postcards?; **acheteur, -euse** nm/f buyer; shopper; *(Comm)* buyer

achever [aʃ(ə)ve] vt to complete, finish; *(blessé)* to finish off; **s'achever** vi to end

acide [asid] adj sour, sharp; *(Chimie)* acid(ic) ▷ nm *(Chimie)* acid; **acidulé, e** adj slightly acid; **bonbons acidulés** acid drops

acier [asje] nm steel; **aciérie** nf steelworks sg

acné [akne] nf acne

acompte [akɔ̃t] nm deposit

à-côté [akote] nm side-issue; *(argent)* extra

à-coup [aku] nm: **par ~s** by fits and starts

acoustique [akustik] nf *(d'une salle)* acoustics pl

acquéreur [akerœr] nm buyer, purchaser

acquérir [akerir] vt to acquire

acquis, e [aki, iz] pp de **acquérir** ▷ nm (accumulated) experience; **son aide nous est ~e** we can count on her help

acquitter [akite] vt (Jur) to acquit; (facture) to pay, settle; **s'acquitter de** vt (devoir) to discharge; (promesse) to fulfil

âcre [akr] adj acrid, pungent

acrobate [akrobat] nm/f acrobat; **acrobatie** nf acrobatics sg

acte [akt] nm act, action; (Théâtre) act; **prendre ~ de** to note, take note of; **faire ~ de candidature** to apply; **faire ~ de présence** to put in an appearance; **acte de naissance** birth certificate

acteur [aktœr] nm actor

actif, -ive [aktif, iv] adj active ▷ nm (Comm) assets pl; (fig): **avoir à son ~** to have to one's credit; **population active** working population

action [aksjɔ̃] nf (gén) action; (Comm) share; **une bonne ~** a good deed; **actionnaire** nm/f shareholder; **actionner** vt (mécanisme) to activate; (machine) to operate

activer [aktive] vt to speed up; **s'activer** vi to bustle about; to hurry up

activité [aktivite] nf activity; **en ~** (volcan) active; (fonctionnaire) in active life

actrice [aktris] nf actress

actualité [aktɥalite] nf (d'un problème) topicality; (événements): **l'~** current events; **actualités** nfpl (Cinéma, TV) the news; **d'~** topical

actuel, le [aktɥɛl] adj (présent) present; (d'actualité) topical; **à l'heure ~le** at the present time; **actuellement** adv at present, at the present time

⚠ Attention à ne pas traduire **actuellement** par **actually**.

acupuncture [akypɔ̃ktyr] nf acupuncture

adaptateur [adaptatœr] nm (Élec) adapter

adapter [adapte] vt to adapt; **s'adapter (à)** (suj: personne) to adapt (to); **~ qch à** (approprier) to adapt sth to; (fit): **~ qch sur/dans/à** (fixer) to fit sth on/into/to

addition [adisjɔ̃] nf addition; (au café) bill; **l'~, s'il vous plaît** could I have the bill, please?; **additionner** vt to add (up)

adepte [adɛpt] nm/f follower

adéquat, e [adekwa(t), at] adj appropriate, suitable

adhérent, e [aderã, ãt] nm/f member

adhérer [adere]: **~ à** vt (coller) to adhere ou stick to; (se rallier à) to join; **adhésif, -ive** adj adhesive, sticky; **ruban adhésif** sticky ou adhesive tape

adieu, x [adjø] excl goodbye ▷ nm farewell

adjectif [adʒɛktif] nm adjective

adjoint, e [adʒwɛ̃, wɛ̃t] nm/f assistant; **adjoint au maire** deputy mayor; **directeur adjoint** assistant manager

admettre [admɛtr] vt (laisser entrer) to admit; (candidat: Scol) to pass; (tolérer) to allow, accept; (reconnaître) to admit, acknowledge

administrateur, -trice [administratœr, tris] nm/f (Comm) director; (Admin) administrator

administration [administrasjɔ̃] nf administration; **l'A~** ≈ the Civil Service

administrer [administre] vt (firme) to manage, run; (biens, remède, sacrement etc) to administer

admirable [admirabl] adj admirable, wonderful

admirateur, -trice [admiratœr, tris] nm/f admirer

admiration [admirasjɔ̃] nf admiration

admirer [admire] vt to admire

admis, e [admi, iz] pp de **admettre**

admissible [admisibl] adj (candidat) eligible; (comportement) admissible, acceptable

ADN sigle m (= acide désoxyribonucléique) DNA

adolescence [adɔlesɑ̃s] nf
adolescence

adolescent, e [adɔlesɑ̃, ɑ̃t] nm/f
adolescent, teenager

adopter [adɔpte] vt to adopt; **adoptif,
-ive** adj (parents) adoptive; (fils, patrie)
adopted

adorable [adɔrabl] adj delightful,
adorable

adorer [adɔre] vt to adore; (Rel) to
worship

adosser [adɔse] vt: ~ **qch à** ou **contre** to
stand with one's back against;
s'adosser à/contre
to lean with one's back against

adoucir [adusir] vt (goût, température)
to make milder; (avec du sucre) to
sweeten; (peau, voix) to soften;
(caractère) to mellow

adresse [adrɛs] nf (domicile)
address; (dextérité) skill, dexterity; ~
électronique email address

adresser [adrese] vt (lettre: expédier)
to send; (: écrire l'adresse sur) to address;
(injure, compliments) to address;
s'adresser à (parler à) to speak to,
address; (s'informer auprès de) to go and
see; (: bureau) to inquire at; (suj: livre,
conseil) to be aimed at; ~ **la parole à** to
speak to, address

adroit, e [adrwa, wat] adj skilful,
skilled

ADSL sigle m (= asymmetrical digital
subscriber line) ADSL, broadband

adulte [adylt] nm/f adult, grown-up
▷ adj (chien, arbre) fully-grown, mature;
(attitude) adult, grown-up

adverbe [adverb] nm adverb

adversaire [adverser] nm/f (Sport,
gén) opponent, adversary

aération [aerasjɔ̃] nf airing; (circulation
de l'air) ventilation

aérer [aere] vt to air; (fig) to lighten

aérien, ne [aerjɛ̃, jen] adj (Aviat) air
cpd, aerial; (câble, métro) overhead; (fig)
light; **compagnie ~ne** airline

aéro... [aero] préfixe: **aérobic** nm
aerobics sg; **aérogare** nf airport
(buildings); (en ville) air terminal;

aéroglisseur nm hovercraft;
aérophagie nf (Méd) wind, aerophagia
(Méd); **aéroport** nm airport; **aérosol**
nm aerosol

affaiblir [afeblir]: **s'affaiblir** vi to
weaken

affaire [afɛr] nf (problème, question)
matter; (criminelle, judiciaire) case;
(scandaleuse etc) affair; (entreprise)
business; (marché, transaction) deal;
business no pl; (occasion intéressante)
bargain; **affaires** nfpl (intérêts publics
et privés) affairs; (activité commerciale)
business sg; (effets personnels) things,
belongings; **ce sont mes ~s** (cela me
concerne) that's my business; **occupe-
toi de tes ~s!** mind your own business!;
ça fera l'~ that will do (nicely); **se tirer
d'~** to sort it ou things out for o.s.; **avoir
~ à** (être en contact) to be dealing with;
les A~s étrangères Foreign Affairs;
affairer: s'affairer vi to busy o.s.,
bustle about

affamé, e [afame] adj starving

affecter [afɛkte] vt to affect; ~ **qch
à** to allocate ou allot sth to; ~ **qn à**
to appoint sb to; (: à diplomate) to post sb to

affectif, -ive [afɛktif, iv] adj
emotional

affection [afɛksjɔ̃] nf affection; (mal)
ailment; **affectionner** vt to be fond of;
affectueux, -euse adj affectionate

affichage [afiʃaʒ] nm billposting;
(électronique) display; **"~ interdit"** "stick
no bills"; **affichage à cristaux liquides**
liquid crystal display, LCD

affiche [afiʃ] nf poster; (officielle) notice;
(Théâtre) bill; **être à l'~** to be on

afficher [afiʃe] vt (affiche) to put up;
(réunion) to put up a notice about;
(électroniquement) to display; (fig) to
exhibit, display; **"défense d'~"** "no bill
posters"; **s'afficher** vt (péj) to flaunt
o.s.; (électroniquement) to be displayed

affilée [afile]: **d'~** adv at a stretch

affirmatif, -ive [afirmatif, iv] adj
affirmative

affirmer [afirme] vt to assert

affligé, e [afliʒe] *adj* distressed, grieved; **~ de** (*maladie, tare*) afflicted with

affliger [afliʒe] *vt* (*peiner*) to distress, grieve

affluence [aflyɑ̃s] *nf* crowds *pl*; **heures d'~** rush hours; **jours d'~** busiest days

affluent [aflyɑ̃] *nm* tributary

affolement [afɔlmɑ̃] *nm* panic

affoler [afɔle] *vt* to throw into a panic; **s'affoler** *vi* to panic

affranchir [afʀɑ̃ʃiʀ] *vt* to put a stamp *ou* stamps on; (*à la machine*) to frank (BRIT), meter (US); (*fig*) to free, liberate; **affranchissement** *nm* postage

affreux, -euse [afʀø, øz] *adj* dreadful, awful

affront [afʀɔ̃] *nm* affront; **affrontement** *nm* clash, confrontation

affronter [afʀɔ̃te] *vt* to confront, face

affût [afy] *nm*: **à l'~ (de)** (*gibier*) lying in wait (for); (*fig*) on the look-out (for)

Afghanistan [afganistɑ̃] *nm*: **l'~** Afghanistan

afin [afɛ̃]: **~ que** *conj* so that, in order that; **~ de faire** in order to do, so as to do

africain, e [afʀikɛ̃, ɛn] *adj* African ▷ *nm/f*: **A~, e** African

Afrique [afʀik] *nf*: **l'~** Africa; **l'Afrique du Nord/Sud** North/South Africa

agacer [agase] *vt* to irritate

âge [ɑʒ] *nm* age; **quel ~ as-tu?** how old are you?; **prendre de l'~** to be getting on (in years); **le troisième ~** (*période*) retirement; (*personnes âgées*) senior citizens; **âgé, e** *adj* old, elderly; **âgé de 10 ans** 10 years old

agence [aʒɑ̃s] *nf* agency, office; (*succursale*) branch; **agence de voyages** travel agency; **agence immobilière** estate agent (BRIT) *ou* real estate (US) agent's (office)

agenda [aʒẽda] *nm* diary; **~ électronique** PDA

> Attention à ne pas traduire *agenda* par le mot anglais *agenda*.

agenouiller [aʒ(ə)nuje]: **s'agenouiller** *vi* to kneel (down)

agent, e [aʒɑ̃, ɑ̃t] *nm/f* (*aussi*: **~(e) de police**) policeman(policewoman); (*Admin*) official, officer; **agent immobilier** estate agent (BRIT), realtor (US)

agglomération [aglɔmeʀasjɔ̃] *nf* town; built-up area; **l'~ parisienne** the urban area of Paris

aggraver [agʀave]: **s'aggraver** *vi* to worsen

agile [aʒil] *adj* agile, nimble

agir [aʒiʀ] *vi* to act; **il s'agit de** (*ça traite de*) it is about; (*il est important de*) it's a matter *ou* question of; **il s'agit de faire** we (*ou you etc*) must do; **de quoi s'agit-il?** what is it about?

agitation [aʒitasjɔ̃] *nf* (*hustle and*) bustle; (*trouble*) agitation, excitement; (*politique*) unrest, agitation

agité, e [aʒite] *adj* fidgety, restless; (*trouble*) agitated, perturbed; (*mer*) rough

agiter [aʒite] *vt* (*bouteille, chiffon*) to shake; (*bras, mains*) to wave; (*préoccuper, exciter*) to perturb

agneau, x [aɲo] *nm* lamb

agonie [agɔni] *nf* mortal agony, death pangs *pl*; (*fig*) death throes *pl*

agrafe [agʀaf] *nf* (*de vêtement*) hook, fastener; (*de bureau*) staple; **agrafer** *vt* to fasten; to staple; **agrafeuse** *nf* stapler

agrandir [agʀɑ̃diʀ] *vt* to enlarge; **s'agrandir** *vi* (*ville, famille*) to grow, expand; (*trou, écart*) to get bigger; **agrandissement** *nm* (*Photo*) enlargement

agréable [agʀeabl] *adj* pleasant, nice

agréé, e [agʀee] *adj*: **concessionnaire ~** registered dealer

agréer [agʀee] *vt* (*requête*) to accept; **~ à** to please, suit; **veuillez ~, Monsieur/Madame, mes salutations distinguées** (*personne nommée*) yours sincerely; (*personne non nommée*) yours faithfully

agrégation [agʀegasjɔ̃] nf highest teaching diploma in France; **agrégé, e** nm/f holder of the agrégation

agrément [agʀemã] nm (accord) consent, approval; (attraits) charm, attractiveness; (plaisir) pleasure

agresser [agʀese] vt to attack; **agresseur** nm aggressor, attacker; (Pol, Mil) aggressor; **agressif, -ive** adj aggressive

agricole [agʀikɔl] adj agricultural; **agriculteur** nm farmer; **agriculture** nf agriculture, farming

agripper [agʀipe] vt to grab, clutch; **s'agripper à** to cling (on) to, clutch, grip

agro-alimentaire [agʀoalimãtɛʀ] nm farm-produce industry

agrumes [agʀym] nmpl citrus fruit(s)

aguets [agɛ] nmpl: **être aux ~** to be on the look out

ai [e] vb voir **avoir**

aide [ed] nm/f assistant; carer ▷ nf assistance, help; (secours financier) aid; **à l'~ de** (avec) with the help ou aid of; **appeler (qn) à l'~** to call for help (from sb); **à l'~!** help!; **aide judiciaire** legal aid; **aide ménagère** = home help (BRIT) ou helper(us); **aide-mémoire** nm inv memoranda page pl; (key facts) handbook; **aide-soignant, e** nm/f auxiliary nurse

aider [ede] vt to help; **~ à qch** to help (towards) sth; **~ qn à faire qch** to help sb to do sth; **pouvez-vous m'~?** can you help me?; **s'aider de** (se servir de) to use, make use of

aïe [aj] excl ouch!

aie etc [ɛ] vb voir **avoir**

aigle [ɛgl] nm eagle

aigre [ɛgʀ] adj sour, sharp; (fig) sharp, cutting; **aigre-doux, -ce** adj (sauce) sweet and sour; **aigreur** nf sourness; sharpness; **aigreurs d'estomac** heartburn sg

aigu, ë [egy] adj (objet, douleur) sharp; (son, voix) high-pitched, shrill; (note) high(-pitched)

aiguille [eguij] nf needle; (de montre) hand; **aiguille à tricoter** knitting needle

aiguiser [egize] vt to sharpen; (fig) to stimulate; (: sens) to excite

ail [aj] nm garlic

aile [ɛl] nf wing; **aileron** nm (de requin) fin; **ailier** nm winger

aille etc [aj] vb voir **aller**

ailleurs [ajœʀ] adv elsewhere, somewhere else; **partout/nulle part ~** everywhere/nowhere else; **d'~** (du reste) moreover, besides; **par ~** (d'autre part) moreover, furthermore

aimable [ɛmabl] adj kind, nice

aimant [ɛmã] nm magnet

aimer [eme] vt to love; (d'amitié, affection, par goût) to like; (souhait): **j'aimerais ...** I would like ...; **j'aime faire du ski** I like skiing; **je t'aime** I love you; **bien ~ qn/qch** to like sb/sth; **j'aime mieux Paul (que Pierre)** I prefer Paul (to Pierre); **j'aimerais mieux faire** I'd much rather do

aine [ɛn] nf groin

aîné, e [ene] adj elder, older; (le plus âgé) eldest, oldest ▷ nm/f oldest child ou one, oldest boy ou son/girl ou daughter

ainsi [ɛ̃si] adv (de cette façon) like this, in this way, thus; (ce faisant) thus ▷ conj thus; so; **~ que** (comme) (just) as; (et aussi) as well as; **pour ~ dire** so to speak; **et ~ de suite** and so on

air [ɛʀ] nm air; (mélodie) tune; (expression) look, air; **prendre l'~** to get some (fresh) air; **avoir l'~** (sembler) to look, appear; **il a l'~ triste/malade** he looks sad/ill; **avoir l'~ de** to look like; **il a l'~ de dormir** he looks as if he's sleeping; **en l'~** (promesses) empty

airbag [ɛʀbag] nm airbag

aisance [ɛzɑ̃s] nf ease; (richesse) affluence

aise [ɛz] nf comfort; **être à l'~** ou **à son ~** to be comfortable; (pas embarrassé) to be at ease; (financièrement) to be comfortably off; **se mettre à l'~** to make o.s. comfortable; **être mal à l'~**

to be uncomfortable; (*gêné*) to be ill at ease; **en faire à son ~** to do as one likes; **aisé, e** *adj* easy; (*assez riche*) well-to-do, well-off

aisselle [ɛsɛl] *nf* armpit

ait [ɛ] *vb voir* **avoir**

ajonc [aʒɔ̃] *nm* gorse *no pl*

ajourner [aʒuRne] *vt* (*réunion*) to adjourn; (*décision*) to defer, postpone

ajouter [aʒute] *vt* to add

alarme [alaRm] *nf* alarm; **donner l'~** to give *ou* raise the alarm; **alarmer** *vt* to alarm; **s'alarmer** *vi* to become alarmed

Albanie [albani] *nf*: **l'~** Albania

album [albɔm] *nm* album

alcool [alkɔl] *nm*: **l'~** alcohol; **un ~** a spirit, a brandy; **bière sans ~** non-alcoholic *ou* alcohol-free beer; **alcool à brûler** methylated spirits (*BRIT*), wood alcohol (*US*); **alcool à 90°** surgical spirit; **alcoolique** *adj, nm/f* alcoholic; **alcoolisé, e** *adj* alcoholic; **une boisson non alcoolisée** a soft drink; **alcoolisme** *nm* alcoholism; **alco(o)test®** *nm* Breathalyser®; (*test*) breath-test

aléatoire [aleatwaR] *adj* uncertain; (*Inform*) random

alentour [alɑ̃tuR] *adv* around, round about; **alentours** *nmpl* (*environs*) surroundings; **aux ~s de** in the vicinity *ou* neighbourhood of, round about; (*temps*) round about

alerte [alɛRt] *adj* agile, nimble; brisk, lively ▷ *nf* alert; warning; **alerte à la bombe** bomb scare; **alerter** *vt* to alert

algèbre [alʒɛbR] *nf* algebra

Alger [alʒe] *n* Algiers

Algérie [alʒeRi] *nf*: **l'~** Algeria; **algérien, ne** *adj* Algerian ▷ *nm/f*: **Algérien, ne** Algerian

algue [alg] *nf* (*gén*) seaweed *no pl*; (*Bot*) alga

alibi [alibi] *nm* alibi

aligner [aliɲe] *vt* to align, line up; (*idées, chiffres*) to string together; (*adapter*): **~ qch sur** to bring sth into

alignment with; **s'aligner** (*soldats etc*) to line up; **s'~ sur** (*Pol*) to align o.s. on

aliment [alimɑ̃] *nm* food; **alimentation** *nf* (*commerce*) food trade; (*magasin*) grocery store; (*régime*) diet; (*en eau etc, de moteur*) supplying; (*Inform*) feeding; **alimenter** *vt* to feed; (*Tech*): **alimenter (en)** to supply (with); to feed (with); (*fig*) to sustain, keep going

allaiter [alete] *vt* to (breast-)feed, nurse; (*suj: animal*) to suckle

allécher [aleʃe] *vt*: **~ qn** to make sb's mouth water; to tempt *ou* entice sb

allée [ale] *nf* (*de jardin*) path; (*en ville*) avenue, drive; **~s et venues** comings and goings

allégé, e [aleʒe] *adj* (*yaourt etc*) low-fat

alléger [aleʒe] *vt* (*voiture*) to make lighter; (*chargement*) to lighten; (*souffrance*) to alleviate, soothe

Allemagne [alman] *nf*: **l'~** Germany; **allemand, e** *adj* German ▷ *nm* (*Ling*) German ▷ *nm/f*: **Allemand, e** German

aller [ale] *nm* (*trajet*) outward journey; (*billet: aussi: ~ simple*) single (*BRIT*) *ou* one-way (*US*) ticket; **~ (et) retour** return (ticket) (*BRIT*), round-trip ticket (*US*) ▷ *vi* (*gén*) to go; **~ à** (*convenir*) to suit; (*suj: forme, pointure etc*) to fit; **~ (bien) avec** (*couleurs, style etc*) to go (well) with; **je vais y ~/me fâcher** I'm going to go/to get angry; **~ chercher qn** to go and get *ou* fetch (*BRIT*) sb; **~ voir** to go and see, go to see; **allez!** come on!; **allons!** come now!; **comment allez-vous?** how are you?; **comment ça va?** how are you?; (*affaires etc*) how are things?; **il va bien/mal** he's well/not well, he's fine/ill; **ça va bien/mal** (*affaires etc*) it's going well/not going well; **~ mieux** to be better; **s'en ~** (*partir*) to be off, go, leave; (*disparaître*) to go away

allergie [alɛRʒi] *nf* allergy

allergique [alɛRʒik] *adj*: **~ à** allergic to; **je suis ~ à la pénicilline** I'm allergic to penicillin

alliance [aljɑ̃s] nf (Mil, Pol) alliance; (bague) wedding ring

allier [alje] vt (Pol, gén) to ally; (fig) to combine; **s'allier** to become allies; to combine

allô [alo] excl hullo, hallo

allocation [alɔkasjɔ̃] nf allowance; **allocation (de) chômage** unemployment benefit; **allocations familiales** = child benefit

allonger [alɔ̃ʒe] vt to lengthen, make longer; (étendre: bras, jambe) to stretch (out); **s'allonger** vi to get longer; (se coucher) to lie down, stretch out; **~ le pas** to hasten one's step(s)

allumage [alymaʒ] nm (Auto) ignition

allume-cigare [alymsigaʀ] nm inv cigar lighter

allumer [alyme] vt (lampe, phare, radio) to put ou switch on; (pièce) to put ou switch the light(s) on; (feu) to light; **s'allumer** vi (lumière, lampe) to come ou go on; **je n'arrive pas à ~ le chauffage** I can't turn the heating on

allumette [alymɛt] nf match

allure [alyʀ] nf (vitesse) speed, pace; (démarche) walk; (aspect, air) look; **avoir de l'~** to have style; **à toute ~** at top speed

allusion [a(l)lyzjɔ̃] nf allusion; (sous-entendu) hint; **faire ~ à** to allude ou refer to; to hint at

MOT-CLÉ

alors [alɔʀ] adv 1 (à ce moment-là) then, at that time; **il habitait alors à Paris** he lived in Paris at that time

2 (par conséquent) then; **tu as fini? alors je m'en vais** have you finished? I'm going then; **et alors?** so what?

▷ conj: **alors que** 1 (au moment où) when, as; **il est arrivé alors que je partais** he arrived as I was leaving

2 (tandis que) whereas, while; **alors que son frère travaillait dur, lui se reposait** while his brother was working hard, HE would rest

3 (bien que) even though; **il a été puni alors qu'il n'a rien fait** he was punished, even though he had done nothing

alourdir [aluʀdiʀ] vt to weigh down, make heavy

Alpes [alp] nfpl: **les ~** the Alps

alphabet [alfabɛ] nm alphabet; (livre) ABC (book)

alpinisme [alpinism] nm mountaineering, climbing

Alsace [alzas] nf Alsace; **alsacien, ne** adj Alsatian ▷ nm/f: **Alsacien, ne** Alsatian

altermondialisme [altɛʀmɔ̃djalism] nm anti-globalism; **altermondialiste** adj, nm/f anti-globalist

alternatif, -ive [altɛʀnatif, iv] adj alternating; **alternative** nf (choix) alternative; **alterner** vi to alternate

altitude [altityd] nf altitude, height

alto [alto] nm (instrument) viola

aluminium [alyminjɔm] nm aluminium (BRIT), aluminum (US)

amabilité [amabilite] nf kindness

amaigrissant, e [amegʀisɑ̃, ɑ̃t] adj (régime) slimming

amande [amɑ̃d] nf (de l'amandier) almond; **amandier** nm almond (tree)

amant [amɑ̃] nm lover

amas [amɑ] nm heap, pile; **amasser** vt to amass

amateur [amatœʀ] nm amateur; **en ~** (péj) amateurishly; **amateur de musique/sport** music/sport lover

ambassade [ɑ̃basad] nf embassy; **l'~ de France** the French Embassy; **ambassadeur, -drice** nm/f ambassador(-dress)

ambiance [ɑ̃bjɑ̃s] nf atmosphere; **il y a de l'~** there's a great atmosphere

ambigu, ë [ɑ̃bigy] adj ambiguous

ambitieux, -euse [ɑ̃bisjø, jøz] adj ambitious

ambition [ɑ̃bisjɔ̃] nf ambition

ambulance [ɑ̃bylɑ̃s] nf ambulance;

appelez une ~! call an ambulance; **ambulancier, -ière** *nm/f* ambulance man(-woman) (BRIT), paramedic (US)

âme [ɑm] *nf* soul; **âme sœur** kindred spirit

amélioration [ameljɔrasjɔ̃] *nf* improvement

améliorer [ameljɔre] *vt* to improve; **s'améliorer** *vi* to improve, get better

aménager [amenaʒe] *vt* (agencer, transformer) to fit out; to lay out; (: quartier, territoire) to develop; (installer) to fix up, put in; **ferme aménagée** converted farmhouse

amende [amɑ̃d] *nf* fine; **faire ~ honorable** to make amends

amener [am(ə)ne] *vt* to bring; (causer) to bring about; **s'amener** *vi* to show up (fam), turn up; **~ qn à faire qch** to lead sb to do sth

amer, amère [amɛʀ] *adj* bitter

américain, e [amerikɛ̃, ɛn] *adj* American ▷ *nm/f*: **A~, e** American

Amérique [amerik] *nf*: **l'~** America; **Amérique centrale/latine** Central/Latin America; **l'Amérique du Nord/Sud** North/South America

amertume [amɛʀtym] *nf* bitterness

ameublement [amœbləmɑ̃] *nm* furnishing; (meubles) furniture

ami, e [ami] *nm/f* friend; (amant/maîtresse) boyfriend/girlfriend ▷ *adj*: **pays/groupe ~** friendly country/group; **petit ~/petite ~** boyfriend/girlfriend

amiable [amjabl]: **à l'~** *adv* (Jur) out of court; (gén) amicably

amiante [amjɑ̃t] *nm* asbestos

amical, e, -aux [amikal, o] *adj* friendly; **amicalement** *adv* in a friendly way; (dans une lettre) (with) best wishes

amincir [amɛ̃siʀ] *vt*: **~ qn** to make sb thinner ou slimmer; (suj: vêtement) to make sb look slimmer

amincissant, e [amɛ̃sisɑ̃, ɑ̃t] *adj*: **régime ~** (slimming) diet; **crème ~e** slimming cream

amiral, -aux [amiral, o] *nm* admiral

amitié [amitje] *nf* friendship; **prendre en ~** to befriend; **faire ou présenter ses ~s à qn** to send sb one's best wishes; **"~s"** (dans une lettre) "(with) best wishes"

amonceler [amɔ̃s(ə)le] *vt* to pile ou heap up; **s'amonceler** *vi* to pile ou heap up; (fig) to accumulate

amont [amɔ̃]: **en ~** *adv* upstream

amorce [amɔʀs] *nf* (sur un hameçon) bait; (explosif) cap; primer; priming; (fig: début) beginning(s), start

amortir [amɔʀtiʀ] *vt* (atténuer: choc) to absorb, cushion; (bruit, douleur) to deaden; (Comm: dette) to pay off; **~ un achat** to make a purchase pay for itself; **amortisseur** *nm* shock absorber

amour [amuʀ] *nm* love; **faire l'~** to make love; **amoureux, -euse** *adj* (regard, tempérament) amorous; (vie, problèmes) love *cpd*; (personne): **être amoureux (de qn)** to be in love (with sb); **tomber amoureux (de qn)** to fall in love (with sb) ▷ *nmpl* courting couple(s); **amour-propre** *nm* self-esteem, pride

ampère [ɑ̃pɛʀ] *nm* amp(ere)

amphithéâtre [ɑ̃fiteɑtʀ] *nm* amphitheatre; (d'université) lecture hall ou theatre

ample [ɑ̃pl] *adj* (vêtement) roomy, ample; (gestes, mouvement) broad; (ressources) ample; **amplement** *adv*: **c'est amplement suffisant** that's more than enough; **ampleur** *nf* (de dégâts, problème) extent

amplificateur [ɑ̃plifikatœʀ] *nm* amplifier

amplifier [ɑ̃plifje] *vt* (fig) to expand, increase

ampoule [ɑ̃pul] *nf* (électrique) bulb; (de médicament) phial; (aux mains, pieds) blister

amusant, e [amyzɑ̃, ɑ̃t] *adj* (divertissant, spirituel) entertaining, amusing; (comique) funny, amusing

amuse-gueule [amyzgœl] *nm inv*

appetizer, snack

amusement [amyzmɑ̃] *nm*
(*divertissement*) amusement; (*jeu etc*)
pastime, diversion

amuser [amyze] *vt* (*divertir*) to
entertain, amuse; (*égayer, faire rire*) to
amuse; **s'amuser** *vi* (*jouer*) to play; (*se
divertir*) to enjoy o.s., have fun; (*fig*) to
mess around

amygdale [amidal] *nf* tonsil

an [ɑ̃] *nm* year; **avoir quinze ans** to be
fifteen (years old); **le jour de l'an, le
premier de l'an, le nouvel an** New
Year's Day

analphabète [analfabɛt] *nm/f*
illiterate

analyse [analiz] *nf* analysis; (*Méd*) test;
analyser *vt* to analyse; to test

ananas [anana(s)] *nm* pineapple

anatomie [anatɔmi] *nf* anatomy

ancêtre [ɑ̃sɛtʁ] *nm/f* ancestor

anchois [ɑ̃ʃwa] *nm* anchovy

ancien, ne [ɑ̃sjɛ̃, jɛn] *adj* old; (*de
jadis, de l'antiquité*) ancient; (*précédent,
ex-*) former, old; (*par l'expérience*)
senior ▷ *nm* (*dans une tribu*) elder;
ancienneté (*Admin*) (length of)
service; (*privilèges obtenus*) seniority

ancre [ɑ̃kʁ] *nf* anchor; **jeter/lever l'~** to
cast/weigh anchor; **ancrer** *vt* (*Constr:
câble etc*) to anchor; (*fig*) to fix firmly

Andorre [ɑ̃dɔʁ] *nf* Andorra

andouille [ɑ̃duj] *nf* (*Culin*) sausage made
of chitterlings; (*fam*) clot, nit

âne [ɑn] *nm* donkey, ass; (*péj*) dunce

anéantir [aneɑ̃tiʁ] *vt* to annihilate,
wipe out; (*fig*) to obliterate, destroy

anémie [anemi] *nf* anaemia;
anémique *adj* anaemic

anesthésie [anɛstezi] *nf* anaesthesia;
faire une ~ locale/générale à qn to
give sb a local/general anaesthetic

ange [ɑ̃ʒ] *nm* angel; **être aux ~s** to be
over the moon

angine [ɑ̃ʒin] *nf* throat infection;
angine de poitrine angina

anglais, e [ɑ̃glɛ, ɛz] *adj* English ▷ *nm/f*:
A~, e Englishman(-woman) ▷ *nm*

(*Ling*) English; **les A~** the English; **filer à
l'~e** to take French leave

angle [ɑ̃gl] *nm* angle; (*coin*) corner;
angle droit right angle

Angleterre [ɑ̃glətɛʁ] *nf*: **l'~** England

anglo... [ɑ̃glɔ] *préfixe* Anglo-, anglo(-);
anglophone *adj* English-speaking

angoisse [ɑ̃gwas] *nf* anguish, distress;
angoissé, e *adj* (*personne*) distressed

anguille [ɑ̃gij] *nf* eel

animal, e, -aux [animal, o] *adj, nm*
animal

animateur, -trice [animatœʁ, tʁis]
nm/f (*de télévision*) host; (*de groupe*)
leader, organizer

animation [animasjɔ̃] *nf* (*voir animé*)
busyness; liveliness; (*Cinéma: technique*)
animation

animé, e [anime] *adj* (*lieu*) busy, lively;
(*conversation, réunion*) lively, animated

animer [anime] *vt* (*ville, soirée*) to liven
up; (*mener*) to lead

anis [ani(s)] *nm* (*Culin*) aniseed; (*Bot*)
anise

ankyloser [ɑ̃kiloze]: **s'ankyloser** *vi*
to get stiff

anneau, x [ano] *nm* (*de rideau, bague*)
ring; (*de chaîne*) link

année [ane] *nf* year

annexe [anɛks] *adj* (*problème*) related;
(*document*) appended; (*salle*) adjoining
▷ *nf* (*bâtiment*) annex(e); (*jointe à une
lettre*) enclosure

anniversaire [anivɛʁsɛʁ] *nm*
birthday; (*d'un événement, bâtiment*)
anniversary

annonce [anɔ̃s] *nf* announcement;
(*signe, indice*) sign; (*aussi: ~ publicitaire*)
advertisement; **les petites ~s** the
classified advertisements, the small
ads

annoncer [anɔ̃se] *vt* to announce; (*être
le signe de*) to herald; **s'~ bien/difficile**
to look promising/difficult

annuaire [anɥɛʁ] *nm* yearbook,
annual; **annuaire téléphonique**
(telephone) directory, phone book

annuel, le [anɥɛl] *adj* annual, yearly

annulation [anylasjɔ̃] nf cancellation

annuler [anyle] vt (rendez-vous, voyage) to cancel; to call off; (jugement) to quash (BRIT), repeal (US); (Math, Physique) to cancel out; **je voudrais ~ ma réservation** I'd like to cancel my reservation

anonymat [anɔnima] nm anonymity; **garder l'~** to remain anonymous

anonyme [anɔnim] adj anonymous; (fig) impersonal

anorak [anɔrak] nm anorak

anorexie [anɔrɛksi] nf anorexia

anormal, e, -aux [anɔrmal, o] adj abnormal

ANPE sigle f (= Agence nationale pour l'emploi) national employment agency

antarctique [ɑ̃tarktik] adj Antarctic ▷ nm: **l'A~** the Antarctic

antenne [ɑ̃tɛn] nf (de radio) aerial; (d'insecte) antenna, feeler; (poste avancé) outpost; (petite succursale) sub-branch; **passer à l'~** to go on the air; **antenne parabolique** satellite dish

antérieur, e [ɑ̃terjœr] adj (dans le temps) previous, earlier; (de devant) front

anti... [ɑ̃ti] préfixe anti...; **antialcoolique** adj anti-alcohol; **antibiotique** nm antibiotic; **antibrouillard** adj: **phare antibrouillard** fog lamp (BRIT) ou light (US)

anticipation [ɑ̃tisipasjɔ̃] nf: **livre/ film d'~** science fiction book/film

anticipé, e [ɑ̃tisipe] adj: **avec mes remerciements ~s** thanking you in advance ou anticipation

anticiper [ɑ̃tisipe] vt (événement, coup) to anticipate, foresee

anti...: anticorps nm antibody; **antidote** nm antidote; **antigel** nm antifreeze; **antihistaminique** nm antihistamine

antillais, e [ɑ̃tijɛ, ɛz] adj West Indian, Caribbean ▷ nm/f: **A~, e** West Indian, Caribbean

Antilles [ɑ̃tij] nfpl: **les ~** the West Indies; **les Grandes/Petites ~** the Greater/Lesser Antilles

antilope [ɑ̃tilɔp] nf antelope

anti...: antimite(s) adj, nm: (produit) **antimite(s)** mothproofer; moth repellent; **antimondialisation** nf anti-globalization; **antipathique** adj unpleasant, disagreeable; **antipelliculaire** adj anti-dandruff; **antiquaire** [ɑ̃tikɛr] nm/f antique dealer

antique [ɑ̃tik] adj antique; (très vieux) ancient, antiquated; **antiquité** nf (objet) antique; **l'Antiquité** Antiquity; **magasin d'antiquités** antique shop

anti...: antirabique adj rabies cpd; **antirouille** adj inv anti-rust cpd; **antisémite** adj anti-Semitic; **antiseptique** adj, nm antiseptic

antivirus [ɑ̃tivirys] nm (Inform) antivirus; **antivol** adj, nm: (dispositif) **antivol** anti-theft device

anxieux, -euse [ɑ̃ksjø, jøz] adj anxious, worried

AOC sigle f (= appellation d'origine contrôlée) label guaranteeing the quality of wine

août [u(t)] nm August

apaiser [apeze] vt (colère, douleur) to soothe; (personne) to calm (down), pacify; **s'apaiser** vi (tempête, bruit) to die down, subside; (personne) to calm down

apercevoir [apɛrsəvwar] vt to see; **s'apercevoir de** vt to notice; **s'~ que** to notice that

aperçu [apɛrsy] nm (vue d'ensemble) general survey

apéritif [aperitif] nm (boisson) aperitif; (réunion) drinks pl

à-peu-près [apøprɛ] (péj) nm inv vague approximation

apeuré, e [apœre] adj frightened, scared

aphte [aft] nm mouth ulcer

apitoyer [apitwaje] vt to move to pity; **s'apitoyer (sur)** to feel pity (for)

aplatir [aplatir] vt to flatten; **s'aplatir** vi to become flatter; (écrasé) to be flattened

aplomb [aplɔ̃] nm (équilibre) balance, equilibrium; (fig) self-assurance; nerve; **d'~** steady

apostrophe [apɔstrɔf] nf (signe) apostrophe

apparaître [aparɛtr] vi to appear

appareil [aparɛj] nm (outil, machine) piece of apparatus, device; (électrique, ménager) appliance; (avion) (aero)plane, aircraft inv; (téléphonique) phone; (dentier) brace (BRIT), braces (US); **"qui est à l'~?"** "who's speaking?"; **dans le plus simple ~** in one's birthday suit; **appareil-(photo)** camera; **appareiller** vi (Navig) to cast off, get under way ▷ vt (assortir) to match up

apparemment [aparamɑ̃] adv apparently

apparence [aparɑ̃s] nf appearance; **en ~** apparently

apparent, e [aparɑ̃, ɑ̃t] adj visible; (évident) obvious; (superficiel) apparent

apparenté, e [aparɑ̃te] adj: **~ à** related to; (fig) similar to

apparition [aparisjɔ̃] nf appearance; (surnaturelle) apparition

appartement [apartǝmɑ̃] nm flat (BRIT), apartment (US)

appartenir [apartǝnir]: **~ à** vt to belong to; **il lui appartient de** it is his duty to

apparu, e [apary] pp de **apparaître**

appât [apɑ] nm (Pêche) bait; (fig) lure, bait

appel [apɛl] nm call; (nominal) roll call; (: Scol) register; (Mil: recrutement) call-up; **faire ~ à** (invoquer) to appeal to; (avoir recours à) to call on; (nécessiter) to call for, require; **faire ou interjeter ~** (Jur) to appeal; **faire l'~** to call the roll; (Scol) to call the register; **sans ~** (fig) final, irrevocable; **faire un ~ de phares** to flash one's headlights; **appel d'offres** (Comm) invitation to tender; **appel (téléphonique)** (tele)phone call

appelé [ap(ǝ)le] nm (Mil) conscript

appeler [ap(ǝ)le] vt to call; (faire venir:

médecin etc) to call, send for; **s'appeler** vi: **elle s'appelle Gabrielle** her name is Gabrielle, she's called Gabrielle; **comment vous appelez-vous?** what's your name?; **comment ça s'appelle?** what is it called?; **être appelé à** (fig) to be destined to

appendicite [apɛ̃disit] nf appendicitis

appesantir [apǝzɑ̃tir]: **s'appesantir** vi to grow heavier; **s'~ sur** (fig) to dwell on

appétissant, e [apetisɑ̃, ɑ̃t] adj appetizing, mouth-watering

appétit [apeti] nm appetite; **bon ~!** enjoy your meal!

applaudir [aplodir] vt to applaud ▷ vi to applaud, clap; **applaudissements** nmpl applause sg, clapping sg

application [aplikasjɔ̃] nf application

appliquer [aplike] vt to apply; (loi) to enforce; **s'appliquer** vi (élève etc) to apply o.s.; **s'~ à** to apply to

appoint [apwɛ̃] nm (extra) contribution ou help; **avoir/faire l'~** to have/give the right change ou money; **chauffage d'~** extra heating

apporter [apɔrte] vt to bring

appréciable [apresjabl] adj appreciable

apprécier [apresje] vt to appreciate; (évaluer) to estimate, assess

appréhender [apreɑ̃de] vt (craindre) to dread; (arrêter) to apprehend

apprendre [aprɑ̃dr] vt to learn; (événement, résultats) to learn of, hear of; **~ qch à qn** (informer) to tell sb (of) sth; (enseigner) to teach sb sth; **~ à faire qch** to learn to do sth; **~ à qn à faire qch** to teach sb to do sth; **apprenti, e** nm/f apprentice; **apprentissage** nm learning; (Comm, Scol: période) apprenticeship

apprêter [aprɛte] vt: **s'~ à faire qch** to get ready to do sth

appris, e [apri, iz] pp de **apprendre**

apprivoiser [aprivwaze] vt to tame

approbation [aprɔbasjɔ̃] nf approval

approcher [aprɔʃe] vi to approach, come near ▷ vt to approach; (*rapprocher*): ~ **qch (de qch)** to bring ou put sth near (to sth); **s'approcher de** to approach, go ou come near to; ~ **de** (*lieu, but*) to draw near to; (*quantité, moment*) to approach

approfondir [aprɔfɔ̃diʀ] vt to deepen; (*question*) to go further into

approprié, e [aprɔpʀije] *adj*: ~ **(à)** appropriate (to), suited to

approprier [aprɔpʀije]: **s'approprier** vt to appropriate, take over; **s'~ en** to stock up with

approuver [apʀuve] vt to agree with; (*trouver louable*) to approve of

approvisionner [apʀɔvizjɔne] vt to supply; (*compte bancaire*) to pay funds into; **s'approvisionner** vi to stock up with

approximatif, -ive [apʀɔksimatif, iv] *adj* approximate, rough; (*termes*) vague

appt *abr* = **appartement**

appui [apɥi] *nm* support; **prendre ~ sur** to lean on; (*objet*) to rest on; **l'~ de la fenêtre** the windowsill, the window ledge

appuyer [apɥije] vt (*poser*): ~ **qch sur/contre** to lean ou rest sth on/against; (*soutenir: personne, demande*) to support, back (up) ▷ vi: ~ **sur** (*bouton*) to press, push; (*mot, détail*) to stress, emphasize; ~ **sur le frein** to brake, to apply the brakes; **s'appuyer sur** to lean on; (*fig: compter sur*) to rely on

après [apʀɛ] *prép* after ▷ *adv* afterwards; **2 heures ~** 2 hours later; ~ **qu'il est ou soit parti** after he left; ~ **avoir fait** after having done; **d'~** (*selon*) according to; ~ **coup** after the event, afterwards; ~ **tout** (*au fond*) after all; **et (puis) ~?** so what?; **après-demain** *adv* the day after tomorrow; **après-midi** *nm ou nf* inv afternoon; **après-rasage** *nm inv* aftershave; **après-shampooing** *nm inv* conditioner; **après-ski** *nm inv* snow boot

après-soleil [apʀɛsɔlɛj] *adj inv* after-sun *cpd* ▷ *nm* after-sun cream ou lotion

apte [apt] *adj* capable; ~ **à qch/faire qch** capable of sth/doing sth; ~ **(au service)** (*Mil*) fit (for service)

aquarelle [akwaʀɛl] *nf* watercolour

aquarium [akwaʀjɔm] *nm* aquarium

arabe [aʀab] *adj* Arabic; (*désert, cheval*) Arabian; (*nation, peuple*) Arab ▷ *nm/f*: **A~** Arab ▷ *nm* (*Ling*) Arabic

Arabie [aʀabi] *nf*: **l'~ (Saoudite)** Saudi Arabia

arachide [aʀaʃid] *nf* (*plante*) groundnut (plant); (*graine*) peanut, groundnut

araignée [aʀene] *nf* spider

arbitraire [aʀbitʀɛʀ] *adj* arbitrary

arbitre [aʀbitʀ] *nm* (*Sport*) referee; (: *Tennis, Cricket*) umpire; (*fig*) arbiter, judge; (*Jur*) arbitrator; **arbitrer** vt to referee; to umpire; to arbitrate

arbre [aʀbʀ] *nm* tree; (*Tech*) shaft

arbuste [aʀbyst] *nm* small shrub

arc [aʀk] *nm* (*arme*) bow; (*Géom*) arc; (*Archit*) arch; **en ~ de cercle** semi-circular

arcade [aʀkad] *nf* arch(way); **arcades** *nfpl* (*série*) arcade *sg*, arches

arc-en-ciel [aʀkãsjɛl] *nm* rainbow

arche [aʀʃ] *nf* arch; **arche de Noé** Noah's Ark

archéologie [aʀkeɔlɔʒi] *nf* arch(a)eology; **archéologue** *nm/f* arch(a)eologist

archet [aʀʃɛ] *nm* bow

archipel [aʀʃipɛl] *nm* archipelago

architecte [aʀʃitɛkt] *nm* architect

architecture [aʀʃitɛktyʀ] *nf* architecture

archives [aʀʃiv] *nfpl* (*collection*) archives

arctique [aʀktik] *adj* Arctic ▷ *nm*: **l'A~** the Arctic

ardent, e [aʀdã, ãt] *adj* (*soleil*) blazing; (*amour*) ardent, passionate; (*prière*) fervent

ardoise [aʀdwaz] *nf* slate

ardu, e [aʀdy] *adj* (*travail*) arduous; (*problème*) difficult

arène [aʀɛn] nf arena; **arènes** nfpl (amphithéâtre) bull-ring sg

arête [aʀɛt] nf (de poisson) bone; (d'une montagne) ridge

argent [aʀʒɑ̃] nm (métal) silver; (monnaie) money; **argent de poche** pocket money; **argent liquide** ready money, (ready) cash; **argenterie** nf silverware

argentin, e [aʀʒɑ̃tɛ̃, in] adj Argentinian, ▷ nm/f: **A~, e** Argentinian

Argentine [aʀʒɑ̃tin] nf: **l'~** Argentina

argentique [aʀʒɑ̃tik] adj (appareil-photo) film cpd

argile [aʀʒil] nf clay

argot [aʀgo] nm slang; **argotique** adj slang cpd; (très familier) slangy

argument [aʀgymɑ̃] nm argument

argumenter [aʀgymɑ̃te] vi to argue

aride [aʀid] adj arid

aristocratie [aʀistɔkʀasi] nf aristocracy; **aristocratique** adj aristocratic

arithmétique [aʀitmetik] adj arithmetic(al) ▷ nf arithmetic

arme [aʀm] nf weapon; (armement) weapons, arms; (blason) (coat of) arms; **~s de destruction massive** weapons of mass destruction; **arme à feu** firearm

armée [aʀme] nf army; **armée de l'air** Air Force; **armée de terre** Army

armer [aʀme] vt to arm; (arme à feu) to cock; (appareil-photo) to wind on; **~ qch de** to reinforce sth with; **s'armer de** to arm o.s. with

armistice [aʀmistis] nm armistice; **l'A~** ≈ Remembrance (BRIT) ou Veterans (US) Day

armoire [aʀmwaʀ] nf (tall) cupboard; (penderie) wardrobe (BRIT), closet (US)

armure [aʀmyʀ] nf armour no pl, suit of armour; **armurerie** nf gunsmith

arnaque [aʀnak] (fam) nf swindling; **c'est de l'~** it's a rip-off; **arnaquer** (fam) vt to swindle

arobase [aʀobaz] nf (symbole) at symbol; **"paul ~ société point fr"** "paul at société dot fr"

aromates [aʀɔmat] nmpl seasoning sg, herbs (and spices)

aromathérapie [aʀɔmateʀapi] nf aromatherapy

aromatisé, e [aʀɔmatize] adj flavoured

arôme [aʀom] nm aroma

arracher [aʀaʃe] vt to pull out; (page etc) to tear off, tear out; (légumes, herbe) to pull up; (bras etc) to tear off; **s'arracher** vt (article recherché) to fight over; **~ qch à qn** to snatch sth from sb; (fig) to wring sth out of sb

arrangement [aʀɑ̃ʒmɑ̃] nm agreement, arrangement

arranger [aʀɑ̃ʒe] vt (gén) to arrange; (réparer) to fix, put right; (régler) différend) to settle, sort out; (convenir à) to suit, be convenient for; **cela m'arrange** that suits me (fine); **s'arranger** vi (se mettre d'accord) to come to an agreement; **je vais m'~** I'll manage; **ça va s'~** it'll sort itself out

arrestation [aʀestasjɔ̃] nf arrest

arrêt [aʀe] nm stopping; (de bus etc) stop; (Jur) judgment, decision; **à l'~** stationary; **tomber en ~ devant** to stop short in front of; **sans ~** (sans interruption) non-stop; (très fréquemment) continually; **arrêt de travail** stoppage (of work)

arrêter [aʀete] vt to stop; (chauffage etc) to turn off, switch off; (fixer: date etc) to appoint, decide on; (criminel, suspect) to arrest; **s'arrêter** vi to stop; **~ de faire** to stop doing; **arrêtez-vous ici/au coin, s'il vous plaît** could you stop here/at the corner, please?

arrhes [aʀ] nfpl deposit sg

arrière [aʀjɛʀ] nm back; (Sport) fullback ▷ adj inv: **siège/roue** = back ou rear seat/wheel; **à l'~** = behind, at the back; **en ~** = behind; (regarder) back, behind; (tomber, aller) backwards; **arrière-goût** nm aftertaste; **arrière-grand-mère** nf great-grandmother; **arrière-grand-père** nm great-grandfather;

arrière-pays nm inv hinterland;
arrière-pensée nf ulterior motive;
mental reservation; **arrière-plan** nm
background; **à l'arrière-plan** in the
background; **arrière-saison** nf late
autumn

arrimer [aʀime] vt to secure;
(cargaison) to stow

arrivage [aʀivaʒ] nm consignment

arrivée [aʀive] nf arrival; (ligne d'arrivée)
finish

arriver [aʀive] vi to arrive; (survenir)
to happen, occur; **il arrive à Paris à
8h** he gets to ou arrives in Paris at 8; **à
quelle heure arrive le train de Lyon?**
what time does the train from Lyons
get in?; **~ à** (atteindre) to reach; **~ à faire
qch** to succeed in doing sth; **en ~ à
(finir par)** to come to; **il arrive que** it
happens that; **il lui arrive de faire** he
sometimes does

arrobase [aʀɔbaz] nf (Inform) @,
'at' sign

arrogance [aʀɔgɑ̃s] nf arrogance

arrogant, e [aʀɔgɑ̃, ɑ̃t] adj arrogant

arrondissement [aʀɔ̃dismɑ̃] nm
(Admin) ≈ district

arroser [aʀoze] vt to water; (victoire) to
celebrate (over a drink); (Culin) to baste;
arrosoir nm watering can

arsenal, -aux [aʀsənal, o] nm (Navig)
naval dockyard; (Mil) arsenal; (fig) gear,
paraphernalia

art [aʀ] nm art

artère [aʀtɛʀ] nf (Anat) artery; (rue)
main road

arthrite [aʀtʀit] nf arthritis

artichaut [aʀtiʃo] nm artichoke

article [aʀtikl] nm article; (Comm)
item, article; **à l'~ de la mort** at the
point of death

articulation [aʀtikylasjɔ̃] nf
articulation; (Anat) joint

articuler [aʀtikyle] vt to articulate

artificiel, le [aʀtifisjɛl] adj artificial

artisan [aʀtizɑ̃] nm artisan, (self-
employed) craftsman; **artisanal, e,
-aux** adj ou made by craftsmen; (péj)

cottage industry cpd; **de fabrication
artisanale** home-made; **artisanat** nm
arts and crafts pl

artiste [aʀtist] nm/f artist; (de variétés)
entertainer; (musicien etc) performer;
artistique adj artistic

as¹ [a] vb voir **avoir**

as² [ɑs] nm ace

ascenseur [asɑ̃sœʀ] nm lift (BRIT),
elevator (US)

ascension [asɑ̃sjɔ̃] nf ascent;
(de montagne) climb; **l'A~** (Rel) the
Ascension

● **ASCENSION**

● The **fête de l'Ascension** is a public
● holiday in France. It always falls on
● a Thursday, usually in May. Many
● French people take the following
● Friday off work too and enjoy a long
● weekend.

asiatique [azjatik] adj Asiatic, Asian
▷ A~ nm/f: **A~** Asian

Asie [azi] nf: **l'~** Asia

asile [azil] nm (refuge) refuge,
sanctuary; (Pol): **droit d'~** (political)
asylum

aspect [aspɛ] nm appearance, look;
(fig) aspect, side; **à l'~ de** at the sight of

asperge [aspɛʀʒ] nf asparagus no pl

asperger [aspɛʀʒe] vt to spray, sprinkle

asphalte [asfalt] nm asphalt

asphyxier [asfiksje] vt to suffocate,
asphyxiate; (fig) to stifle

aspirateur [aspiʀatœʀ] nm vacuum
cleaner; **passer l'~** to vacuum

aspirer [aspiʀe] vt (air) to inhale;
(liquide) to suck (up); (suj: appareil) to
suck up; **~ à** to aspire to

aspirine [aspiʀin] nf aspirin

assagir [asaʒiʀ]: **s'assagir** vi to
quieten down, settle down

assaisonnement [asɛzɔnmɑ̃] nm
seasoning

assaisonner [asɛzɔne] vt to season

assassin [asasɛ̃] nm murderer;

assassin; **assassiner** vt to murder; (esp Pol) to assassinate

assaut [aso] nm assault, attack; **prendre d'~** to storm, assault; **donner l'~ à** to attack

assécher [aseʃe] vt to drain

assemblage [asɑ̃blaʒ] nm (action) assembling; (de couleurs, choses) collection

assemblée [asɑ̃ble] nf (réunion) meeting; (assistance) gathering; (Pol) assembly; **l'A~ nationale** the National Assembly (the lower house of the French Parliament)

assembler [asɑ̃ble] vt (joindre, monter) to assemble, put together; (amasser) to gather (together), collect (together); **s'assembler** vi to gather

asseoir [aswaʀ] vt (malade, bébé) to sit up; (personne debout) to sit down; (autorité, réputation) to establish; **s'asseoir** vi to sit (o.s.) down

assez [ase] adv (suffisamment) enough, sufficiently; (passablement) rather, quite, fairly; **~ de pain/livres** enough ou sufficient bread/books; **vous en avez ~?** have you got enough?; **j'en ai ~!** I've had enough!

assidu, e [asidy] adj (appliqué) assiduous, painstaking; (ponctuel) regular

assied etc [asje] vb voir **asseoir**

assiérai etc [asjeʀe] vb voir **asseoir**

assiette [asjɛt] nf plate; (contenu) plate(ful); **il n'est pas dans son ~** he's not feeling quite himself; **assiette à dessert** dessert plate; **assiette anglaise** assorted cold meats; **assiette creuse** (soup) dish, soup plate; **assiette plate** (dinner) plate

assimiler [asimile] vt to assimilate, absorb; (comparer): **~ qch/qn à** to liken ou compare sth/sb to; **s'assimiler** vr (s'intégrer) to be assimilated

assis, e [asi, iz] pp de **asseoir** ▷ adj sitting (down), seated

assistance [asistɑ̃s] nf (public) audience; (aide) assistance; **enfant de**

l'A~ publique child in care

assistant, e [asistɑ̃, ɑ̃t] nm/f assistant; (d'université) probationary lecturer; **assistant(e) social(e)** social worker

assisté, e [asiste] adj (Auto) power assisted; **~ par ordinateur** computer-assisted; **direction ~e** power steering

assister [asiste] vt (aider) to assist; **~ à** (scène, événement) to witness; (conférence, séminaire) to attend, be at; (spectacle, match) to be at, see

association [asɔsjasjɔ̃] nf association; (Comm) partner

associé, e [asɔsje] nm/f associate; (Comm) partner

associer [asɔsje] vt to associate; **s'associer** vi to join together; **s'~ à qn pour faire** to join (forces) with sb to do; **s'~ à** (couleurs, qualités) to be combined with; (opinions, joie de qn) to share in; **~ qn à** (profits) to give sb a share of; (affaire) to make sb a partner in; (joie, triomphe) to include sb in; **~ qch à** (allier à) to combine sth with

assoiffé, e [aswafe] adj thirsty

assommer [asɔme] vt (étourdir, abrutir) to knock out, stun

Assomption [asɔ̃psjɔ̃] nf: **l'~** the Assumption

◦ **ASSOMPTION**

◦

◦ The **fête de l'Assomption**, more
◦ commonly known as 'le 15 août'
◦ is a national holiday in France.
◦ Traditionally, large numbers of
◦ holidaymakers leave home on 15
◦ August, frequently causing chaos
◦ on the roads.

assorti, e [asɔʀti] adj matched, matching; (varié) assorted; **~ à** matching; **assortiment** nm assortment, selection

assortir [asɔʀtiʀ] vt to match; **~ qch à** to match sth with; **~ qch de** to accompany sth with

assouplir [asupliʀ] vt to make supple;

(fig) to relax; **assouplissant** nm (fabric) softener

assumer [asyme] vt (fonction, emploi) to assume, take on

assurance [asyrɑ̃s] nf (certitude) assurance; (confiance en soi) (self-)confidence; (contrat) insurance (policy); (secteur commercial) insurance; **assurance au tiers** third-party insurance; **assurance maladie** health insurance; **assurance tous risques** (Auto) comprehensive insurance; **assurances sociales** ≈ National Insurance (BRIT), ≈ Social Security (US); **assurance-vie** nf life assurance ou insurance

assuré, e [asyre] adj (certain: réussite, échec) certain, sure; (air) assured; (pas) steady ▷ nm/f insured (person); **assurément** adv assuredly, most certainly

assurer [asyre] vt (Finance) to insure; (victoire etc) to ensure; (frontières, pouvoir) to make secure; (service) to provide, operate; (Comm) to insure o.s. (against); **s'~ de/ que** (vérifier) to make sure of/that; **s'~ (de)** (aide de qn) to secure; **~ à qn que** to assure sb that; **~ qn de** to assure sb of

asthmatique [asmatik] adj, nm/f asthmatic

asthme [asm] nm asthma

asticot [astiko] nm maggot

astre [astr] nm star

astrologie [astrɔlɔʒi] nf astrology

astronaute [astronot] nm/f astronaut

astronomie [astronɔmi] nf astronomy

astuce [astys] nf shrewdness, astuteness; (truc) trick, clever way; **astucieux, -euse** adj clever

atelier [atəlje] nm workshop; (de peintre) studio

athée [ate] adj atheistic ▷ nm/f atheist

Athènes [atɛn] n Athens

athlète [atlɛt] nm/f (Sport) athlete; **athlétisme** nm athletics sg

atlantique [atlɑ̃tik] adj Atlantic ▷ nm: **l'(océan) A~** the Atlantic (Ocean)

atlas [atlɑs] nm atlas

atmosphère [atmɔsfɛr] nf atmosphere

atome [atom] nm atom; **atomique** adj atomic, nuclear

atomiseur [atɔmizœr] nm atomizer

atout [atu] nm trump; (fig) asset

atroce [atrɔs] adj atrocious

attachant, e [ataʃɑ̃, ɑ̃t] adj engaging, lovable, likeable

attache [ataʃ] nf clip, fastener; (fig) tie

attacher [ataʃe] vt to tie up; (étiquette) to attach, tie on; (ceinture) to fasten ▷ vi (poêle, riz) to stick; **s'attacher à** (par affection) to become attached to; **~ qch à** to tie ou attach sth to

attaque [atak] nf attack; (cérébrale) stroke; (d'épilepsie) fit

attaquer [atake] vt to attack ▷ vi to attack; **s'attaquer à** vt (personne) to attack; (problème) to tackle; **~ qn en justice** to bring an action against sb, sue sb

attarder [atarde]: **s'attarder** vi to linger

atteindre [atɛ̃dr] vt to reach; (blesser) to hit; (émouvoir) to affect; **atteint, e** adj (Méd): **être atteint de** to be suffering from; **atteinte** nf: **hors d'atteinte** out of reach; **porter atteinte à** to strike a blow at

attendant [atɑ̃dɑ̃] adv: **en ~** meanwhile, in the meantime

attendre [atɑ̃dr] vt (gén) to wait for; (être destiné ou réservé à) to await, be in store for ▷ vi to wait; **s'attendre à (ce que)** to expect (that); **attendez-moi, s'il vous plaît** wait for me, please; **~ un enfant** to be expecting a baby; **~ de faire/d'être** to wait until one does/is; **attendez qu'il vienne** wait until he comes; **~ qch de** to expect sth of

> **Attention** à ne pas traduire **attendre** par to attend.

attendrir [atɑ̃drir] vt to move (to pity); (viande) to tenderize

attendu, e [atɑ̃dy] adj (visiteur)
expected; (événement) long-awaited; ~
que considering that, since

attentat [atɑ̃ta] nm assassination
attempt; **attentat à la pudeur**
indecent assault no pl; **attentat
suicide** suicide bombing

attente [atɑ̃t] nf wait; (espérance)
expectation

attenter [atɑ̃te]: **~ à** vt (liberté) to
violate; **~ à la vie de qn** to make an
attempt on sb's life

attentif, -ive [atɑ̃tif, iv] adj (auditeur)
attentive; (examen) careful; **~ à**
careful to

attention [atɑ̃sjɔ̃] nf attention;
(prévenance) attention, thoughtfulness
no pl; **à l'~ de** for the attention of;
faire ~ (à) to be careful (of); **faire ~ (à ce
que)** to make sure that; **~!** careful!,
watch out!; **~ à la voiture!** watch
out for that car!; **attentionné, e** adj
thoughtful, considerate

atténuer [atenɥe] vt (douleur) to
alleviate, ease; (couleurs) to soften;
s'atténuer vi to ease; (violence etc)
to abate

atterrir [ateriʀ] vi to land;
atterrissage nm landing

attestation [atɛstasjɔ̃] nf certificate

attirant, e [atiʀɑ̃, ɑ̃t] adj attractive,
appealing

attirer [atiʀe] vt to attract; (appâter) to
lure, entice; **~ qn dans un coin/vers
soi** to draw sb into a corner/towards
one; **~ l'attention de qn** to attract
sb's attention; **~ l'attention de qn
sur** to draw sb's attention to; **s'~ des
ennuis** to bring trouble upon o.s., get
into trouble

attitude [atityd] nf attitude; (position
du corps) bearing

attraction [atʀaksjɔ̃] nf (gén)
attraction; (de cabaret, cirque) number

attrait [atʀɛ] nm appeal, attraction

attraper [atʀape] vt (gén) to catch;
(habitude, amende) to get, pick up;
(fam: duper) to con; **se faire ~** (fam) to

be told off

attrayant, e [atʀɛjɑ̃, ɑ̃t] adj
attractive

attribuer [atʀibɥe] vt (prix) to
award; (rôle, tâche) to allocate, assign;
(imputer): **~ qch à** to attribute sth to;
s'attribuer vt (s'approprier) to claim
for o.s.

attrister [atʀiste] vt to sadden

attroupement [atʀupmɑ̃] nm crowd

attrouper [atʀupe]: **s'attrouper** vi
to gather

au [o] prép +dét = **à +le**

aubaine [obɛn] nf godsend

aube [ob] nf dawn, daybreak; **à l'~** at
dawn ou daybreak

aubépine [obepin] nf hawthorn

auberge [obɛʀʒ] nf inn; **auberge de
jeunesse** youth hostel

aubergine [obɛʀʒin] nf aubergine

aucun, e [okœ̃, yn] dét no, tournure
négative +any; (positif): plus ▷ pron none,
tournure négative +any; (any(one)):
**sans ~
doute** without any doubt; **plus
qu'~ autre** more than any other; **il
le fera mieux qu'~ de nous** he'll do
it better than any of us; **~ des deux**
neither of the two; **~ d'entre eux** none
of them

audace [odas] nf daring, boldness;
(péj) audacity; **audacieux, -euse** adj
daring, bold

au-delà [od(ə)la] adv beyond ▷ nm: **l'~**
the hereafter; **~ de** beyond

au-dessous [odsu] adv underneath;
below; **~ de** under(neath), below;
(limite, somme etc) below, under; (dignité,
condition) below

au-dessus [odsy] adv above; **~ de**
above

au-devant [od(ə)vɑ̃]: **~ de** prép: **aller
~ de** (personne, danger) to go (out) and
meet; (souhaits de qn) to anticipate

audience [odjɑ̃s] nf audience; (Jur:
séance) hearing

audiovisuel, le [odjovizɥɛl] adj
audiovisual

audition [odisjɔ̃] nf (ouïe, écoute)

hearing; (Jur: de témoins) examination; (Mus, Théâtre: épreuve) audition

auditoire [oditwar] nm audience

augmentation [ɔɡmɑ̃tasjɔ̃] nf increase; **augmentation (de salaire)** rise (in salary) (BRIT), (pay) raise (US)

augmenter [ɔɡmɑ̃te] vt (gén) to increase; (salaire, prix) to increase, raise, put up; (employé) to increase the salary of ▷ vi to increase

augure [oɡyr] nm: **de bon/mauvais ~** of good/ill omen

aujourd'hui [oʒurdɥi] adv today

aumône [omon] nf alms sg; **aumônier** [omonje] nm chaplain

auparavant [oparavɑ̃] adv before(hand)

auprès [oprɛ]: **~ de** prép next to, close to; (recourir, s'adresser) to; (en comparaison de) compared with

auquel [okɛl] prép +pron = **à +lequel**

aurai etc [ɔre] vb voir **avoir**

aurons etc [ɔrɔ̃] vb voir **avoir**

aurore [`ʀ] nf dawn, daybreak

ausculter [oskylte] vt to sound (the chest of)

aussi [osi] adv (également) also, too; (de comparaison) as ▷ conj therefore, consequently; **~ fort que** as strong as; **moi ~** me too

aussitôt [osito] adv straight away, immediately; **~ que** as soon as

austère [ostɛr] adj austere

austral, e [ostral] adj southern

Australie [ostrali] nf: **l'~** Australia; **australien, ne** adj Australian ▷ nm/f: **Australien, ne** Australian

autant [otɑ̃] adv (intensité) so much; **je ne savais pas que tu la détestais ~** I didn't know you hated her so much; (comparatif): **~ (que)** as much (as); (nombre): **~ de** as many (as); **~ (de)** so much (ou many); as much (ou many); **~ partir** we (ou you etc) may as well leave; **~ dire que ...** one might as well say that ...; **pour ~** for all that; **d'~ plus/mieux (que)** all the more/the better (since)

autel [otɛl] nm altar

auteur [otœr] nm author

authentique [otɑ̃tik] adj authentic, genuine

auto [oto] nf car

auto...: **autobiographie** nf autobiography; **autobronzant** nm self-tanning cream (or lotion etc); **autobus** nm bus; **autocar** nm coach

autochtone [otɔkton] nm/f native

auto...: **autocollant, e** adj self-adhesive; (enveloppe) self-seal ▷ nm sticker; **autocuiseur** nm pressure cooker; **autodéfense** nf self-defence; **autodidacte** nm/f self-taught person; **auto-école** nf driving school; **autographe** nm autograph

automate [otɔmat] nm (machine) (automatic) machine

automatique [otɔmatik] adj automatic ▷ nm: **l'~** direct dialling

automne [otɔn] nm autumn (BRIT), fall (US)

automobile [otɔmɔbil] adj motor cpd, car cpd ▷ nf (motor) car; **automobiliste** nm/f motorist

autonome [otɔnɔm] adj autonomous; **autonomie** nf autonomy; (Pol) self-government, autonomy

autopsie [otɔpsi] nf post-mortem (examination), autopsy

autoradio [otoradjo] nm car radio

autorisation [otɔrizasjɔ̃] nf permission, authorization; (papiers) permit

autorisé, e [otɔrize] adj (opinion, sources) authoritative

autoriser [otɔrize] vt to give permission for, authorize; (fig) to allow (of)

autoritaire [otɔritɛr] adj authoritarian

autorité [otɔrite] nf authority; **faire ~** to be authoritative; **les ~s** the authorities

autoroute [otorut] nf motorway (BRIT), highway (US); **~ de**

l'information (*Inform*) information
superhighway

○ **AUTOROUTE**

Motorways in France, indicated
by blue road signs with the letter A
followed by a number, are toll roads.
The speed limit is 130 km/h (110 km/
h when it is raining). At the tollgate,
the lanes marked 'réservé' and with
an orange 't' are reserved for people
who subscribe to 'télépéage', an
electronic payment system.

auto-stop [otostɔp] *nm*: **faire de l'~**
to hitch-hike; **prendre qn en ~** to give
sb a lift; **auto-stoppeur, -euse** *nm/f*
hitch-hiker

autour [otur] *adv* around; **~ de** around;
tout ~ all around

○ **MOT-CLÉ**

autre [otr] *adj* **1** (*différent*) other,
different; **je préférerais un autre
verre** I'd prefer another *ou* a different
glass
2 (*supplémentaire*) other; **je voudrais
un autre verre d'eau** I'd like another
glass of water
3: **autre chose** something else; **autre
part** somewhere else; **d'autre part**
on the other hand
▷ *pron*: **un autre** another (one);
nous/vous autres us/you; **d'autres**
others; **l'autre** the other (one); **les
autres** the others; (*autrui*) others; **l'un
et l'autre** both of them; **se détester
l'un l'autre/les uns les autres** to
hate each other *ou* one another; **d'une
semaine à l'autre** from one week to
the next; (*incessamment*) any week now;
entre autres (*personnes*) among others;
(*choses*) among other things

autrefois [otrəfwa] *adv* in the past
autrement [otrəmã] *adv* differently;

(*d'une manière différente*) in another way;
(*sinon*) otherwise; **~ dit** in other words

Autriche [otriʃ] *nf*: **l'~** Austria;
autrichien, ne *adj* Austrian ▷ *nm/f*:
Autrichien, ne Austrian

autruche [otryʃ] *nf* ostrich

aux [o] *prép* +*dét* = **à +les**

auxiliaire [oksiljɛr] *adj*, *nm/f* auxiliary

auxquelles [okɛl] *prép* +*pron* = **à
+lesquelles**

auxquels [okɛl] *prép* +*pron* = **à
+lesquels**

avalanche [avalɑ̃ʃ] *nf* avalanche

avaler [avale] *vt* to swallow

avance [avɑ̃s] *nf* (*de troupes etc*)
advance; progress; (*d'argent*) advance;
(*sur un concurrent*) lead; **avances** *nfpl*
(*amoureuses*) advances; (**être**) **en ~** (*sur
le programme*) (to be) ahead; (*sur un
programme*) (to be) ahead of schedule; **à
l'~, d'~** in advance

avancé, e [avɑ̃se] *adj* advanced;
(*travail*) well on, well under way

avancement [avɑ̃smɑ̃] *nm*
(*professionnel*) promotion

avancer [avɑ̃se] *vi* to move forward,
advance; (*projet, travail*) to make
progress; (*montre, réveil*) to be fast; to
gain ▷ *vt* to move forward, advance;
(*argent*) to advance; (*montre, pendule*)
to put forward; **s'avancer** *vi* to move
forward, advance; (*fig*) to commit o.s.

avant [avɑ̃] *prép, adv* before ▷ *adj inv*:
siège/roue ~ front seat/wheel ▷ *nm*
(*d'un véhicule, bâtiment*) front; (*Sport*:
joueur) forward; **~ qu'il (ne) parte**
before he goes *ou* leaves; **~ de partir**
before leaving; **~ tout** (*surtout*) above
all; **à l'~** (*dans un véhicule*) in (the) front;
en ~ (*se pencher, tomber*) forward(s);
partir en ~ to go on ahead; **en ~ de**
in front of

avantage [avɑ̃taʒ] *nm* advantage;
avantages sociaux fringe benefits;
avantager *vt* (*favoriser*) to favour;
(*embellir*) to flatter; **avantageux, -euse**
adj (*prix*) attractive

avant...: **avant-bras** *nm inv* forearm;
avant-coureur *adj inv*: **signe avant-**

coureur advance indication ou sign;
avant-dernier, -ière adj, nm/f next
to last, last but one; **avant-goût** nm
foretaste; **avant-hier** adv the day
before yesterday; **avant-première**
nf (de film) preview; **avant-veille** nf:
l'avant-veille two days before

avare [avar] adj miserly, avaricious
▷ nm/f miser; **~ de** (compliments etc)
sparing of

avec [avɛk] prép with; (à l'égard de)
to(wards); **et ~ ça?** (dans magasin)
anything else?

avenir [avnir] nm future: **à l'~**
in future; **politicien/métier d'~**
politician/job with prospects ou a
future

aventure [avɑ̃tyr] nf adventure;
(amoureuse) affair; **aventureux, -euse**
adj adventurous, venturesome; (projet)
risky, chancy

avenue [avny] nf avenue

avérer [avere]: **s'avérer** vb +attrib to
prove (to be)

averse [avɛrs] nf shower

averti, e [avɛrti] adj (well-)informed

avertir [avɛrtir] vt: **~ qn** (de qch/que)
to warn sb (of sth/that); (renseigner)
to inform sb (of sth/that); **avertissement**
nm warning; **avertisseur** nm horn,
siren

aveu, x [avø] nm confession

aveugle [avœgl] adj blind ▷ nm/f blind
man/woman

aviation [avjasjɔ̃] nf aviation; (sport)
flying; (Mil) air force

avide [avid] adj eager; (péj) greedy,
grasping

avion [avjɔ̃] nm (aero)plane (BRIT),
(air)plane (US); **aller (quelque part)
en ~** to go (somewhere) by plane, fly
(somewhere); **par ~** by airmail; **avion à
réaction** jet (plane)

aviron [avirɔ̃] nm oar; (sport): **l'~**
rowing

avis [avi] nm opinion; (notification)
notice; **à mon ~** in my opinion;
changer d'~ to change one's mind;

jusqu'à nouvel ~ until further notice

aviser [avize] vt (informer): **~ qn de/que**
to advise ou inform sb of/that ▷ vi
to think about things, assess the
situation; **nous ~ons sur place** we'll
work something out once we're there;
s'~ de qch/que to become suddenly
aware of sth/that; **s'~ de faire** to take
it into one's head to do

avocat, e [avɔka, at] nm/f (Jur)
barrister (BRIT), lawyer ▷ nm (Culin)
avocado (pear); **~ de la défense**
counsel for the defence; **avocat
général** assistant public prosecutor

avoine [avwan] nf oats pl

⊙ MOT-CLÉ

avoir [avwar] nm assets pl, resources
pl; (Comm) credit
  ▷ vt 1 (posséder) to have; **elle a 2
enfants/une belle maison** she has
(got) 2 children/a lovely house; **il a les
yeux bleus** he has (got) blue eyes; **vous
avez du sel?** do you have any salt?;
avoir du courage/de la patience to
be brave/patient
  2 (âge, dimensions) to be: **il a 3 ans** he
is 3 (years old); **le mur a 3 mètres de
haut** the wall is 3 metres high; voir aussi
faim; peur etc
  3 (fam: duper) to do, have; **on vous a
eu!** (dupé) you've been done ou had!;
(fait une plaisanterie) we ou they had
you there
  4: **en avoir après** ou **contre qn** to have
a grudge against sb; **en avoir assez** to
be fed up; **j'en ai pour une demi-heure**
it'll take me half an hour
  5 (obtenir, attraper) to get; **j'ai réussi
à avoir mon train** I managed to
get ou catch my train; **j'ai réussi à
avoir le renseignement qu'il me
fallait** I managed to get (hold of) the
information I needed
  6 (éprouver): **avoir de la peine** to be
ou feel sad
  ▷ vb aux 1 to have; **avoir mangé/dormi**

to have eaten/slept
2 (*avoir +à + infinitif*): **avoir à faire qch**
to have to do sth; **vous n'avez qu'à lui
demander** you only have to ask him
▷ *vb impers* **1**: **il y a** (+ *singulier*) there is; (+
pluriel) there are; **il y avait du café/des
gâteaux** there was coffee/there were
cakes; **qu'y-a-t-il?, qu'est-ce qu'il y a?**
what's the matter?, what is it?; **il doit
y avoir une explication** there must be
an explanation; **il n'y a qu'à ...** we (*ou*
you *etc*) will just have to ...; **il ne peut y
en avoir qu'un** there can only be one
2 (*temporel*): **il y a 10 ans** 10 years ago;
il y a 10 ans/longtemps que je le sais
I've known it for 10 years/a long time; **il
y a 10 ans qu'il est arrivé** it's 10 years
since he arrived

avortement [avɔʀtəmɑ̃] *nm* abortion
avouer [avwe] *vt* (*crime, défaut*) to
confess (to); **~ avoir fait/que** to admit
ou confess to having done/that
avril [avʀil] *nm* April
axe [aks] *nm* axis; (*de roue etc*) axle;
(*fig*) main line; **axe routier** main road,
trunk road (BRIT), highway (US)
ayons *etc* [ɛjɔ̃] *vb voir* **avoir**

bâbord [babɔʀ] *nm*: **à ~** to port, on the
port side
baby-foot [babifut] *nm* table football
bac [bak] *abr m* = **baccalauréat** ▷ *nm*
(*récipient*) tub
baccalauréat [bakalɔʀea] *nm* high
school diploma
bâcler [bakle] *vt* to botch (up)
baffe [baf] (*fam*) *nf* slap, clout
bafouiller [bafuje] *vi, vt* to stammer
bagage [bagaʒ] *nm* piece of luggage;
(*connaissances*) background,
knowledge; **nos ~s ne sont pas arrivés**
our luggage hasn't arrived; **bagage à
main** piece of hand-luggage
bagarre [bagaʀ] *nf* fight, brawl;
bagarrer: se bagarrer *vi* to have a
fight *ou* scuffle, fight
bagnole [baɲɔl] (*fam*) *nf* car
bague [bag] *nf* ring; **bague de
fiançailles** engagement ring
baguette [baget] *nf* stick; (*cuisine
chinoise*) chopstick; (*de chef d'orchestre*)
baton; (*pain*) stick of (French) bread;

baguette magique magic wand
baie [bɛ] nf (Géo) bay; (fruit) berry; **baie (vitrée)** picture window
baignade [bɛɲad] nf bathing; "**~ interdite**" "no bathing"
baigner [bɛɲe] vt (bébé) to bath; **se baigner** vi to have a swim, go swimming ou bathing; **baignoire** nf bath(tub)
bail [baj, bo] (pl **baux**) nm lease
bâiller [bɑje] vi to yawn; (être ouvert) to gape
bain [bɛ̃] nm bath; **prendre un ~** to have a bath; **se mettre dans le ~** (fig) to get into it ou things; **bain de bouche** mouthwash; **bain moussant** bubble bath; **bain de soleil:** **prendre un bain de soleil** to sunbathe; **bain-marie** nm: **faire chauffer au bain-marie** (boîte etc) to immerse in boiling water
baiser [beze] nm kiss ▷ vt (main, front) to kiss; (fam!) to screw (!)
baisse [bes] nf fall, drop; **être en ~** to be falling, be declining
baisser [bese] vt to lower; (radio, chauffage) to turn down ▷ vi to fall, drop, go down; (vue, santé) to fail, dwindle; **se baisser** vi to bend down
bal [bal] nm dance; (grande soirée) ball; **bal costumé** fancy-dress ball
balade [balad] (fam) nf (à pied) walk, stroll; (en voiture) drive; **balader** (fam): **se balader** vi to go for a walk ou stroll; **baladeur** nm personal stereo, Walkman®
balai [balɛ] nm broom, brush
balance [balɑ̃s] nf scales pl; (signe): **la B~** Libra; **balance commerciale** balance of trade
balancer [balɑ̃se] vt to swing; (fam: lancer) to fling, chuck; (: jeter) to chuck out; **se balancer** vi to swing, rock; **se ~ de** (fam) not to care about; **balançoire** nf swing; (sur pivot) seesaw
balayer [baleje] vt (feuilles etc) to sweep up, brush up; (pièce) to sweep; (objections) to sweep aside; (suj: radar) to scan; **balayeur, -euse** nm/f

roadsweeper
balbutier [balbysje] vi, vt to stammer
balcon [balkɔ̃] nm balcony; (Théâtre) dress circle; **avez-vous une chambre avec ~?** do you have a room with a balcony?
Bâle [bal] n Basle, Basel
Baléares [baleaʀ] nfpl: **les ~** the Balearic Islands, the Balearics
baleine [balɛn] nf whale
balise [baliz] nf (Navig) beacon; (marker) buoy; (Aviat) runway light, beacon; (Auto, Ski) sign, marker; **baliser** vt to mark out (with lights etc)
balle [bal] nf (de fusil) bullet; (de sport) ball; (fam: franc) franc
ballerine [bal(ə)ʀin] nf (danseuse) ballet dancer; (chaussure) ballet shoe
ballet [balɛ] nm ballet
ballon [balɔ̃] nm (de sport) ball; (jouet, Aviat) balloon; **ballon de football** football
balnéaire [balneɛʀ] adj seaside cpd; **station ~** seaside resort
balustrade [balystʀad] nf railings pl, handrail
bambin [bɑ̃bɛ̃] nm little child
bambou [bɑ̃bu] nm bamboo
banal, e [banal] adj banal, commonplace; (péj) trite; **banalité** nf banality
banane [banan] nf banana; (sac) waist-bag, bum-bag
banc [bɑ̃] nm seat, bench; (de poissons) shoal; **banc d'essai** (fig) testing ground
bancaire [bɑ̃kɛʀ] adj banking; (chèque, carte) bank cpd
bancal, e [bɑ̃kal] adj wobbly
bandage [bɑ̃daʒ] nm bandage
bande [bɑ̃d] nf (de tissu etc) strip; (Méd) bandage; (motif) stripe; (magnétique etc) tape; (groupe) band; (: péj) bunch; **faire ~ à part** to keep to o.s.; **bande dessinée** comic strip; **bande sonore** sound track
bande-annonce [bɑ̃danɔ̃s] nf trailer
bandeau, x [bɑ̃do] nm headband; (sur les yeux) blindfold
bander [bɑ̃de] vt (blessure) to bandage;

~ les yeux à qn to blindfold sb
bandit [bãdi] nm bandit
bandoulière [bãduljɛʀ] nf: **en ~** (slung ou worn) across the shoulder
Bangladesh [bãɡladɛʃ] nm: **le ~** Bangladesh
banlieue [bãljø] nf suburbs pl; **lignes/ quartiers de ~** suburban lines/areas; **trains de ~** commuter trains
bannir [baniʀ] vt to banish
banque [bãk] nf bank; (activités) banking; **banque de données** data bank
banquet [bãkɛ] nm dinner; (d'apparat) banquet
banquette [bãkɛt] nf seat
banquier [bãkje] nm banker
banquise [bãkiz] nf ice field
baptême [batɛm] nm christening, baptism; **baptême de l'air** first flight
baptiser [batize] vt to baptize, christen
bar [baʀ] nm bar
baraque [baʀak] nf shed; (fam) house; (dans une fête foraine) stall, booth; **baraqué, e** (fam) adj well-built, hefty
barbare [baʀbaʀ] adj barbaric
barbe [baʀb] nf beard; **la ~!** (fam) what a drag ou bore!; **quelle ~!** (fam) what a drag ou bore!; **à la ~ de qn** under sb's nose; **barbe à papa** candy-floss (BRIT), cotton candy (US)
barbelé [baʀbəle] adj, nm: **(fil de fer) ~** barbed wire no pl
barbiturique [baʀbityʀik] nm barbiturate
barbouiller [baʀbuje] vt to daub; **avoir l'estomac barbouillé** to feel queasy
barbu, e [baʀby] adj bearded
barder [baʀde] (fam) vi: **ça va ~** sparks will fly, things are going to get hot
barème [baʀɛm] nm (Scol) scale; (table de référence) table
baril [baʀi(l)] nm barrel; (poudre) keg
bariolé, e [baʀjɔle] adj gaudily-coloured
baromètre [baʀɔmɛtʀ] nm barometer

baron, ne [baʀɔ̃] nm/f baron(ess)
baroque [baʀɔk] adj (Art) baroque; (fig) weird
barque [baʀk] nf small boat
barquette [baʀkɛt] nf (pour repas) tray; (pour fruits) punnet
barrage [baʀaʒ] nm dam; (sur route) roadblock, barricade
barre [baʀ] nf bar; (Navig) helm; (écrite) line, stroke
barreau, x [baʀo] nm bar; (Jur): **le ~** the Bar
barrer [baʀe] vt (route etc) to block; (mot) to cross out; (chèque) to cross (BRIT); (Navig) to steer; **se barrer** (fam) ▷ vi to clear off
barrette [baʀɛt] nf (pour cheveux) (hair) slide (BRIT) ou clip (US)
barricader [baʀikade]: **se barricader** vi to barricade o.s.
barrière [baʀjɛʀ] nf fence; (obstacle) barrier; (porte) gate
barrique [baʀik] nf barrel, cask
bar-tabac [baʀtaba] nm bar (which sells tobacco and stamps)
bas, basse [ba, bas] adj low ▷ nm bottom, lower part; (vêtement) stocking ▷ adv low; (parler) softly; **au ~ mot** at the lowest estimate; **en ~** down below; (d'une liste, d'un mur etc) at/to the bottom; (dans une maison) downstairs; **en ~ de** at the bottom of; **un enfant en ~ âge** a young child; **à ~ ...!** down with ...!
bas-côté [bakote] nm (de route) verge (BRIT), shoulder (US)
basculer [baskyle] vi to fall over, topple (over); (benne) to tip up ▷ vt (contenu) to tip out; (benne) to tip up
base [baz] nf base; (Pol) rank and file; (fondement, principe) basis; **de ~** basic; **à ~ de café** etc coffee etc-based; **base de données** database; **baser** vt to base; **se baser sur** vt (preuves) to base one's argument on
bas-fond [bafɔ̃] nm (Navig) shallow; **bas-fonds** nmpl (fig) dregs
basilic [bazilik] nm (Culin) basil

basket [baskɛt] nm trainer (BRIT), sneaker (US); (aussi: **~-ball**) basketball

basque [bask] adj Basque ▷ nm/f: **B~** Basque; **le Pays Basque** the Basque Country

basse [bas] adj voir **bas** ▷ nf (Mus) bass; **basse-cour** nf farmyard

bassin [basɛ̃] nm (pièce d'eau) pond, pool; (de fontaine;: Géo) basin; (Anat) pelvis; (portuaire) dock

bassine [basin] nf (ustensile) basin; (contenu) bowl(ful)

basson [basɔ̃] nm bassoon

bat [ba] vb voir **battre**

bataille [bataj] nf (Mil) battle; (rixe) fight; **elle avait les cheveux en ~** her hair was a mess

bateau, x [bato] nm boat, ship; **bateau-mouche** nm passenger pleasure boat (on the Seine)

bâti, e [bati] adj: **bien ~** well-built; **terrain ~** piece of land that has been built on

bâtiment [batimɑ̃] nm building; (Navig) ship, vessel; (industrie) building trade

bâtir [batir] vt to build

bâtisse [batis] nf building

bâton [batɔ̃] nm stick; **parler à ~s rompus** to chat about this and that

bats [ba] vb voir **battre**

battement [batmɑ̃] nm (de cœur) beat; (intervalle) interval; **10 minutes de ~** 10 minutes to spare

batterie [batri] nf (Mil, Élec) battery; (Mus) drums pl, drum kit; **batterie de cuisine** pots and pans pl, kitchen utensils pl

batteur [batœr] nm (Mus) drummer; (appareil) whisk

battre [batr] vt to beat; (blé) to thresh; (passer au peigne fin) to scour; (cartes) to shuffle ▷ vi (cœur) to beat; (volets etc) to bang, rattle; **se battre** vi to fight; **~ la mesure** to beat time; **~ son plein** to be at its height, be going full swing; **~ des mains** to clap one's hands

baume [bom] nm balm

bavard, e [bavar, ard] adj (very) talkative; gossipy; **bavarder** vi to chatter; (commérer) to gossip; (divulguer un secret) to blab

baver [bave] vi to dribble; (chien) to slobber; **en ~** (fam) to have a hard time (of it)

bavoir [bavwar] nm bib

bavure [bavyr] nf smudge; (fig) hitch; (policière etc) blunder

bazar [bazar] nm general store; (fam) jumble; **bazarder** (fam) vt to chuck out

BCBG sigle adj (= bon chic bon genre) preppy, smart and trendy

BD sigle f = **bande dessinée**

bd abr = **boulevard**

béant, e [beɑ̃, ɑ̃t] adj gaping

beau, bel, belle [bo, bɛl] (mpl **~x**) adj beautiful, lovely; (homme) handsome; (femme) beautiful ▷ adv: **il fait ~** the weather's fine ▷ nm: **faire le ~** (chien) to sit up and beg; **un ~ jour** one (fine) day; **de plus belle** more than ever, even more; **on a ~ essayer** however hard we try; **bel et bien** well and truly; **le plus ~ c'est que ...** the best of it is that ...

MOT-CLÉ

beaucoup [boku] adv **1** a lot; **il boit beaucoup** he drinks a lot; **il ne boit pas beaucoup** he doesn't drink much ou a lot

2 (suivi de plus, trop etc) much, a lot; **il est beaucoup plus grand** he is much ou a lot taller; **c'est beaucoup plus cher** it's a lot ou much more expensive; **il a beaucoup plus de temps que moi** he has much ou a lot more time than me; **il y a beaucoup plus de touristes ici** there are a lot ou many more tourists here; **beaucoup trop vite** much too fast; **il fume beaucoup trop** he smokes far too much

3: **beaucoup de** (nombre) many, a lot of; (quantité) a lot of; **beaucoup d'étudiants/de touristes** a lot of ou many students/tourists; **beaucoup**

de courage a lot of courage; **il n'a pas beaucoup d'argent** he hasn't got much *ou* a lot of money

4: de beaucoup by far

beau...: beau-fils *nm* son-in-law; (*remariage*) stepson; **beau-frère** *nm* brother-in-law; **beau-père** *nm* father-in-law; (*remariage*) stepfather

beauté [bote] *nf* beauty; **de toute ~** beautiful; **finir qch en ~** to complete sth brilliantly

beaux-arts [bozar] *nmpl* fine arts

beaux-parents [boparã] *nmpl* wife's/ husband's family, in-laws

bébé [bebe] *nm* baby

bec [bɛk] *nm* beak, bill; (*de théière*) spout; (*de casserole*) lip; (*fam*) mouth; **bec de gaz** (*street*) gaslamp

bêche [bɛʃ] *nf* spade; **bêcher** *vt* to dig

bedaine [bədɛn] *nf* paunch

bedonnant, e [bədɔnã, ãt] *adj* potbellied

bée [be] *adj:* **bouche ~** gaping

bégayer [begeje] *vt, vi* to stammer

beige [bɛʒ] *adj* beige

beignet [bɛɲɛ] *nm* fritter

bel [bɛl] *adj voir* **beau**

bêler [bele] *vi* to bleat

belette [bəlɛt] *nf* weasel

belge [bɛlʒ] *adj* Belgian ▷ *nm/f:* **B~** Belgian

Belgique [bɛlʒik] *nf:* **la ~** Belgium

bélier [belje] *nm* ram; (*signe*): **le B~** Aries

belle [bɛl] *adj voir* **beau** ▷ *nf* (*Sport*): **la ~** the decider; **belle-fille** *nf* daughter-in-law; (*remariage*) stepdaughter; **belle-mère** *nf* mother-in-law; stepmother; **belle-sœur** *nf* sister-in-law

belvédère [bɛlvedɛr] *nm* panoramic viewpoint (*or small building there*)

bémol [bemɔl] *nm* (*Mus*) flat

bénédiction [benediksjɔ̃] *nf* blessing

bénéfice [benefis] *nm* (*Comm*) profit; (*avantage*) benefit; **bénéficier de** *vt* to enjoy; (*situation*) to benefit by *ou* from; **bénéfique** *adj* beneficial

Benelux [benelyks] *nm:* **le ~** Benelux, the Benelux countries

bénévole [benevɔl] *adj* voluntary, unpaid

bénin, -igne [benɛ̃, iɲ] *adj* minor, mild; (*tumeur*) benign

bénir [benir] *vt* to bless; **bénit, e** *adj* consecrated; **eau bénite** holy water

benne [bɛn] *nf* skip; (*de téléphérique*) (cable) car; **benne à ordures** (*amovible*) skip

berceau, x [bɛrso] *nm* cradle, crib

bercer [bɛrse] *vt* to rock, cradle; (*suj: musique etc*) to lull; **~ qn de** (*promesses etc*) to delude sb with; **berceuse** *nf* lullaby

béret [berɛ] *nm* (*aussi:* **~ basque**) beret

berge [bɛrʒ] *nf* bank

berger, -ère [bɛrʒe, ɛr] *nm/f* shepherd(-ess); **berger allemand** alsatian (*BRIT*), German shepherd

Berlin [bɛrlɛ̃] *n* Berlin

Bermudes [bɛrmyd] *nfpl:* **les (îles) ~** Bermuda

Berne [bɛrn(ə)] *n* Bern

berner [bɛrne] *vt* to fool

besogne [bəzɔɲ] *nf* work *no pl*, job

besoin [bəzwɛ̃] *nm* need; **avoir ~ de qch/faire qch** to need sth/to do sth; **au ~** if need be; **le ~** (*pauvreté*) need, want; **être dans le ~** to be in need *ou* want; **faire ses ~s** to relieve o.s.

bestiole [bɛstjɔl] *nf* (tiny) creature

bétail [betaj] *nm* livestock, cattle *pl*

bête [bɛt] *nf* animal; (*bestiole*) insect, creature ▷ *adj* stupid, silly; **il cherche la petite ~** he's being pernickety *ou* over fussy; **bête noire** pet hate; **bête sauvage** wild beast *ou* animal

bêtise [betiz] *nf* stupidity; (*action*) stupid thing (to say *ou* do)

béton [betɔ̃] *nm* concrete; **(en) ~** (*alibi, argument*) cast iron; **béton armé** reinforced concrete

betterave [bɛtrav] *nf* beetroot (*BRIT*), beet (*US*); **betterave sucrière** sugar beet sugar beet

Beur [bœʀ] nm/f person of North African origin living in France

beurre [bœʀ] nm butter; **beurrer** vt to butter; **beurrier** nm butter dish

biais [bjɛ] nm (moyen) device, expedient; (aspect) angle; **en ~, de ~** (obliquement) at an angle; **par le ~ de** by means of

bibelot [biblo] nm trinket, curio

biberon [bibʀɔ̃] nm (feeding) bottle; **nourrir au ~** to bottle-feed

bible [bibl] nf bible

biblio... [bibli] préfixe: **bibliobus** nm mobile library van; **bibliothécaire** nm/f librarian; **bibliothèque** nf library; (meuble) bookcase

bic® [bik] nm Biro®

bicarbonate [bikaʀbɔnat] nm: **~ (de soude)** bicarbonate of soda

biceps [bisɛps] nm biceps

biche [biʃ] nf doe

bicolore [bikɔlɔʀ] adj two-coloured

bicoque [bikɔk] (péj) nf shack

bicyclette [bisiklɛt] nf bicycle

bidet [bidɛ] nm bidet

bidon [bidɔ̃] nm can ▷ adj inv (fam) phoney

bidonville [bidɔ̃vil] nm shanty town

bidule [bidyl] (fam) nm thingumajig

⭕ **MOT-CLÉ**

bien [bjɛ̃] nm **1** (avantage, profit): **faire du bien à qn** to do sb good; **dire du bien de** to speak well of; **c'est pour son bien** it's for his own good

2 (possession, patrimoine) possession, property; **son bien le plus précieux** his most treasured possession; **avoir du bien** to have property; **biens (de consommation** etc) (consumer etc) goods

3 (moral): **le bien** good; **distinguer le bien du mal** to tell good from evil

▷ adv **1** (de façon satisfaisante): **elle travaille/mange bien** she works/eats well; **croyant bien faire, je/il ...** thinking I/he was doing the

right thing, I/he ...; **tiens-toi bien!** (assieds-toi correctement) sit up straight!; (debout) stand up straight!; (sois sage) behave yourself!; (prépare-toi) wait for it!; **c'est bien fait!** it serves him (ou her etc) right!

2 (valeur intensive) quite; **bien jeune** quite young; **bien assez** quite enough; **bien mieux** (very) much better; **j'espère bien y aller** I do hope to go; **je veux bien le faire** (concession) I'm quite willing to do it; **il faut bien le faire** it has to be done; **Paul est bien venu, n'est-ce pas?** Paul did come, didn't he?; **où peut-il bien être passé?** where can he have got to?

3 (beaucoup): **bien du temps/des gens** quite a time/a number of people

4 (au moins) at least; **cela fait bien deux ans que je ne l'ai pas vu** I haven't seen him for at least ou a space of two years

▷ adj inv **1** (en bonne forme, à l'aise): **je me sens bien** I feel fine; **je ne me sens pas bien** I don't feel well; **on est bien dans ce fauteuil** this chair is very comfortable

2 (joli, beau) good-looking; **tu es bien dans cette robe** you look good in that dress

3 (satisfaisant) good; **elle est bien, cette maison/secrétaire** it's a good house/she's a good secretary; **c'est bien?** is that ou it O.K.?; **c'est très bien (comme ça)** it's fine (like that)

4 (moralement) right; (: personne) good, nice; (respectable) respectable; **ce n'est pas bien de ...** it's not right to ...; **elle est bien, cette femme** she's a nice woman, she's a good sort; **des gens bien** respectable people

5 (en bons termes): **être bien avec qn** to be on good terms with sb

▷ préfixe: **bien-aimé, e** adj, nm/f beloved; **bien-être** nm well-being; **bienfaisance** nf charity; **bienfait** nm act of generosity, benefaction; (de la science etc) benefit; **bienfaiteur, -trice** *nm/f* benefactor/benefactress; **bien-fondé** *nm* soundness; **bien que** *conj* (al)though; **bien sûr** *adv* certainly

bientôt [bjɛ̃to] *adv* soon; **à ~ see you soon**

bienveillant, e [bjɛ̃vejɑ̃, ɑ̃t] *adj* kindly

bienvenue, e [bjɛ̃vny] *adj* welcome; **bienvenue** *nf*: **souhaiter la bienvenue à** to welcome; **bienvenue à** welcome to

bière [bjɛʀ] *nf* (boisson) beer; (cercueil) bier; **bière blonde** lager; **bière brune** brown ale (BRIT), dark beer (US); **bière (à la) pression** draught beer

bifteck [biftɛk] *nm* steak

bigorneau, x [bigɔʀno] *nm* winkle

bigoudi [bigudi] *nm* curler

bijou, x [biʒu] *nm* (aussi: **~ de banque**) jewel; **bijouterie** *nf* jeweller's (shop); **bijoutier, -ière** *nm/f* jeweller

bikini [bikini] *nm* bikini

bilan [bilɑ̃] *nm* (fig) (net) outcome; (: de victimes) toll; (Comm) balance sheet(s); **un ~ de santé** a (medical) checkup; **faire le ~ de** to assess, review; **déposer son ~** to file a bankruptcy statement

bile [bil] *nf* bile; **se faire de la ~** (fam) to worry o.s. sick

bilieux, -euse [biljø, øz] *adj* bilious; (fig: colérique) testy

bilingue [bilɛ̃g] *adj* bilingual

billard [bijaʀ] *nm* (jeu) billiards sg; (table) billiard table

bille [bij] *nf* (gén) ball; (du jeu de billes) marble

billet [bijɛ] *nm* (aussi: **~ de banque**) (bank)note; (de cinéma, de bus etc) ticket; (courte lettre) note; **billet électronique** e-ticket; **billetterie** *nf* ticket office; **billetterie** *nf* (Banque) cash dispenser

billion [biljɔ̃] *nm* billion (BRIT), trillion (US)

bimensuel, le [bimɑ̃sɥɛl] *adj* bimonthly

bio [bjo] *adj inv* organic

bio... [bjo] *préfixe* bio...; **biochimie**

nf biochemistry; **biographie** *nf* biography; **biologie** *nf* biology; **biologique** *adj* biological; (produits, aliments) organic; **biométrie** *nf* biometrics; **biotechnologie** *nf* biotechnology; **bioterrorisme** *nm* bioterrorism

Birmanie [biʀmani] *nf* Burma

bis [bis] *adv*: **12 ~ 12a** ou A ▷ *excl*, *nm* encore

biscotte [biskɔt] *nf* toasted bread (sold in packets)

biscuit [biskɥi] *nm* biscuit (BRIT), cookie (US)

bise [biz] *nf* (fam: baiser) kiss; (vent) North wind; **grosses ~s (de)** (sur lettre) love and kisses (from)

bisexuel, le [bisɛksɥɛl] *adj* bisexual

bisou [bizu] (fam) *nm* kiss

bissextile [bisɛkstil] *adj*: **année ~** leap year

bistro(t) [bistʀo] *nm* bistro, café

bitume [bitym] *nm* asphalt

bizarre [bizaʀ] *adj* strange, odd

blague [blag] *nf* (propos) joke; (farce) trick; **sans ~!** no kidding!; **blaguer** *vi* to joke

blaireau, x [blɛʀo] *nm* (Zool) badger; (brosse) shaving brush

blâme [blɑm] *nm* blame; (sanction) reprimand; **blâmer** *vt* to blame

blanc, blanche [blɑ̃, blɑ̃ʃ] *adj* white; (non imprimé) blank ▷ *nm/f* white, white man(-woman) ▷ *nm* (couleur) white; (espace non écrit) blank; (aussi: **~ d'œuf**) (egg-)white; (aussi: **~ de poulet**) breast, white meat; (aussi: **vin ~**) white wine; **~ cassé** off-white; **chèque en ~** blank cheque; **à ~** (chauffer) white-hot; (tirer, charger) with blanks; **blanche** *nf* (Mus) minim (BRIT), half-note (US); **blancheur** *nf* whiteness

blanchir [blɑ̃ʃiʀ] *vt* (gén) to whiten; (linge) to launder; (Culin) to blanch; (fig: disculper) to clear ▷ *vi* (cheveux) to go white; **blanchisserie** *nf* laundry

blason [blazɔ̃] *nm* coat of arms

blasphème [blasfɛm] *nm* blasphemy

blazer [blazɛʀ] nm blazer

blé [ble] nm wheat; **blé noir** buckwheat

bled [blɛd] (péj) nm hole

blême [blɛm] adj pale

blessé, e [blese] adj injured ▷ nm/f injured person, casualty

blesser [blese] vt to injure; (délibérément) to wound; (offenser) to hurt; **se blesser** to injure o.s.; **se ~ au pied** to injure one's foot; **blessure** nf (accidentelle) injury; (intentionnelle) wound

bleu, e [blø] adj blue; (bifteck) very rare ▷ nm (couleur) blue; (contusion) bruise; (vêtement: aussi: **~s**) overalls pl; (fromage) blue cheese; **bleu marine** navy blue; **bleuet** nm cornflower

bloc [blɔk] nm (de pierre etc) block; (de papier à lettres) pad; (ensemble) group, block; **serré à ~** tightened right down; **en ~** as a whole; **bloc opératoire** operating ou theatre block; **blocage** nm (des prix) freezing; (Psych) hang-up; **bloc-notes** nm note pad

blog, blogue [blɔg] nm blog; **bloguer** vi to blog

blond, e [blɔ̃, blɔ̃d] adj fair, blond; (sable, blés) golden

bloquer [blɔke] vt (passage) to block; (pièce mobile) to jam; (crédits, compte) to freeze

blottir [blɔtiʀ]: **se blottir** vi to huddle up

blouse [bluz] nf overall

blouson [bluzɔ̃] nm blouson jacket; **blouson noir** (fig) ≈ rocker

bluff [blœf] nm bluff

bobine [bɔbin] nf reel; (Élec) coil

bobo [bobo] abr nm f = bourgeois bohème (fam) boho

bocal, -aux [bɔkal, o] nm jar

bock [bɔk] nm glass of beer

bœuf [bœf] nm ox; (Culin) beef

bof [bɔf] (fam) excl don't care!; (pas terrible) nothing special

bohémien, ne [bɔemjɛ̃, -ɛn] nm/f gipsy

boire [bwaʀ] vt to drink; (s'imprégner de) to soak up; **~ un coup** (fam) to have a drink

bois [bwa] nm wood; **de ~, en ~** wooden; **boisé, e** adj woody, wooded

boisson [bwasɔ̃] nf drink

boîte [bwat] nf box; (fam: entreprise) firm; **aliments en ~** canned ou tinned (BRIT) foods; **boîte à gants** glove compartment; **boîte à ordures** dustbin (BRIT), trashcan (US); **boîte aux lettres** letter box; **boîte d'allumettes** box of matches; (vide) matchbox; **boîte de conserves** can ou tin (BRIT) of food; **boîte (de nuit)** night club; **boîte de vitesses** gear box; **boîte postale** PO Box; **boîte vocale** (Tél) voice mail

boiter [bwate] vi to limp; (fig: raisonnement) to be shaky

boîtier [bwatje] nm case

boive etc [bwav] vb voir **boire**

bol [bɔl] nm bowl; **un ~ d'air** a breath of fresh air; **j'en ai ras le ~** (fam) I'm fed up with this; **avoir du ~** (fam) to be lucky

bombarder [bɔ̃baʀde] vt to bomb; **~ qn de** (cailloux, lettres) to bombard sb with

bombe [bɔ̃b] nf bomb; (atomiseur) (aerosol) spray

⊙ MOT-CLÉ

bon, bonne [bɔ̃, bɔn] adj **1** (agréable, satisfaisant) good; **un bon repas/ restaurant** a good meal/restaurant; **être bon en maths** to be good at maths (BRIT) ou math (US)

2 (charitable): **être bon (envers)** to be good (to)

3 (correct) right; **le bon numéro/ moment** the right number/moment

4 (souhaits): **bon anniversaire!** happy birthday!; **bon voyage!** have a good trip!; **bonne chance!** good luck!; **bonne année!** happy New Year!; **bonne nuit!** good night!

5 (approprié, apte): **bon à/pour** fit to/for; **à quoi bon?** what's the use?

6: **bon enfant** adj inv accommodating,

easy-going; **bonne femme** (péj)
woman; **de bonne heure** early; **bon
marché** adj inv, adv cheap; **bon mot**
witticism; **bon sens** common sense;
bon vivant jovial chap; **bonnes
œuvres** charitable works, charities
▷ nm 1 (billet) voucher; (aussi: **bon
cadeau**) gift voucher; **bon d'essence**
petrol coupon; **bon du Trésor** Treasury
bond
2: **avoir du bon** to have its good points;
pour de bon for good
▷ adv: **il fait bon** it's ou the weather is
fine; **sentir bon** to smell good; **tenir
bon** to stand firm
▷ excl good!; **ah bon?** really?; **bon,
je reste** right then, I'll stay; *voir aussi*
bonne

bonbon [bɔ̃bɔ̃] nm (boiled) sweet
bond [bɔ̃] nm leap; **faire un ~** to leap
in the air
bondé, e [bɔ̃de] adj packed (full)
bondir [bɔ̃diʀ] vi to leap
bonheur [bɔnœʀ] nm happiness;
porter ~ (à qn) to bring (sb) luck; **au
petit ~** haphazardly; **par ~** fortunately
bonhomme [bɔnɔm] (pl
bonshommes) nm fellow; **bonhomme
de neige** snowman
bonjour [bɔ̃ʒuʀ] excl, nm hello; (selon
l'heure) good morning/afternoon; **c'est
simple comme ~!** it's easy as pie!
bonne [bɔn] adj voir **bon** ▷ nf
(domestique) maid
bonnet [bɔnε] nm hat; (de soutien-gorge)
cup; **bonnet de bain** bathing cap
bonsoir [bɔ̃swaʀ] excl good evening
bonté [bɔ̃te] nf kindness no pl
bonus [bɔnys] nm no-claims bonus; (de
DVD) extras pl
bord [bɔʀ] nm (de table, verre, falaise)
edge; (de rivière, lac) bank; (de route) side;
(monter) à ~ (de) (to go) on board; **jeter
par-dessus ~** to throw overboard; **le
commandant de/les hommes du ~**
the ship's master/crew; **au ~ de la mer**
at the seaside; **au ~ de la route** at the

roadside; **être au ~ des larmes** to be on
the verge of tears
bordeaux [bɔʀdo] nm Bordeaux (wine)
▷ adj inv maroon
bordel [bɔʀdεl] nm brothel; (fam!)
bloody mess (!)
border [bɔʀde] vt (être le long de) to line;
(qn dans son lit) to tuck up; (garnir): **~
qch de** to edge sth with
bordure [bɔʀdyʀ] nf border; **en ~ de**
on the edge of
borne [bɔʀn] nf boundary stone; (aussi:
~ kilométrique) kilometre-marker, ≈
milestone; **bornes** nfpl (fig) limits;
dépasser les ~s to go too far
borné, e [bɔʀne] adj (personne) narrow-
minded
borner [bɔʀne] vt: **se ~ à faire** (se
contenter de) to content o.s. with doing;
(se limiter à) to limit o.s. to doing
bosniaque [bɔsnjak] adj Bosnian
▷ nm/f: **B~** Bosnian
Bosnie-Herzégovine
[bɔsniεʀzegɔvin] nf Bosnia-
Herzegovina
bosquet [bɔskε] nm grove
bosse [bɔs] nf (de terrain etc) bump;
(enflure) lump; (du dos, du chameau)
hump; **avoir la ~ des maths** etc (fam) to
have a gift for maths etc; **il a roulé sa ~**
(fam) he's been around
bosser [bɔse] vi (fam) (travailler) to
work; (travailler dur) to slave (away)
bossu, e [bɔsy] nm/f hunchback
botanique [bɔtanik] nf botany ▷ adj
botanic(al)
botte [bɔt] nf (soulier) (high) boot;
(gerbe): **~ de paille** bundle of straw;
botte de radis/d'asperges bunch
of radishes/asparagus; **bottes de
caoutchouc** wellington boots
bottin [bɔtɛ̃] nm directory
bottine [bɔtin] nf ankle boot
bouc [buk] nm goat; (barbe) goatee;
bouc émissaire scapegoat
boucan [bukɑ̃] (fam) nm din, racket
bouche [buʃ] nf mouth; **faire du ~ à ~
qn** to give sb the kiss of life ou mouth-

to-mouth resuscitation (BRIT); **rester ~ bée** to stand open-mouthed; **bouche d'égout** manhole; **bouche d'incendie** fire hydrant; **bouche de métro** métro entrance

bouché, e [buʃe] adj (flacon etc) stoppered; (temps, ciel) overcast; (péj fam: personne) thick (fam); **c'est un secteur ~** there's no future in that area; **avoir le nez ~** to have a blocked(-up) nose; **l'évier est ~** the sink's blocked

bouchée [buʃe] nf mouthful; **bouchées à la reine** chicken vol-au-vents

boucher, -ère [buʃe] nm/f butcher ▷ vt (trou) to fill up; (obstruer) to block (up); **se boucher** vi (tuyau etc) to block up, get blocked up; **j'ai le nez bouché** my nose is blocked; **se ~ le nez** to hold one's nose; **boucherie** (shop); (fig) slaughter

bouchon [buʃɔ̃] nm stopper; (de tube) top; (en liège) cork; (fig: embouteillage) holdup; (Pêche) float

boucle [bukl] nf (forme, figure) loop; (objet) buckle; **boucle de cheveux** curl; **boucle d'oreille** earring

bouclé, e [bukle] adj (cheveux) curly

boucler [bukle] vt (fermer: ceinture etc) to fasten; (terminer) to finish off; (fam: enfermer) to shut away; (quartier) to seal off ▷ vi to curl

bouder [bude] vi to sulk ▷ vt to stay away from

boudin [budɛ̃] nm: **~ (noir)** black pudding; **boudin blanc** white pudding

boue [bu] nf mud

bouée [bwe] nf buoy; **bouée (de sauvetage)** lifebuoy

boueux, -euse [bwø, øz] adj muddy

bouffe [buf] (fam) nf grub (fam), food

bouffée [bufe] nf (de cigarette) puff; **une ~ d'air pur** a breath of fresh air; **bouffée de chaleur** hot flush (BRIT) ou flash (US)

bouffer [bufe] (fam) vi to eat

bouffi, e [bufi] adj swollen

bouger [buʒe] vi to move; (dent etc) to be loose; (s'activer) to get moving ▷ vt

to move; **les prix/les couleurs n'ont pas bougé** prices/colours haven't changed

bougie [buʒi] nf candle; (Auto) spark(ing) plug

bouillabaisse [bujabɛs] nf type of fish soup

bouillant, e [bujã, ãt] adj (qui bout) boiling; (très chaud) boiling (hot)

bouillie [buji] nf (de bébé) cereal; **en ~** (fig) crushed

bouillir [bujiR] vi, vt to boil; **~ d'impatience** to seethe with impatience

bouilloire [bujwaR] nf kettle

bouillon [bujɔ̃] nm (Culin) stock no pl; **bouillonner** vi to bubble; (fig: idées) to bubble up

bouillotte [bujɔt] nf hot-water bottle

boulanger, -ère [bulãʒe, ɛR] nm/f baker; **boulangerie** nf bakery

boule [bul] nf (gén) ball; (de pétanque) bowl; **boule de neige** snowball

boulette [bulet] nf (de viande) meatball

boulevard [bulvaR] nm boulevard

bouleversement [bulvɛRsəmã] nm upheaval

bouleverser [bulvɛRse] vt (émouvoir) to overwhelm; (causer du chagrin) to distress; (pays, vie) to disrupt; (papiers, objets) to turn upside down

boulimie [bulimi] nf bulimia

boulimique [bulimik] adj bulimic

boulon [bulɔ̃] nm bolt

boulot, te [bulo, ɔt] adj plump, tubby ▷ nm (fam: travail) work

boum [bum] nm bang ▷ nf (fam) party

bouquet [bukɛ] nm (de fleurs) bunch (of flowers), bouquet; (de persil etc) bunch; **c'est le ~!** (fam) that takes the biscuit!

bouquin [bukɛ̃] (fam) nm book; **bouquiner** (fam) vi to read

bourdon [buRdɔ̃] nm bumblebee

bourg [buR] nm small market town

bourgeois, e [buRʒwa, waz] (péj) adj ≈ (upper) middle class; **bourgeoisie** nf ≈ upper middle classes pl

bourgeon [buRʒɔ̃] nm bud

Bourgogne [burgɔɲ] nf: **la ~** Burgundy
▷ nm: **bourgogne** burgundy (wine)
bourguignon, ne [burgiɲɔ̃, ɔn] adj of
ou from Burgundy, Burgundian
bourrasque [burask] nf squall
bourratif, -ive [buratif, iv] (fam) adj
filling, stodgy (pej)
bourre [bur] nf (fam: ivre)
plastered, tanked up (BRIT); (rempli): **~
de** crammed full of
bourrer [bure] vt (pipe) to fill; (poêle) to
pack; (valise) to cram (full)
bourru, e [bury] adj surly, gruff
bourse [burs] nf (subvention) grant;
(porte-monnaie) purse; **la B~** the Stock
Exchange
bous [bu] vb voir **bouillir**
bousculade [buskylad] nf (hâte) rush;
(cohue) crush; **bousculer** vt (heurter) to
knock into; (fig) to push, rush
boussole [busɔl] nf compass
bout [bu] vb voir **bouillir** ▷ nm bit; (d'un
bâton etc) tip; (d'une ficelle, table, rue,
période) end; **au ~ de** at the end of, after;
pousser qn à ~ to push sb to the limit;
venir à ~ de to manage to finish; **à ~
portant** (at) point-blank (range)
bouteille [butɛj] nf bottle; (de gaz
butane) cylinder
boutique [butik] nf shop
bouton [butɔ̃] nm button; (sur la
peau) spot; (Bot) bud; **boutonner**
vt to button; **boutonnière** nf
buttonhole; **bouton-pression** nm
press stud
bovin, e [bɔvɛ̃, in] adj bovine; **bovins**
nmpl cattle pl
bowling [bulin] nm (tenpin) bowling;
(salle) bowling alley
boxe [bɔks] nf boxing
BP abr = **boîte postale**
bracelet [braslɛ] nm bracelet
braconnier [brakɔnje] nm poacher
brader [brade] vt to sell off; **braderie**
nf cut-price shop/stall
braguette [bragɛt] nf fly ou flies pl
(BRIT), zipper (us)

brancard [brɑ̃kar] nm (civière)
stretcher; **brancardier** nm stretcher-
bearer
branche [brɑ̃ʃ] nf branch
branché, e [brɑ̃ʃe] (fam) adj trendy
brancher [brɑ̃ʃe] vt to connect (up); (en
mettant la prise) to plug in
brandir [brɑ̃dir] vt to brandish
braquer [brake] vi (Auto) to turn (the
wheel) ▷ vt (revolver etc): **~ qch sur**
to aim sth at, point sth at; (mettre en
colère): **~ qn** to put sb's back up
bras [brɑ] nm arm; **~ dessus, ~ dessous**
arm in arm; **se retrouver avec qch sur
les ~** (fam) to be landed with sth; **bras
droit** (fig) right hand man
brassard [brasar] nm armband
brasse [bras] nf (nage) breast-stroke;
brasse papillon butterfly (stroke)
brassée [brase] nf armful
brasser [brase] vt to mix; **~ qch/
les affaires** to handle a lot of money/
business
brasserie [brasri] nf (restaurant) café-
restaurant; (usine) brewery
brave [brav] adj (courageux) brave; (bon,
gentil) good, kind
braver [brave] vt to defy
bravo [bravo] excl bravo ▷ nm cheer
bravoure [bravur] nf bravery
break [brɛk] nm (Auto) estate car
brebis [brəbi] nf ewe; **brebis galeuse**
black sheep
bredouiller [brəduje] vi, vt to
mumble, stammer
bref, brève [brɛf, ɛv] adj short, brief
▷ adv in short; **d'un ton ~** sharply,
curtly; **en ~** in short, in brief
Brésil [brezil] nm Brazil
Bretagne [brətaɲ] nf Brittany
bretelle [brətɛl] nf (de vêtement, de
sac) strap; (d'autoroute) slip road (BRIT),
entrance/exit ramp (us); **bretelles**
nfpl (pour pantalon) braces (BRIT),
suspenders (us)
breton, ne [brətɔ̃, ɔn] adj Breton
▷ nm/f: **B~, ne** Breton
brève [brɛv] adj voir **bref**

brevet [brəvɛ] nm diploma, certificate; **brevet des collèges** exam taken at the age of 15; **brevet (d'invention)** patent; **breveté, e** adj patented

bricolage [brikɔlaʒ] nm: **le ~** do-it-yourself

bricoler [brikɔle] vi (petits travaux) to do DIY jobs; (passe-temps) to potter about ▷ vt (réparer) to fix up; **bricoleur, -euse** nm/f handyman(-woman), DIY enthusiast

bridge [bridʒ] nm (Cartes) bridge

brièvement [brijɛvmɑ̃] adv briefly

brigade [brigad] nf (Police) squad; (Mil) brigade; **brigadier** nm sergeant

brillamment [brijamɑ̃] adv brilliantly

brillant, e [brijɑ̃, ɑ̃t] adj (remarquable) bright; (luisant) shiny, shining

briller [brije] vi to shine

brin [brɛ̃] nm (de laine, ficelle etc) strand; (fig): **un ~ de** a bit of

brindille [brɛ̃dij] nf twig

brioche [brijɔʃ] nf brioche (bun); (fam: ventre) paunch

brique [brik] nf brick; (de lait) carton

briquet [brikɛ] nm (cigarette) lighter

brise [briz] nf breeze

briser [brize] vt to break; **se briser** vi to break

britannique [britanik] adj British ▷ nm/f: **B~** British person, Briton; **les B~s** the British

brocante [brɔkɑ̃t] nf junk, second-hand goods pl; **brocanteur, -euse** nm/f junkshop owner; junk dealer

broche [brɔʃ] nf brooch; (Culin) spit; (Méd) pin; **à la ~** spit-roasted

broché, e [brɔʃe] adj (livre) paper-backed

brochet [brɔʃɛ] nm pike inv

brochette [brɔʃɛt] nf (ustensile) skewer; (plat) kebab

brochure [brɔʃyʀ] nf pamphlet, brochure, booklet

broder [brɔde] vt to embroider ▷ vi: **~ (sur les faits** ou **une histoire)** to embroider the facts; **broderie** nf embroidery

bronches [brɔ̃ʃ] nfpl bronchial tubes; **bronchite** nf bronchitis

bronze [brɔ̃z] nm bronze

bronzer [brɔ̃ze] vi to get a tan; **se bronzer** to sunbathe

brosse [brɔs] nf brush; **coiffé en ~** with a crewcut; **brosse à cheveux** hairbrush; **brosse à dents** toothbrush; **brosse à habits** clothesbrush; **brosser** vt (nettoyer) to brush; (fig: tableau etc) to paint; **se brosser les dents** to brush one's teeth

brouette [bʀuɛt] nf wheelbarrow

brouillard [bʀujaʀ] nm fog

brouiller [bʀuje] vt (idées, message) to scramble; (idées) to mix up; (rendre trouble) to cloud; (désunir: amis) to set at odds; **se brouiller** vi (vue) to cloud over; (gens): **se ~ (avec)** to fall out (with)

brouillon, ne [bʀujɔ̃, ɔn] adj (sans soin) untidy; (qui manque d'organisation) disorganized ▷ nm draft; (papier) ~ rough paper

broussailles [bʀusaj] nfpl undergrowth sg; **broussailleux, -euse** adj bushy

brousse [bʀus] nf: **la ~** the bush

brouter [bʀute] vi to graze

brugnon [bʀyɲɔ̃] nm (Bot) nectarine

bruiner [bʀɥine] vb impers: **il bruine** it's drizzling, there's a drizzle

bruit [bʀɥi] nm: **un ~** a noise, a sound; (fig: rumeur) a rumour; **le ~** noise; **sans ~** without a sound, noiselessly; **bruit de fond** background noise

brûlant, e [bʀylɑ̃, ɑ̃t] adj burning; (liquide) boiling (hot)

brûlé, e [bʀyle] adj (fig: démasqué) blown ▷ nm: **odeur de ~** smell of burning

brûler [bʀyle] vt to burn; (suj: eau bouillante) to scald; (consommer: électricité, essence) to use; (feu rouge, signal) to go through ▷ vi to burn; (jeu): **tu brûles!** you're getting hot!; **se brûler** to burn o.s.; (s'ébouillanter) to scald o.s.

brûlure [bʀylyʀ] nf (lésion) burn; **brûlures d'estomac** heartburn sg

brume [bʀym] *nf* mist

brun, e [bʀœ̃, bʀyn] *adj* (*gén, bière*) brown; (*cheveux, tabac*) dark; **elle est ~e** she's got dark hair

brunch [bʀœntʃ] *nm* brunch

brushing [bʀœʃiŋ] *nm* blow-dry

brusque [bʀysk] *adj* abrupt

brut, e [bʀyt] *adj* (*minerai, soie*) raw; (*diamant*) rough; (*Comm*) gross; (**pétrole**) ~ crude (oil)

brutal, e, -aux [bʀytal, o] *adj* brutal

Bruxelles [bʀysɛl] *n* Brussels

bruyamment [bʀyjamɑ̃] *adv* noisily

bruyant, e [bʀyjɑ̃, ɑ̃t] *adj* noisy

bruyère [bʀyjɛʀ] *nf* heather

BTS *sigle m* (= *brevet de technicien supérieur*) vocational training certificate taken at the end of a higher education course

bu, e [by] *pp de* **boire**

buccal, e, -aux [bykal, o] *adj*: **par voie ~e** orally

bûche [byʃ] *nf* log; **prendre une ~** (*fig*) to come a cropper; **bûche de Noël** Yule log

bûcher [byʃe] *nm* (*funéraire*) pyre; (*supplice*) stake ▷ *vi* (*fam*) to swot (BRIT), slave (away) ▷ *vt* (*fam*) to swot up (BRIT), slave away at

budget [bydʒɛ] *nm* budget

buée [bye] *nf* (*sur une vitre*) mist

buffet [byfɛ] *nm* (*meuble*) sideboard; (*de réception*) buffet; **buffet de gare** (station) buffet, snack bar

buis [bɥi] *nm* box tree; (*bois*) box(wood)

buisson [bɥisɔ̃] *nm* bush

bulbe [bylb] *nm* (*Bot, Anat*) bulb

Bulgarie [bylgaʀi] *nf* Bulgaria

bulle [byl] *nf* bubble

bulletin [byltɛ̃] *nm* (*communiqué, journal*) bulletin; (*Scol*) report; **bulletin d'informations** news bulletin; **bulletin (de vote)** ballot paper; **bulletin météorologique** weather report

bureau, x [byʀo] *nm* (*meuble*) desk; (*pièce, service*) office; **bureau de change** (foreign) exchange office

ou bureau; **bureau de poste** post office; **bureau de tabac** tobacconist's (shop); **bureaucratie** [byʀokʀasi] *nf* bureaucracy

bus[1] [by] *vb voir* **boire**

bus[2] [bys] *nm bus*; **à quelle heure part le ~?** what time does the bus leave?

buste [byst] *nm* (*torse*) chest; (*seins*) bust

but[1] [by] *vb voir* **boire**

but[2] [by(t)] *nm* (*cible*) target; (*fig*) goal, aim; (*Football etc*) goal; **de ~ en blanc** point-blank; **avoir pour ~ de faire** to aim to do; **dans le ~ de** with the intention of

butane [bytan] *nm* (*camping*) butane; (*usage domestique*) Calor gas®

butiner [bytine] *vi* (*abeilles*) to gather nectar

buvais *etc* [byvɛ] *vb voir* **boire**

buvard [byvaʀ] *nm* blotter

buvette [byvɛt] *nf* bar

C

c' [s] dét voir **ce**

ça [sa] pron (pour désigner) this; (: plus loin) that; (comme sujet indéfini) it; **ça m'étonne que ...** it surprises me that ...; **comment ça va?** how are you?; **ça va?** (d'accord?) O.K.?, all right?; **où ça?** where's that?; **pourquoi ça?** why's that?; **qui ça?** who's that?; **ça alors!** well really!; **ça fait 10 ans (que)** it's 10 years (since); **c'est ça** that's right; **ça y est** that's it

cabane [kaban] nf hut, cabin

cabaret [kabaʀɛ] nm night club

cabillaud [kabijo] nm cod inv

cabine [kabin] nf (de bateau) cabin; (de piscine etc) cubicle; (de camion, train) cab; (d'avion) cockpit; **cabine d'essayage** fitting room; **cabine (téléphonique)** call ou (tele)phone box

cabinet [kabinɛ] nm (petite pièce) closet; (de médecin) surgery (BRIT), office (US); (de notaire etc) office; (: clientèle) practice; (Pol) Cabinet; **cabinets** nmpl (w.-c.) toilet sg; **cabinet de toilette** toilet

câble [kabl] nm cable; **le ~** (TV) cable television, cablevision (US)

cacahuète [kakaɥɛt] nf peanut

cacao [kakao] nm cocoa

cache [kaʃ] nm mask, card (for masking)

cache-cache [kaʃkaʃ] nm: **jouer à ~** to play hide-and-seek

cachemire [kaʃmiʀ] nm cashmere

cacher [kaʃe] vt to hide, conceal; **se cacher** vi (volontairement) to hide; (être caché) to be hidden ou concealed; **~ qch à qn** to hide ou conceal sth from sb

cachet [kaʃɛ] nm (comprimé) tablet; (de la poste) postmark; (rétribution) fee; (fig) style, character

cachette [kaʃɛt] nf hiding place; **en ~** on the sly, secretly

cactus [kaktys] nm cactus

cadavre [kadavʀ] nm corpse, (dead) body

caddie® [kadi] nm (supermarket) trolley (BRIT), (grocery) cart (US)

cadeau, x [kado] nm present, gift; **faire un ~ à qn** to give sb a present ou gift; **faire ~ de qch à qn** to make a present of sth to sb, give sb sth as a present

cadenas [kadna] nm padlock

cadet, te [kadɛ, ɛt] adj younger; (le plus jeune) youngest ▷ nm/f youngest child ou one

cadran [kadʀɑ̃] nm dial; **cadran solaire** sundial

cadre [kadʀ] nm frame; (environnement) surroundings pl ▷ nm/f (Admin) managerial employee, executive; **dans le ~ de** (fig) within the framework ou context of

cafard [kafaʀ] nm cockroach; **avoir le ~** (fam) to be down in the dumps

café [kafe] nm coffee; (bistro) café ▷ adj inv coffee(-coloured); **café au lait** white coffee; **café noir** black coffee; **café tabac** tobacconist's or newsagent's serving coffee and spirits; **cafetière** nf (pot) coffee-pot

cage [kaʒ] *nf* cage; **cage (d'escalier)** stairwell; **cage thoracique** rib cage

cageot [kaʒo] *nm* crate

cagoule [kagul] *nf (passe-montagne)* balaclava

cahier [kaje] *nm* notebook; **cahier de brouillon** jotter (BRIT), rough notebook; **cahier d'exercices** exercise book

caille [kaj] *nf* quail

caillou, X [kaju] *nm* (little) stone; **caillouteux, -euse** *adj (route)* stony

Caire [kɛʀ] *nm:* **le ~** Cairo

caisse [kɛs] *nf* box; *(tiroir où l'on met la recette)* till; *(où l'on paye)* cash desk (BRIT), check-out; *(de banque)* cashier's desk; **caisse d'épargne** savings bank; **caisse de retraite** pension fund; **caisse enregistreuse** cash register; **caissier, -ière** *nm/f* cashier

cake [kɛk] *nm* fruit cake

calandre [kalɑ̃dʀ] *nf* radiator grill

calcaire [kalkɛʀ] *nm* limestone ▷ *adj (eau)* hard; *(Géo)* limestone *cpd*

calcul [kalkyl] *nm* calculation; **le ~** *(Scol)* arithmetic; **calcul (biliaire)** (gall)stone; **calculatrice** *nf* calculator; **calculer** *vt* to calculate, work out; **calculette** *nf* pocket calculator

cale [kal] *nf (de bateau)* hold; *(en bois)* wedge

calé, e [kale] *(fam) adj* clever, bright

caleçon [kalsɔ̃] *nm (d'homme)* boxer shorts; *(de femme)* leggings

calendrier [kalɑ̃dʀije] *nm* calendar; *(fig)* timetable

calepin [kalpɛ̃] *nm* notebook

caler [kale] *vt* to wedge ▷ *vi (moteur, véhicule)* to stall

calibre [kalibʀ] *nm* calibre

câlin, e [kɑlɛ̃, in] *adj* cuddly, cuddlesome; *(regard, voix)* tender

calmant [kalmɑ̃] *nm* tranquillizer, sedative; *(pour la douleur)* painkiller

calme [kalm] *adj* calm, quiet ▷ *nm* calm(ness), quietness; **sans perdre son ~** without losing one's cool *(inf)* ou composure; **calmer** *vt* to calm (down);

(douleur, inquiétude) to ease, soothe; **se calmer** *vi* to calm down

calorie [kalɔʀi] *nf* calorie

camarade [kamaʀad] *nm/f* friend, pal; *(Pol)* comrade

Cambodge [kɑ̃bɔdʒ] *nm:* **le ~** Cambodia

cambriolage [kɑ̃bʀijɔlaʒ] *nm* burglary; **cambrioler** *vt* to burgle (BRIT), burglarize (US); **cambrioleur, -euse** *nm/f* burglar

camelote [kamlɔt] *(fam) nf* rubbish, trash, junk

caméra [kameʀa] *nf (Cinéma, TV)* camera; *(d'amateur)* cine-camera

Cameroun [kamʀun] *nm:* **le ~** Cameroon

caméscope® [kameskɔp] *nm* camcorder®

camion [kamjɔ̃] *nm* lorry (BRIT), truck; **camion de dépannage** breakdown (BRIT) ou tow (US) truck; **camionnette** *nf* (small) van; **camionneur** *nm (chauffeur)* lorry (BRIT) ou truck driver; *(entrepreneur)* haulage contractor (BRIT), trucker (US)

camomille [kamɔmij] *nf* camomile; *(boisson)* camomile tea

camp [kɑ̃] *nm* camp; *(fig)* side

campagnard, e [kɑ̃paɲaʀ, aʀd] *adj* country *cpd*

campagne [kɑ̃paɲ] *nf* country, countryside; *(Mil, Pol, Comm)* campaign; **à la ~** in the country

camper [kɑ̃pe] *vi* to camp ▷ *vt* to sketch; **se ~ devant** to plant o.s. in front of; **campeur, -euse** *nm/f* camper

camping [kɑ̃piŋ] *nm* camping; **faire du ~** to go camping; **(terrain de) camping** campsite, camping site; **camping-car** *nm* camper, motorhome (US); **camping-gaz®** *nm inv* camp(ing) stove

Canada [kanada] *nm:* **le ~** Canada; **canadien, ne** *adj* Canadian ▷ *nm/f:* **Canadien, ne** Canadian; **canadienne** *nf (veste)* fur-lined jacket

canal, -aux [kanal, o] *nm* canal;

(naturel, TV) channel; **canalisation** nf *(tuyau)* pipe

canapé [kanape] nm settee, sofa

canard [kanaʀ] nm duck; *(fam: journal)* rag

cancer [kɑ̃sɛʀ] nm cancer; *(signe):* **le C~** Cancer

cancre [kɑ̃kʀ] nm dunce

candidat, e [kɑ̃dida, at] nm/f candidate; *(à un poste)* applicant, candidate; **candidature** nf *(Pol)* candidature; *(à poste)* application; **poser sa candidature à un poste** to apply for a job

cane [kan] nf *(female)* duck

canette [kanɛt] nf *(de bière)* (flip-top) bottle

canevas [kanva] nm *(Couture)* canvas

caniche [kaniʃ] nm poodle

canicule [kanikyl] nf scorching heat

canif [kanif] nm penknife, pocket knife

canne [kan] nf *(walking)* stick; **canne à pêche** fishing rod; **canne à sucre** sugar cane

cannelle [kanɛl] nf cinnamon

canoë [kanɔe] nm canoe; *(sport)* canoeing; **canoë (kayak)** kayak

canot [kano] nm ding(h)y; **canot de sauvetage** lifeboat; **canot pneumatique** inflatable ding(h)y

cantatrice [kɑ̃tatʀis] nf *(opera)* singer

cantine [kɑ̃tin] nf canteen

canton [kɑ̃tɔ̃] nm district consisting of several communes; *(en Suisse)* canton

caoutchouc [kautʃu] nm rubber; **caoutchouc mousse** foam rubber

cap [kap] nm *(Géo)* cape *(promontoire)* headland; *(fig: tournant)* watershed; *(Navig):* **changer de ~** to change course; **mettre le ~ sur** to head ou steer for

CAP sigle m *(= Certificat d'aptitude professionnelle)* vocational training certificate taken at secondary school

capable [kapabl] adj able, capable; **~ de qch/faire** capable of sth/doing

capacité [kapasite] nf *(compétence)* ability; *(Jur, contenance)* capacity

cape [kap] nf cape, cloak; **rire sous ~** to laugh up one's sleeve

CAPES [kapɛs] sigle m *(= Certificat d'aptitude pédagogique à l'enseignement secondaire)* teaching diploma

capitaine [kapitɛn] nm captain

capital, e, -aux [kapital, o] adj *(œuvre)* major; *(question, rôle)* fundamental ▷ nm capital; *(fig)* stock; **d'une importance ~e** of capital importance; **capitaux** nmpl *(fonds)* capital sg; **capital (social)** authorized capital; **capitale** nf *(ville)* capital; *(lettre)* capital (letter); **capitalisme** nm capitalism; **capitaliste** adj, nm/f capitalist

caporal, -aux [kapoʀal, o] nm lance corporal

capot [kapo] nm *(Auto)* bonnet (BRIT), hood (US)

câpre [kɑpʀ] nf caper

caprice [kapʀis] nm whim, caprice; **faire des ~s** to make a fuss; **capricieux, -euse** adj *(fantasque)* capricious, whimsical; *(enfant)* awkward

Capricorne [kapʀikɔʀn] nm: **le ~** Capricorn

capsule [kapsyl] nf *(de bouteille)* cap; *(Bot etc, spatiale)* capsule

capter [kapte] vt *(ondes radio)* to pick up; *(fig)* to win, capture

captivant, e [kaptivɑ̃, ɑ̃t] adj captivating

capturer [kaptyʀe] vt to capture

capuche [kapyʃ] nf hood

capuchon [kapyʃɔ̃] nm hood; *(de stylo)* cap, top

car [kaʀ] nm coach ▷ conj because, for

carabine [kaʀabin] nf rifle

caractère [kaʀaktɛʀ] nm *(gén)* character; **avoir bon/mauvais ~** to be good-/ill-natured; **en ~s gras** in bold type; **en petits ~s** in small print; **~s d'imprimerie** (block) capitals; **caractériser** [kaʀakteʀize] vt to be characteristic of; **se ~ par** to be characterized ou distinguished by **caractéristique** [kaʀakteʀistik] adj, nf characteristic

carafe[karaf] nf (pour eau, vin ordinaire) carafe

caraïbe[karaib] adj Caribbean ▷ n: **les C~s** the Caribbean (Islands)

carambolage[kaʀɑ̃bɔlaʒ] nm multiple crash, pileup

caramel[kaʀamɛl] nm (bonbon) caramel, toffee; (substance) caramel

caravane[kaʀavan] nf caravan; **caravaning** nm caravanning

carbone[kaʀbɔn] nm carbon; (double) carbon (copy)

carbonique[kaʀbɔnik] adj: **gaz ~** carbon dioxide; **neige ~** dry ice

carbonisé, e[kaʀbɔnize] adj charred

carburant[kaʀbyʀɑ̃] nm (motor) fuel

carburateur[kaʀbyʀatœʀ] nm carburettor

cardiaque[kaʀdjak] adj cardiac, heart cpd ▷ nm/f heart patient; **être ~** to have heart trouble

cardigan[kaʀdigɑ̃] nm cardigan

cardiologue[kaʀdjɔlɔg] nm/f cardiologist, heart specialist

crème[kaʀɛm] nm: **le C~** Lent

carence[kaʀɑ̃s] nf (manque) deficiency

caresse[kaʀɛs] nf caress

caresser[kaʀese] vt to caress; (animal) to stroke

cargaison[kaʀgɛzɔ̃] nf cargo, freight

cargo[kaʀgo] nm cargo boat, freighter

caricature[kaʀikatyʀ] nf caricature

carie[kaʀi] nf: **la ~ (dentaire)** tooth decay; **une ~** a bad tooth

carnaval[kaʀnaval] nm carnival

carnet[kaʀnɛ] nm (calepin) notebook; (de tickets, timbres etc) book; **carnet de chèques** cheque book

carotte[kaʀɔt] nf carrot

carré, e[kaʀe] adj square; (fig: franc) straightforward ▷ nm (Math) square; **mètre/kilomètre ~** square metre/kilometre

carreau, x[kaʀo] nm (par terre) (floor) tile; (au mur) (wall) tile; (de fenêtre) (window) pane; (motif) check, square; (Cartes: couleur) diamonds pl; **tissu à ~x**
checked fabric

carrefour[kaʀfuʀ] nm crossroads sg

carrelage[kaʀlaʒ] nm (sol) (tiled) floor

carrelet[kaʀlɛ] nm (poisson) plaice

carrément[kaʀemɑ̃] adv (franchement) straight out, bluntly; (sans hésiter) straight; (intensif) completely; **c'est ~ impossible** it's completely impossible

carrière[kaʀjɛʀ] nf (métier) career; (de roches) quarry; **militaire de ~** professional soldier

carrosserie[kaʀɔsʀi] nf body, coachwork no pl

carrure[kaʀyʀ] nf build; (fig) stature, calibre

cartable[kaʀtabl] nm satchel, (school)bag

carte[kaʀt] nf (de géographie) map; (marine, du ciel) chart; (d'abonnement, à jouer) card; (au restaurant) menu; (aussi: **~ de visite**) (visiting) card; **pouvez-vous me l'indiquer sur la ~?** can you show me (it) on the map?; **à la ~** (au restaurant) à la carte; **est-ce qu'on peut voir la ~?** can we see the menu?; **donner ~ blanche à qn** to give sb a free rein; **carte bancaire** cash card; **Carte Bleue®** debit card; **carte à puce** smart card; **carte de crédit** credit card; **carte de fidélité** loyalty card; **carte d'identité** identity card; **carte de séjour** residence permit; **carte grise** (Auto) = (car) registration book, logbook; **carte mémoire** (d'appareil-photo numérique) memory card; **carte postale** postcard; **carte routière** road map

carter[kaʀtɛʀ] nm sump

carton[kaʀtɔ̃] nm (matériau) cardboard; (boîte) (cardboard) box; **faire un ~** (fam) to score a hit; **carton (à dessin)** portfolio

cartouche[kaʀtuʃ] nf cartridge; (de cigarettes) carton

cas[kɑ] nm case; **ne faire aucun ~ de** to take no notice of; **en aucun ~** on no account; **au ~ où** in case; **en ~ de** in case of, in the event of; **en ~ de besoin**

if need be; **en tout ~** in any case, at any rate

cascade [kaskad] nf waterfall, cascade

case [kaz] nf (hutte) hut; (compartiment) compartment; (sur un formulaire, de mots croisés etc) box

caser [kaze] (fam) vt (placer) to put (away); (loger) to put up; **se caser** vi (se marier) to settle down; (trouver un emploi) to find a (steady) job

caserne [kazɛʀn] nf barracks pl

casier [kazje] nm (pour courrier) pigeonhole; (compartiment) compartment; (à clef) locker; **casier judiciaire** police record

casino [kazino] nm casino

casque [kask] nm helmet; (chez le coiffeur) (hair-)drier; (pour audition) (head-)phones pl, headset

casquette [kaskɛt] nf cap

casse...: **casse-croûte** nm inv snack; **casse-noix** nm inv nutcrackers pl; **casse-pieds** (fam) adj inv: **il est casse-pieds** he's a pain in the neck

casser [kase] vt to break; (Jur) to quash; **se casser** vi to break; **~ les pieds à qn** (fam: irriter) to get on sb's nerves; **se ~ la tête** (fam) to go to a lot of trouble

casserole [kasʀɔl] nf saucepan

casse-tête [kastɛt] nm inv (difficultés) headache (fig)

cassette [kasɛt] nf (bande magnétique) cassette; (coffret) casket

cassis [kasis] nm blackcurrant

cassoulet [kasule] nm bean and sausage hot-pot

catalogue [katalɔg] nm catalogue

catalytique [katalitik] adj: **pot ~** catalytic convertor

catastrophe [katastʀɔf] nf catastrophe, disaster

catéchisme [kateʃism] nm catechism

catégorie [kategɔʀi] nf category; **catégorique** adj categorical

cathédrale [katedʀal] nf cathedral

catholique [katɔlik] adj, nm/f (Roman) Catholic; **pas très ~** a bit shady ou fishy

cauchemar [koʃmaʀ] nm nightmare

cause [koz] nf cause; (Jur) lawsuit, case; **à ~ de** because of, owing to; **pour ~ de** because of; **(et) pour ~** and for (a very) good reason; **être en ~** (intérêts) to be at stake; **remettre en ~** to challenge; **causer** vt to cause ▷ vi to chat, talk

caution [kosjɔ̃] nf guarantee, security; (Jur) bail (bond); (fig) backing, support; **libéré sous ~** released on bail

cavalier, -ière [kavalje, jɛʀ] adj (désinvolte) offhand ▷ nm/f rider; (au bal) partner ▷ nm (Échecs) knight

cave [kav] nf cellar

CD sigle m (= compact disc) CD

CD-ROM [sedeʀɔm] sigle m CD-ROM

○ MOT-CLÉ

ce, cette [sə, sɛt] (devant nm **cet** + voyelle ou h aspiré; pl **ces**) dét (proximité) this; these pl; (non-proximité) that; those pl; **cette maison(-ci/là)** this/that house; **cette nuit** (qui vient) tonight; (passée) last night
▷ pron 1: **c'est** it's ou it is; **c'est un peintre** he's ou he is a painter; **ce sont des peintres** they're ou they are painters; **c'est le facteur** etc (à la porte) it's the postman; **c'est toi qui lui a parlé** it was you who spoke to him; **qui est-ce?** who is it?; (en désignant) who is he/she?; **qu'est-ce?** what is it?
2: **ce qui, ce que**: **ce qui me plaît, c'est sa franchise** what I like about him ou her is his ou her frankness; **il est bête, ce qui me chagrine** he's stupid, which saddens me; **tout ce qui bouge** everything that ou which moves; **tout ce que je sais** all I know; **ce dont j'ai parlé** what I talked about; **ce que c'est grand!** it's so big!; voir aussi **-ci**; **est-ce que**; **n'est-ce pas**; **c'est-à-dire**

ceci [səsi] pron this

céder [sede] vt (donner) to give up ▷ vi (chaise, barrage) to give way; (personne) to give in; **~ à** to yield to, give in to

CEDEX [sedɛks] *sigle m* (= *courrier d'entreprise à distribution exceptionnelle*) postal service for bulk users

cédille [sedij] *nf* cedilla

ceinture [sɛ̃tyʀ] *nf* belt; (*taille*) waist; **ceinture de sécurité** safety *ou* seat belt

cela [s(ə)la] *pron* that; (*comme sujet indéfini*) it; **~ m'étonne que ...** it surprises me that ...; **quand/où ~?** when/where (was that)?

célèbre [selɛbʀ] *adj* famous; **célébrer** *vt* to celebrate

céleri [sɛlʀi] *nm*: **~(-rave)** celeriac; **céleri en branche** celery

célibataire [selibatɛʀ] *adj* single, unmarried ▷ *nm* bachelor ▷ *nf* unmarried woman

celle, celles [sɛl] *pron voir* **celui**

cellule [selyl] *nf* (*gén*) cell; **~ souche** stem cell

cellulite [selylit] *nf* cellulite

○ **MOT-CLÉ**

celui, celle [səlɥi, sɛl] (*mpl* **ceux**, *fpl* **celles**) *pron* **1: celui-ci/là, celle-ci/là** this one/that one; **ceux-ci, celles-ci** these (ones); **ceux-là, celles-là** those (ones)

2: celui qui bouge the one which *ou* that moves; (*personne*) the one who moves; **celui que je vois** the one (which *ou* that) I see; (*personne*) the one (whom) I see; **celui dont je parle** the one I'm talking about; **celui de mon frère** my brother's; **celui du salon/du dessous** the one (*ou* from) the lounge/below

3 (*valeur indéfinie*): **celui qui veut** whoever wants

cendre [sɑ̃dʀ] *nf* ash; **cendres** *nfpl* (*d'un défunt*) ashes; **sous la ~** (*Culin*) in the embers; **cendrier** *nm* ashtray

censé, e [sɑ̃se] *adj*: **être ~ faire** to be supposed to do

censeur [sɑ̃sœʀ] *nm* (*Scol*) deputy-head

(*BRIT*), vice-principal (*US*)

censure [sɑ̃syʀ] *nf* censorship; **censurer** *vt* (*Cinéma, Presse*) to censor; (*Pol*) to censure

cent [sɑ̃] *num* a hundred, one hundred ▷ *nm* (*US, Canada etc*) cent; (*partie de l'euro*) cent; **centaine** *nf*: **une centaine (de)** about a hundred, a hundred *ou* so; **des centaines (de)** hundreds (of); **centenaire** *adj* hundred-year-old ▷ *nm* (*anniversaire*) centenary; (*monnaie*) cent; **centième** *num* hundredth; **centigrade** *nm* centigrade; **centilitre** *nm* centilitre; **centime** *nm* centime; **centime d'euro** euro cent; **centimètre** *nm* centimetre; (*ruban*) tape measure, measuring tape

central, e, -aux [sɑ̃tʀal, o] *adj* central ▷ *nm*: **~ (téléphonique)** (telephone) exchange; **centrale** *nf* power station; **centrale électrique/nucléaire** power/ nuclear power station

centre [sɑ̃tʀ] *nm* centre; **centre commercial/sportif/culturel** shopping/sports/arts centre; **centre d'appels** call centre; **centre-ville** *nm* town centre, downtown (area) (*US*)

cèpe [sɛp] *nm* (edible) boletus

cependant [s(ə)pɑ̃dɑ̃] *adv* however

céramique [seʀamik] *nf* ceramics *sg*

cercle [sɛʀkl] *nm* circle; **cercle vicieux** vicious circle

cercueil [sɛʀkœj] *nm* coffin

céréale [seʀeal] *nf* cereal

cérémonie [seʀemɔni] *nf* ceremony; **sans ~** (*inviter, manger*) informally

cerf [sɛʀ] *nm* stag

cerf-volant [sɛʀvɔlɑ̃] *nm* kite

cerise [s(ə)ʀiz] *nf* cherry; **cerisier** *nm* cherry tree

cerner [sɛʀne] *vt* (*Mil etc*) to surround; (*fig*: *problème*) to delimit, define

certain, e [sɛʀtɛ̃, ɛn] *adj* certain ▷ *dét* certain; **d'un ~ âge** past one's prime, not so young; **un ~ temps** (quite) some time; **un ~ Georges** someone called Georges; **~s** *pron* some; **certainement** *adv* (*probablement*) most probably *ou*

likely; (bien sûr) certainly, of course
certes [sɛʀt] adv (sans doute)
admittedly; (bien sûr) of course
certificat [sɛʀtifika] nm certificate
certifier [sɛʀtifje] vt: ~ **qch à qn**
to assure sb of sth; **copie certifiée
conforme** certified copy of the original
certitude [sɛʀtityd] nf certainty
cerveau, X [sɛʀvo] nm brain
cervelas [sɛʀvəla] nm saveloy
cervelle [sɛʀvɛl] nf (Anat) brain; (Culin)
brains
ces [se] dét voir **ce**
CES sigle m (= collège d'enseignement
secondaire) ≈ (junior) secondary school
(BRIT)
cesse [sɛs]: **sans ~** adv (tout le temps)
continually, constantly; (sans
interruption) continuously; **il n'a eu de
~ que** he did not rest until; **cesser** vt
to stop ▷ vi to stop, cease; **cesser de
faire** to stop doing; **cessez-le-feu**
inv ceasefire
c'est-à-dire [sɛtadiʀ] adv that is (to say)
cet, cette [sɛt] dét voir **ce**
ceux [sø] pron voir **celui**
chacun, e [ʃakœ̃, yn] pron each;
(indéfini) everyone, everybody
chagrin [ʃagʀɛ̃] nm grief, sorrow; **avoir
du ~** to be grieved
chahut [ʃay] nm uproar; **chahuter** vt
to rag, bait ▷ vi to make an uproar
chaîne [ʃɛn] nf (Radio, TV:
stations) channel; **travail à la ~**
production line work; **réactions
en ~** chain reaction sg; **chaîne de
montagnes** mountain range; **chaîne
(hi-fi)** hi-fi system
chair [ʃɛʀ] nf flesh; **avoir la ~ de poule**
to have goosepimples ou gooseflesh;
bien en ~ plump, well-padded; **en
~ et en os** in the flesh; **~ à saucisse**
sausage meat
chaise [ʃɛz] nf chair; **chaise longue**
deckchair
châle [ʃal] nm shawl
chaleur [ʃalœʀ] nf heat; (fig: accueil)
warmth; **chaleureux, -euse** adj warm

chamailler [ʃamaje]: **se chamailler** vi
to squabble, bicker
chambre [ʃɑ̃bʀ] nf bedroom; (Pol,
Comm) chamber; **faire ~ à part** to sleep
in separate rooms; **je voudrais une ~
pour deux personnes** I'd like a double
room; **chambre à air** (de pneu) (inner)
tube; **chambre à coucher** bedroom;
chambre à un lit/à deux lits (à
l'hôtel) single-/twin-bedded room;
chambre d'amis spare ou guest room;
chambre d'hôte = bed and breakfast;
chambre meublée bedsit(ter) (BRIT),
furnished room; **chambre noire** (Photo)
darkroom
chameau, X [ʃamo] nm camel
chamois [ʃamwa] nm chamois
champ [ʃɑ̃] nm field; **champ de bataille**
battlefield; **champ de courses**
racecourse
champagne [ʃɑ̃paɲ] nm champagne
champignon [ʃɑ̃piɲɔ̃] nm mushroom;
(terme générique) fungus; **champignon
de Paris** ou **de couche** button
mushroom
champion, ne [ʃɑ̃pjɔ̃, jɔn] adj,
nm/f champion; **championnat** nm
championship
chance [ʃɑ̃s] nf: **la ~** luck; **chances** nfpl
(probabilités) chances; **avoir de la ~** to
be lucky; **il a des ~ de réussir** he's got
a good chance of passing; **bonne ~!**
good luck!
change [ʃɑ̃ʒ] nm (devises) exchange
changement [ʃɑ̃ʒmɑ̃] nm change;
changement de vitesses gears pl
changer [ʃɑ̃ʒe] vt (modifier) to change,
alter; (remplacer, Comm) to change ▷ vi
to change, alter; **se changer** vi to
change (o.s.); **~ de** (remplacer: adresse,
nom, voiture etc) to change one's;
(échanger: place, train etc) to change;
~ d'avis to change one's mind; **~ de
vitesse** to change gear; **il faut ~ à Lyon**
you ou we etc have to change in Lyons;
où est-ce que je peux ~ de l'argent?
where can I change some money?
chanson [ʃɑ̃sɔ̃] nf song

chant [ʃɑ̃] nm song; (art vocal) singing; (d'église) hymn

chantage [ʃɑ̃taʒ] nm blackmail; **faire du ~** to use blackmail

chanter [ʃɑ̃te] vt, vi to sing; **si cela lui chante** (fam) if he feels like it; **chanteur, -euse** nm/f singer

chantier [ʃɑ̃tje] nm (building) site; (sur une route) roadworks pl; **mettre en ~** to put in hand; **chantier naval** shipyard

chantilly [ʃɑ̃tiji] nf voir **crème**

chantonner [ʃɑ̃tɔne] vi, vt to sing to oneself, hum

chapeau, x [ʃapo] nm hat; **~!** well done!

chapelle [ʃapɛl] nf chapel

chapitre [ʃapitʀ] nm chapter

chaque [ʃak] dét each, every; (indéfini) every

char [ʃaʀ] nm (Mil): **~ (d'assaut)** tank; **~ à voile** sand yacht

charbon [ʃaʀbɔ̃] nm coal; **charbon de bois** charcoal

charcuterie [ʃaʀkytʀi] nf (magasin) pork butcher's shop and delicatessen; (produits) cooked pork meats pl; **charcutier, -ière** nm/f pork butcher

chardon [ʃaʀdɔ̃] nm thistle

charge [ʃaʀʒ] nf (fardeau) load, burden; (Élec, Mil, Jur) charge; (rôle, mission) responsibility; **charges** nfpl (du loyer) service charges; **à la ~ de** (dépendant de) dependent upon; (aux frais de) chargeable to; **prendre en ~** to take charge of; (suj: véhicule) to take on; (dépenses) to take care of; **charges sociales** social security contributions

chargement [ʃaʀʒəmɑ̃] nm (objets) load

charger [ʃaʀʒe] vt (voiture, fusil, caméra) to load; (batterie) to charge ▷ vi (Mil etc) to charge; **se ~ de** to see to, take care of

chariot [ʃaʀjo] nm trolley; (charrette) waggon

charité [ʃaʀite] nf charity; **faire la ~ à** to give (something) to

charmant, e [ʃaʀmɑ̃, ɑ̃t] adj charming

charme [ʃaʀm] nm charm; **charmer**

vt to charm

charpente [ʃaʀpɑ̃t] nf frame(work); **charpentier** nm carpenter

charrette [ʃaʀɛt] nf cart

charter [ʃaʀtɛʀ] nm (vol) charter flight

chasse [ʃas] nf hunting; (poursuite) chase; (aussi: **~ d'eau**) flush; **prendre en ~** to give chase to; **tirer la ~ (d'eau)** to flush the toilet, pull the chain; **~ à courre** hunting; **chasse-neige** nm inv snowplough (BRIT), snowblow (US); **chasser** vt to hunt; (expulser) to chase away ou out, drive away ou out; **chasseur, -euse** nm/f hunter ▷ nm (avion) fighter

chat¹ [ʃa] nm cat

chat² [tʃat] nm (Internet) chat room

châtaigne [ʃatɛɲ] nf chestnut

châtain [ʃatɛ̃] adj inv (cheveux) chestnut (brown); (personne) chestnut-haired

château, x [ʃato] nm (forteresse) castle; (résidence royale) palace; (manoir) mansion; **château d'eau** water tower; **château fort** stronghold, fortified castle

châtiment [ʃatimɑ̃] nm punishment

chaton [ʃatɔ̃] nm (Zool) kitten

chatouiller [ʃatuje] vt to tickle; **chatouilleux, -euse** adj ticklish

chatte [ʃat] nf (she-)cat

chatter [tʃate] vi (Internet) to chat

chaud, e [ʃo, ʃod] adj (gén) warm; (très chaud) hot; **il fait ~** it's warm; it's hot; **avoir ~** to be warm; to be hot; **ça me tient ~** it keeps me warm; **rester au ~** to stay in the warm

chaudière [ʃodjɛʀ] nf boiler

chauffage [ʃofaʒ] nm heating; **chauffage central** central heating

chauffe-eau [ʃofo] nm inv water-heater

chauffer [ʃofe] vt to heat ▷ vi to heat up, warm up; (trop chauffer: moteur) to overheat; **se chauffer** vi (au soleil) to warm o.s.

chauffeur [ʃofœʀ] nm driver; (privé) chauffeur

45 | chic

chaumière [ʃomjɛʀ] nf (thatched) cottage

chaussée [ʃose] nf road(way)

chausser [ʃose] vt (bottes, skis) to put on; (enfant) to put shoes on; **~ du 38/42** to take size 38/42

chaussette [ʃosɛt] nf sock

chausson [ʃosɔ̃] nm slipper; (de bébé) bootee; **chausson (aux pommes)** (apple) turnover

chaussure [ʃosyʀ] nf shoe; **chaussures basses** flat shoes; **chaussures montantes** ankle boots; **chaussures de ski** ski boots

chauve [ʃov] adj bald; **chauve-souris** nf bat

chauvin, e [ʃovɛ̃, in] adj chauvinistic

chaux [ʃo] nf lime; **blanchi à la ~** whitewashed

chef [ʃɛf] nm head, leader; (de cuisine) chef; **commandant en ~** commander-in-chief; **chef d'accusation** charge; **chef d'entreprise** company head; **chef d'État** head of state; **chef de famille** head of the family; **chef de file** (de parti etc) leader; **chef de gare** station master; **chef d'orchestre** conductor; **chef-d'œuvre** nm masterpiece; **chef-lieu** nm county town

chemin [ʃ(ə)mɛ̃] nm path; (itinéraire, direction, trajet) way; **en ~** on the way; **chemin de fer** railway (BRIT), railroad (US)

cheminée [ʃ(ə)mine] nf chimney; (à l'intérieur) chimney piece, fireplace; (de bateau) funnel

chemise [ʃ(ə)miz] nf shirt; (dossier) folder; **chemise de nuit** nightdress

chemisier [ʃ(ə)mizje] nm blouse

chêne [ʃɛn] nm oak (tree); (bois) oak

chenil [ʃ(ə)nil] nm kennels pl

chenille [ʃ(ə)nij] nf (Zool) caterpillar

chèque [ʃɛk] nm cheque (BRIT), check (US); **est-ce que je peux payer par ~?** can I pay by cheque?; **chèque sans provision** bad cheque; **chèque de voyage** traveller's cheque; **chéquier** [ʃekje] nm cheque book

chic [ʃik] adj inv chic, smart; (fam:

cher, -ère [ʃɛʀ] adj (aimé) dear; (coûteux) expensive, dear ▷ adv: **ça coûte ~** it's expensive

chercher [ʃɛʀʃe] vt to look for; (gloire etc) to seek; **aller ~** to go for, go and fetch; **~ à faire** to try to do; **chercheur, -euse** nm/f researcher, research worker

chéri, e [ʃeʀi] adj beloved, dear; **(mon) ~** darling

cheval, -aux [ʃ(ə)val, o] nm horse; (Auto): **~ (vapeur)** horsepower no pl; **faire du ~** to ride; **à ~** on horseback; **à ~ sur** astride; (fig) overlapping; **cheval de course** racehorse

chevalier [ʃ(ə)valje] nm knight

chevalière [ʃ(ə)valjɛʀ] nf signet ring

chevaux [ʃəvo] nmpl de **cheval**

chevet [ʃ(ə)vɛ] nm: **au ~ de qn** at sb's bedside; **lampe de chevet** bedside lamp

cheveu, -x [ʃ(ə)vø] nm hair; **cheveux** nmpl (chevelure) hair sg; **avoir les ~x courts** to have short hair

cheville [ʃ(ə)vij] nf (Anat) ankle; (de bois) peg; (pour une vis) plug

chèvre [ʃɛvʀ] nf (she-)goat

chèvrefeuille [ʃɛvʀəfœj] nm honeysuckle

chevreuil [ʃəvʀœj] nm roe deer inv; (Culin) venison

🔵 **MOT-CLÉ**

chez [ʃe] prép **1** (à la demeure de) at; (: direction) to; **chez qn** at/to sb's house or place; **je suis chez moi** I'm at home; **je rentre chez moi** I'm going home; **allons chez Nathalie** let's go to Nathalie's

2 (+profession) at; (: direction) to; **chez le boulanger/dentiste** at ou to the baker's/dentist's

3 (dans le caractère, l'œuvre de) in; **chez ce poète** in this poet's work; **c'est ce que je préfère chez lui** that's what I like best about him *généreux*) nice, decent ▷ *nm* stylishness; **~ (alors)!** (*fam*) great!; **avoir le ~ de** to have the knack of

chicorée [ʃikɔʀe] *nf* (*café*) chicory; (*salade*) endive

chien [ʃjɛ̃] *nm* dog; **chien d'aveugle** guide dog; **chien de garde** guard dog

chienne [ʃjɛn] *nf* dog, bitch

chiffon [ʃifɔ̃] *nm* (*piece of*) rag; **chiffonner** *vt* to crumple; (*fam: tracasser*) to concern

chiffre [ʃifʀ] *nm* (*représentant un nombre*) figure, numeral; (*montant, total*) total, sum; **en ~s ronds** in round figures; **chiffre d'affaires** turnover; **chiffrer** *vt* (*dépense*) to put a figure to, assess; (*message*) to (en)code, cipher; **se chiffrer à** to add up to, amount to

chignon [ʃiɲɔ̃] *nm* chignon, bun

Chili [ʃili] *nm*: **le ~** Chile; **chilien, ne** *adj* Chilean ▷ *nm/f*: **Chilien, ne** Chilean

chimie [ʃimi] *nf* chemistry; **chimiothérapie** [ʃimjoterapi] *nf* chemotherapy; **chimique** *adj* chemical; **produits chimiques** chemicals

chimpanzé [ʃɛ̃pɑ̃ze] *nm* chimpanzee

Chine [ʃin] *nf*: **la ~** China; **chinois, e** *adj* Chinese ▷ *nm/f*: **Chinois, e** Chinese ▷ *nm* (*Ling*) Chinese

chiot [ʃjo] *nm* pup(py)

chips [ʃips] *nfpl* crisps (BRIT), (potato) chips (US)

chirurgie [ʃiʀyʀʒi] *nf* surgery; **chirurgie esthétique** plastic surgery; **chirurgien, ne** *nm/f* surgeon

chlore [klɔʀ] *nm* chlorine

choc [ʃɔk] *nm* (*heurt*) impact, shock; (*collision*) crash; (*moral*) shock; (*affrontement*) clash

chocolat [ʃɔkɔla] *nm* chocolate; **chocolat au lait** milk chocolate

chœur [kœʀ] *nm* (*chorale*) choir; (*Opéra, Théâtre*) chorus; **en ~** in chorus

choisir [ʃwaziʀ] *vt* to choose, select

choix [ʃwa] *nm* choice, selection; **avoir le ~** to have the choice; **premier ~** (*Comm*) class one; **de ~** choice, selected;

au ~ as you wish

chômage [ʃomaʒ] *nm* unemployment; **mettre au ~** to make redundant, put out of work; **être au ~** to be unemployed *ou* out of work; **chômeur, -euse** *nm/f* unemployed person

choquer [ʃɔke] *vt* (*offenser*) to shock; (*deuil*) to shake

chorale [kɔʀal] *nf* choir

chose [ʃoz] *nf* thing; **c'est peu de ~** it's nothing (really)

chou, x [ʃu] *nm* cabbage; **mon petit ~** sweetheart; **chou à la crème** choux bun; **chou de Bruxelles** Brussels sprout; **choucroute** *nf* sauerkraut

chouette [ʃwɛt] *nf* owl ▷ *adj* (*fam*) great, smashing

chou-fleur [ʃuflœʀ] *nm* cauliflower

chrétien, ne [kʀetjɛ̃, jɛn] *adj, nm/f* Christian

Christ [kʀist] *nm*: **le ~** Christ; **christianisme** *nm* Christianity

chronique [kʀɔnik] *adj* chronic ▷ *nf* (*de journal*) column, page; (*historique*) chronicle; (*Radio, TV*): **la ~ sportive** the sports review

chronologique [kʀɔnɔlɔʒik] *adj* chronological

chronomètre [kʀɔnɔmɛtʀ] *nm* stopwatch; **chronométrer** *vt* to time

chrysanthème [kʀizɑ̃tɛm] *nm* chrysanthemum

● **CHRYSANTHÈME**
●
● Chrysanthemums are strongly
● associated with funerals in France,
● and therefore should not be given
● as gifts.

chuchotement [ʃyʃɔtmɑ̃] *nm* whisper

chuchoter [ʃyʃɔte] *vt, vi* to whisper

chut [ʃyt] *excl* sh!

chute [ʃyt] *nf* fall; (*déchet*) scrap; **faire une ~ (de 10 m)** to fall (10 m); **chute (d'eau)** waterfall; **chute libre** free fall; **chutes de pluie/neige** rainfall/snowfall

Chypre [ʃipʁ] nm/f Cyprus

-ci [si] *dv voir* **par ▷** *dét:* **ce garçon~** this boy; **ces femmes~** these women

cible [sibl] nf target

ciboulette [sibulɛt] nf (small) chive

cicatrice [sikatʁis] nf scar; **cicatriser** vt to heal

ci-contre [sikɔ̃tʁ] *dv* opposite

ci-dessous [sidəsu] *dv* below

ci-dessus [sidəsy] *dv* above

cidre [sidʁ] nm cider

Cie *dbr* (= *compagnie*) Co.

ciel [sjɛl] nm sky; (*Rel*) heaven

cieux [sjø] nmpl *de* **ciel**

cigale [sigal] nf cicada

cigare [sigaʁ] nm cigar

cigarette [sigaʁɛt] nf cigarette

ci-inclus, e [siɛ̃kly, yz] *adj, dv* enclosed

ci-joint, e [siʒwɛ̃, ɛ̃t] *adj, dv* enclosed

cil [sil] nm (eye)lash

cime [sim] nf top; (*montagne*) peak

ciment [simɑ̃] nm cement

cimetière [simtjɛʁ] nm cemetery; (*d'église*) churchyard

cinéaste [sineast] nm/f film-maker

cinéma [sinema] nm cinema

cinq [sɛ̃k] num five; **cinquantaine** nf: **une cinquantaine (de)** about fifty; **avoir la cinquantaine** (*âge*) to be around fifty; **cinquante** num fifty; **cinquantenaire** *adj, nm/f* fifty-year-old; **cinquième** num fifth ▷ nf (*Scol*) year 8 (*BRIT*), seventh grade (*US*)

cintre [sɛ̃tʁ] nm coat-hanger

cintré, e [sɛ̃tʁe] *adj* (*chemise*) fitted

cirage [siʁaʒ] nm (shoe) polish

circonflexe [siʁkɔ̃flɛks] *adj:* **accent ~** circumflex accent

circonstance [siʁkɔ̃stɑ̃s] nf circumstance; (*occasion*) occasion; **circonstances atténuantes** mitigating circumstances

circuit [siʁkɥi] nm (*Élec, Tech*) circuit; (*trajet*) tour, (round) trip

circulaire [siʁkylɛʁ] *adj, nf* circular

circulation [siʁkylasjɔ̃] nf circulation; (*Auto*): **la ~** (the) traffic

circuler [siʁkyle] vi (*sang, devises*) to circulate; (*véhicules*) to drive (along); (*passants*) to walk along; (*train, bus*) to run; **faire ~** (*nouvelle*) to spread (about), circulate; (*badauds*) to move on

cire [siʁ] nf wax; **ciré** nm oilskin; **cirer** vt to wax, polish

cirque [siʁk] nm circus; (*fig*) chaos, bedlam; **quel ~!** what a carry-on!

ciseau, x [sizo] nm: **~ (à bois)** chisel; **ciseaux** nmpl (*paire de ciseaux*) (pair of) scissors

citadin, e [sitadɛ̃, in] nm/f city dweller

citation [sitasjɔ̃] nf (*d'auteur*) quotation; (*Jur*) summons *sg*

cité [site] nf town; (*plus grande*) city; **cité universitaire** students' residences *pl*

citer [site] vt (*un auteur*) to quote (from); (*nommer*) to name; (*Jur*) to summon

citoyen, ne [sitwajɛ̃, jɛn] nm/f citizen

citron [sitʁɔ̃] nm lemon; **citron pressé** (fresh) lemon juice; **citron vert** lime; **citronnade** nf still lemonade

citrouille [sitʁuj] nf pumpkin

civet [sivɛ] nm: **~ de lapin** rabbit stew

civière [sivjɛʁ] nf stretcher

civil, e [sivil] *adj* (*mariage, poli*) civil; (*non militaire*) civilian; **en ~** in civilian clothes; **dans la ~** in civilian life

civilisation [sivilizasjɔ̃] nf civilization

clair, e [klɛʁ] *adj* light; (*pièce*) light, bright; (*eau, son, fig*) clear ▷ *dv:* **voir ~** to see clearly; **tirer qch au ~** to clear sth up, clarify sth; **mettre au ~** (*notes etc*) to tidy up ▷ nm: **~ de lune** moonlight; **clairement** *dv* clearly

clairière [klɛʁjɛʁ] nf clearing

clandestin, e [klɑ̃dɛstɛ̃, in] *adj* clandestine, secret; (*mouvement*) underground; (*travailleur, immigration*) illegal; **passager ~** stowaway

claque [klak] nf (*gifle*) slap; **claquer** vi (*porte*) to bang, slam; (*fam: mourir*) to snuff it ▷ vt (*porte*) to slam, bang; (*doigts*) to snap; (*fam: dépenser*) to blow; **il claquait des dents** his teeth were chattering; **être claqué** (*fam*) to be dead tired; **se claquer un muscle** to pull ou strain a muscle; **claquettes** nfpl tap-dancing sg; (chaussures) flip-flops

clarinette [klaʀinɛt] nf clarinet

classe [klɑs] nf class; (Scol: local) class(room); (: leçon, élèves) class; **aller en ~** to go to school; **classement** nm (rang: Scol) place; (: Sport) placing; (liste: Scol) class list (in order of merit); (: Sport) placings pl

classer [klɑse] vt (idées, livres) to classify; (papiers) to file; (candidat, concurrent) to grade; (Jur: affaire) to close; **se ~ premier/dernier** to come first/last; (Sport) to finish first/last; **classeur** nm (cahier) file

classique [klasik] adj classical; (sobre: coupe etc) classic(al); (habituel) standard, classic

clavecin [klavsɛ̃] nm harpsichord

clavicule [klavikyl] nf collarbone

clavier [klavje] nm keyboard

clé [kle] nf key; (Mus) clef; (de mécanicien) spanner, wrench (US); **prix ~s en main** (d'une voiture) on-the-road price; **clé de contact** ignition key; **clé USB** USB key

clef [kle] nf = **clé**

clergé [klɛʀʒe] nm clergy

cliché [kliʃe] nm (fig) cliché; (négatif) negative; (photo) print

client, e [klijɑ̃, klijɑ̃t] nm/f (acheteur) customer, client; (d'hôtel) guest, patron; (du docteur) patient; (de l'avocat) client; **clientèle** nf (du magasin) customers pl, clientele; (du docteur, de l'avocat) practice

cligner [kliɲe] vi: **~ des yeux** to blink (one's eyes); **~ de l'œil** to wink; **clignotant** nm (Auto) indicator; **clignoter** vi (étoiles etc) to twinkle; (lumière) to flicker

climat [klima] nm climate

climatisation [klimatizasjɔ̃] nf air conditioning; **climatisé, e** adj air-conditioned

clin d'œil [klɛ̃dœj] nm wink; **en un clin d'œil** in a flash

clinique [klinik] nf private hospital

clip [klip] nm (boucle d'oreille) clip-on; **(vidéo) ~** (pop) video

cliquer [klike] vt to click; **~ sur** to click on

clochard, e [klɔʃaʀ, aʀd] nm/f tramp

cloche [klɔʃ] nf (d'église) bell; (fam) clot; **clocher** nm church tower; (en pointe) steeple ▷ vi (fam) to be ou go wrong; **de clocher** (péj) parochial

cloison [klwazɔ̃] nf partition (wall)

clonage [klɔnaʒ] nm cloning

cloner [klɔne] vt to clone

cloque [klɔk] nf blister

clore [klɔʀ] vt to close

clôture [klotyʀ] nf closure; (barrière) enclosure

clou [klu] nm nail; **clous** nmpl (passage clouté) pedestrian crossing; **pneus à ~s** studded tyres; **le ~ du spectacle** the highlight of the show; **clou de girofle** clove

clown [klun] nm clown

club [klœb] nm club

CNRS sigle m (= Centre nationale de la recherche scientifique) ≈ SERC (BRIT), ≈ NSF (US)

coaguler [kɔagyle] vt, vi (aussi: **se ~**: sang) to coagulate

cobaye [kɔbaj] nm guinea-pig

coca [kɔka] nm Coke®

cocaïne [kɔkain] nf cocaine

coccinelle [kɔksinɛl] nf ladybird (BRIT), ladybug (US)

cocher [kɔʃe] vt to tick off

cochon, ne [kɔʃɔ̃, ɔn] nm pig ▷ adj (fam) dirty, smutty; **cochon d'Inde** guinea pig; **cochonnerie** (fam) nf (saleté) filth; (marchandise) rubbish, trash

cocktail [kɔktɛl] nm cocktail; (réception) cocktail party

cocorico [kɔkɔʀiko] excl, nm cock-a-doodle-do

cocotte [kɔkɔt] nf (en fonte) casserole; **ma ~** (fam) sweetie (pie); **cocotte (minute)®** pressure cooker

code [kɔd] nm code ▷ adj: **phares ~s** dipped lights; **se mettre en ~(s)** to dip one's (head)lights; **code à barres** bar code; **code civil** Common Law; **code de la route** highway code; **code pénal** penal code; **code postal** (numéro) post (BRIT) ou zip (US) code

cœur [kœʀ] nm heart; (Cartes: couleur) hearts pl; (: carte) heart; **avoir bon ~** to be kind-hearted; **avoir mal au ~** to feel sick; **par ~** by heart; **de bon ~** willingly; **cela lui tient à ~** that's (very) close to his heart

coffre [kɔfʀ] nm (meuble) chest; (d'auto) boot (BRIT), trunk (US); **coffre-fort** nm safe; **coffret** nm casket

cognac [kɔɲak] nm brandy, cognac

cogner [kɔɲe] vi to knock; **se ~ contre** to knock ou bump into; **se ~ la tête** to bang one's head

cohérent, e [kɔeʀɑ̃, ɑ̃t] adj coherent, consistent

coiffé, e [kwafe] adj: **~ avec** with tidy/untidy hair; **~ d'un chapeau** wearing a hat

coiffer [kwafe] vt (fig: surmonter) to cover, top; **se coiffer** vi to do one's hair; **~ qn** to do sb's hair; **coiffeur, -euse** nm/f hairdresser; **coiffeuse** nf (table) dressing table; **coiffure** nf (cheveux) hairstyle, hairdo; (art): **la coiffure** hairdressing

coin [kwɛ̃] nm corner; (pour coincer) wedge; **l'épicerie du ~** the local grocer; **dans le ~** (aux alentours) in the area, around about; (habiter) locally; **je ne suis pas du ~** I'm not from here; **au ~ du feu** by the fireside; **regard en ~** sideways glance

coincé, e [kwɛ̃se] adj stuck, jammed; (fig: inhibé) inhibited, hung up (fam)

coïncidence [kɔɛ̃sidɑ̃s] nf coincidence

coing [kwɛ̃] nm quince

col [kɔl] nm (de chemise) collar; (encolure, cou) neck; (de montagne) pass; **col de l'utérus** cervix; **col roulé** polo-neck

colère [kɔlɛʀ] nf anger; **une ~** a fit of anger; **(se mettre) en ~** (to get) angry (with sb); **coléreux, -euse, colérique** adj quick-tempered,

---

irascible

colin [kɔlɛ̃] nm hake

colique [kɔlik] nf diarrhoea

colis [kɔli] nm parcel

collaborer [kɔ(l)labɔʀe] vi to collaborate; **~ à** to collaborate on; (revue) to contribute to

collant, e [kɔlɑ̃, ɑ̃t] adj sticky; (robe etc) clinging, skintight; (péj) clinging ⊳ nm (bas) tights pl; (de danseur) leotard

colle [kɔl] nf glue; (à papiers peints) (wallpaper) paste; (fam: devinette) teaser, riddle; (Scol: fam) detention

collecte [kɔlɛkt] nf collection; **collectif, -ive** adj collective; (visite, billet) group cpd

collection [kɔlɛksjɔ̃] nf collection; (Édition) series; **collectionner** vt to collect; **collectionneur, -euse** nm/f collector

collectivité [kɔlɛktivite] nf group; **collectivités locales** (Admin) local authorities

collège [kɔlɛʒ] nm (école) (secondary) school; (assemblée) body; **collégien** nm schoolboy

collègue [kɔ(l)lɛg] nm/f colleague

coller [kɔle] vt (papier, timbre) to stick (on); (affiche) to stick up; (enveloppe) to stick down; (morceaux) to stick ou glue together; (Comput) to paste; (fam: mettre, fourrer) to stick, shove; (Scol: fam) to keep in ⊳ vi (être collant) to be sticky; (adhérer) to stick; **~ à** to stick to; **être collé à un examen** (fam) to fail an exam

collier [kɔlje] nm (bijou) necklace; (de chien, Tech) collar

colline [kɔlin] nf hill

collision [kɔlizjɔ̃] nf collision, crash; **entrer en ~ (avec)** to collide (with)

collyre [kɔliʀ] nm eye drops

colombe [kɔlɔ̃b] nf dove

Colombie [kɔlɔ̃bi] nf: **la ~** Colombia

colonie [kɔlɔni] nf colony; **colonie (de vacances)** holiday camp (for children)

colonne [kɔlɔn] nf column; **se mettre en ~ par deux** to get into twos;

colonne (vertébrale) spine, spinal column

colorant [kɔlɔʀɑ̃] *nm* colouring

colorer [kɔlɔʀe] *vt* to colour

colorier [kɔlɔʀje] *vt* to colour (in)

coloris [kɔlɔʀi] *nm* colour, shade

colza [kɔlza] *nm* rape(seed)

coma [kɔma] *nm* coma; **être dans le ~** to be in a coma

combat [kɔ̃ba] *nm* fight, fighting *no pl*; **combat de boxe** boxing match; **combattant** *nm*: **ancien combattant** war veteran; **combattre** *vt* to fight; (*épidémie, ignorance*) to combat, fight against

combien [kɔ̃bjɛ̃] *adv* (*quantité*) how much; (*nombre*) how many; **~ de** (*quantité*) how much; (*nombre*) how many; **~ de temps** how long; **~ ça coûte/pèse?** how much does it cost/weigh?; **on est le ~ aujourd'hui?** (*fam*) what's the date today?

combinaison [kɔ̃binɛzɔ̃] *nf* combination; (*astuce*) scheme; (*de femme*) slip; (*de plongée*) wetsuit; (*bleu de travail*) boiler suit (BRIT), coveralls *pl* (US)

combiné [kɔ̃bine] *nm* (*aussi:* **~ téléphonique**) receiver

comble [kɔ̃bl] *adj* (*salle*) packed (full) ▷ *nm* (*du bonheur, plaisir*) height; **combles** *nmpl* (*Constr*) attic *sg*, loft *sg*; **c'est le ~!** that beats everything!

combler [kɔ̃ble] *vt* (*trou*) to fill in; (*besoin, lacune*) to fill; (*déficit*) to make good; (*satisfaire*) to fulfil

comédie [kɔmedi] *nf* comedy; (*fig*) playacting *no pl*; **faire la ~** (*fam*) to make a fuss; **comédie musicale** musical; **comédien, ne** *nm/f* actor(-tress)

comestible [kɔmɛstibl] *adj* edible

comique [kɔmik] *adj* (*drôle*) comical; (*Théâtre*) comic ▷ *nm* (*artiste*) comic, comedian

commandant [kɔmɑ̃dɑ̃] *nm* (*gén*) commander, commandant; (*Navig, Aviat*) captain

commande [kɔmɑ̃d] *nf* (*Comm*)

order; **commandes** *nfpl* (*Aviat etc*) controls; **sur ~** to order; **commander** *vt* (*Comm*) to order; (*diriger, ordonner*) to command; **commander à qn de faire** to command ou order sb to do; **je peux commander, s'il vous plaît?** can I order, please?

 MOT-CLÉ

comme [kɔm] *prép* **1** (*comparaison*) like; **tout comme son père** just like his father; **fort comme un bœuf** as strong as an ox; **joli comme tout** ever so pretty

2 (*manière*) like; **faites-le comme ça** do it like this, do it this way; **comme ci, comme ça** so-so, middling; **comme il faut** (*correctement*) properly

3 (*en tant que*) as a; **donner comme prix** to give as a prize; **travailler comme secrétaire** to work as a secretary

▷ *conj* **1** (*ainsi que*) as; **elle écrit comme elle parle** she writes as she talks; **comme si** as if

2 (*au moment où, alors que*) as; **il est parti comme j'arrivais** he left as I arrived

3 (*parce que, puisque*) as; **comme il était en retard, il ...** as he was late, he ...

▷ *adv*: **comme il est fort/c'est bon!** he's so strong/it's so good!

commencement [kɔmɑ̃smɑ̃] *nm* beginning, start

commencer [kɔmɑ̃se] *vt, vi* to begin, start; **~ à** *ou* **de faire** to begin ou start doing

comment [kɔmɑ̃] *adv* how; **~?** (*que dites-vous*) pardon?; **et ~!** and how!

commentaire [kɔmɑ̃tɛʀ] *nm* (*remarque*) comment, remark; (*exposé*) commentary

commerçant, e [kɔmɛʀsɑ̃, ɑ̃t] *nm/f* shopkeeper, trader

commerce [kɔmɛʀs] *nm* (*activité*) trade, commerce; (*boutique*) business; **~ électronique** e-commerce; **~**

équitable fair trade; **commercial, e, -aux** adj commercial, trading; (péj) commercial; **les commerciaux** the sales people; **commercialiser** vt to market

commissaire [kɔmisɛʀ] nm (de police) ≈ (police) superintendent; **commissaire aux comptes** (Admin) auditor; **commissariat** nm police station

commission [kɔmisjɔ̃] nf (comité, pourcentage) commission; (message): (message) message; (course) errand; **commissions** nfpl (achats) shopping sg

commode [kɔmɔd] adj (pratique) convenient, handy; (facile) easy; (personne): **pas ~** awkward (to deal with) ▷ nf chest of drawers

commun, e [kɔmœ̃, yn] adj common; (pièce) communal, shared; (effort) joint; **ça sort du ~** it's out of the ordinary; **le ~ des mortels** the common run of people; **en ~** (faire) jointly; **mettre en ~** to pool, share; **communs** nmpl (bâtiments) outbuildings; **d'un ~ accord** by mutual agreement

communauté [kɔmynote] nf community

commune [kɔmyn] nf (Admin) commune, ≈ district; (: urbaine) ≈ borough

communication [kɔmynikasjɔ̃] nf communication

communier [kɔmynje] vi (Rel) to receive communion

communion [kɔmynjɔ̃] nf communion

communiquer [kɔmynike] vt (nouvelle, dossier) to pass on, convey; (peur etc) to communicate ▷ vi to communicate; **se communiquer à** (se propager) to spread to

communisme [kɔmynism] nm communism; **communiste** adj, nm/f communist

commutateur [kɔmytatœʀ] nm (Élec) (change-over) switch, commutator

compact, e [kɔpakt] adj (dense) dense;

(appareil) compact

compagne [kɔ̃paɲ] nf companion

compagnie [kɔ̃paɲi] nf (firme, Mil) company; **tenir ~ à qn** to keep sb company; **fausser ~ à qn** to give sb the slip, slip ou sneak away from sb; **compagnie aérienne** airline (company)

compagnon [kɔ̃paɲɔ̃] nm companion

comparable [kɔ̃paʀabl] adj: **~ (à)** comparable (to)

comparaison [kɔ̃paʀɛzɔ̃] nf comparison

comparer [kɔ̃paʀe] vt to compare; **~ qch/qn à** ou **et** (pour choisir) to compare sth/sb with ou and; (pour établir une similitude) to compare sth/sb to

compartiment [kɔ̃paʀtimɑ̃] nm compartment; **un ~ non-fumeurs** a non-smoking compartment (BRIT) ou car (US)

compas [kɔ̃pɑ] nm (Géom) (pair of) compasses pl; (Navig) compass

compatible [kɔ̃patibl] adj compatible

compatriote [kɔ̃patʀijɔt] nm/f compatriot

compensation [kɔ̃pɑ̃sasjɔ̃] nf compensation

compenser [kɔ̃pɑ̃se] vt to compensate for, make up for

compétence [kɔ̃petɑ̃s] nf competence

compétent, e [kɔ̃petɑ̃, ɑ̃t] adj (apte) competent, capable

compétition [kɔ̃petisjɔ̃] nf (gén) competition; (Sport: épreuve) event; **la ~ automobile** motor racing

complément [kɔ̃plemɑ̃] nm complement; (reste) remainder; **complément d'information** (Admin) supplementary ou further information; **complémentaire** adj complementary; (additionnel) supplementary

complet, -ète [kɔ̃plɛ, ɛt] adj complete; (plein: hôtel etc) full ▷ nm (aussi: **~-veston**) suit; **pain complet** wholemeal bread; **complètement** adv completely; **compléter** vt (porter à la quantité voulue) to complete;

(augmenter: connaissances, études) to complement, supplement; *(: garde-robe)* to add to

complexe [kɔ̃plɛks] *adj, nm* complex; **complexe hospitalier/industriel** hospital/industrial complex; **complexé, e** *adj* mixed-up, hung-up

complication [kɔ̃plikasjɔ̃] *nf* complexity, intricacy; *(difficulté, ennui)* complication; **complications** *nfpl* *(Méd)* complications

complice [kɔ̃plis] *nm* accomplice

compliment [kɔ̃plimɑ̃] *nm* *(louange)* compliment; **compliments** *nmpl* *(félicitations)* congratulations

compliqué, e [kɔ̃plike] *adj* complicated, complex; *(personne)* complicated

comportement [kɔ̃pɔʀtəmɑ̃] *nm* behaviour

comporter [kɔ̃pɔʀte] *vt* *(consister en)* to consist of, comprise; *(inclure)* to have; **se comporter** *vi* to behave

composer [kɔ̃poze] *vt* *(musique, texte)* to compose; *(mélange, équipe)* to make up; *(numéro)* to dial; *(constituer)* to make up, form ▷ *vi* *(transiger)* to come to terms; **se composer de** to be composed of, be made up of; **compositeur, -trice** *nm/f* *(Mus)* composer; **composition** *nf* composition; *(Scol)* test

composter [kɔ̃poste] *vt* *(billet)* to punch

▪ **COMPOSTER**

▪ In France you have to punch your ▪ ticket on the platform to validate it ▪ before getting onto the train.

compote [kɔ̃pɔt] *nf* stewed fruit *no pl*; **compote de pommes** stewed apples

compréhensible [kɔ̃pʀeɑ̃sibl] *adj* comprehensible; *(attitude)* understandable

compréhensif, -ive [kɔ̃pʀeɑ̃sif, iv] *adj* understanding

▪ Attention à ne pas traduire ▪ *compréhensif* par *comprehensive*.

comprendre [kɔ̃pʀɑ̃dʀ] *vt* to understand; *(se composer de)* to comprise, consist of

compresse [kɔ̃pʀɛs] *nf* compress

comprimé [kɔ̃pʀime] *nm* tablet

compris, e [kɔ̃pʀi, iz] *pp de* **comprendre** ▷ *adj* *(inclus)* included; **- entre** *(situé)* contained between; **l'électricité -e/non -e, y/non - l'électricité** including/excluding electricity; **100 euros tout -** = 100 euros all inclusive *ou* all in

comptabilité [kɔ̃tabilite] *nf* *(activité)* accounting, accountancy; *(comptes)* accounts *pl*, books *pl*; *(service)* accounts office

comptable [kɔ̃tabl] *nm/f* accountant

comptant [kɔ̃tɑ̃] *adv*: **payer -** to pay cash; **acheter -** to buy for cash

compte [kɔ̃t] *nm* count; *(total, montant)* count, (right) number; *(bancaire, facture)* account; **comptes** *nmpl* *(Finance)* accounts, books; *(fig)* explanation *sg*; **en fin de -** all things considered; **s'en tirer à bon -** to get off lightly; **pour le - de** on behalf of; **pour son propre -** for one's own benefit; **régler un -** *(s'acquitter de qch)* to settle an account; *(se venger)* to get one's own back; **rendre des -s à qn** *(fig)* to be answerable to sb; **tenir - de** to take account of; **travailler à son -** to work for oneself; **rendre - (à qn) de qch** to give (sb) an account of sth; *voir aussi* **rendre**; **compte à rebours** countdown; **compte courant** current account; **compte rendu** report; *(de film, livre)* review; **compte-gouttes** *nm inv* dropper

compter [kɔ̃te] *vt* to count; *(facturer)* to charge for; *(avoir à son actif, comporter)* to have; *(prévoir)* to allow, reckon; *(penser, espérer)*: **- réussir** to expect to succeed ▷ *vi* to count; *(être économe)* to economize; *(figurer)*: **- parmi** to be *ou* rank among; **- sur** to count (up)on;

~ avec qch/qn to reckon ou take account of sth/sb; **sans ~ que** besides which

compteur [kɔ̃tœr] nm meter; **compteur de vitesse** speedometer

comptine [kɔ̃tin] nf nursery rhyme

comptoir [kɔ̃twar] nm (de magasin) counter; (bar) bar

con, ne [kɔ̃, kɔn] (fam!) adj damned ou bloody (BRIT) stupid (!)

concentrer [kɔ̃sɑ̃tre] vt to concentrate; **se concentrer** vi to concentrate

concerner [kɔ̃sɛrne] vt to concern; **en ce qui me concerne** as far as I am concerned

concert [kɔ̃sɛr] nm concert; **de ~** (décider) unanimously

concessionnaire [kɔ̃sesjɔnɛr] nm/f agent, dealer

concevoir [kɔ̃s(ə)vwar] vt (idée, projet) to conceive (of); (comprendre) to understand; (enfant) to conceive; **bien/mal conçu** well-/badly-designed

concierge [kɔ̃sjɛrʒ] nm/f caretaker

concis, e [kɔ̃si, iz] adj concise

conclure [kɔ̃klyr] vt to conclude; **conclusion** nf conclusion

conçois etc [kɔ̃swa] vb voir **concevoir**

concombre [kɔ̃kɔ̃br] nm cucumber

concours [kɔ̃kur] nm competition; (Scol) competitive examination; (assistance) aid, help; **concours de circonstances** combination of circumstances; **concours hippique** horse show

concret, -ète [kɔ̃krɛ, ɛt] adj concrete

conçu, e [kɔ̃sy] pp de **concevoir**

concubinage [kɔ̃kybinaʒ] nm (Jur) cohabitation

concurrence [kɔ̃kyrɑ̃s] nf competition; **faire ~ à** to be in competition with; **jusqu'à ~ de** up to

concurrent, e [kɔ̃kyrɑ̃, ɑ̃t] nm/f (Sport, Écon etc) competitor; (Scol) candidate

condamner [kɔ̃dane] vt (blâmer) to condemn; (Jur) to sentence; (porte, ouverture) to fill in, block up; **~ qn à 2 ans de prison** to sentence sb to 2 years' imprisonment

condensation [kɔ̃dɑ̃sasjɔ̃] nf condensation

condition [kɔ̃disjɔ̃] nf condition; **conditions** nfpl (tarif, prix) terms; (circonstances) conditions; **sans ~s** unconditionally; **à ~ de ou que** provided that; **conditionnel, le** nm conditional (tense)

conditionnement [kɔ̃disjɔnmɑ̃] nm (emballage) packaging

condoléances [kɔ̃dɔleɑ̃s] nfpl condolences

conducteur, -trice [kɔ̃dyktœr, tris] nm/f driver ▷ nm (Élec etc) conductor

conduire [kɔ̃dɥir] vt to drive; (délégation, troupeau) to lead; **se conduire** vi to behave; **~ à** to lead to; **~ qn quelque part** to take sb somewhere; to drive sb somewhere

conduite [kɔ̃dɥit] nf (comportement) behaviour; (d'eau, de gaz) pipe; **sous la ~ de** led by

confection [kɔ̃fɛksjɔ̃] nf (fabrication) making; (Couture): **la ~** the clothing industry

conférence [kɔ̃ferɑ̃s] nf conference; (exposé) lecture; **conférence de presse** press conference

confesser [kɔ̃fese] vt to confess; **confession** nf confession; (culte: catholique etc) denomination

confetti [kɔ̃feti] nm confetti no pl

confiance [kɔ̃fjɑ̃s] nf (en l'honnêteté de qn) confidence, trust; (en la valeur de qch) faith; **avoir ~ en** to have confidence ou faith in, trust; **faire ~ à qn** to trust sb; **mettre qn en ~** to win sb's trust; **confiance en soi** self-confidence

confiant, e [kɔ̃fjɑ̃, jɑ̃t] adj confident; trusting

confidence [kɔ̃fidɑ̃s] nf confidence; **confidentiel, le** adj confidential

confier [kɔ̃fje] vt: **~ à qn** (objet, travail) to entrust to sb; (secret, pensée) to confide to sb; **se ~ à qn** to confide in sb

confirmation[kɔ̃firmasjɔ̃] nf
confirmation

confirmer[kɔ̃firme] vt to confirm

confiserie[kɔ̃fizʀi] nf (magasin)
confectioner's ou sweet shop;
confiseries nfpl (bonbons)
confectionery sg

confisquer[kɔ̃fiske] vt to confiscate

confit, e[kɔ̃fi, it] adj: **fruits ~s**
crystallized fruits; **confit d'oie** nm
conserve of goose

confiture[kɔ̃fityʀ] nf jam

conflit[kɔ̃fli] nm conflict

confondre[kɔ̃fɔ̃dʀ] vt (jumeaux, faits)
to confuse, mix up; (témoin, menteur)
to confound; **se confondre** vi to merge;
se ~ en excuses to apologize profusely

conforme[kɔ̃fɔʀm] adj: **~ à** (loi, règle)
in accordance with; **conformément**
adv: **conformément à** in accordance
with; **conformer** vt: **se conformer à**
to conform to

confort[kɔ̃fɔʀ] nm comfort; **tout ~**
(Comm) with all modern conveniences;
confortable adj comfortable

confronter[kɔ̃frɔ̃te] vt to confront

confus, e[kɔ̃fy, yz] adj (vague)
confused; (embarrassé) embarrassed;
confusion nf (voir confus) confusion;
embarrassment; (voir confondre)
confusion, mixing up

congé[kɔ̃ʒe] nm (vacances) holiday; **en
~** on holiday; **semaine/jour de ~** week/
day off; **prendre ~ de qn** to take one's
leave of sb; **donner son ~ à** to give in
one's notice to; **congé de maladie** sick
leave; **congé de maternité** maternity
leave; **congés payés** paid holiday

congédier[kɔ̃ʒedje] vt to dismiss

congélateur[kɔ̃ʒelatœʀ] nm freezer

congeler[kɔ̃ʒ(ə)le] vt to freeze; **les
produits congelés** frozen foods

congestion[kɔ̃ʒɛstjɔ̃] nf congestion

Congo[kɔ̃go] nm: **le ~** Congo, the
Democratic Republic of the Congo

congrès[kɔ̃gʀɛ] nm congress

conifère[kɔnifɛʀ] nm conifer

conjoint, e[kɔ̃ʒwɛ̃, wɛ̃t] adj joint
▷ nm/f spouse

conjonctivite[kɔ̃ʒɔ̃ktivit] nf
conjunctivitis

conjoncture[kɔ̃ʒɔ̃ktyʀ] nf
circumstances pl; **la ~ actuelle** the
present (economic) situation

conjugaison[kɔ̃ʒygɛzɔ̃] nf (Ling)
conjugation

connaissance[kɔnɛsɑ̃s] nf (savoir)
knowledge no pl; (personne connue)
acquaintance; **être sans ~** to be
unconscious; **perdre/reprendre ~** to
lose/regain consciousness; **à ma/sa
~** to (the best of) my/his knowledge;
faire la ~ de qn to meet sb

connaisseur, -euse[kɔnɛsœʀ, øz]
nm/f connoisseur

connaître[kɔnɛtʀ] vt to know;
(éprouver) to experience; (avoir: succès)
to have, enjoy; **~ de nom/vue** to know
by name/sight; **ils se sont connus à
Genève** (first) met in Geneva; **s'y
~ en qch** to know a lot about sth

connecter[kɔnɛkte] vt to connect; **se
~ à Internet** to log onto the Internet

connerie[kɔnʀi] (fam!) nf stupid thing
(to do/say)

connexion[kɔnɛksjɔ̃] nf connection

connu, e[kɔny] adj (célèbre) well-
known

conquérir[kɔ̃keʀiʀ] vt to conquer;
conquête nf conquest

consacrer[kɔ̃sakʀe] vt (employer) to
devote, dedicate; (Rel) to consecrate; **se
~ à qch** to dedicate ou devote o.s. to sth

conscience[kɔ̃sjɑ̃s] nf conscience;
avoir/prendre ~ de to be/become
aware of; **perdre ~** to lose
consciousness; **avoir bonne/
mauvaise ~** to have a clear/guilty
conscience; **consciencieux, -euse**
adj conscientious; **conscient, e** adj
conscious

consécutif, -ive[kɔ̃sekytif, iv] adj
consecutive; **~ à** following upon

conseil[kɔ̃sɛj] nm (avis) piece of
advice; (assemblée) council; **des ~s**

advice; **prendre ~ (auprès de qn)** to take advice (from sb) **conseil d'administration** board (of directors); **conseil des ministres** ≈ the Cabinet; **conseil municipal** town council

conseiller, -ère [kɔ̃seje, ɛʀ] nm/f adviser ▷ vt (personne) to advise; (méthode, action) to recommend, advise; **~ à qn de** to advise sb to; **pouvez-vous me ~ un bon restaurant?** can you suggest a good restaurant?

consentement [kɔ̃sɑ̃tmɑ̃] nm consent

consentir [kɔ̃sɑ̃tiʀ] vt to agree, consent

conséquence [kɔ̃sekɑ̃s] nf consequence; **en ~ (donc)** consequently; (de façon appropriée) accordingly; **conséquent, e** adj logical, rational; (fam: important) substantial; **par conséquent** consequently

conservateur, -trice [kɔ̃sɛʀvatœʀ, tʀis] nm/f (Pol) conservative; (de musée) curator ▷ nm (pour aliments) preservative

conservatoire [kɔ̃sɛʀvatwaʀ] nm academy

conserve [kɔ̃sɛʀv] nf (gén pl) canned ou tinned (BRIT) food; **en ~** canned, tinned (BRIT)

conserver [kɔ̃sɛʀve] vt (faculté) to retain, keep; (amis, livres) to keep; (préserver, Culin) to preserve

considérable [kɔ̃sideʀabl] adj considerable, significant, extensive

considération [kɔ̃sideʀasjɔ̃] nf consideration; (estime) esteem

considérer [kɔ̃sideʀe] vt to consider; **~ qch comme** to regard sth as

consigne [kɔ̃siɲ] nf (de gare) left luggage (office) (BRIT), checkroom (US); (ordre, instruction) instructions pl; **consigne automatique** left-luggage locker

consister [kɔ̃siste] vi: **~ en/à faire** to consist of/in doing

consoler [kɔ̃sɔle] vt to console

consommateur, -trice [kɔ̃sɔmatœʀ, tʀis] nm/f (Écon) consumer; (dans un café) customer

consommation [kɔ̃sɔmasjɔ̃] nf (boisson) drink; (Écon) consumption; **de ~ (biens, sociétés)** consumer cpd

consommer [kɔ̃sɔme] vt (suj: personne) to eat ou drink, consume; (: voiture, machine) to use, consume; (mariage) to consummate ▷ vi (dans un café) to (have a) drink

consonne [kɔ̃sɔn] nf consonant

constamment [kɔ̃stamɑ̃] adv constantly

constant, e [kɔ̃stɑ̃, ɑ̃t] adj constant; (personne) steadfast

constat [kɔ̃sta] nm (de police, d'accident) report; **~ (à l')amiable** jointly-agreed statement for insurance purposes; **~ d'échec** acknowledgement of failure

constatation [kɔ̃statasjɔ̃] nf (observation) (observed) fact, observation

constater [kɔ̃state] vt (remarquer) to note; (Admin, Jur: attester) to certify

consterner [kɔ̃stɛʀne] vt to dismay

constipé, e [kɔ̃stipe] adj constipated

constitué, e [kɔ̃stitɥe] adj: **~ de** made up ou composed of

constituer [kɔ̃stitɥe] vt (équipe) to set up; (dossier, collection) to put together; (suj: éléments: composer) to make up, constitute; (représenter, être) to constitute; **se ~ prisonnier** to give o.s. up

constructeur, -trice [kɔ̃stʀyktœʀ, tʀis] nm/f manufacturer, builder

constructif, -ive [kɔ̃stʀyktif, iv] adj constructive

construction [kɔ̃stʀyksjɔ̃] nf construction, building

construire [kɔ̃stʀɥiʀ] vt to build, construct

consul [kɔ̃syl] nm consul; **consulat** nm consulate

consultant [kɔ̃syltɑ̃] adj, nm consultant

consultation [kɔ̃syltasjɔ̃] nf consultation; **heures de ~** (Méd) surgery (BRIT) ou office (US) hours

consulter [kɔ̃sylte] vt to consult ▷ vi (médecin) to hold surgery (BRIT), be in (the office) (US)

contact [kɔ̃takt] nm contact; **au ~ de** (air, peau) on contact with; (gens) through contact with; **mettre/ couper le ~** (Auto) to switch on/off the ignition; **entrer en** ou **prendre ~ avec** to get in touch ou contact with; **contacter** vt to contact, get in touch with

contagieux, -euse [kɔ̃taʒjø, jøz] adj infectious; (par le contact) contagious

contaminer [kɔ̃tamine] vt to contaminate

conte [kɔ̃t] nm tale; **conte de fées** fairy tale

contempler [kɔ̃tɑ̃ple] vt to contemplate, gaze at

contemporain, e [kɔ̃tɑ̃pɔʀɛ̃, ɛn] adj, nm/f contemporary

contenir [kɔ̃t(ə)niʀ] vt to contain; (avoir une capacité de) to hold

content, e [kɔ̃tɑ̃, ɑ̃t] adj pleased, glad; **~ de** pleased with; **contenter** vt to satisfy, please; **se contenter de** to content o.s. with

contenu [kɔ̃t(ə)ny] nm (d'un récipient) contents pl; (d'un texte) content

conter [kɔ̃te] vt to recount, relate

conteste [kɔ̃test]: **sans ~** adv unquestionably, indisputably; **contester** vt to question ▷ vi (Pol, gén) to rebel (against established authority)

contexte [kɔ̃tekst] nm context

continent [kɔ̃tinɑ̃] nm continent

continu, e [kɔ̃tiny] adj continuous; **faire la journée -e** to work without taking a full lunch break; **(courant) continu** direct current, DC

continuel, le [kɔ̃tinɥɛl] adj (qui se répète) constant, continual; (continu) continuous

continuer [kɔ̃tinɥe] vt (travail, voyage etc) to continue (with), carry on (with), go on (with); (prolonger: alignement, rue) to continue ▷ vi (vie, bruit) to continue,

go on; **~ à** ou **de faire** to go on ou continue doing

contourner [kɔ̃tuʀne] vt to go round; (difficulté) to get round

contraceptif, -ive [kɔ̃tʀaseptif, iv] adj, nm contraceptive; **contraception** nf contraception

contracté, e [kɔ̃tʀakte] adj tense

contracter [kɔ̃tʀakte] vt (muscle etc) to tense, contract; (maladie, dette) to contract; (assurance) to take out; **se contracter** vi (muscles) to contract

contractuel, le [kɔ̃tʀaktɥɛl] nm/f (agent) traffic warden

contradiction [kɔ̃tʀadiksjɔ̃] nf contradiction; **contradictoire** adj contradictory, conflicting

contraignant, e [kɔ̃tʀɛɲɑ̃, ɑ̃t] adj restricting

contraindre [kɔ̃tʀɛ̃dʀ] vt: **~ qn à faire** to compel sb to do; **contrainte** nf constraint

contraire [kɔ̃tʀɛʀ] adj, nm opposite; **~ à** contrary to; **au ~** on the contrary

contrarier [kɔ̃tʀaʀje] vt (personne: irriter) to annoy; (fig: projets) to thwart, frustrate; **contrariété** nf annoyance

contraste [kɔ̃tʀast] nm contrast

contrat [kɔ̃tʀa] nm contract

contravention [kɔ̃tʀavɑ̃sjɔ̃] nf parking ticket

contre [kɔ̃tʀ] prép against; (en échange) (in exchange) for; **par ~** on the other hand

contrebande [kɔ̃tʀəbɑ̃d] nf (trafic) contraband, smuggling; (marchandise) contraband, smuggled goods pl; **faire la ~ de** to smuggle

contrebas [kɔ̃tʀəba]: **en ~** adv (down) below

contrebasse [kɔ̃tʀəbas] nf (double) bass

contre...: contrecoup nm repercussions pl; **contredire** vt (personne) to contradict; (faits) to refute

contrefaçon [kɔ̃tʀəfasɔ̃] nf forgery

contre...: contre-indication (pl **contre-indications**) nf (Méd) contraindication; **"contre-indication en cas d'eczéma"** should not be used by people with eczema'; **contre-indiqué, e** adj (Méd) contraindicated; (déconseillé) unadvisable, ill-advised

contremaître [kɔ̃tʀəmɛtʀ] nm foreman

contre-plaqué [kɔ̃tʀəplake] nm plywood

contresens [kɔ̃tʀəsɑ̃s] nm (erreur) misinterpretation; (de traduction) mistranslation; **à ~** the wrong way

contretemps [kɔ̃tʀətɑ̃] nm hitch; **à ~** (fig) at an inopportune moment

contribuer [kɔ̃tʀibɥe]: **~ à** vt to contribute towards; **contribution** nf contribution; **mettre à contribution** to call upon; **contributions directes/ indirectes** direct/indirect taxation

contrôle [kɔ̃tʀol] nm checking no pl, check; (des prix) monitoring, control; (test) test, examination; **perdre le ~ de** (véhicule) to lose control of; **contrôle continu** (Scol) continuous assessment; **contrôle d'identité** identity check

contrôler [kɔ̃tʀole] vt (vérifier) to check; (surveiller: opérations) to supervise; (: prix) to monitor, control; (maîtriser, Comm: firme) to control; **contrôleur, -euse** nm/f (de train) (ticket) inspector; (de bus) (bus) conductor(-tress)

controversé, e [kɔ̃tʀovɛʀse] adj (personnage, question) controversial

contusion [kɔ̃tyziɔ̃] nf bruise, contusion

convaincre [kɔ̃vɛ̃kʀ] vt: **~ qn (de qch)** to convince sb (of sth); **~ qn (de faire)** to persuade sb (to do)

convalescence [kɔ̃valesɑ̃s] nf convalescence

convenable [kɔ̃vnabl] adj suitable; (assez bon, respectable) decent

convenir [kɔ̃vniʀ] vi to be suitable; **~ à** to suit; **~ de** (bien-fondé de qch) to admit (to), acknowledge; (date, somme etc) to agree upon; **~ que** (admettre) to admit that; **~ de faire** to agree to do

convention [kɔ̃vɑ̃sjɔ̃] nf convention; **conventions** nfpl (convenances) convention sg; **convention collective** (Écon) collective agreement; **conventionné, e** adj (Admin) applying charges laid down by the state

convenu, e [kɔ̃vny] pp de **convenir**
▷ adj agreed

conversation [kɔ̃vɛʀsasjɔ̃] nf conversation

convertir [kɔ̃vɛʀtiʀ] vt: **~ qn (à)** to convert sb (to); **se convertir (à)** to be converted (to); **~ qch en** to convert sth into

conviction [kɔ̃viksjɔ̃] nf conviction

convienne etc [kɔ̃vjɛn] vb voir **convenir**

convivial, e, -aux [kɔ̃vivjal, jo] adj (Inform) user-friendly

convocation [kɔ̃vɔkasjɔ̃] nf (document) notification to attend; (: Jur) summons sg

convoquer [kɔ̃vɔke] vt (assemblée) to convene; (subordonné) to summon; (candidat) to ask to attend

coopération [kɔɔpeʀasjɔ̃] nf co-operation; (Admin): **la C~** ≈ Voluntary Service Overseas (BRIT), ≈ Peace Corps (US)

coopérer [kɔɔpeʀe] vi: **~ (à)** to co-operate (in)

coordonné, e [kɔɔʀdɔne] adj coordinated; **coordonnées** nfpl (adresse etc) address and telephone number

coordonner [kɔɔʀdɔne] vt to coordinate

copain [kɔpɛ̃] (fam) nm mate, pal; (petit ami) boyfriend

copie [kɔpi] nf copy; (Scol) script, paper; **copier** vt, vi to copy; **copier coller** (Comput) copy and paste; **copier sur** to copy from; **copieur** nm (photo)copier

copieux, -euse [kɔpjø, jøz] adj copious

copine [kɔpin] (fam) nf mate, pal; (petite amie) girlfriend

coq [kɔk] nm cock, rooster

coque[kɔk] nf (de noix, mollusque) shell; (de bateau) hull; **à la ~** (Culin) (soft-)boiled

coquelicot[kɔkliko] nm poppy

coqueluche[kɔklyʃ] nf whooping-cough

coquet, te[kɔkɛ, ɛt] adj appearance-conscious; (logement) smart, charming

coquetier[kɔk(ə)tje] nm egg-cup

coquillage[kɔkijaʒ] nm (mollusque) shellfish inv; (coquille) shell

coquille[kɔkij] nf shell; (Typo) misprint; **coquille St Jacques**scallop

coquin, e[kɔkɛ̃, in] adj mischievous, roguish; (polisson) naughty

cor[kɔr] nm (Mus) horn; (Méd): **~ (au pied)** corn

corail, -aux[kɔraj, o] nm coral no pl

Coran[kɔrɑ̃] nm: **le ~**the Koran

corbeau, x[kɔrbo] nm crow

corbeille[kɔrbɛj] nf basket; **corbeille à papier**waste paper basket ou bin

corde[kɔrd] nf rope; (de violon, raquette) string; (de pendu): **usé jusqu'à la ~** threadbare; **corde à linge**washing ou clothes line; **corde à sauter**skipping rope; **cordes vocales**vocal cords; **cordée** nf (d'alpinistes) rope, roped party

cordialement[kɔrdjalmɑ̃] adv (formule épistolaire) kind regards

cordon[kɔrdɔ̃] nm (cord, string; **cordon de police**cordon; **cordon ombilical**umbilical cord

cordonnerie[kɔrdɔnri] nf shoe repairer's (shop); **cordonnier** nm shoe repairer

Corée[kɔre] nf: **la ~ du Sud/du Nord** South/North Korea

coriace[kɔrjas] adj tough

corne[kɔrn] nf horn; (de cerf) antler

cornée[kɔrne] nf cornea

corneille[kɔrnɛj] nf crow

cornemuse[kɔrnəmyz] nf bagpipes pl

cornet[kɔrnɛ] nm (paper) cone; (de glace) cornet, cone

corniche[kɔrniʃ] nf (route) coast road

cornichon[kɔrniʃɔ̃] nm gherkin

Cornouailles[kɔrnwaj] nf Cornwall

corporel, le[kɔrpɔrɛl] adj bodily; (punition) corporal

corps[kɔr] nm body; **à ~ perdu** headlong; **prendre ~** to take shape; **corps électoral**the electorate; **corps enseignant**the teaching profession

correct, e[kɔrɛkt] adj (exact) acceptable: salaire, hôtel) reasonable, decent; **correcteur, -trice** nm/f (Scol) examiner; **correction** nf (voir corriger) correction; (voir correct) correctness; (coups) thrashing

correspondance[kɔrɛspɔ̃dɑ̃s] nf correspondence; (de train, d'avion) connection; **cours par ~** correspondence course; **vente par ~** mail-order business

correspondant, e[kɔrɛspɔ̃dɑ̃, ɑ̃t] nm/f correspondent; (Tél) person phoning (ou being phoned)

correspondre[kɔrɛspɔ̃dr] vi to correspond, tally; **~ à** to correspond to; **~ avec qn** to correspond with sb

corrida[kɔrida] nf bullfight

corridor[kɔridɔr] nm corridor

corrigé[kɔriʒe] nm (Scol: d'exercice) correct version

corriger[kɔriʒe] vt (devoir) to correct; (punir) to thrash; **~ qn de** (défaut) to cure sb of

corrompre[kɔrɔ̃pr] vt to corrupt; (acheter: témoin etc) to bribe

corruption[kɔrypsjɔ̃] nf corruption; (de témoins) bribery

corse[kɔrs] adj, nm/f Corsican ▷ nf: **la C~** Corsica

corsé, e[kɔrse] adj (café) full-flavoured; (sauce) spicy; (problème) tough

cortège[kɔrtɛʒ] nm procession

cortisone[kɔrtizɔn] nf cortisone

corvée[kɔrve] nf chore, drudgery no pl

cosmétique[kɔsmetik] nm beauty care product

cosmopolite[kɔsmɔpɔlit] adj cosmopolitan

costaud, e[kɔsto, od] (fam) adj strong, sturdy

costume [kɔstym] *nm* (d'homme) suit; (de théâtre) costume; **costumé, e** *adj* dressed up; **bal costumé** fancy dress ball

cote [kɔt] *nf* (en Bourse) quotation; **cote d'alerte** danger ou flood level; **cote de popularité** (popularity) rating

côte [kot] *nf* (rivage) coast(line); (pente) hill; (Anat) rib; (d'un tricot, tissu) rib, ribbing *nq pl*; **~ à ~** side by side; **la Côte (d'Azur)** the (French) Riviera

côté [kote] *nm* (gén) side; (direction) way, direction; **de chaque ~ (de)** on each side (of); **de tous les ~s** from all directions; **de quel ~ - est-il parti?** which way did he go?; **de ce/de l'autre ~** this/the other way; **du ~ de** (provenance) from; (direction) towards; (proximité) near; **de ~** (regarder) sideways; **mettre qch de ~** to put sth aside; **mettre de l'argent de ~** to save some money; **à ~** (right) nearby; (voisins) next door; **à ~ de** beside, next to; (en comparaison) compared to; **être aux ~s de** to be by the side of

Côte d'Ivoire [kotdivwaʀ] *nf*: **la Côte d'Ivoire** Côte d'Ivoire, the Ivory Coast

côtelette [kotlet] *nf* chop

côtier, -ière [kotje, jɛʀ] *adj* coastal

cotisation [kotizasjɔ̃] *nf* subscription, dues *pl*; (pour une pension) contributions *pl*

cotiser [kotize] *vi*: **~ (à)** to pay contributions (to); **se cotiser** *vi* to club together

coton [kotɔ̃] *nm* cotton; **coton hydrophile** cotton wool (BRIT), absorbent cotton (US); **Coton-tige®** *nm* cotton bud

cou [ku] *nm* neck

couchant [kuʃɑ̃] *adj*: **soleil ~** setting sun

couche [kuʃ] *nf* layer; (de peinture, vernis) coat; (de bébé) nappy (BRIT), diaper (US); **couches sociales** social levels ou strata

couché, e [kuʃe] *adj* lying down; (au lit) in bed

coucher [kuʃe] *vt* (personne) to put to bed; (: loger) to put up; (objet) to lay on its side ▷ *vi* to sleep; **~ avec qn** to sleep with sb; **se coucher** *vi* (pour dormir) to go to bed; (pour se reposer) to lie down; (soleil) to set; **coucher de soleil** sunset

couchette [kuʃɛt] *nf* couchette; (pour voyageur, sur bateau) berth

coucou [kuku] *nm* cuckoo

coude [kud] *nm* (Anat) elbow; (de tuyau, de la route) bend; **~ à ~** shoulder to shoulder, side by side

coudre [kudʀ] *vt* (bouton) to sew on ▷ *vi* to sew

couette [kwɛt] *nf* duvet, quilt; **couettes** *nfpl* (cheveux) bunches

couffin [kufɛ̃] *nm* Moses basket

couler [kule] *vi* to flow; run; (fuir: stylo, récipient) to leak; (nez) to run; (sombrer: bateau) to sink ▷ *vt* (cloche, sculpture) to cast; (bateau) to sink; (faire échouer: personne) to bring down

couleur [kulœʀ] *nf* colour (BRIT), color (US); (Cartes) suit; **film/télévision en ~s** colo(u)r film/television; **de ~** (homme, femme: vieilli) colo(u)red

couleuvre [kulœvʀ] *nf* grass snake

coulisses [kulis] *nfpl* (Théâtre) wings; (fig): **dans les ~** behind the scenes

couloir [kulwaʀ] *nm* corridor, passage; (d'avion) aisle; (de bus) gangway; **~ aérien/de navigation** air/shipping lane

coup [ku] *nm* (heurt, choc) knock; (affectif) blow, shock; (agressif) blow; (avec arme à feu) shot; (de l'horloge) stroke; (tennis, golf) stroke; (boxe) blow; (fam: fois) time; **donner un ~ de balai** to give the floor a sweep; **boire un ~** (fam) to have a drink; **être dans le ~** (impliqué) to be in on it; (à la page) to be hip ou trendy; **du ~ ...** as a result; **d'un seul ~** (subitement) suddenly; (à la fois) at one go; **du premier ~** first time; **du même ~** at the same time; **à tous les ~s** (fam) every time; **tenir le ~** to hold out; **après ~** afterwards; **à ~ sûr** definitely, without fail; **~ sur** in quick succession; **sur le ~** outright; **sous le ~ de** (surprise etc) under the influence of luck; **coup de chance** stroke of luck; **coup de coude** nudge (with the elbow); **coup de couteau** stab (of a knife); **coup d'envoi** kick-off; **coup d'essai** first attempt; **coup d'État** coup; **coup de feu** shot; **coup de filet** (Police) haul; **coup de foudre** (fig) love at first sight; **coup de frein** (sharp) braking no pl; **coup de grâce** coup de grâce, death blow; **coup de main**: **donner un coup de main à qn** to give sb a (helping) hand; **coup d'œil** glance; **coup de poing** kick; **coup de poing** punch; **coup de soleil** sunburn no pl; **coup de sonnette** ring of the bell; **coup de téléphone** phone call; **coup de tête** (fig) (sudden) impulse; **coup de théâtre** (fig) dramatic turn of events; **coup de tonnerre** clap of thunder; **coup de vent** gust of wind; **en coup de vent** (rapidement) in a tearing hurry; **coup franc** free kick

coupable [kupabl] adj guilty ▷ nm/f (gén) culprit; (Jur) guilty party

coupe [kup] nf (verre) goblet; (à fruits) dish; (Sport) cup; (de cheveux, de vêtement) cut; (graphique, plan) (cross) section

couper [kupe] vt to cut; (retrancher) to cut (out); (route, courant) to cut (off; (appétit) to take away; (vin à table) to dilute ▷ vi to cut; (prendre un raccourci) to take a short-cut; **se couper** vi (se blesser) to cut o.s.; **~ la parole à qn** to cut sb short; **nous avons été coupés** we've been cut off

couple [kupl] nm couple

couplet [kuple] nm verse

coupole [kupɔl] nf dome

coupon [kupɔ̃] nm (ticket) coupon; (reste de tissu) remnant

coupure [kupyʀ] nf cut; (billet de banque) note; (de journal) cutting; **coupure de courant** power cut

cour [kuʀ] nf (de ferme, jardin) (court)yard; (d'immeuble) back yard; (Jur,

royale) court; **faire la ~ à qn** to court sb; **cour d'assises** court of assizes; **cour de récréation** playground

courage [kuʀaʒ] nm courage, bravery; **courageux, -euse** adj brave, courageous

couramment [kuʀamɑ̃] adv commonly; (parler) fluently

courant, e [kuʀɑ̃, ɑ̃t] adj (fréquent) common; (Comm, gén: normal) standard; (en cours) current ▷ nm current; (fig) movement; (: d'opinion) trend; **être au ~ (de)** (fait, nouvelle) to know (about); **mettre qn au ~ (de)** to tell sb (about); (nouveau travail etc) to teach sb the basics (of); **se tenir au ~ (de)** (techniques etc) to keep o.s. up-to-date (on); **dans le ~ (de)** (pendant) in the course of; **le 10 ~** (Comm) the 10th inst.; **courant d'air** draught; **courant électrique** electric current, power

courbature [kuʀbatyʀ] nf ache

courbe [kuʀb] adj curved ▷ nf curve

coureur, -euse [kuʀœʀ, øz] nm/f (Sport) runner (ou driver); (péj) womanizer; manhunter

courge [kuʀʒ] nf (Culin) marrow; **courgette** nf courgette (BRIT), zucchini (US)

courir [kuʀiʀ] vi to run ▷ vt (Sport: épreuve) to compete in; (risque) to run; (danger) to face; **les magasins** to go round the shops; **le bruit court que** the rumour is going round that

couronne [kuʀɔn] nf crown; (de fleurs) wreath, circlet

courons etc [kuʀɔ̃] vb voir **courir**

courriel [kuʀjel] nm e-mail

courrier [kuʀje] nm mail, post; (lettres à écrire) letters pl; **est-ce que j'ai du ~?** are there any letters for me?; **courrier électronique** e-mail

⚠ Attention à ne pas traduire **courrier** par le mot anglais **courier**.

courroie [kuʀwa] nf strap; (Tech) belt

courrons etc [kuʀɔ̃] vb voir **courir**

cours [kuʀ] nm (leçon) class; (: particulier) lesson; (série de leçons, cheminement) course; (*écoulement*) flow; (Comm: *de devises*) rate; (: *de denrées*) price; **donner libre ~ à** to give free expression to; **avoir ~** (Scol) to have a class ou lecture; **en ~** (*année*) current; (*travaux*) in progress; **en ~ de route** on the way; **au ~ de** in the course of, during; **le ~ de change** the exchange rate; **cours d'eau** waterway; **cours du soir** night school

course [kurs] nf running; (Sport: *épreuve*) race; (*d'un taxi*) journey, trip; (*commission*) errand; **courses** nfpl (*achats*) shopping sg; **faire des ~s** to do some shopping

court, e [kur, kurt] adj short ▷ adv short ▷ nm: **~ (de tennis)** (tennis) court; **à ~ de** short of; **prendre qn de ~** to catch sb unawares; **court-circuit** nm short-circuit

courtoisie [kurtwazi] nf courtesy

couru, e [kury] pp de **courir**

cousais etc [kuzɛ] vb voir **coudre**

couscous [kuskus] nm couscous

cousin, e [kuzɛ̃, in] nm/f cousin

coussin [kusɛ̃] nm cushion

cousu, e [kuzy] pp de **coudre**

coût [ku] nm cost; **le ~ de la vie** the cost of living

couteau, x [kuto] nm knife

coûter [kute] vt, vi to cost; **combien ça coûte?** how much is it?, what does it cost?; **ça coûte trop cher** it's too expensive; **coûte que coûte** at all costs; **coûteux, -euse** adj costly, expensive

coutume [kutym] nf custom

couture [kutyr] nf sewing; (*profession*) dressmaking; (*points*) seam; **couturier** nm fashion designer; **couturière** nf dressmaker

couvent [kuvã] nm (*de sœurs*) convent; (*de frères*) monastery

couver [kuve] vt to hatch; (*maladie*) to be coming down with ▷ vi (*feu*) to smoulder; (*révolte*) to be brewing

couvercle [kuvɛrkl] nm lid; (*de bombe aérosol etc, qui se visse*) cap, top

couvert, e [kuvɛr, ɛrt] pp de **couvrir** ▷ adj (*ciel*) overcast ▷ nm place setting; (*place à table*) place; **couverts** nmpl (*ustensiles*) cutlery sg; **~ de** covered with ou in; **mettre le ~** to lay the table

couverture [kuvɛrtyr] nf blanket; (*de livre, assurance, fig*) cover; (*presse*) coverage

couvre-lit [kuvrəli] nm bedspread

couvrir [kuvrir] vt to cover; **se couvrir** vi (*s'habiller*) to cover up; (*se coiffer*) to put on one's hat; (*ciel*) to cloud over

cow-boy [kɔbɔj] nm cowboy

crabe [krɑb] nm crab

cracher [kraʃe] vi, vt to spit

crachin [kraʃɛ̃] nm drizzle

craie [krɛ] nf chalk

craindre [krɛ̃dr] vt to fear, be afraid of; (*être sensible à: chaleur, froid*) to be easily damaged by

crainte [krɛ̃t] nf fear; **de ~ de/que** for fear of/that; **craintif, -ive** adj timid

crampe [krɑ̃p] nf cramp; **j'ai une ~ à la jambe** I've got cramp in my leg

cramponner [krɑ̃pɔne] vb: **se ~ (à)** to hang ou cling on (to)

cran [krɑ̃] nm (*entaille*) notch; (*de courroie*) hole; (*fam: courage*) guts pl

crâne [krɑn] nm skull

crapaud [krapo] nm toad

craquement [krakmã] nm crack, snap; (*du plancher*) creak, creaking no pl

craquer [krake] vi (*bois, plancher*) to creak; (*fil, branche*) to snap; (*couture*) to come apart; (fig: *accusé*) to break down; (: *fam*) to have a breakdown ▷ vt (*allumette*) to strike; **j'ai craqué** [fam] I couldn't resist it

crasse [kras] nf grime, filth; **crasseux, -euse** adj grimy, filthy

cravache [kravaʃ] nf (*riding*) crop

cravate [kravat] nf tie

crawl [krol] nm crawl; **dos ~é** backstroke

crayon [krɛjɔ̃] nm pencil; **crayon à bille** ball-point pen; **crayon de couleur** crayon, colouring pencil; **crayon-feutre** (pl **crayons-feutres**) nm felt(-tip) pen

création [kʀeasjɔ̃] nf creation

crèche [kʀɛʃ] nf (de Noël) crib; (garderie) crèche, day nursery

crédit [kʀedi] nm (gén) credit; **crédits** nmpl (fonds) funds; **payer/acheter à ~** to pay/buy on credit ou on easy terms; **faire ~ à qn** to give sb credit; **créditer** vt: **créditer un compte (de)** to credit an account (with)

créer [kʀee] vt to create

crémaillère [kʀemajɛʀ] nf: **pendre la ~** to have a house-warming party

crème [kʀɛm] nf cream; (entremets) cream dessert ▷ adj inv cream(-coloured); **un (café) ~** = a white coffee; **crème anglaise** (egg) custard; **crème Chantilly** whipped cream; **crème à raser** shaving cream; **crème solaire** suntan lotion

créneau, x [kʀeno] nm (de fortification) crenel(le); (dans marché) gap, niche; (Auto): **faire un ~** to reverse into a parking space (between two cars alongside the kerb)

crêpe [kʀɛp] nf (galette) pancake ▷ nm (tissu) crêpe; **crêperie** nf pancake shop ou restaurant

crépuscule [kʀepyskyl] nm twilight, dusk

cresson [kʀesɔ̃] nm watercress

creuser [kʀøze] vt (trou, tunnel) to dig; (sol) to make a hole in; (fig) to go (deeply) into; **ça creuse** that gives you a real appetite; **se ~ la cervelle** (fam) to rack one's brains

creux, -euse [kʀø, kʀøz] adj hollow ▷ nm hollow; **heures creuses** slack periods; (électricité, téléphone) off-peak periods; **avoir un ~** (fam) to be hungry

crevaison [kʀəvɛzɔ̃] nf puncture

crevé, e [kʀəve] (fam) adj (fatigué) shattered (BRIT), exhausted

crever [kʀəve] vt (ballon) to burst ▷ vi (pneu) to burst; (automobiliste) to have a puncture (BRIT) ou a flat (tire) (US); (fam) to die

crevette [kʀəvɛt] nf: **~ (rose)** prawn;

crevette grise shrimp

cri [kʀi] nm cry, shout; (d'animal: spécifique) cry, call; **c'est le dernier ~** (fig) it's the latest fashion

criard, e [kʀijaʀ, kʀijaʀd] adj (couleur) garish, loud; (voix) yelling

cric [kʀik] nm (Auto) jack

crier [kʀije] vi (pour appeler) to shout, cry (out); (de douleur etc) to scream, yell ▷ vt (injure) to shout (out), yell (out)

crime [kʀim] nm crime; (meurtre) murder; **criminel, le** nm/f criminal; (assassin) murderer

crin [kʀɛ̃] nm (de cheval) hair no pl

crinière [kʀinjɛʀ] nf mane

crique [kʀik] nf creek, inlet

criquet [kʀikɛ] nm grasshopper

crise [kʀiz] nf crisis; (Méd) attack; (: d'épilepsie) fit; **piquer une ~ de nerfs** to go hysterical; **crise cardiaque** heart attack; **crise de foie** avoir une crise de foie to have really bad indigestion

cristal, -aux [kʀistal, o] nm crystal

critère [kʀitɛʀ] nm criterion

critiquable [kʀitikabl] adj open to criticism

critique [kʀitik] adj critical ▷ nm/f (de théâtre, musique) critic ▷ nf criticism; (Théâtre etc: article) review

critiquer [kʀitike] vt (dénigrer) to criticize; (évaluer) to assess, examine (critically)

croate [kʀɔat] adj Croatian ▷ nm/f: **C~** Croat, Croatian

Croatie [kʀɔasi] nf: **la ~** Croatia

crochet [kʀɔʃɛ] nm hook; (détour) detour; (Tricot: aiguille) crochet hook; (: technique) crochet; **vivre aux ~s de qn** to live ou sponge off sb

crocodile [kʀɔkɔdil] nm crocodile

croire [kʀwaʀ] vt to believe; **se ~ fort** to think one is strong; **~ que** to believe ou think that; **~ à, ~ en** to believe in

croisade [kʀwazad] nf crusade

croisement [kʀwazmɑ̃] nm (carrefour) crossroads sg; (Bio) crossing; (: résultat) crossbreed

croiser [kʀwaze] vt (personne, voiture)

to pass; (route) to cross, cut across; (Bio) to cross; **se croiser** vi (personnes, véhicules) to pass each other; (routes, lettres) (regards) to meet; **~ les jambes/bras** to cross one's legs/fold one's arms

croisière [kʀwazjɛʀ] nf cruise

croissance [kʀwasɑ̃s] nf growth

croissant [kʀwasɑ̃] nm (à manger) croissant; (motif) crescent

croître [kʀwatʀ] vi to grow

croix [kʀwa] nf cross; **la Croix Rouge** the Red Cross

croque-monsieur [kʀɔkməsjø] nm inv toasted ham and cheese sandwich

croquer [kʀɔke] vt (manger) to crunch; (: fruit) to munch; (dessiner) to sketch; **chocolat à croquer** plain dessert chocolate

croquis [kʀɔki] nm sketch

crotte [kʀɔt] nf droppings pl; **crottin** nm dung, manure; (fromage) (small round) cheese (= made of goat's milk)

croustillant, e [kʀustijɑ̃, ɑ̃t] adj crisp

croûte [kʀut] nf crust; (du fromage) rind; (Méd) scab; **en ~** (Culin) in pastry

croûton [kʀutɔ̃] nm (Culin) crouton; (bout du pain) crust, heel

croyant, e [kʀwajɑ̃, ɑ̃t] nm/f believer

CRS sigle fpl (= Compagnies républicaines de sécurité) state security police force ▷ sigle m member of the CRS

cru, e [kʀy] pp de **croire** ▷ adj (non cuit) raw; (lumière, couleur) harsh; (paroles) crude ▷ nm (vignoble) vineyard; (vin) wine; **un grand ~** a great vintage; **jambon ~** Parma ham

crû [kʀy] pp de **croître**

cruauté [kʀyote] nf cruelty

cruche [kʀyʃ] nf pitcher, jug

crucifix [kʀysifi] nm crucifix

crudités [kʀydite] nfpl (Culin) selection of raw vegetables

crue [kʀy] nf (inondation) flood

cruel, le [kʀyɛl] adj cruel

crus etc [kʀy] vb voir **croire**; **croître**

crûs etc [kʀy] vb voir **croître**

crustacés [kʀystase] nmpl shellfish

Cuba [kyba] nf Cuba; **cubain, e** adj Cuban ▷ nm/f: **Cubain, e** Cuban

cube [kyb] nm cube; (jouet) brick; **mètre ~** cubic metre; **2 au ~** 2 cubed

cueillette [kœjɛt] nf picking; (quantité) crop, harvest

cueillir [kœjiʀ] vt (fruits, fleurs) to pick, gather; (fig) to catch

cuiller [kɥijɛʀ], **cuillère** [kɥijɛʀ] nf spoon; **cuiller à café** coffee spoon; (Culin) = teaspoonful; **cuiller à soupe** soup-spoon; (Culin) = tablespoonful; **cuillerée** nf spoonful

cuir [kɥiʀ] nm leather; **cuir chevelu** scalp

cuire [kɥiʀ] vt (aliments) to cook; (au four) to bake ▷ vi to cook; **bien cuit** (viande) well done; **trop cuit** overdone

cuisine [kɥizin] nf (pièce) kitchen; (art culinaire) cookery, cooking; (nourriture) cooking, food; **faire la ~** to cook; **cuisiné, e** adj: **plat cuisiné** ready-made meal ou dish; **cuisiner** vt to cook; (fam) to grill ▷ vi to cook; **cuisinier, -ière** nm/f cook; **cuisinière** nf (poêle) cooker

cuisse [kɥis] nf thigh; (Culin) leg

cuisson [kɥisɔ̃] nf cooking

cuit, e [kɥi, kɥit] pp de **cuire**

cuivre [kɥivʀ] nm copper; **les cuivres** (Mus) the brass

cul [ky] (fam!) nm arse (!)

culminant, e [kylminɑ̃, ɑ̃t] adj: **point ~** highest point

culot [kylo] (fam) nm (effronterie) cheek

culotte [kylɔt] nf (de femme) knickers pl (BRIT), panties pl

culte [kylt] nm (religion) religion; (hommage, vénération) worship; (protestant) service

cultivateur, -trice [kyltivatœʀ, tʀis] nm/f farmer

cultivé, e [kyltive] adj (personne) cultured, cultivated

cultiver [kyltive] vt to cultivate; (légumes) to grow, cultivate

culture [kyltyʀ] nf cultivation; (connaissance etc) culture; **les ~s**

intensives intensive farming; **culture physique** physical training; **culturel, le** adj cultural

cumin [kymɛ̃] nm cumin

cure [kyʀ] nf (Méd) course of treatment; **cure d'amaigrissement** slimming (BRIT) ou weight-loss (US) course; **cure de repos** rest cure

curé [kyʀe] nm parish priest

cure-dent [kyʀdɑ̃] nm toothpick

curieux, -euse [kyʀjø, jøz] adj (indiscret) curious, inquisitive; (étrange) strange, curious ▷ nmpl (badauds) onlookers; **curiosité** nf curiosity; (site) unusual feature

curriculum vitae [kyʀikylɔmvite] nm inv curriculum vitae

cutané, e [kytane] adj skin

cuve [kyv] nf vat; (à mazout etc) tank

cuvée [kyve] nf vintage

cuvette [kyvɛt] nf (récipient) bowl, basin; (Géo) basin

CV sigle m (Auto) = **cheval vapeur**; (Comm) = **curriculum vitae**

cybercafé [sibɛʀkafe] nm Internet café

cyberespace [sibɛʀɛspas] nm cyberspace

cybernaute [sibɛʀnot] nm/f Internet user

cyclable [siklabl] adj: **piste ~** cycle track

cycle [sikl] nm cycle; **cyclisme** nm cycling; **cycliste** nm/f cyclist ▷ adj cycle cpd; **coureur cycliste** racing cyclist

cyclomoteur [siklomotœʀ] nm moped

cyclone [siklon] nm hurricane

cygne [siɲ] nm swan

cylindre [silɛ̃dʀ] nm cylinder; **cylindrée** nf (Auto) (cubic) capacity; **une (voiture à) grosse cylindrée** a big-engined car

cymbale [sɛ̃bal] nf cymbal

cynique [sinik] adj cynical

cystite [sistit] nf cystitis

d

d' [d] prép voir **de**

dactylo [daktilo] nf (aussi: **~graphe**) typist; (aussi: **~graphie**) typing

dada [dada] nm hobby-horse

daim [dɛ̃] nm (fallow) deer inv; (cuir suédé) suede

daltonien, ne [daltɔnjɛ̃, jɛn] adj colour-blind

dame [dam] nf lady; (Cartes, Échecs) queen; **dames** nfpl (jeu) draughts sg (BRIT), checkers sg (US)

Danemark [danmaʀk] nm Denmark

danger [dɑ̃ʒe] nm danger; **être en ~** (personne) to be in danger; **mettre en ~** (personne) to put in danger; (projet, carrière) to jeopardize; **dangereux, -euse** adj dangerous

danois, e [danwa, waz] adj Danish ▷ nm/f: **D~, e** Dane ▷ nm (Ling) Danish

 MOT-CLÉ

dans [dɑ̃] prép **1** (position) in; (à l'intérieur de) inside; **c'est dans le tiroir/le salon**

it's in the drawer/lounge; **dans la boîte** in *ou* inside the box; **je l'ai lu dans le journal** I read it in the newspaper; **marcher dans la ville** to walk about the town

2 (*direction*) into; **elle a couru dans le salon** she ran into the lounge; **monter dans une voiture/le bus** to get into a car/on to the bus

3 (*provenance*) out of, from; **je l'ai pris dans le tiroir/salon** I took it out of *ou* from the drawer/lounge; **boire dans un verre** to drink out of *ou* from a glass

4 (*temps*) in; **dans 2 mois** in 2 months, in 2 months' time

5 (*approximation*) about; **dans les 20 euros** about 20 euros

danse [dãs] *nf*: **la ~** dancing; **une ~** a dance; **la ~ classique** ballet; **danser** *vi*, *vt* to dance; **danseur, euse** *nm/f* ballet dancer; (*au bal etc*) dancer; (: *cavalier*) partner

date [dat] *nf* date; **de longue ~** longstanding; **date de naissance** date of birth; **date limite** deadline; **dater** *vt*, *vi* to date; **dater de** to date from; **à dater de** (as) from

datte [dat] *nf* date

dauphin [dofɛ̃] *nm* (*Zool*) dolphin

davantage [davãtaʒ] *adv* more; (*plus longtemps*) longer; **~ de** more

O MOT-CLÉ

de, d' [də] (*de +le* = **du**, *de +les* = **des**) *prép*

1 (*appartenance*) of; **le toit de la maison** the roof of the house; **la voiture d'Ann/de mes parents** Ann's/my parents' car

2 (*provenance*) from; **il vient de Londres** he comes from London; **elle est sortie du cinéma** she came out of the cinema

3 (*caractérisation, mesure*): **un mur de brique/bureau d'acajou** a brick wall/mahogany desk; **un billet de 50 euros** a 50 euro note; **une pièce de 2 m de large** *ou* **large de 2 m** a room 2m wide,

a 2m-wide room; **un bébé de 10 mois** a 10-month-old baby; **12 mois de crédit/travail** 12 months' credit/work; **être payé 20 euros de l'heure** to be paid 20 euros an *ou* per hour; **augmenter de 10 euros** to increase by 10 euros; **de 14 à 18** from 14 to 18

4 (*moyen*) with; **je l'ai fait de mes propres mains** I did it with my own two hands

5 (*cause*): **mourir de faim** to die of hunger; **rouge de colère** red with fury

6 (*devant infinitif*) to; **il m'a dit de rester** he told me to stay

▷ *dét* **1** (*phrases affirmatives*) some (*souvent omis*); **du vin, de l'eau, des pommes** (some) wine, (some) water, (some) apples; **des enfants sont venus** some children came; **pendant des mois** for months

2 (*phrases interrogatives et négatives*) any; **a-t-il du vin?** has he got any wine?; **il n'a pas de pommes/d'enfants** he hasn't (got) any apples/children, he has no apples/children

dé [de] *nm* (*à jouer*) die *ou* dice; (*aussi*: **dé à coudre**) thimble

déballer [debale] *vt* to unpack

débarcadère [debakadɛʀ] *nm* wharf

débardeur [debaʀdœʀ] *nm* (*maillot*) tank top

débarquer [debaʀke] *vt* to unload, land ▷ *vi* to disembark; (*fig: fam*) to turn up

débarras [debaʀɑ] *nm* (*pièce*) lumber room; (*placard*) junk cupboard; **bon ~!** good riddance!; **débarrasser** *vt* to clear; **se débarrasser de** *vt* to get rid of; **débarrasser qn de** (*vêtements, paquets*) to relieve sb of; **débarrasser (la table)** to clear the table

débat [deba] *nm* discussion, debate; **débattre** [debatʀ] *vt* to discuss, debate; **se débattre** *vi* to struggle

débit [debi] *nm* (*d'un liquide, fleuve*) flow; (*d'un magasin*) turnover (of goods); (*élocution*) delivery; (*bancaire*) debit; **débit de boissons** drinking establishment; **débit de tabac** tobacconist's

déblayer [debleje] vt to clear

débloquer [debloke] vt (prix, crédits) to free

déboîter [debwate] vt (Auto) to pull out; **se ~ le genou** etc to dislocate one's knee etc

débordé, e [debɔrde] adj: **être ~ (de)** (travail, demandes) to be snowed under (with)

déborder [debɔrde] vi to overflow; (lait etc) to boil over; **~ (de) qch** (dépasser) to extend beyond sth; **~ de** (joie, zèle) to be brimming over with ou bursting with

débouché [debuʃe] nm (pour vendre) outlet; (perspective d'emploi) opening

déboucher [debuʃe] vt (évier, tuyau etc) to unblock; (bouteille) to uncork ▷ vi: **~ de** to emerge from; **~ sur** (études) to lead on to

debout [d(ə)bu] adv: **être ~** (personne) to be standing, stand; (: levé, éveillé) to be up; **se mettre ~** to stand up; **se tenir ~** to stand; **~! stand up!** (du lit) get up!; **cette histoire ne tient pas ~** this story doesn't hold water

déboutonner [debutɔne] vt to undo, unbutton

débraillé, e [debraje] adj slovenly, untidy

débrancher [debrãʃe] vt to disconnect; (appareil électrique) to unplug

débrayage [debreʒaʒ] nm (Auto) clutch; **débrayer** vi (Auto) to declutch; (cesser le travail) to stop work

débris [debri] nm fragments; **des ~ de verre** bits of glass

débrouillard, e [debrujar, ard] (fam) adj smart, resourceful

débrouiller [debruje] vt to disentangle, untangle; **se débrouiller** vi to manage; **débrouillez-vous** you'll have to sort things out yourself

début [deby] nm beginning, start; **débuts** nmpl (de carrière) début sg; **~**

juin in early June; **débutant, e** nm/f beginner, novice; **débuter** vi to begin, start; (faire ses débuts) to start out

décaféiné, e [dekafeine] adj decaffeinated

décalage [dekalaʒ] nm gap; **décalage horaire** time difference

décaler [dekale] vt to shift

décapotable [dekapɔtabl] adj convertible

décapsuleur [dekapsylœr] nm bottle-opener

décédé, e [desede] adj deceased

décéder [desede] vi to die

décembre [desãbr] nm December

décennie [deseni] nf decade

décent, e [desã, ãt] adj decent

déception [desɛpsjɔ̃] nf disappointment

décès [desɛ] nm death

décevoir [des(ə)vwar] vt to disappoint

décharge [deʃarʒ] nf (dépôt d'ordures) rubbish tip ou dump; (électrique) electrical discharge; **décharger** vt (marchandise, véhicule) to unload; (tirer) to discharge; **décharger qn de** (responsabilité) to relieve sb of, release sb from

déchausser [deʃose] vt to take off; **se déchausser** vi to take off one's shoes; (dent) to come ou work loose

déchet [deʃɛ] nm (reste) scrap; **déchets** nmpl (ordures) refuse sg, rubbish sg; **~s nucléaires** nuclear waste

déchiffrer [deʃifre] vt to decipher

déchirant, e [deʃirã, ãt] adj heart-rending

déchirement [deʃirmã] nm (chagrin) wrench, heartbreak; (gén pl: conflit) rift, split

déchirer [deʃire] vt to tear; (en morceaux) to tear up; (arracher) to tear out; (fig: conflit) to tear (apart); **se déchirer** vi to tear, rip; **se ~ un muscle** to tear a muscle

déchirure [deʃiryr] nf (accroc) tear, rip; **déchirure musculaire** torn muscle

décidé, e [deside] *adj (personne, air)*
determined; **c'est ~** it's decided;
décidément *adv* really

décider [deside] *vt*: **~ qch** to decide
on sth; **~ de faire/que** to decide to
do/that; **~ qn (à faire qch)** to persuade
sb (to do sth); **se décider (à faire)** to
decide (to do), make up one's mind
(to do); **se ~ pour** to decide on *ou* in
favour of

décimal, e, -aux [desimal, o] *adj*
decimal

décimètre [desimɛtʀ] *nm* decimetre

décisif, -ive [desizif, iv] *adj* decisive

décision [desizjɔ̃] *nf* decision

déclaration [deklaʀasjɔ̃] *nf*
declaration; *(discours: Pol etc)*
statement; **déclaration d'impôts** *ou*
de revenus = tax return; **déclaration
de vol: faire une déclaration de vol** to
report a theft

déclarer [deklaʀe] *vt* to declare; *(décès,
naissance)* to register; **se déclarer** *vi*
(feu) to break out

déclencher [deklɑ̃ʃe] *vt (mécanisme etc)*
to release; *(sonnerie)* to set off; *(attaque,
grève)* to launch; *(provoquer)* to trigger
off; **se déclencher** *vi (sonnerie)* to go off

décliner [dekline] *vi* to decline ▷ *vt*
(invitation) to decline; *(nom, adresse)*
to state

décoiffer [dekwafe] *vt*: **~ qn** to mess
up sb's hair; **je suis toute décoiffée** my
hair is in a real mess

déçois *etc* [deswa] *vb voir* **décevoir**

décollage [dekɔlaʒ] *nm (Aviat)* takeoff

décoller [dekɔle] *vt* to unstick ▷ *vi
(avion)* to take off; **se décoller** *vi* to
come unstuck

décolleté, e [dekɔlte] *adj* low-cut
▷ *nm* low neck(line); *(plongeant)*
cleavage

décolorer [dekɔlɔʀe]: **se décolorer** *vi*
to fade; **se faire ~ les cheveux** to have
one's hair bleached

décommander [dekɔmɑ̃de] *vt* to
cancel; **se décommander** *vi* to cry off

déconcerter [dekɔ̃sɛʀte] *vt* to

disconcert, confound

décongeler [dekɔ̃ʒle] *vt* to thaw

déconner [dekɔne] *(fam) vi* to talk
rubbish

déconseiller [dekɔ̃seje] *vt*: **~ qch (à
qn)** to advise (sb) against sth; **c'est
déconseillé** it's not recommended

décontracté, e [dekɔ̃tʀakte] *adj*
relaxed, laid-back *(fam)*

décontracter [dekɔ̃tʀakte]: **se
décontracter** *vi* to relax

décor [dekɔʀ] *nm* décor; *(paysage)*
scenery; **décorateur** *nm (interior)*
decorator; **décoration** *nf* decoration;
décorer *vt* to decorate

décortiquer [dekɔʀtike] *vt* to shell;
(fig: texte) to dissect

découdre [dekudʀ]: **se découdre** *vi* to
come unstitched

découper [dekupe] *vt (papier, tissu
etc)* to cut up; *(viande)* to carve; *(article)*
to cut out

décourager [dekuʀaʒe] *vt* to
discourage; **se décourager** *vi* to lose
heart, become discouraged

décousu, e [dekuzy] *adj* unstitched;
(fig) disjointed, disconnected

découvert, e [dekuvɛʀ, ɛʀt] *adj (tête)*
bare, uncovered; *(lieu)* open, exposed
▷ *nm (bancaire)* overdraft; **découverte**
nf discovery; **faire la découverte de**
to discover

découvrir [dekuvʀiʀ] *vt* to discover;
(enlever ce qui couvre) to uncover;
(dévoiler) to reveal; **se découvrir** *vi
(chapeau)* to take off one's hat;
(vêtement) to take something off; *(ciel)*
to clear

décrire [dekʀiʀ] *vt* to describe

décrocher [dekʀɔʃe] *vt (détacher)*
to take down; *(téléphone)* to take off
the hook; *(: pour répondre)* to lift the
receiver; *(fam: contrat etc)* to get, land
▷ *vi (fam: abandonner)* to drop out;
(: cesser d'écouter) to switch off

déçu, e [desy] *pp de* **décevoir**

dédaigner [dedeɲe] *vt* to despise,
scorn; *(négliger)* to disregard, spurn;

dédaigneux, -euse adj scornful, disdainful; **dédain** nm scorn, disdain

dedans [dədɑ̃] adv inside; (pas en plein air) indoors, inside ▷ nm inside; **au ~** inside

dédicacer [dedikase] vt: **~ qch (à qn)** to sign (for sb), autograph (for sb)

dédier [dedje] vt: **~ à** to dedicate to

dédommagement [dedɔmaʒmɑ̃] nm compensation

dédommager [dedɔmaʒe] vt: **~ qn (de)** to compensate sb (for)

dédouaner [dedwane] vt to clear through customs

déduire [deduiʀ] vt: **~ qch (de)** (ôter) to deduct sth (from); (conclure) to deduce ou infer sth (from)

défaillance [defajɑ̃s] nf (syncope) blackout; (fatigue) (sudden) weakness no pl; (technique) fault, failure; **défaillance cardiaque** heart failure

défaire [defɛʀ] vt to undo; (installation) to take down, dismantle; **se défaire** vi to come undone; **se ~ de** to get rid of

défait, e [defɛ, ɛt] adj (visage) haggard, ravaged; **se ~** nf defeat

défaut [defo] nm (moral) fault, failing, defect; (tissus) fault, flaw; (manque, carence): **~ de** shortage of; **prendre qn en ~** to catch sb out; **faire ~** (manquer) to be lacking; **à ~ de** for lack ou want of

défavorable [defavɔʀabl] adj unfavourable (BRIT), unfavorable (US)

défavoriser [defavɔʀize] vt to put at a disadvantage

défectueux, -euse [defɛktɥø, øz] adj faulty, defective

défendre [defɑ̃dʀ] vt to defend; (interdire) to forbid; **se défendre** vi to defend o.s.; **~ à qn qch/de faire** to forbid sb sth/to do; **il se défend** (fam: se débrouille) he can hold his own; **se ~ de/contre** (se protéger) to protect o.s. from/against; **se ~ de** (se garder de) to refrain from

défense [defɑ̃s] nf defence; (d'éléphant etc) tusk; **ministre de la ~** Minister of Defence (BRIT), Defence Secretary (US);

"~ de fumer" "no smoking"

défi [defi] nm challenge; **lancer un ~ à qn** to challenge sb; **sur un ton de ~** defiantly

déficit [defisit] nm (Comm) deficit

défier [defje] vt (provoquer) to challenge; (mort, autorité) to defy; **~ qn de faire qch** to challenge ou defy sb to do sth

défigurer [defigyʀe] vt to disfigure

défilé [defile] nm (Géo) (narrow) gorge ou pass; (soldats) parade; (manifestants) procession, march

défiler [defile] vi (troupes) to march past; (sportifs) to parade; (manifestants) to march; (visiteurs) to pour, stream; **faire ~ un document** (Inform) to scroll a document; **se défiler** vi: **il s'est défilé** (fam) he wriggled out of it

définir [definiʀ] vt to define

définitif, -ive [definitif, iv] adj (final) final, definitive; (pour longtemps) permanent, definitive; (refus) definite; **définitive** nf: **en définitive** eventually; (somme toute) in fact; **définitivement** adv (partir, s'installer) for good

déformer [defɔʀme] vt to put out of shape; (pensée, réalité) to distort; **se déformer** vi to lose its shape

défouler [defule]: **se défouler** vi to unwind, let off steam

défunt, e [defœ̃, œ̃t] adj (mort) late before n ▷ nm/f deceased

dégagé, e [degaʒe] adj (route, ciel) clear; **sur un ton ~** casually

dégager [degaʒe] vt (exhaler) to give off; (délivrer) to free, extricate; (désencombrer) to clear; (isoler: idée, aspect) to bring out; **~ qn de** (engagement, parole etc) to release ou free sb from; **se dégager** vi (passage, ciel) to clear

dégâts [dega] nmpl damage sg; **faire des ~** to cause damage

dégel [deʒɛl] nm thaw; **dégeler** vt to thaw (out)

dégivrer [deʒivʀe] vt (frigo) to defrost; (vitres) to de-ice

dégonflé, e [degɔ̃fle] *adj* (*pneu*) flat

dégonfler [degɔ̃fle] *vt* (*pneu, ballon*) to let down, deflate; **se dégonfler** *vi* (*fam*) to chicken out

dégouliner [deguline] *vi* to trickle, drip

dégourdi, e [degurdi] *adj* smart, resourceful

dégourdir [degurdir] *vt*: **se ~ les jambes** to stretch one's legs (*fig*)

dégoût [degu] *nm* disgust, distaste; **dégoûtant, e** *adj* disgusting; **dégoûté, e** *adj* disgusted; **dégoûté de** sick of; **dégoûter** *vt* to disgust; **dégoûter qn de qch** to put sb off sth

dégrader [degrade] *vt* (*Mil: officier*) to degrade; (*abîmer*) to damage, deface; **se dégrader** *vi* (*relations, situation*) to deteriorate

degré [dəgre] *nm* degree

dégressif, -ive [degresif, iv] *adj* on a decreasing scale

dégringoler [degrɛ̃gɔle] *vi* to tumble (down)

déguisement [degizmɑ̃] *nm* (*pour s'amuser*) fancy dress

déguiser [degize]: **se déguiser (en)** *vi* (*se costumer*) to dress up (as); (*pour tromper*) to disguise o.s. (as)

dégustation [degystasjɔ̃] *nf* (*de fromages etc*) sampling; **~ de vins** wine-tasting session

déguster [degyste] *vt* (*vins*) to taste; (*fromages etc*) to sample; (*savourer*) to enjoy, savour

dehors [dəɔr] *adv* outside; (*en plein air*) outdoors ▷ *nm* outside ▷ *nmpl* (*apparences*) appearances; **mettre ou jeter ~** (*expulser*) to throw out; **au ~** outside; **au ~ de** outside; **en ~ de** (*hormis*) apart from

déjà [deʒa] *adv* already; (*auparavant*) before, already

déjeuner [deʒœne] *vi* to (have) lunch; (*le matin*) to have breakfast ▷ *nm* lunch

delà [dəla] *adv*: **en ~ (de), au ~ (de)** beyond

délacer [delase] *vt* (*chaussures*) to undo

délai [delɛ] *nm* (*attente*) waiting period; (*sursis*) extension (of time); (*temps accordé*) time limit; **sans ~** without delay; **dans les ~s** within the time limit

délaisser [delese] *vt* to abandon, desert

délasser [delase] *vt* to relax; **se délasser** *vi* to relax

délavé, e [delave] *adj* faded

délayer [deleje] *vt* (*Culin*) to mix (with water etc); (*peinture*) to thin down

delco(r) [dɛlko] *nm* (*Auto*) distributor

délégué, e [delege] *nm/f* representative

déléguer [delege] *vt* to delegate

délibéré, e [delibere] *adj* (*conscient*) deliberate

délicat, e [delika, at] *adj* delicate; (*plein de tact*) tactful; (*attention*) thoughtful; **délicatement** *adv* delicately; (*avec douceur*) gently

délice [delis] *nm* delight

délicieux, -euse [delisjø, jøz] *adj* (*au goût*) delicious; (*sensation*) delightful

délimiter [delimite] *vt* (*terrain*) to delimit, demarcate

délinquant, e [delɛ̃kɑ̃, -ɑ̃t] *adj, nm/f* delinquent

délirer [delire] *vi* to be delirious; **tu délires!** (*fam*) you're crazy!

délit [deli] *nm* (*criminal*) offence

délivrer [delivre] *vt* (*prisonnier*) to (set) free, release; (*passeport*) to issue

deltaplane(r) [dɛltaplan] *nm* hang-glider

déluge [delyʒ] *nm* (*pluie*) downpour; (*biblique*) Flood

demain [d(ə)mɛ̃] *adv* tomorrow; **~ matin/soir** tomorrow morning/evening

demande [d(ə)mɑ̃d] *nf* (*requête*) request; (*revendication*) demand; (*d'emploi*) application; (*Écon*): **la ~** demand; **"~s d'emploi"** (*annonces*) "situations wanted"

demandé, e [d(ə)mɑ̃de] *adj* (*article etc*): **très ~** (*very*) much in demand

demander [d(ə)mɑ̃de] *vt* to ask for;

(*chemin, heure etc*) to ask; (*nécessiter*) to require, demand; ~ **qch à qn** to ask sb for sth; ~ **un service à qn** to ask sb a favour; ~ **à qn de faire qch** to ask sb to do sth; **je ne demande pas mieux que de ...** I'll be only too pleased to ~; **se ~ si/pourquoi** *etc* to wonder whether/ why *etc*; **demandeur, -euse** *nm/f*: **demandeur d'emploi** job-seeker; **demandeur d'asile** asylum-seeker

démangeaison [demãʒɛzɔ̃] *nf* itching; **avoir des ~s** to be itching

démanger [demãʒe] *vi* to itch

démaquillant [demakijã] *nm* make-up remover

démaquiller [demakije] *vt*: **se ~ démaquiller** to remove one's make-up

démarche [demaʁʃ] *nf* (*allure*) gait, walk; (*intervention*) step; (*fig: intellectuelle*) thought processes *pl*; **faire les ~s nécessaires (pour obtenir qch)** to take the necessary steps (to obtain sth)

démarrage [demaʁaʒ] *nm* start

démarrer [demaʁe] *vi* (*conducteur*) to start (up); (*véhicule*) to move off; (*travaux*) to get moving; **démarreur** *nm* (*Auto*) starter

démêlant [demɛlã] *nm* conditioner

démêler [demele] *vt* to untangle; **démêlés** *nmpl* problems

déménagement [demenaʒmã] *nm* move; **camion de déménagement** removal van

déménager [demenaʒe] (*meubles*) to (re)move ▷ *vi* to move (house); **déménageur** *nm* removal man

démerder [demɛʁde] (*fam*): **se démerder** *vi* to sort things out for o.s.

démettre [demɛtʁ] *vt*: ~ **qn de** (*fonction, poste*) to dismiss sb from; **se ~ l'épaule** *etc* to dislocate one's shoulder *etc*

demeurer [d(ə)mœʁe] *vi* (*habiter*) to live; (*rester*) to remain

demi, e [dəmi] *adj* half ▷ *nm* (*bière*) ≈ half-pint (0,25 litres) ▷ *préfixe*: **~...** half-, semi..., demi-; **trois heures/bouteilles**

et ~es three and a half hours/bottles, three hours/bottles and a half; **il est 2 heures et ~e/midi et ~** it's half past 2/half past 12; **à ~** = half-; **à ~** (e) (*heure*) on the half-hour; **demi-douzaine** *nf* half-dozen, half a dozen; **demi-finale** *nf* semifinal; **demi-frère** *nm* half-brother; **demi-heure** *nf* half-hour, half an hour; **demi-journée** *nf* half-day, half a day; **demi-litre** *nm* half-litre, half a litre; **demi-livre** *nf* half-pound, half a pound; **demi-pension** *nf* (*à l'hôtel*) half-board; **demi-pensionnaire** *nf*: **être demi-pensionnaire** to take school lunches

démis, e [demi, iz] *adj* (*épaule etc*) dislocated

demi-sœur [dəmisœʁ] *nf* half-sister

démission [demisjɔ̃] *nf* resignation; **donner sa ~** to give ou hand in one's notice; **démissionner** *vi* to resign

demi-tarif [dəmitaʁif] *nm* half-price; **voyager à ~** to travel half-fare

demi-tour [dəmituʁ] *nm* about-turn; **faire ~** to turn (and go) back

démocratie [demɔkʁasi] *nf* democracy; **démocratique** *adj* democratic

démodé, e [demɔde] *adj* old-fashioned

demoiselle [d(ə)mwazɛl] *nf* (*jeune fille*) young lady; (*célibataire*) single lady, maiden lady; **demoiselle d'honneur** bridesmaid

démolir [demɔliʁ] *vt* to demolish

démon [demɔ̃] *nm* (*enfant turbulent*) devil, demon; **le D~** the Devil

démonstration [demɔ̃stʁasjɔ̃] *nf* demonstration

démonter [demɔ̃te] *vt* (*machine etc*) to take down, dismantle; **se démonter** (*meuble*) to be dismantled, be taken to pieces; (*personne*) to lose countenance

démontrer [demɔ̃tʁe] *vt* to demonstrate

démouler [demule] *vt* to turn out

démuni, e [demyni] *adj* (*sans argent*) impoverished; **~ de** without

dénicher [deniʃe] (*fam*) *vt* (*objet*) to

unearth; (*restaurant etc*) to discover
dénier [denje] *vt* to deny
dénivellation [denivelasjɔ̃] *nf* (*pente*)
slope
dénombrer [denɔ̃bʀe] *vt* to count
dénomination [denɔminasjɔ̃] *nf*
designation, appellation
dénoncer [denɔ̃se] *vt* to denounce; **se
dénoncer** to give o.s. up, come forward
dénouement [denumɑ̃] *nm* outcome
dénouer [denwe] *vt* to unknot, undo
denrée [dɑ̃ʀe] *nf*: **denrées
alimentaires** foodstuffs
dense [dɑ̃s] *adj* dense; **densité** *nf*
density
dent [dɑ̃] *nf* tooth; **dent de lait/de
sagesse** milk/wisdom tooth; **dentaire**
adj dental; **cabinet dentaire** dental
surgery (BRIT), dentist's office (US)
dentelle [dɑ̃tɛl] *nf* lace *no pl*
dentier [dɑ̃tje] *nm* denture
dentifrice [dɑ̃tifʀis] *nm* toothpaste
dentiste [dɑ̃tist] *nm/f* dentist
dentition [dɑ̃tisjɔ̃] *nf* teeth
dénué, e [denɥe] *adj*: **~ de** devoid of
déodorant [deɔdɔʀɑ̃] *nm* deodorant
déontologie [deɔ̃tɔlɔʒi] *nf* code of
practice
dépannage [depanaʒ] *nm*: **service de
~** (*Auto*) breakdown service
dépanner [depane] *vt* (*voiture,
télévision*) to fix, repair; (*fig*) to bail out,
help out; **dépanneuse** *nf* breakdown
lorry (BRIT), tow truck (US)
dépareillé, e [depaʀeje] *adj* (*collection,
service*) incomplete; (*objet*) odd
départ [depaʀ] *nm* departure; (*Sport*)
start; **au ~** at the start; **la veille de son
~** the day before he leaves/left
département [depaʀtəmɑ̃] *nm*
department

- **DÉPARTEMENT**

- France is divided into 96
- administrative units called
- **départements**. These local
- government divisions are headed

by a state-appointed 'préfet',
and administered by an elected
'Conseil général'. **Départements**
are usually named after prominent
geographical features such as rivers
or mountain ranges.

dépassé, e [depɑse] *adj* superseded,
outmoded; **il est complètement ~**
he's completely out of his depth, he
can't cope
dépasser [depɑse] *vt* (*véhicule,
concurrent*) to overtake; (*endroit*) to
pass, go past; (*somme, limite*) to exceed;
(*fig: en beauté etc*) to surpass, outshine
▷ *vi* (*jupon etc*) to show; **se dépasser**
to excel o.s.
dépaysé, e [depeize] *adj* disoriented
dépaysement [depeizmɑ̃] *nm*
(*changement*) change of scenery
dépêcher [depeʃe]: **se dépêcher** *vi*
to hurry
dépendance [depɑ̃dɑ̃s] *nf*
dependence; (*bâtiment*) outbuilding
dépendre [depɑ̃dʀ]: **~ de** *vt* to depend
on; (*financièrement etc*) to be dependent
on; **ça dépend** it depends
dépens [depɑ̃] *nmpl*: **aux ~ de** at the
expense of
dépense [depɑ̃s] *nf* spending *no pl*,
expense, expenditure *no pl*; **dépenser**
vt to spend; (*énergie*) to expend, use up;
se dépenser *vi* to exert o.s.
dépeupler [depœple]: **se dépeupler** *vi*
to become depopulated
dépilatoire [depilatwaʀ] *adj*: **crème ~**
hair-removing ou depilatory cream
dépister [depiste] *vt* to detect; (*voleur*)
to track down
dépit [depi] *nm* vexation, frustration;
en ~ de in spite of; **en ~ du bon sens**
contrary to all good sense; **dépité, e**
adj vexed, frustrated
déplacé, e [deplɑse] *adj* (*propos*) out of
place, uncalled-for
déplacement [deplɑsmɑ̃] *nm* (*voyage*)
trip, travelling *no pl*; **en ~** away
déplacer [deplase] *vt* (*table, voiture*) to

move, shift; **se déplacer** vi to move; (voyager) to travel; **se ~ une vertèbre** to slip a disc

déplaire [deplɛʀ] vt: **ça me déplaît** I don't like this, I dislike this; **se déplaire** vi to be unhappy; **déplaisant, e** adj disagreeable

dépliant [deplijɑ̃] nm leaflet

déplier [deplije] vt to unfold

déposer [depoze] vt (gén: mettre, poser) to lay ou put down; (à la banque, à la consigne) to deposit; (passager) to drop (off), set down; (roi) to depose; (plainte) to lodge; (marque) to register; **se déposer** vi to settle; **dépositaire** nm/f (Comm) agent; **déposition** nf statement

dépôt [depo] nm (à la banque, sédiment) deposit; (entrepôt) warehouse, store

dépourvu, e [depuʀvy] adj: **~ de** lacking in, without; **prendre qn au ~** to catch sb unprepared

dépression [depʀesjɔ̃] nf depression; **dépression (nerveuse)** (nervous) breakdown

déprimant, e [depʀimɑ̃, ɑ̃t] adj depressing

déprimer [depʀime] vi to be/get depressed

depuis [dəpɥi] prép 1 (point de départ dans le temps) since; **il habite Paris depuis 1983/l'an dernier** he has been living in Paris since 1983/last year; **depuis quand?** since when?; **depuis quand le connaissez-vous?** how long have you known him? 2 (temps écoulé) for; **il habite Paris depuis 5 ans** he has been living in Paris for 5 years; **je le connais depuis 3 ans** I've known him for 3 years 3 (lieu): **il a plu depuis Metz** it's been raining since Metz; **elle a téléphoné depuis Valence** she rang from Valence 4 (quantité, rang) from; **depuis les plus petits jusqu'aux plus grands** from the

youngest to the oldest
▷ adv (temps) since (then); **je ne lui ai pas parlé depuis** I haven't spoken to him since (then); **depuis que** conj (ever) since; **depuis qu'il m'a dit ça** (ever) since he said that to me

député, e [depyte] nm/f (Pol) ≈ Member of Parliament (BRIT), ≈ Member of Congress (US)

dérangement [deʀɑ̃ʒmɑ̃] nm (gêne) trouble; (gastrique etc) disorder; **en ~** (téléphone, machine) out of order

déranger [deʀɑ̃ʒe] vt (personne) to trouble, bother; (projets) to disrupt, upset; (objets, vêtements) to disarrange; **se déranger** vi: **surtout ne vous dérangez pas pour moi** please don't put yourself out on my account; **est-ce que cela vous dérange si ...?** do you mind if ...?

déraper [deʀape] vi (voiture) to skid; (personne, semelles) to slip

dérégler [deʀegle] vt (mécanisme) to put out of order; (estomac) to upset

dérisoire [deʀizwaʀ] adj derisory

dérive [deʀiv] nf: **aller à la ~** (Navig, fig) to drift

dérivé, e [deʀive] nm (Tech) by-product

dermatologue [dɛʀmatɔlɔg] nm/f dermatologist

dernier, -ière [dɛʀnje, jɛʀ] adj last; (le plus récent) latest, last; **lundi/le mois ~** last Monday/month; **c'est le ~ cri** it's the very latest thing; **en ~** last; **ce ~** the latter; **dernièrement** adv recently

dérogation [deʀɔgasjɔ̃] nf (special) dispensation

dérouiller [deʀuje] vt: **se ~ les jambes** to stretch one's legs (fig)

déroulement [deʀulmɑ̃] nm (d'une opération etc) progress

dérouler [deʀule] vt (ficelle) to unwind; **se dérouler** vi (avoir lieu) to take place; (se passer) to go (off); **tout s'est déroulé comme prévu** everything went as planned

dérouter [deʀute] vt (avion, train) to

reroute, divert; (*étonner*) to disconcert, throw (out)

derrière [dɛRjɛR] *adv, prép* behind ▷ *nm* (*d'une maison*) back; (*postérieur*) behind, bottom; **les pattes de** ~ the back ou hind legs; **par** ~ from behind; (*fig*) behind one's back

des [de] *dét voir de* ▷ *prép* +*dét* = **de+les**

dès [dɛ] *prép* from; ~ **que** as soon as; ~ **son retour** as soon as he was (*ou* is) back

désaccord [dezakɔR] *nm* disagreement

désagréable [dezagReabl] *adj* unpleasant

désagrément [dezagRemɑ̃] *nm* annoyance, trouble *no pl*

désaltérer [dezalteRe] *vt*: **se désaltérer** to quench one's thirst

désapprobateur, -trice [dezapRɔbatœR, tRis] *adj* disapproving

désapprouver [dezapRuve] *vt* to disapprove of

désarmant, e [dezaRmɑ̃, ɑ̃t] *adj* disarming

désastre [dezastR] *nm* disaster; **désastreux, -euse** *adj* disastrous

désavantage [dezavɑ̃taʒ] *nm* disadvantage; **désavantager** *vt* to put at a disadvantage

descendre [desɑ̃dR] *vt* (*escalier, montagne*) to go (*ou* come) down; (*valise, paquet*) to take *ou* get down; (*étagère etc*) to lower; (*fam: abattre*) to shoot down ▷ *vi* to go (*ou* come) down; (*passager: s'arrêter*) to get out, alight; ~ **à pied/en voiture** to walk/drive down; ~ **de** (*famille*) to be descended from; ~ **du train** to get out *ou* off the train; ~ **de cheval** to dismount; ~ **d'un arbre** to climb down from a tree; ~ **à l'hôtel** to stay at a hotel

descente [desɑ̃t] *nf* descent, going down; (*chemin*) way down; (*Ski*) downhill (race); **au milieu de la** ~ halfway down; **descente de lit** bedside rug; **descente (de police)** (police) raid

description [dɛskRipsjɔ̃] *nf*

description

déséquilibre [dezekilibR] *nm* (*position*): **en** ~ unsteady; (*fig: des forces, du budget*) imbalance

désert, e [dezɛR, ɛRt] *adj* deserted ▷ *nm* desert; **désertique** *adj* desert *cpd*

désespéré, e [dezɛspeRe] *adj* desperate

désespérer [dezɛspeRe] *vi*: ~ **(de)** to despair (of); **désespoir** *nm* despair; **en désespoir de cause** in desperation

déshabiller [dezabije] *vt* to undress; **se déshabiller** *vi* to undress (o.s.)

déshydraté, e [dezidRate] *adj* dehydrated

désigner [dezine] *vt* (*montrer*) to point out, indicate; (*dénommer*) to denote; (*candidat etc*) to name

désinfectant, e [dezɛ̃fɛktɑ̃, ɑ̃t] *adj, nm* disinfectant

désinfecter [dezɛ̃fɛkte] *vt* to disinfect

désintéressé, e [dezɛ̃teRese] *adj* disinterested, unselfish

désintéresser [dezɛ̃teRese] *vt*: **se (de)** to lose interest (in)

désintoxication [dezɛ̃tɔksikasjɔ̃] *nf*: **faire une cure de** ~ to undergo treatment for alcoholism (*ou* drug addiction)

désinvolte [dezɛ̃vɔlt] *adj* casual, off-hand

désir [deziR] *nm* wish; (*sensuel*) desire; **désirer** *vt* to want, wish for; (*sexuellement*) to desire; **je désire ...** (*formule de politesse*) I would like ...

désister [deziste]: **se désister** *vi* to stand down, withdraw

désobéir [dezɔbeiR] *vi*: ~ **(à qn/qch)** to disobey (sb/sth); **désobéissant, e** *adj* disobedient

désodorisant [dezɔdɔRizɑ̃] *nm* air freshener, deodorizer

désolé, e [dezɔle] *adj* (*paysage*) desolate; **je suis** ~ I'm sorry

désordonné, e [dezɔRdɔne] *adj* untidy

désordre [dezɔRdR] *nm* disorder(liness), untidiness; (*anarchie*) disorder; **en ~** in a mess, untidy

désormais [dezɔʀmɛ] *adv* from now on

desquelles [dekɛl] *prép +pron* = **de +lesquelles**

desquels [dekɛl] *prép +pron* = **de +lesquels**

dessécher [deseʃe]: **se dessécher** *vi* to dry out

desserrer [desere] *vt* to loosen; *(frein)* to release

dessert [desɛʀ] *nm* dessert, pudding

desservir [desɛʀviʀ] *vt (ville, quartier)* to serve; *(débarrasser):* **~ (la table)** to clear the table

dessin [desɛ̃] *nm (œuvre, art)* drawing; *(motif)* pattern, design; **dessin animé** cartoon *(film)*; **dessin humoristique** cartoon; **dessinateur, -trice** *nm/f* drawer; *(de bandes dessinées)* cartoonist; *(industriel)* draughtsman-(woman) (BRIT), draftsman-(woman) (US); **dessiner** *vt* to draw; *(concevoir)* to design; **se dessiner** *vi (forme)* to be outlined; *(fig: solution)* to emerge

dessous [d(ə)su] *adv* underneath, beneath ▷ *nm* underside ▷ *nmpl (sous-vêtements)* underwear *sg*; **en ~, par ~** underneath; **au-~ (de)** below; *(peu digne de)* beneath; **avoir le ~** to get the worst of it; **les voisins du ~** the downstairs neighbours; **dessous-de-plat** *nm inv* tablemat

dessus [d(ə)sy] *adv* on top; *(collé, écrit)* on it ▷ *nm* top; **en ~** above; **par ~** over it ▷ *prép* over; **au-~ (de)** above; **les voisins du ~** the upstairs neighbours; **avoir le ~** to get the upper hand; **sens ~ -dessous** upside down; **dessus-de-lit** *nm inv* bedspread

destin [dɛstɛ̃] *nm* fate; *(avenir)* destiny

destinataire [dɛstinatɛʀ] *nm/f (Postes)* addressee; *(d'un colis)* consignee

destination [dɛstinasjɔ̃] *nf (lieu)* destination; *(usage)* purpose; **à ~ de** bound for, travelling to

destiner [dɛstine] *vt:* **~ qch à qn** *(envisager de donner)* to intend sb to have sth; *(adresser)* to intend sth for sb; **être destiné à** *(usage)* to be meant for; **se ~ à l'enseignement** to intend to become a teacher

détachant [detaʃɑ̃] *nm* stain remover

détacher [detaʃe] *vt (enlever)* to detach, remove; *(délier)* to untie; *(Admin):* **~ qn (auprès de** *ou* **à)** to post sb (to); **se détacher** *vi (se séparer)* to come off; *(: page)* to come out; *(se défaire)* to come undone; **se ~ sur** to stand out against; **se ~ de** *(se désintéresser)* to grow away from

détail [detaj] *nm (Comm):* **le ~** retail; **en ~** in detail; **au ~** *(Comm)* retail; **détaillant** *nm* retailer; **détaillé, e** *adj (plan, explications)* detailed; *(facture)* itemized; **détailler** *vt (expliquer)* to explain in detail

détecter [detɛkte] *vt* to detect

détective [detɛktiv] *nm:* **détective (privé)** private detective

déteindre [detɛ̃dʀ] *vi (au lavage)* to run, lose its colour; **~ sur** *(vêtement)* to run into; *(fig)* to rub off on

détendre [detɑ̃dʀ] *vt (corps, esprit)* to relax; **se détendre** *vi (ressort)* to lose its tension; *(personne)* to relax

détenir [det(ə)niʀ] *vt (record, pouvoir, secret)* to hold; *(prisonnier)* to detain, hold

détente [detɑ̃t] *nf* relaxation

détention [detɑ̃sjɔ̃] *nf (d'armes)* possession; *(captivité)* detention; **détention préventive** custody

détenu, e [det(ə)ny] *nm/f* prisoner

détergent [detɛʀʒɑ̃] *nm* detergent

détériorer [deteʀjɔʀe] *vt* to damage; **se détériorer** *vi* to deteriorate

déterminé, e [detɛʀmine] *adj (résolu)* determined; *(précis)* specific, definite

déterminer [detɛʀmine] *vt (fixer)* to determine; **~ qn à faire qch** to decide sb to do sth; **se ~ à faire qch** to make up one's mind to do sth

détester [detɛste] *vt* to hate, detest

détour [detuʀ] *nm* detour; *(tournant)*

bend, curve; **ça vaut le ~** it's worth the trip; **sans ~** (fig) plainly

détourné, e [deturne] adj (moyen) roundabout

détourner [deturne] vt to divert; (par la force) to hijack; (yeux, tête) to turn away; (de l'argent) to embezzle; **se détourner** vi to turn away

détraquer [detrake] vt to put out of order; (estomac) to upset; **se détraquer** vi (machine) to go wrong

détriment [detrimɑ̃] nm: **au ~ de** to the detriment of

détroit [detrwa] nm strait

détruire [detrɥir] vt to destroy

dette [dɛt] nf debt

DEUG sigle m (= diplôme d'études universitaires générales) diploma taken after 2 years at university

deuil [dœj] nm (perte) bereavement; (période) mourning; **être en ~** to be in mourning

deux [dø] num two; **tous les ~** both; **ses ~ mains** both his hands, his two hands; **~ fois** twice; **deuxième** num second; **deuxièmement** adv secondly; **deux-pièces** nm inv (tailleur) two-piece suit; (de bain) two-piece (swimsuit); (appartement) two-roomed flat (BRIT) ou apartment (US); **deux-points** nm inv colon sg; **deux-roues** nm inv two-wheeled vehicle

devais [dəvɛ] vb voir **devoir**

dévaluation [devalɥasjɔ̃] nf devaluation

devancer [d(ə)vɑ̃se] vt (coureur, rival) to get ahead of; (arriver) to arrive before; (prévenir: questions, désirs) to anticipate

devant [d(ə)vɑ̃] adv in front; (à distance: en avant) ahead ▷ prép in front of; (en avant) ahead of; (avec mouvement: passer) past; (en présence de) before, in front of; (étant donné) in view of ▷ nm front; **prendre les ~s** to make the first move; **les pattes de ~** the front legs, the forelegs; **par ~** (boutonner) at the front; (entrer) the front way; **aller au-~ de**

qn to go out to meet sb; **aller au-~ de** (désirs de qn) to anticipate

devanture [d(ə)vɑ̃tyʀ] nf (étalage) display; (vitrine) (shop) window

développement [dev(ə)lɔpmɑ̃] nm development; **pays en voie de ~** developing countries

développer [dev(ə)lɔpe] vt to develop; **se développer** vi to develop

devenir [dəv(ə)niʀ] vb +attrib to become; **que sont-ils devenus?** what has become of them?

devez [dəve] vb voir **devoir**

déviation [devjasjɔ̃] nf (Auto) diversion (BRIT), detour (US)

devienne etc [dəvjɛn] vb voir **devenir**

deviner [d(ə)vine] vt to guess; (apercevoir) to distinguish; **devinette** nf riddle

devis [d(ə)vi] nm estimate, quotation

devise [dəviz] nf (formule) motto, watchword; **devises** nfpl (argent) currency sg

dévisser [devise] vt to unscrew, undo; **se dévisser** vi to come unscrewed

devoir [d(ə)vwaʀ] nm duty; (Scol) homework no pl; (: en classe) exercise ▷ vt (argent, respect): **~ qch (à qn)** to owe (sb) sth; (+infin: obligation): **il doit le faire** he has to do it, he must do it; (: intention): **le nouveau centre commercial doit ouvrir en mai** the new shopping centre is due to open in May; (: probabilité): **il doit être tard** it must be late; (: fatalité): **cela devait arriver** it was bound to happen; **combien est-ce que je vous dois?** how much do I owe you?

dévorer [devɔʀe] vt to devour

dévoué, e [devwe] adj devoted

dévouer [devwe]: **se dévouer** vi (se sacrifier): **se ~ (pour)** to sacrifice o.s. (for); (se consacrer): **se ~ à** to devote ou dedicate o.s. to

devrai [dəvʀe] vb voir **devoir**

dézipper [dezipe] vt to unzip

diabète [djabɛt] nm diabetes sg; **diabétique** nm/f diabetic

diable [djɑbl] nm devil

diabolo [djabɔlo] nm (boisson) lemonade with fruit cordial

diagnostic [djagnɔstik] nm diagnosis sg; **diagnostiquer** vt to diagnose

diagonal, e, -aux [djagɔnal, o] adj diagonal; **diagonale** nf diagonal; **en diagonale** diagonally

diagramme [djagʀam] nm chart, graph

dialecte [djalɛkt] nm dialect

dialogue [djalɔg] nm dialogue

diamant [djamã] nm diamond

diamètre [djamɛtʀ] nm diameter

diapositive [djapozitiv] nf transparency, slide

diarrhée [djaʀe] nf diarrhoea

dictateur [diktatœʀ] nm dictator; **dictature** nf dictatorship

dictée [dikte] nf dictation

dicter [dikte] vt to dictate

dictionnaire [diksjɔnɛʀ] nm dictionary

dièse [djɛz] nm sharp

diesel [djezɛl] nm diesel ▷ adj inv diesel

diète [djɛt] nf (jeûne) starvation diet; (régime) diet; **diététique: magasin diététique** health food shop (BRIT) ou store (us)

dieu, x [djø] nm (pl -x) god; **D~** God; **mon D~!** good heavens!

différemment [difeʀamã] adv differently

différence [difeʀãs] nf difference; **à la ~ de** unlike; **différencier** vt to differentiate

différent, e [difeʀã, ãt] adj (dissemblable) different; **~ de** different from; (divers) different, various

différer [difeʀe] vt to postpone, put off ▷ vi: **~ (de)** to differ (from)

difficile [difisil] adj difficult; (exigeant) hard to please; **difficilement** adv with difficulty

difficulté [difikylte] nf difficulty; **en ~** (bateau, alpiniste) in difficulties

diffuser [difyze] vt (chaleur) to diffuse;

(émission, musique) to broadcast; (nouvelle) to circulate; (Comm) to distribute

digérer [diʒeʀe] vt to stomach, put up with; (fam: accepter) to stomach, put up with; **digestif** nm (after-dinner) liqueur; **digestion** nf digestion

digne [diɲ] adj dignified; **~ de** worthy of; **~ de foi** trustworthy; **dignité** nf dignity

digue [dig] nf dike, dyke

dilemme [dilɛm] nm dilemma

diligence [diliʒãs] nf stagecoach

diluer [dilɥe] vt to dilute

dimanche [dimãʃ] nm Sunday

dimension [dimãsjɔ̃] nf (grandeur) size; (dimensions) dimensions

diminuer [diminɥe] vt to reduce, decrease; (ardeur etc) to lessen; (dénigrer) to belittle ▷ vi to decrease, diminish; **diminutif** nm (surnom) pet name

dinde [dɛ̃d] nf turkey

dindon [dɛ̃dɔ̃] nm turkey

dîner [dine] nm dinner ▷ vi to have dinner

dingue [dɛ̃g] (fam) adj crazy

dinosaure [dinozɔʀ] nm dinosaur

diplomate [diplɔmat] adj diplomatic ▷ nm diplomat; (fig) diplomatist; **diplomatie** nf diplomacy

diplôme [diplom] nm diploma; **avoir des ~s** to have qualifications; **diplômé, e** adj qualified

dire [diʀ] nm: **au ~ de** according to ▷ vt to say; (secret, mensonge, heure) to tell; **~ qch à qn** to tell sb sth; **~ à qn qu'il fasse** ou **de faire** to tell sb to do; (comm) **on dit que** they say that; **ceci** ou **cela dit** that being said; **si cela lui dit** (plaire) if he fancies it; **que dites-vous de** (penser) what do you think of; **on dirait que** it looks (ou sounds etc) as if; **dis/dites (donc)!** I say!; **se ~ (à soi-même)** to say to o.s.; **se ~ malade** (se prétendre) to claim one is ill; **ça ne se dit pas** (impoli) you shouldn't say that; (pas en usage) you don't say that

direct, e [diʀɛkt] adj direct ▷ nm (TV):

en ~ live; **directement** adv directly

directeur, -trice [dirɛktœʀ, tʀis] nm/f (d'entreprise) director; (de service) manager(-eress); (d'école) head(teacher) (BRIT), principal (US)

direction [dirɛksjɔ̃] nf (sens) direction; (d'entreprise) management; (Auto) steering; **"toutes ~s"** "all routes"

dirent [diʀ] vb voir **dire**

dirigeant, e [diʀiʒɑ̃, ɑ̃t] adj (classe) ruling ▷ nm/f (d'un parti etc) leader

diriger [diʀiʒe] vt (entreprise) to manage, run; (véhicule) to steer; (orchestre) to conduct; (recherches, travaux) to supervise; ~ **sur** (arme) to point ou level ou aim at; ~ **son regard sur** to look in the direction of; **se diriger** vi (s'orienter) to find one's way; **se ~ vers** ou **sur** to make ou head for

dis [di] vb voir **dire**

discerner [disɛʀne] vt to discern, make out

discipline [disiplin] nf discipline; **discipliner** vt to discipline

discontinu, e [diskɔ̃tiny] adj intermittent

discontinuer [diskɔ̃tinɥe] vi: **sans ~** without stopping, without a break

discothèque [diskɔtɛk] nf (boîte de nuit) disco(thèque)

discours [diskuʀ] nm speech

discret, -ète [diskʀɛ, ɛt] adj discreet; (parfum, maquillage) unobtrusive; **discrétion** [diskʀesjɔ̃] nf discretion; **à discrétion** as much as one wants

discrimination [diskʀiminasjɔ̃] nf discrimination; **sans ~** indiscriminately

discussion [diskysjɔ̃] nf discussion

discutable [diskytabl] adj debatable

discuter [diskyte] vt (débattre) to discuss; (contester) to question, dispute ▷ vi to talk; (protester) to argue; ~ **de** to discuss

dise [diz] vb voir **dire**

disjoncteur [disʒɔ̃ktœʀ] nm (Élec) circuit breaker

disloquer [dislɔke]: **se disloquer** vi

(parti, empire) to break up; (cortège) to come apart; (épaule) to be dislocated

disons [dizɔ̃] vb voir **dire**

disparaître [dispaʀɛtʀ] vi to disappear; (se perdre: traditions etc) to die out; **faire ~** (tache) to remove; (douleur) to get rid of

disparition [dispaʀisjɔ̃] nf disappearance; **espèce en voie de ~** endangered species

disparu, e [dispaʀy] nm/f missing person ▷ adj: **être porté ~** to be reported missing

dispensaire [dispɑ̃sɛʀ] nm community clinic

dispenser [dispɑ̃se] vt: ~ **qn de** to exempt sb from

disperser [dispɛʀse] vt to scatter; **se disperser** vi to break up

disponible [dispɔnibl(ə)] adj available

disposé, e [dispoze] adj: **bien/mal ~** (humeur) in a good/bad mood; ~ **à** (prêt à) willing ou prepared to

disposer [dispoze] vt to arrange ▷ vi: **vous pouvez ~** you may leave; ~ **de** to have (at one's disposal); **se ~ à faire** to prepare to do, be about to do

dispositif [dispozitif] nm device; (fig) system, plan of action

disposition [dispozisjɔ̃] nf (arrangement) arrangement, layout; (humeur) mood; **prendre ses ~s** to make arrangements; **avoir des ~s pour la musique** etc to have a special aptitude for music etc; **à la ~ de qn** at sb's disposal; **je suis à votre ~** I am at your service

disproportionné, e [dispʀopoʀsjone] adj disproportionate, out of all proportion

dispute [dispyt] nf quarrel, argument; **disputer** vt (match) to play; (combat) to fight; **se disputer** vi to quarrel

disqualifier [diskalifje] vt to disqualify

disque [disk] nm (Mus) record; (forme, pièce) disc; (Sport) discus; **disque compact** compact disc; **disque dur**

hard disk; **disquette** *nf* floppy disk, diskette

dissertation [disɛrtasjɔ̃] *nf* (Scol) essay

dissimuler [disimyle] *vt* to conceal

dissipé, e [disipe] *adj* (élève) undisciplined, unruly

dissolvant [disɔlvɑ̃] *nm* nail polish remover

dissuader [disɥade] *vt*: **~ qn de faire** to dissuade sb from doing

distance [distɑ̃s] *nf* distance; (fig: écart) gap; **à ~** at ou from a distance; **distancer** X to outdistance

distant, e [distɑ̃, ɑ̃t] *adj* (réservé) distant; **~ de** (lieu) far away from

distillerie [distilki] *nf* distillery

distinct, e [distɛ̃(kt), ɛ̃kt] *adj* distinct; **distinctement** *adv* distinctly, clearly; **distinctif, -ive** *adj* distinctive

distingué, e [distɛ̃ge] *adj* distinguished

distinguer [distɛ̃ge] *vt* to distinguish; **se ~ de** to be distinguished by

distraction [distraksjɔ̃] *nf* (inattention) absent-mindedness; (passe-temps) distraction, entertainment

distraire [distrɛr] *vt* (divertir) to entertain, divert; (déranger) to distract; **se distraire** vi to amuse ou enjoy o.s.; **distrait, e** *adj* absent-minded

distrayant, e [distrɛjɑ̃, ɑ̃t] *adj* entertaining

distribuer [distribɥe] *vt* to distribute, hand out; (Cartes) to deal (out); (courrier) to deliver; **distributeur** *nm* (Comm) distributor; **distributeur (automatique)** (vending) machine; **distributeur de billets** (cash) dispenser

dit, e [di, dit] *pp de* **dire** ▷ *adj* (fixé): **le jour ~** the arranged day; (surnommé): **X, ~ Pierrot** X, known as Pierrot

dites [dit] *vb voir* **dire**

divan [divɑ̃] *nm* divan

divers, e [divɛr, ɛrs] *adj* (varié) diverse, varied; (différent) different, various; **~es**

personnes various ou several people

diversité [divɛrsite] *nf* (variété) diversity

divertir [divɛrtir]: **se divertir** *vi* to amuse ou enjoy o.s.; **divertissement** *nm* distraction, entertainment

diviser [divize] *vt* to divide; **division** *nf* division

divorce [divɔrs] *nm* divorce; **divorcé, e** *nm/f* divorcee; **divorcer** *vi* to get a divorce, get divorced; **divorcer de ou d'avec qn** to divorce sb

divulguer [divylge] *vt* to disclose

dix [dis] *num* ten; **dix-huit** *num* eighteen; **dix-huitième** *num* eighteenth; **dixième** *num* tenth; **dix-neuf** *num* nineteen; **dix-neuvième** *num* nineteenth; **dix-sept** *num* seventeen; **dix-septième** *num* seventeenth

dizaine [dizɛn] *nf*: **une ~ (de)** about ten, ten or so

do [do] *nm* (note) C; (en chantant la gamme) do(h)

docile [dɔsil] *adj* docile

dock [dɔk] *nm* dock; **docker** *nm* docker

docteur [dɔktœr] *nm* doctor; **doctorat** *nm* doctorate

doctrine [dɔktrin] *nf* doctrine

document [dɔkymɑ̃] *nm* document; **documentaire** *adj, nm* documentary; **documentation** *nf* documentation, literature; **documenter** *vt*: **se documenter (sur)** to gather information (on)

dodo [dodo] *nm* (langage enfantin): **aller faire ~** to go to beddy-byes

dogue [dɔg] *nm* mastiff

doigt [dwa] *nm* finger; **à deux ~s de** within an inch of; **un ~ de lait/whiskey** a drop of milk/whisky; **doigt de pied** toe

doit *etc* [dwa] *vb voir* **devoir**

dollar [dɔlar] *nm* dollar

domaine [dɔmɛn] *nm* estate, property; (fig) domain, field

domestique [dɔmɛstik] *adj* domestic ▷ *nm/f* servant, domestic

domicile [dɔmisil] *nm* home, place of residence; **à ~** at home; **livrer à ~** to deliver; **domicilié, e** *adj*: **"domicilié à ..."** "address ..."

dominant, e [dɔminɑ̃, ɑ̃t] *adj* (*opinion*) predominant

dominer [dɔmine] *vt* to dominate; (*sujet*) to master; (*surpasser*) to surpass; (*surplomber*) to tower above, dominate ▷ *vi* to be in the dominant position; **se dominer** *vi* to control o.s.

domino [dɔmino] *nm* domino; **dominos** *nmpl* (*jeu*) dominoes *sg*

dommage [dɔmaʒ] *nm*: **~s** (*dégâts*) damage *no pl*; **c'est ~!** what a shame!; **c'est ~ que** it's a shame *ou* pity that

dompter [dɔ̃(p)te] *vt* to tame; **dompteur, -euse** *nm/f* trainer

DOM-ROM [dɔmʀɔm] *sigle m* (= *départements et régions d'outre-mer*) French overseas departments and regions

don [dɔ̃] *nm* gift; (*charité*) donation; **avoir des ~s pour** to have a gift *ou* talent for; **elle a le ~ de m'énerver** she's got a knack of getting on my nerves

donc [dɔ̃k] *conj* therefore, so; (*après une digression*) so, then

donné, e [dɔne] *adj* (*convenu: lieu, heure*) given; (*pas cher: bien*): **c'est ~** it's a gift; **étant ~ que ...** given that ...; **données** *nfpl* data

donner [dɔne] *vt* to give; (*vieux habits etc*) to give away; (*spectacle*) to put on; **~ qch à qn** to give sb sth, give sth to sb; **~ sur** (*suj: fenêtre, chambre*) to look (out) onto; **ça donne soif/faim** it makes you (feel) thirsty/hungry; **se ~ à fond** to give one's all; **se ~ du mal** to take (great) trouble; **s'en ~ à cœur joie** (*fam*) to have a great time

O **MOT-CLÉ**

dont [dɔ̃] *pron relatif* **1** (*appartenance: objets*) whose, of which; (*appartenance: êtres animés*) whose; **la maison dont le toit est rouge** the house the roof of

which is red, the house whose roof is red; **l'homme dont je connais la sœur** the man whose sister I know

2 (*parmi lesquel(le)s*): **2 livres, dont l'un est ...** 2 books, one of which is ...; **il y avait plusieurs personnes, dont Gabrielle** there were several people, among them Gabrielle; **10 blessés, dont 2 grièvement** 10 injured, 2 of them seriously

3 (*complément d'adjectif, de verbe*): **le fils dont il est si fier** the son he's so proud of; **le pays dont il est originaire** the country he's from; **la façon dont il a fait** the way he did it; **ce dont je parle** what I'm talking about

dopage [dɔpaʒ] *nm* (*Sport*) drug use; (*de cheval*) doping

doré, e [dɔʀe] *adj* golden; (*avec dorure*) gilt, gilded

dorénavant [dɔʀenavɑ̃] *adv* henceforth

dorer [dɔʀe] *vt* to gild; (*faire*) **~** (*Culin*) to brown

dorloter [dɔʀlɔte] *vt* to pamper

dormir [dɔʀmiʀ] *vi* to sleep; (*être endormi*) to be asleep

dortoir [dɔʀtwaʀ] *nm* dormitory

dos [do] *nm* back; (*de livre*) spine; **"voir au ~"** "see over"; **de ~** from the back

dosage [dozaʒ] *nm* mixture

dose [doz] *nf* dose; **doser** *vt* to measure out; **il faut savoir doser ses efforts** you have to be able to pace yourself

dossier [dosje] *nm* (*documents*) file; (*de chaise, banc*) back; (*Presse*) feature; (*Comput*) folder; **un ~ scolaire** a school report

douane [dwan] *nf* customs *pl*; **douanier, -ière** *adj* customs *cpd* ▷ *nm* customs officer

double [dubl] *adj, adv* double ▷ *nm* (**2** *fois plus*): **le ~ (de)** twice as much (*ou* many) (as); (*autre exemplaire*) duplicate, copy; (*sosie*) double; (*Tennis*) doubles *sg*; **en ~ (exemplaire)** in duplicate; **faire ~ emploi** to be redundant; **double-cliquer** *vi* (*Inform*) to double-click

doubler [duble] vt (multiplier par 2) to double; (vêtement) to line; (dépasser) to overtake, pass; (film) to dub; (acteur) to stand in for ▷ vi to double

doublure [dublyr] nf lining; (Cinéma) stand-in

douce [dus] adj voir **doux**; **douceâtre** adj sickly sweet; **doucement** adv gently; (lentement) slowly; **douceur** nf softness; (de quelqu'un) gentleness; (de climat) mildness

douche [duʃ] nf shower; **prendre une ~** to have o.take a shower; **doucher: se doucher** vi to have o.u take a shower

doué, e [dwe] adj gifted, talented; **être ~ pour** to have a gift for

douille [duj] nf (Élec) socket

douillet, te [duje, ɛt] adj cosy; (péj: à la douleur) soft

douleur [dulœr] nf pain; (chagrin) grief, distress; **douloureux, -euse** adj painful

doute [dut] nm doubt; **sans ~** no doubt; (probablement) probably; **sans aucun ~** without a doubt; **douter** vt to doubt; **douter de** (sincérité de qn) to have (one's) doubts about; (réussite) to be doubtful of; **douter que** to doubt if ou whether; **se douter de qch/que** to suspect sth/that; **je m'en doutais** I suspected as much; **douteux, -euse** adj (incertain) doubtful; (péj) dubious-looking

Douvres [duvr] n Dover

doux, douce [du, dus] adj soft; (sucré) sweet; (peu fort: moutarde, clément: climat) mild; (pas brusque) gentle

douzaine [duzɛn] nf (12) dozen; (environ 12): **une ~ (de)** a dozen or so

douze [duz] num twelve; **douzième** num twelfth

dragée [draʒe] nf sugared almond

draguer [drage] vt (rivière) to dredge; (fam) to try to pick up

dramatique [dramatik] adj dramatic; (tragique) tragic ▷ nf (TV) (television) drama

drame [dram] nm drama

drap [dra] nm (de lit) sheet; (tissu) woollen fabric

drapeau, x [drapo] nm flag

drap-housse [draus] nm fitted sheet

dresser [drese] vt (mettre vertical, monter) to put up, erect; (liste) to draw up; (animal) to train; **se dresser** vi (obstacle) to stand; (personne) to draw o.s. up; **~ qn contre qn** to set sb against sb; **~ l'oreille** to prick up one's ears

drogue [drɔg] nf drug; **la ~** drugs pl; **drogué, e** nm/f drug addict; **droguer** vt (victime) to drug; **se droguer** vi (aux stupéfiants) to take drugs; (péj: de médicaments) to dose o.s. up; **droguerie** nf hardware shop; **droguiste** nm keeper/owner of a hardware shop

droit, e [drwa, drwat] adj (non courbe) straight; (vertical) upright, straight; (fig: loyal) upright, straight(forward); (opposé à gauche) right, right-hand ▷ adv straight ▷ nm (prérogative) right; (taxe) duty, tax; (: d'inscription) fee; (Jur): **le ~** law; **avoir le ~ de** to be allowed to; **avoir ~ à** to be entitled to; **être dans son ~** to be within one's rights; **à ~e** on the right; (direction) (to the) right; **droits d'auteur** royalties; **droits d'inscription** enrolment fee; **droite** nf (Pol): **la droite** the right (wing); **droitier, -ière** adj right-handed

drôle [drol] adj funny; **une ~ d'idée** a funny idea

dromadaire [drɔmadɛr] nm dromedary

du [dy] dét voir **de** ▷ prép +dét = **de + le**

dû, due [dy] vb voir **devoir** ▷ adj (somme) owing, owed; (causé par): **dû à** due to ▷ nm due

dune [dyn] nf dune

duplex [dypleks] nm (appartement) split-level apartment, duplex

duquel [dykɛl] prép +pron = **de +lequel**

dur, e [dyr] adj (pierre, siège, travail, problème) hard; (voix, climat) harsh; (sévère) hard, harsh; (cruel) hard(-hearted); (porte, col) stiff; (viande) tough ▷ adv hard ▷ nm (fam:

meneur) tough nut; **~ d'oreille** hard of hearing

durant [dyʀɑ̃] *prép* (*au cours de*) during; (*pendant*) for; **des mois ~** for months

durcir [dyʀsiʀ] *vt, vi* to harden; **se durcir** *vi* to harden

durée [dyʀe] *nf* length; (*d'une pile etc*) life; **de courte ~** (*séjour*) short

durement [dyʀmɑ̃] *adv* harshly

durer [dyʀe] *vi* to last

dureté [dyʀte] *nf* hardness; harshness; stiffness; toughness

durit(r) [dyʀit] *nf* (*car radiator*) hose

duvet [dyvɛ] *nm* down; (*sac de couchage*) down-filled sleeping bag

DVD *sigle m* (= *digital versatile disc*) DVD

dynamique [dinamik] *adj* dynamic; **dynamisme** *nm* dynamism

dynamo [dinamo] *nf* dynamo

dyslexie [dislɛksi] *nf* dyslexia, word-blindness

e

eau, x [o] *nf* water; **eaux** *nfpl* (*Méd*) waters; **prendre l'~** to leak, let in water; **tomber à l'~** (*fig*) to fall through; **eau de Cologne** eau de Cologne; **eau courante** running water; **eau de javel** bleach; **eau de toilette** toilet water; **eau douce** fresh water; **eau gazeuse** sparkling (mineral) water; **eau minérale** mineral water; **eau plate** still water; **eau salée** salt water; **eau-de-vie** *nf* brandy

ébène [ebɛn] *nf* ebony; **ébéniste** *nm* cabinetmaker

éblouir [ebluiʀ] *vt* to dazzle

éboueur [ebwœʀ] *nm* dustman (*BRIT*), garbageman (*US*)

ébouillanter [ebujɑ̃te] *vt* to scald; (*Culin*) to blanch

éboulement [ebulmɑ̃] *nm* rock fall

ébranler [ebʀɑ̃le] *vt* to shake; (*affaiblir*) to weaken; **s'ébranler** *vi* (*partir*) to move off

ébullition [ebylisjɔ̃] *nf* boiling point; **en ~** boiling

écaille [ekaj] nf (de poisson) scale; (matière) tortoiseshell; **écailler** vt (poisson) to scale; **s'écailler** vi to flake ou peel (off)

écart [ekar] nm gap; **à l'~** out of the way; **à l'~ de** away from; **faire un ~** (voiture) to swerve

écarté, e [ekarte] adj (lieu) out-of-the-way, remote; (ouvert): **les jambes ~es** legs apart; **les bras ~s** arms outstretched

écarter [ekarte] vt (séparer) to move apart, separate; (éloigner) to push back, move away; (ouvrir: bras, jambes) to spread, open; (: rideau) to draw (back); (éliminer: candidat, possibilité) to dismiss; **s'écarter** vi to part; (s'éloigner) to move away; **s'~ de** to wander from

échafaudage [eʃafodaʒ] nm scaffolding

échalote [eʃalɔt] nf shallot

échange [eʃɑ̃ʒ] nm exchange; **en ~ de** in exchange ou return for; **échanger** vt: **échanger qch (contre)** to exchange sth (for)

échantillon [eʃɑ̃tijɔ̃] nm sample

échapper [eʃape]: **~ à** vt (gardien) to escape (from); (punition, péril) to escape; **s'échapper** vi to escape; **~ à qn** (détail, sens) to escape sb; (objet qu'on tient) to slip out of sb's hands; **laisser ~** (cri etc) to let out; **l'~ belle** to have a narrow escape

écharde [eʃard] nf splinter (of wood)

écharpe [eʃarp] nf scarf; **avoir le bras en ~** to have one's arm in a sling

échauffer [eʃofe] vt (moteur) to overheat; **s'échauffer** vi (Sport) to warm up; (dans la discussion) to become heated

échéance [eʃeɑ̃s] nf (d'un paiement: date) settlement date; (fig) deadline; **à brève ~** in the short term; **à longue ~** in the long run

échéant [eʃeɑ̃]: **le cas ~** adv if the case arises

échec [eʃɛk] nm failure; (Échecs): **~ et mat/au roi** checkmate/check; **échecs**

nmpl (jeu) chess sg; **tenir en ~** to hold in check

échelle [eʃɛl] nf ladder; (fig, d'une carte) scale

échelon [eʃ(ə)lɔ̃] nm (d'échelle) rung; (Admin) grade; **échelonner** vt to space out

échiquier [eʃikje] nm chessboard

écho [eko] nm echo; **échographie** nf: **passer une échographie** to have a scan

échouer [eʃwe] vi to fail; **s'échouer** vi to run aground

éclabousser [eklabuse] vt to splash

éclair [eklɛr] nm (d'orage) flash of lightning, lightning bolt; (gâteau) éclair

éclairage [eklɛraʒ] nm lighting

éclaircie [eklɛrsi] nf bright interval

éclaircir [eklɛrsir] vt to lighten; (fig: mystère) to clear up; (: point) to clarify; **s'éclaircir** vi (ciel) to clear; **s'~ la voix** to clear one's throat; **éclaircissement** nm (sur un point) clarification

éclairer [eklere] vt (lieu) to light (up); (personne: avec une lampe etc) to light the way for; (fig: problème) to shed light on ▷ vi: **mal/bien** to give a poor/good light; **s'~ à la bougie** to use candlelight

éclat [ekla] nm (de bombe, de verre) fragment; (du soleil, d'une couleur etc) brightness, brilliance; (d'une cérémonie) splendour; (scandale): **faire un ~** to cause a commotion; **éclats de voix** shouts; **éclat de rire** roar of laughter

éclatant, e [eklatɑ̃, ɑ̃t] adj brilliant

éclater [eklate] vi (pneu) to burst; (bombe) to explode; (guerre) to break out; (groupe, parti) to break up; **~ en sanglots/de rire** to burst out sobbing/laughing

écluse [eklyz] nf lock

écœurant, e [ekœrɑ̃, ɑ̃t] adj (gâteau etc) sickly; (fig) sickening

écœurer [ekœre] vt: **~ qn** (nourriture) to make sb feel sick; (conduite, personne) to disgust sb

école [ekɔl] nf school; **aller à l'~** to go

to school; **école maternelle** nursery school; **école primaire** primary (BRIT) ou grade (US) school; **école secondaire** secondary (BRIT) ou high (US) school; **écolier, -ière** nm/f schoolboy(-girl)

écologie [ekɔlɔʒi] nf ecology; **écologique** adj environment-friendly; **écologiste** nm/f ecologist

économe [ekɔnɔm] adj thrifty ▷ nm/f (de lycée etc) bursar (BRIT), treasurer (US)

économie [ekɔnɔmi] nf economy; (gain: d'argent, de temps etc) saving; (science) economics sg; **économies** nfpl (pécule) savings; **économique** adj (avantageux) economical; (Écon) economic; **économiser** vt, vi to save

écorce [ekɔrs] nf bark; (de fruit) peel

écorcher [ekɔrʃe] vt: **s'~ le genou/la main** to graze one's knee/one's hand; **écorchure** nf graze

écossais, e [ekɔsɛ, ɛz] adj Scottish ▷ nm/f: **É-, e** Scot

Écosse [ekɔs] nf: **l'~** Scotland

écouter [ekute] vt to listen to; **s'écouter** (malade) to be a bit of a hypochondriac; **si je m'écoutais** if I followed my instincts; **écouteur** nm (Tél) receiver; **écouteurs** nmpl (casque) headphones pl, headset

écran [ekrã] nm screen; **petit ~** television; **~ total** sunblock

écrasant, e [ekrazã, ãt] adj overwhelming

écraser [ekraze] vt to crush; (piéton) to run over; **s'écraser** vi to crash; **s'~ contre** to crash into

écrémé, e [ekreme] adj (lait) skimmed

écrevisse [ekrəvis] nf crayfish inv

écrire [ekrir] vt to write; **s'écrire** to write to each other; **ça s'écrit comment?** how is it spelt?; **écrit, e** (examen) written paper; **par écrit** in writing

écriteau, x [ekrito] nm notice, sign

écriture [ekrityr] nf writing; **écritures** nfpl (Comm) accounts, books; **l'É- (sainte), les É-s** the Scriptures

écrivain [ekrivɛ̃] nm writer

écrou [ekru] nm nut

écrouler [ekrule]: **s'écrouler** vi to collapse

écru, e [ekry] adj (couleur) off-white, écru

écume [ekym] nf foam

écureuil [ekyrœj] nm squirrel

écurie [ekyri] nf stable

eczéma [ɛgzema] nm eczema

EDF sigle f (= Électricité de France) national electricity company

Édimbourg [edɛ̃bur] n Edinburgh

éditer [edite] vt (publier) to publish; (annoter) to edit; **éditeur, -trice** nm/f publisher; **édition** nf edition; (industrie du livre) publishing

édredon [edredɔ̃] nm eiderdown

éducateur, -trice [edykatœr, tris] nm/f teacher; (en école spécialisée) instructor

éducatif, -ive [edykatif, iv] adj educational

éducation [edykasjɔ̃] nf education; (familiale) upbringing; (manières) (good) manners pl; **éducation physique** physical education

éduquer [edyke] vt to educate; (élever) to bring up

effacer [efase] vt to erase, rub out; **s'effacer** vi (inscription etc) to wear off; (pour laisser passer) to step aside

effarant, e [efarã, ãt] adj alarming

effectif, -ive [efɛktif, iv] adj real ▷ nm (Scol) (pupil) numbers pl; (entreprise) staff, workforce; **effectivement** adv (réellement) actually, really; (en effet) indeed

effectuer [efɛktɥe] vt (opération) to carry out; (trajet) to make

effervescent, e [efɛrvesã, ãt] adj effervescent

effet [efɛ] nm effect; (impression) impression; **effets** nmpl (vêtements etc) things; **faire ~** (médicament) to take effect; **faire de l'~** (impressionner) to make an impression; **faire bon/mauvais ~ sur qn** to make a good/bad impression on sb; **en ~** indeed; **effet de**

serre greenhouse effect
efficace [efikas] *adj* (*personne*)
efficient; (*action, médicament*) effective;
efficacité *nf* efficiency; effectiveness
effondrer [efɔ̃dʀe]: **s'effondrer** *vi* to
collapse
efforcer [efɔʀse]: **s'efforcer de** *vt*: **s'~
de faire** to try hard to do
effort [efɔʀ] *nm* effort
effrayant, e [efʀɛjɑ̃, ɑ̃t] *adj*
frightening
effrayer [efʀeje] *vt* to frighten, scare;
s'~ (de) to be frightened ou scared (by)
effréné, e [efʀene] *adj* wild
effronté, e [efʀɔ̃te] *adj* cheeky
effroyable [efʀwajabl] *adj* horrifying,
appalling
égal, e, -aux [egal, o] *adj* equal;
(*constant: vitesse*) steady ▷ *nm/f* equal;
être ~ à (*prix, nombre*) to be equal to;
ça lui est ~ it's all the same to him,
he doesn't mind; **sans ~** matchless,
unequalled; **d'~ à ~** as equals;
également *adv* equally; (*aussi*) too,
as well; **égaler** *vt* to equal; **égaliser**
vt (*sol, salaires*) to level (out); (*chances*)
to equalize ▷ *vi* (*Sport*) to equalize;
égalité *nf* equality; **être à égalité**
to be level
égard [egaʀ] *nm*: **~s** *mpl* consideration
sg; **à cet ~** in this respect; **par ~ pour**
out of consideration for; **à l'~ de**
towards
égarer [egaʀe] *vt* to mislay; **s'égarer**
vi to get lost, lose one's way; (*objet*) to
go astray
églefin [eɡləfɛ̃] *nm* haddock
église [egliz] *nf* church; **aller à l'~** to
go to church
égoïsme [egɔism] *nm* selfishness;
égoïste *adj* selfish
égout [egu] *nm* sewer
égoutter [egute] *vi* to drip; **s'égoutter**
vi to drip; **égouttoir** *nm* draining
board; (*mobile*) draining rack
égratigner [egʀatiɲe] *vt* to scratch
Égypte [eʒipt] *nf*: **l'~** Egypt;
égyptien, ne *adj* Egyptian ▷ *nm/f*:

Égyptien, ne Egyptian
eh [e] *excl* hey!; **eh bien!** well!
élaborer [elabɔʀe] *vt* to elaborate;
(*projet, stratégie*) to work out; (*rapport*)
to draft
élan [elɑ̃] *nm* (*Zool*) elk, moose; (*Sport*)
run up; (*fig: de tendresse etc*) surge;
prendre de l'~ to gather speed
élancer [elɑ̃se]: **s'élancer** *vi* to dash,
hurl o.s.
élargir [elaʀʒiʀ] *vt* to widen; **s'élargir**
vi to widen; (*vêtement*) to stretch
élastique [elastik] *adj* elastic ▷ *nm* (*de
bureau*) rubber band; (*pour la couture*)
elastic *no pl*
élection [elɛksjɔ̃] *nf* election
électricien, ne [elektʀisjɛ̃, jɛn] *nm/f*
electrician
électricité [elektʀisite] *nf* electricity;
allumer/éteindre l'~ to put on/off
the light
électrique [elektʀik] *adj* electric(al)
électrocuter [elektʀɔkyte] *vt* to
electrocute
électroménager [elektʀɔmenaʒe]
adj, nm: **appareils ~s, l'~** domestic
(electrical) appliances
électronique [elektʀɔnik] *adj*
electronic ▷ *nf* electronics *sg*
élégance [elegɑ̃s] *nf* elegance
élégant, e [elegɑ̃, ɑ̃t] *adj* elegant
élément [elemɑ̃] *nm* element; (*pièce*)
component, part; **élémentaire** *adj*
elementary
éléphant [elefɑ̃] *nm* elephant
élevage [el(ə)vaʒ] *nm* breeding;
(*de bovins*) cattle rearing; **truite d'~**
farmed trout
élevé, e [el(ə)ve] *adj* high; **bien/mal ~**
well-/ill-mannered
élève [elɛv] *nm/f* pupil
élever [el(ə)ve] *vt* (*enfant*) to bring up,
raise; (*animaux*) to breed; (*hausser: taux,
niveau*) to raise; (*édifier: monument*) to
put up, erect; **s'élever** *vi* (*avion*) to go
up; (*niveau, température*) to rise; **s'~ à**
(*suj: frais, dégâts*) to amount to, add up
to; **s'~ contre qch** to rise up against

sth; **~ la voix** to raise one's voice;
éleveur, -euse nm/f breeder
éliminatoire [eliminatwaʀ] nf
(Sport) heat
éliminer [elimine] vt to eliminate
élire [eliʀ] vt to elect
elle [ɛl] pron (sujet) she; (: chose) it;
(complément) her; it; **~s** (sujet) they;
(complément) them; **~-même** herself;
itself; **~s-mêmes** themselves; voir
aussi **il**
éloigné, e [elwaɲe] adj distant, far-off;
(parent) distant
éloigner [elwaɲe] vt (échéance) to put
off, postpone; (soupçons, danger) to
ward off; (objet) **~ qch (de)** to move
ou take sth away (from); (personne):
~ qn (de) to take sb away ou remove
sb (from); **s'éloigner (de)** (personne)
to go away (from); (véhicule) to move
away (from); (affectivement) to grow
away (from)
élu, e [ely] pp de **élire** ▷ nm/f (Pol)
elected representative
Élysée [elize] nm: **(le palais de) l'~**
the Élysée Palace (the French president's
residence)
émail, -aux [emaj, o] nm enamel
e-mail [imɛl] nm e-mail; **envoyer qch
par ~** to e-mail sth
émanciper [emɑ̃sipe] vt: **s'émanciper**
vi (fig) to become emancipated ou
liberated
emballage [ɑ̃balaʒ] nm (papier)
wrapping; (boîte) packaging
emballer [ɑ̃bale] vt to wrap (up); (dans
un carton) to pack (up); (fig: fam) to thrill
(to bits); **s'emballer** vi (moteur) to race;
(cheval) to bolt; (fig: personne) to get
carried away
embarcadère [ɑ̃baʀkadɛʀ] nm
wharf, pier
embarquement [ɑ̃baʀkəmɑ̃] nm (de
passagers) boarding; (de marchandises)
loading
embarquer [ɑ̃baʀke] vt (personne) to
embark; (marchandise) to load; (fam)
to cart off ▷ vi (passager) to board;

s'embarquer vi to board; **s'~ dans**
(affaire, aventure) to embark upon
embarras [ɑ̃baʀa] nm (gêne)
embarrassment; **mettre qn dans
l'~** to put sb in an awkward position;
vous n'avez que l'~ du choix the only
problem is choosing
embarrassant, e [ɑ̃baʀasɑ̃, ɑ̃t] adj
embarrassing
embarrasser [ɑ̃baʀase] vt (encombrer)
to clutter (up); (gêner) to hinder,
hamper; **~ qn** to put sb in an awkward
position; **s'~ de** to burden o.s. with
embaucher [ɑ̃boʃe] vt to take on, hire
embêter [ɑ̃bete] vt to bother;
s'embêter vi (s'ennuyer) to be bored
emblée [ɑ̃ble]: **d'~** adv straightaway
embouchure [ɑ̃buʃyʀ] nf (Géo) mouth
embourber [ɑ̃buʀbe]: **s'embourber** vi
to get stuck in the mud
embouteillage [ɑ̃butejaʒ] nm
traffic jam
embranchement [ɑ̃bʀɑ̃ʃmɑ̃] nm
(routier) junction
embrasser [ɑ̃bʀase] vt to kiss; (sujet:
période) to embrace, encompass
embrayage [ɑ̃bʀejaʒ] nm clutch
embrouiller [ɑ̃bʀuje] vt to muddle up;
(fils) to tangle (up); **s'embrouiller** vi
(personne) to get in a muddle
embruns [ɑ̃bʀœ̃] nmpl sea spray sg
embué, e [ɑ̃bɥe] adj misted up
émeraude [em(ə)ʀod] nf emerald
émerger [emɛʀʒe] vi to emerge; (faire
saillie, aussi fig) to stand out
émeri [em(ə)ʀi] nm: **toile** ou **papier ~**
emery paper
émerveiller [emɛʀveje] vt to fill with
wonder; **s'émerveiller de** to marvel at
émettre [emɛtʀ] vt (son, lumière) to
give out, emit; (message etc: Radio) to
transmit; (billet, timbre, emprunt) to
issue; (hypothèse, avis) to voice, put
forward ▷ vi to broadcast
émeus etc [emø] vb voir **émouvoir**
émeute [emøt] nf riot
émigrer [emigʀe] vi to emigrate
émincer [emɛ̃se] vt to cut into thin

slices

émission [emisjɔ̃] *nf* (*Radio, TV*) programme, broadcast; (*d'un message*) transmission; (*de timbre*) issue

emmêler [ɑ̃mele] *vt* to tangle (up); (*fig*) to muddle up; **s'emmêler** *vi* to get in a tangle

emménager [ɑ̃menaʒe] *vi* to move in; **~ dans** to move into

emmener [ɑ̃m(ə)ne] *vt* to take (with one); (*comme repas, capture*) to take away; **~ qn au cinéma** to take sb to the cinema

emmerder [ɑ̃mɛrde] (*fam!*) *vt* to bug, bother; **s'emmerder** *vi* to be bored stiff

émoticone [emotikon] *nm* smiley

émotif, -ive [emotif, iv] *adj* emotional

émotion [emosjɔ̃] *nf* emotion

émouvoir [emuvwar] *vt* to move; **s'émouvoir** *vi* to be moved; (*s'indigner*) to be roused

empaqueter [ɑ̃pakte] *vt* to parcel up

emparer [ɑ̃pare]: **s'emparer de** (*objet*) to seize, grab; (*comme otage, MIL*) to seize; (*suj: peur etc*) to take hold of

empêchement [ɑ̃pɛʃmɑ̃] *nm* (unexpected) obstacle, hitch

empêcher [ɑ̃peʃe] *vt* to prevent; **~ qn de faire** to prevent *ou* stop sb (from) doing; **il n'empêche que** nevertheless; **il n'a pas pu s'~ de rire** he couldn't help laughing

empereur [ɑ̃prœr] *nm* emperor

empiffrer [ɑ̃pifre]: **s'~** (*fam*) *vi* to stuff o.s.

empiler [ɑ̃pile] *vt* to pile (up)

empire [ɑ̃pir] *nm* empire; (*fig*) influence

empirer [ɑ̃pire] *vi* to worsen, deteriorate

emplacement [ɑ̃plasmɑ̃] *nm* site

emploi [ɑ̃plwa] *nm* (*utilisation*) use; (*Comm, Écon*) employment; (*poste*) job, situation; **mode d'~** directions for use; **emploi du temps** timetable, schedule

employé, e [ɑ̃plwaje] *nm/f* employee; **employé de bureau** office employee *ou* clerk

employer [ɑ̃plwaje] *vt* to use; (*ouvrier, main-d'œuvre*) to employ; **s'~ à qch/à faire** to apply *ou* devote o.s. to doing; **employeur, -euse** *nm/f* employer

empoigner [ɑ̃pwaɲe] *vt* to grab

empoisonner [ɑ̃pwazɔne] *vt* to poison; (*empester: air, pièce*) to stink out; (*fam*): **~ qn** to drive sb mad

emporter [ɑ̃pɔrte] *vt* to take (with one); (*en dérobant ou enlevant, emmener: blessés, voyageurs*) to take away; (*entraîner*) to carry away; **s'emporter** *vi* (*de colère*) to lose one's temper; **l'~ (sur)** to get the upper hand (of); **plats à ~** take-away meals

empreinte [ɑ̃prɛ̃t] *nf*: **~ (de pas)** footprint; **empreintes (digitales)** fingerprints

empressé, e [ɑ̃prese] *adj* attentive

empresser [ɑ̃prese]: **s'empresser** *vi*: **s'~ auprès de qn** to surround sb with attentions; **s'~ de faire** (*se hâter*) to hasten to do

emprisonner [ɑ̃prizɔne] *vt* to imprison

emprunt [ɑ̃prœ̃] *nm* loan

emprunter [ɑ̃prœ̃te] *vt* to borrow; (*itinéraire*) to take, follow

ému, e [emy] *pp de* **émouvoir** ▷ *adj* (*gratitude*) touched; (*compassion*) moved

○ **MOT-CLÉ**

en [ɑ̃] *prép* **1** (*endroit, pays*) in; (*direction*) to: **habiter en France/ville** to live in France/town; **aller en France/ville** to go to France/town

2 (*moment, temps*) in; **en été/juin** in summer/June; **en 3 jours** in 3 days

3 (*moyen*) by; **en avion/taxi** by plane/taxi

4 (*composition*) made of; **c'est en verre** it's (made of) glass; **un collier en argent** a silver necklace

5 (*description, état*): **une femme (habillée) en rouge** a woman (dressed) in red; **peindre qch en rouge** to paint sth red; **en T/étoile** T/star-shaped; **en**

chemise/chaussettes in one's shirt-sleeves/socks; **en soldat** as a soldier; **cassé en plusieurs morceaux** broken into several pieces; **en réparation** being repaired, under repair; **en vacances** on holiday; **en deuil** in mourning; **le même en plus grand** the same but only bigger

6 (avec gérondif): **j'en ai/veux** I have/want some; **en as-tu?** have you got any?; **je n'en veux pas** I don't want any; **j'en ai à** I've got 2; **combien y en a-t-il?** how many (of them) are there?; **j'en ai assez** I've got enough (of it ou them); (j'en ai marre) I've had enough

2 (provenance) from there; **j'en viens** I've come from there

3 (cause): **il en est malade/perd le sommeil** he is ill/can't sleep because of it

4 (complément de nom, d'adjectif, de verbe): **j'en connais les dangers** I know its ou the dangers; **j'en suis fier** I am proud of it ou him ou her ou them; **j'en ai besoin** I need it ou them

encadrer [ɑ̃kadʀe] vt (tableau, image) to frame; (fig: entourer) to surround; (personnel, soldats etc) to train

encaisser [ɑ̃kese] vt (chèque) to cash; (argent) to collect; (fam: coup, défaite) to take

en-cas [ɑ̃ka] nm snack

enceinte [ɑ̃sɛ̃t] adj f ▷ (de 6 mois) (6 months) pregnant ▷ nf (mur) wall; (espace) enclosure; **enceinte (acoustique)** (loud)speaker

encens [ɑ̃sɑ̃] nm incense

enchaîner [ɑ̃ʃene] vt to chain up; (mouvements, séquences) to link (together) ▷ vi to carry on

enchanté, e [ɑ̃ʃɑ̃te] adj (ravi)

delighted; (magique) enchanted; **~ (de faire votre connaissance)** pleased to meet you

enchère [ɑ̃ʃɛʀ] nf bid; **mettre/vendre aux ~s** to put up for (sale by)/sell by auction

enclencher [ɑ̃klɑ̃ʃe] vt (mécanisme) to engage; **s'enclencher** vi to engage

encombrant, e [ɑ̃kɔ̃bʀɑ̃, ɑ̃t] adj cumbersome, bulky

encombrement [ɑ̃kɔ̃bʀəmɑ̃] nm: **être pris dans un ~** to be stuck in a traffic jam

encombrer [ɑ̃kɔ̃bʀe] vt to clutter (up); (gêner) hamper; **s'~ de** (bagages etc) to load ou burden o.s. with

---

MOT-CLÉ

encore [ɑ̃kɔʀ] adv **1** (continuation) still; **il y travaille encore** he's still working on it; **pas encore** not yet

2 (de nouveau) again; **j'irai encore demain** I'll go again tomorrow; **encore une fois** (once) again; **(et puis) quoi encore?** what next?

3 (en plus) more; **encore un peu de viande?** a bit more meat?; **encore deux jours** two more days

4 (intensif) even, still; **encore plus fort/mieux** even louder/better, louder/better still

5 (restriction) even so ou then, only; **encore pourrais-je le faire si ...** even so, I might be able to do it if ...; **si encore** if only

encourager [ɑ̃kuʀaʒe] vt to encourage; **~ qn à faire qch** to encourage sb to do sth

encourir [ɑ̃kuʀiʀ] vt to incur

encre [ɑ̃kʀ] nf ink; **encre de Chine** Indian ink

encyclopédie [ɑ̃siklɔpedi] nf encyclopaedia

endetter [ɑ̃dete]: **s'endetter** vi to get into debt

endive [ɑ̃div] nf chicory no pl

endormi, e [ɑ̃dɔʀmi] *adj* asleep
endormir [ɑ̃dɔʀmiʀ] *vt* to put to
sleep; (*suj: chaleur etc*) to send to sleep;
(*Méd: dent, nerf*) to anaesthetize; (*fig:
soupçons*) to allay; **s'endormir** *vi* to fall
asleep, go to sleep
endroit [ɑ̃dʀwa] *nm* place; (*opposé à
l'envers*) right side; **à l'~** (*vêtement*) the
right way out; (*objet posé*) the right
way round
endurance [ɑ̃dyʀɑ̃s] *nf* endurance
endurant, e [ɑ̃dyʀɑ̃, ɑ̃t] *adj* tough,
hardy
endurcir [ɑ̃dyʀsiʀ] **s'endurcir** *vi*
(*physiquement*) to become tougher;
(*moralement*) to become hardened
endurer [ɑ̃dyʀe] *vt* to endure, bear
énergétique [enɛʀʒetik] *adj* (*aliment*)
energy-giving
énergie [enɛʀʒi] *nf* (*Physique*) energy;
(*Tech*) power; (*morale*) vigour, spirit;
énergique *adj* energetic, vigorous;
(*mesures*) drastic, stringent
énervant, e [enɛʀvɑ̃, ɑ̃t] *adj* irritating,
annoying
énerver [enɛʀve] *vt* to irritate, annoy;
s'énerver *vi* to get excited, get
worked up
enfance [ɑ̃fɑ̃s] *nf* childhood
enfant [ɑ̃fɑ̃] *nm/f* child; **enfantin, e**
adj (*puéril*) childlike; (*langage, jeu etc*)
children's *cpd*
enfer [ɑ̃fɛʀ] *nm* hell
enfermer [ɑ̃fɛʀme] *vt* to shut up; (*à
clef, interner*) to lock up; **s'enfermer** to
shut o.s. away
enfiler [ɑ̃file] *vt* (*vêtement*) to slip on,
slip into; (*perles*) to string; (*aiguille*)
to thread
enfin [ɑ̃fɛ̃] *adv* at last; (*en énumérant*)
lastly; (*toutefois*) still; (*pour conclure*) in a
word; (*somme toute*) after all
enflammer [ɑ̃flame] **s'enflammer** *vi*
to catch fire; (*Méd*) to become inflamed
enflé, e [ɑ̃fle] *adj* swollen
enfler [ɑ̃fle] *vi* to swell (up)
enfoncer [ɑ̃fɔ̃se] *vt* (*clou*) to drive in;
(*faire pénétrer*) **~ qch dans** to push (ou

drive) sth into; (*forcer: porte*) to break
open; **enfoncer** *vi* to sink; **s'~ dans** to
sink into; (*forêt, ville*) to disappear into
enfouir [ɑ̃fwiʀ] *vt* (*dans le sol*) to bury;
(*dans un tiroir etc*) to tuck away
enfuir [ɑ̃fɥiʀ]: **s'enfuir** *vi* to run away
ou off
engagement [ɑ̃gaʒmɑ̃] *nm*
commitment; **sans ~** without
obligation
engager [ɑ̃gaʒe] *vt* (*embaucher*) to take
on; (*: artiste*) to engage; (*commencer*) to
start; (*lier*) to bind, commit; (*impliquer*)
to involve; (*investir*) to invest, lay out;
(*inciter*) to urge; (*introduire: clé*) to insert;
s'engager *vi* (*promettre*) to commit
o.s.; (*Mil*) to enlist; (*débuter: conversation
etc*) to start (up); **s'~ à faire** to
undertake to do; **s'~ dans** (*rue, passage*)
to turn into; (*fig: affaire, discussion*) to
enter into, embark on
engelures [ɑ̃ʒlyʀ] *nfpl* chilblains
engin [ɑ̃ʒɛ̃] *nm* machine; (*outil*)
instrument; (*Auto*) vehicle; (*Aviat*)
aircraft *inv*

▌ Attention à ne pas traduire *engin*
par le mot anglais *engine*.

engloutir [ɑ̃glutiʀ] *vt* to swallow up
engouement [ɑ̃gumɑ̃] *nm* (sudden)
passion
engouffrer [ɑ̃gufʀe] *vt* to swallow up,
devour; **s'engouffrer dans** to rush into
engourdir [ɑ̃guʀdiʀ] *vt* to numb;
(*fig*) to dull, blunt; **s'engourdir** *vi* to
go numb
engrais [ɑ̃gʀɛ] *nm* manure; **engrais
chimique** chemical fertilizer
engraisser [ɑ̃gʀese] *vt* to fatten (up)
engrenage [ɑ̃gʀənaʒ] *nm* gears *pl*,
gearing; (*fig*) chain
engueuler [ɑ̃gœle] (*fam*) *vt* to bawl at
enhardir [ɑ̃aʀdiʀ]: **s'enhardir** *vi* to
grow bolder
énigme [enigm] *nf* riddle
enivrer [ɑ̃nivʀe] *vt*: **s'~** to get drunk
enjamber [ɑ̃ʒɑ̃be] *vt* to stride over
enjeu, x [ɑ̃ʒø] *nm* stakes *pl*
enjoué, e [ɑ̃ʒwe] *adj* playful

enlaidir [ɑ̃lediʀ] vt to make ugly ▷ vi to become ugly

enlèvement [ɑ̃lɛvmɑ̃] nm (rapt) abduction, kidnapping

enlever [ɑ̃l(ə)ve] vt (ôter: gén) to remove; (: vêtements, lunettes) to take off; (emporter: ordures etc) to take away; (kidnapper) to abduct, kidnap; (obtenir: prix, contrat) to win; (prendre): **~ qch à qn** to take sth (away) from sb

enliser [ɑ̃lize]: **s'enliser** vi to sink, get stuck

enneigé, e [ɑ̃neʒe] adj (route, maison) snowed-up; (paysage) snowy

ennemi, e [ɛnmi] adj hostile; (Mil) enemy cpd ▷ nm/f enemy

ennui [ɑ̃nɥi] nm (lassitude) boredom; (difficulté) trouble no pl; **avoir des ~s** to have problems; **ennuyer** vt to bother; (lasser) to bore; **s'ennuyer** vi to be bored; **si cela ne vous ennuie pas** if it's no trouble to you); **ennuyeux, -euse** adj boring, tedious; (embêtant) annoying

énorme [enɔʀm] adj enormous, huge; **énormément** adv enormously; **énormément de neige/gens** an enormous amount of snow/number of people

enquête [ɑ̃kɛt] nf (de journaliste, de police) investigation; (judiciaire, administrative) inquiry; (sondage d'opinion) survey; **enquêter** vi: **enquêter (sur)** to investigate

enragé, e [ɑ̃ʀaʒe] adj (Méd) rabid, with rabies; (fig) fanatical

enrageant, e [ɑ̃ʀaʒɑ̃, ɑ̃t] adj infuriating

enrager [ɑ̃ʀaʒe] vi to be in a rage

enregistrement [ɑ̃ʀ(ə)ʒistʀəmɑ̃] nm recording; **enregistrement des bagages** baggage check-in

enregistrer [ɑ̃ʀ(ə)ʒistʀe] vt (Mus etc) to record; (fig: mémoriser) to make a mental note of; (bagages: à l'aéroport) to check in

enrhumer [ɑ̃ʀyme] vt: **s'~, être enrhumé** to catch a cold

enrichir [ɑ̃ʀiʃiʀ] vt to make rich(er); (fig) to enrich; **s'enrichir** vi to get rich(er)

enrouer [ɑ̃ʀwe]: **s'enrouer** vi to go hoarse

enrouler [ɑ̃ʀule] vt (fil, corde) to wind (up); **s'~ (autour de qch)** to wind (around sth)

enseignant, e [ɑ̃sɛɲɑ̃, ɑ̃t] nm/f teacher

enseignement [ɑ̃sɛɲ(ə)mɑ̃] nm teaching; (Admin) education

enseigner [ɑ̃sɛɲe] vt, vi to teach; **~ qch à qn** to teach sb sth

ensemble [ɑ̃sɑ̃bl] adv together ▷ nm (groupement) set; (vêtements) outfit; (totalité): **l'~ du/de la** the whole ou entire; (unité, harmonie) unity; **impression/idée d'~** overall ou general impression/idea; **dans l'~** (en gros) on the whole

ensoleillé, e [ɑ̃sɔleje] adj sunny

ensuite [ɑ̃sɥit] adv then, next; (plus tard) afterwards, later

entamer [ɑ̃tame] vt (pain, bouteille) to start; (hostilités, pourparlers) to open

entasser [ɑ̃tase] vt (empiler) to pile up, heap up; **s'entasser** vi (s'amonceler) to pile up; **s'~ dans** (personnes) to cram into

entendre [ɑ̃tɑ̃dʀ] vt to hear; (comprendre) to understand; (vouloir dire) to mean; **s'entendre** vi (sympathiser) to get on; (se mettre d'accord) to agree; **j'ai entendu dire que** I've heard (it said) that; **~ parler de** to hear of

entendu, e [ɑ̃tɑ̃dy] adj (réglé) agreed; (au courant: air) knowing; **(c'est) ~** all right, agreed; **bien ~** of course

entente [ɑ̃tɑ̃t] nf understanding; (accord, traité) agreement; **à double ~** (sens) with a double meaning

enterrement [ɑ̃tɛʀmɑ̃] nm (cérémonie) funeral, burial

enterrer [ɑ̃teʀe] vt to bury

entêtant, e [ɑ̃tɛtɑ̃, ɑ̃t] adj heady

en-tête [ɑ̃tɛt] nm heading; **papier à ~** headed notepaper

entêté, e [ɑ̃tete] *adj* stubborn

entêter [ɑ̃tete]: **s'~ (à faire)** *vi* to persist (in doing)

enthousiasme [ɑ̃tuzjasm] *nm* enthusiasm; **enthousiasmer** *vt* to fill with enthusiasm; **s'~ (pour qch)** to get enthusiastic (about sth); **enthousiaste** *adj* enthusiastic

entier, -ère [ɑ̃tje, jɛʀ] *adj* whole; (*total: satisfaction etc*) complete; (*fig: caractère*) unbending ▷ *nm* (Math) whole; **en ~** totally; **lait ~** full-cream milk; **entièrement** *adv* entirely, wholly

entonnoir [ɑ̃tɔnwaʀ] *nm* funnel

entorse [ɑ̃tɔʀs] *nf* (Méd) sprain; (*fig*): **~ au règlement** infringement of the rule

entourage [ɑ̃tuʀaʒ] *nm* circle; (*famille*) circle of family/friends; (*ce qui enclôt*) surround

entourer [ɑ̃tuʀe] *vt* to surround; (*apporter son soutien à*) to rally round; **~ de** to surround with; **s'~ de** to surround o.s. with

entracte [ɑ̃tʀakt] *nm* interval

entraide [ɑ̃tʀɛd] *nf* mutual aid

entrain [ɑ̃tʀɛ̃] *nm* spirit; **avec/sans ~** spiritedly/half-heartedly

entraînement [ɑ̃tʀɛnmɑ̃] *nm* training

entraîner [ɑ̃tʀene] *vt* (*charrier*) to carry ou drag along; (Tech) to drive; (*emmener: personne*) to take (off); (*influencer*) to lead; (Sport) to train; (*impliquer*) to entail; **s'entraîner** *vi* (Sport) to train; **s'~ à qch/à faire** to train o.s. for sth/to do; **~ qn à faire** (*inciter*) to lead sb to do; **entraîneur, -euse** *nm/f* (Sport) coach, trainer ▷ *nm* (Hippisme) trainer

entre [ɑ̃tʀ] *prép* between; (*parmi*) among(st); **l'un d'~ eux/nous** one of them/us; **ils se battent ~ eux** they are fighting among(st) themselves; **~ autres (choses)** among other things; **entrecôte** *nf* entrecôte ou rib steak

entrée [ɑ̃tʀe] *nf* entrance; (*accès: au cinéma etc*) admission; (*billet*) (admission) ticket; (Culin) first course

entre...: entrefilet *nm* paragraph (*short article*); **entremets** *nm* (cream) dessert

entrepôt [ɑ̃tʀəpo] *nm* warehouse

entreprendre [ɑ̃tʀəpʀɑ̃dʀ] *vt* (*se lancer dans*) to undertake; (*commencer*) to begin ou start (upon)

entrepreneur, -euse [ɑ̃tʀəpʀənœʀ, øz] *nm/f*: **entrepreneur (en bâtiment)** (building) contractor

entreprise [ɑ̃tʀəpʀiz] *nf* (*société*) firm, concern; (*action*) undertaking, venture

entrer [ɑ̃tʀe] *vi* to go (ou come) in, enter ▷ *vt* (Inform) to enter, input; (*faire*) **~ qch dans** to get sth into; **~ dans** (*gén*) to enter; (*pièce*) to go (ou come) into; enter; (*club*) to join; (*heurter*) to run into; **~ à l'hôpital** to go into hospital; **faire ~** (*visiteur*) to show in

entre-temps [ɑ̃tʀətɑ̃] *adv* meanwhile

entretenir [ɑ̃tʀət(ə)niʀ] *vt* to maintain; (*famille, maîtresse*) to support, keep; **~ qn (de)** to speak to sb about

entretien [ɑ̃tʀətjɛ̃] *nm* maintenance; (*discussion*) discussion, talk; (*pour un emploi*) interview

entrevoir [ɑ̃tʀəvwaʀ] *vt* (*à peine*) to make out; (*brièvement*) to catch a glimpse of

entrevue [ɑ̃tʀəvy] *nf* (*audience*) interview

entrouvert, e [ɑ̃tʀuvɛʀ, ɛʀt] *adj* half-open

énumérer [enymeʀe] *vt* to list

envahir [ɑ̃vaiʀ] *vt* to invade; (*suj: inquiétude, peur*) to come over; **envahissant, e** (*péj*) *adj* (*personne*) intrusive

enveloppe [ɑ̃v(ə)lɔp] *nf* (*de lettre*) envelope; (*crédits*) budget; **envelopper** *vt* to wrap; (*fig*) to envelop, shroud

enverrai *etc* [ɑ̃veʀe] *vb voir* **envoyer**

envers [ɑ̃vɛʀ] *prép* towards, to ▷ *nm* other side; (*d'une étoffe*) wrong side; **à l'~** (*verticalement*) upside down; (*pull*) back to front; (*chaussettes*) inside out

envie [ɑ̃vi] *nf* (*sentiment*) envy; (*souhait*) desire, wish; **avoir ~ de (faire)** to feel like (doing); (*plus fort*) to want (to do); **avoir ~ que** to wish that; **cette glace me fait ~ I** fancy some of that ice cream; **envier** vt to envy; **envieux, -euse** adj envious

environ [ɑ̃virɔ̃] adv: **~ 3 h/2 km** (around) about 3 o'clock/2 km; voir aussi **environs**

environnant, e [ɑ̃virɔnɑ̃, ɑ̃t] adj surrounding

environnement [ɑ̃virɔnmɑ̃] nm environment

environs [ɑ̃virɔ̃] nmpl surroundings; **aux ~ de** (round) about

envisager [ɑ̃vizaʒe] vt to contemplate, envisage; **~ de faire** to consider doing

envoler [ɑ̃vɔle]: **s'envoler** vi (oiseau) to fly away ou off; (avion) to take off; (papier, feuille) to blow away; (fig) to vanish (into thin air)

envoyé, e [ɑ̃vwaje] nm/f (Pol) envoy; (Presse) correspondent; **envoyé spécial** special correspondent

envoyer [ɑ̃vwaje] vt to send; (lancer) to hurl, throw; **~ chercher** to send for; **~ promener qn** (fam) to send sb packing

épagneul, e [epaɲœl] nm/f spaniel

épais, se [epɛ, ɛs] adj thick; **épaisseur** nf thickness

épanouir [epanwir]: **s'épanouir** vi (fleur) to bloom, open out; (visage) to light up; (personne) to blossom

épargne [eparɲ] nf saving

épargner [eparɲe] vt to save; (ne pas tuer ou endommager) to spare ▷ vi to save; **~ qch à qn** to spare sb sth

éparpiller [eparpije] vt to scatter; **s'éparpiller** vi to scatter; (fig) to dissipate one's efforts

épatant, e [epatɑ̃, ɑ̃t] (fam) adj super

épater [epate] (fam) vt (étonner) to amaze; (impressionner) to impress

épaule [epol] nf shoulder

épave [epav] nf wreck

épée [epe] nf sword

épeler [ep(ə)le] vt to spell

éperon [eprɔ̃] nm spur

épervier [epɛrvje] nm sparrowhawk

épi [epi] nm (de blé, d'orge) ear; (de

maïs) cob

épice [epis] nf spice

épicé, e [epise] adj spicy

épicer [epise] vt to spice

épicerie [episri] nf grocer's shop; (denrées) groceries pl; **épicerie fine** delicatessen; **épicier, -ière** nm/f grocer

épidémie [epidemi] nf epidemic

épiderme [epidɛrm] nm skin

épier [epje] vt to spy on, watch closely

épilepsie [epilɛpsi] nf epilepsy

épiler [epile] vt (jambes) to remove the hair from; (sourcils) to pluck

épinards [epinar] nmpl spinach sg

épine [epin] nf thorn, prickle; (d'oursin etc) spine

épingle [epɛ̃gl] nf pin; **épingle de nourrice** ou **de sûreté** safety pin

épisode [epizɔd] nm episode; **film/roman à ~s** serial; **épisodique** adj occasional

épluche-légumes [eplyʃlegym] nm inv (potato) peeler

éplucher [eplyʃe] vt (fruit, légumes) to peel; (fig) to go over with a fine-tooth comb; **épluchures** nfpl peelings

éponge [epɔ̃ʒ] nf sponge; **éponger** (liquide) to mop up; (surface) to sponge; (fig: déficit) to soak up

époque [epɔk] nf (de l'histoire) age, era; (de l'année, la vie) time; **d'~ (meuble)** period cpd

épouse [epuz] nf wife; **épouser** vt to marry

épousseter [epuste] vt to dust

épouvantable [epuvɑ̃tabl] adj appalling, dreadful

épouvantail [epuvɑ̃taj] nm scarecrow

épouvante [epuvɑ̃t] nf terror; **film d'~** horror film; **épouvanter** vt to terrify

époux [epu] nm husband ▷ nmpl (married) couple

épreuve [eprœv] nf (d'examen) test; (malheur, difficulté) trial, ordeal; (Photo) print; (Typo) proof; (Sport) event; **à toute ~** unfailing; **mettre à l'~** to put to the test

éprouver [epruve] vt (tester) to

test; (marquer, faire souffrir) to afflict, distress; (ressentir) to experience

épuisé, e [epɥize] adj exhausted; (livre) out of print; **épuisement** nm exhaustion

épuiser [epɥize] vt (fatiguer) to exhaust, wear ou tire out; (stock, sujet) to exhaust; **s'épuiser** vi to wear ou tire o.s. out, exhaust o.s.

épuisette [epɥizɛt] nf shrimping net

équateur [ekwatœʀ] nm equator; (la république de) l'É~ Ecuador

équation [ekwasjɔ̃] nf equation

équerre [ekɛʀ] nf (à dessin) (set) square

équilibre [ekilibʀ] nm balance; **garder/perdre l'~** to keep/lose one's balance; **être en ~** to be balanced; **équilibré, e** adj well-balanced; **équilibrer** vt to balance

équipage [ekipaʒ] nm crew

équipe [ekip] nf team; **travailler en ~** to work as a team

équipé, e [ekipe] adj: **bien/mal ~** well-/poorly-equipped

équipement [ekipmɑ̃] nm equipment

équiper [ekipe] vt to equip; **~ qn/qch de** to equip sb/sth with

équipier, -ière [ekipje, jɛʀ] nm/f team member

équitation [ekitasjɔ̃] nf (horse-)riding; **faire de l'~** to go riding

équivalent, e [ekivalɑ̃, ɑ̃t] adj, nm equivalent

équivaloir [ekivalwaʀ]: **~ à** vt to be equivalent to

érable [eʀabl] nm maple

érafler [eʀafle] vt to scratch; **éraflure** nf scratch

ère [ɛʀ] nf era; **en l'an 1050 de notre ~** in the year 1050 A.D.

érection [eʀɛksjɔ̃] nf erection

éroder [eʀɔde] vt to erode

érotique [eʀɔtik] adj erotic

errer [eʀe] vi to wander

erreur [eʀœʀ] nf mistake, error; **faire ~** to be mistaken; **par ~** by mistake

éruption [eʀypsjɔ̃] nf eruption; (Méd) rash

es [ɛ] vb voir **être**

ès [ɛs] prép: **licencié ès lettres/sciences** = Bachelor of Arts/Science

ESB sigle f (= encéphalopathie spongiforme bovine) BSE

escabeau, x [ɛskabo] nm (tabouret) stool; (échelle) stepladder

escalade [ɛskalad] nf climbing no pl; (Pol etc) escalation; **escalader** vt to climb

escale [ɛskal] nf (Navig: durée) call; (endroit) port of call; (Aviat) stop(over); **faire ~ à** (Navig) to put in at; (Aviat) to stop over at; **vol sans ~** nonstop flight

escalier [ɛskalje] nm stairs pl; **dans l'~** ou **les ~s** on the stairs; **escalier mécanique** ou **roulant** escalator

escapade [ɛskapad] nf: **faire une ~** to go on a jaunt; (s'enfuir) to run away ou off

escargot [ɛskaʀgo] nm snail

escarpé, e [ɛskaʀpe] adj steep

esclavage [ɛsklavaʒ] nm slavery

esclave [ɛsklav] nm/f slave

escompte [ɛskɔ̃t] nm discount

escrime [ɛskʀim] nf fencing

escroc [ɛskʀo] nm swindler, conman; **escroquer** vt: **escroquer qch (à qn)** to swindle sb (out of sth); **escroquerie** nf swindle

espace [ɛspas] nm space; **espacer** vt to space out; **s'espacer** vi (visites etc) to become less frequent

espadon [ɛspadɔ̃] nm swordfish inv

espadrille [ɛspadʀij] nf rope-soled sandal

Espagne [ɛspaɲ] nf: **l'~** Spain; **espagnol, e** adj Spanish ▷ nm/f: **Espagnol, e** Spaniard ▷ nm (Ling) Spanish

espèce [ɛspɛs] nf (Bio, Bot, Zool) species inv; (gén) sort, kind, type; (péj): **~ de maladroit/de brute!** you clumsy oaf/you brute!; **espèces** nfpl (Comm) cash sg; **payer en ~** to pay (in) cash

espérance [ɛspeʀɑ̃s] nf hope; **espérance de vie** life expectancy

espérer [ɛspeʀe] vt to hope for;

j'espère (bien) I hope so; **~ que/faire** to hope that/to do

espiègle [ɛspjɛgl] adj mischievous

espion, ne [ɛspjɔ̃, jɔn] nm/f spy; **espionnage** nm espionage, spying; **espionner** vt to spy (up)on

espoir [ɛspwar] nm hope; **dans l'~ de/que** in the hope of that; **reprendre ~** not to lose hope

esprit [ɛspri] nm (intellect) mind; (humour) wit; (mentalité, d'une loi etc, fantôme etc) spirit; **faire de l'~** to try to be witty; **reprendre ses ~s** to come to; **perdre l'~** to lose one's mind

esquimau, de, -x [ɛskimo, od] adj Eskimo ▷ nm/f: **E~, de** Eskimo ▷ nm: **E~® ice** lolly (BRIT), popsicle (US)

essai [ese] nm (tentative) attempt, try; (de produit) testing; (Rugby) try; (Littérature) essay; **à l'~** on a trial basis; **mettre à l'~** to put to the test

essaim [esɛ̃] nm swarm

essayer [eseje] vt to try (vêtement, chaussures) to try (on); (méthode, voiture) to try (out) ▷ vi to try; **~ de faire** to try ou attempt to do

essence [esɑ̃s] nf (de voiture) petrol (BRIT), gas(oline) (US); (extrait de plante) essence; (espèce d'arbre) species inv

essentiel, le [esɑ̃sjɛl] adj essential; **c'est l'~** (ce qui importe) that's the main thing; **l'~ de** the main part of

essieu, x [esjø] nm axle

essor [esɔr] nm (de l'économie etc) rapid expansion

essorer [esɔre] vt (en tordant) to wring (out); (par la force centrifuge) to spin-dry; **essoreuse** nf spin-dryer

essouffler [esufle]: **s'essouffler** vi to get out of breath

essuie-glace [esɥiglas] nm inv windscreen (BRIT) ou windshield (US) wiper

essuyer [esɥije] vt to wipe; (fig: échec) to suffer; **s'essuyer** vi (après le bain) to dry o.s.; **~ la vaisselle** to dry up

est¹ [ɛ] vb voir **être**

est² [ɛst] nm east ▷ adj inv east; (région)

east(ern); **à l'~** in the east; (direction) to the east, east(wards); **à l'~ de** (to the east, east(wards)); **à l'~ de** (to the east) of

est-ce que [ɛskə] adv: **~ c'est cher/ c'était bon?** is it expensive/was it good?; **quand est-ce qu'il part?** when does he leave?, when is he leaving?; voir aussi **que**

esthéticienne [ɛstetisjɛn] nf beautician

esthétique [ɛstetik] adj attractive

estimation [ɛstimasjɔ̃] nf valuation; (chiffre) estimate

estime [ɛstim] nf esteem, regard; **estimer** vt (respecter) to esteem; (expertiser: bijou etc) to value; (évaluer: coût etc) to assess, estimate; (penser): **estimer que/être** to consider that/o.s. to be

estival, e, -aux [ɛstival, o] adj summer cpd

estivant, e [ɛstivɑ̃, ɑ̃t] nm/f (summer) holiday-maker

estomac [ɛstɔma] nm stomach

estragon [ɛstragɔ̃] nm tarragon

estuaire [ɛstɥɛr] nm estuary

et [e] conj and; **et lui?** what about him?; **et alors!** so what!

étable [etabl] nf cowshed

établi [etabli] nm (work)bench

établir [etablir] vt (papiers d'identité, facture) to make out; (liste, programme) to draw up; (entreprise) to set up; (réputation, usage, fait, culpabilité) to establish; **s'établir** vi to be established; **s'~ (à son compte)** to set up in business; **s'~ à/près de** to settle in/near

établissement [etablismɑ̃] nm (entreprise, institution) establishment; **établissement scolaire** school, educational establishment

étage [etaʒ] nm (d'immeuble) storey, floor; **à l'~** upstairs; **au 2ème ~** on the 2nd (BRIT) ou 3rd (US) floor; **c'est à quel ~?** what floor is it on?

étagère [etaʒɛr] nf (rayon) shelf; (meuble) shelves pl

étai [etɛ] nm stay, prop

étain [etɛ̃] nm pewter no pl

étais etc [etɛ] vb voir **être**

étaler [etale] vt (carte, nappe) to spread (out); (peinture) to spread; (échelonner: paiements, vacances) to spread, stagger; (marchandises) to display; (connaissances) to parade; **s'étaler** vi (liquide) to spread out; (fam) to fall flat on one's face; **s'~ sur** (suj: paiements etc) to be spread out over

étalon [etalɔ̃] nm (cheval) stallion

étanche [etɑ̃ʃ] adj (récipient) watertight; (montre, vêtement) waterproof

étang [etɑ̃] nm pond

étant [etɑ̃] vb voir **être**; **donné**

étape [etap] nf stage; (lieu d'arrivée) stopping place; (: Cyclisme) staging point

état [eta] nm (Pol, condition) state; **en mauvais ~** in poor condition; **en ~ (de marche)** in (working) order; **remettre en ~** to repair; **hors d'~** out of order; **être en ~/hors d'~ de faire** to be in a/in no fit state to do; **être dans tous ses ~s** to be in a state; **faire ~ de** (alléguer) to put forward; **l'É~** the State; **état civil** civil status; **état des lieux** inventory of fixtures; **États-Unis** nmpl: **les États-Unis** the United States

etc. [ɛtsetera] adv etc

et c(a)etera [ɛtsetera] adv et cetera, and so on

été [ete] pp de **être** ▷ nm summer

éteindre [etɛ̃dʀ] vt (lampe, lumière, radio) to turn off, switch off; (cigarette, feu) to put out, extinguish; **s'éteindre** vi (feu, lumière) to go out; (mourir) to pass away; **éteint, e** adj (fig) lacklustre, dull; (volcan) extinct

étendre [etɑ̃dʀ] vt (pâte, liquide) to spread; (carte etc) to spread out; (linge) to hang up; (bras, jambes) to stretch out; (fig: agrandir) to extend; **s'étendre** vi (augmenter, se propager) to spread; (terrain, forêt etc) to stretch; (s'allonger) to stretch out; (se coucher) to lie down;

(fig: expliquer) to elaborate

étendu, e [etɑ̃dy] adj extensive

éternel, le [etɛʀnɛl] adj eternal

éternité [etɛʀnite] nf eternity; **ça a duré une ~** it lasted for ages

éternuement [etɛʀnymɑ̃] nm sneeze

éternuer [etɛʀnye] vi to sneeze

êtes [ɛt(z)] vb voir **être**

Éthiopie [etjɔpi] nf: **l'~** Ethiopia

étiez [etje] vb voir **être**

étinceler [etɛ̃s(ə)le] vi to sparkle

étincelle [etɛ̃sɛl] nf spark

étiquette [etikɛt] nf label; (protocole): **l'~** etiquette

étirer [etiʀe]: **s'étirer** vi (personne) to stretch; (convoi, route): **s'~ sur** to stretch out over

étoile [etwal] nf star; **à la belle ~** in the open; **étoile de mer** starfish; **étoile filante** shooting star; **étoilé, e** adj starry

étonnant, e [etɔnɑ̃, ɑ̃t] adj amazing

étonnement [etɔnmɑ̃] nm surprise, amazement

étonner [etɔne] vt to surprise, amaze; **s'étonner que/de** to be amazed that/at; **cela m'~ait (que)** (j'en doute) I'd be very surprised (if)

étouffer [etufe] vt to suffocate; (bruit) to muffle; (scandale) to hush up ▷ vi to suffocate; **s'étouffer** vi (en mangeant etc) to choke; **on étouffe** it's stifling

étourderie [etuʀdʀi] nf (caractère) absent-mindedness no pl; (faute) thoughtless blunder

étourdi, e [etuʀdi] adj (distrait) scatterbrained, heedless

étourdir [etuʀdiʀ] vt (assommer) to stun, daze; (griser) to make dizzy ou giddy; **étourdissement** nm dizzy spell

étrange [etʀɑ̃ʒ] adj strange

étranger, ère [etʀɑ̃ʒe, ɛʀ] adj foreign; (pas de la famille, non familier) strange ▷ nm/f foreigner; stranger ▷ nm: **à l'~** abroad

étrangler [etʀɑ̃gle] vt to strangle; **s'étrangler** vi (en mangeant etc) to choke

être [ɛtʀ] nm being; **être humain** human being
▷ vb +attrib 1 (état, description) to be; **il est instituteur** he is ou he's a teacher; **vous êtes grand/intelligent/fatigué** you are ou you're tall/clever/tired
2 (+à: appartenir) to be; **le livre est à Paul** the book is Paul's ou belongs to Paul; **c'est à moi/eux** it is ou it's mine/theirs
3 (+de: provenance) : **il est de Paris** he is from Paris; (: appartenance) : **il est des nôtres** he is one of us
4 (date) : **nous sommes le 10 janvier** it's the 10th of January (today)
▷ vi to be; **je ne serai pas ici demain** I won't be here tomorrow
▷ vb aux 1 to have; to be; **être arrivé/allé** to have arrived/gone; **il est parti** he has left, he has gone
2 (forme passive) to be; **être fait par** to be made by; **il a été promu** he has been promoted
3 (+à: obligation) : **c'est à réparer** it needs repairing; **c'est à essayer** it should be tried; **il est à espérer que ...** it is ou it's to be hoped that ...
▷ vb impers : **il est** +adjectif it is +adjectif; **il est impossible de le faire** it's impossible to do it
2 (heure, date) : **il est 10 heures** it is ou it's 10 o'clock
3 (emphatique) : **c'est moi** it's me; **c'est à lui de le faire** it's up to him to do it

étrennes [etʀɛn] nfpl Christmas box sg
étrier [etʀije] nm stirrup
étroit, e [etʀwa, wat] adj narrow; (vêtement) tight; (fig: liens, collaboration) close; **à l'~** cramped; **~ d'esprit** narrow-minded
étude [etyd] nf studying; (ouvrage, rapport) study; (Scol: salle de travail) study room; **études** nfpl (Scol) studies; **être à l'~** (projet etc) to be under consideration; **faire des ~s (de droit/**

médecine) to study (law/medicine)
étudiant, e [etydjɑ̃, jɑ̃t] nm/f student
étudier [etydje] vt, vi to study
étui [etɥi] nm case
eu, eue [y] pp de **avoir**
euh [ø] excl er
euro [øʀo] nm euro
Europe [øʀɔp] nf: **l'~** Europe; **européen, ne** adj European ▷ nm/f: **Européen, ne** European
eus etc [y] vb voir **avoir**
eux [ø] pron (sujet) they; (objet) them
évacuer [evakɥe] vt to evacuate
évader [evade]: **s'évader** vi to escape
évaluer [evalɥe] vt (expertiser) to appraise, evaluate; (juger approximativement) to estimate
évangile [evɑ̃ʒil] nm gospel; **É-** Gospel
évanouir [evanwiʀ]: **s'évanouir** vi to faint; (disparaître) to vanish, disappear; **évanouissement** nm (syncope) fainting fit
évaporer [evapɔʀe]: **s'évaporer** vi to evaporate
évasion [evazjɔ̃] nf escape
éveillé, e [eveje] adj awake; (vif) alert, sharp; **éveiller** vt to (a)waken; (soupçons etc) to arouse; **s'éveiller** vi to (a)waken; (fig) to be aroused
événement [evɛnmɑ̃] nm event
éventail [evɑ̃taj] nm fan; (choix) range
éventualité [evɑ̃tɥalite] nf eventuality; possibility; **dans l'~ de** in the event of
éventuel, le [evɑ̃tɥɛl] adj possible
  Attention à ne pas traduire *éventuel* par *eventual.*
éventuellement adv possibly
  Attention à ne pas traduire *éventuellement* par *eventually.*
évêque [evɛk] nm bishop
évidemment [evidamɑ̃] adv (bien sûr) of course; (certainement) obviously
évidence [evidɑ̃s] nf obviousness; (fait) obvious fact; **de toute ~** quite obviously ou evidently; **être en ~** to be clearly visible; **mettre en ~** (fait) to highlight; **évident, e** adj obvious,

evident; **ce n'est pas évident!** (fam) it's not that easy!

évier [evje] nm (kitchen) sink

éviter [evite] vt to avoid; **~ de faire** to avoid doing; **~ qch à qn** to spare sb sth

évoluer [evɔlɥe] vi (enfant, maladie) to develop; (situation, moralement) to evolve, develop; (aller et venir) to move about; **évolution** nf development, evolution

évoquer [evɔke] vt to call to mind, evoke; (mentionner) to mention

ex- [ɛks] préfixe ex-; **son ~mari** her ex-husband; **son ~femme** his ex-wife

exact, e [ɛgza(kt), ɛgzakt] adj exact; (correct) correct; (ponctuel) punctual; **l'heure ~e** the right ou exact time; **exactement** adv exactly

ex aequo [ɛgzeko] adj equally placed; **arriver ~** to finish neck and neck

exagéré, e [ɛgzaʒere] adj (prix etc) excessive

exagérer [ɛgzaʒere] vt to exaggerate ▷ vi to exaggerate; (abuser) to go too far

examen [ɛgzamɛ̃] nm examination; (Scol) exam, examination; **à l'~** under consideration; **examen médical** (medical) examination; (analyse) test

examinateur, -trice [ɛgzaminatœr, tris] nm/f examiner

examiner [ɛgzamine] vt to examine

exaspérant, e [ɛgzasperɑ̃, ɑ̃t] adj exasperating

exaspérer [ɛgzaspere] vt to exasperate

exaucer [ɛgzose] vt (vœu) to grant

excéder [ɛksede] vt (dépasser) to exceed; (agacer) to exasperate

excellent, e [ɛkselɑ̃, ɑ̃t] adj excellent

excentrique [ɛksɑ̃trik] adj eccentric

excepté, e [ɛksɛpte] adj, prép: **les élèves ~s, ~ les élèves** except for the pupils

exception [ɛksɛpsjɔ̃] nf exception; **à l'~ de** except for, with the exception of; (mesure, loi) special, exceptional; **exceptionnel, le** adj exceptional; **exceptionnellement** adv exceptionally

excès [ɛksɛ] nm surplus ▷ nmpl excesses; **faire des ~** to overindulge; **excès de vitesse** speeding no pl; **excessif, -ive** adj excessive

excitant, e [ɛksitɑ̃, ɑ̃t] adj exciting ▷ nm stimulant; **excitation** nf (état) excitement

exciter [ɛksite] vt to excite; (suj: café etc) to stimulate; **s'exciter** vi to get excited

exclamer [ɛksklame]: **s'exclamer** vi to exclaim

exclure [ɛkskly] vt (faire sortir) to expel; (ne pas compter) to exclude, leave out; (rendre impossible) to exclude, rule out; **il est exclu que** it's out of the question that ...; **il n'est pas exclu que ...** it's not impossible that ...; **exclusif, -ive** adj exclusive; **exclusion** nf exclusion; **à l'exclusion de** with the exclusion ou exception of; **exclusivité** nf (Comm) exclusive rights pl; **un film passant en exclusivité à** a film showing only at

excursion [ɛkskyrsjɔ̃] nf (en autocar) excursion, trip; (à pied) walk, hike

excuse [ɛkskyz] nf excuse; **excuses** nfpl (regret) apology sg, apologies; **excuser** vt to excuse; **s'excuser (de)** to apologize (for); **excusez-moi** I'm sorry; (pour attirer l'attention) excuse me

exécuter [ɛgzekyte] vt (tuer) to execute; (tâche etc) to execute, carry out; (Mus: jouer) to perform, execute; **s'exécuter** vi to comply

exemplaire [ɛgzɑ̃plɛr] nm copy

exemple [ɛgzɑ̃pl] nm example; **par ~** for instance, for example; **donner l'~** to set an example

exercer [ɛgzɛrse] vt (pratiquer) to exercise, practise; (influence, contrôle) to exert; (former) to exercise, train; **s'exercer** vi (sportif, musicien) to practise

exercice [ɛgzɛrsis] nm exercise

exhiber [ɛgzibe] vt (montrer: papiers, certificat) to present, produce; (péj) to display, flaunt; **s'exhiber** vi to parade; (suj: exhibitionniste) to expose o.s.; **exhibitionniste** nm/f flasher

exigeant, e [ɛgziʒɑ̃, ɑ̃t] adj demanding; (péj) hard to please

exiger [ɛgziʒe] vt to demand, require

exil [ɛgzil] nm exile; **exiler** vt to exile; **s'exiler** vi to go into exile

existence [ɛgzistɑ̃s] nf existence

exister [ɛgziste] vi to exist; **il existe un/des** there is a/are (some)

exorbitant, e [ɛgzɔrbitɑ̃, ɑ̃t] adj exorbitant

exotique [ɛgzɔtik] adj exotic; **yaourt aux fruits ~s** tropical fruit yoghurt

expédier [ɛkspedje] vt (lettre, paquet) to send; (troupes) to dispatch; (fam: travail etc) to dispose of, dispatch; **expéditeur, -trice** nm/f sender; **expédition** nf sending; (scientifique, sportive, Mil) expedition

expérience [ɛksperjɑ̃s] nf (de la vie) experience; (scientifique) experiment

expérimenté, e [ɛksperimɑ̃te] adj experienced

expérimenter [ɛksperimɑ̃te] vt to test out, experiment with

expert, e [ɛkspɛr, ɛrt] adj, nm expert; **~ en objets d'art** art appraiser; **expert-comptable** ≈ chartered accountant (BRIT), ≈ certified public accountant (US)

expirer [ɛkspire] vi (prendre fin, mourir) to expire; (respirer) to breathe out

explication [ɛksplikasjɔ̃] nf explanation; (discussion) discussion; (dispute) argument

explicite [ɛksplisit] adj explicit

expliquer [ɛksplike] vt to explain; **s'expliquer** to explain (o.s.); **s'~ avec qn** (discuter) to explain o.s. to sb; **son erreur s'explique** one can understand his mistake

exploit [ɛksplwa] nm exploit, feat; **exploitant, e** nm/f: **exploitant (agricole)** farmer; **exploitation** nf exploitation; (d'une entreprise) running; **exploitation agricole** farming

concern; **exploiter** vt (personne, don) to exploit; (entreprise, ferme) to run, operate; (mine) to exploit, work

explorer [ɛksplɔre] vt to explore

exploser [ɛksploze] vi to explode, blow up; (engin explosif) to go off; (personne: de colère) to flare up; **explosif, -ive** adj, nm explosive; **explosion** nf explosion; (de joie, colère) outburst

exportateur, -trice [ɛkspɔrtatœr, tris] adj export cpd, exporting ▷ nm exporter

exportation [ɛkspɔrtasjɔ̃] nf (action) exportation; (produit) export

exporter [ɛkspɔrte] vt to export

exposant [ɛkspozɑ̃] nm exhibitor

exposé, e [ɛkspoze] nm talk ▷ adj: **~ au sud** facing south

exposer [ɛkspoze] vt (marchandise) to display; (peinture) to exhibit, show; (parler de) to explain, set out; (mettre en danger, orienter, Photo) to expose; **s'~ à** (soleil, danger) to expose o.s. to; **exposition** nf (manifestation) exhibition; (Photo) exposure

exprès[1] [ɛksprɛ] adv (délibérément) on purpose; (spécialement) specially; **faire ~ de faire qch** to do sth on purpose

exprès[2], -esse [ɛksprɛs] adj inv (lettre, colis) express

express [ɛksprɛs] adj, nm: **(café) ~** espresso (coffee); **(train) ~** fast train

expressif, -ive [ɛkspresif, iv] adj expressive

expression [ɛkspresjɔ̃] nf expression

exprimer [ɛksprime] vt (sentiment, idée) to express; (jus, liquide) to press out; **s'exprimer** vi (personne) to express o.s

expulser [ɛkspylse] vt to expel; (locataire) to evict; (Sport) to send off

exquis, e [ɛkski, iz] adj exquisite

extasier [ɛkstazje]: **s'extasier sur** vt to go into raptures over

exténuer [ɛkstenɥe] vt to exhaust

extérieur, e [ɛksterjœr] adj (porte, mur etc) outer, outside; (au dehors: escalier, w.-c.) outside; (commerce) foreign; (*influences*) external; (*apparent: calme, gaieté etc*) surface ▷ cpd ▷ **nm** (*d'une maison, d'un récipient etc*) outside, exterior; (*apparence*) exterior; **à l'~** outside; (*à l'étranger*) abroad

externat [ɛkstɛʀna] **nm** day school

externe [ɛkstɛʀn] **adj** external, outer ▷ **nm/f** (*Méd*) non-resident medical student (*BRIT*), extern (*US*); (*Scol*) day pupil

extincteur [ɛkstɛ̃ktœʀ] **nm** (fire) extinguisher

extinction [ɛkstɛ̃ksjɔ̃] **nf**: **extinction de voix** loss of voice

extra [ɛkstʀa] **adj inv** first-rate; (*fam*) fantastic ▷ **nm inv** extra help

extraire [ɛkstʀɛʀ] **vt** to extract; **~ qch de** to extract sth from; **extrait nm** extract; **extrait de naissance** birth certificate

extraordinaire [ɛkstʀaɔʀdinɛʀ] **adj** extraordinary; (*Pol: mesures etc*) special

extravagant, e [ɛkstʀavagɑ̃, ɑ̃t] **adj** extravagant

extraverti, e [ɛkstʀavɛʀti] **adj** extrovert

extrême [ɛkstʀɛm] **adj, nm** extreme; **d'un ~ à l'autre** from one extreme to another; **extrêmement adv** extremely; **Extrême-Orient nm** Far East

extrémité [ɛkstʀemite] **nf** end; (*situation*) straits **pl**, plight; (*geste désespéré*) extreme action; **extrémités nfpl** (*pieds et mains*) extremities

exubérant, e [ɛgzybeʀɑ̃, ɑ̃t] **adj** exuberant

f

F *abr* = **franc**; (*appartement*): **un F2/F3** a one-/two-bedroom flat (*BRIT*) ou apartment (*US*)

fa [fa] **nm inv** (*Mus*) (*en chantant la gamme*) fa

fabricant, e [fabʀikɑ̃, ɑ̃t] **nm/f** manufacturer

fabrication [fabʀikasjɔ̃] **nf** manufacture

fabrique [fabʀik] **nf** factory; **fabriquer vt** to make; (*industriellement*) to manufacture; (*fig*): **qu'est-ce qu'il fabrique?** (*fam*) what is he doing?

fac [fak] (*fam*) **abr f** (*Scol*) = **faculté**

façade [fasad] **nf** front, façade

face [fas] **nf** face; (*fig: aspect*) side ▷ **adj**: **le côté ~** heads; **en ~ de** opposite; (*fig*) in front of; **de ~** (*voir*) face on; **~ à** facing; (*fig*) faced with, in the face of; **faire ~ à** to face; **~ à ~ adv** facing each other ▷ **nm inv** encounter

fâché, e [faʃe] **adj** angry; (*désolé*) sorry

fâcher [faʃe] **vt** to anger; **se fâcher (contre qn) vi** to get angry (with sb);

se ~ avec (se brouiller) to fall out with
facile [fasil] *adj* easy; (*caractère*) easy-going; **facilement** *adv* easily; **facilité** *nf* easiness; (*disposition, don*) aptitude; **facilités** (*possibilités*) facilities; (*Comm*) terms; **faciliter** *vt* to make easier
façon [fasɔ̃] *nf* (*manière*) way; (*d'une robe etc*) making-up, cut; **façons** *nfpl* (*pej*) fuss; **de ~ à/à ce que** so as to/that; **de toute ~** anyway, in any case; **sans ~** (*accepter*) without fuss; **non merci, sans ~** no thanks, honestly
facteur, -trice [faktœʀ] *nm/f* postman(-woman) (*BRIT*), mailman(-woman) (*US*) ▷ *nm* (*Math, fig*: *élément*) factor
facture [faktyʀ] *nf* (*à payer: gén*) bill; (*Comm*) invoice
facultatif, -ive [fakyltatif, iv] *adj* optional
faculté [fakylte] *nf* (*intellectuelle, d'université*) faculty; (*pouvoir, possibilité*) power
fade [fad] *adj* insipid
faible [fɛbl] *adj* weak; (*voix, lumière, vent*) faint; (*rendement, revenu*) low ▷ *nm* (*pour quelqu'un*) weakness, soft spot; **faiblesse** *nf* weakness; **faiblir** *vi* to weaken; (*lumière*) to dim; (*vent*) to drop
faïence [fajɑ̃s] *nf* earthenware *no pl*
faillir [fajiʀ] *vi*: **j'ai failli tomber** I almost *ou* very nearly fell
faillite [fajit] *nf* bankruptcy; **faire ~** to go bankrupt
faim [fɛ̃] *nf* hunger; **avoir ~** to be hungry; **rester sur sa ~** (*aussi fig*) to be left wanting more
fainéant, e [fɛneɑ̃, ɑ̃t] *nm/f* idler, loafer

○ **MOT-CLÉ**

faire [fɛʀ] *vt* 1 (*fabriquer, être l'auteur de*) to make; **faire du vin/une offre/un film** to make wine/an offer/a film; **faire du bruit** to make a noise
2 (*effectuer: travail, opération*) to do; **que faites-vous?** (*quel métier etc*) what do

you do?; (*quelle activité: au moment de la question*) what are you doing?; **faire la lessive** to do the washing
3 (*études*) to do; (*sport, musique*) to play; **faire du droit/du français** to do law/French; **faire du rugby/piano** to play rugby/the piano
4 (*simuler*): **faire le malade/l'innocent** to act the invalid/the innocent
5 (*transformer, avoir un effet sur*): **faire de qn un frustré/avocat** to make sb frustrated/a lawyer; **ça ne me fait rien** (*m'est égal*) I don't care *ou* mind; (*me laisse froid*) it has no effect on me; **ça ne fait rien** it doesn't matter; **faire que** (*impliquer*) to mean that
6 (*calculs, prix, mesures*): **2 et 2 font 4** 2 and 2 are *ou* make 4; **ça fait 10 m/15 euros** it's *ou* that's 10 m/15 euros; **je vous le fais 10 euros** I'll let you have it for 10 euros; **je fais du 40** I take a size 40
7 (*distance*): **faire du 50 (à l'heure)** to do 50 (km an hour); **nous avons fait 1000 km en 2 jours** we did *ou* covered 1000 km in 2 days; **faire l'Europe** to tour *ou* do Europe; **faire les magasins** to go shopping
8: **qu'a-t-il fait de sa valise?** what has he done with his case?
9: **ne faire que**: **il ne fait que critiquer** (*sans cesse*) he (*ever*) does is criticize; (*seulement*) he's only criticizing
10 (*dire*) to say; **"vraiment?" fit-il** "really?" he said
11 (*maladie*) to have; **faire du diabète** to have diabetes *sg*
▷ *vi* 1 (*agir, s'y prendre*) to act, do; **il faut faire vite** we (*ou you etc*) must act quickly; **comment a-t-il fait pour?** how did he manage to?; **faites comme chez vous** make yourself at home
2 (*paraître*) to look; **faire vieux/démodé** to look old/old-fashioned; **ça fait bien** it looks good
▷ *vb substitut* to do; **ne le casse pas comme je l'ai fait** don't break it as I did; **je peux le voir?** — **faites!** can I see

99 | **faire**

it? — please do!
▷ vb impers 1: **il fait beau** etc the weather is fine etc; voir aussi **jour**; **froid** etc
2 (temps écoulé, durée): **ça fait 2 ans qu'il est parti** it's 2 years since he left; **ça fait 2 ans qu'il y est** he's been there for 2 years
▷ vb semi-aux 1: **faire** (+infinitif: action directe) to make; **faire tomber/bouger qch** to make sth fall/move; **faire démarrer un moteur/chauffer de l'eau** to start up an engine/heat some water; **cela fait dormir** it makes you sleep; **faire travailler les enfants** to make the children work ou to get the children to work; **il m'a fait traverser la rue** he helped me to cross the street
2 (indirectement, par un intermédiaire): **faire réparer qch** to get ou have sth repaired; **faire punir les enfants** to have the children punished
se faire vi 1 (être convenable): **cela se fait beaucoup/ne se fait pas** it's done a lot/not done
2: **se faire** +nom ou pron: **se faire une jupe** to make o.s. a skirt; **se faire des amis** to make friends; **se faire du souci** to worry; **il ne s'en fait pas** he doesn't worry
3: **se faire** +adj (devenir): **se faire vieux** to be getting old; **se faire beau** to do o.s. up
4: **se faire à** (s'habituer) to get used to; **je n'arrive pas à me faire à la nourriture/au climat** I can't get used to the food/climate
5: **se faire** +infinitif: **se faire examiner la vue/opérer** to have one's eyes tested/have an operation; **se faire couper les cheveux** to get one's hair cut; **il va se faire tuer/punir** he's going to get himself killed/get punished; **il s'est fait aider** he got somebody to help him; **il s'est fait aider par Simon** he got Simon to help him; **se faire faire un vêtement** to get a garment made for o.s.

6 (impersonnel): **comment se fait-il/faisait-il que?** how is it/was it that?

faire-part [fɛʁpaʁ] nm inv announcement (of birth, marriage etc)
faisan, e [fəzɑ̃, an] nm/f pheasant
faisons [fəzɔ̃] vb voir **faire**
fait, e [fɛ, fɛt] adj (mûr: fromage, melon) ripe ▷ nm (événement) event, occurrence; (réalité, donnée) fact; **être au ~ (de)** to be informed (of); **au ~** (à propos) by the way; **en venir au ~** to get to the point; **du ~ de ceci/qu'il a menti** because of ou on account of this/his having lied; **de ce ~** for this reason; **en fait** in fact; **prendre qn sur le ~** to catch sb in the act; **c'est bien ~ pour lui** (ou eux etc) it serves him (ou them etc) right; **faits divers** news item
faites [fɛt] vb voir **faire**
falaise [falɛz] nf cliff
falloir [falwaʁ] vb impers: **il faut qu'il parte/a fallu qu'il parte** (obligation) he has to ou must leave/had to leave; **il a fallu le faire** it had to be done; **il faudrait qu'elle rentre** she should come ou go back, she ought to come ou go back; **il faut faire attention** you have to be careful; **il me faudrait 100 euros** I would need 100 euros; **il vous faut tourner à gauche après l'église** you have to turn left past the church; **nous avons ce qu'il (nous) faut** we have what we need; **il ne fallait pas** you shouldn't have (done); **comme il faut** (personne) proper; (agir) properly; **s'en falloir vi**: **il s'en est fallu de 100 euros/5 minutes** we/they etc were 100 euros short/5 minutes late (ou early); **il s'en faut de beaucoup qu'il soit** he is far from being; **il s'en est fallu de peu que cela n'arrive** it very nearly happened
famé, e [fame] adj: **mal ~** disreputable, of ill repute
fameux, -euse [famø, øz] adj (illustre) famous; (bon: repas, plat etc) first-rate, first-class; (valeur intensive) real,

downright

familial, e, -aux [familjal, jo] *adj* family *cpd*

familiarité [familjaRite] *nf* familiarity

familier, -ère [familje, jɛR] *adj* (*connu*) familiar; (*atmosphère*) informal, friendly; (*Ling*) informal, colloquial ▷ *nm* regular (visitor)

famille [famij] *nf* family; **il a de la ~ à Paris** he has relatives in Paris

famine [famin] *nf* famine

fanatique [fanatik] *adj* fanatical ▷ *nm/f* fanatic

faner [fane]: **se faner** *vi* to fade

fanfare [fãfaR] *nf* (*orchestre*) brass band; (*musique*) fanfare

fantaisie [fãtezi] *nf* (*spontanéité*) fancy, imagination; (*caprice*) whim ▷ *adj*: **bijou ~** costume jewellery

fantasme [fãtasm] *nm* fantasy

fantastique [fãtastik] *adj* fantastic

fantôme [fãtom] *nm* ghost, phantom

faon [fã] *nm* fawn

FAQ *sigle f* (= *foire aux questions*) FAQ

farce [faRs] *nf* (*viande*) stuffing; (*blague*) (practical) joke; (*Théâtre*) farce; **farcir** *vt* (*viande*) to stuff

farder [faRde]: **se farder** *vi* to make (o.s.) up

farine [faRin] *nf* flour

farouche [faRuʃ] *adj* (*timide*) shy, timid

fart [faRt] *nm* (ski) wax

fascination [fasinasjɔ̃] *nf* fascination

fasciner [fasine] *vt* to fascinate

fascisme [faʃism] *nm* fascism

fasse *etc* [fas] *vb voir* **faire**

fastidieux, -euse [fastidjø, øz] *adj* tedious, tiresome

fatal, e [fatal] *adj* fatal; (*inévitable*) inevitable; **fatalité** *nf* (*destin*) fate; (*coïncidence*) fateful coincidence

fatidique [fatidik] *adj* fateful

fatigant, e [fatigã, ãt] *adj* tiring; (*agaçant*) tiresome

fatigue [fatig] *nf* tiredness, fatigue; **fatigué, e** *adj* tired; **fatiguer** *vt* to tire, make tired; (*fig: agacer*) to annoy ▷ *vi* (*moteur*) to labour, strain; **se fatiguer**

to get tired

fauché, e [foʃe] (*fam*) *adj* broke

faucher [foʃe] *vt* (*herbe*) to cut; (*champs, blés*) to reap; (*fig: véhicule*) to mow down; (*fam: voler*) to pinch

faucon [fokɔ̃] *nm* falcon, hawk

faudra [fodRa] *vb voir* **falloir**

faufiler [fofile]: **se faufiler** *vi*: **se ~ dans** to edge one's way into; **se ~ parmi/entre** to thread one's way among/between

faune [fon] *nf* (*Zool*) wildlife, fauna

fausse [fos] *adj voir* **faux**; **faussement** *adv* (*accuser*) wrongly, wrongfully;

fausser [fose] *vt* (*objet*) to bend, buckle; (*fig*) to distort; **~ compagnie à qn** to give sb the slip

faut [fo] *vb voir* **falloir**

faute [fot] *nf* (*erreur*) mistake, error; (*mauvaise action*) misdemeanour; (*Football etc*) offence; (*Tennis*) fault; **c'est de sa/ma ~** it's his ou her/my fault; **être en ~** to be in the wrong; **~ de** (*temps, argent*) for ou through lack of; **sans ~** without fail; **faute de frappe** typing error; **faute professionnelle** professional misconduct *no pl*

fauteuil [fotœj] *nm* armchair; (*au théâtre*) seat; **fauteuil roulant** wheelchair

fautif, -ive [fotif, iv] *adj* (*responsable*) at fault, in the wrong; (*incorrect*) incorrect, inaccurate; **il se sentait ~** he felt guilty

fauve [fov] *nm* wildcat ▷ *adj* (*couleur*) fawn

faux¹ [fo] *nf* scythe

faux², fausse [fo, fos] *adj* (*inexact*) wrong; (*voix*) out of tune; (*billet*) fake, forged; (*sournois, postiche*) false ▷ *adv* (*Mus*) out of tune ▷ *nm* (*copie*) fake, forgery; **faire ~ bond à qn** to let sb down; **faire un ~ pas** to trip; (*fig*) to make a faux pas; **fausse alerte** false alarm; **fausse couche** miscarriage; **faux frais** *nmpl* extras, incidental expenses; **faux mouvement** awkward movement; **fausse note** wrong note; **faux témoignage** (délit) perjury; **faux-filet** nm sirloin

faveur [favœʀ] nf favour; **traitement de ~** preferential treatment; **en ~ de** in favour of

favorable [favɔʀabl] adj favourable

favori, te [favɔʀi, it] adj, nm/f favourite

favoriser [favɔʀize] vt to favour

fax [faks] nm fax

fécond, e [fekɔ̃, ɔ̃d] adj fertile; **féconder** vt to fertilize

féculent [fekylɑ̃] nm starchy food

fédéral, e, -aux [federal, o] adj federal

fée [fe] nf fairy

feignant, e [fɛɲɑ̃, ɑ̃t] nm/f **=fainéant, e**

feindre [fɛ̃dʀ] vt to feign; **~ de faire** to pretend to do

fêler [fele] vt to crack; **se fêler** vi to crack

félicitations [felisitasjɔ̃] nfpl congratulations

féliciter [felisite] vt: **~ qn (de)** to congratulate sb (on)

félin, e [felɛ̃, in] nm (big) cat

femelle [fəmɛl] adj, nf female

féminin, e [feminɛ̃, in] adj feminine; (sexe) female; (équipe, vêtements etc) women's ▷ nm (Ling) feminine; **féministe** adj feminist

femme [fam] nf woman; (épouse) wife; **femme au foyer** housewife; **femme de chambre** chambermaid; **femme de ménage** cleaning lady

fémur [femyʀ] nm femur, thighbone

fendre [fɑ̃dʀ] vt (couper en deux) to split; (fissurer) to crack; (traverser: foule, air) to cleave through; **se fendre** vi to crack

fenêtre [f(ə)nɛtʀ] nf window

fenouil [fənuj] nm fennel

fente [fɑ̃t] nf (fissure) crack; (de boîte à lettres etc) slit

fer [fɛʀ] nm iron; **fer à cheval** horseshoe; **fer à friser** curling tongs pl; **fer (à repasser)** iron; **fer forgé** wrought iron

ferai etc [fəʀe] vb voir **faire**

fer-blanc [fɛʀblɑ̃] nm tin(plate)

férié, e [feʀje] adj: **jour ~** public holiday

ferions etc [fəʀjɔ̃] vb voir **faire**

ferme [fɛʀm] adj firm ▷ adv (travailler etc) hard ▷ nf (exploitation) farm; (maison) farmhouse

fermé, e [fɛʀme] adj closed, shut; (gaz, eau etc) off; (fig: milieu) exclusive

fermenter [fɛʀmɑ̃te] vi to ferment

fermer [fɛʀme] vt to close, shut; (cesser l'exploitation de) to close down, shut down; (eau, électricité, robinet) to turn off; (aéroport, route) to close ▷ vi to close, shut; (magasin: définitivement) to close down, shut down; **~ à clef** to lock; **se fermer** vi to close, shut

fermeté [fɛʀməte] nf firmness

fermeture [fɛʀmətyʀ] nf closing; (dispositif) catch; **heures de ~** closing times; **fermeture éclair®** ou **à glissière** zip (fastener) (BRIT), zipper (US)

fermier [fɛʀmje] nm farmer

féroce [feʀɔs] adj ferocious, fierce

ferons etc [fəʀɔ̃] vb voir **faire**

ferrer [feʀe] vt (cheval) to shoe

ferroviaire [feʀɔvjɛʀ] adj rail(way) cpd (BRIT), rail(road) cpd (US)

ferry(-boat) [feʀe(-bot)] nm ferry

fertile [fɛʀtil] adj fertile; **~ en incidents** eventful, packed with incidents

fervent, e [fɛʀvɑ̃, ɑ̃t] adj fervent

fesse [fɛs] nf buttock; **fessée** nf spanking

festin [fɛstɛ̃] nm feast

festival [fɛstival] nm festival

festivités [fɛstivite] nfpl festivities

fêtard, e [fɛtaʀ, aʀd] (fam) nm/f high liver, merry-maker

fête [fɛt] nf (religieuse) feast; (publique) holiday; (en famille etc: kermesse) party; (kermesse) fête, fair; (du nom) feast day, name day; **faire la ~** to live it up; **faire ~ à qn** to give sb a warm welcome; **les ~s (de fin d'année)** the festive season; **la salle des ~s** the village hall; **la ~ des Mères/**

Pères Mother's/Father's Day; **fête foraine** (fun) fair; **fêter** vt to celebrate; (*personne*) to have a celebration for

feu, x [fø] nm (*gén*) fire; (*signal lumineux*) light; (*de cuisinière*) ring; **feux** nmpl (Auto) (traffic) lights; **au ~!** (*incendie*) fire!; **à ~ doux/vif** over a slow/brisk heat; **à petit ~** (Culin) over a gentle heat; (*fig*) slowly; **faire ~** to fire; **ne pas faire long ~** not to last long; **prendre ~** to catch fire; **mettre le ~ à** to set fire to; **faire du ~** to make a fire; **avez-vous du ~?** (*pour cigarette*) have you (got) a light?; **feu arrière** rear light; **feu d'artifice** (*spectacle*) fireworks pl; **feu de joie** bonfire; **feu orange/rouge/vert** amber (BRIT) ou yellow (US)/red/green light; **feux de brouillard** fog lights ou lamps; **feux de croisement** dipped (BRIT) ou dimmed (US) headlights; **feux de position** sidelights; **feux de route** headlights

feuillage [fœjaʒ] nm foliage, leaves pl

feuille [fœj] nf (*d'arbre*) leaf; (*de papier*) sheet; **feuille de calcul** spreadsheet; **feuille d'impôts** tax form; **feuille de maladie** medical expenses claim form; **feuille de paye** pay slip

feuillet [fœjɛ] nm leaf

feuilleté, e [fœjte] adj: **pâte ~** flaky pastry

feuilleter [fœjte] vt (*livre*) to leaf through

feuilleton [fœjtɔ̃] nm serial

feutre [føtʁ] nm felt; (*chapeau*) felt hat; (*aussi*: **stylo-~**) felt-tip pen; **feutré, e** adj (*atmosphère*) muffled

fève [fɛv] nf broad bean

février [fevʁije] nm February

fiable [fjabl] adj reliable

fiançailles [fjɑ̃saj] nfpl engagement sg

fiancé, e [fjɑ̃se] nm/f fiancé(e) ⊳ adj: **être ~ (à)** to be engaged (to)

fiancer [fjɑ̃se]: **se fiancer (avec)** vi to become engaged (to)

fibre [fibʁ] nf fibre; **fibre de verre** fibreglass, glass fibre

ficeler [fis(ə)le] vt to tie up

ficelle [fisɛl] nf string no pl; (*morceau*) piece ou length of string

fiche [fiʃ] nf (*pour fichier*) (index) card; (*formulaire*) form; (Élec) plug; **fiche de paye** pay slip

ficher [fiʃe] vt (*dans un fichier*) to file; (Police) to put on file; (*fam*: *faire*) to do; (: *donner*) to give; (: *mettre*) to stick ou shove; **fiche-(moi) le camp!** (*fam*) clear off!; **fiche-moi la paix!** (*fam*) leave me alone!; **se ficher de**: (*fam*: *rire de*) to make fun of; (*être indifférent à*) not to care about

fichier [fiʃje] nm file; **~ joint** (Comput) attachment

fichu, e [fiʃy] pp de **ficher** (*fam*) ⊳ adj (*fam*: *fini*, *inutilisable*) bust, done for; (: *intensif*) wretched, darned ⊳ nm (*foulard*) (head)scarf; **mal ~** (*fam*) feeling lousy

fictif, -ive [fiktif, iv] adj fictitious

fiction [fiksjɔ̃] nf fiction; (*fait imaginé*) invention

fidèle [fidɛl] adj faithful ⊳ nm/f (Rel): **les ~s** (*à l'église*) the congregation sg; **fidélité** nf (*d'un conjoint*) fidelity, faithfulness; (*d'un ami, client*) loyalty

fier¹ [fje]: **se fier à** vt to trust

fier², fière [fjɛʁ] adj proud; **~ de** proud of; **fierté** nf pride

fièvre [fjɛvʁ] nf fever; **avoir de la ~/39 de ~** to have a high temperature/a temperature of 39 °C; **fiévreux, -euse** adj feverish

figer [fiʒe]: **se figer** vi (*huile*) to congeal; (*personne*) to freeze

fignoler [fiɲɔle] (*fam*) vt to polish up

figue [fig] nf fig; **figuier** nm fig tree

figurant, e [figyʁɑ̃, ɑ̃t] nm/f (Théâtre) walk-on; (Cinéma) extra

figure [figyʁ] nf (*visage*) face; (*forme, personnage*) figure; (*illustration*) picture, diagram

figuré, e [figyʁe] adj (*sens*) figurative

figurer [figyʁe] vi to appear ⊳ vt to represent; **se figurer que** to imagine that

fil [fil] nm (*brin, fig*: *d'une histoire*) thread;

(électrique) wire; (d'un couteau) edge; **au ~ des années** with the passing of the years; **au ~ de l'eau** with the stream ou current; **coup de ~** phone call; **donner/recevoir un coup de ~** to make/get ou receive a phone call; **fil de fer** wire; **fil de fer barbelé** barbed wire

file [fil] nf line; (Auto) lane; **en ~ indienne** in single file; **à la ~** (d'affilée) in succession; **file (d'attente)** queue (BRIT), line (US)

filer [file] vt (tissu, toile) to spin; (prendre en filature) to shadow, tail; (fam: donner): **~ qch à qn** to slip sb sth ▷ vi (bas) to run; (aller vite) (fam) to fly past; (fam: partir) to make ou be off; **~ doux** to toe the line

filet [filɛ] nm (Culin) fillet; (d'eau, de sang) trickle; **filet (à provisions)** string bag

filiale [filjal] nf (Comm) subsidiary

filière [filjɛʀ] nf (carrière) path; **suivre la ~** (dans sa carrière) to work one's way up (through the hierarchy)

fille [fij] nf girl; (opposé à fils) daughter; **vieille ~** old maid; **fillette** nf (little) girl

filleul, e [fijœl] nm/f godchild, godson/daughter

film [film] nm (pour photo) (roll of) film; (œuvre) film, picture, movie

fils [fis] nm son; **fils à papa** daddy's boy

filtre [filtʀ] nm filter; **filtrer** vt to filter; (fig: candidats, visiteurs) to screen

fin [fɛ̃] nf end; **fins** nfpl (but) ends; **prendre ~** to come to an end; **mettre ~ à** to put an end to; **à la ~** in the end; **en ~ de compte** in the end; **sans ~** endless; **~ juin** at the end of June; **fin prêt** quite ready

fin², e [fɛ̃, fin] adj (papier, couche, lame) thin; (cheveux, visage) fine; (taille) neat, slim; (esprit, remarque) subtle ▷ adv (couper) finely; **fines herbes** mixed herbs; **avoir la vue/l'ouïe fine** to have keen eyesight/hearing; **repas/vin fin** gourmet meal/fine wine

final, e [final, o] adj final ▷ nm (Mus) finale; **finale** nf final; **quarts de finale** quarter finals; **finalement** adv finally,

in the end; (après tout) after all

finance [finɑ̃s]: **finances** nfpl (situation) finances; (activités) finance sg; **moyennant ~** for a fee; **financer** vt to finance; **financier, -ière** adj financial

finesse [finɛs] nf thinness; (raffinement) fineness; (subtilité) subtlety

fini, e [fini] adj finished; (Math) finite ▷ nm (d'un objet manufacturé) finish

finir [finiʀ] vt to finish ▷ vi to finish, end; **~ par faire** to end up ou finish up doing; **~ de faire** to finish doing; (cesser) to stop doing; **il finit par m'agacer** he's beginning to get on my nerves; **en ~ avec** to be ou have done with; **il va mal ~** he will come to a bad end

finition [finisjɔ̃] nf (résultat) finish

finlandais, e [fɛ̃lɑ̃dɛ, ez] adj Finnish ▷ nm/f: **F~, e** Finn

Finlande [fɛ̃lɑ̃d] nf: **la ~** Finland

finnois, e [finwa, waz] adj Finnish ▷ nm (Ling) Finnish

fioul [fjul] nm fuel oil

firme [fiʀm] nf firm

fis [fi] vb voir **faire**

fisc [fisk] nm tax authorities pl; **fiscal, e, -aux** adj tax cpd, fiscal; **fiscalité** nf tax system

fissure [fisyʀ] nf crack; **fissurer** vt to crack; **se fissurer** vi to crack

fit [fi] vb voir **faire**

fixation [fiksasjɔ̃] nf (attache) fastening; (Psych) fixation

fixe [fiks] adj fixed; (emploi) steady, regular ▷ nm (salaire) basic salary; (téléphone) landline; **à heure ~** at a set time; **menu à prix ~** set menu

fixé, e [fikse] adj: **être ~ (sur)** (savoir à quoi s'en tenir) to have made up one's mind (about)

fixer [fikse] vt (attacher): **~ qch (à/sur)** to fix ou fasten sth (to/onto); (déterminer) to fix, set; (regarder) to stare at; **se fixer** (s'établir) to settle down; **se ~ sur** (suj: attention) to focus on

flacon [flakɔ̃] nm bottle

flageolet [flaʒɔlɛ] nm (Culin) dwarf kidney bean

flagrant, e [flagrɑ̃, ɑ̃t] adj flagrant, blatant; **en ~ délit** in the act

flair [flɛR] nm sense of smell; (fig) intuition; **flairer** vt (humer) to sniff(at); (détecter) to scent

flamand, e [flamɑ̃, ɑ̃d] adj Flemish ▷ nm (Ling) Flemish ▷ nm/f: **F~, e** Fleming

flamant [flamɑ̃] nm flamingo

flambant, e [flɑ̃bɑ̃, ɑ̃t] adv: **~ neuf** brand new

flambé, e [flɑ̃be] adj (Culin) flambé

flambée [flɑ̃be] nf blaze; (fig: des prix) explosion

flamber [flɑ̃be] vi to blaze (up)

flamboyer [flɑ̃bwaje] vi to blaze (up)

flamme [flam] nf flame; (fig) fire, fervour; **en ~s** on fire, ablaze

flan [flɑ̃] nm (Culin) custard tart ou pie

flanc [flɑ̃] nm side; (Mil) flank

flancher [flɑ̃ʃe] (fam) vi to fail, pack up

flanelle [flanɛl] nf flannel

flâner [flɑne] vi to stroll

flanquer [flɑ̃ke] vt to flank; (fam: mettre) to chuck, shove; (: jeter): **~ par terre/à la porte** to fling to the ground/chuck out

flaque [flak] nf (d'eau) puddle; (d'huile, de sang etc) pool

flash [flaʃ] (pl **-es**) nm (Photo) flash; **flash d'information** newsflash

flatter [flate] vt to flatter; **se ~ de qch** to pride o.s. on sth; **flatteur, -euse** adj flattering

flèche [flɛʃ] nf arrow; (de clocher) spire; **monter en ~** (fig) to soar, rocket; **partir en ~** to be off like a shot; **fléchette** nf dart

flétrir [fletRiR] vt: **se flétrir** vi to wither

fleur [flœR] nf flower; (d'un arbre) blossom; **en ~** (arbre) in blossom; **à ~s** flowery

fleuri, e [flœRi] adj (jardin) in flower ou bloom; (tissu, papier) flowery

fleurir [flœRiR] vi (rose) to flower; (arbre) to blossom; (fig) to flourish ▷ vt (tombe) to put flowers on; (chambre) to decorate with flowers

fleuriste [flœRist] nm/f florist

fleuve [flœv] nm river

flexible [fleksibl] adj flexible

flic [flik] (fam: péj) nm cop

flipper [flipœR] nm pinball (machine)

flirter [flœRte] vi to flirt

flocon [flɔkɔ̃] nm flake

flore [flɔR] nf flora

florissant, e [flɔRisɑ̃, ɑ̃t] adj (économie) flourishing

flot [flo] nm flood, stream; **flots** nmpl (de la mer) waves; **être à ~** (Navig) to be afloat; **entrer à ~s** to stream ou pour in

flottant, e [flɔtɑ̃, ɑ̃t] adj (vêtement) loose

flotte [flɔt] nf (Navig) fleet; (fam: eau) water; (: pluie) rain

flotter [flɔte] vi to float; (nuage, odeur) to drift; (drapeau) to fly; (vêtements) to hang loose; (fam: pleuvoir) to rain; **faire ~** to float; **flotteur** nm float

flou, e [flu] adj fuzzy, blurred; (fig) woolly, vague

fluide [flɥid] adj (liquid); (circulation etc) flowing freely ▷ nm fluid

fluor [flyɔR] nm: **dentifrice au ~** fluoride toothpaste

fluorescent, e [flyɔResɑ̃, ɑ̃t] adj fluorescent

flûte [flyt] nf flute; (verre) flute (glass); (pain) (thin) French stick; **~!** drat it!; **flûte traversière/à bec** flute/recorder

flux [fly] nm incoming tide; (écoulement) flow; **le ~ et le reflux** the ebb and flow

foc [fɔk] nm jib

foi [fwa] nf faith; **digne de ~** reliable; **être de bonne/mauvaise ~** to be sincere/insincere; **ma ~ ...** well ...

foie [fwa] nm liver; **crise de ~** stomach upset

foin [fwɛ̃] nm hay; **faire du ~** (fig: fam) to kick up a row

foire [fwaR] nf fair; (fête foraine) (fun) fair; **faire la ~** (fig: fam) to whoop it up; **~ aux questions** (Internet) FAQs; **foire (exposition)** trade fair

fois [fwa] *nf* time; **une/deux ~** once/twice; **2 ~ 2** times 2; **une ~** (*passé*) once; (*futur*) sometime; **une ~ pour toutes** once and for all; **une ~ que** once; **des ~** (*parfois*) sometimes; **à la ~** (*ensemble*) at once

fol [fɔl] *adj voir* **fou**

folie [fɔli] *nf* (*d'une décision, d'un acte*) madness, folly; (*état*) madness, insanity; **la ~ des grandeurs** delusions of grandeur; **faire des ~s** (*en dépenses*) to be extravagant

folklorique [fɔlklɔʀik] *adj* folk *cpd*; (*fam*) weird

folle [fɔl] *adj*, *nf voir* **fou**; **follement** *adv* (*très*) madly, wildly

foncé, e [fɔse] *adj* dark

foncer [fɔse] *vi* to go darker; (*fam: aller vite*) to tear ou belt along; **~ sur** to charge at

fonction [fɔksjɔ] *nf* function; (*emploi, poste*) post, position; **fonctions** *nfpl* (*professionnelles*) duties; **voiture de ~** company car; **en ~ de** (*par rapport à*) according to; **faire ~ de** to serve as; **la ~ publique** the state ou civil (*BRIT*) service; **fonctionnaire** *nm/f* state employee, local authority employee; (*dans l'administration*) = civil servant; **fonctionner** *vi* to work, function

fond [fɔ] *nm* (*d'un récipient, trou*) bottom; (*d'une salle, scène*) back; (*d'un tableau, décor*) background; (*opposé à la forme*) content; (*Sport*): **le ~** long distance (running); **au ~ de** at the bottom of; at the back of; **à ~** (*connaître, soutenir*) thoroughly; (*appuyer, visser*) right down ou home; **à ~ (de train)** (*fam*) full tilt; **dans le ~, au ~** (*en somme*) basically, really; **de ~ en comble** from top to bottom; **fond de teint** foundation (cream); *voir aussi* **fonds**

fondamental, e, -aux [fɔdamɑtal, o] *adj* fundamental

fondant, e [fɔdɑ, ɑt] *adj* (*neige*) melting; (*poire*) that melts in the mouth

fondation [fɔdasjɔ] *nf* founding; (*établissement*) foundation; **fondations** *nfpl* (*d'une maison*) foundations

fondé, e [fɔde] *adj* (*accusation etc*) well-founded; **être ~ à** to have grounds for ou good reason to

fondement [fɔdmɑ] *nm*: **sans ~** (*rumeur etc*) groundless, unfounded

fonder [fɔde] *vt* to found; (*fig*) to base; **se fonder sur** (*suj: personne*) to base o.s. on

fonderie [fɔdʀi] *nf* smelting works *sg*

fondre [fɔdʀ] *vt* (*aussi: faire ~*) to melt; (*dans l'eau*) to dissolve; (*fig: mélanger*) to merge, blend ▷ *vi* (*à la chaleur*) to melt; (*dans l'eau*) to dissolve; (*fig*) to melt away; (*se précipiter*): **~ sur** to swoop down on; **~ en larmes** to burst into tears

fonds [fɔ] *nm* (*Comm*): **~ (de commerce)** business ▷ *nmpl* (*argent*) funds

fondu, e [fɔdy] *adj* (*beurre, neige*) melted; (*métal*) molten; **fondue** *nf* (*Culin*) fondue

font [fɔ] *vb voir* **faire**

fontaine [fɔtɛn] *nf* fountain; (*source*) spring

fonte [fɔt] *nf* melting; (*métal*) cast iron; **la ~ des neiges** (the spring) thaw

foot [fut] (*fam*) *nm* football

football [futbol] *nm* football, soccer; **footballeur** *nm* footballer

footing [futiŋ] *nm* jogging; **faire du ~** to go jogging

forain, e [fɔʀɛ, ɛn] *adj* fairground *cpd* ▷ *nm* (*marchand*) stallholder; (*acteur*) fairground entertainer

forçat [fɔʀsa] *nm* convict

force [fɔʀs] *nf* strength; (*Physique, Mécanique*) force; **forces** *nfpl* (*physiques*) strength *sg*; (*Mil*) forces; **à ~ d'insister** by dint of insisting; as he (*ou* I *etc*) kept on insisting; **de ~** forcibly, by force; **dans la ~ de l'âge** in the prime of life; **les forces de l'ordre** the police *no pl*

forcé, e [fɔʀse] *adj* forced; **c'est ~** (*fam*) it's inevitable; **forcément** *adv* inevitably; **pas forcément** not necessarily

forcer [fɔʀse] vt to force; (voix) to strain ▷ vi (Sport) to overtax o.s.; **~ la dose** (fam) to overdo it; **se ~ (à faire)** to force o.s. (to do)

forestier, -ère [fɔʀεstje, jεʀ] adj forest cpd

forêt [fɔʀε] nf forest

forfait [fɔʀfε] nm (Comm) all-in deal ou price; **déclarer ~** to withdraw; **forfaitaire** adj inclusive

forge [fɔʀʒ] nf forge, smithy; **forgeron** nm (black)smith

formaliser [fɔʀmalize]: **se formaliser** vi: **se ~ (de)** to take offence (at)

formalité [fɔʀmalite] nf formality; **simple ~** mere formality

format [fɔʀma] nm size; **formater** vt (disque) to format

formation [fɔʀmasjɔ̃] nf (développement) forming; (apprentissage) training; **formation permanente** ou **continue** continuing education

forme [fɔʀm] nf (gén) form; (d'un objet) shape, form; **formes** nfpl (bonnes manières) proprieties; (d'une femme) figure sg; **en ~ de poire** pear-shaped, in the shape of a pear; **être en ~** (Sport etc) to be on form; **en bonne et due ~** in due form

formel, le [fɔʀmεl] adj (catégorique) definite, positive; **formellement** adv (absolument) positively; **formellement interdit** strictly forbidden

former [fɔʀme] vt to form; (éduquer) to train; **se former** vi to form

formidable [fɔʀmidabl] adj tremendous

formulaire [fɔʀmylεʀ] nm form

formule [fɔʀmyl] nf (gén) formula; (expression) phrase; **formule de politesse** polite phrase; (en fin de lettre) letter ending

fort, e [fɔʀ, fɔʀt] adj strong; (intensité, rendement) high, great; (corpulent) stout; (doué) good, able ▷ adv (serrer, frapper) hard; (parler) loud(ly); (beaucoup) greatly, very much; (très) very ▷ nm (édifice) fort; (point fort) strong point,

forte; **forte tête** rebel; **forteresse** nf stronghold

fortifiant [fɔʀtifjɑ̃] nm tonic

fortune [fɔʀtyn] nf fortune; **faire ~** to make one's fortune; **de ~** makeshift; **fortuné, e** adj wealthy

forum [fɔʀɔm] nm forum; **~ de discussion** (Internet) message board

fosse [fos] nf (grand trou) pit; (tombe) grave

fossé [fose] nm ditch; (fig) gulf, gap

fossette [fosεt] nf dimple

fossile [fosil] nm fossil

fou (fol), folle [fu, fɔl] adj mad; (déréglé etc) wild, erratic; (fam: extrême, très grand) terrific, tremendous ▷ nm/f madman(-woman) ▷ nm (du roi) jester; **être fou de** to be mad ou crazy about; **avoir le fou rire** to have the giggles

foudre [fudʀ] nf: **la ~** lightning

foudroyant, e [fudʀwajɑ̃, ɑ̃t] adj (progrès) lightning cpd; (succès) stunning; (maladie, poison) violent

fouet [fwε] nm whip; (Culin) whisk; **de plein ~** (se heurter) head on; **fouetter** vt to whip; (crème) to whisk

fougère [fuʒεʀ] nf fern

fougue [fug] nf ardour, spirit; **fougueux, -euse** adj fiery

fouille [fuj] nf search; **fouilles** nfpl (archéologiques) excavations; **fouiller** vt to search; (creuser) to dig ▷ vi to rummage; **fouillis** nm jumble, muddle

foulard [fulaʀ] nm scarf

foule [ful] nf crowd; **la ~** crowds pl; **une ~ de** masses of

foulée [fule] nf stride

fouler [fule] vt to press; (sol) to tread upon; **se ~ la cheville** to sprain one's ankle; **ne pas se ~** not to overexert o.s.; **il ne se foule pas** he doesn't put himself out; **foulure** nf sprain

four [fuʀ] nm oven; (de potier) kiln; (Théâtre: échec) flop

fourche [fuʀʃ] nf pitchfork

fourchette [fuʀʃεt] nf fork; (Statistique) bracket, margin

fourgon [fuʀgɔ̃] nm van; (Rail)

wag(g)on; **fourgonnette** nf (small) van

fourmi [furmi] nf ant; **avoir des ~s dans les jambes/mains** to have pins and needles in one's legs/hands; **fourmilière** nf ant-hill; **fourmiller** vi to swarm

fourneau, X [furno] nm stove

fourni, e [furni] adj (barbe, cheveux) thick; (magasin): **bien ~ (en)** well stocked (with)

fournir [furnir] vt to supply; (preuve, exemple) to provide; (effort) to put in: **~ qch à qn** to supply sth to sb, supply sb with sth; **fournisseur, -euse** nm/f supplier; **fournisseur d'accès à Internet** (Internet) service provider, ISP; **fourniture** nf supply(ing); **fournitures scolaires** school stationery

fourrage [furaʒ] nm fodder

fourré, e [fure] adj (bonbon etc) filled; (manteau etc) fur-lined ▷ nm thicket

fourrer [fure] (fam) vt to stick, shove; **se fourrer dans/sous** to get into/under

fourrière [furjer] nf pound

fourrure [furyr] nf fur; (sur l'animal) coat

foutre [futr] (fam!) vt = **ficher; foutu, e** (fam!) adj = **fichu.**

foyer [fwaje] nm (maison) home; (famille) family; (de cheminée) hearth; (de jeunes etc) (social) club; (résidence) hostel; (salon) foyer; **lunettes à double ~** bi-focals

fracassant, e [frakasɑ̃, ɑ̃t] adj (succès) thundering

fraction [fraksjɔ̃] nf fraction

fracture [fraktyr] nf fracture; **fracture du crâne** fractured skull; **fracturer** vt (coffre, serrure) to break open; (os, membre) to fracture; **se fracturer le crâne** to fracture one's skull

fragile [fraʒil] adj fragile, delicate; (fig) frail; **fragilité** nf fragility

fragment [fragmɑ̃] nm (d'un objet)

fragment, piece

fraîche [frɛʃ] adj voir **frais; fraîcheur** nf coolness; (d'un aliment) freshness; **fraîchir** vi to get cooler; (vent) to freshen

frais, fraîche [frɛ, frɛʃ] adj fresh; (froid) cool ▷ adv (récemment) newly, fresh(ly) ▷ nm: **mettre au ~** to put in a cool place ▷ nmpl (gén) expenses; (Comm) costs; **il fait ~** it's cool; **servir ~** serve chilled; **prendre le ~** to take a breath of cool air; **faire des ~** to go to a lot of expense; **frais de scolarité** school fees (BRIT), tuition (US); **frais généraux** overheads

fraise [frɛz] nf strawberry; **fraise des bois** wild strawberry

framboise [frɑ̃bwaz] nf raspberry

franc, franche [frɑ̃, frɑ̃ʃ] adj (personne) frank, straightforward; (visage) open; (net: refus) clear; (: coupure) clean; (intensif) downright ▷ nm franc

français, e [frɑ̃sɛ, ɛz] adj French ▷ nm/f: **F~, e** Frenchman(-woman) ▷ nm (Ling) French

France [frɑ̃s] nf: **la ~** France; **~ 2, ~ 3** public-sector television channels

● **FRANCE TÉLÉVISION**

● **France 2** and **France 3** are public-
● sector television channels. France
● 2 is a national general interest and
● entertainment channel; France
● 3 provides regional news and
● information as well as programmes
● for the national network.

franche [frɑ̃ʃ] adj voir **franc; franchement** adv frankly; (nettement) definitely; (tout à fait: mauvais etc) downright

franchir [frɑ̃ʃir] vt (obstacle) to clear, get over; (seuil, ligne, rivière) to cross; (distance) to cover

franchise [frɑ̃ʃiz] nf frankness; (douanière) exemption; (Assurances) excess

franc-maçon [fʀɑ̃masɔ̃] nm freemason

franco [fʀɑ̃ko] adv (Comm): ~ **(de port)** postage paid

francophone [fʀɑ̃kɔfɔn] adj French-speaking

franc-parler [fʀɑ̃paʀle] nm inv outspokenness; **avoir son** ~ to speak one's mind

frange [fʀɑ̃ʒ] nf fringe

frangipane [fʀɑ̃ʒipan] nf almond paste

frappant, e [fʀapɑ̃, ɑ̃t] adj striking

frappé, e [fʀape] adj iced

frapper [fʀape] vt to hit, strike; (étonner) to strike; ~ **dans ses mains** to clap one's hands; **frappé de stupeur** dumbfounded

fraternel, le [fʀatɛʀnɛl] adj brotherly, fraternal; **fraternité** nf brotherhood

fraude [fʀod] nf fraud; (Scol) cheating; **passer qch en** ~ to smuggle sth in (ou out); **fraude fiscale** tax evasion

frayeur [fʀejœʀ] nf fright

fredonner [fʀədɔne] vt to hum

freezer [fʀizœʀ] nm freezing compartment

frein [fʀɛ̃] nm brake; **mettre un** ~ **à** (fig) to curb, check; **frein à main** handbrake; **freiner** vi to brake ▷ vt (progrès etc) to check

frêle [fʀɛl] adj frail, fragile

frelon [fʀəlɔ̃] nm hornet

frémir [fʀemiʀ] vi (de peur, d'horreur) to shudder; (de colère) to shake; (feuillage) to quiver

frêne [fʀɛn] nm ash

fréquemment [fʀekamɑ̃] adv frequently

fréquent, e [fʀekɑ̃, ɑ̃t] adj frequent

fréquentation [fʀekɑ̃tasjɔ̃] nf frequenting; **fréquentations** nfpl (relations) company sg; **avoir de mauvaises** ~**s** to keep bad company

fréquenté, e [fʀekɑ̃te] adj: **très** ~ (very) busy; **mal** ~ patronized by disreputable elements

fréquenter [fʀekɑ̃te] vt (lieu) to frequent; (personne) to see; **se fréquenter** to see each other

frère [fʀɛʀ] nm brother

fresque [fʀɛsk] nf (Art) fresco

fret [fʀɛ(t)] nm freight

friand, e [fʀijɑ̃, fʀijɑ̃d] adj: ~ **de** very fond of ▷ nm: ~ **au fromage** cheese puff

friandise [fʀijɑ̃diz] nf sweet

fric [fʀik] (fam) nm cash, bread

friche [fʀiʃ]: **en** ~ adj, adv (lying) fallow

friction [fʀiksjɔ̃] nf (massage) rub, rub-down; (Tech, fig) friction

frigidaire® [fʀiʒidɛʀ] nm refrigerator

frigo [fʀigo] (fam) nm fridge

frigorifique [fʀigɔʀifik] adj refrigerating

frileux, -euse [fʀilø, øz] adj sensitive to (the) cold

frimer [fʀime] (fam) vi to show off

fringale [fʀɛ̃gal] (fam) nf: **avoir la** ~ to be ravenous

fringues [fʀɛ̃g] (fam) nfpl clothes

fripé, e [fʀipe] adj crumpled

frire [fʀiʀ] vt, vi: **faire** ~ to fry

frisé, e [fʀize] adj (cheveux) curly; (personne) curly-haired

frisson [fʀisɔ̃] nm (de froid) shiver; (de peur) shudder; **frissonner** vi (de fièvre, froid) to shiver; (d'horreur) to shudder

frit, e [fʀi, fʀit] pp de **frire**; **frite** nf: (pommes) **frites** chips (BRIT), French fries; **friteuse** nf chip pan; **friteuse électrique** deep fat fryer; **friture** nf (huile) (deep) fat; (plat): **friture** (**de poissons**) fried fish

froid, e [fʀwa, fʀwad] adj, nm cold; **il fait** ~ it's cold; **avoir/prendre** ~ to be/catch cold; **être en** ~ **avec** to be on bad terms with; **froidement** adv (accueillir) coldly; (décider) coolly

froisser [fʀwase] vt to crumple (up), crease; (fig) to hurt, offend; **se froisser** vi to crumple, crease; (personne) to take offence; **se** ~ **un muscle** to strain a muscle

frôler [fʀole] vt to brush against; (suj: projectile) to skim past; (fig) to come very close to

fromage [fʁɔmaʒ] nm cheese; **fromage blanc** soft white cheese

froment [fʁɔmɑ̃] nm wheat

froncer [fʁɔ̃se] vt to gather; **~ les sourcils** to frown

front [fʁɔ̃] nm forehead, brow; (Mil) front; **de ~** (se heurter) head-on; (rouler) together (i.e. 2 or 3 abreast); (simultanément) at once; **faire ~ à** to face up to

frontalier, -ère [fʁɔ̃talje, jɛʁ] adj border cpd, frontier cpd; **~s people** who commute across the border

frontière [fʁɔ̃tjɛʁ] nf frontier, border

frotter [fʁɔte] vi to rub, scrape ▷ vt to rub; (pommes de terre, plancher) to scrub; **~ une allumette** to strike a match

fruit [fʁɥi] nm fruit gen no pl; **fruits de mer** seafood(s); **fruits secs** dried fruit sg; **fruité, e** adj fruity; **fruitier, -ère** adj: **arbre fruitier** fruit tree

frustrer [fʁystʁe] vt to frustrate

fuel(-oil) [fjul(ɔjl)] nm fuel oil; (domestique) heating oil

fugace [fygas] adj fleeting

fugitif, -ive [fyʒitif, iv] adj (fugace) fleeting ▷ nm/f fugitive

fugue [fyg] nf: **faire une ~** to run away, abscond

fuir [fɥiʁ] vt to flee from; (éviter) to shun ▷ vi to run away; (gaz, robinet) to leak

fuite [fɥit] nf flight; (écoulement, divulgation) leak; **être en ~** to be on the run; **mettre en ~** to put to flight

fulgurant, e [fylgyʁɑ̃, ɑ̃t] adj lightning cpd, dazzling

fumé, e [fyme] adj (Culin) smoked; (verre) tinted; **fumée** nf smoke

fumer [fyme] vi to smoke; (soupe) to steam ▷ vt to smoke

fûmes [fym] vb voir **être**

fumeur, -euse [fymœʁ, øz] nm/f smoker

fumier [fymje] nm manure

funérailles [fyneʁaj] nfpl funeral sg

fur [fyʁ]: **au ~ et à mesure** adv as one goes along; **au ~ et à mesure que** as

furet [fyʁɛ] nm ferret

fureter [fyʁ(ə)te] (péj) vi to nose about

fureur [fyʁœʁ] nf fury; **être en ~** to be infuriated; **faire ~** to be all the rage

furie [fyʁi] nf fury; (femme) shrew, vixen; **en ~** (mer) raging; **furieux, -euse** adj furious

furoncle [fyʁɔ̃kl] nm boil

furtif, -ive [fyʁtif, iv] adj furtive

fus [fy] vb voir **être**

fusain [fyzɛ̃] nm (Art) charcoal

fuseau, x [fyzo] nm (pour filer) spindle; (pantalon) (ski) pants; **fuseau horaire** time zone

fusée [fyze] nf rocket

fusible [fyzibl] nm (Élec: fil) fuse wire; (: fiche) fuse

fusil [fyzi] nm (de guerre, à canon rayé) rifle, gun; (de chasse, à canon lisse) shotgun, gun; **fusillade** nf gunfire no pl, shooting no pl; **fusiller** vt to shoot; **fusiller qn du regard** to look daggers at sb

fusionner [fyzjɔne] vi to merge

fût [fy] vb voir **être** ▷ nm (tonneau) barrel, cask

futé, e [fyte] adj crafty; **Bison ~®** TV and radio traffic monitoring service

futile [fytil] adj futile; frivolous

futur, e [fytyʁ] adj, nm future

fuyard, e [fɥijaʁ, aʁd] nm/f runaway

g

Gabon [gabɔ̃] nm: **le ~** Gabon

gâcher [gaʃe] vt (gâter) to spoil; (gaspiller) to waste; **gâchis** nm waste no pl

gaffe [gaf] nf blunder; **faire ~** (fam) to be careful

gage [gaʒ] nm (dans un jeu) forfeit; (fig: de fidélité, d'amour) token; **gages** nmpl (salaire) wages; **mettre en ~** to pawn

gagnant, e [gaɲɑ̃, ɑ̃t] adj: **billet/ numéro ~** winning ticket/number ▷ nm/f winner

gagne-pain [gaɲpɛ̃] nm inv job

gagner [gaɲe] vt (somme d'argent, revenu) to earn; (aller vers, atteindre) to reach; (envahir: sommeil, peur) to overcome; (: mal) to spread to ▷ vi to win; (fig) to gain; **~ du temps/de la place** to gain time/save space; **~ sa vie** to earn one's living

gai, e [ge] adj cheerful; (un peu ivre) merry; **gaiement** adv cheerfully; **gaieté** nf cheerfulness; **de gaieté de cœur** with a light heart

gain [gɛ̃] nm (revenu) earnings pl; (bénéfice: gén pl) profits pl

gala [gala] nm official reception; **de ~** (soirée etc) gala

galant, e [galɑ̃, ɑ̃t] adj (courtois) courteous, gentlemanly; (entreprenant) flirtatious, gallant; (scène, rendez-vous) romantic

galerie [galʀi] nf gallery; (Théâtre) circle; (de voiture) roof rack; (fig: spectateurs) audience; **galerie de peinture** (private) art gallery; **galerie marchande** shopping arcade

galet [galε] nm pebble

galette [galɛt] nf flat cake; **galette des Rois** cake eaten on Twelfth Night

GALETTE DES ROIS

- A **galette des Rois** is a cake eaten on
- Twelfth Night containing a figurine.
- The person who finds it is the king
- (or queen) and gets a paper crown.
- They then choose someone else to be
- their queen (or king).

galipette [galipεt] nf somersault

Galles [gal] nfpl: **le pays de ~** Wales; **gallois, e** adj Welsh ▷ nm (Ling) Welsh; **Gallois, e** nm/f: **Gallois, e** Welshman(-woman) ▷ nm (Ling) Welsh

galon [galɔ̃] nm (Mil) stripe; (décoratif) piece of braid

galop [galo] nm gallop; **galoper** vi to gallop

gambader [gɑ̃bade] vi (animal, enfant) to leap about

gamin, e [gamɛ̃, in] nm/f kid ▷ adj childish

gamme [gam] nf (Mus) scale; (fig) range

gang [gɑ̃g] nm (de criminels) gang

gant [gɑ̃] nm glove; **gant de toilette** face flannel (BRIT), face cloth

garage [gaʀaʒ] nm garage; **garagiste** nm/f garage owner; (employé) garage mechanic

garantie [gaʀɑ̃ti] nf guarantee; **(bon de) ~** guarantee ou warranty slip

garantir [gaʀɑ̃tiʀ] vt to guarantee; **~ à**

qn que to assure sb that

garçon [gaʁsɔ̃] nm boy; (célibataire): **vieux ~** bachelor; **garçon (de café)** (serveur) waiter; **garçon de courses** messenger

garde [gaʁd(ə)] nm (de prisonnier) guard; (de domaine etc) warden; (soldat, sentinelle) guardsman ▷ nf (soldats) guard; **de ~** on duty; **monter la ~** to stand guard; **mettre en ~** to warn; **prendre ~ (à)** to be careful (of); **garde champêtre** nm rural policeman; **garde du corps** nm bodyguard; **garde à vue** nf (Jur) = police custody; **garde-boue** nm inv mudguard; **garde-chasse** nm gamekeeper

garder [gaʁde] vt (conserver) to keep; (surveiller: enfants) to look after; (: immeuble, lieu, prisonnier) to guard; **se garder** vi (aliment: se conserver) to keep; **se ~ de faire** to be careful not to do; **~ le lit/la chambre** to stay in bed/indoors; **pêche/chasse gardée** private fishing/hunting (ground)

garderie [gaʁdəʁi] nf day nursery, crèche

garde-robe [gaʁdəʁɔb] nf wardrobe

gardien, ne [gaʁdjɛ̃, jɛn] nm/f (garde) guard; (de prison) warder; (de domaine, réserve) warden; (de musée etc) attendant; (de phare, cimetière) keeper; (d'immeuble) caretaker; (fig) guardian; **gardien de but** goalkeeper; **gardien de la paix** policeman; **gardien de nuit** night watchman

gare[1] [gaʁ] nf station; **gare routière** bus station

gare[2] [gaʁ] excl: **~ à ...!** mind ...!; **~ à toi!** watch out!

garer [gaʁe] vt to park; **se garer** vi to park

garni, e [gaʁni] adj (plat) served with vegetables (and chips or rice etc)

garniture [gaʁnityʁ] nf (Culin) vegetables pl; **garniture de frein** brake lining

gars [ga] (fam) nm guy

Gascogne [gaskɔɲ] nf Gascony; **le**

golfe de ~ the Bay of Biscay

gas-oil [gazojl] nm diesel (oil)

gaspiller [gaspije] vt to waste

gastronome [gastʁɔnɔm] nm/f gourmet; **gastronomique** adj gastronomic

gâteau, x [gɑto] nm cake; **gâteau sec** biscuit

gâter [gɑte] vt to spoil; **se gâter** vi (dent, fruit) to go bad; (temps, situation) to change for the worse

gâteux, -euse [gɑtø, øz] adj senile

gauche [goʃ] adj left, left-hand; (maladroit) awkward, clumsy ▷ nf (Pol) left (wing); **le bras ~** the left arm; **le côté ~** the left-hand side; **à ~** on the left; (direction) (to the) left; **gaucher, -ère** adj left-handed; **gauchiste** nm/f leftist

gaufre [gofʁ] nf waffle

gaufrette [gofʁɛt] nf wafer

gaulois, e [golwa, waz] adj Gallic ▷ nm/f: **G~, e** Gaul

gaz [gɑz] nm inv gas; **ça sent le ~** I can smell gas, there's a smell of gas

gaze [gɑz] nf gauze

gazette [gazɛt] nf news sheet

gazeux, -euse [gazø, øz] adj (boisson) fizzy; (eau) sparkling

gazoduc [gazɔdyk] nm gas pipeline

gazon [gɑzɔ̃] nm (herbe) grass; (pelouse) lawn

geai [ʒɛ] nm jay

géant, e [ʒeɑ̃, ɑ̃t] adj gigantic; (Comm) giant-size ▷ nm/f giant

geindre [ʒɛ̃dʁ] vi to groan, moan

gel [ʒɛl] nm frost

gélatine [ʒelatin] nf gelatine

gelée [ʒ(ə)le] nf jelly; (gel) frost

geler [ʒ(ə)le] vt, vi to freeze; **il gèle** it's freezing

gélule [ʒelyl] nf (Méd) capsule

Gémeaux [ʒemo] nmpl: **les ~** Gemini

gémir [ʒemiʁ] vi to groan, moan

gênant, e [ʒɛnɑ̃, ɑ̃t] adj (irritant) annoying; (embarrassant) embarrassing

gencive [ʒɑ̃siv] nf gum

gendarme [ʒɑ̃daʁm] nm gendarme;

gendarmerie nf military police force in countryside and small towns; their police station or barracks

gendre [ʒɑ̃dr] nm son-in-law

gêné, e [ʒene] adj embarrassed

gêner [ʒene] vt (incommoder) to bother; (encombrer) to be in the way; (embarrasser): **~ qn** to put sb ill-at-ease; **se gêner** to put o.s. out; **ne vous gênez pas!** don't mind me!

général, e, -aux [ʒeneral, o] adj, nm general; **en ~** usually, in general; **généralement** adv generally; **généraliser** vt, vi to generalize; **se généraliser** vi to become widespread; **généraliste** nm/f general practitioner, G.P.

génération [ʒenerasjɔ̃] nf generation

généreux, -euse [ʒenerø, øz] adj generous

générique [ʒenerik] nm (Cinéma) credits pl

générosité [ʒenerozite] nf generosity

genêt [ʒ(ə)nɛ] nm broom no pl (shrub)

génétique [ʒenetik] adj genetic

Genève [ʒ(ə)nɛv] n Geneva

génial, e, -aux [ʒenjal, jo] adj of genius; (fam: formidable) fantastic, brilliant

génie [ʒeni] nm genius; (Mil): **le ~** the Engineers pl; **génie civil** civil engineering

genièvre [ʒənjɛvr] nm juniper

génisse [ʒenis] nf heifer

génital, e, -aux [ʒenital, o] adj genital; **les parties ~es** the genitals

génoise [ʒenwaz] nf sponge cake

genou, x [ʒ(ə)nu] nm knee; **à ~x** on one's knees; **se mettre à ~x** to kneel down

genre [ʒɑ̃r] nm kind, type, sort; (Ling) gender; **avoir bon ~** to look a nice sort; **avoir mauvais ~** to be coarse-looking; **ce n'est pas son ~** it's not like him

gens [ʒɑ̃] nmpl (f in some phrases) people pl

gentil, le [ʒɑ̃ti, ij] adj kind; (enfant: sage) good; (endroit etc) nice;

gentillesse nf kindness; **gentiment** adv kindly

géographie [ʒeografi] nf geography

géologie [ʒeɔlɔʒi] nf geology

géomètre [ʒeɔmɛtr] nm/f (arpenteur) (land) surveyor

géométrie [ʒeɔmetri] nf geometry; **géométrique** adj geometric

géranium [ʒeranjɔm] nm geranium

gérant, e [ʒerɑ̃, ɑ̃t] nm/f manager(-eress); **gérant d'immeuble** (managing) agent

gerbe [ʒɛrb] nf (de fleurs) spray; (de blé) sheaf

gercé, e [ʒɛrse] adj chapped

gerçure [ʒɛrsyr] nf crack

gérer [ʒere] vt to manage

germain, e [ʒɛrmɛ̃, ɛn] adj: **cousin ~** first cousin

germe [ʒɛrm] nm germ; **germer** vi to sprout; (semence) to germinate

geste [ʒɛst] nm gesture

gestion [ʒɛstjɔ̃] nf management

Ghana [gana] nm: **le ~** Ghana

gibier [ʒibje] nm (animaux) game

gicler [ʒikle] vi to spurt, squirt

gifle [ʒifl] nf slap (in the face); **gifler** vt to slap (in the face)

gigantesque [ʒigɑ̃tɛsk] adj gigantic

gigot [ʒigo] nm leg (of mutton ou lamb)

gigoter [ʒigote] vi to wriggle (about)

gilet [ʒile] nm waistcoat; (pull) cardigan; **gilet de sauvetage** life jacket

gin [dʒin] nm gin; **~-tonic** gin and tonic

gingembre [ʒɛ̃ʒɑ̃br] nm ginger

girafe [ʒiraf] nf giraffe

giratoire [ʒiratwar] adj: **sens ~** roundabout

girofle [ʒirɔfl] nf: **clou de ~** clove

girouette [ʒirwɛt] nf weather vane ou cock

gitan, e [ʒitɑ̃, an] nm/f gipsy

gîte [ʒit] nm (maison) home; (abri) shelter; **gîte (rural)** (country) holiday cottage (BRIT), **gîte** (self-catering accommodation in the country)

givre [ʒivr] nm (hoar) frost; **givré, e** adj

covered in frost; (fam: fou) nuts; **orange givrée** orange sorbet (served in peel)

glace [glas] *nf* ice; (crème glacée) ice cream; (miroir) mirror; (de voiture) window

glacé, e [glase] *adj* (mains, vent, pluie) freezing; (lac) frozen; (boisson) iced

glacer [glase] *vt* to freeze; (gâteau) to ice; (fig:) ~ **qn** (intimider) to chill sb; (paralyser) to make sb's blood run cold

glacial, e [glasjal, jo] *adj* icy

glacier [glasje] *nm* (Géo) glacier; (marchand) ice-cream maker

glacière [glasjɛʀ] *nf* icebox

glaçon [glasɔ̃] *nm* icicle; (pour boisson) ice cube

glaïeul [glajœl] *nm* gladiolus

glaise [glɛz] *nf* clay

gland [glɑ̃] *nm* acorn; (décoration) tassel

glande [glɑ̃d] *nf* gland

glissade [glisad] *nf* (par jeu) slide; (chute) slip; **faire des ~s sur la glace** to slide on the ice

glissant, e [glisɑ̃, ɑ̃t] *adj* slippery

glissement [glismɑ̃] *nm*: **glissement de terrain** landslide

glisser [glise] *vi* (avancer) to glide ou slide along; (coulisser, tomber) to slide; (déraper) to slip; (être glissant) to be slippery ▷ *vt* to slip; **se glisser dans/entre** to slip into/between

global, e, -aux [global, o] *adj* overall

globe [glob] *nm* globe

globule [globyl] *nm* (du sang): **~ blanc/rouge** white/red corpuscle

gloire [glwaʀ] *nf* glory

glousser [gluse] *vi* (poule) to cluck; (rire) to chuckle

glouton, ne [glutɔ̃, ɔn] *adj* gluttonous

gluant, e [glyɑ̃, ɑ̃t] *adj* sticky, gummy

glucose [glykoz] *nm* glucose

glycine [glisin] *nf* wisteria

GO *sigle* (= grandes ondes) LW

goal [gol] *nm* goalkeeper

gobelet [gɔblɛ] *nm* (en étain, verre, argent) tumbler; (d'enfant, de pique-nique) beaker; (à dés) cup

goéland [gɔelɑ̃] *nm* (sea)gull

goélette [gɔelɛt] *nf* schooner

goinfre [gwɛ̃fʀ] *nm* glutton

golf [gɔlf] *nm* golf; (terrain) golf course; **golf miniature** crazy (BRIT) ou miniature golf

golfe [gɔlf] *nm* gulf; (petit) bay

gomme [gɔm] *nf* (à effacer) rubber (BRIT), eraser; **gommer** *vt* to rub out (BRIT), erase

gonflé, e [gɔ̃fle] *adj* swollen; **il est ~** (fam: courageux) he's got some nerve; (impertinent) he's got a nerve

gonfler [gɔ̃fle] *vt* (pneu, ballon: en soufflant) to blow up; (: avec une pompe) to pump up; (nombre, importance) to inflate ▷ *vi* to swell (up); (Culin: pâte) to rise

gonzesse [gɔ̃zɛs] (fam) *nf* chick, bird (BRIT)

gorge [gɔʀʒ] *nf* (Anat) throat; (vallée) gorge; **gorgée** *nf* (petite) sip; (grande) gulp

gorille [gɔʀij] *nm* gorilla; (fam) bodyguard

gosse [gos] (fam) *nm/f* kid

goudron [gudʀɔ̃] *nm* tar; **goudronner** *vt* to tar(mac) (BRIT), asphalt (US)

gouffre [gufʀ] *nm* abyss, gulf

goulot [gulo] *nm* neck; **boire au ~** to drink from the bottle

goulu, e [guly] *adj* greedy

gourde [guʀd] *nf* (récipient) flask; (fam) (clumsy) clot ou oaf ▷ *adj* oafish

gourdin [guʀdɛ̃] *nm* club, bludgeon

gourmand, e [guʀmɑ̃, ɑ̃d] *adj* greedy; **gourmandise** *nf* greed; (bonbon) sweet

gousse [gus] *nf*: **gousse d'ail** clove of garlic

goût [gu] *nm* taste; **avoir bon ~** to taste good; **de bon ~** tasteful; **de mauvais ~** tasteless; **prendre ~ à** to develop a taste ou a liking for

goûter [gute] *vt* (essayer) to taste; (apprécier) to enjoy ▷ *vi* to have (afternoon) tea ▷ *nm* (afternoon) tea; **je peux ~?** can I have a taste?

goutte [gut] *nf* drop; (Méd) gout; (alcool) brandy; **tomber ~ à ~** to drip;

une ~ de whisky a drop of whisky;
goutte-à-goutte nm (Méd) drip
gouttière [gutjɛʀ] nf gutter
gouvernail [guvɛʀnaj] nm rudder;
(barre) helm, tiller
gouvernement [guvɛʀnəmɑ̃] nm
government
gouverner [guvɛʀne] vt to govern
grâce [gʀɑs] nf (charme, Rel) grace;
(faveur) favour; (Jur) pardon; **faire ~ à qn
de qch** to spare sb sth; **demander ~** to
beg for mercy; **~ à** thanks to; **gracieux,
-euse** adj graceful
grade [gʀad] nm rank; **monter en ~** to
be promoted
gradin [gʀadɛ̃] nm tier; step; **gradins**
nmpl (de stade) terracing sg
gradué, e [gʀadye] adj: **verre ~**
measuring jug
graduel, le [gʀaduɛl] adj gradual
graduer [gʀadue] vt (effort etc) to
increase gradually; (règle, verre) to
graduate
graffiti [gʀafiti] nmpl graffiti
grain [gʀɛ̃] nm (gén) grain; (Navig)
squall; **grain de beauté** beauty spot;
grain de café coffee bean; **grain de
poivre** peppercorn
graine [gʀɛn] nf seed
graissage [gʀesaʒ] nm lubrication,
greasing
graisse [gʀes] nf fat; (lubrifiant) grease;
graisser vt to lubricate, grease;
(tacher) to make greasy; **graisseux,
-euse** adj greasy
grammaire [gʀa(m)mɛʀ] nf grammar
gramme [gʀam] nm gramme
grand, e [gʀɑ̃, gʀɑ̃d] adj (haut) tall;
(gros, vaste, large) big, large; (long)
long; (plus âgé) big; (adulte) grown-up;
(important, brillant) great ▷ adv: **~
ouvert** wide open; **au ~ air** in the open
(air); **les grands blessés** the severely
injured; **grand ensemble** housing
scheme; **grand magasin** department
store; **grande personne** grown-up;
grande surface hypermarket; **grandes
écoles** prestigious schools at university

level; **grandes lignes** (Rail) main lines;
grandes vacances summer holidays
(BRIT) ou vacation (US); **grand-chose**
nm/f inv: **pas grand-chose** not
much; **Grande-Bretagne** nf (Great)
Britain; **grandeur** nf (dimension) size;
grandeur nature life-size; **grandiose**
adj imposing; **grandir** vi to grow ▷ vt:
grandir qn (suj: vêtement, chaussure)
to make sb look taller; **grand-mère** nf
grandmother; **grand-peine: à grand-
peine** adv with difficulty; **grand-père**
nm grandfather; **grands-parents** nmpl
grandparents
grange [gʀɑ̃ʒ] nf barn
granit [gʀanit] nm granite
graphique [gʀafik] adj graphic ▷ nm
graph
grappe [gʀap] nf cluster; **grappe de
raisin** bunch of grapes
gras, se [gʀɑ, gʀɑs] adj (viande, soupe)
fatty; (personne) fat; (surface, main)
greasy; (plaisanterie) coarse; (Typo) bold
▷ nm (Culin) fat; **faire la ~se matinée**
to have a lie-in (BRIT), sleep late (US);
grassement adv: **grassement payé**
handsomely paid
gratifiant, e [gʀatifjɑ̃, jɑ̃t] adj
gratifying, rewarding
gratin [gʀatɛ̃] nm (plat) cheese-topped
dish; (croûte) cheese topping; (fam:
élite) upper crust; **gratiné, e** adj (Culin)
au gratin
gratis [gʀatis] adv free
gratitude [gʀatityd] nf gratitude
gratte-ciel [gʀatsjɛl] nm inv
skyscraper
gratter [gʀate] vt (avec un outil) to
scrape; (enlever: avec un outil) to scrape
off; (: avec un ongle) to scratch; (enlever
avec un ongle) to scratch off ▷ vi (irriter)
to be scratchy; (démanger) to itch; **se
gratter** to scratch (o.s.)
gratuit, e [gʀatɥi, ɥit] adj (entrée,
billet) free; (fig) gratuitous
grave [gʀav] adj (maladie, accident)
serious, bad; (sujet, problème) serious,
grave; (air) grave, solemn; (voix, son)

deep, low-pitched; **gravement** adv
seriously; (parler, regarder) gravely
graver [grave] vt (plaque, nom) to
engrave; (CD, DVD) to burn
graveur [gravœr] nm engraver;
graveur de CD/DVD CD/DVD writer
gravier [gravje] nm gravel no pl;
gravillons nmpl loose chippings ou
gravel sg
gravir [gravir] vt to climb (up)
gravité [gravite] nf (de maladie,
d'accident) seriousness; (de sujet,
problème) gravity
graviter [gravite] vi to revolve
gravure [gravyr] nf engraving;
(reproduction) print
gré [gre] nm: **à son ~** to one's liking;
de bon ~ willingly; **contre le ~ de qn**
against sb's will; **de son (plein) ~**
of one's own free will; **bon ~ mal ~** like it
or not; **de ~ ou de force** whether one
likes it or not; **savoir ~ à qn de qch** to
be grateful to sb for sth
grec, grecque [grek] adj Greek;
(classique: vase etc) Grecian ▷ nm/f: **G~,
Grecque** Greek ▷ nm (Ling) Greek
Grèce [gres] nf: **la ~** Greece
greffe [gref] nf (Bot, Méd: de tissu) graft;
(Méd: d'organe) transplant; **greffer** vt
(Bot, Méd: tissu) to graft; (Méd: organe)
to transplant
grêle [grel] adj (very) thin ▷ nf hail;
grêler vb impers: **il grêle** it's hailing;
grêlon [grelɔ̃] nm hailstone
grelot [grelo] nm little bell
grelotter [grelɔte] vi to shiver
grenade [grenad] nf (explosive)
grenade; (Bot) pomegranate;
grenadine nf grenadine
grenier [grenje] nm attic; (de ferme) loft
grenouille [grenuj] nf frog
grès [gre] nm sandstone; (poterie)
stoneware
grève [grev] nf (d'ouvriers) strike; (plage)
shore; **se mettre en/faire ~** to go on/
be on strike; **grève de la faim** hunger
strike; **grève sauvage** wildcat strike
gréviste [grevist] nm/f striker

grièvement [grijevmɑ̃] adv seriously
griffe [grif] nf claw; (de couturier) label;
griffer vt to scratch
grignoter [grinɔte] vt (personne) to
nibble at; (souris) to gnaw at ▷ vi to
nibble
gril [gril] nm steak ou grill pan; **faire
cuire au ~** to grill; **grillade** nf (viande
etc) grill
grillage [grijaʒ] nm (treillis) wire
netting; (clôture) wire fencing
grille [grij] nf (clôture) wire fence;
(portail) (metal) gate; (d'égout) (metal)
grate; (fig) grid
grille-pain [grijpɛ̃] nm inv toaster
griller [grije] vt (pain) to toast; (viande)
to grill; (fig: ampoule etc) to blow; **faire
~** to toast; to grill; (châtaignes) to roast; **~
un feu rouge** to jump the lights
grillon [grijɔ̃] nm cricket
grimace [grimas] nf grimace; (pour
faire rire): **faire des ~s** to pull ou make
faces
grimper [grɛ̃pe] vi, vt to climb
grincer [grɛ̃se] vi (objet métallique) to
grate; (plancher, porte) to creak; **~ des
dents** to grind one's teeth
grincheux, -euse [grɛ̃ʃø, øz] adj
grumpy
grippe [grip] nf flu, influenza; **grippe
aviaire** bird flu; **grippé, e** adj: **être
grippé** to have flu
gris, e [gri, griz] adj grey; (ivre) tipsy
grisaille [grizaj] nf greyness, dullness
griser [grize] vt to intoxicate
grive [griv] nf thrush
Groenland [grɔɛnlɑ̃d] nm Greenland
grogner [grɔɲe] vi to growl; (fig) to
grumble; **grognon, ne** adj grumpy
grommeler [grɔm(ə)le] vi to mutter
to o.s.
gronder [grɔ̃de] vi to rumble; (fig:
révolte) to be brewing ▷ vt to scold; **se
faire ~** to get a telling-off
gros, se [gro, gros] adj big, large;
(obèse) fat; (travaux, dégâts) extensive;
(épais) thick; (rhume, averse) heavy
▷ adv: **risquer/gagner ~** to risk/win

a lot ▷ nm/f fat man/woman ▷ nm (Comm): **le ~** the wholesale business; **le ~ de** the bulk of; **prix de gros** wholesale price; **par ~ temps/grosse mer** in rough weather/heavy seas; **en ~** roughly; (Comm) wholesale; **gros lot** jackpot; **gros mot** swearword; **gros plan** (Photo) close-up; **gros sel** cooking salt; **gros titre** headline; **grosse caisse** big drum

groseille [gʁozɛj] nf: **~ (rouge/blanche)** red/white currant; **groseille à maquereau** gooseberry

grosse [gʁos] adj voir **gros**; **grossesse** nf pregnancy; **grosseur** nf size; (tumeur) lump

grossier, -ière [gʁosje, jɛʁ] adj coarse; (insolent) rude; (dessin) rough; (travail) roughly done; (imitation, instrument) crude; (évident: erreur) gross; **grossièrement** adv (sommairement) roughly; (vulgairement) coarsely; **grossièreté** nf rudeness; (mot): **dire des grossièretés** to use coarse language

grossir [gʁosiʁ] vi (personne) to put on weight ▷ vt (exagérer) to exaggerate; (au microscope) to magnify; (suj: vêtement): **~ qn** to make sb look fatter

grossiste [gʁosist] nm/f wholesaler

grotesque [gʁotɛsk] adj (extravagant) grotesque; (ridicule) ludicrous

grotte [gʁot] nf cave

groupe [gʁup] nm group; **groupe de parole** support group; **groupe sanguin** blood group; **groupe scolaire** school complex; **grouper** vt to group; **se grouper** vi to group

grue [gʁy] nf crane

GSM [ʒeɛsɛm] nm, adj GSM

guenon [gənɔ̃] nf female monkey

guépard [gepaʁ] nm cheetah

guêpe [gɛp] nf wasp

guère [gɛʁ] adv (avec adjectif, adverbe): **ne ... ~** hardly; (avec verbe: pas beaucoup): **ne ... ~** + tournure négative + much; (pas souvent) hardly ever; (pas longtemps) tournure négative + (very) long; **il n'y a**

~ que/de there's hardly anybody (ou anything) but/hardly any; **ce n'est ~ difficile** it's hardly difficult; **nous n'avons ~ le temps** we have hardly any time

guérilla [geʁija] nf guerrilla warfare

guérillero [geʁijeʁo] nm guerrilla

guérir [geʁiʁ] vt (personne, maladie) to cure; (membre, plaie) to heal ▷ vi (malade, maladie) to be cured; (blessure) to heal; **guérison** nf (de maladie) curing; (de membre, plaie) healing; (de malade) recovery; **guérisseur, -euse** nm/f healer

guerre [gɛʁ] nf war; **en ~** at war; **faire la ~ à** to wage war against; **guerre civile/mondiale** civil/world war; **guerrier, -ière** adj warlike ▷ nm/f warrior

guet [gɛ] nm: **faire le ~** to be on the watch ou look-out; **guet-apens** [gɛtapɑ̃] nm ambush; **guetter** vt (épier) to watch (intently); (attendre) to watch (out) for; (hostilement) to be lying in wait for

gueule [gœl] nf (d'animal) mouth; (fam: figure) face; (: bouche) mouth; **ta ~!** (fam) shut up!; **avoir la ~ de bois** (fam) to have a hangover, be hung over; **gueuler** (fam) vi to bawl

gui [gi] nm mistletoe

guichet [giʃɛ] nm (de bureau, banque) counter; **les ~s** (à la gare, au théâtre) the ticket office sg

guide [gid] nm (personne) guide; (livre) guide (book) ▷ nf (éclaireuse) girl guide; **guider** vt to guide

guidon [gidɔ̃] nm handlebars pl

guignol [giɲɔl] nm ≈ Punch and Judy show; (fig) clown

guillemets [gijmɛ] nmpl: **entre ~** in inverted commas

guindé, e [gɛ̃de] adj (personne, air) stiff, starchy; (style) stilted

Guinée [gine] nf Guinea

guirlande [giʁlɑ̃d] nf (fleurs) garland; **guirlande de Noël** tinsel garland

guise [giz] nf: **à votre ~** as you wish ou

please; **en ~ de** by way of
guitare [gitar] *nf* guitar
Guyane [gɥijan] *nf:* **la ~ (française)**
French Guiana
gym [ʒim] *nf (exercices)* gym; **gymnase**
nm gym(nasium); **gymnaste** *nm/f*
gymnast; **gymnastique** *nf* gymnastics
sg; (au réveil etc) keep-fit exercises *pl*
gynécologie [ʒinekɔlɔʒi] *nf*
gynaecology; **gynécologique** *adj*
gynaecological; **gynécologue** *nm/f*
gynaecologist

habile [abil] *adj* skilful; *(malin)* clever;
habileté [abilte] *nf* skill, skilfulness;
cleverness
habillé, e [abije] *adj* dressed; *(chic)*
dressy
habiller [abije] *vt* to dress; *(fournir en
vêtements)* to clothe; *(couvrir)* to cover;
s'habiller *vi* to dress (o.s.); *(se déguiser,
mettre des vêtements chic)* to dress up
habit [abi] *nm* outfit; **habits** *nmpl
(vêtements)* clothes; **habit (de soirée)**
evening dress; *(pour homme)* tails *pl*
habitant, e [abitɑ̃, ɑ̃t] *nm/f*
inhabitant; *(d'une maison)* occupant;
loger chez l'~ to stay with the locals
habitation [abitasjɔ̃] *nf* house;
habitations à loyer modéré (block of)
council flats
habiter [abite] *vt* to live in ▸ *vi:* **~
à/dans** to live in; **où habitez-vous?**
where do you live?
habitude [abityd] *nf* habit; **avoir l'~ de
qch** to be used to sth; **avoir l'~ de faire**
to be in the habit of doing; *(expérience)*

to be used to doing; **d'~** usually; **comme d'~** as usual

habitué, e [abitɥe] *nm/f (de maison)* regular visitor; *(de café)* regular (customer)

habituel, le [abitɥɛl] *adj* usual

habituer [abitɥe] *vt*: **~ qn à** to get sb used to; **s'habituer à** to get used to

'**hache** ['aʃ] *nf* axe

'**hacher** ['aʃe] *vt (viande)* to mince; *(persil)* to chop; '**hachis** *nm* mince *no pl*; '**hachis Parmentier** ≈ shepherd's pie

'**haie** ['ɛ] *nf* hedge; *(Sport)* hurdle

'**haillons** ['ajɔ̃] *nmpl* rags

'**haine** ['ɛn] *nf* hatred

'**haïr** ['aiʀ] *vt* to detest, hate

'**hâlé, e** ['ɑle] *adj* (sun)tanned, sunburnt

haleine [alɛn] *nf* breath; **hors d'~** out of breath; **tenir en ~** *(attention)* to hold spellbound; *(incertitude)* to keep in suspense; **de longue ~** long-term

'**haleter** ['alte] *vi* to pant

'**hall** ['ol] *nm* hall

'**halle** ['al] *nf* (covered) market; **halles** *nfpl (d'une grande ville)* central food market *sg*

hallucination [alysinasjɔ̃] *nf* hallucination

'**halte** ['alt] *nf* stop, break; *(endroit)* stopping place ▷ *excl* stop!; **faire halte** to stop

haltère [altɛʀ] *nm* dumbbell, barbell; **haltères** *nmpl*: **(poids) ~s** *(activité)* weightlifting *sg*; **haltérophilie** *nf* weightlifting

'**hamac** ['amak] *nm* hammock

'**hameau, x** ['amo] *nm* hamlet

hameçon [amsɔ̃] *nm (fish)* hook

'**hanche** ['ãʃ] *nf* hip

'**handball** ['ɑ̃dbal] *nm* handball

handicapé, e ['ɑ̃dikape] *adj* disabled, handicapped ▷ *nm/f* handicapped person; **handicapé mental/physique** mentally/physically handicapped person; **handicapé moteur** person with a movement disorder

'**hangar** ['ɑ̃gaʀ] *nm* shed; *(Aviat)* hangar

'**hanneton** ['antɔ̃] *nm* cockchafer

'**hanter** ['ɑ̃te] *vt* to haunt

'**hantise** ['ɑ̃tiz] *nf* obsessive fear

'**harceler** ['aʀsəle] *vt* to harass; **harceler qn de questions** to plague sb with questions

'**hardi, e** ['aʀdi] *adj* bold, daring

'**hareng** ['aʀɑ̃] *nm* herring; **hareng saur** kipper, smoked herring

'**hargne** ['aʀɲ] *nf* aggressiveness; '**hargneux, -euse** *adj* aggressive

'**haricot** ['aʀiko] *nm* bean; '**haricot blanc** haricot bean; '**haricot vert** green bean; '**haricot rouge** kidney bean

harmonica [aʀmɔnika] *nm* mouth organ

harmonie [aʀmɔni] *nf* harmony; **harmonieux, -euse** *adj* harmonious; *(couleurs, couple)* well-matched

'**harpe** ['aʀp] *nf* harp

'**hasard** ['azaʀ] *nm*: **le hasard** chance, fate; **un hasard** a coincidence; **au hasard** *(aller)* aimlessly; *(choisir)* at random; **par hasard** by chance; **à tout hasard** *(en cas de besoin)* just in case; *(en espérant trouver ce que l'on cherche)* on the off chance (BRIT)

'**hâte** ['ɑt] *nf* haste; **à la hâte** hurriedly, hastily; **en hâte** posthaste, with all possible speed; **avoir hâte de** to be eager *ou* anxious to; '**hâter** *vt* to hasten; **se hâter** *vi* to hurry; '**hâtif, -ive** *adj (travail)* hurried; *(décision, jugement)* hasty

'**hausse** ['os] *nf* rise, increase; **être en hausse** to be going up; '**hausser** *vt* to raise; **hausser les épaules** to shrug (one's shoulders)

'**haut, e** ['o, 'ot] *adj* high; *(grand)* tall ▷ *adv* high ▷ *nm* top (part); **de 3 m de haut** 3 m high, 3 m in height; **des hauts et des bas** ups and downs; **en haut lieu** in high places; **à haute voix, (tout) haut** aloud, out loud; **du haut de** from the top of; **de haut en bas** from top to bottom; **plus haut** higher up, further up; *(dans un texte)* above;

(*parler*) louder; **en haut** (*être/aller*) at/to the top; (*dans une maison*) upstairs; **en haut de** at the top of; **'haut débit** broadband

'hautain, e [otɛ̃, ɛn] *adj* haughty

'hautbois ['obwa] *nm* oboe

'hauteur ['otœʀ] *nf* height; **à la hauteur de** (*accident*) near; (*fig: tâche, situation*) equal to; **à la hauteur** (*fig*) up to it

'haut-parleur *nm* (loud)speaker

Hawaï [awai] *n*: **les îles ~** Hawaii

'Haye ['ɛ] *n*: **la Haye** the Hague

hebdomadaire [ɛbdɔmadɛʀ] *adj, nm* weekly

hébergement [ebɛʀʒəmɑ̃] *nm* accommodation

héberger [ebɛʀʒe] *vt* (*touristes*) to accommodate, lodge; (*amis*) to put up; (*réfugiés*) to take in

hébergeur [ebɛʀʒœʀ] *nm* (Internet) host

hébreu, x [ebʀø] *adj m, nm* Hebrew

Hébrides [ebʀid] *nf*: **les ~** the Hebrides

hectare [ɛktaʀ] *nm* hectare

hein ['ɛ̃] *excl* eh?

'hélas ['elas] *excl* alas! ▷ *adv* unfortunately

'héler [ele] *vt* to hail

hélice [elis] *nf* propeller

hélicoptère [elikɔptɛʀ] *nm* helicopter

helvétique [ɛlvetik] *adj* Swiss

hématome [ematom] *nm* nasty bruise

hémisphère [emisfɛʀ] *nm*: **l'~ nord/sud** the northern/southern hemisphere

hémorragie [emɔʀaʒi] *nf* bleeding no pl, haemorrhage

hémorroïdes [em'ʀid] *nfpl* piles, haemorrhoids

'hennir ['eniʀ] *vi* to neigh, whinny

hépatite [epatit] *nf* hepatitis

herbe [ɛʀb] *nf* grass; (*Culin, Méd*) herb; **~s de Provence** mixed herbs; **en ~** unripe; (*fig*) budding; **herbicide** *nm* weed-killer; **herboriste** *nm/f* herbalist

héréditaire [eʀeditɛʀ] *adj* hereditary

'hérisson ['eʀisɔ̃] *nm* hedgehog

héritage [eʀitaʒ] *nm* inheritance; (*coutumes, système*) heritage, legacy

hériter [eʀite] *vi*: **~ de qch (de qn)** to inherit sth (from sb); **héritier, -ière** *nm/f* heir(-ess)

hermétique [ɛʀmetik] *adj* airtight; watertight; (*fig: obscur*) abstruse; (*: impénétrable*) impenetrable

hermine [ɛʀmin] *nf* ermine

hernie ['ɛʀni] *nf* hernia

héroïne [eʀɔin] *nf* heroine; (*drogue*) heroin

héroïque [eʀɔik] *adj* heroic

'héron ['eʀɔ̃] *nm* heron

'héros ['eʀo] *nm* hero

hésitant, e [ezitɑ̃, ɑ̃t] *adj* hesitant

hésitation [ezitasjɔ̃] *nf* hesitation

hésiter [ezite] *vi*: **~ (à faire)** to hesitate (to do)

hétérosexuel, le [eteʀosɛksɥɛl] *adj* heterosexual

'hêtre ['ɛtʀ] *nm* beech

heure [œʀ] *nf* hour; (*Scol*) period; (*moment*) time; **c'est l'~** it's time; **quelle ~ est-il?** what time is it?; **2 ~s (du matin)** 2 o'clock (in the morning); **être à l'~** to be on time; (*montre*) to be right; **mettre à l'~** to set right; **à une ~ avancée (de la nuit)** at a late hour (of the night); **de bonne ~** early; **à toute ~** at any time; **24 ~s sur 24** round the clock, 24 hours a day; **à l'~ qu'il est** at this time (of day); by now; **sur l'~** at once; **à quelle ~ ouvre le musée/magasin?** what time does the museum/shop open?; **heures de bureau** office hours; **heure de pointe** rush hour; (*téléphone*) peak period; **heures supplémentaires** overtime sg

heureusement [œʀøzmɑ̃] *adv* (*par bonheur*) fortunately, luckily

heureux, -euse [œʀø, øz] *adj* happy; (*chanceux*) lucky, fortunate

'heurt ['œʀ] *nm* (*choc*) collision; (*conflit*) clash

'heurter ['œʀte] *vt* (*mur*) to strike, hit; (*personne*) to collide with

hexagone [ɛgzagɔn] nm hexagon; **l'H~** (la France) France (because of its shape)

hiberner [ibɛʀne] vi to hibernate

hibou, x ['ibu] nm owl

hideux, -euse ['idø, øz] adj hideous

hier [jɛʀ] adv yesterday; **~ matin/midi** yesterday morning/lunchtime; **~ soir** last night, yesterday evening; **toute la journée d'~** all day yesterday; **toute la matinée d'~** all yesterday morning

hiérarchie ['jeʀaʀʃi] nf hierarchy

hindou, e [ɛ̃du] adj Hindu ▷ nm/f: **H~, e** Hindu

hippique [ipik] adj equestrian, horse cpd; **un club ~** a riding centre; **un concours ~** a horse show; **hippisme** nm (horse)riding

hippodrome [ipɔdʀom] nm racecourse

hippopotame [ipɔpɔtam] nm hippopotamus

hirondelle [iʀɔ̃dɛl] nf swallow

hisser ['ise] vt to hoist, haul up

histoire [istwaʀ] nf (science, événements) history; (anecdote, récit, mensonge) story; (affaire) business no pl; **histoires** nfpl (chichis) fuss no pl; (ennuis) trouble sg; **historique** adj historical; (important) historic ▷ nm: **faire l'historique de** to give the background to

'hit-parade ['itpaʀad] nm: **le hit-parade** the charts

hiver [ivɛʀ] nm winter; **hivernal, e, -aux** adj winter cpd; (glacial) wintry; **hiverner** vi to winter

HLM nm ou f (= habitation à loyer modéré) council flat; **des ~** council housing

hobby ['ɔbi] nm hobby

hocher ['ɔʃe] vt: **hocher la tête** to nod; (signe négatif ou dubitatif) to shake one's head

hockey ['ɔkɛ] nm: **hockey (sur glace/gazon)** (ice/field) hockey

hold-up ['ɔldœp] nm inv hold-up

hollandais, e ['ɔlɑ̃dɛ, ɛz] adj Dutch ▷ nm (Ling) Dutch ▷ nm/f: **Hollandais, e** Dutchman(-woman)

'Hollande ['ɔlɑ̃d] nf: **la Hollande** Holland

'homard ['ɔmaʀ] nm lobster

homéopathique [ɔmeɔpatik] adj homoeopathic

homicide [ɔmisid] nm murder; **homicide involontaire** manslaughter

hommage [ɔmaʒ] nm tribute; **rendre ~ à** to pay tribute to

homme [ɔm] nm man; **homme d'affaires** businessman; **homme d'État** statesman; **homme de main** hired man; **homme de paille** stooge; **l'homme de la rue** the man in the street

homo...: homogène adj homogeneous; **homologue** nm/f counterpart; **homologué, e** adj (Sport) ratified; (tarif) authorized; **homonyme** nm (Ling) homonym; (d'une personne) namesake; **homosexuel; homosexuel, le** adj homosexual

'Hong Kong ['ɔ̃gkɔ̃g] n Hong Kong

'Hongrie ['ɔ̃gʀi] nf: **la Hongrie** Hungary; **'hongrois, e** adj Hungarian ▷ nm/f: **Hongrois, e** Hungarian ▷ nm (Ling) Hungarian

honnête [ɔnɛt] adj (intègre) honest; (juste, satisfaisant) fair; **honnêtement** adv honestly; **honnêteté** nf honesty

honneur [ɔnœʀ] nm honour; (mérite) credit; **en l'~ de** in honour of; (événement) on the occasion of; **faire ~ à** (engagements) to honour; (famille) to be a credit to; (fig: repas etc) to do justice to

honorable [ɔnɔʀabl] adj worthy, honourable; (suffisant) decent

honoraire [ɔnɔʀɛʀ] adj honorary; **professeur ~** professor emeritus; **honoraires** nmpl fees

honorer [ɔnɔʀe] vt to honour; (estimer) to hold in high regard; (faire honneur à) to do credit to

'honte ['ɔ̃t] nf shame; **avoir honte de** to be ashamed of; **faire honte à qn** to make sb (feel) ashamed; **'honteux, -euse** adj ashamed; (conduite, acte) shameful, disgraceful

hôpital, -aux [ɔpital, o] nm hospital; **où est l'~ le plus proche?** where is the nearest hospital?

'hoquet [ɔkɛ] nm: **avoir le hoquet** to have (the) hiccoughs

horaire [ɔʀɛʀ] adj hourly ▷ nm timetable, schedule; **horaires** nmpl (d'employé) hours; **horaire souple** flexitime

horizon [ɔʀizɔ̃] nm horizon

horizontal, e, -aux [ɔʀizɔ̃tal, o] adj horizontal

horloge [ɔʀlɔʒ] nf clock; **l'~ parlante** the speaking clock; **horloger, -ère** nm/f watchmaker; clockmaker

'hormis [ˈɔʀmi] prép save

horoscope [ˈɔʀɔskɔp] nm horoscope

horreur [ɔʀœʀ] nf horror; **quelle ~!** how awful!; **avoir ~ de** to loathe or detest; **horrible** adj horrible; **horrifier** vt to horrify

'hors [ˈɔʀ] prép: **hors de** out of; **hors pair** outstanding; **hors de propos** inopportune; **être hors de soi** to be beside o.s.; **hors d'usage** out of service; **'hors-bord** nm inv speedboat (with outboard motor); **'hors-d'œuvre** nm inv hors d'œuvre; **'hors-la-loi** nm inv outlaw; **'hors-service** adj inv out of order; **'hors-taxe** adj (boutique, articles) duty-free

hortensia [ɔʀtɑ̃sja] nm hydrangea

hospice [ɔspis] nm (de vieillards) home

hospitalier, -ière [ɔspitalje, jɛʀ] adj (accueillant) hospitable; (Méd: service, centre) hospital cpd

hospitaliser [ɔspitalize] vt to take/send to hospital, hospitalize

hospitalité [ɔspitalite] nf hospitality

hostie [ɔsti] nf host (Rel)

hostile [ɔstil] adj hostile; **hostilité** nf hostility

hôte [ot] nm (maître de maison) host; (invité) guest

hôtel [otɛl] nm hotel; **aller à l'~** to stay in a hotel; **hôtel de ville** town hall; **hôtel (particulier)** (private) mansion; **hôtellerie** nf hotel business

hôtesse [otɛs] nf hostess; **hôtesse (de l'air)** stewardess, air hostess (BRIT)

'houblon [ˈublɔ̃] nm (Bot) hop; (pour la bière) hops pl

'houille [ˈuj] nf coal; **'houille blanche** hydroelectric power

'houle [ˈul] nf swell; **'houleux, -euse** adj stormy

'hourra [ˈuʀa] excl hurrah!

'housse [ˈus] nf cover

'houx [ˈu] nm holly

'hublot [ˈyblo] nm porthole

'huche [ˈyʃ] nf: **huche à pain** bread bin

'huer [ˈɥe] vt to boo

huile [ɥil] nf oil

huissier [ɥisje] nm usher; (Jur) bailiff

'huit [ˈɥi(t)] num eight; **samedi en huit** a week on Saturday; **dans huit jours** in a week; **'huitaine** nf: **une huitaine (de jours)** a week or so; **'huitième** num eighth

huître [ɥitʀ] nf oyster

humain, e [ymɛ̃, ɛn] adj human; (compatissant) humane ▷ nm (être) human (being); **humanitaire** adj humanitarian; **humanité** nf humanity

humble [œ̃bl] adj humble

'humer [ˈyme] vt (plat) to smell; (parfum) to inhale

humeur [ymœʀ] nf mood; **de bonne/mauvaise ~** in a good/bad mood

humide [ymid] adj damp; (main, yeux) moist; (climat, chaleur) humid; (saison, route) wet

humilier [ymilje] vt to humiliate

humilité [ymilite] nf humility, humbleness

humoristique [ymɔʀistik] adj

humorous

humour [ymur] nm humour; **avoir de l'~** to have a sense of humour; **humour noir** black humour

'huppé, e ['ype] (fam) adj posh

'hurlement ['yʀləmɑ̃] nm howling no pl, howl, yelling no pl, yell

'hurler ['yʀle] vi to howl, yell

'hutte ['yt] nf hut

hydratant, e [idʀatɑ̃, ɑ̃t] adj (crème) moisturizing

hydraulique [idʀolik] adj hydraulic

hydravion [idʀavjɔ̃] nm seaplane

hydrogène [idʀoʒɛn] nm hydrogen

hydroglisseur [idʀoglisœʀ] nm hydroplane

hyène [jɛn] nf hyena

hygiène [iʒjɛn] nf hygiene

hygiénique [iʒjenik] adj hygienic

hymne [imn] nm hymn

hyperlien [ipɛʀljɛ̃] nm hyperlink

hypermarché [ipɛʀmaʀʃe] nm hypermarket

hypermétrope [ipɛʀmetʀɔp] adj long-sighted

hypertension [ipɛʀtɑ̃sjɔ̃] nf high blood pressure

hypnose [ipnoz] nf hypnosis; **hypnotiser** vt to hypnotize

hypocrisie [ipɔkʀizi] nf hypocrisy; **hypocrite** adj hypocritical

hypothèque [ipɔtɛk] nf mortgage

hypothèse [ipotɛz] nf hypothesis

hystérique [isteʀik] adj hysterical

iceberg [ajsbɛʀɡ] nm iceberg

ici [isi] adv here; **jusqu'~** as far as this; (temps) so far; **d'~ demain** by tomorrow; **d'~ là** by then, in the meantime; **d'~ peu** before long

icône [ikon] nf icon

idéal, e, -aux [ideal, o] adj ideal ⊳ nm ideal; **idéaliste** adj idealistic ⊳ nm/f idealist

idée [ide] nf idea; **avoir dans l'~ que** to have an idea that; **se faire des ~s** to imagine things, get ideas into one's head; **avoir des ~s noires** to have black ou dark thoughts; **idées reçues** received wisdom sg

identifier [idɑ̃tifje] vt to identify; **s'identifier** vi: **s'~ avec** ou **à qn/qch** (héros etc) to identify with sb/sth

identique [idɑ̃tik] adj: **~ (à)** identical (to)

identité [idɑ̃tite] nf identity

idiot, e [idjo, idjɔt] adj idiotic ⊳ nm/f idiot

idole [idɔl] nf idol

if [if] nm yew

ignoble [iɲɔbl] adj vile

ignorant, e [iɲɔʀɑ̃, ɑ̃t] adj ignorant; **~ de** ignorant of, not aware of

ignorer [iɲɔʀe] vt not to know; (personne) to ignore

il [il] pron he; (animal, chose, en tournure impersonnelle) it; **il fait froid** it's cold; **Pierre est-il arrivé?** has Pierre arrived?; **il a gagné** he won; voir aussi **avoir**

île [il] nf island; **l'Île Maurice** Mauritius; **les îles anglo-normandes** the Channel Islands; **les îles britanniques** the British Isles

illégal, e, -aux [i(l)legal, o] adj illegal

illimité, e [i(l)limite] adj unlimited

illisible [i(l)lizibl] adj illegible; (roman) unreadable

illogique [i(l)lɔʒik] adj illogical

illuminer [i(l)lymine] vt to light up; (monument, rue: pour une fête) to illuminate; (: au moyen de projecteurs) to floodlight

illusion [i(l)lyzjɔ̃] nf illusion; **se faire des ~s** to delude o.s.; **faire ~** to delude ou fool people

illustration [i(l)lystrasjɔ̃] nf illustration

illustré, e [i(l)lystre] adj illustrated ▷ nm comic

illustrer [i(l)lystre] vt to illustrate; **s'illustrer** to become famous, win fame

ils [il] pron they

image [imaʒ] nf (gén) picture; (métaphore) image; **image de marque** brand image; (fig) public image; **imagé, e** adj (texte) full of imagery; (langage) colourful

imaginaire [imaʒinɛʀ] adj imaginary

imagination [imaʒinasjɔ̃] nf imagination; **avoir de l'~** to be imaginative

imaginer [imaʒine] vt to imagine; (inventer: expédient) to devise, think up; **s'imaginer** vt (se figurer: scène etc) to imagine, picture; **s'~ que** to imagine that

imbécile [ɛ̃besil] adj idiotic ▷ nm/f idiot

imbu, e [ɛ̃by] adj: **~ de** full of

imitateur, -trice [imitatœʀ, tʀis] nm/f (gén) imitator; (Music-Hall) impersonator

imitation [imitasjɔ̃] nf imitation; (de personnalité) impersonation

imiter [imite] vt to imitate; (contrefaire) to forge; (ressembler à) to look like

immangeable [ɛ̃mɑ̃ʒabl] adj inedible

immatriculation [imatʀikylasjɔ̃] nf registration

○ **IMMATRICULATION**

○ The last two numbers on vehicle
○ licence plates show which
○ 'département' of France the vehicle
○ is registered in. For example, a car
○ registered in Paris has the number 75
○ on its licence plates.

immatriculer [imatʀikyle] vt to register; **faire/se faire ~** to register

immédiat, e [imedja, at] adj immediate ▷ nm: **dans l'~** for the time being; **immédiatement** adv immediately

immense [i(m)mɑ̃s] adj immense

immerger [imɛʀʒe] vt to immerse, submerge

immeuble [imœbl] nm building; (à usage d'habitation) block of flats

immigration [imigʀasjɔ̃] nf immigration

immigré, e [imigʀe] nm/f immigrant

imminent, e [iminɑ̃, ɑ̃t] adj imminent

immobile [i(m)mɔbil] adj still, motionless

immobilier, -ière [imɔbilje, jɛʀ] adj property cpd ▷ nm: **l'~** the property business

immobiliser [imɔbilize] vt (gén) to immobilize; (circulation, véhicule, affaires) to bring to a standstill; **s'immobiliser** (personne) to stand still; (machine, véhicule) to come to a halt

immoral, e, -aux [i(m)mɔʀal, o] *adj* immoral

immortel, le [imɔʀtɛl] *adj* immortal

immunisé, e [im(m)ynize] *adj*: **~ contre** immune to

immunité [imynite] *nf* immunity

impact [ɛ̃pakt] *nm* impact

impair, e [ɛ̃pɛʀ] *adj* odd ▷ *nm* faux pas, blunder

impardonnable [ɛ̃paʀdɔnabl] *adj* unpardonable, unforgivable

imparfait, e [ɛ̃paʀfɛ, ɛt] *adj* imperfect

impartial, e, -aux [ɛ̃paʀsjal, o] *adj* impartial, unbiased

impasse [ɛ̃pas] *nf* dead end, cul-de-sac; *(fig)* deadlock

impassible [ɛ̃pasibl] *adj* impassive

impatience [ɛ̃pasjɑ̃s] *nf* impatience

impatient, e [ɛ̃pasjɑ̃, jɑ̃t] *adj* impatient; **impatienter: s'impatienter** *vi* to get impatient

impeccable [ɛ̃pekabl] *adj (parfait)* perfect; *(propre)* impeccable; *(fam)* smashing

impensable [ɛ̃pɑ̃sabl] *adj (événement hypothétique)* unthinkable; *(événement qui a eu lieu)* unbelievable

impératif, -ive [ɛ̃peʀatif, iv] *adj* imperative ▷ *nm (Ling)* imperative; **impératifs** *nmpl (exigences: d'une fonction, d'une charge)* requirements; *(: de la mode)* demands

impératrice [ɛ̃peʀatʀis] *nf* empress

imperceptible [ɛ̃pɛʀsɛptibl] *adj* imperceptible

impérial, e, -aux [ɛ̃peʀjal, jo] *adj* imperial

impérieux, -euse [ɛ̃peʀjø, jøz] *adj (caractère, ton)* imperious; *(obligation, besoin)* pressing, urgent

impérissable [ɛ̃peʀisabl] *adj* undying

imperméable [ɛ̃pɛʀmeabl] *adj* waterproof; *(fig)*: **~ à** impervious to ▷ *nm* raincoat

impertinent, e [ɛ̃pɛʀtinɑ̃, ɑ̃t] *adj* impertinent

impitoyable [ɛ̃pitwajabl] *adj* pitiless, merciless

implanter [ɛ̃plɑ̃te]: **s'implanter** *vi* to be set up

impliquer [ɛ̃plike] *vt* to imply; **~ qn (dans)** to implicate sb (in)

impoli, e [ɛ̃pɔli] *adj* impolite, rude

impopulaire [ɛ̃pɔpylɛʀ] *adj* unpopular

importance [ɛ̃pɔʀtɑ̃s] *nf* importance; *(de somme)* size; *(de retard, dégâts)* extent; **sans ~** unimportant

important, e [ɛ̃pɔʀtɑ̃, ɑ̃t] *adj* important; *(en quantité: somme, retard)* considerable, sizeable; *(: dégâts)* extensive; *(péj: airs, ton)* self-important ▷ *nm*: **l'~** the important thing

importateur, -trice [ɛ̃pɔʀtatœʀ, tʀis] *nm/f* importer

importation [ɛ̃pɔʀtasjɔ̃] *nf* importation; *(produit)* import

importer [ɛ̃pɔʀte] *vt (Comm)* to import; *(maladies, plantes)* to introduce ▷ *vi (être important)* to matter; **il importe qu'il fasse** it's important that he should do; **peu m'importe** *(je n'ai pas de préférence)* I don't mind; *(je m'en moque)* I don't care; **peu importe (que)** it doesn't matter (if); *voir aussi* **n'importe**

importun, e [ɛ̃pɔʀtœ̃, yn] *adj* irksome, importunate; *(arrivée, visite)* inopportune, ill-timed ▷ *nm* intruder; **importuner** *vt* to bother

imposant, e [ɛ̃pozɑ̃, ɑ̃t] *adj* imposing

imposer [ɛ̃poze] *vt (taxer)* to tax; **s'imposer** *(être nécessaire)* to be imperative; **~ qch à qn** to impose sth on sb; **en ~ à** to impress; **s'~ comme** to emerge as; **s'~ par** to win recognition through

impossible [ɛ̃posibl] *adj* impossible; **il m'est ~ de le faire** it is impossible for me to do it, I can't possibly do it; **faire l'~** to do one's utmost

imposteur [ɛ̃postœʀ] *nm* impostor

impôt [ɛ̃po] *nm* tax; **impôt foncier** land tax; **impôt sur le chiffre d'affaires** corporation (BRIT) ou corporate (US) tax; **impôt sur le revenu** income tax; **impôts locaux** rates, local taxes (US),

~ council tax (BRIT)

impotent, e [ɛ̃pɔtɑ̃, ɑ̃t] adj disabled
impraticable [ɛ̃pratikabl] adj (projet)
impracticable, unworkable; (piste)
impassable

imprécis, e [ɛ̃presi, iz] adj imprecise
imprégner [ɛ̃preɲe] vt (tissu)
to impregnate; (lieu, air) to fill;
s'imprégner de (fig) to absorb
imprenable [ɛ̃prənabl] adj (forteresse)
impregnable; **vue ~** unimpeded
outlook

impression [ɛ̃presjɔ̃] nf impression;
(d'un ouvrage, tissu) printing; **faire
bonne/mauvaise ~** to make a good/
bad impression; **impressionnant, e**
adj (imposant) impressive; (bouleversant)
upsetting; **impressionner** vt (frapper)
to impress; (bouleverser) to upset

imprévisible [ɛ̃previzibl] adj
unforeseeable

imprévu, e [ɛ̃prevy] adj unforeseen,
unexpected ▷ nm (incident) unexpected
incident; **des vacances pleines d'~**
holidays full of surprises; **en cas d'~** if
anything unexpected happens; **sauf ~**
unless anything unexpected crops up

imprimante [ɛ̃primɑ̃t] nf printer;
imprimante (à) laser laser printer
imprimé [ɛ̃prime] nm (formulaire)
printed form; (Postes) printed matter
no pl; (tissu) printed fabric; **~ à fleur**
floral print

imprimer [ɛ̃prime] vt to print; (publier)
to publish; **imprimerie** nf printing;
(établissement) printing works sg;
imprimeur nm printer

impropre [ɛ̃prɔpr] adj inappropriate;
~ à unfit for

improviser [ɛ̃prɔvize] vt, vi to
improvise

improviste [ɛ̃prɔvist]: **à l'~** adv
unexpectedly, without warning

imprudence [ɛ̃prydɑ̃s] nf (d'une
personne, d'une action) carelessness no
pl; (d'une remarque) imprudence no pl;
commettre une ~ to do something
foolish

imprudent, e [ɛ̃prydɑ̃, ɑ̃t] adj
(conducteur, geste, action) careless;
(remarque) unwise, imprudent; (projet)
foolhardy

impuissant, e [ɛ̃pɥisɑ̃, ɑ̃t] adj
helpless; (sans effet) ineffectual;
(sexuellement) impotent

impulsif, -ive [ɛ̃pylsif, iv] adj
impulsive

impulsion [ɛ̃pylsjɔ̃] nf (Élec, instinct)
impulse; (élan, influence) impetus

inabordable [inabɔrdabl] adj (cher)
prohibitive

inacceptable [inakseptabl] adj
unacceptable

inaccessible [inaksesibl] adj
inaccessible; **~ à** impervious to

inachevé, e [ina∫(ə)ve] adj unfinished

inactif, -ive [inaktif, iv] adj inactive;
(remède) ineffective; (Bourse: marché)
slack

inadapté, e [inadapte] adj (gén): **~ à**
not adapted to, unsuited to; (Psych)
maladjusted

inadéquat, e [inadekwa(t), kwat] adj
inadequate

inadmissible [inadmisibl] adj
inadmissible

inadvertance [inadvɛrtɑ̃s]: **par ~** adv
inadvertently

inanimé, e [inanime] adj (matière)
inanimate; (évanoui) unconscious; (sans
vie) lifeless

inanition [inanisjɔ̃] nf: **tomber d'~** to
faint with hunger (and exhaustion)

inaperçu, e [inapɛrsy] adj: **passer ~** to
go unnoticed

inapte [inapt] adj: **~ à** incapable of;
(Mil) unfit for

inattendu, e [inatɑ̃dy] adj
unexpected

inattentif, -ive [inatɑ̃tif, iv] adj
inattentive; **~ à** (dangers, détails)
heedless of; **inattention** nf lack of
attention; **une faute ou une erreur
d'inattention** a careless mistake

inaugurer [inogyre] vt (monument) to
unveil; (exposition, usine) to open; (fig)

to inaugurate

inavouable [inavwabl] *adj* shameful; (*bénéfices*) undisclosable

incalculable [ɛ̃kalkylabl] *adj* incalculable

incapable [ɛ̃kapabl] *adj* incapable; **~ de faire** incapable of doing; (*empêché*) unable to do

incapacité [ɛ̃kapasite] *nf* (*incompétence*) incapability; (*impossibilité*) incapacity; **dans l'~ de faire** unable to do

incarcérer [ɛ̃karsere] *vt* to incarcerate, imprison

incassable [ɛ̃kasabl] *adj* unbreakable

incendie [ɛ̃sɑ̃di] *nm* fire; **incendie criminel** arson *no pl*; **incendie de forêt** forest fire; **incendier** *vt* (*mettre le feu à*) to set fire to, set alight; (*brûler complètement*) to burn down

incertain, e [ɛ̃sɛrtɛ̃, ɛn] *adj* uncertain; (*temps*) unsettled; (*imprécis: contours*) indistinct, blurred; **incertitude** *nf* uncertainty

incessamment [ɛ̃sesamɑ̃] *adv* very shortly

incident [ɛ̃sidɑ̃] *nm* incident; **incident de parcours** minor hitch *or* setback; **incident technique** technical difficulties *pl*

incinérer [ɛ̃sinere] *vt* (*ordures*) to incinerate; (*mort*) to cremate

incisive [ɛ̃siziv] *nf* incisor

inciter [ɛ̃site] *vt*: **~ qn à (faire) qch** to encourage sb to (do) sth; (*à la révolte etc*) to incite sb to do sth

incivilité [ɛ̃sivilite] *nf* (*grossièreté*) incivility; **incivilités** *nfpl* antisocial behaviour *sg*

inclinable [ɛ̃klinabl] *adj*: **siège à dossier ~** reclining seat

inclination [ɛ̃klinasjɔ̃] *nf* (*penchant*) inclination

incliner [ɛ̃kline] *vt* (*pencher*) to tilt ▷ *vi*: **~ à qch/à faire** to incline towards sth/doing; **s'incliner** *vr* (*se pencher*) to bow; **s'~ devant** (*par respect*) to pay one's respects

inclure [ɛ̃klyr] *vt* to include; (*joindre à un envoi*) to enclose

inclus, e [ɛ̃kly, -yz] *pp de* **inclure** ▷ *adj* included; (*joint à un envoi*) enclosed ▷ *adv*: **est-ce que le service est ~?** is service included?; **jusqu'au 10 mars ~** until 10th March inclusive

incognito [ɛ̃kɔɲito] *adv* incognito ▷ *nm*: **garder l'~** to remain incognito

incohérent, e [ɛ̃kɔerɑ̃, ɑ̃t] *adj* (*comportement*) inconsistent; (*geste, langage, texte*) incoherent

incollable [ɛ̃kɔlabl] *adj* (*riz*) non-stick; **il est ~** (*fam*) he's got all the answers

incolore [ɛ̃kɔlɔr] *adj* colourless

incommoder [ɛ̃kɔmode] *vt* (*chaleur, odeur*): **~ qn** to bother sb

incomparable [ɛ̃kɔ̃parabl] *adj* incomparable

incompatible [ɛ̃kɔ̃patibl] *adj* incompatible

incompétent, e [ɛ̃kɔ̃petɑ̃, ɑ̃t] *adj* incompetent

incomplet, -ète [ɛ̃kɔ̃plɛ, ɛt] *adj* incomplete

incompréhensible [ɛ̃kɔ̃preɑ̃sibl] *adj* incomprehensible

incompris, e [ɛ̃kɔ̃pri, iz] *adj* misunderstood

inconcevable [ɛ̃kɔ̃s(ə)vabl] *adj* inconceivable

inconfortable [ɛ̃kɔ̃fɔrtabl(ə)] *adj* uncomfortable

incongru, e [ɛ̃kɔ̃gry] *adj* unseemly

inconnu, e [ɛ̃kɔny] *adj* unknown ▷ *nm/f* stranger ▷ *nm*: **l'~** the unknown; **inconnue** *nf* unknown factor

inconsciemment [ɛ̃kɔ̃sjamɑ̃] *adv* unconsciously

inconscient, e [ɛ̃kɔ̃sjɑ̃, jɑ̃t] *adj* unconscious; (*irréfléchi*) thoughtless, reckless; (*sentiment*) subconscious ▷ *nm* (*Psych*): **l'~** the unconscious; **~ de** unaware of

inconsidéré, e [ɛ̃kɔ̃sidere] *adj* ill-considered

inconsistant, e [ɛ̃kɔ̃sistɑ̃, ɑ̃t] *adj* (*fig*) flimsy, weak

inconsolable [ɛ̃kɔ̃sɔlabl] *adj*
inconsolable

incontestable [ɛ̃kɔ̃tɛstabl] *adj*
indisputable

incontinent, e [ɛ̃kɔ̃tinɑ̃, ɑ̃t] *adj*
incontinent

incontournable [ɛ̃kɔ̃turnabl] *adj*
unavoidable

incontrôlable [ɛ̃kɔ̃trolabl]
adj unverifiable; *(irrépressible)*
uncontrollable

inconvénient [ɛ̃kɔ̃venjɑ̃] *nm*
disadvantage, drawback; **si vous n'y
voyez pas d'**– if you have no objections

incorporer [ɛ̃kɔrpɔre] *vt*: **~ (à)** to
mix in (with); **~ (dans)** *(paragraphe
etc)* to incorporate (in); *(Mil: appeler)*
to recruit (into); **il a très bien su s'~
à notre groupe** he very easily
incorporated himself into our group

incorrect, e [ɛ̃kɔrɛkt] *adj (impropre,
inconvenant)* improper; *(défectueux)*
faulty; *(inexact)* incorrect; *(impoli)*
impolite; *(déloyal)* underhand

incorrigible [ɛ̃kɔriʒibl] *adj*
incorrigible

incrédule [ɛ̃kredyl] *adj* incredulous;
(Rel) unbelieving

incroyable [ɛ̃krwajabl] *adj* incredible

incruster [ɛ̃kryste] *vt (Art)* to inlay;
s'incruster *vi (invité)* to take root

inculpé, e [ɛ̃kylpe] *nm/f* accused

inculper [ɛ̃kylpe] *vt*: **~ (de)** to charge
(with)

inculquer [ɛ̃kylke] *vt*: **~ qch à** to
inculcate sth in ou instil sth into

Inde [ɛ̃d] *nf*: **l'~** India

indécent, e [ɛ̃desɑ̃, ɑ̃t] *adj* indecent

indécis, e [ɛ̃desi, iz] *adj (par nature)*
indecisive; *(temporairement)* undecided

indéfendable [ɛ̃defɑ̃dabl] *adj*
indefensible

indéfini, e [ɛ̃defini] *adj (imprécis,
incertain)* undefined; *(illimité, Ling)*
indefinite; **indéfiniment** *adv*
indefinitely; **indéfinissable** *adj*
indefinable

indélébile [ɛ̃delebil] *adj* indelible

indélicat, e [ɛ̃delika, at] *adj* tactless

indemne [ɛ̃dɛmn] *adj* unharmed;
indemniser *vt*: **indemniser qn (de)** to
compensate sb (for)

indemnité [ɛ̃dɛmnite] *nf*
(dédommagement) compensation *no pl*;
(allocation) allowance; **indemnité de
licenciement** redundancy payment

indépendamment [ɛ̃depɑ̃damɑ̃]
adv independently; **~ de** independently
of; irrespective of; *(en plus de)* over
and above

indépendance [ɛ̃depɑ̃dɑ̃s] *nf*
independence

indépendant, e [ɛ̃depɑ̃dɑ̃, ɑ̃t] *adj*
independent; **~ de** independent of;
travailleur ~ self-employed worker

indescriptible [ɛ̃dɛskriptibl] *adj*
indescribable

indésirable [ɛ̃dezirabl] *adj*
undesirable

indestructible [ɛ̃dɛstryktibl] *adj*
indestructible

indéterminé, e [ɛ̃detɛrmine] *adj
(date, cause, nature)* unspecified; *(forme,
longueur, quantité)* indeterminate

index [ɛ̃dɛks] *nm (doigt)* index finger;
(d'un livre etc) index; **mettre à l'~** to
blacklist

indicateur [ɛ̃dikatœr] *nm (Police)*
informer; *(Tech)* gauge, indicator ⊳ *adj*:
panneau ~ signpost; **indicateur des
chemins de fer** railway timetable;
indicateur de rues street directory

indicatif, -ive [ɛ̃dikatif, iv] *adj*: **à titre
~** for (your) information ⊳ *nm (Ling)*
indicative; *(Radio)* theme *ou* signature
tune; *(Tél)* dialling code (BRIT), area
code (US); **quel est l'~ de ...** what's the
code for ...?

indication [ɛ̃dikasjɔ̃] *nf* indication;
(renseignement) information *no
pl*; **indications** *nfpl (directives)*
instructions

indice [ɛ̃dis] *nm (marque, signe)*
indication, sign; *(Police: signe d'une
enquête)* clue; *(Jur: présomption)* piece
of evidence; *(Science, Écon, Tech)* index;

~ de protection (sun protection) factor
indicible [ɛ̃disibl] adj inexpressible
indien, ne [ɛ̃djɛ̃, jɛn] adj Indian
  ▷ nm/f: **I~, ne** Indian
indifféremment [ɛ̃difeʀamɑ̃] adv
  (sans distinction) equally (well)
indifférence [ɛ̃difeʀɑ̃s] nf indifference
indifférent, e [ɛ̃difeʀɑ̃, ɑ̃t] adj (peu
  intéressé) indifferent; **ça m'est ~** it
  doesn't matter to me; **elle m'est ~e**
  I am indifferent to her
indigène [ɛ̃diʒɛn] adj native,
  indigenous; (des gens du pays) local
  ▷ nm/f native
indigeste [ɛ̃diʒɛst] adj indigestible
indigestion [ɛ̃diʒɛstjɔ̃] nf indigestion
  no pl; **avoir une ~** to have indigestion
indigne [ɛ̃diɲ] adj unworthy
indigner [ɛ̃diɲe] vt: **s'~ de qch** to get
  annoyed about sth; **s'~ contre qn** to
  get annoyed with sb
indiqué, e [ɛ̃dike] adj (date, lieu)
  agreed; (traitement) appropriate;
  (conseillé) advisable
indiquer [ɛ̃dike] vt (suj: pendule, aiguille)
  to show; (: étiquette, panneau) to show,
  indicate; (renseigner sur) to point out,
  tell; (déterminer: date, lieu) to give, state;
  (signaler, dénoter) to indicate, point
  to; **~ qch/qn à qn** (montrer du doigt) to
  point sth/sb out to sb; (faire connaître:
  médecin, restaurant) to tell sb of sth/sb;
  pourriez-vous m'~ les toilettes/
  l'heure? could you direct me to the
  toilets/tell me the time?
indiscipliné, e [ɛ̃disipline] adj
  undisciplined
indiscret, -ète [ɛ̃diskʀɛ, ɛt] adj
  indiscreet
indiscutable [ɛ̃diskytabl] adj
  indisputable
indispensable [ɛ̃dispɑ̃sabl] adj
  indispensable, essential
indisposé, e [ɛ̃dispoze] adj indisposed
indistinct, e [ɛ̃distɛ̃(kt), ɛ̃kt] adj
  indistinct; **indistinctement** adv (voir,
  prononcer) indistinctly; (sans distinction)
  indiscriminately

individu [ɛ̃dividy] nm individual;
  individuel, le adj (gén) individual;
  (responsabilité, propriété, liberté)
  personal; **chambre individuelle** single
  room; **maison individuelle** detached
  house
indolore [ɛ̃dolɔʀ] adj painless
Indonésie [ɛ̃donezi] nf Indonesia
indu, e [ɛ̃dy] adj: **à une heure ~e** at
  some ungodly hour
indulgent, e [ɛ̃dylʒɑ̃, ɑ̃t] adj (parent,
  regard) indulgent; (juge, examinateur)
  lenient
industrialisé, e [ɛ̃dystʀijalize] adj
  industrialized
industrie [ɛ̃dystʀi] nf industry;
  industriel, le adj industrial ▷ nm
  industrialist
inébranlable [inebʀɑ̃labl] adj (masse,
  colonne) solid; (personne, certitude, foi)
  unshakeable
inédit, e [inedi, it] adj (correspondance,
  livre) hitherto unpublished; (spectacle,
  moyen) novel, original; (film) unreleased
inefficace [inefikas] adj (remède,
  moyen) ineffective; (machine, employé)
  inefficient
inégal, e, -aux [inegal, o] adj
  unequal; (irrégulier) uneven; **inégalable**
  adj matchless; **inégalé, e** adj (record)
  unequalled; (beauté) unrivalled;
  inégalité nf inequality
inépuisable [inepɥizabl] adj
  inexhaustible
inerte [inɛʀt] adj (immobile) lifeless;
  (sans réaction) passive
inespéré, e [inɛspeʀe] adj
  unexpected, unhoped-for
inestimable [inɛstimabl] adj
  priceless; (fig: bienfait) invaluable
inévitable [inevitabl] adj
  unavoidable; (fatal, habituel) inevitable
inexact, e [inegza(kt), akt] adj
  inaccurate
inexcusable [inɛkskyzabl] adj
  unforgivable
inexplicable [inɛksplikabl] adj
  inexplicable

in extremis [inɛkstremis] adv at the last minute ▷ adj last-minute

infaillible [ɛ̃fajibl] adj infallible

infarctus [ɛ̃farktys] nm: ~ **(du myocarde)** coronary (thrombosis)

infatigable [ɛ̃fatigabl] adj tireless

infect, e [ɛ̃fɛkt] adj revolting; (personne) obnoxious; (temps) foul

infecter [ɛ̃fɛkte] vt (atmosphère, eau) to contaminate; (Méd) to infect; **s'infecter** to become infected ou septic; **infection** nf infection; (puanteur) stench

inférieur, e [ɛ̃ferjœr] adj lower; (en qualité, intelligence) inferior; ~ **à** (somme, quantité) less ou smaller than; (moins bon que) inferior to

infernal, e, -aux [ɛ̃fɛrnal, o] adj (insupportable: chaleur, rythme) infernal; (: enfant) horrid; (satanique, effrayant) diabolical

infidèle [ɛ̃fidɛl] adj unfaithful

infiltrer [ɛ̃filtre]: **s'infiltrer** vr: **s'~ dans** to get into; (liquide) to seep through; (fig: groupe, ennemi) to infiltrate

infime [ɛ̃fim] adj minute, tiny

infini, e [ɛ̃fini] adj infinite ▷ nm infinity; **à l'~** endlessly; **infiniment** adv infinitely; **infinité** nf: **une infinité de** an infinite number of

infinitif [ɛ̃finitif] nm infinitive

infirme [ɛ̃firm] adj disabled ▷ nm/f disabled person

infirmerie [ɛ̃firməri] nf medical room

infirmier, -ière [ɛ̃firmje] nm/f nurse; **infirmière chef** sister

infirmité [ɛ̃firmite] nf disability

inflammable [ɛ̃flamabl] adj (in)flammable

inflation [ɛ̃flasjɔ̃] nf inflation

influençable [ɛ̃flyɑ̃sabl] adj easily influenced

influence [ɛ̃flyɑ̃s] nf influence; **influencer** vt to influence; **influent, e** adj influential

informaticien, ne [ɛ̃fɔrmatisjɛ̃, jɛn] nm/f computer scientist

information [ɛ̃fɔrmasjɔ̃] nf (renseignement) piece of information; (Presse, TV: nouvelle) item of news; (diffusion de renseignements, Inform) information; (Jur) inquiry, investigation; **informations** nfpl (TV) news sg

informatique [ɛ̃fɔrmatik] nf (technique) data processing; (science) computer science ▷ adj computer cpd; **informatiser** to computerize

informer [ɛ̃fɔrme] vt: ~ **qn (de)** to inform sb (of): **s'informer** vr: **s'~ (de/si)** to inquire ou find out (about/ whether): **s'~ sur** to inform o.s. about

infos [ɛ̃fo] nfpl: **les ~** the news sg

infraction [ɛ̃fraksjɔ̃] nf offence; ~ **à** violation ou breach of; **être en ~** to be in breach of the law

infranchissable [ɛ̃frɑ̃ʃisabl] adj impassable; (fig) insuperable

infrarouge [ɛ̃fraruʒ] adj infrared

infrastructure [ɛ̃frastryktyr] nf (Aviat, Mil) ground installations pl; (Écon: touristique etc) infrastructure

infuser [ɛ̃fyze] vt, vi (thé) to brew; (tisane) to infuse; **infusion** nf (tisane) herb tea

ingénier [ɛ̃ʒenje]: **s'ingénier** vi: **s'~ à faire** to strive to do

ingénierie [ɛ̃ʒeniri] nf engineering

ingénieur [ɛ̃ʒenjœr] nm engineer; **ingénieur du son** sound engineer

ingénieux, -euse [ɛ̃ʒenjø, jøz] adj ingenious, clever

ingrat, e [ɛ̃gra, at] adj (personne) ungrateful; (travail, sujet) thankless; (visage) unprepossessing

ingrédient [ɛ̃gredjɑ̃] nm ingredient

inhabité, e [inabite] adj uninhabited

inhabituel, e [inabituel] adj unusual

inhibition [inibisjɔ̃] nf inhibition

inhumain, e [inymɛ̃, ɛn] adj inhuman

inimaginable [inimaʒinabl] adj unimaginable

ininterrompu, e [inɛ̃terɔ̃py] adj (file, série) unbroken; (flot, vacarme) uninterrupted, non-stop; (effort) unremitting, continuous; (suite, ligne) unbroken

initial, e, -aux [inisjal, jo] *adj* initial; **initiales** *nfpl* (d'un nom, sigle etc) initials

initiation [inisjasjɔ̃] *nf:* ~ **à** introduction to

initiative [inisjativ] *nf* initiative

initier [inisje] *vt:* ~ **qn à** to initiate sb into; (faire découvrir: art, jeu) to introduce sb to

injecter [ɛ̃ʒɛkte] *vt* to inject; **injection** *nf* injection; **à injection** (Auto) fuel injection *cpd*

injure [ɛ̃ʒyʀ] *nf* insult, abuse *no pl*; **injurier** *vt* to insult, abuse; **injurieux, -euse** *adj* abusive, insulting

injuste [ɛ̃ʒyst] *adj* unjust, unfair; **injustice** *nf* injustice

inlassable [ɛ̃lasabl] *adj* tireless

inné, e [i(n)ne] *adj* innate, inborn

innocent, e [inɔsɑ̃, ɑ̃t] *adj* innocent; **innocenter** *vt* to clear, prove innocent

innombrable [i(n)nɔ̃bʀabl] *adj* innumerable

innover [inɔve] *vi* to break new ground

inoccupé, e [inɔkype] *adj* unoccupied

inodore [inɔdɔʀ] *adj* (gaz) odourless; (fleur) scentless

inoffensif, -ive [inɔfɑ̃sif, iv] *adj* harmless, innocuous

inondation [inɔ̃dasjɔ̃] *nf* flood

inonder [inɔ̃de] *vt* to flood; ~ **de** to flood with

inopportun, e [inɔpɔʀtœ̃ yn] *adj* ill-timed, untimely

inoubliable [inublijabl] *adj* unforgettable

inouï, e [inwi] *adj* unheard-of, extraordinary

inox [inɔks] *nm* stainless steel

inquiet, -ète [ɛ̃kjɛ, ɛkjɛt] *adj* anxious; **inquiétant, e** *adj* worrying, disturbing; **inquiéter** *vt* to worry; **s'inquiéter** to worry; **s'inquiéter de** to worry about; (s'enquérir de) to inquire about; **inquiétude** *nf* anxiety

insaisissable [ɛ̃sezisabl] *adj* (fugitif, ennemi) elusive; (différence, nuance)

imperceptible

insalubre [ɛ̃salybʀ] *adj* insalubrious

insatisfait, e [ɛ̃satisfɛ, ɛt] *adj* (non comblé) unsatisfied; (mécontent) dissatisfied

inscription [ɛ̃skʀipsjɔ̃] *nf* inscription; (immatriculation) enrolment

inscrire [ɛ̃skʀiʀ] *vt* (marquer: sur son calepin etc) to note ou write down; (: sur un mur, une affiche etc) to write; (: dans la pierre, le métal) to inscribe; (mettre: sur une liste, un budget etc) to put down; **s'inscrire** (pour une excursion etc) to put one's name down; **s'~ (à)** (club, parti) to join; (université) to register ou enrol (at); (examen, concours) to register (for); ~ **qn à** (club, parti) to enrol sb at

insecte [ɛ̃sɛkt] *nm* insect; **insecticide** *nm* insecticide

insensé, e [ɛ̃sɑ̃se] *adj* mad

insensible [ɛ̃sɑ̃sibl] *adj* (nerf, membre) numb; (dur, indifférent) insensitive

inséparable [ɛ̃sepaʀabl] *adj* inseparable ▷ *nm:* ~**s** (oiseaux) lovebirds

insigne [ɛ̃siɲ] *nm* (d'un parti, club) badge; (d'une fonction) insignia ▷ *adj* distinguished

insignifiant, e [ɛ̃siɲifjɑ̃, ɑ̃t] *adj* insignificant; trivial

insinuer [ɛ̃sinɥe] *vt* to insinuate; **s'insinuer dans** (fig) to worm one's way into

insipide [ɛ̃sipid] *adj* insipid

insister [ɛ̃siste] *vi* to insist; (continuer à sonner) to keep on trying; ~ **sur** (détail, sujet) to lay stress on

insolation [ɛ̃sɔlasjɔ̃] *nf* (Méd) sunstroke *no pl*

insolent, e [ɛ̃sɔlɑ̃, ɑ̃t] *adj* insolent

insolite [ɛ̃sɔlit] *adj* strange, unusual

insomnie [ɛ̃sɔmni] *nf* insomnia *no pl*; **avoir des ~s** to sleep badly, not be able to sleep

insouciant, e [ɛ̃susjɑ̃, jɑ̃t] *adj* carefree; ~ **du danger** heedless of (the) danger

insoupçonnable [ɛ̃supsɔnabl] *adj* unsuspected; (personne) above suspicion

insoupçonné, e [ɛ̃supsɔne] adj
unsuspected

insoutenable [ɛ̃sut(ə)nabl] adj
(argument) untenable; (chaleur)
unbearable

inspecter [ɛ̃spɛkte] vt to inspect;
inspecteur, -trice nm/f inspector;
inspecteur d'Académie (regional)
director of education; **inspecteur
des finances** = tax inspector (BRIT),
= Internal Revenue Service agent
(US); **inspecteur (de police)** (police)
inspector; **inspection** nf inspection

inspirer [ɛ̃spire] vt (gén) to inspire ▷ vi
(aspirer) to breathe in; **s'inspirer** vr: **s'~
de** to be inspired by

instable [ɛ̃stabl] adj unstable; (meuble,
équilibre) unsteady; (temps) unsettled

installation [ɛ̃stalasjɔ̃] nf (mise en
place) installation; **installations** nfpl
(de sport, dans un camping) facilities;
l'installation électrique wiring

installer [ɛ̃stale] vt (loger, placer) to put;
(meuble, gaz, électricité) to put in; (rideau,
étagère, tente) to put up; (appartement)
to fit out; **s'installer** (s'établir: artisan,
dentiste etc) to set o.s. up; (se loger) to
settle; (emménager) to settle in; (sur
un siège, à un emplacement) to settle
(down); (fig: maladie, grève) to take a
firm hold

instance [ɛ̃stɑ̃s] nf (Admin: autorité)
authority; **affaire en ~** matter pending;
être en ~ de divorce to be awaiting
a divorce

instant [ɛ̃stɑ̃] nm moment, instant;
dans un ~ in a moment; **à l'~** this
instant; **je l'ai vu à l'~** I've just this
minute seen him, I saw him a moment
ago; **pour l'~** for the moment, for the
time being

instantané, e [ɛ̃stɑ̃tane] adj (lait, café)
instant; (explosion, mort) instantaneous
▷ nm snapshot

instar [ɛ̃staʀ]: **à l'~ de** prép following
the example of, like

instaurer [ɛ̃stɔʀe] vt to institute;

(couvre-feu) to impose; **s'instaurer** vr
(paix) to be established; (doute) to set in

instinct [ɛ̃stɛ̃] nm instinct;
instinctivement adv instinctively

instituer [ɛ̃stitɥe] vt to establish

institut [ɛ̃stity] nm institute; **institut
de beauté** beauty salon; **Institut
universitaire de technologie**
≈ polytechnic

instituteur, -trice [ɛ̃stitytœʀ, tʀis]
nm/f (primary school) teacher

institution [ɛ̃stitysjɔ̃] nf institution;
(collège) private school; **institutions**
nfpl (structures politiques et sociales)
institutions

instructif, -ive [ɛ̃stʀyktif, iv] adj
instructive

instruction [ɛ̃stʀyksjɔ̃] nf
(enseignement, savoir) education;
(Jur) (preliminary) investigation and
hearing; (directive) order; **instructions** nfpl (ordres, mode
d'emploi) instructions; **instruction
civique** civics sg

instruire [ɛ̃stʀɥiʀ] vt (élèves) to teach;
(recrues) to train; (Jur: affaire) to conduct
the investigation for; **s'instruire** to
educate o.s.; **instruit, e** adj educated

instrument [ɛ̃stʀymɑ̃] nm
instrument; **instrument à cordes/à
vent** stringed/wind instrument;
instrument de mesure measuring
instrument; **instrument de musique**
musical instrument; **instrument de
travail** (working) tool

insu [ɛ̃sy] nm: **à l'~ de qn** without sb
knowing (it)

insuffisant, e [ɛ̃syfizɑ̃, ɑ̃t] adj (en
quantité) insufficient; (en qualité)
inadequate; (sur une copie) poor

insulaire [ɛ̃sylɛʀ] adj island cpd;
(attitude) insular

insuline [ɛ̃sylin] nf insulin

insulte [ɛ̃sylt] nf insult; **insulter** vt
to insult

insupportable [ɛ̃sypɔʀtabl] adj
unbearable

insurmontable [ɛ̃syʀmɔ̃tabl] adj
(difficulté) insuperable; (aversion)

unconquerable

intact, e [ɛ̃takt] *adj* intact

intarissable [ɛ̃taʀisabl] *adj*
inexhaustible

intégral, e, -aux [ɛ̃tegʀal, o] *adj*
complete; **texte ~** unabridged
version; **bronzage ~** all-over tan;
intégralement *adv* in full; **intégralité**
nf whole; **dans son intégralité** in
full; **intégrant, e** *adj*: **faire partie
intégrante de** to be an integral part of

intègre [ɛ̃tegʀ] *adj* upright

intégrer [ɛ̃tegʀe] : **s'intégrer** *vr*: **s'~ à**
ou **dans qch** to become integrated into
sth; **bien s'~** to fit in

intégrisme [ɛ̃tegʀism] *nm*
fundamentalism

intellectuel, le [ɛ̃telɛktɥɛl] *adj*
intellectual ▷ *nm/f* intellectual; (*péj*)
highbrow

intelligence [ɛ̃teliʒɑ̃s] *nf* intelligence;
(*compréhension*): **l'~ de** the
understanding of; (*complicité*): **regard
d'~** glance of complicity; (*accord*): **vivre
en bonne ~ avec qn** to be on good
terms with sb

intelligent, e [ɛ̃teliʒɑ̃, ɑ̃t] *adj*
intelligent

intelligible [ɛ̃teliʒibl] *adj* intelligible

intempéries [ɛ̃tɑ̃peʀi] *nfpl* bad
weather *sg*

intenable [ɛ̃t(ə)nabl] *adj* (*chaleur*)
unbearable

intendant, e [ɛ̃tɑ̃dɑ̃] *nm/f* (*Mil*)
quartermaster; (*Scol*) bursar

intense [ɛ̃tɑ̃s] *adj* intense; **intensif,
-ive** *adj* intensive; **un cours intensif** a
crash course

intenter [ɛ̃tɑ̃te] *vt*: **~ un procès contre**
ou **à** to start proceedings against

intention [ɛ̃tɑ̃sjɔ̃] *nf* intention; (*Jur*)
intent; **avoir l'~ de faire** to intend
to do; **à l'~ de** for; (*renseignement*) for
the benefit of; (*film, ouvrage*) aimed
at; **à cette ~** with this aim in view;
intentionné, e *adj*: **bien intentionné**
well-meaning *ou* -intentioned; **mal
intentionné** ill-intentioned

interactif, -ive [ɛ̃tɛʀaktif, iv] *adj*
(*Comput*) interactive

intercepter [ɛ̃tɛʀsɛpte] *vt* to
intercept; (*lumière, chaleur*) to cut off

interchangeable [ɛ̃tɛʀʃɑ̃ʒabl] *adj*
interchangeable

interdiction [ɛ̃tɛʀdiksjɔ̃] *nf* ban;
interdiction de fumer no smoking

interdire [ɛ̃tɛʀdiʀ] *vt* to forbid; (*Admin*)
to ban, prohibit; (: *journal, livre*) to ban;
~ à qn de faire to forbid sb to do; (*suj:
empêchement*) to prevent sb from doing

interdit, e [ɛ̃tɛʀdi, it] *pp de* **interdire**
▷ *adj* (*stupéfait*) taken aback; **film ~ aux
moins de 18/12 ans** ≈ 18-/12A-rated
film; **stationnement ~** "no parking"

intéressant, e [ɛ̃teʀesɑ̃, ɑ̃t] *adj*
interesting; (*avantageux*) attractive

intéressé, e [ɛ̃teʀese] *adj* (*parties*)
involved, concerned; (*amitié, motifs*)
self-interested

intéresser [ɛ̃teʀese] *vt* (*captiver*) to
interest; (*toucher*) to be of interest to;
(*Admin: concerner*) to affect, concern;
s'intéresser *vr*: **s'~ à** to be interested in

intérêt [ɛ̃teʀɛ] *nm* interest; (*égoïsme*)
self-interest; **tu as ~ à accepter** it's
in your interest to accept; **tu as ~ à te
dépêcher** you'd better hurry

intérieur, e [ɛ̃teʀjœʀ] *adj* (*mur, escalier,
poche*) inside; (*commerce, politique*)
domestic; (*cour, calme, vie*) inner;
(*navigation*) inland ▷ *nm*: **l'~** (*d'une
maison, d'un récipient etc*) the inside;
(*d'un pays, aussi: décor, mobilier*) the
interior; **à l'~ (de)** inside; **ministère
de l'~e** ≈ Home Office (*BRIT*),
≈ Department of the Interior (*US*);
intérieurement *adv* inwardly

intérim [ɛ̃teʀim] *nm* interim period;
faire de l'~ to temp; **assurer l'~ (de)** to
deputize (for); **par ~** interim

intérimaire [ɛ̃teʀimɛʀ] *adj* (*directeur,
ministre*) acting; (*secrétaire, personnel*)
temporary ▷ *nm/f* (*secrétaire*)
temporary secretary, temp (*BRIT*)

interlocuteur, -trice [ɛ̃tɛʀlɔkytœʀ,
tʀis] *nm/f* speaker; **son ~** the person he

was speaking to

intermédiaire [ɛ̃tɛʀmedjɛʀ] adj intermediate; (solution) temporary ▷ nm/f intermediary; (Comm) middleman; **sans ~** directly; **par l'~ de** through

interminable [ɛ̃tɛʀminabl] adj endless

intermittence [ɛ̃tɛʀmitɑ̃s] nf: **par ~** sporadically, intermittently

internat [ɛ̃tɛʀna] nm boarding school

international, e, -aux [ɛ̃tɛʀnasjɔnal, o] adj, nm/f international

internaute [ɛ̃tɛʀnot] nm/f Internet user

interne [ɛ̃tɛʀn] adj internal ▷ nm/f (Scol) boarder; (Méd) houseman

Internet [ɛ̃tɛʀnɛt] nm: **l'~** the Internet

interpeller [ɛ̃tɛʀpəle] vt (appeler) to call out to; (apostropher) to shout at; (Police, Pol) to question; (concerner) to concern

interphone [ɛ̃tɛʀfɔn] nm intercom; (d'immeuble) entry phone

interposer [ɛ̃tɛʀpoze] vt: **s'interposer** to intervene; **par personnes interposées** through a third party

interprète [ɛ̃tɛʀpʀɛt] nm/f interpreter; (porte-parole) spokesperson; **pourriez-vous nous servir d'~?** could you act as our interpreter?

interpréter [ɛ̃tɛʀpʀete] vt to interpret; (jouer) to play; (chanter) to sing

interrogatif, -ive [ɛ̃tɛʀɔgatif, iv] adj (Ling) interrogative

interrogation [ɛ̃tɛʀɔgasjɔ̃] nf question; (action) questioning; **écrite/orale** (Scol) written/oral test

interrogatoire [ɛ̃tɛʀɔgatwaʀ] nm (Police) questioning no pl; (Jur, aussi fig) cross-examination

interroger [ɛ̃tɛʀɔʒe] vt to question; (Inform) to consult; (Scol) to test

interrompre [ɛ̃tɛʀɔ̃pʀ] vt (gén) to interrupt; (négociations) to break off;

(match) to stop; **s'interrompre** to break off; **interrupteur** nm switch; **interruption** nf interruption; (pause) break; **sans interruption** without stopping; **interruption (volontaire) de grossesse** termination (of pregnancy)

intersection [ɛ̃tɛʀsɛksjɔ̃] nf intersection

intervalle [ɛ̃tɛʀval] nm (espace) space; (de temps) interval; **dans l'~** in the meantime; **à deux jours d'~** two days apart

intervenir [ɛ̃tɛʀvəniʀ] vi (gén) to intervene; **~ auprès de qn** to intervene with sb; **intervention** nf intervention; (discours) speech; **intervention chirurgicale** (Méd) (surgical) operation

interview [ɛ̃tɛʀvju] nf interview

intestin [ɛ̃tɛstɛ̃] nm intestine

intime [ɛ̃tim] adj intimate; (vie) private; (conviction) inmost; (dîner, cérémonie) quiet ▷ nm/f close friend; **un journal ~** a diary

intimider [ɛ̃timide] vt to intimidate

intimité [ɛ̃timite] nf: **dans l'~** in private; (sans formalités) with only a few friends, quietly

intolérable [ɛ̃tɔleʀabl] adj intolerable

intox [ɛ̃tɔks] (fam) nf brainwashing

intoxication [ɛ̃tɔksikasjɔ̃] nf: **intoxication alimentaire** food poisoning

intoxiquer [ɛ̃tɔksike] vt to poison; (fig) to brainwash

intraitable [ɛ̃tʀɛtabl] adj inflexible, uncompromising

intransigeant, e [ɛ̃tʀɑ̃ziʒɑ̃, ɑ̃t] adj intransigent

intrépide [ɛ̃tʀepid] adj dauntless

intrigue [ɛ̃tʀig] nf (scénario) plot;

intriguer vt to puzzle, intrigue

introduction [ɛ̃tʀɔdyksjɔ̃] nf introduction

introduire [ɛ̃tʀɔdɥiʀ] vt to introduce; (visiteur) to show in; (aiguille, clef): **~ qch dans** to insert ou introduce sth into; **s'introduire** vr (techniques, usages) to be introduced; **s'~ (dans)** to get in(to); (dans un groupe) to get o.s. accepted (into)

introuvable [ɛ̃truvabl] adj which cannot be found; (Comm) unobtainable

intrus, e [ɛ̃try, yz] nm/f intruder

intuition [ɛ̃tɥisjɔ̃] nf intuition

inusable [inyzabl] adj hard-wearing

inutile [inytil] adj useless; (superflu) unnecessary; **inutilement** adv unnecessarily; **inutilisable** adj unusable

invalide [ɛ̃valid] adj disabled ▷ nm: **~ de guerre** disabled ex-serviceman

invariable [ɛ̃varjabl] adj invariable

invasion [ɛ̃vazjɔ̃] nf invasion

inventaire [ɛ̃vɑ̃tɛr] nm inventory; (Comm: liste) stocklist; (: opération) stocktaking no pl

inventer [ɛ̃vɑ̃te] vt to invent; (subterfuge) to devise, invent; (histoire, excuse) to make up, invent; **inventeur** nm inventor; **inventif, -ive** adj inventive; **invention** nf invention

inverse [ɛ̃vɛrs] adj opposite ▷ nm: **l'~** the opposite; **dans l'ordre ~** in the reverse order; **en sens ~** in (ou from) the opposite direction; **dans le sens ~ des aiguilles d'une montre** anticlockwise; **tu t'es trompé, c'est l'~** you've got it wrong, it's the other way round; **inversement** adv conversely; **inverser** vt to invert, reverse; (Élec) to reverse

investir [ɛ̃vɛstir] vt to invest; **~ qn de** (d'une fonction, d'un pouvoir) to vest ou to invest sb with; **s'investir** vr: **s'~ dans** (Psych) to put a lot into; **investissement** nm investment

invisible [ɛ̃vizibl] adj invisible

invitation [ɛ̃vitasjɔ̃] nf invitation

invité, e [ɛ̃vite] nm/f guest

inviter [ɛ̃vite] vt to invite; **~ qn à faire qch** to invite sb to do sth

invivable [ɛ̃vivabl] adj unbearable

involontaire [ɛ̃vɔlɔ̃tɛr] adj (mouvement) involuntary; (insulte) unintentional; (complice) unwitting

invoquer [ɛ̃vɔke] vt (Dieu, muse) to call

upon, invoke; (prétexte) to put forward (as an excuse); (loi, texte) to refer to

invraisemblable [ɛ̃vrɛsɑ̃blabl] adj (fait, nouvelle) unlikely, improbable; (insolence, habit) incredible

iode [jɔd] nm iodine

irai etc [ire] vb voir **aller**

Irak [irak] nm Iraq; **irakien, ne** adj Iraqi ▷ nm/f: **Irakien, ne** Iraqi

Iran [irɑ̃] nm Iran; **iranien, ne** adj Iranian ▷ nm/f: **Iranien, ne** Iranian

irions etc [irjɔ̃] vb voir **aller**

iris [iris] nm iris

irlandais, e [irlɑ̃dɛ, ɛz] adj Irish ▷ nm/f: **I~, e** Irishman(-woman)

Irlande [irlɑ̃d] nf Ireland; **la République d'~** the Irish Republic; **la mer d'~** the Irish Sea; **Irlande du Nord** Northern Ireland

ironie [irɔni] nf irony; **ironique** adj ironical; **ironiser** vi to be ironical

irons etc [irɔ̃] vb voir **aller**

irradier [iradje] vt to irradiate

irraisonné, e [irezɔne] adj irrational

irrationnel, le [irasjɔnɛl] adj irrational

irréalisable [irealizabl] adj unrealizable; (projet) impracticable

irrécupérable [irekyperabl] adj beyond repair; (personne) beyond redemption

irréel, le [ireɛl] adj unreal

irréfléchi, e [irefleʃi] adj thoughtless

irrégularité [iregylarite] nf irregularity; (de travail, d'effort, de qualité) unevenness no pl

irrégulier, ière [iregylje, jɛr] adj irregular; (travail, effort, qualité) uneven; (élève, athlète) erratic

irrémédiable [iremedjabl] adj irreparable

irremplaçable [irɑ̃plasabl] adj irreplaceable

irréparable [ireparabl] adj (objet) beyond repair; (dommage etc) irreparable

irréprochable [ireprɔʃabl] adj irreproachable, beyond reproach;

(tenue) impeccable

irrésistible [irezistibl] *adj* irresistible; *(besoin, désir, preuve, logique)* compelling; *(amusant)* hilarious

irrésolu, e [irezɔly] *adj (personne)* irresolute; *(problème)* unresolved

irrespectueux, -euse [irɛspɛktyø, øz] *adj* disrespectful

irresponsable [irɛspɔ̃sabl] *adj* irresponsible

irriguer [irige] *vt* to irrigate

irritable [iritabl] *adj* irritable

irriter [irite] *vt* to irritate

irruption [irypsjɔ̃] *nf*: **faire ~ (chez qn)** to burst in (on sb)

Islam [islam] *nm*: **l'~** Islam; **islamique** *adj* Islamic; **islamophobie** *nf* Islamophobia

Islande [islɑ̃d] *nf* Iceland

isolant, e [izɔlɑ̃, ɑ̃t] *adj* insulating; *(insonorisant)* soundproofing

isolation [izɔlasjɔ̃] *nf* insulation; **~ acoustique** soundproofing

isolé, e [izɔle] *adj* isolated; *(contre le froid)* insulated

isoler [izɔle] *vt* to isolate; *(prisonnier)* to put in solitary confinement; *(ville)* to cut off, isolate; *(contre le froid)* to insulate; **s'isoler** *vi* to isolate o.s.

Israël [israɛl] *nm* Israel; **israélien, ne** *adj* Israeli ▷ *nm/f*: **Israélien, ne** Israeli; **israélite** *adj* Jewish ▷ *nm/f*: **Israélite** Jew (Jewess)

issu, e [isy] *adj*: **~ de** *(né de)* descended from; *(résultant de)* stemming from; **issue** *nf (ouverture, sortie)* exit; *(solution)* way out, solution; *(dénouement)* outcome; **à l'issue de** at the conclusion *ou* close of; **voie sans issue** dead end; **issue de secours** emergency exit

Italie [itali] *nf* Italy; **italien, ne** *adj* Italian ▷ *nm/f*: **Italien, ne** Italian ▷ *nm (Ling)* Italian

italique [italik] *nm*: **en ~** in italics

itinéraire [itinerɛr] *nm* itinerary, route; **itinéraire bis** alternative route

IUT *sigle m* = **Institut universitaire de technologie**

IVG *sigle f* (= interruption volontaire de grossesse) abortion

ivoire [ivwar] *nm* ivory

ivre [ivr] *adj* drunk; **~ de** *(colère, bonheur)* wild with; **ivrogne** *nm/f* drunkard

j

j' [ʒ] pron voir **je**

jacinthe [ʒasɛ̃t] nf hyacinth

jadis [ʒadis] adv long ago

jaillir [ʒajiʁ] vi (liquide) to spurt out; (cris, réponses) to burst forth

jais [ʒɛ] nm jet; **(d'un noir) de ~** jet-black

jalousie [ʒaluzi] nf jealousy; (store) slatted blind

jaloux, -ouse [ʒalu, uz] adj jealous; **être ~ de** to be jealous of

jamaïquain, e [ʒamaikɛ̃, -ɛn] adj Jamaican ▷ nm/f **J~, e** Jamaican

Jamaïque [ʒamaik] nf: **la ~** Jamaica

jamais [ʒamɛ] adv never; (sans négation) ever; **ne ... ~** never; **je ne suis ~ allé en Espagne** I've never been to Spain; **si vous passez dans la région, venez nous voir** if you happen to be/if you're ever in this area, come and see us; **à ~ for ever**

jambe [ʒɑ̃b] nf leg

jambon [ʒɑ̃bɔ̃] nm ham

jante [ʒɑ̃t] nf (wheel) rim

janvier [ʒɑ̃vje] nm January

Japon [ʒapɔ̃] nm Japan; **japonais, e** adj Japanese ▷ nm/f **Japonais, e** Japanese ▷ nm (Ling) Japanese

jardin [ʒaʁdɛ̃] nm garden; **jardin d'enfants** nursery school; **jardinage** nm gardening; **jardiner** vi to do some gardening; **jardinier, -ière** nm/f gardener; **jardinière** nf planter; (de fenêtre) window box; **jardinière de légumes** (Culin) mixed vegetables

jargon [ʒaʁgɔ̃] nm gibberish; (langue professionnelle) jargon

jarret [ʒaʁɛ] nm back of knee; (Culin) knuckle, shin

jauge [ʒoʒ] nf (instrument) gauge; **jauge (de niveau) d'huile** (Auto) dipstick

jaune [ʒon] adj, nm yellow ▷ adv (fam): **rire ~** to laugh on the other side of one's face; **jaune d'œuf** (egg) yolk; **jaunir** vi, vt to turn yellow; **jaunisse** nf jaundice

Javel [ʒavɛl] nf voir **eau**

javelot [ʒavlo] nm javelin

je, j' [ʒə] pron I

jean [dʒin] nm jeans pl

Jésus-Christ [ʒezykʁi(st)] n Jesus Christ; **600 avant/après ~** ou **J.-C.** 600 B.C./A.D.

jet [ʒɛ] nm (lancer: action) throwing no pl; (: résultat) throw; (jaillissement: d'eau) jet; (: de sang) spurt; **jet d'eau** spray

jetable [ʒətabl] adj disposable

jetée [ʒəte] nf jetty; (grande) pier

jeter [ʒ(ə)te] vt (gén) to throw; (se défaire de) to throw away ou out; **~ qch à qn** to throw sth to sb; (de façon agressive) to throw sth at sb; **~ un coup d'œil (à)** to take a look (at); **~ un sort à qn** to cast a spell on sb; **se ~ sur qn** to rush at sb; **se ~ dans** (suj: fleuve) to flow into

jeton [ʒətɔ̃] nm (de jeu) counter

jette etc [ʒɛt] vb voir **jeter**

jeu, x [ʒø] nm (divertissement, Tech: d'une pièce) play; (Tennis: partie, Football etc: façon de jouer) game; (Théâtre etc) acting; (série d'objets, jouet) set; (Cartes) hand; (au casino): **le ~** gambling; **remettre en ~** (Football) to throw in; **être en ~** (fig) to be at stake; **entrer/mettre en ~** (fig) to come/bring into play; **jeu de cartes** pack of cards; **jeu d'échecs** chess set; **jeu de hasard** game of chance; **jeu de mots** pun; **jeu de société** board game; **jeu télévisé** television quiz; **jeu vidéo** video game

jeudi [ʒødi] nm Thursday

jeun [ʒœ̃]: **à ~** adv on an empty stomach; **être à ~** to have eaten nothing; **rester à ~** not to eat anything

jeune [ʒœn] adj young; **jeunes** nmpl: **les ~s** young people; **jeune fille** girl; **jeune homme** young man; **jeunes gens** young people

jeûne [ʒøn] nm fast

jeunesse [ʒœnɛs] nf youth; (aspect) youthfulness

joaillier, -ière [ʒɔaje, -jɛʀ] nm/f jeweller

jogging [dʒɔgiɲ] nm jogging; (survêtement) tracksuit; **faire du ~** to go jogging

joie [ʒwa] nf joy

joindre [ʒwɛ̃dʀ] vt to join; (à une lettre): **~ qch à** to enclose sth with; (contacter) to contact, get in touch with; **se ~ à qch** to join in sth; **se ~ à qn** to join in sth; **se ~ à qch** to join in sth

joint, e [ʒwɛ̃, ɛt] adj: **pièce ~e** (de lettre) enclosure; (de mail) attachment ▷ nm joint; (ligne) join; **joint de culasse** cylinder head gasket

joli, e [ʒɔli] adj pretty, attractive; **une ~e somme/situation** a tidy sum/a nice little job; **c'est du ~!** (ironique) that's very nice!; **c'est bien ~, mais ...** that's all very well but ...

jonc [ʒɔ̃] nm (bot) rush

jonction [ʒɔ̃ksjɔ̃] nf junction

jongleur, -euse [ʒɔ̃glœʀ, øz] nm/f juggler

jonquille [ʒɔ̃kij] nf daffodil

Jordanie [ʒɔʀdani] nf: **la ~** Jordan

joue [ʒu] nf cheek

jouer [ʒwe] vt to play; (somme d'argent, réputation) to stake, wager; (simuler: sentiment) to affect, feign ▷ vi to play; (Théâtre, Cinéma) to act; (au casino) to

gamble; (bois, porte: se voiler) to warp; (clef, pièce: avoir du jeu) to be loose; **~ sur** (miser) to gamble on; **~ de** (Mus) to play; **~ à** (jeu, sport, roulette) to play; **~ un tour à qn** to play a trick on sb; **~ serré** to play a close game; **~ la comédie** (fig) to put on an act; **à toi/nous de ~** it's your/our go ou turn; **bien joué!** well done!; **on joue Hamlet au théâtre X** Hamlet is on at the X theatre

jouet [ʒwɛ] nm toy; **être le ~ de** (illusion etc) to be the victim of

joueur, -euse [ʒwœʀ, øz] nm/f player; **être beau/mauvais ~** to be a good/bad loser

jouir [ʒwiʀ] vi (sexe: fam) to come ▷ vt: **~ de** to enjoy

jour [ʒuʀ] nm day; (opposé à la nuit) day, daytime; (clarté) daylight; (fig: aspect) light; (ouverture) gap; **de ~** (crème, service) day cpd; **travailler de ~** to work during the day; **voyager de ~** to travel by day; **au ~ le ~** from day to day; **de nos ~s** these days; **du ~ au lendemain** overnight; **il fait ~** it's daylight; **au grand ~** (fig) in the open; **mettre au ~** to disclose; **mettre à ~** to update; **donner le ~ à** to give birth to; **voir le ~** to be born; **le ~ J** D-day; **jour férié** public holiday; **jour ouvrable** working day

journal, -aux [ʒuʀnal, o] nm (news)paper; (spécialisé) journal; (intime) diary; **journal de bord** log; **journal parlé/télévisé** radio/ television news sg

journalier, -ière [ʒuʀnalje, jɛʀ] adj daily; (banal) everyday

journalisme [ʒuʀnalism] nm journalism; **journaliste** nm/f journalist

journée [ʒuʀne] nf day; **faire la ~ continue** to work over lunch

joyau, x [ʒwajo] nm gem, jewel

joyeux, -euse [ʒwajø, øz] adj joyful, merry; **~ Noël!** merry Christmas!; **~ anniversaire!** happy birthday!

jubiler [ʒybile] vi to be jubilant, exult

judas [ʒyda] nm (trou) spy-hole

judiciaire [ʒydisjɛʀ] adj judicial

judicieux, -euse [ʒydisjø, jøz] adj judicious

judo [ʒydo] nm judo

juge [ʒyʒ] nm judge; **juge d'instruction** examining (BRIT) ou committing (US) magistrate; **juge de paix** justice of the peace

jugé [ʒyʒe] nm: **au ~** adv by guesswork

jugement [ʒyʒmɑ̃] nm judgement; (Jur: au pénal) sentence; (: au civil) decision

juger [ʒyʒe] vt to judge; (estimer) to consider; **~ qn/qch satisfaisant** to consider sb/sth (to be) satisfactory; **~ bon de faire** to see fit to do

juif, -ive [ʒɥif, ʒɥiv] adj Jewish ▷ nm/f: **J~, ive** Jew (Jewess)

juillet [ʒɥijɛ] nm July

● **14 JUILLET**

● **Le 14 juillet** is a national holiday
● in France and commemorates the
● storming of the Bastille during the
● French Revolution. Throughout
● the country there are celebrations,
● which feature parades, music,
● dancing and firework displays. In
● Paris a military parade along the
● Champs-Élysées is attended by the
● President.

juin [ʒɥɛ̃] nm June

jumeau, -elle, x [ʒymo, ɛl] adj, nm/f twin

jumeler [ʒym(ə)le] vt to twin

jumelle [ʒymɛl] adj, nf voir **jumeau**; **jumelles** nfpl (appareil) binoculars

jument [ʒymɑ̃] nf mare

jungle [ʒɔ̃gl] nf jungle

jupe [ʒyp] nf skirt

jupon [ʒypɔ̃] nm waist slip

juré, e [ʒyʀe] nm/f juror ▷ adj: **ennemi ~** sworn enemy

jurer [ʒyʀe] vt (obéissance etc) to swear, vow ▷ vi (dire des jurons) to swear, curse; (dissoner): **~ (avec)** to clash (with); **~ de faire/que** to swear to do/that; **~ de**

qch (s'en porter garant) to swear to sth

juridique [ʒyʀidik] adj legal

juron [ʒyʀɔ̃] nm curse, swearword

jury [ʒyʀi] nm jury; (Art, Sport) panel of judges; (Scol) board of examiners

jus [ʒy] nm juice; (de viande) gravy, (meat) juice; **jus de fruit** fruit juice

jusque [ʒysk]: **jusqu'à** prép (endroit) as far as, (up) to; (moment) until, till; (limite) up to; **~ sur/dans** up to; (y compris) even on/in; **jusqu'à ce que** until; **jusqu'à présent** ou **maintenant** so far; **jusqu'où?** how far?

justaucorps [ʒystokɔʀ] nm leotard

juste [ʒyst] adj (équitable) just, fair; (légitime) just; (exact) right; (pertinent) apt; (étroit) tight; (insuffisant) on the short side ▷ adv rightly, correctly; (chanter) in tune; (exactement, seulement) just; **~ assez/au-dessus** just enough/above; **au ~** exactly; **le ~ milieu** the happy medium; **c'était ~** it was a close thing; **pouvoir tout ~ faire** to be only just able to do; **justement** adv justly; (précisément) just, precisely; **justesse** nf (précision) accuracy; (d'une remarque) aptness; (d'une opinion) soundness; **de justesse** only just

justice [ʒystis] nf (équité) fairness, justice; (Admin) justice; **rendre ~ à qn** to do sb justice

justificatif, -ive [ʒystifikatif, iv] adj (document) supporting; **pièce justificative** written proof

justifier [ʒystifje] vt to justify; **~ de** to prove

juteux, -euse [ʒytø, øz] adj juicy

juvénile [ʒyvenil] adj youthful

kiwi [kiwi] *nm* kiwi
klaxon [klaksɔn] *nm* horn; **klaxonner**
  vi, vt to hoot (BRIT), honk (US)
km *abr* = **kilomètre**
km/h *abr* (= *kilomètres/heure*) ≈ mph
K.-O. (*fam*) *adj inv* shattered, knackered
Kosovo [kɔsɔvo] *nm* Kosovo
Koweit, Kuweit [kɔwɛt] *nm*: **le ~**
  Kuwait
k-way® [kawɛ] *nm* (lightweight nylon)
  cagoule
kyste [kist] *nm* cyst

K [ka] *nm* (*Inform*) K
kaki [kaki] *adj inv* khaki
kangourou [kãguru] *nm* kangaroo
karaté [karate] *nm* karate
kascher [kaʃɛr] *adj* kosher
kayak [kajak] *nm* canoe, kayak; **faire
  du ~** to go canoeing
képi [kepi] *nm* kepi
kermesse [kɛrmɛs] *nf* fair; (*fête de
  charité*) bazaar, (charity) fête
kidnapper [kidnape] *vt* to kidnap
kilo [kilo] *nm* = **kilogramme**
kilo...: **kilogramme** *nm* kilogramme;
  kilométrage *nm* number of kilometres
  travelled, ≈ mileage; **kilomètre** *nm*
  kilometre; **kilométrique** *adj* (*distance*)
  in kilometres
kinésithérapeute [kineziterapøt]
  nm/f physiotherapist
kiosque [kjɔsk] *nm* kiosk, stall
kir [kir] *nm* kir (*white wine with
  blackcurrant liqueur*)
kit [kit] *nm* kit; **~ piéton** *ou* **mains libres**
  hands-free kit; **en ~** in kit form

l' [l] art déf voir **le**

la [la] art déf voir **le** ▷ nm (Mus) A; (en chantant la gamme) la

là [la] adv there; (ici) here; (dans le temps) then; **elle n'est pas là** she isn't here; **c'est là que** this is where; **là où** where; **de là** (fig) hence; **par là** (fig) by that; voir aussi **-ci**; **ce**; **celui**; **là-bas** adv there

l' [l] art déf voir **le**

la [la] art déf voir **le** ▷ nm (Mus) A; (en chantant la gamme) la

là [la] adv there; (ici) here; (dans le temps) then; **elle n'est pas là** she isn't here; **c'est là que** this is where; **là où** where; **de là** (fig) hence; **par là** (fig) by that; voir aussi **-ci**; **ce**; **celui**; **là-bas** adv there

laboratoire [labɔratwar] nm laboratory; **laboratoire de langues** language laboratory

laborieux, -euse [labɔrjø, jøz] adj (tâche) laborious

labourer vt to plough

labyrinthe [labiʀɛ̃t] nm labyrinth, maze

lac [lak] nm lake

lacet [lasɛ] nm (de chaussure) lace; (de route) sharp bend; (piège) snare

lâche [lɑʃ] adj (poltron) cowardly; (desserré) loose, slack ▷ nm/f coward

lâcher [lɑʃe] vt to let go of; (ce qui tombe, abandonner) to drop; (oiseau, animal: libérer) to release, set free; (fig: mot,

remarque) to let slip, come out with ▷ vi (freins) to fail; ~ **les amarres** (Navig) to cast off (the moorings); ~ **prise** to let go

lacrymogène [lakrimɔʒɛn] adj: **gaz ~** teargas

lacune [lakyn] nf gap

là-dedans [ladədɑ̃] adv inside (there), in it; (fig) in that

là-dessous [ladsu] adv underneath, under there; (fig) behind that

là-dessus [ladsy] adv on there; (fig: sur ces mots) at that point; (: à ce sujet) about that

lagune [lagyn] nf lagoon

là-haut [lao] adv up there

laid, e [lɛ, lɛd] adj ugly; **laideur** nf ugliness no pl

lainage [lɛnaʒ] nm (vêtement) woollen garment; (étoffe) woollen material

laine [lɛn] nf wool

laïque [laik] adj lay, civil; (Scol) state cpd ▷ nm/f layman(-woman)

laisse [lɛs] nf (de chien) lead, leash; **tenir en ~** to keep on a lead ou leash

laisser [lese] vt to leave ▷ vb aux: ~ **qn faire** to let sb do; **se ~ aller** to let o.s. go; **laisse-toi faire** let me (ou him etc) do it; **laisser-aller** nm carelessness, slovenliness; **laissez-passer** nm inv pass

lait [lɛ] nm milk; **frère/sœur de ~** foster brother/sister; **lait concentré/ condensé** condensed/evaporated milk; **lait écrémé/entier** skimmed/ full-cream (BRIT) ou whole milk; **laitage** nm dairy product; **laiterie** nf dairy; **laitier, -ière** adj dairy cpd ▷ nm/f milkman (dairywoman)

laiton [lɛtɔ̃] nm brass

laitue [lety] nf lettuce

lambeau, x [lɑ̃bo] nm scrap; **en ~x** in tatters, tattered

lame [lam] nf blade; (vague) wave; (lamelle) strip; **lame de fond** ground swell no pl; **lame de rasoir** razor blade; **lamelle** nf thin strip ou blade

lamentable [lamɑ̃tabl] adj appalling

lamenter [lamɑ̃te] vb: **se ~ (sur)** to

moan (over)

lampadaire [lɑ̃padɛʀ] nm (de salon) standard lamp; (dans la rue) street lamp

lampe [lɑ̃p] nf lamp; (Tech) valve; **lampe à bronzer** sun lamp; **lampe à pétrole** oil lamp; **lampe de poche** torch (BRIT), flashlight (US); **lampe halogène** halogen lamp

lance [lɑ̃s] nf spear; **lance d'incendie** fire hose

lancée [lɑ̃se] nf: **être/continuer sur sa ~** to be under way/keep going

lancement [lɑ̃smɑ̃] nm launching

lance-pierres [lɑ̃spjɛʀ] nm inv catapult

lancer [lɑ̃se] nm (Sport) throwing no pl, throw ▷ vt to throw; (émettre, projeter) to throw out, send out; (produit, fusée, bateau, artiste) to launch; (injure) to hurl, fling; **se lancer** vi (prendre de l'élan) to build up speed; (se précipiter): **se ~ sur** ou **contre** to rush at; **se ~ dans** (discussion) to launch into; (aventure) to embark on; **~ qch à qn** to throw sth to sb; (de façon agressive) to throw sth at sb; **~ un cri** ou **un appel** to shout ou call out; **lancer du poids** putting the shot

landau [lɑ̃do] nm pram (BRIT), baby carriage (US)

lande [lɑ̃d] nf moor

langage [lɑ̃gaʒ] nm language

langouste [lɑ̃gust] nf crayfish inv; **langoustine** nf Dublin Bay prawn

langue [lɑ̃g] nf (Anat, Culin) tongue; (Ling) language; **tirer la ~ (à)** to stick one's tongue out (at); **de ~ française** French-speaking; **quelles ~s parlez-vous?** what languages do you speak?; **langue maternelle** native language, mother tongue; **langues vivantes** modern languages

langueur [lɑ̃gœʀ] nf languidness

languir [lɑ̃giʀ] vi to languish; (conversation) to flag; **faire ~ qn** to keep sb waiting

lanière [lanjɛʀ] nf (de fouet) lash; (de sac, bretelle) strap

lanterne [lɑ̃tɛʀn] nf (portable) lantern; (électrique) light, lamp; (de voiture) (side)light

laper [lape] vt to lap up

lapidaire [lapidɛʀ] adj (fig) terse

lapin [lapɛ̃] nm rabbit; (peau) rabbitskin; (fourrure) cony; **poser un ~ à qn** (fam) to stand sb up

Laponie [laponi] nf Lapland

laps [laps] nm: **~ de temps** space of time, time no pl

laque [lak] nf (vernis) lacquer; (pour cheveux) hair spray

laquelle [lakɛl] pron voir **lequel**

larcin [laʀsɛ̃] nm theft

lard [laʀ] nm (bacon) (streaky) bacon; (graisse) fat

lardon [laʀdɔ̃] nm: **~s** chopped bacon

large [laʀʒ] adj wide, broad; (fig) generous ▷ adv: **calculer/voir ~** to allow extra/think big ▷ nm (largeur): **5 m de ~** 5 m wide ou in width; (mer): **le ~** the open sea; **au ~ de** off; **large d'esprit** broad-minded; **largement** adv widely; (de loin) greatly; (au moins) easily; (généreusement) generously; **c'est largement suffisant** that's ample; **largesse** nf generosity; **largesses** nfpl (dons) liberalities; **largeur** nf (qu'on mesure) width; (impression visuelle) wideness, width; (d'esprit) broadness

larguer [laʀge] vt to drop; **~ les amarres** to cast off (the moorings)

larme [laʀm] nf tear; (fam: goutte): **une ~ de** a drop of; **en ~s** in tears; **larmoyer** vi (yeux) to water; (se plaindre) to whimper

larvé, e [laʀve] adj (fig) latent

laryngite [laʀɛ̃ʒit] nf laryngitis

las, lasse [lɑ, lɑs] adj weary

laser [lazɛʀ] nm (rayon) laser (beam); **chaîne** ou **platine ~** laser disc (player); **disque ~** laser disc

lasse [lɑs] adj voir **las**

lasser [lɑse] vt to weary, tire; **se lasser de** vt to grow weary ou tired of

latéral, e, -aux [lateʀal, o] adj side cpd, lateral

latin, e [latɛ̃, in] adj Latin ▷ nm/f: **L~, L~e** Latin ▷ nm (Ling) Latin

latitude [latityd] nf latitude

lauréat, e [lɔrea, at] nm/f winner

laurier [lɔrje] nm (Bot) laurel; **feuille de ~** (Culin) bay leaf

lavable [lavabl] adj washable

lavabo [lavabo] nm washbasin; **lavabos** nmpl (toilettes) toilet sg

lavage [lavaʒ] nm washing no pl, wash; **lavage de cerveau** brainwashing no pl

lavande [lavɑ̃d] nf lavender

lave [lav] nf lava no pl

lave-linge [lavlɛ̃ʒ] nm inv washing machine

laver [lave] vt to wash; (tache) to wash off; **se laver** vi to have a wash, wash; **se ~ les mains/dents** to wash one's hands/clean one's teeth; **~ la vaisselle/le linge** to wash the dishes/clothes; **~ qn de** (accusation) to clear sb of; **laverie** nf: **laverie (automatique)** launderette; **lavette** nf dish cloth; (fam) drip; **laveur, -euse** nm/f cleaner; **lave-vaisselle** nm inv dishwasher; **lavoir** nm wash house; (évier) sink

laxatif, -ive [laksatif, iv] adj, nm laxative

layette [lejet] nf baby clothes

○ **MOT-CLÉ**

le [lə], **la, l'** (pl **les**) art déf **1** the; **le livre/la pomme/l'arbre** the book/the apple/the tree; **les étudiants** the students

2 (noms abstraits): **le courage/l'amour/la jeunesse** courage/love/youth

3 (indiquant la possession): **se casser la jambe** etc to break one's leg; **levez la main** put your hand up; **avoir les yeux gris/le nez rouge** to have grey eyes/a red nose

4 (temps): **le matin/soir** in the morning/evening; mornings/evenings; **le jeudi** etc (d'habitude) on Thursdays etc; (ce jeudi là etc) on (the) Thursday

5 (distribution, évaluation) a, an; **10**

euros le mètre/kilo 10 euros a ou per metre/kilo; **le tiers/quart de a** third/quarter of

▷ pron **1** (personne: mâle) him; (: femelle) her; (: pluriel) them; **je le/la/les vois** I can see him/her/them

2 (animal, chose: singulier) it; (: pluriel) them; **je le** (ou **la**) **vois** I can see it; **je les vois** I can see them

3 (remplaçant une phrase): **je ne le savais pas** I didn't know (about it); **il était riche et ne l'est plus** he was once rich but no longer is

lécher [leʃe] vt to lick; (laper: lait, eau) to lick ou lap up; **se ~ les doigts/lèvres** to lick one's fingers/lips; **lèche-vitrines** nm: **faire du lèche-vitrines** to go window-shopping

leçon [l(ə)sɔ̃] nf lesson; **faire la ~ à** (fig) to give a lecture to; **leçons de conduite** driving lessons; **leçons particulières** private lessons ou tuition sg (BRIT)

lecteur, -trice [lɛktœr, tris] nm/f reader; (d'université) foreign language assistant ▷ nm (Tech): **~ de cassettes/CD/DVD** cassette/CD/DVD player; **lecteur de disquette(s)** disk drive; **lecteur MP3** MP3 player

lecture [lɛktyr] nf reading
Attention à ne pas traduire **lecture** par le mot anglais **lecture**.

ledit [lədi], **ladite** (mpl **lesdits**, fpl **lesdites**) dét the aforesaid

légal, e, -aux [legal, o, od] adj legal; **légaliser** vt to legalize; **légalité** nf law

légendaire [leʒɑ̃dɛr] adj legendary

légende [leʒɑ̃d] nf (mythe) legend; (de carte, plan) key; (de dessin) caption

léger, -ère [leʒe, ɛr] adj light; (bruit, retard) slight; (personne: superficiel) thoughtless; (: volage) free and easy; **à la légère** (parler, agir) rashly, thoughtlessly; **légèrement** adv (s'habiller, bouger) lightly; (un peu) slightly; **manger légèrement** to eat a light meal; **légèreté** nf lightness; (d'une remarque) flippancy

législatif, -ive [leʒislatif, iv] adj
legislative; **les** nfpl general
election sg

légitime [leʒitim] adj (Jur) lawful,
legitimate; (fig) rightful, legitimate; **en
état de ~ défense** in self-defence

legs [leg] nm legacy

léguer [lege] vt: **~ qch à qn** (Jur) to
bequeath sth to sb

légume [legym] nm vegetable;
légumes secs pulses; **légumes verts**
green vegetables, greens

lendemain [lɑ̃dmɛ̃] nm: **le ~** the next
ou following day; **le ~ matin/soir** the
next ou following morning/evening; **le
~ de** the day after

lent, e [lɑ̃, lɑ̃t] adj slow; **lentement** adv
slowly; **lenteur** nf slowness no pl

lentille [lɑ̃tij] nf (Optique) lens sg;
(Culin) lentil; **lentilles de contact**
contact lenses

léopard [leɔpar] nm leopard

lèpre [lɛpr] nf leprosy

○ **MOT-CLÉ**

lequel, laquelle [ləkɛl, lakɛl] (mpl
lesquels, fpl **lesquelles**) (à + lequel =
auquel, de + lequel = **duquel** etc) pron
1 (interrogatif) which, which one; **lequel
des deux?** which one?
2 (relatif: personne: sujet) who; (: objet,
après préposition) whom; (: chose) which
▷ adj: **auquel cas** in which case

les [le] dét voir **le**

lesbienne [lɛsbjɛn] nf lesbian

léser [leze] vt to wrong

lésiner [lezine] vi: **ne pas ~ sur les
moyens** (pour mariage etc) to push the
boat out

lésion [lezjɔ̃] nf lesion, damage no pl

lessive [lesiv] nf (poudre) washing
powder; (linge) washing no pl, wash;
lessiver vt to wash; (fam: fatiguer) to
tire out, exhaust

lest [lɛst] nm ballast

leste [lɛst] adj sprightly, nimble

lettre [lɛtr] nf letter; **lettres** nfpl
(littérature) literature sg; (Scol) arts
(subjects); **à la ~** literally; **en toutes ~s**
in full; **lettre piégée** letter bomb

leucémie [løsemi] nf leukaemia

○ **MOT-CLÉ**

leur [lœr] adj possessif their; **leur
maison** their house; **leurs amis** their
friends
▷ pron **1** (objet indirect) (to) them; **je leur
ai dit la vérité** I told them the truth;
je le leur ai donné I gave it to them, I
gave them it
2 (possessif): **le(la) leur, les leurs** theirs

levain [ləvɛ̃] nm leaven

levé, e [ləve] adj: **être ~** to be up; **levée**
nf (Postes) collection

lever [l(ə)ve] vt (vitre, bras etc) to raise;
(soulever de terre, supprimer: interdiction,
siège) to lift; (impôts, armée) to levy ▷ vi
to rise ▷ nm: **au ~** on getting up; **se
lever** vi to get up; (soleil) to rise; (jour)
to break; (brouillard) to lift; **ça se ~**
(temps) it's going to clear up; **lever de
soleil** sunrise; **lever du jour** daybreak

levier [ləvje] nm lever

lèvre [lɛvr] nf lip

lévrier [levrije] nm greyhound

levure [l(ə)vyr] nf yeast; **levure
chimique** baking powder

lexique [lɛksik] nm vocabulary;
(glossaire) lexicon

lézard [lezar] nm lizard

lézarde [lezard] nf crack

liaison [ljɛzɔ̃] nf (rapport) connection;
(transport) link; (amoureuse) affair;
(Phonétique) liaison; **entrer/être en ~
avec** to get/be in contact with

liane [ljan] nf creeper

liasse [ljas] nf wad, bundle

Liban [libɑ̃] nm: **le ~** the Lebanon

libeller [libele] vt (chèque, mandat): **~
(au nom de)** to make out (to); (lettre)
to word

libellule [libelyl] nf dragonfly

libéral, e, -aux [liberal, o] adj, nm/f liberal; **profession ~e** (liberal) profession

libérer [libeʀe] vt (délivrer) to free, liberate; (relâcher: prisonnier) to discharge, release; (: d'inhibitions) to liberate; (gaz) to release; **se libérer** vi (de rendez-vous) to get out of previous engagements

liberté [libɛʀte] nf freedom; (loisir) free time; **libertés** nfpl (privautés) liberties; **mettre/être en ~** to set/be free; **en ~ provisoire/surveillée/conditionnelle** on bail/probation/parole

libraire [libʀɛʀ] nm/f bookseller

librairie [libʀeʀi] nf bookshop

> Attention à ne pas traduire *librairie* par *library*.

libre [libʀ] adj free; (route, voie) clear; (place, salle) free; (ligne) not engaged; (Scol) non-state; (: de faire free from sth to do; **la place est ~?** is this seat free?; **libre arbitre** free will; **libre-échange** nm free trade; **libre-service** nm self-service store

Libye [libi] nf: **la ~** Libya

licence [lisɑ̃s] nf (permis) permit; (diplôme) degree; (liberté) liberty; **licencié, e** nm/f (Scol): **licencié ès lettres/en droit** ≈ Bachelor of Arts/Law

licenciement [lisɑ̃simɑ̃] nm redundancy

licencier [lisɑ̃sje] vt (débaucher) to make redundant, lay off; (renvoyer) to dismiss

licite [lisit] adj lawful

lie [li] nf dregs pl, sediment

lié, e [lje] adj: **très ~ avec** very friendly with ou close to

Liechtenstein [liʃtɛnʃtain] nm: **le ~** Liechtenstein

liège [ljɛʒ] nm cork

lien [ljɛ̃] nm (corde, fig: affectif) bond; (rapport) link, connection; **lien de parenté** family tie; **lien hypertexte** hyperlink

lier [lje] vt (attacher) to tie up; (joindre)

to link up; (fig: unir, engager) to bind; **~ conversation (avec)** to strike up a conversation (with); **~ connaissance avec** qn to get to know

lierre [ljɛʀ] nm ivy

lieu, x [ljø] nm place; **lieux** nmpl (locaux) premises; (endroit: d'un accident etc) scene sg; **en ~ sûr** in a safe place; **en premier ~** in the first place; **en dernier ~** lastly; **avoir ~** to take place; **tenir ~ de** to serve as; **donner ~ à** to give rise to; **au ~ de** instead of; **arriver/être sur les ~x** to arrive at/be on the scene; **lieu commun** cliché; **lieu-dit** (pl **lieux-dits**) nm locality

lieutenant [ljøt(ə)nɑ̃] nm lieutenant

lièvre [ljɛvʀ] nm hare

ligament [ligamɑ̃] nm ligament

ligne [liɲ] nf (gén) line; (Transports: liaison) service; (: trajet) route; (silhouette) figure; **garder la ~** to keep one's figure; **entrer en ~ de compte** to come into it; **en ~** (Inform) online; **~ fixe** (Tél) land line (phone)

lignée [liɲe] nf line, lineage

ligoter [ligɔte] vt to tie up

ligue [lig] nf league

lilas [lila] nm lilac

limace [limas] nf slug

limande [limɑ̃d] nf dab

lime [lim] nf file; **lime à ongles** nail file; **limer** vt to file

limitation [limitasjɔ̃] nf: **limitation de vitesse** speed limit

limite [limit] nf (de terrain) boundary; (partie ou point extrême) limit; **à la ~** (au pire) if the worst comes (ou came) to the worst; **vitesse/charge ~** maximum speed/load; **cas ~** borderline case; **date ~** deadline; **date ~ de vente/consommation** sell-by/best-before date; **limiter** vt to limit, restrict; (délimiter) to border; **limitrophe** adj border cpd

limoger [limɔʒe] vt to dismiss

limon [limɔ̃] nm silt

limonade [limɔnad] nf lemonade

lin [lɛ̃] nm (tissu) linen

linceul [lɛ̃sœl] nm shroud
linge [lɛ̃ʒ] nm (serviettes etc) linen;
(lessive) washing; (aussi: ~ **de corps**)
underwear; **lingerie** nf lingerie,
underwear
lingot [lɛ̃go] nm ingot
linguistique [lɛ̃gɥistik] adj linguistic
  ▷ nf linguistics sg
lion, ne [ljɔ̃, ljɔn] nm/f lion (lioness);
(signe): **le L~** Leo; **lionceau, x** nm
lion cub
liqueur [likœr] nf liqueur
liquidation [likidasjɔ̃] nf (vente) sale
liquide [likid] adj liquid ▷ nm liquid;
(Comm): **en ~** in ready money ou cash;
je n'ai pas de ~ I haven't got any cash;
liquider vt to liquidate; (Comm: articles)
to clear, sell off
lire [lir] nf (monnaie) lira ▷ vt, vi to read
lis [lis] nm = **lys**
Lisbonne [lizbɔn] n Lisbon
lisible [lizibl] adj legible
lisière [lizjɛr] nf (de forêt) edge
lisons [lizɔ̃] vb voir **lire**
lisse [lis] adj smooth
liste [list] nf list; **faire la ~ de** to list;
liste de mariage wedding (present)
list; **liste électorale** electoral roll;
listing nm (Inform) printout
lit [li] nm bed; **petit ~, ~ à une place**
single bed; **grand ~, ~ à deux places**
double bed; **faire son ~** to make one's
bed; **aller/se mettre au ~** to go to/get
into bed; **lit de camp** campbed; **lit
d'enfant** cot (BRIT), crib (US)
literie [litri] nf bedding, bedclothes pl
litige [litiʒ] nm dispute
litre [litr] nm litre
littéraire [literɛr] adj literary ▷ nm/f
arts student; **elle est très ~** she's very
literary
littéral, e, -aux [literal, o] adj literal
littérature [literatyr] nf literature
littoral, e, -aux [litɔral, o] nm coast
livide [livid] adj livid, pallid
livraison [livrɛzɔ̃] nf delivery
livre [livr] nm book ▷ nf (monnaie)
pound; (poids) half a kilo, = pound; **livre**
de poche paperback
livré, e [livre] adj: **~ à soi-même** left to
o.s. ou one's own devices
livrer [livre] vt (Comm) to deliver;
(otage, coupable) to hand over; (secret,
information) to give away; **se livrer
à** (se confier) to confide in; (se rendre,
s'abandonner) to give o.s. up to; (faire:
pratiques, actes) to indulge in; (enquête)
to carry out
livret [livre] nm booklet; (d'opéra)
libretto; **livret de caisse d'épargne**
(savings) bank-book; **livret de famille**
(official) family record book; **livret
scolaire** (school) report book
livreur, -euse [livrœr, øz] nm/f
delivery boy ou man/girl ou woman
local, e, -aux [lɔkal] adj local ▷ nm
(salle) premises pl; voir aussi **locaux**;
localité nf locality
locataire [lɔkatɛr] nm/f tenant; (de
chambre) lodger
location [lɔkasjɔ̃] nf (par le locataire,
le loueur) renting; (par le propriétaire)
renting out, letting; (Théâtre)
booking office; **"~ de voitures"** "car
rental"; **habiter en ~** to live in rented
accommodation; **prendre une ~ (pour
les vacances)** to rent a house etc (for
the holidays)

> Attention à ne pas traduire location
> par le mot anglais location.

locomotive [lɔkɔmɔtiv] nf
locomotive, engine
locution [lɔkysjɔ̃] nf phrase
loge [lɔʒ] nf (Théâtre: d'artiste) dressing
room; (: de spectateurs) box; (de concierge,
franc-maçon) lodge
logement [lɔʒmɑ̃] nm
accommodation no pl (BRIT),
accommodations pl (US); (appartement)
flat (BRIT), apartment (US); (Pol, Admin):
le ~ housing no pl
loger [lɔʒe] vt to accommodate ▷ vi to
live; **être logé, nourri** to have board
and lodging; **se loger** vr: **trouver à
se ~** to find somewhere to live; **se ~
dans** (suj: balle, flèche) to lodge itself in;

logeur, -euse nm/f landlord(-lady)

logiciel [lɔʒisjɛl] nm software

logique [lɔʒik] adj logical ▷ nf logic

logo [logo] nm logo

loi [lwa] nf law; **faire ~** to lay down the law

loin [lwɛ̃] adv far; (dans le temps: futur) a long way off; (: passé) a long time ago; **plus ~** further; **de ~** far from; **c'est d'ici?** is it far from here?; **au ~** far off; **de ~** from a distance; (fig: de beaucoup) by far

lointain, e [lwɛ̃tɛ̃, ɛn] adj faraway, distant; (dans le futur, passé) distant; (cause, parent) remote, distant ▷ nm: **dans le ~** in the distance

loir [lwaʀ] nm dormouse

Loire [lwaʀ] nf: **la ~** the (River) Loire

loisir [lwaziʀ] nm: **heures de ~** spare time; **loisirs** nmpl (temps libre) leisure sg; (activités) leisure activities; **avoir le ~ de faire** to have the time ou opportunity to do; **à ~** at leisure

londonien, ne [lɔ̃dɔnjɛ̃, jɛn] adj London cpd, of London ▷ nm/f: **L~, ne** Londoner

Londres [lɔ̃dʀ] n London

long, longue [lɔ̃, lɔ̃g] adj long ▷ adv: **en savoir ~** to know a great deal ▷ nm: **de 3 m de ~** 3 m long, 3 m in length; **ne pas faire ~ feu** not to last long; **(tout) le ~ de** (all) along; **tout au ~ de** (année, vie) throughout; **de ~ en large** (marcher) to and fro, up and down; voir aussi **longue**

longer [lɔ̃ʒe] vt to go (ou walk ou drive) along(side); (suj: mur, route) to border

longiligne [lɔ̃ʒiliɲ] adj long-limbed

longitude [lɔ̃ʒityd] nf longitude

longtemps [lɔ̃tɑ̃] adv for a long time, (for) long; **avant ~** before long; **pour ou pendant ~** for a long time; **mettre ~ à faire** to take a long time to do; **il en a pour ~?** will he be long?

longue [lɔ̃g] adj voir **long** ▷ nf: **à la ~** in the end; **longuement** adv (longtemps) for a long time; (en détail) at length

longueur [lɔ̃gœʀ] nf length;

longueurs nfpl (fig: d'un film etc) tedious parts; **en ~** lengthwise; **tirer en ~** to drag on; **à ~ de journée** all day long

loquet [lɔkɛ] nm latch

lorgner [lɔʀɲe] vt to eye; (fig) to have one's eye on

lors [lɔʀ]: **~ de** prép at the time of; during

lorsque [lɔʀsk] conj when, as

losange [lɔzɑ̃ʒ] nm diamond

lot [lo] nm (part) share; (de loterie) prize; (fig: destin) fate, lot; (Comm, Inform) batch; **le gros ~** the jackpot

loterie [lɔtʀi] nf lottery

lotion [lɔsjɔ̃] nf lotion; **lotion après rasage** aftershave (lotion)

lotissement [lɔtismɑ̃] nm housing development; (parcelle) plot, lot

loto [lɔto] nm lotto

lotte [lɔt] nf monkfish

louanges [lwɑ̃ʒ] nfpl praise sg

loubard [lubaʀ] (fam) nm lout

louche [luʃ] adj shady, fishy, dubious ▷ nf ladle; **loucher** vi to squint

louer [lwe] vt (maison: suj: propriétaire) to let, rent (out); (: locataire) to rent; (voiture etc: entreprise) to hire out (BRIT), rent (out); (: locataire) to hire, rent; (réserver) to book; (faire l'éloge de) to praise; **"à ~"** "to let" (BRIT), "for rent" (US); **je voudrais ~ une voiture** I'd like to hire (BRIT) ou rent (US) a car

loup [lu] nm wolf; **jeune ~** young go-getter

loupe [lup] nf magnifying glass; **à la ~** in minute detail

louper [lupe] (fam) vt (manquer) to miss; (examen) to flunk

lourd, e [luʀ, luʀd] adj, adv heavy; **c'est trop ~** it's too heavy; **~ de** (conséquences, menaces) charged with; **il fait ~** the weather is close, it's sultry; **lourdaud, e** (péj) adj clumsy; **lourdement** adv heavily

loutre [lutʀ] nf otter

louveteau, x [luv(ə)to] nm wolf-cub; (scout) cub (scout)

louvoyer [luvwaje] vi (fig) to hedge,

evade the issue

loyal, e, -aux [lwajal, o] adj (fidèle) loyal, faithful; (fair-play) fair; **loyauté** nf loyalty, faithfulness; fairness

loyer [lwaje] nm rent

lu, e [ly] pp de **lire**

lubie [lybi] nf whim, craze

lubrifiant [lybrifjã] nm lubricant

lubrifier [lybrifje] vt to lubricate

lubrique [lybrik] adj lecherous

lucarne [lykarn] nf skylight

lucide [lysid] adj lucid; (accidenté) conscious

lucratif, -ive [lykratif, iv] adj lucrative, profitable; **à but non ~** non profit-making

lueur [lyœr] nf (pâle) (faint) light; (chatoyante) glimmer no pl; (fig) glimmer; gleam

luge [ly3] nf sledge (BRIT), sled (US)

lugubre [lygybr] adj gloomy, dismal

MOT-CLÉ

lui [lɥi] pron 1 (objet indirect: mâle) (to) him; (: femelle) (to) her; (: chose, animal) (to) it; **je lui ai parlé** I have spoken to him (ou to her); **il lui a offert un cadeau** he gave him (ou her) a present
2 (après préposition, comparatif: personne) him; (: chose, animal) it; **elle est contente de lui** she is pleased with him; **je la connais mieux que lui** I know her better than he does; I know her better than I know him; **ce livre est à lui** this book is his, this is his book; **c'est à lui de jouer** it's his turn ou go
3 (sujet, forme emphatique) he; **lui, il est à Paris** HE is in Paris; **c'est lui qui l'a fait** HE did it
4 (objet, forme emphatique) him; **c'est lui que j'attends** I'm waiting for HIM
5: **lui-même** himself; itself

luire [lɥir] vi to shine; (en rougeoyant) to glow

lumière [lymjɛr] nf light; **mettre en ~** (fig) to highlight; **lumière du jour**

daylight

luminaire [lyminɛr] nm lamp, light

lumineux, -euse [lyminø, øz] adj luminous; (éclairé) illuminated; (ciel, couleur) bright; (rayon) of light, light cpd; (fig: regard) radiant

lunatique [lynatik] adj whimsical, temperamental

lundi [lœdi] nm Monday; **on est ~** it's Monday; **le(s) ~(s)** on Mondays; **"à ~"** "see you on Monday"; **lundi de Pâques** Easter Monday

lune [lyn] nf moon; **lune de miel** honeymoon

lunette [lynɛt] nf: **~s** nfpl glasses, spectacles; (protectrices) goggles; **lunette arrière** (Auto) rear window; **lunettes de soleil** sunglasses; **lunettes noires** dark glasses

lustre [lystr] nm (de plafond) chandelier; (fig: éclat) lustre; **lustrer** vt to shine

luth [lyt] nm lute

lutin [lytɛ] nm imp, goblin

lutte [lyt] nf (conflit) struggle; (sport) wrestling; **lutter** vi to fight, struggle

luxe [lyks] nm luxury; **de ~** luxury cpd

Luxembourg [lyksãbur] nm: **le ~** Luxembourg

luxer [lykse] vt: **se ~ l'épaule** to dislocate one's shoulder

luxueux, -euse [lyksɥø, øz] adj luxurious

lycée [lise] nm ≈ secondary school; **lycéen, ne** nm/f secondary school pupil

Lyon [ljɔ] n Lyons

lyophilisé, e [ljofilize] adj (café) freeze-dried

lyrique [lirik] adj lyrical; (Opéra) lyric; **artiste ~** opera singer

lys [lis] nm lily

m

M *abr* = **Monsieur**

m' [m] *pron voir* **me**

ma [ma] *adj voir* **mon**

macaron [makaʀɔ̃] *nm (gâteau)* macaroon; *(insigne)* (round) badge

macaronis [makaʀɔni] *nmpl* macaroni *sg*; **~ au fromage** *ou* **en gratin** macaroni cheese (BRIT), macaroni and cheese (US)

macédoine [masedwan] *nf:* **~ de fruits** fruit salad; **~ de légumes** mixed vegetables; **la M~** Macedonia

macérer [maseʀe] *vi, vt* to macerate; *(dans du vinaigre)* to pickle

mâcher [mɑʃe] *vt* to chew; **ne pas ~ ses mots** not to mince one's words

machin [maʃɛ̃] *(fam) nm* thing(umajig); *(personne):* **M~(e)** *nm(f)* what's-his-(*ou* her)-name

machinal, e, -aux [maʃinal, o] *adj* mechanical, automatic

machination [maʃinasjɔ̃] *nf* frame-up

machine [maʃin] *nf* machine; *(locomotive)* engine; **machine à laver/coudre** washing/sewing machine; **machine à sous** fruit machine

mâchoire [mɑʃwaʀ] *nf* jaw

mâchonner [mɑʃɔne] *vt* to chew (at)

maçon [masɔ̃] *nm* builder; *(poseur de briques)* bricklayer; **maçonnerie** *nf (murs)* brickwork; *(pierres)* masonry, stonework

Madagascar [madagaskaʀ] *nf* Madagascar

Madame [madam] *(pl* **Mesdames**) *nf:* **~ Dupont** Mrs Dupont; **occupez-vous de ~/Monsieur/Mademoiselle** please serve this lady/gentleman/(young) lady; **bonjour ~/Monsieur/Mademoiselle** good morning; *(ton déférent)* good morning Madam/Sir/Madam; *(le nom est connu)* good morning Mrs/Mr/Miss X; **~/Monsieur/Mademoiselle!** *(pour appeler)* Madam/Sir/Miss!; **~/Monsieur/Mademoiselle** *(sur lettre)* Dear Madam/Sir/Madam; **chère ~/ cher Monsieur/chère Mademoiselle** Dear Mrs/Mr/Miss X; **Mesdames** Ladies; **mesdames, mesdemoiselles, messieurs** ladies and gentlemen

madeleine [madlɛn] *nf* madeleine, small sponge cake

Mademoiselle [madmwazɛl] *(pl* **Mesdemoiselles**) *nf* Miss; *voir aussi* **Madame**

madère [madɛʀ] *nm* Madeira (wine)

Madrid [madʀid] *n* Madrid

magasin [magazɛ̃] *nm (boutique)* shop; *(entrepôt)* warehouse; **en ~** *(Comm)* in stock

magazine [magazin] *nm* magazine

Maghreb [magʀɛb] nm: **le ~** North Africa; **maghrébin, e** adj North African ▷ nm/f: **Maghrébin, e** North African

magicien, ne [maʒisjɛ̃, jɛn] nm/f magician

magie [maʒi] nf magic; **magique** adj magic; (enchanteur) magical

magistral, e, -aux [maʒistʀal, o] adj (œuvre, adresse) masterly; (ton) authoritative; **cours ~** lecture

magistrat [maʒistʀa] nm magistrate

magnétique [maɲetik] adj magnetic

magnétophone [maɲetɔfɔn] nm tape recorder; **magnétophone à cassettes** cassette recorder

magnétoscope [maɲetɔskɔp] nm video-tape recorder

magnifique [maɲifik] adj magnificent

magret [magʀɛ] nm: **~ de canard** duck steaklet

mai [mɛ] nm May

MAI

- **Le premier mai** is a public holiday in France and commemorates the trades union demonstrations in the United States in 1886 when workers demanded their right to an eight-hour working day. Sprigs of lily of the valley are traditionally exchanged.
- **Le 8 mai** is also a public holiday and commemorates the surrender of the German army to Eisenhower on 7 May, 1945. It is marked by parades of ex-servicemen and ex-servicewomen in most towns.

maigre [mɛgʀ] adj (very) thin, skinny; (viande) lean; (fromage) low-fat; (végétation) thin, sparse; (fig) poor, meagre, skimpy; **jours ~s** days of abstinence, fish days; **maigreur** nf thinness; **maigrir** vi to get thinner, lose weight; **maigrir de 2 kilos** to lose 2 kilos

mail [mɛl] nm e-mail

maille [maj] nf stitch; **maille à l'endroit/à l'envers** plain/purl stitch

maillet [maje] nm mallet

maillon [majɔ̃] nm link

maillot [majo] nm (aussi: **~ de corps**) vest; (de sportif) jersey; **maillot de bain** swimming ou bathing (BRIT) costume, swimsuit; (d'homme) (swimming ou bathing (BRIT)) trunks pl

main [mɛ̃] nf hand; **à la ~** (tenir, avoir) in one's hand; (faire, tricoter etc) by hand; **se donner la ~** to hold hands; **donner** ou **tendre la ~ à qn** to hold out one's hand to sb; **se serrer la ~** to shake hands; **serrer la ~ à qn** to shake hands with sb; **sous la ~** to ou at hand; **haut les ~s!** hands up!; **attaque à ~ armée** armed attack; **à remettre en ~s propres** to be delivered personally; **mettre la dernière ~ à** to put the finishing touches to; **se faire/perdre la ~** to get one's hand in/lose one's touch; **avoir qch bien en ~** to have (got) the hang of sth; **main-d'œuvre** nf manpower, labour; **mainmise** nf (fig): **mainmise sur** complete hold on; **mains libres** adj inv (téléphone, kit) hands-free

maint, e [mɛ̃, mɛ̃t] adj many a; **~s** many; **à ~es reprises** time and (time) again

maintenant [mɛ̃t(ə)nɑ̃] adv now; (actuellement) nowadays

maintenir [mɛ̃t(ə)niʀ] vt (retenir, soutenir) to hold back; (contenir: foule etc) to hold back; (conserver, affirmer) to maintain; **se maintenir** vi (prix) to keep steady; (amélioration) to persist

maintien [mɛ̃tjɛ̃] nm (sauvegarde) maintenance; (attitude) bearing

maire [mɛʀ] nm mayor; **mairie** nf (bâtiment) town hall; (administration) town council

mais [mɛ] conj but; **~ non!** of course not!; **~ enfin** but after all; (indignation) look here!

maïs [mais] nm maize (BRIT), corn (US)

maison [mɛzɔ̃] nf house; (chez-soi)

home; (Comm) firm ▷ adj inv (Culin) home-made; (fig) in-house, own; **à la ~** at home; (direction) home; **maison de repos** convalescent home; **maison de retraite** old people's home; **maison close** ou **de passe** brothel; **maison de santé** mental home; **maison des jeunes** ≈ youth club; **maison mère** parent company

maître, -esse [mɛtʀ, mɛtʀɛs] nm/f master (mistress); (Scol) teacher, schoolmaster(-mistress); (peintre etc) master; (titre): **M~** Maître, term of address gen for a barrister ▷ adj (principal, essentiel) main; **être ~ de** (soi, situation) to be in control of; **une ~sse femme** a managing woman; **maître chanteur** blackmailer; **maître d'école** schoolmaster; **maître d'hôtel** (domestique) butler; (d'hôtel) head waiter; **maître nageur** lifeguard; **maîtresse** (f) (amante) mistress; **maîtresse (d'école)** teacher, (school)mistress; **maîtresse de maison** hostess; (ménagère) housewife

maîtrise [mɛtʀiz] nf (aussi: **~ de soi**) self-control, self-possession; (habileté) skill, mastery; (suprématie) mastery, command; (diplôme) ≈ master's degree; **maîtriser** vt (cheval, incendie) to (bring under) control; (sujet) to master; (émotion) to control, master; **se maîtriser** to control o.s.

majestueux, -euse [maʒɛstɥø, øz] adj majestic

majeur, e [maʒœʀ] adj (important) major; (Jur) of age ▷ nm (doigt) middle finger; **en ~e partie** for the most part; **la ~e partie de** most of

majorer [maʒɔʀe] vt to increase

majoritaire [maʒɔʀitɛʀ] adj majority cpd

majorité [maʒɔʀite] nf (gén) majority; (parti) party in power; **en ~** mainly; **avoir la ~** to have the majority

majuscule [maʒyskyl] adj, nf: **(lettre) ~** capital (letter)

mal [mal, mo] (pl **maux**) nm (opposé

au bien) evil; (tort, dommage) harm; (douleur physique) pain, ache; (maladie) illness, sickness no pl ▷ adv badly ▷ adj bad, wrong; **être ~ à l'aise** to be uncomfortable; **être ~ avec qn** to be on bad terms with sb; **il a ~ compris** he misunderstood; **se sentir** ou **se trouver ~** to feel ill ou unwell; **dire/penser du ~ de** to speak/think ill of; **ne voir aucun ~ à** to see nothing wrong in; **faire ~ à qn** to hurt sb; **se faire ~** to hurt o.s.; **avoir du ~ à faire qch** to have trouble doing sth; **se donner du ~ pour faire qch** to go to a lot of trouble to do sth; **ça fait ~** it hurts; **j'ai ~ au dos** my back hurts; **avoir ~ à la tête/à la gorge/aux dents** to have a headache/a sore throat/toothache; **avoir le ~ du pays** to be homesick; voir aussi **cœur; maux; mal de mer** seasickness; **mal en point** in a bad state

malade [malad] adj ill, sick; (poitrine, jambe) bad; (plante) diseased ▷ nm/f invalid, sick person; (à l'hôpital etc) patient; **tomber ~** to fall ill; **être ~ du cœur** to have heart trouble ou a bad heart; **malade mental** mentally ill person; **maladie** nf (spécifique) disease, illness; (mauvaise santé) illness, sickness; **maladif, -ive** adj sickly; (curiosité, besoin) pathological

maladresse [maladʀɛs] nf clumsiness no pl; (gaffe) blunder

maladroit, e [maladʀwa, wat] adj clumsy

malaise [malɛz] nm (Méd) feeling of faintness; (fig) uneasiness, malaise; **avoir un ~** to feel faint

Malaisie [malɛzi] nf: **la ~** Malaysia

malaria [malaʀja] nf malaria

malaxer [malakse] vt (pétrir) to knead; (mélanger) to mix

malbouffe [malbuf] (fam) nf: **la ~** junk food

malchance [malʃɑ̃s] nf misfortune, ill luck no pl; **par ~** unfortunately; **malchanceux, -euse** adj unlucky

mâle [mɑl] adj (aussi Élec, Tech) male; (viril: voix, traits) manly ▷ nm male

malédiction [malediksjɔ̃] nf curse

mal...: **malentendant, e** nm/f: **les malentendants** the hard of hearing; **malentendu** nm misunderstanding; **il y a eu un malentendu** there's been a misunderstanding; **malfaçon** nf fault; **malfaisant, e** adj evil, harmful; **malfaiteur** nm lawbreaker, criminal; (voleur) burglar, thief; **malfamé, e** adj disreputable

malgache [malgaʃ] adj Madagascan, Malagasy ▷ nm/f: **M~** Madagascan, Malagasy ▷ nm (Ling) Malagasy

malgré [malgre] prép in spite of, despite; **~ tout** all the same

malheur [malœʀ] nm (situation) adversity, misfortune; (événement) misfortune; (: très grave) disaster, tragedy; **faire un ~** to be a smash hit; **malheureusement** adv unfortunately; **malheureux, -euse** adj (triste) unhappy, miserable; (infortuné, regrettable) unfortunate; (malchanceux) unlucky; (insignifiant) wretched ▷ nm poor soul

malhonnête [malɔnɛt] adj dishonest; **malhonnêteté** nf dishonesty

malice [malis] nf mischievousness; (méchanceté): **par ~** out of malice ou spite; **sans ~** guileless; **malicieux, -euse** adj mischievous

Attention à ne pas traduire *malicieux* par *malicious*.

malin, -igne [malɛ̃, malin] adj (futé: f gén: aussi: **maline**) smart, shrewd; (Méd) malignant

malingre [malɛ̃gʀ] adj puny

malle [mal] nf trunk; **mallette** nf (small) suitcase; (porte-documents) attaché case

malmener [malmǝne] vt to manhandle; (fig) to give a rough handling to

malodorant, e [malɔdɔʀɑ̃, ɑ̃t] adj foul-ou ill-smelling

malpoli, e [malpɔli] adj impolite

malsain, e [malsɛ̃, ɛn] adj unhealthy

malt [malt] nm malt

Malte [malt] nf Malta

maltraiter [maltʀete] vt to manhandle, ill-treat

malveillance [malvejɑ̃s] nf (animosité) ill will; (intention de nuire) malevolence

malversation [malvɛʀsasjɔ̃] nf embezzlement

maman [mamɑ̃] nf mum(my), mother

mamelle [mamɛl] nf teat

mamelon [mamlɔ̃]5] nm (Anat) nipple

mamie [mami] (fam) nf granny

mammifère [mamifɛʀ] nm mammal

mammouth [mamut] nm mammoth

manche [mɑ̃ʃ] nf (de vêtement) sleeve; (d'un jeu, tournoi) round; (Géo): **la M~** the Channel ▷ nm (d'outil, casserole) handle; (de pelle, pioche etc) shaft; **à ~s courtes/longues** short-/long-sleeved; **manche à balai** broomstick; (Inform, Aviat) joystick nm inv

manchette [mɑ̃ʃɛt] nf (de chemise) cuff; (coup) forearm blow; (titre) headline

manchot [mɑ̃ʃo] nm one-armed man; armless man; (Zool) penguin

mandarine [mɑ̃daʀin] nf mandarin (orange), tangerine

mandat [mɑ̃da] nm (postal) postal ou money order; (d'un député etc) mandate; (procuration) power of attorney, proxy; (Police) warrant; **mandat d'arrêt** warrant for arrest; **mandat de perquisition** search warrant; **mandataire** nm/f (représentant) representative; (Jur) proxy

manège [manɛʒ] nm riding school; (à la foire) roundabout, merry-go-round; (fig) game, ploy

manette [manɛt] nf lever, tap; **manette de jeu** joystick

mangeable [mɑ̃ʒabl] adj edible, eatable

mangeoire [mɑ̃ʒwaʀ] nf trough, manger

manger [mɑ̃ʒe] vt to eat; (ronger: suj: rouille etc) to eat into ou away ▷ vi to eat; **donner à ~ à** (enfant) to feed; **est-**

ce qu'on peut ~ quelque chose? can we have something to eat?

mangue [mɑ̃g] nf mango

maniable [manjabl] adj (voiture, voilier) easy to handle

maniaque [manjak] adj finicky, fussy ▷ nm/f (méticuleux) fusspot; (fou) maniac

manie [mani] nf (tic) odd habit; (obsession) mania; **avoir la ~ de** to be obsessive about

manier [manje] vt to handle

manière [manjɛʀ] nf (façon) way, manner; **manières** nfpl (attitude) manners; (chichis) fuss sg; **de ~ à** so as to; **de cette ~** in this way ou manner; **d'une certaine ~** in a way; **de toute ~** in any case; **d'une ~ générale** generally speaking, as a general rule

maniéré, e [manjeʀe] adj affected

manifestant, e [manifɛstɑ̃, ɑ̃t] nm/f demonstrator

manifestation [manifɛstasjɔ̃] nf (de joie, mécontentement) expression, demonstration; (symptôme) outward sign; (culturelle etc) event; (Pol) demonstration

manifeste [manifɛst] adj obvious, evident ▷ nm manifesto; **manifester** vt (volonté, intentions) to show, indicate; (joie, peur) to express, show ▷ vi to demonstrate; **se manifester** vi (émotion) to show ou express itself; (difficultés) to arise; (symptômes) to appear

manigancer [manigɑ̃se] vt to plot

manipulation [manipylasjɔ̃] nf handling; (Pol, génétique) manipulation

manipuler [manipyle] vt to handle; (fig) to manipulate

manivelle [manivɛl] nf crank

mannequin [mankɛ̃] nm (Couture) dummy; (Mode) model

manœuvre [manœvʀ] nf (gén) manœuvre (BRIT), maneuver (US) ▷ nm labourer; **manœuvrer** vt to manœuvre (BRIT), maneuver (US); (levier, machine) to operate ▷ vi to manoeuvre

manoir [manwaʀ] nm manor ou country house

manque [mɑ̃k] nm (insuffisance): **~ de** lack of; (vide) emptiness, gap; (Méd) withdrawal; **être en état de ~** to suffer withdrawal symptoms

manqué, e [mɑ̃ke] adj failed; **garçon ~** tomboy

manquer [mɑ̃ke] vi (faire défaut) to be lacking; (être absent) to be missing; (échouer) to fail ▷ vt to miss ▷ vb impers: **il (nous) manque encore 10 euros** we are still 10 euros short; **il manque des pages (au livre)** there are some pages missing (from the book); **il/cela me manque** I miss him/this; **~ à** (règles etc) to be in breach of, fail to observe; **~ de** to lack; **je ne ~ai pas de le lui dire** I'll be sure to tell him; **il a manqué (de) se tuer** he very nearly got killed

mansarde [mɑ̃saʀd] nf attic; **mansardé, e** adj: **chambre mansardée** attic room

manteau, x [mɑ̃to] nm coat

manucure [manykyʀ] nf manicurist

manuel, le [manɥɛl] adj manual ▷ nm (ouvrage) manual, handbook

manufacture [manyfaktyʀ] nf factory; **manufacturé, e** adj manufactured

manuscrit, e [manyskʀi, it] adj handwritten ▷ nm manuscript

manutention [manytɑ̃sjɔ̃] nf (Comm) handling

mappemonde [mapmɔ̃d] nf (plane) map of the world; (sphère) globe

maquereau, x [makʀo] nm (Zool) mackerel inv; (fam) pimp

maquette [makɛt] nf (à échelle réduite) (scale) model; (d'une page illustrée) paste-up

maquillage [makijaʒ] nm making up; (crème etc) make-up

maquiller [makije] vt (personne, visage) to make up; (truquer: passeport, statistique) to fake; (: voiture volée) to do over (respray etc); **se maquiller** vi to make up (one's face)

maquis [maki] nm (Géo) scrub; (Mil)
maquis, underground fighting no pl

maraîcher, -ère [maʀɛʃe, ɛʀ] adj:
cultures maraîchères market
gardening sg ▷ nm/f market gardener

marais [maʀɛ] nm marsh, swamp

marasme [maʀasm] nm stagnation,
slump

marathon [maʀatɔ̃] nm marathon

marbre [maʀbʀ] nm marble

marc [maʀ] nm (de raisin, pommes) marc

marchand, e [maʀʃɑ̃, ɑ̃d] nm/f
shopkeeper, tradesman(-woman); (au
marché) stallholder; (de vins, charbon)
merchant ▷ adj: **prix/valeur ~(e)**
market price/value; **marchand de
fruits** fruiterer (BRIT), fruit seller (US);
marchand de journaux newsagent;
marchand de légumes greengrocer
(BRIT), produce dealer (US); **marchand
de poissons** fishmonger (BRIT), fish
seller (US); **marchander** vi to bargain,
haggle; **marchandise** nf goods pl,
merchandise no pl

marche [maʀʃ] nf (d'escalier) step;
(activité) walking; (promenade, trajet,
allure) walk; (démarche) gait; (Mil etc,
Mus) march; (fonctionnement)
running; (des événements) course; **dans
le sens de la ~** (Rail) facing the engine;
en ~ (monter etc) while the vehicle is
moving ou in motion; **mettre en ~** to
start; **se mettre en ~** (personne) to get
moving; (machine) to start; **être en état
de ~** to be in working order; **marche
à suivre** (correct) procedure; **marche
arrière** reverse (gear); **faire marche
arrière** to reverse; (fig) to backtrack,
back-pedal

marché [maʀʃe] nm market;
(transaction) bargain, deal; **faire du
~ noir** to buy and sell on the black
market; **marché aux puces** flea
market

marcher [maʀʃe] vi to walk; (Mil) to
march; (aller: voiture, train, affaires) to
go; (prospérer) to go well; (fonctionner) to

work, run; (fam: consentir) to go along,
agree; (: croire naïvement) to be taken
in; **faire ~ qn** (taquiner) to pull sb's leg;
(tromper) to lead sb up the garden path;
comment est-ce que ça marche?
how does this work?; **marcheur, -euse**
nm/f walker

mardi [maʀdi] nm Tuesday; **Mardi gras**
Shrove Tuesday

mare [maʀ] nf pond; (flaque) pool

marécage [maʀekaʒ] nm marsh,
swamp; **marécageux, -euse** adj
marshy

maréchal, -aux [maʀeʃal, o] nm
marshal

marée [maʀe] nf tide; (poissons) fresh
(sea) fish; **marée haute/basse** high/
low tide; **marée noire** oil slick

marelle [maʀɛl] nf: **(jouer à) la ~** (to
play) hopscotch

margarine [maʀgaʀin] nf margarine

marge [maʀʒ] nf margin; **en ~ de** (fig)
on the fringe of; **marge bénéficiaire**
profit margin

marginal, e, -aux [maʀʒinal, o] nm/f
(original) eccentric; (déshérité) dropout

marguerite [maʀgəʀit] nf
marguerite, (oxeye) daisy;
(d'imprimante) daisy-wheel

mari [maʀi] nm husband

mariage [maʀjaʒ] nm marriage; (noce)
wedding; **mariage civil/religieux**
registry office (BRIT) ou civil/religious
church wedding

marié, e [maʀje] adj married ▷ nm
(bride)groom; **les ~s** the bride and
groom; **les (jeunes) ~s** the newly-weds

marier [maʀje] vt to marry; (fig)
to blend; **se ~ (avec)** to marry, get
married (to)

marin, e [maʀɛ̃, in] adj sea cpd, marine
▷ nm sailor

marine [maʀin] adj voir **marin** ▷ adj
inv navy (blue) ▷ nm (Mil) marine ▷ nf
navy; **marine marchande** merchant
navy

mariner [maʀine] vt: **faire ~** to
marinade

marionnette [marjɔnɛt] nf puppet

maritalement [maritalmɑ̃] adv: **vivre ~** to live as husband and wife

maritime [maritim] adj sea cpd; maritime

mark [mark] nm mark

marmelade [marməlad] nf stewed fruit, compote; **marmelade d'oranges** marmalade

marmite [marmit] nf (cooking-)pot

marmonner [marmɔne] vt, vi to mumble, mutter

marmotter [marmɔte] vt to mumble

Maroc [marɔk] nm: **le ~** Morocco; **marocain, e** [marɔkɛ̃, ɛn] adj Moroccan ▷ nm/f: **Marocain, e** Moroccan

maroquinerie [marɔkinri] nf (articles) fine leather goods pl; (boutique) shop selling fine leather goods

marquant, e [markɑ̃, ɑ̃t] adj outstanding

marque [mark] nf mark; (Comm: de nourriture) brand; (: de voiture, produits manufacturés) make; (de disques) label; **de ~** (produits) high-class; (visiteur etc) distinguished, well-known; **une grande ~ de vin** a well-known brand of wine; **marque de fabrique** trademark; **marque déposée** registered trademark

marquer [marke] vt to mark; (inscrire) to write down; (bétail) to brand; (Sport: but etc) to score; (: joueur) to mark; (accentuer: taille etc) to emphasize; (manifester: refus, intérêt) to show ▷ vi (événement) to stand out, be outstanding; (Sport) to score; **~ les points** to keep the score

marqueterie [markətri] nf inlaid work, marquetry

marquis [marki] nm marquis, marquess

marraine [marɛn] nf godmother

marrant, e [marɑ̃, ɑ̃t] (fam) adj funny

marre [mar] (fam) adv: **en avoir ~ de** to be fed up with

marrer [mare]: **se ~** (fam) vi to have a (good) laugh

marron [marɔ̃] nm (fruit) chestnut ▷ adj inv brown; **marrons glacés** candied chestnuts; **marronnier** nm chestnut (tree)

mars [mars] nm March

Marseille [marsɛj] n Marseilles

marteau, x [marto] nm hammer; **être ~** (fam) to be nuts; **marteau-piqueur** nm pneumatic drill

marteler [martəle] vt to hammer

martien, ne [marsjɛ̃, jɛn] adj Martian, of ou from Mars

martyr, e [martir] nm/f martyr ▷ adj: **enfants ~s** battered children; **martyre** nm martyrdom; (fig: sens affaibli) agony, torture; **martyriser** vt (Rel) to martyr; (fig) to bully; (enfant) to batter, beat

marxiste [marksist] adj, nm/f Marxist

mascara [maskara] nm mascara

masculin, e [maskylɛ̃, in] adj masculine; (sexe, population) male; (équipe, vêtements) men's; (viril) manly ▷ nm masculine

masochiste [mazɔʃist] adj masochistic

masque [mask] nm mask; **masque de beauté** face pack ou mask; **masque de plongée** diving mask; **masquer** vt (cacher: paysage, porte) to hide, conceal; (dissimuler: vérité, projet) to mask, obscure

massacre [masakr] nm massacre, slaughter; **massacrer** vt to massacre, slaughter; (fam: texte etc) to murder

massage [masaʒ] nm massage

masse [mas] nf mass; (Élec) earth; (maillet) sledgehammer; (péj): **la ~** the masses pl; **une ~ de** (fam) masses ou loads of; **en ~** adv (acheter) in bulk; (en foule) en masse ▷ adj (exécutions, production) mass cpd

masser [mase] vt (assembler: gens) to gather; (pétrir) to massage; **se masser** vi (foule) to gather; **masseur, -euse** nm/f masseur(-euse)

massif, -ive [masif, iv] adj (porte) solid, massive; (visage) heavy, large;

(bois, or) solid; (dose) massive; (déportations etc) mass cpd ▷ nm (montagneux) massif; (de fleurs) clump, bank; **le M~ Central** the Massif Central

massue [masy] nf club, bludgeon

mastic [mastik] nm (pour vitres) putty; (pour fentes) filler

mastiquer [mastike] vt (aliment) to chew, masticate

mat, e [mat] adj (couleur, métal) mat(t); (bruit, son) dull ▷ adj inv (Échecs): **être ~** to be checkmate

mât [mɑ] nm (Navig) mast; (poteau) pole, post

match [matʃ] nm match; **faire ~ nul** to draw; **match aller** first leg; **match retour** second leg, return match

matelas [mat(ə)lɑ] nm mattress; **matelas pneumatique** air bed ou mattress

matelot [mat(ə)lo] nm sailor, seaman

mater [mate] vt (personne) to bring to heel, subdue; (révolte) to put down

matérialiser [materjalize]: **se matérialiser** vi to materialize

matérialiste [materjalist] adj materialistic

matériau [materjo] nm material; **matériaux** nmpl material(s)

matériel, le [materjɛl] adj material ▷ nm equipment no pl; (de camping etc) gear no pl; (Inform) hardware

maternel, le [matɛrnɛl] adj (amour, geste) motherly, maternal; (grand-père, oncle) maternal; **maternelle** nf (aussi: **école maternelle**) (state) nursery school

maternité [matɛrnite] nf (établissement) maternity hospital; (état de mère) motherhood, maternity; (grossesse) pregnancy; **congé de ~** maternity leave

mathématique [matematik] adj mathematical; **mathématiques** nfpl (science) mathematics sg

maths [mat] (fam) nfpl maths

matière [matjɛr] nf matter; (Comm, Tech) material, matter no pl; (fig: d'un

livre etc) subject matter, material; (Scol) subject; **en ~ de** as regards; **matières grasses** fat content sg; **matières premières** raw materials

Matignon [matiɲɔ̃] nm: **(l'hôtel) ~** the French Prime Minister's residence

matin [matɛ̃] nm, adv morning; **le ~** (pendant le matin) in the morning; **demain/hier/dimanche ~** tomorrow/yesterday/Sunday morning; **tous les ~s** every morning; **une heure du ~** one o'clock in the morning; **du ~ au soir** from morning till night; **de bon** ou **grand ~** early in the morning; **matinal, e, -aux** adj (toilette, gymnastique) morning cpd; **être matinal** (personne) to be up early; to be an early riser; **matinée** nf morning; (spectacle) matinée

matou [matu] nm tom(cat)

matraque [matrak] nf (de policier) truncheon (BRIT), billy (US)

matricule [matrikyl] nm (Mil) regimental number; (Admin) reference number

matrimonial, e, -aux [matrimonjal, jo] adj marital, marriage cpd

maudit, e [modi, -it] (fam) adj (satané) blasted, confounded

maugréer [mogree] vi to grumble

maussade [mosad] adj sullen; (temps) gloomy

mauvais, e [mɔvɛ, ɛz] adj bad; (faux): **le ~ numéro/moment** the wrong number/moment; (méchant, malveillant) malicious; spiteful ▷ adv: **il fait ~** the weather is bad; **sentir ~** to have a nasty smell, smell nasty; **la mer est ~e** the sea is rough; **mauvais joueur** bad loser; **mauvaise herbe** weed; **mauvaise langue** gossip, scandalmonger (BRIT); **mauvaise plaisanterie** nasty trick

mauve [mov] adj mauve

maux [mo] nmpl de **mal**

maximum [maksimɔm] adj, nm maximum; **au ~** (le plus possible) as much as one can; (tout au plus) at the (very) most ou maximum; **faire le ~** to do one's level best

mayonnaise [majɔnɛz] nf mayonnaise

mazout [mazut] nm (fuel) oil

me, m' [m(ə)] pron (direct: téléphoner, attendre etc) me; (indirect: parler, donner etc) (to) me; (réfléchi) myself

mec [mɛk] (fam) nm bloke, guy

mécanicien, ne [mekanisjɛ̃, jɛn] nm/f mechanic; (Rail) (train ou engine) driver; **pouvez-vous nous envoyer un ~?** can you send a mechanic?

mécanique [mekanik] adj mechanical ▷ nf (science) mechanics sg; (mécanisme) mechanics; **ennui ~** engine trouble no pl

mécanisme [mekanism] nm mechanism

méchamment [meʃamɑ̃] adv nastily, maliciously, spitefully

méchanceté [meʃɑ̃ste] nf nastiness, maliciousness; **dire des ~s à qn** to say spiteful things to sb

méchant, e [meʃɑ̃, ɑ̃t] adj nasty, malicious, spiteful; (enfant: pas sage) naughty; (animal) vicious

mèche [mɛʃ] nf (de cheveux) lock; (de lampe, bougie) wick; (d'un explosif) fuse; **se faire faire des ~s** to have highlights put in one's hair; **de ~ avec** in league with

méchoui [meʃwi] nm barbecue of a whole roast sheep

méconnaissable [mekɔnɛsabl] adj unrecognizable

méconnaître [mekɔnɛtʀ] vt (ignorer) to be unaware of; (mésestimer) to misjudge

mécontent, e [mekɔ̃tɑ̃, ɑ̃t] adj: **~ (de)** discontented ou dissatisfied ou displeased (with); (contrarié) annoyed (at); **mécontentement** nm dissatisfaction, discontent, displeasure; (irritation) annoyance

Mecque [mɛk] nf: **la ~** Mecca

médaille [medaj] nf medal

médaillon [medajɔ̃] nm (bijou) locket

médecin [medsɛ̃] nm doctor

médecine [med(ə)sin] nf medicine

média [medja] nmpl: **les ~** the media; **médiatique** adj media cpd

médical, e, -aux [medikal, o] adj medical; **passer une visite ~e** to have a medical

médicament [medikamɑ̃] nm medicine, drug

médiéval, e, -aux [medjeval, o] adj medieval

médiocre [medjɔkʀ] adj mediocre, poor

méditer [medite] vi to meditate

Méditerranée [mediteʀane] nf: **la (mer) ~** the Mediterranean (Sea); **méditerranéen, ne** adj Mediterranean ▷ nm/f: **Méditerranéen, ne** native ou inhabitant of a Mediterranean country

méduse [medyz] nf jellyfish

méfait [mefɛ] nm (faute) misdemeanour, wrongdoing; **méfaits** nmpl (ravages) ravages, damage sg

méfiance [mefjɑ̃s] nf mistrust, distrust

méfiant, e [mefjɑ̃, jɑ̃t] adj mistrustful, distrustful

méfier [mefje]: **se méfier** vi to be wary; to be careful; **se ~ de** to mistrust, distrust, be wary of

mégaoctet [megaɔktɛ] nm megabyte

mégarde [megaʀd] nf: **par ~** (accidentellement) accidentally; (par erreur) by mistake

mégère [meʒɛʀ] nf shrew

mégot [mego] (fam) nm cigarette end

meilleur, e [mɛjœʀ] adj, adv better ▷ nm: **le ~** the best; **le ~ des deux** the better of the two; **il fait ~ qu'hier** it's better weather than yesterday; **meilleur marché** (inv) cheaper

mél [mɛl] nm e-mail

mélancolie [melɑ̃kɔli] nf melancholy, gloom; **mélancolique** adj melancholic, melancholy

mélange [melɑ̃ʒ] nm mixture;

mélanger vt to mix; (vins, couleurs) to blend; (mettre en désordre) to mix up, muddle (up)

mêlée [mele] nf melee, scramble; (Rugby) scrum(mage)

mêler [mele] vt (unir) to mix; (embrouiller) to muddle (up), mix up; **se mêler** vi to mix, mingle; **se ~ à** (personne: se joindre) to join; (: s'associer à) to mix with; **se ~ de** (suj: personne) to meddle with, interfere in; **mêle-toi de ce qui te regarde ou de tes affaires!** mind your own business!

mélodie [melɔdi] nf melody; **mélodieux, -euse** adj melodious

melon [m(ə)lɔ̃] nm (Bot) (honeydew) melon; (aussi: **chapeau ~**) bowler (hat)

membre [mɑ̃bʀ] nm (Anat) limb; (personne, pays, élément) member ▷ adj member cpd

mémé [meme] (fam) nf granny

O **MOT-CLÉ**

même [mɛm] adj 1 (avant le nom) same; **en même temps** at the same time; **ils ont les mêmes goûts** they have the same ou similar tastes

2 (après le nom: renforcement): **il est la loyauté même** he is loyalty itself; **ce sont ses paroles mêmes** these are his very words

▷ pron: **le(la) même** the same one ▷ adv 1 (renforcement): **il n'a même pas pleuré** he didn't even cry; **même lui l'a dit** even HE said it; **ici même** at this very place; **même si** even if

2: **à même: à même la bouteille** straight from the bottle; **à même la peau** next to the skin; **être à même de faire** to be in a position to do, be able to do

3: **de même: faire de même** to do likewise; **lui de même** so does (ou did ou is) he; **de même que** just as; **il en va de même pour** the same goes for

mémoire [memwaʀ] nf memory ▷ nm

(Scol) dissertation, paper; **mémoires** nmpl (souvenirs) memoirs; **à la ~ de** to the ou in memory of; **de ~** from memory; **mémoire morte** read-only memory, ROM; **mémoire vive** random access memory, RAM

mémorable [memɔʀabl] adj memorable, unforgettable

menace [mənas] nf threat; **menacer** vt to threaten

ménage [menaʒ] nm (travail) housework; (couple) (married) couple; (famille, Admin) household; **faire le ~** to do the housework; **ménagement** nm care and attention; **ménager, -ère** adj household cpd, domestic ▷ vt (traiter: personne) to handle with tact; (utiliser) to use sparingly; (prendre soin de) to take (great) care of, look after; (organiser) to arrange; **ménagère** nf housewife

mendiant, e [mɑ̃djɑ̃, jɑ̃t] nm/f beggar

mendier [mɑ̃dje] vi to beg ▷ vt to beg (for)

mener [m(ə)ne] vt to lead; (enquête) to conduct; (affaires) to manage ▷ vi: **~ à/dans** (emmener) to take to/into; **~ qch à bien** to see sth through (to a successful conclusion), complete sth successfully

meneur, -euse [mənœʀ, øz] nm/f leader; (péj) agitator

méningite [menɛ̃ʒit] nf meningitis no pl

ménopause [menopoz] nf menopause

menottes [mənɔt] nfpl handcuffs

mensonge [mɑ̃sɔ̃ʒ] nm lie; (action) lying no pl; **mensonger, -ère** adj lying

mensualité [mɑ̃sɥalite] nf (traite) monthly payment

mensuel, le [mɑ̃sɥɛl] adj monthly

mensurations [mɑ̃syʀasjɔ̃] nfpl measurements

mental, e, -aux [mɑ̃tal, o] adj mental; **mentalité** nf mentality

menteur, -euse [mɑ̃tœʀ, øz] nm/f liar

menthe [mɑ̃t] nf mint

mention [mɑ̃sjɔ̃] nf (annotation) note,

comment; (Scol) grade; **~ bien** = grade B, = good pass; (Université) = upper 2nd class pass (BRIT), = pass with (high) honors (US); (Admin): **"rayer les ~s inutiles"** "delete as appropriate"; **mentionner** vt to mention

mentir [mɑ̃tiʀ] vi to lie

menton [mɑ̃tɔ̃] nm chin

menu, e [məny] adj (personne) slim, slight; (frais, détail) minor ▷ adv (couper, hacher) very fine ▷ nm menu; **~ touristique/gastronomique** economy/gourmet's menu

menuiserie [mənɥizʀi] nf (métier) joinery, carpentry; (passe-temps) woodwork; **menuisier** nm joiner, carpenter

méprendre [mepʀɑ̃dʀ]: **se méprendre** vi: **se ~ sur** to be mistaken (about)

mépris [mepʀi] nm (dédain) contempt, scorn; **au ~ de** regardless of, in defiance of; **méprisable** adj contemptible, despicable; **méprisant, e** adj scornful; **méprise** nf mistake, error; **mépriser** vt to scorn, despise; (gloire, danger) to scorn, spurn

mer [mɛʀ] nf sea; (marée) tide; **en ~** at sea; **en haute** ou **pleine ~** off shore, on the open sea; **la ~ du Nord/Rouge/ Noire/Morte** the North/Red/Black/ Dead Sea

mercenaire [mɛʀsənɛʀ] nm mercenary, hired soldier

mercerie [mɛʀsəʀi] nf (boutique) haberdasher's shop (BRIT), notions store (US)

merci [mɛʀsi] excl thank you ▷ nf: **à la ~ de qn/qch** at sb's mercy/the mercy of sth; **~ beaucoup** thank you very much; **~ de** thank you for; **sans ~** merciless(ly)

mercredi [mɛʀkʀədi] nm Wednesday; **~ des Cendres** Ash Wednesday; voir aussi **lundi**

mercure [mɛʀkyʀ] nm mercury

merde [mɛʀd] (fam!) nf shit (!) ▷ excl (bloody) hell (!)

mère [mɛʀ] nf mother; **mère célibataire** single parent, unmarried mother; **mère de famille** housewife, mother

merguez [mɛʀgɛz] nf merguez sausage (type of spicy sausage from N Africa)

méridional, e, -aux [meʀidjɔnal, o] adj southern ▷ nm/f Southerner

meringue [məʀɛ̃g] nf meringue

mérite [meʀit] nm merit; **avoir du ~ (à faire qch)** to deserve credit (for doing sth); **mériter** vt to deserve

merle [mɛʀl] nm blackbird

merveille [mɛʀvɛj] nf marvel, wonder; **faire ~** to work wonders; **à ~** perfectly, wonderfully; **merveilleux, -euse** adj marvellous, wonderful

mes [me] adj voir **mon**

mésange [mezɑ̃ʒ] nf tit(mouse)

mésaventure [mezavɑ̃tyʀ] nf misadventure, misfortune

Mesdames [medam] nfpl de **Madame**

Mesdemoiselles [medmwazɛl] nfpl de **Mademoiselle**

mesquin, e [mɛskɛ̃, in] adj mean, petty; **mesquinerie** nf meanness; (procédé) mean trick

message [mesaʒ] nm message; **est-ce que je peux laisser un ~?** can I leave a message?; **~ SMS** text message; **messager, -ère** nm/f messenger; **messagerie** nf (Internet): **messagerie électronique** e-mail; **messagerie vocale** (service) voice mail; **messagerie instantanée** instant messenger

messe [mɛs] nf mass; **aller à la ~** to go to mass

Messieurs [mesjø] nmpl de **Monsieur**

mesure [m(ə)zyʀ] nf (évaluation, dimension) measurement; (récipient) measure; (Mus: cadence) time, tempo; (: division) bar; (retenue) moderation; (disposition) measure, step; **sur ~** (costume) made-to-measure; **dans la ~ où** insofar as, inasmuch as; **à ~ que** as; **être en ~ de** to be in a position to; **dans une certaine ~** to a certain extent

mesurer [məzyʀe] vt to measure; (juger) to weigh up, assess; (modérer: ses *paroles etc)* to moderate

métal, -aux [metal, o] *nm* metal;
métallique *adj* metallic

météo [meteo] *nf (bulletin)* weather
report

météorologie [meteɔʀɔlɔʒi] *nf*
meteorology

méthode [metɔd] *nf (livre,*
ouvrage) manual, tutor

méticuleux, -euse [metikylø, øz] *adj*
meticulous

métier [metje] *nm (profession: gén)*
job; *(: manuel: base; artisanal)* craft;
(technique, expérience) (acquired) skill *ou*
technique; *(aussi: ~ à tisser)* (weaving)
loom

métis, se [metis] *adj, nm/f* half-caste,
half-breed

métrage [metʀaʒ] *nm:* **long/moyen/**
court ~ full-length/medium-length/
short film

mètre [mɛtʀ] *nm* metre; *(règle)* (metre)
rule; *(ruban)* tape measure; **métrique**
adj metric

métro [metʀo] *nm* underground (BRIT),
subway

métropole [metʀɔpɔl] *nf (capitale)*
metropolis; *(pays)* home country

mets [mɛ] *nm* dish

metteur [metœʀ] *nm:* **~ en scène**
(Théâtre) producer; *(Cinéma)* director

MOT-CLÉ

mettre [mɛtʀ] *vt* **1** *(placer)* to put;
mettre en bouteille/en sac to bottle/
put in bags *ou* sacks
2 *(vêtements: revêtir)* to put on; *(: porter)*
to wear; **mets ton gilet** put your
cardigan on *ou* put; **je ne mets plus mon**
manteau I no longer wear my coat
3 *(faire fonctionner: chauffage, électricité)*
to put on; *(: réveil, minuteur)* to set;
(installer: gaz, eau) to put in, lay on;
mettre en marche to start up
4 *(consacrer):* **mettre du temps à faire**
qch to take time to do sth *ou* over sth
5 *(noter, écrire)* to say, put (down);

qu'est-ce qu'il a mis sur la carte?
what did he say *ou* write on the card?;
mettez au pluriel ... put ... into the
plural
6 *(supposer):* **mettons que ...** let's
suppose *ou* say that ...
7: **y mettre du sien** to pull one's weight
se mettre *vi* **1** *(se placer):* **vous pouvez**
vous mettre là you can sit *(ou* stand)
there; **où ça se met?** where does it
go?; **se mettre au lit** to get into bed;
se mettre au piano to sit down at the
piano; **se mettre de l'encre sur les**
doigts to get ink on one's fingers
2 *(s'habiller):* **se mettre en maillot de**
bain to get into *ou* put on a swimsuit;
n'avoir rien à se mettre to have
nothing to wear
3: **se mettre à** to begin, start; **se**
mettre à faire to begin *ou* start doing
ou to do; **se mettre au piano** to start
learning the piano; **se mettre au**
régime to go on a diet; **se mettre**
au travail/à l'étude to get down to
work/one's studies

meuble [mœbl] *nm* piece of furniture;
des ~s furniture; **meublé** *nm* furnished
flatlet (BRIT) *ou* room; **meubler** *vt* to
furnish

meuf [mœf] *nf (fam)* woman

meugler [møgle] *vi* to low, moo

meule [møl] *nf (de foin, blé)* stack; *(de*
fromage) round; *(à broyer)* millstone

meunier [mønje] *nm* miller

meurs *etc* [mœʀ] *vb voir* **mourir**

meurtre [mœʀtʀ] *nm* murder;
meurtrier, -ière *adj (arme etc)* deadly;
(fureur, instincts) murderous ▷ *nm/f*
murderer(-ress)

meurtrir [mœʀtʀiʀ] *vt* to bruise; *(fig)*
to wound

meus *etc* [mø] *vb voir* **mouvoir**

meute [møt] *nf* pack

mexicain, e [mɛksikɛ̃, ɛn] *adj*
Mexican ▷ *nm/f:* **M~, e** Mexican
Mexico [mɛksiko] *n* Mexico City
Mexique [mɛksik] *nm:* **le ~** Mexico

mi [mi] nm (Mus) E; (en chantant la gamme) mi ▷ préfixe: **mi...** half(-); mid-; **à la mi-janvier** in mid-January; **à mi-jambes/corps** (up ou down) to the knees/waist; **à mi-hauteur** halfway up

miauler [mjole] vi to mew

miche [miʃ] nf round ou cob loaf

mi-chemin [miʃmɛ̃]: **à ~** adv halfway, midway

mi-clos, e [miklo, kloz] adj half-closed

micro [mikro] nm mike, microphone; (Inform) micro

microbe [mikrɔb] nm germ, microbe

micro...: **micro-onde** nf: **four à micro-ondes** microwave oven; **micro-ordinateur** nm microcomputer; **microscope** nm microscope; **microscopique** adj microscopic

midi [midi] nm midday, noon; (moment du déjeuner) lunchtime; (sud) south; **à ~** at 12 (o'clock) ou midday ou noon; **le M~** the South (of France), the Midi

mie [mi] nf crumb (of the loaf)

miel [mjɛl] nm honey; **mielleux, -euse** adj (personne) unctuous, syrupy

mien, ne [mjɛ̃, mjɛn] pron: **le(la) ~(ne), les ~(ne)s** mine; **les ~s** my family

miette [mjɛt] nf (de pain, gâteau) crumb; (fig: de la conversation etc) scrap; **en ~s** in pieces ou bits

O **MOT-CLÉ**

mieux [mjø] adv **1** (d'une meilleure façon): **mieux (que)** better (than); **elle travaille/mange mieux** she works/eats better; **aimer mieux** to prefer; **elle va mieux** she is better; **de mieux en mieux** better and better
2 (de la meilleure façon) best; **ce que je connais le mieux** what I know best; **les livres les mieux faits** the best-made books
▷ adj **1** (plus à l'aise, en meilleure forme) better; **se sentir mieux** to feel better; **2** (plus satisfaisant) better; **c'est mieux ainsi** it's better like this; **c'est le mieux**

des deux it's the better of the two; **le(la) mieux, les mieux** the best; **demandez-lui, c'est le mieux** ask him, it's the best thing
3 (plus joli) better-looking; **il est mieux que son frère** (plus beau) he's better-looking than his brother; (plus gentil) he's nicer than his brother; **il est mieux sans moustache** he looks better without a moustache
4: **au mieux** at best; **au mieux avec** on the best of terms with; **pour le mieux** for the best
▷ nm **1** (progrès) improvement
2: **de mon/ton mieux** as best I/you can (ou could); **faire de son mieux** to do one's best

mignon, ne [miɲɔ̃, ɔn] adj sweet, cute

migraine [migʁɛn] nf headache; (Méd) migraine

mijoter [miʒɔte] vt to simmer; (préparer avec soin) to cook lovingly; (fam: tramer) to plot, cook up ▷ vi to simmer

milieu, x [miljø] nm (centre) middle; (Bio, Géo) environment; (entourage social) milieu; (provenance) background; (pègre): **le ~** the underworld; **au ~ de** in the middle of; **au beau ou en plein ~ (de)** right in the middle (of); **un juste ~** a happy medium

militaire [militɛʁ] adj military, army cpd ▷ nm serviceman

militant, e [militɑ̃, ɑ̃t] adj, nm/f militant

militer [milite] vi to be a militant

mille [mil] num a ou one thousand ▷ nm (mesure): **~ (marin)** nautical mile; **mettre dans le ~** (fig) to be bang on target; **millefeuille** nm cream ou vanilla slice; **millénaire** nm millennium ▷ adj thousand-year-old; (fig) ancient; **mille-pattes** nm inv centipede

millet [mijɛ] nm millet

milliard [miljaʁ] nm milliard, thousand million (BRIT), billion (US); **milliardaire** nm/f multimillionaire

(BRIT), billionaire (US)

millier [milje] nm thousand; **un ~ (de)** a thousand or so, about a thousand; **par ~s** in (their) thousands, by the thousand

milligramme [miligram] nm milligramme

millimètre [milimɛtʀ] nm millimetre

million [miljɔ̃] nm million; **deux ~s de** two million; **millionnaire** nm/f millionaire

mime [mim] nm/f (acteur) mime(r) ▷ nm (art) mime, miming; **mimer** vt to mime; (singer) to mimic, take off

minable [minabl] adj (décrépit) shabby(-looking); (médiocre) pathetic

mince [mɛ̃s] adj thin; (personne, taille) slim, slender; (fig: profit, connaissances) slight, small, weak ▷ excl: **~ alors!** drat it!, darn it! (US); **minceur** nf thinness; (d'une personne) slimness, slenderness; **mincir** vi to get slimmer

mine [min] nf (physionomie) expression, look; (allure) exterior, appearance; (de crayon) lead; (gisement, explosif, fig: source) mine; **avoir bonne ~** (personne) to look well; (ironique) to look an utter idiot; **avoir mauvaise ~** to look unwell ou poorly; **faire ~ de faire** to make a pretence of doing; **~ de rien** although you wouldn't think so

miner [mine] vt (saper) to undermine, erode; (Mil) to mine

minerai [minʀɛ] nm ore

minéral, e, -aux [mineral, o] adj, nm mineral

minéralogique [mineralɔʒik] adj: **plaque ~** number (BRIT) ou license (US) plate; **numéro ~** registration (BRIT) ou license (US) number

minet, te [minɛ, ɛt] nm/f (chat) pussy-cat; (péj) young trendy

mineur, e [minœʀ] adj minor ▷ nm/f (Jur) minor, person under age ▷ nm (travailleur) miner

miniature [minjatyʀ] adj, nf miniature

minibus [minibys] nm minibus

minier, -ière [minje, jɛʀ] adj mining

mini-jupe [miniʒyp] nf mini-skirt

minime [minim] adj minor, minimal

minimessage [minimesaʒ] nm text message

minimiser [minimize] vt to minimize; (fig) to play down

minimum [minimɔm] adj, nm minimum; **au ~** (au moins) at the very least

ministère [ministɛʀ] nm (aussi Rel) ministry; (cabinet) government

ministre [ministʀ] nm (aussi Rel) minister; **ministre d'État** senior minister ou secretary

Minitel® [minitɛl] nm videotext terminal and service

◦ **MINITEL®**
◦
◦ Minitel® is a public information
◦ system provided by France-Télécom
◦ to telephone subscribers since
◦ the early 80s. Among the services
◦ available are a computerized
◦ telephone directory and information
◦ on travel timetables, stock-market
◦ news and situations vacant.
◦ Subscribers pay for their time on
◦ screen as part of their phone bill.
◦ Although this information is now
◦ also available on the Internet, the
◦ special Minitel® screens, terminals
◦ and keyboards are still very much a
◦ part of French daily life.

minoritaire [minɔʀitɛʀ] adj minority

minorité [minɔʀite] nf minority; **être en ~** to be in the ou a minority

minuit [minɥi] nm midnight

minuscule [minyskyl] adj minute, tiny ▷ nf: (lettre) **~** small letter

minute [minyt] nf minute; **à la ~** (just) this instant; (faire) there and then; **minuter** vt to time; **minuterie** nf time switch

minutieux, -euse [minysjø, jøz] adj (personne) meticulous; (travail) minutely detailed

mirabelle [miʀabɛl] nf (cherry) plum

miracle [miʀakl] nm miracle

mirage [miʀaʒ] nm mirage

mire [miʀ] nf: **point de ~** (fig) focal point

miroir [miʀwaʀ] nm mirror

miroiter [miʀwate] vi to sparkle, shimmer; **faire ~ qch à qn** to paint sth in glowing colours for sb, dangle sth in front of sb's eyes

mis, e [mi, miz] pp de **mettre** ▷ adj: **bien ~** well-dressed

mise [miz] nf (argent: au jeu) stake; (tenue) clothing, attire; **être de ~** to be acceptable ou in season; **mise à jour** updating; **mise au point** (fig) clarification; **mise de fonds** capital outlay; **mise en plis** set; **mise en scène** production

miser [mize] vt (enjeu) to stake, bet; **~ sur** (cheval, numéro) to bet on; (fig) to bank ou count on

misérable [mizeʀabl] adj (lamentable, malheureux) pitiful, wretched; (pauvre) poverty-stricken; (insignifiant, mesquin) miserable ▷ nm/f wretch

misère [mizɛʀ] nf (extreme) poverty, destitution; **misères** nfpl (malheurs) woes, miseries; (ennuis) little troubles; **salaire de ~** starvation wage

missile [misil] nm missile

mission [misjɔ̃] nf mission; **partir en ~** (Admin, Pol) to go on an assignment; **missionnaire** nm/f missionary

mité, e [mite] adj moth-eaten

mi-temps [mitɑ̃] nf inv (Sport: période) half; (: pause) half-time; **à ~** part-time

miteux, -euse [mitø, øz] adj (lieu) seedy

mitigé, e [mitiʒe] adj: **sentiments ~s** mixed feelings

mitoyen, ne [mitwajɛ̃, jɛn] adj (mur) common, party; cpd: **maisons ~nes** semi-detached houses; (plus de deux) terraced (BRIT) ou row (US) houses

mitrailler [mitʀaje] vt to machine-gun; (fig) to pelt, bombard;

(: photographier) to take shot after shot of; **mitraillette** nf submachine gun; **mitrailleuse** nf machine gun

mi-voix [mivwa]: **à ~** adv in a low ou hushed voice

mixage [miksaʒ] nm (Cinéma) (sound) mixing

mixer [miksœʀ] nm (food) mixer

mixte [mikst] adj (gén) mixed; (Scol) mixed, coeducational; **cuisinière ~** combined gas and electric cooker (BRIT) ou stove (US)

mixture [mikstyʀ] nf mixture; (fig) concoction

Mlle (pl **~s**) abr = **Mademoiselle**

MM abr = **Messieurs**

Mme (pl **~s**) abr = **Madame**

mobile [mɔbil] adj mobile; (pièce de machine) moving ▷ nm (motif) motive; (œuvre d'art) mobile; (téléphone) ~ mobile (phone)

mobilier, -ière [mɔbilje, jɛʀ] nm furniture

mobiliser [mɔbilize] vt to mobilize

mocassin [mɔkasɛ̃] nm moccasin

moche [mɔʃ] (fam) adj (laid) ugly; (mauvais) rotten

modalité [mɔdalite] nf form, mode

mode [mɔd] nf fashion ▷ nm (manière) form, mode; (Ling) mood; (Mus, Inform) mode; **à la ~** fashionable, in fashion; **mode d'emploi** directions pl (for use); **mode de paiement** method of payment; **mode de vie** lifestyle

modèle [mɔdɛl] adj, nm model; (qui pose: de peintre) sitter; **modèle déposé** registered design; **modèle réduit** small-scale model; **modeler** vt to model

modem [mɔdɛm] nm modem

modéré, e [mɔdeʀe] adj, nm/f moderate

modérer [mɔdeʀe] vt to moderate; **se modérer** vi to restrain o.s.

moderne [mɔdɛʀn] adj modern ▷ nm (style) modern style; (meubles) modern furniture; **moderniser** vt to modernize

modeste [mɔdɛst] adj modest;

modestie nf modesty

modifier [mɔdifje] vt to modify, alter;
se modifier vi to alter

modique adj modest

module [mɔdyl] nm module

moelle [mwal] nf marrow

moelleux, -euse [mwalø, øz] adj soft;
(*gâteau*) light and moist

mœurs [mœʀ] nfpl (*conduite*) morals;
(*manières*) manners; (*pratiques sociales,
mode de vie*) habits

moi [mwa] pron me; (*emphatique*): ~,
je ... for my part, I ...; (*réponse*): **c'est
~ qui l'ai fait** I did it, it was me who
did it; **apporte-le-~** bring it to me; **à ~**
mine; (*dans un jeu*) my turn; **moi-même**
pron myself; (*emphatique*) I myself

moindre [mwɛdʀ] adj lesser; lower;
le(la) ~, les ~ the least, the slightest;
merci — c'est la ~ des choses! thank
you — it's a pleasure!

moine [mwan] nm monk, friar

moineau, x [mwano] nm sparrow

⊙ **MOT-CLÉ**

moins [mwɛ] adv 1 (*comparatif*):
moins (que) less (than); **moins grand
que** less tall than, not as tall as; **il a
3 ans de moins que moi** he's 3 years
younger than me; **moins je travaille,
mieux je me porte** the less I work, the
better I feel

2 (*superlatif*): **le moins** (the) least; **c'est
ce que j'aime le moins** it's what I like
(the) least; **le(la) moins doué(e)** the
least gifted; **au moins, du moins** at
least; **pour le moins** at the very least

3: **moins de** (*quantité*) less (than);
(*nombre*) fewer (than); **moins de
sable/d'eau** less sand/water; **moins
de livres/gens** fewer books/people;
moins de 2 ans less than 2 years;
moins de midi not yet midday

4: **de moins, en moins: 100 euros/3
jours de moins** 100 euros/3 days less;
3 livres en moins 3 books fewer;
3 books too few; de l'argent en moins

less money; **le soleil en moins** but for
the sun, minus the sun; **de moins en
moins** less and less

5: **à moins de, à moins que** unless;
à moins de faire unless we do (*ou* he
does *etc*); **à moins que tu ne fasses**
unless you do; **à moins qu'il n'y ait un accident**
unless there's an accident

▷ *prép*: **4 moins 2** 4 minus 2; **il est
moins 5** it's 5 to; **il fait moins 5** it's 5
(degrees) below (freezing), it's minus 5

mois [mwa] nm month

moisi [mwazi] nm mould, mildew;
odeur de ~ musty smell; **moisir** vi to
go mouldy; **moisissure** nf mould no pl

moisson [mwasɔ̃] nf harvest;
moissonner vt to harvest, reap;
moissonneuse nf (*machine*) harvester

moite [mwat] adj sweaty, sticky

moitié [mwatje] nf half; **la ~ half; la
~ de** half (of); **la ~ du temps** half the
time; **à la ~ de** halfway through; **à ~**
(*avant le verbe*) half; (*avant l'adjectif*)
half-; **à ~ prix** (at) half-price

molaire [mɔlɛʀ] nf molar

mole [mɔl] adj voir **mou; mollement**
adv (*péj: travailler*) sluggishly; (*protester*)
feebly

mollet [mɔlɛ] nm calf ▷ adj m: **œuf ~**
soft-boiled egg

molletonné, e [mɔltɔne] adj
fleece-lined

mollir [mɔliʀ] vi (*fléchir*) to relent;
(*substance*) to go soft

mollusque [mɔlysk] nm mollusc

môme [mom] (*fam*) nm/f (*enfant*) brat

moment [mɔmɑ̃] nm moment; **ce
n'est pas le ~ this is not the (right)
time; au même ~ at the same time;
(*instant*) at the same moment; pour un
bon ~ for a good while; pour le ~ for the
moment, for the time being; au ~ de
at the time of; au ~ où just as; à tout ~
(*peut arriver etc*) at any time *ou* moment;
(*constamment*) constantly, continually;

en ce ~ at the moment; at present; **sur le ~** at the time; **par ~s** now and then, at times; **d'un ~ à l'autre** any time (now); **du ~ où que** seeing that, since; **momentané, e** adj temporary, momentary; **momentanément** adv (court instant) for a short while

momie [mɔmi] nf mummy

mon, ma [mɔ̃, ma] (pl **mes**) adj my

Monaco [mɔnako] nm Monaco

monarchie [mɔnaʀʃi] nf monarchy

monastère [mɔnastɛʀ] nm monastery

mondain, e [mɔ̃dɛ̃, ɛn] adj (vie) society cpd

monde [mɔ̃d] nm world; (haute société): **le ~** (high) society; **il y a du ~** (beaucoup de gens) there are a lot of people; (quelques personnes) there are some people; **beaucoup/peu de ~** many/few people; **mettre au ~** to bring into the world; **pas le moins du ~** not in the least; **mondial, e, -aux** adj (population) world (influence) world-wide; **mondialement** adv throughout the world; **mondialisation** nf globalization

monégasque [mɔnegask] adj Monegasque, of ou from Monaco ▷ nm/f: **M~** Monegasque, person from ou inhabitant of Monaco

monétaire [mɔnetɛʀ] adj monetary

moniteur, -trice [mɔnitœʀ, tʀis] nm/f (Sport) instructor(-tress); (de colonie de vacances) supervisor ▷ nm (écran) monitor

monnaie [mɔnɛ] nf (Écon, gén: moyen d'échange) currency; (petites pièces): **avoir de la ~** to have (some) change; **une pièce de ~** a coin; **faire de la ~** to get (some) change; **avoir/faire la ~ de 20 euros** to have change of/get change for 20 euros; **rendre à qn la ~ (sur 20 euros)** to give sb the change (out of ou from 20 euros); **gardez la ~** keep the change; **désolé, je n'ai pas de ~** sorry, I don't have any change; **avez-vous de la ~?** do you have any change?

monologue [mɔnɔlɔg] nm monologue, soliloquy; **monologuer** vi to soliloquize

monopole [mɔnɔpɔl] nm monopoly

monotone [mɔnɔtɔn] adj monotonous

Monsieur [məsjø] (pl **Messieurs**) titre Mr ▷ nm (homme quelconque): **un/le monsieur** a/the gentleman; **~, ...** (en tête de lettre) Dear Sir, ...; voir aussi **Madame**

monstre [mɔ̃stʀ] nm monster ▷ adj (fam: colossal) monstrous; **un travail ~** a fantastic amount of work; **monstrueux, -euse** adj monstrous

mont [mɔ̃] nm: **par ~s et par vaux** up hill and down dale; **le Mont Blanc** Mont Blanc

montage [mɔ̃taʒ] nm (assemblage: d'appareil) assembly; (Photo) photomontage; (Cinéma) editing

montagnard, e [mɔ̃taɲaʀ, aʀd] adj mountain cpd ▷ nm/f mountain-dweller

montagne [mɔ̃taɲ] nf (cime) mountain; (région): **la ~** the mountains pl; **montagnes russes** big dipper sg, switchback sg; **montagneux, -euse** adj mountainous; (basse montagne) hilly

montant, e [mɔ̃tɑ̃, ɑ̃t] adj rising; **pull à col ~** high-necked jumper ▷ nm (somme, total) (sum) total, total amount; (de fenêtre) upright; (de lit) post

monte-charge [mɔ̃tʃaʀʒ] nm inv goods lift, hoist

montée [mɔ̃te] nf (des prix, hostilités) rise; (escalade) climb; (côte) hill; **au milieu de la ~** halfway up

monter [mɔ̃te] vt (escalier, côte) to go (ou come) up; (valise, paquet) to take (ou bring) up; (étagère) to raise; (tente, échafaudage) to put up; (machine) to assemble; (Cinéma) to edit; (Théâtre) to put on, stage; (société etc) to set up ▷ vi to go (ou come) up; (prix, niveau, température) to go up, rise; (passager) to get on; **~ à cheval** (faire du cheval) to ride (a horse); **~ sur** to climb up onto; **~**

sur ou **à un arbre/une échelle** to climb (up) a tree/ladder; **se monter à** (frais etc) to add up to, to come to

montgolfière [mɔ̃gɔlfjɛʀ] nf hot-air balloon

montre [mɔ̃tʀ] nf watch; **contre la ~** (Sport) against the clock

Montréal [mɔ̃ʀeal] n Montreal

montrer [mɔ̃tʀe] vt to show; **~ qch à qn** to show sb sth; **pouvez-vous me ~ où c'est?** can you show me where it is?

monture [mɔ̃tyʀ] nf (cheval) mount; (de lunettes) frame; (d'une bague) setting

monument [mɔnymɑ̃] nm monument; **monument aux morts** war memorial

moquer [mɔke]: **se moquer de** vt to make fun of, laugh at; (ne pas se désintéresser de) not to care about; (tromper): **se ~ de qn** to take sb for a ride

moquette [mɔkɛt] nf fitted carpet

moqueur, -euse [mɔkœʀ, øz] adj mocking

moral, e, -aux [mɔʀal, o] adj moral ▷ nm morale; **avoir le ~** (fam) to be in good spirits; **avoir le ~ à zéro** (fam) to be really down; **morale** nf (mœurs) morals pl; (valeurs) moral standards pl, morality; (d'une fable etc) moral; **faire la morale à** to lecture, preach at; **moralité** nf morality; (de fable) moral

morceau, x [mɔʀso] nm piece, bit; (d'une œuvre) passage, extract; (Mus) piece; (Culin: de viande) cut; (de sucre) lump; **mettre en ~x** to pull to pieces ou bits; **manger un ~** to have a bite (to eat)

morceler [mɔʀsəle] vt to break up, divide up

mordant, e [mɔʀdɑ̃, ɑ̃t] adj (ton, remarque) scathing, cutting; (ironie, froid) biting ▷ nm (style) bite, punch

mordiller [mɔʀdije] vt to nibble at, chew at

mordre [mɔʀdʀ] vt to bite ▷ vi (poisson) to bite; **~ sur** (fig) to go over into, overlap into; **~ à l'hameçon** to bite, rise to the bait

mordu, e [mɔʀdy] (fam) nm/f enthusiast; **un ~ de jazz** a jazz fanatic

morfondre [mɔʀfɔ̃dʀ]: **se morfondre** vi to mope

morgue [mɔʀg] nf (arrogance) haughtiness; (lieu: de la police) morgue; (: à l'hôpital) mortuary

morne [mɔʀn] adj dismal, dreary

morose [mɔʀoz] adj sullen, morose

mors [mɔʀ] nm bit

morse [mɔʀs] nm (Zool) walrus; (Tél) Morse (code)

morsure [mɔʀsyʀ] nf bite

mort¹ [mɔʀ] nf death

mort², e [mɔʀ, mɔʀt] pp de **mourir** ▷ adj dead ▷ nm/f (défunt) dead man ou woman; (victime): **il y a eu plusieurs ~s** several people were killed, there were several killed; **~ de peur/fatigue** frightened to death/dead tired

mortalité [mɔʀtalite] nf mortality, death rate

mortel, le [mɔʀtɛl] adj (poison) deadly, lethal; (accident, blessure) fatal; (silence, ennemi) deadly; (péché) mortal; (fam: ennuyeux) deadly boring

mort-né, e [mɔʀne] adj (enfant) stillborn

mortuaire [mɔʀtɥeʀ] adj: **avis ~** death announcement

morue [mɔʀy] nf (Zool) cod inv

mosaïque [mɔzaik] nf mosaic

Moscou [mɔsku] n Moscow

mosquée [mɔske] nf mosque

mot [mo] nm word; (message) line, note; **~ à ~** word for word; **mot de passe** password; **mots croisés** crossword (puzzle) sg

motard [mɔtaʀ] nm biker; (policier) motorcycle cop

motel [mɔtɛl] nm motel

moteur, -trice [mɔtœʀ, tʀis] adj (Anat, Physiol) motor; (Tech) driving; (Auto): **à 4 roues motrices** 4-wheel drive ▷ nm engine, motor; **à ~** power-driven, motor cpd; **moteur de recherche** search engine

motif [mɔtif] nm (cause) motive;

(décoratif) design, pattern, motif; **sans ~** groundless

motivation [mɔtivasjɔ̃] nf motivation

motiver [mɔtive] vt to motivate; (justifier) to justify, account for

moto [mɔto] nf motorbike; **motocycliste** nm/f motorcyclist

motorisé, e [mɔtɔrize] adj (personne) having transport ou a car

motrice [mɔtris] adj voir **moteur**

motte [mɔt] nf: **~ de terre** lump of earth, clod (of earth); **motte de beurre** lump of butter

mou (mol), molle [mu, mɔl] adj soft; (personne) lethargic; (protestations) weak ▷ nm: **avoir du mou** to be slack

mouche [muʃ] nf fly

moucher [muʃe]: **se moucher** vi to blow one's nose

moucheron [muʃʀɔ̃] nm midge

mouchoir [muʃwaʀ] nm handkerchief, hanky; **mouchoir en papier** tissue, paper hanky

moudre [mudʀ] vt to grind

moue [mu] nf pout; **faire la ~** to pout; (fig) to pull a face

mouette [mwɛt] nf (sea)gull

moufle [mufl] nf (gant) mitt(en)

mouillé, e [muje] adj wet

mouiller [muje] vt (humecter) to wet, moisten; (tremper): **~ qn/qch** to make sb/sth wet ▷ vi (Navig) to lie ou be at anchor; **se mouiller** to get wet; (fam: prendre des risques) to commit o.s.

moulant, e [mulɑ̃, ɑ̃t] adj figure-hugging

moule [mul] nf mussel ▷ nm (Culin) mould; **moule à gâteaux** nm cake tin (BRIT) ou pan (US)

mouler [mule] vt (suj: vêtement) to hug, fit closely round

moulin [mulɛ̃] nm mill; **moulin à café** coffee mill; **moulin à eau** watermill; **moulin à légumes** (vegetable) shredder; **moulin à paroles** (fig) chatterbox; **moulin à poivre** pepper mill; **moulin à vent** windmill

moulinet [mulinɛ] nm (de canne à pêche) reel; (mouvement): **faire des ~s avec qch** to whirl sth around

moulinette® [mulinɛt] nf (vegetable) shredder

moulu, e [muly] pp de **moudre**

mourant, e [muʀɑ̃, ɑ̃t] adj dying

mourir [muʀiʀ] vi to die; (civilisation) to die out; **~ de froid/faim** to die of exposure/hunger; **~ de faim/d'ennui** (fig) to be starving/be bored to death; **~ d'envie de faire** to be dying to do

mousse [mus] nf (Bot) moss; (de savon) lather; (écume: sur eau, bière) froth, foam; (Culin) mousse ▷ nm (Navig) ship's boy; **mousse à raser** shaving foam

mousseline [muslin] nf muslin; **pommes ~** mashed potatoes

mousser [muse] vi (bière, détergent) to foam; (savon) to lather; **mousseux, -euse** adj frothy ▷ nm: **(vin) mousseux** sparkling wine

mousson [musɔ̃] nf monsoon

moustache [mustaʃ] nf moustache; **moustaches** nfpl (du chat) whiskers pl; **moustachu, e** adj with a moustache

moustiquaire [mustikɛʀ] nf mosquito net

moustique [mustik] nm mosquito

moutarde [mutaʀd] nf mustard

mouton [mutɔ̃] nm sheep inv; (peau) sheepskin; (Culin) mutton

mouvement [muvmɑ̃] nm movement; (fig: impulsion) gesture; **avoir un bon ~** to make a nice gesture; **en ~** in motion; on the move; **mouvementé, e** adj (vie, poursuite) eventful; (réunion) turbulent

mouvoir [muvwaʀ]: **se mouvoir** vi to move

moyen, ne [mwajɛ̃, jɛn] adj average; (tailles, prix) medium; (de grandeur moyenne) medium-sized; (façon) means sg, way; **moyens** nmpl (capacités) means; **très ~** (résultats) pretty poor; **je n'en ai pas les ~s** I can't afford it; **au ~ de** by means of; **par tous les ~s** by every possible means, every possible way; **par ses propres ~s** all by oneself; **moyen âge** Middle Ages pl; **moyen de transport** means of transport

moyennant [mwajenɑ̃] prép (somme) for; (service, conditions) in return for; (travail, effort) with

moyenne [mwajɛn] nf average; (Math) mean; (Scol) pass mark; **en ~** on (an) average; **moyenne d'âge** average age

Moyen-Orient [mwajɛnɔʀjɑ̃] nm: **le ~** the Middle East

moyeu, x [mwajø] nm hub

MST sigle f (= maladie sexuellement transmissible) STD

mû, mue [my] pp de **mouvoir**

muer [mɥe] vi (oiseau, mammifère) to moult; (serpent) to slough; (jeune garçon): **il mue** his voice is breaking

muet, te [mɥɛ, mɥɛt] adj dumb; (fig): **~ d'admiration** etc speechless with admiration etc; (Cinéma) silent ▷ nm/f mute

mufle [myfl] nm muzzle; (fam: goujat) boor

mugir [myʒiʀ] vi (taureau) to bellow; (vache) to low; (fig) to howl

muguet [mygɛ] nm lily of the valley

mule [myl] nf (Zool) (she-)mule

mulet [mylɛ] nm (Zool) (he-)mule

multinational, e [myltinasjɔnal] nf multinational

multiple [myltipl] adj multiple, numerous; (varié) many, manifold; **multiplication** nf multiplication; **multiplier** vt to multiply; **se multiplier** vi to multiply

municipal, e, -aux [mynisipal, o] adj (élections, stade) municipal; (conseil) town cpd; **piscine/bibliothèque ~e** public swimming pool/library; **municipalité** nf (ville) municipality; (conseil) town council

munir [myniʀ] vt: **~ qch de** to equip sth with; **se ~ de** to arm o.s. with

munitions [mynisjɔ̃] nfpl ammunition sg

mur [myʀ] nm wall; **mur du son** sound barrier

mûr, e [myʀ] adj ripe; (personne) mature

muraille [myʀɑj] nf (high) wall

mural, e, -aux [myʀal, o] adj wall cpd; (art) mural

mûre [myʀ] nf blackberry

muret [myʀɛ] nm low wall

mûrir [myʀiʀ] vi (fruit, blé) to ripen; (abcès) to come to a head; (fig: idée, personne) to mature ▷ vt (projet) to nurture; (personne) to (make) mature

murmure [myʀmyʀ] nm murmur; **murmurer** vi to murmur

muscade [myskad] nf (aussi: **noix (de) ~**) nutmeg

muscat [myska] nm (raisins) muscat grape; (vin) muscatel (wine)

muscle [myskl] nm muscle; **musclé, e** adj muscular; (fig) strong-arm

museau, x [myzo] nm muzzle; (Culin) brawn

musée [myze] nm museum; (de peinture) art gallery

museler [myz(ə)le] vt to muzzle; **muselière** nf muzzle

musette [myzɛt] nf (sac) lunchbag

musical, e, -aux [myzikal, o] adj musical

music-hall [myzikol] nm (salle) variety theatre; (genre) variety

musicien, ne [myzisjɛ̃, jɛn] adj musical ▷ nm/f musician

musique [myzik] nf music

● **FÊTE DE LA MUSIQUE**
●
● The **Fête de la Musique** is a music
● festival which takes place every year
● on 21 June. Throughout France, local
● musicians perform free of charge in
● parks, streets and squares.

musulman, e [myzylmɑ̃, an] adj, nm/f Moslem, Muslim

mutation [mytasjɔ̃] nf (Admin) transfer

muter [myte] vt to transfer, move

mutilé, e [mytile] nm/f disabled

person (through loss of limbs)
mutiler [mytile] vt to mutilate, maim
mutin, e [mytɛ̃, in] adj (air, ton)
mischievous, impish ▷ nm/f (Mil,
Navig) mutineer; **mutinerie** nf mutiny
mutisme [mytism] nm silence
mutuel, le [mytɥɛl] adj mutual;
mutuelle nf voluntary insurance
premiums for back-up health cover
myope [mjɔp] adj short-sighted
myosotis [mjɔzotis] nm forget-
me-not
myrtille [miʀtij] nf bilberry
mystère [mistɛʀ] nm mystery;
mystérieux, -euse adj mysterious
mystifier [mistifje] vt to fool
mythe [mit] nm myth
mythologie [mitɔlɔʒi] nf mythology

n' [n] adv voir **ne**
nacre [nakʀ] nf mother of pearl
nage [naʒ] nf swimming; (manière) style
of swimming, stroke; **traverser/
s'éloigner à la ~** to swim across/away;
en ~ bathed in sweat; **nageoire** nf fin;
nager vi to swim; **nageur, -euse** nm/f
swimmer
naïf, -ïve [naif, naiv] adj naïve
nain, e [nɛ̃, nɛn] nm/f dwarf
naissance [nesɑ̃s] nf birth; **donner ~ à**
to give birth to; (fig) to give rise to; **lieu
de ~** place of birth
naître [nɛtʀ] vi to be born; (fig): **~ de**
to arise from, be born out of; **il est né en
1960** he was born in 1960; **faire ~** (fig) to
give rise to, arouse
naïveté [naivte] nf naïvety
nana [nana] (fam) nf (fille) chick, bird
(BRIT)
nappe [nap] nf tablecloth; (de pétrole,
gaz) layer; **napperon** nm table-mat
naquit etc [naki] vb voir **naître**
narguer [naʀge] vt to taunt

narine [naʀin] nf nostril

natal, e [natal] adj native; **natalité** nf birth rate

natation [natasjɔ̃] nf swimming

natif, -ive [natif, iv] adj native

nation [nasjɔ̃] nf nation; **national, e, -aux** adj national; **nationale** nf: **(route) nationale** ≈ A road (BRIT), ≈ state highway (US); **nationaliser** vt to nationalize; **nationalisme** nm nationalism; **nationalité** nf nationality

natte [nat] nf (cheveux) plait; (tapis) mat

naturaliser [natyralize] vt to naturalize

nature [natyr] nf nature ▷ adj, adv (Culin) plain, without seasoning or sweetening; (café, thé) black, without sugar; (yaourt) natural; **payer en ~** to pay in kind; **nature morte** still life; **naturel, le** adj (gén, aussi enfant) natural ▷ nm (absence d'affectation) naturalness; (caractère) disposition, nature; **naturellement** adv naturally; (bien sûr) of course

naufrage [nofʀaʒ] nm (ship)wreck; **faire ~** to be shipwrecked

nausée [noze] nf nausea; **avoir la ~** to feel sick

nautique [notik] adj nautical, water cpd: **sports ~s** water sports

naval, e [naval] adj naval; (industrie) shipbuilding

navet [navɛ] nm turnip; (péj: film) rubbishy film

navette [navɛt] nf shuttle; **faire la ~ (entre)** to go to and fro ou shuttle (between)

navigateur [navigatœʀ] nm (Navig) seafarer; (Inform) browser

navigation [navigasjɔ̃] nf navigation, sailing

naviguer [navige] vi to navigate, sail; **~ sur Internet** to browse the Internet

navire [naviʀ] nm ship

navrer [navʀe] vt to upset, distress; **je suis navré** I'm so sorry

ne, n' [n(ə)] adv voir **pas; plus; jamais** etc; (sans valeur négative: non traduit): **c'est plus loin que je ne le croyais** it's further than I imagined

né, e [ne] pp (voir **naître**): **né en 1960** born in 1960; **née Scott** née Scott

néanmoins [neɑ̃mwɛ̃] adv nevertheless

néant [neɑ̃] nm nothingness; **réduire à ~** to bring to nought; (espoir) to dash

nécessaire [neseseʀ] adj necessary ▷ nm necessary; (sac) kit; **je vais faire le ~** I'll see to it; **nécessaire de couture** sewing kit; **nécessaire de toilette** toilet bag; **nécessité** nf necessity; **nécessiter** vt to require

nectar [nɛktaʀ] nm nectar

néerlandais, e [neɛʀlɑ̃dɛ, ɛz] adj Dutch

nef [nɛf] nf (d'église) nave

néfaste [nefast] adj (nuisible) harmful; (funeste) ill-fated

négatif, -ive [negatif, iv] adj negative ▷ nm (Photo) negative

négligé, e [negliʒe] adj (en désordre) slovenly ▷ nm (tenue) negligee

négligeable [negliʒabl] adj negligible

négligent, e [negliʒɑ̃, ɑ̃t] adj careless, negligent

négliger [negliʒe] vt (tenue) to be careless about; (avis, précautions) to disregard; (épouse, jardin) to neglect; **~ de faire** to fail to do, not bother to do

négociant, e [negɔsjɑ̃, jɑ̃t] nm/f merchant

négociation [negɔsjasjɔ̃] nf negotiation

négocier [negɔsje] vi, vt to negotiate

nègre [nɛgʀ] nm (péj) (écrivain) ghost (writer)

neige [nɛʒ] nf snow; **neiger** vi to snow

nénuphar [nenyfaʀ] nm water-lily

néon [neɔ̃] nm neon

néo-zélandais, e [neozelɑ̃dɛ, ɛz] adj New Zealand cpd ▷ nm/f: **Néo-Zélandais, e** New Zealander

Népal [nepal] nm: **le ~** Nepal

nerf [nɛʀ] nm nerve; **être sur les ~s**

to be all keyed up; **nerveux, -euse** adj nervous; (irritable) touchy, nervy; (voiture) nippy, responsive; **nervosité** nf excitability, tenseness; (irritabilité passagère) irritability, nerviness

n'est-ce pas? [nɛspɑ] adv isn't it?, won't you? etc, selon le verbe qui précède

Net [nɛt] nm (Internet): **le ~** the Net

net, nette adj (sans équivoque, distinct) clear; (évident: amélioration, différence) marked, distinct; (propre) neat, clean; (Comm: prix, salaire) net ▷ adv (refuser) flatly ▷ nm: **mettre au ~** to copy out; **s'arrêter ~** to stop dead; **nettement** adv clearly, distinctly; (incontestablement) decidedly; **netteté** nf clearness

nettoyage [netwajaʒ] nm cleaning; **nettoyage à sec** dry cleaning

nettoyer [netwaje] vt to clean

neuf¹ [nœf] num nine

neuf², neuve [nœf, nœv] adj new; **remettre à ~** to do up (as good as new), refurbish; **quoi de ~?** what's new?

neutre [nøtʀ] adj neutral; (Ling) neuter

neuve [nœv] adj voir **neuf⁹**

neuvième [nœvjɛm] num ninth

neveu, x [n(ə)vø] nm nephew

New York [njujɔʀk] n New York

nez [ne] nm nose; **~ à ~ avec** face to face with; **avoir du ~** to have flair

ni [ni] conj: **ni … ni** neither … nor; **je n'aime ni les lentilles ni les épinards** I like neither lentils nor spinach; **il n'a dit ni oui ni non** he didn't say either yes or no; **elles ne sont venues ni l'une ni l'autre** neither of them came; **il n'a rien vu ni entendu** he didn't see or hear anything

niche [niʃ] nf (du chien) kennel; (de mur) recess, niche; **nicher** vi to nest

nid [ni] nm nest; **nid de poule** pothole

nièce [njɛs] nf niece

nier [nje] vt to deny

Nil [nil] nm: **le ~** the Nile

n'importe [nɛpɔʀt] adv: **n'importe qui/quoi/où** anybody/anything/anywhere; **n'importe quand** any time;

n'importe quel/quelle any; **n'importe lequel/laquelle** any (one); **n'importe comment** (sans soin) carelessly

niveau, x [nivo] nm (des élèves, études) standard; **niveau de vie** standard of living

niveler [niv(ə)le] vt to level

noble [nɔbl] adj noble; **noblesse** nf nobility; (d'une action etc) nobleness

noce [nɔs] nf wedding; (gens) wedding party (ou guests pl); **faire la ~** (fam) to go on a binge; **noces d'argent/d'or/de diamant** silver/golden/diamond wedding (anniversary)

nocif, -ive [nɔsif, iv] adj harmful

nocturne [nɔktyʀn] adj nocturnal ▷ nf late-night opening

Noël [nɔɛl] nm Christmas

nœud [nø] nm knot; (ruban) bow; **nœud papillon** bow tie

noir, e [nwaʀ] adj black; (obscur, sombre) dark ▷ nm/f black man/woman ▷ nm: **dans le ~** in the dark; **travail au ~** moonlighting; **travailler au ~** to work on the side; **noircir** vt, vi to blacken; **noire** nf (Mus) crotchet (BRIT), quarter note (US)

noisette [nwazɛt] nf hazelnut

noix [nwa] nf walnut; (Culin): **une ~ de beurre** a knob of butter; **à la ~** (fam) worthless; **noix de cajou** cashew nut; **noix de coco** coconut; **noix muscade** nutmeg

nom [nɔ̃] nm name; (Ling) noun; **nom de famille** surname; **nom de jeune fille** maiden name

nomade [nɔmad] nm/f nomad

nombre [nɔ̃bʀ] nm number; **venir en ~** to come in large numbers; **depuis ~ d'années** for many years; **au ~ de mes amis** among my friends; **nombreux, -euse** adj many, numerous; (avec nom sg: foule etc) large; **peu nombreux** few; **de nombreux cas** many cases

nombril [nɔ̃bʀi(l)] nm navel

nommer [nɔme] vt to name; (élire) to appoint, nominate; **se nommer: il se**

nomme Pascal his name's Pascal, he's called Pascal

non [nɔ̃] adv (réponse) no; (avec loin, sans, seulement) not; **~ (pas) que** not that; **moi ~ plus** neither do I, I don't either; **c'est bon ~?** (exprimant le doute) it's good, isn't it?; **je pense que ~** I don't think so

non alcoolisé, e [nɔ̃alkɔlize] adj non alcoholic

nonchalant, e [nɔ̃ʃalɑ̃, ɑ̃t] adj nonchalant

non-fumeur, -euse [nɔ̃fymœʀ, øz] nm/f non-smoker

non-sens [nɔ̃sɑ̃s] nm absurdity

nord [nɔʀ] nm North ▷ adj northern; north; **au ~** (situation) in the north; (direction) to the north; **au ~ de** (to the) north of; **nord-africain, e** adj North-African ▷ nm/f: **Nord-Africain, e** North African; **nord-est** nm North-East; **nord-ouest** nm North-West

normal, e, -aux [nɔʀmal, o] adj normal; **c'est tout à fait ~** it's perfectly natural; **vous trouvez ça ~?** does it seem right to you?; **normale** nf: **la normale** the norm, the average; **normalement** adv (en général) normally

normand, e [nɔʀmɑ̃, ɑ̃d] adj of Normandy ▷ nm/f: **N~, e** (de Normandie) Norman

Normandie [nɔʀmɑ̃di] nf Normandy

norme [nɔʀm] nf norm; (Tech) standard

Norvège [nɔʀvɛʒ] nf Norway; **norvégien, ne** adj Norwegian ▷ nm/f: **Norvégien, ne** Norwegian ▷ nm (Ling) Norwegian

nos [no] adj voir **notre**

nostalgie [nɔstalʒi] nf nostalgia; **nostalgique** adj nostalgic

notable [nɔtabl] adj (fait) notable, noteworthy; (marqué) noticeable, marked ▷ nm prominent citizen

notaire [nɔtɛʀ] nm solicitor

notamment [nɔtamɑ̃] adv in particular, among others

note [nɔt] nf (écrite, Mus) note; (Scol) mark (BRIT), grade; (facture) bill; **note de service** memorandum

noter [nɔte] vt (écrire) to write down; (remarquer) to note, notice; (devoir) to mark, grade

notice [nɔtis] nf summary, short article; (brochure) leaflet, instruction book

notifier [nɔtifje] vt: **~ qch à qn** to notify sb of sth, notify sth to sb

notion [nɔsjɔ̃] nf notion, idea

notoire [nɔtwaʀ] adj widely known; (en mal) notorious

notre [nɔtʀ] adj (pl **nos**) our

nôtre [nɔtʀ] pron: **le ~, la ~, les ~s** ours ▷ adj ours; **les ~s** ours; (alliés etc) our own people; **soyez des ~s** join us

nouer [nwe] vt to tie, knot; (fig: alliance etc) to strike up

noueux, -euse [nwø, øz] adj gnarled

nourrice [nuʀis] nf (gardienne) child-minder

nourrir [nuʀiʀ] vt to feed; (fig: espoir) to harbour, nurse; **nourrissant, e** adj nourishing, nutritious; **nourrisson** nm (unweaned) infant; **nourriture** nf food

nous [nu] pron (sujet) we; (objet) us; **nous-mêmes** pron ourselves

nouveau (nouvel), -elle, x [nuvo, nuvɛl] adj new ▷ nm: **y a-t-il du nouveau?** is there anything new on this? ▷ nm/f (new pupil (ou employee); **de nouveau, à nouveau** again; **nouveau venu, nouvelle venue** newcomer; **nouveaux mariés** newly-weds; **nouveau-né, e** nm/f newborn baby; **nouveauté** nf novelty; (objet) new thing ou article

nouvel [nuvɛl] adj voir **nouveau**; **Nouvel An** New Year

nouvelle [nuvɛl] adj voir **nouveau** ▷ nf (piece) of news sg; (Littérature) short story; **les ~s** (Presse, TV) the news; **je suis sans ~s de lui** I haven't heard from him; **Nouvelle-Calédonie** nf New Caledonia; **Nouvelle-Zélande** nf New Zealand

novembre[nɔvɑ̃bʀ] nm November

● NOVEMBRE

● **Le 11 novembre** is a public holiday in France commemorating the signing of the armistice, near Compiègne, at the end of World War I.

noyade[nwajad] nf drowning no pl
noyau, x[nwajo] nm (de fruit) stone; (Bio, Physique) nucleus; (fig: centre) core
noyer[nwaje] nm walnut (tree); (bois) walnut ▷ vt to drown; (moteur) to flood; **se noyer** vi to be drowned, drown; (suicide) to drown o.s.
nu, e[ny] adj naked; (membres) naked, bare; (pieds, mains, chambre, fil électrique) bare ▷ nm (Art) nude; **tout nu** stark naked; **se mettre nu** to strip
nuage[nɥaʒ] nm cloud; **nuageux, -euse** adj cloudy
nuance[nɥɑ̃s] nf (de couleur, sens) shade; **il y a une ~ (entre)** there's a slight difference (between); **nuancer** vt (opinion) to bring some reservations ou qualifications to
nucléaire[nykleɛʀ] adj nuclear ▷ nm: **le ~** nuclear energy
nudiste[nydist] nm/f nudist
nuée[nɥe] nf: **une ~ de** a cloud ou host ou swarm of
nuire[nɥiʀ] vi to be harmful; **~ à** to harm, do damage to; **nuisible** adj harmful; **animal nuisible** pest
nuit[nɥi] nf night; **il fait ~** it's dark; **cette ~** (hier) last night; (aujourd'hui) tonight; **de ~** (vol, service) night cpd; **nuit blanche** sleepless night
nul, nulle[nyl] adj (aucun) no; (minime) nil, non-existent; (non valable) null; (péj): **être ~ (en)** to be useless ou hopeless (at) ▷ pron none, no one; **match** ou **résultat ~** draw; **~le part** nowhere; **nullement** adv by no means
numérique[nymeʀik] adj numerical; (affichage, son, télévision) digital
numéro[nymeʀo] nm number;

(spectacle) act, turn; (Presse) issue, number; **numéro de téléphone** (tele)phone number; **numéro vert** ≈ freefone® number (BRIT), ≈ toll-free number (US); **numéroter** vt to number
nuque[nyk] nf nape of the neck
nu-tête[nytɛt] adj inv, adv bareheaded
nutritif, -ive[nytʀitif, iv] adj (besoins, valeur) nutritional; (nourrissant) nutritious
nylon[nilɔ̃] nm nylon

O

oasis [ɔazis] nf oasis
obéir [ɔbeir] vi to obey; **~ à** to obey; **obéissance** nf obedience; **obéissant, e** adj obedient
obèse [ɔbɛz] adj obese; **obésité** nf obesity
objecter [ɔbʒɛkte] vt: **~ que** to object that; **objecteur** nm: **objecteur de conscience** conscientious objector
objectif, -ive [ɔbʒɛktif, iv] adj objective ▷ nm objective; (Photo) lens sg, objective
objection [ɔbʒɛksjɔ̃] nf objection
objectivité [ɔbʒɛktivite] nf objectivity
objet [ɔbʒɛ] nm object; (d'une discussion, recherche) subject; **être ou faire l'~ de** (discussion) to be the subject of; (soins) to be given ou shown; **sans ~** purposeless; (craintes) groundless; **(bureau des) ~s trouvés** lost property sg (BRIT), lost-and-found sg (US); **objet d'art** objet d'art; **objets de valeur** valuables; **objets personnels** personal items

obligation [ɔbligasjɔ̃] nf obligation; (Comm) bond, debenture; **obligatoire** adj compulsory, obligatory; **obligatoirement** adv necessarily; (fam: sans aucun doute) inevitably
obliger [ɔbliʒe] vt (contraindre): **~ qn à faire** to force ou oblige sb to do; **je suis bien obligé (de le faire)** I have to (do it)
oblique [ɔblik] adj oblique; **en ~** diagonally
oblitérer [ɔblitere] vt (timbre-poste) to cancel
obnubiler [ɔbnybile] vt to obsess
obscène [ɔpsɛn] adj obscene
obscur, e [ɔpskyr] adj dark; (méconnu) obscure; **obscurcir** vt to darken; (fig) to obscure; **s'obscurcir** vi to grow dark; **obscurité** nf darkness; **dans l'obscurité** in the dark, in darkness
obsédé, e [ɔpsede] nm/f: **un ~ de jazz** a jazz fanatic; **obsédé sexuel** sex maniac
obséder [ɔpsede] vt to obsess, haunt
obsèques [ɔpsɛk] nfpl funeral sg
observateur, -trice [ɔpsɛrvatœr, tris] adj observant, perceptive ▷ nm/f observer
observation [ɔpsɛrvasjɔ̃] nf observation; (d'un règlement etc) observance; (reproche) reproof; **être en ~** (Méd) to be under observation
observatoire [ɔpsɛrvatwar] nm observatory
observer [ɔpsɛrve] vt (regarder) to observe, watch; (scientifiquement; aussi règlement etc) to observe; (surveiller) to watch; (remarquer) to observe, notice; **faire ~ qch à qn** (dire) to point out sth to sb
obsession [ɔpsesjɔ̃] nf obsession
obstacle [ɔpstakl] nm obstacle; (Équitation) jump, hurdle; **faire ~ à** (projet) to hinder, put obstacles in the path of
obstiné, e [ɔpstine] adj obstinate
obstiner [ɔpstine]: **s'obstiner** vi to insist, dig one's heels in; **s'~ à faire** to persist (obstinately) in doing
obstruer [ɔpstrye] vt to block,

obstruct

obtenir [ɔptənir] *vt* to obtain, get; (*résultat*) to achieve, obtain; **~ de pouvoir faire** to obtain permission to do

obturateur [ɔptyratœʀ] *nm* (*Photo*) shutter

obus [ɔby] *nm* shell

occasion [ɔkazjɔ̃] *nf* (*aubaine, possibilité*) opportunity; (*circonstance*) occasion; (*Comm: article non neuf*) secondhand buy; (*: acquisition avantageuse*) bargain; **à plusieurs ~s** on several occasions; **à l'~** sometimes, on occasions; **d'~** secondhand; **occasionnel, le** *adj* (*non régulier*) occasional

occasionner [ɔkazjɔne] *vt* to cause

occident [ɔksidɑ̃] *nm*: **l'O~** the West; **occidental, e, -aux** *adj* western; (*Pol*) Western ▷ *nm/f* Westerner

occupation [ɔkypasjɔ̃] *nf* occupation

occupé, e [ɔkype] *adj* (*personne*) busy; (*place, sièges*) taken; (*toilettes*) engaged; (*Mil, Pol*) occupied; **la ligne est ~e** the line's engaged (BRIT) *ou* busy (US)

occuper [ɔkype] *vt* to occupy; (*poste*) to hold; **s'occuper de** (*être responsable de*) to be in charge of; (*se charger de: affaire*) to take charge of, deal with; (*: clients etc*) to attend to; **s'~ (à qch)** to occupy o.s. *ou* keep o.s. busy (with sth)

occurrence [ɔkyʀɑ̃s] *nf*: **en l'~** in this case

océan [ɔseɑ̃] *nm* ocean

octet [ɔktɛ] *nm* byte

octobre [ɔktɔbʀ] *nm* October

oculiste [ɔkylist] *nm/f* eye specialist

odeur [ɔdœʀ] *nf* smell

odieux, -euse [ɔdjø, jøz] *adj* hateful

odorant, e [ɔdɔʀɑ̃, ɑ̃t] *adj* sweet-smelling, fragrant

odorat [ɔdɔʀa] *nm* (sense of) smell

œil [œj] (*pl* **yeux**) *nm* eye; **avoir un ~ au beurre noir** *ou* **poché** to have a black eye; **à l'~** (fam) for free; **à l'~ nu** with the naked eye; **ouvrir l'~** (fig) to keep one's eyes open *ou* an eye out; **fermer**

les yeux (sur) (fig) to turn a blind eye (to); **les yeux fermés** (*aussi fig*) with one's eyes shut

œillères [œjɛʀ] *nfpl* blinkers (BRIT), blinders (US)

œillet [œjɛ] *nm* (*Bot*) carnation

œuf [œf, *pl* ø] *nm* egg; **œuf à la coque** boiled egg; **œuf au plat** fried egg; **œuf dur** hard-boiled egg; **œuf de Pâques** Easter egg; **œufs brouillés** scrambled eggs

œuvre [œvʀ] *nf* (*tâche*) task, undertaking; (*livre, tableau etc*) work; (*ensemble de la production artistique*) works *pl* ▷ *nm* (*Constr*): **le gros ~** the shell; **mettre en ~** (*moyens*) to make use of; **œuvre de bienfaisance** charity; **œuvre d'art** work of art

offense [ɔfɑ̃s] *nf* insult; **offenser** *vt* to offend, hurt; **s'offenser de qch** to take offence (BRIT) *ou* offense (US) at sth

offert, e [ɔfɛʀ, ɛʀt] *pp de* **offrir**

office [ɔfis] *nm* (*agence*) bureau, agency; (*Rel*) service ▷ *nm ou nf* (*pièce*) pantry; **faire ~ de** to act as; **d'~** automatically; **office du tourisme** tourist bureau

officiel, le [ɔfisjɛl] *adj, nm/f* official

officier [ɔfisje] *nm* officer

officieux, -euse [ɔfisjø, jøz] *adj* unofficial

offrande [ɔfʀɑ̃d] *nf* offering

offre [ɔfʀ] *nf* offer; (*aux enchères*) bid; (*Admin: soumission*) tender; (*Écon*): **l'~ et la demande** supply and demand; **"~s d'emploi"** "situations vacant"; **offre d'emploi** job advertised; **offre publique d'achat** takeover bid

offrir [ɔfʀiʀ] *vt*: **~ (à qn)** to offer (to sb); (*faire cadeau de*) to give (to sb); **s'offrir** *vt* (*vacances, voiture*) to treat o.s. to; **~ (à qn) de faire qch** to offer to do sth (for sb); **~ à boire à qn** (*chez soi*) to offer sb a drink; **je vous offre un verre** I'll buy you a drink

OGM *sigle m* (= *organisme génétiquement modifié*) GMO

oie [wa] *nf* (*Zool*) goose

oignon [ɔɲɔ̃] *nm* onion; (*de tulipe*)

etc) bulb

oiseau, x [wazo] nm bird; **oiseau de proie** bird of prey

oisif, -ive [wazif, iv] adj idle

oléoduc [ɔleɔdyk] nm (oil) pipeline

olive [ɔliv] nf (Bot) olive; **olivier** nm olive (tree)

OLP sigle f (= Organisation de libération de la Palestine) PLO

olympique [ɔlɛ̃pik] adj Olympic

ombragé, e [ɔ̃bʀaʒe] adj shaded, shady

ombre [ɔ̃bʀ] nf (espace non ensoleillé) shade; (ombre portée, tache) shadow; **à l'~** in the shade; **dans l'~** (fig) in the dark; **ombre à paupières** eyeshadow

omelette [ɔmlɛt] nf omelette; **omelette norvégienne** baked Alaska

omettre [ɔmɛtʀ] vt to omit, leave out

omoplate [ɔmɔplat] nf shoulder blade

MOT-CLÉ

on [ɔ̃] pron 1 (indéterminé) one, you, one: **on peut le faire ainsi** you ou one can do it like this, it can be done like this 2 (quelqu'un): **on les a attaqués** they were attacked; **on vous demande au téléphone** there's a phone call for you, you're wanted on the phone 3 (nous) we: **on va y aller demain** we're going tomorrow 4 (les gens) they; **autrefois, on croyait ...** they used to believe ... 5 **on ne peut plus** adv: **on ne peut plus stupide** as stupid as can be

oncle [ɔ̃kl] nm uncle

onctueux, -euse [ɔ̃ktɥø, øz] adj creamy, smooth

onde [ɔ̃d] nf wave; **~s courtes/ moyennes** short/medium wave sg; **grandes ~s** long wave sg

ondée [ɔ̃de] nf shower

on-dit [ɔ̃di] nm inv rumour

onduler [ɔ̃dyle] vi to undulate; (cheveux) to wave

onéreux, -euse [ɔneʀø, øz] adj costly

ongle [ɔ̃gl] nm nail

ont [ɔ̃] vb voir **avoir**

ONU sigle f (= Organisation des Nations Unies) UN

onze [ɔ̃z] num eleven; **onzième** num eleventh

OPA sigle f = **offre publique d'achat**

opaque [ɔpak] adj opaque

opéra [ɔpeʀa] nm opera; (édifice) opera house

opérateur, -trice [ɔpeʀatœʀ, tʀis] nm/f operator; **opérateur (de prise de vues)** cameraman

opération [ɔpeʀasjɔ̃] nf operation; (Comm) deal

opératoire [ɔpeʀatwaʀ] adj (choc etc) post-operative

opérer [ɔpeʀe] vt (personne) to operate on; (faire, exécuter) to carry out, make ▷ vi (remède: faire effet) to act, work; (Méd) to operate; **s'opérer** vi (avoir lieu) to occur, take place; **se faire ~** to have an operation

opérette [ɔpeʀɛt] nf operetta, light opera

opinion [ɔpinjɔ̃] nf opinion; **l'opinion (publique)** public opinion

opportun, e [ɔpɔʀtœ̃ yn] adj timely, opportune; **opportuniste** nm/f opportunist

opposant, e [ɔpozɑ̃, ɑ̃t] nm/f opponent

opposé, e [ɔpoze] adj (direction) opposite; (faction) opposing; (opinions, intérêts) conflicting; (contre): **~ à** opposed to, against ▷ nm: **l'~** the other ou opposite side (ou direction); (contraire) the opposite; **à l'~** (fig) on the other hand; **à l'~ de** (fig) contrary to, unlike

opposer [ɔpoze] vt (personnes, équipes) to oppose; (couleurs) to contrast; **s'opposer** vi (équipes) to confront each other; (opinions) to conflict; (couleurs, styles) to contrast; **s'~ à** (interdire) to oppose; **~ qch à** (comme obstacle, défense) to set sth against; (comme objection) to put sth forward against

opposition [ɔpozisjɔ̃] nf opposition; **par ~ à** as opposed to; **entrer en ~ avec** to come into conflict with; **faire ~ à un chèque** to stop a cheque

oppressant, e [ɔpʀesɑ̃, ɑ̃t] adj oppressive

oppresser [ɔpʀese] vt to oppress; **oppression** nf oppression

opprimer [ɔpʀime] vt to oppress

opter [ɔpte] vi: **~ pour** to opt for

opticien, ne [ɔptisjɛ̃, jɛn] nm/f optician

optimisme [ɔptimism] nm optimism; **optimiste** nm/f optimist ▷ adj optimistic

option [ɔpsjɔ̃] nf option; **matière à ~** (Scol) optional subject

optique [ɔptik] adj (nerf) optic; (verres) optical ▷ nf (fig: manière de voir) perspective

or [ɔʀ] nm gold ▷ conj now, but; **en or** (objet) gold cpd; **une affaire en or** a real bargain; **il croyait gagner or il a perdu** he was sure he would win and yet he lost

orage [ɔʀaʒ] nm (thunder)storm; **orageux, -euse** adj stormy

oral, e, -aux [ɔʀal, o] adj, nm oral; **par voie ~e** (Méd) orally

orange [ɔʀɑ̃ʒ] nf orange ▷ adj inv orange; **orangé, e** adj orangey, orange-coloured; **orangeade** nf orangeade; **oranger** nm orange tree

orateur [ɔʀatœʀ] nm speaker

orbite [ɔʀbit] nf (Anat) (eye-)socket; (Physique) orbit

Orcades [ɔʀkad] nfpl: **les ~** the Orkneys, the Orkney Islands

orchestre [ɔʀkɛstʀ] nm orchestra; (de jazz) band; (places) stalls pl (BRIT), orchestra (US)

orchidée [ɔʀkide] nf orchid

ordinaire [ɔʀdinɛʀ] adj ordinary; (qualité) standard; (péj: commun) common ▷ nm ordinary; (menus) everyday fare ▷ nf (essence): ~ two-star (petrol) (BRIT), ~ regular gas (US); **d'~** usually, normally; **comme à l'~** as usual

ordinateur [ɔʀdinatœʀ] nm computer; **ordinateur individuel** ou **personnel** personal computer; **ordinateur portable** laptop (computer)

ordonnance [ɔʀdɔnɑ̃s] nf (Méd) prescription; (Mil) orderly, batman (BRIT); **pouvez-vous me faire une ~?** can you write me a prescription?

ordonné, e [ɔʀdɔne] adj tidy, orderly

ordonner [ɔʀdɔne] vt (agencer) to organize, arrange; (donner un ordre): **~ à qn de faire** to order sb to do; (Rel) to ordain; (Méd) to prescribe

ordre [ɔʀdʀ] nm order; (propreté et soin) orderliness, tidiness; (nature): **d'~ pratique** of a practical nature; **ordres** nmpl (Rel) holy orders; **mettre en ~** to tidy (up), put in order; **par ~ alphabétique/d'importance** in alphabetical order or order of importance; **à l'~ de qn** payable to sb; **être aux ~s de qn/sous les ~s de qn** to be at sb's disposal/under sb's command; **jusqu'à nouvel ~** until further notice; **de premier ~** first-rate; **ordre du jour** (d'une réunion) agenda; **à l'ordre du jour** (fig) topical; **ordre public** law and order

ordure [ɔʀdyʀ] nf filth no pl; **ordures** nfpl (balayures, déchets) rubbish sg, refuse sg; **ordures ménagères** household refuse

oreille [ɔʀɛj] nf ear; **avoir de l'~** to have a good ear (for music)

oreiller [ɔʀeje] nm pillow

oreillons [ɔʀɛjɔ̃] nmpl mumps sg

ores [ɔʀ]: **d'~ et déjà** adv already

orfèvrerie [ɔʀfɛvʀəʀi] nf goldsmith's (ou silversmith's) trade; (ouvrage) gold (ou silver) plate

organe [ɔʀgan] nm organ; (porte-parole) representative, mouthpiece

organigramme [ɔʀganigʀam] nm (tableau hiérarchique) organization chart; (schéma) flow chart

organique [ɔʀganik] adj organic

organisateur, -trice [ɔʀganizatœʀ,

tris] nm/f organizer
organisation [ɔrganizasjɔ̃] nf
organization; **Organisation des
Nations Unies** United Nations
(Organization)
organiser [ɔrganize] vt to organize;
(*mettre sur pied: service etc*) to set up;
s'organiser to get organized
organisme [ɔrganism] nm (*Bio*)
organism; (*corps, Admin*) body
organiste [ɔrganist] nm/f organist
orgasme [ɔrgasm] nm orgasm, climax
orge [ɔrʒ] nf barley
orgue [ɔrg] nm organ
orgueil [ɔrgœj] nm pride; **orgueilleux,
-euse** adj proud
oriental, e, -aux [ɔrjɑ̃tal, -o] adj
(*langue, produit*) oriental; (*frontière*)
eastern
orientation [ɔrjɑ̃tasjɔ̃] nf (*de
recherches*) orientation; (*d'une maison
etc*) aspect; (*d'un journal*) leanings pl;
avoir le sens de l'~ to have a (good)
sense of direction; **orientation
professionnelle** careers advisory
service
orienté, e [ɔrjɑ̃te] adj (fig: *article,
journal*) slanted; **bien/mal ~**
(*appartement*) well/badly positioned; **~
au sud** facing south, with a southern
aspect
orienter [ɔrjɑ̃te] vt (*tourner: antenne*)
to direct, turn; (*personne, recherches*)
to direct; (fig: *élève*) to orientate;
s'orienter (*se repérer*) to find one's
bearings; **s'~ vers** (fig) to turn towards
origan [ɔrigɑ̃] nm oregano
originaire [ɔriʒinɛr] adj: **être ~ de** to
be a native of
original, e, -aux [ɔriʒinal, o] adj
original; (*bizarre*) eccentric ▷ nm/f
eccentric ▷ nm (*document etc, Art*)
original
origine [ɔriʒin] nf origin; **origines** nfpl
(*d'une personne*) origins; **d'~** (*pays*) of
origin; **d'~ suédoise** of Swedish origin;
(*pneus etc*) original; **à l'~** originally;
originel, le adj original

orme [ɔrm] nm elm
ornement [ɔrnəmɑ̃] nm ornament
orner [ɔrne] vt to decorate, adorn
ornière [ɔrnjɛr] nf rut
orphelin, e [ɔrfəlɛ̃, in] adj orphan(ed)
▷ nm/f orphan; **orphelin de
mère/de père** motherless/fatherless;
orphelinat nm orphanage
orteil [ɔrtɛj] nm toe; **gros ~** big toe
orthographe [ɔrtɔgraf] nf spelling
ortie [ɔrti] nf (stinging) nettle
os [ɔs] nm bone; **os à moelle**
marrowbone
osciller [ɔsile] vi (*au vent etc*) to rock;
(fig): **~ entre** to waver ou fluctuate
between
osé, e [oze] adj daring, bold
oseille [ozɛj] nf sorrel
oser [oze] vi, vt to dare; **~ faire** to dare
(to) do
osier [ozje] nm willow; **d'~, en ~**
wicker(work)
osseux, -euse [ɔsø, øz] adj bony;
(*tissu, maladie, greffe*) bone cpd
otage [ɔtaʒ] nm hostage; **prendre qn
comme ~** to take sb hostage
OTAN sigle f (= Organisation du traité de
l'Atlantique Nord) NATO
otarie [ɔtari] nf sea-lion
ôter [ote] vt to remove; (*soustraire*)
to take away; **~ qch à qn** to take sth
(away) from sb; **~ qch de** to remove
sth from
otite [ɔtit] nf ear infection
ou [u] conj or; **ou ... ou** either ... or; **ou
bien** or (else)

🔵 **MOT-CLÉ**

où [u] pron relatif 1 (*position, situation*)
where, that (*souvent omis*); **la chambre
où il était** the room (that) he was in,
the room where he was; **la ville où
je l'ai rencontré** the town where I
met him; **la pièce d'où il est sorti** the
room he came out of; **le village d'où
je viens** the village I come from; **les
villes par où il est passé** the towns he

went through

2 (temps, état) that (souvent omis); **le jour où il est parti** the day (that) he left; **au prix où c'est** at the price it is
▷ adv 1 (interrogation) where; **où est-il/va-t-il?** where is he/is he going?; **par où?** which way?; **d'où vient que ...?** how come ...?

2 (position) where; **je sais où il est** I know where he is; **où que l'on aille** wherever you go

ouate ['wat] nf cotton wool (BRIT), cotton (US)

oubli [ubli] nm (acte): **l'~ de** forgetting; (trou de mémoire) lapse of memory; (négligence) omission, oversight; **tomber dans l'~** to sink into oblivion

oublier [ublije] vt to forget; (laisser quelque part: chapeau etc) to leave behind; (ne pas revenir: erreurs etc) to miss; **j'ai oublié ma clé/mon passeport** I've forgotten my key/my passport

ouest [west] nm west ▷ adj inv west; (région) western; **à l'~** in the west; (direction) (to the) west, westwards; **à l'~ de** (to the) west of

ouf ['uf] excl phew!

oui ['wi] adv yes

ouï-dire ['widir]: **par ~** adv by hearsay

ouïe [wi] nf hearing; **ouïes** nfpl (de poisson) gills

ouragan [uʀagɑ̃] nm hurricane

ourlet [uʀlɛ] nm hem

ours [uʀs] nm bear; **ours blanc/brun** polar/brown bear; **ours (en peluche)** teddy bear

oursin [uʀsɛ̃] nm sea urchin

ourson [uʀsɔ̃] nm (bear-)cub

ouste [ust] excl hop it!

outil [uti] nm tool; **outiller** vt to equip

outrage [utʀaʒ] nm insult; **outrage à la pudeur** indecent behaviour no pl

outrance [utʀɑ̃s]: **à ~** adv excessively, to excess

outre [utʀ] prép besides ▷ adv: **passer ~ à** to disregard, take no notice of; **en ~** besides, moreover; **~ mesure** to excess;

(manger, boire) immoderately; **outre-Atlantique** adv across the Atlantic; **outre-mer** adv overseas

ouvert, e [uvɛʀ, ɛʀt] adj (robinet, gaz etc) on; **ouvertement** adv openly; **ouverture** nf opening; (Mus) overture; **heures d'ouverture** (Comm) opening hours; **ouverture d'esprit** open-mindedness

ouvrable [uvʀabl] adj: **jour ~** working day, weekday

ouvrage [uvʀaʒ] nm (tâche, de tricot etc) work no pl; (texte, livre) work

ouvre-boîte(s) [uvʀəbwat] nm inv tin (BRIT) ou can opener

ouvre-bouteille(s) [uvʀəbutɛj] nm inv bottle-opener

ouvreuse [uvʀøz] nf usherette

ouvrier, -ière [uvʀije, ijɛʀ] nm/f worker ▷ adj working-class; (conflit) industrial; (mouvement) labour cpd: **classe ouvrière** working class

ouvrir [uvʀiʀ] vt (gén) to open; (brèche, passage, Méd: abcès) to open up; (commencer l'exploitation de, créer) to open (up); (eau, électricité, chauffage, robinet) to turn on ▷ vi to open; to open up; **s'ouvrir** vi to open; **s'ouvrir à qn** to open one's heart to sb; **est-ce ouvert au public?** is it open to the public?; **quand est-ce que le musée est ouvert?** when is the museum open?; **à quelle heure ouvrez-vous?** what time do you open?; **~ l'appétit à qn** to whet sb's appetite

ovaire [ovɛʀ] nm ovary

ovale [oval] adj oval

OVNI [ovni] sigle m (= objet volant non identifié) UFO

oxyder [okside]: **s'oxyder** vi to become oxidized

oxygène [oksiʒɛn] nm oxygen

oxygéné, e [oksiʒene] adj: **eau ~e** hydrogen peroxide

ozone [ozon] nf ozone; **la couche d'~** the ozone layer

p

pacifique [pasifik] *adj* peaceful ▷ *nm*: **le P~**, **l'océan P~** the Pacific (Ocean)

pack [pak] *nm* pack

pacotille [pakɔtij] *nf* cheap junk

PACS *sigle m* (= *pacte civil de solidarité*) contract of civil partnership; **pacser**: **se pacser** *vi* to sign a contract of civil partnership

pacte [pakt] *nm* pact, treaty

pagaille [pagaj] *nf* mess, shambles *sg*

page [paʒ] *nf* page ▷ *nm* page (boy); **à la ~** (*fig*) up-to-date; **page d'accueil** (*Inform*) home page; **page Web** (*Inform*) web page

paiement [pemɑ̃] *nm* payment

païen, ne [pajɛ̃, pajɛn] *adj, nm/f* pagan, heathen

paillasson [pajasɔ̃] *nm* doormat

paille [paj] *nf* straw

pain [pɛ̃] *nm* (*substance*) bread; (*unité*) loaf (of bread); (*morceau*): **~ de savon** *etc* bar of soap *etc*; **pain au chocolat** chocolate-filled pastry; **pain aux raisins** currant bun; **pain bis/complet**

brown/wholemeal (*BRIT*) *ou* wholewheat (*US*) bread; **pain d'épice** ≈ gingerbread; **pain de mie** sandwich loaf; **pain grillé** toast

pair, e [pɛʀ] *adj* (*nombre*) even ▷ *nm* peer; **aller de ~** to go hand in hand *ou* together; **jeune fille au ~** au pair; **paire** *nf* pair

paisible [pezibl] *adj* peaceful, quiet

paix [pɛ] *nf* peace; **faire/avoir la ~** to make/have peace; **fiche-lui la ~!** (*fam*) leave him alone!

Pakistan [pakistɑ̃] *nm*: **le ~** Pakistan

palais [palɛ] *nm* palace; (*Anat*) palate

pâle [pɑl] *adj* pale; **bleu ~** pale blue

Palestine [palɛstin] *nf*: **la ~** Palestine

palette [palɛt] *nf* (*de peintre*) palette; (*produits*) range

pâleur [palœʀ] *nf* paleness

palier [palje] *nm* (*d'escalier*) landing; (*fig*) level, plateau; **par ~s** in stages

pâlir [paliʀ] *vi* to turn *ou* go pale; (*couleur*) to fade

pallier [palje] *vt* to offset, make up for

palme [palm] *nf* (*de plongeur*) flipper; **palmé, e** *adj* (*pattes*) webbed

palmier [palmje] *nm* palm tree; (*gâteau*) heart-shaped biscuit made of flaky pastry

pâlot, te [palo, ɔt] *adj* pale, peaky

palourde [paluʀd] *nf* clam

palper [palpe] *vt* to feel, finger

palpitant, e [palpitɑ̃, ɑ̃t] *adj* thrilling

palpiter [palpite] *vi* (*cœur*, *pouls*) to beat; (: *plus fort*) to pound, throb

paludisme [palydism] *nm* malaria

pamphlet [pɑ̃flɛ] *nm* lampoon, satirical tract

pamplemousse [pɑ̃pləmus] *nm* grapefruit

pan [pɑ̃] *nm* section, piece ▷ *excl* bang!

panache [panaʃ] *nm* plume; (*fig*) spirit, panache

panaché, e [panaʃe] *adj*: **glace ~e** mixed-flavour ice cream ▷ *nm* (*bière*) shandy

pancarte [pɑ̃kaʀt] *nf* sign, notice

pancréas [pɑ̃kʀeas] *nm* pancreas

pané, e [pane] adj fried in breadcrumbs

panier [panje] nm basket; **mettre au
~** to chuck away; **panier à provisions**
shopping basket; **panier-repas** nm
packed lunch

panique [panik] nf, adj panic;
paniquer vi to panic

panne [pan] nf breakdown; **être/
tomber en ~** to have broken down/
break down; **être en ~ d'essence** ou
sèche to have run out of petrol (BRIT)
ou gas (US); **ma voiture est en ~** my car
has broken down; **panne d'électricité**
ou **de courant** power cut ou failure

panneau, x [pano] nm (écriteau) sign,
notice; **panneau d'affichage** notice
board; **panneau de signalisation**
roadsign; **panneau indicateur**
signpost

panoplie [panɔpli] nf (jouet) outfit;
(fig) array

panorama [panɔʀama] nm panorama

panse [pɑ̃s] nf paunch

pansement [pɑ̃smɑ̃] nm dressing,
bandage; **pansement adhésif** sticking
plaster

pantacourt [pɑ̃takuʀ] nm three-
quarter length trousers pl

pantalon [pɑ̃talɔ̃] nm trousers pl,
pair of trousers; **pantalon de ski** ski
pants pl

panthère [pɑ̃tɛʀ] nf panther

pantin [pɑ̃tɛ̃] nm puppet

pantoufle [pɑ̃tufl] nf slipper

paon [pɑ̃] nm peacock

papa [papa] nm dad(dy)

pape [pap] nm pope

paperasse [papʀas] (péj) nf bumf
no pl, papers pl; **paperasserie** [péj]
nf paperwork no pl; (tracasserie) red
tape no pl

papeterie [papetʀi] nf (magasin)
stationer's (shop)

papi nm (fam) granddad

papier [papje] nm paper; (article)
article; **papiers** nmpl (aussi: **~s
d'identité**) (identity) papers; **papier
à lettres** writing paper, notepaper;

papier (d')aluminium aluminium
(BRIT) ou aluminum (US) foil, tinfoil;
papier calque tracing paper; **papier de
verre** sandpaper; **papier hygiénique**
ou **(de) toilette** toilet paper; **papier
journal** newspaper; **papier peint**
wallpaper

papillon [papijɔ̃] nm butterfly; (fam:
contravention) (parking) ticket; **papillon
de nuit** moth

papillote [papijɔt] nf: **en ~** cooked
in tinfoil

papoter [papɔte] vi to chatter

paquebot [pak(ə)bo] nm liner

pâquerette [pɑkʀɛt] nf daisy

Pâques [pɑk] nm, nfpl Easter

paquet [pake] nm packet; (colis) parcel;
(fig: tas): **~ de** pile ou heap of; **un ~ de
cigarettes, s'il vous plaît** a packet of
cigarettes, please; **paquet-cadeau** nm:
**pouvez-vous me faire un paquet-
cadeau, s'il vous plaît?** can you
gift-wrap it for me, please?

par [paʀ] prép by; **finir** etc **~** to end etc
with; **~ amour** out of love; **passer ~
Lyon/la côte** to go via ou through
Lyons/along the coast; **~ la fenêtre**
(jeter, regarder) out of the window; **3 ~
jour/personne** 3 a ou per day/person; **2
~ 2** in twos; **~ ici** this way; (dans le coin)
round here; **~-ci, ~-là** here and there; **~
temps de pluie** in wet weather

parabolique [paʀabɔlik] adj: **antenne
~** parabolic ou dish aerial

parachute [paʀaʃyt] nm parachute;
parachutiste nm/f parachutist; (Mil)
paratrooper

parade [paʀad] nf (spectacle, défilé)
parade; (Escrime, Boxe) parry

paradis [paradi] *nm* heaven, paradise
paradoxe [paradɔks] *nm* paradox
paraffine [parafin] *nf* paraffin
parages [paraʒ] *nmpl*: **dans les ~ (de)** in the area *ou* vicinity (of)
paragraphe [paragraf] *nm* paragraph
paraître [parɛtr] *vb* +*attrib* to seem, look, appear ▷ *vi* to appear; (*être visible*) to show; (*Presse, Édition*) to be published, come out, appear ▷ *vb impers*: **il paraît que** it seems *ou* appears that, they say that
parallèle [paralɛl] *adj* parallel; (*non officiel*) unofficial ▷ *nm* (*comparaison*): **faire un ~ entre** to draw a parallel between ▷ *nf* parallel (line)
paralyser [paralize] *vt* to paralyse
paramédical, e, -aux [paramedikal, o] *adj*: **personnel ~** paramedics *pl*, paramedical workers *pl*
paraphrase [parafraz] *nf* paraphrase
parapluie [paraplɥi] *nm* umbrella
parasite [parazit] *nm* parasite; **parasites** *nmpl* (*Tél*) interference *sg*
parasol [parasɔl] *nm* parasol, sunshade
paratonnerre [paratɔnɛr] *nm* lightning conductor
parc [park] *nm* (*public*) park, gardens *pl*; (*de château etc*) grounds *pl*; (*d'enfant*) playpen; **parc à thème** theme park; **parc d'attractions** amusement park; **parc de stationnement** car park
parcelle [parsɛl] *nf* fragment, scrap; (*de terrain*) plot, parcel
parce que [pars(ə)kə] *conj* because
parchemin [parʃəmɛ̃] *nm* parchment
parc(o)mètre [park(ɔ)mɛtr] *nm* parking meter
parcourir [parkurir] *vt* (*trajet, distance*) to cover; (*article, livre*) to skim *ou* glance through; (*lieu*) to go all over, travel up and down; (*suj: frisson*) to run through
parcours [parkur] *nm* (*trajet*) journey; (*itinéraire*) route
par-dessous [pard(ə)su] *prép, adv*

under(neath)
pardessus [pardəsy] *nm* overcoat
par-dessus [pard(ə)sy] *prép* over (the top of) ▷ *adv* over (the top); **le marché** on top of all that; **~ tout** above all; **en avoir ~ la tête** to have had enough
par-devant [pard(ə)vɑ̃] *adv* (*passer*) round the front
pardon [pardɔ̃] *nm inv* forgiveness *no pl* ▷ *excl* sorry!; (*pour interpeller etc*) excuse me!; **demander ~ à qn (de)** to apologize to sb (for); **je vous demande ~** I'm sorry; (*pour interpeller*) excuse me;
pardonner *vt* to forgive; **pardonner qch à qn** to forgive sb for sth
pare...: pare-brise *nm inv* windscreen (*BRIT*), windshield (*US*); **pare-chocs** *nm inv* bumper; **pare-feu** *nm inv* (*de foyer*) fireguard; (*Inform*) firewall
pareil, le [parɛj] *adj* (*identique*) the same, alike; (*similaire*) similar; (*tel*): **un courage/livre ~** such courage/a book, courage/a book like this; **de ~s livres** such books; **faire ~** to do the same (thing); **~ à** the same as; (*similaire*) similar to; **sans ~** unparalleled, unequalled
parent, e [parɑ̃, ɑ̃t] *nm/f*: **un(e) ~(e)** a relative *ou* relation; **parents** *nmpl* (*père et mère*) parents; **parenté** *nf* (*lien*) relationship
parenthèse [parɑ̃tɛz] *nf* (*ponctuation*) bracket, parenthesis; (*digression*) parenthesis, digression; **entre ~s** in brackets; (*fig*) incidentally
paresse [parɛs] *nf* laziness; **paresseux, -euse** *adj* lazy
parfait, e [parfɛ, ɛt] *adj* perfect ▷ *nm* (*Ling*) perfect (tense); **parfaitement** *adv* perfectly ▷ *excl* (most) certainly
parfois [parfwa] *adv* sometimes
parfum [parfœ̃] *nm* (*produit*) perfume, scent; (*odeur: de fleur*) scent, fragrance; (*goût*) flavour; **quels ~s avez-vous?** what flavours do you have?; **parfumé, e** *adj* (*fleur, fruit*) fragrant; (*femme*) perfumed; **parfumé au café** coffee-

flavoured; **parfumer** vt (suj: odeur, bouquet) to perfume; (crème, gâteau) to flavour; **parfumerie** nf (produits) perfumes pl; (boutique) perfume shop

pari [paʀi] nm bet; **parier** vt to bet

Paris [paʀi] n Paris; **parisien, ne** adj Parisian; (Géo, Admin) Paris cpd ▷ nm/f: **Parisien, ne** Parisian

parité [paʀite] nf (Pol): **~ hommes-femmes** balanced representation of men and women

parjure [paʀʒyʀ] nm perjury

parking [paʀkiŋ] nm (lieu) car park

Attention à ne pas traduire *parking* par le mot anglais *parking*.

parlant, e [paʀlɑ̃, ɑ̃t] adj (regard) eloquent; (Cinéma) talking

parlement [paʀləmɑ̃] nm parliament; **parlementaire** adj parliamentary ▷ nm/f member of parliament

parler [paʀle] vi to speak, talk; (avouer) to talk; **~ (à qn) de** to talk ou speak (to sb) about; **~ le/en français** to speak French/in French; **~ affaires** to talk business; **sans ~ de** (fig) not to mention, to say nothing of; **tu parles!** (fam: bien sûr) you bet!; **parlez-vous français?** do you speak French?; **je ne parle pas anglais** I don't speak English; **est-ce que je peux ~ à …?** can I speak to …?

parloir [paʀlwaʀ] nm (de prison, d'hôpital) visiting room

parmi [paʀmi] prép among(st)

paroi [paʀwa] nf wall; (cloison) partition

paroisse [paʀwas] nf parish

parole [paʀɔl] nf (faculté): **la ~** speech; (mot, promesse) word; **paroles** nfpl (Mus) words, lyrics; **tenir ~** to keep one's word; **prendre la ~** to speak; **demander la ~** to ask for permission to speak; **je te crois sur ~** I'll take your word for it

parquet [paʀkɛ] nm (parquet) floor; (Jur): **le ~** the Public Prosecutor's department

parrain [paʀɛ̃] nm godfather;

parrainer vt (suj: entreprise) to sponsor

pars [paʀ] vb voir **partir**

parsemer [paʀsəme] vt (suj: feuilles, papiers) to be scattered over; **~ qch de** to scatter sth with

part [paʀ] nf (qui revient à qn) share; (fraction, partie) part; **à ~** adv (séparément) separately; (de côté) aside ▷ prép apart from, except for; **prendre ~ à** (débat etc) to take part in; (soucis, douleur de qn) to share in; **faire ~ de qch à qn** to announce sth to sb, inform sb of sth; **pour ma ~** as for me, as far as I'm concerned; **à ~ entière** full; **de la ~ de** (au nom de) on behalf of; (donné par) from; **de toute(s) ~(s)** from all sides ou quarters; **de ~ et d'autre** on both sides, on either side; **d'une ~ … d'autre part** ~ on the one hand … on the other hand; **d'autre ~** (de plus) moreover; **faire la ~ des choses** to make allowances

partage [paʀtaʒ] nm (fractionnement) dividing up; (répartition) sharing (out) no pl, share-out

partager [paʀtaʒe] vt to share; (distribuer, répartir) to share (out); (morceler, diviser) to divide (up); **se partager** vt (héritage etc) to share between themselves (ou ourselves)

partenaire [paʀtənɛʀ] nm/f partner

parterre [paʀtɛʀ] nm (de fleurs) (flower) bed; (Théâtre) stalls pl

parti [paʀti] nm (Pol) party; (décision) course of action; (personne à marier) match; **tirer ~ de** to take advantage of, turn to good account; **prendre ~ (pour/contre)** to take sides ou a stand (for/against); **parti pris** bias

partial, e, -aux [paʀsjal, jo] adj biased, partial

participant, e [paʀtisipɑ̃, ɑ̃t] nm/f participant; (à un concours) entrant

participation [paʀtisipasjɔ̃] nf participation; (financière) contribution

participer [paʀtisipe]: **~ à** vt (course, réunion) to take part in; (frais etc) to contribute to; (chagrin, succès de qn) to share (in)

particularité [partikylarite] *nf*
(distinctive) characteristic

particulier, -ière [partikylje, jɛʁ]
adj (*spécifique*) particular; (*personnel, privé*)
private; (*étrange*) peculiar, odd ▷ *nm*
(*individu: Admin*) private individual; **~ à**
peculiar to; **en ~** (*surtout*) in particular,
particularly; (*en privé*) in private;
particulièrement *adv* particularly

partie [paʁti] *nf* (*gén*) part; (*Jur etc:
protagonistes*) party; (*de cartes, tennis etc*)
game; **une ~ de pêche** a fishing party
ou trip; **en ~** partly, in part; **faire ~ de**
(*suj: chose*) to be part of; **prendre qn à ~**
to take sb to task; **en grande ~** largely,
in the main; **partie civile** (*Jur*) party
claiming damages in a criminal case

partiel, le [paʁsjɛl] *adj* partial ▷ *nm*
(*Scol*) class exam

partir [paʁtiʁ] *vi* (*gén*) to go; (*quitter*)
to go, leave; (*tache*) to go, come out; **~**
de (*lieu: quitter*) to leave; (: *commencer*
à) to start from; **~ pour/à** (*lieu, pays*
etc) to leave for/go off to; **à ~ de** from;
le train/le bus part à quelle heure?
what time does the train/bus leave?

partisan, e [paʁtizɑ̃, an] *nm/f*
partisan ▷ *adj*: **être ~ de qch/de faire**
to be in favour of sth/doing

partition [paʁtisjɔ̃] *nf* (*Mus*) score

partout [paʁtu] *adv* everywhere; **~**
où il allait everywhere *ou* wherever
he went

paru [paʁy] *pp de* **paraître**

parution [paʁysjɔ̃] *nf* publication

parvenir [paʁvəniʁ]: **~ à** *vt* (*atteindre*)
to reach; (*réussir*): **~ à faire** to manage
to do, succeed in doing; **faire ~ qch à**
qn to have sth sent to sb

pas¹ [pɑ] *nm* (*enjambée, Danse*) step;
(*allure, mesure*) pace; (*bruit*) (foot)step;
(*trace*) footprint; **~ à ~** step by step;
au ~ at walking pace; **marcher à**
grands ~ to stride along; **à ~ de loup**
stealthily; **faire les cent ~** to pace up
and down; **faire le premier ~** to make
the first move; **sur le ~ de la porte** on
the doorstep

MOT-CLÉ

pas² [pɑ] *adv* **1** (*en corrélation avec*
ne, non etc) not; **il ne pleure pas**
(*habituellement*) he does not *ou* doesn't
cry; (*maintenant*) he's not *ou* isn't crying;
il n'a pas pleuré/ne pleurera pas he
did not *ou* didn't/will not *ou* won't cry;
ils n'ont pas de voiture/d'enfants
they don't have *ou* haven't got a car/any
children; **il m'a dit de ne pas le faire** he
told me not to do it; **non pas que ...**
not that ...

2 (*employé sans ne etc*): **pas moi** not
me, *ou* I don't (*ou* can't *etc*); **elle travaille,**
(mais) lui pas *ou* **pas lui** she works but
he doesn't *ou* does not; **une pomme**
pas mûre an unripe apple; **pas du**
tout not at all; **pas de sucre, merci**
no sugar, thanks; **ceci est à vous ou**
pas? is this yours or not?, is this yours
or not?

3: **pas mal** (*joli: personne, maison*) not
bad; **pas mal fait** not badly done *ou*
made; **comment ça va? — pas mal**
how are things? — not bad; **pas mal de**
quite a lot of

passage [pɑsaʒ] *nm* (*fait de passer*)
voir **passer**; (*lieu, prix de la traversée,*
extrait) passage; (*chemin*) way; **de ~**
(*touristes*) passing through; **passage à**
niveau level crossing; **passage clouté**
pedestrian crossing; **passage interdit**
no entry; **passage souterrain** subway
(*BRIT*), underpass

passager, -ère [pɑsaʒe, ɛʁ] *adj*
passing ▷ *nm/f* passenger

passant, e [pɑsɑ̃, ɑ̃t] *adj* (*rue, endroit*)
busy ▷ *nm/f* passer-by; **en ~** in passing

passe [pɑs] *nf* (*Sport, Navig*) pass; **être**
en ~ de faire to be on the way to doing;
être dans une mauvaise ~ to be going
through a rough patch

passé, e [pɑse] *adj* (*révolu*) past; (*dernier:*
semaine etc) last; (*couleur*) faded ▷ *prép*

after ▷ *nm* past; (*Ling*) past (tense); **~ de mode** out of fashion; **passé composé** perfect (tense); **passé simple** past historic (tense)

passe-partout [pɑspaʀtu] *nm inv* master *ou* skeleton key ▷ *adj inv* all-purpose

passeport [pɑspɔʀ] *nm* passport

passer [pɑse] *vi* (*aller*) to go; (*voiture, piétons: défiler*) to pass (by), go by; (*facteur, laitier etc*) to come, call; (*pour rendre visite*) to call ou drop in; (*film, émission*) to be on; (*temps, jours*) to pass, go by; (*couleur*) to fade; (*mode*) to die out; (*douleur*) to pass, go away; (*Scol*): **~ dans la classe supérieure** to go up to the next class ▷ *vt* (*frontière, rivière etc*) to cross; (*douane*) to go through; (*examen*) to sit, take; (*visite médicale etc*) to have; (*journée, temps*) to spend; (*enfiler: vêtement*) to slip on; (*film, pièce*) to show, put on; (*disque*) to play, put on; (*commande*) to place; (*marché, accord*) to agree on; **se passer** *vi* (*avoir lieu: scène, action*) to take place; (*se dérouler: entretien etc*) to go by; (*s'écouler: semaine etc*) to pass, go by; (*arriver*) **que s'est-il passé?** what happened?; **~ qch à qn** (*sel etc*) to pass sth to sb; (*prêter*) to lend sb sth; (*lettre, message*) to pass sth on to sb; (*tolérer*) to let sb get away with sth; **~ par** to go through; **~ avant qch/qn** (*fig*) to come before sth/sb; **~ un coup de fil à qn** (*fam*) to give sb a ring; **laisser ~** (*air, lumière, personne*) to let through; (*occasion*) to let slip, miss; (*erreur*) to overlook; **~ à la radio/télévision** to be on the radio/on television; **~ à table** to sit down to eat; **~ au salon** to go into the sitting-room; **~ son tour** to miss one's turn; **~ la seconde** (*Auto*) to change into second; **~ le balai/l'aspirateur** to sweep up/hoover; **je vous passe M. Dupont** (*je vous mets en communication avec lui*) I'm putting you through to Mr Dupont; (*je lui passe l'appareil*) here is Mr Dupont, I'll hand you over to Mr Dupont; **se ~ de** to go ou

do without

passerelle [pɑsʀɛl] *nf* footbridge; (*de navire, avion*) gangway

passe-temps [pɑstɑ̃] *nm inv* pastime

passif, -ive [pasif, iv] *adj* passive

passion [pasjɔ̃] *nf* passion; **passionnant, e** *adj* fascinating; **passionné, e** *adj* (*personne*) passionate; (*récit*) impassioned; **être passionné de** to have a passion for; **passionner** *vt* (*personne*) to fascinate, grip

passoire [paswaʀ] *nf* sieve; (*à légumes*) colander; (*à thé*) strainer

pastèque [pastɛk] *nf* watermelon

pasteur [pastœʀ] *nm* (*protestant*) minister, pastor

pastille [pastij] *nf* (*à sucer*) lozenge, pastille

patate [patat] *nf* (*fam: pomme de terre*) spud; **patate douce** sweet potato

patauger [patoʒe] *vi* to splash about

pâte [pɑt] *nf* (*à tarte*) pastry; (*à pain*) dough; (*à frire*) batter; **pâtes** *nfpl* (*macaroni etc*) pasta *sg*; **pâte à modeler** modelling clay, Plasticine® (*BRIT*); **pâte brisée** shortcrust pastry; **pâte d'amandes** almond paste, marzipan; **pâte de fruits** crystallized fruit *no pl*; **pâte feuilletée** puff ou flaky pastry

pâté [pɑte] *nm* (*charcuterie*) pâté; (*tache*) ink blot; **pâté de maisons** block (of houses); **pâté (de sable)** sandpie; **pâté en croûte** pork pie

pâtée [pɑte] *nf* mash, feed

patente [patɑ̃t] *nf* (*Comm*) trading licence

paternel, le [patɛʀnɛl] *adj* (*amour, soins*) fatherly; (*ligne, autorité*) paternal

pâteux, -euse [pɑtø, øz] *adj* pasty; (*langue*) coated

pathétique [patetik] *adj* moving

patience [pasjɑ̃s] *nf* patience

patient, e [pasjɑ̃, ɑ̃t] *adj, nm/f* patient; **patienter** *vi* to wait

patin [patɛ̃] *nm* skate; (*sport*) skating; **patins (à glace)** (ice) skates; **patins à roulettes** roller skates

patinage [patinaʒ] *nm* skating

patiner [patine] vi to skate; (roue, voiture) to spin; **se patiner** vi (meuble, cuir) to acquire a sheen; **patineur, -euse** nm/f skater; **patinoire** nf skating rink, (ice) rink

pâtir [patir]: **~ de** vt to suffer because of

pâtisserie [patisri] nf (boutique) cake shop; (gâteau) cake, pastry; (à la maison) pastry- ou cake-making, baking; **pâtissier, -ière** nm/f pastrycook

patois [patwa] nm dialect, patois

patrie [patri] nf homeland

patrimoine [patrimwan] nm (culture) heritage

- **JOURNÉES DU PATRIMOINE**
-
- Once a year, important public
- buildings are open to the public for
- a weekend. During these **Journées
- du Patrimoine**, there are guided
- visits and talks based on a particular
- theme.

patriotique [patrijotik] adj patriotic

patron, ne [patrɔ̃, ɔn] nm/f boss; (Rel) patron saint ▷ nm (Couture) pattern; **patronat** [patrɔna] nm employers pl; **patronner** vt to sponsor, support

patrouille [patruj] nf patrol

patte [pat] nf (jambe) leg; (pied: de chien, chat) paw; (: d'oiseau) foot

pâturage [patyraʒ] nm pasture

paume [pom] nf palm

paumé, e [pome] (fam) nm/f drop-out

paupière [popjɛr] nf eyelid

pause [poz] nf (arrêt) break; (en parlant, Mus) pause

pauvre [povr] adj poor; **les pauvres** nmpl the poor; **pauvreté** nf (état) poverty

pavé, e [pave] adj (cour) paved; (chaussée) cobbled ▷ nm (bloc) paving stone; cobblestone

pavillon [pavijɔ̃] nm (de banlieue) small (detached) house; (drapeau) flag

payant, e [pejɑ̃, ɑ̃t] adj (spectateurs etc) paying; (fig: entreprise) profitable; (effort) which pays off; **c'est ~** you have to pay, there is a charge

paye [pɛj] nf pay, wages pl

payer [peje] vt (créancier, employé, loyer) to pay; (achat, réparations, fig: faute) to pay for ▷ vi to pay; (métier) to be well-paid; (tactique etc) to pay off; **il me l'a fait - 10 euros** he charged me 10 euros for it; **~ qch à qn** to buy sth for sb, buy sb sth; **se - la tête de qn** (fam) to take the mickey out of sb; **est-ce que je peux ~ par carte de crédit?** can I pay by credit card?

pays [pei] nm country; (région) region; **du ~** local

paysage [peizaʒ] nm landscape

paysan, ne [peizɑ̃, an] nm/f farmer; (péj) peasant ▷ adj (agricole) farming; (rural) country

Pays-Bas [peiba] nmpl: **les ~** the Netherlands

PC nm (Inform) PC

PDA sigle m (= personal digital assistant) PDA

PDG sigle m = **président directeur général**

péage [peaʒ] nm toll; (endroit) tollgate

peau, x [po] nf skin; **gants de ~** fine leather gloves; **être bien/mal dans sa ~** to be quite at ease/ill-at-ease; **peau de chamois** (chiffon) chamois leather, shammy

pêche [pɛʃ] nf (fruit) peach; (sport, activité) fishing; (poissons pêchés) catch; **pêche à la ligne** (en rivière) angling

péché [peʃe] nm sin

pécher [peʃe] vi (Rel) to sin

pêcher [peʃe] nm peach tree ▷ vi to go fishing ▷ vt (attraper) to catch; (être pêcheur de) to fish for

pécheur, -eresse [peʃœr, peʃrɛs] nm/f sinner

pêcheur [peʃœr] nm fisherman; (à la ligne) angler

pédagogie [pedagɔʒi] nf educational methods pl, pedagogy; **pédagogique**

adj educational

pédale [pedal] *nf* pedal

pédalo [pedalo] *nm* pedal-boat

pédant, e [pedɑ̃, ɑ̃t] (*péj*) *adj* pedantic

pédestre [pedɛstʀ] *adj*: **randonnée ~** ramble; **sentier ~** pedestrian footpath

pédiatre [pedjatʀ] *nm/f* paediatrician, child specialist

pédicure [pedikyʀ] *nm/f* chiropodist

pègre [pɛgʀ] *nf* underworld

peigne [pɛɲ] *nm* comb; **peigner** *vt* to comb (the hair of); **se peigner** *vi* to comb one's hair; **peignoir** *nm* dressing gown; **peignoir de bain** bathrobe

peindre [pɛ̃dʀ] *vt* to paint; (*fig*) to portray, depict

peine [pɛn] *nf* (*affliction*) sorrow, sadness *no pl*; (*mal, effort*) trouble *no pl*, (*difficulté*) difficulty; (*Jur*) sentence; **avoir de la ~** to be sad; **faire de la ~ à qn** to distress *ou* upset sb; **prendre la ~ de faire** to go to the trouble of doing; **se donner de la ~** to make an effort; **ce n'est pas la ~ de faire** there's no point in doing, it's not worth doing; **à ~** scarcely, barely; **à ~... que** hardly ... than, no sooner ... than; **peine capitale** capital punishment; **peine de mort** death sentence *ou* penalty; **peiner** *vi* (*personne*) to work hard; (*moteur, voiture*) to labour ▷ *vt* to grieve, sadden

peintre [pɛ̃tʀ] *nm* painter; **peintre en bâtiment** painter (and decorator)

peinture [pɛ̃tyʀ] *nf* painting; (*matière*) paint; (*surfaces peintes: aussi*: **~s**) paintwork; **"~ fraîche"** "wet paint"

péjoratif, -ive [peʒɔʀatif, iv] *adj* pejorative, derogatory

Pékin [pekɛ̃] *n* Beijing

pêle-mêle [pɛlmɛl] *adv* higgledy-piggledy

peler [pəle] *vt, vi* to peel

pèlerin [pɛlʀɛ̃] *nm* pilgrim

pèlerinage [pɛlʀinaʒ] *nm* pilgrimage

pelle [pɛl] *nf* shovel; (*d'enfant, de terrassier*) spade

pellicule [pelikyl] *nf* film; **pellicules**

nfpl (*Méd*) dandruff *sg*; **je voudrais une ~ de 36 poses** I'd like a 36-exposure film

pelote [p(ə)lɔt] *nf* (*de fil, laine*) ball; **pelote basque** pelota

peloton [p(ə)lɔtɔ̃] *nm* group, squad; (*Cyclisme*) pack

pelotonner [p(ə)lɔtɔne]: **se pelotonner** *vi* to curl (o.s.) up

pelouse [p(ə)luz] *nf* lawn

peluche [p(ə)lyʃ] *nf*: (**animal en**) **~** fluffy animal, soft toy; **chien/lapin en ~** fluffy dog/rabbit

pelure [p(ə)lyʀ] *nf* peeling, peel *no pl*

pénal, e, -aux [penal, o] *adj* penal; **pénalité** *nf* penalty

penchant [pɑ̃ʃɑ̃] *nm* (*tendance*) tendency, propensity; (*faible*) liking, fondness

pencher [pɑ̃ʃe] *vi* to lean, lean over ▷ *vt* to tilt; **se pencher** *vi* to lean over; (*se baisser*) to bend down; **se ~ sur** (*fig: problème*) to look into; **~ pour** to be inclined to favour

pendant [pɑ̃dɑ̃] *prép* (*au cours de*) during; (*indique la durée*) for; **~ que** while

pendentif [pɑ̃dɑ̃tif] *nm* pendant

penderie [pɑ̃dʀi] *nf* wardrobe

pendre [pɑ̃dʀ] *vt, vi* to hang; (*se suicider*) to hang o.s.; **~ qch à** (*mur*) to hang sth (up) on; (*plafond*) to hang sth (up) from

pendule [pɑ̃dyl] *nf* clock ▷ *nm* pendulum

pénétrer [penetʀe] *vi, vt* to penetrate; **~ dans** to enter

pénible [penibl] *adj* (*travail*) hard; (*sujet*) painful; (*personne*) tiresome; **péniblement** *adv* with difficulty

péniche [peniʃ] *nf* barge

pénicilline [penisilin] *nf* penicillin

péninsule [penɛ̃syl] *nf* peninsula

pénis [penis] *nm* penis

pénitence [penitɑ̃s] *nf* (*peine*) penance; (*repentir*) penitence; **pénitencier** *nm* penitentiary

pénombre [penɔ̃bʀ] *nf* (*faible clarté*) half-light; (*obscurité*) darkness

pensée [pɑ̃se] *nf* thought; (*démarche,*

doctrine) thinking no pl; (fleur) pansy; **en ~** in one's own

penser [pɑ̃se] vi, vt to think; **~ à** (ami, vacances) to think of ou about; (réfléchir à: problème, offre) to think about ou over; (prévoir) to think of; **faire ~ à** to remind one of; **~ faire qch** to be thinking of doing sth, intend to do sth; **pensif, -ive** adj pensive, thoughtful

pension [pɑ̃sjɔ̃] nf (allocation) pension; (prix du logement) board and lodgings; bed and board; (école) boarding school; **pension alimentaire** (de divorce) maintenance allowance, alimony; **pension complète** full board; **pension de famille** boarding house, guesthouse; **pensionnaire** nmf (Scol) boarder; **pensionnat** nm boarding school

pente [pɑ̃t] nf slope; **en ~** sloping

Pentecôte [pɑ̃tkot] nf: **la ~** Whitsun (BRIT), Pentecost

pénurie [penyʀi] nf shortage

pépé [pepe] (fam) nm grandad

pépin [pepɛ̃] nm (Bot: graine) pip; (ennui) snag, hitch

pépinière [pepinjɛʀ] nf nursery

perçant, e [pɛʀsɑ̃, ɑ̃t] adj (cri) piercing, shrill; (regard) piercing

percepteur, -trice [pɛʀsɛptœʀ, tʀis] nm/f tax collector

perception [pɛʀsɛpsjɔ̃] nf perception; (bureau) tax office

percer [pɛʀse] vt to pierce; (ouverture etc) to make; (mystère, énigme) to penetrate ▷ vi to break through; **perceuse** nf drill

percevoir [pɛʀsəvwaʀ] vt (distinguer) to perceive, detect; (taxe, impôt) to collect; (revenu, indemnité) to receive

perche [pɛʀʃ] nf (bâton) pole

percher [pɛʀʃe] vt, vi to perch; **se percher** vi to perch; **perchoir** nm perch

perçois etc [pɛʀswa] vb voir **percevoir**

perçu, e [pɛʀsy] pp de **percevoir**

percussion [pɛʀkysjɔ̃] nf percussion

percuter [pɛʀkyte] vt to strike; (suj:

véhicule) to crash into

perdant, e [pɛʀdɑ̃, ɑ̃t] nm/f loser

perdre [pɛʀdʀ] vt to lose; (gaspiller: temps, argent) to waste; (personne: moralement etc) to ruin ▷ vi to lose; (sur une vente etc) to lose out; **se perdre** vi (s'égarer) to get lost, lose one's way; (denrées) to go to waste; **j'ai perdu mon portefeuille/passeport** I've lost my wallet/passport; **je me suis perdu** (et je le suis encore) I'm lost; (et je ne le suis plus) I got lost

perdrix [pɛʀdʀi] nf partridge

perdu, e [pɛʀdy] pp de **perdre** ▷ adj (isolé) out-of-the-way; (Comm: emballage) non-returnable; (malade): **il est ~** there's no hope left for him; **à vos moments ~s** in your spare time

père [pɛʀ] nm father; **père de famille** father; **le père Noël** Father Christmas

perfection [pɛʀfɛksjɔ̃] nf perfection; **à la ~** to perfection; **perfectionné, e** adj sophisticated; **perfectionner** vt to improve, perfect; **se perfectionner en anglais** to improve one's English

perforer [pɛʀfɔʀe] vt (poinçonner) to punch

performant, e [pɛʀfɔʀmɑ̃, ɑ̃t] adj: **très ~** high-performance cpd

perfusion [pɛʀfyzjɔ̃] nf: **faire une ~ à qn** to put sb on a drip

péril [peʀil] nm peril

périmé, e [peʀime] adj (Admin) out-of-date, expired

périmètre [peʀimɛtʀ] nm perimeter

période [peʀjɔd] nf period; **périodique** adj periodic ▷ nm periodical; **garniture** ou **serviette périodique** sanitary towel (BRIT) ou napkin (US)

périphérique [peʀifeʀik] adj (quartiers) outlying ▷ nm (Auto): **boulevard ~** ring road (BRIT), beltway (US)

périr [peʀiʀ] vi to die, perish

périssable [peʀisabl] adj perishable

perle [pɛʀl] nf pearl; (de plastique, métal, sueur) bead

permanence [pɛʀmanɑ̃s] nf

permanence; (local) (duty) office;
assurer une ~ (service public, bureaux)
to operate ou maintain a basic service;
être de ~ to be on call ou duty; **en ~**
continuously

permanent, e [pɛʀmanɑ̃, ɑ̃t] adj
permanent; (spectacle) continuous;
permanente nf perm

perméable [pɛʀmeabl] adj (terrain)
permeable; **~ à** (fig) receptive ou open to

permettre [pɛʀmɛtʀ] vt to allow,
permit; **~ à qn de faire/qch** to allow
sb to do/sth; **se ~ de faire** to take the
liberty of doing

permis [pɛʀmi] nm permit, licence;
permis de conduire driving licence
(BRIT), driver's license (US); **permis de
construire** planning permission (BRIT),
building permit (US); **permis de séjour**
residence permit; **permis de travail**
work permit

permission [pɛʀmisjɔ̃] nf permission;
(Mil) leave; **avoir la ~ de faire** to have
permission to do; **en ~** on leave

Pérou [peʀu] nm Peru

perpétuel, le [pɛʀpetɥɛl] adj
perpetual; **perpétuité** nf: **à perpétuité**
for life; **être condamné à perpétuité**
to receive a life sentence

perplexe [pɛʀplɛks] adj perplexed,
puzzled

perquisitionner [pɛʀkizisjɔne] vi to
carry out a search

perron [peʀɔ̃] nm steps pl (leading to
entrance)

perroquet [peʀɔkɛ] nm parrot

perruche [peʀyʃ] nf budgerigar (BRIT),
budgie (BRIT), parakeet (US)

perruque [peʀyk] nf wig

persécuter [pɛʀsekyte] vt to
persecute

persévérer [pɛʀseveʀe] vi to
persevere

persil [pɛʀsi] nm parsley

Persique [pɛʀsik] adj: **le golfe ~**
the (Persian) Gulf

persistant, e [pɛʀsistɑ̃, ɑ̃t] adj
persistent

persister [pɛʀsiste] vi to persist; **~ à
faire qch** to persist in doing sth

personnage [pɛʀsɔnaʒ] nm (individu)
character, individual; (célébrité)
important person; (de roman, film)
character; (Peinture) figure

personnalité [pɛʀsɔnalite] nf
personality; (personnage) prominent
figure

personne [pɛʀsɔn] nf person ▷ pron
nobody, no one; (avec négation en
anglais) anybody, anyone; **personne
âgée** elderly person; **personnel, le** adj
personal; (égoïste) selfish ▷ nm staff,
personnel; **personnellement** adv
personally

perspective [pɛʀspɛktiv] nf (Art)
perspective; (vue) view; (point de vue)
viewpoint, angle; (chose envisagée)
prospect; **en ~** in prospect

perspicace [pɛʀspikas] adj clear-
sighted, gifted with (ou showing)
insight; **perspicacité** nf clear-
sightedness

persuader [pɛʀsɥade] vt: **~ qn (de
faire)** to persuade sb (to do); **persuasif,
-ive** adj persuasive

perte [pɛʀt] nf loss; (de temps) waste;
(fig: morale) ruin; **à ~ de vue** as far as the
eye can (ou could) see; **pertes blanches**
(vaginal) discharge sg

pertinent, e [pɛʀtinɑ̃, ɑ̃t] adj apt,
relevant

perturbation [pɛʀtyʀbasjɔ̃] nf:
perturbation (atmosphérique)
atmospheric disturbance

perturber [pɛʀtyʀbe] vt to disrupt;
(Psych) to perturb, disturb

pervers, e [pɛʀvɛʀ, ɛʀs] adj perverted

pervertir [pɛʀvɛʀtiʀ] vt to pervert

pesant, e [pəzɑ̃, ɑ̃t] adj heavy; (fig:
présence) burdensome

pèse-personne [pɛzpɛʀsɔn] nm
(bathroom) scales pl

peser [pəze] vt to weigh ▷ vi to weigh;
(fig: avoir de l'importance) to carry
weight; **~ lourd** to be heavy

pessimiste [pesimist] adj pessimistic

▷ nm/f pessimist

peste [pɛst] nf plague

pétale [petal] nm petal

pétanque [petɑ̃k] nf type of bowls

● PÉTANQUE

● **Pétanque** is a version of the game
● of 'boules', played on a variety of
● hard surfaces. Standing with their
● feet together, players throw steel
● bowls at a wooden jack. **Pétanque**
● originated in the South of France
● and is still very much associated
● with that area.

pétard [petar] nm banger (BRIT),
firecracker

péter [pete] vi (fam: casser) to bust;
(fam!) to fart (!)

pétillant, e [petijɑ̃, ɑ̃t] adj (eau etc)
sparkling

pétiller [petije] vi (feu) to crackle;
(champagne) to bubble; (yeux) to sparkle

petit, e [p(ə)ti, it] adj small; (avec
nuance affective) little; (voyage) short,
little; (bruit etc) faint, slight ▷ nm/f
(petit enfant) little boy/girl, child; petits
nmpl (d'un animal) young no pl; **faire de
~s** to have kittens ou puppies etc); **la
classe des ~s** the infant class; **les tout-
~s** the little ones, the tiny tots (fam); **~ à
~** bit by bit, gradually; **petit ami**
boyfriend/girlfriend; **petit déjeuner**
breakfast; **le petit déjeuner est à
quelle heure?** what time is breakfast?;
petit four petit four; **petit pain** (bread)
roll; **les petites annonces** the small
ads; **petits pois** (garden) peas; **petite-
fille** nf granddaughter; **petit-fils** nm
grandson

pétition [petisjɔ̃] nf petition

petits-enfants [pətizɑ̃fɑ̃] nmpl
grandchildren

pétrin [petrɛ̃] nm (fig): **dans le ~** (fam)
in a jam ou fix

pétrir [petrir] vt to knead

pétrole [petrol] nm oil; (pour lampe,

réchaud etc) paraffin (oil); **pétrolier,
-ière** nm oil tanker

⚠ Attention à ne pas traduire *pétrole*
par le mot anglais *petrol*.

○ MOT-CLÉ

peu [pø] adv **1** (modifiant verbe, adjectif,
adverbe): **il boit peu** he doesn't drink
(very) much; **il est peu bavard** he's
not very talkative; **peu avant/après**
shortly before/afterwards

2 (modifiant nom): **peu de: peu de
gens/d'arbres** few ou not (very) many
people/trees; **il a peu d'espoir** he
hasn't (got) much hope, he has little
hope; **pour peu de temps** for (only) a
short while

3: **peu à peu** little by little; **à peu près**
just about, more or less; **à peu près
10 kg/10 euros** approximately 10
kg/10 euros

▷ pron **1**: **le peu de gens qui** the few
people who; **le peu de sable qui** what
little sand, the little sand which

2: **un peu** a little; **un petit peu** a little
bit; **un peu d'espoir** a little hope;
elle est un peu bavarde she's quite
ou rather talkative; **un peu plus de**
slightly more than; **un peu moins de**
slightly less than; (avec pluriel) slightly
fewer than

▷ pron: **peu le savent** few know (it); **de
peu** (only) just

peuple [pœpl] nm people; **peupler** vt
(pays, région) to populate; (étang) to
stock; (suj: hommes, poissons) to inhabit

peuplier [pøplije] nm poplar (tree)

peur [pœr] nf fear; **avoir ~ (de/de
faire/que)** to be frightened ou afraid
(of/of doing/that); **faire ~ à** to
frighten; **de ~ de/que** for fear of/that;
peureux, -euse adj fearful, timorous

peut [pø] vb voir **pouvoir**

peut-être [pøtɛtr] adv perhaps,
maybe; **~ que** perhaps, maybe; **~ bien
qu'il fera/est** he may well do/be

phare [faʀ] nm (en mer) lighthouse; (de véhicule) headlight

pharmacie [faʀmasi] nf (magasin) chemist's (BRIT), pharmacy; (de salle de bain) medicine cabinet; **pharmacien, ne** nm/f pharmacist, chemist (BRIT)

phénomène [fenɔmɛn] nm phenomenon

philosophe [filɔzɔf] nm/f philosopher ▷ adj philosophical

philosophie [filɔzɔfi] nf philosophy

phobie [fɔbi] nf phobia

phoque [fɔk] nm seal

phosphorescent, e [fɔsfɔresã, ãt] adj luminous

photo [fɔto] nf photo(graph); **prendre en ~** to take a photo of; **pourriez-vous nous prendre en ~, s'il vous plaît?** would you take a picture of us, please?; **faire de la ~** to take photos; **photo d'identité** passport photograph; **photocopie** nf photocopy; **photocopier** vt to photocopy; **photocopieuse** nf photocopier; **photographe** nm/f photographer; **photographie** nf (technique) photography; (cliché) photograph; **photographier** vt to photograph

phrase [fʀaz] nf sentence

physicien, ne [fizisjɛ̃, jɛn] nm/f physicist

physique [fizik] adj physical ▷ nm physique ▷ nf physics sg; **au ~ physically; physiquement** adv physically

pianiste [pjanist] nm/f pianist

piano [pjano] nm piano; **pianoter** vi to tinkle away (at the piano)

pic [pik] nm (instrument) pick(axe); (montagne) peak; (Zool) woodpecker; **à ~** vertically; (fig: tomber, arriver) just at the right time

pichet [piʃɛ] nm jug

picorer [pikɔʀe] vt to peck

pie [pi] nf magpie

pièce [pjɛs] nf (d'un logement) room; (Théâtre) play; (de machine) part; (de monnaie) coin; (document) document; (fragment, de collection) piece; **dix euros ~** ten euros each; **vendre à la ~** to sell separately; **travailler à la ~** to do piecework; **un maillot une ~** a one-piece swimsuit; **un deux-~s cuisine** a two-room(ed) flat (BRIT) ou apartment (US) with kitchen; **pièce à conviction** exhibit; **pièce d'eau** ornamental lake ou pond; **pièce de rechange** spare (part); **pièce d'identité: avez-vous une pièce d'identité?** have you got any (means of) identification?; **pièce jointe** (Comput) attachment; **pièce montée** tiered cake; **pièces détachées** spares, (spare) parts; **pièces justificatives** supporting documents

pied [pje] nm foot; (de table) leg; (de lampe) base; **~s nus** ou **nus-~s** barefoot; **à ~** on foot; **au ~ de la lettre** literally; **avoir ~** to be able to touch the bottom, not to be out of one's depth; **avoir le ~ marin** to be a good sailor; **sur ~** (debout, rétabli) up and about; **mettre sur ~** (entreprise) to set up; **c'est le ~** (fam) it's brilliant; **mettre les ~s dans le plat** (fam) to put one's foot in it; **il se débrouille comme un ~** (fam) he's completely useless; **pied-noir** nm Algerian-born Frenchman

piège [pjɛʒ] nm trap; **prendre au ~** to trap; **piéger** vt (avec une bombe) to booby-trap; **lettre/voiture piégée** letter-/car-bomb

piercing [pjɛʀsiŋ] nm body piercing

pierre [pjɛʀ] nf stone; **pierre tombale** tombstone; **pierreries** nfpl gems, precious stones

piétiner [pjetine] vi (trépigner) to stamp (one's foot); (fig) to be at a standstill ▷ vt to trample on

piéton, ne [pjetɔ̃, ɔn] nm/f pedestrian; **piétonnier, -ière** adj: **rue** ou **zone piétonnière** pedestrian precinct

pieu, x [pjø] nm post; (pointu) stake

pieuvre [pjœvʀ] nf octopus

pieux, -euse [pjø, pjøz] adj pious

pigeon [piʒɔ̃] nm pigeon

piger [piʒe] (fam) vi, vt to understand

pigiste [piʒist] nm/f freelance(r)

pignon [piɲɔ̃] nm (de mur) gable

pile [pil] nf (tas) pile; (Élec) battery
  ▷ adv (fam: s'arrêter etc) dead; **à deux heures ~** at two on the dot; **jouer à ~ ou face** to toss up (for it); **~ ou face?** heads or tails?

piler [pile] vt to crush, pound

pilier [pilje] nm pillar

piller [pije] vt to pillage, plunder, loot

pilote [pilɔt] nm pilot; (de voiture) driver
  ▷ adj pilot cpd; **pilote de course** racing driver; **pilote de ligne** airline pilot; **piloter** vt (avion) to pilot, fly; (voiture) to drive

pilule [pilyl] nf pill; **prendre la ~** to be on the pill

piment [pimã] nm (aussi: **~ rouge**) chilli; (fig) spice, piquancy; **~ doux** pepper, capsicum; **pimenté, e** adj (plat) hot, spicy

pin [pɛ̃] nm pine

pinard [pinaʀ] nm (fam) (cheap) wine, plonk (BRIT)

pince [pɛ̃s] nf (outil) pliers pl; (de homard, crabe) pincer, claw; (Couture: pli) dart; **pince à épiler** tweezers pl; **pince à linge** clothes peg (BRIT) ou pin (US)

pincé, e [pɛ̃se] adj (air) stiff

pinceau, x [pɛ̃so] nm (paint)brush

pincer [pɛ̃se] vt to pinch; (fam) to nab

pinède [pinɛd] nf pinewood, pine forest

pingouin [pɛ̃gwɛ̃] nm penguin

ping-pong® [piŋpɔŋ] nm table tennis

pinson [pɛ̃sɔ̃] nm chaffinch

pintade [pɛ̃tad] nf guinea-fowl

pion [pjɔ̃] nm (Échecs) pawn; (Dames) piece; (Scol) supervisor

pionnier [pjɔnje] nm pioneer

pipe [pip] nf pipe; **fumer la ~** to smoke a pipe

piquant, e [pikã, ãt] adj (barbe, rosier etc) prickly; (saveur, sauce) hot, pungent; (détail) titillating; (froid) biting ▷ nm (épine) thorn, prickle; (fig) spiciness, spice

pique [pik] nf pike; (fig) cutting remark

  ▷ nm (Cartes) spades pl

pique-nique [piknik] nm picnic; **pique-niquer** vi to have a picnic

piquer [pike] vt (suj: guêpe, fourmi, orties) to sting; (: moustique) to bite; (: barbe) to prick; (: froid) to bite; (Méd) to give a jab to; (: chien, chat) to put to sleep; (intérêt) to arouse; (fam: voler) to pinch ▷ vi (avion) to go into a dive

piquet [pike] nm (pieu) post, stake; (de tente) peg

piqûre [pikyʀ] nf (d'épingle) prick; (d'ortie) sting; (de moustique) bite; (Méd) injection, shot (US); **faire une ~ à qn** to give sb an injection

pirate [piʀat] nm, adj pirate; **pirate de l'air** hijacker

pire [piʀ] adj worse; (superlatif): **le(la) ~ ...** the worst ... ▷ nm: **le ~ (de)** the worst (of); **au ~** at (the very) worst

pis [pi] nm (de vache) udder ▷ adj, adv worse; **de mal en ~** from bad to worse

piscine [pisin] nf (swimming) pool; **piscine couverte** indoor (swimming) pool

pissenlit [pisãli] nm dandelion

pistache [pistaʃ] nf pistachio (nut)

piste [pist] nf (d'un animal, sentier) track, trail; (indice) lead; (de stade) track; (de cirque) ring; (de danse) floor; (de patinage) rink; (de ski) run; (Aviat) runway; **piste cyclable** cycle track

pistolet [pistɔlɛ] nm (arme) pistol, gun; (à peinture) spray gun; **pistolet-mitrailleur** nm submachine gun

piston [pistɔ̃] nm (Tech) piston; **avoir du ~** (fam) to have friends in the right places; **pistonner** vt (candidat) to pull strings for

piteux, -euse [pitø, øz] adj pitiful, sorry (avant le nom); **en ~ état** in a sorry state

pitié [pitje] nf pity; **il me fait ~** I feel sorry for him; **avoir ~ de** (compassion) to pity, feel sorry for; (merci) to have pity ou mercy on

pitoyable [pitwajabl] adj pitiful

pittoresque [pitɔʀɛsk] adj

picturesque

PJ sigle f (= police judiciaire) ≈ CID (BRIT), ≈ FBI (US)

placard [plakaʀ] nm (armoire) cupboard; (affiche) poster, notice

place [plas] nf (emplacement, classement) place; (de ville, village) square; (espace libre) room, space; (de parking) space; (siège: de train, cinéma, voiture) seat; (emploi) job; **en** ~ (mettre) in its place; **sur** ~ on the spot; **faire** ~ **à** to give way to; **ça prend de la** ~ it takes up a lot of room ou space; **à la** ~ **de** in place of, instead of; **à votre** ~ ... if I were you ...; **je voudrais réserver deux** ~**s** I'd like to book two seats; **la** ~ **est prise?** is this seat taken?; **se mettre à la** ~ **de qn** to put o.s. in sb's place ou in sb's shoes

placé, e [plase] adj: **haut** ~ (fig) high-ranking; **être bien/mal** ~ (spectateur) to have a good/poor seat; (concurrent) to be in a good/bad position; **il est bien** ~ **pour le savoir** he is in a position to know

placement [plasmɑ̃] nm (Finance) investment; **agence** ou **bureau de** ~ employment agency

placer [plase] vt to place; (convive, spectateur) to seat; (argent) to place, invest; **se** ~ **au premier rang** to go and stand (ou sit) in the first row

plafond [plafɔ̃] nm ceiling

plage [plaʒ] nf beach; **plage arrière** (Auto) parcel ou back shelf

plaider [plede] vi (avocat) to plead ▷ vt to plead; ~ **pour** (fig) to speak for; **plaidoyer** nm (Jur) speech for the defence; (fig) plea

plaie [plɛ] nf wound

plaignant, e [plɛɲɑ̃, ɑ̃t] nm/f plaintiff

plaindre [plɛ̃dʀ] vt to pity, feel sorry for; **se plaindre** vi (gémir) to moan; (protester): **se** ~ **(à qn) (de)** to complain (to sb) (about); (souffrir): **se** ~ **de** to complain of

plaine [plɛn] nf plain

plain-pied [plɛ̃pje] adv: **de** ~ **(avec)** on the same level (as)

plainte [plɛ̃t] nf (gémissement) moan, groan; (doléance) complaint; **porter** ~ to lodge a complaint

plaire [plɛʀ] vi to be a success, be successful; **ça plaît beaucoup aux jeunes** it's very popular with young people; ~ **à**: **cela me plaît** I like it; **se** ~ **quelque part** to like being somewhere ou like it somewhere; **s'il vous plaît** please

plaisance [plezɑ̃s] nf (aussi: **navigation de** ~) (pleasure) sailing, yachting

plaisant, e [plezɑ̃, ɑ̃t] adj pleasant; (histoire, anecdote) amusing

plaisanter [plezɑ̃te] vi to joke; **plaisanterie** nf joke

plaisir [pleziʀ] nm pleasure; **faire** ~ **à qn** (délibérément) to be nice to sb, please sb; **ça me fait** ~ I like (doing) it; **j'espère que ça te fera** ~ I hope you'll like it; **pour le** ~ for pleasure

plaît [plɛ] vb voir **plaire**

plan, e [plɑ̃, an] adj flat ▷ nm plan; (fig) level, plane; (Cinéma) shot; **au premier/second** ~ in the foreground/middle distance; **à l'arrière-** ~ in the background; **plan d'eau** lake

planche [plɑ̃ʃ] nf (pièce de bois) plank, (wooden) board; (illustration) plate; **planche à repasser** ironing board; **planche (à roulettes)** skateboard; **planche (à voile)** (sport) windsurfing

plancher [plɑ̃ʃe] nm floor; floorboards pl ▷ vi (fam) to work hard

planer [plane] vi to glide; (fam: rêveur) to have one's head in the clouds; ~ **sur** (fig: danger) to hang over

planète [planɛt] nf planet

planeur [planœʀ] nm glider

planifier [planifje] vt to plan

planning [planiŋ] nm programme, schedule; **planning familial** family planning

plant [plɑ̃] nm seedling, young plant

plante [plɑ̃t] nf plant; **la plante du pied** the sole (of the foot); **plante verte** ou **d'appartement** house plant

planter [plɑ̃te] vt (plante) to plant; (enfoncer) to hammer ou drive in; (tente) to put up, pitch; (fam: personne) to dump; **se planter** (fam: se tromper) to get it wrong

plaque [plak] nf plate; (de verglas, d'eczéma) patch; (avec inscription) plaque; **plaque chauffante** hotplate; **plaque de chocolat** bar of chocolate; **plaque tournante** (fig) centre

plaqué, e [plake] adj: **~ or/argent** gold-/silver-plated

plaquer [plake] vt (Rugby) to bring down; (fam: laisser tomber) to drop

plaquette [plakɛt] nf (de chocolat) bar; (beurre) pack(et); **plaquette de frein** brake pad

plastique [plastik] adj, nm plastic; **plastiquer** vt to blow up (with a plastic bomb)

plat, e [pla, -at] adj flat; (cheveux) straight; (style) flat, dull ▷ nm (récipient, Culin) dish; (d'un repas) course; **à ~ ventre** face down; **à ~** (pneu, batterie) flat; (fam: personne) dead beat; **plat cuisiné** pre-cooked meal; **plat de résistance** main course; **plat du jour** dish of the day

platane [platan] nm plane tree

plateau, x [plato] nm (support) tray; (Géo) plateau; (Ciné) set; **plateau à fromages** cheese board

plate-bande [platbɑ̃d] nf flower bed

plate-forme [platfɔrm] nf platform; **plate-forme de forage/pétrolière** drilling/oil rig

platine [platin] nm platinum ▷ nf (d'un tourne-disque) turntable; **platine laser** compact disc ou CD player

plâtre [plɑtr] nm (matériau, statue) plaster; (statue) plaster statue; (Méd) (plaster) cast; **avoir un bras dans le ~** to have an arm in plaster

plein, e [plɛ̃, plɛn] adj full ▷ nm: **faire le ~ (d'essence)** to fill up (with petrol); **à ~es mains** (ramasser) in handfuls; **à ~ temps** full-time; **en ~ air** in the open air; **en ~ soleil** in direct sunlight; **en ~e**

nuit/rue in the middle of the night/street; **en ~ jour** in broad daylight; **le ~, s'il vous plaît** fill it up, please

pleurer [plœre] vi to cry; (yeux) to water ▷ vt to mourn (for); **~ sur** to lament (over), to bemoan

pleurnicher [plœrniʃe] vi to snivel, whine

pleurs [plœr] nmpl: **en ~** in tears

pleut [plø] vb voir **pleuvoir**

pleuvoir [pløvwar] vb impers to rain ▷ vi (coups) to rain down; (critiques, invitations) to shower down; **il pleut** it's raining; **il pleut des cordes** it's pouring (down), it's raining cats and dogs

pli [pli] nm fold; (de jupe) pleat; (de pantalon) crease

pliant, e [plijɑ̃, plijɑ̃t] adj folding

plier [plije] vt to fold; (pour ranger) to fold up; (genou, bras) to bend ▷ vi to bend; (fig) to yield; **se ~ à** to submit to

plisser [plise] vt (jupe) to put pleats in; (yeux) to screw up; (front) to crease

plomb [plɔ̃] nm (métal) lead; (d'une cartouche) (lead) shot; (Pêche) sinker; (Élec) fuse; **sans ~** (essence etc) unleaded

plomberie [plɔ̃bri] nf plumbing

plombier [plɔ̃bje] nm plumber

plonge [plɔ̃ʒ] nf washing-up

plongeant, e [plɔ̃ʒɑ̃, ɑ̃t] adj (vue) from above; (décolleté) plunging

plongée [plɔ̃ʒe] nf (Sport) diving no pl; (sans scaphandre) skin diving; **~ sous-marine** diving

plongeoir [plɔ̃ʒwar] nm diving board

plongeon [plɔ̃ʒɔ̃] nm dive

plonger [plɔ̃ʒe] vi to dive ▷ vt: **~ qch dans** to plunge sth into; **se ~ dans** (études, lecture) to bury ou immerse o.s. in; **plongeur nm** diver

plu [ply] pp de **plaire**; de **pleuvoir**

pluie [plɥi] nf rain

plume [plym] nf feather; (pour écrire) (pen) nib; (fig) pen

plupart [plypar]: **la ~** pron the majority, most (of them); **la ~ des** most, the majority of; **la ~ du temps/d'entre nous** most of the time/of us;

pour la – for the most part, mostly

pluriel [plyʀjɛl] *nm* plural

plus¹ [ply] *vb voir* **plaire**

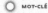

MOT-CLÉ

plus² [ply] *adv* **1** *(forme négative)*: **ne ...
plus** no more, no longer; **je n'ai plus
d'argent** I've got no more money *ou*
no money left; **il ne travaille plus** he's
no longer working, he doesn't work
any more

2 [ply, plyz + *voyelle*] *(comparatif)* more,
...+er; *(superlatif)*: **le plus** the most,
the ...+est; **plus grand/intelligent
(que)** bigger/more intelligent (than);
le plus grand/intelligent the biggest/
most intelligent; **tout au plus** at the
very most

3 [plys, plyz + *voyelle*] *(davantage)*
more; **il travaille plus (que)** he works
more (than); **plus il travaille, plus il
est heureux** the more he works, the
happier he is; **plus de 10 personnes/3
heures** more than *ou* over 10 people/3
hours; **3 heures de plus que** 3 hours
more than; **de plus** what's more,
moreover; **il a 3 ans de plus que moi**
he's 3 years older than me; **3 kilos
en plus** 3 kilos more; **de plus en plus**
more and more; **en plus de** in
addition to; **de plus en plus** more and
more; **plus ou moins** more or less; **ni
plus ni moins** no more, no less
▷ *prép* [plys]: **4 plus 2** 4 plus 2

plusieurs [plyzjœʀ] *dét, pron* several;
ils sont ~ there are several of them

plus-value [plyvaly] *nf (bénéfice)*
surplus

plutôt [plyto] *adv* rather; **je préfère
~ celui-ci** I'd rather have this one; **~
que (de) faire** rather than *ou* instead
of doing

pluvieux, -euse [plyvjø, jøz] *adj*
rainy, wet

PME sigle f (= *petite(s) et moyenne(s)
entreprise(s))* small business(es)

PMU sigle m (= *Pari mutuel urbain*) system

of betting on horses; *(café)* betting agency

PNB sigle m (= *produit national brut*) GNP

pneu [pnø] *nm* tyre (BRIT), tire (US); **j'ai
un ~ crevé** I've got a flat tyre

pneumonie [pnømɔni] *nf* pneumonia

poche [pɔʃ] *nf* pocket; *(sous les yeux)*
bag, pouch; **argent de ~** pocket money

pochette [pɔʃɛt] *nf (d'aiguilles etc)* case;
(mouchoir) breast pocket handkerchief;
(sac à main) clutch bag; **pochette de
disque** record sleeve

poêle [pwal] *nm* stove ▷ *nf*: **~ (à frire)**
frying pan

poème [pɔɛm] *nm* poem

poésie [pɔezi] *nf (poème)* poem; *(art)*:
la ~ poetry

poète [pɔɛt] *nm* poet

poids [pwa] *nm* weight; *(Sport)*
shot; **vendre au ~** to sell by weight;
perdre/prendre du ~ to lose/put on
weight; **poids lourd** *(camion)* lorry
(BRIT), truck (US)

poignant, e [pwaɲɑ̃, ɑ̃t] *adj* poignant

poignard [pwaɲaʀ] *nm* dagger;
poignarder *vt* to stab, knife

poigne [pwaɲ] *nf* grip; **avoir de la ~**
(fig) to rule with a firm hand

poignée [pwaɲe] *nf (de sel etc, fig)*
handful; *(de couvercle, porte)* handle;
poignée de main handshake

poignet [pwaɲɛ] *nm (Anat)* wrist; *(de
chemise)* cuff

poil [pwal] *nm (Anat)* hair; *(de pinceau,
brosse)* bristle; *(de tapis)* strand; *(pelage)*
coat; **à ~** *(fam)* starkers; **au ~** *(fam)*
hunky-dory; **poilu, e** *adj* hairy

poinçonner [pwɛ̃sɔne] *vt (bijou)* to
hallmark; *(billet)* to punch

poing [pwɛ̃] *nm* fist; **coup de ~** punch

point [pwɛ̃] *nm (endroit)* spot;
(marque, signe) dot; *(: de ponctuation)*
full stop, period (US); *(Couture, Tricot)*
stitch ▷ *adv* = **pas¹**; **faire le ~** *(fig)* to
take stock (of the situation); **sur le
~ de faire** (just) about to do; **à tel ~
que** so much so that; **mettre au ~**
(procédé) to develop; *(affaire)* to settle; **à ~**
(Culin: viande) medium; **à ~ (nommé)**

just at the right time; **deux ~s** colon; **point de côté** stitch (*pain*); **point d'exclamation/d'interrogation** exclamation/question mark; **point de repère** landmark; (*dans le temps*) point of reference; **point de vente** retail outlet; **point de vue** viewpoint; (*fig: opinion*) point of view; **point faible** weak spot; **point final** full stop, period (*us*); **point mort: au point mort** (*Auto*) in neutral; **points de suspension** suspension points

pointe [pwɛt] *nf* point; (*clou*) tack; (*fig*): **une ~ de** a hint of; **être à la ~ de** (*fig*) to be in the forefront of; **sur la ~ des pieds** on tiptoe; **en ~** pointed, tapered; **de ~** (*technique etc*) precise; **heures de ~** peak hours

pointer [pwɛte] *vt* (*diriger: canon, doigt*): **~ sur qch** to point at sth ▷ *vi* (*employé*) to clock in

pointillé [pwɛtije] *nm* (*trait*) dotted line

pointilleux, -euse [pwɛtijø, øz] *adj* particular, pernickety

pointu, e [pwɛty] *adj* pointed; (*voix*) shrill; (*analyse*) precise

pointure [pwɛtyʀ] *nf* size

point-virgule [pwɛ̃viʀgyl] *nm* semi-colon

poire [pwaʀ] *nf* pear; (*fam: péj*) mug

poireau, x [pwaʀo] *nm* leek

poirier [pwaʀje] *nm* pear tree

pois [pwa] *nm* (*Bot*) pea; (*sur une étoffe*) dot, spot; **~ chiche** chickpea; **à ~** (*cravate etc*) spotted, polka-dot *cpd*

poison [pwazɔ̃] *nm* poison

poisseux, -euse [pwasø, øz] *adj* sticky

poisson [pwasɔ̃] *nm* fish *gén inv*; (*Astrol*): **P~s** Pisces; **~ d'avril** April fool; (*blague*) April Fool's Day trick; *see note*; **poisson rouge** goldfish; **poissonnerie** *nf* fish-shop; **poissonnier, -ière** *nm/f* fishmonger (*BRIT*), fish merchant (*us*)

◗ **POISSON D'AVRIL**

◗ The traditional April Fools' Day prank
◗ in France involves attaching a cut-

◗ out paper fish, known as a 'poisson
◗ d'avril', to the back of one's victim,
◗ without being caught.

poitrine [pwatʀin] *nf* chest; (*seins*) bust, bosom; (*Culin*) breast

poivre [pwavʀ] *nm* pepper

poivron [pwavʀɔ̃] *nm* pepper, capsicum

polaire [pɔlɛʀ] *adj* polar

pôle [pol] *nm* (*Géo, Élec*) pole; **le ~ Nord/Sud** the North/South Pole

poli, e [pɔli] *adj* polite; (*lisse*) smooth

police [pɔlis] *nf* police; **police judiciaire** ≈ Criminal Investigation Department (*BRIT*), ≈ Federal Bureau of Investigation (*us*); **police secours** ≈ emergency services *pl* (*BRIT*), ≈ paramedics *pl* (*us*); **policier, -ière** *adj* police *cpd* ▷ *nm* policeman; (*aussi*: **roman policier**) detective novel

polir [pɔliʀ] *vt* to polish

politesse [pɔlites] *nf* politeness

politicien, ne [pɔlitisjɛ̃, jɛn] (*péj*) *nm/f* politician

politique [pɔlitik] *adj* political ▷ *nf* politics *sg*; (*mesures, méthode*) policies *pl*

politiquement [pɔlitikmɑ̃] *adv* politically; **~ correct** politically correct

pollen [pɔlɛn] *nm* pollen

polluant, e [pɔlɥɑ̃, ɑ̃t] *adj* polluting ▷ *nm* (*produit*) ~ pollutant; **non ~** non-polluting

polluer [pɔlɥe] *vt* to pollute; **pollution** *nf* pollution

polo [pɔlo] *nm* (*chemise*) polo shirt

Pologne [pɔlɔɲ] *nf* **la ~** Poland; **polonais, e** *adj* Polish ▷ *nm/f*: **Polonais, e** Pole ▷ *nm* (*Ling*) Polish

poltron, ne [pɔltʀɔ̃, ɔn] *adj* cowardly

polycopier [pɔlikɔpje] *vt* to duplicate

Polynésie [pɔlinezi] *nf*: **la ~** Polynesia; **la ~ française** French Polynesia

polyvalent, e [pɔlivalɑ̃, ɑ̃t] *adj* (*rôle*) varied; (*salle*) multi-purpose

pommade [pɔmad] *nf* ointment, cream

pomme [pɔm] *nf* apple; **tomber**

dans les ~s (fam) to pass out; **pomme d'Adam** Adam's apple; **pomme de pin** pine ou fir cone; **pomme de terre** potato

pommette [pɔmɛt] nf cheekbone

pommier [pɔmje] nm apple tree

pompe [pɔ̃p] nf pump; (faste) pomp (and ceremony); **pompe (à essence)** petrol pump; **pompes funèbres** funeral parlour sg, undertaker's sg; **pomper** vt to pump; (aspirer) to pump up; (absorber) to soak up

pompeux, -euse [pɔ̃pø, øz] adj pompous

pompier [pɔ̃pje] nm fireman

pompiste [pɔ̃pist] nm/f petrol (BRIT) ou gas (US) pump attendant

poncer [pɔ̃se] vt to sand (down)

ponctuation [pɔ̃ktɥasjɔ̃] nf punctuation

ponctuel, le [pɔ̃ktɥɛl] adj punctual

pondéré, e [pɔ̃deʀe] adj level-headed, composed

pondre [pɔ̃dʀ] vt to lay

poney [pɔnɛ] nm pony

pont [pɔ̃] nm bridge; (Navig) deck; **faire le ~** to take the extra day off; see note; **pont suspendu** suspension bridge; **pont-levis** nm drawbridge

○ **PONT**

○ The expression 'faire le pont' refers
○ to the practice of taking a Monday
○ or Friday off to make a long weekend
○ if a public holiday falls on a Tuesday
○ or Thursday. The French commonly
○ take an extra day off work to give
○ four consecutive days' holiday at
○ l'Ascension', le 14 juillet' and 'le
○ 15 août'.

pop [pɔp] adj inv pop

populaire [pɔpylɛʀ] adj popular; (manifestation) mass cpd; (milieux, quartier) working-class; (expression) vernacular

popularité [pɔpylaʀite] nf popularity

population [pɔpylasjɔ̃] nf population

populeux, -euse [pɔpylø, øz] adj densely populated

porc [pɔʀ] nm pig; (Culin) pork

porcelaine [pɔʀsəlɛn] nf porcelain, china; piece of china/ware

porc-épic [pɔʀkepik] nm porcupine

porche [pɔʀʃ] nm porch

porcherie [pɔʀʃəʀi] nf pigsty

pore [pɔʀ] nm pore

porno [pɔʀno] adj porno ▷ nm porn

port [pɔʀ] nm harbour, port; (ville) port; (de l'uniforme etc) wearing; (pour lettre) postage; (pour colis, aussi: posture) carriage; **port d'arme** (Jur) carrying of a firearm; **port payé** postage paid

portable [pɔʀtabl] adj (portatif) portable; (téléphone) mobile ▷ nm (Comput) laptop (computer); (téléphone) mobile (phone)

portail [pɔʀtaj] nm gate

portant, e [pɔʀtɑ̃, ɑ̃t] adj: **bien/mal ~** in good/poor health

portatif, -ive [pɔʀtatif, iv] adj portable

porte [pɔʀt] nf door; (de ville, jardin) gate; **mettre à la ~** to throw out; **porte-avions** nm inv aircraft carrier; **porte-bagages** nm inv luggage rack; **porte-bonheur** nm inv lucky charm; **porte-clefs** nm inv key ring; **porte-documents** nm inv attaché ou document case

porté, e [pɔʀte] adj: **être ~ à faire** to be inclined to do; **être ~ sur qch** to be keen on sth; **portée** nf (d'une arme) range; (fig: effet) impact, import; (: capacité) scope, capability; (de chatte etc) litter; (Mus) stave, staff; **à/hors de portée (de)** within/out of reach (of); **à portée de (la) main** within (arm's) reach; **à la portée de qn** (fig) at sb's level; **à la portée de qn** at sb's capabilities

porte...: **portefeuille** nm wallet; **portemanteau, x** nm (cintre) coat hanger; (au mur) coat rack; **porte-monnaie** nm inv purse; **porte-parole** nm inv spokesman

porter [pɔʀte] vt to carry; (sur soi: vêtement, barbe, bague) to wear; (fig: responsabilité etc) to bear, carry; (inscription, nom, fruits) to bear; (coup) to deal; (attention) to turn; (apporter): **~ qch à qn** to take sth to sb ▷ vi (voix) to carry; (coup, argument) to hit home; **se porter** vi (se sentir): **se ~ bien/mal** to be well/unwell; **~ sur** (recherches) to be concerned with; **se faire ~ malade** to report sick

porteur, -euse [pɔʀtœʀ, øz] nm/f (de bagages) porter; (de chèque) bearer

porte-voix [pɔʀtəvwa] nm inv megaphone

portier [pɔʀtje] nm doorman

portière [pɔʀtjɛʀ] nf door

portion [pɔʀsjɔ̃] nf (part) portion, share; (partie) portion, section

porto [pɔʀto] nm port (wine)

portrait [pɔʀtʀɛ] nm (peinture) portrait; (photo) photograph; **portrait-robot** nm Identikit® ou photo-fit® picture

portuaire [pɔʀtɥɛʀ] adj port cpd, harbour cpd

portugais, e [pɔʀtygɛ, ɛz] adj Portuguese ▷ nm/f: **P~, e** Portuguese ▷ nm (Ling) Portuguese

Portugal [pɔʀtygal] nm: **le ~** Portugal

pose [poz] nf (de moquette) laying; (attitude, d'un modèle) pose; (Photo) exposure

posé, e [poze] adj serious

poser [poze] vt to put; (installer: moquette, carrelage) to lay; (rideaux, papier peint) to hang; (question) to ask; (principe, conditions) to lay or set down; (difficulté) to pose; (formuler: problème) to formulate ▷ vi (modèle) to pose; **se poser** vi (oiseau, avion) to land; (question) to arise: **~ qch (sur)** (déposer) to put sth down (on); **~ qch sur/quelque part** (placer) to put sth on/somewhere; **~ sa candidature à un poste** to apply for a post

positif, -ive [pozitif, iv] adj positive

position [pozisjɔ̃] nf position; **prendre**

~ (fig) to take a stand

posologie [pozɔlɔʒi] nf dosage

posséder [pɔsede] vt to own, possess; (qualité, talent) to have, possess; (sexuellement) to possess; **possession** nf ownership no pl, possession; **prendre possession de qch** to take possession of sth

possibilité [pɔsibilite] nf possibility; **possibilités** nfpl (potentiel) potential sg

possible [pɔsibl] adj possible; (projet, entreprise) feasible ▷ nm: **faire son ~** to do all one can, do one's utmost; **le plus/moins de livres** as many/few books as possible; **le plus vite ~** as quickly as possible; **aussitôt/dès que ~** as soon as possible

postal, e, -aux [pɔstal, o] adj postal

poste¹ [pɔst] nf (service) post, postal service; (administration, bureau) post office; **mettre à la ~** to post; **poste restante** poste restante (BRIT), general delivery (US)

poste² [pɔst] nm (fonction, Mil) post; (Tél) extension; (de radio etc) set; **poste (de police)** police station; **poste de secours** first-aid post; **poste d'essence** filling station; **poste d'incendie** fire point; **poste de pilotage** cockpit, flight deck

poster [pɔste] vt to post; **où est-ce je peux ~ ces cartes postales?** where can I post these cards?

postérieur, e [pɔsteʀjœʀ] adj (date) later; (partie) back ▷ nm (fam) behind

postuler [pɔstyle] vi: **~ à ou pour un emploi** to apply for a job

pot [po] nm (en verre) jar; (en terre) pot; (en plastique, carton) carton; (en métal) tin; (fam: chance) luck; **avoir du ~** (fam) to be lucky; **boire ou prendre un ~** (fam) to have a drink; **petit ~ (pour bébé)** (jar of) baby food; **~ catalytique** catalytic converter; **pot d'échappement** exhaust pipe

potable [pɔtabl] adj: **eau (non) ~** (non-)drinking water

potage [pɔtaʒ] nm soup; **potager,**

-ère adj: **(jardin) potager** kitchen ou vegetable garden

pot-au-feu [potofø] nm inv (beef) stew

pot-de-vin [podvɛ̃] nm bribe

pote [pɔt] (fam) nm pal

poteau, x [pɔto] nm post; **poteau indicateur** signpost

potelé, e [pɔt(ə)le] adj plump, chubby

potentiel, le [pɔtɑ̃sjɛl] adj, nm potential

poterie [pɔtri] nf pottery; (objet) piece of pottery

potier, -ière [pɔtje, jɛʀ] nm/f potter

potiron [pɔtiʀɔ̃] nm pumpkin

pou, x [pu] nm louse

poubelle [pubɛl] nf (dust)bin

pouce [pus] nm thumb

poudre [pudʀ] nf powder; (fard) (face) powder; (explosif) gunpowder; **en ~: café en ~** instant coffee; **lait en ~** dried ou powdered milk; **poudreuse** nf powder snow; **poudrier** nm (powder) compact

pouffer [pufe] vi: **~ (de rire)** to burst out laughing

poulailler [pulaje] nm henhouse

poulain [pulɛ̃] nm foal; (fig) protégé

poule [pul] nf hen; (Culin) (boiling) fowl; **poule mouillée** coward

poulet [pulɛ] nm chicken; (fam) cop

poulie [puli] nf pulley

pouls [pu] nm pulse; **prendre le ~ de qn** to feel sb's pulse

poumon [pumɔ̃] nm lung

poupée [pupe] nf doll

pour [puʀ] prép ou ▷ nm: **le ~ et le contre** the pros and cons; **~ faire** (so as) to do, in order to do; **~ avoir fait** for having done; **~ que** so that, in order that; **fermé ~ (cause de) travaux** closed for renovations ou alterations; **c'est ~ ça que ...** that's why ...; **~ quoi faire?** what for?; **~ 20 euros d'essence** 20 euros' worth of petrol; **~ cent** per cent; **~ ce qui est de** as of

pourboire [puʀbwaʀ] nm tip; **combien de ~ est-ce qu'il faut laisser?**

how much should I tip?

pourcentage [puʀsɑ̃taʒ] nm percentage

pourchasser [puʀʃase] vt to pursue

pourparlers [puʀpaʀle] nmpl talks, negotiations

pourpre [puʀpʀ] adj crimson

pourquoi [puʀkwa] adv, conj why ▷ nm inv: **le ~ (de)** the reason (for)

pourrai etc [puʀe] vb voir **pouvoir**

pourri, e [puʀi] adj rotten

pourrir [puʀiʀ] vi to rot; (fruit) to go rotten ou bad ▷ vt to rot; (fig) to spoil thoroughly; **pourriture** nf rot

poursuite [puʀsɥit] nf pursuit, chase; **poursuites** nfpl (Jur) legal proceedings

poursuivre [puʀsɥivʀ] vt to pursue, chase (after); (obséder) to haunt; (Jur) to bring proceedings against, prosecute; (: au civil) to sue; (but) to strive towards; (continuer: études etc) to carry on with, continue; **se poursuivre** vi to go on, continue

pourtant [puʀtɑ̃] adv yet; **c'est ~ facile** (and) yet it's easy

pourtour [puʀtuʀ] nm perimeter

pourvoir [puʀvwaʀ] vt: **~ qch/qn de** to equip sth/sb with ▷ vi: **~ à** to provide for; **pourvu, e** adj: **pourvu de** equipped with; **pourvu que** (si) provided that, so long as; (espérons que) let's hope (that)

pousse [pus] nf growth; (bourgeon) shoot

poussée [puse] nf thrust; (d'acné) eruption; (fig: prix) upsurge

pousser [puse] vt to push; (émettre: cri, soupir) to give; (stimuler: élève) to urge on; (poursuivre: études, discussion) to carry on (further) ▷ vi to push; (croître) to grow; **se pousser** vi to move over; **~ qn à** (inciter) to urge sb to; (acculer) to drive sb to; **faire ~** (plante) to grow

poussette [pusɛt] nf push chair (BRIT), stroller (US)

poussière [pusjɛʀ] nf dust; **poussiéreux, -euse** adj dusty

poussin [pusɛ̃] nm chick
poutre [putʀ] nf beam

 MOT-CLÉ

pouvoir [puvwaʀ] nm power; (Pol:
dirigeants): **le pouvoir** those in power;
les pouvoirs publics the authorities;
pouvoir d'achat purchasing power
▷ vb semi-aux **1** (être en état de) can,
be able to; **je ne peux pas le réparer**
I can't ou I am not able to repair it;
déçu de ne pas pouvoir le faire
disappointed not to be able to do it
2 (avoir la permission) can, may, be
allowed to; **vous pouvez aller au
cinéma** you can ou may go to the
pictures
3 (probabilité, hypothèse) may, might,
could; **il a pu avoir un accident** he
may ou might ou could have had an
accident; **il aurait pu le dire!** he might
ou could have said (so)!
▷ vb impers may, might, could; **il peut
arriver que** it may ou might ou could
happen that; **il pourrait pleuvoir** it
might rain
▷ vt can, be able to; **j'ai fait tout ce que
j'ai pu** I did all I could; **je n'en peux plus**
(épuisé) I'm exhausted; (à bout) I can't
take any more
▷ vi: **se pouvoir: il se peut que** it may
ou might be that; **cela se pourrait**
that's quite possible

prairie [pʀeʀi] nf meadow
praline [pʀalin] nf sugared almond
praticable [pʀatikabl] adj passable,
practicable
pratiquant, e [pʀatikɑ̃, ɑ̃t] nm/f
(regular) churchgoer
pratique [pʀatik] nf practice ▷ adj
practical; **pratiquement** adv (pour ainsi
dire) practically, virtually; **pratiquer**
vt to practise; (l'équitation, la pêche)
to go in for; (le golf, football) to play;
(intervention, opération) to carry out
pré [pʀe] nm meadow

préalable [pʀealabl] adj preliminary;
au ~ beforehand
préambule [pʀeɑ̃byl] nm preamble;
(fig) prelude; **sans ~** straight away
préau [pʀeo] nm (Scol) covered
playground
préavis [pʀeavi] nm notice
précaution [pʀekosjɔ̃] nf precaution;
avec ~ cautiously; **par ~** as a
precaution
précédemment [pʀesedamɑ̃] adv
before, previously
précédent, e [pʀesedɑ̃, ɑ̃t] adj
previous ▷ nm precedent; **sans ~**
unprecedented; **le jour ~** the day
before, the previous day
précéder [pʀesede] vt to precede
prêcher [pʀeʃe] vt to preach
précieux, euse [pʀesjø, øz] adj
precious; (aide, conseil) invaluable
précipice [pʀesipis] nm drop, chasm
précipitamment [pʀesipitamɑ̃] adv
hurriedly, hastily
précipitation [pʀesipitasjɔ̃] nf (hâte)
haste
précipité, e [pʀesipite] adj hurried,
hasty
précipiter [pʀesipite] vt (hâter: départ)
to hasten; (faire tomber): **~ qn/qch du
haut de** to throw ou hurl sb/sth off ou
from; **se précipiter** vi to speed up; **se ~
sur/vers** to rush at/towards
précis, e [pʀesi, iz] adj (mesures) accurate, precise; **à 4 heures
~es** at 4 o'clock sharp; **précisément**
adv precisely; **préciser** vt (expliquer)
to be more specific about, clarify;
(spécifier) to state, specify; **se préciser**
vi to become clear(er); **précision**
nf precision; (détail) point ou detail;
demander des précisions to ask for
further explanation
précoce [pʀekɔs] adj early; (enfant)
precocious
préconçu, e [pʀekɔ̃sy] adj
preconceived
préconiser [pʀekɔnize] vt to advocate
prédécesseur [pʀedesesœʀ] nm
predecessor

predecessor

prédilection [pʁedileksjɔ̃] nf: **avoir une ~ pour** to be partial to

prédire [pʁediʁ] vt to predict

prédominer [pʁedɔmine] vi to predominate

préface [pʁefas] nf preface

préfecture [pʁefɛktyʁ] nf prefecture; **préfecture de police** police headquarters pl

préférable [pʁefeʁabl] adj preferable

préféré, e [pʁefeʁe] adj, nm/f favourite

préférence [pʁefeʁɑ̃s] nf preference; **de ~** preferably

préférer [pʁefeʁe] vt: **~ qn/qch (à)** to prefer sb/sth (to), like sb/sth better (than); **~ faire** to prefer to do; **je préférerais du thé** I would rather have tea, I'd prefer tea

préfet [pʁefɛ] nm prefect

préhistorique [pʁeistɔʁik] adj prehistoric

préjudice [pʁeʒydis] nm (matériel) loss; (moral) harm no pl; **porter ~ à** to harm, be detrimental to; **au ~ de** at the expense of

préjugé [pʁeʒyʒe] nm prejudice; **avoir un ~ contre** to be prejudiced ou biased against

prélasser [pʁelase]: **se prélasser** vi to lounge

prélèvement [pʁelɛvmɑ̃] nm (montant) deduction; **faire un ~ de sang** to take a blood sample

prélever [pʁel(ə)ve] vt (échantillon) to take; **~ (sur)** (montant) to deduct (from); (argent: sur son compte) to withdraw (from)

prématuré, e [pʁematyʁe] adj premature ▷ nm premature baby

premier, -ière [pʁəmje, jɛʁ] adj first; (rang) front; (fig: objectif) basic; **le ~ venu** the first person to come along; **de ~ ordre** first-rate; **Premier ministre** Prime Minister; **première** nf (Scol) year 12 (BRIT), eleventh grade (US); (Aviat, Rail etc) first class; **premièrement** adv firstly

prémonition [pʁemɔnisjɔ̃] nf premonition

prenant, e [pʁənɑ̃, ɑ̃t] adj absorbing, engrossing

prénatal, e [pʁenatal] adj (Méd) antenatal

prendre [pʁɑ̃dʁ] vt to take; (repas) to have; (se procurer) to get; (malfaiteur, poisson) to catch; (passager) to pick up; (personnel) to take on; (traiter: personne) to handle; (voix, ton) to put on; (ôter): **~ qch à** to take sth from; (coincer): **se ~ les doigts dans** to get one's fingers caught in ▷ vi (liquide, ciment) to set; (greffe, vaccin) to take; (feu: foyer) to go; (se diriger): **~ à gauche** to turn (to the) left; **~ froid** to catch cold; **se ~ pour** to think one is; **s'en ~ à** to attack; **se ~ d'amitié pour** to befriend; **s'y ~** (procéder) to set about it

preneur [pʁənœʁ] nm: **être/trouver ~** to be willing to buy/find a buyer

prénom [pʁenɔ̃] nm first ou Christian name

préoccupation [pʁeɔkypasjɔ̃] nf (souci) concern; (idée fixe) preoccupation

préoccuper [pʁeɔkype] vt (inquiéter) to worry; (absorber) to preoccupy; **se ~ de** to be concerned with

préparatifs [pʁepaʁatif] nmpl preparations

préparation [pʁepaʁasjɔ̃] nf preparation

préparer [pʁepaʁe] vt to prepare; (café, thé) to make; (examen) to prepare for; (voyage, entreprise) to plan; **se préparer** vi (orage, tragédie) to brew, be in the air; **~ qch à qn** (surprise etc) to have sth in store for sb; **se ~ (à qch/faire)** to prepare (o.s.) ou get ready (for sth/to do)

prépondérant, e [pʁepɔ̃deʁɑ̃, ɑ̃t] adj major, dominating

préposé, e [pʁepoze] nm/f employee; (facteur) postman

préposition [pʁepozisjɔ̃] nf preposition

près [prɛ] adv near, close; **~ de** near (to), close to; (environ) nearly, almost; **de ~** closely; **à 5 kg** ~ to within about 5 kg; **il n'est pas à 10 minutes ~** he can spare 10 minutes; **est-ce qu'il y a une banque ~ d'ici?** is there a bank nearby?

présage [prezaʒ] nm omen

presbyte [prɛsbit] adj long-sighted

presbytère [prɛsbiter] nm presbytery

prescription [prɛskripsjɔ̃] nf prescription

prescrire [prɛskrir] vt to prescribe

présence [prezɑ̃s] nf presence; (au bureau, à l'école) attendance

présent, e [prezɑ̃, ɑ̃t] adj, nm present; **à ~ (que)** now (that)

présentation [prezɑ̃tasjɔ̃] nf presentation; (de nouveau venu) introduction; (allure) appearance; **faire les ~s** to do the introductions

présenter [prezɑ̃te] vt to present; (excuses, condoléances) to offer; (invité, conférencier): **~ qn (à)** to introduce sb (to) ▷ vi: **~ bien** to have a pleasing appearance; **se présenter** vi (occasion) to arise; **se ~ à** (examen) to sit; (élection) to stand at, run for; **je vous présente Nadine** this is Nadine, could I introduce you to Nadine?

préservatif [prezɛrvatif] nm condom, sheath

préserver [prezɛrve] vt: **~ de** (protéger) to protect from

président [prezidɑ̃] nm (Pol) president; (d'une assemblée, Comm) chairman; **président directeur général** chairman and managing director; **présidentielles** nfpl presidential elections

présider [prezide] vt to preside over; (dîner) to be the guest of honour at

presque [prɛsk] adv almost, nearly; **~ personne** hardly anyone; **~ rien** hardly anything; **~ pas** hardly (at all); **~ pas (de)** hardly any

presqu'île [prɛskil] nf peninsula

pressant, e [prɛsɑ̃, ɑ̃t] adj urgent

presse [prɛs] nf press; (affluence):

heures de ~ busy times

pressé, e [prɛse] adj in a hurry; (travail) urgent; **orange ~e** freshly-squeezed orange juice

pressentiment [prɛsɑ̃timɑ̃] nm foreboding, premonition

pressentir [prɛsɑ̃tir] vt to sense

presse-papiers [prɛspapje] nm inv paperweight

presser [prɛse] vt (fruit, éponge) to squeeze; (bouton) to press; (allure) to speed up; (inciter): **~ qn de faire** to urge ou press sb to do ▷ vi to be urgent; **se presser** vi (se hâter) to hurry (up); **se ~ contre qn** to squeeze up against sb; **le temps presse** there's not much time; **rien ne presse** there's no hurry

pressing [prɛsiŋ] nm (magasin) dry-cleaner's

pression [prɛsjɔ̃] nf pressure; (bouton) press stud; (fam: bière) draught beer; **faire ~ sur** to put pressure on; **sous ~** pressurized, under pressure; (fig) under pressure; **pression artérielle** blood pressure

prestataire [prɛstater] nm/f supplier

prestation [prɛstasjɔ̃] nf (allocation) benefit; (d'une entreprise) service provided; (d'un artiste) performance

prestidigitateur, -trice [prɛstidiʒitatœr, tris] nm/f conjurer

prestige [prɛstiʒ] nm prestige; **prestigieux, -euse** adj prestigious

présumer [prezyme] vt: **~ que** to presume ou assume that

prêt, e [prɛ, prɛt] adj ready ▷ nm (somme) loan; **quand est-ce que mes photos seront ~es?** when will my photos be ready?; **prêt-à-porter** nm ready-to-wear ou off-the-peg (BRIT) clothes pl

prétendre [pretɑ̃dr] vt (affirmer): **~ que** to claim that; (avoir l'intention de): **~ faire qch** to intend to do sth; **prétendu, e** adj (supposé) so-called

⚠ Attention à ne pas traduire **prétendre** par to pretend.

prétentieux, -euse [pretɑ̃sjø, jøz]

adj pretentious

prétention [pʀetɑ̃sjɔ̃] *nf* claim; *(vanité)* pretentiousness

prêter [pʀete] *vt (livres, argent)*: ~ **qch (à)** to lend sth (to); *(supposer)*: ~ **à qn** *(caractère, propos)* to attribute to sb; **pouvez-vous me ~ de l'argent?** can you lend me some money?

prétexte [pʀetɛkst] *nm* pretext, excuse; **sous aucun ~** on no account; **prétexter** *vt* to give as a pretext *ou* an excuse

prêtre [pʀɛtʀ] *nm* priest

preuve [pʀœv] *nf* proof; *(indice)* evidence *no pl*; **faire ~ de** to show; **faire ses ~s** to prove o.s. *(ou itself)*

prévaloir [pʀevalwaʀ] *vi* to prevail

prévenant, e [pʀev(ə)nɑ̃, ɑ̃t] *adj* thoughtful, kind

prévenir [pʀev(ə)niʀ] *vt (éviter: catastrophe etc)* to avoid, prevent; *(anticiper: désirs, besoins)* to anticipate; ~ **qn (de)** *(avertir)* to warn sb (about); *(informer)* to tell ou inform sb (about)

préventif, -ive [pʀevɑ̃tif, iv] *adj* preventive

prévention [pʀevɑ̃sjɔ̃] *nf* prevention; **prévention routière** road safety

prévenu, e [pʀev(ə)ny] *nm/f (Jur)* defendant, accused

prévision [pʀevizjɔ̃] *nf*: ~**s** predictions; *(Écon)* forecast *sg*; **en ~ de** in anticipation of; **prévisions météorologiques** weather forecast *sg*

prévoir [pʀevwaʀ] *vt (anticiper)* to foresee; *(s'attendre à)* to expect, reckon on; *(organiser: voyage etc)* to plan; *(envisager)* to allow; **comme prévu** as planned; **prévoyant, e** *adj* gifted with *(ou showing)* foresight; **prévu, e** *pp de* **prévoir**

prier [pʀije] *vi* to pray ▷ *vt (Dieu)* to pray to; *(implorer)* to beg; *(demander)*: ~ **qn de faire** to ask sb to do; **se faire ~** to need coaxing *ou* persuading; **je vous en prie** *(allez-y)* please do; *(de rien)* don't mention it; **prière** *nf* prayer; **"prière de ..."** "please ..."

primaire [pʀimɛʀ] *adj* primary ▷ *nm (Scol)* primary education

prime [pʀim] *nf (bonus)* bonus; *(subvention)* premium; *(Comm: cadeau)* free gift; *(Assurances, Bourse)* premium ▷ *adj*: **de ~ abord** at first glance; **primer** *vt (récompenser)* to award a prize to ▷ *vi* to dominate; to be most important

primevère [pʀimvɛʀ] *nf* primrose

primitif, -ive [pʀimitif, iv] *adj* primitive; *(originel)* original

prince [pʀɛ̃s] *nm* prince; **princesse** *nf* princess

principal, e, -aux [pʀɛ̃sipal, o] *adj* principal, main ▷ *nm (Scol)* principal, head (master); *(essentiel)* main thing

principe [pʀɛ̃sip] *nm* principle; **par ~** on principle; **en ~** *(habituellement)* as a rule; *(théoriquement)* in principle

printemps [pʀɛ̃tɑ̃] *nm* spring

priorité [pʀijɔʀite] *nf* priority; *(Auto)* right of way; **priorité à droite** right of way to vehicles coming from the right

pris, e [pʀi, pʀiz] *pp de* **prendre** ▷ *adj (place)* taken; *(mains)* full; *(personne)* busy; **avoir le nez/la gorge ~(e)** to have a stuffy nose/a hoarse throat; **être ~ de panique** to be panic-stricken

prise [pʀiz] *nf (d'une ville)* capture; *(Pêche, Chasse)* catch; *(point d'appui ou pour empoigner)* hold; *(Élec: fiche)* plug; *(: femelle)* socket; **être aux ~s avec** to be grappling with; **prise de courant** power point; **prise de sang** blood test; **prise multiple** adaptor

priser [pʀize] *vt (estimer)* to prize, value

prison [pʀizɔ̃] *nf* prison; **aller/être en ~** to go to/be in prison ou jail; **prisonnier, -ière** *nm/f* prisoner ▷ *adj* captive

privé, e [pʀive] *adj* private; *(en punition)*: **tu es ~ de télé!** no TV for you! ▷ *nm (Comm)* private sector; **en ~**, **~ in private**

priver [pʀive] *vt*: ~ **qn de** to deprive sb of; **se priver de** to go ou do without

privilège [pʀivilɛʒ] *nm* privilege

prix [pʀi] *nm* price; *(récompense, Scol)* prize; **hors de ~** exorbitantly priced;

à aucun ~ not at any price; **à tout ~** at all costs

probable [pʀɔbabl] *adj* likely, probable; **probablement** *adv* probably

problème [pʀɔblɛm] *nm* problem

procédé [pʀɔsede] *nm* (*méthode*) process; (*comportement*) behaviour *no pl*

procéder [pʀɔsede] *vi* to proceed; (*moralement*) to behave; **~ à** to carry out

procès [pʀɔsɛ] *nm* trial; (*poursuites*) proceedings *pl*; **être en ~ avec** to be involved in a lawsuit with

processus [pʀɔsesys] *nm* process

procès-verbal, -aux [pʀɔsɛvɛʀbal, o] *nm* (*de réunion*) minutes *pl*; (*aussi*: **P.-V.**) parking ticket

prochain, e [pʀɔʃɛ̃, ɛn] *adj* next; (*proche: départ, arrivée*) impending ▷ *nm* fellow man; **la ~e fois/semaine ~e** next time/week; **prochainement** *adv* soon, shortly

proche [pʀɔʃ] *adj* nearby; (*dans le temps*) imminent; (*parent, ami*) close; **proches** *nmpl* (*parents*) close relatives; **être ~ (de)** to be near, be close (to)

proclamer [pʀɔklame] *vt* to proclaim

procuration [pʀɔkyʀasjɔ̃] *nf* proxy

procurer [pʀɔkyʀe] *vt*: **~ qch à qn** (*fournir*) to obtain sth for sb; (*causer: plaisir etc*) to bring sb sth; **se procurer** *vt* to get; **procureur** *nm* public prosecutor

prodige [pʀɔdiʒ] *nm* marvel, wonder; (*personne*) prodigy; **prodiguer** *vt* (*soins, attentions*) to lavish; **~ qch à qn** to give sb sth

producteur, -trice [pʀɔdyktœʀ, tʀis] *nm/f* producer

productif, -ive [pʀɔdyktif, iv] *adj* productive

production [pʀɔdyksjɔ̃] *nf* production; (*rendement*) output

productivité [pʀɔdyktivite] *nf* productivity

produire [pʀɔdɥiʀ] *vt* to produce; **se produire** *vi* (*événement*) to happen, occur; (*acteur*) to perform, appear

produit [pʀɔdɥi] *nm* product;

produit chimique chemical; **produits agricoles** farm produce *sg*; **produits de beauté** beauty products, cosmetics; **produits d'entretien** cleaning products

prof [pʀɔf] (*fam*) *nm* teacher

proférer [pʀɔfeʀe] *vt* to utter

professeur, e [pʀɔfesœʀ] *nm/f* teacher; (*de faculté*) (university) lecturer; (: *titulaire d'une chaire*) professor

profession [pʀɔfesjɔ̃] *nf* occupation; **~ libérale** (liberal) profession; **sans ~** unemployed; **professionnel, le** *adj, nm/f* professional

profil [pʀɔfil] *nm* profile; **de ~** in profile

profit [pʀɔfi] *nm* (*avantage*) benefit, advantage; (*Comm, Finance*) profit; **au ~ de** in aid of; **tirer ~ de** to profit from; **profitable** *adj* (*utile*) beneficial; (*lucratif*) profitable; **profiter** *vi*: **profiter de** (*situation, vacances, jeunesse etc*) to take advantage of; (*vacances, jeunesse etc*) to make the most of

profond, e [pʀɔfɔ̃, ɔ̃d] *adj* deep; (*sentiment, intérêt*) profound; **profondément** *adv* deeply; **il dort profondément** he is sound asleep; **profondeur** *nf* depth; **l'eau à quelle profondeur?** how deep is the water?

programme [pʀɔgʀam] *nm* programme; (*Scol*) syllabus, curriculum; (*Inform*) program; **programmer** *vt* (*émission*) to schedule; (*Inform*) to program; **programmeur, -euse** *nm/f* programmer

progrès [pʀɔgʀɛ] *nm* progress *no pl*; **faire des ~** to make progress; **progresser** *vi* to progress; **progressif, -ive** *adj* progressive

proie [pʀwa] *nf* prey *no pl*

projecteur [pʀɔʒɛktœʀ] *nm* (*pour film*) projector; (*de théâtre, cirque*) spotlight

projectile [pʀɔʒɛktil] *nm* missile

projection [pʀɔʒɛksjɔ̃] *nf* projection; (*séance*) showing

projet [pʀɔʒɛ] *nm* plan; (*ébauche*) draft; **projet de loi** bill; **projeter** *vt* (*envisager*) to plan; (film, photos) to project; (ombre, lueur) to throw, cast; (jeter) to throw up (ou off ou out)

prolétaire [pʀɔletɛʀ] adj, nmf proletarian

prolongement [pʀɔlɔ̃ʒmɑ̃] nm extension; **dans le ~ de** running on from

prolonger [pʀɔlɔ̃ʒe] vt (débat, séjour) to prolong; (délai, billet, rue) to extend; **se prolonger** vi to go on

promenade [pʀɔm(ə)nad] nf walk (ou drive ou ride); **faire une ~** to go for a walk; **une ~ en voiture/à vélo** a drive/(bicycle) ride

promener [pʀɔm(ə)ne] vt (chien) to take out for a walk; (doigts, regard): **~ qch sur** to run sth over; **se promener** vi to go for (ou be out for) a walk

promesse [pʀɔmɛs] nf promise

promettre [pʀɔmɛtʀ] vt to promise ▷ vi to be ou look promising; **~ à qn de faire** to promise sb that one will do

promiscuité [pʀɔmiskɥite] nf (chambre) lack of privacy

promontoire [pʀɔmɔ̃twaʀ] nm headland

promoteur, -trice [pʀɔmɔtœʀ, tʀis] nm/f: **promoteur (immobilier)** property developer (BRIT), real estate promoter (us)

promotion [pʀɔmɔsjɔ̃] nf promotion; **en ~** on special offer

promouvoir [pʀɔmuvwaʀ] vt to promote

prompt, e [pʀɔ̃(pt), pʀɔ̃(p)t] adj swift, rapid

prôner [pʀone] vt (préconiser) to advocate

pronom [pʀɔnɔ̃] nm pronoun

prononcer [pʀɔnɔ̃se] vt to pronounce; (dire) to utter; (discours) to deliver; **se prononcer** vi to be pronounced; **comment est-ce que ça se prononce?** how do you pronounce ou say it?; **se ~ (sur)** (se décider) to reach a decision (on ou about), give a verdict (on); **prononciation** nf pronunciation

pronostic [pʀɔnɔstik] nm (Méd) prognosis; (fig: aussi: **~s**) forecast

propagande [pʀɔpagɑ̃d] nf propaganda

propager [pʀɔpaʒe] vt to spread; **se propager** vi to spread

prophète [pʀɔfɛt] nm prophet

prophétie [pʀɔfesi] nf prophecy

propice [pʀɔpis] adj favourable

proportion [pʀɔpɔʀsjɔ̃] nf proportion; **toute(s) ~(s) gardée(s)** making due allowance(s)

propos [pʀɔpo] nm (intention) intention, aim; (sujet): **à quel ~?** what about? ▷ nmpl (paroles) talk no pl, remarks; **à ~ de** about, regarding; **à tout ~** for the slightest thing ou reason; **à ~** by the way; (opportunément) at the right moment

proposer [pʀɔpoze] vt to propose; **~ qch (à qn)** (suggérer) to suggest sth (to sb), propose sth (to sb); (offrir) to offer (sb) sth; **se ~ (pour faire)** to offer one's services (to sb); **proposition** (suggestion) nf proposal, suggestion; (Ling) clause

propre [pʀɔpʀ] adj clean; (net) neat, tidy; (possessif) own; (sens) literal; (particulier): **~ à** peculiar to; (approprié): **~ à** suitable for ▷ nm: **recopier au ~** to make a fair copy of; **proprement** adv (avec propreté) cleanly; **le village proprement dit** the village itself; **à proprement parler** strictly speaking; **propreté** nf cleanliness

propriétaire [pʀɔpʀijetɛʀ] nmf owner; (pour le locataire) landlord(-lady)

propriété [pʀɔpʀijete] nf property; (droit) ownership

propulser [pʀɔpylse] vt to propel

prose [pʀoz] nf (style) prose

prospecter [pʀɔspɛkte] vt to prospect; (Comm) to canvass

prospectus [pʀɔspɛktys] nm leaflet

prospère [pʀɔspɛʀ] adj prosperous; **prospérer** vi to prosper

prosterner [pʀɔstɛʀne]: **se prosterner** vi to bow low, prostrate o.s.

prostituée [pʀɔstitɥe] nf prostitute

prostitution [pʀɔstitysjɔ̃] nf prostitution

protecteur, -trice [pʀɔtɛktœʀ, tʀis] adj protective; (air, ton: péj) patronizing ▷ nm/f protector

protection [pʀɔtɛksjɔ̃] nf protection; (d'un personnage influent: aide) patronage

protéger [pʀɔteʒe] vt to protect; **se ~ de/contre** to protect o.s. from

protège-slip [pʀɔtɛʒslip] nm panty liner

protéine [pʀɔtein] nf protein

protestant, e [pʀɔtɛstɑ̃, ɑ̃t] adj, nm/f Protestant

protestation [pʀɔtɛstasjɔ̃] nf (plainte) protest

protester [pʀɔteste] vi: ~ (contre) to protest (against ou about); ~ de (son innocence) to protest

prothèse [pʀɔtɛz] nf: **prothèse dentaire** denture

protocole [pʀɔtɔkɔl] nm (fig) etiquette

proue [pʀu] nf bow(s pl), prow

prouesse [pʀues] nf feat

prouver [pʀuve] vt to prove

provenance [pʀɔv(ə)nɑ̃s] nf origin; **avion en ~ de** plane (arriving) from

provenir [pʀɔv(ə)niʀ]: ~ **de** vt to come from

proverbe [pʀɔvɛʀb] nm proverb

province [pʀɔvɛ̃s] nf province

proviseur [pʀɔvizœʀ] nm ≈ head(teacher) (BRIT), ≈ principal (US)

provision [pʀɔviʒjɔ̃] nf (réserve) stock, supply; **provisions** nfpl (vivres) provisions, food no pl

provisoire [pʀɔvizwaʀ] adj temporary; **provisoirement** adv temporarily

provocant, e [pʀɔvɔkɑ̃, ɑ̃t] adj provocative

provoquer [pʀɔvɔke] vt (défier) to provoke; (causer) to cause, bring about; (inciter): ~ **qn à** to incite sb to

proxénète [pʀɔksenɛt] nm procurer

proximité [pʀɔksimite] nf nearness,

closeness; (dans le temps) imminence, closeness; **à ~** near ou close by; **à - de** near (to), close to

prudemment [pʀydamɑ̃] adv carefully; wisely, sensibly

prudence [pʀydɑ̃s] nf carefulness; **avec ~** carefully; **par ~** as a precaution

prudent, e [pʀydɑ̃, ɑ̃t] adj (pas téméraire) careful; (: en général) safety-conscious; (sage, conseillé) wise, sensible; **c'est plus ~** it's wiser

prune [pʀyn] nf plum

pruneau, x [pʀyno] nm prune

prunier [pʀynje] nm plum tree

PS sigle m = **parti socialiste**

pseudonyme [psødɔnim] nm (gén) fictitious name; (d'écrivain) pseudonym, pen name

psychanalyse [psikanaliz] nf psychoanalysis

psychiatre [psikjatʀ] nm/f psychiatrist; **psychiatrique** adj psychiatric

psychique [psiʃik] adj psychological

psychologie [psikɔlɔʒi] nf psychology; **psychologique** adj psychological; **psychologue** nm/f psychologist

pu [py] pp de **pouvoir**

puanteur [pɥɑ̃tœʀ] nf stink, stench

pub [pyb] nf (fam: annonce) ad, advert; (pratique) advertising

public, -ique [pyblik] adj public; (école, instruction) state cpd ▷ nm public; (assistance) audience; **en ~** in public

publicitaire [pyblisitɛʀ] adj advertising cpd; (film) publicity cpd

publicité [pyblisite] nf (méthode, profession) advertising; (annonce) advertisement; (révélations) publicity

publier [pyblije] vt to publish

publipostage [pyblipɔstaʒ] nm mailing m

publique [pyblik] adj voir **public**

puce [pys] nf flea; (Inform) chip; **carte à ~** smart card; **(marché aux) ~s** flea market sg

pudeur [pydœʀ] nf modesty; **pudique**

adj (chaste) modest; *(discret)* discreet

puer [pɥe] *(péj)* vi to stink

puéricultrice [pɥerikyltris] *nf* p(a)ediatric nurse

puéril, e [pɥeril] *adj* childish

puis [pɥi] *vb voir* **pouvoir** ▷ *adv* then

puiser [pɥize] *vt:* **~ (dans)** to draw (from)

puisque [pɥisk] *conj* since

puissance [pɥisɑ̃s] *nf* power; **en ~** *adj* potential

puissant, e [pɥisɑ̃, ɑ̃t] *adj* powerful

puits [pɥi] *nm* well

pull(-over) [pyl(ɔvɛr)] *nm* sweater

pulluler [pylyle] *vi* to swarm

pulpe [pylp] *nf* pulp

pulvériser [pylverize] *vt:* to pulverize; *(liquide)* to spray

punaise [pynɛz] *nf (Zool)* bug; *(clou)* drawing pin (BRIT), thumbtack (US)

punch [pɔ̃ʃ] *nm (boisson)* punch

punir [pynir] *vt* to punish; **punition** *nf* punishment

pupille [pypij] *nf (Anat)* pupil ▷ *nm/f (enfant)* ward

pupitre [pypitr] *nm (Scol)* desk

pur, e [pyr] *adj* pure; *(vin)* undiluted; *(whisky)* neat; **en ~e perte** to no avail; **c'est de la folie ~e** it's sheer madness

purée [pyre] *nf:* **~ (de pommes de terre)** mashed potatoes *pl;* **purée de marrons** chestnut purée

purement [pyrmɑ̃] *adv* purely

purgatoire [pyrgatwar] *nm* purgatory

purger [pyrʒe] *vt (Méd, Pol)* to purge; *(Jur: peine)* to serve

pur-sang [pyrsɑ̃] *nm inv* thoroughbred

pus [py] *nm* pus

putain [pytɛ̃] *(fam!)* *nf* whore (!)

puzzle [pœzl] *nm* jigsaw (puzzle)

P.-V. [peve] *sigle m = procès-verbal*

pyjama [piʒama] *nm* pyjamas *pl (BRIT),* pajamas *pl (US)*

pyramide [piramid] *nf* pyramid

Pyrénées [pirene] *nfpl:* **les ~** the Pyrenees

q

QI *sigle m (= quotient intellectuel)* IQ

quadragénaire [k(w)adraʒenɛr] *nm/f* man/woman in his/her forties

quadruple [k(w)adrypl] *nm:* **le ~ de** four times as much as

quai [ke] *nm (de port)* quay; *(de gare)* platform; **être à ~** *(navire)* to be alongside; **de quel ~ part le train pour Paris?** which platform does the Paris train go from?

qualification [kalifikasjɔ̃] *nf (aptitude)* qualification

qualifier [kalifje] *vt* to qualify; **se qualifier** *vi* to qualify; **~ qch/qn de** to describe sth/sb as

qualité [kalite] *nf* quality

quand [kɑ̃] *conj, adv* when; **~ je serai riche** when I'm rich; **~ même** all the same; **~ même, il exagère!** really, he overdoes it!; **~ bien même** even though

quant [kɑ̃]: **~ à** *prép (pour ce qui est de)* as for, as to; *(au sujet de)* regarding

quantité [kɑ̃tite] *nf* quantity, amount; *(grand nombre):* **une** *ou* **des ~(s)** de a great deal of

quarantaine [kaʀɑ̃tɛn] nf (Méd)
quarantine; **avoir la ~** (âge) to be
around forty; **avoir ~ (de)** forty or so,
about forty

quarante [kaʀɑ̃t] num forty

quart [kaʀ] nm (fraction) quarter;
(surveillance) watch; **un ~ de vin** a
quarter litre of wine; **le ~ de** a quarter
of; **quart d'heure** quarter of an hour;
quarts de finale quarter finals

quartier [kaʀtje] nm (de ville) district,
area; (de bœuf) (de fruit) piece;
cinéma de ~ local cinema; **avoir ~
libre** (fig) to be free; **quartier général**
headquarters pl

quartz [kwaʀts] nm quartz

quasi [kazi] adv almost, nearly;
quasiment adv almost, nearly;
quasiment jamais hardly ever

quatorze [katɔʀz] num fourteen

quatorzième [katɔʀzjɛm] num
fourteenth

quatre [katʀ] num four; **à ~ pattes** on
all fours; **se mettre en ~ pour qn** to go
out of one's way for sb; **~ à ~** (monter,
descendre) four at a time; **quatre-vingt-
dix** num ninety; **quatre-vingts** num
eighty; **quatrième** num fourth ▷ nf
(Scol) year 9 (BRIT), eighth grade (US)

quatuor [kwatɥɔʀ] nm quartet(te)

MOT-CLÉ

que [kə] conj 1 (introduisant complétive)
that; **il sait que tu es là** he knows
(that) you're here; **je veux que tu
acceptes** I want you to accept; **il a dit
que oui** he said he would (ou it was so)
2 (reprise d'autres conjonctions): **quand
il rentrera et qu'il aura mangé** when
he gets back and (when) he has eaten;
si vous y allez et que vous ... if you go
there and if you ...
3 (en tête de phrase: hypothèse, souhait
etc): **qu'il le veuille ou non** whether
he likes it or not; **qu'il fasse ce qu'il
voudra!** let him do as he pleases!

4 (après comparatif) than, as; voir aussi
plus; **aussi**; **autant** etc
5 (seulement): **ne ... que** only; **il ne boit
que de l'eau** he only drinks water
6 (temps): **il y a 4 ans qu'il est parti**
it is 4 years since he left; **il a left 4
years ago**
▷ adv (exclamation): **qu'il ou qu'est-ce
qu'il est bête/court vite!** he's so
silly!/he runs so fast!; **que de livres!**
what a lot of books!
▷ pron 1 (relatif: personne) whom; (:
chose) that, which; **l'homme que je
vois** the man (whom) I see; **le livre
que tu vois** the book (that ou which)
you see; **un jour que j'étais ...** a day
when I was ...
2 (interrogatif) what; **que fais-tu?**,
qu'est-ce que tu fais? what are you
doing?; **qu'est-ce que c'est?** what
is it?, what's that?; **que faire?** what
can one do?

Québec [kebɛk] n: **le ~** Quebec;
québecois, e adj Quebec ▷ nm/f:
Québécois, e Quebecker ▷ nm (Ling)
Quebec French

MOT-CLÉ

quel, quelle [kɛl] adj 1 (interrogatif:
personne) who; (: chose) what; **quel est
cet homme?** who is this man?; **quel
est ce livre?** what is this book?; **quel
livre/homme?** what book/man?;
(parmi un certain choix) which book/
man?; **quels acteurs préférez-vous?**
which actors do you prefer?; **dans
quels pays êtes-vous allé?** which ou
what countries did you go to?
2 (exclamatif): **quelle surprise!** what
a surprise!
3: **quel que soit le coupable** whoever
is guilty; **quel que soit votre avis**
whatever your opinion

quelconque [kɛlkɔ̃k] adj (indéfini): **un
ami/prétexte ~** some friend/pretext

or other; (*médiocre: repas*) indifferent, poor; (*laid: personne*) plain-looking

○ **MOT-CLÉ**

quelque [kɛlk] adj **1** (*au singulier*) some; (*au pluriel*) a few, some; (*tournure interrogative*) any; **quelque espoir** some hope; **il a quelques amis** he has a few ou some friends; **a-t-il quelques amis?** does he have any friends?; **les quelques livres qui** the few books which; **20 kg et quelque(s)** a bit over 20 kg
2: **quelque ... que** (*+sub*) **quelque livre qu'il choisisse** whatever (*ou* whichever) book he chooses
3: **quelque chose** something; (*tournure interrogative*) anything; **quelque chose d'autre** something else; anything else; **quelque part** somewhere; anywhere; **en quelque sorte** as it were
▷ adv **1** (*environ*): **quelque 100 mètres** some 100 metres
2: **quelque peu** rather, somewhat

quelquefois [kɛlkəfwa] adv sometimes

quelques-uns, -unes [kɛlkəzœ̃, yn] pron a few, some

quelqu'un [kɛlkœ̃] pron someone, somebody; (*+ tournure interrogative*) anyone, anybody; **quelqu'un d'autre** someone ou somebody else; (*+ tournure interrogative*) anybody else

qu'en dira-t-on [kɑ̃diratɔ̃] nm inv: **le qu'en dira-t-on** gossip, what people say

querelle [kəɛl] nf quarrel; **quereller: se quereller** vi to quarrel

qu'est-ce que [kɛskə] vb + conj voir **que**

qu'est-ce qui [kɛski] vb + conj voir **qui**

question [kɛstjɔ̃] nf question; (*fig*) matter, issue; **il a été ~ de** we (*ou* they) spoke about; **de quoi est-il ~?** what is it about?; **il n'en est pas ~** there's no question of it; **en ~** in question; **hors de ~** out of the question; **remettre**

en ~ to question; **questionnaire** nm questionnaire; **questionner** vt to question

quête [kɛt] nf collection; (*recherche*) quest, search; **faire la ~** (*à l'église*) to take the collection; (*artiste*) to pass the hat round

quetsche [kwɛtʃ] nf kind of dark-red plum

queue [kø] nf tail; (*fig: du classement*) bottom; (: *de poêle*) handle; (: *de fruit, feuille*) stalk; (: *de train, colonne, file*) rear; **faire la ~** to queue (up) (*BRIT*), line up (*US*); **queue de cheval** ponytail; **queue de poisson** (*Auto*): **faire une queue de poisson à qn** to cut in front of sb

○ **MOT-CLÉ**

qui [ki] pron **1** (*interrogatif: personne*) who; (: *chose*): **qu'est-ce qui est sur la table?** what is on the table?; **qui est-ce qui?** who?; **qui est-ce que?** who?; **à qui est ce sac?** whose bag is this?; **à qui parlais-tu?** who were you talking to?, to whom were you talking?; **chez qui allez-vous?** whose house are you going to?
2 (*relatif: personne*) who; (*+prép*) whom; **l'ami de qui je vous ai parlé** the friend I told you about; **la dame chez qui je suis allé** the lady whose house I went to
3 (*sans antécédent*): **amenez qui vous voulez** bring who you like; **qui que ce soit** whoever it may be

quiconque [kikɔ̃k] pron (*celui qui*) whoever, anyone who; (*n'importe qui*) anyone, anybody

quille [kij] nf (*jeu de*) ~**s** skittles sg (*BRIT*), bowling (*US*)

quincaillerie [kɛ̃kajʁi] nf (*ustensiles*) hardware; (*magasin*) hardware shop

quinquagénaire [kɛ̃kaʒenɛʁ] nm/f man/woman in his/her fifties

quinquennat [kɛ̃kena] nm five year term of office (*of French President*)

quinte [kɛ̃t] nf: **~ (de toux)** coughing fit

quintuple [kɛ̃typl] nm: **le ~ de** five times as much as

quinzaine [kɛ̃zɛn] nf: **une ~ (de)** about fifteen, fifteen or so; **une ~ (de jours)** a fortnight (BRIT), two weeks

quinze [kɛ̃z] num fifteen; **dans ~ jours** in a fortnight('s time), in two weeks('time)

quinzième [kɛ̃zjɛm] num fifteenth

quiproquo [kipʀɔko] nm misunderstanding

quittance [kitɑ̃s] nf (reçu) receipt

quitte [kit] adj: **être ~ envers qn** to be no longer in sb's debt; (fig) to be quits with sb; **~ à faire** even if it means doing

quitter [kite] vt to leave; (vêtement) to take off; **se quitter** vi (couples, interlocuteurs) to part; **ne quittez pas** (au téléphone) hold the line

qui-vive [kiviv] nm: **être sur le ~** to be on the alert

⬤ MOT-CLÉ

quoi [kwa] pron interrog 1 what; **quoi de neuf?** what's new?; **quoi?** (qu'est-ce que tu dis?) what?
2 (avec prép): **à quoi tu penses?** what are you thinking about?; **de quoi parlez-vous?** what are you talking about?; **à quoi bon?** what's the use?
▷ pron rel: **as-tu de quoi écrire?** do you have anything to write with?; **il n'y a pas de quoi** (please) don't mention it; **il n'y a pas de quoi rire** there's nothing to laugh about
▷ pron (locutions): **quoi qu'il arrive** whatever happens; **quoi qu'il en soit** be that as it may; **quoi que ce soit** anything at all
▷ excl what!

quoique [kwak] conj (al)though

quotidien, ne [kɔtidjɛ̃, jɛn] adj daily; (banal) everyday ▷ nm (journal) daily (paper); **quotidiennement** adv daily

---

r

r. abr = **route**; **rue**

rab [ʀab] (fam) nm (nourriture) extra; **est-ce qu'il y a du ~?** are there any seconds?

rabâcher [ʀabaʃe] vt to keep on repeating

rabais [ʀabɛ] nm reduction, discount; **rabaisser** vt (dénigrer) to belittle; (rabattre: prix) to reduce

Rabat [ʀaba(t)] n Rabat

rabattre [ʀabatʀ] vt (couvercle, siège) to pull down; (déduire) to reduce; **se rabattre** vi (se refermer: couvercle) to fall shut; (véhicule, coureur) to cut in; **se sur** to fall back on

rabbin [ʀabɛ̃] nm rabbi

rabougri, e [ʀabugʀi] adj stunted

raccommoder [ʀakɔmɔde] vt to mend, repair

raccompagner [ʀakɔ̃paɲe] vt to take ou see back

raccord [ʀakɔʀ] nm link; (retouche) touch up; **raccorder** vt to join (up), link up; (suj: pont etc) to connect, link

raccourci [Rakursi] nm short cut

raccourcir [RakursiR] vt to shorten
▷ vi (jours) to grow shorter, draw in

raccrocher [RakROʃe] vt (tableau) to hang back up; (récepteur) to put down
▷ vi (Tél) to hang up, ring off

race [Ras] nf race; (d'animaux, fig) breed;
de ~ purebred, pedigree

rachat [Raʃa] nm buying; (du même objet) buying back

racheter [Raʃ(ə)te] vt (article perdu) to buy another; (après avoir vendu) to buy back; (d'occasion) to buy; (Comm: part, firme) to buy out; (davantage): **~ du lait/3 œufs** to buy more milk/another 3 eggs ou 3 more eggs; **se racheter** vi (fig) to make amends

racial, e, -aux [Rasjal, jo] adj racial

racine [Rasin] nf root; **racine carrée/cubique** square/cube root

racisme [Rasism] nm racism

raciste [Rasist] adj, nm/f racist

racket [Raket] nm racketeering no pl

raclée [Rɑkle] (fam) nf hiding, thrashing

racler [Rɑkle] vt (surface) to scrape; **se ~ la gorge** to clear one's throat

racontars [RakɔtaR] nmpl story, lie

raconter [Rakɔte] vt: **~ (à qn)** (décrire) to relate (to sb), tell (sb) about; (dire de mauvaise foi) to tell (sb); **~ une histoire** to tell a story

radar [RadaR] nm radar

rade [Rad] nf (natural) harbour; **rester en ~** (fig) to be left stranded

radeau, x [Rado] nm raft

radiateur [RadjatœR] nm radiator, heater; (Auto) radiator; **radiateur électrique** electric heater ou fire

radiation [Radjɑsjɔ] nf (Physique) radiation

radical, e, -aux [Radikal, o] adj radical

radieux, -euse [Radjø, jøz] adj radiant

radin, e [Radɛ̃, in] (fam) adj stingy

radio [Radjo] nf (Méd) X-ray
▷ nm radio operator; **à la ~ on** the radio; **radioactif, -ive** adj radioactive;

radiocassette nm cassette radio, radio cassette player; **radiographie** nf radiography; (photo) X-ray photograph; **radiophonique** adj radio cpd; **radioréveil** (pl **radios-réveils**) nm radio alarm clock

radis [Radi] nm radish

radoter [Radɔte] vi to ramble on

radoucir [RadusiR]: **se radoucir** vi (temps) to become milder; (se calmer) to calm down

rafale [Rafal] nf (vent) gust (of wind); (tir) burst of gunfire

raffermir [RafɛRmiR] vt to firm up

raffiner [Rafine] vt to refine; **raffinerie** nf refinery

raffoler [Rafɔle]: **~ de** vt to be very keen on

rafle [Rɑfl] nf (de police) raid; **rafler** (fam) vt to swipe, nick

rafraîchir [RafReʃiR] vt (atmosphère, température) to cool (down); (aussi: **mettre à ~**) to chill; (fig: rénover) to brighten up; **se rafraîchir** vi (temps) to grow cooler; (en se lavant) to freshen up; (en buvant) to refresh o.s.; **rafraîchissant, e** adj refreshing; **rafraîchissement** nm (boisson) cool drink; **rafraîchissements** nmpl (boissons, fruits etc) refreshments

rage [Raʒ] nf (Méd): **la ~** rabies; (fureur) rage, fury; **faire ~** to rage; **rage de dents** (raging) toothache

ragot [Rago] (fam) nm malicious gossip no pl

ragoût [Ragu] nm stew

raide [Rɛd] adj stiff; (câble) taut, tight; (escarpé) steep; (droit: cheveux) straight; (fam: sans argent) flat broke; (osé) daring, bold ▷ adv (en pente) steeply; **~ mort** stone dead; **raideur** nf (rigidité) stiffness; **avec raideur** (répondre) stiffly, abruptly; (marcher) stiffly; **se raidir** vi (tissu) to stiffen; (personne) to tense up; (: se préparer moralement) to brace o.s.; (fig: position) to harden

raie [Rɛ] nf (Zool) skate, ray; (rayure) stripe; (des cheveux) parting

raifort [ʀɛfɔʀ] nm horseradish

rail [ʀɑj] nm rail; (chemins de fer) railways pl; **par ~** by rail

railler [ʀɑje] vt to scoff at, jeer at

rainure [ʀenyʀ] nf groove

raisin [ʀezɛ̃] nm (aussi: **~s**) grapes pl; **raisins secs** raisins

raison [ʀezɔ̃] nf reason; **avoir ~** to be right; **donner ~ à qn** to agree with sb; (événement) to prove sb right; **perdre la ~** to become insane; **se faire une ~** to learn to live with it; **~ de plus** all the more reason; **à plus forte ~** all the more so; **en ~ de** because of; **à ~ de** at the rate of; **sans ~** for no reason; **raison sociale** corporate name; **raisonnable** adj reasonable, sensible

raisonnement [ʀezɔnmɑ̃] nm (façon de réflexion) reasoning; (argumentation) argument

raisonner [ʀezɔne] vi (penser) to reason; (argumenter, discuter) to argue ▷ vt (personne) to reason with

rajeunir [ʀaʒœniʀ] vt (suj: coiffure, robe): **~ qn** to make sb look younger; (fig: personnel) to inject new blood into ▷ vi to become (ou look) younger

rajouter [ʀaʒute] vt to add

rajuster [ʀaʒyste] vt (vêtement) to straighten, tidy; (salaires) to adjust

ralenti [ʀalɑ̃ti] nm: **au ~** (fig) at a slower pace; **tourner au ~** (Auto) to tick over, idle

ralentir [ʀalɑ̃tiʀ] vt to slow down

râler [ʀale] vi to groan; (fam) to grouse, moan (and groan)

rallier [ʀalje] vt (rejoindre) to rejoin; (gagner à sa cause) to win over

rallonge [ʀalɔ̃ʒ] nf (de table) (extra) leaf

rallonger [ʀalɔ̃ʒe] vt to lengthen

rallye [ʀali] nm rally; (Pol) march

ramassage [ʀamasaʒ] nm: **ramassage scolaire** school bus service

ramasser [ʀamase] vt (objet tombé ou par terre, fam) to pick up; (recueillir: copies, ordures) to collect; (récolter) to gather; **ramassis** (péj) nm (de voyous) bunch; (d'objets) jumble

rambarde [ʀɑ̃baʀd] nf guardrail

rame [ʀam] nf (aviron) oar; (de métro) train; (de papier) ream

rameau, x [ʀamo] nm (small) branch; **les Rameaux** (Rel) Palm Sunday sg

ramener [ʀam(ə)ne] vt to bring back; (reconduire) to take back; **~ qch à** (réduire à) to reduce sth to

ramer [ʀame] vi to row

ramollir [ʀamɔliʀ] vt to soften; **se ramollir** vi to go soft

rampe [ʀɑ̃p] nf (d'escalier) banister(s pl); (dans un garage) ramp; (Théâtre): **la ~** the footlights pl; **rampe de lancement** launching pad

ramper [ʀɑ̃pe] vi to crawl

rancard [ʀɑ̃kaʀ] (fam) nm (rendez-vous) date

rancart [ʀɑ̃kaʀ] nm: **mettre au ~** (fam) to scrap

rance [ʀɑ̃s] adj rancid

rancœur [ʀɑ̃kœʀ] nf rancour

rançon [ʀɑ̃sɔ̃] nf ransom

rancune [ʀɑ̃kyn] nf grudge, rancour; **garder ~ à qn (de qch)** to bear sb a grudge (for sth); **sans ~!** no hard feelings!; **rancunier, -ière** adj vindictive, spiteful

randonnée [ʀɑ̃dɔne] nf (pédestre) walk, ramble; (: en montagne) hike, hiking ou **~ pédestre**; **la ~** (activité) hiking, walking; **une ~ à cheval** a pony trek

rang [ʀɑ̃] nm (rangée) row; (grade, classement) rank; **rangs** nmpl (Mil) ranks; **se mettre en ~s** to line up ou form rows; **au premier ~** in the first row; (fig) ranking first

rangé, e [ʀɑ̃ʒe] adj (vie) well-ordered; (personne) steady

rangée [ʀɑ̃ʒe] nf row

ranger [ʀɑ̃ʒe] vt (mettre de l'ordre dans) to tidy up; (classer, grouper) to order, arrange; (mettre à sa place) to put away; (fig: classer): **~ qn/qch parmi** to rank sb/sth among; **se ranger** vi (véhicule, conducteur) to pull over ou in; (piéton) to step aside; (s'assagir) to settle down; **se ~ à** (avis) to come round to

ranimer [ʀanime] vt (personne) to bring round; (douleur, souvenir) to revive; (feu) to rekindle

rapace [ʀapas] nm bird of prey

râpe [ʀɑp] nf (Culin) grater; **râper** vt (Culin) to grate

rapide [ʀapid] adj fast; (prompt: coup d'œil, mouvement) quick ▷ nm express (train); (de cours d'eau) rapid; **rapidement** adv fast; quickly

rapiécer [ʀapjese] vt to patch

rappel [ʀapɛl] nm (Théâtre) curtain call; (Méd: vaccination) booster; (deuxième avis) reminder; **rappeler** vt to call back; (ambassadeur, Mil) to recall; (faire se souvenir): **rappeler qch à qn** to remind sb of sth; **se rappeler** (se souvenir de) to remember, recall; **pouvez-vous rappeler plus tard?** can you call back later?

rapport [ʀapɔʀ] nm (lien, analogie) connection; (compte rendu) report; (profit) yield, return; **rapports** nmpl (entre personnes, pays) relations; **avoir ~ à** to have something to do with; **être/se mettre en ~ avec qn** to be/get in touch with sb; **par ~ à** in relation to; **rapports (sexuels)** (sexual) intercourse sg; **rapport qualité-prix** value (for money)

rapporter [ʀapɔʀte] vt (rendre, ramener) to bring back; (bénéfice) to yield, bring in; (mentionner, répéter) to report ▷ vi (investissement) to give a good return ou yield; (activité) to be very profitable; **se ~ à** to relate to

rapprochement [ʀapʀɔʃmɑ̃] nm (de nations) reconciliation; (rapport) parallel

rapprocher [ʀapʀɔʃe] vt (deux objets) to bring closer together; (fig: ennemis, partis ou) to bring together; (comparer) to establish a parallel between; (chaise d'une table): **~ qch (de)** to bring sth closer to ou nearer; **se ~ de** to come closer to; (présenter une analogie avec) to be close to

raquette [ʀakɛt] nf (de tennis) racket;

(de ping-pong) bat

rare [ʀɑʀ] adj rare; **se faire ~** to become scarce; **rarement** adv rarely, seldom

ras, e [ʀɑ, ʀɑz] adj (poil, herbe) short; (tête) close-cropped ▷ adv short; **en ~e campagne** in open country; **à ~ bords** to the brim; **en avoir ~ le bol** (fam) to be fed up

raser [ʀaze] vt (barbe, cheveux) to shave off; (menton, personne) to shave; (fam: ennuyer) to bore; (démolir) to raze (to the ground); (frôler) to graze, skim; **se raser** vi to shave; (fam) to be bored (to tears); **rasoir** nm razor

rassasier [ʀasazje] vt: **être rassasié** to have eaten one's fill

rassemblement [ʀasɑ̃bləmɑ̃] nm (groupe) gathering; (Pol) union

rassembler [ʀasɑ̃ble] vt (réunir) to assemble, gather; (documents, notes) to gather together, collect; **se rassembler** vi to gather

rassurer [ʀasyʀe] vt to reassure; **se rassurer** vi to reassure o.s.; **rassure-toi** don't worry

rat [ʀa] nm rat

rate [ʀat] nf spleen

raté, e [ʀate] adj (tentative) unsuccessful, failed ▷ nm/f (fam: personne) failure

râteau, x [ʀɑto] nm rake

rater [ʀate] vi (affaire, projet etc) to go wrong, fail ▷ vt (fam: cible, train, occasion) to miss; (plat) to spoil; (fam: examen) to fail; **nous avons raté notre train** we missed our train

ration [ʀasjɔ̃] nf ration

RATP sigle f (= Régie autonome des transports parisiens) Paris transport authority

rattacher [ʀataʃe] vt (animal, cheveux) to tie up again; (fig: relier): **~ qch à** to link sth with

rattraper [ʀatʀape] vt (fugitif) to recapture; (empêcher de tomber) to catch (hold of); (atteindre, rejoindre) to catch up with; (réparer: erreur) to make up for; **se rattraper** vi to make up for it;

(à) (se raccrocher) to stop o.s. falling (by catching hold of)

rature [ratyr] nf deletion, erasure

rauque [Rok] adj (voix) hoarse

ravages [Rava3] nmpl: **faire des ~** to wreak havoc

ravi, e [Ravi] adj: **être ~ de/que** to be delighted with/that

ravin [Ravɛ̃] nm gully, ravine

ravir [Ravir] vt (enchanter) to delight; **à ~** adv beautifully

raviser [Ravize]: **se raviser** vi to change one's mind

ravissant, e [Ravisɑ̃, ɑ̃t] adj delightful

ravisseur, -euse [Ravisœr, øz] nm/f abductor, kidnapper

ravitailler [Ravitaje] vt (en vivres, munitions) to provide with fresh supplies; (avion) to refuel; **se ~ (en)** to get fresh supplies of

raviver [Ravive] vt (feu, douleur) to revive; (couleurs) to brighten up

rayé, e [Reje] adj (à rayures) striped

rayer [Reje] vt (érafler) to scratch; (barrer) to cross out; (d'une liste) to cross off

rayon [Rejɔ̃] nm (de soleil etc) ray; (Géom) radius; (de roue) spoke; (étagère) shelf; (de grand magasin) department; **dans un ~ de** within a radius of; **rayon de soleil** sunbeam; **rayons X** X-rays

rayonnement [Rejɔnmɑ̃] nm (fig: d'une culture) influence

rayonner [Rejɔne] vi (fig) to shine forth; (personne: de joie, de beauté) to be radiant; (touriste) to go touring (from one base)

rayure [Rejyr] nf (motif) stripe; (éraflure) scratch; **à ~s** striped

raz-de-marée [Radmare] nm inv tidal wave

ré [Re] nm (Mus) D; (en chantant la gamme) re

réaction [Reaksjɔ̃] nf reaction

réadapter [Readapte]: **se réadapter (à)** vi to readjust (to)

réagir [Reaʒir] vi to react

réalisateur, -trice [RealizatœR, tRis]

nm/f (TV, Cinéma) director

réalisation [Realizasjɔ̃] nf realization; (cinéma) production; **en cours de ~** under way

réaliser [Realize] vt (projet, opération) to carry out, realize; (rêve, souhait) to realize, fulfil; (exploit) to achieve; (film) to produce; (se rendre compte de) to realize; **se réaliser** vi to be realized

réaliste [Realist] adj realistic

réalité [Realite] nf reality; **en ~** in (actual) fact; **dans la ~** in reality

réanimation [Reanimasjɔ̃] nf resuscitation; **service de ~** intensive care unit

rébarbatif, -ive [Rebarbatif, iv] adj forbidding

rebattu, e [R(ə)baty] adj hackneyed

rebelle [Rəbɛl] nm/f rebel ▷ adj (troupes) rebel; (enfant) rebellious; (mèche etc) unruly

rebeller [R(ə)bele]: **se rebeller** vi to rebel

rebondir [R(ə)bɔ̃dir] vi (ballon: au sol) to bounce; (: contre un mur) to rebound; (fig) to get moving again

rebord [R(ə)bɔr] nm edge; **le ~ de la fenêtre** the windowsill

rebours [R(ə)bur]: **à ~** adv the wrong way

rebrousser [R(ə)bruse] vt: **~ chemin** to turn back

rebuter [Rəbyte] vt to put off

récalcitrant, e [Rekalsitrɑ̃, ɑ̃t] adj refractory

récapituler [Rekapityle] vt to recapitulate, sum up

receler [R(ə)səle] vt (produit d'un vol) to receive; (fig) to conceal; **receleur, -euse** nm/f receiver

récemment [Resamɑ̃] adv recently

recensement [R(ə)sɑ̃smɑ̃] nm (population) census

recenser [R(ə)sɑ̃se] vt (population) to take a census of; (inventorier) to list

récent, e [Resɑ̃, ɑ̃t] adj recent

récépissé [Resepise] nm receipt

récepteur [ReseptœR] nm receiver

réception [resɛpsjɔ̃] nf receiving no pl; (accueil) reception, welcome; (bureau) reception desk; (réunion mondaine) reception, party; **réceptionniste** nm/f receptionist

recette [r(ə)sɛt] nf recipe; (Comm) takings pl; **recettes** nfpl (Comm: rentrées) receipts; **faire ~** (spectacle, exposition) to be a winner

recevoir [r(ə)səvwar] vt to receive; (client, patient) to see; **être reçu** (à un examen) to pass

rechange [r(ə)ʃɑ̃ʒ]: **de ~** adj (pièces, roue) spare; (fig: solution) alternative; **des vêtements de ~** a change of clothes

recharge [r(ə)ʃarʒ] nf refill; **rechargeable** adj (stylo etc) refillable; **recharger** vt (stylo) to refill; (batterie) to recharge

réchaud [reʃo] nm (portable) stove

réchauffer [reʃofe] vt (plat) to reheat; (mains, personne) to warm; **se réchauffer** vi (température) to get warmer; (personne) to warm o.s. (up)

rêche [rɛʃ] adj rough

recherche [r(ə)ʃɛrʃ] nf (action) search; (raffinement) studied elegance; (scientifique etc): **la ~** research; **recherches** nfpl (de la police) investigations; (scientifiques) research sg; **la ~ de** the search for; **être à la ~ de qch** to be looking for sth

recherché, e [r(ə)ʃɛrʃe] adj (rare, demandé) much sought-after; (raffiné: style) mannered; (: tenue) elegant

rechercher [r(ə)ʃɛrʃe] vt (objet égaré, personne) to look for; (causes, nouveau procédé) to try to find; (bonheur, compliments) to seek

rechute [r(ə)ʃyt] nf (Méd) relapse

récidiver [residive] vi to commit a subsequent offence; (fig) to do it again

récif [resif] nm reef

récipient [resipjɑ̃] nm container

réciproque [resiprɔk] adj reciprocal

récit [resi] nm story; **récital** nm recital; **réciter** vt to recite

réclamation [reklamasjɔ̃] nf complaint; (service des) **~s** complaints department

réclame [reklam] nf ad, advert(isement); **en ~** on special offer; **réclamer** vt to ask for; (revendiquer) to claim, demand ▷ vi to complain

réclusion [reklyzjɔ̃] nf imprisonment

recoin [rəkwɛ̃] nm nook, corner

reçois etc [rəswa] vb voir **recevoir**

récolte [rekɔlt] nf harvesting, gathering; (produits) harvest, crop; **récolter** vt to harvest, gather (in); (fig) to collect

recommandé [r(ə)kɔmɑ̃de] nm (Postes): **en ~** by registered mail

recommander [r(ə)kɔmɑ̃de] vt to recommend; (Postes) to register

recommencer [r(ə)kɔmɑ̃se] vt (reprendre: lutte, séance) to resume, start again; (refaire: travail, explications) to start afresh, start (over) again ▷ vi to start again; (récidiver) to do it again

récompense [rekɔ̃pɑ̃s] nf reward; (prix) award; **récompenser** vt: **récompenser qn (de ou pour)** to reward sb (for)

réconcilier [rekɔ̃silje] vt to reconcile; **se réconcilier (avec)** to make up (with)

reconduire [r(ə)kɔ̃dɥir] vt (raccompagner) to take ou see back; (renouveler) to renew

réconfort [rekɔ̃fɔr] nm comfort; **réconforter** vt (consoler) to comfort

reconnaissance [r(ə)kɔnɛsɑ̃s] nf (gratitude) gratitude, gratefulness; (action de reconnaître) recognition; (Mil) reconnaissance, recce; **reconnaissant, e** adj grateful; **je vous serais reconnaissant de bien vouloir ...** I would be most grateful if you would (kindly) ...

reconnaître [r(ə)kɔnɛtr] vt to recognize; (Mil: lieu) to reconnoitre; (Jur: enfant, torts) to acknowledge; **~ que** to admit ou acknowledge that; **~ qn/qch à** (l'identifier grâce à) to recognize sb/sth by; **reconnu, e** adj (indiscuté, connu) recognized

reconstituer [R(ə)kɔ̃stitɥe] vt (événement, accident) to reconstruct; (fresque, vase brisé) to piece together, reconstitute

reconstruire [R(ə)kɔ̃stRɥiR] vt to rebuild

reconvertir [R(ə)kɔ̃vɛRtiR]: **se reconvertir dans** vr (un métier, une branche) to go into

record [R(ə)kɔR] nm, adj record

recoupement [R(ə)kupmɑ̃] nm: **par ~** by cross-checking

recouper [R(ə)kupe]: **se recouper** vi (témoignages) to tie up/match up

recourber [R(ə)kuRbe]: **se recourber** vi to curve (up), bend (up)

recourir [R(ə)kuRiR]: **~ à** vt (ami, agence) to turn ou appeal to; (force, ruse, emprunt) to resort to

recours [R(ə)kuR] nm: **avoir ~ à** = **recourir à**; **en dernier ~** as a last resort

recouvrer [R(ə)kuvRe] vt (vue, santé etc) to recover, regain

recouvrir [R(ə)kuvRiR] vt (couvrir à nouveau) to re-cover; (couvrir entièrement, aussi fig) to cover

récréation [RekReasjɔ̃] nf (Scol) break

recroqueviller [R(ə)kRɔk(ə)vije]: **se recroqueviller** vi (personne) to huddle up

recrudescence [R(ə)kRydesɑ̃s] nf fresh outbreak

recruter [R(ə)kRyte] vt to recruit

rectangle [Rɛktɑ̃gl] nm rectangle; **rectangulaire** adj rectangular

rectificatif [Rɛktifikatif] nm correction

rectifier [Rɛktifje] vt (calcul, adresse, paroles) to correct; (erreur) to rectify

rectiligne [Rɛktilin] adj straight

recto [Rɛkto] nm front (of a page); **~ verso** on both sides (of the page)

reçu, e [R(ə)sy] pp de **recevoir** ▷ adj (candidat) successful; (admis, consacré) accepted ▷ nm (Comm) receipt; **je peux**

avoir un ~, s'il vous plaît? can I have a receipt, please?

recueil [Rəkœj] nm collection; **recueillir** vt to collect; (voix, suffrages) to win; (accueillir: réfugiés, chat) to take in; **se recueillir** vi to gather one's thoughts, meditate

recul [R(ə)kyl] nm (éloignement) distance; (déclin) decline; **être en ~** to be on the decline; **avec du ~** with hindsight; **avoir un mouvement de ~** to recoil; **prendre du ~** to stand back; **reculé, e** adj remote; **reculer** vi to move back, back away; (Auto) to reverse, back (up); (fig) to be on the decline ▷ vt to move back; (véhicule) to reverse, back (up); (date, décision) to postpone; **reculer devant** (danger, difficulté) to shrink from; **reculons**: **à reculons** adv backwards

récupérer [RekypeRe] vt to recover, get back; (heures de travail) to make up; (déchets) to salvage ▷ vi to recover

récurer [RekyRe] vt to scour; **poudre à ~** scouring powder

reçut [Rəsy] vb voir **recevoir**

recycler [R(ə)sikle] vt (Tech) to recycle; **se recycler** vi to retrain

rédacteur, -trice [RedaktœR, tRis] nm/f (journaliste) writer; subeditor; (d'ouvrage de référence) compiler, editor

rédaction [Redaksjɔ̃] nf writing; (rédacteurs) editorial staff; (Scol: devoir) essay, composition

redescendre [R(ə)desɑ̃dR] vi to go back down ▷ vt (pente etc) to go down

rédiger [Rediʒe] vt to write; (contrat) to draw up

redire [R(ə)diR] vt to repeat; **trouver à ~ à** to find fault with

redoubler [R(ə)duble] vi (tempête, violence) to intensify; (Scol) to repeat a year; **~ de patience/prudence** to be doubly patient/careful

redoutable [R(ə)dutabl] adj formidable, fearsome

redouter [R(ə)dute] vt to dread

redressement [R(ə)dRɛsmɑ̃] nm

(économique) recovery

redresser [ʀ(ə)dʀese] vt *(relever)* to set upright; *(pièce tordue)* to straighten out; *(situation, économie)* to put right; **se redresser** vi *(personne)* to sit (ou stand) up (straight); *(économie)* to recover

réduction [ʀedyksjɔ̃] nf reduction; **y a-t-il une ~ pour les étudiants?** is there a reduction for students?

réduire [ʀedɥiʀ] vt to reduce; *(prix, dépenses)* to cut, reduce; **réduit** nm *(pièce)* tiny room

rééducation [ʀeedykasjɔ̃] nf *(d'un membre)* re-education; *(de délinquants, d'un blessé)* rehabilitation

réel, le [ʀeel] adj real; **réellement** adv really

réexpédier [ʀeekspedje] vt *(à l'envoyeur)* to return, send back; *(au destinataire)* to send on, forward

refaire [ʀ(ə)fɛʀ] vt to do again; *(faire de nouveau: sport)* to take up again; *(réparer, restaurer)* to do up

réfectoire [ʀefɛktwaʀ] nm refectory

référence [ʀefeʀɑ̃s] nf reference; **références** nfpl *(recommandations)* reference sg

référer [ʀefeʀe]: **se référer à** vt to refer to

refermer [ʀ(ə)fɛʀme] vt to close ou shut again; **se refermer** vi *(porte)* to close ou shut (again)

refiler [ʀ(ə)file] vt *(fam)* to palm off

réfléchi, e [ʀefleʃi] adj *(caractère)* thoughtful; *(action)* well-thought-out; *(Ling)* reflexive; **c'est tout ~** my mind's made up

réfléchir [ʀefleʃiʀ] vt to reflect ▷ vi to think; **~ à** to think about

reflet [ʀ(ə)flɛ] nm reflection; *(sur l'eau etc)* sheen no pl, glint; **refléter** vt to reflect; **se refléter** vi to be reflected

réflexe [ʀeflɛks] nm, adj reflex

réflexion [ʀeflɛksjɔ̃] nf *(de la lumière etc)* reflection; *(fait de penser)* thought; *(remarque)* remark; **~ faite, à la ~** on reflection

réflexologie [ʀeflɛksɔlɔʒi] nf reflexology

réforme [ʀefɔʀm] nf reform; *(Rel)*: **la R~** the Reformation; **réformer** vt to reform; *(Mil)* to declare unfit for service

refouler [ʀ(ə)fule] vt *(envahisseurs)* to drive back; *(larmes)* to force back; *(désir, colère)* to repress

refrain [ʀ(ə)fʀɛ̃] nm refrain, chorus

refréner, réfréner [ʀefʀene] vt to curb, check

réfrigérateur [ʀefʀiʒeʀatœʀ] nm refrigerator, fridge

refroidir [ʀ(ə)fʀwadiʀ] vt to cool; *(fig: personne)* to put off ▷ vi to cool (down); **se refroidir** vi *(temps)* to get cooler ou colder; *(fig: ardeur)* to cool (off); **refroidissement** nm *(grippe etc)* chill

refuge [ʀ(ə)fyʒ] nm refuge; **réfugié, e** adj, nm/f refugee; **réfugier: se réfugier** vi to take refuge

refus [ʀ(ə)fy] nm refusal; **ce n'est pas de ~** I won't say no, it's welcome; **refuser** vt to refuse; *(Scol: candidat)* to fail; **refuser qch à qn** to refuse sb sth; **refuser du monde** to have to turn people away; **se refuser à faire** to refuse to do

regagner [ʀ(ə)ɡaɲe] vt *(faveur)* to win back; *(lieu)* to get back to

régal [ʀeɡal] nm treat; **régaler: se régaler** vi to have a delicious meal; *(fig)* to enjoy o.s.

regard [ʀ(ə)ɡaʀ] nm *(coup d'œil)* look, glance; *(expression)* look (in one's eye); **au ~ de** *(loi, morale)* from the point of view of; **en ~ de** in comparison with

regardant, e [ʀ(ə)ɡaʀdɑ̃, ɑ̃t] adj *(économe)* tight-fisted; **peu ~ (sur)** very free (about)

regarder [ʀ(ə)ɡaʀde] vt to look at; *(film, télévision, match)* to watch; *(concerner)* to concern ▷ vi to look; **ne pas ~ à la dépense** to spare no expense; **~ qn/qch comme** to regard sb/sth as

régie [ʀeʒi] nf *(Comm, Industrie)* state-owned company; *(Théâtre, Cinéma)* production; *(Radio, TV)* control room

régime [ʀeʒim] nm (Pol) régime; (Méd) diet; (Admin: carcéral, fiscal etc) system; (de bananes, dattes) bunch; **se mettre au/suivre un ~** to go on/be on a diet

régiment [ʀeʒimã] nm regiment

région [ʀeʒjɔ̃] nf region; **régional, e, -aux** adj regional

régir [ʀeʒiʀ] vt to govern

régisseur [ʀeʒisœʀ] nm (d'un domaine) steward; (Cinéma, TV) assistant director; (Théâtre) stage manager

registre [ʀaʒistʀ] nm register

réglage [ʀeglaʒ] nm adjustment

règle [ʀegl] nf (instrument) ruler; (loi) rule; **règles** nfpl (menstruation) period sg; **en ~** (papiers d'identité) in order; **en ~ générale** as a (general) rule

réglé, e [ʀegle] adj (vie) well-ordered; (arrangé) settled

règlement [ʀegləmã] nm (paiement) settlement; (arrêté) regulation; (règles, statuts) regulations pl, rules pl; **réglementaire** adj conforming to the regulations; (tenue) regulation cpd; **réglementation** nf (règles) regulations; **réglementer** vt to regulate

régler [ʀegle] vt (conflit, facture) to settle; (personne) to settle up with; (mécanisme, machine) to regulate, adjust; (thermostat etc) to set, adjust

réglisse [ʀeglis] nf liquorice

règne [ʀeɲ] nm (d'un roi etc, fig) reign; **le ~ végétal/animal** the vegetable/animal kingdom; **régner** vi (roi) to rule, reign; (fig) to reign

regorger [ʀ(ə)ɡɔʀʒe] vi: **~ de** to overflow with, be bursting with

regret [ʀ(ə)ɡʀɛ] nm regret; **à ~** with regret; **sans ~** with no regrets; **regrettable** adj regrettable; **regretter** vt to regret; (personne) to miss; **je regrette mais ...** I'm sorry but ...

regrouper [ʀ(ə)ɡʀupe] vt (grouper) to group together; (contenir) to include, comprise; **se regrouper** vi to gather (together)

régulier, -ière [ʀegylje, jɛʀ] adj (gén)

regular; (vitesse, qualité) steady; (égal: couche, ligne) even; (Transports: ligne, service) scheduled, regular; (légal) lawful, in order; (honnête) straight, on the level; **régulièrement** adv regularly; (uniformément) evenly

rehausser [ʀaose] vt (relever) to heighten, raise; (fig: souligner) to set off, enhance

rein [ʀɛ̃] nm kidney; **reins** nmpl (dos) back sg

reine [ʀɛn] nf queen

reine-claude [ʀɛnklod] nf greengage

réinscriptible [ʀeɛ̃skʀiptibl] adj (CD, DVD) rewritable

réinsertion [ʀeɛ̃sɛʀsjɔ̃] nf (de délinquant) reintegration, rehabilitation

réintégrer [ʀeɛ̃tegʀe] vt (lieu) to return to; (fonctionnaire) to reinstate

rejaillir [ʀ(ə)ʒajiʀ] vi to splash up; **~ sur** (fig: scandale) to rebound on; (: gloire) to be reflected on

rejet [ʀaʒɛ] nm rejection; **rejeter** vt (relancer) to throw back; (écarter) to reject; (déverser) to throw out, discharge; (vomir) to bring out throw up; **rejeter la responsabilité de qch sur qn** to lay the responsibility for sth at sb's door

rejoindre [ʀ(ə)ʒwɛ̃dʀ] vt (famille, régiment) to rejoin, return to; (lieu) to get (back) to; (suj: route etc) to meet, join; (rattraper) to catch up (with); **se rejoindre** vi to meet; **je te rejoins à la gare** I'll see ou meet you at the station

réjouir [ʀeʒwiʀ] vt to delight; **se ~ (de qch/de faire)** to be delighted (about sth/to do); **réjouissances** nfpl (fête) festivities

relâche [ʀəlɑʃ] nm ou nf: **sans ~** without respite ou a break; **relâché, e** adj loose, lax; **relâcher** vt (libérer) to release; (desserrer) to loosen; **se relâcher** vi (discipline) to become slack ou lax; (élève etc) to slacken off

relais [ʀ(ə)lɛ] nm (Sport): **(course de) ~** relay (race); **prendre le ~ (de)** to take over (from); **relais routier** ≈ transport café (BRIT), ≈ truck stop (US)

relancer [R(ə)lɑ̃se] vt (balle) to throw back; (moteur) to restart; (fig) to boost, revive; (harceler): **~ qn** to pester sb

relatif, -ive [R(ə)latif, iv] adj relative

relation [R(ə)lasjɔ̃] nf (rapport) relation(ship); (connaissance) acquaintance; **relations** nfpl (rapports) relations; (connaissances) connections; **être/entrer en ~(s) avec** to be/get in contact with

relaxer [Rəlakse]: **se relaxer** vi to relax

relayer [R(ə)leje] vt (collaborateur, coureur etc) to relieve; (inf) to turn up; (style) to elevate; (plat, sauce) **se relayer** vi (dans une activité) to take it in turns

reléguer [R(ə)lege] vt to relegate

relevé, e [Rəl(ə)ve] adj (manches) rolled-up; (sauce) highly-seasoned ⊳ nm (de compteur) reading; **relevé bancaire** ou **de compte** bank statement

relève [Rəlɛv] nf (personne) relief; **prendre la ~** to take over

relever [Rəl(ə)ve] vt (meuble) to stand up again; (personne tombée) to help up; (vitre, niveau de vie) to raise; (inf) to turn up; (style) to elevate; (plat, sauce) to season; (sentinelle, équipe) to relieve; (fautes) to pick out; (défi) to accept, take up; (noter: adresse etc) to take down, note; (: plan) to sketch; (compteur) to read; (ramasser: cahiers) to collect, take in; **se relever** vi (se remettre debout) to get up; **~ de** (maladie) to be recovering from; (être du ressort de) to be a matter for; (fig) to pertain to; **~ qn de** (fonctions) to relieve sb of; **~ la tête** to look up

relief [Rəljɛf] nm relief; **mettre en ~** (fig) to bring out, highlight

relier [Rəlje] vt to link up; (livre) to bind; **~ qch à** to link sth to

religieux, -euse [R(ə)liʒjø, jøz] adj religious ⊳ nm monk

religion [R(ə)liʒjɔ̃] nf religion

relire [R(ə)liʀ] vt (à nouveau) to reread, read again; (vérifier) to read over

reluire [R(ə)lɥiʀ] vi to gleam

remanier [R(ə)manje] vt to reshape,

recast; (Pol) to reshuffle

remarquable [R(ə)maRkabl] adj remarkable

remarque [R(ə)maRk] nf remark; (écrite) note

remarquer [R(ə)maRke] vt (voir) to notice; **se remarquer** vi to be noticeable; **faire ~ (à qn) que** to point out (to sb) that; **faire ~ qch (à qn)** to point sth out (to sb); **remarquez, ...** mind you ...; **se faire ~** to draw attention to o.s.

rembourrer [Rɑ̃buRe] vt to stuff

remboursement [Rɑ̃buRsəmɑ̃] nm (de dette, d'emprunt) repayment; (de frais) refund; **rembourser** vt to pay back, repay; (frais, billet etc) to refund; **se faire rembourser** to get a refund

remède [R(ə)mɛd] nm (médicament) medicine; (traitement, fig) remedy, cure

remémorer [R(ə)memoRe]: **se remémorer** vt to recall, recollect

remerciements [Rəmɛrsimɑ̃] nmpl thanks; **(avec) tous mes ~** (with) grateful ou many thanks

remercier [R(ə)mɛRsje] vt to thank; (congédier) to dismiss; **~ qn de/d'avoir fait** to thank sb for/for having done

remettre [R(ə)mɛtR] vt (replacer) to put back; (vêtement) to put back on; (ajouter) to add; (ajourner): **~ qch (à)** to postpone sth (until); **se remettre** vi: **se ~ (de)** to recover (from); **~ qch à qn** (donner: lettre, clé etc) to hand over sth to sb; (: prix, décoration) to present sb with; **se ~ à faire qch** to start doing sth again; **s'en ~ à** to leave it (up) to

remise [R(ə)miz] nf (rabais) discount; (local) shed; **remise de peine** reduction of sentence; **remise des prix** prize-giving; **remise en cause** ou **question** calling into question, challenging; **remise en jeu** (Football) throw-in

remontant [R(ə)mɔ̃tɑ̃] nm tonic, pick-me-up

remonte-pente [R(ə)mɔ̃tpɑ̃t] nm ski-lift

remonter [R(ə)mɔ̃te] vi to go back

up; (prix, température) to go up again
▷ vt (pente) to go up; (fleuve) to sail (ou
swim etc) up; (manches, pantalon) to
roll up; (col) to turn up; (niveau, limite)
to raise; (fig: personne) to buck up;
(qch de démonté) to put back together,
reassemble; (montre) to wind up; **~ le
moral à qn** to raise sb's spirits; **~ à**
(dater de) to date ou go back to

remords [R(ə)mɔR] nm remorse no pl;
avoir des ~ to feel remorse

remorque [R(ə)mɔRk] nf trailer;
remorquer vt to tow; **remorqueur**
nm tug(boat)

remous [Rəmu] nm (d'un navire)
(back)wash no pl; (de rivière) swirl, eddy
▷ nmpl (fig) stir sg

remparts [RɑpaR] nmpl walls,
ramparts

remplaçant, e [Rɑplasɑ, ɑt] nm/f
replacement, stand-in; (Scol) supply
teacher

remplacement [Rɑplasmɑ] nm
replacement; **faire des ~s** (professeur) to
do supply teaching; (secrétaire) to temp

remplacer [Rɑplase] vt to replace; **~
qch/qn par** to replace sth/sb with

rempli, e [Rɑpli] adj (emploi du temps)
full, busy; **~ de** full of, filled with

remplir [RɑpliR] vt to fill (up);
(questionnaire) to fill out ou up;
(obligations, fonction, condition) to fulfil;
se remplir vi to fill up

remporter [RɑpɔRte] vt (marchandise)
to take away; (fig) to win, achieve

remuant, e [Rəmɥɑ, ɑt] adj restless

remue-ménage [R(ə)mymenaʒ] nm
inv commotion

remuer [Rəmɥe] vt to move; (café,
sauce) to stir ▷ vi to move; **se remuer**
vi to move; (fam: s'activer) to get a move on

rémunérer [RemyneRe] vt to
remunerate

renard [RənaR] nm fox

renchérir [RɑʃeRiR] vi (fig): **~ (sur)** (en
paroles) to add something (to)

rencontre [RɑkɔtR] nf meeting;
(imprévue) encounter; **aller à la ~ de qn**

to go and meet sb; **rencontrer** vt to
meet; (mot, expression) to come across;
(difficultés) to meet with; **se rencontrer**
vi to meet

rendement [Rɑdmɑ] nm (d'un
travailleur, d'une machine) output; (d'un
champ) yield

rendez-vous [Rɑdevu] nm
appointment; (d'amoureux) date;
(lieu) meeting place; **donner ~ à qn**
to arrange to meet sb; **avoir/
prendre ~ (avec)** to have/make an
appointment (with); **j'ai ~ avec ...**
I have an appointment with ...; **je
voudrais prendre ~** I'd like to make an
appointment

rendre [RɑdR] vt (restituer) to give back,
return; (invitation) to return, repay;
(vomir) to bring up; (exprimer, traduire) to
render; (faire devenir): **~ qn célèbre/qch
possible** to make sb famous/sth
possible; **se rendre** vi (capituler) to
surrender, give o.s. up; (aller): **se rendre
quelque part** to go somewhere; **~ la
monnaie à qn** to give sb his change; **se
~ compte de qch** to realize sth

rênes [REn] nfpl reins

renfermé, e [RɑfERme] adj (fig)
withdrawn ▷ nm: **sentir le ~** to smell
stuffy

renfermer [RɑfERme] vt to contain

renforcer [RɑfɔRse] vt to
reinforce; **renfort: renforts** nmpl
reinforcements; **à grand renfort de**
with a great deal of

renfrogné, e [RɑfRɔɲe] adj sullen

renier [Rənje] vt (personne) to disown,
repudiate; (foi) to renounce

renifler [Rənifle] vi, vt to sniff

renne [REn] nm reindeer inv

renom [Rɑnɔ] nm reputation; (célébrité)
renown; **renommé, e** adj celebrated,
renowned; **renommée** nf fame

renoncer [R(ə)nɔse]: **~ à** vt to give up; **~
à faire** to give up the idea of doing

renouer [Rənwe] vt: **~ avec** (habitude)
to take up again

renouveler [R(ə)nuv(ə)le] vt to

renew: (exploit, méfait) to repeat; **se
renouveler** vi (incident) to recur,
happen again; **renouvellement** nm
(remplacement) renewal
rénover [ʀenɔve] vt (immeuble) to
renovate, do up; (quartier) to redevelop
renseignement [ʀɑ̃sɛɲmɑ̃] nm
information no pl, piece of information;
(guichet des) ~s information office;
(service des) ~s (Tél) directory
enquiries (BRIT), information (US)
renseigner [ʀɑ̃seɲe] vt: **~ qn (sur)**
to give information to sb (about); **se
renseigner** vi to ask for information,
make inquiries
rentabilité [ʀɑ̃tabilite] nf profitability
rentable [ʀɑ̃tabl] adj profitable
rente [ʀɑ̃t] nf private income; (pension)
pension
rentrée [ʀɑ̃tʀe] nf: **~ (d'argent)** cash
no pl coming in; **la ~ (des classes)** the
start of the new school year
rentrer [ʀɑ̃tʀe] vi (revenir chez soi) to
go (ou come) (back) home; (entrer de
nouveau) to go (ou come) back in; (entrer)
to go (ou come) in; (air, clou: pénétrer) to
go in; (revenu) to come in ▷ vt to bring
in; (véhicule) to put away; (chemise dans
pantalon etc) to tuck in; (griffes) to draw
in; **~ le ventre** to pull in one's stomach;
~ dans (heurter) to crash into; **~ dans
l'ordre** to be back to normal; **~ dans
ses frais** to recover one's expenses;
je rentre mardi I'm going ou coming
home on Tuesday
renverse [ʀɑ̃vɛʀs]: **à la ~** adv
backwards
renverser [ʀɑ̃vɛʀse] vt (faire tomber:
chaise, verre) to knock over, overturn;
(liquide, contenu) to spill, upset; (piéton)
to knock down; (retourner) to turn
upside down; (: ordre des mots etc)
to reverse; (fig: gouvernement etc) to
overthrow; (fam: stupéfier) to bowl over;
se renverser vi (verre, vase) to fall over;
(contenu) to spill
renvoi [ʀɑ̃vwa] nm (d'employé)
dismissal; (d'élève) expulsion; (référence)

221 | repérer

cross-reference; (éructation) belch;
renvoyer vt to send back; (congédier) to
dismiss; (élève: définitivement) to expel;
(lumière) to reflect; (ajourner): **renvoyer
qch (à)** to put sth off ou postpone
sth (until)
repaire [ʀ(ə)pɛʀ] nm den
répandre [ʀepɑ̃dʀ] vt (renverser) to
spill; (étaler, diffuser) to spread; (odeur)
to give off; **se répandre** vi to spread; (se
propager) to spread; **répandu, e** adj
(opinion, usage) widespread
réparation [ʀepaʀasjɔ̃] nf repair
réparer [ʀepaʀe] vt to repair; (fig:
offense) to make up for, atone for;
(: oubli, erreur) to put right; **où est-ce
que je peux le faire ~?** where can I
get it fixed?
repartie [ʀepaʀti] nf retort; **avoir de
la ~** to be quick at repartee
repartir [ʀ(ə)paʀtiʀ] vi to leave again;
(voyageur) to set off again; (fig) to get
going again; **~ à zéro** to start from
scratch (again)
répartir [ʀepaʀtiʀ] vt (pour attribuer)
to share out; (pour disperser, disposer)
to divide up; (poids) to distribute; **se
répartir** vt (travail, rôles) to share out
between themselves; **répartition** nf
(des richesses etc) distribution
repas [ʀ(ə)pa] nm meal
repassage [ʀ(ə)pasaʒ] nm ironing
repasser [ʀ(ə)pase] vi to come (ou
go) back ▷ vt (vêtement, tissu) to iron;
(examen) to retake, resit; (film) to show
again; (leçon: revoir) to go over (again)
repentir [ʀəpɑ̃tiʀ] nm repentance;
se repentir vi to repent; **se ~ d'avoir fait
qch** (regretter) to regret having done sth
répercussions [ʀepɛʀkysjɔ̃] nfpl (fig)
repercussions
répercuter [ʀepɛʀkyte]: **se répercuter**
vi (bruit) to reverberate; (fig): **se ~ sur**
to have repercussions on
repère [ʀ(ə)pɛʀ] nm mark; (monument,
événement) landmark
repérer [ʀ(ə)peʀe] vt (fam: erreur,
personne) to spot; (: endroit) to locate; **se**

repérer vi to find one's way about

répertoire [ʀepɛʀtwaʀ] nm (liste) (alphabetical) list; (carnet) index notebook; (Inform) folder, directory; (d'un artiste) repertoire

répéter [ʀepete] vt to repeat; (préparer: leçon) to learn, go over; (Théâtre) to rehearse; **se répéter** vi (redire) to repeat o.s.; (se reproduire) to be repeated, recur; **pouvez-vous ~, s'il vous plaît?** can you repeat that, please?

répétition [ʀepetisjɔ̃] nf repetition; (Théâtre) rehearsal; **~ générale** (final) dress rehearsal

répit [ʀepi] nm respite; **sans ~** without letting up

replier [ʀ(ə)plije] vt (rabattre) to fold down ou over; **se replier** vi (troupes, armée) to withdraw, fall back; (sur soi-même) to withdraw into o.s.

réplique [ʀeplik] nf (repartie, fig) reply; (Théâtre) line; (copie) replica, **répliquer** vi to reply; (riposter) to retaliate

répondeur [ʀepɔ̃dœʀ] nm: **~ (automatique)** (Tél) answering machine

répondre [ʀepɔ̃dʀ] vi to answer, reply; (freins) to respond; **~ à** to reply to, answer; (affection, salut) to return; (provocation) to respond to; (correspondre à: besoin) to answer; (: conditions) to meet; (: description) to match; (avec impertinence) **~ à qn** to answer sb back; **~ de** to answer for

réponse [ʀepɔ̃s] nf answer, reply; **en ~ à** in reply to

reportage [ʀ(ə)pɔʀtaʒ] nm report

reporter[1] [ʀəpɔʀtɛʀ] nm reporter

reporter[2] [ʀəpɔʀte] vt (ajourner): **~ qch (à)** to postpone sth (until); (transférer): **~ qch sur** to transfer sth to; **se reporter à** (époque) to think back to; (document) to refer to

repos [ʀ(ə)po] nm rest; (tranquillité) peace and quiet; (Mil): **~!** stand at ease; **ce n'est pas de tout ~** it's no picnic!

reposant, e [ʀ(ə)pozɑ̃, ɑ̃t] adj restful

reposer [ʀ(ə)poze] vt (verre, livre) to put down; (délasser) to rest ▷ vi: **laisser ~** (pâte) to leave to stand; **se reposer** vi to rest; **se ~ sur qn** to rely on sb; **~ sur** (fig) to rest on

repoussant, e [ʀ(ə)pusɑ̃, ɑ̃t] adj repulsive

repousser [ʀ(ə)puse] vi to grow again ▷ vt to repel, repulse; (offre) to turn down, reject; (personne) to push back; (différer) to put back

reprendre [ʀ(ə)pʀɑ̃dʀ] vt (objet prêté, donné) to take back; (prisonnier, ville) to recapture; (firme, entreprise) to take over; (le travail) to resume; (emprunter: argument, idée) to take up, use; (refaire: article etc) to go over again; (vêtement) to alter; (réprimander) to tell off; (corriger) to correct; (chercher): **je viendrai te ~ à 4 h** I'll come and fetch you at 4; (se resservir de): **~ du pain/un œuf** to take (ou eat) more bread/another egg ▷ vi (classes, pluie) to start (up) again; (activités, travaux, combats) to resume, start (up) again; (affaires) to pick up; (dire): **reprit-il** he went on; **~ des forces** to recover one's strength; **~ courage** to take new heart; **~ la route** to resume one's journey, set off again; **~ haleine** ou **son souffle** to get one's breath back

représentant, e [ʀ(ə)pʀezɑ̃tɑ̃, ɑ̃t] nm/f representative

représentation [ʀ(ə)pʀezɑ̃tasjɔ̃] nf (symbole, image) representation; (spectacle) performance

représenter [ʀ(ə)pʀezɑ̃te] vt to represent; (donner: pièce, opéra) to perform; **se représenter** vt (se figurer) to imagine

répression [ʀepʀesjɔ̃] nf repression

réprimer [ʀepʀime] vt (émotions) to suppress; (peuple etc) to repress

repris [ʀ(ə)pʀi] nm: **~ de justice** ex-prisoner, ex-convict

reprise [ʀ(ə)pʀiz] nf (recommencement) resumption; (économique) recovery; (TV) repeat; (Comm) trade-in, part exchange; (raccommodage) mend; **à plusieurs ~s** on several occasions

repriser [R(ə)pRize] vt (chaussette, lainage) to darn; (tissu) to mend

reproche [R(ə)pRɔʃ] nm (remontrance) reproach; **faire des ~s à qn** to reproach sb; **sans ~(s)** beyond reproach; **reprocher** vt: **reprocher qch à qn** to reproach ou blame sb for sth; **reprocher qch à** (critiquer) to have sth against

reproduction [R(ə)pRɔdyksjɔ̃] nf reproduction

reproduire [R(ə)pRɔdɥiR] vt to reproduce; **se reproduire** vi (Bio) to reproduce; (recommencer) to recur, re-occur

reptile [Rɛptil] nm reptile

république [Repyblik] nf republic

répugnant, e [Repyɲɑ̃, ɑ̃t] adj disgusting

répugner [Repyɲe]: **~ à** vt : **~ à qn** to repel ou disgust sb; **~ à faire** to be loath ou reluctant to do

réputation [Repytasjɔ̃] nf reputation; **réputé, e** adj renowned

requérir [RakeRiR] vt (nécessiter) to require, call for

requête [Rakɛt] nf request

requin [Rakɛ̃] nm shark

requis, e [Raki, iz] adj required

RER sigle m (= réseau express régional) Greater Paris high-speed train service

rescapé, e [Reskape] nm/f survivor

rescousse [Reskus] nf: **aller à la ~ de qn** to go to sb's aid ou rescue

réseau, x [Rezo] nm network

réservation [RezɛRvasjɔ̃] nf booking, reservation; **j'ai confirmé ma ~ par fax/e-mail** I confirmed my booking by fax/e-mail

réserve [RezɛRv] nf (retenue) reserve; (entrepôt) storeroom; (restriction, d'Indiens) reservation; (de pêche, chasse) preserve; **de ~** (provisions etc) in reserve

réservé, e [RezɛRve] adj reserved; **chasse/pêche ~e** private hunting/fishing

réserver [RezɛRve] vt to reserve;

(chambre, billet etc) to book, reserve; (fig: destiner) to have in store; (garder): **~ qch pour/à** to keep ou save sth for; **je voudrais ~ une chambre pour deux personnes** I'd like to book a double room; **j'ai réservé une table au nom de ...** I booked a table in the name of ...

réservoir [RezɛRvwaR] nm tank

résidence [Rezidɑ̃s] nf residence; **résidence secondaire** second home; **résidence universitaire** hall of residence (BRIT), dormitory (US); **résidentiel, le** adj residential; **résider** vi: **résider à/dans/en** to reside in; **résider dans** (fig) to lie in

résidu [Rezidy] nm residue no pl

résigner [Reziɲe]: **se résigner** vi: **~ (à qch/à faire)** to resign o.s. (to sth/to doing)

résilier [Rezilje] vt to terminate

résistance [Rezistɑ̃s] nf resistance; (de réchaud, bouilloire: fil) element

résistant, e [Rezistɑ̃, ɑ̃t] adj (personne) robust, tough; (matériau) strong, hard-wearing

résister [Reziste] vi to resist; **~ à** (assaut, tentation) to resist; (supporter: gel etc) to withstand; (désobéir à) to stand up to, oppose

résolu, e [Rezɔly] pp de **résoudre** ▷ adj: **être ~ à qch/faire** to be set upon sth/doing

résolution [Rezɔlysjɔ̃] nf (fermeté, décision) resolution; (d'un problème) solution

résolve etc [Rezɔlv] vb voir **résoudre**

résonner [Rezɔne] vi (cloche, pas) to reverberate, resound; (salle) to be resonant

résorber [RezɔRbe]: **se résorber** vi (fig: chômage) to be reduced; (: déficit) to be absorbed

résoudre [RezudR] vt to solve; **se ~ à faire** to bring o.s. to do

respect [Rɛspɛ] nm respect; **tenir en ~** to keep at bay; **présenter ses ~s à qn** to pay one's respects to sb; **respecter** vt to respect; **respectueux, -euse** adj respectful

respiration [ʀɛspiʀasjɔ̃] nf
breathing no pl

respirer [ʀɛspiʀe] vi to breathe; (fig: se détendre) to get one's breath; (: se rassurer) to breathe again ▷ vt to breathe (in), inhale; (manifester: santé, calme etc) to exude

resplendir [ʀɛsplɑ̃diʀ] vi to shine; (fig): ~ (de) to be radiant (with)

responsabilité [ʀɛspɔ̃sabilite] nf responsibility; (légale) liability

responsable [ʀɛspɔ̃sabl] adj responsible ▷ nm/f (coupable) person responsible; (personne compétente) person in charge; (de parti, syndicat) official; ~ de responsible for

ressaisir [ʀ(ə)seziʀ]: **se ressaisir** vi to regain one's self-control

ressasser [ʀ(ə)sase] vt to keep going over

ressemblance [ʀ(ə)sɑ̃blɑ̃s] nf resemblance, similarity, likeness

ressemblant, e [ʀ(ə)sɑ̃blɑ̃, ɑ̃t] adj (portrait) lifelike, true to life

ressembler [ʀ(ə)sɑ̃ble] ▷ vb: ~ à vt to be like, resemble; (visuellement) to look like; **se ressembler** vi to be (ou look) alike

ressentiment [ʀ(ə)sɑ̃timɑ̃] nm resentment

ressentir [ʀ(ə)sɑ̃tiʀ] vt to feel; **se ~ de** to feel (ou show) the effects of

resserrer [ʀ(ə)seʀe] vt (nœud, boulon) to tighten (up); (fig: liens) to strengthen

resservir [ʀ(ə)seʀviʀ] vt to do ou serve again; ~ **qn (d'un plat)** to give sb a second helping (of a dish); **se ~ de** (plat) to take a second helping of (outil etc) to use again

ressort [ʀəsɔʀ] nm (pièce) spring; (énergie) spirit; (recours): **en dernier** ~ as a last resort; (compétence): **être du ~ de** to fall within the competence of

ressortir [ʀəsɔʀtiʀ] vi to go (ou come) out (again); (contraster) to stand out; ~ **de** to emerge from; **faire** ~ (fig: souligner) to bring out

ressortissant, e [ʀ(ə)sɔʀtisɑ̃, ɑ̃t] nm/f national

ressources [ʀ(ə)suʀs] nfpl (moyens) resources

ressusciter [ʀesysite] vt (fig) to revive, bring back ▷ vi to rise (from the dead)

restant, e [ʀɛstɑ̃, ɑ̃t] adj remaining ▷ nm: **le ~ (de)** the remainder (of); **un ~ de** (de trop) some left-over

restaurant [ʀɛstɔʀɑ̃] nm restaurant; **pouvez-vous m'indiquer un bon ~?** can you recommend a good restaurant?

restauration [ʀɛstɔʀasjɔ̃] nf restoration; (hôtellerie) catering; **restauration rapide** fast food

restaurer [ʀɛstɔʀe] vt to restore; **se restaurer** vi to have something to eat

reste [ʀɛst] nm (restant): **le ~ (de)** the rest of; (de trop): **un ~ (de)** some left-over; **restes** nmpl (nourriture) left-overs; (d'une cité etc, dépouille mortelle) remains; **du ~, au ~** besides, moreover

rester [ʀɛste] vi to stay, remain; (subsister) to remain, be left; (durer) to last, live on ▷ vb impers: **il reste du pain/2 œufs** there's some bread/there are 2 eggs left (over); **restons-en là** let's leave it at that; **il me reste assez de temps** I have enough time left; **il ne reste plus qu'à ...** I've just got to ...

restituer [ʀɛstitɥe] vt (objet, somme): ~ **qch (à qn)** to return sth (to sb)

restreindre [ʀɛstʀɛ̃dʀ] vt to restrict, limit

restriction [ʀɛstʀiksjɔ̃] nf restriction

résultat [ʀezylta] nm result; **résultats** nmpl (d'examen, d'élection) results pl

résulter [ʀezylte]: ~ **de** vt to result from, be the result of

résumé [ʀezyme] nm summary, résumé; **en** ~ in brief; (pour conclure) to sum up

résumer [ʀezyme] vt (texte) to summarize; (récapituler) to sum up

⚠ Attention à ne pas traduire **résumer** par **to resume**.

résurrection [ʀezyʀɛksjɔ̃] nf

resurrection

rétablir [ʀetabliʀ] vt to restore, re-establish; **se rétablir** vi (guérir) to recover; (silence, calme) to return, be restored; **rétablissement** nm restoring; (guérison) recovery

retaper [ʀ(ə)tape] (fam) vt (maison, voiture etc) to do up; (revigorer) to buck up

retard [ʀ(ə)taʀ] nm (d'une personne attendue) lateness no pl; (sur l'horaire, un programme) delay; (fig: scolaire, mental etc) backwardness; **en ~ (de 2 heures)** (2 hours) late; **avoir du ~** to be late; (sur un programme) to be behind (schedule); **prendre du ~** (train, avion) to be delayed; **sans ~** without delay; **désolé d'être en ~** sorry I'm late; **le vol a deux heures de ~** the flight is two hours late

retardataire [ʀ(ə)taʀdatɛʀ] nm/f latecomer

retardement [ʀ(ə)taʀdəmɑ̃]: **à ~** adj delayed action cpd; **bombe à ~** time bomb

retarder [ʀ(ə)taʀde] vt to delay; (montre) to put back ▷ vi (montre) to be slow; **~ qn (d'une heure)** (sur un horaire) to delay sb (an hour); **~ qch (de 2 jours)** (départ, date) to put sth back (2 days)

retenir [ʀət(ə)niʀ] vt (garder, retarder) to keep, detain; (maintenir: objet qui glisse, fig: colère, larmes) to hold back; (se rappeler) to remember; (réserver) to reserve; (accepter: proposition etc) to accept; (fig: empêcher d'agir): **~ qn (de faire)** to hold sb back (from doing); (prélever): **~ qch (sur)** to deduct sth (from); **se retenir** vi (se raccrocher): **se ~ à** to hold onto; (se contenir): **se ~ de faire** to restrain o.s. from doing; **son souffle** to hold one's breath

retentir [ʀ(ə)tɑ̃tiʀ] vi to ring out; **retentissant, e** adj resounding

retenue [ʀat(ə)ny] nf (prélèvement) deduction; (Scol) detention; (modération) (self-)restraint

réticence [ʀetisɑ̃s] nf hesitation, reluctance no pl; **réticent, e** adj

hesitant, reluctant

rétine [ʀetin] nf retina

retiré, e [ʀ(ə)tiʀe] adj (vie) secluded; (lieu) remote

retirer [ʀ(ə)tiʀe] vt (vêtement, lunettes) to take off, remove; (argent, plainte) to withdraw; (reprendre: bagages, billets) to collect, pick up; (extraire): **~ qch de** to take sth out of, remove sth from

retomber [ʀ(ə)tɔ̃be] vi (à nouveau) to fall again; (atterrir: après un saut etc) to land; (échoir): **~ sur qn** to fall on sb

rétorquer [ʀetɔʀke] vt: **~ (à qn) que** to retort (to sb) that

retouche [ʀ(ə)tuʃ] nf (sur vêtement) alteration; **retoucher** vt (photographie) to touch up; (texte, vêtement) to alter

retour [ʀ(ə)tuʀ] nm return; **au ~** (en route) on the way back; **à mon ~** when I get/got back; **être de ~ (de)** to be back (from); **par ~ du courrier** by return of post; **quand serons-nous de ~?** when do we get back?

retourner [ʀ(ə)tuʀne] vt (dans l'autre sens: matelas, crêpe etc) to turn (over); (: sac, vêtement) to turn inside out; (fam: bouleverser) to shake; (renvoyer, restituer): **~ qch à qn** to return sth to sb ▷ vi (aller, revenir): **~ quelque part/à** to go back ou return somewhere/to; **se retourner** vi (tourner la tête) to turn round; **~ à** (état, activité) to return to, go back to; **se ~ contre** (fig) to turn against

retrait [ʀ(ə)tʀɛ] nm (d'argent) withdrawal; **en ~** set back; **retrait du permis (de conduire)** disqualification from driving (BRIT), revocation of driver's license (US)

retraite [ʀ(ə)tʀɛt] nf (d'un employé) retirement; (revenu) pension; (d'une armée, Rel) retreat; **prendre sa ~** to retire; **retraite anticipée** early retirement; **retraité, e** adj retired ▷ nm/f pensioner

retrancher [ʀ(ə)tʀɑ̃ʃe] vt (nombre, somme): **~ qch de** to take ou deduct sth from; **se ~ derrière/dans** to take refuge behind/in

rétrécir [ʀetʀesiʀ] vt (vêtement) to take in ▷ vi to shrink; **se rétrécir** (route, vallée) to narrow

rétro [ʀetʀo] adj inv: **la mode ~** the nostalgia vogue

rétroprojecteur [ʀetʀopʀɔʒɛktœʀ] nm overhead projector

rétrospective [ʀetʀospɛktiv] nf (Art) retrospective; (Cinéma) season, retrospective; **rétrospectivement** adv in retrospect

retrousser [ʀ(ə)tʀuse] vt to roll up

retrouvailles [ʀ(ə)tʀuvaj] nfpl reunion sg

retrouver [ʀ(ə)tʀuve] vt (fugitif, objet perdu) to find; (calme, santé) to regain; (revoir) to see again; (rejoindre) to meet (again), join; **se retrouver** vi to meet; (s'orienter) to find one's way; **se ~ quelque part** to find o.s. somewhere; **s'y ~** (y voir clair) to make sense of it; (rentrer dans ses frais) to break even; **je ne retrouve plus mon portefeuille** I can't find my wallet (BRIT) ou billfold (US)

rétroviseur [ʀetʀovizœʀ] nm (rear-view) mirror

réunion [ʀeynjɔ̃] nf (séance) meeting

réunir [ʀeyniʀ] vt (rassembler) to gather together; (inviter: amis, famille) to have round; (cumuler: qualités etc) to combine; (rapprocher: ennemis) to bring together (again), reunite; (rattacher: parties) to join (together); **se réunir** vi to meet

réussi, e [ʀeysi] adj successful

réussir [ʀeysiʀ] vi to succeed, be successful; (à un examen) to pass ▷ vt to make a success of; **~ à faire** to succeed in doing; **~ à qn** (être bénéfique à) to agree with sb; **réussite** nf success; (Cartes) patience

revaloir [ʀ(ə)valwaʀ] vt: **je vous revaudrai cela** I'll repay you some day; (en mal) I'll pay you back for this

revanche [ʀ(ə)vɑ̃ʃ] nf revenge; (sport) revenge match; **en ~** on the other hand

rêve [ʀɛv] nm dream; **de ~** dream cpd;

faire un ~ to have a dream

réveil [ʀevɛj] nm waking up no pl; (fig) awakening; (pendule) alarm (clock); **au ~** on waking up; **réveiller** vt (personne) to wake up; (fig) to awaken, revive; **se réveiller** vi to wake up; pouvez-vous **me réveiller à 7 heures, s'il vous plaît?** could I have an alarm call at 7am, please?

réveillon [ʀevɛjɔ̃] nm Christmas Eve; (de la Saint-Sylvestre) New Year's Eve; **réveillonner** vi to celebrate Christmas Eve (ou New Year's Eve)

révélateur, -trice [ʀevelatœʀ, tʀis] adj: **~ (de qch)** revealing (sth)

révéler [ʀevele] vt to reveal; **se révéler** vi to be revealed, reveal itself ▷ vb +attrib: **se ~ difficile/aisé** to prove difficult/easy

revenant, e [ʀ(ə)vənɑ̃, ɑ̃t] nm/f ghost

revendeur, -euse [ʀ(ə)vɑ̃dœʀ, øz] nm/f (détaillant) retailer; (de drogue) (drug-)dealer

revendication [ʀ(ə)vɑ̃dikasjɔ̃] nf claim, demand

revendiquer [ʀ(ə)vɑ̃dike] vt to claim, demand; (responsabilité) to claim

revendre [ʀ(ə)vɑ̃dʀ] vt (d'occasion) to resell; (détailler) to sell; **à ~** (en abondance) to spare

revenir [ʀəvniʀ] vi to come back; (coûter): **~ cher/à 100 euros (à qn)** to cost (sb) a lot/100 euros; **~ à** (reprendre: études, projet) to return to, go back to; (équivaloir à) to amount to; **~ à qn** (part, honneur) to go to sb, be sb's; (souvenir, nom) to come back to sb; **~ sur** (question, sujet) to go back over; (engagement) to go back on; **~ à soi** to come round; **n'en pas ~**: **je n'en reviens pas** I can't get over it; **~ sur ses pas** to retrace one's steps; **cela revient à dire que/au même** it amounts to saying that/the same thing; **faire ~** (Culin) to brown

revenu [ʀəv(ə)ny] nm income; **revenus** nmpl income sg

rêver [ʀeve] vt, vi to dream; **~ de/à** to dream of

réverbère [ʀevɛʀbɛʀ] nm street lamp ou light; **réverbérer** vt to reflect

revers [ʀ(ə)vɛʀ] nm (de feuille, main) back; (d'étoffe) wrong side; (de pièce, médaille) back, reverse; (Tennis, Ping-Pong) backhand; (de veste) lapel; (fig: échec) setback

revêtement [ʀ(ə)vɛtmɑ̃] nm (des sols) flooring; (de chaussée) surface

revêtir [ʀ(ə)vetiʀ] vt (habit) to don, put on; (prendre: importance, apparence) to take on; **~ qch de** to cover sth with

rêveur, -euse [ʀɛvœʀ, øz] adj dreamy ▷ nm/f dreamer

revient [ʀ(ə)vjɛ̃] vb voir **revenir**

revigorer [ʀ(ə)vigɔʀe] vt (air frais) to invigorate, brace up; (repas, boisson) to revive, buck up

revirement [ʀ(ə)viʀmɑ̃] nm change of mind; (d'une situation) reversal

réviser [ʀevize] vt to revise; (machine) to overhaul, service

révision [ʀevizjɔ̃] nf revision; (de voiture) servicing no pl

revivre [ʀ(ə)vivʀ] vi (reprendre des forces) to come alive again ▷ vt (épreuve, moment) to relive

revoir [ʀəvwaʀ] vt to see again; (réviser) to revise ▷ nm: **au ~** goodbye

révoltant, e [ʀevɔltɑ̃, ɑ̃t] adj revolting, appalling

révolte [ʀevɔlt] nf rebellion, revolt

révolter [ʀevɔlte] vt to revolt, outrage; **se révolter (contre)** to rebel (against)

révolu, e [ʀevɔly] adj past; (Admin): **âgé de 18 ans ~s** over 18 years of age

révolution [ʀevɔlysjɔ̃] nf revolution; **révolutionnaire** adj, nm/f revolutionary

revolver [ʀevɔlvɛʀ] nm gun; (à barillet) revolver

révoquer [ʀevɔke] vt (fonctionnaire) to dismiss; (arrêt, contrat) to revoke

revue [ʀ(ə)vy] nf review; (périodique) review, magazine; (de music-hall) variety show; **passer en ~** (mentalement) to go through

rez-de-chaussée [ʀed(ə)ʃose] nm inv ground floor

RF sigle f = **République française**

Rhin [ʀɛ̃] nm Rhine

rhinocéros [ʀinɔseʀɔs] nm rhinoceros

Rhône [ʀon] nm Rhone

rhubarbe [ʀybaʀb] nf rhubarb

rhum [ʀɔm] nm rum

rhumatisme [ʀymatism] nm rheumatism no pl

rhume [ʀym] nm cold; **rhume de cerveau** head cold; **le rhume des foins** hay fever

ricaner [ʀikane] vi (avec méchanceté) to snigger; (bêtement) to giggle

riche [ʀiʃ] adj rich; (personne, pays) rich, wealthy; **~ en** rich in; **richesse** nf wealth; (fig: de sol, musée etc) richness; **richesses** nfpl (ressources, argent) wealth sg; (fig: trésors) treasures

ricochet [ʀikɔʃɛ] nm: **faire des ~s** to skip stones

ride [ʀid] nf wrinkle

rideau, x [ʀido] nm curtain; **rideau de fer** (boutique) metal shutter(s)

rider [ʀide] vt to wrinkle; **se rider** vi to become wrinkled

ridicule [ʀidikyl] adj ridiculous ▷ nm: **le ~** ridicule; **ridiculiser** vt to ridicule; **se ridiculiser** vt to make a fool of o.s.

 MOT-CLÉ

rien [ʀjɛ̃] pron 1: **(ne) ... rien** nothing, tournure négative + anything; **qu'est-ce que vous avez? — rien** what have you got? — nothing; **il n'a rien dit/fait** he said/did nothing, he hasn't said/done anything; **n'avoir peur de rien** to be afraid ou frightened of nothing, not to be afraid ou frightened of anything; **il n'a rien** (n'est pas blessé) he's all right; **ça ne fait rien** it doesn't matter; **de rien!** not at all!

2: **rien de:** **rien d'intéressant** nothing interesting; **rien d'autre** nothing else; **rien du tout** nothing at all

3: **rien que** just, only; nothing but; **rien que pour lui faire plaisir** only ou just to please him; **rien que la vérité** nothing but the truth; **rien que cela** that alone ▷ *nm*: **un petit rien** (*cadeau*) a little something; **des riens** trivia *pl*; **un rien de** a hint of; **en un rien de temps** in no time at all

rieur, -euse [ʀ(i)jœʀ, ʀ(i)jøz] *adj* cheerful

rigide [ʀiʒid] *adj* stiff; (*fig*) rigid; strict

rigoler [ʀiɡɔle] *vi* (*fam: rire*) to laugh; (*s'amuser*) to have (some) fun; (*plaisanter*) to be joking *ou* kidding; **rigolo, -ote** (*fam*) *adj* funny ▷ *nm/f* comic; (*péj*) fraud, phoney

rigoureusement [ʀiɡuʀøzmɑ̃] *adv* (*vrai*) absolutely; (*interdit*) strictly

rigoureux, -euse [ʀiɡuʀø, øz] *adj* rigorous; (*hiver*) hard, harsh

rigueur [ʀiɡœʀ] *nf* rigour; **"tenue de soirée de ~"** "formal dress only"; **à la ~** at a pinch; **tenir ~ à qn de qch** to hold sth against sb

rillettes [ʀijɛt] *nfpl* potted meat (*made from pork or goose*)

rime [ʀim] *nf* rhyme

rinçage [ʀɛ̃saʒ] *nm* rinsing (out); (*opération*) rinse

rincer [ʀɛ̃se] *vt* to rinse; (*récipient*) to rinse out

ringard, e [ʀɛ̃ɡaʀ, aʀd] (*fam*) *adj* old-fashioned

riposter [ʀipɔste] *vi* to retaliate ▷ *vt*: **~ que** to retort that

rire [ʀiʀ] *vi* to laugh; (*se divertir*) to have fun ▷ *nm* laugh; **le ~** laughter; **~ de** to laugh at; **pour ~** (*pas sérieusement*) for a joke *ou* a laugh

risible [ʀizibl] *adj* laughable

risque [ʀisk] *nm* risk; **le ~** danger; **à ses ~s et périls** at his own risk; **risqué, e** *adj* risky; (*plaisanterie*) risqué, daring; **risquer** *vt* (*vie*) to risk; (*allusion, question*) to venture, hazard; **ça ne risque rien** it's quite safe; **risquer de: il risque de se tuer** he could get himself killed; **ce qui risque de se produire** what might *ou* could well happen; **il ne risque pas**

de recommencer there's no chance of him doing that again; **se risquer à faire** (*tenter*) to venture *ou* dare to do

rissoler [ʀisɔle] *vi, vt*: **(faire) ~** to brown

ristourne [ʀistuʀn] *nf* discount

rite [ʀit] *nm* rite; (*fig*) ritual

rivage [ʀivaʒ] *nm* shore

rival, e, -aux [ʀival, o] *adj, nm/f* rival; **rivaliser** *vi*: **rivaliser avec** (*personne*) to rival, vie with; **rivalité** *nf* rivalry

rive [ʀiv] *nf* shore; (*de fleuve*) bank; **riverain, e** *nm/f* (*de rivière*) riverside *ou* (*de lakeside*) resident; (*d'une route*) local resident

rivière [ʀivjɛʀ] *nf* river

riz [ʀi] *nm* rice; **rizière** *nf* paddy-field, ricefield

RMI *sigle m* (= *revenu minimum d'insertion*) ≈ income support (BRIT), ≈ welfare (US)

RN *sigle f* = **route nationale**

robe [ʀɔb] *nf* dress; (*de juge*) robe; (*pelage*) coat; **robe de chambre** dressing gown; **robe de mariée** wedding dress; **robe de soirée** evening dress

robinet [ʀɔbinɛ] *nm* tap (BRIT), faucet (US)

robot [ʀɔbo] *nm* robot; **robot de cuisine** food processor

robuste [ʀɔbyst] *adj* robust, sturdy; **robustesse** *nf* robustness, sturdiness

roc [ʀɔk] *nm* rock

rocade [ʀɔkad] *nf* bypass

rocaille [ʀɔkaj] *nf* loose stones *pl*; (*jardin*) rockery, rock garden

roche [ʀɔʃ] *nf* rock

rocher [ʀɔʃe] *nm* rock

rocheux, -euse [ʀɔʃø, øz] *adj* rocky

rodage [ʀɔdaʒ] *nm*: **en ~** running in

rôder [ʀode] *vi* to roam about; (*de façon suspecte*) to lurk (about *ou* around); **rôdeur, -euse** *nm/f* prowler

rogne [ʀɔɲ] (*fam*) *nf*: **être en ~** to be in a temper

rogner [ʀɔɲe] *vt* to clip; **~ sur** (*fig*) to cut down *ou* back on

rognons [ʀɔɲɔ̃] *nmpl* (*Culin*) kidneys

roi [ʀwa] *nm* king; **la fête des Rois, les**

Rois Twelfth Night

rôle [ʀol] nm role, part

rollers [ʀɔlœʀ] nmpl Rollerblades®

romain, e [ʀɔmɛ̃, ɛn] adj Roman ▷ nm/f: **R~, e** Roman

roman, e [ʀɔmɑ̃, an] adj (Archit) Romanesque ▷ nm novel: **roman policier** detective story

romancer [ʀɔmɑ̃se] vt (agrémenter) to romanticize; **romancier, -ière** nm/f novelist; **romanesque** adj (amours, aventures) storybook cpd; (sentimental: personne) romantic

roman-feuilleton [ʀɔmɑ̃fœjtɔ̃] nm serialized novel

romanichel, le [ʀɔmaniʃɛl] (péj) nm/f gipsy

romantique [ʀɔmɑ̃tik] adj romantic

romarin [ʀɔmaʀɛ̃] nm rosemary

Rome [ʀɔm] n Rome

rompre [ʀɔ̃pʀ] vt to break; (entretien, fiançailles) to break off ▷ vi (fiancés) to break it off; **se rompre** vi to break; **rompu, e** adj (fourbu) exhausted

ronces [ʀɔ̃s] nfpl brambles

ronchonner [ʀɔ̃ʃɔne] (fam) vi to grouse, grouch

rond, e [ʀɔ̃, ʀɔ̃d] adj round; (joues, mollets) well-rounded; (fam: ivre) tight ▷ nm (cercle) ring; (fam: sou): **je n'ai plus un ~** I haven't a penny left; **en ~** (s'asseoir, danser) in a ring; **ronde** nf (gén: de surveillance) rounds pl, patrol; (danse) round (dance); (Mus) semibreve (BRIT), whole note (US); **à la ronde** (alentour): **à 10 km à la ronde** for 10 km round; **rondelet, te** adj plump

rondelle [ʀɔ̃dɛl] nf (tranche) slice, round; (Tech) washer

rond-point [ʀɔ̃pwɛ̃] nm roundabout

ronflement [ʀɔ̃fləmɑ̃] nm snore, snoring

ronfler [ʀɔ̃fle] vi to snore; (moteur, poêle) to hum

ronger [ʀɔ̃ʒe] vt to gnaw (at); (suj: vers, rouille) to eat into; **se ~ les ongles** to bite one's nails; **se ~ les sangs** to worry o.s. sick; **rongeur** nm rodent

ronronner [ʀɔ̃ʀɔne] vi to purr

rosbif [ʀɔsbif] nm: **du ~** roasting beef; (cuit) roast beef

rose [ʀoz] nf rose ▷ adj pink; **rose bonbon** adj inv candy pink

rosé, e [ʀoze] adj pinkish; **(vin) ~** rosé

roseau, x [ʀozo] nm reed

rosée [ʀoze] nf dew

rosier [ʀozje] nm rosebush, rose tree

rossignol [ʀɔsiɲɔl] nm (Zool) nightingale

rotation [ʀɔtasjɔ̃] nf rotation

roter [ʀɔte] (fam) vi to burp, belch

rôti [ʀoti] nm: **du ~** roasting meat; (cuit) roast meat; **un ~ de bœuf/porc** a joint of beef/pork

rotin [ʀɔtɛ̃] nm rattan (cane); **fauteuil en ~** cane (arm)chair

rôtir [ʀotiʀ] vi, vt (aussi: **faire ~**) to roast; **rôtisserie** nf (restaurant) steakhouse; (traiteur) roast meat shop; **rôtissoire** nf (roasting) spit

rotule [ʀɔtyl] nf kneecap

rouage [ʀwaʒ] nm cog (wheel), gearwheel; **les ~s de l'État** the wheels of State

roue [ʀu] nf wheel; **roue de secours** spare wheel

rouer [ʀwe] vt: **~ qn de coups** to give sb a thrashing

rouge [ʀuʒ] adj, nm/f red ▷ nm red; **(vin) ~** red wine; **sur la liste ~** ex-directory (BRIT), unlisted (US); **passer au ~** (signal) to go red; (automobiliste) to go through a red light; **rouge à joue** blusher; **rouge (à lèvres)** lipstick; **rouge-gorge** nm robin (redbreast)

rougeole [ʀuʒɔl] nf measles sg

rougeoyer [ʀuʒwaje] vi to glow red

rouget [ʀuʒɛ] nm mullet

rougeur [ʀuʒœʀ] nf redness; (Méd: tache) red blotch

rougir [ʀuʒiʀ] vi to turn red; (de honte, timidité) to blush, flush; (de plaisir, colère) to flush

rouille [ʀuj] nf rust; **rouillé, e** adj rusty; **rouiller** vt to rust ▷ vi to rust, go rusty

roulant, e [ʀulɑ̃, ɑ̃t] adj (meuble) on

wheels; (*tapis etc*) moving; **escalier ~** escalator

rouleau, x [ʀulo] *nm* roll; (*à mise en plis, à peinture, vague*) roller; **rouleau à pâtisserie** rolling pin

roulement [ʀulmɑ̃] *nm* (*rotation*) rotation; (*bruit*) rumbling *no pl*, rumble; **travailler par ~** to work on a rota (BRIT) *ou* rotation (US) basis; **roulement (à billes)** ball bearings *pl*; **roulement de tambour** drum roll

rouler [ʀule] *vt* to roll; (*papier, tapis*) to roll up; (*Culin: pâte*) to roll out; (*fam: duper*) to do, con ▷ *vi* (*bille, boule*) to roll; (*voiture, train*) to go, run; (*automobiliste*) to drive; (*bateau*) to roll; **se ~ dans** (*boue*) to roll in; (*couverture*) to wrap o.s. (up) in

roulette [ʀulɛt] *nf* (*de table, fauteuil*) castor; (*de dentiste*) drill; (*jeu*) roulette; **à ~s** on castors; **ça a marché comme sur des ~s** (*fam*) it went off very smoothly

roulis [ʀuli] *nm* roll(ing)

roulotte [ʀulɔt] *nf* caravan

roumain, e [ʀumɛ̃, ɛn] *adj* Rumanian ▷ *nm/f:* **R~, e** Rumanian

Roumanie [ʀumani] *nf* Rumania

rouquin, e [ʀukɛ̃, in] (*péj*) *nm/f* redhead

rouspéter [ʀuspete] (*fam*) *vi* to moan

rousse [ʀus] *adj voir* **roux**

roussir [ʀusiʀ] *vt* to scorch ▷ *vi* (*Culin*): **faire ~** to brown

route [ʀut] *nf* road; (*fig: chemin*) way; (*itinéraire, parcours*) route; (*fig: voie*) road, path; **il y a 3 h de ~** it's a 3-hour ride *ou* journey; **en ~** on the way; **en ~!** let's go!; **mettre en ~** to start up; **se mettre en ~** to set off; **quelle ~ dois-je prendre pour aller à ...?** which road do I take for ...?; **route nationale** ≈ A road (BRIT), ≈ state highway (US); **routier, -ière** *adj* road *cpd* ▷ *nm* (*camionneur*) (long-distance) lorry (BRIT) *ou* truck (US) driver; (*restaurant*) ≈ transport café (BRIT), ≈ truck stop (US)

routine [ʀutin] *nf* routine; **routinier, -ière** (*péj*) *adj* (*activité*) humdrum;

(*personne*) addicted to routine

rouvrir [ʀuvʀiʀ] *vt, vi* to reopen, open again; **se rouvrir** *vi* to reopen, open again

roux, rousse [ʀu, ʀus] *adj* red; (*personne*) red-haired ▷ *nm/f* redhead

royal, e, -aux [ʀwajal, o] *adj* royal; (*cadeau etc*) fit for a king

royaume [ʀwajom] *nm* kingdom; (*fig*) realm; **le Royaume-Uni** the United Kingdom

royauté [ʀwajote] *nf* (*régime*) monarchy

ruban [ʀybɑ̃] *nm* ribbon; **ruban adhésif** adhesive tape

rubéole [ʀybeɔl] *nf* German measles *sg*, rubella

rubis [ʀybi] *nm* ruby

rubrique [ʀybʀik] *nf* (*titre, catégorie*) heading; (*Presse: article*) column

ruche [ʀyʃ] *nf* hive

rude [ʀyd] *adj* (*au toucher*) rough; (*métier, tâche*) hard, tough; (*climat*) severe, harsh; (*bourru*) harsh, rough; (*fruste: manières*) rugged; (*fam: fameux*) jolly good; **rudement** (*fam*) *adv* (*très*) terribly

rudimentaire [ʀydimɑ̃tɛʀ] *adj* rudimentary, basic

rudiments [ʀydimɑ̃] *nmpl*: **avoir des ~ d'anglais** to have a smattering of English

rue [ʀy] *nf* street

ruée [ʀɥe] *nf* rush

ruelle [ʀɥɛl] *nf* alley(-way)

ruer [ʀɥe] *vi* (*cheval*) to kick out; **se ruer** *vi*: **se ~ sur** to pounce on; **se ~ vers/dans/hors de** to rush *ou* dash towards/into/out of

rugby [ʀygbi] *nm* rugby (football)

rugir [ʀyʒiʀ] *vi* to roar

rugueux, -euse [ʀygø, øz] *adj* rough

ruine [ʀɥin] *nf* ruin; **ruiner** *vt* to ruin; **ruineux, -euse** *adj* ruinous

ruisseau, x [ʀɥiso] *nm* stream, brook

ruisseler [ʀɥis(ə)le] *vi* to stream

rumeur [ʀymœʀ] *nf* (*nouvelle*) rumour; (*bruit confus*) rumbling

ruminer [ʀymine] *vt* (*herbe*) to ruminate; (*fig*) to ruminate on *ou* over, chew over

rupture [ʀyptyʀ] *nf* (*séparation*, *désunion*) break-up, split; (*de négociations etc*) breakdown; (*de contrat*) breach; (*dans continuité*) break

rural, e, -aux [ʀyʀal, o] *adj* rural, country *cpd*

ruse [ʀyz] *nf*: **la ~** cunning, craftiness; (*pour tromper*) trickery; **une ~** a trick, a ruse; **rusé, e** *adj* cunning, crafty

russe [ʀys] *adj* Russian ▷ *nm/f*: **R~** Russian ▷ *nm* (*Ling*) Russian

Russie [ʀysi] *nf*: **la ~** Russia

rustine® [ʀystin] *nf* rubber repair patch (for bicycle tyre)

rustique [ʀystik] *adj* rustic

rythme [ʀitm] *nm* rhythm; (*vitesse*) rate; (: *de la vie*) pace, tempo; **rythmé, e** *adj* rhythmic(al)

S

s' [s] *pron voir* **se**

sa [sa] *adj voir* **son¹**

sable [sabl] *nm* sand

sablé [sable] *nm* shortbread biscuit

sabler [sable] *vt* (*contre le verglas*) to grit; **~ le champagne** to drink champagne

sabot [sabo] *nm* clog; (*de cheval*) hoof; **sabot de frein** brake shoe

saboter [sabɔte] *vt* to sabotage; (*bâcler*) to make a mess of, botch

sac [sak] *nm* bag; (*à charbon etc*) sack; **mettre à ~** to sack; **sac à dos** rucksack; **sac à main** handbag; **sac de couchage** sleeping bag; **sac de voyage** travelling bag

saccadé, e [sakade] *adj* jerky; (*respiration*) spasmodic

saccager [sakaʒe] *vt* (*piller*) to sack; (*dévaster*) to create havoc in

saccharine [sakaʀin] *nf* saccharin

sachet [saʃɛ] *nm* (*small*) bag; (*de sucre*, *café*) sachet; **du potage en ~** packet soup; **sachet de thé** tea bag

sacoche [sakɔʃ] nf (gén) bag; (de bicyclette) saddlebag
sacré, e [sakʀe] adj sacred; (fam: satané) blasted; (: fameux): **un ~ toupet** a heck of a cheek
sacrement [sakʀəmɑ̃] nm sacrament
sacrifice [sakʀifis] nm sacrifice;
sacrifier vt to sacrifice
sacristie [sakʀisti] nf (catholique) sacristy; (protestante) vestry
sadique [sadik] adj sadistic
safran [safʀɑ̃] nm saffron
sage [saʒ] adj wise; (enfant) good
sage-femme [saʒfam] nf midwife
sagesse [saʒɛs] nf wisdom
Sagittaire [saʒitɛʀ] nm: **le ~** Sagittarius
Sahara [saaʀa] nm: **le ~** the Sahara (desert)
saignant, e [sɛɲɑ̃, ɑ̃t] adj (viande) rare
saigner [seɲe] vi to bleed ▷ vt to bleed; (animal) to kill (by bleeding); **~ du nez** to have a nosebleed
saillir [sajiʀ] vi to project, stick out; (veine, muscle) to bulge
sain, e [sɛ̃, sɛn] adj healthy; (lecture) safe and sound, unharmed; **~ d'esprit** sound in mind, sane
saindoux [sɛ̃du] nm lard
saint, e [sɛ̃, sɛ̃t] adj holy ▷ nm/f saint; **le Saint Esprit** the Holy Spirit ou Ghost; **la Sainte Vierge** the Blessed Virgin; **la Saint-Sylvestre** New Year's Eve; **sainteté** nf holiness
sais etc [se] vb voir **savoir**
saisie [sezi] nf seizure; **saisie (de données)** (data) capture
saisir [seziʀ] vt to take hold of, grab; (fig: occasion) to seize; (comprendre) to grasp; (entendre) to get, catch; (données) to capture; (Culin) to fry quickly; (Jur: biens, publication) to seize; **saisissant, e** adj startling, striking
saison [sɛzɔ̃] nf season; **haute/basse/morte ~** high/low/slack season; **saisonnier, -ière** adj seasonal
salade [salad] nf (Bot) lettuce etc; (Culin) (green) salad; (fam: confusion)

tangle, muddle; **salade composée** mixed salad; **salade de fruits** fruit salad; **saladier** nm (salad) bowl
salaire [salɛʀ] nm (annuel, mensuel) salary; (hebdomadaire, journalier) pay, wages pl; **salaire minimum interprofessionnel de croissance** index-linked guaranteed minimum wage
salarié, e [salaʀje] nm/f salaried employee; wage-earner
salaud [salo] nm (fam!) sod (!), bastard (!)
sale [sal] adj dirty, filthy; (fig: mauvais) nasty
salé, e [sale] adj (mer, goût) salty; (Culin: amandes, beurre etc) salted; (: gâteaux) savoury; (fam: grivois) spicy; (: facture) steep
saler [sale] vt to salt
saleté [salte] nf (état) dirtiness; (crasse) dirt, filth; (tache etc) dirt no pl; (fam: méchanceté) dirty trick; (: camelote) rubbish no pl; (: obscénité) filthy thing (to say)
salière [saljɛʀ] nf saltcellar
salir [saliʀ] vt to (make) dirty; (fig: quelqu'un) to soil the reputation of; **se salir** vi to get dirty; **salissant, e** adj (tissu) which shows the dirt; (travail) dirty, messy
salle [sal] nf room; (d'hôpital) ward; (de restaurant) dining room; (d'un cinéma) auditorium; (: public) audience; **salle à manger** dining room; **salle d'attente** waiting room; **salle de bain(s)** bathroom; **salle de classe** classroom; **salle de concert** concert hall; **salle d'eau** shower-room; **salle d'embarquement** (à l'aéroport) departure lounge; **salle de jeux** (pour enfants) playroom; **salle de séjour** living room; **salle des ventes** saleroom
salon [salɔ̃] nm lounge, sitting room; (mobilier) lounge suite; (exposition) exhibition, show; **salon de coiffure** hairdressing salon; **salon de thé** tearoom
salope [salɔp] nf (fam!) bitch (!);

saloperie (fam!) nf (action) dirty trick; (chose sans valeur) rubbish no pl
salopette [salɔpɛt] nf dungarees pl; (d'ouvrier) overall(s)
salsifis [salsifi] nm salsify
salubre [salybʀ] adj healthy, salubrious
saluer [salɥe] vt (pour dire bonjour, fig) to greet; (pour dire au revoir) to take one's leave; (Mil) to salute
salut [saly] nm (geste) wave; (parole) greeting; (Mil) salute; (sauvegarde) safety; (Rel) salvation ▷ excl (fam: bonjour) hi (there); (: au revoir) see you, bye
salutations [salytasjɔ̃] nfpl greetings; **Veuillez agréer, Monsieur, mes ~ distinguées** yours faithfully
samedi [samdi] nm Saturday
SAMU [samy] sigle m (= service d'assistance médicale d'urgence) ≈ ambulance (service) (BRIT), ≈ paramedics pl (US)
sanction [sɑ̃ksjɔ̃] nf sanction; **sanctionner** vt (loi, usage) to sanction; (punir) to punish
sandale [sɑ̃dal] nf sandal
sandwich [sɑ̃dwi(t)ʃ] nm sandwich; **je voudrais un ~ au jambon/fromage** I'd like a ham/cheese sandwich
sang [sɑ̃] nm blood; **en ~** covered in blood; **se faire du mauvais ~** to fret, get in a state; **sang-froid** nm calm, sangfroid; **de sang-froid** in cold blood; **sanglant, e** adj bloody
sangle [sɑ̃gl] nf strap
sanglier [sɑ̃glije] nm (wild) boar
sanglot [sɑ̃glo] nm sob; **sangloter** vi to sob
sangsue [sɑ̃sy] nf leech
sanguin, e [sɑ̃gɛ̃, in] adj blood cpd
sanitaire [saniteʀ] adj health cpd; **sanitaires** nmpl (lieu) bathroom sg
sans [sɑ̃] prép without; **un pull ~ manches** a sleeveless jumper; **~ faute** without fail; **~ arrêt** without a break; **~ ça** (fam) otherwise; **~ qu'il s'en aperçoive** without him

ou his noticing; **sans-abri** nmpl homeless; **sans-emploi** nm/f inv unemployed person; **les sans-emploi** the unemployed; **sans-gêne** adj inv inconsiderate
santé [sɑ̃te] nf health; **en bonne ~** in good health; **boire à la ~ de qn** to drink (to) sb's health; **à ta/votre ~!** cheers!
saoudien, ne [saudjɛ̃, jɛn] adj Saudi Arabian ▷ nm/f: **S~, ne** Saudi Arabian
saoul, e [su, sul] adj = **soûl**
saper [sape] vt to undermine, sap
sapeur-pompier [sapœʀpɔ̃pje] nm fireman
saphir [safiʀ] nm sapphire
sapin [sapɛ̃] nm fir (tree); (bois) fir; **sapin de Noël** Christmas tree
sarcastique [saʀkastik] adj sarcastic
Sardaigne [saʀdɛɲ] nf: **la ~** Sardinia
sardine [saʀdin] nf sardine
SARL sigle f (= société à responsabilité limitée) ≈ plc (BRIT), ≈ Inc. (US)
sarrasin [saʀazɛ̃] nm buckwheat
satané, e [satane] (fam) adj confounded
satellite [satelit] nm satellite
satin [satɛ̃] nm satin
satire [satiʀ] nf satire; **satirique** adj satirical
satisfaction [satisfaksjɔ̃] nf satisfaction
satisfaire [satisfɛʀ] vt to satisfy; **~ à** (conditions) to meet; **satisfaisant, e** adj (acceptable) satisfactory; **satisfait, e** adj satisfied; **satisfait de** happy ou satisfied with
saturer [satyʀe] vt to saturate
sauce [sos] nf sauce; (avec un rôti) gravy; **sauce tomate** tomato sauce; **saucière** nf sauceboat
saucisse [sosis] nf sausage
saucisson [sosisɔ̃] nm (slicing) sausage
sauf, sauve [sof, sov] adj unharmed, unhurt; (fig: honneur) intact, saved ▷ prép except; **laisser la vie sauve à qn** to spare sb's life; **~ si** (à moins que) unless; **~ erreur** if I'm not mistaken;

~ **avis contraire** unless you hear to the contrary

sauge [soʒ] nf sage

saugrenu, e [sogrəny] adj preposterous

saule [sol] nm willow (tree)

saumon [somɔ̃] nm salmon inv

saupoudrer [sopudre] vt: ~ **qch de** to sprinkle sth with

saur [sɔʀ] adj m: **hareng ~** smoked herring, kipper

saut [so] nm jump; (discipline sportive) jumping; **faire un ~ chez qn** to pop over to sb's (place); **saut à l'élastique** bungee jumping; **saut à la perche** pole vaulting; **saut en hauteur/longueur** high/long jump; **saut périlleux** somersault

sauter [sote] vi to jump, leap; (exploser) to blow up, explode; (: fusibles) to blow; (se détacher) to pop out (ou off) ▷ vt to jump (over), leap (over); (fig: omettre) to skip, miss (out); **faire ~** to blow up; (Culin) to sauté; **à la corde** to skip; **~ au cou de qn** to fly into sb's arms; **~ sur une occasion** to jump at an opportunity; **~ aux yeux** to be (quite) obvious

sauterelle [sotʀɛl] nf grasshopper

sautiller [sotije] vi (oiseau) to hop; (enfant) to skip

sauvage [sovaʒ] adj (gén) wild; (peuplade) savage; (farouche: personne) unsociable; (barbare) wild, savage; (non officiel) unauthorized, unofficial; **faire du camping ~** to camp in the wild ▷ nm/f savage; (timide) unsociable type

sauve [sov] adj f voir **sauf**

sauvegarde [sovgard] nf safeguard; (Inform) backup; **sauvegarder** vt to safeguard; (Inform: enregistrer) to save; (: copier) to back up

sauve-qui-peut [sovkipø] excl run for your life!

sauver [sove] vt to save; (porter secours à) to rescue; (récupérer) to salvage, rescue; **se sauver** vi (s'enfuir) to run away; (fam: partir) to be off; **sauvetage**

nm rescue; **sauveteur** nm rescuer; **sauvette**: **à la sauvette** adv (se marier etc) hastily, hurriedly; **sauveur** nm saviour (BRIT), savior (US)

savant, e [savɑ̃, ɑ̃t] adj scholarly, learned ▷ nm scientist

saveur [savœʀ] nf flavour; (fig) savour

savoir [savwaʀ] vt to know; (être capable de): **il sait nager** he can swim ▷ nm knowledge; **se savoir** vi (être connu) to be known; **je ne sais pas** I don't know; **je ne sais pas parler français** I don't speak French; **savez-vous où je peux ...?** do you know where I can ...?; **je n'en sais rien** I (really) don't know; **à ~ that** is, namely; **faire ~ qch à qn** to let sb know sth; **pas que je sache** not as far as I know

savon [savɔ̃] nm (produit) soap; (morceau) bar of soap; (fam): **passer un ~ à qn** to give sb a good dressing-down; **savonner** vt to soap; **savonnette** nf bar of soap

savourer [savure] vt to savour; **savoureux, -euse** adj tasty; (fig: anecdote) spicy, juicy

saxo(phone) [sakso(fɔn)] nm sax(ophone)

scabreux, -euse [skabʀø, øz] adj risky; (indécent) improper, shocking

scandale [skɑ̃dal] nm scandal; **faire un ~** (scène) to make a scene; (Jur) to create a disturbance; **faire ~** to scandalize people; **scandaleux, -euse** adj scandalous, outrageous

scandinave [skɑ̃dinav] adj Scandinavian ▷ nm/f: **S~** Scandinavian

Scandinavie [skɑ̃dinavi] nf Scandinavia

scarabée [skarabe] nm beetle

scarlatine [skaʀlatin] nf scarlet fever

scarole [skaʀɔl] nf endive

sceau, x [so] nm seal

sceller [sele] vt to seal

scénario [senarjo] nm scenario

scène [sɛn] nf (gén) scene; (estrade, fig: théâtre) stage; **entrer en ~** to come on stage; **mettre en ~** (Théâtre) to stage;

(Cinéma) to direct; **faire une ~ (à qn)** to make a scene (with sb); **scène de ménage** domestic scene

sceptique [sɛptik] *adj* sceptical

schéma [ʃema] *nm (diagramme)* diagram, sketch; **schématique** *adj* diagrammatic(al), schematic *(fig)* oversimplified

sciatique [sjatik] *nf* sciatica

scie [si] *nf* saw

sciemment [sjamɑ̃] *adv* knowingly

science [sjɑ̃s] *nf* science; *(savoir)* knowledge; **sciences humaines/ sociales** social sciences; **sciences naturelles** *(Scol)* natural science *sg,* biology *sg;* **sciences po** political science *ou* studies *pl;* **science-fiction** *nf* science fiction; **scientifique** *adj* scientific ▷ *nm/f* scientist; *(étudiant)* science student

scier [sje] *vt* to saw; *(retrancher)* to saw off; **scierie** *nf* sawmill

scintiller [sɛ̃tije] *vi* to sparkle; *(étoile)* to twinkle

sciure [sjyʀ] *nf:* **~ (de bois)** sawdust

sclérose [skleʀoz] *nf:* **sclérose en plaques** multiple sclerosis

scolaire [skɔlɛʀ] *adj* school *cpd;* **scolariser** *vt* to provide with schooling/schools; **scolarité** *nf* schooling

scooter [skutœʀ] *nm* (motor) scooter

score [skɔʀ] *nm* score

scorpion [skɔʀpjɔ̃] *nm (signe):* **le S-** Scorpio

scotch [skɔtʃ] *nm (whisky)* scotch, whisky; **S-®** *(adhésif)* Sellotape® *(BRIT),* Scotch® tape *(US)*

scout, e [skut] *adj, nm* scout

script [skʀipt] *nm (écriture)* printing; *(Cinéma)* shooting script

scrupule [skʀypyl] *nm* scruple

scruter [skʀyte] *vt* to scrutinize; *(l'obscurité)* to peer into

scrutin [skʀytɛ̃] *nm (vote)* ballot; *(ensemble des opérations)* poll

sculpter [skylte] *vt* to sculpt; *(bois)* to carve; **sculpteur** *nm* sculptor;

sculpture *nf* sculpture

SDF *sigle m:* **sans domicile fixe** homeless person; **les ~** the homeless

⬤ MOT-CLÉ

se [sə], **s'** *pron* 1 *(emploi réfléchi)* oneself; *(: masc)* himself; *(: fém)* herself; *(: sujet non humain)* itself; *(: pl)* themselves; **se savonner** to soap o.s.

2 *(réciproque)* one another, each other; **ils s'aiment** they love one another *ou* each other

3 *(passif):* **cela se répare facilement** it is easily repaired

4 *(possessif):* **se casser la jambe/se laver les mains** to break one's leg/ wash one's hands

séance [seɑ̃s] *nf (d'assemblée)* meeting, session; *(de tribunal)* sitting, session; *(musicale, Cinéma, Théâtre)* performance

seau, x [so] *nm* bucket, pail

sec, sèche [sɛk, sɛʃ] *adj* dry; *(raisins, figues)* dried; *(cœur: insensible)* hard, cold ▷ *nm:* **tenir au ~** to keep in a dry place ▷ *adv* hard; **je le bois ~** I drink it straight *ou* neat; **à ~ (puits)** dried up

sèche [sɛʃ] *adj f voir* **sec**; **sèche-cheveux** *nm inv* hair-drier; **sèche-linge** *nm inv* tumble dryer; **sèchement** *adv (répondre)* drily

sécher [seʃe] *vt* to dry; *(dessécher: peau, blé)* to dry (out); *(: étang)* to dry up; *(fam: cours)* to skip ▷ *vi* to dry; to dry out; to dry up; *(fam: candidat)* to be stumped; **se sécher** *(après le bain)* to dry o.s.; **sécheresse** *nf* dryness; *(absence de pluie)* drought; **séchoir** *nm* drier

second, e [s(ə)gɔ̃, ɔ̃d] *adj* second ▷ *nm (assistant)* second in command; *(Navig)* first mate ▷ *nf (Scol)* year 11 *(BRIT),* tenth grade *(US)*; *(Aviat, Rail etc)* second class; **voyager en ~e** to travel second-class; **secondaire** *adj* secondary; **seconde²** *nf* second; **seconder** *vt* to assist

secouer [s(ə)kwe] vt to shake; (passagers) to rock; (traumatiser) to shake (up)

secourir [s(ə)kuʀiʀ] vt (venir en aide à) to assist, aid; **secourisme** nm first aid; **secouriste** nm/f first aid worker

secours [s(ə)kuʀ] nm help, aid, assistance ▷ nmpl aid sg; **au ~!** help!; **appeler au ~** to shout ou call for help; **porter ~ à qn** to give sb assistance, help sb; **les premiers ~** first aid sg

○ **ÉQUIPES DE SECOURS**

○ Emergency phone numbers can
○ be dialled free from public phones.
○ For the police ('la police') dial 17; for
○ medical services ('le SAMU') dial
○ 15; for the fire brigade ('les sapeurs
○ pompiers'), dial 18.

secousse [s(ə)kus] nf jolt, bump; (électrique) shock; (fig: psychologique) jolt, shock

secret, -ète [səkʀɛ, ɛt] adj secret; (fig: renfermé) reticent, reserved ▷ nm secret; (discrétion absolue): **le ~** secrecy; **en ~** in secret, secretly; **secret professionnel** professional secrecy

secrétaire [s(ə)kʀetɛʀ] nm/f secretary ▷ nm (meuble) writing desk; **secrétaire de direction** private ou personal secretary; **secrétaire d'État** junior minister; **secrétariat** nm (profession) secretarial work; (bureau) office; (: d'organisation internationale) secretariat

secteur [sɛktœʀ] nm sector; (zone) area; (Élec): **branché sur ~** plugged into the mains (supply)

section [sɛksjɔ̃] nf section; (de parcours d'autobus) fare stage; (Mil: unité) platoon; **sectionner** vt to sever

sécu [seky] abr f = **sécurité sociale**

sécurité [sekyʀite] nf (absence de danger) safety; (absence de troubles) security; **système de ~** security system; **être en ~** to be safe; **la sécurité routière** road safety; **la sécurité sociale** ≈ (the) Social Security (BRIT), ≈ Welfare (US)

sédentaire [sedɑ̃tɛʀ] adj sedentary

séduction [sedyksjɔ̃] nf seduction; (charme, attrait) appeal, charm

séduire [sedɥiʀ] vt to charm; (femme: abuser de) to seduce; **séduisant, e** adj (femme) seductive; (homme, offre) very attractive

ségrégation [segʀegasjɔ̃] nf segregation

seigle [sɛgl] nm rye

seigneur [sɛɲœʀ] nm lord

sein [sɛ̃] nm breast; (entrailles) womb; **au ~ de** (équipe, institution) within

séisme [seism] nm earthquake

seize [sɛz] num sixteen; **seizième** num sixteenth

séjour [seʒuʀ] nm stay; (pièce) living room; **séjourner** vi to stay

sel [sɛl] nm salt; (fig: piquant) spice

sélection [selɛksjɔ̃] nf selection; **sélectionner** vt to select

self-service [sɛlfsɛʀvis] adj, nm self-service

selle [sɛl] nf saddle; **selles** nfpl (Méd) stools; **seller** vt to saddle

selon [s(ə)lɔ̃] prép according to; (en se conformant à) in accordance with; **~ que** according to whether; **~ moi** as I see it

semaine [s(ə)mɛn] nf week; **en ~** during the week, on weekdays

semblable [sɑ̃blabl] adj similar; (de ce genre): **de ~s mésaventures** such mishaps ▷ nm fellow creature ou man; **~ à** similar to, like

semblant [sɑ̃blɑ̃] nm: **un ~ de ...** a semblance of ...; **faire ~ (de faire)** to pretend (to do)

sembler [sɑ̃ble] vb +attrib to seem ▷ vb impers: **il semble (bien) que/inutile de** it (really) seems ou appears that/ useless to; **il me semble que** it seems to me that; **comme bon lui semble** as he sees fit

semelle [s(ə)mɛl] nf sole; (intérieure) insole, inner sole

semer [s(ə)me] vt to sow; (fig: éparpiller) to scatter; (: confusion) to spread; (fam: poursuivants) to lose, shake off; **semé de** (difficultés) riddled with

semestre [s(ə)mɛstʀ] nm half-year; (Scol) semester

séminaire [seminɛʀ] nm seminar

semi-remorque [səmiʀəmɔʀk] nm articulated lorry (BRIT), semi(trailer) (us)

semoule [s(ə)mul] nf semolina

sénat [sena] nm senate; **sénateur** nm senator

Sénégal [senegal] nm: **le ~** Senegal

sens [sɑ̃s] nm (Physiol.) sense; (signification) meaning, sense; (direction) direction; **à mon ~** to my mind; **dans le ~ des aiguilles d'une montre** clockwise; **dans le ~ contraire des aiguilles d'une montre** anticlockwise; **dans le mauvais ~** (aller) the wrong way, in the wrong direction; **le bon ~** common sense; **sens dessus dessous** upside down; **sens interdit/unique** one-way street

sensation [sɑ̃sasjɔ̃] nf sensation; **à ~** (péj) sensational; **faire ~** to cause ou create a sensation; **sensationnel, le** adj (fam) fantastic, terrific

sensé, e [sɑ̃se] adj sensible

sensibiliser [sɑ̃sibilize] vt: **~ qn à** to make sb sensitive to

sensibilité [sɑ̃sibilite] nf sensitivity

sensible [sɑ̃sibl] adj sensitive; (aux sens) perceptible; (appréciable: différence, progrès) appreciable, noticeable; **~ à** sensitive to; **sensiblement** adv (à peu près): **ils sont sensiblement du même âge** they are approximately the same age; **sensiblerie** nf sentimentality

⚠ Attention à ne pas traduire sensible par le mot anglais *sensible*.

sensuel, le [sɑ̃sɥɛl] adj (personne) sensual; (musique) sensuous

sentence [sɑ̃tɑ̃s] nf (jugement) sentence

sentier [sɑ̃tje] nm path

sentiment [sɑ̃timɑ̃] nm feeling; **recevez mes ~s respectueux**

(personne nommée) yours sincerely; (personne non nommée) yours faithfully; **sentimental, e, -aux** adj sentimental; (vie, aventure) love cpd

sentinelle [sɑ̃tinɛl] nf sentry

sentir [sɑ̃tiʀ] vt (par l'odorat) to smell; (par le goût) to taste; (au toucher, fig) to feel; (répandre une odeur de) to smell of; (: ressemblance) to smell like ▸ vi to smell; **~ mauvais** to smell bad; **se ~ bien** to feel good; **se ~ mal** (être indisposé) to feel unwell ou ill; **se ~ le courage/la force de faire** to feel brave/strong enough to do; **il ne peut pas le ~** (fam) he can't stand him; **je ne me sens pas bien** I don't feel well

séparation [separasjɔ̃] nf separation; (cloison) division, partition

séparé, e [separe] adj (distinct) separate; (époux) separated; **séparément** adv separately

séparer [separe] vt to separate; (désunir) to drive apart; (détacher): **~ qch de** to pull sth (off) from; **se séparer** vi (époux, amis) to separate, part; (se diviser: route etc) to divide; **se ~ de** (époux) to separate ou part from; (employé, objet personnel) to part with

sept [sɛt] num seven; **septante** (BELGIQUE, SUISSE) adj inv seventy

septembre [sɛptɑ̃bʀ] nm September

septicémie [sɛptisemi] nf blood poisoning, septicaemia

septième [sɛtjɛm] num seventh

séquelles [sekɛl] nfpl after-effects; (fig) aftermath

serbe [sɛʀb(ə)] adj Serbian

Serbie [sɛʀbi] nf: **la ~** Serbia

serein, e [səʀɛ̃, ɛn] adj serene

sergent [sɛʀʒɑ̃] nm sergeant

série [seʀi] nf series nv; (de clés, casseroles, outils) set; (catégorie: Sport) rank; **en ~** in quick succession; (Comm) mass cpd; **de ~** (voiture) standard; **hors ~** (Comm) custom-built; **série noire** (crime) thriller

sérieusement [seʀjøzmɑ̃] adv seriously

sérieux, -euse [serjø, jøz] adj serious; (élève, employé) reliable, dependable; (client, maison) reliable, dependable ▷ nm seriousness; (d'une entreprise etc) reliability; **garder son ~** to keep a straight face; **prendre qch/qn au ~** to take sth/sb seriously

serin [s(ə)Rɛ̃] nm canary

seringue [s(ə)Rɛ̃g] nf syringe

serment [sɛRmɑ̃] nm (juré) oath; (promesse) pledge, vow

sermon [sɛRmɔ̃] nm sermon

séropositif, -ive [seRopozitif, iv] adj (Méd) HIV positive

serpent [sɛRpɑ̃] nm snake; **serpenter** vi to wind

serpillière [sɛRpijɛR] nf floorcloth

serre [sɛR] nf (Agr) greenhouse; **serres** nfpl (griffes) claws, talons

serré, e [seRe] adj (habits) tight; (fig: lutte, match) tight, close-fought; (passagers etc) (tightly) packed; (réseau) dense; **avoir le cœur ~** to have a heavy heart

serrer [seRe] vt (tenir) to grip ou hold tight; (comprimer, coincer) to squeeze; (poings, mâchoires) to clench; (suj: vêtement) to be too tight for; (ceinture, nœud, vis) to tighten ▷ vi: **~ à droite** to keep ou get over to the right

serrure [seRyR] nf lock; **serrurier** nm locksmith

sert etc [sɛR] vb voir **servir**

servante [sɛRvɑ̃t] nf (maid)servant

serveur, -euse [sɛRvœR, øz] nm/f waiter (waitress)

serviable [sɛRvjabl] adj obliging, willing to help

service [sɛRvis] nm service; (assortiment de vaisselle) set, service; (bureau: de la vente etc) department, section; (travail) duty; **premier ~** (série de repas) first sitting; **être de ~** to be on duty; **faire le ~** to serve; **rendre un ~ à qn** to do sb a favour; (objet: s'avérer utile) to come in handy ou handy for sb; **mettre en ~** to put into service ou operation; **~ compris/non compris**

service included/not included; **hors ~** out of order; **service après vente** after sales service; **service d'ordre** police (ou stewards) in charge of maintaining order; **service militaire** military service; see note; **services secrets** secret service sg

● **SERVICE MILITAIRE**

● Until 1997, French men over the age
● of 18 who were passed as fit, and
● who were not in full-time higher
● education, were required to do
● ten months' "service militaire".
● Conscientious objectors were
● required to do two years' community
● service.
● Since 1997, military service has been
● suspended in France. However, all
● sixteen-year-olds, both male and
● female, are required to register for
● a compulsory one-day training
● course, the "JAPD" ("journée d'appel
● de préparation à la défense"), which
● covers basic information on the
● principles and organization of
● defence in France, and also advises
● on career opportunities in the
● military and in the voluntary sector.
● Young people must attend the
● training day before their eighteenth
● birthday.

serviette [sɛRvjɛt] nf (de table) (table) napkin, serviette; (de toilette) towel; (porte-documents) briefcase; **serviette hygiénique** sanitary towel

servir [sɛRviR] vt to serve; (au restaurant) to wait on; (au magasin) to serve, attend to ▷ vi (Tennis) to serve; (Cartes) to deal; **se servir** vi (prendre d'un plat) to help o.s.; **vous êtes servi?** are you being served?; **~ à qn** (diplôme, livre) to be of use to sb; **~ à qch/faire** (outil etc) to be used for sth/doing; **ça ne sert à rien** it's no use; **~ (à qn) de** to serve as (for sb); **se ~ de** (plat) to help o.s. to;

(voiture, outil, relations) to use; **sers-toi!** help yourself!

serviteur [sɛʀvitœʀ] nm servant

ses [se] adj voir **son'**

seuil [sœj] nm doorstep; (fig) threshold

seul, e [sœl] adj (sans compagnie) alone; (unique) **un ~ livre** only one book, a single book ▷ adv (vivre) alone, on one's own ▷ nm, nf: **il en reste un(e) ~(e)** there's only one left; **le ~ livre** the only book; **parler tout ~** to talk to oneself; **faire qch (tout) ~** to do sth (all) on one's own (all) by oneself; **à lui (tout) ~** single-handed, on his own; **se sentir ~** to feel lonely; **seulement** adv only; **non seulement ... mais aussi ou encore** not only ... but also

sève [sɛv] nf sap

sévère [sevɛʀ] adj severe

sexe [sɛks] nm sex; (organes génitaux) genitals, sex organs; **sexuel, le** adj sexual

shampooing [ʃɑ̃pwɛ̃] nm shampoo

Shetland [ʃetlɑ̃d] n: **les îles ~** the Shetland Islands, Shetland

short [ʃɔʀt] nm (pair of) shorts pl

⬤ MOT-CLÉ

si [si] adv 1 (oui) yes; **"Paul n'est pas venu" — "si!"** "Paul hasn't come" — "yes, he has!"; **je vous assure que si** I assure you he did ou she is etc
2 (tellement) so; **si gentil/rapidement** so kind/fast; **(tant et) si bien que** so much so that; **si rapide qu'il soit** however fast he may be
▷ conj if; **si tu veux** if you want; **je me demande si** I wonder if ou whether; **si seulement** if only
▷ nm (Mus) B; (en chantant la gamme) ti

Sicile [sisil] nf: **la ~** Sicily

SIDA [sida] sigle m (= syndrome immuno-déficitaire acquis) AIDS sg

sidéré, e [sideʀe] adj staggered

sidérurgie [sideʀyʀʒi] nf steel industry

239 | **signifier**

siècle [sjɛkl] nm century

siège [sjɛʒ] nm seat; (d'entreprise) head office; (d'organisation) headquarters pl; (Mil) siege; **siège social** registered office; **siéger** vi to sit

sien, ne [sjɛ̃, sjɛn] pron: **le(la) ~(ne), les ~(ne)s** (homme) his; (femme) hers; (chose, animal) its

sieste [sjɛst] nf (afternoon) snooze ou nap; **faire la ~** to have a snooze ou nap

sifflement [sifləmɑ̃] nm: **un ~** whistle

siffler [sifle] vi (gén) to whistle; (en respirant) to wheeze; (serpent, vapeur) to hiss ▷ vt (chanson) to whistle; (chien etc) to whistle for; (fille) to whistle at; (pièce, orateur) to hiss, boo; (fin du match, départ) to blow one's whistle for; (fam: verre) to guzzle

sifflet [siflɛ] nm whistle; **coup de ~** whistle

siffloter [siflɔte] vi, vt to whistle

sigle [sigl] nm acronym

signal, -aux [siɲal, o] nm signal; (indice, écriteau) sign; **donner le ~ de** to give the signal for; **signal d'alarme** alarm signal; **signalement** nm description, particulars pl

signaler [siɲale] vt to indicate; (personne: faire un signe) to signal; (vol, perte) to report; (faire remarquer): **~ qch à qn/(à qn) que** to point out sth to sb/(to sb) that; **je voudrais ~ un vol** I'd like to report a theft

signature [siɲatyʀ] nf signature; (action) signing

signe [siɲ] nm sign; (Typo) mark; **faire un ~ de la main** to give a sign with one's hand; **faire ~ à qn** (fig: contacter) to get in touch with sb; **faire ~ à qn d'entrer** to motion (to) sb to come in; **signer** vt to sign; **se signer** vi to cross o.s.; **où dois-je signer?** where do I sign?

significatif, -ive [siɲifikatif, iv] adj significant

signification [siɲifikasjɔ̃] nf meaning

signifier [siɲifje] vt (vouloir dire) to mean; (faire connaître): **~ qch (à qn)** to make sth known (to sb)

silence [silɑ̃s] *nm* silence; *(Mus)* rest; **garder le ~** to keep silent, say nothing; **silencieux, -euse** *adj* quiet, silent ▷ *nm* silencer

silhouette [silwɛt] *nf* outline, silhouette; *(allure)* figure

sillage [sijaʒ] *nm* wake

sillon [sijɔ̃] *nm* furrow; *(de disque)* groove; **sillonner** *vt* to criss-cross

simagrées [simaɡʀe] *nfpl* fuss *sg*

similaire [similɛʀ] *adj* similar; **similicuir** *nm* imitation leather; **similitude** *nf* similarity

simple [sɛ̃pl] *adj* simple; *(non multiple)* single ▷ *nm*: **~ messieurs/dames** men's/ladies' singles *sg* ▷ *nm/f*: **~ d'esprit** simpleton

simplicité [sɛ̃plisite] *nf* simplicity; **en toute ~** quite simply

simplifier [sɛ̃plifje] *vt* to simplify

simuler [simyle] *vt* to sham, simulate

simultané, e [simyltane] *adj* simultaneous

sincère [sɛ̃sɛʀ] *adj* sincere; **sincèrement** *adv* sincerely; *(pour parler franchement)* honestly, really; **sincérité** *nf* sincerity

Singapour [sɛ̃ɡapuʀ] *nm* Singapore

singe [sɛ̃ʒ] *nm* monkey; *(de grande taille)* ape; **singer** *vt* to ape, mimic; **singeries** *nfpl* antics

singulariser [sɛ̃ɡylaʀize]: **se singulariser** *vi* to call attention to o.s.

singularité [sɛ̃ɡylaʀite] *nf* peculiarity

singulier, -ière [sɛ̃ɡylje, jɛʀ] *adj* remarkable, singular ▷ *nm* singular

sinistre [sinistʀ] *adj* sinister ▷ *nm* *(incendie)* blaze; *(catastrophe)* disaster; *(Assurances)* damage *(giving rise to a claim)*; **sinistré, e** *adj* disaster-stricken ▷ *nm/f* disaster victim

sinon [sinɔ̃] *conj* *(autrement, sans quoi)* otherwise, or else; *(sauf)* except, other than; *(si ce n'est)* if not

sinueux, -euse [sinyø, øz] *adj* winding

sinus [sinys] *nm* *(Anat)* sinus; *(Géom)*

sine; **sinusite** *nf* sinusitis

sirène [siʀɛn] *nf* siren; **sirène d'alarme** fire alarm; *(en temps de guerre)* air-raid siren

sirop [siʀo] *nm* *(à diluer: de fruit etc)* syrup; *(pharmaceutique)* syrup, mixture; **~ pour la toux** cough mixture

siroter [siʀote] *vt* to sip

sismique [sismik] *adj* seismic

site [sit] *nm* *(paysage, environnement)* setting; *(d'une ville etc: emplacement)* site; **site (pittoresque)** beauty spot; **sites touristiques** places of interest; **site Web** *(Inform)* website

sitôt [sito] *adv*: **~ parti** as soon as he *etc* had left; **~ que** as soon as; **pas de ~** not for a long time

situation [sitɥasjɔ̃] *nf* situation; *(d'un édifice, d'une ville)* position, location; **situation de famille** marital status

situé, e [sitɥe] *adj* situated

situer [sitɥe] *vt* to site, situate; *(en pensée)* to set, place; **se situer** *vi* to be situated

six [sis] *num* six; **sixième** *num* sixth ▷ *nf* *(Scol)* year 7 (BRIT), sixth grade (US)

skaï® [skaj] *nm* Leatherette®

ski [ski] *nm* *(objet)* ski; *(sport)* skiing; **faire du ~** to ski; **ski de fond** cross-country skiing; **ski nautique** water-skiing; **ski de piste** downhill skiing; **ski de randonnée** cross-country skiing; **skier** *vi* to ski; **skieur, -euse** *nm/f* skier

slip [slip] *nm* *(sous-vêtement)* pants *pl*, briefs *pl*; *(de bain: d'homme)* trunks *pl*; *(: du bikini)* (bikini) briefs *pl*

slogan [slɔɡã] *nm* slogan

Slovaquie [slɔvaki] *nf*: **la ~** Slovakia

SMIC [smik] *nm* **= salaire minimum interprofessionnel de croissance**

smoking [smɔkiŋ] *nm* dinner *ou* evening suit

SMS *sigle m* (= *short message service*) *(service)* SMS; *(message)* text message

SNCF *sigle f* (= *Société nationale des chemins de fer français*) French railways

snob [snɔb] *adj* snobbish ▷ *nm/f* snob; **snobisme** *nm* snobbery, snobbishness

sobre [sɔbʀ] *adj* (*personne*) temperate, abstemious; (*élégance, style*) sober

sobriquet [sɔbʀikɛ] *nm* nickname

social, e, -aux [sɔsjal, jo] *adj* social

socialisme [sɔsjalism] *nm* socialism; **socialiste** *nm/f* socialist

société [sɔsjete] *nf* society; (*sportive*) club; (*Comm*) company; **la ~ de consommation** the consumer society; **société anonyme** ≈ limited (BRIT) ou incorporated (US) company

sociologie [sɔsjɔlɔʒi] *nf* sociology

socle [sɔkl] *nm* (*de colonne, statue*) plinth, pedestal; (*de lampe*) base

socquette [sɔkɛt] *nf* ankle sock

sœur [sœʀ] *nf* sister; (*religieuse*) nun, sister

soi [swa] *pron* oneself; **en ~** (*intrinsèquement*) in itself; **cela va de ~** that ou it goes without saying; **soi-disant** *adj inv* so-called ▷ *adv* supposedly

soie [swa] *nf* silk; **soierie** *nf* (*tissu*) silk

soif [swaf] *nf* thirst; **avoir ~** to be thirsty; **donner ~ à qn** to make sb thirsty

soigné, e [swaɲe] *adj* (*tenue*) well-groomed, neat; (*travail*) careful, meticulous

soigner [swaɲe] *vt* (*malade, maladie*: suj: *docteur*) to treat; (suj: *infirmière, mère*) to nurse, look after; (*travail, détails*) to take care over; (*jardin, invités*) to look after; **soigneux, -euse** *adj* (*propre*) tidy, neat; (*appliqué*) painstaking, careful

soi-même [swamɛm] *pron* oneself

soin [swɛ̃] *nm* (*application*) care; (*propreté, ordre*) tidiness, neatness; **soins** *nmpl* (*à un malade, blessé*) treatment *sg*, medical attention *sg*; (*hygiène*) care *sg*; **prendre ~ de** to take care of, look after; **prendre ~ de faire** to take care to do; **les premiers ~s** first aid *sg*

soir [swaʀ] *nm* evening; **ce ~** this evening, tonight; **à ce ~!** I see you this evening (ou tonight)!; **sept/dix heures du ~** seven in the evening/ten at

night; **demain ~** tomorrow evening, tomorrow night; **soirée** *nf* evening; (*réception*) party

soit [swa] *vb voir* **être** ▷ *conj* (*à savoir*) namely; (*ou*): **~ ... ~ ...** either ... or; **~ que ... ~ que ou que** whether ... or whether

soit [swat] *adv* so be it, very well

soixantaine [swasɑ̃tɛn] *nf*: **une ~ (de)** sixty or so, about sixty; **avoir la ~** (*âge*) to be around sixty

soixante [swasɑ̃t] *num* sixty;
soixante-dix *num* seventy

soja [sɔʒa] *nm* soya; (*graines*) soya beans *pl*; **germes de ~** beansprouts

sol [sɔl] *nm* ground; (*de logement*) floor; (*Agr*) soil; (*Mus*) G; (: *en chantant la gamme*) so(h)

solaire [sɔlɛʀ] *adj* (*énergie etc*) solar; (*crème etc*) sun *cpd*

soldat [sɔlda] *nm* soldier

solde [sɔld] *nf* pay ▷ *nm* (*Comm*) balance; **soldes** *nm ou f pl* (*articles*) sale goods; (*vente*) sales; **en ~** at sale price; **solder** *vt* (*marchandise*) to sell at sale price, sell off

sole [sɔl] *nf* sole *inv* (*fish*)

soleil [sɔlɛj] *nm* sun; (*lumière*) sun(light); (*temps ensoleillé*) sun(shine); **il fait du ~** it's sunny; **au ~** in the sun

solennel, le [sɔlanɛl] *adj* solemn

solfège [sɔlfɛʒ] *nm* musical theory

solidaire [sɔlidɛʀ] *adj*: **être ~s** to show solidarity, stand ou stick together; **être ~ de** (*collègues*) to stand by; **solidarité** *nf* solidarity; **par solidarité (avec)** in sympathy (with)

solide [sɔlid] *adj* solid; (*mur, maison, meuble*) solid, sturdy; (*connaissances, argument*) sound; (*personne, estomac*) robust, sturdy ▷ *nm* solid

soliste [sɔlist] *nm/f* soloist

solitaire [sɔlitɛʀ] *adj* (*sans compagnie*) solitary, lonely; (*lieu*) lonely ▷ *nm/f* (*ermite*) recluse; (*fig: ours*) loner

solitude [sɔlityd] *nf* loneliness; (*tranquillité*) solitude

solliciter [sɔlisite] *vt* (*personne*) to appeal to; (*emploi, faveur*) to seek

sollicitude [sɔlisityd] nf concern
soluble [sɔlybl] adj soluble
solution [sɔlysjɔ̃] nf solution; **solution de facilité** easy way out
solvable [sɔlvabl] adj solvent
sombre [sɔ̃bʀ] adj dark; (fig) gloomy; **sombrer** vi (bateau) to sink; **sombrer dans** (misère, désespoir) to sink into
sommaire [sɔmɛʀ] adj (simple) basic; (expéditif) summary ▷ nm summary
somme [sɔm] nf (Math) sum; (quantité) amount; (argent) sum, amount ▷ nm: **faire un ~** to have a (short) nap; **en ~** in all; **~ toute** all in all
sommeil [sɔmɛj] nm sleep; **avoir ~** to be sleepy; **sommeiller** vi to doze
sommet [sɔmɛ] nm top; (d'une montagne) summit, top; (fig: de la perfection, gloire) height
sommier [sɔmje] nm (bed) base
somnambule [sɔmnɑ̃byl] nm/f sleepwalker
somnifère [sɔmnifɛʀ] nm sleeping drug no pl (ou pill)
somnoler [sɔmnɔle] vi to doze
somptueux, -euse [sɔ̃ptɥø, øz] adj sumptuous
son¹, sa [sɔ̃, sa] (pl **ses**) adj (antécédent humain: mâle) his; (: femelle) her; (: valeur indéfinie) one's, his/her; (antécédent non humain) its
son² [sɔ̃] nm sound; (de blé) bran
sondage [sɔ̃daʒ] nm: **sondage (d'opinion)** (opinion) poll
sonde [sɔ̃d] nf (Navig) lead ou sounding line; (Méd) probe; (Tech: de forage) borer, driller
sonder [sɔ̃de] vt (Navig) to sound; (Tech) to bore, drill; (fig: personne) to sound out; **~ le terrain** (fig) to test the ground
songe [sɔ̃ʒ] nm dream; **songer** vi: **songer à** (penser à) to think over; (envisager) to consider, think of; **songer que** to think that; **songeur, -euse** adj pensive
sonnant, e [sɔnɑ̃, ɑ̃t] adj: **à 8 heures ~es** on the stroke of 8
sonné, e [sɔne] adj (fam) cracked; **il est**

midi ~ it's gone twelve
sonner [sɔne] vi to ring ▷ vt (cloche) to ring; (glas, tocsin) to sound; (portier, infirmière) to ring for; **~ faux** (instrument) to sound out of tune; (rire) to ring false
sonnerie [sɔnʀi] nf (son) ringing; (sonnette) bell; (de portable) ringtone; **sonnerie d'alarme** alarm bell
sonnette [sɔnɛt] nf bell; **sonnette d'alarme** alarm bell
sonore [sɔnɔʀ] adj (voix) sonorous, ringing; (salle) resonant; (film, signal) sound cpd; **sonorisation** nf (équipement: de salle de conférences) public address system, P.A. system; (: de discothèque) sound system; **sonorité** nf (de piano, violon) tone; (d'une salle) acoustics pl
sophistiqué, e [sɔfistike] adj sophisticated
sorbet [sɔʀbɛ] nm water ice, sorbet
sorcier [sɔʀsje] nm sorcerer
sordide [sɔʀdid] adj (lieu) squalid; (action) sordid
sort [sɔʀ] nm (destinée) fate; (condition) lot; (magique) curse, spell; **tirer au ~** to draw lots
sortie [sɔʀti] nf (issue) way out, exit; (remarque drôle) sally; (promenade) outing; (le soir: au restaurant etc) night out; (Comm: d'un disque) release; (: d'un livre) publication; (: d'un modèle) launching; **où est la ~?** where's the exit?; **sortie de bain** (vêtement) bathrobe
sortilège [sɔʀtilɛʒ] nm (magic) spell
sortir [sɔʀtiʀ] vi (gén) to go out; (partir, se promener, aller au spectacle) to go out; (numéro gagnant) to come up ▷ vt (gén) to take out; (produit, modèle) to bring out; (fam: dire) to come out with; **~ avec qn** to be going out with sb; **s'en ~** (malade) to pull through;

(d'une difficulté etc) to get through; **~ de** (endroit) to go (ou come) out of, leave; (provenir de) to come from; (compétence) to be outside

sosie [sɔzi] nm double

sot, sotte [so, sɔt] adj silly, foolish ▷ nm/f fool; **sottise** nf (caractère) silliness, foolishness; (action) silly ou foolish thing

sou [su] nm: **près de ses ~s** tight-fisted; **sans le ~** penniless

soubresaut [subrəso] nm start; (cahot) jolt

souche [suʃ] nf (d'arbre) stump; (de carnet) counterfoil (BRIT), stub

souci [susi] nm (inquiétude) worry; (préoccupation) concern; (Bot) marigold; **se faire du ~** to worry; **soucier: se soucier de** vt to care about; **soucieux, -euse** adj concerned, worried

soucoupe [sukup] nf saucer; **soucoupe volante** flying saucer

soudain, e [sudɛ̃, ɛn] adj (douleur, mort) sudden ▷ adv suddenly, all of a sudden

Soudan [sudɑ̃] nm: **le ~** Sudan

soude [sud] nf soda

souder [sude] vt (avec fil à souder) to solder; (par soudure autogène) to weld; (fig) to bind together

soudure [sudyʀ] nf soldering; welding; (joint) soldered joint; weld

souffle [sufl] nm (en expirant) breath; (en soufflant) puff, blow; (respiration) breathing; (d'explosion, de ventilateur) blast; (du vent) blowing; **être à bout de ~** to be out of breath; **un ~ d'air** a breath of air

soufflé, e [sufle] adj (fam: stupéfié) staggered ▷ nm (Culin) soufflé

souffler [sufle] vi (gén) to blow; (haleter) to puff and blow ▷ vt (feu, bougie) to blow out; (chasser: poussière etc) to blow away; (Tech: verre) to blow; (dire): **~ qch à qn** to whisper sth to sb

souffrance [sufʀɑ̃s] nf suffering; **en ~** (affaire) pending

souffrant, e [sufʀɑ̃, ɑ̃t] adj unwell

souffre-douleur [sufʀədulœʀ] nm inv butt, underdog

souffrir [sufʀiʀ] vi to suffer, be in pain ▷ vt to suffer, endure; (supporter) to bear, stand; **~ de** (maladie, froid) to suffer from; **elle ne peut pas le ~** she can't stand ou bear him

soufre [sufʀ] nm sulphur

souhait [swɛ] nm wish; **tous nos ~s pour la nouvelle année** our best wishes for the New Year; **à vos ~s!** bless you!; **souhaitable** adj desirable

souhaiter [swete] vt to wish for; **~ la bonne année à qn** to wish sb a happy New Year; **~ que** to hope that

soûl, e [su, sul] adj drunk ▷ nm: **tout son ~** to one's heart's content

soulagement [sulaʒmɑ̃] nm relief

soulager [sulaʒe] vt to relieve

soûler [sule] vt: **~ qn** to get sb drunk; (suj: boisson) to make sb drunk; (fig) to make sb's head spin ou reel; **se soûler** vi to get drunk

soulever [sul(ə)ve] vt to lift; (poussière) to send up; (enthousiasme) to arouse; (question, débat) to raise; **se soulever** vi (peuple) to rise up; (personne couchée) to lift o.s. up

soulier [sulje] nm shoe

souligner [suliɲe] vt to underline; (fig) to emphasize, stress

soumettre [sumɛtʀ] vt (pays) to subject, subjugate; (rebelle) to put down, subdue; **~ qch à qn** (projet etc) to submit sth to sb; **se soumettre (à)** to submit (to)

soumis, e [sumi, iz] adj submissive; **soumission** nf submission

soupçon [supsɔ̃] nm suspicion; (petite quantité): **un ~ de** a hint ou touch of; **soupçonner** vt to suspect; **soupçonneux, -euse** adj suspicious

soupe [sup] nf soup

souper [supe] vi to have supper ▷ nm supper

soupeser [supəze] vt to weigh in one's hand(s); (fig) to weigh up

soupière [supjɛʀ] nf (soup) tureen

soupir [supiʀ] nm sigh; **pousser un**

~ de soulagement to heave a sigh of relief

soupirer [supiʀe] vi to sigh

souple [supl] adj supple; (fig: règlement, caractère) flexible; (: démarche, taille) lithe, supple; **souplesse** nf suppleness; (de caractère) flexibility

source [suʀs] nf (point d'eau) spring; (d'un cours d'eau, fig) source; **de bonne ~** on good authority

sourcil [suʀsij] nm (eye)brow; **sourciller** vi: **sans sourciller** without turning a hair ou batting an eyelid

sourd, e [suʀ, suʀd] adj deaf; (bruit) muffled; (douleur) dull ▷ nm/f deaf person; **faire la ~e oreille** to turn a deaf ear; **sourdine** nf (Mus) mute; **en sourdine** softly, quietly; **sourd-muet, sourde-muette** adj deaf-and-dumb ▷ nm/f deaf-mute

souriant, e [suʀjɑ̃, jɑ̃t] adj cheerful

sourire [suʀiʀ] nm smile ▷ vi to smile; **~ à qn** to smile at sb; (fig: plaire à) to appeal to sb; (suj: chance) to smile on sb; **garder le ~** to keep smiling

souris [suʀi] nf mouse

sournois, e [suʀnwa, waz] adj deceitful, underhand

sous [su] prép under; **~ la pluie** in the rain; **~ terre** underground; **~ peu** shortly, before long; **sous-bois** nm inv undergrowth

souscrire [suskʀiʀ]: **~ à** vt to subscribe to

sous...: sous-directeur, -trice nm/f assistant manager(-manageress); **sous-entendre** vt to imply, infer; **sous-entendu, e** adj implied ▷ nm innuendo, insinuation; **sous-estimer** vt to underestimate; **sous-jacent, e** adj underlying; **sous-louer** vt to sublet; **sous-marin, e** adj (flore, faune) submarine; (pêche) underwater ▷ nm submarine; **sous-pull** nm thin poloneck jersey; **soussigné, e** adj: **je soussigné** I the undersigned; **sous-sol** nm basement; **sous-titre** nm subtitle

soustraction [sustʀaksjɔ̃] nf subtraction

soustraire [sustʀɛʀ] vt to subtract, take away; (dérober): **~ qch à qn** to remove sth from sb; **se soustraire à** (autorité etc) to elude, escape from

sous...: sous-traitant nm subcontractor; **sous-traiter** vt to sub-contract; **sous-vêtements** nmpl underwear sg

soutane [sutan] nf cassock, soutane

soute [sut] nf hold

soutenir [sut(ə)niʀ] vt to support; (assaut, choc) to stand up to, withstand; (intérêt, effort) to keep up; (assurer): **~ que** to maintain that; **soutenu, e** adj (efforts) sustained, unflagging; (style) elevated

souterrain, e [suteʀɛ̃, ɛn] adj underground ▷ nm underground passage

soutien [sutjɛ̃] nm support; **soutien-gorge** nm bra

soutirer [sutiʀe] vt: **~ qch à qn** to squeeze ou get sth out of sb

souvenir [suv(ə)niʀ] nm (réminiscence) memory; (objet) souvenir ▷ vb: **se ~ de** to remember; **se ~ que** to remember that; **en ~ de** in memory ou remembrance of; **avec mes affectueux/meilleurs ~s, ...** with love from, .../regards, ...

souvent [suvɑ̃] adv often; **peu ~** seldom, infrequently

souverain, e [suv(ə)ʀɛ̃, ɛn] nm/f sovereign, monarch

soyeux, -euse [swajø, øz] adj silky

spacieux, -euse [spasjø, jøz] adj spacious, roomy

spaghettis [spageti] nmpl spaghetti sg

sparadrap [spaʀadʀa] nm sticking plaster (BRIT), Bandaid® (US)

spatial, e, -aux [spasjal, jo] adj (Aviat) space cpd

speaker, ine [spikœʀ, kʀin] nm/f announcer

spécial, e, -aux [spesjal, jo] adj special; (bizarre) peculiar; **spécialement** adv especially, particularly; (tout exprès) specially; **spécialiser: se spécialiser** vi to specialize; **spécialiste** nm/f specialist; **spécialité** nf speciality; (branche) special field

spécifier [spesifje] vt to specify, state

spécimen [spesimɛn] nm specimen

spectacle [spɛktakl] nm (scène) sight; (représentation) show; (industrie) show business; **spectaculaire** adj spectacular

spectateur, -trice [spɛktatœʀ, tʀis] nm/f (Cinéma etc) member of the audience; (Sport) spectator; (d'un événement) onlooker, witness

spéculer [spekyle] vi to speculate

spéléologie [speleɔlɔʒi] nf potholing

sperme [spɛʀm] nm semen, sperm

sphère [sfɛʀ] nf sphere

spirale [spiʀal] nf spiral

spirituel, le [spiʀitɥɛl] adj spiritual; (fin, piquant) witty

splendide [splɑ̃did] adj splendid

spontané, e [spɔ̃tane] adj spontaneous; **spontanéité** nf spontaneity

sport [spɔʀ] nm sport ▷ adj inv (vêtement) casual; **faire du ~** to do sport; **sports d'hiver** winter sports; **sportif, -ive** adj (journal, association, épreuve) sports cpd; (allure, démarche) athletic; (attitude, esprit) sporting

spot [spɔt] nm (lampe) spot(light); (annonce) **spot (publicitaire)** commercial (break)

square [skwaʀ] nm public garden(s)

squelette [skəlɛt] nm skeleton; **squelettique** adj scrawny

SRAS [sʀas] sigle m (= syndrome respiratoire aigu sévère) SARS

Sri Lanka [sʀilɑ̃ka] nm: **le ~** Sri Lanka

stabiliser [stabilize] vt to stabilize

stable [stabl] adj stable, steady

stade [stad] nm (Sport) stadium; (phase, niveau) stage

stage [staʒ] nm (cours) training course; **~ de formation (professionnelle)** vocational (training) course; **~ de**

perfectionnement advanced training course; **stagiaire** nm/f, adj trainee

 Attention à ne pas traduire **stage** par le mot anglais **stage**.

stagner [stagne] vi to stagnate

stand [stɑ̃d] nm (d'exposition) stand; (de foire) stall; **stand de tir** (à la foire, Sport) shooting range

standard [stɑ̃daʀ] adj inv standard ▷ nm switchboard; **standardiste** nm/f switchboard operator

standing [stɑ̃diŋ] nm standing; **de grand ~** luxury

starter [staʀtɛʀ] nm (Auto) choke

station [stasjɔ̃] nf station; (de bus) stop; (de villégiature) resort; **station de ski** ski resort; **station de taxis** taxi rank (BRIT) ou stand (US); **stationnement** nm parking; **stationner** vi to park; **station-service** nf service station

statistique [statistik] nf (science) statistics sg; (rapport, étude) statistic ▷ adj statistical

statue [staty] nf statue

statu quo [statykwo] nm status quo

statut [staty] nm status; **statuts** nmpl (Jur, Admin) statutes; **statutaire** adj statutory

Sté abr = **société**

steak [stɛk] nm steak; **~ haché** hamburger

sténo(graphie) [steno(gʀafi)] nf shorthand

stérile [steʀil] adj sterile

stérilet [steʀilɛ] nm coil, loop

stériliser [steʀilize] vt to sterilize

stimulant [stimylɑ̃] nm (fig) stimulus, incentive; (physique) stimulant

stimuler [stimyle] vt to stimulate

stipuler [stipyle] vt to stipulate

stock [stɔk] nm stock; **stocker** vt to stock

stop [stɔp] nm (Auto: écriteau) stop sign; (: feu arrière) brake-light; **faire du ~** (fam) to hitch(hike); **stopper** vt, vi to stop, halt

store [stɔʀ] nm blind; (de magasin)

shade, awning

strabisme [stʀabism] nm squinting

strapontin [stʀapɔ̃tɛ̃] nm jump ou foldaway seat

stratégie [stʀateʒi] nf strategy; **stratégique** adj strategic

stress [stʀɛs] nm stress; **stressant, e** adj stressful; **stresser** vt: **stresser qn** to make sb (feel) tense

strict, e [stʀikt] adj strict; (tenue, décor) severe, plain; **le ~ nécessaire/ minimum** the bare essentials/ minimum

strident, e [stʀidɑ̃, ɑ̃t] adj shrill, strident

strophe [stʀɔf] nf verse, stanza

structure [stʀyktyʀ] nf structure; **~s d'accueil** reception facilities

studieux, -euse [stydjø, jøz] adj studious

studio [stydjo] nm (logement) (one-roomed) flatlet (BRIT) ou apartment (US); (d'artiste, TV etc) studio

stupéfait, e [stypefɛ, ɛt] adj astonished

stupéfiant, e [stypefjɑ̃, jɑ̃t] adj (étonnant) stunning, astounding ▷ nm (Méd) drug, narcotic

stupéfier [stypefje] vt (étonner) to stun, astonish

stupeur [stypœʀ] nf astonishment

stupide [stypid] adj stupid; **stupidité** nf stupidity; (parole, acte) stupid thing (to do ou say)

style [stil] nm style

stylé, e [stile] adj well-trained

styliste [stilist] nm/f designer

stylo [stilo] nm: **~ (à encre)** (fountain) pen; **stylo (à) bille** ball-point pen

su, e [sy] pp de **savoir** ▷ nm: **au su de** with the knowledge of

suave [sɥav] adj sweet

subalterne [sybaltɛʀn] adj (employé, officier) junior; (rôle) subordinate, subsidiary ▷ nm/f subordinate

subconscient [sybkɔ̃sjɑ̃] nm subconscious

subir [sybiʀ] vt (affront, dégâts) to suffer;

(opération, châtiment) to undergo

subit, e [sybi, it] adj sudden; **subitement** adv suddenly, all of a sudden

subjectif, -ive [sybʒɛktif, iv] adj subjective

subjonctif [sybʒɔ̃ktif] nm subjunctive

subjuguer [sybʒyge] vt to captivate

submerger [sybmɛʀʒe] vt to submerge; (fig) to overwhelm

subordonné, e [sybɔʀdɔne] adj, nm/f subordinate

subrepticement [sybʀɛptismɑ̃] adv surreptitiously

subside [sybzid] nm grant

subsidiaire [sybzidjɛʀ] adj: **question ~** deciding question

subsister [sybziste] vi (rester) to remain, subsist; (survivre) to live on

substance [sypstɑ̃s] nf substance

substituer [sypstitɥe] vt: **~ qn/qch à** to substitute sb/sth for; **se ~ à qn** (évincer) to substitute o.s. for sb

substitut [sypstity] nm (succédané) substitute

subterfuge [sybtɛʀfyʒ] nm subterfuge

subtil, e [syptil] adj subtle

subvenir [sybvəniʀ]: **~ à** vt to meet

subvention [sybvɑ̃sjɔ̃] nf subsidy, grant; **subventionner** vt to subsidize

suc [syk] nm (Bot) sap; (de viande, fruit) juice

succéder [syksede]: **~ à** vt to succeed; **se succéder** vi (accidents, années) to follow one another

succès [syksɛ] nm success; **avoir du ~** to be a success, be successful; **à ~** successful; **succès de librairie** bestseller

successeur [syksesœʀ] nm successor

successif, -ive [syksesif, iv] adj successive

succession [syksesjɔ̃] nf (série, Pol) succession; (Jur: patrimoine) estate, inheritance

succomber [sykɔ̃be] vi to die, succumb; (fig): **~ à** to succumb to

succulent, e [sykylɑ̃, ɑ̃t] adj (repas,

mets) delicious

succursale [sykyʀsal] nf branch

sucer [syse] vt to suck; **sucette** nf (bonbon) lollipop; (de bébé) dummy (BRIT), pacifier (US)

sucre [sykʀ] nm (substance) sugar; (morceau) lump of sugar, sugar lump ou cube; **sucre d'orge** barley sugar; **sucre en morceaux/cristallisé/en poudre** lump/granulated/caster sugar; **sucre glace** icing sugar, confectioner's sugar (US); **sucré, e** adj (produit alimentaire) sweetened; (au goût) sweet; **sucrer** vt (thé, café) to sweeten, put sugar in; **sucreries** nfpl (bonbons) sweets, sweet things; **sucrier** nm (récipient) sugar bowl

sud [syd] nm: **le ~** the south ▷ adj inv south; (côte) south, southern; **au ~** (situation) in the south; (direction) to the south; **au ~ de** (to the) south of; **sud-africain, e** adj South African ▷ nm/f: **Sud-Africain, e** South African; **sud-américain, e** adj South American ▷ nm/f: **Sud-Américain, e** South American; **sud-est** nm, adj inv south-east; **sud-ouest** nm, adj inv south-west

Suède [sɥɛd] nf: **la ~** Sweden; **suédois, e** adj Swedish ▷ nm/f: **Suédois, e** Swede ▷ nm (Ling) Swedish

suer [sɥe] vi to sweat; (suinter) to ooze; **sueur** nf sweat; **en sueur** sweating, in a sweat; **donner des sueurs froides à qn** to put sb in(to) a cold sweat

suffire [syfiʀ] vi (être assez): **~ (à qn/ pour qch/pour faire)** to be enough ou sufficient (for sb/for sth/to do); **il suffit d'une négligence ...** it only takes one act of carelessness ...; **il suffit qu'on oublie pour que ...** one only needs to forget for ...; **ça suffit!** that's enough!

suffisamment [syfizamã] adv sufficiently, enough; **~ de** sufficient, enough

suffisant, e [syfizã, ãt] adj sufficient; (résultats) satisfactory; (vaniteux) self-important, bumptious

suffixe [syfiks] nm suffix

suffoquer [syfɔke] vt to choke, suffocate; (stupéfier) to stagger, astound ▷ vi to choke, suffocate

suffrage [syfʀaʒ] nm (Pol: voix) vote

suggérer [syɡʒeʀe] vt to suggest; **suggestion** nf suggestion

suicide [sɥisid] nm suicide; **suicider: se suicider** vi to commit suicide

suie [sɥi] nf soot

suisse [sɥis] adj Swiss ▷ nm: **S~** Swiss pl inv ▷ nf: **la S~** Switzerland; **la S~ romande/allemande** French-speaking/German-speaking Switzerland

suite [sɥit] nf (continuation: d'énumération etc) rest, remainder; (: de feuilleton) continuation; (: film: etc sur le même thème) sequel; (série) series, succession; (conséquence) result; (ordre, liaison logique) coherence; (appartement, Mus) suite; (escorte) retinue, suite; **suites** nfpl (d'une maladie etc) effects; **prendre la ~ de** (directeur etc) to succeed, take over from; **donner ~ à** (requête, projet) to follow up; **faire ~ à** to follow; **(faisant) ~ à votre lettre du ...** further to your letter of the ...; **de ~** (d'affilée) in succession; (immédiatement) at once; **par la ~** afterwards, subsequently; **à la ~** one after the other; **à la ~ de** (derrière) behind; (en conséquence de) following

suivant, e [sɥivã, ãt] adj next, following ▷ prép (selon) according to; **au ~!** next!

suivi, e [sɥivi] adj (effort, qualité) consistent; (cohérent) coherent; **très/ peu ~** (cours) well-/poorly-attended

suivre [sɥivʀ] vt (gén) to follow; (Scol: cours) to attend; (comprendre) to keep up with; (Comm: article) to continue to stock ▷ vi to follow; (élève: assimiler) to keep up; **se suivre** vi (accidents etc) to follow one after the other; **faire ~** (lettre) to forward; **"à ~"** to be continued"

sujet, te [syʒe, ɛt] adj: **être ~ à** (vertige etc) to be liable ou subject to ▷ nm/f

(*d'un souverain*) subject ▷ *nm* subject;
au ~ de about; **sujet de conversation**
topic *ou* subject of conversation;
sujet d'examen (*Scol*) examination
question

super [sypɛʀ] (*fam*) *adj inv* terrific,
great, fantastic, super

superbe [sypɛʀb] *adj* magnificent,
superb

superficie [sypɛʀfisi] *nf* (surface) area

superficiel, le [sypɛʀfisjɛl] *adj*
superficial

superflu, e [sypɛʀfly] *adj* superfluous

supérieur, e [sypeʀjœʀ] *adj* (*lèvre,
étages, classes*) upper; (*niveau,
température, niveau, enseignement*): **~ (à)**
higher (than); (*meilleur: qualité, produit*):
~ (à) superior (to); (*excellent, hautain*)
superior ▷ *nm, nf* superior; **supériorité**
nf superiority

supermarché [sypɛʀmaʀʃe] *nm*
supermarket

superposer [sypɛʀpoze] *vt* (*faire
chevaucher*) to superimpose; **lits
superposés** bunk beds

superpuissance [sypɛʀpɥisɑ̃s] *nf*
super-power

superstitieux, -euse [sypɛʀstisjø,
jøz] *adj* superstitious

superviser [sypɛʀvize] *vt* to
supervise

supplanter [syplɑ̃te] *vt* to supplant

suppléant, e [sypleɑ̃, -ɑ̃t] *adj*
(*professeur*) supply *cpd*; (*juge,
fonctionnaire*) deputy *cpd* ▷ *nm/f*
(*professeur*) supply teacher

suppléer [syplee] *vt* (*ajouter: mot
manquant etc*) to supply, provide;
(*compenser: lacune*) to fill in; **~ à** to
make up for

supplément [syplemɑ̃] *nm*
supplement; (*de frites etc*) extra portion;
un ~ de travail extra *ou* additional
work; **payer un ~** to pay an additional
charge; **le vin est en ~** wine is extra;
supplémentaire *adj* additional,
further; (*train, bus*) relief *cpd*, extra

supplications [syplikasjɔ̃] *nfpl* pleas,

entreaties

supplice [syplis] *nm* torture *no pl*

supplier [syplije] *vt* to implore,
beseech

support [sypɔʀ] *nm* support;
(*publicitaire*) medium; (*audio-visuel*)
aid

supportable [sypɔʀtabl] *adj* (*douleur*)
bearable

supporter[1] [sypɔʀtɛʀ] *nm* supporter,
fan

supporter[2] [sypɔʀte] *vt* (*conséquences,
épreuve*) to bear, endure; (*défauts,
personne*) to put up with; (*suj: chose:
chaleur etc*) to withstand; (: *personne:
chaleur, vin*) to be able to take

> Attention à ne pas traduire
> *supporter* par **to support**.

supposer [sypoze] *vt* to suppose;
(*impliquer*) to presuppose; **à ~ que**
supposing (that)

suppositoire [sypozitwaʀ] *nm*
suppository

suppression [sypʀesjɔ̃] *nf* (*voir
supprimer*) cancellation; removal;
deletion

supprimer [sypʀime] *vt* (*congés,
service d'autobus etc*) to cancel; (*emplois,
privilèges, témoin gênant*) to do away
with; (*cloison, cause, anxiété*) to remove;
(*clause, mot*) to delete

suprême [sypʀɛm] *adj* supreme

 MOT-CLÉ

sur [syʀ] *prép* **1** (*position*) on; (*par-dessus*)
over; (*au-dessus*) above; **pose-le sur
la table** put it on the table; **je n'ai
pas d'argent sur moi** I haven't any
money on me

2 (*direction*) towards; **en allant sur
Paris** going towards Paris; **sur votre
droite** on ou to your right

3 (*à propos de*) on, about; **un livre/une
conférence sur Balzac** a book/lecture
on ou about Balzac

4 (*proportion*) out of; **un sur 10** one in
10; (*Scol*) one out of 10

5 (*mesures*) by; **4 m sur 2** 4 m by 2

6 (*succession*): **avoir accident sur accident** to have one accident after the other

sûr, e [syʀ] *adj* sure, certain; (*digne de confiance*) reliable; (*sans danger*) safe; (*diagnostic, goût*) reliable; **le plus ~ est de** the safest thing is to; **sûr de soi** self-assured, self-confident

surcharge [syʀʃaʀʒ] *nf* (*de passagers, marchandises*) excess load; **surcharger** *vt* to overload

surcroît [syʀkʀwa] *nm*: **un ~ de** additional *+nom*; **par ou de ~** moreover; **en ~** in addition

surdité [syʀdite] *nf* deafness

sûrement [syʀmɑ̃] *adv* (*certainement*) certainly; (*sans risques*) safely

surenchère [syʀɑ̃ʃɛʀ] *nf* (*aux enchères*) higher bid; **surenchérir** *vi* to bid higher; (*fig*) to try and outbid each other

surestimer [syʀɛstime] *vt* to overestimate

sûreté [syʀte] *nf* (*sécurité*) safety; (*exactitude: de renseignements etc*) reliability; (*d'un geste*) steadiness; **mettre en ~** to put in a safe place; **pour plus de ~** as an extra precaution, to be on the safe side

surf [sœʀf] *nm* surfing

surface [syʀfas] *nf* surface; (*superficie*) surface area; **une grande ~** a supermarket; **faire ~** to surface; **en ~** near the surface; (*fig*) superficially

surfait, e [syʀfɛ, ɛt] *adj* overrated

surfer [syʀfe] *vi*: **~ sur Internet** to surf ou browse the Internet

surgelé, e [syʀʒəle] *adj* (deep-)frozen ▷ *nm*: **les ~s** (deep-)frozen food

surgir [syʀʒiʀ] *vi* to appear suddenly; (*fig: problème, conflit*) to arise

sur...: **surhumain, e** *adj* superhuman; **sur-le-champ** *adv* immediately; **surlendemain** *nm*: **le surlendemain (soir)** two days later (in the evening); **le surlendemain de** two days after; **surmenage** *nm* overwork(ing);

surmener: se surmener *vi* to overwork

surmonter [syʀmɔ̃te] *vt* (*vaincre*) to overcome; (*être au-dessus de*) to top

surnaturel, le [syʀnatyʀɛl] *adj, nm* supernatural

surnom [syʀnɔ̃] *nm* nickname

surnombre [syʀnɔ̃bʀ] *nm*: **être en ~** to be too many (ou one too many)

surpeuplé, e [syʀpœple] *adj* overpopulated

surplace [syʀplas] *nm*: **faire du ~** to mark time

surplomber [syʀplɔ̃be] *vt, vi* to overhang

surplus [syʀply] *nm* (*Comm*) surplus; (*reste*): **~ de bois** wood left over

surprenant, e [syʀpʀənɑ̃, ɑ̃t] *adj* amazing

surprendre [syʀpʀɑ̃dʀ] *vt* (*étonner*) to surprise; (*tomber sur: intrus etc*) to catch; (*entendre*) to overhear

surpris, e [syʀpʀi, iz] *adj*: **~ (de/que)** surprised (at/that); **surprise** *nf* surprise; **faire une surprise à qn** to give sb a surprise; **surprise-partie** *nf* party

sursaut [syʀso] *nm* start, jump; **~ de** (*énergie, indignation*) sudden fit ou burst of; **en ~** with a start; **sursauter** *vi* to (give a) start, jump

sursis [syʀsi] *nm* (*Jur: gén*) suspended sentence; (*fig*) reprieve

surtout [syʀtu] *adv* (*avant tout, d'abord*) above all; (*spécialement, particulièrement*) especially; **~, ne dites rien!** whatever you do don't say anything!; **~ pas!** certainly ou definitely not!; **~ que ...** especially as ...

surveillance [syʀvɛjɑ̃s] *nf* watch; (*Police, Mil*) surveillance; **sous ~ médicale** under medical supervision

surveillant, e [syʀvɛjɑ̃, ɑ̃t] *nm/f* (*de prison*) warder; (*Scol*) monitor

surveiller [syʀveje] *vt* (*enfant, élèves, bagages*) to watch, keep an eye on; (*prisonnier, suspect*) to keep (a) watch on; (*territoire, bâtiment*) to (keep) watch over; (travaux, cuisson) to supervise; (Scol: examen) to invigilate; **son langage/sa ligne** to watch one's language/figure

survenir [syʀvəniʀ] vi (incident, retards) to occur, arise; (événement) to take place

survêtement [syʀvɛtmɑ̃] nm tracksuit

survie [syʀvi] nf survival; **survivant, e** nm/f survivor; **survivre** vi to survive; **survivre à** (accident etc) to survive

survoler [syʀvɔle] vt to fly over; (fig: livre) to skim through

survolté, e [syʀvɔlte] adj (fig) worked up

sus [sy(s)]: **en ~ de** prép in addition to, over and above; **en ~** in addition

susceptible [syseptibl] adj touchy, sensitive; **~ de faire** (hypothèse) liable to do

susciter [sysite] vt (admiration) to arouse; (ennuis): **~ (à qn)** to create (for sb)

suspect, e [syspɛ(kt), ɛkt] adj suspicious; (témoignage, opinions) suspect ▷ nm/f suspect; **suspecter** vt to suspect; (honnêteté de qn) to question, have one's suspicions about

suspendre [syspɑ̃dʀ] vt (accrocher: vêtement): **~ qch (à)** to hang sth up (on); (interrompre, démettre) to suspend

suspendu, e [syspɑ̃dy] adj (accroché): **~ à** hanging on (ou from); (perché): **au-dessus de** suspended over

suspens [syspɑ̃]: **en ~** adv (affaire) in abeyance; **tenir en ~** to keep in suspense

suspense [syspɛns, syspɑ̃s] nm suspense

suspension [syspɑ̃sjɔ̃] nf suspension; (lustre) light fitting ou fitment

suture [sytyʀ] nf (Méd): **point de ~** stitch

svelte [svɛlt] adj slender, svelte

SVP abr (= s'il vous plaît) please

sweat [swit] nm (fam) sweatshirt

sweat-shirt [switʃœʀt] (pl **-s**) nm sweatshirt

syllabe [si(l)lab] nf syllable

symbole [sɛ̃bɔl] nm symbol; **symbolique** adj symbolic(al); (geste, offrande) token cpd; **symboliser** vt to symbolize

symétrique [simetʀik] adj symmetrical

sympa [sɛ̃pa] (fam) adj inv nice; **sois ~, prête-le moi** be a pal and lend it to me

sympathie [sɛ̃pati] nf (inclination) liking; (affinité) friendship; (condoléances) sympathy; **j'ai beaucoup de ~ pour lui** I like him a lot; **sympathique** adj nice, friendly

⚠ Attention à ne pas traduire *sympathique* par *sympathetic*.

sympathisant, e [sɛ̃patizɑ̃, ɑ̃t] nm/f sympathizer

sympathiser [sɛ̃patize] vi (voisins etc: s'entendre) to get on (BRIT) ou along (US) (well)

symphonie [sɛ̃fɔni] nf symphony

symptôme [sɛ̃ptom] nm symptom

synagogue [sinagɔg] nf synagogue

syncope [sɛ̃kɔp] nf (Méd): blackout; **tomber en ~** to faint, pass out

syndic [sɛ̃dik] nm (d'immeuble) managing agent

syndical, e, -aux [sɛ̃dikal, o] adj (trade) union cpd; **syndicaliste** nm/f trade unionist

syndicat [sɛ̃dika] nm (d'ouvriers, employés) (trade) union; **syndicat d'initiative** tourist office; **syndiqué, e** adj belonging to a (trade) union; **syndiquer: se syndiquer** vi to form a trade union; (adhérer) to join a trade union

synonyme [sinɔnim] adj synonymous ▷ nm synonym; **~ de** synonymous with

syntaxe [sɛ̃taks] nf syntax

synthèse [sɛ̃tɛz] nf synthesis

synthétique [sɛ̃tetik] adj synthetic

Syrie [siʀi] nf: **la ~** Syria

systématique [sistematik] adj systematic

système [sistɛm] nm system; **le ~ D** resourcefulness

t

t' [t] pron voir **te**

ta [ta] adj voir **ton'**

tabac [taba] nm tobacco; (magasin) tobacconist's (shop)

tabagisme [tabaʒism] nm: **tabagisme passif** passive smoking

table [tabl] nf (table; **à ~!** dinner etc is ready!; **se mettre à ~** to sit down to eat; **mettre la ~** to lay the table; **une ~ pour 4, s'il vous plaît** a table for 4, please; **table à repasser** ironing board; **table de cuisson** hob; **table de nuit** ou **de chevet** bedside table; **table des matières** (table of) contents pl; **table d'orientation** viewpoint indicator; **table roulante** trolley (BRIT), tea wagon (US)

tableau, x [tablo] nm (peinture) painting; (reproduction, fig) picture; (panneau) board; (schéma) table, chart; **tableau d'affichage** notice board; **tableau de bord** dashboard; (Aviat) instrument panel; **tableau noir** blackboard

tablette [tablɛt] nf (planche) shelf; **tablette de chocolat** bar of chocolate

tablier [tablije] nm apron

tabou [tabu] nm taboo

tabouret [taburɛ] nm stool

tac [tak] nm: **il m'a répondu du ~ au ~** he answered me right back

tache [taʃ] nf (saleté) stain, mark; (Art, de couleur, lumière) spot; **tache de rousseur** freckle

tâche [taʃ] nf task

tacher [taʃe] vt to stain, mark

tâcher [taʃe] vi: **~ de faire** to try ou endeavour to do

tacheté, e [taʃte] adj spotted

tact [takt] nm tact; **avoir du ~** to be tactful

tactique [taktik] adj tactical ▷ nf (technique) tactics sg; (plan) tactic

taie [tɛ] nf: **~ (d'oreiller)** pillowslip, pillowcase

taille [taj] nf cutting; (d'arbre etc) pruning; (milieu du corps) waist; (hauteur) height; (grandeur) size; **de ~ à faire** capable of doing; **de ~** sizeable; **taille-crayon(s)** nm pencil sharpener

tailler [taje] vt (pierre, diamant) to cut; (arbre, plante) to prune; (vêtement) to cut out; (crayon) to sharpen

tailleur [tajœʀ] nm (couturier) tailor; (vêtement) suit; **en ~** (assis) cross-legged

taillis [taji] nm copse

taire [tɛʀ] vi: **faire ~ qn** to make sb be quiet; **se taire** vi to be silent ou quiet; **taisez-vous!** be quiet!

Taïwan [tajwan] nf Taiwan

talc [talk] nm talc, talcum powder

talent [talã] nm talent

talkie-walkie [tokiwoki] nm walkie-talkie

talon [talɔ̃] nm heel; (de chèque, billet) stub, counterfoil (BRIT); **talons plats/ aiguilles** flat/stiletto heels

talus [taly] nm embankment

tambour [tɑ̃buʀ] nm (Mus, aussi Tech) drum; (musicien) drummer; (porte) revolving door(s pl); **tambourin** nm tambourine

Tamise[tamiz] nf: **la ~** the Thames

tamisé, e[tamize] adj (fig) subdued, soft

tampon[tɑ̃pɔ̃] nm (de coton, d'ouate) wad, pad; (amortisseur) buffer; (bouchon) plug, stopper; (cachet, timbre) stamp; (mémoire) ~ (Inform) buffer; **tampon (hygiénique)** tampon; **tamponner** vt (timbres) to stamp; (heurter) to crash ou ram into; **tamponneuse** adj f: **autos tamponneuses** dodgems

tandem[tɑ̃dɛm] nm tandem

tandis[tɑ̃di]: **~ que** conj while

tanguer[tɑ̃ge] vi to pitch (and toss)

tant[tɑ̃] adv so much; **~ de** (sable, eau) so much; (gens, livres) so many; **~ que** as long as; (autant que) as much as; **~ mieux** that's great; (avec une certaine réserve) so much the better; **~ pis** too bad; (conciliant) never mind; **~ bien que mal** as well as can be expected

tante[tɑ̃t] nf aunt

tantôt[tɑ̃to] adv (parfois): **~ ... ~** now ... now; (cet après-midi) this afternoon

taon[tɑ̃] nm horsefly

tapage[tapaʒ] nm uproar, din

tapageur, -euse[tapaʒœr, øz] adj noisy; (voyant) loud, flashy

tape[tap] nf slap

tape-à-l'œil[tapalœj] adj inv flashy, showy

taper[tape] vt (porte) to bang, slam; (enfant) to slap; (dactylographier) to type (out); (fam: emprunter): **~ qn de 10 euros** to touch sb for 10 euros ▷ vi (soleil) to beat down; **se taper** vt (repas) to put away; (fam: corvée) to get landed with; **~ sur qn** to thump sb; (fig) to run sb down; **~ sur un clou** to hit a nail; **~ sur la table** to bang on the table; **~ à** (porte etc) to knock on; **~ dans** (se servir) to dig into; **~ des mains/pieds** to clap one's hands/stamp one's feet; **~ (à la machine)** to type

tapi, e[tapi] adj (blotti) crouching; (caché) hidden away

tapis[tapi] nm carpet; (petit) rug; **tapis de sol** (de tente) groundsheet;

tapis de souris (Inform) mouse mat; **tapis roulant** (pour piétons) moving walkway; (pour bagages) carousel

tapisser[tapise] vt (avec du papier peint) to paper; (recouvrir): **~ qch (de)** to cover sth (with); **tapisserie** nf (tenture, broderie) tapestry; (papier peint) wallpaper; **tapissier-décorateur** nm interior decorator

tapoter[tapote] vt (joue, main) to pat; (objet) to tap

taquiner[takine] vt to tease

tard[tar] adv late; **plus ~** later (on); **au plus ~** at the latest; **sur le ~** late in life; **il est trop ~** it's too late

tarder[tarde] vi (chose) to be a long time coming; (personne): **~ à faire** to delay doing; **il me tarde d'être** I am longing to be; **sans (plus) ~** without (further) delay

tardif, -ive[tardif, iv] adj late

tarif[tarif] nm: **~ des consommations** price list; **~s postaux/douaniers** postal/customs rates; **~ des taxis** taxi fares; **~ plein/réduit** (train) full/reduced fare; (téléphone) peak/off-peak rate

tarir[tarir] vi to dry up, run dry

tarte[tart] nf tart; **~ aux fraises** strawberry tart; **~ Tatin** apple upside-down tart

tartine[tartin] nf slice of bread; **tartine de miel** slice of bread and honey; **tartiner** vt to spread; **fromage à tartiner** cheese spread

tartre[tartr] nm (des dents) tartar; (de bouilloire) fur, scale

tas[tɑ] nm heap, pile; (fig): **un ~ de** heaps of, lots of; **en ~** in a heap ou pile; **formé sur le ~** trained on the job

tasse[tɑs] nf cup; **tasse à café** coffee cup

tassé, e[tase] adj: **bien ~** (café etc) strong

tasser[tase] vt (terre, neige) to pack down; (entasser): **~ qch dans** to cram sth into; **se tasser** vi (se serrer) to squeeze up; (s'affaisser) to settle; (fig) to settle down

tâter [tate] vt to feel; (fig) to try out; **se tâter** (hésiter) to be in two minds; **~ de** (prison etc) to have a taste of

tatillon, ne [tatijɔ̃, ɔn] adj pernickety

tâtonnement [tɑtɔnmɑ̃] nm: **par ~s** (fig) by trial and error

tâtonner [tɑtɔne] vi to grope one's way along

tâtons [tɑtɔ̃]: **à ~** adv: **chercher/ avancer à ~** to grope around for/grope one's way forward

tatouage [tatwaʒ] nm tattoo

tatouer [tatwe] vt to tattoo

taudis [todi] nm hovel, slum

taule [tol] (fam) nf nick (fam), prison

taupe [top] nf mole

taureau, x [tɔʀo] nm bull; (signe): **le T~** Taurus

taux [to] nm rate; (d'alcool) level; **taux d'intérêt** interest rate

taxe [taks] nf tax; (douanière) duty; **toutes ~s comprises** inclusive of tax; **la boutique hors ~s** the duty-free shop; **taxe à la valeur ajoutée** value-added tax; **taxe de séjour** tourist tax

taxer [takse] vt (personne) to tax; (produit) to put a tax on, tax

taxi [taksi] nm taxi; (chauffeur: fam) taxi driver; **pouvez-vous m'appeler un ~, s'il vous plaît?** can you call me a taxi, please?

Tchécoslovaquie [tʃekɔslɔvaki] nf Czechoslovakia; **tchèque** adj Czech ▷ nm/f: **Tchèque** Czech ▷ nm (Ling) Czech; **la République tchèque** the Czech Republic

Tchétchénie [tʃetʃeni] nf: **la ~** Chechnya

te, t' [tə] pron you; (réfléchi) yourself

technicien, ne [tɛknisjɛ̃, jɛn] nm/f technician

technico-commercial, e, -aux [tɛknikɔkɔmɛʀsjal, jo] adj: **agent ~** sales technician

technique [tɛknik] adj technical ▷ nf technique; **techniquement** adv technically

techno [tɛkno] nf (Mus) techno (music)

technologie [tɛknɔlɔʒi] nf technology; **technologique** adj technological

teck [tɛk] nm teak

tee-shirt [tiʃœʀt] nm T-shirt, tee-shirt

teindre [tɛ̃dʀ] vt to dye; **se ~ les cheveux** to dye one's hair; **teint, e** adj dyed ▷ nm (du visage) complexion; (momentané) colour ▷ nf shade; **grand teint** colourfast

teinté, e [tɛ̃te] adj: **~ de** (fig) tinged with

teinter [tɛ̃te] vt (verre, papier) to tint; (bois) to stain

teinture [tɛ̃tyʀ] nf dye; **teinture d'iode** tincture of iodine; **teinturerie** nf dry cleaner's; **teinturier** nm dry cleaner

tel, telle [tɛl] adj (pareil) such; (comme): **~ un/des** like a/like ...; (indéfini) such and such a; (intensif): **un ~/de ~s ...** such (a)/such ...; **rien de ~** nothing like it; **~ que** like, such as; **~ quel** as it is ou stands (ou comme etc); **venez ~ jour** come on such-and-such a day

télé [tele] (fam) nf TV; **à la ~** on TV ou telly

télé...: **télécabine** nf (benne) cable car; **télécarte** nf phonecard; **téléchargeable** adj downloadable; **téléchargement** (action) downloading; (fichier) download; **télécharger** vt to download; **télécommande** nf remote control; **télécopieur** nm fax machine; **télédistribution** nf cable TV; **télégramme** nm telegram; **télégraphier** vt to telegraph, cable; **téléguider** vt to radio-control; **télématique** nf telematics sg; **téléobjectif** nm telephoto lens sg; **télépathie** nf telepathy; **téléphérique** nm cable car

téléphone [telefɔn] nm telephone; **avoir le ~** to be on the (tele)phone; **au ~** on the phone; **téléphoner** vi to make a phone call; **téléphoner à** to phone,

call up; **est-ce que je peux téléphoner d'ici?** can I make a call from here?; **téléphonique** adj (tele)phone cpd
télé... téléréalité nf reality TV
télescope [teleskɔp] nm telescope
télescoper [teleskɔpe] vt to smash up; **se télescoper** (véhicules) to concertina
télé... téléscripteur nm teleprinter; **télésiège** nm chairlift; **téléski** nm ski-tow; **téléspectateur, -trice** nm/f (television) viewer; **télétravail** nm telecommuting; **télévente** nf telesales; **téléviseur** nm television set; **télévision** nf television; **à la télévision** on television; **télévision numérique** digital TV; **télévision par câble/satellite** cable/satellite television
télex [teleks] nm telex
telle [tel] adj voir **tel**; **tellement** adv (tant) so much; (si) so; **tellement de** (sable, eau) so much; (gens, livres) so many; **il s'est endormi tellement il était fatigué** he was so tired (that) he fell asleep; **pas tellement** not (all) that much; not (all) that +adjectif
téméraire [temerɛr] adj reckless, rash
témoignage [temwaɲaʒ] nm (Jur: déclaration) testimony no pl, evidence no pl; (rapport, récit) account; (fig: d'affection etc: cadeau) token, mark; (: geste) gesture
témoigner [temwaɲe] vt (intérêt, gratitude) to show ▷ vi (Jur) to testify, give evidence; **~ de** to bear witness to, to testify to
témoin [temwɛ̃] nm witness ▷ adj: **appartement ~** show flat (BRIT); **être ~ de** to witness; **témoin oculaire** eyewitness
tempe [tɑ̃p] nf temple
tempérament [tɑ̃peramɑ̃] nm temperament, disposition; **à ~** (vente) on deferred (payment) terms; (achat) by instalments, hire purchase cpd
température [tɑ̃peratyr] nf temperature; **avoir** ou **faire de la ~** to be running ou have a temperature

tempête [tɑ̃pɛt] nf storm; **tempête de sable/neige** sand/snowstorm
temple [tɑ̃pl] nm temple; (protestant) church
temporaire [tɑ̃pɔrɛr] adj temporary
temps [tɑ̃] nm (atmosphérique) weather; (durée) time; (époque) time, times pl; (Ling) tense; (Mus) beat; (Tech) stroke; **un ~ de chien** (fam) rotten weather; **quel ~ fait-il?** what's the weather like?; **il fait beau/mauvais ~** the weather is fine/bad; **avoir le ~/tout son ~** to have time/plenty of time; **en ~ de paix/guerre** in peacetime/wartime; **en ~ utile** ou **voulu** in due time ou course; **ces derniers ~** lately; **dans quelque ~** in a (little) while; **de ~ en ~, de ~ à autre** from time to time; **à ~** (partir, arriver) in time; **à ~ complet, à plein ~** full-time; **à ~ partiel, à mi-~** part-time; **dans le ~** at one time; **temps d'arrêt** pause, halt; **temps libre** free ou spare time; **temps mort** (Comm) slack period
tenable [t(ə)nabl] adj bearable
tenace [tənas] adj persistent
tenant, e [tənɑ̃, ɑ̃t] nm/f (Sport): **~ du titre** title-holder
tendance [tɑ̃dɑ̃s] nf tendency; (opinions) leanings pl, sympathies pl; (évolution) trend; **avoir ~ à** to have a tendency to, tend to
tendeur [tɑ̃dœr] nm (attache) elastic strap
tendre [tɑ̃dr] adj tender; (bois, roche, couleur) soft ▷ vt (élastique, peau) to stretch; (corde) to tighten; (muscle) to tense; (fig: piège) to set, lay; (donner): **~ qch à qn** to hold sth out to sb; (offrir) to offer sb sth; **se tendre** vi (corde) to tighten; (relations) to become strained; **~ à qch/à faire** to tend towards sth/to do; **~ l'oreille** to prick up one's ears; **~ la main/le bras** to hold out one's hand/stretch out one's arm; **tendrement** adv tenderly; **tendresse** nf tenderness
tendu, e [tɑ̃dy] pp de **tendre** ▷ adj (corde) tight; (muscles) tensed; (relations) strained

ténèbres [tenɛbʀ] *nfpl* darkness *sg*

teneur [tənœʀ] *nf* content; (*d'une lettre*) terms *pl*, content

tenir [t(ə)niʀ] *vt* to hold; (*magasin, hôtel*) to run; (*promesse*) to keep ▷ *vi* to hold; (*neige, gel*) to last; **se tenir** *vi* (*avoir lieu*) to be held, take place; (*être: personne*) to stand; **~ à** (*personne, objet*) to be attached to; (*réputation*) to care about; **~ à faire** to be determined to do; **~ de** (*ressembler à*) to take after; **ça ne tient qu'à lui** it is entirely up to him; **~ qn pour** to regard sb as; **~ qch de qn** (*histoire*) to have heard *ou* learnt sth from sb; (*qualité, défaut*) to have inherited *ou* got sth from sb; **~ dans** to fit into; **~ compte de qch** to take sth into account; **~ les comptes** to keep the books; **~ bon** to stand fast; **~ le coup** to hold out; **~ au chaud** (*café, plat*) to keep hot; **un manteau qui tient chaud** a warm coat; **tiens/tenez, voilà le stylo** there's the pen!; **tiens, voilà Alain!** look, here's Alain!; **tiens?** (*surprise*) really?; **se ~ droit** to stand (*ou* sit) up straight; **bien se ~** to behave well; **se ~ à qch** to hold on to sth; **s'en ~ à qch** to confine o.s. to sth

tennis [tenis] *nm* tennis; (*court*) tennis court ▷ *nm ou fpl* (*aussi:* **chaussures de ~**) tennis *ou* gym shoes; **tennis de table** table tennis; **tennisman** *nm* tennis player

tension [tɑ̃sjɔ̃] *nf* tension; (*Méd*) blood pressure; **avoir de la ~** to have high blood pressure

tentation [tɑ̃tasjɔ̃] *nf* temptation

tentative [tɑ̃tativ] *nf* attempt

tente [tɑ̃t] *nf* tent

tenter [tɑ̃te] *vt* (*éprouver, attirer*) to tempt; (*essayer*): **~ qch/de faire** to attempt *ou* try sth/to do; **~ sa chance** to try one's luck

tenture [tɑ̃tyʀ] *nf* hanging

tenu, e [t(ə)ny] *pp de* **tenir** ▷ *adj* (*maison, comptes*): **bien ~** well-kept; (*obligé*): **~ de faire** obliged to do ▷ *nf* (*vêtements*) clothes *pl*; (*comportement*)

(good) manners *pl*, good behaviour; (*d'une maison*) upkeep; **en petite ~e** scantily dressed *ou* clad

ter [tɛʀ] *adj*: **16** *~* **16b** *ou* B

terme [tɛʀm] *nm* term; (*fin*) end; **à court/long ~** *adj* short-/long-term ▷ *adv* in the short/long term; **avant ~** (*Méd*) prematurely; **mettre un ~ à** to put an end *ou* a stop to; **en bons ~s** on good terms

terminaison [tɛʀminɛzɔ̃] *nf* (*Ling*) ending

terminal, -aux [tɛʀminal, o] *nm* terminal; **terminale** *nf* (*Scol*) = year 13 (*BRIT*) = twelfth grade (*US*)

terminer [tɛʀmine] *vt* to finish; **se terminer** *vi* to end; **quand est-ce que le spectacle se termine?** when does the show finish?

terne [tɛʀn] *adj* dull

ternir [tɛʀniʀ] *vt* to dull; (*fig*) to sully, tarnish; **se ternir** *vi* to become dull

terrain [teʀɛ̃] *nm* (*sol, fig*) ground; (*Comm: étendue de terre*) land *no pl*; (*parcelle*) plot (of land); (*à bâtir*) site; **sur le ~** (*fig*) on the field; **terrain d'aviation** airfield; **terrain de camping** campsite; **terrain de football/rugby** football/ rugby pitch (*BRIT*) *ou* field (*US*); **terrain de golf** golf course; **terrain de jeu** games field; (*pour les petits*) playground; **terrain de sport** sports ground; **terrain vague** waste ground *no pl*

terrasse [teʀas] *nf* terrace; **à la ~** (*café*) outside; **terrasser** *vt* (*adversaire*) to floor; (*suj: maladie etc*) to strike down

terre [tɛʀ] *nf* (*gén, aussi Élec*) earth; (*substance*) soil, earth; (*opposé à mer*) land *no pl*; (*contrée*) land; **terres** *nfpl* (*terrains*) lands, land *sg*; **en ~** (*pipe, poterie*) clay *cpd*; **à ~** *ou* **par ~** (*mettre, être, s'asseoir*) on the ground (*ou* floor); (*jeter, tomber*) to the ground, down; **terre à terre** *adj inv* (*considération, personne*) down-to-earth; **terre cuite** terracotta; **la terre ferme** dry land; **terre glaise** clay

terreau [teʀo] *nm* compost

terre-plein [tɛʀplɛ̃] *nm* platform; (*sur chaussée*) central reservation

terrestre [tɛʀɛstʀ] *adj* (*surface*) earth's, of the earth; (*Bot, Zool, Mil*) land *cpd*; (*Rel*) earthly

terreur [tɛʀœʀ] *nf* terror no *pl*

terrible [tɛʀibl] *adj* terrible, dreadful; (*fam*) terrific; **pas ~** nothing special

terrien, ne [tɛʀjɛ̃, jɛn] *adj*: **propriétaire ~** landowner ▷ *nm/f* (*non martien etc*) earthling

terrier [tɛʀje] *nm* burrow, hole; (*chien*) terrier

terrifier [tɛʀifje] *vt* to terrify

terrine [tɛʀin] *nf* (*récipient*) terrine; (*Culin*) pâté

territoire [tɛʀitwaʀ] *nm* territory

terroriser [tɛʀɔʀize] *vt* to terrorize

terrorisme [tɛʀɔʀism] *nm* terrorism; **terroriste** *nm/f* terrorist

tertiaire [tɛʀsjɛʀ] *adj* tertiary ▷ *nm* (*Écon*) service industries *pl*

tes [te] *adj voir* **ton**

test [tɛst] *nm* test

testament [tɛstamɑ̃] *nm* (*Jur*) will; (*Rel*) Testament; (*fig*) legacy

tester [tɛste] *vt* to test

testicule [tɛstikyl] *nm* testicle

tétanos [tetanɔs] *nm* tetanus

têtard [tɛtaʀ] *nm* tadpole

tête [tɛt] *nf* head; (*cheveux*) hair no *pl*; (*visage*) face; **de ~** (*comme adj: wagon etc*) front *cpd*; (*comme adj: calculer*) in one's head, mentally; **perdre la ~** (*fig: s'affoler*) to lose one's head; (: *devenir fou*) to go off one's head; **tenir ~ à qn** to stand up to sb; **la ~ en bas** with one's head down; **la ~ la première** (*tomber*) headfirst; **faire une ~** (*Football*) to head the ball; **faire la ~** (*fig*) to sulk; **en ~** at the front; (*Sport*) in the lead; **à la ~ de** at the head of; **à ~ reposée** in a more leisurely moment; **n'en faire qu'à sa ~** to do as one pleases; **en avoir par-dessus la ~** to be fed up; **en ~ à ~** in private, alone together; **de la ~ aux pieds** from head to toe; **tête de lecture** (playback) head; **tête de liste** (*Pol*) chief candidate; **tête**

de mort skull and crossbones; **tête de série** (*Tennis*) seeded player, seed; **tête de Turc** (*fig*) whipping boy (BRIT); butt; **tête-à-queue** *nm inv*: **faire une tête-à-queue** to spin round

téter [tete] *vt*: **~ (sa mère)** to suck at one's mother's breast, feed

tétine [tetin] *nf* teat; (*sucette*) dummy (BRIT), pacifier (US)

têtu, e [tety] *adj* stubborn, pigheaded

texte [tɛkst] *nm* text; (*morceau choisi*) passage

textile [tɛkstil] *adj* textile *cpd* ▷ *nm* textile; **le ~** the textile industry

Texto® [tɛksto] *nm* text message

texture [tɛkstyʀ] *nf* texture

TGV *sigle m* (= *train à grande vitesse*) high-speed train

thaïlandais, e [tajlɑ̃dɛ, ɛz] *adj* Thai ▷ *nm/f*: **T~,** e Thai

Thaïlande [tajlɑ̃d] *nf* Thailand

thé [te] *nm* tea; **~ au citron** lemon tea; **~ au lait** tea with milk; **prendre le ~** to have tea; **faire le ~** to make the tea

théâtral, e, -aux [teatʀal, o] *adj* theatrical

théâtre [teatʀ] *nm* theatre; (*péj: simulation*) playacting; (*site: lieu*): **le ~ de** the scene of; **faire du ~** to act

théière [tejɛʀ] *nf* teapot

thème [tɛm] *nm* theme; (*Scol: traduction*) prose (composition)

théologie [teɔlɔʒi] *nf* theology

théorie [teɔʀi] *nf* theory; **théorique** *adj* theoretical

thérapie [teʀapi] *nf* therapy

thermal, e, -aux [tɛʀmal, o] *adj*: **station ~e** spa; **cure ~e** water cure

thermomètre [tɛʀmɔmɛtʀ] *nm* thermometer

thermos® [tɛʀmos] *nm ou nf*: **(bouteille) thermos** vacuum ou Thermos® flask

thermostat [tɛʀmɔsta] *nm* thermostat

thèse [tɛz] *nf* thesis

thon [tɔ̃] *nm* tuna (fish)

thym [tɛ̃] *nm* thyme

Tibet [tibɛ] nm: **le ~** Tibet

tibia [tibja] nm shinbone, tibia; (partie antérieure de la jambe) shin

TIC sigle fpl (= technologies de l'information et de la communication) ICT sg

tic [tik] nm tic, (nervous) twitch; (de langage etc) mannerism

ticket [tikɛ] nm ticket; **ticket de caisse** receipt; **je peux avoir un ticket de caisse, s'il vous plaît?** can I have a receipt, please?

tiède [tjɛd] adj lukewarm; (vent, air) mild, warm; **tiédir** vi to cool; (se réchauffer) to grow warmer

tien, ne [tjɛ̃, tjɛn] pron: **le(la) ~(ne)**, **les ~(ne)s** yours; **à la ~ne!** cheers!

tiens [tjɛ̃] vb, excl voir **tenir**

tiercé [tjɛrse] nm system of forecast betting giving first 3 horses

tiers, tierce [tjɛr, tjɛrs] adj third ▷ nm (Jur) third party; (fraction) third; **le tiers monde** the Third World

tige [tiʒ] nf stem; (baguette) rod

tignasse [tiɲas] (péj) nf mop of hair

tigre [tigr] nm tiger; **tigré, e** adj (rayé) striped; (tacheté) spotted; (chat) tabby; **tigresse** nf tigress

tilleul [tijœl] nm lime (tree), linden (tree); (boisson) lime-blossom) tea

timbre [tɛ̃br] nm (tampon) stamp; (aussi: **~-poste**) (postage) stamp; (Mus: de voix, instrument) timbre, tone

timbré, e [tɛ̃bre] (fam) adj cracked

timide [timid] adj shy; (timoré) timid; **timidement** adv shyly; timidly; **timidité** nf shyness; timidity

tintamarre [tɛ̃tamar] nm din, uproar

tinter [tɛ̃te] vi to ring, chime; (argent, clefs) to jingle

tique [tik] nf (parasite) tick

tir [tir] nm (sport) shooting; (fait ou manière de tirer) firing ou (of a rifle); (rafale) fire; (stand) shooting gallery; **tir à l'arc** archery

tirage [tiraʒ] nm (action) printing; (Photo) print; (de journal) circulation; (de livre: nombre d'exemplaires) (print) run; (: édition) edition; (de loterie) draw; **par ~**

au sort by drawing lots

tire [tir] nf: **vol à la ~** pickpocketing

tiré, e [tire] adj (traits) drawn; **~ par les cheveux** far-fetched

tire-bouchon [tirbuʃɔ̃] nm corkscrew

tirelire [tirlir] nf moneybox

tirer [tire] vt (gén) to pull; (trait, rideau, carte, conclusion, chèque) to draw; (langue) to stick out; (en faisant feu: balle, coup) to fire; (: animal) to shoot; (journal, livre, photo) to print; (Football: corner etc) to take ▷ vi (faire feu) to fire; (faire du tir, Football) to shoot; **~ sur** (corde) to pull at; (faire feu sur) to shoot at ou fire at; (pipe) to draw on; (approcher de: couleur) to verge ou border on; **~ à l'arc/la carabine** to shoot with a bow and arrow/with a rifle; **~ à sa fin** to be drawing to a close; **~ qch au clair** to clear sth up; **~ au sort** to draw lots; **~ parti de** to take advantage of; **~ profit de** to profit from; **~ les cartes** to read ou tell the cards

tiret [tirɛ] nm dash

tireur [tirœr] nm gunman; **tireur d'élite** marksman

tiroir [tirwar] nm drawer; **tiroir-caisse** nm till

tisane [tizan] nf herb tea

tisser [tise] vt to weave

tissu [tisy] nm fabric, material, cloth no pl; (Anat, Bio) tissue; **tissu-éponge** nm (terry) towelling no pl

titre [titr] nm (gén) title; (de journal) headline; (diplôme) qualification; (Comm) security; **en ~** (champion) official; **à juste ~** rightly; **à quel ~?** on what grounds?; **à aucun ~** on no account; **au même ~ (que)** in the same way (as); **à ~ d'information** for (your) information; **à ~ gracieux** free of charge; **à ~ d'essai** on a trial basis; **à ~ privé** in a private capacity;

titre de propriété title deed; **titre de transport** ticket

tituber [titybe] vi to stagger (along)

titulaire [titylɛʀ] adj (Admin) with tenure ▷ nm/f (de permis) holder; **être ~ de** (diplôme, permis) to hold

toast [tost] nm slice ou piece of toast; (de bienvenue) (welcoming) toast; **porter un ~ à qn** to propose ou drink a toast to sb

toboggan [tɔbɔgɑ̃] nm slide; (Auto) flyover

toc [tɔk] excl: **~, ~** knock knock ▷ nm: **en ~** fake

tocsin [tɔksɛ̃] nm alarm (bell)

tohu-bohu [tɔybɔy] nm hubbub

toi [twa] pron you

toile [twal] nf (tableau) canvas; **de ou en ~** (pantalon) cotton; (sac) canvas; **la T~** (Internet) the Web; **toile cirée** oilcloth; **toile d'araignée** cobweb; **toile de fond** (fig) backdrop

toilette [twalɛt] nf (habits) outfit; **toilettes** nfpl (w.-c.) toilet sg; **faire sa ~** to have a wash, get washed; **articles de ~** toiletries; **où sont les ~s?** where's the toilet?

toi-même [twamɛm] pron yourself

toit [twa] nm roof; **toit ouvrant** sunroof

toiture [twatyʀ] nf roof

Tokyo [tɔkjo] n Tokyo

tôle [tol] nf (plaque) steel ou iron sheet; **tôle ondulée** corrugated iron

tolérable [tɔleʀabl] adj tolerable

tolérant, e [tɔleʀɑ̃, ɑ̃t] adj tolerant

tolérer [tɔleʀe] vt to tolerate; (Admin: hors taxe etc) to allow

tollé [tɔ(l)le] nm outcry

tomate [tɔmat] nf tomato; **~s farcies** stuffed tomatoes

tombe [tɔ̃b] nf (sépulture) grave; (avec monument) tomb

tombeau, x [tɔ̃bo] nm tomb

tombée [tɔ̃be] nf: **à la ~ de la nuit** ou **du jour** at nightfall

tomber [tɔ̃be] vi to fall; (fièvre, vent) to drop; **laisser ~** (objet) to drop;

(personne) to let down; (activité) to give up; **laisse ~!** forget it!; **faire ~** to knock over; **~ sur** (rencontrer) to bump into; **~ de fatigue/sommeil** to drop from exhaustion/be falling asleep on one's feet; **ça tombe bien** that's come at the right time; **il est bien tombé** he's been lucky; **à l'eau** (projet) to fall through; **~ en panne** to break down

tombola [tɔ̃bɔla] nf raffle

tome [tom] nm volume

ton¹, ta [tɔ̃, ta] (pl **tes**) adj your

ton² [tɔ̃] nm (gén) tone; (couleur) shade, tone; **de bon ~** in good taste

tonalité [tɔnalite] nf (au téléphone) dialling tone

tondeuse [tɔ̃døz] nf (à gazon) (lawn)mower; (du coiffeur) clippers pl; (pour les moutons) shears pl

tondre [tɔ̃dʀ] vt (pelouse, herbe) to mow; (haie) to cut, clip; (mouton, toison) to shear; (cheveux) to crop

tongs [tɔ̃g] nfpl flip-flops

tonifier [tɔnifje] vt (peau, organisme) to tone up

tonique [tɔnik] adj fortifying ▷ nm tonic

tonne [tɔn] nf metric ton, tonne

tonneau, x [tɔno] nm (à vin, cidre) barrel; **faire des ~x** (voiture, avion) to roll over

tonnelle [tɔnɛl] nf bower, arbour

tonner [tɔne] vi to thunder; **il tonne** it is thundering, there's some thunder

tonnerre [tɔnɛʀ] nm thunder

tonus [tɔnys] nm energy

top [tɔp] nm: **au 3ème ~** at the 3rd stroke ▷ adj: **~ secret** top secret

topinambour [tɔpinɑ̃buʀ] nm Jerusalem artichoke

torche [tɔʀʃ] nf torch

torchon [tɔʀʃɔ̃] nm cloth; (à vaisselle) tea towel ou cloth

tordre [tɔʀdʀ] vt (chiffon) to wring; (barre, fig: visage) to twist; **se tordre** vi: **se ~ le poignet/la cheville** to twist one's wrist/ankle; **se ~ de douleur/rire** to be doubled up with pain/laughter;

tordu, e [tɔʀdy] *adj* bent; (*fig*) crazy

tornade [tɔʀnad] *nf* tornado

torrent [tɔʀɑ̃] *nm* mountain stream

torsade [tɔʀsad] *nf*: **un pull à ~s** a cable sweater

torse [tɔʀs] *nm* chest; (*Anat, Sculpture*) torso; **~ nu** stripped to the waist

tort [tɔʀ] *nm* (*défaut*) fault; **torts** *nmpl* (*Jur*) fault *sg*; **avoir ~** to be wrong; **être dans son ~** to be in the wrong; **donner ~ à qn** to lay the blame on sb; **causer du ~ à qn** to harm sb; **à ~** wrongly; **à ~ et à travers** wildly

torticolis [tɔʀtikɔli] *nm* stiff neck

tortiller [tɔʀtije] *vt* to twist; (*moustache*) to twirl; **se tortiller** *vi* to wriggle; (*en dansant*) to wiggle

tortionnaire [tɔʀsjɔnɛʀ] *nm* torturer

tortue [tɔʀty] *nf* tortoise; (*d'eau douce*) terrapin; (*d'eau de mer*) turtle

tortueux, -euse [tɔʀtɥø, øz] *adj* (*rue*) twisting; (*fig*) tortuous

torture [tɔʀtyʀ] *nf* torture; **torturer** *vt* to torture; (*fig*) to torment

tôt [to] *adv* early; **~ ou tard** sooner or later; **si ~** so early; (*déjà*) so soon; **plus ~** earlier; **au plus ~** at the earliest

total, e, -aux [tɔtal, o] *adj, nm* total; **au ~** in total; (*fig*) on the whole; **faire le ~** to work out the total; **totalement** *adv* totally; **totaliser** *vt* to total; **totalitaire** *adj* totalitarian; **totalité** *nf*: **la totalité de** (*of*) (the whole +*sg*); **en totalité** entirely

toubib [tubib] (*fam*) *nm* doctor

touchant, e [tuʃɑ̃, ɑ̃t] *adj* touching

touche [tuʃ] *nf* (*de piano, de machine à écrire*) key; (*de téléphone*) button; (*Peinture etc*) stroke, touch; (*fig: de nostalgie*) touch; (*Football: aussi*: **remise en ~**) throw-in; (*aussi*: **ligne de ~**) touch-line; **touche dièse** (*de téléphone, clavier*) hash key

toucher [tuʃe] *nm* touch ▶ *vt* to touch; (*palper*) to feel; (*atteindre: d'un coup de feu etc*) to hit; (*concerner*) to concern, affect; (*contacter*) to reach, contact; (*recevoir: récompense*) to receive, get; (*: salaire*) to

draw, get; (*: chèque*) to cash; **se toucher** (*être en contact*) to touch; **au ~** to the touch; **à ~** to touch; (*concerner*) to have to do with, concern; **je vais lui en ~ un mot** I'll have a word with him about it; **~ au but** (*fig*) to near one's goal; **~ à sa fin** to be drawing to a close

touffe [tuf] *nf* tuft

touffu, e [tufy] *adj* thick, dense

toujours [tuʒuʀ] *adv* always; (*encore*) still; (*constamment*) forever; **~ plus** more and more; **pour ~** forever; **~ est-il que** the fact remains that; **essaie ~** (*you can*) try anyway

toupie [tupi] *nf* (spinning) top

tour¹ [tuʀ] *nf* tower; (*immeuble*) high-rise block (*BRIT*) ou building (*US*); (*Échecs*) castle, rook; **tour de contrôle** *nf* control tower; **la tour Eiffel** the Eiffel Tower

tour² [tuʀ] *nm* (*excursion*) trip; (*à pied*) stroll, walk; (*en voiture*) run, ride; (*Sport: aussi*: **~ de piste**) lap; (*d'être servi ou de jouer etc*) turn; (*de roue etc*) revolution; (*Pol: aussi*: **~ de scrutin**) ballot; (*ruse, de prestidigitation*) trick; (*de potier*) wheel; (*à bois, métaux*) lathe; (*circonférence*): **de 3 m de ~** 3 m round, with a circumference ou girth of 3 m; **faire le ~ de** to go round; (*à pied*) to walk round; **c'est au ~ de Renée** it's Renée's turn; **à ~ de rôle**, **à ~** in turn; **tour de chant** *nm* song recital; **tour de force** tour de force; **tour de garde** *nm* spell of duty; **tour d'horizon** *nm* (*fig*) general survey; **tour de taille/tête** *nm* waist/head measurement; **un 33 tours** an LP; **un 45 tours** a single

tourbe [tuʀb] *nf* peat

tourbillon [tuʀbijɔ̃] *nm* whirlwind; (*d'eau*) whirlpool; (*fig*) whirl, swirl; **tourbillonner** *vi* to whirl (round)

tourelle [tuʀɛl] *nf* turret

tourisme [tuʀism] *nm* tourism; **agence de ~** tourist agency; **faire du ~** to go touring; (*en visitant*) to go sightseeing; **touriste** *nm/f* tourist; **touristique** *adj* tourist *cpd*; (*région*) touristic

tourment [tuʀmã] nm torment;
tourmenter vt to torment; **se
tourmenter** to fret, worry o.s.

tournage [tuʀnaʒ] nm (Cinéma)
shooting

tournant [tuʀnã] nm (de route) bend;
(fig) turning point

tournée [tuʀne] nf (du facteur etc)
round; (d'artiste, politicien) tour; (au café)
round (of drinks)

tourner [tuʀne] vt to turn; (sauce,
mélange) to stir; (Cinéma: faire les prises
de vues) to shoot; (: produire) to make
▷ vi to turn; (moteur) to run; (taximètre)
to tick away; (lait etc) to turn (sour); **se
tourner** vi to turn round; **tournez à
gauche/droite au prochain carrefour**
turn left/right at the next junction;
mal ~ to go wrong; **~ autour de** to go
round; (péj) to hang round; **~ à/en** to
turn into; **~ qn en ridicule** to ridicule
sb; **le dos à** (mouvement) to turn one's
back on; (position) to have one's back
to; **~ de l'œil** to pass out; **se ~ vers** to
turn towards; (fig) to turn to; **se ~ les
pouces** to twiddle one's thumbs

tournesol [tuʀnəsɔl] nm sunflower

tournevis [tuʀnəvis] nm screwdriver

tournoi [tuʀnwa] nm tournament

tournure [tuʀnyʀ] nf (Ling) turn of
phrase; (évolution): **la ~ de qch** the way
sth is developing; **tournure d'esprit**
turn ou cast of mind

tourte [tuʀt] nf pie

tourterelle [tuʀtəʀɛl] nf turtledove

tous [tu] adj, pron voir **tout**

Toussaint [tusɛ̃] nf: **la ~** All Saints' Day

tousser [tuse] vi to cough

○ MOT-CLÉ

tout, e [tu, tut] (mpl **tous**, fpl **toutes**)
adj 1 (avec article singulier) all; **tout le
lait** all the milk; **toute la nuit** all night,
the whole night; **tout le livre** the whole
book; **tout un pain** a whole loaf; **tout
le temps** all the time; the whole time;
tout le monde everybody; **c'est tout
le contraire** it's quite the opposite
2 (avec article pluriel) every, all; **tous les
livres** all the books; **toutes les nuits**
every night; **toutes les fois** every time;
toutes les trois/deux semaines every
third/other ou second week, every
three/two weeks; **tous les deux** both
ou each of us (ou them ou you); **toutes
les trois** all three of us (ou them ou you)
3 (sans article): **à tout âge** at any age;
pour toute nourriture, il avait ... his
only food was ...

▷ pron everything, all; **il a tout fait**
he's done everything; **je les vois tous**
I can see them all ou all of them; **nous y
sommes tous allés** all of us went, we
all went; **c'est tout** that's all; **en tout**
in all; **tout ce qu'il sait** all he knows
▷ nm whole; **le tout** all of it (ou them);
le tout est de ... the main thing is to ...;
pas du tout not at all

▷ adv 1 (très, complètement) very; **tout
près** very near; **le tout premier** the
very first; **tout seul** all alone; **le livre
tout entier** the whole book; **tout
en haut** right at the top; **tout droit**
straight ahead
2: **tout en** while; **tout en travaillant**
while working, as he etc works ou worked
3: **tout d'abord** first of all; **tout à
coup** suddenly; **tout à fait** absolutely; **tout
à l'heure** a short while ago; (futur) in a
short while, shortly; (passé) a short while ago; **à tout à l'heure!**
see you later!; **tout de même** all the
same; **tout de suite** immediately,
straight away; **tout simplement**
quite simply

toutefois [tutfwa] adv however

toutes [tut] *adj, pron voir* **tout**

tout-terrain [tuterɛ̃] *adj*: **vélo ~** mountain bike; **véhicule ~** four-wheel drive

toux [tu] *nf* cough

toxicomane [tɔksikɔman] *nm/f* drug addict

toxique [tɔksik] *adj* toxic

trac [tʀak] *nm* (*au théâtre, en public*) stage fright; (*aux examens*) nerves *pl*; **avoir le ~** (*au théâtre, en public*) to have stage fright; (*aux examens*) to be feeling nervous

tracasser [tʀakase] *vt* to worry, bother; **se tracasser** to worry

trace [tʀas] *nf* (*empreintes*) tracks *pl*; (*marques, aussi fig*) mark; (*quantité infime, indice, vestige*) trace; **traces de pas** footprints

tracer [tʀase] *vt* to draw; (*piste*) to open up

tract [tʀakt] *nm* tract, pamphlet

tracteur [tʀaktœʀ] *nm* tractor

traction [tʀaksjɔ̃] *nf*: **~ avant/arrière** front-wheel/rear-wheel drive

tradition [tʀadisjɔ̃] *nf* tradition; **traditionnel, le** *adj* traditional

traducteur, -trice [tʀadyktœʀ, tʀis] *nm/f* translator

traduction [tʀadyksjɔ̃] *nf* translation

traduire [tʀadɥiʀ] *vt* to translate; (*exprimer*) to convey; **~ qn en justice** to bring sb before the courts; **pouvez-vous me ~ ceci?** can you translate this for me?

trafic [tʀafik] *nm* traffic; **trafic d'armes** arms dealing; **trafiquant, e** *nm/f* trafficker; (*d'armes*) dealer; **trafiquer** (*péj*) *vt* (*vin*) to doctor; (*moteur, document*) to tamper with

tragédie [tʀaʒedi] *nf* tragedy; **tragique** *adj* tragic

trahir [tʀaiʀ] *vt* to betray; **trahison** *nf* betrayal; (*Jur*) treason

train [tʀɛ̃] *nm* (*Rail*) train; (*allure*) pace; **être en ~ de faire qch** to be doing sth; **c'est bien le ~ pour ...?** is this the train for ...?; **train d'atterrissage**

undercarriage; **train de vie** lifestyle; **train électrique** (*jouet*) (electric) train set

traîne [tʀɛn] *nf* (*de robe*) train; **être à la ~** to lag behind

traîneau, x [tʀɛno] *nm* sleigh, sledge

traîner [tʀene] *vt* (*remorque*) to pull; (*enfant, chien*) to drag ou trail along ▷ *vi* (*robe, manteau*) to trail; (*être en désordre*) to lie around; (*aller lentement*) to dawdle (along); (*vagabonder, aller lentement*) to hang about; (*durer*) to drag on; **se traîner** *vi*: **se ~ par terre** to crawl (on the ground); **~ les pieds** to drag one's feet

train-train [tʀɛ̃tʀɛ̃] *nm* humdrum routine

traire [tʀeʀ] *vt* to milk

trait [tʀɛ] *nm* (*ligne*) line; (*de dessin*) stroke; (*caractéristique*) feature, trait; **traits** *nmpl* (*du visage*) features; **d'un ~** (*boire*) in one gulp; **de ~** (*animal*) draught; **avoir ~ à** to concern; **trait d'union** hyphen

traitant, e [tʀɛtɑ̃, ɑ̃t] *adj* (*shampooing*) medicated; **votre médecin ~** your usual ou family doctor

traite [tʀɛt] *nf* (*Comm*) draft; (*Agr*) milking; **d'une ~** without stopping

traité [tʀete] *nm* treaty

traitement [tʀɛtmɑ̃] *nm* treatment; (*salaire*) salary; **traitement de données** data processing; **traitement de texte** word processing; (*logiciel*) word processing package

traiter [tʀete] *vt* to treat; (*qualifier*): **~ qn d'idiot** to call sb a fool ▷ *vi* to deal; **~ de** to deal with

traiteur [tʀɛtœʀ] *nm* caterer

traître, -esse [tʀɛtʀ, tʀɛtʀɛs] *adj* (*dangereux*) treacherous ▷ *nm* traitor

trajectoire [tʀaʒɛktwaʀ] *nf* path

trajet [tʀaʒɛ] *nm* (*parcours, voyage*) journey; (*itinéraire*) route; (*distance à parcourir*) distance; **il y a une heure de ~** the journey takes one hour

trampoline [tʀɑ̃pɔlin] *nm* trampoline

tramway [tʀamwɛ] *nm* tram(way);

(voiture) tram(car) (BRIT), streetcar (US)

tranchant, e [tʀɑ̃ʃɑ̃, ɑ̃t] adj sharp; (fig) peremptory ▷ nm (d'un couteau) cutting edge; (de la main) edge; **à double ~** double-edged

tranche [tʀɑ̃ʃ] nf (morceau) slice; (arête) edge; **~ d'âge/de salaires** age/wage bracket

tranché, e [tʀɑ̃ʃe] adj (couleurs) distinct; (opinions) clear-cut

trancher [tʀɑ̃ʃe] vt to cut, sever ▷ vi to take a decision; **~ avec** to contrast sharply with

tranquille [tʀɑ̃kil] adj quiet; (rassuré) easy in one's mind, with one's mind at rest; **se tenir ~** (enfant) to be quiet; **laisse-moi/laisse-ça ~** leave me/it alone; **avoir la conscience ~** to have a clear conscience; **tranquillisant** nm tranquillizer; **tranquillité** nf peace (and quiet); (d'esprit) peace of mind

transférer [tʀɑ̃sfeʀe] vt to transfer; **transfert** nm transfer

transformation [tʀɑ̃sfɔʀmasjɔ̃] nf change, alteration; (radicale) transformation; (Rugby) conversion; **transformations** nfpl (travaux) alterations

transformer [tʀɑ̃sfɔʀme] vt to change; (radicalement) to transform; (vêtement) to alter; (matière première, appartement, Rugby) to convert; **(se) ~ en** to turn into

transfusion [tʀɑ̃sfyzjɔ̃] nf: **~ sanguine** blood transfusion

transgénique [tʀɑ̃sʒenik] adj transgenic

transgresser [tʀɑ̃sgʀese] vt to contravene

transi, e [tʀɑ̃zi] adj numb (with cold), chilled to the bone

transiger [tʀɑ̃ziʒe] vi to compromise

transit [tʀɑ̃zit] nm transit; **transiter** vi to pass in transit

transition [tʀɑ̃zisjɔ̃] nf transition; **transitoire** adj transitional

transmettre [tʀɑ̃smɛtʀ] vt (passer): **~ qch à qn** to pass sth on to sb;

(Tech, Tél, Méd) to transmit; (TV, Radio: retransmettre) to broadcast; **transmission** nf transmission

transparent, e [tʀɑ̃spaʀɑ̃, ɑ̃t] adj transparent

transpercer [tʀɑ̃spɛʀse] vt (froid, pluie) to go through, pierce; (balle) to go through

transpiration [tʀɑ̃spiʀasjɔ̃] nf perspiration

transpirer [tʀɑ̃spiʀe] vi to perspire

transplanter [tʀɑ̃splɑ̃te] vt (Méd, Bot) to transplant

transport [tʀɑ̃spɔʀ] nm transport; **transports en commun** public transport sg; **transporter** vt to carry, move; (Comm) to transport, convey; **transporteur** nm haulage contractor (BRIT), trucker (US)

transvaser [tʀɑ̃svaze] vt to decant

transversal, e, -aux [tʀɑ̃svɛʀsal, o] adj (rue) which runs across; **coupe ~e** cross section

trapèze [tʀapɛz] nm (au cirque) trapeze

trappe [tʀap] nf trap door

trapu, e [tʀapy] adj squat, stocky

traquenard [tʀaknaʀ] nm trap

traquer [tʀake] vt to track down; (harceler) to hound

traumatiser [tʀomatize] vt to traumatize

travail, -aux [tʀavaj, o] nm (gén) work; (tâche, métier) work to do, job; (Écon, Méd) labour; **être sans ~** (employé) to be unemployed; voir aussi **travaux**; **travail (au) noir** moonlighting

travailler [tʀavaje] vi to work; (bois) to warp ▷ vt (bois, métal) to work; (objet d'art, discipline) to work on; **cela le travaille** it is on his mind; **travailleur, -euse** adj hard-working ▷ nm/f worker; **travailleur social** social worker; **travailliste** adj ≈ Labour cpd

travaux [tʀavo] nmpl (de réparation, agricoles etc) work sg; (sur route) roadworks pl; (de construction) building work; **travaux des champs** farmwork sg; **travaux dirigés** (Scol) tutorial sg; **travaux forcés** hard labour no pl; **travaux manuels** (Scol) handicrafts; **travaux ménagers** housework no pl; **travaux pratiques** (Scol) practical work; (en laboratoire) lab work

travers [tʀavɛʀ] nm fault, failing; **en ~ (de)** across; **au ~ (de)/à ~** through; **de ~** (nez, bouche) crooked; (chapeau) askew; **comprendre de ~** to misunderstand; **regarder de ~** (fig) to look askance at

traverse [tʀavɛʀs] nf (de voie ferrée) sleeper; **chemin de ~** shortcut

traversée [tʀavɛʀse] nf crossing; **combien de temps dure la ~?** how long does the crossing take?

traverser [tʀavɛʀse] vt (gén) to cross; (ville, tunnel, aussi: percer, fig) to go through; (suj: ligne, trait) to run across

traversin [tʀavɛʀsɛ̃] nm bolster

travesti [tʀavɛsti] nm transvestite

trébucher [tʀebyʃe] vi: **~ (sur)** to stumble (over), trip (against)

trèfle [tʀɛfl] nm (Bot) clover; (Cartes: couleur) clubs pl; (: carte) club; **~ à quatre feuilles** four-leaf clover

treize [tʀɛz] num thirteen; **treizième** num thirteenth

tréma [tʀema] nm diaeresis

tremblement [tʀɑ̃bləmɑ̃] nm: **tremblement de terre** earthquake

trembler [tʀɑ̃ble] vi to tremble, shake; **~ de** (froid, fièvre) to shiver ou tremble with; (peur) to shake ou tremble with; **pour qn** to fear for sb

trémousser [tʀemuse]: **se trémousser** vi to jig about, wriggle about

trempé, e [tʀɑ̃pe] adj soaking (wet), drenched; (Tech) tempered

tremper [tʀɑ̃pe] vt to soak, drench; (aussi: **faire ~, mettre à ~**) to soak; (plonger): **~ qch dans** to dip sth in(to) ▷ vi to soak; (fig): **~ dans** to be involved ou have a hand in; **se tremper** vi to have a quick dip

tremplin [tʀɑ̃plɛ̃] nm springboard; (Ski) ski-jump

trentaine [tʀɑ̃tɛn] nf: **une ~ (de)** thirty or so, about thirty; **avoir la ~** (âge) to be around thirty

trente [tʀɑ̃t] num thirty; **être son ~ et un** to be wearing one's Sunday best; **trentième** num thirtieth

trépidant, e [tʀepidɑ̃, ɑ̃t] adj (fig: rythme) pulsating; (: vie) hectic

trépigner [tʀepiɲe] vi to stamp (one's feet)

très [tʀɛ] adv very; much +pp, highly +pp

trésor [tʀezɔʀ] nm treasure; **Trésor (public)** public revenue; **trésorerie** nf (gestion) accounts pl; (bureaux) accounts department; **difficultés de trésorerie** cash problems, shortage of cash ou funds; **trésorier, -ière** nm/f treasurer

tressaillir [tʀesajiʀ] vi to shiver, shudder

tressauter [tʀesote] vi to start, jump

tresse [tʀɛs] nf braid, plait; **tresser** vt (cheveux) to braid, plait; (fil, jonc) to plait; (corbeille) to weave; (corde) to twist

tréteau, x [tʀeto] nm trestle

treuil [tʀœj] nm winch

trêve [tʀɛv] nf (Mil, Pol) truce; (fig) respite; **~ de ...** enough of this ...

tri [tʀi] nm: **faire le ~ (de)** to sort out; **le (bureau de) ~** (Postes) the sorting office

triangle [tʀijɑ̃gl] nm triangle; **triangulaire** adj triangular

tribord [tʀibɔʀ] nm: **à ~** to starboard, on the starboard side

tribu [tʀiby] nf tribe

tribunal, -aux [tʀibynal, o] nm (Jur) court; (Mil) tribunal

tribune [tʀibyn] nf (estrade) platform, rostrum; (débat) forum; (d'église, de tribunal) gallery; (de stade) stand

tribut [tʀiby] nm tribute

tributaire [tʀibytɛʀ] adj: **être ~ de** to be dependent on

tricher [tʀiʃe] vi to cheat; **tricheur, -euse** nm/f cheat(er)

tricolore [tʀikɔlɔʀ] adj three-coloured; (français) red, white and blue

tricot [tʀiko] *nm* (*technique, ouvrage*) knitting *no pl*; (*vêtement*) jersey, sweater; **~ de peau** vest; **tricoter** *vt* to knit

tricycle [tʀisikl] *nm* tricycle

trier [tʀije] *vt* to sort out; (*Postes, fruits*) to sort

trimestre [tʀimɛstʀ] *nm* (*Scol*) term; (*Comm*) quarter; **trimestriel, le** *adj* quarterly; (*Scol*) end-of-term

trinquer [tʀɛ̃ke] *vi* to clink glasses

triomphe [tʀijɔ̃f] *nm* triumph; **triompher** *vi* to triumph, win; **triompher de** to triumph over, overcome

tripes [tʀip] *nfpl* (*Culin*) tripe *sg*

triple [tʀipl] *adj* triple ▷ *nm*: **le ~ (de)** (*comparaison*) three times as much (as); **en ~ exemplaire** in triplicate; **tripler** *vi, vt* to triple, treble

triplés, -ées [tʀiple] *nm/fpl* triplets

tripoter [tʀipote] *vt* to fiddle with

triste [tʀist] *adj* sad; (*couleur, temps, journée*) dreary; (*péj*): **~ personnage/ affaire** sorry individual/affair; **tristesse** *nf* sadness

trivial, e, -aux [tʀivjal, jo] *adj* coarse, crude; (*commun*) mundane

troc [tʀɔk] *nm* barter

trognon [tʀɔɲɔ̃] *nm* (*de fruit*) core; (*de légume*) stalk

trois [tʀwɑ] *num* three; **troisième** *num* third ▷ *nf* (*Scol*) year 10 (*BRIT*), ninth grade (*US*); **le troisième âge** (*période de vie*) one's retirement years; (*personnes âgées*) senior citizens *pl*

trombe [tʀɔ̃b] *nf*: **des ~s d'eau** a downpour; **en ~** like a whirlwind

trombone [tʀɔ̃bɔn] *nm* (*Mus*) trombone; (*de bureau*) paper clip

trompe [tʀɔ̃p] *nf* (*d'éléphant*) trunk; (*Mus*) trumpet, horn

tromper [tʀɔ̃pe] *vt* to deceive; (*vigilance, poursuivants*) to elude; **se tromper** *vi* to make a mistake, be mistaken; **se ~ de voiture/jour** to take the wrong car/get the day wrong; **se ~ de 3 cm/20 euros** to be out by 3 cm/20

euros; **je me suis trompé de route** I took the wrong road

trompette [tʀɔ̃pɛt] *nf* trumpet; **en ~** (*nez*) turned-up

trompeur, -euse [tʀɔ̃pœʀ, øz] *adj* deceptive

tronc [tʀɔ̃] *nm* (*Bot, Anat*) trunk; (*d'église*) collection box

tronçon [tʀɔ̃sɔ̃] *nm* section; **tronçonner** *vt* to saw up; **tronçonneuse** *nf* chainsaw

trône [tʀon] *nm* throne

trop [tʀo] *adv* (*+vb*) too much; (*+adjectif, adverbe*) too; **~ (nombreux)** too many; **~ peu (nombreux)** too few; **~ (souvent)** too often; **~ (longtemps)** (for) too long; **~ de** (*nombre*) too many; (*quantité*) too much; **de ~, en ~: des livres en ~** a few books too many; **du lait en ~** too much milk; **3 livres/3 euros de ~** 3 books too many/3 euros too much; **ça coûte ~ cher** it's too expensive

tropical, e, -aux [tʀopikal, o] *adj* tropical

tropique [tʀopik] *nm* tropic

trop-plein [tʀoplɛ̃] *nm* (*tuyau*) overflow *ou* outlet (pipe); (*liquide*) overflow

troquer [tʀoke] *vt*: **~ qch contre** to barter *ou* trade sth for; (*fig*) to swap sth for

trot [tʀo] *nm* trot; **trotter** *vi* to trot

trottinette [tʀotinɛt] *nf* (child's) scooter

trottoir [tʀotwaʀ] *nm* pavement (*BRIT*), sidewalk (*US*); **faire le ~** (*péj*) to walk the streets; **trottoir roulant** moving walkway, travellator

trou [tʀu] *nm* hole; (*fig*) gap; (*Comm*) deficit; **trou d'air** air pocket; **trou de mémoire** blank, lapse of memory

troublant, e [tʀublɑ̃, ɑ̃t] *adj* disturbing

trouble [tʀubl] *adj* (*liquide*) cloudy; (*image, photo*) blurred; (*affaire*) shady, murky ▷ *adv*: **voir ~** to have blurred vision ▷ *nm* agitation; **troubles** *nmpl* (*Pol*) disturbances, troubles, unrest *sg*;

trouble-fête *nm* spoilsport

troubler [tʀuble] *vt* to disturb; (*liquide*) to make cloudy; (*intriguer*) to intrigue; **se troubler** *vi* (*personne*) to become flustered *ou* confused

trouer [tʀue] *vt* to make a hole (*ou* holes) in

trouille [tʀuj] (*fam*) *nf*: **avoir la ~** to be scared to death

troupe [tʀup] *nf* troop; **troupe (de théâtre)** (theatrical) company

troupeau, x [tʀupo] *nm* (*de moutons*) flock; (*de vaches*) herd

trousse [tʀus] *nf* case, kit; (*d'écolier*) pencil case; **aux ~s de** (*fig*) on the heels *ou* tail of; **trousse à outils** toolkit; **trousse de toilette** toilet bag

trousseau, x [tʀuso] *nm* (*de mariée*) trousseau; **trousseau de clefs** bunch of keys

trouvaille [tʀuvaj] *nf* find

trouver [tʀuve] *vt* to find; (*rendre visite*): **aller/venir ~ qn** to go/come and see sb; **se trouver** *vi* (*être*) to be; **je trouve que** I find *ou* think that; **~ à boire/critiquer** to find something to drink/criticize; **se ~ mal** to pass out

truand [tʀyɑ̃] *nm* gangster; **truander** *vt*: **se faire truander** to be swindled

truc [tʀyk] *nm* (*astuce*) way, trick; (*de cinéma, prestidigitateur*) trick; effect; (*chose*) thing, thingumajig; **avoir le ~** to have the knack; **c'est pas mon ~** (*fam*) it's not really my thing

truffe [tʀyf] *nf* truffle; (*nez*) nose

truffé, e [tʀyfe] *adj* (*Culin*) garnished with truffles; **~ de** (*fig: citations*) peppered with; (: *fautes*) riddled with; (: *pièges*) bristling with

truie [tʀɥi] *nf* sow

truite [tʀɥit] *nf* trout

truquage [tʀyka3] *nm* special effects *pl*

truquer [tʀyke] *vt* (*élections, serrure, dés*) to fix

TSVP *sigle* (= *tournez svp*) PTO

TTC *sigle* (= *toutes taxes comprises*) inclusive of tax

tu¹ [ty] *pron* you; **dire tu à qn** to use the "tu" form to sb

tu², e [ty] *pp de* **taire**

tuba [tyba] *nm* (*Mus*) tuba; (*Sport*) snorkel

tube [tyb] *nm* tube; (*chanson*) hit

tuberculose [tybεʀkyloz] *nf* tuberculosis

tuer [tɥe] *vt* to kill; **se tuer** *vi* to be killed; (*suicide*) to kill o.s.; **se ~ au travail** (*fig*) to work o.s. to death; **tuerie** *nf* slaughter *no pl*

tue-tête [tytεt]: **à ~** *adv* at the top of one's voice

tueur [tɥœʀ] *nm* killer; **tueur à gages** hired killer

tuile [tɥil] *nf* tile; (*fam*) spot of bad luck, blow

tulipe [tylip] *nf* tulip

tuméfié, e [tymefje] *adj* puffed-up, swollen

tumeur [tymœʀ] *nf* growth, tumour

tumulte [tymylt] *nm* commotion; **tumultueux, -euse** *adj* stormy, turbulent

tunique [tynik] *nf* tunic

Tunis [tynis] *n* Tunis

Tunisie [tynizi] *nf*: **la ~** Tunisia; **tunisien, ne** *adj* Tunisian ▷ *nm/f*: **Tunisien, ne** Tunisian

tunnel [tynεl] *nm* tunnel; **le ~ sous la Manche** the Channel Tunnel

turbulent, e [tyʀbylɑ̃, ɑ̃t] *adj* boisterous, unruly

turc, turque [tyʀk] *adj* Turkish ▷ *nm/f*: **T~, Turque** Turk/Turkish woman ▷ *nm* (*Ling*) Turkish

turf [tyʀf] *nm* racing; **turfiste** *nm/f* racegoer

Turquie [tyʀki] *nf*: **la ~** Turkey

turquoise [tyʀkwaz] *nf* turquoise ▷ *adj* inv turquoise

tutelle [tytεl] *nf* (*Jur*) guardianship; (*Pol*) trusteeship; **sous la ~ de** (*fig*) under the supervision of

tuteur [tytœʀ] *nm* (*Jur*) guardian; (*de plante*) stake, support

tutoyer [tytwaje] *vt*: **~ qn** to address

sb as "tu"

tuyau, x [tɥijo] *nm* pipe; *(flexible)* tube; *(fam)* tip; **tuyau d'arrosage** hosepipe; **tuyau d'échappement** exhaust pipe; **tuyauterie** *nf* piping *no pl*

TVA *sigle f* (= *taxe à la valeur ajoutée*) VAT

tympan [tɛ̃pɑ̃] *nm* (*Anat*) eardrum

type [tip] *nm* type; *(fam)* chap, guy ▷ *adj* typical, classic

typé, e [tipe] *adj* ethnic

typique [tipik] *adj* typical

tyran [tiʁɑ̃] *nm* tyrant; **tyrannique** *adj* tyrannical

tzigane [dzigan] *adj* gipsy, tzigane

ulcère [ylsɛʁ] *nm* ulcer

ultérieur, e [ylteʁjœʁ] *adj* later, subsequent; **remis à une date ~e** postponed to a later date; **ultérieurement** *adv* later, subsequently

ultime [yltim] *adj* final

 MOT-CLÉ

un, une [œ̃, yn] *art indéf* a; *(devant voyelle)* an; **un garçon/vieillard** a boy/an old man; **une fille** a girl ▷ *pron* one; **l'un des meilleurs** one of the best; **l'un ..., l'autre** (the) one ..., the other; **les uns ..., les autres** some ..., others; **l'un et l'autre** both (of them); **l'un ou l'autre** either (of them); **l'un l'autre** each other; **les uns les autres** one another; **pas un seul** not a single one; **un par un** one by one ▷ *num* one; **un pamplemousse seulement** one grapefruit only, just

one grapefruit
▷ *nf*: **la une** (*Presse*) the front page

unanime [ynanim] *adj* unanimous;
unanimité *nf*: **à l'unanimité**
unanimously

uni, e [yni] *adj* (*ton, tissu*) plain; (*surface*)
smooth, even; (*famille*) close(-knit);
(*pays*) united

unifier [ynifje] *vt* to unite, unify

uniforme [ynifɔʀm] *adj* uniform;
(*surface, ton*) even ▷ *nm* uniform;
uniformiser *vt* (*systèmes*) to
standardize

union [ynjɔ̃] *nf* union; **union de
consommateurs** consumers'
association; **union libre** (*en concubinage*): **vivre en
union libre** (*en concubinage*) to cohabit;
Union européenne European Union;
Union soviétique Soviet Union

unique [ynik] *adj* (*seul*) only;
(*exceptionnel*) unique; (*le même*): **un
prix/système** ~ a single price/system;
fils/fille ~ only son/daughter,
only child; **sens** ~ one-way street;
uniquement *adv* only, solely; (*juste*)
only, merely

unir [yniʀ] *vt* (*nations*) to unite; (*en
mariage*) to unite, join together; **s'unir**
vi to unite; (*en mariage*) to be joined
together

unitaire [yniteʀ] *adj*: **prix** ~ unit price

unité [ynite] *nf* unit; (*harmonie,
cohésion*) unity

univers [yniveʀ] *nm* universe;
universel, le *adj* universal

universitaire [yniveʀsiteʀ] *adj*
university *cpd*; (*diplôme, études*)
academic, university *cpd* ▷ *nm/f*
academic

université [yniveʀsite] *nf* university

urbain, e [yʀbɛ̃, ɛn] *adj* urban, city
cpd, town *cpd*; **urbanisme** *nm* town
planning

urgence [yʀʒɑ̃s] *nf* urgency; (*Méd etc*)
emergency; **d'**~ *adj* emergency *cpd*
▷ *adv* as a matter of urgency; (**service
des**) ~**s** casualty

urgent, e [yʀʒɑ̃, ɑ̃t] *adj* urgent

urine [yʀin] *nf* urine; **urinoir** *nm*
(*public*) urinal

urne [yʀn] *nf* (*électorale*) ballot box;
(*vase*) urn

urticaire [yʀtikeʀ] *nf* nettle rash

us [ys] *nmpl*: **us et coutumes** (habits
and) customs

usage [yzaʒ] *nm* (*emploi, utilisation*) use;
(*coutume*) custom; **à l'**~ with use; **à l'**~
de (*pour*) for (use of); **en** ~ in use; **hors
d'**~ out of service; **à** ~ **interne** (*Méd*) to
be taken (internally); **à** ~ **externe** (*Méd*)
for external use only; **usagé, e** *adj* (*usé*)
worn; **usager, -ère** *nm/f* user

usé, e [yze] *adj* worn; (*banal: argument
etc*) hackneyed

user [yze] *vt* (*outil*) to wear down;
(*vêtement*) to wear out; (*matière*) to wear
away; (*consommer: charbon etc*) to use;
s'user *vi* (*tissu, vêtement*) to wear out;
~ **de** (*moyen, procédé*) to use, employ;
~ **de** (*droit*) to exercise

usine [yzin] *nf* factory

usité, e [yzite] *adj* common

ustensile [ystɑ̃sil] *nm* implement;
ustensile de cuisine kitchen utensil

usuel, le [yzɥɛl] *adj* everyday, common

usure [yzyʀ] *nf* wear

utérus [yteʀys] *nm* uterus, womb

utile [ytil] *adj* useful

utilisation [ytilizasjɔ̃] *nf* use

utiliser [ytilize] *vt* to use

utilitaire [ytiliteʀ] *adj* utilitarian

utilité [ytilite] *nf* usefulness *no pl*; **de
peu d'**~ of little use *ou* help

utopie [ytɔpi] *nf* utopia

V

va [va] *vb voir* **aller**

vacance [vakɑ̃s] *nf* (*Admin*) vacancy; **vacances** *nfpl* holiday(s pl (*BRIT*)), vacation *sg* (*US*); **les grandes ~s** the summer holidays; **prendre des/ses ~s** to take a holiday/one's holiday(s); **aller en ~s** to go on holiday; **je suis ici en ~s** I'm here on holiday; **vacancier, -ière** *nm/f* holiday-maker

vacant, e [vakɑ̃, ɑ̃t] *adj* vacant

vacarme [vakarm] *nm* (*bruit*) racket

vaccin [vaksɛ̃] *nm* vaccine; (*opération*) vaccination; **vaccination** *nf* vaccination; **vacciner** *vt* to vaccinate; **être vacciné contre qch** (*fig*) to be cured of sth

vache [vaʃ] *nf* (*Zool*) cow; (*cuir*) cowhide ▷ *adj* (*fam*) rotten, mean; **vachement** (*fam*) *adv* (*très*) really; (*pleuvoir, travailler*) a hell of a lot; **vacherie** *nf* (*action*) dirty trick; (*remarque*) nasty remark

vaciller [vasije] *vi* to sway, wobble; (*bougie, lumière*) to flicker; (*fig*) to be failing, falter

va-et-vient [vaevjɛ̃] *nm inv* (*de personnes, véhicules*) comings and goings *pl*, to-ings and fro-ings *pl*

vagabond [vagabɔ̃] *nm* (*rôdeur*) tramp, vagrant; (*voyageur*) wanderer; **vagabonder** *vi* to roam, wander

vagin [vaʒɛ̃] *nm* vagina

vague [vag] *nf* wave ▷ *adj* vague; (*regard*) faraway; (*manteau, robe*) loose(-fitting); (*quelconque*) **un ~ bureau/cousin** some office/cousin or other; **vague de fond** ground swell; **vague de froid** cold spell

vaillant, e [vajɑ̃, ɑ̃t] *adj* (*courageux*) gallant; (*robuste*) hale and hearty

vain, e [vɛ̃, vɛn] *adj* vain; **en ~** in vain

vaincre [vɛ̃kʀ] *vt* to defeat; (*fig*) to conquer, overcome; **vaincu, e** *nm/f* defeated party; **vainqueur** *nm* victor; (*Sport*) winner

vaisseau, x [vɛso] *nm* (*Anat*) vessel; (*Navig*) ship, vessel; **vaisseau spatial** spaceship

vaisselier [vɛsalje] *nm* dresser

vaisselle [vɛsɛl] *nf* (*service*) crockery; (*plats etc à laver*) (dirty) dishes *pl*; **faire la ~** to do the washing-up (*BRIT*) *ou* the dishes

valable [valabl] *adj* valid; (*acceptable*) decent, worthwhile

valet [valɛ] *nm* manservant; (*Cartes*) jack

valeur [valœʀ] *nf* (*gén*) value; (*mérite*) worth, merit; (*Comm: titre*) security; **valeurs** *nfpl* (*morales*) values; **mettre en ~** (*détail*) to highlight; (*objet décoratif*) to show off to advantage; **avoir de la ~** to be valuable; **sans ~** worthless; **prendre de la ~** to go up *ou* gain in value

valide [valid] *adj* (*en bonne santé*) fit; (*valable*) valid; **valider** *vt* to validate

valise [valiz] *nf* (suit)case; **faire ses ~s** to pack one's bags

vallée [vale] *nf* valley

vallon [valɔ̃] *nm* small valley

valoir [valwaʀ] *vi* (*être valable*) to hold, apply ▷ *vt* (*prix, valeur, effort*) to be worth; (*causer*): **~ qch à qn** to earn sb sth; **se valoir** vi to be of equal merit; (*péj*) to be two of a kind; **faire ~** (*droits, prérogatives*) to assert; **se faire ~** to make the most of o.s.; **à ~ sur** to be deducted from; **vaille que vaille** somehow or other; **cela ne me dit rien qui vaille** I don't like the look of it at all; **ce climat ne me vaut rien** this climate doesn't suit me; **~ le coup** ou **la peine** to be worth the trouble ou worth it; **~ mieux: il vaut mieux se taire** it's better to say nothing; **ça ne vaut rien** it's worthless; **que vaut ce candidat?** how good is this applicant?

valse [vals] nf waltz

vandalisme [vãdalism] nm vandalism

vanille [vanij] nf vanilla

vanité [vanite] nf vanity; **vaniteux, -euse** adj vain, conceited

vanne [van] nf gate; (*fig*) joke

vannerie [vanri] nf basketwork

vantard, e [vãtaʀ, aʀd] adj boastful

vanter [vãte] vt to speak highly of, praise; **se vanter** vi to boast, brag; **se ~ de** to pride o.s. on; (*péj*) to boast of

vapeur [vapœʀ] nf steam; (*émanation*) vapour, fumes pl; **vapeurs** nfpl (*bouffées*) vapours; **à ~** steam-powered, steam cpd; **cuit à la ~** steamed; **vaporeux, -euse** adj (*flou*) hazy, misty; (*léger*) filmy; **vaporisateur** nm spray; **vaporiser** vt (*parfum etc*) to spray

varappe [vaʀap] nf rock climbing

vareuse [vaʀøz] nf (*blouson*) pea jacket; (*d'uniforme*) tunic

variable [vaʀjabl] adj variable; (*temps, humeur*) changeable; (*divers: résultats*) varied, various

varice [vaʀis] nf varicose vein

varicelle [vaʀisɛl] nf chickenpox

varié, e [vaʀje] adj varied; (*divers*) various; **hors d'œuvre ~s** selection of hors d'œuvres

varier [vaʀje] vi to vary; (*temps, humeur*) to change ▷ vt to vary; **variété** nf variety; **variétés** nfpl: **spectacle/ émission de variétés** variety show

variole [vaʀjɔl] nf smallpox

Varsovie [vaʀsɔvi] n Warsaw

vas [va] vb voir **aller**; **~-y!** [vazi] go on!

vase [vaz] nm vase ▷ nf silt, mud; **vaseux, -euse** adj silty, muddy; (*fig: confus*) woolly, hazy; (: *fatigué*) woozy

vasistas [vazistas] nm fanlight

vaste [vast] adj vast, immense

vautour [votuʀ] nm vulture

vautrer [votʀe] vb: **se ~ dans/sur** to wallow in/sprawl on

va-vite [vavit]: **à la ~** adv in a rush ou hurry

VDQS sigle (= vin délimité de qualité supérieure) label guaranteeing the quality of wine

veau, x [vo] nm (Zool) calf; (Culin) veal; (peau) calfskin

vécu, e [veky] pp de **vivre**

vedette [vədɛt] nf (artiste etc) star; (canot) motor boat; (police) launch

végétal, e, -aux [veʒetal, o] adj vegetable ▷ nm vegetable, plant; **végétalien, ne** adj, nm/f vegan

végétarien, ne [veʒetaʀjɛ̃, jɛn] adj, nm/f vegetarian; **avez-vous des plats ~s?** do you have any vegetarian dishes?

végétation [veʒetasjɔ̃] nf vegetation; **végétations** nfpl (Méd) adenoids

véhicule [veikyl] nm vehicle; **véhicule utilitaire** commercial vehicle

veille [vɛj] nf (état) wakefulness; (jour): **la ~ (de)** the day before; **la ~ au soir** the previous evening; **à la ~ de** on the eve of; **la ~ de Noël** Christmas Eve; **la ~ du jour de l'An** New Year's Eve

veillée [veje] nf (soirée) evening; (réunion) evening gathering; **veillée (funèbre)** wake

veiller [veje] vi to stay up ▷ vt (malade, mort) to watch over, sit up with; **~ à** to attend to, see to; **~ à ce que** to make sure that; **~ sur** to watch over; **veilleur** nm: **veilleur de nuit** night watchman; **veilleuse** nf (lampe) night light; (Auto) sidelight; (flamme) pilot light

veinard, e [venaʀ, aʀd] nm/f lucky devil

veine [vɛn] nf (Anat, du bois etc) vein;
(filon) vein, seam; (fam: chance): **avoir
de la ~** to be lucky

véliplanchiste [veliplɑ̃ʃist] nm/f
windsurfer

vélo [velo] nm bike, cycle; **faire du ~** to
go cycling; **vélomoteur** nm moped

velours [v(ə)lur] nm velvet; **velours
côtelé** corduroy; **velouté, e** adj velvety
▷ nm: **velouté de tomates** cream of
tomato soup

velu, e [vəly] adj hairy

vendange [vɑ̃dɑ̃ʒ] nf (aussi: **~s**) grape
harvest; **vendanger** vi to harvest
the grapes

vendeur, -euse [vɑ̃dœr, øz] nm/f
shop assistant ▷ nm (Jur) vendor, seller

vendre [vɑ̃dr] vt to sell; **~ qch à qn** to
sell sb sth; **"à ~"** "for sale"

vendredi [vɑ̃dredi] nm Friday;
vendredi saint Good Friday

vénéneux, -euse [venenø, øz] adj
poisonous

vénérien, ne [venerjɛ̃, jɛn] adj
venereal

vengeance [vɑ̃ʒɑ̃s] nf vengeance no pl,
revenge no pl

venger [vɑ̃ʒe] vt to avenge; **se venger**
vi to avenge o.s.; **se ~ de qch** to avenge
o.s. for sth, take one's revenge for sth;
se ~ de qn to take revenge on sb; **se ~
sur** to take revenge on

venimeux, -euse [vənimø, øz] adj
poisonous, venomous; (fig: haineux)
venomous, vicious

venin [vənɛ̃] nm venom, poison

venir [v(ə)nir] vi to come; **~ de** to come
from; **~ de faire: je viens d'y aller/de
le voir** I've just been there/seen him;
s'il vient à pleuvoir if it should rain;
j'en viens à croire que I have come to
believe that; **où veux-tu en ~?** what
are you getting at?; **faire ~** (docteur,
plombier) to call (out)

vent [vɑ̃] nm wind; **il y a du ~** it's windy;
c'est du ~ it's all hot air; **dans le ~**
(fam) trendy

vente [vɑ̃t] nf sale; **la ~** (activité) selling;

(secteur) sales pl; **mettre en ~** (produit)
to put on sale; (maison, objet personnel)
to put up for sale; **vente aux enchères**
auction sale; **vente de charité**
jumble sale

venteux, -euse [vɑ̃tø, øz] adj windy

ventilateur [vɑ̃tilatœr] nm fan

ventiler [vɑ̃tile] vt to ventilate

ventouse [vɑ̃tuz] nf (de caoutchouc)
suction pad

ventre [vɑ̃tr] nm (Anat) stomach;
(légèrement péj) belly; (utérus) womb;
avoir mal au ~ to have stomach ache
(BRIT) ou a stomach ache (US)

venu, e [v(ə)ny] pp de **venir** ▷ adj: **bien
~** timely; **mal ~** out of place; **être mal
~ à** ou **de faire** to have no grounds for
doing, be in no position to do

ver [ver] nm worm; (des fruits etc)
maggot; (du bois) woodworm no pl; voir
aussi **vers**; **ver à soie** silkworm; **ver de
terre** earthworm; **ver luisant** glow-
worm; **ver solitaire** tapeworm

verbe [verb] nm verb

verdâtre [verdɑtr] adj greenish

verdict [verdik(t)] nm verdict

verdir [verdir] vi, vt to turn green;
verdure nf greenery

véreux, -euse [verø, øz] adj worm-
eaten; (malhonnête) shady, corrupt

verge [verʒ] nf (Anat) penis

verger [verʒe] nm orchard

verglacé, e [verglase] adj icy,
iced-over

verglas [vergla] nm (black) ice

véridique [veridik] adj truthful

vérification [verifikasjɔ̃] nf (action)
checking no pl; (contrôle) check

vérifier [verifje] vt to check;
(corroborer) to confirm, bear out

véritable [veritabl] adj real; (ami,
amour) true; **un ~ désastre** an absolute
disaster

vérité [verite] nf truth; **en ~** really,
actually

verlan [verlɑ̃] nm (fam) (back) slang

vermeil, le [vermej] adj ruby red

vermine [vermin] nf vermin pl

vermoulu, e [vɛʀmuly] *adj* worm-eaten

verni, e [vɛʀni] *adj* (*fam*) lucky; **cuir ~** patent leather

vernir [vɛʀniʀ] *vt* (*bois, tableau, ongles*) to varnish; (*poterie*) to glaze; **vernis** *nm* (*enduit*) varnish; glaze; (*fig*) veneer; **vernis à ongles** nail polish *ou* varnish; **vernissage** *nm* (*d'une exposition*) preview

vérole [veʀɔl] *nf* (*variole*) smallpox

verre [vɛʀ] *nm* glass; (*de lunettes*) lens *sg*; **boire** *ou* **prendre un ~** to have a drink; **verres de contact** contact lenses; **verrière** *nf* (*paroi vitrée*) glass wall; (*toit vitré*) glass roof

verrou [veʀu] *nm* (*targette*) bolt; **mettre qn sous les ~s** to put sb behind bars; **verrouillage** *nm* locking; **verrouillage centralisé** central locking; **verrouiller** *vt* (*porte*) to bolt; (*ordinateur*) to lock

verrue [veʀy] *nf* wart

vers [vɛʀ] *nm* line ▷ *nmpl* (*poésie*) verse *sg* ▷ *prép* (*en direction de*) toward(s); (*près de*) around (about); (*temporel*) about, around

versant [vɛʀsɑ̃] *nm* slopes *pl*, side

versatile [vɛʀsatil] *adj* fickle, changeable

verse [vɛʀs] : **à ~** *adv*: **il pleut à ~** it's pouring (with rain)

Verseau [vɛʀso] *nm*: **le ~** Aquarius

versement [vɛʀsəmɑ̃] *nm* payment; **en 3 ~s** in 3 instalments

verser [vɛʀse] *vt* (*liquide, grains*) to pour; (*larmes, sang*) to shed; (*argent*) to pay; **~ qch sur un compte** to pay sth into an account

version [vɛʀsjɔ̃] *nf* version; (*Scol*) translation (*into the mother tongue*); **film en ~ originale** film in the original language

verso [vɛʀso] *nm* back; **voir au ~** see over(leaf)

vert, e [vɛʀ, vɛʀt] *adj* green; (*vin*) young; (*vigoureux*) sprightly ▷ *nm* green; **les V~s** (*Pol*) the Greens

vertèbre [vɛʀtɛbʀ] *nf* vertebra

vertement [vɛʀtəmɑ̃] *adv* (*réprimander*) sharply

vertical, e, -aux [vɛʀtikal, o] *adj* vertical; **verticale** *nf* vertical; **à la verticale** vertically; **verticalement** *adv* vertically

vertige [vɛʀtiʒ] *nm* (*peur du vide*) vertigo; (*étourdissement*) dizzy spell; (*fig*) fever; **vertigineux, -euse** *adj* breathtaking

vertu [vɛʀty] *nf* virtue; **en ~ de** in accordance with; **vertueux, -euse** *adj* virtuous

verve [vɛʀv] *nf* witty eloquence; **être en ~** to be in brilliant form

verveine [vɛʀvɛn] *nf* (*Bot*) verbena, vervain; (*infusion*) verbena tea

vésicule [vezikyl] *nf* vesicle; **vésicule biliaire** gall-bladder

vessie [vesi] *nf* bladder

veste [vɛst] *nf* jacket; **veste droite/croisée** single-/double-breasted jacket

vestiaire [vɛstjɛʀ] *nm* (*au théâtre etc*) cloakroom; (*de stade etc*) changing-room (*BRIT*); locker-room (*US*)

vestibule [vɛstibyl] *nm* hall

vestige [vɛstiʒ] *nm* relic; (*fig*) vestige; **vestiges** *nmpl* (*de ville*) remains

vestimentaire [vɛstimɑ̃tɛʀ] *adj* (*détail*) of dress; (*élégance*) sartorial; **dépenses ~s** clothing expenditure

veston [vɛstɔ̃] *nm* jacket

vêtement [vɛtmɑ̃] *nm* garment, item of clothing; **vêtements** *nmpl* clothes

vétérinaire [veteʀinɛʀ] *nm/f* vet, veterinary surgeon

vêtir [vetiʀ] *vt* to clothe, dress

vêtu, e [vety] *pp de* **vêtir** ▷ *adj*: **~ de** dressed in, wearing

vétuste [vetyst] *adj* ancient, timeworn

veuf, veuve [vœf, vœv] *adj* widowed ▷ *nm* widower

veuve [vœv] *nf* widow

vexant, e [vɛksɑ̃, ɑ̃t] *adj* (*contrariant*) annoying; (*blessant*) hurtful

vexation [vɛksasjɔ̃] *nf* humiliation

vexer [vɛkse] vt: **~ qn** to hurt sb's feelings; **se vexer** vi to be offended

viable [vjabl] adj viable; (économie, industrie etc) sustainable

viande [vjɑ̃d] nf meat; **je ne mange pas de ~** I don't eat meat

vibrer [vibʀe] vi to vibrate; (son, voix) to be vibrant; (fig) to be stirred; **faire ~** (cause) to vibrate; (fig) to stir, thrill

vice [vis] nm vice; (défaut) fault ⊳ préfixe: **~...** vice-; **vice de forme** legal flaw ou irregularity

vicié, e [visje] adj (air) polluted, tainted; (Jur) invalidated

vicieux, -euse [visjø, jøz] adj (pervers) lecherous; (rétif) unruly ⊳ nm/f lecher

vicinal, e, -aux [visinal, o] adj: **chemin ~** by-road, byway

victime [viktim] nf victim; (d'accident) casualty

victoire [viktwaʀ] nf victory

victuailles [viktɥaj] nfpl provisions

vidange [vidɑ̃ʒ] nf (d'un fossé, réservoir) emptying; (Auto) oil change; (de lavabo: bonde) waste outlet; **vidanges** nfpl (matières) sewage sg; **vidanger** vt to empty

vide [vid] adj empty ⊳ nm (Physique) vacuum; (espace) (empty) space, gap; (futilité, néant) void; **avoir peur du ~** to be afraid of heights; **emballé sous ~** vacuum packed; **à ~** (sans occupants) empty; (sans charge) unladen

vidéo [video] nf video ⊳ adj: **cassette ~** video cassette; **jeu ~** video game; **vidéoclip** nm music video; **vidéoconférence** nf videoconference

vide-ordures [vidɔʀdyʀ] nm inv (rubbish) chute

vider [vide] vt to empty; (Culin: volaille, poisson) to gut, clean out; **se vider** vi to empty; **~ les lieux** to quit ou vacate the premises; **videur** nm (de boîte de nuit) bouncer, doorman

vie [vi] nf life; **être en ~** to be alive; **sans ~** lifeless; **à ~** for life; **que faites-vous dans la ~?** what do you do?

vieil [vjɛj] adj m voir **vieux**; **vieillard**

nm old man; **vieille** adj, nf voir **vieux**; **vieilleries** nfpl old things; **vieillesse** nf old age; **vieillir** vi (prendre de l'âge) to grow old; (population, vin) to age; (doctrine, auteur) to become dated ⊳ vt to age; **vieillissement** nm growing old; ageing

Vienne [vjɛn] nf Vienna

viens [vjɛ̃] vb voir **venir**

vierge [vjɛʀʒ] adj virgin; (page) clean, blank ⊳ nf virgin; (signe): **la V~** Virgo

Vietnam, Viet-Nam [vjɛtnam] nm Vietnam; **vietnamien, ne** adj Vietnamese ⊳ nm/f: **Vietnamien, ne** Vietnamese

vieux, vieil, vieille [vjø, vjɛj] adj old ⊳ nm/f old man (woman); **les vieux** nmpl old people; **un petit ~** a little old man; **mon ~/ma vieille** (fam) old man/girl; **prendre un coup de ~** to take years on; **vieux garçon** bachelor; **vieux jeu** adj inv old-fashioned

vif, vive [vif, viv] adj (animé) lively; (alerte, brusque, aigu) sharp; (lumière, couleur) bright; (air) crisp; (vent, émotion) keen; (fort: regret, déception) great, deep; (vivant): **brûlé ~** burnt alive; **de vive voix** personally; **avoir l'esprit ~** to be quick-witted; **piquer qn au ~** to cut sb to the quick; **à ~** (plaie) open; **avoir les nerfs à ~** to be on edge

vigne [viɲ] nf (plante) vine; (plantation) vineyard; **vigneron** nm wine grower

vignette [viɲɛt] nf (Admin) ≈ (road) tax disc (BRIT), ≈ license plate sticker (US); (de médicament) price label (used for reimbursement)

vignoble [viɲɔbl] nm (plantation) vineyard; (vignes d'une région) vineyards pl

vigoureux, -euse [viguʀø, øz] adj vigorous, robust

vigueur [vigœʀ] nf vigour; **entrer en ~** to come into force; **en ~** current

vilain, e [vilɛ̃, ɛn] adj (laid) ugly; (affaire, blessure) nasty; (pas sage: enfant) naughty; **vilain mot** naughty ou bad word

villa [villa] nf (detached) house; **~ en multipropriété** time-share villa

village [vilaʒ] nm village; **villageois, e** adj village cpd ▷ nm/f villager

ville [vil] nf town; (importante) city; (administration): **la ~** the (town) council, the local authority; **ville d'eaux** spa; **ville nouvelle** new town

vin [vɛ̃] nm wine; **avoir le ~ gai** to get happy after a few drinks; **vin d'honneur** reception (with wine and snacks); **vin de pays** local wine; **vin ordinaire** ou **de table** table wine

vinaigre [vinɛgʀ] nm vinegar; **vinaigrette** nf vinaigrette, French dressing

vindicatif, -ive [vɛ̃dikatif, iv] adj vindictive

vingt [vɛ̃] num twenty; **~-quatre heures sur ~-quatre** twenty-four hours a day, round the clock; **vingtaine** nf: **une vingtaine (de)** about twenty, twenty or so; **vingtième** num twentieth

vinicole [vinikɔl] adj wine cpd, wine-growing

vinyle [vinil] nm vinyl

viol [vjɔl] nm (d'une femme) rape; (d'un lieu sacré) violation

violacé, e [vjɔlase] adj purplish, mauvish

violemment [vjɔlamɑ̃] adv violently

violence [vjɔlɑ̃s] nf violence

violent, e [vjɔlɑ̃, ɑ̃t] adj violent; (remède) drastic

violer [vjɔle] vt (femme) to rape; (sépulture, loi, traité) to violate

violet, te [vjɔlɛ, ɛt] adj, nm purple, mauve; **violette** nf (fleur) violet

violon [vjɔlɔ̃] nm violin; (fam: prison) lock-up; **violon d'Ingres** hobby; **violoncelle** nm cello; **violoniste** nm/f violinist

vipère [vipɛʀ] nf viper, adder

virage [viraʒ] nm (d'un véhicule) turn; (d'une route, piste) bend

virée [vire] nf trip; (à pied) walk; (longue) walking tour; (dans les cafés) tour

virement [virmɑ̃] nm (Comm) transfer

virer [vire] vt (Comm): **~ qch (sur)** to transfer sth (into); (fam: expulser): **~ qn** to kick sb out ▷ vi to turn; (Chimie) to change colour; **~ au bleu/rouge** to turn blue/red; **~ de bord** to tack

virevolter [virvɔlte] vi to twirl around

virgule [virgyl] nf comma; (Math) point

viril, e [viril] adj (propre à l'homme) masculine; (énergique, courageux) manly, virile

virtuel, le [virtɥɛl] adj potential; (théorique) virtual

virtuose [virtɥoz] nm/f (Mus) virtuoso; (gén) master

virus [virys] nm virus

vis¹ [vi] vb voir **voir**; **vivre**

vis² [vis] nf screw

visa [viza] nm (sceau) stamp; (validation de passeport) visa

visage [vizaʒ] nm face

vis-à-vis [vizavi] prép: **~ de qn** to(wards) sb; **en ~** facing each other

visées [vize] nfpl (intentions) designs

viser [vize] vi to aim at; (concerner) to be aimed ou directed at; (apposer un visa sur) to stamp, visa; **~ à qch/faire** to aim at sth/at doing ou to do

visibilité [vizibilite] nf visibility

visible [vizibl] adj visible; (disponible): **est-il ~?** can he see me?, will he see visitors?

visière [vizjɛʀ] nf (de casquette) peak; (qui s'attache) eyeshade

vision [vizjɔ̃] nf vision; (sens) (eye)sight, vision; (fait de voir): **la ~ de** the sight of; **visionneuse** nf viewer

visiophone [vizjɔfɔn] nm videophone

visite [vizit] nf visit; **~ médicale** medical examination; **~ accompagnée** ou **guidée** guided tour; **la ~ guidée commence à quelle heure?** what time does the guided tour start?; **faire une ~ à qn** to call on sb, pay sb a visit; **rendre ~ à qn** to visit sb, pay sb a visit; **être en ~ (chez qn)** to be visiting (sb); **avoir**

de la ~ to have visitors; **heures de ~**
(*hôpital, prison*) visiting hours
visiter [vizite] *vt* to visit; **visiteur,
-euse** *nm/f* visitor
vison [vizɔ̃] *nm* mink
visser [vise] *vt*: **~ qch** (*fixer, serrer*) to
screw sth on
visuel, le [vizɥɛl] *adj* visual
vital, e, -aux [vital, o] *adj* vital
vitamine [vitamin] *nf* vitamin
vite [vit] *adv* (*rapidement*) quickly, fast;
(*sans délai*) quickly; (*sous peu*) soon; **~!**
quick!; **faire ~** to be quick; **le temps
passe ~** time flies
vitesse [vites] *nf* speed; (*Auto: dispositif*)
gear; **prendre de la ~** to pick up or
gather speed; **à toute ~** at full or top
speed; **en ~** (*rapidement*) quickly; (*en
hâte*) in a hurry

● **LIMITE DE VITESSE**

○ The speed limit in France is 50 km/h
○ in built-up areas, 90 km/h on main
○ roads, and 130 km/h on motorways
○ (110 km/h when it is raining).

viticulteur [vitikyltœʀ] *nm* wine
grower
vitrage [vitraʒ] *nm*: **double ~** double
glazing
vitrail, -aux [vitraj, o] *nm* stained-
glass window
vitre [vitʀ] *nf* (*window*) pane; (*de
portière, voiture*) window; **vitré, e** *adj*
glass *cpd*
vitrine [vitʀin] *nf* (*shop*) window;
(*petite armoire*) display cabinet; **en ~** in
the window

vivable [vivabl] *adj* (*personne*) livable-
with; (*maison*) fit to live in
vivace [vivas] *adj* (*arbre, plante*) hardy;
(*fig*) indestructible, inveterate
vivacité [vivasite] *nf* liveliness,
vivacity
vivant, e [vivã, ãt] *adj* (*qui vit*) living,
alive; (*animé*) lively; (*preuve, exemple*)
living ▷ *nm*: **du ~ de qn** in sb's lifetime;

les ~s the living
vive [viv] *adj* voir **vif** ▷ *vb* voir **vivre**
▷ *excl*: **~ le roi!** long live the king!;
vivement *adv* deeply ▷ *excl*: **vivement
les vacances!** roll on the holidays!
vivier [vivje] *nm* (*étang*) fish tank;
(*réservoir*) fishpond
vivifiant, e [vivifjã, jãt] *adj*
invigorating
vivoter [vivɔte] *vi* (*personne*) to scrape
a living, get by; (*fig: affaire etc*) to
struggle along
vivre [vivʀ] *vi, vt* to live; (*période*) to live
through; **vivres** *nmpl* provisions, food
supplies; **~ de** to live on; **il vit encore**
he is still alive; **se laisser ~** to take life
as it comes; **ne plus ~** (*être anxieux*) to
live on one's nerves; **il a vécu** (*eu une vie
aventureuse*) he has seen life; **être facile
à ~** to be easy to get on with; **faire ~ qn**
(*pourvoir à sa subsistance*) to provide (a
living) for sb
vlan [vlã] *excl* wham!, bang!
VO [veo] *nf*: **film en VO** film in the
original version; **en VO sous-titrée** in
the original version with subtitles
vocabulaire [vɔkabulɛʀ] *nm*
vocabulary
vocation [vɔkasjɔ̃] *nf* vocation, calling
vœu, x [vø] *nm* wish; (*promesse*) vow;
faire ~ de to take a vow of; **tous nos ~x
de bonne année, meilleurs ~x** best
wishes for the New Year
vogue [vɔg] *nf* fashion, vogue; **en ~** in
fashion, in vogue
voici [vwasi] *prép* (*pour introduire,
désigner*) here is +*sg*, here are +*pl*; **et
~ que ~** and now it (ou he) ...; *voir
aussi* **voilà**
voie [vwa] *nf* way; (*Rail*) track, line;
(*Auto*) lane; **être en bonne ~** to be
going well; **mettre qn sur la ~** to
put sb on the right track; **pays en
~ de développement** developing
country; **être en ~ d'achèvement/de
rénovation** to be nearing completion/
in the process of renovation; **par ~
buccale ou orale** orally; **route à ~**

unique single-track road; **route à 2/3 ~s** 2-/3-lane road; **voie de garage** (Rail) siding; **voie express** expressway; **voie ferrée** track; railway line (BRIT), railroad (US); **la voie lactée** the Milky Way; **la voie publique** the public highway

voilà [vwala] *prép* (en désignant) there is +sg, there are +pl; **les ~ ou voici** here ou there they are; **en ~ un** here's one, there's one; **voici mon frère et ~ ma sœur** this is my brother and that's my sister; **~ ou voici deux ans** two years ago; **~ ou voici deux ans que** it's two years since; **et ~!** there we are!; **~ tout** that's that; **~ ou voici** (en offrant etc) there ou here you are; **tiens! ~ Paul** look! there's Paul

voile [vwal] *nm* veil; (tissu léger) net ▷ *nf* sail; (sport) sailing; **voiler** *vt* to veil; (fausser: roue) to buckle; (: bois) to warp; **se voiler** *vi* (lune, regard) to mist over; (voix) to become husky; (roue, disque) to buckle; (planche) to warp; **voilier** *nm* sailing ship; (de plaisance) sailing boat; **voilure** *nf* (de voilier) sails pl

voir [vwaʀ] *vi*, *vt* to see; **se voir** *vi* (être visible) to show; (se fréquenter) to see each other; (se produire) to happen; **cela se voit** (c'est visible) that's obvious; it shows; **faire ~ qch à qn** to show sb sth; **en faire ~ à qn** (fig) to give sb a hard time; **ne pas pouvoir ~ qn** not to be able to stand sb; **voyons!** let's see now; (indignation etc) come on!; **ça n'a rien à ~ avec lui** that has nothing to do with him

voire [vwaʀ] *adv* even

voisin, e [vwazɛ̃, in] *adj* (proche) neighbouring; (contigu) next; (ressemblant) connected ▷ *nm/f* neighbour; **voisinage** *nm* (proximité) proximity; (environs) vicinity; (quartier, voisins) neighbourhood

voiture [vwatyʀ] *nf* car; (wagon) coach, carriage; **voiture de course** racing car; **voiture de sport** sports car

voix [vwa] *nf* voice; (Pol) vote; **à haute ~**

aloud; **à ~ basse** in a low voice; **à 2/4 ~** (Mus) in 2/4 parts; **avoir ~ au chapitre** to have a say in the matter

vol [vɔl] *nm* (d'oiseau, d'avion) flight; (larcin) theft; **~ régulier** scheduled flight; **à ~ d'oiseau** as the crow flies; **au ~: attraper qch au ~** to catch sth as it flies past; **en ~** in flight; **je voudrais signaler un ~** I'd like to report a theft; **vol à main armée** armed robbery; **vol à voile** gliding; **vol libre** hang-gliding

volage [vɔlaʒ] *adj* fickle

volaille [vɔlaj] *nf* (oiseaux) poultry pl; (viande) poultry no pl; (oiseau) fowl

volant, e [vɔlɑ̃, ɑ̃t] *adj* voir **feuille** etc ▷ *nm* (d'automobile) (steering) wheel; (de commande) wheel; (objet lancé) shuttlecock; (bande de tissu) flounce

volcan [vɔlkɑ̃] *nm* volcano

volée [vɔle] *nf* (Tennis) volley; **à la ~: rattraper à la ~** to catch sth in mid-air; **à toute ~** (sonner les cloches) vigorously; (lancer un projectile) with full force

voler [vɔle] *vi* (avion, oiseau, fig) to fly; (voleur) to steal ▷ *vt* (objet) to steal; (personne) to rob; **~ qch à qn** to steal sth from sb; **on m'a volé mon portefeuille** my wallet (BRIT) ou billfold (US) has been stolen; **il ne l'a pas volé!** he asked for it!

volet [vɔle] *nm* (de fenêtre) shutter; (de feuillet, document) section

voleur, -euse [vɔlœʀ, øz] *nm/f* thief ▷ *adj* thieving; **"au ~!"** "stop thief!"

volontaire [vɔlɔ̃teʀ] *adj* (acte, enrôlement, prisonnier) voluntary; (oubli) intentional; (caractère, personne: décidé) self-willed ▷ *nm/f* volunteer

volonté [vɔlɔ̃te] *nf* (faculté de vouloir) will; (énergie, fermeté) will (power); (souhait, désir) wish; **à ~** as much as one likes; **bonne ~** goodwill, willingness; **mauvaise ~** lack of goodwill, unwillingness

volontiers [vɔlɔ̃tje] *adv* (avec plaisir) willingly, gladly; (habituellement, souvent) readily, willingly; **voulez-vous boire quelque chose? — ~!** I would you like something to drink? — yes, please!

volt [vɔlt] nm volt

volte-face [vɔltəfas] nf inv: **faire ~** to turn round

voltige [vɔltiʒ] nf (Équitation) trick riding; (au cirque) acrobatics sg; **voltiger** vi to flutter (about)

volubile [vɔlybil] adj voluble

volume [vɔlym] nm volume; (Géom: solide) solid; **volumineux, -euse** adj voluminous, bulky

volupté [vɔlypte] nf sensual delight ou pleasure

vomi [vɔmi] nm vomit; **vomir** vi to vomit, be sick ▷ vt to bring up; (fig) to belch out, spew out; (exécrer) to loathe, abhor

vorace [vɔras] adj voracious

vos [vo] adj voir **votre**

vote [vɔt] nm vote; **vote par correspondance/procuration** postal/ proxy vote; **voter** vi to vote ▷ vt (projet de loi) to vote for; (loi, réforme) to pass

votre [vɔtʀ] (pl **vos**) adj your

vôtre [votʀ] pron: **le ~, la ~, les ~s** yours; **les ~s** (fig) your family ou folks; **à la ~** (toast) your (good) health!

vouer [vwe] vt: **~ sa vie à** (étude, cause etc) to devote one's life to; **une amitié éternelle à qn** to vow undying friendship to sb

○ **MOT-CLÉ**

vouloir [vulwaʀ] nm: **le bon vouloir de qn** sb's goodwill; sb's pleasure ▷ vt 1 (exiger, désirer) to want; **vouloir faire/que qn fasse** to want to do/sb to do; **voulez-vous du thé?** would you like ou do you want some tea?; **que me veut-il?** what does he want with me?; **sans le vouloir** (involontairement) without meaning to, unintentionally; **je voudrais ceci/faire** I would ou I'd like this/to do; **le hasard a voulu que …** as fate would have it …; **la tradition veut que …** it is a tradition that …

2 (consentir): **je veux bien** (bonne volonté) I'll be happy to; (concession) fair enough, that's fine; **je peux le faire, si vous voulez** I can do it if you like; **oui, si on veut** (en quelque sorte) yes, if you like; **veuillez attendre** please wait; **veuillez agréer …** (formule épistolaire: personne nommée) yours sincerely; (personne non nommée) yours faithfully

3: **en vouloir à qn** to bear sb a grudge; **s'en vouloir (de)** to be annoyed with o.s. (for); **il en veut à mon argent** he's after my money

4: **vouloir de: l'entreprise ne veut plus de lui** the firm doesn't want him any more; **elle ne veut pas de son aide** she doesn't want his help

5: **vouloir dire** to mean

voulu, e [vuly] adj (requis) required, requisite; (délibéré) deliberate, intentional; voir aussi **vouloir**

vous [vu] pron you; (objet indirect) (to) you; (réfléchi: sg) yourself; (: pl) yourselves; (réciproque) each other ▷ nm: **employer le ~** (vouvoyer) to use the "vous" form; **~-même** yourself; **~-mêmes** yourselves

vouvoyer [vuvwaje] vt: **~ qn** to address sb as "vous"

voyage [vwajaʒ] nm journey, trip; (fait de voyager): **le ~** travel(ling); **partir/être en ~** to go off/be away on a journey ou trip; **faire bon ~** to have a good journey; **votre ~ s'est bien passé?** how was your journey?; **voyage d'affaires/ d'agrément** business/pleasure trip; **voyage de noces** honeymoon; **nous sommes en voyage de noces** we're on honeymoon; **voyage organisé** package tour

voyager [vwajaʒe] vi to travel; **voyageur, -euse** nm/f traveller; (passager) passenger; **voyageur de commerce** sales representative, commercial traveller

voyant, e [vwajɑ̃, ɑ̃t] adj (couleur) loud, gaudy ▷ nm (signal) (warning) light

voyelle [vwajɛl] nf vowel

voyou [vwaju] nm hooligan

vrac [vʁak]: **en ~** adv (au détail) loose; (en gros) in bulk; (en désordre) in a jumble

vrai, e [vʁɛ] adj (véridique: récit, faits) true; (non factice, authentique) real; **à ~ dire** to tell the truth; **vraiment** adv really; **vraisemblable** adj likely; (excuse) convincing; **vraisemblablement** adj probably; **vraisemblance** nf likelihood; (romanesque) verisimilitude

vrombir [vʁɔ̃biʁ] vi to hum

VRP sigle m (= voyageur, représentant, placier) sales rep (fam)

VTT sigle m (= vélo tout-terrain) mountain bike

vu, e [vy] pp de **voir** ▷ adj: **bien/mal vu** (fig: personne) popular/unpopular; (: chose) approved/disapproved of ▷ prép (en raison de) in view of; **vu que** in view of the fact that

vue [vy] nf (fait de voir): **la ~ de** the sight of; (sens, faculté) (eye)sight; (panorama, image, photo) view; **vues** nfpl (idées) views; (dessein) designs; (: chose) out of sight; **avoir en ~** to have in mind; **tirer à ~** to shoot on sight; **à ~ d'œil** visibly; **à première ~** at first sight; **de ~** by sight; **perdre de ~** to lose sight of; **en ~ (visible)** in sight; (célèbre) in the public eye; **en ~ de faire** with a view to doing; **perdre la ~** to lose one's (eye)sight; **avoir ~ sur** (suj: fenêtre) to have a view of; **vue d'ensemble** overall view

vulgaire [vylgɛʁ] adj (grossier) vulgar, coarse; (ordinaire) commonplace, mundane; (péj: quelconque): **de ~s touristes** common tourists; (Bot, Zool: non latin) common; **vulgariser** vt to popularize

vulnérable [vylneʁabl] adj vulnerable

W

wagon [vagɔ̃] nm (de voyageurs) carriage; (de marchandises) truck, wagon; **wagon-lit** nm sleeper, sleeping car; **wagon-restaurant** nm restaurant ou dining car

wallon, ne [walɔ̃, ɔn] adj Walloon ▷ nm (Ling) Walloon ▷ nm/f: **W~, ne** Walloon

watt [wat] nm watt

w-c sigle mpl (= water-closet(s)) toilet

Web [wɛb] nm inv: **le ~** (the World Wide) Web; **webmaster** [-mastœʁ], **webmestre** [-mɛstʁ] nm/f webmaster

week-end [wikɛnd] nm weekend

western [wɛstɛʁn] nm western

whisky [wiski] (pl **whiskies**) nm whisky

xénophobe [gzenɔfɔb] *adj* xenophobic ▷ *nm/f* xenophobe
xérès [gzeʀɛs] *nm* sherry
xylophone [gzilɔfɔn] *nm* xylophone

y [i] *adv* (*à cet endroit*) there; (*dessus*) on it (*ou* them); (*dedans*) in it (*ou* them) ▷ *pron* (*about ou on ou of*) it (*d'après le verbe employé*); **j'y pense** i'm thinking about it; **ça y est!** that's it!; *voir aussi* **aller; avoir**
yacht [jɔt] *nm* yacht
yaourt [jauʀt] *nm* yoghurt; **~ nature/ aux fruits** plain/fruit yogurt
yeux [jø] *nmpl de* **œil**
yoga [jɔga] *nm* yoga
yoghourt [jɔguʀt] *nm* = **yaourt**
yougoslave [jugɔslav] (*Histoire*) *adj* Yugoslav(ian) ▷ *nm/f*: **Y~** Yugoslav
Yougoslavie [jugɔslavi] *nf* (*Histoire*) Yugoslavia; **l'ex-~** the former Yugoslavia

Z

≈ restricted parking area; **zone industrielle** industrial estate
zoo [zo(o)] nm zoo
zoologie [zɔɔlɔʒi] nf zoology; **zoologique** adj zoological
zut [zyt] excl dash (it)! (BRIT), nuts! (US)

zapper [zape] vi to zap
zapping [zapiŋ] nm: **faire du ~** to flick through the channels
zèbre [zɛbʀ(ə)] nm (Zool) zebra; **zébré, e** adj striped, streaked
zèle [zɛl] nm zeal; **faire du ~** (péj) to be over-zealous; **zélé, e** adj zealous
zéro [zeʀo] nm zero, nought (BRIT); **au-dessous de ~** below zero (Centigrade) ou freezing; **partir de ~** to start from scratch; **trois (buts) à ~** 3 (goals to) nil
zeste [zɛst] nm peel, zest
zézayer [zezeje] vi to have a lisp
zigzag [zigzag] nm zigzag; **zigzaguer** vi to zigzag
Zimbabwe [zimbabwe] nm: **le ~** Zimbabwe
zinc [zɛ̃g] nm (Chimie) zinc
zipper [zipe] vt (Inform) to zip
zizi [zizi] nm (langage enfantin) willy
zodiaque [zɔdjak] nm zodiac
zona [zona] nm shingles sg
zone [zon] nf zone, area; (fam: quartiers pauvres): **la ~** the slums; **zone bleue**

A [eɪ] n (Mus) la m

 KEYWORD

a [eɪ, ə] (before vowel or silent h **an**) indef art **1** un(e); **a book** un livre; **an apple** une pomme; **she's a doctor** elle est médecin

2 (instead of the number "one") un(e); **a year ago** il y a un an; **a hundred/ thousand** etc **pounds** cent/mille etc livres

3 (in expressing ratios, prices etc): **3 a day/week** 3 par jour/semaine; **10 km an hour** 10 km à l'heure; **£5 a person** 5£ par personne; **30p a kilo** 30p le kilo

A2 n (BRIT: Scol) deuxième partie de l'examen équivalent au baccalauréat

A.A. n abbr (BRIT: = Automobile Association) ≈ ACF m, (= Alcoholics Anonymous) AA

A.A.A. n abbr (= American Automobile Association) ≈ ACF m

aback [əˈbæk] adv: **to be taken ~** être déconcentané(e)

abandon [əˈbændən] vt abandonner

abattoir [ˈæbətwɑː'] n (BRIT) abattoir m

abbey [ˈæbɪ] n abbaye f

abbreviation [əbriːvɪˈeɪʃən] n abréviation f

abdomen [ˈæbdəmən] n abdomen m

abduct [æbˈdʌkt] vt enlever

abide [əˈbaɪd] vt souffrir, supporter; **I can't ~ it/him** je ne le supporte pas; **abide by** vt fus observer, respecter

ability [əˈbɪlɪtɪ] n compétence f, capacité f; (skill) talent m

able [ˈeɪbl] adj compétent(e); **to be ~ to do sth** pouvoir faire qch, être capable de faire qch

abnormal [æbˈnɔːməl] adj anormal(e)

aboard [əˈbɔːd] adv à bord ▷ prep à bord de; (train) dans

abolish [əˈbɒlɪʃ] vt abolir

abolition [æbəˈlɪʃən] n abolition f

abort [əˈbɔːt] vt (Med) faire avorter; (Comput, fig) abandonner; **abortion** [əˈbɔːʃən] n avortement m; **to have an abortion** se faire avorter

 KEYWORD

about [əˈbaut] adv **1** (approximately) environ, à peu près; **about a hundred/ thousand** etc environ cent/mille etc, une centaine (de)/un millier (de) etc; **it takes about 10 hours** ça prend environ or à peu près 10 heures; **at about 2 o'clock** vers 2 heures; **I've just about finished** j'ai presque fini

2 (referring to place) çà et là, de-ci de-là; **to run about** courir çà et là; **to walk about** se promener, aller et venir; **they left all their things lying about** ils ont laissé se traîner toutes leurs affaires

3: **to be about to do sth** être sur le point de faire qch

▷ prep **1** (relating to) au sujet de, à propos de; **a book about London** un livre sur Londres; **what is it about?** de quoi s'agit-il?; **we talked about it** nous en avons parlé; **what** or **how about doing this?** et si nous faisions ceci? 2 (referring to place) dans; **to walk about the town** se promener dans la ville

above [ə'bʌv] adv au-dessus ▷ prep au-dessus de; (more than) plus de; **mentioned ~** mentionné ci-dessus; **~ all** par-dessus tout, surtout

abroad [ə'brɔːd] adv à l'étranger

abrupt [ə'brʌpt] adj (steep, blunt) abrupt(e); (sudden, gruff) brusque

abscess ['æbsɪs] n abcès m

absence ['æbsəns] n absence f

absent ['æbsənt] adj absent(e); **absent-minded** adj distrait(e)

absolute ['æbsəluːt] adj absolu(e); **absolutely** [æbsə'luːtlɪ] adv absolument

absorb [əb'zɔːb] vt absorber; **to be ~ed in a book** être plongé(e) dans un livre; **absorbent cotton** n (US) coton m hydrophile; **absorbing** adj absorbant(e); (book, film etc) captivant(e)

abstain [əb'steɪn] vi: **to ~ (from)** s'abstenir (de)

abstract ['æbstrækt] adj abstrait(e)

absurd [əb'səːd] adj absurde

abundance [ə'bʌndəns] n abondance f

abundant [ə'bʌndənt] adj abondant(e)

abuse n [ə'bjuːs] (insults) insultes fpl, injures fpl; (ill-treatment) mauvais traitements mpl; (of power etc) abus m ▷ vt [ə'bjuːz] (insult) insulter; (ill-treat) malmener; (power etc) abuser de; **abusive** adj grossier(-ière), injurieux(-euse)

abysmal [ə'bɪzməl] adj (ignorance etc) sans bornes

academic [ækə'demɪk] adj universitaire; (person: scholarly) intellectuel(-le); (pej: issue) oiseux(-euse), purement théorique ▷ n universitaire m/f; **academic year** n

(University) année f universitaire; (Scol) année scolaire

academy [ə'kædəmɪ] n (learned body) académie f; (school) collège m; **~ of music** conservatoire m

accelerate [æk'seləreɪt] vt, vi accélérer; **acceleration** [æksələ'reɪʃən] n accélération f; **accelerator** n (BRIT) accélérateur m

accent ['æksɛnt] n accent m

accept [ək'sɛpt] vt accepter; **acceptable** adj acceptable; **acceptance** n acceptation f

access ['æksɛs] n accès m; **to have ~ to** (information, library etc) avoir accès à, pouvoir utiliser or consulter; (person) avoir accès auprès de; **accessible** [æk'sɛsəbl] adj accessible

accessory [æk'sɛsərɪ] n accessoire m; **~ to** (Law) accessoire à

accident ['æksɪdənt] n accident m; (chance) hasard m; **I've had an ~** j'ai eu un accident; **by ~** (by chance) par hasard; (not deliberately) accidentellement; **accidental** [æksɪ'dɛntl] adj accidentel(le); **accidentally** [æksɪ'dɛntəlɪ] adv accidentellement; **Accident and Emergency Department** n (BRIT) service m des urgences; **accident insurance** n assurance f accident

acclaim [ə'kleɪm] vt acclamer ▷ n acclamations fpl

accommodate [ə'kɔmədeɪt] vt loger, recevoir; (oblige, help) obliger; (car etc) contenir

accommodation (US **accommodations**) [əkɔmə'deɪʃən(z)] n(pl) logement m

accompaniment [ə'kʌmpənɪmənt] n accompagnement m

accompany [ə'kʌmpənɪ] vt accompagner

accomplice [ə'kʌmplɪs] n complice m/f

accomplish [ə'kʌmplɪʃ] vt accomplir; **accomplishment** n (skill: gen pl) talent m; (completion) accomplissement m;

(achievement) réussite f

accord [əˈkɔːd] n accord m ▷ vt accorder; **of his own ~** de son plein gré; **accordance** n: **in accordance with** conformément à; **according: according to** prep selon; **accordingly** adv *(appropriately)* en conséquence; *(as a result)* par conséquent

account [əˈkaunt] n *(Comm)* compte m; *(report)* compte rendu, récit m; **accounts** npl *(Comm: records)* comptabilité f, comptes; **of no ~** sans importance; **on ~** en compte; **to buy sth on ~** acheter qch à crédit; **on no ~** en aucun cas; **on ~ of** à cause de; **to take into ~, take ~ of** tenir compte de; **account for** vt fus *(explain)* expliquer, rendre compte de; *(represent)* représenter; **accountable** adj: **accountable (to)** responsable *(devant)*; **accountant** n comptable m/f; **account number** n numéro m de compte

accumulate [əˈkjuːmjuleɪt] vt accumuler, amasser ▷ vi s'accumuler, s'amasser

accuracy [ˈækjurəsɪ] n exactitude f, précision f

accurate [ˈækjurɪt] adj exact(e), précis(e); *(device)* précis; **accurately** adv avec précision

accusation [ækjuˈzeɪʃən] n accusation f

accuse [əˈkjuːz] vt: **~ sb (of sth)** accuser qn *(de qch)*; **accused** n *(Law)* accusé(e)

accustomed [əˈkʌstəmd] adj: **~ to** habitué(e) or accoutumé(e) à

ace [eɪs] n as m

ache [eɪk] n mal m, douleur f ▷ vi *(be sore)* faire mal, être douloureux(-euse); **my head ~s** j'ai mal à la tête

achieve [əˈtʃiːv] vt *(aim)* atteindre; *(victory, success)* remporter, obtenir; **achievement** n exploit m, réussite f; *(of aims)* réalisation f

acid [ˈæsɪd] adj, n acide (m)

acknowledge [əkˈnɒlɪdʒ] vt *(also: ~*

receipt of) accuser réception de; *(fact)* reconnaître; **acknowledgement** n *(of letter)* accusé m de réception

acne [ˈæknɪ] n acné m

acorn [ˈeɪkɔːn] n gland m

acoustic [əˈkuːstɪk] adj acoustique

acquaintance [əˈkweɪntəns] n connaissance f

acquire [əˈkwaɪə] vt acquérir; **acquisition** [ækwɪˈzɪʃən] n acquisition f

acquit [əˈkwɪt] vt acquitter; **to ~ o.s. well** s'en tirer très honorablement

acre [ˈeɪkə] n acre f (= 4047 m²)

acronym [ˈækrənɪm] n acronyme m

across [əˈkrɒs] prep *(on the other side)* de l'autre côté de; *(crosswise)* en travers de ▷ adv de l'autre côté; en travers; **to run/swim ~** traverser en courant/à la nage; **~ from** en face de

acrylic [əˈkrɪlɪk] adj, n acrylique (m)

act [ækt] n acte m, action f; *(Theat: part of play)* acte; *(: of performer)* numéro m; *(Law)* loi f ▷ vi agir; *(Theat)* jouer; *(pretend)* jouer la comédie ▷ vt *(role)* jouer, tenir; **to catch sb in the ~** prendre qn sur le fait or en flagrant délit; **to ~ as** servir de; **act up** *(inf)* ▷ vi *(person)* se conduire mal; *(knee, back, injury)* jouer des tours; *(machine)* être capricieux(-ieuse); **acting** adj suppléant(e), par intérim ▷ n *(activity)*: **to do some acting** faire du théâtre *(or du cinéma)*

action [ˈækʃən] n action f; *(Mil)* combat(s) m(pl); *(Law)* procès m, action en justice; **out of ~** hors de combat; *(machine etc)* hors d'usage; **to take ~** agir, prendre des mesures; **action replay** n *(BRIT TV)* ralenti m

activate [ˈæktɪveɪt] vt *(mechanism)* actionner, faire fonctionner

active [ˈæktɪv] adj actif(-ive); *(volcano)* en activité; **actively** adv activement; *(discourage)* vivement

activist [ˈæktɪvɪst] n activiste m/f

activity [ækˈtɪvɪtɪ] n activité f; **activity holiday** n vacances actives

actor ['æktə'] n acteur m

actress ['æktrɪs] n actrice f

actual ['æktjuəl] adj réel(le), véritable; (emphatic use) lui-même (elle-même).
  Be careful not to translate **actual** by the French word **actuel**.

actually ['æktjuəlɪ] adv réellement, véritablement; (in fact) en fait
  Be careful not to translate **actually** by the French word **actuellement**.

acupuncture ['ækjupʌŋktʃə'] n acuponcture f

acute [ə'kju:t] adj aigu(ë); (mind, observer) pénétrant(e)

A.D. adv abbr (= Anno Domini) ap. J.-C.

ad [æd] n abbr = **advertisement**

adamant ['ædəmənt] adj inflexible

adapt [ə'dæpt] vt adapter ▷ vi: **to ~ (to)** s'adapter (à); **adapter, adaptor** n (Elec)adaptateur m; (for several plugs) prise f multiple

add [æd] vt ajouter; (figures: also: **to ~ up**) additionner ▷ vi (fig): **it doesn't ~ up** cela ne rime à rien; **add up to** vt fus (Math) s'élever à; (fig: mean) signifier

addict ['ædɪkt] n toxicomane m/f; (fig) fanatique m/f; **addicted** [ə'dɪktɪd] adj: **to be addicted to** (drink, drugs) être adonné(e) à; (fig: football etc) être un(e) fanatique de; **addiction** [ə'dɪkʃən] n (Med) dépendance f; **addictive** [ə'dɪktɪv] adj qui crée une dépendance

addition [ə'dɪʃən] n (adding up) addition f; (thing added) ajout m; **in ~** de plus, de surcroît; **in ~ to** en plus de; **additional** adj supplémentaire

additive ['ædɪtɪv] n additif m

address [ə'drɛs] n adresse f; (talk) discours m, allocution f ▷ vt adresser; (speak to) s'adresser à; **my ~ is ...** mon adresse, c'est ...; **address book** n carnet m d'adresses

adequate ['ædɪkwɪt] adj (enough) suffisant(e); (satisfactory) satisfaisant(e)

adhere [əd'hɪə'] vi: **to ~ to** adhérer à; (fig: rule, decision) se tenir à

adhesive [əd'hi:zɪv] n adhésif m;

adhesive tape n (BRIT) ruban m adhésif; (US Med) sparadrap m

adjacent [ə'dʒeɪsənt] adj adjacent(e), contigu(ë); **~ to** adjacent à

adjective ['ædʒɛktɪv] n adjectif m

adjoining [ə'dʒɔɪnɪŋ] adj voisin(e), adjacent(e), attenant(e)

adjourn [ə'dʒə:n] vt ajourner ▷ vi suspendre la séance; lever la séance; clore la session

adjust [ə'dʒʌst] vt (machine) ajuster, régler; (prices, wages) rajuster ▷ vi: **to ~ (to)** s'adapter (à); **adjustable** adj réglable; **adjustment** n (of machine) ajustage m, réglage m; (of prices, wages) rajustement m; (of person) adaptation f

administer [əd'mɪnɪstə'] vt administrer; **administration** [ədmɪnɪs'treɪʃən] n (management) administration f; (government) gouvernement m; **administrative** [əd'mɪnɪstrətɪv] adj administratif(-ive)

administrator [əd'mɪnɪstreɪtə'] n administrateur(-trice)

admiral ['ædmərəl] n amiral m

admiration [ædmə'reɪʃən] n admiration f

admire [əd'maɪə'] vt admirer; **admirer** n (fan) admirateur(-trice)

admission [əd'mɪʃən] n admission f; (to exhibition, night club etc) entrée f; (confession) aveu m

admit [əd'mɪt] vt laisser entrer; admettre; (agree) reconnaître, admettre; (crime) reconnaître avoir commis; **"children not ~ted"** "entrée interdite aux enfants"; **admit to** vt fus reconnaître, avouer; **admittance** n admission f, (droit m d')entrée f; **admittedly** adv il faut en convenir

adolescent [ædəu'lɛsnt] adj, n adolescent(e)

adopt [ə'dɔpt] vt adopter; **adopted** adj adoptif(-ive), adopté(e); **adoption** [ə'dɔpʃən] n adoption f

adore [ə'dɔ:'] vt adorer

adorn [ə'dɔ:n] vt orner

Adriatic (Sea) [eɪdrɪˈætɪk-] n, adj: **the Adriatic (Sea)** la mer Adriatique, l'Adriatique f

adrift [əˈdrɪft] adv à la dérive

adult [ˈædʌlt] n adulte m/f ▷ adj (grown-up) adulte; (for adults) pour adultes; **adult education** f éducation f des adultes

adultery [əˈdʌltərɪ] n adultère m

advance [ədˈvɑːns] n avance f ▷ vt avancer ▷ vi s'avancer; **in** ~ en avance, d'avance; **to make ~s to sb** (gen) faire des propositions à qn; (amorously) faire des avances à qn; ~ **booking** location f; ~ **notice**, ~ **warning** préavis m; (verbal) avertissement m; **do I need to book in ~?** est-ce qu'il faut réserver à l'avance?; **advanced** adj avancé(e); (Scol: studies) supérieur(e)

advantage [ədˈvɑːntɪdʒ] n (also Tennis) avantage m; **to take ~ of** (person) exploiter; (opportunity) profiter de

advent [ˈædvənt] n avènement m, venue f; **A~** (Rel) avent m

adventure [ədˈventʃəʳ] n aventure f; **adventurous** [ədˈventʃərəs] adj aventureux(-euse)

adverb [ˈædvɜːb] n adverbe m

adversary [ˈædvəsərɪ] n adversaire m/f

adverse [ˈædvɜːs] adj adverse; (effect) négatif(-ive); (weather, publicity) mauvais(e); (wind) contraire

advert [ˈædvɜːt] n abbr (BRIT) = **advertisement**

advertise [ˈædvətaɪz] vi faire de la publicité or de la réclame; (in classified ads etc) mettre une annonce ▷ vt faire de la publicité or de la réclame pour; (in classified ads etc) mettre une annonce pour vendre; **to ~ for** (staff) recruter par (voie d')annonce; **advertisement** [ədˈvɜːtɪsmənt] n (Comm) publicité f, réclame f; (in classified ads etc) annonce f; **advertiser** n annonceur m; **advertising** n publicité f

advice [ədˈvaɪs] n conseils mpl; (notification) avis m; **a piece of ~** un

conseil; **to take legal ~** consulter un avocat

advisable [ədˈvaɪzəbl] adj recommandable, indiqué(e)

advise [ədˈvaɪz] vt conseiller; **to ~ sb of sth** aviser or informer qn de qch; **to ~ against sth/doing sth** déconseiller qch/conseiller de ne pas faire qch; **adviser**, **advisor** n conseiller(-ère); **advisory** adj consultatif(-ive)

advocate n [ˈædvəkɪt] (lawyer) avocat (plaidant); (upholder) défenseur m, avocat(e) ▷ vt [ˈædvəkeɪt] recommander, prôner; **to be an ~ of** être partisan(e) de

Aegean [iːˈdʒiːən] n, adj: **the ~ (Sea)** la mer Égée, l'Égée f

aerial [ˈɛərɪəl] n antenne f ▷ adj aérien(ne)

aerobics [ɛəˈrəubɪks] n aérobic m

aeroplane [ˈɛərəpleɪn] n (BRIT) avion m

aerosol [ˈɛərəsɔl] n aérosol m

affair [əˈfɛəʳ] n affaire f; (also: **love ~**) liaison f; aventure f

affect [əˈfɛkt] vt affecter; (subj: disease) atteindre; **affected** adj affecté(e)

affection [əˈfɛkʃən] n affection f; **affectionate** adj affectueux(-euse)

afflict [əˈflɪkt] vt affliger

affluent [ˈæfluənt] adj (person, family, surroundings) aisé(e), riche; **the ~ society** la société d'abondance

afford [əˈfɔːd] vt (behaviour) se permettre; (provide) fournir, procurer; **can we ~ a car?** avons-nous de quoi acheter une voiture?; **affordable** adj abordable

Afghanistan [æfˈɡænɪstæn] n Afghanistan m

afraid [əˈfreɪd] adj effrayé(e); **to be ~ of or to** avoir peur de; **I am ~ that** je crains que + sub; **I'm ~ so/not** oui/non, malheureusement

Africa [ˈæfrɪkə] n Afrique f; **African** adj africain(e) ▷ n Africain(e); **African-American** adj afro-américain(e) ▷ n Afro-Américain(e)

after [ˈɑːftəʳ] prep, adv après ▷ conj

après que; **it's quarter ~ two** (us) il est deux heures et quart; **~ having done/~ he left** après avoir fait/après son départ; **to name sb ~ sb** donner à qn le nom de qn; **to ask ~ sb** demander des nouvelles de qn; **what/who are you ~?** que/qui cherchez-vous?; **~ you!** après vous!; **~ all** après tout; **after-effects** npl (of disaster, radiation, drink etc) répercussions fpl; (of illness) séquelles fpl, suites fpl; **aftermath** n conséquences fpl; **afternoon** n après-midi m or f; **after-shave (lotion)** n lotion f après-rasage; **aftersun (lotion/cream)** n après-soleil m or f; **afterwards** (us **afterward**) adv après

again [ə'gɛn] adv de nouveau, encore (une fois); **to do sth ~** refaire qch; **~ and ~** à plusieurs reprises

against [ə'gɛnst] prep contre; (compared to) par rapport à

age [eɪdʒ] n âge m ▷ vt, vi vieillir; **he is 20 years of ~** il a 20 ans; **to come of ~** atteindre sa majorité; **it's been ~s since I saw you** ça fait une éternité que je ne t'ai pas vu; **~d 10** âgé(e) de 10 ans; **age group** n tranche f d'âge; **age limit** n limite f d'âge

agency ['eɪdʒənsɪ] n agence f

agenda [ə'dʒɛndə] n ordre m du jour

> Be careful not to translate agenda by the French word agenda.

agent ['eɪdʒənt] n agent m; (firm) concessionnaire m

aggravate ['ægrəveɪt] vt (situation) aggraver; (annoy) exaspérer, agacer

aggression [ə'grɛʃən] n agression f

aggressive [ə'grɛsɪv] adj agressif(-ive)

agile ['ædʒaɪl] adj agile

agitated ['ædʒɪteɪtɪd] adj inquiet(-ète)

AGM n abbr (= annual general meeting) AG f

ago [ə'gəu] adv: **2 days ~** il y a 2 jours; **not long ~** il n'y a pas longtemps; **how long ~?** il y a combien de temps (de cela)?

agony ['ægənɪ] n (pain) douleur f atroce; (distress) angoisse f; **to be in ~**

souffrir le martyre

agree [ə'griː] vt (price) convenir de ▷ vi: **to ~ with** (person) être d'accord avec; (statements etc) concorder avec; (Ling) s'accorder avec; **to ~ to do** accepter de or consentir à faire; **to ~ to sth** consentir à qch; **to ~ that** (admit) convenir or reconnaître que; **garlic doesn't ~ with me** je ne supporte pas l'ail; **agreeable** adj (pleasant) agréable; (willing) consentant(e), d'accord; **agreed** adj (time, place) convenu(e); **agreement** n accord m; **in agreement** d'accord

agricultural [ægrɪ'kʌltʃərəl] adj agricole

agriculture ['ægrɪkʌltʃə'] n agriculture f

ahead [ə'hɛd] adv en avant; devant; **go right or straight ~** (direction) allez tout droit; **go ~!** (permission) allez-y!; **~ of** devant; (fig: schedule etc) en avance sur; **~ of time** en avance

aid [eɪd] n aide f; (device) appareil m ▷ vt aider; **in ~ of** en faveur de

aide [eɪd] n (person) assistant(e)

AIDS [eɪdz] n abbr (= acquired immune (or immuno-)deficiency syndrome) SIDA m

ailing ['eɪlɪŋ] adj (person) souffreteux(euse); (economy) malade

ailment ['eɪlmənt] n affection f

aim [eɪm] vt: **to ~ sth (at)** (gun, camera) braquer or pointer qch (sur); (missile) lancer qch (à or contre or en direction de); (remark, blow) destiner or adresser qch (à) ▷ vi (also: **to take ~**) viser ▷ n (objective) but m; (skill): **his ~ is bad** il vise mal; **to ~ at** viser; (fig) viser à; **to ~ to do** avoir l'intention de faire

ain't [eɪnt] (inf) = **am not**; **aren't**; **isn't**

air [ɛə'] n air m ▷ vt aérer; (idea, grievance, views) mettre sur le tapis ▷ cpd (currents, attack etc) aérien(ne); **to throw sth into the ~** (ball etc) jeter qch en l'air; **by ~** par avion; **to be on the ~** (Radio, TV: programme) être diffusé(e); (: station) émettre; **airbag** n airbag m; **airbed** n (BRIT) matelas *m* pneumatique; **airborne** *adj* (*plane*) en vol; **as soon as the plane was airborne** dès que l'avion eut décollé; **air-conditioned** *adj* climatisé(e), à air conditionné; **air conditioning** *n* climatisation *f*; **aircraft** *n inv* avion *m*; **airfield** *n* terrain *m* d'aviation; **Air Force** *n* Armée *f* de l'air; **air hostess** *n* (BRIT) hôtesse *f* de l'air; **airing cupboard** *n* (BRIT) placard qui contient la chaudière et dans lequel on met le linge à sécher; **airlift** *n* pont aérien; **airline** *n* ligne aérienne, compagnie aérienne; **airliner** *n* avion *m* de ligne; **airmail** *n*: **by airmail** par avion; **airplane** *n* (US) avion *m*; **airport** *n* aéroport *m*; **air raid** *n* attaque aérienne; **airsick** *adj*: **to be airsick** avoir le mal de l'air; **airspace** *n* espace *m* aérien; **airstrip** *n* terrain *m* d'atterrissage; **air terminal** *n* aérogare *f*; **airtight** *adj* hermétique; **air-traffic controller** *n* aiguilleur *m* du ciel; **airy** *adj* bien aéré(e); (*manners*) dégagé(e)

aisle [aɪl] *n* (*of church: central*) allée *f* centrale; (: *side*) nef *f* latérale, bas-côté *m*; (*in theatre, supermarket*) allée; (*on plane*) couloir *m*; **aisle seat** *n* place *f* côté couloir

ajar [ə'dʒɑːʳ] *adj* entrouvert(e)

à la carte [ælæˈkɑːt] *adv* à la carte

alarm [ə'lɑːm] *n* alarme *f* ▷ *vt* alarmer; **alarm call** *n* coup *m* de fil pour réveiller; **could I have an alarm call at 7 am, please?** pouvez-vous me réveiller à 7 heures, s'il vous plaît?; **alarm clock** *n* réveille-matin *m inv*, réveil *m*; **alarmed** *adj* (*frightened*) alarmé(e); (*protected by an alarm*) protégé(e) par un système d'alarme; **alarming** *adj* alarmant(e)

Albania [ælˈbeɪnɪə] *n* Albanie *f*

albeit [ɔːlˈbiːɪt] *conj* bien que + *sub*, encore que + *sub*

album [ˈælbəm] *n* album *m*

alcohol [ˈælkəhɒl] *n* alcool *m*; **alcohol-free** *adj* sans alcool; **alcoholic** [ælkəˈhɒlɪk] *adj*, *n* alcoolique (*m/f*)

alcove [ˈælkəʊv] *n* alcôve *f*

ale [eɪl] *n* bière *f*

alert [ə'lɜːt] *adj* alerte, vif (vive); (*watchful*) vigilant(e) ▷ *n* alerte *f* ▷ *vt* alerter; **on the ~** sur le qui-vive; (*Mil*) en état d'alerte

algebra [ˈældʒɪbrə] *n* algèbre *m*

Algeria [ælˈdʒɪərɪə] *n* Algérie *f*

Algerian [ælˈdʒɪərɪən] *adj* algérien(ne) ▷ *n* Algérien(ne)

Algiers [ælˈdʒɪəz] *n* Alger

alias [ˈeɪlɪəs] *adv* alias ▷ *n* faux nom, nom d'emprunt

alibi [ˈælɪbaɪ] *n* alibi *m*

alien [ˈeɪlɪən] *n* (*from abroad*) étranger(-ère); (*from outer space*) extraterrestre ▷ *adj*: **~ (to)** étranger(-ère) (à); **alienate** *vt* aliéner; (*subj: person*) s'aliéner

alight [ə'laɪt] *adj* en feu ▷ *vi* mettre pied à terre; (*passenger*) descendre; (*bird*) se poser

align [ə'laɪn] *vt* aligner

alike [ə'laɪk] *adj* semblable, pareil(le) ▷ *adv* de même; **to look ~** se ressembler

alive [ə'laɪv] *adj* vivant(e); (*active*) plein(e) de vie

KEYWORD

all [ɔːl] *adj* (*singular*) tout(e); (*plural*) tous (toutes); **all day** toute la journée; **all night** toute la nuit; **all men** tous les hommes; **all five** tous les cinq; **all the books** tous les livres; **all his life** toute sa vie

▷ *pron* 1 tout; **I ate it all, I ate all of it** j'ai tout mangé; **all of us went** nous y sommes tous allés; **all of the boys went** tous les garçons y sont allés; **is that all?** c'est tout?; (*in shop*) ce sera tout?

2 (*in phrases*): **above all** surtout, par-dessus tout; **after all** après tout; **at all: not at all** (*in answer to question*) pas du tout; (*in answer to thanks*) je vous en prie!; **I'm not at all tired** je ne suis pas du tout fatigué(e); **anything at all will**

do n'importe quoi fera l'affaire; **all in all** tout bien considéré, en fin de compte ▷ *adv*: **all alone** tout(e) seul(e); **it's not as hard as all that** ce n'est pas si difficile que ça; **all the more/the better** d'autant plus/mieux; **all but** presque, pratiquement; **the score is 2 all** le score est de 2 partout

Allah ['ælə] n Allah m

allegation [ælɪ'ɡeɪʃən] n allégation f

alleged [ə'ledʒd] adj prétendu(e);

allegedly adv à ce que l'on prétend, paraît-il

allegiance [ə'liːdʒəns] n fidélité f, obéissance f

allergic [ə'ləːdʒɪk] adj: **~ to** allergique à; **I'm ~ to penicillin** je suis allergique à la pénicilline

allergy ['ælədʒɪ] n allergie f

alleviate [ə'liːvɪeɪt] vt soulager, adoucir

alley ['ælɪ] n ruelle f

alliance [ə'laɪəns] n alliance f

allied ['ælaɪd] adj allié(e)

alligator ['ælɪɡeɪtə] n alligator m

all-in ['ɔːlɪn] adj, adv (BRIT: charge) tout compris

allocate ['æləkeɪt] vt (share out) répartir, distribuer; **to ~ sth to** (duties) assigner or attribuer qch à; (sum, time) allouer qch à

allot [ə'lɒt] vt (share out) répartir, distribuer; **to ~ sth to** (time) allouer qch à; (duties) assigner qch à

all-out ['ɔːlaut] adj (effort etc) total(e) ▷ adv: **all out** à fond

allow [ə'lau] vt (practice, behaviour) permettre, autoriser; (sum to spend etc) accorder, allouer; (sum, time estimated) compter, prévoir; (claim, goal) admettre; (concede): **to ~ that** convenir que; **to ~ sb to do** permettre à qn de faire, autoriser qn à faire; **he is ~ed to ...** on lui permet de ...; **allow for** vt fus tenir compte de; **allowance** n (money received) allocation f; (: from parent etc) subside m; (: for expenses) indemnité f; (us: pocket money) argent m

de poche; (Tax) somme f déductible du revenu imposable, abattement m; **to make allowances for** (person) essayer de comprendre; (thing) tenir compte de

all right adv (feel, work) bien; (as answer) d'accord

ally ['ælaɪ] allié m ▷ vt [ə'laɪ]: **to ~ o.s. with** s'allier avec

almighty [ɔːl'maɪtɪ] adj tout(e)-puissant(e); (tremendous) énorme

almond ['aːmənd] n amande f

almost ['ɔːlməust] adv presque

alone [ə'ləun] adj, adv seul(e); **to leave sb ~** laisser qn tranquille; **to leave sth ~** ne pas toucher à qch; **let ~ ...** sans parler de ...; encore moins ...

along [ə'lɒŋ] prep le long de ▷ adv: **is he coming ~ with us?** vient-il avec nous?; **he was hopping/limping ~** il venait or avançait en sautillant/boitant; **~ with** avec, en plus de; (person) en compagnie de; **all ~** (all the time) depuis le début; **alongside** prep (along) le long de; (beside) à côté de ▷ adv bord à bord; côte à côte

aloof [ə'luːf] adj distant(e) ▷ adv: **to stand ~** se tenir à l'écart or à distance

aloud [ə'laud] adv à haute voix

alphabet ['ælfəbɛt] n alphabet m

Alps [ælps] npl: **the ~** les Alpes fpl

already [ɔːl'rɛdɪ] adv déjà

alright [ɔːl'raɪt] adv (BRIT) = **all right**

also ['ɔːlsəu] adv aussi

altar ['ɔltə] n autel m

alter ['ɔltə] vt, vi changer; **alteration** [ɔltə'reɪʃən] n changement m, modification f; **alterations** npl (Sewing) retouches fpl; (Archit) modifications fpl

alternate adj [ɔl'təːnɪt] alterné(e), alternant(e), alternatif(-ive); (us) = **alternative** ▷ vi ['ɔltəːneɪt] alterner; **to ~ with** alterner avec; **on ~ days** un jour sur deux, tous les deux jours

alternative [ɔl'təːnətɪv] adj (solution, plan) autre, de remplacement; (lifestyle) parallèle ▷ n (choice) alternative f; (other possibility) autre possibilité f;

~ medicine médecine alternative, médecine douce; **alternatively** adv: **alternatively one could ...** une autre or l'autre solution serait de ...

although [ɔːlˈðəʊ] conj bien que + sub

altitude [ˈæltɪtjuːd] n altitude f

altogether [ɔːltəˈɡeðəᵊ] adv entièrement, tout à fait; (on the whole) tout compte fait; (in all) en tout

aluminium [æljuˈmɪnɪəm] (BRIT **aluminum**) [əˈluːmɪnəm] (US) n aluminium m

always [ˈɔːlweɪz] adv toujours

Alzheimer's (disease) [ˈæltshaɪməz-] n maladie f d'Alzheimer

am [æm] vb see **be**

a.m. adv abbr (= ante meridiem) du matin

amalgamate [əˈmælɡəmeɪt] vt, vi fusionner

amass [əˈmæs] vt amasser

amateur [ˈæmətəᵊ] n amateur m

amaze [əˈmeɪz] vt stupéfier; **to be ~d (at)** être stupéfait(e) (de); **amazed** adj stupéfait(e); **amazement** n surprise f, étonnement m; **amazing** adj étonnant(e), incroyable; (bargain, offer) exceptionnel(le)

Amazon [ˈæməzən] n (Geo) Amazone f

ambassador [æmˈbæsədəᵊ] n ambassadeur m

amber [ˈæmbəᵊ] n ambre m; **at ~** (BRIT Aut) à l'orange

ambiguous [æmˈbɪɡjuəs] adj ambigu(ë)

ambition [æmˈbɪʃən] n ambition f; **ambitious** [æmˈbɪʃəs] adj ambitieux(-euse)

ambulance [ˈæmbjʊləns] n ambulance f; **call an ~!** appelez une ambulance!

ambush [ˈæmbʊʃ] n embuscade f ▷ vt tendre une embuscade à

amen [ˈɑːˈmɛn] excl amen

amend [əˈmɛnd] vt (law) amender; (text) corriger; **to make ~s** réparer ses torts, faire amende honorable; **amendment** n (to law) amendement m; (to text) correction f

amenities [əˈmiːnɪtɪz] npl aménagements mpl, équipements mpl

America [əˈmɛrɪkə] n Amérique f; **American** adj américain(e) ▷ n Américain(e); **American football** n (BRIT) football m américain

amicable [ˈæmɪkəbl] adj amical(e); (Law) à l'amiable

amid(st) [əˈmɪd(st)] prep parmi, au milieu de

ammunition [æmjuˈnɪʃən] n munitions fpl

amnesty [ˈæmnɪstɪ] n amnistie f

among(st) [əˈmʌŋ(st)] prep parmi, entre

amount [əˈmaʊnt] n (sum of money) somme f; (total) montant m; (quantity) quantité f; nombre m ▷ vi: **to ~ to** (total) s'élever à; (be same as) équivaloir à, revenir à

amp(ère) [æmp(ɛəᵊ)] n ampère m

ample [ˈæmpl] adj ample, spacieux(-euse); (enough): **this is ~** c'est largement suffisant; **to have ~ time/ room** avoir bien assez de temps/place

amplifier [ˈæmplɪfaɪəᵊ] n amplificateur m

amputate [ˈæmpjuteɪt] vt amputer

Amtrak [ˈæmtræk] (US) n société mixte de transports ferroviaires interurbains pour voyageurs

amuse [əˈmjuːz] vt amuser; **amusement** n amusement m; (pastime) distraction f; **amusement arcade** n salle f de jeu; **amusement park** n parc m d'attractions

amusing [əˈmjuːzɪŋ] adj amusant(e), divertissant(e)

an [æn, ən, n] indef art see **a**

anaemia [əˈniːmɪə] (US **anemia**) n anémie f

anaemic [əˈniːmɪk] (US **anemic**) adj anémique

anaesthetic [ænɪsˈθɛtɪk] (US **anesthetic**) n anesthésique m

analog(ue) [ˈænələɡ] adj (watch, computer) analogique

analogy [əˈnælədʒɪ] n analogie f

analyse ['ænəlaɪz] (*us* **analyze**) *vt* analyser; **analysis** (*pl* **analyses**) [ə'næləsɪs, -siːz] *n* analyse *f*; **analyst** ['ænəlɪst] *n* (*political analyst etc*) analyste *m/f*; (*us*) psychanalyste *m/f*

analyze ['ænəlaɪz] *vt* (*us*) = **analyse**

anarchy ['ænəkɪ] *n* anarchie *f*

anatomy [ə'nætəmɪ] *n* anatomie *f*

ancestor ['ænsɪstə*] *n* ancêtre *m*, aïeul *m*

anchor ['æŋkə*] *n* ancre *f* ▷ *vi* (*also:* **to drop ~**) jeter l'ancre, mouiller ▷ *vt* mettre à l'ancre; (*fig*): **to ~ sth to** fixer qch à

anchovy ['æntʃəvɪ] *n* anchois *m*

ancient ['eɪnʃənt] *adj* ancien(ne), antique; (*person*) d'un âge vénérable; (*car*) antédiluvien(ne)

and [ænd] *conj* et; **~ so on** et ainsi de suite; **try ~ come** tâchez de venir; **come ~ sit here** venez vous asseoir ici; **he talked ~ talked** il a parlé pendant des heures; **better ~ better** de mieux en mieux; **more ~ more** de plus en plus

Andorra [æn'dɔːrə] *n* (principauté *f* d')Andorre *f*

anemia *etc* [ə'niːmɪə] (*us*) = **anaemia** *etc*

anesthetic [ænɪs'θetɪk] (*us*) = **anaesthetic**

angel ['eɪndʒəl] *n* ange *m*

anger ['æŋgə*] *n* colère *f*

angina [æn'dʒaɪnə] *n* angine *f* de poitrine

angle ['æŋgl] *n* angle *m*; **from their ~** de leur point de vue

angler ['æŋglə*] *n* pêcheur(-euse) à la ligne

Anglican ['æŋglɪkən] *adj*, *n* anglican(e)

angling ['æŋglɪŋ] *n* pêche *f* à la ligne

angrily ['æŋgrɪlɪ] *adv* avec colère

angry ['æŋgrɪ] *adj* en colère, furieux(-euse); (*wound*) enflammé(e); **to be ~ with sb/at sth** être furieux contre qn/de qch; **to get ~** se fâcher, se mettre en colère

anguish ['æŋgwɪʃ] *n* angoisse *f*

animal ['ænɪməl] *n* animal *m* ▷ *adj*

animal(e)

animated ['ænɪmeɪtɪd] *adj* animé(e)

animation [ænɪ'meɪʃən] *n* (*of person*) entrain *m*; (*of street, Cine*) animation *f*

aniseed ['ænɪsiːd] *n* anis *m*

ankle ['æŋkl] *n* cheville *f*

annex ['æneks] *n* (*brit: also:* **~e**) annexe *f* ▷ *vt* [ə'neks] annexer

anniversary [ænɪ'vəːsərɪ] *n* anniversaire *m*

announce [ə'naʊns] *vt* annoncer; (*birth, death*) faire part de; **announcement** *n* annonce *f*; (*for births etc: in newspaper*) avis *m* de faire-part; (*: letter, card*) faire-part *m*; **announcer** *n* (*Radio, TV: between programmes*) speaker(ine); (*: in a programme*) présentateur(-trice)

annoy [ə'nɔɪ] *vt* agacer, ennuyer, contrarier; **don't get ~ed!** ne vous fâchez pas!; **annoying** *adj* agaçant(e), contrariant(e)

annual ['ænjuəl] *adj* annuel(le) ▷ *n* (*Bot*) plante annuelle; (*book*) album *m*; **annually** *adv* annuellement

annum ['ænəm] *n see* **per**

anonymous [ə'nɒnɪməs] *adj* anonyme

anorak ['ænəræk] *n* anorak *m*

anorexia [ænə'reksɪə] *n* (*also:* **~ nervosa**) anorexie *f*

anorexic [ænə'reksɪk] *adj*, *n* anorexique (*m/f*)

another [ə'nʌðə*] *adj*: **~ book** (*one more*) un autre livre, encore un livre, un livre de plus; (*a different one*) un autre livre ▷ *pron* un(e) autre, encore un(e), un(e) de plus; *see also* **one**

answer ['ɑːnsə*] *n* réponse *f*; (*to problem*) solution *f* ▷ *vi* répondre ▷ *vt* (*reply to*) répondre à; (*problem*) résoudre; (*prayer*) exaucer; **in ~ to your letter** suite à *or* en réponse à votre lettre; **to ~ the phone** répondre (au téléphone); **to ~ the bell** *or* **the door** aller *or* venir ouvrir (la porte); **answer back** *vi* répondre, répliquer; **answerphone** *n* (*esp brit*) répondeur *m* (téléphonique)

ant [ænt] n fourmi f

Antarctic [ænt'ɑːktɪk] n: **the ~** l'Antarctique f

antelope ['æntɪləʊp] n antilope f

antenatal ['æntɪ'neɪtl] adj prénatal(e)

antenna (pl **-e**) [æn'tenə, -niː] n antenne f

anthem ['ænθəm] n: **national ~** hymne national

anthology [æn'θɒlədʒɪ] n anthologie f

anthrax ['ænθræks] n anthrax m

anthropology [ænθrə'pɒlədʒɪ] n anthropologie f

anti ['æntɪ] prefix anti-; **antibiotic** ['æntɪbaɪ'ɒtɪk] n antibiotique m; **antibody** ['æntɪbɒdɪ] n anticorps m

anticipate [æn'tɪsɪpeɪt] vt s'attendre à, prévoir; (wishes, request) aller au devant de, devancer; **anticipation** [æntɪsɪ'peɪʃən] n attente f

anticlimax ['æntɪ'klaɪmæks] n déception f

anticlockwise ['æntɪ'klɒkwaɪz] (BRIT) adv dans le sens inverse des aiguilles d'une montre

antics ['æntɪks] npl singeries fpl

anti: antidote ['æntɪdəʊt] n antidote m, contrepoison m; **antifreeze** ['æntɪfriːz] n antigel m; **anti-globalization** n antimondialisation f; **antihistamine** [æntɪ'hɪstəmɪn] n antihistaminique m; **antiperspirant** [æntɪ'pɜːspɪrənt] n déodorant m

antique [æn'tiːk] n (ornament) objet m d'art ancien; (furniture) meuble ancien ▷ adj ancien(ne); **antique shop** n magasin m d'antiquités

antiseptic [æntɪ'septɪk] adj, n antiseptique m

antisocial ['æntɪ'səʊʃəl] adj (unfriendly) peu liant(e), insociable; (against society) antisocial(e)

antlers ['æntləz] npl bois mpl, ramure f

anxiety [æŋ'zaɪətɪ] n anxiété f; (keenness): **~ to do** grand désir or impatience f de faire

anxious ['æŋkʃəs] adj (très) inquiet(-ète); (always worried)

anxieux(-euse); (worrying) angoissant(e); (keen): **~ to do/that** qui tient beaucoup à faire/à ce que + sub; impatient(e) de faire/que + sub

KEYWORD

any ['enɪ] adj **1** (in questions etc: singular) du, de l', de la; (: plural) des; **do you have any butter/children/ink?** avez-vous du beurre/des enfants/de l'encre?

2 (with negative) de, d'; **I don't have any money/books** je n'ai pas d'argent/de livres

3 (no matter which) n'importe quel(le); (each and every) tout(e), chaque; **choose any book you like** vous pouvez choisir n'importe quel livre; **any teacher you ask will tell you** n'importe quel professeur vous le dira

4 (in phrases): **in any case** de toute façon; **any day now** un jour à l'autre; **at any moment** à tout moment, d'un instant à l'autre; **at any rate** en tout cas; **any time** n'importe quand; **he might come (at) any time** il pourrait venir n'importe quand; **come (at) any time** venez quand vous voulez

▷ pron **1** (in questions etc) en; **have you got any?** est-ce que vous en avez?; **can any of you sing?** est-ce que parmi vous il y en a qui savent chanter?

2 (with negative) en; **I don't have any (of them)** je n'en ai pas, je n'en ai aucun

3 (no matter which one(s)) n'importe lequel (or laquelle); (anybody) n'importe qui; **take any of those books (you like)** vous pouvez prendre n'importe lequel de ces livres

▷ adv **1** (in questions etc): **do you want any more soup/sandwiches?** voulez-vous encore de la soupe/des sandwichs?; **are you feeling any better?** est-ce que vous vous sentez mieux?

2 (with negative): **I can't hear him any more** je ne l'entends plus; **don't wait any longer** n'attendez pas plus longtemps; **anybody** pron n'importe qui; (in interrogative sentences) quelqu'un; (in negative sentences): **I don't see anybody** je ne vois personne; **if anybody should phone ...** si quelqu'un téléphone ...; **anyhow** adv quoi qu'il en soit; (haphazardly) n'importe comment; **do it anyhow you like** faites-le comme vous voulez; **she leaves things just anyhow** elle laisse tout traîner; **I shall go anyhow** j'irai de toute façon; **anyone** pron = **anybody**; **anything** pron (no matter what) n'importe quoi; (in questions) quelque chose; (with negative) ne ... rien; **can you see anything?** tu vois quelque chose?; **if anything happens to me ...** s'il m'arrive quoi que ce soit ...; **you can say anything you like** vous pouvez dire ce que vous voulez; **anything will do** n'importe quoi fera l'affaire; **he'll eat anything** il mange de tout; **anytime** adv (at any moment) d'un moment à l'autre; (whenever) n'importe quand; **anyway** adv de toute façon; **anyway, I couldn't come even if I wanted to** de toute façon, je ne pouvais pas venir même si je le voulais; **I shall go anyway** j'irai quand même; **why are you phoning, anyway?** au fait, pourquoi tu me téléphones?; **anywhere** adv n'importe où; (in interrogative sentences) quelque part; (in negative sentences): **I can't see him anywhere** je ne le vois nulle part; **can you see him anywhere?** tu le vois quelque part?; **put the books down anywhere** pose les livres n'importe où; **anywhere in the world** n'importe où dans le monde

apart [ə'pɑːt] adv (to one side) à part; de côté; à l'écart; (separately) séparément; **to take/pull** = démonter; **10 miles/a long way** = à 10 miles/très éloignés l'un de l'autre; **~ from** prep à part, excepté

apartment [ə'pɑːtmənt] n (us)

appartement m, logement m; (room) chambre f; **apartment building** n (us) immeuble m; maison divisée en appartements

apathy ['æpəθɪ] n apathie f, indifférence f

ape [eɪp] n (grand) singe ▷ vt singer

aperitif [ə'pɛrɪtɪf] n apéritif m

aperture ['æpətʃjʊə'] n orifice m, ouverture f; (Phot) ouverture f (du diaphragme)

APEX ['eɪpɛks] n abbr (Aviat: = advance purchase excursion) APEX m

apologize [ə'pɒlədʒaɪz] vi: **to ~ (for sth to sb)** s'excuser (of auprès de qn), présenter des excuses (à qn pour qch)

apology [ə'pɒlədʒɪ] n excuses fpl

apostrophe [ə'pɒstrəfɪ] n apostrophe f

appal [ə'pɔːl] (us **appall**) vt consterner, atterrer, horrifier; **appalling** adj épouvantable; (stupidity) consternant(e)

apparatus [æpə'reɪtəs] n appareil m, dispositif m; (in gymnasium) agrès mpl

apparent [ə'pærənt] adj apparent(e); **apparently** adv apparemment

appeal [ə'piːl] vi (Law) faire or interjeter appel ▷ n (Law) appel m; (request) appel; prière f; (charm) attrait m, charme m; **to ~ for** demander (instamment); **to ~ to** (beg) faire appel à; (be attractive) plaire à; **it doesn't ~ to me** cela ne m'attire pas; **appealing** adj (attractive) attrayant(e)

appear [ə'pɪə'] vi apparaître, se montrer; (Law) comparaître; (publication) paraître, sortir, être publié(e); (seem) paraître, sembler; **it would ~ that** il semble que; **to ~ in Hamlet** jouer dans Hamlet; **to ~ on TV** passer à la télé; **appearance** n apparition f; parution f; (look, aspect) apparence f, aspect m

appendices [ə'pendɪsiːz] npl of **appendix**

appendicitis [əpendɪ'saɪtɪs] n appendicite f

appendix (pl **appendices**) [ə'pendɪks,

-siːz] n appendice m

appetite ['æpɪtaɪt] n appétit m

appetizer ['æpɪtaɪzəʳ] n (food) amuse-gueule m; (drink) apéritif m

applaud [ə'plɔːd] vt, vi applaudir

applause [ə'plɔːz] n applaudissements mpl

apple ['æpl] n pomme f; **apple pie** n tarte f aux pommes

appliance [ə'plaɪəns] n appareil m

applicable [ə'plɪkəbl] adj applicable; **to be ~** (relevant) valoir pour

applicant ['æplɪkənt] n: **~ (for)** candidat(e) (à)

application [æplɪ'keɪʃən] n application f; (for a job, a grant etc) demande f; candidature f; **application form** n formulaire m de demande

apply [ə'plaɪ] vt: **to ~ (to)** (paint, ointment) appliquer (sur); (law, etc) appliquer (à) ▷ vi: **to ~ to** (ask) s'adresser à; (be suitable for, relevant to) s'appliquer à ▷ **to ~ (for)** (permit, grant) faire une demande (en vue d'obtenir), (job) poser sa candidature (pour), faire une demande d'emploi (concernant); **to ~ o.s. to** s'appliquer à

appoint [ə'pɔɪnt] vt (to post) nommer, engager; (date, place) fixer, désigner; **appointment** n (to post) nomination f; (job) poste m; (arrangement to meet) rendez-vous m; **to have an appointment** avoir un rendez-vous; **to make an appointment (with)** prendre rendez-vous (avec); **I'd like to make an appointment** je voudrais prendre rendez-vous

appraisal [ə'preɪzl] n évaluation f

appreciate [ə'priːʃɪeɪt] vt (like) apprécier, faire cas de; (be grateful for) être reconnaissant(e) de; (be aware of) comprendre, se rendre compte de ▷ vi (Finance) prendre de la valeur; **appreciation** [əprɪːʃɪ'eɪʃən] n appréciation f; (gratitude) reconnaissance f; (Finance) hausse f, valorisation f

apprehension [æprɪ'hɛnʃən] n

appréhension f, inquiétude f

apprehensive [æprɪ'hɛnsɪv] adj inquiet(-ète), appréhensif(-ive)

apprentice [ə'prɛntɪs] n apprenti m

approach [ə'prəutʃ] vi approcher ▷ vt (come near) approcher de; (ask, apply to) s'adresser à; (subject, passer-by) aborder ▷ n approche f; accès m, abord m; démarche f (intellectuelle)

appropriate [ə'prəupriɪt] (tool etc) qui convient, approprié(e); (moment, remark) opportun(e) ▷ vt [ə'prəuprɪeɪt] (take) s'approprier

approval [ə'pruːvəl] n approbation f; **on ~** (Comm) à l'examen

approve [ə'pruːv] vt approuver; **approve of** vt fus (thing) approuver; (person): **they don't ~ of her** ils n'ont pas bonne opinion d'elle

approximate [ə'prɔksɪmɪt] adj approximatif(-ive); **approximately** adv approximativement

Apr. abbr = **April**

apricot ['eɪprɪkɔt] n abricot m

April ['eɪprəl] n avril m; **April Fools' Day** n le premier avril

- **APRIL FOOLS' DAY**

  April Fools' Day est le 1er avril, à l'occasion duquel on fait des farces de toutes sortes. Les victimes de ces farces sont les "April fools". Traditionnellement, on n'est censé faire des farces que jusqu'à midi.

apron ['eɪprən] n tablier m

apt [æpt] adj (suitable) approprié(e); (likely): **~ to do** susceptible de faire; ayant tendance à faire

aquarium [ə'kwɛərɪəm] n aquarium m

Aquarius [ə'kwɛərɪəs] n le Verseau

Arab ['ærəb] n Arabe m/f ▷ adj arabe

Arabia [ə'reɪbɪə] n Arabie f; **Arabian** adj arabe; **Arabic** ['ærəbɪk] adj, n arabe (m)

arbitrary ['ɑːbɪtrərɪ] adj arbitraire

arbitration [ɑːbɪ'treɪʃən] n

arbitrage m

arc [ɑːk] n arc m

arcade [ɑːˈkeɪd] n arcade f; (passage with shops) passage m, galerie f; (with games) salle f de jeu

arch [ɑːtʃ] n arche f; (of foot) cambrure f, voûte f plantaire ▷ vt arquer, cambrer

archaeology [ɑːkɪˈɒlədʒɪ] (us **archeology**) n archéologie f

archbishop [ɑːtʃˈbɪʃəp] n archevêque m

archeology [ɑːkɪˈɒlədʒɪ] (us) = **archaeology**

architect [ˈɑːkɪtɛkt] n architecte m

architectural [ɑːkɪˈtɛktʃərəl] adj architectural(e); **architecture** n architecture f

archive [ˈɑːkaɪv] n (often pl) archives fpl

Arctic [ˈɑːktɪk] adj arctique ▷ n: **the ~** l'Arctique m

are [ɑːʳ] vb see **be**

area [ˈɛərɪə] n (Geom) superficie f; (zone) région f; (: smaller) secteur m; (in room) coin m; (knowledge, research) domaine m; **area code** (us) n (Tel) indicatif m de zone

arena [əˈriːnə] n arène f

aren't [ɑːnt] = **are not**

Argentina [ɑːdʒənˈtiːnə] n Argentine f; **Argentinian** [ɑːdʒənˈtɪnɪən] adj argentin(e) ▷ n Argentin(e)

arguably [ˈɑːgjuəblɪ] adv: **it is ~ ...** on peut soutenir que c'est ...

argue [ˈɑːgjuː] vi (quarrel) se disputer; (reason) argumenter; **to ~ that** objecter or alléguer que, donner comme argument que

argument [ˈɑːgjumənt] n (quarrel) dispute f, discussion f; (reasons) argument m

Aries [ˈɛərɪz] n le Bélier

arise (pt **arose**, pp **~n**) [əˈraɪz, əˈrəʊz, əˈrɪzn] vi survenir, se présenter

arithmetic [əˈrɪθmətɪk] n arithmétique f

arm [ɑːm] n bras m ▷ vt armer; **arms** npl (weapons, Heraldry) armes fpl; **~ in ~** bras dessus bras dessous; **armchair** n fauteuil m

armed [ɑːmd] adj armé(e); **armed forces** npl: **the armed forces** les forces armées; **armed robbery** n vol m à main armée

armour (us **armor**) [ˈɑːməʳ] n armure f; (Mil: tanks) blindés mpl

armpit [ˈɑːmpɪt] n aisselle f

armrest [ˈɑːmrɛst] n accoudoir m

army [ˈɑːmɪ] n armée f

A road (BRIT) ≈ route nationale

aroma [əˈrəʊmə] n arôme m; **aromatherapy** n aromathérapie f

arose [əˈrəʊz] pt of **arise**

around [əˈraʊnd] adv (tout) autour; (nearby) dans les parages ▷ prep autour de; (near) près de; (fig: about) environ; (: date, time) vers; **is he ~?** est-il dans les parages or là?

arouse [əˈraʊz] vt (sleeper) éveiller; (curiosity, passions) éveiller, susciter; (anger) exciter

arrange [əˈreɪndʒ] vt arranger; **to ~ to do sth** prévoir de faire qch; **arrangement** n arrangement m; **arrangements** npl (plans etc) arrangements mpl, dispositions fpl

array [əˈreɪ] n (of objects) déploiement m, étalage m

arrears [əˈrɪəz] npl arriéré m; **to be in ~ with one's rent** devoir un arriéré de loyer

arrest [əˈrɛst] vt arrêter; (sb's attention) retenir, attirer ▷ n arrestation f; **under ~** en état d'arrestation

arrival [əˈraɪvl] n arrivée f; **new ~** nouveau venu/nouvelle venue; (baby) nouveau-né(e)

arrive [əˈraɪv] vi arriver; **arrive at** vt fus (decision, solution) parvenir à

arrogance [ˈærəgəns] n arrogance f

arrogant [ˈærəgənt] adj arrogant(e)

arrow [ˈærəʊ] n flèche f

arse [ɑːs] n (BRIT inf!) cul m (!)

arson [ˈɑːsn] n incendie criminel

art [ɑːt] n art m; **Arts** npl (Scol) les lettres fpl; **art college** n école f des beaux-arts

artery ['ɑːtərɪ] n artère f

art gallery n musée m d'art; (saleroom) galerie f de peinture

arthritis [ɑːθraɪtɪs] n arthrite f

artichoke ['ɑːtɪtʃəuk] n artichaut m; **Jerusalem** ~ topinambour m

article ['ɑːtɪkl] n article m

articulate adj [ɑː'tɪkjulɪt] (person) qui s'exprime clairement et aisément; (speech) bien articulé(e), prononcé(e) clairement ▷ vb [ɑː'tɪkjuleɪt] ▷ vi articuler, parler distinctement ▷ vt articuler

artificial [ɑːtɪ'fɪʃəl] adj artificiel(le)

artist ['ɑːtɪst] n artiste m/f; **artistic** [ɑː'tɪstɪk] adj artistique

art school n = école f des beaux-arts

🔑 **KEYWORD**

as [æz] conj 1 (time: moment) comme, alors que; à mesure que; **he came in as I was leaving** il est arrivé comme je partais; **as the years went by** à mesure que les années passaient; **as from tomorrow** à partir de demain 2 (since, because) comme, puisque; **he left early as he had to be home by 10** comme il or puisqu'il devait être de retour avant 10h, il est parti de bonne heure

3 (referring to manner, way) comme; **do as you wish** faites comme vous voudrez; **as she said** comme elle le disait ▷ adv 1 (in comparisons): **as big as** aussi grand que; **twice as big as** deux fois plus grand que; **as much or many as** autant que; **as much money/many books as** autant d'argent/de livres que; **as soon as** dès que

2 (concerning): **as for or to that** quant à cela, pour ce qui est de cela

3: **as if or though** comme si; **he looked as if he was ill** il avait l'air d'être malade; see also **long**; **such**; **well** ▷ prep (in the capacity of) en tant que, en qualité de; **he works as a driver** il travaille comme chauffeur; **as**

chairman of the company, he ... en tant que président de la société, il ...; **he gave me it as a present** il me l'a offert, il m'en a fait cadeau

a.s.a.p. abbr **= as soon as possible**

asbestos [æz'bɛstəs] n asbeste m, amiante m

ascent [ə'sɛnt] n (climb) ascension f

ash [æʃ] n (dust) cendre f; (also: ~ **tree**) frêne m

ashamed [ə'feɪmd] adj honteux(-euse), confus(e); **to be ~ of** avoir honte de

ashore [ə'ʃɔː] adv à terre

ashtray ['æʃtreɪ] n cendrier m

Ash Wednesday n mercredi m des Cendres

Asia ['eɪʃə] n Asie f; **Asian** n (from Asia) Asiatique m/f; (BRIT: from Indian subcontinent) Indo-Pakistanais(-e) ▷ adj asiatique; indo-pakistanais(-e)

aside [ə'saɪd] adv de côté; à l'écart ▷ n aparté m

ask [ɑːsk] vt demander; (invite) inviter; **to ~ sb sth/to do sth** demander à qn qch/de faire qch; **to ~ sb about sth** questionner qn au sujet de qch; se renseigner auprès de qn au sujet de qch; **to ~ (sb) a question** poser une question (à qn); **to ~ sb out to dinner** inviter qn au restaurant; **ask for** vt fus demander; **it's just ~ing for trouble** or **for it** ce serait chercher des ennuis

asleep [ə'sliːp] adj endormi(e); **to fall ~** s'endormir

AS level n abbr (= Advanced Subsidiary level) première partie de l'examen équivalent au baccalauréat

asparagus [əs'pærəgəs] n asperges fpl

aspect ['æspɛkt] n aspect m; (direction in which a building etc faces) orientation f, exposition f

aspirations [æspə'reɪʃənz] npl (hopes, ambition) aspirations fpl

aspire [əs'paɪə] vi: **to ~ to** aspirer à

aspirin ['æsprɪn] n aspirine f

ass [æs] n âne m; (inf) imbécile m/f; (us

infl) cul *m* (!)

assassin [əˈsæsɪn] *n* assassin *m*;
assassinate *vt* assassiner

assault [əˈsɔːlt] *n* (Mil) assaut *m*; (gen:
attack) agression *f* ▷ *vt* attaquer;
(*sexually*) violenter

assemble [əˈsɛmbl] *vt* assembler ▷ *vi*
s'assembler, se rassembler

assembly [əˈsɛmblɪ] *n* (*meeting*)
rassemblement *m*; (*parliament*)
assemblée *f*; (*construction*)
assemblage *m*

assert [əˈsəːt] *vt* affirmer, déclarer;
(*authority*) faire valoir; (*innocence*)
protester de; **assertion** [əˈsəːʃən] *n*
assertion *f*, affirmation *f*

assess [əˈsɛs] *vt* évaluer, estimer; (*tax,
damages*) établir ou fixer le montant de;
(*person*) juger la valeur de; **assessment**
n évaluation *f*, estimation *f*; (*of tax*)
fixation *f*

asset [ˈæsɛt] *n* avantage *m*, atout *m*;
(*person*) atout; **assets** *npl* (Comm)
capital *m*; avoir(s) *m*(*pl*); actif *m*

assign [əˈsaɪn] *vt* (*date*) fixer, arrêter; **to
~ sth to** (*task*) assigner qch à; (*resources*)
affecter qch à; **assignment** *n* (*task*)
mission *f*; (*homework*) devoir *m*

assist [əˈsɪst] *vt* aider, assister;
assistance *n* aide *f*, assistance *f*;
assistant *n* assistant(e), adjoint(e);
(BRIT: *also*: **shop assistant**)
vendeur(-euse)

associate *adj*, *n* [əˈsəʊʃɪt] associé(e)
▷ *vb* [əˈsəʊʃɪeɪt] ▷ *vt* associer ▷ *vi*: **to ~
with sb** fréquenter qn

association [əsəʊsɪˈeɪʃən] *n*
association *f*

assorted [əˈsɔːtɪd] *adj* assorti(e)

assortment [əˈsɔːtmənt] *n*
assortiment *m*; (*of people*) mélange *m*

assume [əˈsjuːm] *vt* supposer;
(*responsibilities etc*) assumer; (*attitude,
name*) prendre, adopter

assumption [əˈsʌmpʃən] *n*
supposition *f*, hypothèse *f*; (*of power*)
assomption *f*, prise *f*

assurance [əˈʃʊərəns] *n* assurance *f*

assure [əˈʃʊəʳ] *vt* assurer

asterisk [ˈæstərɪsk] *n* astérisque *m*

asthma [ˈæsmə] *n* asthme *m*

astonish [əˈstɒnɪʃ] *vt* étonner,
stupéfier; **astonished** *adj* étonné(e);
to be astonished at être étonné(e)
de; **astonishing** *adj* étonnant(e),
stupéfiant(e); **I find it astonishing
that** ... je trouve incroyable que ... + *sub*;
astonishment *n* (grand) étonnement,
stupéfaction *f*

astound [əˈstaʊnd] *vt* stupéfier,
sidérer

astray [əˈstreɪ] *adv*: **to go ~** s'égarer;
(*fig*) quitter le droit chemin; **to lead ~**
(*morally*) détourner du droit chemin

astrology [əˈstrɒlədʒɪ] *n* astrologie *f*

astronaut [ˈæstrənɔːt] *n*
astronaute *m/f*

astronomer [əˈstrɒnəməʳ] *n*
astronome *m*

astronomical [æstrəˈnɒmɪkl] *adj*
astronomique

astronomy [əˈstrɒnəmɪ] *n*
astronomie *f*

astute [əsˈtjuːt] *adj* astucieux(-euse),
malin(-igne)

asylum [əˈsaɪləm] *n* asile *m*; **asylum
seeker** [-siːkə] *n* demandeur(-euse)
d'asile

KEYWORD

at [æt] *prep* **1** (*referring to position,
direction*) à; **at the top** au sommet; **at
home/school** à la maison *or* chez soi/à
l'école; **at the baker's** à la boulangerie,
chez le boulanger; **to look at sth**
regarder qch
2 (*referring to time*): **at 4 o'clock** à 4
heures; **at Christmas** à Noël; **at night**
la nuit; **at times** par moments, parfois
3 (*referring to rates, speed etc*) à; **at £1
a kilo** une livre le kilo; **two at a time**
deux à la fois; **at 50 km/h** à 50 km/h
4 (*referring to manner*): **at a stroke** d'un
seul coup; **at peace** en paix
5 (*referring to activity*): **to be at work** (*in*

the office etc) être au travail; (working) travailler; **to play at cowboys** jouer aux cowboys; **to be good at sth** être bon en qch

6 (referring to cause): **shocked/surprised/annoyed at sth** choqué par/étonné de/agacé par qch; **I went at his suggestion** j'y suis allé sur son conseil

7 (symbol) arobase f

ate [eɪt] pt of **eat**

atheist ['eɪθɪɪst] n athée m/f

Athens ['æθɪnz] n Athènes

athlete ['æθliːt] n athlète m/f

athletic [æθ'lɛtɪk] adj athlétique; **athletics** n athlétisme m

Atlantic [ət'læntɪk] adj atlantique ▷ n: **the ~ (Ocean)** l'(océan m) Atlantique m

atlas ['ætləs] n atlas m

A.T.M. n abbr (= Automated Telling Machine) guichet m automatique

atmosphere ['ætməsfɪə] n (air) atmosphère f; (fig: of place etc) atmosphère f, ambiance f

atom ['ætəm] n atome m; **atomic** [ə'tɒmɪk] adj atomique; **atom(ic) bomb** n bombe f atomique

A to Z® n (map) plan m des rues

atrocity [ə'trɒsɪtɪ] n atrocité f

attach [ə'tætʃ] vt (gen) attacher; (document, letter) joindre; **to be ~ed to sb/sth** (to like) être attaché à qn/qch; **attachment** n (tool) accessoire m; (Comput) fichier m joint; (love): **attachment (to)** affection f (pour), attachement m (à)

attack [ə'tæk] vt attaquer; (task etc) s'attaquer à ▷ n attaque f; **heart ~** crise f cardiaque; **attacker** n attaquant m, agresseur m

attain [ə'teɪn] vt (also: **to ~ to**) parvenir à, atteindre; (knowledge) acquérir

attempt [ə'tɛmpt] n tentative f ▷ vt essayer, tenter

attend [ə'tɛnd] vt (course) suivre; (meeting, talk) assister à; (school, church) aller à, fréquenter; (patient) soigner;

s'occuper de; **attend to** vt fus (needs, affairs etc) s'occuper de; (customer) s'occuper de, servir; **attendance** n (being present) présence f; (people present) assistance f; **attendant** n employé(e), gardien(ne) m/f ▷ adj concomitant(e), qui accompagne or s'ensuit

> Be careful not to translate **to attend** by the French word **attendre**.

attention [ə'tɛnʃən] n attention f ▷ excl (Mil) garde-à-vous!; **for the ~ of** (Admin) à l'attention de

attic ['ætɪk] n grenier m, combles mpl

attitude ['ætɪtjuːd] n attitude f

attorney [ə'tɜːnɪ] n (US: lawyer) avocat m; **Attorney General** n (BRIT) ≈ procureur général; (US) ≈ garde m des Sceaux, ministre m de la Justice

attract [ə'trækt] vt attirer; **attraction** [ə'trækʃən] n (gen pl: pleasant things) attraction f, attrait m; (Physics) attraction f; (fig: towards sb, sth) attirance f; **attractive** adj séduisant(e), attrayant(e)

attribute n ['ætrɪbjuːt] attribut m ▷ vt [ə'trɪbjuːt]: **to ~ sth to** attribuer qch à

aubergine ['əʊbəʒiːn] n aubergine f

auburn ['ɔːbən] adj auburn inv, châtain roux inv

auction ['ɔːkʃən] n (also: **sale by ~**) vente f aux enchères ▷ vt (also: **to sell by ~**) vendre aux enchères

audible ['ɔːdɪbl] adj audible

audience ['ɔːdɪəns] n (people) assistance f, public m; (on radio) auditeurs mpl; (at theatre) spectateurs mpl; (interview) audience f

audit ['ɔːdɪt] vt vérifier

audition [ɔː'dɪʃən] n audition f

auditor ['ɔːdɪtə] n vérificateur m des comptes

auditorium [ɔːdɪ'tɔːrɪəm] n auditorium m, salle f de concert or de spectacle

Aug. abbr = **August**

August ['ɔːɡəst] n août m

aunt [ɑːnt] n tante f; **auntie, aunty** n diminutive of **aunt**

au pair ['əʊ'peə'] n (also: ~ **girl**) jeune fille f au pair

aura ['ɔːrə] n atmosphère f; (of person) aura f

austerity [ɒs'terɪtɪ] n austérité f

Australia [ɒs'treɪlɪə] n Australie f; **Australian** adj australien(ne) ▷ n Australien(ne)

Austria ['ɒstrɪə] n Autriche f; **Austrian** adj autrichien(ne) ▷ n Autrichien(ne)

authentic [ɔː'θentɪk] adj authentique

author ['ɔːθə'] n auteur m

authority [ɔː'θɒrɪtɪ] n autorité f; (permission) autorisation (formelle); **the authorities** les autorités fpl, l'administration f

authorize ['ɔːθəraɪz] vt autoriser

auto ['ɔːtəʊ] n (us) auto f, voiture f; **autobiography** [ɔːtəbaɪ'ɒɡrəfɪ] n autobiographie f; **autograph** ['ɔːtəɡrɑːf] n autographe m ▷ vt signer, dédicacer; **automatic** [ɔːtə'mætɪk] adj automatique ▷ n (gun) automatique m; (car) voiture f à transmission automatique; **automatically** adv automatiquement; **automobile** ['ɔːtəməbiːl] n (us) automobile f; **autonomous** [ɔː'tɒnəməs] adj autonome; **autonomy** [ɔː'tɒnəmɪ] n autonomie f

autumn ['ɔːtəm] n automne m

auxiliary [ɔːɡ'zɪlɪərɪ] adj, n auxiliaire (m/f)

avail [ə'veɪl] vt: **to ~ o.s. of** user de; profiter de ▷ n: **to no ~** sans résultat, en vain, en pure perte

availability [əveɪlə'bɪlɪtɪ] n disponibilité f

available [ə'veɪləbl] adj disponible

avalanche ['ævəlɑːnʃ] n avalanche f

Ave. abbr = **avenue**

avenue ['ævənjuː] n avenue f; (fig) moyen m

average ['ævərɪdʒ] n moyenne f ▷ adj moyen(ne) ▷ vt (a certain figure) atteindre or faire etc en moyenne; **on ~** en moyenne

avert [ə'vɜːt] vt (danger) prévenir, écarter; (one's eyes) détourner

avid ['ævɪd] adj avide

avocado [ævə'kɑːdəʊ] n (brit: also: ~ **pear**) avocat m

avoid [ə'vɔɪd] vt éviter

await [ə'weɪt] vt attendre

awake [ə'weɪk] adj éveillé(e) ▷ vb (pt **awoke**, pp **awoken**) ▷ vt éveiller ▷ vi s'éveiller; **to be ~** être éveillé(e)

award [ə'wɔːd] n (for bravery) récompense f; (prize) prix m; (Law: damages) dommages-intérêts mpl ▷ vt (prize) décerner; (Law: damages) accorder

aware [ə'weə'] adj: **~ of** (conscious) conscient(e) de; (informed) au courant de; **to become ~ of/that** prendre conscience de/que; se rendre compte de/que; **awareness** n conscience f, connaissance f

away [ə'weɪ] adv (a) loin; (movement): **she went ~** elle est partie ▷ adj (not in, not here) absent(e); **far ~** (au) loin; **two kilometres ~** à (une distance de) deux kilomètres, à deux kilomètres de distance; **two hours ~ by car** à deux heures de voiture en voiture; **the holiday was two weeks ~** il restait deux semaines jusqu'aux vacances; **he's ~ for a week** il est parti (pour) une semaine; **to take sth ~ from sb** prendre qch à qn; **to take sth ~ from sth** (subtract) ôter qch de qch; **to work/pedal ~** travailler/pédaler à cœur joie; **to fade ~** (colour) s'estomper; (sound) s'affaiblir

awe [ɔː] n respect mêlé de crainte, effroi mêlé d'admiration; **awesome** ['ɔːsəm] (us) adj (inf: excellent) génial(e)

awful ['ɔːfəl] adj affreux(-euse); **an ~ lot of** énormément de; **awfully** adv (very) terriblement, vraiment

awkward ['ɔːkwəd] adj (clumsy) gauche, maladroit(e); (inconvenient) peu pratique; (embarrassing) gênant

awoke [ə'wəʊk] pt of **awake**

awoken [ə'wəʊkən] pp of **awake**

siège m/roue f arrière inv; ~ **payments/
rent** arriéré m de paiements/loyer; ~
garden/room jardin/pièce sur l'arrière
▷ *adv* (*not forward*) en arrière; (*returned*)
he's ~ il est rentré, il est de retour;
he ran ~ il est revenu en courant;
(*restitution*): **throw the ball** ~ renvoie
la balle; **can I have it** ~? puis-je le
ravoir?, peux-tu me le rendre?; (*again*):
he called ~ il a rappelé; **back down**
vi rabattre de ses prétentions; **back
out** *vi* (*of promise*) se dédire; **back up**
vt (*person*) soutenir; (*Comput*) faire une
copie de sauvegarde de; **backache** *n*
mal *m* au dos; **backbencher** (BRIT) *n*
membre du parlement sans portefeuille;
backbone *n* colonne vertébrale,
épine dorsale; **backdoor** *n* porte f de
derrière; **backfire** *vi* (*Aut*) pétarader;
(*plans*) mal tourner; **backgammon** *n*
trictrac *m*; **background** *n* arrière-plan
m; (*of events*) situation f, conjoncture
f; (*basic knowledge*) éléments *mpl* de
base; (*experience*) formation f; **family
background** milieu familial; **backing**
n (*fig*) soutien *m*, appui *m*; **backlog** *n*:
backlog of work travail *m* en retard;
backpack *n* sac *m* à dos; **backpacker**
n randonneur(-euse); **backslash** *n*
barre oblique inversée; **backstage**
adv dans les coulisses; **backstroke** *n*
dos crawlé; **backup** *adj* (*train, plane*)
supplémentaire; (*Comput*) copie f
de sauvegarde ▷ *n* (*support*) appui *m*,
soutien *m*; (*Comput*: *also*: **backup file**
sauvegarde f; **backward** *adj* (*movement*)
en arrière; (*person, country*) arriéré(e),
attardé(e); **backwards** *adv* (*move,
go*) en arrière; (*read a list*) à l'envers;
(*fall*) à la renverse; (*walk*) à
reculons; **backyard** *n* arrière-cour f

bacon ['beɪkən] *n* bacon *m*, lard *m*

bacteria [bæk'tɪərɪə] *npl* bactéries *fpl*

bad [bæd] *adj* mauvais(e); (*child*)
vilain(e); (*mistake, accident*) grave;
(*meat, food*) gâté(e), avarié(e); **his** ~ **leg**
sa jambe malade; **to go** ~ (*meat, food*) se
gâter; (*milk*) tourner

bade [bæd] *pt* of **bid**

badge [bædʒ] *n* insigne *m*; (*of
policeman*) plaque f; (*stick-on, sew-on*)
badge *m*

badger ['bædʒə*r*] *n* blaireau *m*

badly ['bædlɪ] *adv* (*work, dress etc*)
mal; **to reflect** ~ **on sb** donner une
mauvaise image de qn; ~ **wounded**
grièvement blessé; **he needs it** ~ il en
a absolument besoin; ~ **off** *adj, adv*
dans la gêne

bad-mannered ['bæd'mænəd] *adj*
mal élevé(e)

badminton ['bædmɪntən] *n*
badminton *m*

bad-tempered ['bæd'tempəd] *adj* (*by
nature*) ayant mauvais caractère; (*on one
occasion*) de mauvaise humeur

bag [bæg] *n* sac *m*; ~**s of** (*inf*: *lots of*)
des tas de; **baggage** *n* bagages *mpl*;
baggage allowance *n* franchise f
de bagages; **baggage reclaim** *n* (*at
airport*) livraison f des bagages; **baggy**
adj avachi(e), qui fait des poches;
bagpipes *npl* cornemuse f

bail [beɪl] *n* caution f ▷ *vt* (*prisoner*:
also: **grant** ~ **to**) mettre en liberté sous
caution; (*boat*: *also*: ~ **out**) écoper; **to
be released on** ~ être libéré(e) sous
caution; **bail out** (*prisoner*) payer la
caution de

bait [beɪt] *n* appât *m* ▷ *vt* appâter; (*fig*:
tease) tourmenter

bake [beɪk] *vt* (faire) cuire au four
▷ *vi* (*bread etc*) cuire (au four); (*make
cakes etc*) faire de la pâtisserie; **baked
beans** *npl* haricots blancs à la sauce
tomate; **baked potato** *n* pomme f
de terre en robe des champs; **baker** *n*
boulanger *m*; **bakery** *n* boulangerie f;
baking *n* (*process*) cuisson f; **baking
powder** *n* levure f (chimique)

balance ['bæləns] *n* équilibre *m*;
(*Comm*: *sum*) solde *m*; (*remainder*) reste
m; (*scales*) balance f ▷ *vt* mettre ou
faire tenir en équilibre; (*pros and cons*)
peser; (*budget*) équilibrer; (*account*)
balancer; (*compensate*) compenser,

axe [æks] (US **ax**) n hache f ▷ vt (project etc) abandonner; (jobs) supprimer
axle ['æksl] n essieu m
ay(e) [aɪ] excl (yes) oui
azalea [ə'zeɪlɪə] n azalée f

B [biː] n (Mus): **B** si m
B.A. abbr (Scol) = **Bachelor of Arts**
baby ['beɪbɪ] n bébé m; **baby carriage** n (US) voiture f d'enfant; **baby-sit** vi garder les enfants; **baby-sitter** n baby-sitter m/f; **baby wipe** n lingette f (pour bébé)
bachelor ['bætʃələʳ] n célibataire m; **B~ of Arts/Science (BA/BSc)** = licencié(e) ès or en lettres/sciences
back [bæk] n (of person, horse) dos m; (of hand) dos, revers m; (of house) derrière m; (of car, train) arrière m; (of chair) dossier m; (of page) verso m; (of crowd): **can the people at the ~ hear me properly?** est-ce que les gens du fond peuvent m'entendre?; (Football) arrière m; **~ to front** à l'envers ▷ vt (financially) soutenir (financièrement); (candidate: also: **~ up**) soutenir, appuyer; (horse: at races) parier or miser sur; (car) (faire) reculer ▷ vi reculer; (car etc) faire marche arrière ▷ adj (in compounds) de derrière, à l'arrière; **~ seat/wheel** (Aut)

contrebalancer; **~ of trade/payments** balance commerciale/des comptes or paiements; **balanced** adj (personality, diet) équilibré(e); (report) objectif(-ive); **balance sheet** n bilan m

balcony ['bælkənɪ] n balcon m; **do you have a room with a ~?** avez-vous une chambre avec balcon?

bald [bɔːld] adj chauve; (tyre) lisse

ball [bɔːl] n boule f; (football) ballon m; (for tennis, golf) balle f; (dance) bal m; **to play ~** jouer au ballon (or à la balle); (fig) coopérer

ballerina [bælə'riːnə] n ballerine f

ballet ['bæleɪ] n ballet m; (art) danse f (classique); **ballet dancer** n danseur(-euse) de ballet

balloon [bə'luːn] n ballon m

ballot ['bælət] n scrutin m

ballpoint (pen) ['bɔːlpɔɪnt-] n stylo m à bille

ballroom ['bɔːlrum] n salle f de bal

Baltic [bɔːltɪk] n: **the ~ (Sea)** la (mer) Baltique

bamboo [bæm'buː] n bambou m

ban [bæn] n interdiction f ▷ vt interdire

banana [bə'nɑːnə] n banane f

band [bænd] n bande f; (at a dance) orchestre m; (Mil) musique f, fanfare f

bandage ['bændɪdʒ] n bandage m, pansement m ▷ vt (wound, leg) mettre un pansement or un bandage sur

Band-Aid® ['bændeɪd] n (us) pansement adhésif

B. & B. n abbr = **bed and breakfast**

bandit ['bændɪt] n bandit m

bang [bæŋ] n détonation f; (of door) claquement m; (blow) coup (violent) m ▷ vt frapper (violemment); (door) claquer ▷ vi détoner; claquer

Bangladesh [bæŋglə'deʃ] n Bangladesh m

Bangladeshi [bæŋglə'deʃɪ] adj du Bangladesh ▷ n habitant(e) du Bangladesh

bangle ['bæŋgl] n bracelet m

bangs [bæŋz] npl (us: fringe) frange f

banish ['bænɪʃ] vt bannir

banister(s) ['bænɪstə(z)] n(pl) rampe f (d'escalier)

banjo (pl **-es** or **~s**) ['bændʒəu] n banjo m

bank [bæŋk] n banque f; (of river, lake) bord m, rive f; (of earth) talus m, remblai m ▷ vi (Aviat) virer sur l'aile; **bank on** vt fus miser or tabler sur; **bank account** n compte m en banque; **bank balance** n solde m bancaire; **bank card** (BRIT) n carte f d'identité bancaire; **bank charges** npl (BRIT) frais mpl de banque; **banker** n banquier m; **bank holiday** n (BRIT) jour férié (où les banques sont fermées); voir encadré; **banking** n opérations fpl bancaires; profession f de banquier; **bank manager** n directeur m d'agence (bancaire); **banknote** n billet m de banque

⊙ **BANK HOLIDAY**

⊙
⊙ Le terme **bank holiday** s'applique
⊙ au Royaume-Uni aux jours fériés
⊙ pendant lesquels banques et
⊙ commerces sont fermés. Les
⊙ principaux **bank holidays** à part
⊙ Noël et Pâques se situent au mois
⊙ de mai et fin août, et contrairement
⊙ aux pays de tradition catholique, ne
⊙ coïncident pas nécessairement avec
⊙ une fête religieuse.

bankrupt ['bæŋkrʌpt] adj en faillite; **to go ~** faire faillite; **bankruptcy** n faillite f

bank statement n relevé m de compte

banner ['bænə'] n bannière f

bannister(s) ['bænɪstə(z)] n(pl) = **banister(s)**

banquet ['bæŋkwɪt] n banquet m, festin m

baptism ['bæptɪzəm] n baptême m

baptize [bæp'taɪz] vt baptiser

bar [bɑːʳ] n (pub) bar m; (counter) comptoir m, bar m; (rod: of metal etc) barre f; (of window etc) barreau m; (of chocolate)

tablette f, plaque f; (fig: obstacle)
obstacle m; (Mus) mesure f ▷ vt (road)
barrer; (person) exclure; (activity)
interdire; **~ of soap** savonnette
f; **behind ~s** (prisoner) derrière les
barreaux; **the B~** (Law) le barreau; **~
none** sans exception

barbaric [baːˈbærɪk] adj barbare

barbecue [ˈbaːbɪkjuː] n barbecue m

barbed wire [ˈbaːbd-] n fil m de fer
barbelé

barber [ˈbaːbəʳ] n coiffeur m (pour
hommes); **barber's (shop)** (us **barber
(shop)**) n salon m de coiffure (pour
hommes)

bar code n code m à barres, code-
barre m

bare [bɛəʳ] adj nu(e) ▷ vt mettre à nu,
dénuder; (teeth) montrer; **barefoot** adj,
adv nu-pieds; (les) pieds nus; **barely**
adv à peine

bargain [ˈbaːgɪn] n (transaction)
marché m; (good buy) affaire f, occasion
f ▷ vi (haggle) marchander; (negotiate)
négocier, traiter; **into the ~** par-dessus
le marché; **bargain for** vt fus (inf): **he
got more than he ~ed for!** il en a eu
pour son argent!

barge [baːdʒ] n péniche f; **barge in** vi
(walk in) faire irruption; (interrupt talk)
intervenir mal à propos

bark [baːk] n (of tree) écorce f; (of dog)
aboiement m ▷ vi aboyer

barley [ˈbaːlɪ] n orge f

barmaid [ˈbaːmeɪd] n serveuse f (de
bar), barmaid f

barman [ˈbaːmən] n serveur m (de bar),
barman m

barn [baːn] n grange f

barometer [bəˈrɔmɪtəʳ] n baromètre m

baron [ˈbærən] n baron m; **baroness**
n baronne f

barracks [ˈbærəks] npl caserne f

barrage [ˈbæraːʒ] n (Mil) tir m de
barrage; (dam) barrage m; (of criticism)
feu m

barrel [ˈbærəl] n tonneau m; (of gun)

canon m

barren [ˈbærən] adj stérile

barrette [bəˈrɛt] (us) n barrette f

barricade [bærɪˈkeɪd] n barricade f

barrier [ˈbærɪəʳ] n barrière f

barring [ˈbaːrɪŋ] prep sauf

barrister [ˈbærɪstəʳ] n (BRIT) avocat
(plaidant)

barrow [ˈbærəʊ] n (cart) charrette
f à bras

bartender [ˈbaːtɛndəʳ] n (US) serveur
m (de bar), barman m

base [beɪs] n base f ▷ vt (opinion, belief):
to ~ sth on baser or fonder qch sur ▷ adj
vil(e), bas(se)

baseball [ˈbeɪsbɔːl] n base-ball m;
baseball cap n casquette f de base-ball

Basel [ˈbaːl] = **Bâle**

basement [ˈbeɪsmənt] n sous-sol m

bases [ˈbeɪsiːz] npl of **basis**

bash [bæʃ] vt (inf) frapper, cogner

basic [ˈbeɪsɪk] adj (precautions, rules)
élémentaire; (principles, research)
fondamental; (vocabulary, salary) de
base; (minimal) réduit au minimum,
rudimentaire; **basically** adv (in fact) en
fait; (essentially) fondamentalement;
basics npl: **the basics** l'essentiel m

basil [ˈbæzl] n basilic m

basin [ˈbeɪsn] n (vessel, also Geo) cuvette
f, bassin m; (BRIT: for food) bol m; (also:
wash~) lavabo m

basis (pl **bases**) [ˈbeɪsɪs, -siːz] n base
f; **on a part-time/trial ~** à temps
partiel/à l'essai

basket [ˈbaːskɪt] n corbeille f; (with
handle) panier m; **basketball** n
basket-ball m

Basle [baːl] = **Bâle**

Basque [bæsk] adj basque ▷ n Basque
m/f; **the ~ Country** le Pays basque

bass [beɪs] n (Mus) basse f

bastard [ˈbaːstəd] n enfant naturel(le),
bâtard(e); (inf!) salaud m (!)

bat [bæt] n chauve-souris f; (for baseball
etc) batte f; (BRIT: for table tennis)
raquette f ▷ vt: **he didn't ~ an eyelid** il
n'a pas sourcillé ni bronché

batch [bætʃ] *n (of bread)* fournée *f*; *(of papers)* liasse *f*; *(of applicants, letters)* paquet *m*

bath [*pl* **~s**] [bɑːθ, bɑːðz] *n* bain *m*; *(bathtub)* baignoire *f* ▷ *vt* baigner, donner un bain à; **to have a ~** prendre un bain; *see also* **baths**

bathe [beɪð] *vi* se baigner ▷ *vt* baigner; *(wound etc)* laver

bathing ['beɪðɪŋ] *n* baignade *f*; **bathing costume** *(us* **bathing suit)** *n* maillot *m* (de bain)

bath: **bathrobe** *n* peignoir *m* de bain; **bathroom** *n* salle *f* de bains; **baths** [bɑːðz] *npl (BRIT: also:* **swimming baths)** piscine *f*; **bath towel** *n* serviette *f* de bain; **bathtub** *n* baignoire *f*

baton ['bætən] *n* bâton *m*; *(Mus)* baguette *f*; *(club)* matraque *f*

batter ['bætə*r*] *vt* battre ▷ *n* pâte *f* à frire; **battered** *adj (hat, pan)* cabossé(e); **battered wife/child** épouse/enfant maltraité(e) or martyr(e)

battery ['bætərɪ] *n (for torch, radio)* pile *f*; *(Aut, Mil)* batterie *f*; **battery farming** *n* élevage *m* en batterie

battle ['bætl] *n* bataille *f*, combat *m* ▷ *vi* se battre, lutter; **battlefield** *n* champ *m* de bataille

bay [beɪ] *n (of sea)* baie *f*; *(BRIT: for parking)* place *f* de stationnement; *(: for loading)* aire *f* de chargement; **B~ of Biscay** golfe *m* de Gascogne; **to hold sb at ~** tenir qn à distance or en échec

bay leaf *n* laurier *m*

bazaar [bə'zɑː*r*] *n (shop, market)* bazar *m*; *(sale)* vente *f* de charité

BBC *n abbr (= British Broadcasting Corporation)* office *m* de la radiodiffusion et télévision britannique

B.C. *adv abbr (= before Christ)* av. J.-C.

○ **KEYWORD**

be [biː] *(pt* **was**, **were**, *pp* **been)** *aux vb* **1** *(with present participle: forming continuous tenses):* **what are you doing?** que faites-vous?; **they're coming tomorrow** ils viennent demain; **I've been waiting for you for 2 hours** je t'attends depuis 2 heures

2 *(with pp: forming passives)* être; **to be killed** être tué(e); **the box had been opened** la boîte avait été ouverte; **he was nowhere to be seen** on ne le voyait nulle part

3 *(in tag questions):* **it was fun, wasn't it?** c'était drôle, n'est-ce pas?; **he's good-looking, isn't he?** il est beau, n'est-ce pas?; **she's back, is she?** elle est rentrée, n'est-ce pas or alors?

4 *(+to +infinitive):* **the house is to be sold** *(necessity)* la maison doit être vendue; *(future)* la maison va être vendue; **he's not to open it** il ne doit pas l'ouvrir

▷ *vi* **+ complement 1** *(gen)* être; **I'm English** je suis anglais(e); **I'm tired** je suis fatigué(e); **I'm hot/cold** j'ai chaud/froid; **he's a doctor** il est médecin; **be careful/good/quiet!** faites attention/soyez sages/taisez-vous!; **2 and 2 are 4** 2 et 2 font 4

2 *(of health):* **how are you?** comment allez-vous?; **I'm better now** je vais mieux maintenant; **he's very ill** il est très malade

3 *(of age):* **how old are you?** quel âge avez-vous?; **I'm sixteen (years old)** j'ai seize ans

4 *(cost)* coûter; **how much was the meal?** combien a coûté le repas?; **that'll be £5, please** ça fera 5 livres, s'il vous plaît; **this shirt is £17** cette chemise coûte 17 livres

▷ *vi* **1** *(exist, occur etc)* être, exister; **the prettiest girl that ever was** la fille la plus jolie qui ait jamais existé; **is there a God?** y a-t-il un dieu?; **be that as it may** quoi qu'il en soit; **so be it** soit

2 *(referring to place)* être, se trouver; **I won't be here tomorrow** je ne serai pas là demain

3 *(referring to movement)* aller; **where have you been?** où êtes-vous allé(s)?

▷ *impers vb* **1** (*referring to time*) être; **it's 5 o'clock** il est 5 heures; **it's the 28th of April** c'est le 28 avril
2 (*referring to distance*): **it's 10 km to the village** le village est à 10 km
3 (*referring to the weather*) faire; **it's too hot/cold** il fait trop chaud/froid; **it's windy today** il y a du vent aujourd'hui
4 (*emphatic*): **it's me/the postman** c'est moi/le facteur; **it was Maria who paid the bill** c'est Maria qui a payé la note

beach [biːtʃ] *n* plage *f* ▷ *vt* échouer
beacon ['biːkən] *n* (*lighthouse*) fanal *m*; (*marker*) balise *f*
bead [biːd] *n* perle *f*; (*of dew, sweat*) goutte *f*; **beads** *npl* (*necklace*) collier *m*
beak [biːk] *n* bec *m*
beam [biːm] *n* (*Archit*) poutre *f*; (*of light*) rayon *m* ▷ *vi* rayonner
bean [biːn] *n* haricot *m*; (*of coffee*) grain *m*; **beansprouts** *npl* pousses *fpl* or germes *mpl* de soja
bear [bɛəʳ] *n* ours *m* ▷ *vb* (*pt* **bore**, *pp* **borne**) ▷ *vt* porter; (*endure*) supporter, rapporter ▷ *vi*: **to ~ right/left** obliquer à droite/gauche, se diriger vers la droite/gauche
beard [bɪəd] *n* barbe *f*
bearer ['bɛərəʳ] *n* porteur *m*; (*of passport etc*) titulaire *m/f*
bearing ['bɛərɪŋ] *n* maintien *m*, allure *f*; (*connection*) rapport *m*; (*Tech*): **(ball) bearings** *npl* roulement *m* (à billes)
beast [biːst] *n* bête *f*; (*inf: person*) brute *f*
beat [biːt] *n* battement *m*; (*Mus*) temps *m*, mesure *f*; (*of policeman*) ronde *f* ▷ *vt*, *vi* (*pt* ~, *pp* ~**en**) battre; **off the ~en track** hors des chemins or sentiers battus; **to ~ it** (*inf*) ficher le camp; **beat up** *vt* (*inf: person*) tabasser; **beating** *n* raclée *f*
beautiful ['bjuːtɪful] *adj* beau (belle); **beautifully** *adv* admirablement
beauty ['bjuːtɪ] *n* beauté *f*; **beauty parlour** (*us* **beauty parlor**) [-'paːləʳ] *n* institut *m* de beauté; **beauty salon** *n* institut *m* de beauté; **beauty spot**

n (*on skin*) grain *m* de beauté; (*BRIT Tourism*) site naturel (d'une grande beauté)
beaver ['biːvəʳ] *n* castor *m*
became [bɪ'keɪm] *pt of* **become**
because [bɪ'kɔz] *conj* parce que; **~ of** *prep* à cause de
beckon ['bɛkən] *vt* (*also*: **~ to**) faire signe (de venir) à
become [bɪ'kʌm] *vi* devenir; **to ~ fat/thin** grossir/maigrir; **to ~ angry** se mettre en colère
bed [bɛd] *n* lit *m*; (*of flowers*) parterre *m*; (*of coal, clay*) couche *f*; (*of sea, lake*) fond *m*; **to go to ~** aller se coucher; **bed and breakfast** *n* (*terms*) chambre et petit déjeuner; (*place*) ≈ chambre *f* d'hôte; *voir encadré*; **bedclothes** *npl* couvertures *fpl* et draps *mpl*; **bedding** *n* literie *f*; **bed linen** *n* draps *mpl* de lit (*et taies fpl d'oreillers*), literie *f*; **bedroom** *n* chambre *f* (à coucher); **bedside** *n*: **at sb's bedside** au chevet de qn; **bedside lamp** *n* lampe *f* de chevet; **bedside table** *n* table *f* de chevet; **bedsit(ter)** *n* (*BRIT*) chambre meublée, studio *m*; **bedspread** *n* couvre-lit *m*, dessus-de-lit *m*; **bedtime** *n*: **it's bedtime** c'est l'heure de se coucher

bee [biː] *n* abeille *f*
beech [biːtʃ] *n* hêtre *m*
beef [biːf] *n* bœuf *m*; **roast ~** rosbif *m*; **beefburger** *n* hamburger *m*;

Beefeater *n* hallebardier *m* (de la tour de Londres)

been [biːn] *pp of* **be**

beer [bɪəʳ] *n* bière *f*; **beer garden** *n* (BRIT) jardin *m* d'un pub (où l'on peut emmener ses consommations)

beet [biːt] *n* (vegetable) betterave *f*; (US: also: **red ~**) betterave (potagère)

beetle ['biːtl] *n* scarabée *m*, coléoptère *m*

beetroot ['biːtruːt] *n* (BRIT) betterave *f*

before [bɪ'fɔːʳ] *prep* (of time) avant; (of space) devant ▷ *conj* avant que + *sub*; avant de ▷ *adv* avant; **~ going** avant de partir; **~ she goes** avant qu'elle (ne) parte; **the week ~** la semaine précédente or d'avant; **I've never seen it ~** c'est la première fois que je le vois; **beforehand** *adv* au préalable, à l'avance

beg [bɛg] *vi* mendier ▷ *vt* mendier; (forgiveness, mercy etc) demander; (entreat) supplier; **to ~ sb to do sth** supplier qn de faire qch; see also **pardon**

began [bɪ'gæn] *pt of* **begin**

beggar ['bɛgəʳ] *n* mendiant(e)

begin [bɪ'gɪn] (*pt* **began**, *pp* **begun**) *vt*, *vi* commencer; **to ~ doing** or **to do sth** commencer à faire qch; **beginner** *n* débutant(e); **beginning** *n* commencement *m*, début *m*

begun [bɪ'gʌn] *pp of* **begin**

behalf [bɪ'hɑːf] *n*: **on ~ of**, (US) **in ~ of** (representing) de la part de; (for benefit of) pour le compte de; **on my/his ~** de ma/sa part

behave [bɪ'heɪv] *vi* se conduire, se comporter; (well: also: **~ o.s.**) se conduire bien or comme il faut; **behaviour** (US **behavior**) *n* comportement *m*, conduite *f*

behind [bɪ'haɪnd] *prep* derrière; (time) en retard sur; (supporting) **to be ~ sb** soutenir qn ▷ *adv* derrière; en retard ▷ *n* derrière *m*; **~ the scenes** dans les coulisses; **to be ~ (schedule) with sth** être en retard dans qch

beige [beɪʒ] *adj* beige

Beijing ['beɪ'dʒɪŋ] *n* Pékin

being ['biːɪŋ] *n* être *m*; **to come into ~** prendre naissance

belated [bɪ'leɪtɪd] *adj* tardif(-ive)

belch [bɛltʃ] *vi* avoir un renvoi, roter ▷ *vt* (also: **~ out**: smoke etc) vomir, cracher

Belgian ['bɛldʒən] *adj* belge, de Belgique ▷ *n* Belge *m/f*

Belgium ['bɛldʒəm] *n* Belgique *f*

belief [bɪ'liːf] *n* (opinion) conviction *f*; (trust, faith) foi *f*

believe [bɪ'liːv] *vt*, *vi* croire, estimer; **to ~ in** (God) croire en; (ghosts, method) croire à; (Rel) croyant(e); **believer** *n* (in idea, activity) partisan(e); (Rel) croyant(e)

bell [bɛl] *n* cloche *f*; (small) clochette *f*, grelot *m*; (on door) sonnette *f*; (electric) sonnerie *f*

bellboy ['bɛlbɔɪ] (US **bellhop** ['bɛlhɔp]) *n* groom *m*, chasseur *m*

bellow ['bɛləu] *vi* (bull) meugler; (person) brailler

bell pepper *n* (esp US) poivron *m*

belly ['bɛlɪ] *n* ventre *m*; **belly button** (inf) *n* nombril *m*

belong [bɪ'lɔŋ] *vi*: **to ~ to** appartenir à; (club etc) faire partie de; **this book ~s here** ce livre va ici, la place de ce livre est ici; **belongings** *npl* affaires *fpl*, possessions *fpl*

beloved [bɪ'lʌvɪd] *adj* (bien-)aimé(e), chéri(e)

below [bɪ'ləu] *prep* sous, au-dessous de ▷ *adv* en dessous; en contre-bas; **see ~** voir plus bas or plus loin or ci-dessous

belt [bɛlt] *n* ceinture *f*; (Tech) courroie *f* ▷ *vt* (thrash) donner une raclée à; **beltway** *n* (US Aut) route *f* de ceinture; (: motorway) périphérique *m*

bemused [bɪ'mjuːzd] *adj* médusé(e)

bench [bɛntʃ] *n* banc *m*; (in workshop) établi *m*; **the B~** (Law: judges) la magistrature, la Cour

bend [bɛnd] *vb* (*pt*, *pp* **bent**) ▷ *vt* courber; (leg, arm) plier ▷ *vi* se courber ▷ *n* (BRIT: in road) virage *m*, tournant *m*; (in pipe, river) coude *m*; **bend down** *vi* se baisser; **bend over** vi se pencher

beneath [bɪ'ni:θ] prep sous, au-dessous de; (unworthy of) indigne de ▷ adv dessous, au-dessous, en bas

beneficial [benɪ'fɪʃəl] adj: **~ (to)** salutaire (pour), bénéfique (à)

benefit ['benɪfɪt] n avantage m, profit m; (allowance of money) allocation f ▷ vt faire du bien à, profiter à ▷ vi: **he'll ~ from it** cela lui fera du bien, il y gagnera or s'en trouvera bien

Benelux ['benɪlʌks] n Bénélux m

benign [bɪ'naɪn] adj (person, smile) bienveillant(e), affable; (Med) bénin(-igne)

bent [bent] pt, pp of **bend** ▷ n inclination f, penchant m ▷ adj: **to be ~ on** être résolu(e) à

bereaved [bɪ'ri:vd] n: **the ~** la famille du disparu

beret ['bereɪ] n béret m

Berlin [bə:'lɪn] n Berlin

Bermuda [bə:'mju:də] n Bermudes fpl

Bern [bə:n] n Berne

berry ['berɪ] n baie f

berth [bə:θ] n (bed) couchette f; (for ship) poste m d'amarrage, mouillage m ▷ vi (in harbour) venir à quai; (at anchor) mouiller

beside [bɪ'saɪd] prep à côté de; (compared with) auprès de; **that's ~ the point** ça n'a rien à voir; **to be ~ o.s. (with anger)** être hors de soi; **besides** adv en outre, de plus ▷ prep en plus de; (except) excepté

best [best] adj meilleur(e) ▷ adv le mieux; **the ~ part of** (quantity) le plus clair de, la plus grande partie de; **at ~** au mieux; **to make the ~ of sth** s'accommoder de qch (du mieux que l'on peut); **to do one's ~** faire de son mieux; **to the ~ of my knowledge** pour autant que je sache; **to the ~ of my ability** du mieux que je pourrai; **best-before date** n date f de limite d'utilisation or de consommation; **best man** (irreg) n garçon m d'honneur; **bestseller** n best-seller m, succès m

de librairie

bet [bet] n pari m ▷ vt, vi (pt, pp ~ or ~**ted**) parier; **to ~ sb sth** parier qch à qn

betray [bɪ'treɪ] vt trahir

better ['betə*] adj meilleur(e) ▷ adv mieux ▷ vt améliorer ▷ n: **to get the ~ of** triompher de, l'emporter sur; **you had ~ do it** vous feriez mieux de le faire; **he thought ~ of it** il s'est ravisé; **to get ~** (Med) aller mieux; (improve) s'améliorer

betting ['betɪŋ] n paris mpl; **betting shop** n (BRIT) bureau m de paris

between [bɪ'twi:n] prep entre ▷ adv au milieu, dans l'intervalle

beverage ['bevərɪdʒ] n boisson f (gén sans alcool)

beware [bɪ'weə*] vi: **to ~ (of)** prendre garde (à); **"~ of the dog"** "(attention) chien méchant"

bewildered [bɪ'wɪldəd] adj dérouté(e), ahuri(e)

beyond [bɪ'jɔnd] prep (in space, time) au-delà de; (exceeding) au-dessus de ▷ adv au-delà; **~ doubt** hors de doute; **~ repair** irréparable

bias ['baɪəs] n (prejudice) préjugé m, parti pris m; (preference) prévention f; **bias(s)ed** adj partial(e), montrant un parti pris

bib [bɪb] n bavoir m

Bible ['baɪbl] n Bible f

bicarbonate of soda [baɪ'kɑ:bənɪt-] n bicarbonate m de soude

biceps ['baɪseps] n biceps m

bicycle ['baɪsɪkl] n bicyclette f; **bicycle pump** n pompe f à vélo

bid [bɪd] n offre f; (at auction) enchère f; (attempt) tentative f ▷ vb (pt ~ or **bade**, pp ~ or **~den**) ▷ vi faire une enchère or offre ▷ vt faire une enchère or offre de; **to ~ sb good day** souhaiter le bonjour à qn; **bidder** n: **the highest bidder** le plus offrant

bidet ['bi:deɪ] n bidet m

big [bɪg] adj (in height: person, building, tree) grand(e); (in bulk, amount: person, parcel, book) gros(se); **bigheaded** adj prétentieux(-euse); **big toe** n gros orteil

bike [baɪk] n vélo m; **bike lane** n piste f cyclable

bikini [bɪˈkiːnɪ] n bikini m

bilateral [baɪˈlætərl] adj bilatéral(e)

bilingual [baɪˈlɪŋgwəl] adj bilingue

bill [bɪl] n note f, facture f; (in restaurant) addition f, note f; (Pol) projet m de loi; (us: banknote) billet m (de banque); (notice) affiche f; (of bird) bec m; **put it on my** ~ mettez-le sur mon compte; **"post no ~s"** "défense d'afficher"; **to fit** or **fill the** ~ (fig) faire l'affaire; **billboard** (us) n panneau m d'affichage; **billfold** [ˈbɪlfəʊld] n (us) portefeuille m

billiards [ˈbɪljədz] n (jeu m de) billard m

billion [ˈbɪljən] n (BRIT) billion m (million de millions); (us) milliard m

bin [bɪn] n boîte f; (BRIT: also: **dust-**, **litter** ~) poubelle f; (for coal) coffre m

bind (pt, pp **bound**) [baɪnd, baʊnd] vt attacher; (book) relier; (oblige) obliger, contraindre ▷ n (inf: nuisance) scie f

binge [bɪndʒ] n (inf): **to go on a** ~ faire la bringue

bingo [ˈbɪŋgəʊ] n sorte de jeu de loto pratiqué dans des établissements publics

binoculars [bɪˈnɔkjuləz] npl jumelles fpl

bio... [baɪə] prefix: **biochemistry**

n biochimie f; **biodegradable** [ˈbaɪəʊdɪˈgreɪdəbl] adj biodégradable; **biography** [baɪˈɔgrəfɪ] n biographie f; **biological** adj biologique; **biology** [baɪˈɔlədʒɪ] n biologie f; **biometric** [baɪəˈmetrɪk] adj biométrique

birch [bəːtʃ] n bouleau m

bird [bəːd] n oiseau m; (BRIT inf: girl) nana f; **bird flu** n grippe f aviaire; **bird of prey** n oiseau m de proie; **birdwatching** n ornithologie f (d'amateur)

Biro® [ˈbaɪərəʊ] n stylo m à bille

birth [bəːθ] n naissance f; **to give** ~ **to** donner naissance à, mettre au monde; (subj: animal) mettre bas; **birth certificate** n acte m de naissance; **birth control** n (policy) limitation f des naissances; (methods) méthode(s) contraceptive(s); **birthday** n anniversaire m ▷ cpd (cake, card etc) d'anniversaire; **birthmark** n envie f, tache f de vin; **birthplace** n lieu m de naissance

biscuit [ˈbɪskɪt] n (BRIT) biscuit m; (us) petit pain au lait

bishop [ˈbɪʃəp] n évêque m; (Chess) fou m

bistro [ˈbiːstrəʊ] n petit restaurant m, bistrot m

bit [bɪt] pt of **bite** ▷ n morceau m; (Comput) bit m, élément m binaire; (of tool) mèche f; (of horse) mors m; **a** ~ **of** un peu de; **a** ~ **mad/dangerous** un peu fou/risqué; ~ **by** ~ petit à petit

bitch [bɪtʃ] n (dog) chienne f; (infl) salope f (!), garce f

bite [baɪt] vt, vi (pt **bit**, pp **bitten**) mordre; (insect) piquer ▷ n morsure f; (insect bite) piqûre f; (mouthful) bouchée f; **let's have a** ~ (**to eat**) mangeons un morceau; **to** ~ **one's nails** se ronger les ongles

bitten [ˈbɪtn] pp of **bite**

bitter [ˈbɪtəʳ] adj amer(-ère); (criticism) cinglant(e); (icy: weather, wind) glacial(e) ▷ n (BRIT: beer) bière f (à forte teneur en houblon)

bizarre [bɪˈzɑːʳ] adj bizarre

black [blæk] *adj* noir(e) ▷ *n* (*colour*) noir *m*; (*person*): **B~** noir(e) ▷ *vt* (*BRIT Industry*) boycotter; **to give sb a ~ eye** pocher l'œil à qn, faire un œil au beurre noir à qn; **to be in the ~** (*in credit*) avoir un compte créditeur; **~ and blue** (*bruised*) couvert(e) de bleus; **black out** *vi* (*faint*) s'évanouir; **blackberry** *n* mûre *f*; **blackbird** *n* merle *m*; **blackboard** *n* tableau noir; **black coffee** *n* café noir; **blackcurrant** *n* cassis *m*; **black ice** *n* verglas *m*; **blackmail** *n* chantage *m* ▷ *vt* faire chanter, soumettre au chantage; **black market** *n* marché noir; **blackout** *n* panne *f* d'électricité; (*in wartime*) black-out *m*; (*TV*) interruption *f* d'émission; (*fainting*) syncope *f*; **black pepper** *n* poivre noir; **black pudding** *n* boudin (noir); **Black Sea** *n*: **the Black Sea** la mer Noire

bladder ['blædə^r] *n* vessie *f*

blade [bleɪd] *n* lame *f*; (*of propeller*) pale *f*; **a ~ of grass** un brin d'herbe

blame [bleɪm] *n* faute *f*, blâme *m* ▷ *vt*: **to ~ sb/sth for sth** attribuer à qn/qch la responsabilité de qch; reprocher qch à qn/qch; **I'm not to ~** ce n'est pas ma faute

bland [blænd] *adj* (*taste, food*) doux (douce), fade

blank [blæŋk] *adj* blanc (blanche); (*look*) sans expression, dénué(e) d'expression ▷ *n* espace *m* vide, blanc *m*; (*cartridge*) cartouche *f* à blanc; **his mind was a ~** il avait la tête vide

blanket ['blæŋkɪt] *n* couverture *f*; (*of snow, cloud*) couche *f*

blast [blɑːst] *n* explosion *f*; (*shock wave*) souffle *m*; (*of air, steam*) bouffée *f* ▷ *vt* faire sauter ou exploser

blatant ['bleɪtənt] *adj* flagrant(e), criant(e)

blaze [bleɪz] *n* (*fire*) incendie *m*; (*fig*) flamboiement *m*; (*fire*) flamber; (*fig*) flamboyer, resplendir ▷ *vt*: **to ~ a trail** (*fig*) montrer la voie; **in a ~ of publicity** à grand renfort de publicité

blazer ['bleɪzə^r] *n* blazer *m*

bleach [bliːtʃ] *n* (*also*: **household ~**) eau *f* de Javel ▷ *vt* (*linen*) blanchir; **bleachers** *npl* (*us Sport*) gradins *mpl* (*en plein soleil*)

bleak [bliːk] *adj* morne, désolé(e); (*weather*) triste, maussade; (*smile*) lugubre; (*prospect, future*) morose

bled [bled] *pt, pp* of **bleed**

bleed (*pt, pp* **bled**) [bliːd, bled] *vt* saigner; (*brakes, radiator*) purger ▷ *vi* saigner; **my nose is ~ing** je saigne du nez

blemish ['blemɪʃ] *n* défaut *m*; (*on reputation*) tache *f*

blend [blend] *n* mélange *m* ▷ *vt* mélanger ▷ *vi* (*colours etc: also*: **~ in**) se mélanger, se fondre, s'allier; **blender** *n* (*Culin*) mixeur *m*

bless (*pt, pp* **~ed** *or* **blest**) [bles, blest] *vt* bénir; **~ you!** (*after sneeze*) à tes souhaits!; **blessing** *n* bénédiction *f*; (*godsend*) bienfait *m*

blew [bluː] *pt* of **blow**

blight [blaɪt] *vt* (*hopes etc*) anéantir, briser

blind [blaɪnd] *adj* aveugle ▷ *n* (*for window*) store *m* ▷ *vt* aveugler; **the blind** *npl* les aveugles *mpl*; **blind alley** *n* impasse *f*; **blindfold** *n* bandeau *m* ▷ *adj, adv* les yeux bandés ▷ *vt* bander les yeux à

blink [blɪŋk] *vi* cligner des yeux; (*light*) clignoter

bliss [blɪs] *n* félicité *f*, bonheur *m* sans mélange

blister ['blɪstə^r] *n* (*on skin*) ampoule *f*, cloque *f*; (*on paintwork*) boursouflure *f* ▷ *vi* (*paint*) se boursoufler, se cloquer

blizzard ['blɪzəd] *n* blizzard *m*, tempête *f* de neige

bloated ['bləutɪd] *adj* (*face*) bouffi(e); (*stomach, person*) gonflé(e)

blob [blɒb] *n* (*drop*) goutte *f*; (*stain, spot*) tache *f*

block [blɒk] *n* bloc *m*; (*in pipes*) obstruction *f*; (*toy*) cube *m*; (*of buildings*) pâté *m* (de maisons) ▷ *vt* bloquer;

(fig) faire obstacle à; **the sink is ~ed** l'évier est bouché; **~ of flats** *(BRIT)* immeuble *(locatif)*; **mental ~** blocage *m*; **block up** *vt* boucher; **blockade** [blɔ'keɪd] *n* blocus *m* ▷ *vt* faire le blocus de; **blockage** *n* obstruction *f*; **blockbuster** *n (film, book)* grand succès; **block capitals** *npl* majuscules *fpl* d'imprimerie; **block letters** *npl* majuscules *fpl*

blog [blɔg] *n* blog *m*, blogue *m*

bloke [bləuk] *n (BRIT inf)* type *m*

blond(e) [blɔnd] *adj*, *n* blond(e)

blood [blʌd] *n* sang *m*; **blood donor** *n* donneur(-euse) de sang; **blood group** *n* groupe sanguin; **blood poisoning** *n* empoisonnement *m* du sang; **blood pressure** *n* tension *(artérielle)*; **bloodshed** *n* effusion *f* de sang, carnage *m*; **bloodshot** *adj*: **bloodshot eyes** yeux injectés de sang; **bloodstream** *n* sang *m*, système sanguin; **blood test** *n* analyse *f* de sang; **blood transfusion** *n* transfusion *f* de sang; **blood type** *n* groupe sanguin; **blood vessel** *n* vaisseau sanguin; **bloody** *adj* sanglant(e); *(BRIT inf!)*: **this bloody ...** ce foutu ..., ce putain de ... (!) ▷ *adv*: **bloody strong/good** *(BRIT inf!)* vachement or sacrément fort/bon

bloom [blu:m] *n* fleur *f* ▷ *vi* être en fleur

blossom ['blɔsəm] *n* fleur(s) *f(pl)* ▷ *vi* être en fleurs; *(fig)* s'épanouir

blot [blɔt] *n* tache *f* ▷ *vt* tacher; *(ink)* sécher

blouse [blauz] *n (feminine garment)* chemisier *m*, corsage *m*

blow [bləu] *n* coup *m* ▷ *vb (pt* **blew***, pp* **~n***)* ▷ *vi* souffler ▷ *vt (instrument)* jouer de; *(fuse)* faire sauter; **to ~ one's nose** se moucher; **blow away** *vt* chasser, faire s'envoler; **blow out** *vi (fire, flame)* s'éteindre; *(tyre)* éclater; *(fuse)* sauter; **blow up** *vi* exploser, sauter ▷ *vt* faire sauter; *(tyre)* gonfler; *(Phot)* agrandir; **blow-dry** *n (hairstyle)* brushing *m*

blown [bləun] *pp of* **blow**

blue [blu:] *adj* bleu(e); *(depressed)* triste; **~ film/joke** film *m*/histoire *f* pornographique; **out of the ~** *(fig)* à l'improviste, sans qu'on s'y attende; **bluebell** *n* jacinthe *f* des bois; **blueberry** *n* myrtille *f*, airelle *f*; **blue cheese** *n (fromage)* bleu *m*; **blues** *npl*: **the blues** *(Mus)* le blues; **to have the blues** *(inf: feeling)* avoir le cafard; **bluetit** *n* mésange bleue

bluff [blʌf] *vi* bluffer ▷ *n* bluff *m*; **to call sb's ~** mettre qn au défi d'exécuter ses menaces

blunder ['blʌndə'] *n* gaffe *f*, bévue *f* ▷ *vi* faire une gaffe or une bévue

blunt [blʌnt] *adj (knife)* émoussé(e), peu tranchant(e); *(pencil)* mal taillé(e); *(person)* brusque, ne mâchant pas ses mots

blur [blə:'] *n (shape)*: **to become a ~** devenir flou ▷ *vt* brouiller, rendre flou(e); **blurred** *adj* flou(e)

blush [blʌʃ] *vi* rougir ▷ *n* rougeur *f*; **blusher** *n* rouge *m* à joues

board [bɔ:d] *n (wooden)* planche *f*; *(on wall)* panneau *m*; *(for chess etc)* plateau *m*; *(cardboard)* carton *m*; *(committee)* conseil *m*, comité *m*; *(in firm)* conseil d'administration; *(Naut, Aviat)*: **on ~** à bord ▷ *vt (ship)* monter à bord de; *(train)* monter dans; **full ~** *(BRIT)* pension complète; **half ~** *(BRIT)* demi-pension *f*; **~ and lodging** *n* chambre *f* avec pension; **to go by the ~** *(hopes, principles)* être abandonné(e); **board game** *n* jeu *m* de société; **boarding card** *n (Aviat, Naut)* carte *f* d'embarquement; **boarding pass** *n (BRIT)* = **boarding card**; **boarding school** *n* internat *m*, pensionnat *m*; **board room** *n* salle *f* du conseil d'administration

boast [bəust] *vi*: **to ~ (about or of)** se vanter (de)

boat [bəut] *n* bateau *m*; *(small)* canot *m*; barque *f*

bob [bɔb] *vi (boat, cork on water: also:* **~**

up and down) danser, se balancer

bobby pin ['bɒbɪ] n (US) pince f à cheveux

body ['bɒdɪ] n corps m; (of car) carrosserie f; (fig: society) organe m, organisme m; **body-building** n body-building m, culturisme m; **bodyguard** n garde m du corps; **bodywork** n carrosserie f

bog [bɒg] n tourbière f ▷ vt: **to get ~ged down (in)** (fig) s'enliser (dans)

bogus ['bəʊgəs] adj bidon inv; fantôme

boil [bɔɪl] vt (faire) bouillir ▷ vi bouillir ▷ n (Med) furoncle m; **to come to the** or (US) **a ~** bouillir; **boil down to** vi (fig): **to ~ down to** se réduire or ramener à; **boil over** vi déborder; **boiled egg** n œuf m à la coque; **boiled potatoes** n pommes fpl à l'anglaise or à l'eau; **boiler** n chaudière f; **boiling** ['bɔɪlɪŋ] adj: **I'm boiling (hot)** (inf) je crève de chaud; **boiling point** n point m d'ébullition

bold [bəʊld] adj hardi(e), audacieux(-euse); (pej) effronté(e); (outline, colour) franc (franche), tranché(e), marqué(e)

bollard ['bɒləd] n (BRIT Aut) borne f lumineuse or de signalisation

bolt [bəʊlt] n verrou m; (with nut) boulon m ▷ adv: **~ upright** droit(e) comme un piquet ▷ vt verrouiller; (food) engloutir ▷ vi se sauver, filer (comme une flèche); (horse) s'emballer

bomb [bɒm] n bombe f ▷ vt bombarder; **bombard** [bɒm'bɑːd] vt bombarder; **bomber** n (Aviat) bombardier m; (terrorist) poseur m de bombes; **bomb scare** n alerte f à la bombe

bond [bɒnd] n lien m; (binding promise) engagement m, obligation f; (Finance) obligation; **bonds** npl (chains) chaînes fpl; **in ~** (of goods) en entrepôt

bone [bəʊn] n os m; (of fish) arête f ▷ vt désosser; ôter les arêtes de

bonfire ['bɒnfaɪə] n feu m (de joie); (for rubbish) feu

bonnet ['bɒnɪt] n bonnet m; (BRIT: of a country) frontière f; **borderline** (fig

car) capot m

bonus ['bəʊnəs] n (money) prime f; (advantage) avantage m

boo [buː] excl hou!, peuh! ▷ vt huer

book [bʊk] n livre m; (of stamps, tickets etc) carnet m; (Comm): **books** npl comptes mpl, comptabilité f ▷ vt (ticket) prendre; (seat, room) réserver; (football player) prendre le nom de, donner un carton à; **I ~ed a table in the name of ...** j'ai réservé une table au nom de ...; **book in** vi (BRIT: at hotel) prendre sa chambre; **book up** vt réserver; **the hotel is ~ed up** l'hôtel est complet; **bookcase** n bibliothèque f (meuble); **booking** (BRIT) réservation f. **I confirmed my booking by fax/e-mail** j'ai confirmé ma réservation par fax/e-mail; **booking office** n (BRIT) bureau m de location; **book-keeping** n comptabilité f; **booklet** n brochure f; **bookmaker** n bookmaker m; **bookmark** n (for book) marque-page m; (Comput) signet m; **bookseller** n libraire m/f; **bookshelf** n (single) étagère f (à livres); (bookcase) bibliothèque f; **bookshop, bookstore** n librairie f

boom [buːm] n (noise) grondement m; (in prices, population) forte augmentation; (busy period) boom m, vague f de prospérité ▷ vi gronder; prospérer

boost [buːst] n stimulant m, remontant m ▷ vt stimuler

boot [buːt] n botte f; (for hiking) chaussure f (de marche); (ankle boot) bottine f; (BRIT: of car) coffre m ▷ vt (Comput) lancer, mettre en route; **to ~ (in addition)** par-dessus le marché, en plus

booth [buːð] n (at fair) baraque (foraine); (of telephone etc) cabine f; (also: **voting ~**) isoloir m

booze [buːz] (inf) n boissons fpl alcooliques, alcool m

border ['bɔːdə] n bordure f; bord m; (of a country) frontière f; **borderline** (fig ligne f de démarcation

bore [bɔːʳ] pt of **bear** ▷ vt (person) ennuyer, raser; (hole) percer; (well, tunnel) creuser ▷ n (person) raseur(-euse); (boring thing) barbe f; (of gun) calibre m; **bored** adj: **to be bored** s'ennuyer; **boredom** n ennui m

boring ['bɔːrɪŋ] adj ennuyeux(-euse)

born [bɔːn] adj: **to be ~** naître; **I was ~ in 1960** je suis né en 1960

borne [bɔːn] pp of **bear**

borough ['bʌrə] n municipalité f

borrow ['bɔrəu] vt: **to ~ sth (from sb)** emprunter qch (à qn)

Bosnia(-Herzegovina) ['bɔsnɪə(hɜːtsəˈɡəʊvɪːnə)] n Bosnie-Herzégovine f; **Bosnian** ['bɔznɪən] adj bosniaque, bosnien(ne) ▷ n Bosniaque m/f, Bosnien(ne)

bosom ['buzəm] n poitrine f; (fig) sein m

boss [bɔs] n patron(ne) ▷ vt (also: **~ about, ~ around**) mener à la baguette; **bossy** adj autoritaire

both [bəuθ] adj les deux, l'un(e) et l'autre ▷ pron: **~ (of them)** les deux, tous (toutes) (les) deux, l'un(e) et l'autre; **~ of us went, we ~ went** nous y sommes allés tous les deux ▷ adv: **~ A and B** A et B

bother ['bɔðəʳ] vt (worry) tracasser; (needle, bait) importuner, ennuyer; (disturb) déranger ▷ vi (also: **~ o.s.**) se tracasser, se faire du souci ▷ n (trouble) ennuis mpl; **to ~ doing** prendre la peine de faire; **don't ~** ce n'est pas la peine; **it's no ~** aucun problème

bottle ['bɔtl] n bouteille f; (baby's) biberon m; (of perfume, medicine) flacon m ▷ vt mettre en bouteille(s); **bottle bank** n conteneur m (de bouteilles); **bottle-opener** n ouvre-bouteille m

bottom ['bɔtəm] n (of container, sea) fond m; (buttocks) derrière m; (of page, list) bas m; (of mountain, tree, hill) pied m ▷ adj (shelf, step) du bas

bought [bɔːt] pt, pp of **buy**

boulder ['bəuldəʳ] n gros rocher (gén lisse, arrondi)

bounce [bauns] vi (ball) rebondir; (cheque) être refusé (étant sans provision) ▷ vt faire rebondir ▷ n (rebound) rebond m; **bouncer** n (inf: at dance, club) videur m

bound [baund] pt, pp of **bind** ▷ n (gen pl) limite f; (leap) bond m ▷ vi (leap) bondir ▷ vt (limit) borner ▷ adj: **to be ~ to do sth** (obliged) être obligé(e) or avoir obligation de faire qch; **he's ~ to fail** (likely) il est sûr d'échouer, son échec est inévitable or assuré; **~ by** (law, regulation) engagé(e) par; **~ for à** destination de; **out of ~s** dont l'accès est interdit

boundary ['baundrɪ] n frontière f

bouquet ['bukeɪ] n bouquet m

bourbon ['buəbən] n (us: also: **~ whiskey**) bourbon m

bout [baut] n période f; (of malaria etc) accès m, crise f, attaque f; (Boxing etc) combat m, match m

boutique [buːˈtiːk] n boutique f

bow¹ [bəu] n nœud m; (weapon) arc m; (Mus) archet m

bow² [bau] n (with body) révérence f, inclination f (du buste or corps); (Naut: also: **~s**) proue f ▷ vi faire une révérence, s'incliner

bowels [bauəlz] npl intestins mpl; (fig) entrailles fpl

bowl [bəul] n (for eating) bol m; (for washing) cuvette f; (ball) boule f ▷ vi (Cricket) lancer (la balle); **bowler** n (Cricket) lanceur m (de la balle); (BRIT: also: **bowler hat**) (chapeau m) melon m; **bowling** n (game) jeu m de boules, jeu de quilles; **bowling alley** n bowling m; **bowling green** n terrain m de boules (gazonné et carré); **bowls** n (jeu m de) boules fpl

bow tie [bau-] n nœud m papillon

box [bɔks] n boîte f; (also: **cardboard ~**) carton m; (Theat) loge f ▷ vt mettre en boîte ▷ vi boxer, faire de la boxe; **boxer** ['bɔksəʳ] n (person) boxeur m; **boxer shorts** npl caleçon m; **boxing** ['bɔksɪŋ] n (sport) boxe f; **Boxing Day**

n (BRIT) le lendemain de Noël; *voir encadré*; **boxing gloves** *npl* gants *mpl* de boxe; **boxing ring** *n* ring *m*; **box junction** *n* (BRIT Aut) zone *f* (de carrefour) d'accès réglementé; **box office** *n* bureau *m* de location

● **BOXING DAY**

● **Boxing Day** est le lendemain de Noël, férié en Grande-Bretagne. Ce nom vient d'une coutume du XIXe siècle qui consistait à donner des cadeaux de Noël (dans des boîtes) à ses employés etc le 26 décembre.

boy [bɔɪ] *n* garçon *m*; **boy band** *n* boys band *m*

boycott ['bɔɪkɔt] *n* boycottage *m* ▷ *vt* boycotter

boyfriend ['bɔɪfrɛnd] *n* (petit) ami

bra [brɑː] *n* soutien-gorge *m*

brace [breɪs] *n* (support) attache *f*, agrafe *f*; (BRIT: also: **~s**: on teeth) appareil *m* (dentaire); (tool) vilebrequin *m* ▷ *vt* (support) consolider, soutenir; **braces** *npl* (BRIT: for trousers) bretelles *fpl*; **to ~ o.s.** (fig) se préparer mentalement

bracelet ['breɪslɪt] *n* bracelet *m*

bracket ['brækɪt] *n* (Tech) tasseau *m*, support *m*; (group) classe *f*, tranche *f*; (also: **brace ~**) accolade *f*; (also: **round ~**) parenthèse *f*; (also: **square ~**) crochet *m* ▷ *vt* mettre entre parenthèses; **in ~s** entre parenthèses ou crochets

brag [bræg] *vi* se vanter

braid [breɪd] *n* (trimming) galon *m*; (of hair) tresse *f*, natte *f*

brain [breɪn] *n* cerveau *m*; **brains** *npl* (intellect, food) cervelle *f*

braise [breɪz] *vt* braiser

brake [breɪk] *n* frein *m* ▷ *vt*, *vi* freiner; **brake light** *n* feu *m* de stop

bran [bræn] *n* son *m*

branch [brɑːntʃ] *n* branche *f*; (Comm) succursale *f*; (: of bank) agence *f*; **branch off** *vi* (road) bifurquer; **branch out** *vi* diversifier ses activités

brand [brænd] *n* marque (commerciale) ▷ *vt* (cattle) marquer (au fer rouge); **brand name** *n* nom *m* de marque; **brand-new** *adj* tout(e) neuf (neuve), flambant neuf (neuve)

brandy ['brændɪ] *n* cognac *m*

brash [bræʃ] *adj* effronté(e)

brass [brɑːs] *n* cuivre *m* (jaune), laiton *m*; **the ~** (Mus) les cuivres; **brass band** *n* fanfare *f*

brat [bræt] *n* (pej) mioche *m/f*, môme *m/f*

brave [breɪv] *adj* courageux(-euse), brave ▷ *vt* braver, affronter; **bravery** *n* bravoure *f*, courage *m*

brawl [brɔːl] *n* rixe *f*, bagarre *f*

Brazil [brə'zɪl] *n* Brésil *m*; **Brazilian** *adj* brésilien(ne) ▷ *n* Brésilien(ne)

breach [briːtʃ] *vt* ouvrir une brèche dans ▷ *n* (gap) brèche *f*; (breaking): **~ of contract** rupture *f* de contrat; **~ of the peace** attentat *m* à l'ordre public

bread [brɛd] *n* pain *m*; **breadbin** *n* (BRIT) boîte *f* ou huche *f* à pain; **breadbox** *n* (US) boîte *f* ou huche *f* à pain; **breadcrumbs** *npl* miettes *fpl* de pain; (Culin) chapelure *f*, panure *f*

breadth [brɛtθ] *n* largeur *f*

break [breɪk] (*pt* **broke**, *pp* **broken**) *vt* casser, briser; (promise) rompre; (law) violer ▷ *se* casser, se briser; (weather) tourner; (storm) éclater; (day) se lever ▷ *n* (gap) brèche *f*; (fracture) cassure *f*; (rest) interruption *f*, arrêt *m*; (: short) pause *f*; (: at school) récréation *f*; (chance) chance *f*, occasion *f* favorable; **to ~ one's leg** *etc* se casser la jambe *etc*; **to ~ a record** battre un record; **to ~ the news to sb** annoncer la nouvelle à qn; **break down** *vt* (door etc) enfoncer; (figures, data) décomposer, analyser ▷ *vi* s'effondrer; (Med) faire une dépression (nerveuse); (Aut) tomber en panne; **my car has broken down** ma voiture est en panne; **break in** *vt* (horse etc) dresser ▷ *vi* (burglar) entrer par effraction; (interrupt) interrompre; **break into** *vt fus* (house) s'introduire ou pénétrer par effraction dans; **break off** vi (speaker) s'interrompre; (branch) se rompre ▷ vt (talks, engagement) rompre; **break out** vi éclater, se déclarer; (prisoner) s'évader; **to ~ out in spots** se couvrir de boutons; **break up** vi (partnership) cesser, prendre fin; (marriage) se briser; (crowd, meeting) se séparer; (ship) se disloquer; (Scol: pupils) être en vacances; (line) couper; **the line's** or **you're ~ing up** ça coupe ▷ vt fracasser, casser; (fight etc) interrompre, faire cesser; (marriage) disloquer; **breakdown** n (Aut) panne f; (in communications, marriage) rupture f; (Med: also: **nervous breakdown**) dépression (nerveuse); (of figures) ventilation f, répartition f; **breakdown truck** (US **breakdown van**) n dépanneuse f

breakfast ['brekfəst] n petit déjeuner m; **what time is ~?** le petit déjeuner est à quelle heure?

break: break-in n cambriolage m; **breakthrough** n percée f

breast [brest] n (of woman) sein m; (chest) poitrine f; (of chicken, turkey) blanc m; **breast-feed** vt, vi (irreg: like **feed**) allaiter; **breast-stroke** n brasse f

breath [brɛθ] n haleine f, souffle m; **to take a deep ~** respirer à fond; **out of ~** à bout de souffle, essoufflé(e)

Breathalyser® ['brɛθəlaɪzə*] (BRIT) n alcootest m

breathe [briːð] vt, vi respirer; **breathe in** vi inspirer ▷ vt aspirer; **breathe out** vt, vi expirer; **breathing** n respiration f

breath: breathless adj essoufflé(e), haletant(e); **breathtaking** adj stupéfiant(e), à vous couper le souffle; **breath test** n alcootest m

bred [bred] pt, pp of **breed**

breed [briːd] (pt, pp **bred**) vt élever, faire l'élevage de ▷ vi se reproduire ▷ n race f, variété f

breeze [briːz] n brise f

breezy ['briːzɪ] adj (day, weather) venteux(-euse); (manner) désinvolte; (person) jovial(e)

brew [bruː] vt (tea) faire infuser; (beer) brasser ▷ vi (fig) se préparer, couver; **brewery** n brasserie f (fabrique)

bribe [braɪb] n pot-de-vin m ▷ vt acheter; soudoyer; **bribery** n corruption f

bric-a-brac ['brɪkəbræk] n bric-à-brac m

brick [brɪk] n brique f; **bricklayer** n maçon m

bride [braɪd] n mariée f, épouse f; **bridegroom** n marié m, époux m; **bridesmaid** n demoiselle f d'honneur

bridge [brɪdʒ] n pont m; (Naut) passerelle f (de commandement); (of nose) arête f; (Cards, Dentistry) bridge m ▷ vt (gap) combler

bridle ['braɪdl] n bride f

brief [briːf] adj bref (brève) ▷ n (Law) dossier m, cause f; (gen) tâche f ▷ vt mettre au courant; **briefs** npl slip m; **briefcase** n serviette f, porte-documents m inv; **briefing** n instructions fpl; (Press) briefing m; **briefly** adv brièvement

brigadier [brɪgə'dɪə*] n brigadier général

bright [braɪt] adj brillant(e); (room, weather) clair(e); (person: clever) intelligent(e), doué(e); (: cheerful) gai(e); (idea) génial(e); (colour) vif (vive)

brilliant ['brɪljənt] adj brillant(e); (light, sunshine) éclatant(e); (inf: great) super

brim [brɪm] n bord m

brine [braɪn] n (Culin) saumure f

bring (pt, pp **brought**) [brɪŋ, brɔːt] vt (thing) apporter; (person) amener; **bring about** vt provoquer, entraîner; **bring back** vt rapporter; (person) ramener; **bring down** vt (lower) abaisser; (shoot down) abattre; (government) faire s'effondrer; **bring in** vt (person) faire entrer; (object) rentrer; (Pol: legislation) introduire; (produce: income) rapporter; **bring on** vt (illness, attack) provoquer; (player, substitute) amener; **bring out** vt sortir; (meaning) faire ressortir, mettre en relief; **bring up** vt élever; (carry up) monter; (question) soulever; (food: vomit) vomir, rendre

brink [brɪŋk] n bord m

brisk [brɪsk] adj vif (vive); (abrupt) brusque; (trade etc) actif(-ive)

bristle ['brɪsl] n poil m ▷ vi se hérisser

Brit [brɪt] n abbr (inf = British person) Britannique m/f

Britain ['brɪtən] n (also: **Great ~**) la Grande-Bretagne

British ['brɪtɪʃ] adj britannique ▷ npl: **the ~** les Britanniques mpl; **British Isles** npl: **the British Isles** les îles fpl Britanniques

Briton ['brɪtən] n Britannique m/f

Brittany ['brɪtənɪ] n Bretagne f

brittle ['brɪtl] adj cassant(e), fragile

B road n (BRIT) n route départementale

broad [brɔːd] adj large; (distinction) général(e); (accent) prononcé(e); **in ~ daylight** en plein jour; **broadband** n transmission f à haut débit; **broad bean** n fève f; **broadcast** n émission f ▷ vb (pt, pp **broadcast**) ▷ vt (Radio) radiodiffuser; (TV) téléviser ▷ vi émettre; **broaden** vt élargir; **to broaden one's mind** élargir ses horizons ▷ vi s'élargir; **broadly** adv en gros, généralement; **broad-minded** adj large d'esprit

broccoli ['brɔkəlɪ] n brocoli m

brochure ['brəʊʃjʊəʳ] n prospectus m, dépliant m

broil [brɔɪl] (US) vt rôtir

broiler ['brɔɪləʳ] n (fowl) poulet m (à rôtir); (US: grill) gril m

broke [brəʊk] pt of **break** ▷ adj (inf) fauché(e)

broken ['brəʊkn] pp of **break** ▷ adj (stick, leg etc) cassé(e); (machine: also: **~ down**) fichu(e); **in ~ French/English** dans un français/anglais approximatif or hésitant

broker ['brəʊkəʳ] n courtier m

bronchitis [brɔŋ'kaɪtɪs] n bronchite f

bronze [brɔnz] n bronze m

brooch [brəʊtʃ] n broche f

brood [bruːd] n couvée f ▷ vi (person)

méditer (sombrement), ruminer

broom [brum] n balai m; (Bot) genêt m

Bros. abbr (Comm: = brothers) Frères

broth [brɔθ] n bouillon m de viande et de légumes

brothel ['brɔθl] n maison close, bordel m

brother ['brʌðəʳ] n frère m; **brother-in-law** n beau-frère m

brought [brɔːt] pt, pp of **bring**

brow [brau] n front m; (eyebrow) sourcil m; (of hill) sommet m

brown [braun] adj brun(e), marron inv; (hair) châtain inv; (tanned) bronzé(e) ▷ n (colour) brun m, marron m ▷ vt brunir; (Culin) faire dorer, faire roussir; **brown bread** n pain m bis

Brownie ['braunɪ] n jeannette f éclaireuse (cadette)

brown rice n riz m complet

brown sugar n cassonade f

browse [brauz] vi (in shop) regarder (sans acheter); **to ~ through a book** feuilleter un livre; **browser** n (Comput) navigateur m

bruise [bruːz] n bleu m, ecchymose f, contusion f ▷ vt contusionner, meurtrir

brunette [bruː'nɛt] n (femme) brune

brush [brʌʃ] n brosse f; (for painting) pinceau m; (for shaving) blaireau m; (quarrel) accrochage m, prise f de bec ▷ vt brosser; (also: **~ past**, **~ against**) effleurer, frôler

Brussels ['brʌslz] n Bruxelles

Brussels sprout [-spraut] n chou m de Bruxelles

brutal ['bruːtl] adj brutal(e)

B.Sc. n abbr = **Bachelor of Science**

BSE n abbr (= bovine spongiform encephalopathy) ESB f, BSE f

bubble ['bʌbl] n bulle f ▷ vi bouillonner, faire des bulles; (sparkle, fig) pétiller; **bubble bath** n bain moussant; **bubble gum** n chewing-gum m; **bubblejet printer** ['bʌbldʒɛt-] n imprimante f à bulle d'encre

buck [bʌk] n mâle m (d'un lapin, lièvre,

daim etc); (*us inf*) dollar *m* ▷ *vi* ruer, lancer une ruade; **to pass the ~ (to sb)** se décharger de la responsabilité (sur qn)

bucket ['bʌkɪt] *n* seau *m*

buckle ['bʌkl] *n* boucle *f* ▷ *vt* (*belt etc*) boucler, attacher ▷ *vi* (*warp*) tordre, gauchir; (: *wheel*) se voiler

bud [bʌd] *n* bourgeon *m*; (*of flower*) bouton *m* ▷ *vi* bourgeonner; (*flower*) éclore

Buddhism ['budɪzəm] *n* bouddhisme *m*

Buddhist ['budɪst] *adj* bouddhiste ▷ *n* Bouddhiste *m/f*

buddy ['bʌdɪ] *n* (*us*) copain *m*

budge [bʌdʒ] *vt* faire bouger ▷ *vi* bouger

budgerigar ['bʌdʒərɪgɑ:'] *n* perruche *f*

budget ['bʌdʒɪt] *n* budget *m* ▷ *vi*: **to ~ for sth** inscrire qch au budget

budgie ['bʌdʒɪ] *n* = **budgerigar**

buff [bʌf] *adj* (*couleur*) chamois *m* ▷ *n* (*inf*: *enthusiast*) mordu(e)

buffalo (*pl* **~** *or* **~es**) ['bʌfələu] *n* (*BRIT*) buffle *m*; (*us*) bison *m*

buffer ['bʌfə'] *n* tampon *m*; (*Comput*) mémoire *f* tampon

buffet *n* ['bufeɪ] (*food BRIT*: *bar*) buffet *m* ▷ *vt* ['bʌfɪt] secouer, ébranler; **buffet car** (*BRIT Rail*) voiture-bar *f*

bug [bʌg] *n* (*bedbug etc*) punaise *f*; (*esp us*: *any insect*) insecte *m*, bestiole *f*; (*fig*: *germ*) virus *m*, microbe *m*; (*spy device*) dispositif *m* d'écoute (électronique), micro clandestin; (*Comput*: *of program*) erreur *f* ▷ *vt* (*room*) poser des micros dans; (*inf*: *annoy*) embêter

buggy ['bʌgɪ] *n* poussette *f*

build [bɪld] *n* (*of person*) carrure *f*, charpente *f* ▷ *vt* (*pt*, *pp* **built**) construire, bâtir; **build up** *vt* accumuler, amasser; (*business*) développer; (*reputation*) bâtir; **builder** *n* entrepreneur *m*; **building** *n* (*trade*) construction *f*; (*structure*) bâtiment *m*, construction *f*; (: *residential*, *offices*) immeuble *m*; **building site** *n* chantier

m (de construction); **building society** *n* (*BRIT*) société *f* de crédit immobilier

built [bɪlt] *pt*, *pp of* **build**; **built-in** *adj* (*cupboard*) encastré(e); (*device*) incorporé(e); intégré(e); **built-up** *adj*: **built-up area** zone urbanisée

bulb [bʌlb] *n* (*Bot*) bulbe *m*, oignon *m*; (*Elec*) ampoule *f*

Bulgaria [bʌl'geərɪə] *n* Bulgarie *f*; **Bulgarian** *adj* bulgare ▷ *n* Bulgare *m/f*

bulge [bʌldʒ] *n* renflement *m*, gonflement *m* ▷ *vi* faire saillie; présenter un renflement; (*pocket*, *file*): **to be bulging with** être plein(e) à craquer de

bulimia [bə'lɪmɪə] *n* boulimie *f*

bulimic [bju:'lɪmɪk] *adj*, *n* boulimique (*m/f*)

bulk [bʌlk] *n* masse *f*, volume *m*; **in ~** (*Comm*) en gros, en vrac; **the ~ of** la plus grande *or* grosse partie de; **bulky** *adj* volumineux(-euse), encombrant(e)

bull [bul] *n* taureau *m*; (*male elephant*, *whale*) mâle *m*

bulldozer ['buldəuzə'] *n* bulldozer *m*

bullet ['bulɪt] *n* balle *f* (*de fusil etc*)

bulletin ['bulɪtɪn] *n* bulletin *m*, communiqué *m*; (*also*: **news ~**) (bulletin d'informations *fpl*; **bulletin board** *n* (*Comput*) messagerie *f* (électronique)

bullfight ['bulfaɪt] *n* corrida *f*, course *f* de taureaux; **bullfighter** *n* torero *m*; **bullfighting** *n* tauromachie *f*

bully ['bulɪ] *n* brute *f*, tyran *m* ▷ *vt* tyranniser, rudoyer

bum [bʌm] *n* (*inf*: *BRIT*: *backside*) derrière *m*; (: *esp us*: *tramp*) vagabond(e), traîne-savates *m/f inv*; (: *idler*) glandeur *m*

bumblebee ['bʌmblbi:] *n* bourdon *m*

bump [bʌmp] *n* (*blow*) coup *m*, choc *m*; (*jolt*) cahot *m*; (*on road etc*, *on head*) bosse *f* ▷ *vt* heurter, cogner; (*car*) emboutir; **bump into** *vt fus* rentrer dans, tamponner; (*inf*: *meet*) tomber sur; **bumper** *n* pare-chocs *m inv* ▷ *adj*: **bumper crop/harvest** récolte *f*/ moisson exceptionnelle; **bumpy** *adj* (*road*) cahoteux(-euse); **it was a**

bumpy flight/ride on a été secoués dans l'avion/la voiture

bun [bʌn] n (cake) petit gâteau; (bread) petit pain au lait; (of hair) chignon m

bunch [bʌntʃ] n (of flowers) bouquet m; (of keys) trousseau m; (of bananas) régime m; (of people) groupe m; **bunches** npl (in hair) couettes fpl; **~ of grapes** grappe f de raisin

bundle ['bʌndl] n paquet m ▷ vt (also: **~ up**) faire un paquet de; (put): **to ~ sth/sb into** fourrer ou enfourner qch/qn dans

bungalow ['bʌŋɡələu] n bungalow m

bungee jumping ['bʌndʒiː'dʒʌmpɪŋ] n saut m à l'élastique

bunion ['bʌnjən] n oignon m (au pied)

bunk [bʌŋk] n couchette f; **bunk beds** npl lits superposés

bunker ['bʌŋkə'] n (coal store) soute f à charbon; (Mil, Golf) bunker m

bunny ['bʌnɪ] n (also: **~ rabbit**) lapin m

buoy [bɔɪ] n bouée f; **buoyant** adj (ship) flottable; (carefree) gai(e), plein(e) d'entrain; (Comm: market, economy) actif(-ive)

burden ['bəːdn] n fardeau m, charge f ▷ vt charger; (oppress) accabler, surcharger

bureau (pl **-x**) ['bjuərəu, -z] n (BRIT: writing desk) bureau m, secrétaire m; (US: chest of drawers) commode f; (office) bureau, office m

bureaucracy [bjuə'rɔkrəsɪ] n bureaucratie f

bureaucrat ['bjuərəkræt] n bureaucrate m/f, rond-de-cuir m

bureau de change [-də'ʃɑ̃ʒ] (pl **bureaux de change**) n bureau m de change

bureaux ['bjuərəuz] npl of **bureau**

burger ['bəːgə'] n hamburger m

burglar ['bəːglə'] n cambrioleur m; **burglar alarm** n sonnerie f d'alarme; **burglary** n cambriolage m

Burgundy ['bəːgəndɪ] n Bourgogne f

burial ['bɛrɪəl] n enterrement m

burn [bəːn] vt, vi (pt, pp **-ed** or **-t**) brûler

▷ n brûlure f; **burn down** vt incendier, détruire par le feu; (work for writer etc): **to ~ o.s. out** s'user (à force de travailler); **burning** adj (building, forest) en flammes; (issue, question) brûlant(e); (ambition) dévorant(e)

Burns' Night [bəːnz-] n fête écossaise à la mémoire du poète Robert Burns

- **BURNS NIGHT**

- **Burns Night** est une fête qui a lieu
- le 25 janvier, à la mémoire du poète
- écossais Robert Burns (1759 - 1796),
- à l'occasion de laquelle les Écossais
- partout dans le monde organisent
- un souper, en général arrosé de
- whisky. Le plat principal est toujours
- le haggis, servi avec de la purée de
- pommes de terre et de la purée de
- rutabagas. On apporte le haggis au
- son des cornemuses et au cours du
- repas on lit des poèmes de Burns et
- on chante ses chansons.

burnt [bəːnt] pt, pp of **burn**

burp [bəːp] (inf) n rot m ▷ vi roter

burrow ['bʌrəu] n terrier m (of rabbit) creuser un terrier; (rummage) fouiller

burst [bəːst] (pt, pp **-**) vt faire éclater; (river: banks etc) rompre ▷ vi éclater; (tyre) crever ▷ n explosion f; (also: **~ pipe**) fuite f (due à une rupture); **a ~ of enthusiasm/energy** accès d'enthousiasme/d'énergie; **to ~ into flames** s'enflammer soudainement; **to ~ out laughing** éclater de rire; **to ~ into tears** fondre en larmes; **to ~ open** vi s'ouvrir violemment ou soudainement; **to be ~ing with** (container) être plein(e) (à craquer) de, regorger de; (fig) être débordant(e) de; **burst into** vt fus (room etc) faire irruption dans

bury ['bɛrɪ] vt enterrer

bus (pl **-es**) [bʌs, 'bʌsɪz] n autobus m; **bus conductor** n receveur(-euse) m/f de bus

bush [buʃ] n buisson m; (scrub land)

brousse f; **to beat about the ~** tourner autour du pot

business ['bɪznɪs] n (matter, firm) affaire f; (trading) affaires fpl; (job, duty) travail m; **to be away on ~** être en déplacement d'affaires; **it's none of my ~** cela ne me regarde pas, ce ne sont pas mes affaires; **he means ~** (inf) il ne plaisante pas, il est sérieux; **business class** n (on plane) classe f affaires; **businesslike** adj sérieux(-euse), efficace; **businessman** (irreg) n homme m d'affaires; **business trip** n voyage m d'affaires; **businesswoman** (irreg) n femme f d'affaires

busker ['bʌskəʳ] n (BRIT) artiste ambulant(e)

bus: bus pass n carte f de bus; **bus shelter** n abribus m; **bus station** n gare routière; **bus-stop** n arrêt m d'autobus

bust [bʌst] n buste m; (measurement) tour m de poitrine ▷ adj (inf: broken) fichu(e), fini(e); **to go ~** faire faillite

bustling ['bʌslɪŋ] adj (town) très animé(e)

busy ['bɪzɪ] adj occupé(e); (shop, street) très fréquenté(e); (US: telephone, line) occupé ▷ vt: **to ~ o.s.** s'occuper; **busy signal** n (US) tonalité f occupé inv

KEYWORD

but [bʌt] conj mais; **I'd love to come, but I'm busy** j'aimerais venir mais je suis occupé; **he's not English but French** il n'est pas anglais mais français; **but that's far too expensive!** mais c'est bien trop cher!
▷ prep (apart from, except) sauf, excepté; **nothing but** rien d'autre que; **we've had nothing but trouble** nous n'avons eu que des ennuis; **no-one but him can do it** lui seul peut le faire; **who but a lunatic would do such a thing?** qui sinon un fou ferait une chose pareille?; **but for you/your help** sans toi/ton aide; **anything but that** tout sauf or

---

317 | by

excepté ça, tout mais pas ça
▷ adv (just, only) ne ... que; **she's but a child** elle n'est qu'une enfant; **had I but known** si seulement j'avais su; **I can but try** je peux toujours essayer; **all but finished** pratiquement terminé

butcher ['bʊtʃəʳ] n boucher m ▷ vt massacrer; (cattle etc for meat) tuer; **butcher's (shop)** n boucherie f
butler ['bʌtləʳ] n maître m d'hôtel
butt [bʌt] n (cask) gros tonneau; (of gun) crosse f; (of cigarette) mégot m; (BRIT fig: target) cible f ▷ vt donner un coup de tête à
butter ['bʌtəʳ] n beurre m ▷ vt beurrer; **buttercup** n bouton m d'or
butterfly ['bʌtəflaɪ] n papillon m; (Swimming: also: ~ **stroke**) brasse f papillon
buttocks ['bʌtəks] npl fesses fpl
button ['bʌtn] n bouton m; (US: badge) pin m ▷ vt (also: ~ **up**) boutonner ▷ vi se boutonner
buy [baɪ] (pt, pp bought) vt acheter ▷ n achat m; **to ~ sb sth/sth from sb** acheter qch à qn; **to ~ sb a drink** offrir un verre or à boire à qn; **can I ~ you a drink?** je vous offre un verre?; **where can I ~ some postcards?** où est-ce que je peux acheter des cartes postales?; **buy out** vt (partner) désintéresser; **buy up** vt acheter en bloc, rafler; **buyer** n acheteur(-euse) m/f
buzz [bʌz] n bourdonnement m; (inf: phone call): **to give sb a ~** passer un coup de fil à qn ▷ vi bourdonner; **buzzer** n timbre m électrique

KEYWORD

by [baɪ] prep **1** (referring to cause, agent) par, de; **killed by lightning** tué par la foudre; **surrounded by a fence** entouré d'une barrière; **a painting by Picasso** un tableau de Picasso
2 (referring to method, manner, means): **by bus/car** en autobus/voiture; **by train**

par le ou en train; **to pay by cheque** payer par chèque; **by moonlight/candlelight** à la lueur de la lune/d'une bougie; **by saving hard, he ...** à force d'économiser, il ...

3 (via, through) par; **we came by Dover** nous sommes venus par Douvres

4 (close to, past) à côté de; **the house by the school** la maison à côté de l'école; **a holiday by the sea** des vacances au bord de la mer; **she went by me** elle est passée à côté de moi; **I go by the post office every day** je passe devant la poste tous les jours

5 (with time: not later than) avant; (: during): **by daylight** à la lumière du jour; **by night** la nuit, de nuit; **by 4 o'clock** avant 4 heures; **by this time tomorrow** d'ici demain à la même heure; **by the time I got here it was too late** lorsque je suis arrivé il était déjà trop tard

6 (amount) à; **by the kilo/metre** au kilo/au mètre; **paid by the hour** payé à l'heure

7 (Math: measure): **to divide/multiply by 3** diviser/multiplier par 3; **a room 3 metres by 4** une pièce de 3 mètres sur 4; **it's broader by a metre** c'est plus large d'un mètre

8 (according to) d'après, selon; **it's 3 o'clock by my watch** il est 3 heures à ma montre; **it's all right by me** je n'ai rien contre

9: **(all) by oneself** etc tout(e) seul(e)
▷ adv **1** see **go**; **pass** etc

2: **by and by** un peu plus tard, bientôt; **by and large** dans l'ensemble

bye(-bye) ['baɪ('baɪ)] excl au revoir!, salut!

by-election ['baɪɪlɛkʃən] n (BRIT) élection (législative) partielle

bypass ['baɪpɑːs] n rocade f; (Med) pontage m ▷ vt éviter

byte [baɪt] n (Comput) octet m

C [siː] n (Mus): **C** do m

cab [kæb] n taxi m; (of train, truck) cabine f

cabaret ['kæbəreɪ] n (show) spectacle m de cabaret

cabbage ['kæbɪdʒ] n chou m

cabin ['kæbɪn] n (house) cabane f, hutte f; (on ship) cabine f; (on plane) compartiment m; **cabin crew** n (Aviat) équipage m

cabinet ['kæbɪnɪt] n (Pol) cabinet m; (furniture) petit meuble à tiroirs et rayons; (also: **display** ~) vitrine f, petite armoire vitrée; **cabinet minister** n ministre m (membre du cabinet)

cable ['keɪbl] n câble m ▷ vt câbler, télégraphier; **cable car** n téléphérique m; **cable television** n télévision f par câble

cactus (pl **cacti**) ['kæktəs, -taɪ] n cactus m

café ['kæfeɪ] n ≈ café(-restaurant) m (sans alcool)

cafeteria [kæfɪ'tɪərɪə] n cafétéria f

caffein(e) ['kæfi:n] n caféine f
cage [keɪdʒ] n cage f
cagoule [kə'gu:l] n K-way® m
Cairo ['kaɪərəʊ] n le Caire
cake [keɪk] n gâteau m; **~ of soap** savonnette f
calcium ['kælsɪəm] n calcium m
calculate ['kælkjʊleɪt] vt calculer; (estimate: chances, effect) évaluer; **calculation** [kælkjʊ'leɪʃən] n calcul m; **calculator** n calculatrice f
calendar ['kæləndə'] n calendrier m
calf (pl **calves**) [kɑ:f, kɑ:vz] n (of cow) veau m; (of other animals) petit m; (also: **~skin**) veau m, vachette f; (Anat) mollet m
calibre (US **caliber**) ['kælɪbə'] n calibre m
call [kɔ:l] vt appeler; (meeting) convoquer ▷ vi appeler; (visit: also: **~ in, ~ round**) passer ▷ n (shout) appel m, cri m; (also: **telephone ~**) coup m de téléphone; **to be on ~** être de permanence; **to be ~ed** s'appeler; **can I make a ~ from here?** est-ce que je peux téléphoner d'ici?; **call back** vi (return) repasser ▷ vt (Tel) rappeler ▷ vt (Tel) rappeler; **can you ~ back later?** pouvez-vous rappeler plus tard?; **call for** vt fus (demand) demander; (fetch) passer prendre; **call in** vt (doctor, expert, police) appeler, faire venir; **call off** vt annuler; **call on** vt fus (visit) rendre visite à, passer voir; (request): **to ~ on sb to do** inviter qn à faire; **call out** vi pousser un cri or des cris; **call up** vt (Mil) appeler, mobiliser; (Tel) appeler; **callbox** n (BRIT) cabine f téléphonique; **call centre** (US **call center**) n centre m d'appels; **caller** n (Tel) personne f qui appelle; (visitor) visiteur m
callous ['kæləs] adj dur(e), insensible
calm [kɑ:m] adj calme ▷ n calme m ▷ vt calmer; **calm down** vi se calmer, s'apaiser ▷ vt calmer, apaiser; **calmly** ['kɑ:mlɪ] adv calmement, avec calme
Calor gas® ['kælə'-] n (BRIT) butane m,

butagaz® m
calorie ['kælərɪ] n calorie f
calves [kɑ:vz] npl of **calf**
Cambodia [kæm'bəʊdɪə] n Cambodge m
camcorder ['kæmkɔ:də'] n caméscope m
came [keɪm] pt of **come**
camel ['kæməl] n chameau m
camera ['kæmərə] n appareil-photo m; (Cine, TV) caméra f; **in ~** à huis clos, en privé; **cameraman** n caméraman m; **camera phone** n téléphone m avec appareil photo numérique intégré
camouflage ['kæməflɑ:ʒ] n camouflage m ▷ vt camoufler
camp [kæmp] n camp m ▷ vi camper ▷ adj (man) efféminé(e)
campaign [kæm'peɪn] n (Mil, Pol etc) campagne f ▷ vi (also fig) faire campagne; **campaigner** n: **campaigner for** partisan(e) de; **campaigner against** opposant(e) à
camp: **campbed** n (BRIT) lit m de camp; **camper** n campeur(-euse); (vehicle) camping-car m; **campground** (US) n (terrain m de) camping m; **camping** n camping m; **to go camping** faire du camping; **campsite** n (terrain m de) camping m
campus ['kæmpəs] n campus m
can¹ [kæn] n (of milk, oil, water) bidon m; (tin) boîte f (de conserve) ▷ vt mettre en conserve

○ **KEYWORD**

can² [kæn] (negative **cannot, can't,** conditional and pt **could**) aux vb 1 (be able to) pouvoir; **you can do it if you try** vous pouvez le faire si vous essayez; **I can't hear you** je ne t'entends pas
2 (know how to) savoir; **I can swim/ play tennis/drive** je sais nager/jouer au tennis/conduire; **can you speak French?** parlez-vous français?
3 (may) pouvoir; **can I use your phone?** puis-je me servir de votre téléphone?

4 (expressing disbelief, puzzlement etc): **it can't be true!** ce n'est pas possible!; **what can we want?** qu'est-ce qu'il peut bien vouloir?

5 (expressing possibility, suggestion etc): **he could be in the library** il est peut-être dans la bibliothèque; **she could have been delayed** il se peut qu'elle ait été retardée

Canada ['kænədə] n Canada m; **Canadian** [kə'neɪdɪən] adj canadien(ne) ▷ n Canadien(ne)
canal [kə'næl] n canal m
canary [kə'nɛərɪ] n canari m, serin m
cancel ['kænsəl] vt annuler; (train) supprimer; (party, appointment) décommander; (cross out) barrer, rayer; (cheque) faire opposition à; **I would like to ~ my booking** je voudrais annuler ma réservation; **cancellation** [kænsə'leɪʃən] n annulation f; suppression f
Cancer ['kænsə'] n (Astrology) le Cancer
cancer ['kænsə'] n cancer m
candidate ['kændɪdeɪt] n candidat(e)
candle ['kændl] n bougie f; (in church) cierge m; **candlestick** n (also: **candle holder**) bougeoir m; (bigger, ornate) chandelier m
candy ['kændɪ] n sucre candi; (us) bonbon m; **candy bar** (us) n barre f chocolatée; **candyfloss** n (Brit) barbe f à papa
cane [keɪn] n (for baskets, chairs etc) rotin m ▷ vt (Brit Scol) donner des coups de bâton à
canister ['kænɪstə'] n boîte f (gén en métal); (of gas) bombe f
cannabis ['kænəbɪs] n (drug) cannabis m
canned ['kænd] adj (food) en boîte, en conserve; (inf: music) enregistré(e); (Brit inf: drunk) bourré(e); (us inf: worker) mis(e) à la porte
cannon (pl ~ or ~s) ['kænən] n (gun) canon m
cannot ['kænɔt] = **can not**

canoe [kə'nu:] n pirogue f; (Sport) canoë m; **canoeing** n (sport) canoë m
canon ['kænən] n (clergyman) chanoine m; (standard) canon m
can-opener [-'aupnə'] n ouvre-boîte m
can't [kɑ:nt] = **can not**
canteen [kæn'ti:n] n (eating place) cantine f; (Brit: of cutlery) ménagère f
canter ['kæntə'] vi aller au petit galop
canvas ['kænvəs] n toile f
canvass ['kænvəs] vi (Pol): **to ~ for** faire campagne pour ▷ vt (citizens, opinions) sonder
canyon ['kænjən] n cañon m, gorge f (profonde)
cap [kæp] n casquette f; (for swimming) bonnet m de bain; (of pen) capuchon m; (of bottle) capsule f; (contraceptive: also: **Dutch ~**) diaphragme m ▷ vt (outdo) surpasser; (put limit on) plafonner
capability [keɪpə'bɪlɪtɪ] n aptitude f, capacité f
capable ['keɪpəbl] adj capable
capacity [kə'pæsɪtɪ] n (of container) capacité f, contenance f; (ability) aptitude f
cape [keɪp] n (garment) cape f; (Geo) cap m
caper ['keɪpə'] n (Culin: gen pl) câpre f; (prank) farce f
capital ['kæpɪtl] n (also: **~ city**) capitale f; (money) capital m; (also: **~ letter**) majuscule f; **capitalism** n capitalisme m; **capitalist** adj, n capitaliste m/f; **capital punishment** n peine capitale
Capitol ['kæpɪtl] n: **the ~** le Capitole
Capricorn ['kæprɪkɔ:n] n le Capricorne
capsize [kæp'saɪz] vt faire chavirer ▷ vi chavirer
capsule ['kæpsju:l] n capsule f
captain ['kæptɪn] n capitaine m
caption ['kæpʃən] n légende f
captivity [kæp'tɪvɪtɪ] n captivité f
capture ['kæptʃə'] vt (prisoner, animal) capturer; (town) prendre; (attention) capter; (Comput) saisir ▷ n capture f; (of

data) saisie f de données

car [kɑːʳ] n voiture f, auto f; (us Rail) wagon m, voiture

carafe [kəˈræf] n carafe f

caramel [ˈkærəməl] n caramel m

carat [ˈkærət] n carat m

caravan [ˈkærəvæn] n caravane f; **caravan site** n (BRIT) camping m pour caravanes

carbohydrate [kɑːbəuˈhaɪdreɪt] n hydrate m de carbone; (food) féculent m

carbon [ˈkɑːbən] n carbone m; **carbon dioxide** [-daɪˈɔksaɪd] n gaz m carbonique, dioxyde m de carbone; **carbon monoxide** [-mɔˈnɔksaɪd] n oxyde m de carbone

car boot sale n voir encadré

> **CAR BOOT SALE**
>
> Type de brocante très populaire, où chacun vide sa cave ou son grenier. Les articles sont présentés dans des coffres de voitures et la vente a souvent lieu sur un parking ou dans un chemin. Les brocanteurs d'un jour doivent s'acquitter d'une petite contribution pour participer à la vente.

carburettor (us **carburetor**) [kɑːbjuˈretəʳ] n carburateur m

card [kɑːd] n carte f; (material) carton m; **cardboard** n carton m; **card game** n jeu m de cartes

cardigan [ˈkɑːdɪgən] n cardigan m

cardinal [ˈkɑːdɪnl] adj cardinal(e); (importance) capital(e) ▷ n cardinal m

cardphone [ˈkɑːdfəun] n téléphone m à carte (magnétique)

care [kɛəʳ] n soin m, attention f; (worry) souci m ▷ vi: **to ~ about** (feel interest for) se soucier de, s'intéresser à; (person: love) être attaché à; **to ~ for** vt fus (like) aimer

career [kəˈrɪəʳ] n carrière f ▷ vi (also: ~ along) aller à toute allure

care: **carefree** adj sans souci, insouciant(e); **careful** adj soigneux(-euse); (cautious) prudent(e); **(be) careful!** (fais) attention!; **carefully** adv avec soin, soigneusement; prudemment; **careless** adj négligent(e); (heedless) insouciant(e); **carelessness** n manque m de soin, négligence f; insouciance f; **carer** [ˈkɛərəʳ] n (professional) travailleur social; (unpaid) personne qui s'occupe d'un proche qui est malade; **caretaker** n gardien(ne), concierge m/f

car-ferry [ˈkɑːferɪ] n (on sea) ferry(-boat) m; (on river) bac m

cargo (pl **-es**) [ˈkɑːgəu] n cargaison f, chargement m

car hire n (BRIT) location f de voitures

Caribbean [kærɪˈbiːən] adj, n: **the ~ (Sea)** la mer des Antilles ou des Caraïbes

caring [ˈkɛərɪŋ] adj (person) bienveillant(e); (society, organization) humanitaire

carnation [kɑːˈneɪʃən] n œillet m

carnival [ˈkɑːnɪvl] n (public celebration) carnaval m; (us: funfair) fête foraine

carol [ˈkærəl] n: **(Christmas) ~** chant m de Noël

carousel [kærəˈsel] n (for luggage) carrousel m; (us) manège m

car park (BRIT) n parking m, parc m de stationnement

carpenter [ˈkɑːpɪntəʳ] n charpentier m; (joiner) menuisier m

carpet [ˈkɑːpɪt] n tapis m ▷ vt recouvrir (d'un tapis); **fitted ~** (BRIT) moquette f

car rental n (us) location f de voitures

carriage [ˈkærɪdʒ] n (BRIT Rail)

wagon m; (horse-drawn) voiture f; (of goods) transport m; (: cost) port m; **carriageway** n (BRIT: part of road) chaussée f

carrier ['kærɪə'] n transporteur m, camionneur m; (company) entreprise f de transport; (Med) porteur(-euse); **carrier bag** n (BRIT) sac m en papier or en plastique

carrot ['kærət] n carotte f

carry ['kærɪ] vt (subj: person) porter; (: vehicle) transporter; (involve: responsibilities etc) impliquer, comporter; (Med: disease) être porteur de ▷ vi (sound) porter; **to get carried away** (fig) s'emballer, s'enthousiasmer; **carry on** vi (continue) continuer ▷ vt (: conduct: business) diriger; (: conversation) entretenir; (continue: business, conversation) continuer; **carry on with sth/doing** continuer qch/à faire; **carry out** vt (orders) exécuter; (investigation) effectuer

cart [kɑːt] n charrette f ▷ vt (inf) transporter

carton ['kɑːtən] n (box) carton m; (of yogurt) pot m (en carton)

cartoon [kɑː'tuːn] n (Press) dessin m (humoristique); (satirical) caricature f; (comic strip) bande dessinée; (Cine) dessin animé

cartridge ['kɑːtrɪdʒ] n (for gun, pen) cartouche f

carve [kɑːv] vt (meat: also: ~ **up**) découper; (wood, stone) tailler, sculpter; **carving** n (in wood etc) sculpture f

car wash n station f de lavage (de voitures)

case [keɪs] n cas m; (Law) affaire f, procès m; (box) caisse f, boîte f; (for glasses) étui m; (BRIT: also: **suit~**) valise f; **in ~ of** en cas de; **in ~ he** au cas où il; **just in ~** à tout hasard; **in any ~** en tout cas, de toute façon

cash [kæʃ] n argent m; (Comm) (argent m) liquide m ▷ vt encaisser; **to pay (in) ~** payer (en argent) comptant or en espèces; **~ with order/on delivery**

(Comm) payable or paiement à la commande/livraison; **I haven't got any** – je n'ai pas de liquide; **cashback** n (discount) remise f; (at supermarket etc) retrait m (à la caisse); **cash card** n carte f de retrait; **cash desk** n (BRIT) caisse f; **cash dispenser** n distributeur m automatique de billets

cashew [kæ'ʃuː] n (also: ~ **nut**) noix f de cajou

cashier [kæ'ʃɪə'] n caissier(-ère)

cashmere ['kæʃmɪə'] n cachemire m

cash point n distributeur m automatique de billets

cash register n caisse enregistreuse

casino [kə'siːnəu] n casino m

casket ['kɑːskɪt] n coffret m; (us: coffin) cercueil m

casserole ['kæsərəul] n (pot) cocotte f; (food) ragoût m (en cocotte)

cassette [kæ'sɛt] n cassette f; **cassette player** n lecteur m de cassettes

cast [kɑːst] (vb: pt, pp ~) vt (throw) jeter; (shadow: lit) projeter; (: fig) jeter; (glance) jeter ▷ n (Theat) distribution f; (also: **plaster ~**) plâtre m; **to ~ sb as Hamlet** attribuer à qn le rôle d'Hamlet; **to ~ one's vote** voter, exprimer son suffrage; **to ~ doubt on** jeter un doute sur; **cast off** vi (Naut) larguer les amarres; (Knitting) arrêter les mailles

castanets [kæstə'nɛts] npl castagnettes fpl

caster sugar ['kɑːstə-] n (BRIT) sucre m semoule

cast-iron ['kɑːstaɪən] adj (lit) de or en fonte; (fig: will: will) de fer; (alibi) en béton

castle ['kɑːsl] n château m; (fortress) château-fort m; (Chess) tour f

casual ['kæʒjul] adj (by chance) de hasard, fait(e) au hasard, fortuit(e); (irregular: work etc) temporaire; (unconcerned) désinvolte; **~ wear** vêtements mpl sport inv

casualty ['kæʒjultɪ] n accidenté(e), blessé(e); (dead) victime f, mort(e); (BRIT: Med: department) urgences fpl

cat [kæt] n chat m

Catalan ['kætələn] *adj* catalan(e)

catalogue (*US* **catalog**) ['kætəlɒg] *n* catalogue *m* ▷ *vt* cataloguer

catalytic converter [kætə'lɪtɪkkən'vɜːtə'] *n* pot *m* catalytique

cataract ['kætərækt] *n* (*also Med*) cataracte *f*

catarrh [kə'tɑː'] *n* rhume *m* chronique, catarrhe *f*

catastrophe [kə'tæstrəfɪ] *n* catastrophe *f*

catch [kætʃ] (*pt, pp* **caught**) *vt* attraper; (*person: by surprise*) prendre, surprendre; (*understand*) saisir; (*get entangled*) accrocher ▷ *vi* (*fire*) prendre; (*get entangled*) s'accrocher ▷ *n* (*fish etc*) prise *f*; (*hidden problem*) attrape *f*; (*Tech*) loquet *m*; cliquet *m*; **to ~ sb's attention** *or* **eye** attirer l'attention de qn; **to ~ fire** prendre feu; **to ~ sight of** apercevoir; **catch up** *vi* (*with work*) se rattraper, combler son retard ▷ *vt* (*also:* **~ up with**) rattraper; **catching** ['kætʃɪŋ] *adj* (*Med*) contagieux(-euse)

category ['kætɪgərɪ] *n* catégorie *f*

cater ['keɪtə'] *vi*: **to ~ for** (*BRIT: needs*) satisfaire, pourvoir à; (: *readers, consumers*) s'adresser à, pourvoir aux besoins de; (*Comm: parties etc*) préparer des repas pour

caterpillar ['kætəpɪlə'] *n* chenille *f*

cathedral [kə'θiːdrəl] *n* cathédrale *f*

Catholic ['kæθəlɪk] (*Rel*) *adj* catholique ▷ *n* catholique *m/f*

Catseye® ['kæts'aɪ] *n* (*BRIT Aut*) (clou m à) cataciptre *m*

cattle ['kætl] *npl* bétail *m*, bestiaux *mpl*

catwalk ['kætwɔːk] *n* passerelle *f*; (*for models*) podium *m* (*de défilé de mode*)

caught [kɔːt] *pt, pp of* **catch**

cauliflower ['kɒlɪflauə'] *n* chou-fleur *m*

cause [kɔːz] *n* cause *f* ▷ *vt* causer

caution ['kɔːʃən] *n* prudence *f*; (*warning*) avertissement *m* ▷ *vt* avertir, donner un avertissement à; **cautious** *adj* prudent(e)

cave [keɪv] *n* caverne *f*, grotte *f*; **cave in** *vi* (*roof etc*) s'effondrer

caviar(e) ['kævɪɑː'] *n* caviar *m*

cavity ['kævɪtɪ] *n* cavité *f*; (*Med*) carie *f*

cc *abbr* (= *cubic centimetre*) cm³; (*on letter etc*) = **carbon copy**

CCTV *n abbr* = **closed-circuit television**

CD *n abbr* (= *compact disc*) CD *m*; **CD burner** *n* graveur *m* de CD; **CD player** *n* platine *f* laser; **CD-ROM** [siːdiː'rɒm] *n abbr* (= *compact disc read-only memory*) CD-ROM *m inv*; **CD writer** *n* graveur *m* de CD

cease [siːs] *vt, vi* cesser; **ceasefire** *n* cessez-le-feu *m*

cedar ['siːdə'] *n* cèdre *m*

ceilidh ['keɪlɪ] *n* bal *m* folklorique écossais *or* irlandais

ceiling ['siːlɪŋ] *n* (*also fig*) plafond *m*

celebrate ['sɛlɪbreɪt] *vt, vi* célébrer; **celebration** [sɛlɪ'breɪʃən] *n* célébration *f*

celebrity [sɪ'lɛbrɪtɪ] *n* célébrité *f*

celery ['sɛlərɪ] *n* céleri *m* (*en branches*)

cell [sɛl] *n* (*gen*) cellule *f*; (*Elec*) élément *m* (*de pile*)

cellar ['sɛlə'] *n* cave *f*

cello ['tʃɛləu] *n* violoncelle *m*

Cellophane® ['sɛləfeɪn] *n* cellophane® *f*

cellphone ['sɛlfəun] *n* téléphone *m* cellulaire

Celsius ['sɛlsɪəs] *adj* Celsius *inv*

Celtic ['kɛltɪk, 'sɛltɪk] *adj* celte, celtique

cement [sə'mɛnt] *n* ciment *m*

cemetery ['sɛmɪtrɪ] *n* cimetière *m*

censor ['sɛnsə'] *n* censeur *m* ▷ *vt* censurer; **censorship** *n* censure *f*

census ['sɛnsəs] *n* recensement *m*

cent [sɛnt] *n* (*unit of dollar, euro*) cent *m* (= *un centième du dollar, de l'euro*); *see also* **per**

centenary [sɛn'tiːnərɪ] (*US* **centennial** [sɛn'tɛnɪəl]) *n* centenaire *m*

center ['sɛntə'] (*US*) = **centre**

centi... [sɛntɪ] *prefix*: **centigrade** *adj* centigrade; **centimetre** (*US*

centimeter) n centimètre m;
centipede ['sɛntɪpiːd] n mille-
pattes m inv
central ['sɛntrəl] adj central(e);
Central America n Amérique centrale;
central heating n chauffage central;
central reservation n (BRIT Aut) terre-
plein central
centre (US center) ['sɛntəʳ] n centre m
▷ vt centrer; centre-forward n (Sport)
avant-centre m; centre-half n (Sport)
demi-centre m
century ['sɛntjʊrɪ] n siècle m; in the
twentieth ~ au vingtième siècle
CEO n abbr (US) = chief executive
officer
ceramic [sɪˈræmɪk] adj céramique
cereal ['siːrɪəl] n céréale f
ceremony ['sɛrɪmənɪ] n cérémonie f;
to stand on ~ faire des façons
certain ['səːtən] adj certain(e);
to make ~ of s'assurer de; for ~
certainement, sûrement; certainly
adv certainement; certainty n
certitude f
certificate [səˈtɪfɪkɪt] n certificat m
certify ['səːtɪfaɪ] vt certifier; (award
diploma to) conférer un diplôme etc
à; (declare insane) déclarer malade
mental(e)
cf. abbr (= compare) cf., voir
CFC n abbr (= chlorofluorocarbon) CFC m
chain [tʃeɪn] n (gen) chaîne f ▷ vt
(also: ~ up) enchaîner, attacher (avec
une chaîne); chain-smoke vi fumer
cigarette sur cigarette
chair [tʃɛəʳ] n chaise f; (armchair)
fauteuil m; (of university) chaire f; (of
meeting) présidence f ▷ vt (meeting)
présider; chairlift n télésiège m;
chairman n président m; chairperson
n président(e); chairwoman n
présidente f
chalet ['ʃæleɪ] n chalet m
chalk [tʃɔːk] n craie f; chalkboard (US)
n tableau noir
challenge ['tʃælɪndʒ] n défi m ▷ vt
défier; (statement, right) mettre en

question, contester; to ~ sb to do
mettre qn au défi de faire; challenging
adj (task, career) qui représente un défi
ou une gageure; (tone, look) de défi,
provocateur(-trice)
chamber ['tʃeɪmbəʳ] n chambre f; (BRIT
Law: gen pl) cabinet m; ~ of commerce
chambre de commerce; chambermaid
n femme f de chambre
champagne [ʃæmˈpeɪn] n
champagne m
champion ['tʃæmpɪən] n (also of cause)
champion(ne); championship n
championnat m
chance [tʃɑːns] n (luck) hasard m;
(opportunity) occasion f, possibilité f;
(hope, likelihood) chance f; (risk) risque
m ▷ vt (risk) risquer ▷ adj fortuit(e), de
hasard; to take a ~ prendre un risque;
by ~ par hasard; to ~ it risquer le coup,
essayer
chancellor ['tʃɑːnsələʳ] n chancelier m;
Chancellor of the Exchequer
[-ɪksˈtʃɛkəʳ] (BRIT) n chancelier m de
l'Échiquier
chandelier [ʃændəˈlɪəʳ] n lustre m
change [tʃeɪndʒ] vt (alter, replace:
Comm: money) changer; (switch,
substitute: hands, trains, clothes,
one's name etc) changer de ▷ vi (gen)
changer; (change clothes) se changer;
(be transformed): to ~ into se changer
or transformer en ▷ n changement
m; (money) monnaie f; to ~ gear (Aut)
changer de vitesse; to ~ one's mind
changer d'avis; a ~ of clothes des
vêtements de rechange; for a ~ pour
changer; do you have ~ for £10? vous
avez la monnaie de 10 livres?; where
can I ~ some money? où est-ce que je
peux changer de l'argent?; keep the
~! gardez la monnaie!; change over
vi (swap) échanger; (change: drivers
etc) changer; (change: sides: players etc)
changer de côté; to ~ over from sth
to sth passer de qch à qch; changeable
adj (weather) variable; change
machine n distributeur m de monnaie;

changing room n (BRIT: in shop) salon m d'essayage; (: Sport) vestiaire m

channel ['tʃænl] n (TV) chaîne f; (waveband, groove, fig: medium) canal m; (of river, sea) chenal m ▷ vt canaliser; **the (English) C~** la Manche; **Channel Islands** npl: **the Channel Islands** les îles fpl Anglo-Normandes; **Channel Tunnel** n: **the Channel Tunnel** le tunnel sous la Manche

chant [tʃɑːnt] n chant m; (Rel) psalmodie f ▷ vt chanter; scander

chaos ['keɪɒs] n chaos m

chaotic [keɪˈɒtɪk] adj chaotique

chap [tʃæp] n (BRIT inf: man) type m

chapel ['tʃæpl] n chapelle f

chapped [tʃæpt] adj (skin, lips) gercé(e)

chapter ['tʃæptə*] n chapitre m

character ['kærɪktə*] n caractère m; (in novel, film) personnage m; (eccentric person) numéro m, phénomène m; **characteristic** ['kærɪktə'rɪstɪk] adj, n caractéristique (f); **characterize** ['kærɪktəraɪz] vt caractériser

charcoal ['tʃɑːkəʊl] n charbon m de bois; (Art) charbon

charge [tʃɑːdʒ] n (accusation) accusation f; (Law) inculpation f; (cost) prix (demandé) ▷ vt (gun, battery, Mil: enemy) charger; (customer, sum) faire payer ▷ vi foncer; **charges** npl (costs) frais mpl; (Comm Tel): **to reverse the ~s** téléphoner en PCV; **to take a ~ of** se charger de; **to be in ~ of** être responsable de, s'occuper de; **to ~ sb (with)** (Law) inculper qn (de); **charge card** n carte f de client (émise par un grand magasin); **charger** n (also: **battery charger**) chargeur m

charismatic [kærɪzˈmætɪk] adj charismatique

charity ['tʃærɪtɪ] n charité f; (organization) institution f charitable or de bienfaisance, œuvre f (de charité); **charity shop** n (BRIT) boutique vendant des articles d'occasion au profit d'une organisation caritative

charm [tʃɑːm] n charme m; (on bracelet)

breloque f ▷ vt charmer, enchanter; **charming** adj charmant(e)

chart [tʃɑːt] n tableau m, diagramme m; graphique m; (map) carte marine ▷ vt dresser or établir la carte de; (sales, progress) établir la courbe de; **charts** npl (Mus) hit-parade m; **to be in the ~s** (record, pop group) figurer au hit-parade

charter ['tʃɑːtə*] vt (plane) affréter ▷ n (document) charte f; **chartered accountant** n (BRIT) expert-comptable m; **charter flight** n charter m

chase [tʃeɪs] vt poursuivre, pourchasser; (also: **~ away**) chasser ▷ n poursuite f, chasse f

chat [tʃæt] vi (also: **have a ~**) bavarder, causer; (on Internet) chatter ▷ n conversation f, bavardage m; **chat up** vt (BRIT inf: girl) baratiner; **chat room** n (Internet) forum m de discussion; **chat show** n (BRIT) talk-show m

chatter ['tʃætə*] vi (person) bavarder, papoter ▷ n bavardage m, papotage m; **my teeth are ~ing** je claque des dents

chauffeur ['ʃəʊfə*] n chauffeur m (de maître)

chauvinist ['ʃəʊvɪnɪst] n (also: **male ~**) phallocrate m, macho m; (nationalist) chauvin(e)

cheap [tʃiːp] adj bon marché inv, pas cher (chère); (reduced: ticket) à prix réduit; (: fare) réduit(e); (joke) facile, d'un goût douteux; (poor quality) à bon marché, de qualité médiocre ▷ adv à bon marché, pour pas cher; **can you recommend a ~ hotel/restaurant, please?** pourriez-vous m'indiquer un hôtel/restaurant bon marché?; **cheap day return** n billet m d'aller et retour réduit (valable pour la journée); **cheaply** adv à bon marché, à bon compte

cheat [tʃiːt] vi tricher; (in exam) copier ▷ vt tromper, duper; (rob): **to ~ sb out of sth** escroquer qch à qn ▷ n tricheur(-euse) m/f; escroc m; **cheat on** vt fus tromper

Chechnya [tʃɪtʃˈnjɑː] n Tchétchénie f

check [tʃɛk] vt vérifier; (passport, ticket) contrôler; (halt) enrayer; (restrain) maîtriser ▷ vi (official etc) se renseigner ▷ n vérification f, contrôle m; (pattern) carreaux mpl; **to ~ with sb** demander à qn; **check in** vi (in hotel) remplir sa fiche (d'hôtel); (at airport) se présenter à l'enregistrement ▷ vt (luggage) (faire) enregistrer; **check off** vt (tick off) cocher; **check out** vi (in hotel) régler sa note ▷ vt (investigate: story) vérifier (qch); **check up** vi: **to ~ up on sth** vérifier (qch); **to ~ up on sb** se renseigner sur le compte de qn; **checkbook** (us) n = **chequebook**; **checked** adj (pattern, cloth) à carreaux; **checkers** n (us) jeu m de dames; **check-in** n (also: **check-in desk**: at airport) enregistrement m; **checking account** n (us) compte courant; **checklist** n liste f de contrôle; **checkmate** n échec et mat m; **checkout** n (in supermarket) caisse f; **checkpoint** n contrôle m; **checkroom** (us) n consigne f; **checkup** n (Med) examen médical, check-up m

cheddar [ˈtʃɛdəʳ] n (also: **~ cheese**) cheddar m

cheek [tʃiːk] n joue f; (impudence) toupet m, culot m; **what a ~!** quel toupet!; **cheekbone** n pommette f; **cheeky** adj effronté(e), culotté(e)

cheer [tʃɪəʳ] vt acclamer, applaudir; (gladden) réjouir, réconforter ▷ vi applaudir ▷ n (gen pl) acclamations fpl, applaudissements mpl; bravos mpl, hourras mpl; **~s!** à la vôtre!; **cheer up** vi se dérider, reprendre courage ▷ vt remonter le moral à or de, dérider, égayer; **cheerful** adj gai(e), joyeux(-euse)

cheerio [tʃɪərɪˈəu] excl (BRIT) salut!, au revoir!

cheerleader [ˈtʃiːəliːdəʳ] n membre d'un groupe de majorettes qui chantent et dansent pour soutenir leur équipe pendant les matchs de football américain

cheese [tʃiːz] n fromage m; **cheeseburger** n cheeseburger m; **cheesecake** n tarte f au fromage

chef [ʃɛf] n chef (cuisinier)

chemical [ˈkɛmɪkl] adj chimique ▷ n produit m chimique

chemist [ˈkɛmɪst] n (BRIT: pharmacist) pharmacien(ne); (scientist) chimiste m/f; **chemistry** n chimie f; **chemist's (shop)** n (BRIT) pharmacie f

cheque (us **check**) [tʃɛk] n chèque m; **chequebook** (us **checkbook**) n chéquier m, carnet m de chèques; **cheque card** n (BRIT) carte f (d'identité) bancaire

cherry [ˈtʃɛrɪ] n cerise f; (also: **~ tree**) cerisier m

chess [tʃɛs] n échecs mpl

chest [tʃɛst] n poitrine f; (box) coffre m, caisse f

chestnut [ˈtʃɛsnʌt] n châtaigne f; (also: **~ tree**) châtaignier m

chest of drawers n commode f

chew [tʃuː] vt mâcher; **chewing gum** n chewing-gum m

chic [ʃiːk] adj chic inv, élégant(e)

chick [tʃɪk] n poussin m; (inf) pépée f

chicken [ˈtʃɪkɪn] n poulet m; (inf: coward) poule mouillée; **chicken out** vi (inf) se dégonfler; **chickenpox** n varicelle f

chickpea [ˈtʃɪkpiː] n pois m chiche

chief [tʃiːf] n chef m ▷ adj principal(e); **chief executive** (us **chief executive officer**) n directeur(-trice) général(e); **chiefly** adv principalement, surtout

child (pl **~ren**) [tʃaɪld, ˈtʃɪldrən] n enfant m/f; **child abuse** n maltraitance d'enfants; (sexual) abus m sexuels sur des enfants; **child benefit** n (BRIT) = allocations familiales; **childbirth** n accouchement m; **child-care** n (for working parents) garde f des enfants (pour les parents qui travaillent); **childhood** n enfance f; **childish** adj puéril(e), enfantin(e); **child minder** n (BRIT) garde f d'enfants; **children** [ˈtʃɪldrən] npl of **child**

Chile [ˈtʃɪlɪ] n Chili m

chill [tʃɪl] n (of water) froid m; (of air) fraîcheur f; (Med) refroidissement m, coup m de froid ▷ vt (person) faire frissonner; (Culin) mettre au frais, rafraîchir; **chill out** vi (inf: esp us) se relaxer

chil(l)i [ˈtʃɪlɪ] n Chine f

chilly [ˈtʃɪlɪ] adj froid(e), glacé(e); (sensitive to cold) frileux(-euse)

chimney [ˈtʃɪmnɪ] n cheminée f

chimpanzee [tʃɪmpænˈziː] n chimpanzé m

chin [tʃɪn] n menton m

China [ˈtʃaɪnə] n Chine f

china [ˈtʃaɪnə] n (material) porcelaine f; (crockery) vaisselle f en) porcelaine

Chinese [tʃaɪˈniːz] adj chinois(e) ▷ n (pl inv) Chinois(e); (Ling) chinois m

chip [tʃɪp] n (gen pl: Culin: BRIT) frite f; (: us: also: **potato ~**) chip m; (of wood) copeau m; (of glass, stone) éclat m; (also: **micro-**) puce f; (in gambling) fiche f ▷ vt (cup, plate) ébrécher; **chip shop** n (BRIT) friterie f

○ **CHIP SHOP**
○
○ Un **chip shop**, que l'on appelle
○ également en "fish-and-chip shop",
○ est un magasin où l'on vend des plats
○ à emporter. Les **chip shops** sont
○ d'ailleurs à l'origine des "takeaways".
○ On y achète en particulier du
○ poisson frit et des frites, mais
○ on y trouve également des plats
○ traditionnels britanniques ("steak
○ pies", saucisses, etc). Tous les plats
○ étaient à l'origine emballés dans du
○ papier journal. Dans certains de ces
○ magasins, on peut s'asseoir pour
○ consommer sur place.

chiropodist [kɪˈrɒpədɪst] n (BRIT) pédicure m/f

chisel [ˈtʃɪzl] n ciseau m

chives [tʃaɪvz] npl ciboulette f, civette f

chlorine [ˈklɔːriːn] n chlore m

choc-ice [ˈtʃɒkaɪs] n (BRIT) esquimau® m

chocolate [ˈtʃɒklɪt] n chocolat m

choice [tʃɔɪs] n choix m ▷ adj de choix

choir [ˈkwaɪəʳ] n chœur m, chorale f

choke [tʃəuk] vi étouffer ▷ vt étrangler; étouffer; (block) boucher, obstruer ▷ n (Aut) starter m

cholesterol [kəˈlɛstərɒl] n cholestérol m

choose (pt **chose**, pp **chosen**) [tʃuːz, tʃəuz, ˈtʃəuzn] vt choisir; **to ~ to do** décider de faire, juger bon de faire

chop [tʃɒp] vt (wood) couper (à la hache); (Culin: also: **~ up**) couper (fin), émincer, hacher (en morceaux) ▷ n (Culin) côtelette f; **chop down** vt (tree) abattre; **chop off** vt trancher; **chopsticks** [ˈtʃɒpstɪks] npl baguettes fpl

chord [kɔːd] n (Mus) accord m

chore [tʃɔːʳ] n travail m de routine; **household ~s** travaux mpl du ménage

chorus [ˈkɔːrəs] n chœur m; (repeated part of song, also fig) refrain m

chose [tʃəuz] pt of **choose**

chosen [ˈtʃəuzn] pp of **choose**

Christ [kraɪst] n Christ m

christen [ˈkrɪsn] vt baptiser; **christening** n baptême m

Christian [ˈkrɪstɪən] adj, n chrétien(ne); **Christianity** [krɪstɪˈænɪtɪ] n christianisme m; **Christian name** n prénom m

Christmas [ˈkrɪsməs] n Noël m or f; **happy** or **merry ~!** joyeux Noël!; **Christmas card** n carte f de Noël; **Christmas carol** n chant m de Noël; **Christmas Day** n le jour de Noël; **Christmas Eve** n la veille de Noël; la nuit de Noël; **Christmas pudding** n (esp BRIT) Christmas m pudding; **Christmas tree** n arbre m de Noël

chrome [krəum] n chrome m

chronic [ˈkrɒnɪk] adj chronique

chrysanthemum [krɪˈsænθəməm] n chrysanthème m

chubby [ˈtʃʌbɪ] adj potelé(e),

rondelet(te)

chuck [tʃʌk] vt (inf) lancer, jeter; (BRIT: also: **~ up**: job) lâcher; **chuck out** vt (inf: person) flanquer dehors or à la porte; (: rubbish etc) jeter

chuckle ['tʃʌkl] vi glousser

chum [tʃʌm] n copain (copine)

chunk [tʃʌŋk] n gros morceau

church [tʃɜːtʃ] n église f; **churchyard** n cimetière m

churn [tʃɜːn] n (for butter) baratte f; (also: **milk ~**) (grand) bidon à lait

chute [ʃuːt] n goulotte f; (also: **rubbish ~**) vide-ordures m inv; (BRIT: children's slide) toboggan m

chutney ['tʃʌtnɪ] n chutney m

CIA n abbr (= Central Intelligence Agency) CIA f

CID n abbr (= Criminal Investigation Department) ≈ P.J. f

cider ['saɪdə'] n cidre m

cigar [sɪ'gɑː'] n cigare m

cigarette [sɪgə'ret] n cigarette f; **cigarette lighter** n briquet m

cinema ['sɪnəmə] n cinéma m

cinnamon ['sɪnəmən] n cannelle f

circle ['sɜːkl] n cercle m; (in cinema) balcon m ▷ vi faire or décrire des cercles ▷ vt (surround) entourer, encercler; (move round) faire le tour de, tourner autour de

circuit ['sɜːkɪt] n circuit m; (lap) tour m

circular ['sɜːkjulə'] adj circulaire ▷ n circulaire f; (as advertisement) prospectus m

circulate ['sɜːkjuleɪt] vi circuler ▷ vt faire circuler; **circulation** [sɜːkju'leɪʃən] n circulation f; (of newspaper) tirage m

circumstances ['sɜːkəmstənsɪz] npl circonstances fpl; (financial condition) moyens mpl, situation financière

circus ['sɜːkəs] n cirque m

cite [saɪt] vt citer

citizen ['sɪtɪzn] n (Pol) citoyen(ne); (resident): **the ~s of this town** les habitants de cette ville; **citizenship** n citoyenneté f; (BRIT: Scol) ≈ éducation

f civique

citrus fruits ['sɪtrəs-] npl agrumes mpl

city ['sɪtɪ] n (grande) ville f; **the C~** la Cité de Londres (centre des affaires); **city centre** n centre-ville m; **city technology college** n (BRIT) établissement m d'enseignement technologique (situé dans un quartier défavorisé)

civic ['sɪvɪk] adj civique; (authorities) municipal(e)

civil ['sɪvɪl] adj civil(e); (polite) poli(e), civil(e); **civilian** [sɪ'vɪlɪən] adj, n civil(e)

civilization [sɪvɪlaɪ'zeɪʃən] n civilisation f

civilized ['sɪvɪlaɪzd] adj civilisé(e); (fig) où règnent les bonnes manières

civil: **civil law** n code civil; (study) droit civil; **civil rights** npl droits mpl civiques; **civil servant** n fonctionnaire m/f; **Civil Service** n fonction publique, administration f; **civil war** n guerre civile

CJD n abbr (= Creutzfeldt-Jakob disease) MCJ f

claim [kleɪm] vt (rights etc) revendiquer; (compensation) réclamer; (assert) déclarer, prétendre ▷ vi (for insurance) faire une déclaration de sinistre ▷ n revendication f; prétention f; (right) droit m; **(insurance) ~** demande f d'indemnisation, déclaration f de sinistre; **claim form** n (gen) formulaire m de demande

clam [klæm] n palourde f

clamp [klæmp] n crampon m; (on workbench) valet m; (on car) sabot m de Denver ▷ vt attacher; (car) mettre un sabot à; **clamp down on** vt fus sévir contre, prendre des mesures draconiennes à l'égard de

clan [klæn] n clan m

clap [klæp] vi applaudir

claret ['klærət] n (vin m de) bordeaux m (rouge)

clarify ['klærɪfaɪ] vt clarifier

clarinet [klærɪ'net] n clarinette f

clarity ['klærɪtɪ] n clarté f

clash [klæʃ] n (sound) choc m, fracas m; (with police) affrontement m; (fig) conflit m ▷ vi se heurter; être ou entrer en conflit; (colours) jurer; (dates, events) tomber en même temps

clasp [klɑːsp] n (of necklace, bag) fermoir m ▷ vt serrer, étreindre

class [klɑːs] n (gen) classe f; (group, category) catégorie f ▷ vt classer, classifier

classic ['klæsɪk] adj classique ▷ n (author, work) classique m; **classical** adj classique

classification [klæsɪfɪ'keɪʃən] n classification f

classify ['klæsɪfaɪ] vt classifier, classer

classmate ['klɑːsmeɪt] n camarade m/f de classe

classroom ['klɑːsrum] n (salle f de) classe f; **classroom assistant** n assistant(-e) d'éducation

classy ['klɑːsɪ] (inf) adj classe (inf)

clatter ['klætə*] n cliquetis m ▷ vi cliqueter

clause [klɔːz] n clause f; (Ling) proposition f

claustrophobic [klɔːstrə'fəubɪk] adj (person) claustrophobe; (place) où l'on se sent claustrophobe

claw [klɔː] n griffe f; (of bird of prey) serre f; (of lobster) pince f

clay [kleɪ] n argile f

clean [kliːn] adj propre; (clear, smooth) net(te); (record, reputation) sans tache; (joke, story) correct(e) ▷ vt nettoyer; **clean up** vt nettoyer; (fig) remettre de l'ordre dans; **cleaner** n (person) nettoyeur(-euse), femme f de ménage; (product) détachant m; **cleaner's** n (also: **dry cleaner's**) teinturier m; **cleaning** n nettoyage m

cleanser ['klɛnzə*] n (for face) démaquillant m

clear [klɪə*] adj clair(e); (glass, plastic) transparent(e); (road, way) libre, dégagé(e); (profit, majority) net(te); (conscience) tranquille; (skin) frais (fraîche); (sky) dégagé(e) ▷ vt (road)

dégager, déblayer; (table) débarrasser; (room etc: of people) faire évacuer; (cheque) compenser; (Law: suspect) innocenter; (obstacle) franchir or sauter sans heurter ▷ vi (weather) s'éclaircir; (fog) se dissiper ▷ adv: **~ of** à distance de, à l'écart de; **to ~ the table** débarrasser la table, desservir; **clear away** vt (things, clothes etc) enlever, retirer; **to ~ away the dishes** débarrasser la table; **clear up** vt ranger, mettre en ordre; (mystery) éclaircir, résoudre; **clearance** n (removal) déblayage m; (permission) autorisation f; **clear-cut** adj précis(e), nettement défini(e); **clearing** n (in forest) clairière f; **clearly** adv clairement; (obviously) de toute évidence; **clearway** n (Brit) route f à stationnement interdit

clench [klɛntʃ] vt serrer

clergy ['klɜːdʒɪ] n clergé m

clerk [klɑːk, us klɜːrk] n (Brit) employé(e) de bureau; (us: salesman, woman) vendeur(-euse)

clever ['klɛvə*] adj (intelligent) intelligent(e); (skilful) habile, adroit(e); (device, arrangement) ingénieux(-euse), astucieux(-euse)

cliché ['kliːʃeɪ] n cliché m

click [klɪk] vi (Comput) cliquer ▷ vt: **to ~ one's tongue** faire claquer sa langue; **to ~ one's heels** claquer des talons; **to ~ on an icon** cliquer sur une icône

client ['klaɪənt] n client(e)

cliff [klɪf] n falaise f

climate ['klaɪmɪt] n climat m; **climate change** n changement m climatique

climax ['klaɪmæks] n apogée m, point culminant; (sexual) orgasme m

climb [klaɪm] vi grimper, monter; (plane) prendre de l'altitude ▷ vt (stairs) monter; (mountain) escalader; (tree) grimper à ▷ n montée f, escalade f; **to ~ over a wall** passer par dessus un mur; **climb down** vi (re)descendre; (Brit fig) rabattre de ses prétentions; **climber** n (also: **rock climber**) grimpeur(-euse), varappeur(-euse); (plant) plante grimpante; **climbing** n (also: **rock climbing**) escalade f, varappe f

clinch [klɪntʃ] vt (deal) conclure, sceller

cling (pt, pp **clung**) [klɪŋ, klʌŋ] vi: **to ~ (to)** se cramponner (à), s'accrocher (à); (clothes) coller (à)

Clingfilm® ['klɪŋfɪlm] n film m alimentaire

clinic ['klɪnɪk] n clinique f; centre médical

clip [klɪp] n (for hair) barrette f; (also: **paper ~**) trombone m; (TV, Cinema) clip m ▷ vt (also: **~ together**) papers) attacher; (hair, nails) couper; (hedge) tailler; **clipping** n (from newspaper) coupure f de journal

cloak [kləʊk] n (large) grande cape ▷ vt (fig) masquer, cacher; **cloakroom** n (for coats etc) vestiaire m; (BRIT: W.C.) toilettes fpl

clock [klɒk] n (large) horloge f; (small) pendule f; **clock in** or **on** vi (with card) pointer (en arrivant); (start work) commencer à travailler; **clock off** or **out** (BRIT) vi (with card) pointer (en partant); (leave work) quitter le travail; **clockwise** adv dans le sens des aiguilles d'une montre; **clockwork** n rouages mpl, mécanisme m; (of clock) mouvement m (d'horlogerie) ▷ adj (toy, train) mécanique

clog [klɒg] n sabot m ▷ vt boucher, encrasser ▷ vi (also: **~ up**) se boucher, s'encrasser

clone [kləʊn] n clone m ▷ vt cloner

close¹ [kləʊs] adj (near): **~ (to)** près (de), proche (de); (contact, link, watch) étroit(e); (examination) attentif(-ive), minutieux(-euse); (contest) serré(e); (weather) lourd(e), étouffant(e) ▷ adv près, à proximité; **~ to** prep près de; **~ by, ~ at hand** adj, adv tout(e) près; **~ a friend** un ami intime; **to have a ~ shave** (fig) l'échapper belle

close² [kləʊz] vt fermer ▷ vi (shop etc) fermer; (lid, door etc) se fermer; (end) se terminer, se conclure ▷ n (end)

conclusion f; **what time do you ~?** à quelle heure fermez-vous?; **close down** vi fermer (définitivement); **closed** adj (shop etc) fermé(e)

closely ['kləʊslɪ] adv (examine, watch) de près

closet ['klɒzɪt] n (cupboard) placard m, réduit m

close-up [kləʊsʌp] n gros plan

closing time n heure f de fermeture

closure ['kləʊʒə'] n fermeture f

clot [klɒt] n (of blood, milk) caillot m; (inf: person) ballot m ▷ vi (: external bleeding) se coaguler

cloth [klɒθ] n (material) tissu m, étoffe f; (BRIT: also: **tea~**) torchon m; lavette f; (also: **table~**) nappe f

clothes [kləʊðz] npl vêtements mpl, habits mpl; **clothes line** n corde f (à linge); **clothes peg** (US **clothes pin**) n pince f à linge

clothing ['kləʊðɪŋ] n = **clothes**

cloud [klaʊd] n nuage m; **cloud over** vi se couvrir; (fig) s'assombrir; **cloudy** adj nuageux(-euse), couvert(e); (liquid) trouble

clove [kləʊv] n clou m de girofle; **a ~ of garlic** une gousse d'ail

clown [klaʊn] n clown m ▷ vi (also: **~ about, ~ around**) faire le clown

club [klʌb] n (society) club m; (weapon) massue f, matraque f; (also: **golf ~**) club ▷ vt matraquer ▷ vi: **to ~ together** s'associer; **clubs** npl (Cards) trèfle m; **club class** n (Aviat) classe f club

clue [klu:] n indice m; (in crosswords) définition f; **I haven't a ~** je n'en ai pas la moindre idée

clump [klʌmp] n: **~ of trees** bouquet m d'arbres

clumsy ['klʌmzɪ] adj (person) gauche, maladroit(e); (object) malcommode, peu maniable

clung [klʌŋ] pt, pp of **cling**

cluster ['klʌstə'] n (petit) groupe m; (of flowers) grappe f ▷ vi se rassembler

clutch [klʌtʃ] n (Aut) embrayage m; (grasp): **~es** étreinte f, prise f ▷ vt (grasp) agripper; (*hold tightly*) serrer fort; (*hold on to*) se cramponner à

cm *abbr* (= *centimetre*) cm

Co. *abbr* = **company, county**

c/o *abbr* (= *care of*) c/o, aux bons soins de

coach [kəʊtʃ] *n* (*bus*) autocar m; (*horse-drawn*) diligence f; (*of train*) voiture f, wagon m; (*Sport: trainer*) entraîneur(-euse); (*school: tutor*) répétiteur(-trice) ▷ *vt* (*Sport*) entraîner; (*student*) donner des leçons particulières à; **coach station** (BRIT) n gare routière; **coach trip** n excursion f en car

coal [kəʊl] *n* charbon m

coalition [kəʊəˈlɪʃən] *n* coalition f

coarse [kɔːs] *adj* grossier(-ère), rude; (*vulgar*) vulgaire

coast [kəʊst] *n* côte f ▷ *vi* (*car, cycle*) descendre en roue libre; **coastal** *adj* côtier(-ère); **coastguard** n garde-côte m; **coastline** n côte f, littoral m

coat [kəʊt] *n* manteau m; (*of animal*) pelage m, poil m; (*of paint*) couche f ▷ *vt* couvrir, enduire; **coat hanger** n cintre m; **coating** n couche f, enduit m

coax [kəʊks] *vt* persuader par des cajoleries

cob [kɔb] *n see* **corn**

cobbled [ˈkɔbld] *adj* pavé(e)

cobweb [ˈkɔbwɛb] *n* toile f d'araignée

cocaine [kəˈkeɪn] *n* cocaïne f

cock [kɔk] *n* (*rooster*) coq m; (*male bird*) mâle m ▷ *vt* (*gun*) armer; **cockerel** n jeune coq m

cockney [ˈkɔknɪ] *n* cockney m/f (*habitant des quartiers populaires de l'East End de Londres*) = faubourien(ne)

cockpit [ˈkɔkpɪt] *n* (*in aircraft*) poste m de pilotage, cockpit m

cockroach [ˈkɔkrəʊtʃ] *n* cafard m, cancrelat m

cocktail [ˈkɔkteɪl] *n* cocktail m

cocoa [ˈkəʊkəʊ] *n* cacao m

coconut [ˈkəʊkənʌt] *n* noix f de coco

C.O.D. *abbr* = **cash on delivery**

cod [kɔd] *n* morue fraîche, cabillaud m

code [kəʊd] *n* code m; (*Tel: area code*) indicatif m

coeducational [ˈkəʊɛdjuˈkeɪʃənl] *adj* mixte

coffee [ˈkɔfɪ] *n* café m; **coffee bar** (BRIT) café m; **coffee bean** n grain m de café; **coffee break** n pause-café f; **coffee maker** n cafetière f; **coffeepot** n cafetière f; **coffee shop** n café m; **coffee table** n (petite) table basse

coffin [ˈkɔfɪn] *n* cercueil m

cog [kɔg] *n* (*wheel*) roue dentée; (*tooth*) dent f (d'engrenage)

cognac [ˈkɔnjæk] *n* cognac m

coherent [kəʊˈhɪərənt] *adj* cohérent(e)

coil [kɔɪl] *n* rouleau m, bobine f; (*contraceptive*) stérilet m ▷ *vt* enrouler

coin [kɔɪn] *n* pièce f de monnaie ▷ *vt* (*word*) inventer

coincide [kəʊɪnˈsaɪd] *vi* coïncider; **coincidence** [kəʊˈɪnsɪdəns] n coïncidence f

Coke® [kəʊk] *n* coca m

coke [kəʊk] *n* (*coal*) coke m

colander [ˈkɔləndə] *n* passoire f (à légumes)

cold [kəʊld] *adj* froid(e) ▷ *n* froid m; (*Med*) rhume m; **it's ~** il fait froid; **to be ~** (*person*) avoir froid; **to catch a ~** s'enrhumer, attraper un rhume; **in ~ blood** de sang-froid; **cold cuts** (us) npl viandes froides; **cold sore** n bouton m de fièvre

coleslaw [ˈkəʊlslɔː] *n* sorte de salade de chou cru

colic [ˈkɔlɪk] *n* colique(s) f(pl)

collaborate [kəˈlæbəreɪt] *vi* collaborer

collapse [kəˈlæps] *vi* s'effondrer, s'écrouler; (*Med*) avoir un malaise ▷ *n* effondrement m, écroulement m; (*of government*) chute f

collar [ˈkɔlə] *n* (*of coat, shirt*) col m; (*for dog*) collier m; **collarbone** n clavicule f

colleague [ˈkɔliːg] *n* collègue m/f

collect [kəˈlɛkt] *vt* rassembler; (*pick up*) ramasser; (*as a hobby*) collectionner; (BRIT: *call for*) (passer) prendre; (*mail*) faire la levée de, ramasser; (*money owed*) encaisser; (donations, subscriptions) recueillir ▷ vi (people) se rassembler; (dust, dirt) s'amasser; **to call ~** (US Tel) téléphoner en PCV; **collection** [kə'lɛkʃən] n collection f; (of mail) levée f; (for money) collecte f, quête f; **collective** [kə'lɛktɪv] adj collectif(-ive); **collector** n collectionneur m

college ['kɒlɪdʒ] n collège m; (of technology, agriculture etc) institut m

collide [kə'laɪd] vi: **to ~ (with)** entrer en collision (avec)

collision [kə'lɪʒən] n collision f, heurt m

cologne [kə'ləʊn] n (also: **eau de ~**) eau f de cologne

colon ['kəʊlən] n (sign) deux-points mpl; (Med) côlon m

colonel ['kɜːnl] n colonel m

colonial [kə'ləʊnɪəl] adj colonial(e)

colony ['kɒlənɪ] n colonie f

colour etc (us **color** etc) ['kʌlə*] n couleur f ▷ vt colorer; (dye) teindre; (paint) peindre; (with crayons) colorier; (news) fausser, exagérer ▷ vi (blush) rougir; **I'd like a different ~** je le voudrais dans un autre coloris; **colour in** vt colorier; **colour-blind** adj daltonien(ne); **coloured** adj coloré(e); (photo) en couleur; **colour film** n (for camera) pellicule f(en) couleur; **colourful** adj coloré(e), vif (vive); (personality) pittoresque, haut(e) en couleurs; **colouring** n colorant m; (complexion) teint m; **colour television** n télévision f(en) couleur

column ['kɒləm] n colonne f; (fashion column, sports column etc) rubrique f

coma ['kəʊmə] n coma m

comb [kəʊm] n peigne m ▷ vt (hair) peigner; (area) ratisser, passer au peigne fin

combat ['kɒmbæt] n combat m ▷ vt combattre, lutter contre

combination [kɒmbɪ'neɪʃən] n (gen) combinaison f

combine vb [kəm'baɪn] ▷ vt combiner ▷ vi s'associer; (Chem) se combiner ▷ n

['kɒmbaɪn] (Econ) trust m; **to ~ sth with sth** (one quality with another) joindre ou allier qch à qch

come (pt **came**, pp ~) [kʌm, keɪm] vi 1 (movement towards) venir; **to ~ running** arriver en courant; **~ here!** viens ici!; **~ with me** suivez-moi

2 (arrive) arriver; **to ~ home** rentrer (chez soi ou à la maison); **we've just ~ from Paris** nous arrivons de Paris

3 (reach): **to ~ to** (decision etc) parvenir à, arriver à; **the bill came to £40** la note s'est élevée à 40 livres

4 (occur): **an idea came to me** il m'est venu une idée

5 (be, become): **to ~ loose/undone** se défaire/desserrer; **I've ~ to like him** j'ai fini par bien l'aimer; **come across** vt fus rencontrer par hasard, tomber sur; **come along** vi (BRIT: pupil, work) faire des progrès, avancer; **come back** vi revenir; **come down** vi descendre; (prices) baisser; (buildings) s'écrouler; (: be demolished) être démoli(e); **come from** vt fus (source) venir de; (place) venir de, être originaire de; **come in** vi entrer; (train) arriver; (fashion) entrer en vogue; (on deal etc) participer; **come off** vi (button) se détacher; (attempt) réussir; **come on** vi (lights, electricity) s'allumer; (central heating) se mettre en marche; (pupil, work, project) faire des progrès, avancer; **~ on!** viens!; allons!, allez!; **come out** vi sortir; (sun) se montrer; (book) paraître; (stain) s'enlever; (strike) cesser le travail, se mettre en grève; **come round** vi (after faint, operation) revenir à soi, reprendre connaissance; **come to** vi revenir à soi; **come up** vi monter; (sun) se lever; (problem) se poser; (event) survenir; (in conversation) être soulevé; **come up with** vt fus (money) fournir; **he came up with an idea** il a proposé quelque chose

comeback ['kʌmbæk] n (Theat etc) rentrée f

comedian [kə'miːdɪən] n (comic) comique m; (Theat) comédien m
comedy ['kɒmɪdɪ] n comédie f; (humour) comique m
comet ['kɒmɪt] n comète f
comfort ['kʌmfət] n confort m, bien-être m; (solace) consolation f, réconfort m ▷ vt consoler, réconforter; **comfortable** adj confortable; (person) à l'aise; (financially) aisé(e); (patient) dont l'état est stationnaire; **comfort station** n (US) toilettes fpl
comic ['kɒmɪk] adj (also: **~al**) comique ▷ n (person) comique m; (BRIT: magazine) magazine m de bandes dessinées or de BD; (: for adults) illustré m; **comic book** n (US) (for children) magazine m de bandes dessinées or de BD; (for adults) illustré m; **comic strip** n bande dessinée
comma ['kɒmə] n virgule f
command [kə'mɑːnd] n ordre m, commandement m; (Mil: authority) commandement m; (mastery) maîtrise f ▷ vt (troops) commander; **to ~ sb to do** donner l'ordre or commander à qn de faire; **commander** n (Mil) commandant m
commemorate [kə'meməreɪt] vt commémorer
commence [kə'mɛns] vt, vi commencer; **commencement** (US) n (University) remise f des diplômes
commend [kə'mɛnd] vt louer; (recommend) recommander
comment ['kɒmɛnt] n commentaire m ▷ vi: **to ~ on** faire des remarques sur; **"no ~"** "je n'ai rien à déclarer"; **commentary** ['kɒməntərɪ] n commentaire m; (Sport) reportage m (en direct); **commentator** ['kɒmənteɪtə'] n commentateur m; (Sport) reporter m
commerce ['kɒmɜːs] n commerce m
commercial [kə'mɜːʃəl] adj commercial(e) ▷ n (Radio, TV) annonce f publicitaire, spot m (publicitaire); **commercial break** n (Radio, TV) spot m

(publicitaire)
commission [kə'mɪʃən] n (committee, fee) commission f ▷ vt (work of art) commander, charger un artiste de l'exécution de; **out of ~** (machine) hors service; **commissioner** n (Police) préfet m (de police)
commit [kə'mɪt] vt (act) commettre; (resources) consacrer; (to sb's care) confier (à); **to ~ o.s. (to do)** s'engager (à faire); **to ~ suicide** se suicider; **commitment** n engagement m; (obligation) responsabilité(s) (fpl)
committee [kə'mɪtɪ] n comité m, commission f
commodity [kə'mɒdɪtɪ] n produit m, marchandise f, article m
common ['kɒmən] adj (gen) commun(e); (usual) courant(e) ▷ n terrain communal; **commonly** adv communément, généralement; couramment; **commonplace** adj banal(e), ordinaire; **Commons** npl (BRIT Pol): **the (House of) Commons** la chambre des Communes; **common sense** n bon sens; **Commonwealth** n: **the Commonwealth** le Commonwealth
communal ['kɒmjuːnl] adj (life) communautaire; (for common use) commun(e)
commune n ['kɒmjuːn] (group) communauté f ▷ vi [kə'mjuːn]: **to ~ with** (nature) communier avec
communicate [kə'mjuːnɪkeɪt] vt communiquer, transmettre ▷ vi: **to ~ (with)** communiquer (avec)
communication [kəmjuːnɪ'keɪʃən] n communication f
communion [kə'mjuːnɪən] n (also: **Holy C~**) communion f
communism ['kɒmjunɪzəm] n communisme m; **communist** adj, n communiste m/f
community [kə'mjuːnɪtɪ] n communauté f; **community centre** (US **community center**) n foyer socio-éducatif, centre m de loisirs;

community service n ≈ travail m d'intérêt général, TIG m

commute [kə'mju:t] vi faire le trajet journalier (de son domicile à un lieu de travail assez éloigné) ▷ vt (Law) commuer; **commuter** n banlieusard(e) (qui fait un trajet journalier pour se rendre à son travail)

compact adj {kəm'pækt} compact(e) ▷ n ['kɔmpækt] (also: **powder ~**) poudrier m; **compact disc** n disque compact; **compact disc player** n lecteur m de disques compacts

companion [kəm'pænjən] n compagnon/compagne

company ['kʌmpənɪ] n compagnie f; **to keep sb ~** tenir compagnie à qn; **company car** n voiture f de fonction; **company director** n administrateur(-trice)

comparable ['kɔmpərəbl] adj comparable

comparative [kəm'pærətɪv] adj (study) comparatif(-ive); (relative) relatif(-ive); **comparatively** adv (relatively) relativement

compare [kəm'pɛə'] vt: **to ~ sth/sb with** or **to** comparer qch/qn avec or à ▷ vi: **to ~ (with)** se comparer (à); être comparable (à); **comparison** [kəm'pærɪsn] n comparaison f

compartment [kəm'pɑ:tmənt] n (also Rail) compartiment m; **a non-smoking ~** un compartiment non-fumeurs

compass ['kʌmpəs] n boussole f; **compasses** npl (Math) compas m

compassion [kəm'pæʃən] n compassion f, humanité f

compatible [kəm'pætɪbl] adj compatible

compel [kəm'pɛl] vt contraindre, obliger; **compelling** adj (fig: argument) irrésistible

compensate ['kɔmpənseɪt] vt indemniser, dédommager ▷ vi: **to ~ for** compenser; **compensation** [kɔmpən'seɪʃən] n compensation

f; (money) dédommagement m, indemnité f

compete [kəm'pi:t] vi (take part) concourir; (vie): **to ~ (with)** rivaliser (avec), faire concurrence (à)

competent ['kɔmpɪtənt] adj compétent(e), capable

competition [kɔmpɪ'tɪʃən] n (contest) compétition f, concours m; (Econ) concurrence f

competitive [kəm'pɛtɪtɪv] adj (Econ) concurrentiel(le); (sports) de compétition; (person) qui a l'esprit de compétition

competitor [kəm'pɛtɪtə'] n concurrent(e)

complacent [kəm'pleɪsnt] adj (too) content(e) de soi

complain [kəm'pleɪn] vi: **to ~ (about)** se plaindre (de); (in shop etc) réclamer (au sujet de); **complaint** n plainte f; (in shop etc) réclamation f; (Med) affection f

complement ['kɔmplɪmənt] n complément m; (esp of ship's crew etc) effectif complet ▷ vt (enhance) compléter; **complementary** [kɔmplɪ'mɛntərɪ] adj complémentaire

complete [kəm'pli:t] adj complet(-ète); (finished) achevé(e) ▷ vt achever, parachever; (set, group) compléter; (a form) remplir; **completely** adv complètement; **completion** [kəm'pli:ʃən] n achèvement m; (of contract) exécution f

complex ['kɔmplɛks] adj complexe ▷ n (Psych; buildings etc) complexe m

complexion [kəm'plɛkʃən] n (of face) teint m

compliance [kəm'plaɪəns] n (submission) docilité f; (agreement): **~ with** le fait de se conformer à; **in ~ with** en conformité avec, conformément à

complicate ['kɔmplɪkeɪt] vt compliquer; **complicated** adj compliqué(e); **complication** [kɔmplɪ'keɪʃən] n complication f

compliment n ['kɔmplɪmənt] compliment m ▷ vt ['kɔmplɪmənt]

complimenter; **complimentary**
[kɒmplɪ'mɛntərɪ] adj flatteur(-euse);
(free) à titre gracieux
comply [kəm'plaɪ] vi: **to ~ with** se
soumettre à, se conformer à
component [kəm'pəʊnənt] adj
composant(e), constituant(e) ▷ n
composant m, élément m
compose [kəm'pəʊz] vt composer;
(form): **to be ~d of** se composer de; **to ~
o.s.** se calmer, se maîtriser; **composer**
n (Mus) compositeur m; **composition**
[kɒmpə'zɪʃən] n composition f
composure [kəm'pəʊʒə*] n calme m,
maîtrise f de soi
compound ['kɒmpaʊnd] n (Chem,
Ling) composé m; (enclosure) enclos m,
enceinte f ▷ adj composé(e); (fracture)
compliqué(e)
comprehension [kɒmprɪ'hɛnʃən] n
compréhension f
comprehensive [kɒmprɪ'hɛnsɪv]
adj (très) complet(-ète); **~ policy**
(Insurance) assurance f tous risques;
comprehensive (school) n (BRIT)
école secondaire non sélective avec
circulation d'une section à l'autre, ≈ CES m

> Be careful not to translate
> *comprehensive* by the French word
> *compréhensif*.

compress vt [kəm'prɛs] comprimer;
(text, information) condenser ▷ n
['kɒmprɛs] (Med) compresse f
comprise [kəm'praɪz] vt (also: **be ~
of**) comprendre; (constitute) constituer,
représenter
compromise ['kɒmprəmaɪz] n
compromis m ▷ vt compromettre ▷ vi
transiger, accepter un compromis
compulsive [kəm'pʌlsɪv] adj (Psych)
compulsif(-ive); (book, film etc)
captivant(e)
compulsory [kəm'pʌlsərɪ] adj
obligatoire
computer [kəm'pju:tə*] n
ordinateur m; **computer game** n jeu
m vidéo; **computer-generated** adj
de synthèse; **computerize** vt (data)

traiter par ordinateur; (system, office)
informatiser; **computer programmer**
n programmeur(-euse); **computer
programming** n programmation f;
computer science n informatique f;
computer studies npl informatique f;
computing [kəm'pju:tɪŋ] n
informatique f
con [kɒn] vt duper; (cheat) escroquer ▷ n
escroquerie f
conceal [kən'si:l] vt cacher, dissimuler
concede [kən'si:d] vt concéder ▷ vi
céder
conceited [kən'si:tɪd] adj
vaniteux(-euse), suffisant(e)
conceive [kən'si:v] vt, vi concevoir
concentrate ['kɒnsəntreɪt] vi se
concentrer ▷ vt concentrer
concentration [kɒnsən'treɪʃən] n
concentration f
concept ['kɒnsɛpt] n concept m
concern [kən'sɜ:n] n affaire f;
(Comm) entreprise f, firme f; (anxiety)
inquiétude f, souci m ▷ vt (worry)
inquiéter; (involve) concerner; (relate
to) se rapporter à; **to be ~ed (about)**
s'inquiéter (de), être inquiet(-ète) (au
sujet de); **concerning** prep en ce qui
concerne, à propos de
concert ['kɒnsət] n concert m; **concert
hall** n salle f de concert
concerto [kən'tʃə:təʊ] n concerto m
concession [kən'sɛʃən] n (compromise)
concession f; (reduced price) réduction
f; **tax ~** dégrèvement fiscal; **"~s"** tarif
réduit
concise [kən'saɪs] adj concis(e)
conclude [kən'klu:d] vt conclure;
conclusion [kən'klu:ʒən] n
conclusion f
concrete ['kɒŋkri:t] n béton m ▷ adj
concret(-ète); (Constr) en béton
concussion [kən'kʌʃən] n (Med)
commotion (cérébrale)
condemn [kən'dɛm] vt condamner
condensation [kɒndɛn'seɪʃən] n
condensation f
condense [kən'dɛns] vi se condenser

▷ vt condenser

condition [kənˈdɪʃən] n condition f; (disease) maladie f ▷ vt déterminer, conditionner; **on ~ that** à condition que + sub, à condition que; **conditional** [kənˈdɪʃənl] adj conditionnel(le); **conditioner** n (for hair) baume démêlant; (for fabrics) assouplissant m

condo [ˈkɒndəu] n (us inf) = **condominium**

condom [ˈkɒndəm] n préservatif m

condominium [kɒndəˈmɪnɪəm] n (us: building) immeuble m (en copropriété); (: rooms) appartement m (dans un immeuble en copropriété)

condone [kənˈdəun] vt fermer les yeux sur, approuver (tacitement)

conduct n [ˈkɒndʌkt] conduite f ▷ vt [kənˈdʌkt] conduire; (manage) mener, diriger; (Mus) diriger; **to ~ o.s.** se conduire, se comporter; **conducted tour** (BRIT) n voyage organisé; (of building) visite guidée; **conductor** n (of orchestra) chef m d'orchestre; (on bus) receveur m; (us: on train) chef m de train; (Elec) conducteur m

cone [kəun] n cône m; (for ice-cream) cornet m; (Bot) pomme f de pin, cône

confectionery [kənˈfekʃənrɪ] n (sweets) confiserie f

confer [kənˈfɜː*] vt: **to ~ sth on** conférer qch à ▷ vi conférer, s'entretenir

conference [ˈkɒnfərns] n conférence f

confess [kənˈfes] vt confesser, avouer ▷ vi (admit sth) avouer; (Rel) se confesser; **confession** [kənˈfeʃən] n confession f

confide [kənˈfaɪd] vi: **to ~ in** s'ouvrir à, se confier à

confidence [ˈkɒnfɪdns] n confiance f; (also: **self-~**) assurance f, confiance en soi; (secret) confidence f; **in ~ (speak, write)** en confidence, confidentiellement; **confident** adj (self-assured) sûr(e) de soi; (sure) sûr(e); **confidential** [kɒnfɪˈdenʃəl] adj confidentiel(le)

confine [kənˈfaɪn] vt limiter, borner;

(shut up) confiner, enfermer; **confined** adj (space) restreint(e), réduit(e)

confirm [kənˈfɜːm] vt (report, Rel) confirmer; (appointment) ratifier; **confirmation** [kɒnfəˈmeɪʃən] n confirmation f; ratification f

confiscate [ˈkɒnfɪskeɪt] vt confisquer

conflict n [ˈkɒnflɪkt] conflit m, lutte f ▷ vi [kənˈflɪkt] (opinions) s'opposer, se heurter

conform [kənˈfɔːm] vi: **to ~ (to)** se conformer (à)

confront [kənˈfrʌnt] vt (two people) confronter; (enemy, danger) affronter, faire face à; (problem) faire face à; **confrontation** [kɒnfrənˈteɪʃən] n confrontation f

confuse [kənˈfjuːz] vt (person) troubler; (situation) embrouiller; (one thing with another) confondre; **confused** adj (person) dérouté(e), désorienté(e); (situation) embrouillé(e); **confusing** adj peu clair(e), déroutant(e); **confusion** [kənˈfjuːʒən] n confusion f

congestion [kənˈdʒestʃən] n (Med) congestion f; (fig: traffic) encombrement m

congratulate [kənˈgrætjuleɪt] vt: **to ~ sb (on)** féliciter qn (de); **congratulations** [kəngrætjuˈleɪʃənz] npl: **congratulations (on)** félicitations fpl (pour) ▷ excl: **congratulations!** (toutes mes) félicitations!

congregation [kɒngrɪˈgeɪʃən] n assemblée f (des fidèles)

congress [ˈkɒngres] n congrès m; (Pol): **C~** Congrès m; **congressman** n membre m du Congrès; **congresswoman** n membre m du Congrès

conifer [ˈkɒnɪfə*] n conifère m

conjugate [ˈkɒndʒugeɪt] vt conjuguer

conjugation [kɒndʒəˈgeɪʃən] n conjugaison f

conjunction [kənˈdʒʌŋkʃən] n conjonction f; **in ~ with** avec (conjointement) avec

conjure [ˈkʌndʒə*] vi faire des tours de

passe-passe

connect [kəˈnɛkt] vt joindre, relier;
(Elec) connecter; (Tel: caller) mettre
en connexion; (: subscriber) brancher;
(fig) établir un rapport entre, faire un
rapprochement entre ▷ vi (train): **to ~
with** assurer la correspondance avec;
to be ~ed with avoir un rapport avec;
(have dealings with) avoir des rapports
avec, être en relation avec; **connecting
flight** n (vol m de) correspondance
f; **connection** [kəˈnɛkʃən] n
relation f, lien m; (Elec) connexion
f; (Tel) communication f; (train etc)
correspondance f

conquer [ˈkɔŋkəʳ] vt conquérir;
(feelings) vaincre, surmonter

conquest [ˈkɔŋkwɛst] n conquête f

cons [kɔnz] npl see **convenience**; **pro**

conscience [ˈkɔnʃəns] n conscience f

conscientious [kɔnʃɪˈɛnʃəs] adj
consciencieux(-euse)

conscious [ˈkɔnʃəs] adj conscient(e);
(deliberate: insult, error) délibéré(e);
consciousness n conscience f; (Med)
connaissance f

consecutive [kənˈsɛkjutɪv] adj
consécutif(-ive); **on three ~ occasions**
trois fois de suite

consensus [kənˈsɛnsəs] n
consensus m

consent [kənˈsɛnt] n consentement m
▷ vi: **to ~ (to)** consentir (à)

consequence [ˈkɔnsɪkwəns] n
suites fpl, conséquence f; (significance)
importance f

consequently [ˈkɔnsɪkwəntlɪ] adv
par conséquent, donc

conservation [kɔnsəˈveɪʃən] n
préservation f, protection f; (also:
nature ~) défense f de l'environnement

conservative [kənˈsəːvətɪv] adj
conservateur(-trice); (cautious)
prudent(e); **Conservative** adj, n (BRIT
Pol) conservateur(-trice)

conservatory [kənˈsəːvətrɪ] n (room)
jardin m d'hiver; (Mus) conservatoire m

consider [kənˈsɪdəʳ] vt (study)

considérer, réfléchir à; (take into
account) penser à, prendre en
considération; (regard, judge)
considérer, estimer; **to ~ doing sth**
envisager de faire qch; **considerable**
adj considérable; **considerably**
adv nettement; **considerate** adj
prévenant(e), plein(e) d'égards;
consideration [kənsɪdəˈreɪʃən] n
considération f; (reward) rétribution
f, rémunération f; **considering** prep:
considering (that) étant donné (que)

consignment [kənˈsaɪnmənt] n
arrivage m, envoi m

consist [kənˈsɪst] vi: **to ~ of** consister
en, se composer de

consistency [kənˈsɪstənsɪ] n
(thickness) consistance f; (fig)
cohérence f

consistent [kənˈsɪstənt] adj logique,
cohérent(e)

consolation [kɔnsəˈleɪʃən] n
consolation f

console¹ [kənˈsəul] vt consoler

console² [ˈkɔnsəul] n console f

consonant [ˈkɔnsənənt] n consonne f

conspicuous [kənˈspɪkjuəs] adj
voyant(e), qui attire l'attention

conspiracy [kənˈspɪrəsɪ] n
conspiration f, complot m

constable [ˈkʌnstəbl] n (BRIT) ≈ agent
m de police, gendarme m; **chief ~**
≈ préfet m de police

constant [ˈkɔnstənt] adj constant(e);
incessant(e); **constantly** adv
constamment, sans cesse

constipated [ˈkɔnstɪpeɪtɪd]
adj constipé(e); **constipation**
[kɔnstɪˈpeɪʃən] n constipation f

constituency [kənˈstɪtjuənsɪ] n (Pol:
area) circonscription électorale;
(: electors) électorat m

constitute [ˈkɔnstɪtjuːt] vt constituer

constitution [kɔnstɪˈtjuːʃən] n
constitution f

constraint [kənˈstreɪnt] n contrainte f

construct [kənˈstrʌkt] vt construire;
construction [kənˈstrʌkʃən] n

construction f; **constructive** adj
constructif(-ive)

consul ['kɒnsl] n consul m; **consulate**
['kɒnsjulɪt] n consulat m

consult [kən'sʌlt] vt consulter;
consultant n (Med) médecin
consultant; (other specialist) consultant
m, (expert-)conseil m; **consultation**
[kɒnsəl'teɪʃən] n consultation f;
consulting room n (BRIT) cabinet m de
consultation

consume [kən'sju:m] vt consommer;
(subj: flames, hatred, desire) consumer;
consumer n consommateur(-trice)

consumption [kən'sʌmpʃən] n
consommation f

cont. abbr (= continued) suite

contact ['kɒntækt] n contact m;
(person) connaissance f, relation f ▷ vt
se mettre en contact or en rapport
avec; **contact lenses** npl verres mpl
de contact

contagious [kən'teɪdʒəs] adj
contagieux(-euse)

contain [kən'teɪn] vt contenir;
to ~ o.s. se contenir, se maîtriser;
container n récipient m; (for shipping
etc) conteneur m

contaminate [kən'tæmɪneɪt] vt
contaminer

cont'd abbr (= continued) suite

contemplate ['kɒntəmpleɪt] vt
contempler; (consider) envisager

contemporary [kən'tempərərɪ] adj
contemporain(e); (design, wallpaper)
moderne ▷ n contemporain(e)

contempt [kən'tempt] n mépris m,
dédain m; **~ of court** (Law) outrage m à
l'autorité de la justice

contend [kən'tend] vt: **to ~ that**
soutenir or prétendre que ▷ vi: **to ~
with** (compete) rivaliser avec; (struggle)
lutter avec

content [kən'tent] adj content(e),
satisfait(e) ▷ vt contenter, satisfaire
▷ n ['kɒntent] contenu m; (of fat,
moisture) teneur f; **contents** npl (of
container etc) contenu m; **(table of) ~s**

table f des matières; **contented** adj
content(e), satisfait(e)

contest n ['kɒntest] combat m, lutte f;
(competition) concours m ▷ vt [kən'test]
contester, discuter; (compete for)
disputer; (Law) attaquer; **contestant**
[kən'testənt] n concurrent(e); (in fight)
adversaire m/f

context ['kɒntekst] n contexte m

continent ['kɒntɪnənt] n continent
m; **the C~** (BRIT) l'Europe continentale;
continental [kɒntɪ'nentl] adj
continental(e); **continental breakfast**
n café (or thé) complet; **continental
quilt** n (BRIT) couette f

continual [kən'tɪnjuəl] adj
continuel(le); **continually** adv
continuellement, sans cesse

continue [kən'tɪnju:] vi continuer ▷ vt
continuer; (start again) reprendre

continuity [kɒntɪ'nju:ɪtɪ] n continuité
f; (TV etc) enchaînement m

continuous [kən'tɪnjuəs] adj
continu(e), permanent(e); (Ling)
progressif(-ive); **continuous
assessment** (BRIT) n contrôle
continu; **continuously** adv (repeatedly)
continuellement; (uninterruptedly) sans
interruption

contour ['kɒntuə'] n contour m, profil
m; (also: **~ line**) courbe f de niveau

contraception [kɒntrə'sepʃən] n
contraception f

contraceptive [kɒntrə'septɪv]
adj contraceptif(-ive),
anticonceptionnel(le) ▷ n
contraceptif m

contract n ['kɒntrækt] contrat m ▷ vb
[kən'trækt] ▷ vi (become smaller) se
contracter, se resserrer ▷ vt contracter;
(Comm): **to ~ to do sth** s'engager (par
contrat) à faire qch; **contractor** n
entrepreneur m

contradict [kɒntrə'dɪkt] vt contredire;
contradiction [kɒntrə'dɪkʃən] n
contradiction f

contrary[1] ['kɒntrərɪ] adj contraire,
opposé(e) ▷ n contraire m; **on the ~** au

contraire; **unless you hear to the ~**
sauf avis contraire

contrary² [kən'trɛəri] adj (perverse)
contrariant(e), entêté(e)

contrast n ['kɒntrɑːst] contraste
m ▷ vt [kən'trɑːst] mettre en
contraste, contraster; **in ~ to** or **with**
contrairement à, par opposition à

contribute [kən'trɪbjuːt] vi
contribuer ▷ vt: **to ~ £10/an article
to** donner 10 livres/un article à; **to
~ to** (gen) contribuer à; (newspaper)
collaborer à; (discussion) prendre part
à; **contribution** [kɒntrɪ'bjuːʃən]
n contribution f; (for social
security) cotisation f; (to publication)
article m; **contributor** n (to newspaper)
collaborateur(-trice); (of money, goods)
donateur(-trice)

control [kən'trəul] vt (process,
machinery) commander; (temper)
maîtriser; (disease) enrayer ▷ n
maîtrise f; (power) autorité f; **controls**
npl (of machine etc) commandes fpl;
(on radio) boutons mpl de réglage; **to
be in ~ of** être maître de, maîtriser;
(in charge of) être responsable de;
everything is under ~ j'ai (or il a etc) la
situation en main; **the car went out
of ~** j'ai (or il a etc) perdu le contrôle du
véhicule; **control tower** n (Aviat) tour
f de contrôle

controversial [kɒntrə'vəːʃl] adj
discutable, controversé(e)

controversy ['kɒntrəvəːsi] n
controverse f, polémique f

convenience [kən'viːniəns] n
commodité f; **at your ~** quand or
comme cela vous convient; **all modern
~s, all mod cons** (BRIT) avec tout le
confort moderne, tout confort

convenient [kən'viːniənt] adj
commode

convent ['kɒnvənt] n couvent m

convention [kən'vɛnʃən] n
convention f; (custom) usage m;
conventional adj conventionnel(le)

conversation [kɒnvə'seɪʃən] n

conversation f

conversely [kɒn'vəːsli] adv
inversement, réciproquement

conversion [kən'vəːʃən] n conversion
f; (BRIT: of house) transformation
f, aménagement m; (Rugby)
transformation f

convert vt [kən'vəːt] (Rel, Comm)
convertir; (alter) transformer; (house)
aménager ▷ n ['kɒnvəːt] converti(e);
convertible adj convertible ▷ n
(voiture f) décapotable f

convey [kən'veɪ] vt transporter;
(thanks) transmettre; (idea)
communiquer; **conveyor belt** n
convoyeur m tapis roulant

convict vt [kən'vɪkt] déclarer (or
reconnaître) coupable ▷ n ['kɒnvɪkt]
forçat m, convict m; **conviction**
[kən'vɪkʃən] n (Law) condamnation f;
(belief) conviction f

convince [kən'vɪns] vt convaincre,
persuader; **convinced** adj: **convinced
of/that** convaincu(e) de/que;
convincing adj persuasif(-ive),
convaincant(e)

convoy ['kɒnvɔɪ] n convoi m

cook [kuk] vt (faire) cuire ▷ vi
cuire; (person) faire la cuisine ▷ n
cuisinier(-ière); **cookbook** n livre m de
cuisine; **cooker** n cuisinière f; **cookery**
n cuisine f; **cookery book** (BRIT)
= **cookbook**; **cookie** n (us) biscuit m,
petit gâteau sec; **cooking** n cuisine f

cool [kuːl] adj frais (fraîche); (not afraid)
calme; (unfriendly) froid(e); (inf: trendy)
cool inv (inf); (: great) super inv (inf)
▷ vt, vi rafraîchir, refroidir; **cool down**
vi refroidir; (fig: person, situation) se
calmer; **cool off** vi (become calmer) se
calmer; (lose enthusiasm) perdre son
enthousiasme

cop [kɒp] n (inf) flic m

cope [kəup] vi s'en sortir, tenir le coup;
to ~ with (problem) faire face à

copper ['kɒpə'] n cuivre m; (BRIT: inf:
policeman) flic m

copy ['kɒpi] n copie f; (book etc)

exemplaire m ▷ vt copier; (imitate) imiter; **copyright** n droit m d'auteur, copyright m

coral ['kɒrəl] n corail m

cord [kɔːd] n corde f; (fabric) velours côtelé; (Elec) cordon m (d'alimentation), fil m (électrique); **cordless** adj sans fil

corduroy ['kɔːdərɔɪ] n velours côtelé

core [kɔːʳ] n (of fruit) trognon m, cœur m; (fig: of problem etc) cœur m ▷ vt enlever le trognon or le cœur de

coriander [kɒrɪ'ændəʳ] n coriandre f

cork [kɔːk] n (material) liège m; (of bottle) bouchon m; **corkscrew** n tire-bouchon m

corn [kɔːn] n (Brit: wheat) blé m; (us: maize) maïs m; (on foot) cor m; **~ on the cob** (Culin) épi m de maïs au naturel

corned beef ['kɔːnd-] n corned-beef m

corner ['kɔːnəʳ] n coin m; (in road) tournant m, virage m; (Football) corner m ▷ vt (trap: prey) acculer; (fig) coincer; (Comm: market) accaparer ▷ vi prendre un virage; **corner shop** (Brit) n magasin m du coin

cornflakes ['kɔːnfleɪks] npl cornflakes mpl

cornflour ['kɔːnflauəʳ] n (Brit) farine f de maïs, maïzena f ®

cornstarch ['kɔːnstɑːtʃ] n (us) farine f de maïs, maïzena f ®

Cornwall ['kɔːnwəl] n Cornouailles f

coronary ['kɒrənərɪ] n: **~ (thrombosis)** infarctus m (du myocarde), thrombose f coronaire

coronation [kɒrə'neɪʃən] n couronnement m

coroner ['kɒrənəʳ] n coroner m, officier de police judiciaire chargé de déterminer les causes d'un décès

corporal ['kɔːpərl] n caporal m, brigadier m ▷ adj: **~ punishment** châtiment corporel

corporate ['kɔːpərɪt] adj (action, ownership) en commun; (Comm) de la société

corporation [kɔːpə'reɪʃən] n (of town) municipalité f, conseil municipal; (Comm) société f

corps [kɔːʳ, pl kɔːz] n corps m; **the diplomatic ~** le corps diplomatique; **the press ~** la presse

corpse [kɔːps] n cadavre m

correct [kə'rɛkt] adj (accurate) correct(e), exact(e); (proper) correct, convenable ▷ vt corriger; **correction** [kə'rɛkʃən] n correction f

correspond [kɒrɪs'pɒnd] vi correspondre; **to ~ to sth** (be equivalent to) correspondre à qch; **correspondence** n correspondance f; **correspondent** n correspondant(e); **corresponding** adj correspondant(e)

corridor ['kɒrɪdɔːʳ] n couloir m, corridor m

corrode [kə'rəud] vt corroder, ronger ▷ vi se corroder

corrupt [kə'rʌpt] adj corrompu(e); (Comput) altéré(e) ▷ vt corrompre; (Comput) altérer; **corruption** n corruption f; (Comput) altération f (de données)

Corsica ['kɔːsɪkə] n Corse f

cosmetic [kɒz'mɛtɪk] n produit m de beauté, cosmétique m ▷ adj (fig: reforms) symbolique, superficiel(le); **cosmetic surgery** n chirurgie f esthétique

cosmopolitan [kɒzmə'pɒlɪtən] adj cosmopolite

cost [kɒst] n coût m ▷ vb (pt, pp ~) ▷ vi coûter ▷ vt établir or calculer le prix de revient de; **costs** npl (Comm) frais mpl; (Law) dépens mpl; **how much does it ~?** combien ça coûte?; **to ~ sb time/effort** demander du temps/un effort à qn; **it ~ him his life/job** ça lui a coûté la vie/son emploi; **at all ~s** coûte que coûte, à tout prix

co-star ['kəustɑːʳ] n partenaire m/f

costly ['kɒstlɪ] adj coûteux(-euse)

cost of living n coût m de la vie

costume ['kɒstjuːm] n costume m; (Brit: also: **swimming ~**) maillot m

(de bain)

cosy (us **cozy**) ['kəʊzɪ] adj (room, bed) douillet(te); **to be ~** (person) être bien (au chaud)

cot [kɒt] n (BRIT: child's) lit m d'enfant, petit lit; (us: campbed) lit de camp

cottage ['kɒtɪdʒ] n petite maison à la campagne, cottage m; **cottage cheese** n fromage blanc (maigre)

cotton ['kɒtn] n coton m; (thread) fil m (de coton); **cotton on** vi (inf): **to ~ (on (to sth))** piger (qch); **cotton bud** (BRIT) n coton-tige ® m; **cotton candy** (us) n barbe f à papa; **cotton wool** (BRIT) n ouate f, coton m hydrophile

couch [kautʃ] n canapé m; divan m

cough [kɒf] vi tousser ▷ n toux f; **I've got a ~** j'ai la toux; **cough mixture, cough syrup** n sirop m pour la toux

could [kʊd] pt of **can**²; **couldn't** = **could not**

council ['kaunsl] n conseil m; **city or town ~** conseil municipal; **council estate** n (BRIT) (quartier m or zone f de) logements loués à/par la municipalité; **council house** n (BRIT) maison f (à loyer modéré) louée par la municipalité; **councillor** n (us **councilor**) conseiller(-ère); **council tax** n (BRIT) impôts locaux

counsel ['kaunsl] n conseil m; (lawyer) avocat(e) ▷ vt: **to ~ (sb to do sth)** conseiller (à qn de faire qch); **counselling** (us **counseling**) n (Psych) aide psychosociale; **counsellor** (us **counselor**) n conseiller(-ère); (us Law) avocat m

count [kaunt] vt, vi compter ▷ n compte m; (nobleman) comte m; **count in** vt (inf): **to ~ sb in on sth** inclure qn dans qch; **count on** vt fus compter sur; **countdown** n compte m à rebours

counter ['kauntə'] n comptoir m; (in post office, bank) guichet m; (in game) jeton m ▷ vt aller à l'encontre de, opposer ▷ adv: **to ~ to** à l'encontre de; contrairement à; **counterclockwise** (us) adv en sens inverse des aiguilles

d'une montre

counterfeit ['kauntəfɪt] n faux m, contrefaçon f ▷ vt contrefaire ▷ adj faux(fausse)

counterpart ['kauntəpɑːt] n (of person) homologue m/f

countess ['kauntɪs] n comtesse f

countless ['kauntlɪs] adj innombrable

country ['kʌntrɪ] n pays m; (native land) patrie f; (as opposed to town) campagne f; (region) région f, pays; **country and western (music)** n musique f country; **country house** n manoir m, (petit) château; **countryside** n campagne f

county ['kauntɪ] n comté m

coup [kuː, pl kuːz] n (achievement) beau coup; (also: ~ **d'état**) coup d'État

couple ['kʌpl] n couple m; **a ~ of** (two) deux; (a few) deux ou trois

coupon ['kuːpɒn] n (voucher) bon m de réduction; (detachable form) coupon m détachable, coupon-réponse m

courage ['kʌrɪdʒ] n courage m; **courageous** [kə'reɪdʒəs] adj courageux(-euse)

courgette [kuə'ʒet] n (BRIT) courgette f

courier ['kurɪə'] n messager m, courrier m; (for tourists) accompagnateur(-trice)

course [kɔːs] n cours m; (of ship) route f; (for golf) terrain m; (part of meal) plat m; **of ~** adv bien sûr; **(no,) of ~ not!** bien sûr que non!, évidemment que non!; **~ of treatment** (Med) traitement m

court [kɔːt] n cour f; (Law) cour, tribunal m; (Tennis) court m ▷ vt (woman) courtiser, faire la cour à; **to take ~** actionner or poursuivre en justice

courtesy ['kəːtəsɪ] n courtoisie f, politesse f; **(by) ~ of** avec l'aimable autorisation de; **courtesy bus, courtesy coach** n navette gratuite

court: **court-house** ['kɔːthaus] n (us) palais m de justice; **courtroom** ['kɔːtrum] n salle f de tribunal; **courtyard** ['kɔːtjɑːd] n cour f

cousin ['kʌzn] n cousin(e); **first ~** cousin(e) germain(e)

cover ['kʌvə'] vt couvrir; (Press: report

on) faire un reportage sur; (feelings, mistake) cacher; (include) englober; (discuss) traiter ▷ n (of book, Comm) couverture f; (of pan) couvercle m; (over furniture) housse f; (shelter) abri m; **covers** npl (on bed) couvertures fpl; **to take ~** se mettre à l'abri; **under ~** à l'abri; **under ~ of darkness** à la faveur de la nuit; **under separate ~** (Comm) sous pli séparé; **cover up** vi: **to ~ up for sb** (fig) couvrir qn; **coverage** n (in media) reportage m; **cover charge** n couvert m (supplément à payer); **cover-up** n tentative f pour étouffer une affaire

cow [kau] n vache f ▷ vt effrayer, intimider

coward ['kauəd] n lâche m/f; **cowardly** adj lâche

cowboy ['kaubɔɪ] n cow-boy m

cozy ['kəuzɪ] adj (US) = **cosy**

crab [kræb] n crabe m

crack [kræk] n (split) fente f, fissure f; (in cup, bone) fêlure f; (in wall) lézarde f; (noise) craquement m, coup (sec); (Drugs) crack m ▷ vt fendre, fissurer; fêler; lézarder; (whip) faire claquer; (nut) casser; (problem) résoudre; (code) déchiffrer ▷ cpd (athlete) de première classe, d'élite; **crack down on** vt fus (crime) sévir contre, réprimer; **cracked** adj (cup, bone) fêlé(e); (broken) cassé(e); (wall) lézardé(e); (surface) craquelé(e); (inf) toqué(e), timbré(e); **cracker** n (also: **Christmas cracker**) pétard m; (biscuit) biscuit (salé), craquelin m

crackle ['krækl] vi crépiter, grésiller

cradle ['kreɪdl] n berceau m

craft [krɑːft] n métier (artisanal); (cunning) ruse f, astuce f; (boat: pl inv) embarcation f, barque f; (plane: pl inv) appareil m; **craftsman** (irreg) n artisan m, ouvrier (qualifié); **craftsmanship** n métier m, habileté f

cram [kræm] vt (fill): **to ~ sth with** bourrer qch de; (put): **to ~ sth into** fourrer qch dans ▷ vi (for exams) bachoter

cramp [kræmp] n crampe f; **I've got ~ in my leg** j'ai une crampe à la jambe; **cramped** adj à l'étroit, très serré(e)

cranberry ['krænbərɪ] n canneberge f

crane [kreɪn] n grue f

crap [kræp] n (inf: nonsense) conneries fpl (!); (: excrement) merde f (!)

crash [kræʃ] n (noise) fracas m; (of car, plane) collision f; (of business) faillite f ▷ vt (plane) écraser ▷ vi (plane) s'écraser; (two cars) se percuter, s'emboutir; (business) s'effondrer; **to ~ into** se jeter or se fracasser contre; **crash course** n cours intensif; **crash helmet** n casque (protecteur)

crate [kreɪt] n cageot m; (for bottles) caisse f

crave [kreɪv] vt, vi: **to ~ (for)** avoir une envie irrésistible de

crawl [krɔːl] vi ramper; (vehicle) avancer au pas ▷ n (Swimming) crawl m

crayfish ['kreɪfɪʃ] n (pl inv: freshwater) écrevisse f; (saltwater) langoustine f

crayon ['kreɪən] n crayon m (de couleur)

craze [kreɪz] n engouement m

crazy ['kreɪzɪ] adj fou (folle); **to be ~ about sb/sth** (inf) être fou de qn/qch

creak [kriːk] vi (hinge) grincer; (floor, shoes) craquer

cream [kriːm] n crème f ▷ adj (colour) crème inv; **cream cheese** n fromage m à la crème, fromage blanc; **creamy** adj crémeux(-euse)

crease [kriːs] n pli m ▷ vt froisser, chiffonner ▷ vi se froisser, se chiffonner

create [kriː'eɪt] vt créer; **creation** [kriː'eɪʃən] n création f; **creative** adj créatif(-ive); **creator** n créateur(-trice)

creature ['kriːtʃər] n créature f

crèche [krɛʃ] n garderie f, crèche f

credentials [krɪ'dɛnʃlz] npl (references) références fpl; (identity papers) pièce f d'identité

credibility [krɛdɪ'bɪlɪtɪ] n crédibilité f

credible ['krɛdɪbl] adj digne de foi, crédible

credit ['krɛdɪt] n crédit m; (recognition)

honneur m; (Scol) unité f de valeur ▷ vt (Comm) créditer; (believe: also: **give ~ to**) ajouter foi à, croire; **credits** npl (Cine) générique m; **to be in ~** (person, bank account) être créditeur(-trice); **to ~ sb with** (fig) prêter or attribuer à qn; **credit card** n carte f de crédit; **do you take credit cards?** acceptez-vous les cartes de crédit?

creek [kriːk] n (inlet) crique f, anse f; (us: stream) ruisseau m, petit cours d'eau

creep (pt, pp **crept**) [kriːp, krɛpt] vi ramper

cremate [krɪˈmeɪt] vt incinérer

crematorium (pl **crematoria**) [krɛməˈtɔːrɪəm, -ˈtɔːrɪə] n four m crématoire

crept [krɛpt] pt, pp of **creep**

crescent [ˈkrɛsnt] n croissant m; (street) rue f (en arc de cercle)

cress [krɛs] n cresson m

crest [krɛst] n crête f; (of coat of arms) timbre m

crew [kruː] n équipage m; (Cine) équipe f (de tournage); **crew-neck** n col ras

crib [krɪb] n lit m d'enfant; (for baby) berceau m ▷ vt (inf) copier

cricket [ˈkrɪkɪt] n (insect) grillon m, cri-cri m inv; (game) cricket m; **cricketer** n joueur m de cricket

crime [kraɪm] n crime m; **criminal** [ˈkrɪmɪnl] adj, n criminel(le)

crimson [ˈkrɪmzn] adj cramoisi(e)

cringe [krɪndʒ] vi avoir un mouvement de recul

cripple [ˈkrɪpl] n boiteux(-euse), infirme m/f ▷ vt (person) estropier, paralyser; (ship, plane) immobiliser; (production, exports) paralyser

crisis (pl **crises**) [ˈkraɪsɪs, -siːz] n crise f

crisp [krɪsp] adj croquant(e), craquant(e); (weather) vif (vive); (manner etc) brusque; **crisps** (brit) npl (pommes fpl) chips fpl; **crispy** adj croustillant(e)

criterion (pl **criteria**) [kraɪˈtɪərɪən, -ˈtɪərɪə] n critère m

critic [ˈkrɪtɪk] n critique m/f; **critical** adj critique; **criticism** [ˈkrɪtɪsɪzəm]

n critique f; **criticize** [ˈkrɪtɪsaɪz] vt critiquer

Croat [ˈkrəuæt] adj, n = **Croatian**

Croatia [krəuˈeɪʃə] n Croatie f; **Croatian** adj croate ▷ n Croate m/f; (Ling) croate m

crockery [ˈkrɔkərɪ] n vaisselle f

crocodile [ˈkrɔkədaɪl] n crocodile m

crocus [ˈkrəukəs] n crocus m

croissant [ˈkrwasɑ̃] n croissant m

crook [kruk] n escroc m; (of shepherd) houlette f; **crooked** [ˈkrukɪd] adj courbé(e), tordu(e); (action) malhonnête

crop [krɔp] n (produce) culture f; (amount produced) récolte f; (riding crop) cravache f ▷ vt (hair) tondre; **crop up** vi surgir, se présenter, survenir

cross [krɔs] n croix f; (Biol) croisement m ▷ vt (street also) traverser; (arms, legs, Biol) croiser; (cheque) barrer ▷ adj en colère, fâché(e); **cross off** or **out** vt barrer, rayer; **cross over** vi traverser; **cross-Channel ferry** [ˈkrɔsˈtʃænl-] n ferry m qui fait la traversée de la Manche; **crosscountry (race)** n cross (-country)-m; **crossing** n (sea passage) traversée f; (also: **pedestrian crossing**) passage clouté; **how long does the crossing take?** combien de temps dure la traversée?; **crossing guard** (us) n contractuel qui fait traverser la rue aux enfants; **crossroads** n carrefour m; **crosswalk** n (us) passage clouté; **crossword** n mots mpl croisés

crotch [krɔtʃ] n (of garment) entrejambe m; (Anat) entrecuisse m

crouch [krautʃ] vi s'accroupir; (hide) se tapir; (before springing) se ramasser

crouton [ˈkruːtɔn] n croûton m

crow [krəu] n (bird) corneille f; (of cock) chant du coq, cocorico m ▷ vi (cock) chanter

crowd [kraud] n foule f ▷ vt bourrer, remplir ▷ vi affluer, s'attrouper, s'entasser; **crowded** adj bondé(e), plein(e)

crown [kraun] n couronne f; (of head)

sommet *m* de la tête; (*of hill*) sommet *m* ▷ vt (*also tooth*) couronner; **crown jewels** *npl* joyaux *mpl* de la Couronne

crucial ['kru:ʃl] *adj* crucial(e), décisif(-ive)

crucifix ['kru:sɪfɪks] *n* crucifix *m*

crude [kru:d] *adj* (*materials*) brut(e); non raffiné(e); (*basic*) rudimentaire, sommaire; (*vulgar*) cru(e), grossier(-ière); **crude (oil)** *n* (pétrole) brut *m*

cruel ['kruəl] *adj* cruel(le); **cruelty** *n* cruauté *f*

cruise [kru:z] *n* croisière *f* ▷ vi (*ship*) croiser; (*car*) rouler; (*aircraft*) voler

crumb [krʌm] *n* miette *f*

crumble ['krʌmbl] *vt* émietter ▷ vi (*plaster etc*) s'effriter; (*land, earth*) s'ébouler; (*building*) s'écrouler, crouler; (*fig*) s'effondrer

crumpet ['krʌmpɪt] *n* petite crêpe (épaisse)

crumple ['krʌmpl] *vt* froisser, friper

crunch [krʌntʃ] *vt* croquer; (*underfoot*) faire craquer, écraser; faire crisser ▷ *n* (*fig*) instant *m* or moment *m* critique, moment *m* de vérité; **crunchy** *adj* croquant(e), croustillant(e)

crush [krʌʃ] *n* (*crowd*) foule *f*, cohue *f*; (*love*): **to have a ~ on sb** avoir le béguin pour qn; (*drink*): **lemon ~** citron pressé ▷ vt écraser; (*crumple*) froisser; (*grind, break up*): garlic, ice) piler; (: *grapes*) presser; (*hopes*) anéantir

crust [krʌst] *n* croûte *f*; **crusty** *adj* (*bread*) croustillant(e); (*inf*: *person*) revêche, bourru(e)

crutch [krʌtʃ] *n* béquille *f*; (*also*: **crotch**) entrejambe *m*

cry [kraɪ] *vi* pleurer; (*shout*: *also*: **~ out**) crier ▷ *n* cri *m*; **cry out** *vi* (*call out, shout*) pousser un cri ▷ vt crier

crystal ['krɪstl] *n* cristal *m*

cub [kʌb] *n* petit *m* (d'un animal); (*also*: **~ scout**) louveteau *m*

Cuba ['kju:bə] *n* Cuba *m*

cube [kju:b] *n* cube *m* ▷ vt (*Math*) élever au cube

cubicle ['kju:bɪkl] *n* (*in hospital*) box *m*; (*at pool*) cabine *f*

cuckoo ['kuku:] *n* coucou *m*

cucumber ['kju:kʌmbə'] *n* concombre *m*

cuddle ['kʌdl] *vt* câliner, caresser ▷ vi se blottir l'un contre l'autre

cue [kju:] *n* queue *f* de billard; (*Theat etc*) signal *m*

cuff [kʌf] *n* (BRIT: *of shirt, coat etc*) poignet *m*, manchette *f*; (*US*: *on trousers*) revers *m*; (*blow*) gifle *f*; **off the ~** *adv* à l'improviste; **cufflinks** *n* boutons *m* de manchette

cuisine [kwɪˈziːn] *n* cuisine *f*

cul-de-sac ['kʌldəsæk] *n* cul-de-sac *m*, impasse *f*

cull [kʌl] *vt* sélectionner ▷ *n* (*of animals*) abattage sélectif

culminate ['kʌlmɪneɪt] *vi*: **to ~ in** finir or se terminer par; (*lead to*) mener à

culprit ['kʌlprɪt] *n* coupable *m/f*

cult [kʌlt] *n* culte *m*

cultivate ['kʌltɪveɪt] *vt* cultiver

cultural ['kʌltʃərəl] *adj* culturel(le)

culture ['kʌltʃə'] *n* culture *f*

cumin ['kʌmɪn] *n* (*spice*) cumin *m*

cunning ['kʌnɪŋ] *n* ruse *f*, astuce *f* ▷ *adj* rusé(e), malin(-igne); (*clever*: *device, idea*) astucieux(-euse)

cup [kʌp] *n* tasse *f*; (*prize, event*) coupe *f*; (*of bra*) bonnet *m*

cupboard ['kʌbəd] *n* placard *m*

cup final *n* (BRIT *Football*) finale *f* de la coupe

curator [kjuə'reɪtə'] *n* conservateur *m* (d'un musée etc)

curb [kɜ:b] *vt* refréner, mettre un frein à ▷ *n* (*fig*) frein *m*; (*US*) bord *m* du trottoir

curdle [kɜ:dl] *vi* (se) cailler

cure [kjuə'] *vt* guérir; (*Culin*: salt) saler; (: *smoke*) fumer; (: *dry*) sécher ▷ *n* remède *m*

curfew ['kɜːfjuː] *n* couvre-feu *m*

curiosity [kjuərɪˈɔsɪtɪ] *n* curiosité *f*

curious ['kjuərɪəs] *adj* curieux(-euse); **I'm ~ about him** il m'intrigue

curl [kɜːl] *n* boucle *f* (de cheveux) ▷ vt,

vi boucler; (*tightly*) friser; **curl up** *vi* s'enrouler; (*person*) se pelotonner; **curler** *n* bigoudi *m*, rouleau *m*; **curly** *adj* bouclé(e); (*tightly curled*) frisé(e)

currant ['kʌrnt] *n* raisin *m* de Corinthe, raisin sec; (*fruit*) groseille *f*

currency ['kʌrnsɪ] *n* monnaie *f*; **to gain ~** (*fig*) s'accréditer

current ['kʌrnt] *n* courant *m* ▷ *adj* (*common*) courant(e); (*tendency, price, event*) actuel(le); **current account** *n* (BRIT) compte courant; **current affairs** *npl* (questions *fpl* d')actualité *f*; **currently** *adv* actuellement

curriculum (*pl* **-s** *or* **curricula** [kə'rɪkjuləm, -lə] *n* programme *m* d'études; **curriculum vitae** [-'viːtaɪ] *n* curriculum vitae (CV) *m*

curry ['kʌrɪ] *n* curry *m* ▷ *vt*: **to ~ favour with** chercher à gagner la faveur or à s'attirer les bonnes grâces de; **curry powder** *n* poudre *f* de curry

curse [kəːs] *vi* jurer, blasphémer ▷ *vt* maudire ▷ *n* (*spell*) malédiction *f*; (*problem, scourge*) fléau *m*; (*swearword*) juron *m*

cursor ['kəːsə*ʳ*] *n* (Comput) curseur *m*

curt [kəːt] *adj* brusque, sec(-sèche)

curtain ['kəːtn] *n* rideau *m*

curve [kəːv] *n* courbe *f*; (*in the road*) tournant *m*, virage *m* ▷ *vi* se courber; (*road*) faire une courbe; **curved** *adj* courbe

cushion ['kuʃən] *n* coussin *m* ▷ *vt* (*fall, shock*) amortir

custard ['kʌstəd] *n* (*for pouring*) crème anglaise

custody ['kʌstədɪ] *n* (*of child*) garde *f*; (*for offenders*): **to take sb into ~** placer qn en détention préventive

custom ['kʌstəm] *n* coutume *f*, usage *m*; (Comm) clientèle *f*

customer ['kʌstəmə*ʳ*] *n* client(e)

customized ['kʌstəmaɪzd] *adj* personnalisé(e); (*car etc*) construit(e) sur commande

customs ['kʌstəmz] *npl* douane *f*; **customs officer** *n* douanier *m*

cut [kʌt] *vb* (*pt, pp* ~) ▷ *vt* couper; (*meat*) découper; (*reduce*) réduire ▷ *vi* couper ▷ *n* (*gen*) coupure *f*; (*of clothes*) coupe *f*; (*in salary etc*) réduction *f*; (*of meat*) morceau *m*; **to ~ a tooth** percer une dent; **to ~ one's finger** se couper le doigt; **to get one's hair ~** se faire couper les cheveux; **I've ~ myself** je me suis coupé; **cut back** *vt* (*plants*) tailler; (*production, expenditure*) réduire; **cut down** *vt* (*tree*) abattre; (*reduce*) réduire; **cut off** *vt* couper; (*fig*) isoler; **cut out** *vt* (*picture etc*) découper; (*remove*) supprimer; **cut up** *vt* découper; **cutback** *n* réduction *f*

cute [kjuːt] *adj* mignon(ne), adorable

cutlery ['kʌtlərɪ] *n* couverts *mpl*

cutlet ['kʌtlɪt] *n* côtelette *f*

cut-price ['kʌt'praɪs] (*us* **cut-rate** ['kʌt'reɪt]) *adj* au rabais, à prix réduit

cutting ['kʌtɪŋ] (*fig*) cinglant(e) ▷ *n* (BRIT: *from newspaper*) coupure *f* (de journal); (*from plant*) bouture *f*

CV *n abbr* = **curriculum vitae**

cwt *abbr* = **hundredweight(s)**

cyberspace ['saɪbəspeɪs] *n* cyberespace *m*

cycle ['saɪkl] *n* cycle *m*; (*bicycle*) bicyclette *f*, vélo *m* ▷ *vi* faire de la bicyclette; **cycle hire** *n* location *f* de vélos; **cycle lane, cycle path** *n* piste *f* cyclable; **cycling** *n* cyclisme *m*; **cyclist** *n* cycliste *m/f*

cyclone ['saɪkləun] *n* cyclone *m*

cylinder ['sɪlɪndə*ʳ*] *n* cylindre *m*

cymbals ['sɪmblz] *npl* cymbales *fpl*

cynical ['sɪnɪkl] *adj* cynique

Cypriot ['sɪprɪət] *adj* cypriote, chypriote ▷ *n* Cypriote *m/f*, Chypriote *m/f*

Cyprus ['saɪprəs] *n* Chypre *f*

cyst [sɪst] *n* kyste *m*; **cystitis** [sɪs'taɪtɪs] *n* cystite *f*

czar [zaːʳ] *n* tsar *m*

Czech [tʃɛk] *adj* tchèque ▷ *n* Tchèque *m/f*; (Ling) tchèque *m*; **Czech Republic** *n*: **the Czech Republic** la République tchèque

d

D [di:] n (Mus): **D** ré m

dab [dæb] vt (eyes, wound) tamponner; (paint, cream) appliquer (par petites touches or rapidement)

dad, daddy [dæd, 'dædɪ] n papa m

daffodil ['dæfədɪl] n jonquille f

daft [dɑ:ft] adj (inf) idiot(e), stupide

dagger ['dægə*] n poignard m

daily ['deɪlɪ] adj quotidien(ne), journalier(-ière) ▷ adv tous les jours

dairy ['dɛərɪ] n (shop) crémerie f, laiterie f; (on farm) laiterie f; **dairy produce** n produits laitiers

daisy ['deɪzɪ] n pâquerette f

dam [dæm] n (wall) barrage m; (water) réservoir m, lac m de retenue ▷ vt endiguer

damage ['dæmɪdʒ] n dégâts mpl, dommages mpl; (fig) tort m ▷ vt endommager, abîmer; (fig) faire du tort à; **damages** npl (Law) dommages-intérêts mpl

damn [dæm] vt condamner; (curse) maudire ▷ n (inf): **I don't give a ~** je

m'en fous ▷ adj (inf: also: **~ed**): **this ~ ...** ce sacré or foutu ...; ▷ **~ (it)!** zut!

damp [dæmp] adj humide ▷ n humidité f ▷ vt (also: **~en**: cloth, rag) humecter; (: enthusiasm etc) refroidir

dance [dɑ:ns] n danse f; (ball) bal m ▷ vi danser; **dance floor** n piste f de danse; **dancer** n danseur(-euse); **dancing** n danse f

dandelion ['dændɪlaɪən] n pissenlit m

dandruff ['dændrəf] n pellicules fpl

D & T n abbr (BRIT: Scol) = **design and technology**

Dane [deɪn] n Danois(e)

danger ['deɪndʒə*] n danger m; **~!** (on sign) danger!; **in ~** en danger; **he was in ~ of falling** il risquait de tomber; **dangerous** adj dangereux(-euse)

dangle ['dæŋgl] vt balancer ▷ vi pendre, se balancer

Danish ['deɪnɪʃ] adj danois(e) ▷ n (Ling) danois m

dare [dɛə*] vt: **to ~ sb to do** défier qn or mettre qn au défi de faire ▷ vt: **to ~ (to) do sth** oser faire qch; **I ~ say he'll turn up** il est probable qu'il viendra; **daring** adj hardi(e), audacieux(-euse) ▷ n audace f, hardiesse f

dark [dɑ:k] adj (night, room) obscur(e), sombre; (colour, complexion) foncé(e), sombre ▷ n: **in the ~** dans le noir; **to be in the ~ about** (fig) ignorer tout de; **after ~** après la tombée de la nuit; **darken** vt obscurcir, assombrir ▷ vi s'obscurcir, s'assombrir; **darkness** n obscurité f; **darkroom** n chambre noire

darling ['dɑ:lɪŋ] adj, n chéri(e)

darn [dɑ:n] vt (sewing) repriser

dart [dɑ:t] n fléchette f; (in sewing) pince f ▷ vi: **to ~ towards** se précipiter or s'élancer vers; **dartboard** n cible f (de jeu de fléchettes); **darts** n jeu m de fléchettes

dash [dæʃ] n (sign) tiret m; (small quantity) goutte f, larme f ▷ vt (throw) jeter or lancer violemment; (hopes) anéantir ▷ vi: **to ~ towards** se précipiter or se ruer vers

dashboard ['dæʃbɔːd] n (Aut) tableau m de bord

data ['deɪtə] npl données fpl; **database** n base f de données; **data processing** n traitement m (électronique) de l'information

date [deɪt] n date f; (with sb) rendez-vous m; (fruit) datte f ▷ vt dater; (person) sortir avec; **~ of birth** date de naissance; **to ~** adv à ce jour; **out of ~** périmé(e); **up to ~** à la page, mis(e) à jour, moderne; **dated** adj démodé(e)

daughter ['dɔːtəʳ] n fille f; **daughter-in-law** n belle-fille f, bru f

daunting ['dɔːntɪŋ] adj décourageant(e), intimidant(e)

dawn [dɔːn] n aube f, aurore f ▷ vi (day) se lever, poindre; **it ~ed on him that ...** il lui vint à l'esprit que ...

day [deɪ] n jour m; (as duration) journée f; (period of time, age) époque f, temps m; **the ~ before** la veille, le jour précédent; **the ~ after, the following ~** le lendemain, le jour suivant; **the ~ before yesterday** avant-hier; **the ~ after tomorrow** après-demain; **by ~** de jour; **day-care centre** ['deɪkɛə-] n (for elderly etc) centre m d'accueil de jour; (for children) garderie f; **daydream** vi rêver (tout éveillé); **daylight** n (lumière f du) jour m; **day return** n (BRIT) billet m d'aller-retour (valable pour la journée); **daytime** n jour m, journée f; **day-to-day** adj (routine, expenses) journalier(-ière); **day trip** n excursion f (d'une journée)

dazed [deɪzd] adj abruti(e)

dazzle ['dæzl] vt éblouir, aveugler; **dazzling** adj (light) aveuglant(e), éblouissant(e); (fig) éblouissant(e)

DC abbr (Elec) = **direct current**

dead [dɛd] adj mort(e); (numb) engourdi(e), insensible; (battery) à plat ▷ adv (completely) absolument, complètement; (exactly) juste; **he was shot ~** il a été tué d'un coup de revolver; **~ tired** éreinté(e), complètement fourbu(e); **to stop ~** s'arrêter pile or net;

the line is ~ (Tel) la ligne est coupée; **dead end** n impasse f; **deadline** n date for heure f limite; **deadly** adj mortel(le); (weapon) meurtrier(-ière); **Dead Sea** n: **the Dead Sea** la mer Morte

deaf [dɛf] adj sourd(e); **deafen** vt rendre sourd(e); **deafening** adj assourdissant(e)

deal [diːl] n affaire f, marché m ▷ vt (pt, pp **~t**) (blow) porter; (cards) donner, distribuer; **a great ~ of** beaucoup de; **deal with** vt fus (handle) s'occuper or se charger de; (be about: book etc) traiter de; **dealer** n (Comm) marchand m; (Cards) donneur de; **dealings** npl (in goods, shares) opérations fpl, transactions fpl; (relations) relations fpl, rapports mpl

dealt [dɛlt] pt, pp of **deal**

dean [diːn] n (Rel, BRIT Scol) doyen m; (us Scol) conseiller principal (conseillère principale) d'éducation

dear [dɪəʳ] adj cher (chère); (expensive) cher, coûteux(-euse) ▷ n: **my ~** mon cher (ma chère) ▷ excl: **~ me!** mon Dieu!; **D~ Sir/Madam** (in letter) Monsieur/Madame; **D~ Mr/Mrs X** Cher Monsieur X (Chère Madame X); **dearly** adv (love) tendrement; (pay) cher

death [dɛθ] n mort f; (Admin) décès m; **death penalty** n peine f de mort; **death sentence** n condamnation f à mort

debate [dɪ'beɪt] n discussion f, débat m ▷ vt discuter, débattre

debit ['dɛbɪt] n débit m ▷ vt: **to ~ a sum to sb** or **to sb's account** porter une somme au débit de qn, débiter qn d'une somme; **debit card** n carte f de paiement

debris ['dɛbriː] n débris mpl, décombres mpl

debt [dɛt] n dette f; **to be in ~** avoir des dettes, être endetté(e)

début ['deɪbjuː] n début(s) m(pl)

Dec. abbr (= December) déc

decade ['dɛkeɪd] n décennie f, décade f

decaffeinated [diːˈkæfɪneɪtɪd] adj décaféiné(e)

decay [dɪˈkeɪ] n (of building) délabrement m; (also: **tooth ~**) carie f (dentaire) ▷ vi (rot) se décomposer, pourrir; (: teeth) se carier

deceased [dɪˈsiːst] n: **the ~** le (la) défunt(e)

deceit [dɪˈsiːt] n tromperie f, supercherie f; **deceive** [dɪˈsiːv] vt tromper

December [dɪˈsɛmbə*] n décembre m

decency [ˈdiːsənsɪ] n décence f

decent [ˈdiːsənt] adj (proper) décent(e), convenable

deception [dɪˈsɛpʃən] n tromperie f

deceptive [dɪˈsɛptɪv] adj trompeur(-euse)

decide [dɪˈsaɪd] vt (subj: person) décider; (question, argument) trancher, régler ▷ vi se décider, décider; **to ~ to do/that** décider de faire/que; **to ~ on** décider, se décider pour

decimal [ˈdɛsɪməl] adj décimal(e) ▷ n décimale f

decision [dɪˈsɪʒən] n décision f

decisive [dɪˈsaɪsɪv] adj décisif(-ive); (manner, person) décidé(e), catégorique

deck [dɛk] n (Naut) pont m; (record deck) platine f; (of cards) jeu m; (of bus): **top ~** impériale f; **deckchair** n chaise longue

declaration [dɛkləˈreɪʃən] n déclaration f

declare [dɪˈklɛə*] vt déclarer

decline [dɪˈklaɪn] n (decay) déclin m; (lessening) baisse f ▷ vt refuser, décliner ▷ vi décliner; (business) baisser

decorate [ˈdɛkəreɪt] vt (adorn, give a medal to) décorer; (paint and paper) peindre et tapisser; **decoration** [dɛkəˈreɪʃən] n (medal etc, adornment) décoration f; **decorator** n peintre m en bâtiment

decrease [ˈdiːkriːs] n diminution f ▷ vt, vi [diːˈkriːs] diminuer

decree [dɪˈkriː] n (Pol, Rel) décret m; (Law) arrêt m, jugement m

dedicate [ˈdɛdɪkeɪt] vt consacrer; (book

etc) dédier; **dedicated** adj (person) dévoué(e); (Comput) spécialisé(e), dédié(e); **Dedicated word processor** station f de traitement de texte; **dedication** [dɛdɪˈkeɪʃən] n (devotion) dévouement m; (in book) dédicace f

deduce [dɪˈdjuːs] vt déduire, conclure

deduct [dɪˈdʌkt] vt: **to ~ sth (from)** déduire qch (de), retrancher qch (de); **deduction** [dɪˈdʌkʃən] n (deducting, deducing) déduction f; (from wage etc) prélèvement m, retenue f

deed [diːd] n action f, acte m; (Law) acte notarié, contrat M

deem [diːm] vt (formal) juger, estimer

deep [diːp] adj profond(e); (voice) grave ▷ adv: **spectators stood 20 ~** il y avait 20 rangs de spectateurs; **4 metres ~** de 4 mètres de profondeur; **how ~ is the water?** l'eau a quelle profondeur?; **deep-fry** vt faire frire (dans une friteuse); **deeply** adv profondément; (regret, interested) vivement

deer [dɪə*] n (pl inv): **(red) ~** cerf m; **(fallow) ~** daim m; **(roe) ~** chevreuil m

default [dɪˈfɔːlt] n (Comput: also: **~ value**) valeur f par défaut; **by ~** (Law) par défaut, par contumace; (Sport) par forfait

defeat [dɪˈfiːt] n défaite f ▷ vt (team, opponents) battre

defect n [ˈdiːfɛkt] défaut m ▷ vi [dɪˈfɛkt]: **to ~ to the enemy/the West** passer à l'ennemi/l'Ouest; **defective** [dɪˈfɛktɪv] adj défectueux(-euse)

defence (us **defense**) [dɪˈfɛns] n défense f

defend [dɪˈfɛnd] vt défendre; **defendant** n défendeur(-deresse); (in criminal case) accusé(e), prévenu(e); **defender** n défenseur m

defense [dɪˈfɛns] (us) = **defence**

defensive [dɪˈfɛnsɪv] adj défensif(-ive) ▷ n: **on the ~** sur la défensive

defer [dɪˈfəː*] vt (postpone) différer, ajourner

defiance [dɪˈfaɪəns] n défi m; **in ~ of** au mépris de; **defiant** [dɪˈfaɪənt] adj provocant(e), de défi; (person) rebelle, intraitable

deficiency [dɪ'fɪʃənsɪ] n (lack) insuffisance f; (: Med) carence f; (flaw) faiblesse f; **deficient** [dɪ'fɪʃənt] adj (inadequate) insuffisant(e); **to be deficient in** manquer de

deficit ['defɪsɪt] n déficit m

define [dɪ'faɪn] vt définir

definite ['defɪnɪt] adj (fixed) défini(e), (bien) déterminé(e); (clear, obvious) net(te), manifeste; (certain) sûr(e); **he was ~ about it** il a été catégorique; **definitely** adv sans aucun doute

definition [defɪ'nɪʃən] n définition f; (clearness) netteté f

deflate [di:'fleɪt] vt dégonfler

deflect [dɪ'flɛkt] vt détourner, faire dévier

defraud [dɪ'frɔːd] vt: **to ~ sb of sth** escroquer qch à qn

defrost [di:'frɒst] vt (fridge) dégivrer; (frozen food) décongeler

defuse [di:'fjuːz] vt désamorcer

defy [dɪ'faɪ] vt défier; (efforts etc) résister à; **it defies description** cela défie toute description

degree [dɪ'griː] n degré m; (Scol) diplôme m (universitaire); **a (first) ~ in maths** (BRIT) une licence en maths; **by ~s** (gradually) par degrés; **to some ~, to a certain ~** jusqu'à un certain point, dans une certaine mesure

dehydrated [di:haɪ'dreɪtɪd] adj déshydraté(e); (milk, eggs) en poudre

de-icer ['diː'aɪsə] n dégivreur m

delay [dɪ'leɪ] vt retarder; (payment) différer ▷ vi s'attarder ▷ n délai m, retard m; **to be ~ed** être en retard

delegate n ['delɪgɪt] délégué(e) ▷ vt ['delɪgeɪt] déléguer

delete [dɪ'liːt] vt rayer, supprimer; (Comput) effacer

deli ['delɪ] n épicerie fine

deliberate adj [dɪ'lɪbərɪt] (intentional) délibéré(e); (slow) mesuré(e) ▷ vi [dɪ'lɪbəreɪt] délibérer, réfléchir; **deliberately** adv (on purpose) exprès, délibérément

delicacy ['delɪkəsɪ] n délicatesse f; (choice food) mets fin ou délicat, friandise f

delicate ['delɪkɪt] adj délicat(e)

delicatessen [delɪkə'tesn] n épicerie fine

delicious [dɪ'lɪʃəs] adj délicieux(-euse)

delight [dɪ'laɪt] n (grande) joie, grand plaisir m ▷ vt enchanter; **she's a ~ to work with** c'est un plaisir de travailler avec elle; **to take ~ in** prendre grand plaisir à; **delighted** adj: **delighted (at or with sth)** ravi(e) (de qch); **to be delighted to do sth/that** être enchanté(e) ou ravi(e) de faire qch/que; **delightful** adj (person) adorable; (meal, evening) merveilleux(-euse)

delinquent [dɪ'lɪŋkwənt] adj, n délinquant(e)

deliver [dɪ'lɪvə] vt (mail) distribuer; (goods) livrer; (message) remettre; (speech) prononcer; (Med: baby) mettre au monde; **delivery** n (of mail) distribution f; (of goods) livraison f; (of speaker) élocution f; (Med) accouchement m; **to take delivery of** prendre livraison de

delusion [dɪ'luːʒən] n illusion f

de luxe [də'lʌks] adj de luxe

delve [delv] vi: **to ~ into** fouiller dans

demand [dɪ'mɑːnd] vt réclamer, exiger ▷ n exigence f; (claim) revendication f; (Econ) demande f; **in ~** demandé(e), recherché(e); **on ~** sur demande; **demanding** adj (person) exigeant(e); (work) astreignant(e)

| Be careful not to translate **to demand** by the French word **demander**.

demise [dɪ'maɪz] n décès m

demo ['deməu] n abbr (inf) = demonstration (protest) manif f; (Comput) démonstration f

democracy [dɪ'mɒkrəsɪ] n démocratie f; **democrat** ['deməkræt] n démocrate m/f; **democratic** [demə'krætɪk] adj démocratique

demolish [dɪ'mɒlɪʃ] vt démolir
demolition [demə'lɪʃən] n démolition f
demon ['di:mən] n démon m
demonstrate ['demənstreɪt] vt démontrer, prouver; (show) faire une démonstration de ▷ vi: **to ~ (for/against)** manifester (en faveur de/contre); **demonstration** [demən'streɪʃən] n démonstration f; (Pol etc) manifestation f; **demonstrator** n (Pol etc) manifestant•e
demote [dɪ'məut] vt rétrograder
den [dɛn] n (of lion) tanière f; (room) repaire m
denial [dɪ'naɪəl] n (of accusation) démenti m; (of rights, guilt, truth) dénégation f
denim ['dɛnɪm] n jean m; **denims** npl (blue-)jeans mpl
Denmark ['dɛnmɑːk] n Danemark m
denomination [dɪnɒmɪ'neɪʃən] n (money) valeur f; (Rel) confession f
denounce [dɪ'nauns] vt dénoncer
dense [dɛns] adj dense; (inf: stupid) obtus•e
density ['dɛnsɪtɪ] n densité f; **single-/double-~ disk** (Comput) disquette f (à) simple/double densité
dent [dɛnt] n bosse f ▷ vt (also: **make a ~ in**) cabosser
dental ['dɛntl] adj dentaire; **dental floss** [-flɒs] n fil m dentaire; **dental surgery** n cabinet m de dentiste
dentist ['dɛntɪst] n dentiste m/f
dentures ['dɛntʃəz] npl dentier msg
deny [dɪ'naɪ] vt nier; (refuse) refuser
deodorant [di:'əudərənt] n déodorant m
depart [dɪ'pɑːt] vi partir; **to ~ from** (fig: differ from) s'écarter de
department [dɪ'pɑːtmənt] n (Comm) rayon m; (Scol) section f; (Pol) ministère m, département m; **department store** n grand magasin
departure [dɪ'pɑːtʃə] n départ m; (fig): **a new ~** une nouvelle voie; **departure**

lounge n salle f de départ
depend [dɪ'pɛnd] vi: **to ~ (up)on** dépendre de; (rely on) compter sur; **it ~s** cela dépend; **~ing on the result ...** selon le résultat ...; **dependant** n personne f à charge; **dependent** adj: **to be dependent (on)** dépendre (de) ▷ n = **dependant**
depict [dɪ'pɪkt] vt (in picture) représenter; (in words) (dé)peindre, décrire
deport [dɪ'pɔːt] vt déporter, expulser
deposit [dɪ'pɒzɪt] n (Chem, Comm, Geo) dépôt m; (of ore, oil) gisement m; (part payment) arrhes fpl, acompte m; (on bottle etc) consigne f; (for hired goods etc) cautionnement m, garantie f ▷ vt déposer; **deposit account** n compte m sur livret
depot ['dɛpəu] n dépôt m; (us: Rail) gare f
depreciate [dɪ'priːʃɪeɪt] vi se déprécier, se dévaloriser
depress [dɪ'prɛs] vt déprimer; (press down) appuyer sur, abaisser; (wages etc) faire baisser; **depressed** adj (person) déprimé•e; (area) en déclin, touché•e par le sous-emploi; **depressing** adj déprimant•e; **depression** [dɪ'prɛʃən] n dépression f
deprive [dɪ'praɪv] vt: **to ~ sb of** priver qn de; **deprived** adj déshérité•e
dept. abbr (= department) dép, dépt
depth [dɛpθ] n profondeur f; **to be in the ~s of despair** être au plus profond du désespoir; **to be out of one's ~** (BRIT: swimmer) ne plus avoir pied; (fig) être dépassé•e; nager
deputy ['dɛpjuti] n (second in command) adjoint•e; (Pol) député m; (us: also: **~ sheriff**) shérif adjoint ▷ adj: **~ head** (Scol) directeur(-trice) adjoint•e, sous-directeur(-trice)
derail [dɪ'reɪl] vt: **to be ~ed** dérailler
derelict ['dɛrɪlɪkt] adj abandonné•e, à l'abandon
derive [dɪ'raɪv] vt: **to ~ sth from** tirer qch de; trouver qch dans ▷ vi: **to ~ from**

provenir de, dériver de

descend [dɪˈsɛnd] vt, vi descendre;
to ~ from descendre de, être issu(e)
de; **to ~ to** s'abaisser à; **descendant** n
descendant(e); **descent** n descente f;
(origin) origine f

describe [dɪsˈkraɪb] vt décrire;
description [dɪsˈkrɪpʃən] n
description f; (sort) sorte f, espèce f

desert n [ˈdɛzət] désert m ▷ vb
[dɪˈzəːt] ▷ vt déserter, abandonner
▷ vi (Mil) déserter; **deserted** [dɪˈzəːtɪd]
adj désert(e)

deserve [dɪˈzəːv] vt mériter

design [dɪˈzaɪn] n (sketch) plan m,
dessin m; (layout, shape) conception f,
ligne f; (pattern) dessin, motif(s) m(pl);
(of dress, car) modèle m; (art) design m,
stylisme m; (intention) dessein m ▷ vt
dessiner; (plan) concevoir; **design and
technology** n (BRIT: Scol) technologie f

designate vt [ˈdɛzɪgneɪt] désigner
▷ adj [ˈdɛzɪgnɪt] désigné(e)

designer [dɪˈzaɪnəʳ] n (Archit,
Art) dessinateur(-trice); (Industry)
concepteur m, designer m; (Fashion)
styliste m/f

desirable [dɪˈzaɪərəbl] adj (property,
location, purchase) attrayant(e)

desire [dɪˈzaɪəʳ] n désir m ▷ vt désirer,
vouloir

desk [dɛsk] n (in office) bureau m;
(for pupil) pupitre m; (BRIT: in shop,
restaurant) caisse f; (in hotel, at airport)
réception f; **desk-top publishing**
[ˈdɛsktɔp-] n publication assistée par
ordinateur, PAO f

despair [dɪsˈpɛəʳ] n désespoir m ▷ vi: **to
~ of** désespérer de

despatch [dɪsˈpætʃ] n, vt = **dispatch**

desperate [ˈdɛspərɪt] adj désespéré(e);
(fugitive) prêt(e) à tout; **to be ~ for sth/
to do sth** avoir désespérément besoin
de qch/de faire qch; **desperately** adv
désespérément; (very) terriblement,
extrêmement; **desperation**
[dɛspəˈreɪʃən] n désespoir m; **in
(sheer) desperation** en désespoir

de cause

despise [dɪsˈpaɪz] vt mépriser

despite [dɪsˈpaɪt] prep malgré, en
dépit de

dessert [dɪˈzəːt] n dessert m;
dessertspoon n cuiller f à dessert

destination [dɛstɪˈneɪʃən] n
destination f

destined [ˈdɛstɪnd] adj: **~ for London** à
destination de Londres

destiny [ˈdɛstɪnɪ] n destinée f, destin m

destroy [dɪsˈtrɔɪ] vt détruire; (injured
horse) abattre; (dog) faire piquer

destruction [dɪsˈtrʌkʃən] n
destruction f

destructive [dɪsˈtrʌktɪv] adj
destructeur(-trice)

detach [dɪˈtætʃ] vt détacher; **detached**
adj (attitude) détaché(e); **detached
house** n pavillon m maison(nette)
(individuelle)

detail [ˈdiːteɪl] n détail m ▷ vt raconter
en détail, énumérer; **in ~** en détail;
detailed adj détaillé(e)

detain [dɪˈteɪn] vt retenir; (in captivity)
détenir

detect [dɪˈtɛkt] vt déceler, percevoir;
(Med, Police) dépister; (Mil, Radar,
Tech) détecter; **detection** [dɪˈtɛkʃən]
n découverte f; **detective** n policier
m; **private detective** détective privé;
detective story n roman policier

detention [dɪˈtɛnʃən] n détention f;
(Scol) retenue f, consigne f

deter [dɪˈtəːʳ] vt dissuader

detergent [dɪˈtəːdʒənt] n détersif m,
détergent m

deteriorate [dɪˈtɪərɪəreɪt] vi se
détériorer, se dégrader

determination [dɪtəːmɪˈneɪʃən] n
détermination f

determine [dɪˈtəːmɪn] vt déterminer;
to ~ to do résoudre de faire, se
déterminer à faire; **determined** adj
(person) déterminé(e), décidé(e);
determined to do bien décidé à faire

deterrent [dɪˈtɛrənt] n effet m de
dissuasion; force f de dissuasion

detest [dɪ'tɛst] vt détester, avoir horreur de

detour ['di:tuǝʳ] n détour m; (us Aut: diversion) déviation f

detract [dɪ'trækt] vt: **to ~ from** (quality, pleasure) diminuer; (news) accablant(e); (reputation) porter atteinte à

detrimental [dɛtrɪ'mɛntl] adj: **~ to** préjudiciable à, nuisible à

devastating ['dɛvǝsteɪtɪŋ] adj dévastateur(-trice); (news) accablant(e)

develop [dɪ'vɛlǝp] vt (gen) développer; (disease) commencer à souffrir de; (resources) mettre en valeur, exploiter; (land) aménager ▷ vi se développer; (situation, disease: evolve) évoluer; (facts, symptoms: appear) se manifester, se produire; **can you ~ this film?** pouvez-vous développer cette pellicule?; **developing country** n pays m en voie de développement; **development** n développement m; (of land) exploitation f; (new fact, event) rebondissement m, fait(s) nouveau(x)

device [dɪ'vaɪs] n (apparatus) appareil m, dispositif m

devil ['dɛvl] n diable m; démon m

devious ['di:vɪǝs] adj (person) sournois(e), dissimulé(e)

devise [dɪ'vaɪz] vt imaginer, concevoir

devote [dɪ'vǝut] vt: **to ~ sth to** consacrer qch à; **devoted** adj dévoué(e); (book etc) très attaché(e) à; (book etc) être consacré(e) à; **devotion** n dévouement m, attachement m; (Rel) dévotion f, piété f

devour [dɪ'vauǝʳ] vt dévorer

devout [dɪ'vaut] adj pieux(-euse), dévot(e)

dew [dju:] n rosée f

diabetes [daɪǝ'bi:ti:z] n diabète m

diabetic [daɪǝ'bɛtɪk] n diabétique m/f ▷ adj (person) diabétique

diagnose [daɪǝg'nǝuz] vt diagnostiquer

diagnosis (pl **diagnoses**) [daɪǝg'nǝusɪs, -si:z] n diagnostic m

diagonal [daɪ'ægǝnl] adj diagonal(e) ▷ n diagonale f

diagram ['daɪǝgræm] n diagramme m, schéma m

dial ['daɪǝl] n cadran m ▷ vt (number) faire, composer

dialect ['daɪǝlɛkt] n dialecte m

dialling code ['daɪǝlɪŋ-] (us **dial code**) n indicatif m (téléphonique); **what's the ~ for Paris?** quel est l'indicatif de Paris?

dialling tone ['daɪǝlɪŋ-] (us **dial tone**) n tonalité f

dialogue (us **dialog**) ['daɪǝlɔg] n dialogue m

diameter [daɪ'æmɪtǝʳ] n diamètre m

diamond ['daɪǝmǝnd] n diamant m; (shape) losange m; **diamonds** npl (Cards) carreau m

diaper ['daɪǝpǝʳ] n (us) couche f

diarrhoea (us **diarrhea**) [daɪǝ'ri:ǝ] n diarrhée f

diary ['daɪǝrɪ] n (daily account) journal m; (book) agenda m

dice [daɪs] n (pl inv) dé m ▷ vt (Culin) couper en dés or en cubes

dictate [dɪk'teɪt] vt dicter; **dictation** [dɪk'teɪʃǝn] n dictée f

dictator [dɪk'teɪtǝʳ] n dictateur m

dictionary ['dɪkʃǝnrɪ] n dictionnaire m

did [dɪd] pt of **do**

didn't [dɪdnt] = **did not**

die [daɪ] vi mourir; **to be dying for sth** avoir une envie folle de qch; **to be dying to do sth** mourir d'envie de faire qch; **die down** vi se calmer, s'apaiser; **die out** vi disparaître, s'éteindre

diesel ['di:zl] n (vehicle) diesel m; (also: **~ oil**) carburant m diesel, gas-oil m

diet ['daɪǝt] n alimentation f; (restricted food) régime m ▷ vi (also: **be on a ~**) suivre un régime

differ ['dɪfǝʳ] vi: **to ~ from sth** (be different) être différent(e) de qch, différer de qch; **to ~ from sb over sth** ne pas être d'accord avec qn au sujet de qch; **difference** n différence f; (quarrel) différend m, désaccord m; **different**

adj différent(e); **differentiate** [ˌdɪfəˈrenʃɪeɪt] *vi*: **to differentiate between** faire une différence entre; **differently** *adv* différemment

difficult [ˈdɪfɪkəlt] *adj* difficile; **difficulty** *n* difficulté *f*

dig [dɪg] *vt* (*pt, pp* **dug**) (*hole*) creuser; (*garden*) bêcher ▷ *n* (*prod*) coup *m* de coude; (*fig: remark*) coup de griffe *or* de patte; (*Archaeology*) fouille *f*; **to ~ one's nails into** enfoncer ses ongles dans; **dig up** *vt* déterrer

digest *vt* [daɪˈdʒest] digérer ▷ *n* [ˈdaɪdʒest] sommaire *m*, résumé *m*; **digestion** [dɪˈdʒestʃən] *n* digestion *f*

digit [ˈdɪdʒɪt] *n* (*number*) chiffre *m* (*de o à 9*); (*finger*) doigt *m*; **digital** *adj* (*system, recording, radio*) numérique, digital(e); (*watch*) à affichage numérique *or* digital; **digital camera** *n* appareil *m* photo numérique; **digital TV** *n* télévision *f* numérique

dignified [ˈdɪgnɪfaɪd] *adj* digne

dignity [ˈdɪgnɪtɪ] *n* dignité *f*

digs [dɪgz] *npl* (*BRIT inf*) piaule *f*, chambre meublée

dilemma [daɪˈlemə] *n* dilemme *m*

dill [dɪl] *n* aneth *m*

dilute [daɪˈluːt] *vt* diluer

dim [dɪm] *adj* (*light, eyesight*) faible; (*memory, outline*) vague, indécis(e); (*room*) sombre; (*inf: stupid*) borné(e), obtus(e) ▷ *vt* (*light*) réduire, baisser; (*US Aut*) mettre en code, baisser

dime [daɪm] *n* (*US*) pièce *f* de 10 cents

dimension [daɪˈmenʃən] *n* dimension *f*

diminish [dɪˈmɪnɪʃ] *vt, vi* diminuer

din [dɪn] *n* vacarme *m*

dine [daɪn] *vi* dîner; **diner** *n* (*person*) dîneur(-euse); (*US: eating place*) petit restaurant

dinghy [ˈdɪŋgɪ] *n* youyou *m*; (*inflatable*) canot *m* pneumatique; (*also: **sailing ~***) voilier *m*, dériveur *m*

dingy [ˈdɪndʒɪ] *adj* miteux(-euse), minable

dining car [ˈdaɪnɪŋ-] *n* (*BRIT*) voiture-

restaurant *f*, wagon-restaurant *m*

dining room [ˈdaɪnɪŋ-] *n* salle *f* à manger

dining table [ˈdaɪnɪŋ-] *n* table *f* de (la) salle à manger

dinner [ˈdɪnəʳ] *n* (*evening meal*) dîner *m*; (*lunch*) déjeuner *m*; (*public*) banquet *m*; **dinner jacket** *n* smoking *m*; **dinner party** *n* dîner *m*; **dinner time** *n* (*evening*) heure *f* du dîner; (*midday*) heure du déjeuner

dinosaur [ˈdaɪnəsɔːʳ] *n* dinosaure *m*

dip [dɪp] *n* (*slope*) déclivité *f*; (*in sea*) baignade *f*, bain *m*; (*Culin*) ≈ sauce *f* ▷ *vt* tremper, plonger; (*BRIT Aut: lights*) mettre en code, baisser ▷ *vi* plonger

diploma [dɪˈpləʊmə] *n* diplôme *m*

diplomacy [dɪˈpləʊməsɪ] *n* diplomatie *f*

diplomat [ˈdɪpləmæt] *n* diplomate *m*; **diplomatic** [dɪpləˈmætɪk] *adj* diplomatique

dipstick [ˈdɪpstɪk] *n* (*BRIT Aut*) jauge *f* de niveau d'huile

dire [daɪəʳ] *adj* (*poverty*) extrême; (*awful*) affreux(-euse)

direct [daɪˈrekt] *adj* direct(e) ▷ *vt* (*tell way*) diriger, orienter; (*letter, remark*) adresser; (*Cine, TV*) réaliser; (*Theat*) mettre en scène; (*order*): **to ~ sb to do sth** ordonner à qn de faire qch ▷ *adv* directement; **can you ~ me to ...?** pouvez-vous m'indiquer le chemin de ...?; **direct debit** *n* (*BRIT Banking*) prélèvement *m* automatique

direction [dɪˈrekʃən] *n* direction *f*; **directions** *npl* (*to a place*) indications *fpl*; **~s for use** mode *m* d'emploi; **sense of ~** sens *m* de l'orientation

directly [dɪˈrektlɪ] *adv* (*in straight line*) directement, tout droit; (*at once*) tout de suite, immédiatement

director [dɪˈrektəʳ] *n* directeur *m*; (*Theat*) metteur *m* en scène; (*Cine, TV*) réalisateur(-trice)

directory [dɪˈrektərɪ] *n* annuaire *m*; (*Comput*) répertoire *m*; **directory enquiries** (*US* **directory assistance**) *n*

(Tel: service) renseignements mpl

dirt [də:t] n saleté f; (mud) boue f; **dirty**
adj sale; (joke) cochon(ne) ▷ vt salir

disability [dɪsə'bɪlɪtɪ] n invalidité f,
infirmité f

disabled [dɪs'eɪbld] adj handicapé(e);
(maimed) mutilé(e)

disadvantage [dɪsəd'vɑ:ntɪdʒ] n
désavantage m, inconvénient m

disagree [dɪsə'gri:] vi (differ) ne pas
concorder; (be against, think otherwise):
to ~ (with) ne pas être d'accord
(avec); **disagreeable** adj désagréable;
disagreement n désaccord m,
différend m

disappear [dɪsə'pɪə*] vi disparaître;
disappearance n disparition f

disappoint [dɪsə'pɔɪnt] vt décevoir;
disappointed adj déçu(e);
disappointing adj décevant(e);
disappointment n déception f

disapproval [dɪsə'pru:vəl] n
désapprobation f

disapprove [dɪsə'pru:v] vi: **to ~ of**
désapprouver

disarm [dɪs'ɑ:m] vt désarmer;
disarmament [dɪs'ɑ:məmənt] n
désarmement m

disaster [dɪ'zɑ:stə*] n catastrophe
f, désastre m; **disastrous** adj
désastreux(-euse)

disbelief ['dɪsbə'li:f] n incrédulité f

disc [dɪsk] n disque m; (Comput) = **disk**

discard [dɪs'kɑ:d] vt (old things) se
débarrasser de; (fig) écarter, renoncer à

discharge vt [dɪs'tʃɑ:dʒ] (duties)
s'acquitter de; (waste etc) déverser;
décharger; (patient) renvoyer (chez lui);
(employee, soldier) congédier, licencier
▷ n ['dɪstʃɑ:dʒ] (Elec, Med) émission f;
(dismissal) renvoi m; licenciement m

discipline ['dɪsɪplɪn] n discipline f ▷ vt
discipliner; (punish) punir

disc jockey n disque-jockey m (DJ)

disclose [dɪs'kləuz] vt révéler,
divulguer

disco ['dɪskəu] n abbr discothèque f

discoloured [dɪs'kʌləd] (us

discolored) adj décoloré(e), jauni(e)

discomfort [dɪs'kʌmfət] n malaise
m, gêne f; (lack of comfort) manque m
de confort

disconnect [dɪskə'nekt] vt (Elec, Radio)
débrancher; (gas, water) couper

discontent [dɪskən'tent] n
mécontentement m

discontinue [dɪskən'tɪnju:] vt cesser,
interrompre; **"-d"** (Comm) "fin de série"

discount n ['dɪskaunt] remise f, rabais
m ▷ vt [dɪs'kaunt] (report etc) ne pas
tenir compte de

discourage [dɪs'kʌrɪdʒ] vt décourager

discover [dɪs'kʌvə*] vt découvrir;
discovery n découverte f

discredit [dɪs'kredɪt] vt (idea) mettre
en doute; (person) discréditer

discreet [dɪ'skri:t] adj discret(-ète)

discrepancy [dɪ'skrepənsɪ] n
divergence f, contradiction f

discretion [dɪ'skreʃən] n discrétion f;
at the ~ of à la discrétion de

discriminate [dɪ'skrɪmɪneɪt] vi: **to ~
between** établir une distinction entre,
faire une différence entre; **to ~ against**
pratiquer une discrimination contre;
discrimination [dɪskrɪmɪ'neɪʃən]
n discrimination f; (judgment)
discernement m

discuss [dɪs'kʌs] vt discuter de; (debate)
discuter; **discussion** [dɪs'kʌʃən] n
discussion f

disease [dɪ'zi:z] n maladie f

disembark [dɪsɪm'bɑ:k] vt, vi
débarquer

disgrace [dɪs'greɪs] n honte f;
(disfavour) disgrâce f ▷ vt déshonorer,
couvrir de honte; **disgraceful** adj
scandaleux(-euse), honteux(-euse)

disgruntled [dɪs'grʌntld] adj
mécontent(e)

disguise [dɪs'gaɪz] n déguisement m
▷ vt déguiser; **in ~** déguisé(e)

disgust [dɪs'gʌst] n dégoût m, aversion
f ▷ vt dégoûter, écœurer

disgusted [dɪs'gʌstɪd] adj dégoûté(e),
écœuré(e)

disgusting [dɪsˈɡʌstɪŋ] *adj* dégoûtant(e)

dish [dɪʃ] *n* plat *m*; **to do** *or* **wash the ~es** faire la vaisselle; **dishcloth** *n* (*for drying*) torchon *m*; (*for washing*) lavette *f*

dishonest [dɪsˈɔnɪst] *adj* malhonnête

dishtowel [ˈdɪʃtaʊəl] *n* (us) torchon *m* (à vaisselle)

dishwasher [ˈdɪʃwɔʃəʳ] *n* lave-vaisselle *m*

disillusion [dɪsɪˈluːʒən] *vt* désabuser, désenchanter

disinfectant [dɪsɪnˈfɛktənt] *n* désinfectant *m*

disintegrate [dɪsˈɪntɪɡreɪt] *vi* se désintégrer

disk [dɪsk] *n* (Comput) disquette *f*; **single-/double-sided** *n* disquette une face/double face; **disk drive** *n* lecteur *m* de disquette; **diskette** *n* (Comput) disquette *f*

dislike [dɪsˈlaɪk] *n* aversion *f*, antipathie *f* ▷ *vt* ne pas aimer

dislocate [ˈdɪsləkeɪt] *vt* disloquer, déboîter

disloyal [dɪsˈlɔɪəl] *adj* déloyal(e)

dismal [ˈdɪzml] *adj* (*gloomy*) lugubre, maussade; (*very bad*) lamentable

dismantle [dɪsˈmæntl] *vt* démonter

dismay [dɪsˈmeɪ] *n* consternation *f* ▷ *vt* consterner

dismiss [dɪsˈmɪs] *vt* congédier, renvoyer; (*idea*) écarter; (Law) rejeter; **dismissal** *n* renvoi *m*

disobedient [dɪsəˈbiːdɪənt] *adj* désobéissant(e), indiscipliné(e)

disobey [dɪsəˈbeɪ] *vt* désobéir à

disorder [dɪsˈɔːdəʳ] *n* désordre *m*; (*rioting*) désordres *mpl*; (Med) troubles *mpl*

disorganized [dɪsˈɔːɡənaɪzd] *adj* désorganisé(e)

disown [dɪsˈəʊn] *vt* renier

dispatch [dɪsˈpætʃ] *vt* expédier, envoyer ▷ *n* envoi *m*, expédition *f*; (Mil, Press) dépêche *f*

dispel [dɪsˈpɛl] *vt* dissiper, chasser

dispense [dɪsˈpɛns] *vt* (*medicine*)

préparer (et vendre); **dispense with** *vt fus* se passer de; **dispenser** *n* (*device*) distributeur *m*

disperse [dɪsˈpəːs] *vt* disperser ▷ *vi* se disperser

display [dɪsˈpleɪ] *n* (*of goods*) étalage *m*; affichage *m*; (Comput: *information*) visualisation *f*; (: *device*) visuel *m*; (*of feeling*) manifestation *f* ▷ *vt* montrer; (*goods*) mettre à l'étalage, exposer; (*results, departure times*) afficher; (*pej*) faire étalage de

displease [dɪsˈpliːz] *vt* mécontenter, contrarier

disposable [dɪsˈpəʊzəbl] *adj* (*pack etc*) jetable; (*income*) disponible

disposal [dɪsˈpəʊzl] *n* (*of rubbish*) évacuation *f*, destruction *f*; (*of property etc: by selling*) vente *f*; (: *by giving away*) cession *f*; **at one's ~** à sa disposition

dispose [dɪsˈpəʊz] *vi*: **~ of** (*unwanted goods*) se débarrasser de, se défaire de; (*problem*) expédier; **disposition** [dɪspəˈzɪʃən] *n* disposition *f*; (*temperament*) naturel *m*

disproportionate [dɪsprəˈpɔːʃənət] *adj* disproportionné(e)

dispute [dɪsˈpjuːt] *n* discussion *f*; (*also*: **industrial ~**) conflit *m* ▷ *vt* (*question*) contester; (*matter*) discuter

disqualify [dɪsˈkwɔlɪfaɪ] *vt* (Sport) disqualifier; **to ~ sb for sth/from doing** rendre qn inapte à qch/à faire

disregard [dɪsrɪˈɡɑːd] *vt* ne pas tenir compte de

disrupt [dɪsˈrʌpt] *vt* (*plans, meeting, lesson*) perturber, déranger; **disruption** [dɪsˈrʌpʃən] *n* perturbation *f*, dérangement *m*

dissatisfaction [dɪssætɪsˈfækʃən] *n* mécontentement *m*, insatisfaction *f*

dissatisfied [dɪsˈsætɪsfaɪd] *adj*: **~ (with)** insatisfait(e) (de)

dissect [dɪˈsɛkt] *vt* disséquer

dissent [dɪˈsɛnt] *n* dissentiment *m*, différence f d'opinion

dissertation [dɪsəˈteɪʃən] *n* (Scol) mémoire *m*

dissolve [dɪ'zɔlv] vt dissoudre ▷ vi se dissoudre, fondre; **to ~ in(to) tears** fondre en larmes

distance ['dɪstns] n distance f; **in the ~** au loin

distant ['dɪstnt] adj lointain(e), éloigné(e); (manner) distant(e), froid(e)

distil (us **distill**) [dɪs'tɪl] vt distiller; **distillery** n distillerie f

distinct [dɪs'tɪŋkt] adj distinct(e); (clear) marqué(e); **as ~ from** par opposition à; **distinction** [dɪs'tɪŋkʃən] n distinction f; (in exam) mention f très bien; **distinctive** adj distinctif(-ive)

distinguish [dɪs'tɪŋgwɪʃ] vt distinguer; **to ~ o.s.** se distinguer; **distinguished** adj (eminent, refined) distingué(e)

distort [dɪs'tɔːt] vt déformer

distract [dɪs'trækt] vt distraire, déranger; **distracted** adj (not concentrating) distrait(e); (worried) affolé(e); **distraction** [dɪs'trækʃən] n distraction f

distraught [dɪs'trɔːt] adj éperdu(e)

distress [dɪs'trɛs] n détresse f ▷ vt affliger; **distressing** adj douloureux(-euse), pénible

distribute [dɪs'trɪbjuːt] vt distribuer; **distribution** [dɪstrɪ'bjuːʃən] n distribution f; **distributor** n (gen: Tech) distributeur m; (Comm) concessionnaire m/f

district ['dɪstrɪkt] n (of country) région f; (of town) quartier m; (Admin) district m; **district attorney** n (us) ≈ procureur de la République

distrust [dɪs'trʌst] n méfiance f, doute m ▷ vt se méfier de

disturb [dɪs'təːb] vt troubler; (inconvenience) déranger; **disturbance** n dérangement m; (political etc) troubles mpl; **disturbed** adj (worried, upset) agité(e), troublé(e); **to be emotionally disturbed** avoir des problèmes affectifs; **disturbing** adj troublant(e), inquiétant(e)

ditch [dɪtʃ] n fossé m; (for irrigation)

rigole f ▷ vt (inf) abandonner; (person) plaquer

ditto ['dɪtəu] adv idem

dive [daɪv] n plongeon m; (of submarine) plongée f ▷ vi plonger; **to ~ into** (bag etc) plonger la main dans; (place) se précipiter dans; **diver** n plongeur m

diverse [daɪ'vəːs] adj divers(e)

diversion [daɪ'vəːʃən] n (BRIT Aut) déviation f; (distraction, Mil) diversion f

diversity [daɪ'vəːsɪtɪ] n diversité f, variété f

divert [daɪ'vəːt] vt (BRIT: traffic) dévier; (plane) dérouter; (train, river) détourner

divide [dɪ'vaɪd] vt diviser; (separate) séparer ▷ vi se diviser; **divided highway** (us) n route f à quatre voies

divine [dɪ'vaɪn] adj divin(e)

diving ['daɪvɪŋ] n plongée (sous-marine); **diving board** n plongeoir m

division [dɪ'vɪʒən] n division f; (separation) séparation f; (Comm) service m

divorce [dɪ'vɔːs] n divorce m ▷ vt divorcer d'avec; **divorced** adj divorcé(e); **divorcee** [dɪvɔː'siː] n divorcé(e)

D.I.Y. adj, n abbr (BRIT) = **do-it-yourself**

dizzy ['dɪzɪ] adj: **I feel ~** la tête me tourne, j'ai la tête qui tourne

DJ n abbr = **disc jockey**

DNA n abbr (= deoxyribonucleic acid) ADN m

 KEYWORD

do [duː] (pt **did**, pp **done**) n (inf: party etc) soirée f, fête f

▷ vb **1** (in negative constructions) non traduit; **I don't understand** je ne comprends pas

2 (to form questions) non traduit; **didn't you know?** vous ne le saviez pas?; **what do you think?** qu'en pensez-vous?

3 (for emphasis, in polite expressions): **people do make mistakes sometimes** on peut toujours se tromper; **she does seem rather late** je

trouve qu'elle est bien en retard; **do sit down/help yourself** asseyez-vous/servez-vous je vous en prie; **do take care!** faites bien attention à vous!
4 (used to avoid repeating vb): **she swims better than I do** elle nage mieux que moi; **do you agree? - yes, I do/no I don't** vous êtes d'accord? - oui/non; **she lives in Glasgow - so do I** elle habite Glasgow - moi aussi; **he didn't like it and neither did we** il n'a pas aimé ça, et nous non plus; **who broke it? - I did** qui l'a cassé? - c'est moi; **he asked me to help him and I did** il m'a demandé de l'aider, et c'est ce que j'ai fait
5 (in question tags): **you like him, don't you?** vous l'aimez bien, n'est-ce pas?; **I don't know him, do I?** je ne crois pas le connaître
▷ **vt 1** (gen: carry out, perform etc) faire; (visit: city, museum) faire, visiter; **what are you doing tonight?** qu'est-ce que vous faites ce soir?; **what do you do?** (job) que faites-vous dans la vie?; **what can I do for you?** que puis-je faire pour vous?; **to do the cooking/washing-up** faire la cuisine/la vaisselle; **to do one's teeth/hair/nails** se brosser les dents/se coiffer/se faire les ongles
2 (Aut etc: distance) faire; (: speed) faire du; **we've done 200 km already** nous avons déjà fait 200 km; **the car was doing 100** la voiture faisait du 100 (à l'heure); **he can do 100 in that car** il peut faire du 100 (à l'heure) dans cette voiture-là
▷ **vi 1** (act, behave) faire; **do as I do** faites comme moi
2 (get on, fare) marcher; **the firm is doing well** l'entreprise marche bien; **he's doing well/badly at school** ça marche bien/mal pour lui à l'école; **how do you do?** comment allez-vous?; (on being introduced) enchanté(e)!
3 (suit) aller; **will it do?** est-ce que ça ira?
4 (be sufficient) suffire, aller; **will £10**

do? est-ce que 10 livres suffiront?; **that'll do** ça suffit, ça ira; **that'll do!** (in annoyance) ça va or suffit comme ça!; **to make do (with)** se contenter (de)
do up vt (laces, dress) attacher; (buttons) boutonner; (zip) fermer; (renovate: room) refaire; (: house) remettre à neuf
do with vt fus (need): **I could do with a drink/some help** quelque chose à boire/un peu d'aide ne serait pas de refus; **it could do with a wash** ça ne lui ferait pas de mal d'être lavé; (be connected with): **that has nothing to do with you** cela ne vous concerne pas; **I won't have anything to do with it** je ne veux pas m'en mêler
do without vi s'en passer; **if you're late for tea then you'll do without** si vous êtes en retard pour le dîner il faudra vous en passer
▷ **vt** fus se passer de; **I can do without a car** je peux me passer de voiture

dock [dɔk] n dock m; (wharf) quai m; (Law) banc m des accusés ▷ vi se mettre à quai; (Space) s'arrimer; **docks** npl (Naut) docks

doctor ['dɔktə*] n médecin m, docteur m; (PhD etc) docteur ▷ vt (drink) frelater; **call a ~!** appelez un docteur or un médecin!; **Doctor of Philosophy (PhD)** n (degree) doctorat m; (person) titulaire m/f d'un doctorat

document ['dɔkjumənt] n document m; **documentary** [dɔkju'mɛntərɪ] adj, n documentaire m; **documentation** [dɔkjumən'teɪʃən] n documentation f

dodge [dɔdʒ] n truc m; combine f ▷ vt esquiver, éviter

dodgy ['dɔdʒɪ] adj (inf: uncertain) douteux(-euse); (: shady) louche

does [dʌz] vb see **do**

doesn't ['dʌznt] = **does not**

dog [dɔg] n chien(ne) m ▷ vt (follow closely) suivre de près; (fig: memory etc) poursuivre, harceler; **doggy bag** ['dɔgɪ-] n petit sac pour emporter les restes

do-it-yourself [ˈduːɪtjɔːˈsɛlf] n
bricolage m

dole [dəul] n (BRIT: payment) allocation f
de chômage; **the ~** au chômage

doll [dɔl] n poupée f

dollar [ˈdɔləʳ] n dollar m

dolphin [ˈdɔlfɪn] n dauphin m

dome [dəum] n dôme m

domestic [dəˈmɛstɪk] adj (duty,
happiness) familial(e); (policy,
affairs, flight) intérieur(e); (animal)
domestique; **domestic appliance** n
appareil ménager

dominant [ˈdɔmɪnənt] adj
dominant(e)

dominate [ˈdɔmɪneɪt] vt dominer

domino [ˈdɔmɪnəu] (pl **-es**) n
domino m; **dominoes** n (game)
dominos mpl

donate [dəˈneɪt] vt faire don de,
donner; **donation** [dəˈneɪʃən] n
donation f, don m

done [dʌn] pp of **do**

donkey [ˈdɔŋkɪ] n âne m

donor [ˈdəunəʳ] n (of blood etc)
donneur(-euse); (to charity)
donateur(-trice); **donor card** n carte f
de don d'organes

don't [dəunt] = do not

donut [ˈdəunʌt] (US) n = **doughnut**

doodle [ˈduːdl] vi griffonner, gribouiller

doom [duːm] n (fate) destin m ▷ vt: **to
be ~ed to failure** être voué(e) à l'échec

door [dɔːʳ] n porte f; (Rail, car) portière f;
doorbell n sonnette f; **door handle**
n poignée f de porte; (of car) poignée
de portière; **doorknob** n poignée for
bouton m de porte; **doorstep** n pas
m de (la) porte, seuil m; **doorway** n
(embrasure f de) porte f

dope [dəup] n (inf: drug) drogue f;
(: person) andouille f ▷ vt (horse etc)
doper

dormitory [ˈdɔːmɪtrɪ] n (BRIT) dortoir
m; (us: hall of residence) résidence f
universitaire

DOS [dɔs] n abbr (= disk operating system)
DOS m

dosage [ˈdəusɪdʒ] n dose f; dosage m;
(on label) posologie f

dose [dəus] n dose f

dot [dɔt] n point m; (on material) pois m
▷ vt: **~ted with** parsemé(e) de; **on the
~** à l'heure tapante; **dotcom** [ˈdɔtˈkɔm]
n point com m, pointcom m; **dotted
line** [ˈdɔtɪd-] n ligne pointillée; **to sign
on the dotted line** signer à l'endroit
indiqué or sur la ligne pointillée

double [ˈdʌbl] adj double ▷ adv (twice):
to cost ~ (sth) coûter le double
(de qch) or deux fois plus (que qch) ▷ n
double m; (Cine) doublure f ▷ vt
doubler; (fold) plier en deux ▷ vi
doubler; **on the ~, at the ~** au pas
de course; **double back** vi (person)
revenir sur ses pas; **double bass** n
contrebasse f; **double bed** n grand
lit; **double-check** vt, vi revérifier;
double-click vi (Comput) double-
cliquer; **double-cross** vt doubler,
trahir; **doubledecker** n autobus m à
impériale; **double glazing** n (BRIT)
double vitrage m; **double room** n
chambre f pour deux; doubles n
(Tennis) double m; **double yellow
lines** npl (BRIT: Aut) double bande jaune
marquant l'interdiction de stationner

doubt [daut] n doute m ▷ vt douter
de; **~ no** sans doute; **to ~ that** douter
que + sub; **doubtful** adj douteux(-euse);
(person) incertain(e); **doubtless** adv
sans doute, sûrement

dough [dəu] n pâte f; **doughnut** (US
donut) n beignet m

dove [dʌv] n colombe f

Dover [ˈdəuvəʳ] n Douvres

down [daun] n (fluff) duvet m ▷ adv
en bas, vers le bas; (on the ground) par
terre ▷ prep en bas de; (along) le long
de ▷ vt (inf: drink) siffler; **to walk ~ a
hill** descendre une colline; **to run ~ the
street** descendre la rue en courant;
~ with X! à bas X!; **down-and-out** n
(tramp) clochard(e); **downfall** n chute
f, ruine f; **downhill** adv: **to go downhill**
descendre; (business) péricliter

Downing Street ['daʊnɪŋ-] n (BRIT):
10 ~ résidence du Premier ministre

● DOWNING STREET

● **Downing Street** est une rue de
Westminster (à Londres) où se
trouvent la résidence officielle
du Premier ministre et celle du
ministre des Finances. Le nom
Downing Street est souvent utilisé
pour désigner le gouvernement
britannique.

down: download vt (Comput)
télécharger; **downright** adj (lie etc)
effronté(e); (refusal) catégorique

Down's syndrome [daʊnz-] n
trisomie f

down: downstairs adv (on or to
ground floor) au rez-de-chaussée; (on
or to floor below) à l'étage inférieur;
down-to-earth adj terre à terre inv;
downtown adv en ville; **down under**
adv en Australie ou Nouvelle Zélande;
downward ['daʊnwəd] adj, adv vers
le bas; **downwards** ['daʊnwədz] adv
vers le bas

doz. abbr = **dozen**

doze [dəʊz] vi sommeiller

dozen ['dʌzn] n douzaine f; **a ~ books**
une douzaine de livres; **~s of** des
centaines de

Dr. abbr (= doctor) Dr; (in street names)
= **drive**

drab [dræb] adj terne, morne

draft [drɑːft] n (us letter, school
work) brouillon m; (of literary work)
ébauche f; (Comm) traite f; (us: call-up)
conscription f ▷ vt faire le brouillon de;
(Mil: send) détacher; see also **draught**

drag [dræg] vt traîner; (river) draguer
▷ vi traîner ▷ n (inf) casse-pieds m/f;
(women's clothing): **in ~** (en) travesti;
to ~ and drop (Comput) glisser-poser

dragon ['drægn] n dragon m

dragonfly ['drægənflaɪ] n libellule f

drain [dreɪn] n égout m; (on resources)

saignée f ▷ vt (land, marshes) drainer,
assécher; (vegetables) égoutter;
(reservoir etc) vider ▷ vi (water) s'écouler;
drainage n (system) système m
d'égouts; (act) drainage m; **drainpipe** n
tuyau m d'écoulement

drama ['drɑːmə] n (art) théâtre m, art
m dramatique; (play) pièce f; (event)
drame m; **dramatic** [drə'mætɪk]
adj (Theat) dramatique; (impressive)
spectaculaire

drank [dræŋk] pt of **drink**

drape [dreɪp] vt draper; **drapes** npl (us)
rideaux mpl

drastic ['dræstɪk] adj (measures)
d'urgence, énergique; (change)
radical(e)

draught (us **draft**) [drɑːft] n courant m
d'air; (of beer): **on ~** (beer) à la pression; **draught
beer** n bière f (à la) pression; **draughts**
n (BRIT: game) (jeu m de) dames fpl

draw [drɔː] (vb: pt **drew**, pp **~n**) vt tirer;
(picture) dessiner; (attract) attirer; (line,
circle) tracer; (money) retirer; (object)
toucher ▷ vi (Sport) faire match nul ▷ n
match nul; (lottery) loterie f; (: picking
of ticket) tirage m au sort; **draw out**
vi (lengthen) s'allonger ▷ vt (money)
retirer; **draw up** vi (stop) s'arrêter
▷ vt (document) établir, dresser; (plan)
formuler, dessiner; (chair) approcher;
drawback n inconvénient m,
désavantage m

drawer [drɔːʳ] n tiroir m

drawing ['drɔːɪŋ] n dessin m; **drawing
pin** n (BRIT) punaise f; **drawing room**
n salon m

drawn [drɔːn] pp of **draw**

dread [drɛd] n épouvante f, effroi m ▷ vt
redouter, appréhender; **dreadful** adj
épouvantable, affreux(-euse)

dream [driːm] n rêve m ▷ vt, vi (pt,
pp **~ed** or **~t**) rêver; **dreamer** n
rêveur(-euse)

dreamt [drɛmt] pt, pp of **dream**

dreary ['drɪərɪ] adj triste; monotone

drench [drɛntʃ] vt tremper

dress [drɛs] n robe f; (clothing)

habillement m, tenue f ▷ vt habiller; (wound) panser ▷ vt (ball) s'habiller; **dress up** vi s'habiller; (in fancy dress) se déguiser; **dress circle** n (BRIT) premier balcon; **dresser** n (furniture) vaisselier m; (: US) coiffeuse f, commode f; **dressing** n (Med) pansement m; (Culin) sauce f, assaisonnement m; **dressing gown** n (BRIT) robe f de chambre; **dressing room** n (Theat) loge f; (Sport) vestiaire m; **dressing table** n coiffeuse f; **dressmaker** n couturière f

drew [dru:] pt of **draw**

dribble ['drɪbl] vi (baby) baver ▷ vt (ball) dribbler

dried [draɪd] adj (fruit, beans) sec (sèche); (eggs, milk) en poudre

drier ['draɪəʳ] n = **dryer**

drift [drɪft] n (of current etc) force f; direction f; (of snow) rafale f; coulée f; (: on ground) congère f; (general meaning) sens général m; (of boat) aller à la dérive, dériver; (sand, snow) s'amonceler, s'entasser

drill [drɪl] n perceuse f; (bit) foret m; (of dentist) roulette f, fraise f; (Mil) exercice m ▷ vt percer; (troops) entraîner ▷ vi (for oil) faire un or des forage(s)

drink [drɪŋk] n boisson f; (alcoholic) verre m ▷ vt, vi (pt **drank**, pp **drunk**) boire; **to have a ~** boire quelque chose, boire un verre; **a ~ of water** un verre d'eau; **would you like a ~?** tu veux boire quelque chose?; **drink-driving** n conduite f en état d'ivresse; **drinker** n buveur(-euse) m/f; **drinking water** n eau f potable

drip [drɪp] n (drop) goutte f; (Med: device) goutte-à-goutte m inv; (: liquid) perfusion f ▷ vi tomber goutte à goutte; (tap) goutter

drive [draɪv] n promenade f or trajet m en voiture; (also: **~way**) allée f; (energy) dynamisme m, énergie f; (push) effort (concerté); campagne f; (Comput: also: **disk ~**) lecteur m de disquette ▷ vb (pt **drove**, pp **~n**) ▷ vt conduire; (nail)

enfoncer; (push) chasser, pousser; (Tech: motor) actionner; entraîner ▷ vi (be at the wheel) conduire; (travel by car) aller en voiture; **left-/right-hand ~** (Aut) conduite f à gauche/droite; **to ~ sb mad** rendre qn fou (folle); **drive out** vt (force out) chasser; **drive-in** adj, n (esp US) drive-in m

driven ['drɪvn] pp of **drive**

driver ['draɪvəʳ] n conducteur(-trice) m/f; (of taxi, bus) chauffeur m; **driver's license** n (US) permis m de conduire

driveway ['draɪvweɪ] n allée f

driving ['draɪvɪŋ] n conduite f; **driving instructor** n moniteur m d'auto-école; **driving lesson** n leçon f de conduite; **driving licence** n (BRIT) permis m de conduire; **driving test** n examen m du permis de conduire

drizzle ['drɪzl] n bruine f, crachin m

droop [dru:p] vi (flower) commencer à se faner; (shoulders, head) tomber

drop [drɒp] n (of liquid) goutte f; (fall) baisse f; (also: **parachute ~**) saut m ▷ vt laisser tomber; (voice, eyes, price) baisser; (passenger) déposer ▷ vi tomber; **drop in** vi (inf: visit): **to ~ in (on)** faire un saut (chez), passer (chez); **drop off** vi (sleep) s'assoupir ▷ vt (passenger) déposer; **drop out** vi (withdraw) se retirer; (student etc) abandonner; décrocher

drought [draut] n sécheresse f

drove [drəuv] pt of **drive**

drown [draun] vt noyer ▷ vi se noyer

drowsy ['drauzɪ] adj somnolent(e)

drug [drʌg] n médicament m; (narcotic) drogue f ▷ vt droguer; **to be on ~s** se droguer; **drug addict** n toxicomane m/f; **drug dealer** n revendeur(-euse) m/f de drogue; **druggist** n (US) pharmacien(ne) m/f-droguiste; **drugstore** n (US) pharmacie-droguerie f, drugstore m

drum [drʌm] n tambour m; (for oil, petrol) bidon m; **drums** npl (Mus) batterie f; **drummer** n (joueur m de) tambour m

drunk [drʌŋk] *pp* of **drink** ▷ *adj* ivre,
soûl(e) ▷ *n* (*also:* **~ard**) ivrogne *m/f*;
to get ~ se soûler; **drunken** *adj* ivre,
soûl(e); (*rage, stupor*) ivrogne, d'ivrogne

dry [draɪ] *adj* sec (sèche); (*day*) sans
pluie ▷ *vt* sécher; (*clothes*) faire sécher
▷ *vi* sécher; **dry off** *vi, vt* sécher; **dry up**
vi (*river, supplies*) se tarir; **dry-cleaner's**
n teinturerie *f*; **dry-cleaning** *n* (*process*)
nettoyage *m* à sec; **dryer** *n* (*tumble-
dryer*) sèche-linge *m* inv; (*for hair*) sèche-
cheveux *m* inv

DSS *n abbr* (BRIT) = **Department of
Social Security**

DTP *n abbr* (= *desktop publishing*) PAO *f*

dual ['djuəl] *adj* double; **dual
carriageway** *n* (BRIT) route *f* à quatre
voies

dubious ['djuːbɪəs] *adj* hésitant(e),
incertain(e); (*reputation, company*)
douteux(-euse)

duck [dʌk] *n* canard *m* ▷ *vi* se baisser
vivement, baisser subitement la tête

due [djuː] *adj* (*money, payment*) dû
(due); (*expected*) attendu(e); (*fitting*)
qui convient ▷ *adv*: **~ north** droit vers
le nord; **~ to** (*because of*) en raison de;
(*caused by*) dû à; **the train is ~ at 8 a.m.**
le train est attendu à 8 h; **she is ~ back
tomorrow** elle doit rentrer demain; **he
is ~ £10** on lui doit 10 livres; **to give sb
his** *or* **her ~** être juste envers qn

duel ['djuəl] *n* duel *m*

duet [djuːˈɛt] *n* duo *m*

dug [dʌɡ] *pt, pp* of **dig**

duke [djuːk] *n* duc *m*

dull [dʌl] *adj* (*boring*) ennuyeux(-euse);
(*not bright*) morne, terne; (*sound,
pain*) sourd(e); (*weather, day*) gris(e),
maussade ▷ *vt* (*pain, grief*) atténuer;
(*mind, senses*) engourdir

dumb [dʌm] *adj* muet(te); (*stupid*) bête

dummy ['dʌmɪ] *n* (*tailor's model*)
mannequin *m*; (*mock-up*) factice *m*,
maquette *f*; (BRIT: *for baby*) tétine *f* ▷ *adj*
faux (fausse), factice

dump [dʌmp] *n* (*also:* **rubbish ~**)
décharge (publique); (*inf: place*) trou *m*

▷ *vt* (*put down*) déposer; déverser; (*get
rid of*) se débarrasser de; (Comput) lister

dumpling ['dʌmplɪŋ] *n* boulette *f*
(de pâte)

dune [djuːn] *n* dune *f*

dungarees [dʌŋɡəˈriːz] *npl* bleu(s)
m(pl); (*for child, woman*) salopette *f*

dungeon ['dʌndʒən] *n* cachot *m*

duplex ['djuːplɛks] *n* (US: *also:*
~ apartment) duplex *m*

duplicate *n* ['djuːplɪkət] double *m*
▷ *vt* ['djuːplɪkeɪt] faire un double de;
(*on machine*) polycopier; **in ~** en deux
exemplaires, en double

durable ['djuərəbl] *adj* durable;
(*clothes, metal*) résistant(e), solide

duration [djuəˈreɪʃən] *n* durée *f*

during ['djuərɪŋ] *prep* pendant, au
cours de

dusk [dʌsk] *n* crépuscule *m*

dust [dʌst] *n* poussière *f* ▷ *vt*
(*furniture*) essuyer, épousseter;
(*cake etc*): **to ~ with** saupoudrer de;
dustbin *n* (BRIT) poubelle *f*; **duster**
n chiffon *m*; **dustman** *n* (BRIT: *irreg*)
boueux *m*, éboueur *m*; **dustpan**
n pelle *f* à poussière; **dusty** *adj*
poussiéreux(-euse)

Dutch [dʌtʃ] *adj* hollandais(e),
néerlandais(e) ▷ *n* (Ling) hollandais *m*,
néerlandais *m* ▷ *adv*: **to go ~** or **dutch**
(*inf*) partager les frais; **the Dutch**
npl les Hollandais, les Néerlandais;
Dutchman (*irreg*) *n* Hollandais *m*;
Dutchwoman (*irreg*) *n* Hollandaise *f*

duty ['djuːtɪ] *n* devoir *m*; (*tax*) droit *m*,
taxe *f*; **on ~** de service; (*at night etc*) de
garde; **off ~** libre, pas de service or de
garde; **duty-free** *adj* exempté(e) de
douane, hors-taxe

duvet ['duːveɪ] *n* (BRIT) couette *f*

DVD *n abbr* (= *digital versatile or video disc*)
DVD *m*; **DVD burner** *n* graveur *m* de
DVD; **DVD player** *n* lecteur *m* de DVD;
DVD writer *n* graveur *m* de DVD

dwarf (*pl* **dwarves**) [dwɔːf, dwɔːvz] *n*
nain(e) *f* ▷ *vt* écraser

dwell (*pt, pp* **dwelt**) [dwɛl, dwɛlt] *vi*

demeurer; **dwell on** vt fus s'étendre sur
dwelt [dwɛlt] pt, pp of **dwell**
dwindle ['dwɪndl] vi diminuer,
décroître
dye [daɪ] n teinture f ▷ vt teindre
dying ['daɪɪŋ] adj mourant(e),
agonisant(e)
dynamic [daɪ'næmɪk] adj dynamique
dynamite ['daɪnəmaɪt] n dynamite f
dyslexia [dɪs'lɛksɪə] n dyslexie f
dyslexic [dɪs'lɛksɪk] adj, n dyslexique
m/f

E [iː] n (Mus): **E** mi m
E111 n abbr (= form E111) formulaire m E111
each [iːtʃ] adj chaque ▷ pron chacun(e);
~ **other** l'un l'autre; **they hate ~ other**
ils se détestent (mutuellement); **they
have 2 books ~** ils ont 2 livres chacun;
they cost £5 ~ ils coûtent 5 livres
(la) pièce
eager ['iːgər] adj (person, buyer)
empressé(e); (keen: pupil, worker)
enthousiaste; **to be ~ to do sth**
(impatient) brûler de faire qch; (keen)
désirer vivement faire qch; **to be ~ for**
(event) désirer vivement; (vengeance,
affection, information) être avide de
eagle ['iːgl] n aigle m
ear [ɪər] n oreille f; (of corn) épi m;
earache n mal m aux oreilles; **eardrum**
n tympan m
earl [əːl] n comte m
earlier ['əːlɪər] adj (date etc) plus
rapproché(e); (edition etc) plus
ancien(ne), antérieur(e) ▷ adv plus tôt
early ['əːlɪ] adv tôt, de bonne heure;

(*ahead of time*) en avance; (*near the beginning*) au début ⊳ adj précoce, qui se manifeste (*or* se fait) tôt *or* de bonne heure; premier(-ière); (*reply*) rapide; (*death*) prématuré(e); (*work*) de jeunesse; **to have an ~ night/start** se coucher/ partir tôt *or* de bonne heure; **in the ~ spring/19th century** au début du printemps/ 19ème siècle; **early retirement** *n* retraite anticipée

earmark ['ɪəmɑːk] *vt*: **to ~ sth for** réserver *or* destiner qch à

earn [əːn] *vt* gagner; (*Comm*: *yield*) rapporter; **to ~ one's living** gagner sa vie

earnest ['əːnɪst] *adj* sérieux(-euse) ⊳ *n*: **in ~** *adv* sérieusement, pour de bon

earnings ['əːnɪŋz] *npl* salaire *m*; gains *mpl*; (*of company etc*) profits *mpl*, bénéfices *mpl*

ear: earphones *npl* écouteurs *mpl*; **earplugs** *npl* boules *fpl* Quiès®; (*to keep out water*) protège-tympans *mpl*; **earring** *n* boucle *f* d'oreille

earth [əːθ] *n* (*gen, also* BRIT *Elec*) terre *f* ⊳ *vt* (BRIT *Elec*) relier à la terre; **earthquake** *n* tremblement *m* de terre, séisme *m*

ease [iːz] *n* facilité *f*, aisance *f*; (*comfort*) bien-être *m* ⊳ *vt* (*soothe*: *mind*) tranquilliser; (*reduce*: *pain, problem*) atténuer; (: *tension*) réduire; (*loosen*) relâcher, détendre; (*help*: *pass*) **to ~ sth in/out** faire pénétrer/sortir qch délicatement *or* avec douceur, faciliter la pénétration/la sortie de qch; **at ~** à l'aise; (*Mil*) au repos

easily ['iːzɪlɪ] *adv* facilement; (*by far*) de loin

east [iːst] *n* est *m* ⊳ *adj* (*wind*) d'est; (*side*) est *inv* ⊳ *adv* à l'est, vers l'est; **the E~** l'Orient *m*; (*Pol*) les pays *mpl* de l'Est; **eastbound** *adj* en direction de l'est; (*carriageway*) est *inv*

Easter ['iːstə'] *n* Pâques *fpl*; **Easter egg** *n* œuf *m* de Pâques

eastern ['iːstən] *adj* de l'est, oriental(e)

Easter Sunday *n* le dimanche de Pâques

easy ['iːzɪ] *adj* facile; (*manner*) aisé(e) ⊳ *adv*: **to take it** *or* **things ~** (*rest*) ne pas se fatiguer; (*not worry*) ne pas (trop) s'en faire; **easy-going** *adj* accommodant(e), facile à vivre

eat (*pt* **ate**, *pp* **~en**) [iːt, eɪt, 'iːtn] *vt*, *vi* manger; **can we have something to ~?** est-ce qu'on peut manger quelque chose?; **eat out** *vi* manger au restaurant

eavesdrop ['iːvzdrɔp] *vi*: **to ~ (on)** écouter de façon indiscrète

e-book ['iːbuk] *n* livre *m* électronique

e-business ['iːbɪznɪs] *n* (*company*) entreprise *f* électronique; (*commerce*) commerce *m* électronique

EC *n abbr* (= *European Community*) CE *f*

eccentric [ɪk'sɛntrɪk] *adj*, *n* excentrique *m/f*

echo, echoes ['ɛkəu] *n* écho *m* ⊳ *vt* répéter ⊳ *vi* résonner; faire écho

eclipse [ɪ'klɪps] *n* éclipse *f*

eco-friendly [iːkəu'frɛndlɪ] *adj* non nuisible à *or* qui ne nuit pas à l'environnement

ecological [iːkə'lɔdʒɪkəl] *adj* écologique

ecology [ɪ'kɔlədʒɪ] *n* écologie *f*

e-commerce [iːkɔmɜːs] *n* commerce *m* électronique

economic [iːkə'nɔmɪk] *adj* économique; (*profitable*) rentable; **economical** *adj* économique; (*person*) économe; **economics** *n* (*Scol*) économie *f* politique ⊳ *npl* (*of project etc*) côté *m or* aspect *m* économique

economist [ɪ'kɔnəmɪst] *n* économiste *m/f*

economize [ɪ'kɔnəmaɪz] *vi* économiser, faire des économies

economy [ɪ'kɔnəmɪ] *n* économie *f*; **economy class** *n* (*Aviat*) classe *f* touriste; **economy class syndrome** *n* syndrome *m* de la classe économique

ecstasy ['ɛkstəsɪ] *n* extase *f*; (*Drugs*)

ecstasy m; **ecstatic** [ɛks'tætɪk] adj extatique, en extase

eczema ['ɛksɪmə] n eczéma m

edge [ɛdʒ] n bord m; (of knife etc) tranchant m, fil m ▷ vt border; **on ~** (fig) crispé(e), tendu(e)

edgy ['ɛdʒɪ] adj crispé(e), tendu(e)

edible ['ɛdɪbl] adj comestible; (meal) mangeable

Edinburgh ['ɛdɪnbərə] n Édimbourg

edit ['ɛdɪt] vt (text, book) éditer; (report) préparer; (film) monter; (magazine) diriger; (newspaper) être le rédacteur or la rédactrice en chef de; **edition** [ɪ'dɪʃən] n édition f; **editor** n (of newspaper) rédacteur(-trice), rédacteur(-trice) en chef; (of sb's work) éditeur(-trice); (also: **film editor**) monteur(-euse); **political/ foreign editor** rédacteur politique/au service étranger; **editorial** [ɛdɪ'tɔ:rɪəl] adj de la rédaction, éditorial(e) ▷ n éditorial m

educate ['ɛdjukeɪt] vt (teach) instruire; (bring up) éduquer; **educated** ['ɛdjukeɪtɪd] adj (person) cultivé(e)

education [ɛdju'keɪʃən] n éducation f; (studies) études fpl; (teaching) enseignement m, instruction f; **educational** adj pédagogique; (institution) scolaire; (game, toy) éducatif(-ive)

eel [i:l] n anguille f

eerie ['ɪərɪ] adj inquiétant(e), spectral(e), surnaturel(le)

effect [ɪ'fɛkt] n effet m ▷ vt effectuer; **effects** npl (property) effets, affaires fpl; **to take ~** (Law) entrer en vigueur, prendre effet; (drug) agir, faire son effet; **in ~** en fait; **effective** adj efficace; (actual) véritable; **effectively** adv efficacement; (in reality) effectivement, en fait

efficiency [ɪ'fɪʃənsɪ] n efficacité f; (of machine, car) rendement m

efficient [ɪ'fɪʃənt] adj efficace; (machine, car) d'un bon rendement; **efficiently** adv efficacement

effort ['ɛfət] n effort m; **effortless** adj sans effort, aisé(e); (achievement) facile

e.g. adv abbr (= exempli gratia) par exemple, p. ex.

egg [ɛg] n œuf m; **hard-boiled/soft-boiled ~** œuf dur/à la coque; **eggcup** n coquetier m; **egg plant** (US) n aubergine f; **eggshell** n coquille f d'œuf; **egg white** n blanc m d'œuf; **egg yolk** n jaune m d'œuf

ego ['i:gəu] n (self-esteem) amour-propre m; (Psych) moi m

Egypt ['i:dʒɪpt] n Égypte f; **Egyptian** [ɪ'dʒɪpʃən] adj égyptien(ne) ▷ n Égyptien(ne)

Eiffel Tower ['aɪfəl-] n tour f Eiffel

eight [eɪt] num huit; **eighteen** num dix-huit; **eighteenth** num dix-huitième; **eighth** num huitième; **eightieth** ['eɪtɪɪθ] num quatre-vingtième

eighty ['eɪtɪ] num quatre-vingt(s)

Eire ['ɛərə] n République f d'Irlande

either ['aɪðə*] adj l'un ou l'autre; (both, each) chaque ▷ pron: **~ (of them)** l'un ou l'autre ▷ adv non plus ▷ conj: **~ good or bad** soit bon soit mauvais; **on ~ side** de chaque côté; **I don't like ~** je n'aime ni l'un ni l'autre; **no, I don't ~** moi non plus; **which bike do you want? ~ will do** quel vélo voulez-vous? - n'importe lequel; **answer with ~ yes or no** répondez par oui ou par non

eject [ɪ'dʒɛkt] vt (tenant etc) expulser; (object) éjecter
elaborate adj [ɪ'læbərɪt] compliqué(e), recherché(e), minutieux(-euse) ▷ vb [ɪ'læbəreɪt] ▷ vt élaborer ▷ vi entrer dans les détails
elastic [ɪ'læstɪk] adj, n élastique (m); **elastic band** n (BRIT) élastique m
elbow ['ɛlbəu] n coude m
elder ['ɛldə] adj aîné(e) ▷ n (tree) sureau m; **one's ~s** ses aînés; **elderly** adj âgé(e) ▷ npl: **the elderly** les personnes âgées
eldest ['ɛldɪst] adj, n: **the ~ (child)** l'aîné(e) (des enfants)
elect [ɪ'lɛkt] vt élire; (choose): **to ~ to do** choisir de faire ▷ adj: **the president ~** le président désigné; **election** n élection f; **electoral** adj électoral(e); **electorate** n électorat m
electric [ɪ'lɛktrɪk] adj électrique; **electrical** adj électrique; **electric blanket** n couverture chauffante; **electric fire** n (BRIT) radiateur m électrique; **electrician** [ɪlɛk'trɪʃən] n électricien m; **electricity** [ɪlɛk'trɪsɪtɪ] n électricité f; **electric shock** n choc m or décharge f électrique; **electrify** [ɪ'lɛktrɪfaɪ] vt (Rail) électrifier; (audience) électriser
electronic [ɪlɛk'trɒnɪk] adj électronique; **electronic mail** n courrier m électronique; **electronics** n électronique f
elegance ['ɛlɪgəns] n élégance f
elegant ['ɛlɪgənt] adj élégant(e)
element ['ɛlɪmənt] n (gen) élément m; (of heater, kettle etc) résistance f
elementary [ɛlɪ'mɛntərɪ] adj élémentaire; (school, education) primaire; **elementary school** n (US) école f primaire
elephant ['ɛlɪfənt] n éléphant m
elevate ['ɛlɪveɪt] vt élever
elevator ['ɛlɪveɪtə] n (in warehouse etc) élévateur m, monte-charge m inv; (US: lift) ascenseur m
eleven [ɪ'lɛvn] num onze; **eleventh**

num onzième
eligible ['ɛlɪdʒəbl] adj éligible; (for membership) admissible; **an ~ young man** un beau parti; **to be ~ for sth** remplir les conditions requises pour qch
eliminate [ɪ'lɪmɪneɪt] vt éliminer
elm [ɛlm] n orme m
eloquent ['ɛləkwənt] adj éloquent(e)
else [ɛls] adv: **something ~** quelque chose d'autre, autre chose; **somewhere ~** ailleurs, autre part; **everywhere ~** partout ailleurs; **everyone ~** tous les autres; **nothing ~** rien d'autre; **where ~?** à quel autre endroit?; **little ~** pas grand-chose d'autre; **elsewhere** adv ailleurs, autre part
elusive [ɪ'lu:sɪv] adj insaisissable
e-mail ['i:meɪl] n abbr (= electronic mail) e-mail m, courriel m ▷ vt: **to ~ sb** envoyer un e-mail or un courriel à qn; **e-mail address** n adresse f e-mail
embankment [ɪm'bæŋkmənt] n (of road, railway) remblai m, talus m; (of river) berge f, quai m; (dyke) digue f
embargo, embargoes [ɪm'bɑ:gəu] n (Comm, Naut) embargo m; (prohibition) interdiction f
embark [ɪm'bɑ:k] vi embarquer ▷ vt embarquer; **to ~ on** (journey etc) commencer, entreprendre; (fig) se lancer or s'embarquer dans
embarrass [ɪm'bærəs] vt embarrasser, gêner; **embarrassed** adj gêné(e); **embarrassing** adj gênant(e), embarrassant(e); **embarrassment** n embarras m, gêne f; (embarrassing thing, person) source f d'embarras
embassy ['ɛmbəsɪ] n ambassade f
embrace [ɪm'breɪs] vt embrasser, étreindre; (include) embrasser ▷ vi s'embrasser, s'étreindre ▷ n étreinte f
embroider [ɪm'brɔɪdə] vt broder; **embroidery** n broderie f
embryo ['ɛmbrɪəu] n (also fig) embryon m
emerald ['ɛmərəld] n émeraude f

emerge [ɪˈmɜːdʒ] vi apparaître; (from room, car) surgir; (from sleep, imprisonment) sortir

emergency [ɪˈmɜːdʒənsɪ] n (crisis) cas m d'urgence; (Med) urgence f; **in an ~** en cas d'urgence; **state of ~** état m d'urgence; **emergency brake** (us) n frein m à main; **emergency exit** n sortie f de secours; **emergency landing** n atterrissage forcé; **emergency room** n (us: Med) urgences fpl; **emergency services** npl: **the emergency services** (fire, police, ambulance) les services mpl d'urgence

emigrate [ˈɛmɪɡreɪt] vi émigrer; **emigration** [ɛmɪˈɡreɪʃən] n émigration f

eminent [ˈɛmɪnənt] adj éminent(e)

emissions [ɪˈmɪʃənz] npl émissions fpl

emit [ɪˈmɪt] vt émettre

emotion [ɪˈməʊʃən] n sentiment m; **emotional** adj (person) émotif(-ive), très sensible; (needs) affectif(-ive); (scene) émouvant(e); (tone, speech) qui fait appel aux sentiments

emperor [ˈɛmpərər] n empereur m

emphasis (pl -ases) [ˈɛmfəsɪs, -siːz] n accent m; **to lay** or **place ~ on sth** (fig) mettre l'accent sur, insister sur

emphasize [ˈɛmfəsaɪz] vt (syllable, word, point) appuyer or insister sur; (feature) souligner, accentuer

empire [ˈɛmpaɪər] n empire m

employ [ɪmˈplɔɪ] vt employer; **employee** [ɪmplɔɪˈiː] n employé(e); **employer** n employeur(-euse); **employment** n emploi m; **employment agency** n agence f or bureau m de placement

empower [ɪmˈpaʊər] vt: **to ~ sb to do** autoriser or habiliter qn à faire

empress [ˈɛmprɪs] n impératrice f

emptiness [ˈɛmptɪnɪs] n vide m; (of area) aspect m désertique

empty [ˈɛmptɪ] adj vide; (street, area) désert(e); (threat, promise) en l'air, vain(e) ▷ vt vider ▷ vi se vider; (liquid) s'écouler; **empty-handed** adj les mains vides

EMU n abbr (= European Monetary Union) UME f

emulsion [ɪˈmʌlʃən] n émulsion f; (also: **~ paint**) peinture mate

enable [ɪˈneɪbl] vt: **to ~ sb to do** permettre à qn de faire

enamel [ɪˈnæməl] n émail m; (also: **~ paint**) (peinture f) laque f

enchanting [ɪnˈtʃɑːntɪŋ] adj ravissant(e), enchanteur(-eresse)

encl. abbr (on letters etc: = enclosed) ci-joint(e); (= enclosure) P.J.

enclose [ɪnˈkləʊz] vt (land) clôturer; (space, object) entourer; (letter etc): **to ~ (with)** joindre (à); **please find ~d** veuillez trouver ci-joint

enclosure [ɪnˈkləʊʒər] n enceinte f

encore [ɔŋˈkɔː] excl, n bis (m)

encounter [ɪnˈkaʊntər] n rencontre f ▷ vt rencontrer

encourage [ɪnˈkʌrɪdʒ] vt encourager; **encouragement** n encouragement m; **encouraging** [ɪnˈkʌrɪdʒɪŋ] adj encourageant(e)

encyclop(a)edia [ɛnsaɪkləʊˈpiːdɪə] n encyclopédie f

end [ɛnd] n fin f; (of table, street, rope etc) bout m, extrémité f ▷ vt terminer; (also: **bring to an ~, put an ~ to**) mettre fin à ▷ vi se terminer, finir; **in the ~** finalement; **on ~** (object) debout, dressé(e); **to stand on ~** (hair) se dresser sur la tête; **for hours on ~** pendant des heures (et des heures); **end up** vi: **to ~ up in** (condition) finir or se terminer par; (place) finir or aboutir à

endanger [ɪnˈdeɪndʒər] vt mettre en danger; **an ~ed species** une espèce en voie de disparition

endearing [ɪnˈdɪərɪŋ] adj attachant(e)

endeavour [ɪnˈdɛvər] (us **endeavor**) n effort m; (attempt) tentative f ▷ vt: **to ~ to do** tenter or s'efforcer de faire

ending [ˈɛndɪŋ] n dénouement m, conclusion f; (Ling) terminaison f

endless [ˈɛndlɪs] adj sans fin, interminable

endorse [ɪn'dɔːs] vt (cheque) endosser; (approve) appuyer, approuver, sanctionner; **endorsement** n (approval) appui m, aval m; (: BRIT on driving licence) contravention f (portée du permis de conduire)

endurance [ɪn'djuərəns] n endurance f

endure [ɪn'djuə'] vt (bear) supporter, endurer ▷ vi (last) durer

enemy ['enəmɪ] adj, n ennemi(e)

energetic [enə'dʒetɪk] adj énergique; (activity) très actif(-ive), qui fait se dépenser (physiquement)

energy ['enədʒɪ] n énergie f

enforce [ɪn'fɔːs] vt (law) appliquer, faire respecter

engaged [ɪn'geɪdʒd] adj (BRIT: busy, in use) occupé(e); (betrothed) fiancé(e); **to get ~** se fiancer; **the line's ~** la ligne est occupée; **engaged tone** n (BRIT Tel) tonalité f occupé inv

engagement [ɪn'geɪdʒmənt] n (undertaking) obligation f, engagement m; (appointment) rendez-vous m inv; (to marry) fiançailles fpl; **engagement ring** n bague f de fiançailles

engaging [ɪn'geɪdʒɪŋ] adj engageant(e), attirant(e)

engine ['endʒɪn] n (Aut) moteur m; (Rail) locomotive f

　Be careful not to translate **engine** by the French word **engin**.

engineer [endʒɪ'nɪə'] n ingénieur m; (BRIT: repairer) dépanneur m; (Navy, US Rail) mécanicien m; **engineering** n engineering m, ingénierie f; (of bridges, ships) génie m; (of machine) mécanique f

England ['ɪŋglənd] n Angleterre f

English ['ɪŋglɪʃ] adj anglais(e) ▷ n (Ling) anglais m; **the ~** npl les Anglais; **English Channel** n: **the English Channel** la Manche; **Englishman** (irreg) n Anglais m; **Englishwoman** (irreg) n Anglaise f

engrave [ɪn'greɪv] vt graver

engraving [ɪn'greɪvɪŋ] n gravure f

enhance [ɪn'hɑːns] vt rehausser,

mettre en valeur

enjoy [ɪn'dʒɔɪ] vt aimer, prendre plaisir à; (have benefit of: health, fortune) jouir de; (: success) connaître; **to ~ o.s.** s'amuser; **enjoyable** adj agréable; **enjoyment** n plaisir m

enlarge [ɪn'lɑːdʒ] vt accroître; (Phot) agrandir ▷ vi: **to ~ on** (subject) s'étendre sur; **enlargement** n (Phot) agrandissement m

enlist [ɪn'lɪst] vt recruter; (support) s'assurer ▷ vi s'engager

enormous [ɪ'nɔːməs] adj énorme

enough [ɪ'nʌf] adj: **~ time/books** assez or suffisamment de temps/livres ▷ adv: **big ~** assez or suffisamment grand ▷ pron: **have you got ~?** (en) avez-vous assez?; **~ to eat** assez à manger; **that's ~, thanks** cela suffit or c'est assez, merci; **I've had ~ of him** j'en ai assez de lui; **he has not worked ~** il n'a pas assez or suffisamment travaillé, il n'a pas travaillé assez or suffisamment; **... which, funnily or oddly ~ ...** qui, chose curieuse

enquire [ɪn'kwaɪə'] vt, vi = **inquire**

enquiry [ɪn'kwaɪərɪ] n = **inquiry**

enrage [ɪn'reɪdʒ] vt mettre en fureur or en rage, rendre furieux(-euse)

enrich [ɪn'rɪtʃ] vt enrichir

enrol (US **enroll**) [ɪn'rəul] vt inscrire ▷ vi s'inscrire; **enrolment** (US **enrollment**) n inscription f

en route [ɒn'ruːt] adv en route, en chemin

en suite [ɒn'swiːt] adj: **with ~ bathroom** avec salle de bains en attenante

ensure [ɪn'ʃuə'] vt assurer, garantir

entail [ɪn'teɪl] vt entraîner, nécessiter

enter ['entə'] vt (room) entrer dans, pénétrer dans; (club, army) entrer à; (competition) s'inscrire à or pour; (sb for a competition) (faire) inscrire; (write down) inscrire, noter; (Comput) entrer, introduire ▷ vi entrer

enterprise ['entəpraɪz] n (company, undertaking) entreprise f; (initiative)

(esprit m d')initiative f; **free ~** libre
entreprise; **private ~** entreprise privée;
enterprising adj entreprenant(e),
dynamique; (scheme) audacieux(-euse)
entertain [ɛntəˈteɪn] vt amuser,
distraire; (invite) recevoir (à dîner);
(idea, plan) envisager; **entertainer** n
artiste m/f de variétés; **entertaining**
adj amusant(e), distrayant(e);
entertainment n (amusement)
distraction f, divertissement m,
amusement m; (show) spectacle m
enthusiasm [ɪnˈθuːzɪæzəm] n
enthousiasme m
enthusiast [ɪnˈθuːzɪæst] n
enthousiaste m/f; **enthusiastic**
[ɪnθuːzɪˈæstɪk] adj enthousiaste;
to be enthusiastic about être
enthousiasmé(e) par
entire [ɪnˈtaɪə] adj (tout) entier(-ère);
entirely adv entièrement,
complètement
entitle [ɪnˈtaɪtl] vt: **to ~ sb to sth**
donner droit à qch à qn; **entitled** adj
(book) intitulé(e); **to be entitled to do**
avoir le droit de faire
entrance n [ˈɛntrns] entrée f ▷ vt
[ɪnˈtrɑːns] enchanter, ravir; **where's
the ~?** où est l'entrée?; **to gain ~ to**
(university etc) être admis à; **entrance
examination** n examen m d'entrée
or d'admission; **entrance fee** n (to
museum etc) prix m d'entrée; (to join club
etc) droit m d'inscription; **entrance
ramp** n (US Aut) bretelle f d'accès;
entrant n (in race etc) participant(e),
concurrent(e); (BRIT: in exam)
candidat(e)
entrepreneur [ˈɔntrəprəˈnəː] n
entrepreneur m
entrust [ɪnˈtrʌst] vt: **to ~ sth to**
confier qch à
entry [ˈɛntrɪ] n entrée f; (in register,
diary) inscription f; **"no ~"** défense
d'entrer, "entrée interdite"; (Aut)
"sens interdit"; **entry phone** n (BRIT)
interphone m (à l'entrée d'un immeuble)
envelope [ˈɛnvələup] n enveloppe f

envious [ˈɛnvɪəs] adj envieux(-euse)
environment [ɪnˈvaɪərnmənt]
n (social, moral) milieu m; (natural
world): **the ~** l'environnement m;
environmental [ɪnvaɪərnˈmɛntl]
adj (of surroundings) du milieu;
(issue, disaster) écologique;
environmentally [ɪnvaɪərnˈmɛntlɪ]
adv: **environmentally sound/friendly**
qui ne nuit pas à l'environnement
envisage [ɪnˈvɪzɪdʒ] vt (foresee) prévoir
envoy [ˈɛnvɔɪ] n envoyé(e); (diplomat)
ministre m plénipotentiaire
envy [ˈɛnvɪ] n envie f ▷ vt envier; **to ~ sb
sth** envier qch à qn
epic [ˈɛpɪk] n épopée f ▷ adj épique
epidemic [ɛpɪˈdɛmɪk] n épidémie f
epilepsy [ˈɛpɪlɛpsɪ] n épilepsie f;
epileptic adj, n épileptique m/f;
epileptic fit n crise f d'épilepsie
episode [ˈɛpɪsəud] n épisode m
equal [ˈiːkwl] adj égal(e) ▷ vt égaler;
~ to (task) à la hauteur de; **equality**
[iːˈkwɔlɪtɪ] n égalité f; **equalize**
vt, vi (Sport) égaliser; **equally** adv
également; (share) en parts égales;
(treat) de la même façon; (pay) autant;
(just as) tout aussi
equation [ɪˈkweɪʃən] n (Math)
équation f
equator [ɪˈkweɪtə] n équateur m
equip [ɪˈkwɪp] vt équiper; **to ~ sb/sth
with** équiper or munir qn/qch de;
equipment n équipement m; (electrical
etc) appareillage m, installation f
equivalent [ɪˈkwɪvələnt] adj
équivalent(e) ▷ n équivalent m; **to be ~
to** équivaloir à, être équivalent(e) à
ER abbr (BRIT: = Elizabeth Regina) la reine
Élisabeth; (US Med: = emergency room)
urgences fpl
era [ˈɪərə] n ère f, époque f
erase [ɪˈreɪz] vt effacer; **eraser** n
gomme f
erect [ɪˈrɛkt] adj droit(e) ▷ vt
construire; (monument) ériger, élever;
(tent etc) dresser; **erection** [ɪˈrɛkʃən]
n (Physiol) érection f; (of building)

construction f

ERM n abbr (= Exchange Rate Mechanism) mécanisme m des taux de change

erode [ɪˈrəʊd] vt éroder; (metal) ronger

erosion [ɪˈrəʊʒən] n érosion f

erotic [ɪˈrɒtɪk] adj érotique

errand [ˈɛrnd] n course f, commission f

erratic [ɪˈrætɪk] adj irrégulier(-ière), inconstant(e)

error [ˈɛrə*] n erreur f

erupt [ɪˈrʌpt] vi entrer en éruption; (fig) éclater; **eruption** [ɪˈrʌpʃən] n éruption f; (of anger, violence) explosion f

escalate [ˈɛskəleɪt] vi s'intensifier; (costs) monter en flèche

escalator [ˈɛskəleɪtə*] n escalier roulant

escape [ɪˈskeɪp] n évasion f, fuite f; (of gas etc) fuite f ▷ vi s'échapper, fuir; (from jail) s'évader; (fig) s'en tirer; (leak) s'échapper ▷ vt échapper à; **to ~ from** (person) échapper à; (place) s'échapper de; (fig) fuir; **his name ~s me** son nom m'échappe

escort vt [ɪˈskɔːt] escorter ▷ n [ˈɛskɔːt] (Mil) escorte f

especially [ɪˈspɛʃlɪ] adv (particularly) particulièrement; (above all) surtout

espionage [ˈɛspɪənɑːʒ] n espionnage m

essay [ˈɛseɪ] n (Scol) dissertation f; (Literature) essai m

essence [ˈɛsns] n essence f; (Culin) extrait m

essential [ɪˈsɛnʃl] adj essentiel(le); (basic) fondamental(e); **essentials** npl éléments essentiels; **essentially** adv essentiellement

establish [ɪˈstæblɪʃ] vt établir; (business) fonder, créer; (one's power etc) asseoir, affermir; **establishment** n établissement m; (founding) création f; (institution) établissement m; **the Establishment** les pouvoirs établis; l'ordre établi

estate [ɪˈsteɪt] n (land) domaine m, propriété f; (Law) biens mpl, succession f; (BRIT: also: **housing ~**)

lotissement m; **estate agent** n (BRIT) agent immobilier; **estate car** n (BRIT) break m

estimate n [ˈɛstɪmət] estimation f; (Comm) devis m ▷ vb [ˈɛstɪmeɪt] ▷ vt estimer

etc abbr (= et cetera) etc

eternal [ɪˈtəːnl] adj éternel(le)

eternity [ɪˈtəːnɪtɪ] n éternité f

ethical [ˈɛθɪkl] adj moral(e); **ethics** [ˈɛθɪks] n éthique f ▷ npl moralité f

Ethiopia [iːˈθɪəʊpɪə] n Éthiopie f

ethnic [ˈɛθnɪk] adj ethnique; (clothes, food) folklorique, exotique, propre aux minorités ethniques non-occidentales; **ethnic minority** n minorité f ethnique

e-ticket [ˈiːtɪkɪt] n billet m électronique

etiquette [ˈɛtɪkɛt] n convenances fpl, étiquette f

EU n abbr (= European Union) UE f

euro [ˈjʊərəʊ] n (currency) euro m

Europe [ˈjʊərəp] n Europe f; **European** [jʊərəˈpɪːən] adj européen(ne) ▷ n Européen(ne); **European Community** n Communauté européenne; **European Union** n Union européenne

Eurostar® [ˈjʊərəʊstɑː*] n Eurostar® m

evacuate [ɪˈvækjueɪt] vt évacuer

evade [ɪˈveɪd] vt échapper à; (question etc) éluder; (duties) se dérober à

evaluate [ɪˈvæljueɪt] vt évaluer

evaporate [ɪˈvæpəreɪt] vi s'évaporer; (fig: hopes, fear) s'envoler; (anger) se dissiper

eve [iːv] n: **on the ~ of** à la veille de

even [ˈiːvn] adj (level, smooth) régulier(-ière); (equal) égal(e); (number) pair(e) ▷ adv même; **~ if** même si + indic; **~ though** alors même que + cond; **~ more** encore plus; **~ faster** encore plus vite; **~ so** quand même; **not ~** pas même; **~ he was there** même lui était là; **~ on Sundays** même le dimanche; **to get ~ with sb** prendre sa revanche sur qn

evening [ˈiːvnɪŋ] n soir m; (as duration,

event) soirée f; **in the ~** le soir; **evening class** n cours m du soir; **evening dress** n (man's) tenue f de soirée, smoking m; (woman's) robe f de soirée

event [ɪˈvɛnt] adj événement m; (Sport) épreuve f; **in the ~ of** en cas de; **eventful** adj mouvementé(e)

eventual [ɪˈvɛntʃuəl] adj final(e)

> Be careful not to translate *eventual* by the French word **éventuel**.

eventually [ɪˈvɛntʃuəlɪ] adv finalement

> Be careful not to translate *eventually* by the French word **éventuellement**.

ever [ˈɛvəʳ] adv jamais; (at all times) toujours; (in questions): **why ~ not?** mais enfin, pourquoi pas?; **the best ~** le meilleur qu'on ait jamais vu; **have you ~ seen it?** l'as-tu déjà vu?, as-tu eu l'occasion or t'est-il arrivé de le voir?; **~ since** (as adv) depuis; (as conj) depuis que; **~ so pretty** si joli; **evergreen** n arbre m à feuilles persistantes

KEYWORD

every [ˈɛvrɪ] adj 1 (each) chaque; **every one of them** tous (sans exception); **every shop in town was closed** tous les magasins en ville étaient fermés 2 (all possible) tous (toutes) les; **I gave you every assistance** j'ai fait tout mon possible pour vous aider; **I have every confidence in him** j'ai entièrement or pleinement confiance en lui; **we wish you every success** nous vous souhaitons beaucoup de succès

3 (showing recurrence) tous les; **every day** tous les jours, chaque jour; **every other car** une voiture sur deux; **every other/third day** tous les deux/trois jours; **every now and then** de temps en temps; **everybody = everyone**; **everyday** adj (expression) courant(e), d'usage courant; (use) courant; (clothes, life) de tous les jours; (occurrence,

problem) quotidien(ne); **everyone** pron tout le monde, tous pl; **everything** pron tout; **everywhere** adv partout; **everywhere you go you meet ...** où qu'on aille, on rencontre ...

evict [ɪˈvɪkt] vt expulser

evidence [ˈɛvɪdns] n (proof) preuve(s) f(pl); (of witness) témoignage m; (sign): **to show ~ of** donner des signes de; **to give ~** témoigner, déposer

evident [ˈɛvɪdnt] adj évident(e); **evidently** adv de toute évidence; (apparently) apparemment

evil [ˈiːvl] adj mauvais(e) ⊳ n mal m

evoke [ɪˈvəuk] vt évoquer

evolution [iːvəˈluːʃən] n évolution f

evolve [ɪˈvɔlv] vt élaborer ⊳ vi évoluer, se transformer

ewe [juː] n brebis f

ex [ɛks] n (inf): **my ex** mon ex

ex- [ɛks] prefix ex-

exact [ɪgˈzækt] adj exact(e) ⊳ vt: **to ~ sth (from)** (signature, confession) extorquer qch (à); (apology) exiger qch (de); **exactly** adv exactement

exaggerate [ɪgˈzædʒəreɪt] vt, vi exagérer; **exaggeration** [ɪgzædʒəˈreɪʃən] n exagération f

exam [ɪgˈzæm] n abbr (Scol) =**examination**

examination [ɪgzæmɪˈneɪʃən] n (Scol, Med) examen m; **to take or sit an ~** (BRIT) passer un examen

examine [ɪgˈzæmɪn] vt (gen) examiner; (Scol, Law: person) interroger; **examiner** n examinateur(-trice)

example [ɪgˈzɑːmpl] n exemple m; **for ~** par exemple

exasperated [ɪgˈzɑːspəreɪtɪd] adj exaspéré(e)

exasperation [ɪgˈzɑːspəreɪʃən] adj exaspéré(e)

excavate [ˈɛkskəveɪt] vt (site) fouiller, excaver; (object) mettre au jour

exceed [ɪkˈsiːd] vt dépasser; (one's powers) outrepasser; **exceedingly** adv extrêmement

excel [ɪkˈsɛl] vi exceller ⊳ vt surpasser; **to ~ o.s.** se surpasser

excellence ['eksələns] n excellence f
excellent ['eksələnt] adj excellent(e)
except [ɪk'sept] prep (also: **~ for, ~ing**)
sauf, excepté, à l'exception de ▷ vt
excepter; **~ if/when** sauf si/quand;
~ that excepté que, si ce n'est que;
exception [ɪk'sepʃən] n exception
f; **to take exception to** s'offusquer
de; **exceptional** [ɪk'sepʃənl] adj
exceptionnel(le); **exceptionally**
[ɪk'sepʃənəlɪ] adv exceptionnellement
excerpt ['eksɜ:pt] n extrait m
excess [ɪk'ses] n excès m; **excess
baggage** n excédent m de bagages;
excessive adj excessif(-ive)
exchange [ɪks'tʃeɪndʒ] n échange m;
(also: **telephone ~**) central m ▷ vt
(for) échanger (contre); **could I ~ this,
please?** est-ce que je peux échanger
ceci, s'il vous plaît?; **exchange rate** n
taux m de change
excite [ɪk'saɪt] vt exciter; **excited** adj
(tout (toute)) excité(e); **to get excited**
s'exciter; **excitement** n excitation f;
exciting adj passionnant(e)
exclaim [ɪk'skleɪm] vi s'exclamer;
exclamation [eksklə'meɪʃən] n
exclamation f; **exclamation mark**
(us **exclamation point**) n point m
d'exclamation
exclude [ɪk'sklu:d] vt exclure
excluding [ɪk'sklu:dɪŋ] prep: **~ VAT** la
TVA non comprise
exclusion [ɪk'sklu:ʒən] n exclusion f
exclusive [ɪk'sklu:sɪv] adj
exclusif(-ive); (club, district) sélect(e);
(item of news) en exclusivité; **~ of VAT**
TVA non comprise; **exclusively** adv
exclusivement
excruciating [ɪk'skru:ʃieɪtɪŋ]
adj (pain) atroce, déchirant(e);
(embarrassing) pénible
excursion [ɪk'skɜ:ʃən] n excursion f
excuse n [ɪk'skju:s] excuse f ▷ vt
[ɪk'skju:z] (forgive) excuser; **to ~ sb
from** (activity) dispenser qn de; **~ me!**
excusez-moi, pardon!; **now if you
will ~ me, ...** maintenant, si vous (le)

permettez ...
ex-directory ['eksdɪ'rektərɪ] adj (BRIT)
sur la liste rouge
execute ['eksɪkju:t] vt exécuter;
execution [eksɪ'kju:ʃən] n exécution f
executive [ɪg'zekjutɪv] n (person) cadre
m; (managing group) bureau m; (Pol)
exécutif m ▷ adj exécutif(-ive); (position,
job) de cadre
exempt [ɪg'zempt] adj: **~ from**
exempté(e) or dispensé(e) de ▷ vt: **to ~
sb from** exempter or dispenser qn de
exercise ['eksəsaɪz] n exercice m ▷ vt
exercer; (patience etc) faire preuve de;
(dog) promener ▷ vi (also: **to take ~**)
prendre de l'exercice; **exercise book**
n cahier m
exert [ɪg'zɜ:t] vt exercer, employer; **to
~ o.s.** se dépenser; **exertion** [ɪg'zɜ:ʃən]
n effort m
exhale [eks'heɪl] vt exhaler ▷ vi expirer
exhaust [ɪg'zɔ:st] n (also: **~ fumes**)
gaz mpl d'échappement; (also: **~ pipe**)
tuyau m d'échappement ▷ vt épuiser;
exhausted adj épuisé(e); **exhaustion**
[ɪg'zɔ:stʃən] n épuisement m; **nervous
exhaustion** fatigue nerveuse
exhibit [ɪg'zɪbɪt] n (Art) pièce f or objet
m exposé(e); (Law) pièce à conviction
▷ vt (Art) exposer; (courage, skill) faire
preuve de; **exhibition** [eksɪ'bɪʃən] n
exposition f
exhilarating [ɪg'zɪləreɪtɪŋ] adj
grisant(e), stimulant(e)
exile ['eksaɪl] n exil m; (person) exilé(e)
▷ vt exiler
exist [ɪg'zɪst] vi exister; **existence** n
existence f; **existing** adj actuel(le)
exit ['eksɪt] n sortie f ▷ vi (Comput,
Theat) sortir; **where's the ~?** où est la
sortie?; **exit ramp** n (us Aut) bretelle
f d'accès
exotic [ɪg'zɔtɪk] adj exotique
expand [ɪk'spænd] vt (area) agrandir;
(quantity) accroître ▷ vi (trade, etc) se
développer, s'accroître; (gas, metal)
se dilater
expansion [ɪk'spænʃən] n (territorial,

economic) expansion f; (*of trade, influence etc*) développement m; (*of production*) accroissement m; (*of population*) croissance f; (*of gas, metal*) expansion, dilatation f

expect [ɪk'spɛkt] vt (*anticipate*) s'attendre à, s'attendre à ce que + *sub*; (*count on*) compter sur, escompter; (*require*) demander, exiger; (*suppose*) supposer; (*await: also baby*) attendre ▷ vi: **to be ~ing** (*pregnant woman*) être enceinte; **expectation** [ɛkspɛk'teɪʃən] n (*hope*) attente f, espérance(s) f(pl); (*belief*) attente

expedition [ɛkspə'dɪʃən] n expédition f

expel [ɪk'spɛl] vt chasser, expulser; (*Scol*) renvoyer, exclure

expenditure [ɪk'spɛndɪtʃəʳ] n (*act of spending*) dépense f; (*money spent*) dépenses fpl

expense [ɪk'spɛns] n (*high cost*) coût m; (*spending*) dépense f, frais mpl; **expenses** npl frais mpl; dépenses; **at the ~ of** (*fig*) aux dépens de; **expense account** n (*note*f des) frais mpl

expensive [ɪk'spɛnsɪv] adj cher (chère), coûteux(-euse); **it's too ~ça** coûte trop cher

experience [ɪk'spɪərɪəns] n expérience f ▷ vt connaître; (*feeling*) éprouver; **experienced** adj expérimenté(e)

experiment [ɪk'spɛrɪmənt] n expérience f ▷ vi faire une expérience; **experimental** [ɪkspɛrɪ'mɛntl] adj expérimental(e)

expert ['ɛkspɜːt] adj expert(e) ▷ n expert m; **expertise** [ɛkspə'tiːz] n (grande) compétence

expire [ɪk'spaɪəʳ] vi expirer; **expiry** n expiration f; **expiry date** n date f d'expiration; (*on label*) à utiliser avant _

explain [ɪk'spleɪn] vt expliquer; **explanation** [ɛksplə'neɪʃən] n explication f

explicit [ɪk'splɪsɪt] adj explicite; (*definite*) formel(le)

explode [ɪk'spləud] vi exploser

exploit n ['ɛksplɔɪt] exploit m ▷ vt [ɪk'splɔɪt] exploiter; **exploitation** [ɛksplɔɪ'teɪʃən] n exploitation f

explore [ɪk'splɔːʳ] vt explorer; (*possibilities*) étudier, examiner; **explorer** n explorateur(-trice)

explosion [ɪk'spləuʒən] n explosion f; **explosive** [ɪk'spləusɪv] adj explosif(-ive) ▷ n explosif m

export vt [ɛk'spɔːt] exporter ▷ n ['ɛkspɔːt] exportation f ▷ cpd d'exportation; **exporter** n exportateur m

expose [ɪk'spəuz] vt exposer; (*unmask*) démasquer, dévoiler; **exposed** adj (*land, house*) exposé(e); **exposure** [ɪk'spəuʒəʳ] n exposition f; (*publicity*) couverture f; (*Phot: speed*) (temps m de) pose f; (*: shot*) pose; **to die of exposure** (*Med*) mourir de froid

express [ɪk'sprɛs] adj (*definite*) formel(le), exprès(-esse); (BRIT: *letter etc*) exprès inv ▷ n (*train*) rapide m ▷ vt exprimer; **expression** [ɪk'sprɛʃən] n expression f; **expressway** n (us) voie f express (à plusieurs files)

exquisite [ɛk'skwɪzɪt] adj exquis(e)

extend [ɪk'stɛnd] vt (*visit, street*) prolonger, remettre; (*building*) agrandir; (*offer*) présenter, offrir; (*hand, arm*) tendre ▷ vi (*land*) s'étendre; **extension** n (*of visit, street*) prolongation f; (*building*) annexe f; (*telephone: in offices*) poste m; (*: in private house*) téléphone m supplémentaire; **extension cable, extension lead** n (*Elec*) rallonge f; **extensive** adj étendu(e), vaste; (*damage, alterations*) considérable; (*inquiries*) approfondi(e)

extent [ɪk'stɛnt] n étendue f; **to some ~** dans une certaine mesure; **to the ~ of ...** au point de ...; **to what ~?** dans quelle mesure?, jusqu'à quel point?; **to such an ~ that ...** à tel point que ...

exterior [ɛk'stɪərɪəʳ] adj extérieur(e) ▷ n extérieur m

external [ɛk'stɜːnl] adj externe

extinct [ɪkˈstɪŋkt] adj (volcano) éteint(e); (species) disparu(e); **extinction** n extinction f

extinguish [ɪkˈstɪŋgwɪʃ] vt éteindre

extra [ˈekstrə] adj supplémentaire, de plus (in addition) en plus ▷ n supplément m; (perk) à-coté m; (Cine, Theat) figurant(e)

extract vt [ɪkˈstrækt] extraire; (tooth) arracher; (money, promise) soutirer ▷ n [ˈekstrækt] extrait m

extradite [ˈekstrədaɪt] vt extrader

extraordinary [ɪkˈstrɔːdɪnrɪ] adj extraordinaire

extravagance [ɪkˈstrævəgəns] n (excessive spending) prodigalités fpl; (thing bought) folie f, dépense excessive; **extravagant** adj extravagant(e); (in spending: person) prodigue, dépensier(-ière); (: tastes) dispendieux(-euse)

extreme [ɪkˈstriːm] adj, n extrême (m); **extremely** adv extrêmement

extremist [ɪkˈstriːmɪst] adj, n extrémiste m/f

extrovert [ˈekstrəvɜːt] n extraverti(e)

eye [aɪ] n œil m ((yeux) pl); (of needle) trou m, chas m ▷ vt examiner; **to keep an ~ on** surveiller; **eyeball** n globe m oculaire; **eyebrow** n sourcil m; **eyedrops** npl gouttes fpl pour les yeux; **eyelash** n cil m; **eyelid** n paupière f; **eyeliner** n eye-liner m; **eyeshadow** n ombre f à paupières; **eyesight** n vue f; **eye witness** n témoin m oculaire

f

F [ef] n (Mus): **F** fa m

fabric [ˈfæbrɪk] n tissu m

fabulous [ˈfæbjʊləs] adj fabuleux(-euse); (inf: super) formidable, sensationnel(le)

face [feɪs] n visage m, figure f; (expression) air m; (of clock) cadran m; (of cliff) paroi f; (of mountain) face f; (of building) façade f ▷ vt faire face à; (facts etc) accepter; **~ down** (person) à plat ventre; (card) face en dessous; **to lose/save ~** perdre/sauver la face; **to pull a ~** faire une grimace; **in the ~ of** (difficulties etc) face à, devant; **on the ~ of it** à première vue; **~ to ~** face à face; **face up to** vt fus faire face à, affronter; **face cloth** n (BRIT) gant m de toilette; **face pack** n (BRIT) masque m (de beauté)

facial [ˈfeɪʃl] adj facial(e) ▷ n soin complet du visage

facilitate [fəˈsɪlɪteɪt] vt faciliter

facilities [fəˈsɪlɪtɪz] npl installations fpl, équipement m; **credit ~** facilités de paiement

fact [fækt] n fait m; **in ~** en fait

faction ['fækʃən] n faction f

factor ['fæktə*] n facteur m; (of sun cream) indice m (de protection); **I'd like a ~ 15 suntan lotion** je voudrais une crème solaire d'indice 15

factory ['fæktərɪ] n usine f, fabrique f

factual ['fæktjuəl] adj basé(e) sur les faits

faculty ['fækəltɪ] n faculté f; (us: teaching staff) corps enseignant

fad [fæd] n (personal) manie f; (craze) engouement m

fade [feɪd] vi se décolorer, passer; (light, sound) s'affaiblir; (flower) se faner; **fade away** vi (sound) s'affaiblir

fag [fæg] n (BRIT inf: cigarette) clope f

Fahrenheit ['fɑːrənhaɪt] n Fahrenheit m inv

fail [feɪl] vt (exam) échouer à; (candidate) recaler; (subj: courage, memory) faire défaut à ▷ vi échouer; (eyesight, health, light: also: **be ~ing**) baisser, s'affaiblir; (brakes) lâcher; **to ~ to do sth** (neglect) négliger de or ne pas faire qch; (be unable) ne pas arriver or parvenir à faire qch; **without ~** à coup sûr; sans faute; **failing** n défaut m ▷ prep faute de; **failing that** à défaut, sinon; **failure** ['feɪljə*] n échec m; (person) raté(e) f; (mechanical etc) défaillance f

faint [feɪnt] adj faible; (recollection) vague; (mark) à peine visible ▷ n évanouissement m ▷ vi s'évanouir; **to feel ~** défaillir; **faintest** adj: **I haven't the faintest idea** je n'ai pas la moindre idée; **faintly** adv faiblement; (vaguely) vaguement

fair [fɛə*] adj équitable, juste; (hair) blond(e); (skin, complexion) pâle, blanc (blanche); (weather) beau (belle); (good enough) assez bon(ne); (sizeable) considérable, assez bon ▷ adv: **to play ~** jouer franc jeu ▷ n foire f; (BRIT: funfair) fête (foraine); **fairground** n champ m de foire; **fair-haired** adj (person) aux cheveux clairs, blond(e); **fairly** adv

(justly) équitablement; (quite) assez; **fair trade** n commerce m équitable; **fairway** n (Golf) fairway m

fairy ['fɛərɪ] n fée f; **fairy tale** n conte m de fées

faith [feɪθ] n foi f; (trust) confiance f; (sect) culte m, religion f; **faithful** adj fidèle; **faithfully** adv fidèlement; **yours faithfully** (BRIT: in letters) veuillez agréer l'expression de mes salutations les plus distinguées

fake [feɪk] n (painting etc) faux m; (person) imposteur m ▷ adj faux (fausse) ▷ vt (emotions) simuler; (painting) faire un faux de

falcon ['fɔːlkən] n faucon m

fall [fɔːl] n chute f; (decrease) baisse f; (us: autumn) automne m ▷ vi (pt fell, pp **-en**) tomber; (price, temperature, dollar) baisser; **falls** npl (waterfall) chute f d'eau, cascade f; **to ~ flat** vi (on one's face) tomber de tout son long; s'étaler; (joke) tomber à plat; (plan) échouer; **fall apart** vi (object) tomber en morceaux; **fall down** vi (person) tomber; (building) s'effondrer, s'écrouler; **fall for** vt fus (trick) se laisser prendre à; (person) tomber amoureux(-euse) de; **fall off** vi tomber; (diminish) baisser, diminuer; **fall out** vi (friends etc) se brouiller; (hair, teeth) tomber; **fall over** vi tomber (par terre); **fall through** vi (plan, project) tomber à l'eau

fallen ['fɔːlən] pp of **fall**

fallout ['fɔːlaut] n retombées f (radioactives)

false [fɔːls] adj; **under ~ pretences** sous un faux prétexte; **false alarm** n fausse alerte; **false teeth** npl (BRIT) fausses dents, dentier m

fame [feɪm] n renommée f, renom m

familiar [fə'mɪlɪə*] adj familier(-ière); **to be ~ with sth** connaître qch; **familiarize** [fə'mɪlɪəraɪz] vt: **to familiarize o.s. with** se familiariser avec

family ['fæmɪlɪ] n famille f; **family doctor** n médecin m de famille; **family**

planning n planning familial

famine ['fæmɪn] n famine f

famous ['feɪməs] adj célèbre

fan [fæn] n (folding) éventail m;
(Elec) ventilateur m; (person) fan m,
admirateur(-trice); (Sport) supporter
m/f ▷ vt éventer; (fire, quarrel) attiser

fanatic [fə'nætɪk] n fanatique m/f

fan belt n courroie f de ventilateur

fan club n fan-club m

fancy ['fænsɪ] n (whim) fantaisie f,
envie f; (imagination) imagination
f ▷ adj (luxury) de luxe; (elaborate:
jewellery, packaging) fantaisie inv ▷ vt
(feel like, want) avoir envie de; (imagine)
imaginer; **to take a ~ to** se prendre
d'affection pour; s'enticher de; **he
fancies her** elle lui plaît; **fancy dress** n
déguisement m, travesti m

fan heater n (BRIT) radiateur soufflant

fantasize ['fæntəsaɪz] vi fantasmer

fantastic [fæn'tæstɪk] adj fantastique

fantasy ['fæntəsɪ] n imagination f,
fantaisie f; (unreality) fantasme m

fanzine ['fænziːn] n fanzine m

FAQ n abbr (= frequently asked question)
FAQ f inv, faq f inv

far [fɑː*] adj (distant) lointain(e),
éloigné(e) ▷ adv loin; **the ~ side/end**
l'autre côté/bout; **it's not ~ (from
here)** ce n'est pas loin (d'ici); **~ away,
~ off** au loin, dans le lointain; **~ better**
beaucoup mieux; **~ from** loin de; **by ~**
de loin, de beaucoup; **go as ~ as the
bridge** allez jusqu'au pont; **as ~ as I
know** pour autant que je sache; **how ~
is it to ...?** combien y a-t-il jusqu'à ...?;
how ~ have you got with your work?
où en êtes-vous dans votre travail?

farce [fɑːs] n farce f

fare [fɛə*] n (on trains, buses) prix m du
billet; (in taxi) prix de la course; (food)
table f, chère f; **half ~** demi-tarif; **full
~** plein tarif

Far East n: **the ~** l'Extrême-Orient m

farewell [fɛə'wɛl] excl, n adieu m

farm [fɑːm] n ferme f ▷ vt cultiver;
farmer n fermier(-ière); **farmhouse**

n (maison f de) ferme f; **farming** n
agriculture f; (of animals) élevage m;
farmyard n cour f de ferme

far-reaching ['fɑː'riːtʃɪŋ] adj d'une
grande portée

fart [fɑːt] (inf!) vi péter

farther ['fɑːðə*] adv plus loin ▷ adj plus
eloigné(e), plus lointain(e)

farthest ['fɑːðɪst] superlative of **far**

fascinate ['fæsɪneɪt] vt fasciner,
captiver; **fascinated** adj fasciné(e)

fascinating ['fæsɪneɪtɪŋ] adj
fascinant(e)

fascination [fæsɪ'neɪʃən] n
fascination f

fascist ['fæʃɪst] adj, n fasciste m/f

fashion ['fæʃən] n (manner)
façon f, manière f ▷ vt façonner; **in
~** à la mode; **out of ~** démodé(e);
fashionable adj à la mode; **fashion
show** n défilé m de mannequins or
de mode

fast [fɑːst] adj rapide; (clock): **to be ~**
avancer; (dye, colour) grand or bon teint
inv ▷ adv vite, rapidement; (stuck, held)
solidement ▷ n jeûne m ▷ vi jeûner; **~
asleep** profondément endormi

fasten ['fɑːsn] vt attacher, fixer;
(coat) attacher, fermer ▷ vi se fermer,
s'attacher

fast food n fast food m, restauration
f rapide

fat [fæt] adj gros(se) ▷ n graisse f; (on
meat) gras m; (for cooking) matière
grasse

fatal ['feɪtl] adj (mistake) fatal(e); (injury)
mortel(le); **fatality** [fə'tælɪtɪ] n (road
death etc) victime f, décès m; **fatally** adv
fatalement; (injured) mortellement

fate [feɪt] n destin m; (of person) sort m

father ['fɑːðə*] n père m; **Father
Christmas** n le Père Noël; **father-in-
law** n beau-père m

fatigue [fə'tiːg] n fatigue f

fattening ['fætnɪŋ] adj (food) qui
fait grossir

fatty ['fætɪ] adj (food) gras(se) ▷ n (inf)
gros (grosse)

faucet ['fɔːsɪt] n (us) robinet m

fault [fɔːlt] n faute f; (defect) défaut m; (Geo) faille f ▷ vt trouver des défauts à, prendre en défaut; **it's my ~** c'est de ma faute; **to find ~ with** trouver à redire à, à critiquer à; **at ~** fautif(-ive), coupable; **faulty** adj défectueux(-euse)

fauna ['fɔːnə] n faune f

favour etc (us **favor** etc) ['feɪvə'] n faveur f; (help) service m ▷ vt (proposition) être en faveur de; (pupil etc) favoriser; (team, horse) donner gagnant; **to do sb a ~** rendre un service à qn; **in ~ of** en faveur de; **to find ~ with sb** trouver grâce aux yeux de qn; **favourable** adj favorable; **favourite** ['feɪvrɪt] adj, n favori(te)

fawn [fɔːn] n (deer) faon m ▷ adj (also: **~-coloured**) fauve ▷ vi: **to ~ (up)on** flatter servilement

fax [fæks] n (document) télécopie f; (machine) télécopieur m ▷ vt envoyer par télécopie

FBI n abbr (us: = Federal Bureau of Investigation) FBI m

fear [fɪə'] n crainte f, peur f ▷ vt craindre; **for ~ of** de peur de; **~ that** de peur que + sub or de + infinitive; **fearful** adj craintif(-ive); (sight, noise) affreux(-euse); **fearless** adj intrépide

feasible ['fiːzəbl] adj faisable, réalisable

feast [fiːst] n festin m, banquet m; (Rel: also: **~ day**) fête f ▷ vi festoyer

feat [fiːt] n exploit m, prouesse f

feather ['feðə'] n plume f

feature ['fiːtʃə'] n caractéristique f; (article) chronique f, rubrique f ▷ vt (film) avoir pour vedette(s); (subj: film) avoir pour vedette ▷ vi figurer (en bonne place); **features** npl (of face) traits mpl; **a (special) ~ on sth/sb** un reportage sur qch/qn; **feature film** n long métrage

Feb. abbr (= February) fév

February ['februərɪ] n février m

fed [fed] pt, pp of **feed**

federal ['fedərəl] adj fédéral(e)

federation [fedə'reɪʃən] n fédération f

fed up adj: **to be ~ (with)** en avoir marre or plein le dos (de)

fee [fiː] n rémunération f; (of doctor, lawyer) honoraires mpl; (of school, college etc) frais mpl de scolarité; (for examination) droits mpl

feeble ['fiːbl] n (of animal) nourriture f, pâture f; (on printer) mécanisme m d'alimentation f ▷ vt (pt, pp **fed**) (person) nourrir; (BRIT: baby: breastfeed) allaiter; (: with bottle) donner le biberon à; (horse etc) donner à manger à; (machine) alimenter; (data etc) entrer; **to ~ sth into** enregistrer qch dans; **feedback** n (Elec) effet m Larsen; (from person) réactions fpl

feel [fiːl] n (sensation) sensation f; (impression) impression f ▷ vt (pt, pp **felt**) (touch) toucher; (explore) tâter, palper; (cold, pain) sentir; (grief, anger) ressentir, éprouver; (think, believe): **to ~ (that)** trouver que; **to ~ hungry/cold** avoir faim/froid; **to ~ lonely/better** se sentir seul/mieux; **I don't ~ well** je ne me sens pas bien; **it ~s soft** c'est doux au toucher; **to ~ like** (want) avoir envie de; **feeling** n (physical) sensation f; (emotion, impression) sentiment m; **to hurt sb's feelings** froisser qn

feet [fiːt] npl of **foot**

fell [fel] pt of **fall** ▷ vt (tree) abattre

fellow ['feləu] n type m; (comrade) compagnon m; (of learned society) membre m ▷ cpd: **their ~ prisoners/students** leurs camarades prisonniers/étudiants; **fellow citizen** n concitoyen(ne); **fellow countryman** n (irreg) compatriote m; **fellow men** npl semblables mpl; **fellowship** n (society) association f; (comradeship) amitié f, camaraderie f; (Scol) sorte de bourse universitaire

felony ['felənɪ] n crime m, forfait m

felt [felt] pt, pp of **feel** ▷ n feutre m; **felt-tip** n (also: **felt-tip pen**) stylo-feutre m

female ['fiːmeɪl] n (Zool) femelle f;

(pej: woman) bonne femme ▷ adj (Biol) femelle; (sex, character) féminin(e); (vote etc) des femmes

feminine ['femɪnɪn] adj féminin(e)

feminist ['femɪnɪst] n féministe m/f

fence [fens] n barrière f ▷ vi faire de l'escrime; **fencing** n (sport) escrime m

fend [fend] vi: **to ~ for o.s.** se débrouiller (tout seul); **fend off** vt (attack etc) parer; (questions) éluder

fender ['fendə'] n garde-feu m inv; (on boat) défense f; (us: of car) aile f

fennel ['fenl] n fenouil m

ferment vi [fə'ment] fermenter ▷ n ['fɜːment] (fig) agitation f, effervescence f

fern [fɜːn] n fougère f

ferocious [fə'rəuʃəs] adj féroce

ferret ['ferɪt] n furet m

ferry ['ferɪ] n (small) bac m; (large: also: **~boat**) ferry(-boat m) m ▷ vt transporter

fertile ['fɜːtaɪl] adj fertile; (Biol) fécond(e); **fertilize** ['fɜːtɪlaɪz] vt fertiliser; (Biol) féconder; **fertilizer** n engrais m

festival ['festɪvəl] n (Rel) fête f; (Art, Mus) festival m

festive ['festɪv] adj de fête; **the ~ season** (BRIT: Christmas) la période des fêtes

fetch [fetʃ] vt aller chercher; (BRIT: sell for) rapporter

fête [feɪt] n fête f, kermesse f

fetus ['fiːtəs] n (US) = **foetus**

feud [fjuːd] n querelle f, dispute f

fever ['fiːvə'] n fièvre f; **feverish** adj fiévreux(-euse), fébrile

few [fjuː] adj (not many) peu de ▷ pron peu; **a ~** (as adj) quelques; (as pron) quelques-uns(-unes); **quite a ~ ...** adj un certain nombre de ..., pas mal de ...; **in the past ~** these derniers jours; **fewer** adj moins de; (as pron) moins nombreux; **fewest** adj le moins nombreux

fiancé [fɪ'ɑːŋseɪ] n fiancé m; **fiancée** n fiancée f

fiasco [fɪ'æskəu] n fiasco m

fib [fɪb] n bobard m

fibre (us **fiber**) ['faɪbə'] n fibre f; **fibreglass** (us **Fiberglass**®) n fibre f de verre

fickle ['fɪkl] adj inconstant(e), volage, capricieux(-euse)

fiction ['fɪkʃən] n romans mpl, littérature f romanesque; (invention) fiction f; **fictional** adj fictif(-ive)

fiddle ['fɪdl] n (Mus) violon m; (cheating) combine f, escroquerie f ▷ vt (BRIT: accounts) falsifier, maquiller; **fiddle with** vt fus tripoter

fidelity [fɪ'delɪtɪ] n fidélité f

fidget ['fɪdʒɪt] vi se trémousser, remuer

field [fiːld] n champ m; (fig) domaine m, champ; (Sport: ground) terrain m; **field marshal** n maréchal m

fierce [fɪəs] adj (look, animal) féroce, sauvage; (wind, attack, person) (très) violent(e); (fighting, enemy) acharné(e)

fifteen [fɪf'tiːn] num quinze; **fifteenth** num quinzième

fifth [fɪfθ] num cinquième

fiftieth ['fɪftɪɪθ] num cinquantième

fifty ['fɪftɪ] num cinquante; **fifty-fifty** adv moitié-moitié ▷ adj: **to have a fifty-fifty chance (of success)** avoir une chance sur deux (de réussir)

fig [fɪg] n figue f

fight [faɪt] n (between persons) bagarre f; (argument) dispute f; (Mil) combat m; (against cancer etc) lutte f ▷ vb (pt, pp **fought**); ▷ vt se battre contre; (cancer, alcoholism, emotion) combattre, lutter contre; (election) se présenter à ▷ vi se battre; (argue) se disputer; (fig): **to ~ (for/against)** lutter (pour/contre); **fight back** vi rendre les coups; (after illness) reprendre le dessus ▷ vt (tears) réprimer; **fight off** vt repousser; (disease, sleep, urge) lutter contre; **fighting** n combats mpl; (brawls) bagarres fpl

figure ['fɪgə'] n (Drawing, Geom) figure f; (number) chiffre m; (body, outline) silhouette f; (person's shape) ligne f, formes fpl; (person) personnage m

▷ vt (us: think) supposer ▷ vi (appear) figurer; (us: make sense) s'expliquer; **figure out** (understand) arriver à comprendre; (plan) calculer

file [faɪl] n (tool) lime f; (dossier m; (folder) dossier, chemise f; (: binder) classeur m; (Comput) fichier m; (row) file f ▷ vt (nails, wood) limer; (papers) classer; (Law: claim) faire enregistrer; déposer; **filing cabinet** n classeur m (meuble)

Filipino [fɪlɪˈpiːnəu] adj philippin(e) ▷ n (person) Philippin(e)

fill [fɪl] vt remplir; (vacancy) pourvoir à ▷ n: **to eat one's** ~ manger à sa faim; **to ~ with** remplir de; **fill in** vt (hole) boucher; (form) remplir; **fill out** vt (form, receipt) remplir; **fill up** vt remplir ▷ vi (Aut) faire le plein

fillet [ˈfɪlɪt] n filet m; **fillet steak** n filet m de bœuf, tournedos m

filling [ˈfɪlɪŋ] n (Culin) garniture f, farce f; (for tooth) plombage m; **filling station** n station-service f, station d'essence

film [fɪlm] n film m; (Phot) pellicule f, film; (of powder, liquid) couche f, pellicule ▷ vt (scene) filmer ▷ vi tourner; **I'd like a 36-exposure** ~ je voudrais une pellicule de 36 poses; **film star** n vedette f de cinéma

filter [ˈfɪltə] n filtre m ▷ vt filtrer; **filter lane** n (BRIT Aut: at traffic lights) voie f de dégagement; (: on motorway) voie f de sortie

filth [fɪlθ] n saleté f; **filthy** adj sale, dégoûtant(e); (language) ordurier(-ière), grossier(-ière)

fin [fɪn] n (of fish) nageoire f; (of shark) aileron m; (of diver) palme f

final [ˈfaɪnl] adj final(e), dernier(-ière); (decision, answer) définitif(-ive) ▷ n (BRIT Sport) finale f; **finals** npl (Scol) examens mpl de dernière année; (us Sport) finale f; **finale** [fɪˈnɑːlɪ] n finale m; **finalist** n (Sport) finaliste m/f; **finalize** vt mettre au point; **finally** adv (eventually) enfin, finalement; (lastly) en dernier lieu

finance [faɪˈnæns] n finance f ▷ vt financer; **finances** npl finances fpl; **financial** [faɪˈnænʃəl] adj financier(-ière); **financial year** n année f budgétaire

find [faɪnd] vt (pt, pp **found**) trouver; (lost object) retrouver ▷ n trouvaille f, découverte f; **to ~ sb guilty** (Law) déclarer qn coupable; **find out** vt se renseigner sur; (truth, secret) découvrir; (person) démasquer ▷ vi: **to ~ out about** (make enquiries) se renseigner sur; (by chance) apprendre; **findings** npl (Law) conclusions fpl, verdict m; (of report) constatations fpl

fine [faɪn] adj (weather) beau (belle); (excellent) excellent(e); (thin, subtle, not coarse) fin(e); (acceptable) bien inv ▷ adv (well) très bien; (small) fin, finement ▷ n (Law) amende f, contravention f ▷ vt (Law) condamner à une amende; donner une contravention à; **he's** ~ il va bien; **the weather is** ~ il fait beau; **fine arts** npl beaux-arts mpl

finger [ˈfɪŋgə] n doigt m ▷ vt palper, toucher; **index** ~ index m; **fingernail** n ongle m (de la main); **fingerprint** n empreinte digitale; **fingertip** n bout m du doigt

finish [ˈfɪnɪʃ] n fin f; (Sport) arrivée f; (polish etc) finition f ▷ vt finir, terminer ▷ vi finir, se terminer; **to ~ doing sth** finir de faire qch; **to ~ third** arriver or terminer troisième; **when does the show** ~? quand est-ce que le spectacle se termine?; **finish off** vt finir, terminer; (kill) achever; **finish up** vi, vt finir

Finland [ˈfɪnlənd] n Finlande f; **Finn** n Finnois(e), Finlandais(e); **Finnish** adj finnois(e), finlandais(e) ▷ n (Ling) finnois m

fir [fəː] n sapin m

fire [faɪə] n feu m; (accidental) incendie m; (heater) radiateur m ▷ vt (discharge): **to ~ a gun** tirer un coup de feu; (fig: interest) enflammer, animer; (inf: dismiss) mettre à la porte, renvoyer ▷ vi

(shoot) tirer, faire feu; ~! au feu!; **on** = en
feu; **to set** ~ **to sth**, **set sth on** ~ mettre
le feu à qch; **fire alarm** n avertisseur
m d'incendie; **firearm** n arme f à feu;
fire brigade n (us **fire department**)
(régiment m de sapeurs-)pompiers
mpl; **fire engine** n (BRIT) pompe f
à incendie; **fire escape** n escalier
m de secours; **fire exit** n issue f or
sortie f de secours; **fire extinguisher**
n extincteur m; **fireman** (irreg) n
pompier m; **fireplace** n cheminée f;
fire station n caserne f de pompiers;
fire truck (us) n = **fire engine**; **firewall**
n (Internet) pare-feu m; **firewood** n bois
m de chauffage; **fireworks** npl (display)
feu(x) m(pl) d'artifice

firm [fəːm] adj ferme ▷ n compagnie f,
firme f; **firmly** adv fermement

first [fəːst] adj premier(-ière) ▷ adv
(before other people) le premier, la
première; (before other things) en
premier, d'abord; (when listing reasons
etc) en premier lieu, premièrement; (in
the beginning) au début ▷ n (person: in
race) premier(-ière); (Aut) première f;
**the ~ of
January** le premier janvier; **at** ~ au
commencement, au début; ~ **of all** tout
d'abord, pour commencer; **first aid** n
premiers secours or soins; **first-aid kit**
n trousse f à pharmacie; **first-class** adj
(ticket etc) de première classe; (excellent)
excellent(e), exceptionnel(le); (post)
en tarif prioritaire; **first-hand** adj
de première main; **first lady** n (us)
femme f du président; **firstly** adv
premièrement, en premier lieu; **first
name** n prénom m; **first-rate** adj
excellent(e)

fiscal ['fɪskl] adj fiscal(e); **fiscal year** n
exercice financier

fish [fɪʃ] n (pl inv) poisson m ▷ vt, vi
pêcher; ~ **and chips** poisson frit et
frites; **fisherman** (irreg) n pêcheur m;
fish fingers npl (BRIT) bâtonnets de
poisson (congelés); **fishing** n pêche
f; **to go fishing** aller à la pêche;

fishing boat n barque f de pêche;
fishing line n ligne f (de pêche);
fishmonger n (BRIT) marchand m de
poisson; **fishmonger's (shop)** n (BRIT)
poissonnerie f; **fish sticks** npl (us)
= **fish fingers**; **fishy** adj (inf) suspect(e),
louche

fist [fɪst] n poing m

fit [fɪt] adj (Med, Sport) en (bonne) forme;
(proper) convenable; approprié(e) ▷ vt
(subj: clothes) aller à; (put in, attach)
installer, poser; (equip) équiper, garnir,
munir; (suit) convenir à ▷ vi (clothes)
aller; (parts) s'adapter; (in space, gap)
entrer, s'adapter ▷ n (Med) accès m,
crise f; (of anger) accès; (of hysterics,
jealousy) crise; ~ **to** (ready to) en état de;
~ **for** (worthy) digne de; (capable) apte
à; **to keep** ~ se maintenir en forme;
this dress is a tight/good ~ cette robe
est un peu juste/(me) va très bien; **a
~ of coughing** une quinte de toux;
by ~**s and starts** par à-coups; **fit in** vi
(add up) cadrer; (integrate) s'intégrer;
(to new situation) s'adapter; **fitness**
n (Med) forme f physique; **fitted** adj
(jacket, shirt) ajusté(e); **fitted carpet**
n moquette f; **fitted kitchen** n (BRIT)
cuisine équipée; **fitted sheet** n drap-
housse m; **fitting** adj approprié(e)
▷ n (of dress) essayage m; (of piece of
equipment) pose f, installation f; **fitting
room** n (in shop) cabine f d'essayage;
fittings npl installations fpl

five [faɪv] num cinq; **fiver** n (inf: BRIT)
billet de cinq livres; (: us) billet de
cinq dollars

fix [fɪks] vt (date, amount etc) fixer; (sort
out) arranger; (mend) réparer; (make
ready: meal, drink) préparer ▷ n: **to be
in a** ~ être dans le pétrin; **fix up** vt
(meeting) arranger; **to** ~ **sb up with sth**
faire avoir qch à qn; **fixed** adj (prices
etc) fixe; **fixture** n installation f (fixe);
(Sport) rencontre f (au programme)

fizzy ['fɪzɪ] adj pétillant(e),
gazeux(-euse)

flag [flæg] n drapeau m; (also: ~**stone**)

flair [flɛəʳ] n flair m

flak [flæk] n (Mil) tir antiaérien; (inf: criticism) critiques fpl

flake [fleɪk] n (of rust, paint) écaille f; (of snow, soap powder) flocon m ▷ vi (also: **~ off**) s'écailler

flamboyant [flæm'bɔɪənt] adj flamboyant(e), éclatant(e); (person) haut(e) en couleur

flame [fleɪm] n flamme f

flamingo [flə'mɪŋɡəu] n flamant m (rose)

flammable ['flæməbl] adj inflammable

flan [flæn] n (BRIT) tarte f

flank [flæŋk] n flanc m ▷ vt flanquer

flannel ['flænl] n (BRIT: also: **face ~**) gant m de toilette; (fabric) flanelle f

flap [flæp] n (of pocket, envelope) rabat m; (of wings) battre (de) ▷ vi (sail, flag) claquer

flare [flɛəʳ] n (signal) signal lumineux; (Mil) fusée éclairante; (in skirt etc) évasement m; **flares** npl (trousers) pantalon m à pattes d'éléphant; **flare up** vi s'embraser; (fig: person) se mettre en colère, s'emporter; (: revolt) éclater

flash [flæʃ] n éclair m; (also: **news ~**) flash m (d'information); (Phot) flash m ▷ vt (switch on) allumer (brièvement); (direct): **to ~ sth at** braquer qch sur; (send: message) câbler; (smile) lancer ▷ vi briller; jeter des éclairs; (light on ambulance etc) clignoter; **a ~ of lightning** un éclair; **in a ~** en un clin d'œil; **to ~ one's headlights** faire un appel de phares; **he ~ed by or past** il passa (devant nous) comme un éclair; **flashback** n flashback m, retour m en arrière; **flashbulb** n ampoule f de flash; **flashlight** n lampe f de poche

flask [flɑːsk] n flacon m, bouteille f; (also: **vacuum ~**) bouteille f thermos®

flat [flæt] adj plat(e); (tyre) dégonflé(e), à plat; (beer) éventé(e); (battery) à plat;

(denial) catégorique; (Mus) bémol inv; (: voice) faux (fausse) ▷ n (BRIT: apartment) appartement m; (Aut) crevaison f, pneu crevé; (Mus) bémol m; **~ out** (work) sans relâche; (race) à fond; **flatten** vt (also: **flatten out**) aplatir; (crop) coucher; (house, city) raser

flatter ['flætəʳ] vt flatter; **flattering** adj flatteur(-euse); (clothes etc) seyant(e)

flaunt [flɔːnt] vt faire étalage de

flavour etc (us **flavor** etc) ['fleɪvəʳ] n goût m, saveur f; (of ice cream etc) parfum m ▷ vt parfumer, aromatiser; **vanilla-~ed** à l'arôme de vanille, vanillé(e); **what ~s do you have?** quels parfums avez-vous?; **flavouring** n arôme m (synthétique)

flaw [flɔː] n défaut m; **flawless** adj sans défaut

flea [fliː] n puce f; **flea market** n marché m aux puces

flee [pt, pp **fled**] [fliː, fled] vt fuir, s'enfuir de ▷ vi fuir, s'enfuir

fleece [fliːs] n (of sheep) toison f; (top) (laine f) polaire f ▷ vt (inf) voler, filouter

fleet [fliːt] n flotte f; (of lorries, cars etc) parc m; convoi m

fleeting ['fliːtɪŋ] adj fugace, fugitif(-ive); (visit) très bref (brève)

Flemish ['flɛmɪʃ] adj flamand(e) ▷ n (Ling) flamand m; **the ~** npl les Flamands

flesh [flɛʃ] n chair f

flew [fluː] pt of **fly**

flex [flɛks] n fil m or câble m électrique (souple) ▷ vt (knee) fléchir; (muscles) tendre; **flexibility** n flexibilité f; **flexible** adj flexible; (person, schedule) souple; **flexitime** (us **flextime**) n horaire m variable or à la carte

flick [flɪk] n petit coup m; (with finger) chiquenaude f ▷ vt donner un petit coup à; (switch) appuyer sur; **flick through** vt fus feuilleter

flicker ['flɪkəʳ] vi (light, flame) vaciller

flies [flaɪz] npl of **fly**

flight [flaɪt] n vol m; (escape) fuite f; (also: **~ of steps**) escalier m; **flight**

attendant n steward m, hôtesse f de l'air

flimsy ['flɪmzɪ] adj peu solide; (clothes) trop léger(-ère); (excuse) pauvre, mince

flinch [flɪntʃ] vi tressaillir; **to ~ from** se dérober à, reculer devant

fling [flɪŋ] vt (pt, pp **flung**) jeter, lancer

flint [flɪnt] n silex m; (in lighter) pierre f (à briquet)

flip [flɪp] vt (throw) donner une chiquenaude à; (switch) appuyer sur; (us: pancake) faire sauter; **to ~ sth over** retourner qch

flip-flops ['flɪpflɒps] npl (esp BRIT) tongs fpl

flipper ['flɪpə*r*] n (of animal) nageoire f; (for swimmer) palme f

flirt [flɜːt] vi flirter ▷ n flirteur(-euse)

float [fləʊt] n flotteur m; (in procession) char m; (sum of money) réserve f ▷ vi flotter

flock [flɒk] n (of sheep) troupeau m; (of birds) vol m; (of people) foule f

flood [flʌd] n inondation f; (of letters, refugees etc) flot m ▷ vt inonder ▷ vi (place) être inondé; (people): **to ~ into** envahir; **flooding** n inondation f; **floodlight** n projecteur m

floor [flɔː*r*] n sol m; (storey) étage m; (of sea, valley) fond m ▷ vt (knock down) terrasser; (baffle) désorienter; **ground ~**, (us) **first ~** rez-de-chaussée m; **first ~**, (us) **second ~** premier étage; **what is it on?** c'est à quel étage?; **floorboard** n planche f (du plancher); **flooring** n sol m; (wooden) plancher m; (covering) revêtement m de sol; **floor show** n spectacle m de variétés

flop [flɒp] n fiasco m ▷ vi (fail) faire fiasco; (fall) s'affaler, s'effondrer; **floppy** adj lâche, flottant(e) ▷ n (Comput: also: **floppy disk**) disquette f

flora ['flɔːrə] n flore f

floral ['flɔːrl] adj floral(e); (dress) à fleurs

florist ['flɒrɪst] n fleuriste m/f; **florist's (shop)** n magasin m or boutique f de fleuriste

flotation [fləʊ'teɪʃən] n (of shares)

émission f; (of company) lancement m (en Bourse)

flour ['flaʊə*r*] n farine f

flourish ['flʌrɪʃ] vi prospérer ▷ n (gesture) moulinet m

flow [fləʊ] n (of water, traffic etc) écoulement m; (tide, influx) flux m; (of blood, Elec) circulation f; (of river) courant m ▷ vi couler; (traffic): **to ~ into** s'écouler; (robes, hair) flotter

flower ['flaʊə*r*] n fleur f ▷ vi fleurir; **flower bed** n plate-bande f; **flowerpot** n pot m (à fleurs)

flown [fləʊn] pp of **fly**

fl. oz. abbr = **fluid ounce**

flu [fluː] n grippe f

fluctuate ['flʌktjʊeɪt] vi varier, fluctuer

fluent ['fluːənt] adj (speech, style) coulant(e), aisé(e); **he speaks ~ French, he's ~ in French** il parle le français couramment

fluff [flʌf] n duvet m; (on jacket, carpet) peluche f; **fluffy** adj duveteux(-euse); (toy) en peluche

fluid ['fluːɪd] n fluide m; (in diet) liquide m ▷ adj fluide; **fluid ounce** n (BRIT) = 0.028 l; 0.05 pints

fluke [fluːk] n coup m de veine

flung [flʌŋ] pt, pp of **fling**

fluorescent [flʊə'rɛsnt] adj fluorescent(e)

fluoride ['flʊəraɪd] n fluor m

flurry ['flʌrɪ] n (of snow) rafale f, bourrasque f; **a ~ of activity** une affairement soudain

flush [flʌʃ] n (on face) rougeur f; (fig: of youth etc) éclat m ▷ vt nettoyer à grande eau ▷ vi rougir ▷ adj (level): **~ with** au ras de, de niveau avec; **to ~ the toilet** tirer la chasse (d'eau)

flute [fluːt] n flûte f

flutter ['flʌtə*r*] n (of panic, excitement) agitation f; (of wings) battement m ▷ vi (bird) battre des ailes, voleter

fly [flaɪ] n (insect) mouche f; (on trousers: also: **flies**) braguette f ▷ vb (pt **flew**, pp **flown**) ▷ vt (plane) piloter; (passengers, *cargo*) transporter (par avion); *(distance)* parcourir ▷ vi voler; *(passengers)* aller en avion; *(escape)* s'enfuir, fuir; *(flag)* se déployer; **fly away, fly off** vi s'envoler; **fly-drive** n formule f avion plus voiture; **flying** n *(activity)* aviation f; *(action)* vol m ▷ adj: **flying visit** visite f éclair inv; **with flying colours** haut la main; **flying saucer** n soucoupe volante; **flyover** n *(BRIT: overpass)* pont routier

FM abbr (Radio: = frequency modulation) FM

foal [fəʊl] n poulain m

foam [fəʊm] n écume f; *(on beer)* mousse f; *(also: ~ rubber)* caoutchouc m mousse ▷ vi *(liquid)* écumer; *(soapy water)* mousser

focus ['fəʊkəs] n (pl **-es**) foyer m; *(of interest)* centre m ▷ vt *(field glasses etc)* mettre au point ▷ vi: **to ~ (on)** *(with camera)* régler la mise au point (sur); *(with eyes)* fixer son regard (sur); *(fig: concentrate)* se concentrer; **out of/in ~** *(picture)* flou(e)/net(te); *(camera)* pas au point/au point

foetus (us **fetus**) ['fiːtəs] n fœtus m

fog [fɒg] n brouillard m; **foggy** adj: **it's foggy** il y a du brouillard; **fog lamp** (us **fog light**) n (Aut) phare m anti-brouillard

foil [fɔɪl] vt déjouer, contrecarrer ▷ n feuille f de métal; *(kitchen foil)* papier m d'alu(minium); **to act as a ~ to** *(fig)* servir de repoussoir or de faire-valoir à

fold [fəʊld] n *(bend, crease)* pli m; (Agr) parc m à moutons; *(fig)* bercail m ▷ vt plier; **to ~ one's arms** croiser les bras; **fold up** vi *(map etc)* se plier, se replier; *(business)* fermer boutique ▷ vt *(map etc)* plier, replier; **folder** n *(for papers)* chemise f; *(: binder)* classeur m; (Comput) dossier m; **folding** adj *(chair, bed)* pliant(e)

foliage ['fəʊlɪɪdʒ] n feuillage m

folk [fəʊk] npl gens mpl ▷ cpd folklorique; **folks** npl *(inf: parents)* famille f, parents mpl; **folklore**

['fəʊklɔː'] n folklore m; **folk music** n musique f folklorique; *(contemporary)* musique folk, folk m; **folk song** n chanson f folklorique; *(contemporary)* chanson folk inv

follow ['fɒləʊ] vt suivre ▷ vi suivre; *(result)* s'ensuivre; **to ~ suit** *(fig)* faire de même; **follow up** vt *(letter, offer)* donner suite à; *(case)* suivre; **follower** n disciple m/f, partisan(e); **following** adj suivant(e) ▷ n partisans mpl, disciples mpl; **follow-up** n suite f; *(on file, case)* suivi m

fond [fɒnd] adj *(memory, look)* tendre, affectueux(-euse); *(hopes, dreams)* un peu fou (folle); **to be ~ of** aimer beaucoup

food [fuːd] n nourriture f; **food mixer** n mixeur m; **food poisoning** n intoxication f alimentaire; **food processor** n robot m de cuisine; **food stamp** n (us) bon m de nourriture *(pour indigents)*

fool [fuːl] n idiot(e); (Culin) mousse f de fruits ▷ vt berner, duper; **fool about, fool around** vi *(pej: waste time)* traînailler, glandouiller; *(: behave foolishly)* faire l'idiot or l'imbécile; **foolish** adj idiot(e), stupide; *(rash)* imprudent(e); **foolproof** adj *(plan etc)* infaillible

foot (pl **feet**) [fʊt, fiːt] n pied m; *(of animal)* patte f; *(measure)* pied (= 30.48 cm; 12 inches) ▷ vt *(bill)* payer; **on ~** à pied; **footage** n (Cine: length) ≈ métrage m; *(: material)* séquences fpl; **foot-and-mouth (disease)** [fʊtənd'maʊθ-] n fièvre aphteuse; **football** n *(ball)* ballon m (de football); *(sport: BRIT)* football m; *(: us)* football américain; **footballer** n (BRIT) = **football player**; **football match** n (BRIT) match m de foot(ball); **football player** n footballeur(-euse), joueur(-euse) de football; *(us)* joueur(-euse) de football américain; **footbridge** n passerelle f; **foothills** npl contreforts mpl; **foothold** n prise f (de pied); **footing** n *(fig)* position f; **to lose**

one's footing perdre pied; **footnote**
n note f (en bas de page); **footpath**
n sentier m; **footprint** n trace f (de
pied); **footstep** n pas m; **footwear** n
chaussures fpl

O **KEYWORD**

for [fɔːʳ] prep 1 (indicating destination,
intention, purpose) pour; **the train for
London** le train pour (or à destination
de) Londres; **he left for Rome** il est
parti pour Rome; **he went for the
paper** il est allé chercher le journal; **is
this for me?** c'est pour moi?; **it's time
for lunch** c'est l'heure du déjeuner;
what's it for? ça sert à quoi?; **what for?**
(why) pourquoi?; (to what end) pour quoi
faire?, à quoi bon?; **for sale** à vendre; **to
pray for peace** prier pour la paix
2 (on behalf of, representing) pour;
the MP for Hove le député de Hove;
to work for sb/sth travailler pour
qn/qch; **I'll ask him for you** je vais lui
demander pour toi; **G for George** G
comme Georges
3 (because of) pour; **for this reason**
pour cette raison; **for fear of being
criticized** de peur d'être critiqué
4 (with regard to) pour; **it's cold for
July** il fait froid pour juillet; **a gift for
languages** un don pour les langues
5 (in exchange for) pour; **I sold it for £5** je l'ai
vendu 5 livres; **to pay 50 pence for a
ticket** payer un billet 50 pence
6 (in favour of) pour; **are you for or
against us?** êtes-vous pour ou contre
nous?; **I'm all for it** je suis tout à fait
pour; **vote for X** votez pour X
7 (referring to distance) pendant, sur;
there are roadworks for 5 km il y a
des travaux sur or pendant 5 km; **we
walked for miles** nous avons marché
pendant des kilomètres
8 (referring to time) pendant; depuis;
pour; **he was away for 2 years** il a
été absent pendant 2 ans; **she will be
away for a month** elle sera absente

(pendant) un mois; **it hasn't rained for
3 weeks** ça fait 3 semaines qu'il ne pleut
pas, il ne pleut pas depuis 3 semaines;
I have known her for years je la
connais depuis des années; **can you do
it for tomorrow?** est-ce que tu peux le
faire pour demain?
9 (with infinitive clauses): **it is not for
me to decide** ce n'est pas à moi de
décider; **it would be best for you to
leave** le mieux serait que vous partiez;
there is still time for you to do it vous
avez encore le temps de le faire; **for
this to be possible ...** pour que cela
soit possible ...
10 (in spite of): **for all that** malgré cela,
néanmoins; **for all his work/efforts**
malgré tout son travail/tous ses
efforts; **for all his complaints, he's
very fond of her** il a beau se plaindre, il
l'aime beaucoup
▷ conj (since, as: rather formal) puisque

forbid (pt **forbad(e)**, pp **~den**) [fəˈbɪd,
-ˈbæd, -ˈbɪdn] vt défendre, interdire; **to
~ sb to do** défendre or interdire à qn de
faire; **forbidden** adj défendu(e)
force [fɔːs] n force f ▷ vt forcer; (push)
pousser (de force); **to ~ o.s. to do** se
forcer à faire; **in ~** (being used: rule, law,
prices) en vigueur; (in large numbers) en
force; **forced** adj forcé(e); **forceful** adj
énergique

ford [fɔːd] n gué m
fore [fɔːʳ] n: **to the ~** en évidence;
forearm n avant-bras m inv; **forecast**
n prévision f; (also: **weather forecast**)
prévisions fpl météorologiques, météo
f ▷ vt (irreg: like **cast**) prévoir; **forecourt**
n (of garage) devant m; **forefinger** n
index m; **forefront** n: **in the forefront
of** au premier rang or plan de;
foreground n premier plan; **forehead**
[ˈfɔrɪd] n front m

foreign [ˈfɔrɪn] adj étranger(-ère);
(trade) extérieur(e); (travel) à l'étranger;
foreign currency n devises
étrangères; **foreigner** n étranger(-ère);

foreign exchange n (system) change m; (money) devises fpl; **Foreign Office** n (BRIT) ministère m des Affaires étrangères; **Foreign Secretary** n (BRIT) ministre m des Affaires étrangères

fore: foreman (irreg) n (in construction) contremaître m; **foremost** adj le (la) plus en vue, premier(-ière) ▷ adv: **first and foremost** avant tout, tout d'abord; **forename** n prénom m

forensic [fəˈrɛnsɪk] adj: ~ **medicine** médecine légale

foresee (pt **foresaw**, pp ~**n**) [fɔːˈsiː, -ˈsɔː, -ˈsiːn] vt prévoir; **foreseeable** adj prévisible

forest [ˈfɒrɪst] n forêt f; **forestry** n sylviculture f

forever [fəˈrɛvəʳ] adv pour toujours; (fig: endlessly) continuellement

foreword [ˈfɔːwəːd] n avant-propos m inv

forfeit [ˈfɔːfɪt] vt perdre

forgave [fəˈgeɪv] pt of **forgive**

forge [fɔːdʒ] n forge f ▷ vt (signature) contrefaire; (wrought iron) forger; **to ~ money** (BRIT) fabriquer de la fausse monnaie; **forger** n faussaire m; **forgery** n faux m, contrefaçon f

forget (pt **forgot**, pp **forgotten**) [fəˈgɛt, -ˈgɒt, -ˈgɒtn] vt, vi oublier; **I've forgotten my key/passport** j'ai oublié ma clé/mon passeport; **forgetful** adj distrait(e), étourdi(e)

forgive (pt **forgave**, pp ~**n**) [fəˈgɪv, -ˈgeɪv, -ˈgɪvn] vt pardonner; **to ~ sb for sth/for doing sth** pardonner qch à qn/à qn de faire qch

forgot [fəˈgɒt] pt of **forget**

forgotten [fəˈgɒtn] pp of **forget**

fork [fɔːk] n (for eating) fourchette f; (for gardening) fourche f; (of roads) bifurcation f ▷ vi (road) bifurquer

forlorn [fəˈlɔːn] adj (deserted) abandonné(e); (hope, attempt) désespéré(e)

form [fɔːm] n forme f; (Scol) classe f; (questionnaire) formulaire m ▷ vt former; (habit) contracter; **to ~ part** of sth faire partie de qch; **on top ~** en pleine forme

formal [ˈfɔːməl] adj (offer, receipt) en bonne et due forme; (person) cérémonieux(-euse); (occasion, dinner) officiel(le); (garden) à la française; (clothes) de soirée; **formality** [fɔːˈmælɪtɪ] n formalité f

format [ˈfɔːmæt] n format m ▷ vt (Comput) formater

formation [fɔːˈmeɪʃən] n formation f

former [ˈfɔːməʳ] adj ancien(ne); (before n) précédent(e); **the ~ ... the latter** le premier ... le second, celui-là ... celui-ci; **formerly** adv autrefois

formidable [ˈfɔːmɪdəbl] adj redoutable

formula [ˈfɔːmjulə] n formule f

fort [fɔːt] n fort m

forthcoming [fɔːθˈkʌmɪŋ] adj qui va paraître or avoir lieu prochainement; (character) ouvert(e), communicatif(-ive); (available) disponible

fortieth [ˈfɔːtɪɪθ] num quarantième

fortify [ˈfɔːtɪfaɪ] vt (city) fortifier; (person) remonter

fortnight [ˈfɔːtnaɪt] n (BRIT) quinzaine f, quinze jours mpl; **fortnightly** adj bimensuel(le) ▷ adv tous les quinze jours

fortress [ˈfɔːtrɪs] n forteresse f

fortunate [ˈfɔːtʃənɪt] adj heureux(-euse); (person) chanceux(-euse); **it is ~ that** c'est une chance que, il est heureux que; **fortunately** adv heureusement, par bonheur

fortune [ˈfɔːtʃən] n chance f; (wealth) fortune f; **fortune-teller** n diseuse f de bonne aventure

forty [ˈfɔːtɪ] num quarante

forum [ˈfɔːrəm] n forum m, tribune f

forward [ˈfɔːwəd] adj (movement, position) en avant, vers l'avant; (not shy) effronté(e); (in time) en avance ▷ adv (also: ~**s**) en avant f n (Sport) avant m ▷ vt (letter) faire suivre; (parcel, goods) expédier; (fig) promouvoir, favoriser; **to move ~** avancer; **forwarding address** n adresse f de réexpédition

forward slash n barre f oblique

fossil ['fɔsl] adj, n fossile m

foster ['fɔstə*] vt (encourage) encourager, favoriser; (child) élever (sans adopter); **foster child** n enfant élevé dans une famille d'accueil

foster parent n parent qui élève un enfant sans l'adopter

fought [fɔ:t] pt, pp of **fight**

foul [faul] adj (weather, smell, food) infect(e); (language) ordurier(-ière) ▷ n (Football) faute f ▷ vt (subj: dog etc) salir, encrasser; **he's got a ~ temper** il a un caractère de chien; **foul play** n (Law) acte criminel

found [faund] pt, pp of **find** ▷ vt (establish) fonder; **foundation** [faun'deɪʃən] n (act) fondation f; (base) fondement m; (also: **~ cream**) fond m de teint; **foundations** npl (of building) fondations fpl

founder ['faundə*] n fondateur m ▷ vi couler, sombrer

fountain ['fauntɪn] n fontaine f; **fountain pen** n stylo m (à encre)

four [fɔ:*] num quatre; **on all ~s** à quatre pattes; **four-letter word** n obscénité f, gros mot; **four-poster** n (also: **four-poster bed**) lit m à baldaquin; **fourteen** num quatorze; **fourteenth** num quatorzième; **fourth** num quatrième ▷ n (Aut: also: **fourth gear**) quatrième f; **four-wheel drive** n (Aut: car) voiture f à quatre roues motrices

fowl [faul] n volaille f

fox [fɔks] n renard m ▷ vt mystifier

foyer ['fɔɪeɪ] n (in hotel) vestibule m; (Theat) foyer m

fraction ['frækʃən] n fraction f

fracture ['fræktʃə*] n fracture f ▷ vt fracturer

fragile ['frædʒaɪl] adj fragile

fragment ['frægmənt] n fragment m

fragrance ['freɪgrəns] n parfum m

frail [freɪl] adj fragile, délicat(e);

(person) frêle

frame [freɪm] n (of building) charpente f; (of human, animal) charpente, ossature f; (of picture) cadre m; (of door, window) encadrement m, chambranle m; (of spectacles: also: **~s**) monture f ▷ vt (picture) encadrer; **~ of mind** disposition f d'esprit; **framework** n structure f

France [fra:ns] n la France

franchise ['fræntʃaɪz] n (Pol) droit m de vote; (Comm) franchise f

frank [fræŋk] adj franc (franche) ▷ vt (letter) affranchir; **frankly** adv franchement

frantic ['fræntɪk] adj (hectic) frénétique; (distraught) hors de soi

fraud [frɔ:d] n supercherie f, fraude f, tromperie f; (person) imposteur m

fraught [frɔ:t] adj (tense: person) très tendu(e); (: situation) pénible; **~ with** (difficulties etc) chargé(e) de, plein(e) de

fray [freɪ] n effiloché ▷ vi s'effilocher

freak [fri:k] n (eccentric person) phénomène m; (unusual event) hasard m extraordinaire; (pej: fanatic): **health food ~** fana m/f ou obsédé(e) de l'alimentation saine ▷ adj (storm) exceptionnel(le); (accident) bizarre

freckle ['frekl] n tache f de rousseur

free [fri:] adj libre; (gratis) gratuit(e) ▷ vt (prisoner etc) libérer; (jammed object or person) dégager; **is this seat ~?** la place est libre?; **~ (of charge)** gratuitement; **freedom** n liberté f; **Freefone®** n numéro vert; **free gift** n prime f; **free kick** n (Sport) coup franc; **freelance** adj (journalist etc) indépendant(e), free-lance inv ▷ adv en free-lance; **freely** adv librement; (liberally) libéralement; **Freepost®** n (BRIT) port payé; **free-range** adj (egg) de ferme; (chicken) fermier; **freeway** n (US) autoroute f; **free will** n libre arbitre m; **of one's own free will** de son plein gré

freeze [fri:z] vb (pt **froze**, pp **frozen**) ▷ vi geler ▷ vt geler; (food) congeler; (prices, salaries) bloquer, geler ▷ n gel m;

(of prices, salaries) blocage m; **freezer** n congélateur m; **freezing (cold)** (room etc) glacial(e); (person, hands) gelé(e), glacé(e) ▷ n: **3 degrees below freezing** 3 degrés au-dessous de zéro; **it's freezing** il fait un froid glacial; **freezing point** n point m de congélation

freight [freɪt] n (goods) fret m, cargaison f; (money charged) fret, prix m du transport; **freight train** n (us) train m de marchandises

French [frɛntʃ] adj français(e) ▷ n (Ling) français m; **the ~** npl les Français; **what's the ~ (word) for ...?** comment dit-on ... en français?; **French bean** n (BRIT) haricot vert; **French bread** n pain m français; **French dressing** n (Culin) vinaigrette f; **French fried potatoes** (us **French fries**) npl (pommes de terre fpl) frites fpl; **Frenchman** (irreg) n Français m; **French stick** n ≈ baguette f; **French window** n porte-fenêtre f; **Frenchwoman** (irreg) n Française f

frenzy ['frɛnzɪ] n frénésie f

frequency ['friːkwənsɪ] n fréquence f

frequent adj ['friːkwənt] fréquent(e) ▷ vt ['frɪkwɛnt] fréquenter; **frequently** ['friːkwəntlɪ] adv fréquemment

fresh [frɛʃ] adj frais (fraîche); (new) nouveau (nouvelle); (cheeky) familier(-ière), culotté(e); **freshen** vi (wind, air) fraîchir; **freshen up** vi faire un brin de toilette; **fresher** n (BRIT University: inf) bizuth m, étudiant(e) de première année; **freshly** adv nouvellement, récemment; **freshman** (us: irreg) n = **fresher**; **freshwater** adj (fish) d'eau douce

fret [frɛt] vi s'agiter, se tracasser

Fri abbr (= Friday) ve

friction ['frɪkʃən] n friction f, frottement m

Friday ['fraɪdɪ] n vendredi m

fridge [frɪdʒ] n (BRIT) frigo m, frigidaire® m

fried [fraɪd] adj frit(e); **~ egg** œuf m sur le plat

friend [frɛnd] n ami(e); **friendly** adj amical(e); (kind) sympathique, gentil(le); (place) accueillant(e); (Pol: country) ami(e) ▷ n (also: **friendly match**) match amical; **friendship** n amitié f

fries [fraɪz] (esp us) npl **French fried potatoes**

frigate ['frɪgɪt] n frégate f

fright [fraɪt] n peur f, effroi m; **to give sb a ~** faire peur à qn; **to take ~** prendre peur, s'effrayer; **frighten** vt effrayer, faire peur à; **frightened** adj: **to be frightened (of)** avoir peur (de); **frightening** adj effrayant(e); **frightful** adj affreux(-euse)

frill [frɪl] n (of dress) volant m; (of shirt) jabot m

fringe [frɪndʒ] n (BRIT: of hair) frange f; (edge: of forest etc) bordure f

Frisbee® ['frɪzbɪ] n Frisbee® m

fritter ['frɪtə*] n beignet m

frivolous ['frɪvələs] adj frivole

fro [frəu] see **to**

frock [frɔk] n robe f

frog [frɔg] n grenouille f; **frogman** (irreg) n homme-grenouille m

○ KEYWORD

from [frɔm] prep **1** (indicating starting place, origin etc) de; **where do you come from?**, **where are you from?** d'où venez-vous?; **where has he come from?** d'où arrive-t-il?; **from London to Paris** de Londres à Paris; **to escape from sb/sth** échapper à qn/qch; **a letter/telephone call from my sister** une lettre/un appel de ma sœur; **to drink from the bottle** boire à (même) la bouteille; **tell him from me that ...** dites-lui de ma part que ...

2 (indicating time) (à partir) de; **from one o'clock to or until or till two** d'une heure à deux heures; **from January (on)** à partir de janvier

3 (indicating distance) de; **the hotel is one kilometre from the beach** l'hôtel est à un kilomètre de la plage

4 (indicating price, number etc) de; **prices range from £10 to £50** les prix varient entre 10 livres et 50 livres; **the interest rate was increased from 9% to 10%** le taux d'intérêt est passé de 9% à 10%

5 (indicating difference) de; **he can't tell red from green** il ne peut pas distinguer le rouge du vert; **to be different from sb/sth** être différent de qn/qch

6 (because of, on the basis of): **from what he says** d'après ce qu'il dit; **weak from hunger** affaibli par la faim

front [frʌnt] n (of house, dress) devant m; (of coach, train) avant m; (promenade: also: **sea ~**) bord m de mer; (Mil, Pol, Meteorology) front m; (fig: appearances) contenance f, façade f ▷ adj de devant; (seat, wheel) avant ▷inv ▷ **in ~ (of)** devant; **front door** n porte f d'entrée; (of car) portière f avant; **frontier** ['frʌntɪə*] n frontière f; **front page** n première page f; **front-wheel drive** n traction f avant

frost [frɔst] n gel m, gelée f; (also: **hoar~**) givre m; **frostbite** n gelures fpl; **frosting** n (esp us: on cake) glaçage m; **frosty** adj (window) couvert(e) de givre; (weather, welcome) glacial(e)

froth [frɔθ] n mousse f; écume f

frown [fraun] n froncement m de sourcils f ▷ vi froncer les sourcils

froze [frəʊz] pt of **freeze**

frozen ['frəʊzn] pp of **freeze** ▷ adj (food) congelé(e); (very cold: person; Comm: assets) gelé(e)

fruit [fruːt] n (pl inv) fruit m; **fruit juice** n jus m de fruit; **fruit machine** n (BRIT) machine f à sous; **fruit salad** n salade f de fruits

frustrate [frʌs'treɪt] vt frustrer; **frustrated** adj frustré(e)

fry (pt, pp **fried**) [fraɪ, -d] vt (faire) frire;

small ~ le menu fretin; **frying pan** n poêle f (à frire)

ft. abbr = **foot**; **feet**

fudge [fʌdʒ] n (Culin) sorte de confiserie à base de sucre, de beurre et de lait

fuel [fjuəl] n (for heating) combustible m; (for engine) carburant m; **fuel tank** n (in vehicle) réservoir m de or à carburant

fulfil (us **fulfill**) [ful'fɪl] vt (function, condition) remplir; (order) exécuter; (wish, desire) satisfaire, réaliser

full [ful] adj plein(e); (details, hotel, bus) complet(-ète); (busy: day) chargé(e); (skirt) ample, large ▷ adv: **to know ~ well that** savoir fort bien que; **I'm ~ (up)** j'ai bien mangé; **~ employment/ fare** plein emploi/tarif; **a ~ two hours** deux bonnes heures; **at ~ speed** à toute vitesse; **in ~** (reproduce, quote, pay) intégralement; (write name etc) en toutes lettres; **full-length** (portrait) en pied; (coat) long(ue); **full-length film** long métrage; **full moon** n pleine lune; **full-scale** adj (attack) grandeur nature inv; (search, retreat) complet(-ète), total(e); **full stop** n point m; **full-time** adj, adv (work) à plein temps; **fully** adv entièrement, complètement; (at least)

fumble ['fʌmbl] vi fouiller, tâtonner; **fumble with** vt fus tripoter

fume [fjuːm] vi (rage) rager; **fumes** npl vapeurs fpl, émanations fpl, gaz mpl

fun [fʌn] n amusement m, divertissement m; **to have ~** s'amuser; **for ~** pour rire; **to make ~ of** se moquer de

function ['fʌŋkʃən] n fonction f; (reception, dinner) cérémonie f, soirée officielle f ▷ vi fonctionner

fund [fʌnd] n caisse f, fonds m; (source, store) source f, mine f; **funds** npl (money) fonds mpl

fundamental [fʌndə'mentl] adj fondamental(e)

funeral ['fjuːnərəl] n enterrement m, obsèques fpl (more formal occasion); **funeral director** n entrepreneur m des pompes funèbres; **funeral parlour** ['pɑ:lər] n (BRIT) dépôt m mortuaire

funfair ['fʌnfɛər] n (BRIT) fête (foraine)

fungus (pl **fungi**) ['fʌŋgəs, -gaɪ] n champignon m; (mould) moisissure f

funnel ['fʌnl] n entonnoir m; (of ship) cheminée f

funny ['fʌnɪ] adj amusant(e), drôle; (strange) curieux(-euse), bizarre

fur [fɜːʳ] n fourrure f; (BRIT: in kettle etc) (dépôt m de) tartre m; **fur coat** n manteau m de fourrure

furious ['fjuərɪəs] adj furieux(-euse); (effort) acharné(e)

furnish ['fɜːnɪʃ] vt meubler; (supply) fournir; **furnishings** npl mobilier m, articles mpl d'ameublement

furniture ['fɜːnɪtʃəʳ] n meubles mpl, mobilier m; **piece of ~** meuble m

furry ['fɜːrɪ] adj (animal) à fourrure; (toy) en peluche

further ['fɜːðəʳ] adj supplémentaire, autre; nouveau (nouvelle) ▷ adv plus loin; (more) davantage; (moreover) de plus ▷ vt faire avancer or progresser, promouvoir; **further education** n enseignement m postscolaire (recyclage, formation professionnelle); **furthermore** adv de plus, en outre

furthest ['fɜːðɪst] superlative of **far**

fury ['fjuərɪ] n fureur f

fuse (US **fuze**) [fjuːz] n fusible m; (for bomb etc) amorce f, détonateur m ▷ vt, vi (metal) fondre; (BRIT: Elec): **to ~ the lights** faire sauter les fusibles or les plombs; **fuse box** n boîte f à fusibles

fusion ['fjuːʒən] n fusion f

fuss [fʌs] n (anxiety, excitement) chichis mpl, façons fpl; (commotion) tapage m; (complaining, trouble) histoire(s) f(pl); **to make a ~** faire des façons (or des histoires); **to make a ~ of sb** dorloter qn; **fussy** adj (person) tatillon(ne), difficile, chichiteux(-euse); (dress, style) tarabiscoté(e)

future ['fjuːtʃəʳ] adj futur(e) ▷ n avenir m; (Ling) futur m; **futures** npl (Comm) opérations fpl à terme; **in (the) ~** à l'avenir

fuze [fjuːz] n, vt, vi (US) = **fuse**

fuzzy ['fʌzɪ] adj (Phot) flou(e); (hair) crépu(e)

g

G [dʒi:] n (Mus): **G** sol m

g. abbr (= gram) g

gadget ['gædʒɪt] n gadget m

Gaelic ['geɪlɪk] adj, n (Ling) gaélique (m)

gag [gæg] n (on mouth) bâillon m; (joke) gag m ▷ vt (prisoner etc) bâillonner

gain [geɪn] n (improvement) gain m; (profit) gain, profit m ▷ vt gagner ▷ vi (watch) avancer; **to ~ from/by** gagner de/à; **to ~ on sb** (catch up) rattraper qn; **to ~ 3lbs (in weight)** prendre 3 livres; **to ~ ground** gagner du terrain

gal. abbr = **gallon**

gala ['gɑ:lə] n gala m

galaxy ['gæləksɪ] n galaxie f

gale [geɪl] n coup m de vent

gall bladder ['gɔ:l-] n vésicule f biliaire

gallery ['gælərɪ] n (also: **art ~**) musée m; (: private) galerie f; (: in theatre) dernier balcon

gallon ['gæln] n gallon m (BRIT = 4.543 l; US = 3.785 l)

gallop ['gæləp] n galop m ▷ vi galoper

gallstone ['gɔ:lstəun] n calcul m (biliaire)

gamble ['gæmbl] n pari m, risque calculé ▷ vt, vi jouer; **to ~ on** (fig) miser sur; **gambler** n joueur m; **gambling** n jeu m

game [geɪm] n jeu m; (event) match m; (of tennis, chess, cards) partie f; (Hunting) gibier m ▷ adj (willing): **to be ~ (for)** être prêt(e) (à or pour); **big ~** gros gibier; **games** npl (Scol) sport m; (sport event) jeux; **games console** ['geɪmz-] n console f de jeux vidéo; **game show** n jeu télévisé

gammon ['gæmən] n (bacon) quartier m de lard fumé; (ham) jambon fumé or salé

gang [gæŋ] n bande f; (of workmen) équipe f

gangster ['gæŋstə'] n gangster m, bandit m

gap [gæp] n trou m; (in time) intervalle m; (difference): **~ (between)** écart m (entre)

gape [geɪp] vi (person) être or rester bouche bée; (hole, shirt) être ouvert(e)

gap year n année que certains étudiants prennent pour voyager ou pour travailler avant d'entrer à l'université

garage ['gærɑ:ʒ] n garage m; **garage sale** n vide-grenier m

garbage ['gɑ:bɪdʒ] n (US: rubbish) ordures fpl, détritus mpl; (inf: nonsense) âneries fpl; **garbage can** n (US) poubelle f, boîte f à ordures; **garbage collector** n (US) éboueur m

garden ['gɑ:dn] n jardin m; **gardens** npl (public) jardin public; (private) parc m; **garden centre** (BRIT) n pépinière f, jardinerie f; **gardener** n jardinier m; **gardening** n jardinage m

garlic ['gɑ:lɪk] n ail m

garment ['gɑ:mənt] n vêtement m

garnish ['gɑ:nɪʃ] (Culin) vt garnir ▷ n décoration f

garrison ['gærɪsn] n garnison f

gas [gæs] n gaz m; (US: gasoline) essence f ▷ vt asphyxier; **I can smell ~** ça sent le gaz; **gas cooker** n (BRIT) cuisinière f à

gaz; **gas cylinder** n bouteille f de gaz;
gas fire n (BRIT) radiateur m à gaz

gasket ['ɡæskɪt] n (Aut) joint m de
culasse

gasoline ['ɡæsəliːn] n (US) essence f

gasp [ɡɑːsp] n halètement m; (of shock
etc): **she gave a small ~ of pain** la
douleur lui coupa le souffle ▷ vi haleter;
(fig) avoir le souffle coupé

gas: **gas pedal** n (US) accélérateur m;
gas station n (US) station-service f;
gas tank n (US Aut) réservoir m
d'essence

gate [ɡeɪt] n (of garden) portail m; (of
field, at level crossing) barrière f; (of
building, town, at airport) porte f

gateau (pl -x) ['ɡætəʊ, -z] n gros
gâteau m à la crème

gatecrash ['ɡeɪtkræʃ] vt s'introduire
sans invitation dans

gateway ['ɡeɪtweɪ] n porte f

gather ['ɡæðə'] vt (flowers, fruit)
cueillir; (pick up) ramasser; (assemble:
objects) rassembler; (: people) réunir;
(: information) recueillir; (understand)
comprendre; (Sewing) froncer ▷ vi
(assemble) se rassembler; **to ~ speed**
prendre de la vitesse; **gathering** n
rassemblement m

gauge [ɡeɪdʒ] n (instrument) jauge f ▷ vt
jauger; (fig) juger de

gave [ɡeɪv] pt of **give**

gay [ɡeɪ] adj (homosexual)
homosexuel(le); (colour) gai, vif (vive)

gaze [ɡeɪz] n regard m fixe ▷ vi: **to ~ at**
vt fixer du regard

GB abbr = **Great Britain**

GCSE n abbr (BRIT: = General Certificate of
Secondary Education) examen passé à l'âge
de 16 ans sanctionnant les connaissances
de l'élève

gear [ɡɪə'] n matériel m, équipement
m; (Tech) engrenage m; (Aut) vitesse
f ▷ vt (fig: adapt) adapter; **top** or (US)
high/low ~ quatrième or cinquième/
première vitesse; **in** ~ en prise; **gear up**
vi: **to ~ up (to do)** se préparer (à faire);
gear box n boîte f de vitesse; **gear**

lever n levier m de vitesse; **gear shift**
(US) n = **gear lever**; **gear stick** (BRIT) n
= **gear lever**

geese [ɡiːs] npl of **goose**

gel [dʒel] n gelée f

gem [dʒem] n pierre précieuse

Gemini ['dʒemɪnaɪ] n les Gémeaux mpl

gender ['dʒendə'] n genre m; (person's
sex) sexe m

gene [dʒiːn] n (Biol) gène m

general ['dʒenərl] n général m ▷ adj
général(e); **in ~** en général; **general
anaesthetic** (US **general anesthetic**)
n anesthésie générale; **general
election** n élection(s) législative(s);
generalize vi généraliser; **generally**
adv généralement; **general
practitioner** n généraliste m/f;
general store n épicerie f

generate ['dʒenəreɪt] vt engendrer;
(electricity) produire

generation [dʒenə'reɪʃən] n
génération f; (of electricity etc)
production f

generator ['dʒenəreɪtə'] n
générateur m

generosity [dʒenə'rɒsɪtɪ] n
générosité f

generous ['dʒenərəs] adj
généreux(-euse); (copious)
copieux(-euse)

genetic [dʒɪ'nɛtɪk] adj génétique; **~
engineering** ingénierie m génétique; **~
fingerprinting** système m d'empreinte
génétique; **genetically modified** adj
(food etc) génétiquement modifié m;
genetics n génétique f

Geneva [dʒɪ'niːvə] n Genève

genitals ['dʒenɪtlz] npl organes
génitaux

genius ['dʒiːnɪəs] n génie m

gent [dʒent] n abbr (BRIT inf)
= **gentleman**

gentle ['dʒentl] adj doux (douce);
(breeze, touch) léger(-ère)

gentleman (irreg) ['dʒentlmən]
n monsieur m; (well-bred man)
gentleman m

gently ['dʒɛntlɪ] adv doucement

gents [dʒɛnts] n W.-C. mpl (pour hommes)

genuine ['dʒɛnjuɪn] adj véritable, authentique; (person, emotion) sincère; **genuinely** adv sincèrement, vraiment

geographic(al) [dʒɪə'græfɪk(l)] adj géographique

geography [dʒɪ'ɔgrəfɪ] n géographie f

geology [dʒɪ'ɔlədʒɪ] n géologie f

geometry [dʒɪ'ɔmətrɪ] n géométrie f

geranium [dʒɪ'reɪnɪəm] n géranium m

geriatric [dʒɛrɪ'ætrɪk] adj gériatrique
▷ n patient(e) gériatrique

germ [dʒəːm] n (Med) microbe m

German ['dʒəːmən] adj allemand(e)
▷ n Allemand(e); (Ling) allemand m;
German measles n rubéole f

Germany ['dʒəːmənɪ] n Allemagne f

gesture ['dʒɛstʃər] n geste m

get [gɛt] (pt, pp **got**, pp **gotten** (us)) vi
1 (become, be) devenir; **to get old/tired** devenir vieux/fatigué, vieillir/se fatiguer; **to get drunk** s'enivrer; **to get dirty** se salir; **to get married** se marier; **when do I get paid?** quand est-ce que je serai payé?; **it's getting late** il se fait tard
2 (go): **to get to/from** aller à/de; **to get home** rentrer chez soi; **how did you get here?** comment es-tu arrivé ici?
3 (begin) commencer or se mettre à; **to get to know sb** apprendre à connaître qn; **I'm getting to like him** je commence à l'apprécier; **let's get going** or **started** allons-y
4 (modal aux vb): **you've got to do it** il faut que vous le fassiez; **I've got to tell the police** je dois le dire à la police
▷ vt 1: **to get sth done** (do) faire qch; (have done) faire faire qch; **to get one's hair cut** se faire couper les cheveux; **to get the car going** or **to go** (faire) démarrer la voiture; **to get sb to do sth** faire faire qch à qn
2 (obtain: money, permission, results) obtenir, avoir; (buy) acheter; (find: job, flat) trouver; (fetch: person, doctor, object) aller chercher; **to get sth for sb** procurer qch à qn; **get me Mr Jones, please** (on phone) passez-moi Mr Jones, s'il vous plaît; **can I get you a drink?** est-ce que je peux vous servir à boire?
3 (receive: present, letter) recevoir, avoir; (acquire: reputation) avoir; (prize) obtenir; **what did you get for your birthday?** qu'est-ce que tu as eu pour ton anniversaire?; **how much did you get for the painting?** combien avez-vous vendu le tableau?
4 (catch) prendre, saisir, attraper; (hit: target etc) atteindre; **to get sb by the arm/throat** prendre or saisir or attraper qn par le bras/à la gorge; **get him!** arrête-le!; **the bullet got him in the leg** il a pris la balle dans la jambe
5 (take, move): **to get sth to sb** faire parvenir qch à qn; **do you think we'll get it through the door?** on arrivera à le faire passer par la porte?
6 (catch, take: plane, bus etc) prendre; **where do I get the train for Birmingham?** où prend-on le train pour Birmingham?
7 (understand) comprendre, saisir; (hear) entendre; **I've got it!** j'ai compris!; **I don't get your meaning** je ne vois or comprends pas ce que vous voulez dire; **I didn't get your name** je n'ai pas entendu votre nom
8 (have, possess): **to have got** avoir; **how many have you got?** vous en avez combien?
9 (illness) avoir; **I've got a cold** j'ai le rhume; **she got pneumonia and died** elle a fait une pneumonie et elle en est morte

get away vi partir, s'en aller; (escape) s'échapper

get away with vt fus (punishment) en être quitte pour; (crime etc) se faire pardonner

get back vi (return) rentrer
▷ vt récupérer, recouvrer; **when do we get back?** quand serons-nous de retour?
get in vi entrer; (arrive home) rentrer; (train) arriver
get into vt fus entrer dans; (car, train etc) monter dans; (clothes) mettre, enfiler, endosser; **to get into bed/a rage** se mettre au lit/en colère
get off vi (from train etc) descendre; (depart: person, car) s'en aller
▷ vt (remove: clothes, stain) enlever
▷ vt fus (train, bus) descendre de; **where do I get off?** où est-ce que je dois descendre?
get on vi (at exam etc) se débrouiller; (agree): **to get on (with)** s'entendre (avec); **how are you getting on?** comment ça va?
▷ vt fus monter dans; (horse) monter sur
get out vi sortir; (of vehicle) descendre
▷ vt sortir
get out of vt fus sortir de; (duty etc) échapper à, se soustraire à
get over vt fus (illness) se remettre de
get through vi (Tel) avoir la communication; **to get through to sb** atteindre qn
get up vi (rise) se lever
▷ vt fus monter

getaway ['gɛtəweɪ] n fuite f
Ghana ['gɑːnə] n Ghana m
ghastly ['gɑːstlɪ] adj atroce, horrible
ghetto ['gɛtəu] n ghetto m
ghost [gəust] n fantôme m, revenant m
giant ['dʒaɪənt] n géant(e) b adj géant(e), énorme
gift [gɪft] n cadeau m; (donation, talent) don m; **gifted** adj doué(e); **gift shop** (US **gift store**) n boutique f de cadeaux; **gift token, gift voucher** n chèque-cadeau m
gig [gɪg] n (inf: concert) concert m
gigabyte ['dʒɪgəbaɪt] n gigaoctet m
gigantic [dʒaɪˈgæntɪk] adj gigantesque

giggle ['gɪgl] vi pouffer, ricaner sottement
gills [gɪlz] npl (of fish) ouïes fpl, branchies fpl
gilt [gɪlt] n dorure f b adj doré(e)
gimmick ['gɪmɪk] n truc m
gin [dʒɪn] n gin m
ginger ['dʒɪndʒə*] n gingembre m
gipsy ['dʒɪpsɪ] n = **gypsy**
giraffe [dʒɪˈrɑːf] n girafe f
girl [gəːl] n fille f, fillette f; (young unmarried woman) jeune fille; (daughter) fille; **an English ~** une jeune Anglaise; **girl band** n girls band m; **girlfriend** n (of girl) amie f; (of boy) petite amie; **Girl Guide** n (BRIT) éclaireuse f; (Roman Catholic) guide f; **Girl Scout** n (US) = **Girl Guide**
gist [dʒɪst] n essentiel m
give [gɪv] vb (pt **gave**, pp **~n**) b vt donner b vi (break) céder; (stretch: fabric) se prêter; **to ~ sb sth, ~ sth to sb** donner qch à qn; (gift) offrir qch à qn; (message) transmettre qch à qn; **to ~ sb a cry/sigh** pousser un cri/un soupir; **give away** vt donner; (give free) faire cadeau de; (betray) donner, trahir; (disclose) révéler; **give back** vt rendre; **give in** vi céder b vt donner; **give out** vt (food etc) distribuer; **give up** vi renoncer b vt renoncer à; **to ~ up smoking** arrêter de fumer; **to ~ o.s. up** se rendre
given ['gɪvn] pp of **give** b adj (fixed: time, amount) donné(e), déterminé(e)
▷ conj: **~ the circumstances ...** étant donné les circonstances ...; vu les circonstances ...; **~ that ...** étant donné que ...
glacier ['glæsɪə*] n glacier m
glad [glæd] adj content(e); **gladly** ['glædlɪ] adv volontiers
glamorous ['glæmərəs] adj (person) séduisant(e); (job) prestigieux(-euse)
glamour (US **glamor**) ['glæmə*] n éclat m, prestige m
glance [glɑːns] n coup d'œil b vi: **to ~**

at jeter un coup d'œil à

gland [glænd] *n* glande *f*

glare [gleə*r*] *n* (of anger) regard furieux; (of light) lumière éblouissante; (of publicity) feux *mpl* ▷ *vi* briller d'un éclat aveuglant; **to ~ at** lancer un regard ou des regards furieux à; **glaring** *adj* (mistake) criant(e), qui saute aux yeux

glass [glɑːs] *n* verre *m*; **glasses** *npl* (spectacles) lunettes *fpl*

glaze [gleɪz] *vt* (door) vitrer; (pottery) vernir ▷ *n* vernis *m*

gleam [gliːm] *vi* luire, briller

glen [glɛn] *n* vallée *f*

glide [glaɪd] *vi* glisser; (Aviat, bird) planer; **glider** *n* (Aviat) planeur *m*

glimmer ['glɪmə*r*] *n* lueur *f*

glimpse [glɪmps] *n* vision passagère, aperçu *m* ▷ *vt* entrevoir, apercevoir

glint [glɪnt] *vi* étinceler

glisten ['glɪsn] *vi* briller, luire

glitter ['glɪtə*r*] *vi* scintiller, briller

global ['gləʊbl] *adj* (world-wide) mondial(e); (overall) global(e); **globalization** *n* mondialisation *f*; **global warming** *n* réchauffement *m* de la planète

globe [gləʊb] *n* globe *m*

gloom [gluːm] *n* obscurité *f*; (sadness) tristesse *f*, mélancolie *f*; **gloomy** *adj* (person) morose; (place, outlook) sombre

glorious ['glɔːrɪəs] *adj* glorieux(-euse); (beautiful) splendide

glory ['glɔːrɪ] *n* gloire *f*; splendeur *f*

gloss [glɔs] *n* (shine) brillant *m*, vernis *m*; (also: **~ paint**) peinture brillante ou laquée

glossary ['glɔsərɪ] *n* glossaire *m*, lexique *m*

glossy ['glɔsɪ] *adj* brillant(e), luisant(e) ▷ *n* (also: **~ magazine**) revue *f* de luxe

glove [glʌv] *n* gant *m*; **glove compartment** *n* (Aut) boîte *f* à gants, vide-poches *m inv*

glow [gləʊ] *vi* rougeoyer; (face) rayonner; (eyes) briller

glucose ['gluːkəʊs] *n* glucose *m*

glue [gluː] *n* colle *f* ▷ *vt* coller

GM *abbr* (= genetically modified) génétiquement modifié(e)

gm *abbr* (= gram) g

GMO *n abbr* (= genetically modified organism) OGM *m*

GMT *abbr* (= Greenwich Mean Time) GMT

gnaw [nɔː] *vt* ronger

go [gəʊ] *vb* (*pt* **went**, *pp* **gone**) ▷ *vi* aller; (depart) partir, s'en aller; (work) marcher; (break) céder; (time) passer; (be sold): **to go for £10** se vendre 10 livres; (become): **to go pale/mouldy** pâlir/moisir ▷ *n* (*pl* **goes**): **to have a go (at)** essayer (de faire); **to be on the go** être en mouvement; **whose go is it?** à qui est-ce de jouer?; **he's going to do it** il va le faire, il est sur le point de le faire; **to go for a walk** aller se promener; **to go dancing/shopping** aller danser/faire les courses; **to go and see sb**, **go to see sb** aller voir qn; **how did it go?** comment est-ce que ça s'est passé?; **to go round the back/by the shop** passer par derrière/devant le magasin; **... to go** (*us: food*) ... à emporter; **go ahead** *vi* (take place) avoir lieu; (get going) y aller; **go away** *vi* partir, s'en aller; **go back** *vi* rentrer; revenir; (go again) retourner; **go by** *vi* (years, time) passer, s'écouler ▷ *vt* fus s'en tenir à; (believe) en croire; **go down** *vi* descendre; (number, price, amount) baisser; (ship) couler; (sun) se coucher ▷ *vt fus* descendre; **go for** *vt fus* (fetch) aller chercher; (like) aimer; (attack) s'en prendre à; attaquer; **go in** *vi* entrer; **go into** *vt fus* entrer dans; (investigate) étudier, examiner; (embark on) se lancer dans; **go off** *vi* partir, s'en aller; (food) se gâter; (milk) tourner; (bomb) sauter; (alarm clock) sonner; (alarm) se déclencher; (lights etc) s'éteindre; (event) se dérouler ▷ *vt fus* ne plus aimer; **the gun went off** le coup est parti; **go on** *vi* continuer; (happen) se passer; (lights) s'allumer ▷ *vt fus*: **to go on doing** continuer à faire; **go out** *vi* sortir; (fire, light) s'éteindre;

(tide) descendre; **to go out with sb** sortir avec qn; **go over** vi, **go over vt** fus (check) revoir, vérifier; **go past vt** fus: **to go past sth** passer devant qch; **go round** vi (circulate: news, rumour) circuler; (revolve) tourner; (suffice) suffire (pour tout le monde); (visit): **to go round to sb's** passer chez qn; aller chez qn; (make a detour) faire un détour (par); **to go round (by)** faire un détour (par); **go through vt** fus (town etc) traverser; (search through) fouiller; (suffer) subir; **go up** vi monter; (price) augmenter ▷ **vt** fus gravir; **go with vt** fus aller avec; **go without vt** fus se passer de

go-ahead ['gəʊəhed] adj dynamique, entreprenant(e) ▷ n feu vert

goal [gəʊl] n but m; **goalkeeper** n gardien m de but; **goal-post** n poteau m de but

goat [gəʊt] n chèvre f

gobble ['gɔbl] vt (also: **~ down, ~ up**) engloutir

god [gɔd] n dieu m; **G~** Dieu; **godchild** n filleul(e); **goddaughter** n filleule f; **goddess** n déesse f; **godfather** n parrain m; **godmother** n marraine f; **godson** n filleul m

goggles ['gɔglz] npl (for skiing etc) lunettes (protectrices); (for swimming) lunettes de piscine

going ['gəʊɪŋ] n (conditions) état m du terrain ▷ adj: **the ~ rate** le tarif (en vigueur)

gold [gəʊld] n or m ▷ adj en or; (reserves) d'or; **golden** adj (made of gold) en or; (in colour) doré(e); **goldfish** n poisson m rouge; **goldmine** n mine f d'or; **gold-plated** adj plaqué(e) or inv

golf [gɔlf] n golf m; **golf ball** n balle f de golf; (on typewriter) boule f; **golf club** n club m de golf; (stick) crosse f de golf; **golf course** n terrain m de golf; **golfer** n joueur(-euse) de golf

gone [gɔn] pp of **go**

gong [gɔŋ] n gong m

good [gʊd] adj bon(ne); (kind) gentil(le); (child) sage; (weather) beau (belle) ▷ n

bien m; **goods** npl marchandise f, articles mpl; **~!** bon!, très bien!; **to be ~ at** être bon en; **to be ~ for** être bon pour; **it's no ~ complaining** cela ne sert à rien de se plaindre; **to make ~** (deficit) combler; (losses) compenser; **for ~** (for ever) pour de bon, une fois pour toutes; **would you be ~ enough to ...?** auriez-vous la bonté or l'amabilité de ...?; **is this any ~?** (will it do?) est-ce que ceci fera l'affaire?, est-ce que cela peut vous rendre service?; (what's it like?) qu'est-ce que ça vaut?; **a ~ deal (of)** beaucoup (de); **a ~ many** beaucoup (de); **~ morning/afternoon!** bonjour!; **~ evening!** bonsoir!; **~ night!** bonsoir!; (on going to bed) bonne nuit!; **goodbye** excl au revoir!; **to say goodbye to sb** dire au revoir à qn; **Good Friday** n Vendredi saint; **good-looking** adj beau (belle), bien inv; **good-natured** adj (person) qui a un bon naturel; **goodness** n (of person) bonté f; (of food) valeur f; **for goodness sake!** je vous en prie!; **goodness gracious!** mon Dieu!; **goods train** n (BRIT) train m de marchandises; **goodwill** n bonne volonté

goose (pl **geese**) [guːs, giːs] n oie f

gooseberry ['gʊzbərɪ] n groseille f à maquereau; **to play ~** (BRIT) tenir la chandelle

goose bumps, goose pimples npl chair f de poule

gorge [gɔːdʒ] n gorge f ▷ vt: **to ~ o.s. (on)** se gorger (de)

gorgeous ['gɔːdʒəs] adj splendide, superbe

gorilla [gəˈrɪlə] n gorille m

gosh (inf) [gɔʃ] excl mince alors!

gospel ['gɔspl] n évangile m

gossip ['gɔsɪp] n (chat) bavardages mpl; (malicious) commérage m, cancans mpl; (person) commère f ▷ vi bavarder; cancaner, faire des commérages; **gossip column** n (Press) échos mpl

got [gɔt] pt, pp of **get**

gotten ['gɔtn] (US) pp of **get**

gourmet ['gʊəmeɪ] n gourmet m,

gastronome m/f

govern ['gʌvn] vt gouverner;
(influence) déterminer; **government**
n gouvernement m; (BRIT: ministers)
ministère m; **governor** n (of colony,
state, bank) gouverneur m; (of school,
hospital etc) administrateur(-trice);
(BRIT: of prison) directeur(-trice)

gown [gaun] n robe f; (of teacher, BRIT:
of judge) toge f

G.P. n abbr (Med) = **general practitioner**

grab [græb] vt saisir, empoigner ▷ vi: to
~ **at** essayer de saisir

grace [greis] n grâce f ▷ vt (honour)
honorer; (adorn) orner; **5 days' ~**
un répit de 5 jours; **graceful** adj
gracieux(-euse), élégant(e); **gracious**
['greiʃəs] adj bienveillant(e)

grade [greid] n (Comm: quality) qualité
f; (size) calibre m; (type) catégorie
f; (in hierarchy) grade m, échelon m;
(Scol) note f; (: class) classe
f; (: gradient) pente f ▷ vt classer; (by
size) calibrer; **grade crossing** n (US)
passage m à niveau; **grade school** n
(US) école f primaire

gradient ['greidiənt] n inclinaison
f, pente f

gradual ['grædjuəl] adj graduel(le),
progressif(-ive); **gradually** adv peu à
peu, graduellement

graduate n ['grædjuit] diplômé(e)
d'université; (US: of high school)
diplômé(e) de fin d'études ▷ vi
['grædjueit] obtenir un diplôme
d'université (or de fin d'études);
graduation [grædju'eiʃən] n
cérémonie f de remise des diplômes

graffiti [grə'fi:ti] npl graffiti mpl

graft [grɑːft] n (Agr, Med) greffe f;
(bribery) corruption f ▷ vt greffer; **hard
~** (inf) boulot acharné

grain [grein] n (single piece) grain m; (no
pl: cereals) céréales fpl; (US: corn) blé m

gram [græm] n gramme m

grammar ['græmə'] n grammaire f;
grammar school n (BRIT) = lycée m

gramme [græm] n = **gram**

gran (inf) [græn] n (BRIT) mamie f (inf),
mémé f (inf)

grand [grænd] adj magnifique,
splendide; (gesture etc) noble; **grandad**
(inf) n = **granddad**; **grandchild** (pl
~**ren**) n petit-fils m, petite-fille f;
grandchildren npl petits-enfants;
granddad n (inf) papy m (inf), papi
m (inf); **pépé** m (inf); **granddaughter**
n petite-fille f; **grandfather** n
grand-père m; **grandma** n (inf)
= **grandmother**; **grandmother** n grand-
mère f; **grandpa** n (inf) = **granddad**;
grandparents npl grands-parents mpl;
grand piano n piano m à queue; **Grand
Prix** ['grɑ̃:'pri:] n (Aut) grand prix
automobile; **grandson** n petit-fils m

granite ['grænit] n granit m

granny ['græni] n (inf) = **gran**

grant [grɑːnt] vt accorder; (a request)
accéder à; (admit) concéder ▷ n (Scol)
bourse f; (Admin) subside m, subvention
f; **to take sth for ~ed** considérer qch
comme acquis; **to take sb for ~ed**
considérer qn comme faisant partie
du décor

grape [greip] n raisin m

grapefruit ['greipfru:t] n
pamplemousse m

graph [grɑːf] n graphique m, courbe f;
graphic ['græfik] adj graphique; (vivid)
vivant(e); **graphics** n (art) arts mpl
graphiques; (process) graphisme m
▷ npl (drawings) illustrations fpl

grasp [grɑːsp] vt saisir ▷ n (grip) prise f;
(fig) compréhension f, connaissance f

grass [grɑːs] n herbe f; (lawn) gazon m;
grasshopper n sauterelle f

grate [greit] n grille f de cheminée ▷ vi
grincer ▷ vt (Culin) râper

grateful ['greitful] adj
reconnaissant(e)

grater ['greitə'] n râpe f

gratitude ['grætitju:d] n gratitude f

grave [greiv] n tombe f ▷ adj grave,
sérieux(-euse)

gravel ['grævl] n gravier m

gravestone ['greivstəun] n pierre

tombale

graveyard ['greɪvjɑːd] n cimetière m

gravity ['grævɪtɪ] n (Physics) gravité f; pesanteur f; (seriousness) gravité

gravy ['greɪvɪ] n jus m (de viande), sauce f (au jus de viande)

gray [greɪ] adj (us) = **grey**

graze [greɪz] vi paître, brouter ▷ vt (touch lightly) frôler, effleurer; (scrape) écorcher ▷ n écorchure f

grease [griːs] n (fat) graisse f; (lubricant) lubrifiant m ▷ vt graisser; lubrifier; **greasy** adj gras(se), graisseux(-euse); (hands, clothes) graisseux

great [greɪt] adj grand(e); (heat, pain etc) très fort(e), intense; (inf) formidable; **Great Britain** n Grande-Bretagne f; **great-grandfather** n arrière-grand-père m; **great-grandmother** n arrière-grand-mère f; **greatly** adv très, grandement; (with verbs) beaucoup

Greece [griːs] n Grèce f

greed [griːd] n (also: **-iness**) avidité f; (for food) gourmandise f; **greedy** adj avide; (for food) gourmand(e)

Greek [griːk] adj grec (grecque) ▷ n Grec (Grecque); (Ling) grec m

green [griːn] adj vert(e); (inexperienced) (bien) jeune, naïf(-ive); (ecological: product etc) écologique ▷ n (colour) vert m; (on golf course) green m; (stretch of grass) pelouse f; **greens** npl (vegetables) légumes verts; **green card** n (Aut) carte verte; (us: work permit) permis m de travail; **greengage** n reine-claude f; **greengrocer** n (BRIT) marchand m de fruits et légumes; **greengrocer's (shop)** n magasin m de fruits et légumes; **greenhouse** n serre f; **greenhouse effect** n: **the greenhouse effect** l'effet m de serre

Greenland ['griːnlənd] n Groenland m

green salad n salade verte

greet [griːt] vt accueillir; (greeting) saluer; **greeting** n salutation f; **Christmas/birthday greetings** souhaits mpl de Noël/de bon anniversaire; **greeting(s) card** n carte f de vœux

grew [gruː] pt of **grow**

grey (us **gray**) [greɪ] adj gris(e); (dismal) sombre; **grey-haired** adj aux cheveux gris; **greyhound** n lévrier m

grid [grɪd] n grille f; (Elec) réseau m; **gridlock** n (traffic jam) embouteillage m

grief [griːf] n chagrin m, douleur f

grievance ['griːvəns] n doléance f, grief m; (cause for complaint) grief

grieve [griːv] vi avoir du chagrin; se désoler ▷ vt faire de la peine à, affliger; **to ~ for sb** pleurer qn

grill [grɪl] n (on cooker) gril m; (also: **mixed ~**) grillade(s) f(pl) ▷ vt (BRIT) griller; (inf: question) cuisiner

grille [grɪl] n grillage m; (Aut) calandre f

grim [grɪm] adj sinistre, lugubre; (serious, stern) sévère

grime [graɪm] n crasse f

grin [grɪn] n large sourire m ▷ vi sourire

grind [graɪnd] vb (pt, pp **ground**) ▷ vt écraser; (coffee, pepper etc) moudre; (us: meat) hacher ▷ n (work) corvée f

grip [grɪp] n (handclasp) poigne f; (control) prise f; (handle) poignée f; (holdall) sac m de voyage ▷ vt saisir, empoigner; (viewer, reader) captiver; **to come to ~s with** se colleter avec, en venir aux prises avec; **to ~ the road** (Aut) adhérer à la route; **gripping** adj prenant(e), palpitant(e)

grit [grɪt] n gravillon m; (courage) cran m ▷ vt (road) sabler; **to ~ one's teeth** serrer les dents

grits [grɪts] npl (us) gruau m de maïs

groan [grəun] n (of pain) gémissement m ▷ vi gémir

grocer ['grəusə] n épicier m; **groceries** npl provisions fpl; **grocer's (shop)**, **grocery** n épicerie f

groin [grɔɪn] n aine f

groom [gruːm] n (for horses) palefrenier m; (also: **bride~**) marié m ▷ vt (horse) panser; (fig): **to ~ sb for** former qn pour

groove [gruːv] n sillon m, rainure f

grope [grəup] vi tâtonner; **to ~ for** chercher à tâtons

gross [grəʊs] *adj* grossier(-ière); (Comm) brut(e); **grossly** *adv* (greatly) très, grandement

grotesque [grə'tesk] *adj* grotesque

ground [graʊnd] *pt, pp of* **grind** ▷ *n* sol *m*, terre *f*; (land) terrain *m*, terres *fpl*; (Sport) terrain; (reason: gen pl) raison *f*; (us: also: ~ **wire**) terre *f* ▷ *vt* (plane) empêcher de décoller, retenir au sol; (us Elec) équiper d'une prise de terre; **grounds** *npl* (gardens etc) parc *m*, domaine *m*; (of coffee) marc *m*; **on the ~**, **to the ~** par terre; **to gain/lose ~** gagner/perdre du terrain; **ground floor** *n* (BRIT) rez-de-chaussée *m*; **groundsheet** *n* (BRIT) tapis *m* de sol; **groundwork** *n* préparation *f*

group [gruːp] *n* groupe *m* ▷ *vt* (also: ~ **together**) grouper ▷ *vi* (also: ~ **together**) se grouper

grouse [graʊs] *n* (pl inv: bird) grouse *f* (sorte de coq de bruyère) ▷ *vi* (complain) rouspéter, râler

grovel ['grɔvl] *vi* (fig): **to ~ (before)** ramper (devant)

grow (pt **grew**, pp ~n) [grəʊ, gruː, grəʊn] *vi* (plant) pousser, croître; (person: increase) grandir; (increase) augmenter, se développer; (become) devenir; **to ~ rich/weak** s'enrichir/s'affaiblir ▷ *vt* cultiver, faire pousser; (hair, beard) laisser pousser; **grow on** *vt fus*: **that painting is ~ing on me** je finirai par aimer ce tableau; **grow up** *vi* grandir

growl [graʊl] *vi* grogner

grown [grəʊn] *pp of* **grow**; **grown-up** *n* adulte *m/f*, grande personne

growth [grəʊθ] *n* croissance *f*, développement *m*; (what has grown) pousse *f*, poussée *f*; (Med) grosseur *f*, tumeur *f*

grub [grʌb] *n* larve *f*; (inf: food) bouffe *f*

grubby ['grʌbɪ] *adj* crasseux(-euse)

grudge [grʌdʒ] *n* rancune *f* ▷ *vt*: **to ~ sb sth** (in giving) donner qch à qn à contre-cœur; (resent) reprocher qch à qn; **to bear sb a ~ (for)** garder rancune or en vouloir à qn (de)

gruelling (us **grueling**) ['grʊəlɪŋ] *adj* exténuant(e)

gruesome ['gruːsəm] *adj* horrible

grumble ['grʌmbl] *vi* rouspéter, ronchonner

grumpy ['grʌmpɪ] *adj* grincheux(-euse)

grunt [grʌnt] *vi* grogner

guarantee [gærən'tiː] *n* garantie *f* ▷ *vt* garantir

guard [gɑːd] *n* garde *f*; (one man) garde *m*; (BRIT Rail) chef *m* de train; (safety device: on machine) dispositif *m* de sûreté; (also: **fire~**) garde-feu *m inv* ▷ *vt* garder, surveiller; (protect): **to ~ sb/sth (against** or **from)** protéger qn/qch (contre); **to be on one's ~** (fig) être sur ses gardes; **guardian** *n* gardien(ne); (of minor) tuteur(-trice)

guerrilla [gə'rɪlə] *n* guérillero *m*

guess [ges] *vi* deviner ▷ *vt* deviner; (estimate) évaluer; (us) croire, penser ▷ *n* supposition *f*, hypothèse *f*; **to take** or **have a ~** essayer de deviner

guest [gest] *n* invité(e); (in hotel) client(e); **guest house** *n* pension *f*; **guest room** *n* chambre *f* d'amis

guidance ['gaɪdəns] *n* (advice) conseils *mpl*

guide [gaɪd] *n* (person) guide *m/f*; (book) guide *m*; (also: **Girl G~**) éclaireuse *f*; (Roman Catholic) guide *f* ▷ *vt* guider; **is there an English-speaking ~?** est-ce que l'un des guides parle anglais?; **guidebook** *n* guide *m*; **guide dog** *n* chien *m* d'aveugle; **guided tour** *n* visite guidée; **what time does the guided tour start?** la visite guidée commence à quelle heure?; **guidelines** *npl* (advice) instructions générales, conseils *mpl*

guild [gɪld] *n* (History) corporation *f*; (sharing interests) cercle *m*, association *f*

guilt [gɪlt] *n* culpabilité *f*; **guilty** *adj* coupable

guinea pig ['gɪnɪ-] *n* cobaye *m*

guitar [gɪ'tɑː] *n* guitare *f*; **guitarist** *n* guitariste *m/f*

gulf [gʌlf] *n* golfe *m*; (abyss) gouffre *m*

gull [gʌl] *n* mouette *f*

gulp [gʌlp] vi avaler sa salive; (from emotion) avoir la gorge serrée, s'étrangler ▷ vt (also: **~ down**) avaler

gum [gʌm] n (Anat) gencive f; (glue) colle f; (also: **chewing-~**) chewing-gum m ▷ vt coller

gun [gʌn] n (small) revolver m, pistolet m; (rifle) fusil m, carabine f; (cannon) canon m; **gunfire** n fusillade f; **gunman** (irreg) n bandit armé; **gunpoint** n: **at gunpoint** sous la menace du pistolet (or fusil); **gunpowder** n poudre f à canon; **gunshot** n coup m de feu

gush [gʌʃ] vi jaillir; (fig) se répandre en effusions

gust [gʌst] n (of wind) rafale f

gut [gʌt] n intestin m, boyau m; **guts** npl (Anat) boyaux mpl; (inf: courage) cran m

gutter ['gʌtə'] n (of roof) gouttière f; (in street) caniveau m

guy [gaɪ] n (inf: man) type m; (also: **~rope**) corde f; (figure) effigie de Guy Fawkes

Guy Fawkes' Night [gaɪ'fɔːks-] n voir encadré

○ **GUY FAWKES' NIGHT**
○
○ **Guy Fawkes' Night**, que l'on
○ appelle également "bonfire night",
○ commémore l'échec du complot (le
○ "Gunpowder Plot") contre James Ist
○ et son parlement le 5 novembre 1605.
○ L'un des conspirateurs, Guy Fawkes,
○ avait été surpris dans les caves du
○ parlement alors qu'il s'apprêtait à y
○ mettre le feu. Chaque année pour le
○ 5 novembre, les enfants préparent à
○ l'avance une effigie de Guy Fawkes
○ et ils demandent aux passants "un
○ penny pour le guy" avec lequel ils
○ pourront s'acheter des fusées de feu
○ d'artifice. Beaucoup de gens font
○ encore un feu dans leur jardin sur
○ lequel ils brûlent le "guy".

gym [dʒɪm] n (also: **~nasium**) gymnase m; (also: **~nastics**) gym f; **gymnasium**

n gymnase m; **gymnast** n gymnaste m/f; **gymnastics** n, npl gymnastique f; **gym shoes** npl chaussures fpl de gym(nastique)

gynaecologist (us gynecologist) [gaɪnɪ'kɔlədʒɪst] n gynécologue m/f

gypsy ['dʒɪpsɪ] n gitan(e), bohémien(ne)

h

haberdashery [ˈhæbəˈdæʃərɪ] n (BRIT) mercerie f

habit [ˈhæbɪt] n habitude f; (costume: Rel) habit m

habitat [ˈhæbɪtæt] n habitat m

hack [hæk] vt hacher, tailler ▷ n (pej: writer) nègre m; **hacker** n (Comput) pirate m (informatique)

had [hæd] pt, pp of **have**

haddock (pl **~** or **~s**) [ˈhædək] n églefin m; **smoked ~** haddock m

hadn't [ˈhædnt] = **had not**

haemorrhage (US **hemorrhage**) [ˈhɛmərɪdʒ] n hémorragie f

haemorrhoids (US **hemorrhoids**) [ˈhɛmərɔɪdz] npl hémorroïdes fpl

haggle [ˈhægl] vi marchander

Hague [heɪg] n: **The ~** La Haye

hail [heɪl] n grêle f ▷ vt (call) héler; (greet) acclamer ▷ vi grêler; **hailstone** n grêlon m

hair [hɛər] n cheveux mpl; (on body) poils mpl; (of animal) pelage m; (single hair: on head) cheveu m; (: on body, of animal) poil m; **to do one's ~** se coiffer; **hairband** n (elasticated) bandeau m; (plastic) serre-tête m; **hairbrush** n brosse f à cheveux; **haircut** n coupe f (de cheveux); **hairdo** n coiffure f; **hairdresser** n coiffeur(-euse); **hairdresser's** n salon m de coiffure, coiffeur m; **hair dryer** n sèche-cheveux m, séchoir m; **hair gel** n gel m pour cheveux; **hair spray** n laque f (pour les cheveux); **hairstyle** n coiffure f; **hairy** adj poilu(e), chevelu(e); (inf: frightening) effrayant(e)

hake (pl **~** or **~s**) [heɪk] n colin m, merlu m

half [hɑːf] n (pl **halves**) moitié f; (of beer: also: **~ pint**) ≈ demi m; (Rail, bus: also: **~ fare**) demi-tarif m; (Sport: of match) mi-temps f ▷ adj demi(e) ▷ adv (à) moitié, à demi; **~ an hour** une demi-heure; **~ a dozen** une demi-douzaine; **~ a pound** une demi-livre, ≈ 250 g; **two and a ~** deux et demi; **to cut sth in ~** couper qch en deux; **half board** n (BRIT: in hotel) demi-pension f; **half-brother** n demi-frère m; **half day** n demi-journée f; **half fare** n demi-tarif m; **half-hearted** adj tiède, sans enthousiasme; **half-hour** n demi-heure f; **half-price** adj à moitié prix ▷ adv (also: **at half-price**) à moitié prix; **half term** n (BRIT Scol) vacances fpl de demi-trimestre); **half-time** n mi-temps f; **halfway** adv à mi-chemin; **halfway through sth** au milieu de qch

hall [hɔːl] n salle f; (entrance way: big) hall m; (small) entrée f; (us: corridor) couloir m; (mansion) château m, manoir m

hallmark [ˈhɔːlmɑːk] n poinçon m; (fig) marque f

hallo [həˈləʊ] excl = **hello**

hall of residence n (BRIT) pavillon m or résidence f universitaire

Halloween, Hallowe'en [ˈhæləʊˈiːn] n veille f de la Toussaint; voir encadré

HALLOWEEN

Selon la tradition, **Halloween** est la nuit des fantômes et des sorcières. En Écosse et aux États-Unis surtout (et de plus en plus en Angleterre) les enfants, pour fêter **Halloween**, se déguisent ce soir-là et ils vont ainsi de porte en porte en demandant de petits cadeaux (du chocolat, une pomme etc).

hallucination [həluːsɪˈneɪʃən] n hallucination f

hallway ['hɔːlweɪ] n (entrance) vestibule m; (corridor) couloir m

halo ['heɪləʊ] n (of saint etc) auréole f

halt [hɔːlt] n halte f, arrêt m ▷ vt faire arrêter; (progress etc) interrompre ▷ vi faire halte, s'arrêter

halve [hɑːv] vt (apple etc) partager or diviser en deux; (reduce by half) réduire de moitié

halves [hɑːvz] npl of **half**

ham [hæm] n jambon m

hamburger ['hæmbəːɡəʳ] n hamburger m

hamlet ['hæmlɪt] n hameau m

hammer ['hæməʳ] n marteau m ▷ vt (nail) enfoncer; (fig) éreinter, démolir ▷ vi (at door) frapper à coups redoublés; **to ~ a point home to sb** faire rentrer qch dans la tête de qn

hammock ['hæmək] n hamac m

hamper ['hæmpəʳ] vt gêner ▷ n panier m (d'osier)

hamster ['hæmstəʳ] n hamster m

hamstring ['hæmstrɪŋ] n (Anat) tendon m du jarret

hand [hænd] n main f; (of clock) aiguille f; (handwriting) écriture f; (at cards) jeu m; (worker) ouvrier(-ière) m ▷ vt passer, donner; **to give sb a ~** donner un coup de main à qn; **at ~** à portée de la main; **in ~** (situation) en main; (work) en cours; **to be on ~** (person) être disponible; (emergency services) se tenir prêt(e) (à intervenir); **to ~** (information etc) sous

la main, à portée de la main; **on the one ~ ...**, **on the other ~** d'une part ..., d'autre part; **hand down** vt passer; (tradition, heirloom) transmettre; (us: sentence, verdict) prononcer; **hand in** vt remettre; **hand out** vt distribuer; **hand over** vt remettre; (powers etc) transmettre; **handbag** n sac m à main; **hand baggage** n = **hand luggage**; **handbook** n manuel m; **handbrake** n frein m à main; **handcuffs** fpl menottes fpl; **handful** n poignée f

handicap ['hændɪkæp] n handicap m ▷ vt handicaper; **mentally/physically ~ped** handicapé(e) mentalement/ physiquement

handkerchief ['hæŋkətʃɪf] n mouchoir m

handle ['hændl] n (of door etc) poignée f; (of cup etc) anse f; (of knife etc) manche m; (of saucepan) queue f; (for winding) manivelle f ▷ vt toucher, manier; (deal with) s'occuper de; (treat: people) prendre; **"~ with care"** "fragile"; **to fly off the ~** s'énerver; **handlebar(s)** n(pl) guidon m

hand: **hand luggage** n bagages mpl à main; **handmade** adj fait(e) à la main; **handout** n (money) aide f, don m; (leaflet) prospectus m; (at lecture) polycopié m; **hands-free** adj (phone) mains libres inv ▷ n (also: **hands-free kit**) kit m mains libres inv

handsome ['hænsəm] adj beau (belle); (profit) considérable

handwriting ['hændraɪtɪŋ] n écriture f

handy ['hændɪ] adj (person) adroit(e); (close at hand) sous la main; (convenient) pratique

hang (pt, pp **hung**) [hæŋ, hʌŋ] vt accrocher; (criminal: pt, pp **~ed**) pendre ▷ vi pendre; (hair, drapery) tomber ▷ n: **to get the ~ of (doing) sth** (inf) attraper le coup pour faire qch; **hang about** vi traîner; **hang around** vi traîner; **hang down** vi pendre; **hang on** vi (wait) attendre; **hang out** vt (washing) étendre (dehors) ▷ vi (inf: live) habiter, percher; (: spend time) traîner; **hang round** vi = **hang around**; **hang up** vi (Tel) raccrocher ▷ vt (coat, painting etc) accrocher, suspendre

hanger ['hæŋə^r] n cintre m, portemanteau m

hang-gliding ['hæŋglaɪdɪŋ] n vol m libre ou sur aile delta

hangover ['hæŋəuvə^r] n (after drinking) gueule f de bois

hankie, hanky ['hæŋkɪ] n abbr = **handkerchief**

happen ['hæpən] vi arriver, se passer, se produire; **what's ~ing?** que se passe-t-il?; **she ~ed to be free** il s'est trouvé (or elle se trouvait) qu'elle était libre; **as it ~s** justement

happily ['hæpɪlɪ] adv heureusement; (cheerfully) joyeusement

happiness ['hæpɪnɪs] n bonheur m

happy ['hæpɪ] adj heureux(-euse); ~ **with** (arrangements etc) satisfait(e) de; **to be ~ to do** faire volontiers; ~ **birthday!** bon anniversaire!

harass ['hærəs] vt accabler, tourmenter; **harassment** n tracasseries fpl

harbour (us **harbor**) ['hɑ:bə^r] n port m ▷ vt héberger, abriter; (hopes, suspicions) entretenir

hard [hɑ:d] adj dur(e); (question, problem) difficile; (facts, evidence) concret(-ète) ▷ adv (work) dur; (think, try) sérieusement; **to look ~ at** regarder fixement; (thing) regarder de près; **no ~ feelings!** sans rancune!; **to be ~ of hearing** être dur(e) d'oreille; **to be ~ done by** être traité(e) injustement; **hardback** n livre relié; **hardboard** n Isorel® m; **hard disk** n (Comput) disque dur; **harden** vt durcir; (fig) endurcir ▷ vi (substance) durcir

hardly ['hɑ:dlɪ] adv (scarcely) à peine; (harshly) durement; ~ **anywhere/ever** presque nulle part/jamais

hard: hardship n (difficulties) épreuves fpl; (deprivation) privations fpl; **hard**

shoulder n (BRIT Aut) accotement stabilisé; **hard-up** adj (inf) fauché(e); **hardware** n quincaillerie f; (Comput, Mil) matériel m; **hardware shop** (us **hardware store**) n quincaillerie f; **hard-working** adj travailleur(-euse), consciencieux(-euse)

hardy ['hɑ:dɪ] adj robuste; (plant) résistant(e) au gel

hare [hɛə^r] n lièvre m

harm [hɑ:m] n mal m; (wrong) tort m ▷ vt (person) faire du mal ou du tort à; (thing) endommager; **out of ~'s way** à l'abri du danger, en lieu sûr; **harmful** adj nuisible; **harmless** adj inoffensif(-ive)

harmony ['hɑ:mənɪ] n harmonie f

harness ['hɑ:nɪs] n harnais m ▷ vt (horse) harnacher; (resources) exploiter

harp [hɑ:p] n harpe f ▷ vi: **to ~ on about** revenir toujours sur

harsh [hɑ:ʃ] adj dur(e); (severe) sévère; (unpleasant: sound) discordant(e); (: light) cru(e)

harvest ['hɑ:vɪst] n (of corn) moisson f; (of fruit) récolte f; (of grapes) vendange f ▷ vt moissonner; récolter; vendanger

has [hæz] vb see **have**

hasn't ['hæznt] = **has not**

hassle ['hæsl] n (inf: fuss) histoire(s) f(pl)

haste [heɪst] n hâte f, précipitation f; **hasten** ['heɪsn] vt hâter, accélérer ▷ vi se hâter, s'empresser; **hastily** adv à la hâte; (leave) précipitamment; **hasty** adj (decision, action) hâtif(-ive); (departure, escape) précipité(e)

hat [hæt] n chapeau m

hatch [hætʃ] n (Naut: also: ~**way**) écoutille f; (BRIT: also: **service ~**) passe-plats m inv ▷ vi éclore

hatchback ['hætʃbæk] n (Aut) modèle m avec hayon arrière

hate [heɪt] vt haïr, détester ▷ n haine f; **hatred** ['heɪtrɪd] n haine f

haul [hɔ:l] vt traîner, tirer ▷ n (of fish) prise f; (of stolen goods) butin m

haunt [hɔ:nt] vt (subj: ghost, fear)

hanter; (: person) fréquenter ▷ n
repaire m; (: person) fréquenter ▷ n
hanté(e); (look) égaré(e), hagard(e)

⊙ **KEYWORD**

have [hæv] (pt, pp **had**) aux vb **1** (gen)
avoir; être; **to have eaten/slept** avoir
mangé/dormi; **to have arrived/gone**
être arrivé(e)/allé(e); **having finished**
or **when he had finished, he left**
quand il a eu fini, il est parti; **we've
already eaten** nous avons déjà mangé
2 (in tag questions): **you've done it,
haven't you?** vous l'avez fait, n'est-ce
pas?
3 (in short answers and questions): **no I
haven't!/yes we have!** mais non!/
mais si!; **so I have!** ah oui, oui c'est
vrai!; **I've been there before, have
you?** j'y suis déjà allé, et vous?
▷ modal aux vb (be obliged): **to have
(got) to do sth** devoir faire qch, être
obligé(e) de faire qch; **she has (got)
to do it** elle doit le faire, il faut qu'elle
le fasse; **you haven't to tell her** vous
n'êtes pas obligé de le lui dire; (must not)
ne le lui dites surtout pas; **do you have
to book?** il faut réserver?
▷ vt **1** (possess) avoir; **he has (got) blue
eyes/dark hair** il a les yeux bleus/les
cheveux bruns
2 (referring to meals etc): **to have
breakfast** prendre le petit déjeuner; **to
have dinner/lunch** dîner/déjeuner; **to
have a drink** prendre un verre; **to have
a cigarette** fumer une cigarette
3 (receive) avoir, recevoir; (obtain) avoir;
may I have your address? puis-je
avoir votre adresse?; **you can have it
for £5** vous pouvez l'avoir pour 5 livres;
I must have it for tomorrow il me
le faut pour demain; **to have a baby**
avoir un bébé
4 (maintain, allow): **I won't have it!** ça
ne se passera pas comme ça; **we can't
have that** nous ne tolérerons pas ça
5 (by sb else): **to have sth done** faire

faire qch; **to have one's hair cut** se
faire couper les cheveux; **to have sb do
sth** faire faire qch à qn
6 (experience, suffer) avoir; **to have a
cold/flu** avoir un rhume/la grippe;
to have an operation se faire opérer;
she had her bag stolen elle s'est fait
voler son sac
7 (+noun): **to have a swim/walk** nager/
se promener; **to have a bath/shower**
prendre un bain/une douche; **let's
have a look** regardons; **to have a
meeting** se réunir; **to have a party**
organiser une fête; **let me have a try**
laissez-moi essayer

haven ['heɪvn] n port m; (fig) havre m
haven't ['hævnt] = **have not**
havoc ['hævək] n ravages mpl
Hawaii [hə'waɪɪ] n (îles fpl) Hawaï m
hawk [hɔːk] n faucon m
hawthorn ['hɔːθɔːn] n aubépine f
hay [heɪ] n foin m; **hay fever** n rhume
des foins; **haystack** n meule f de foin
hazard ['hæzəd] n (risk) danger m,
risque m ▷ vt risquer, hasarder;
hazardous adj hasardeux(-euse),
risqué(e); **hazard warning lights** npl
(Aut) feux mpl de détresse
haze [heɪz] n brume f
hazel [heɪzl] n (tree) noisetier m
▷ adj (eyes) noisette inv; **hazelnut** n
noisette f
hazy ['heɪzɪ] adj brumeux(-euse);
(idea) vague

he [hiː] pron il; **it is he who ...** c'est lui
qui ...; **here he is** le voici

head [hɛd] n tête f; (leader) chef m; (of
school) directeur(-trice); (of secondary
school) proviseur m ▷ vt (list) être
en tête de; (group, company) être à
la tête de; **~s or tails** pile ou face;
~ first la tête la première; **~ over heels
in love** follement or éperdument
amoureux(-euse); **to ~ the ball** faire
une tête; **head for** vt fus se diriger vers;
(disaster) aller à; **head off** vt (threat,
danger) détourner; **headache** n mal m

de tête; **to have a headache** avoir mal à la tête; **heading** n titre m; (subject title) rubrique f; **headlamp** (BRIT) n =**headlight**; **headlight** n phare m; **headline** n titre m; **head office** n siège m, bureau m central; **headphones** npl casque m (à écouteurs); **headquarters** npl (of business) bureau or siège central; (Mil) quartier général; **headroom** n (in car) hauteur f de plafond; (under bridge) hauteur limite; **headscarf** n foulard m; **headset** n =**headphones**; **headteacher** n directeur(-trice), (of secondary school) proviseur m; **head waiter** n maître m d'hôtel

heal [hiːl] vt, vi guérir

health [hɛlθ] n santé f; **health care** n services médicaux; **health centre** n (BRIT) centre m de santé; **health food** n aliment(s) naturel(s); **Health Service** n: **the Health Service** (BRIT) = la Sécurité Sociale; **healthy** adj (person) en bonne santé; (climate, food, attitude etc) sain(e)

heap [hiːp] n tas m ▷ vt (also: ~ **up**) entasser, amonceler; **she ~ed her plate with cakes** elle a chargé son assiette de gâteaux; **~s (of)** (inf: lots) des tas (de)

hear (pt, pp ~**d**) [hɪə, hɜːd] vt entendre; (news) apprendre ▷ vi entendre; **to ~ about** entendre parler de; (have news of) avoir des nouvelles de; **to ~ from sb** recevoir des nouvelles de qn

heard [hɜːd] pt, pp of **hear**

hearing ['hɪərɪŋ] n (sense) ouïe f; (of witnesses) audition f; (of a case) audience f; **hearing aid** n appareil m acoustique

hearse [hɜːs] n corbillard m

heart [hɑːt] n cœur m; **hearts** npl (Cards) cœur m; **at ~** au fond; **by ~** (learn, know) par cœur; **to lose/take ~** perdre/prendre courage; **heart attack** n crise f cardiaque; **heartbeat** n battement m de cœur; **heartbroken** adj: **to be heartbroken** avoir beaucoup de chagrin; **heartburn** n brûlures f pl d'estomac; **heart disease** n maladie

f cardiaque

hearth [hɑːθ] n foyer m, cheminée f

heartless adj (person) sans cœur, insensible; (treatment) cruel(le)

hearty ['hɑːtɪ] adj chaleureux(-euse); (appetite) solide; (dislike) cordial(e); (meal) copieux(-euse)

heat [hiːt] n chaleur f; (Sport: also: **qualifying ~**) éliminatoire f ▷ vt chauffer; **heat up** vi (liquid) chauffer; (room) se réchauffer ▷ vt réchauffer; **heated** adj chauffé(e); (fig) passionné(e), échauffé(e), excité(e); **heater** n appareil m de chauffage; radiateur m; (in car) chauffage m; (water heater) chauffe-eau m

heather ['hɛðə'] n bruyère f

heating ['hiːtɪŋ] n chauffage m

heatwave ['hiːtweɪv] n vague f de chaleur

heaven ['hɛvn] n ciel m, paradis m; (fig) paradis; **heavenly** adj céleste, divin(e)

heavily ['hɛvɪlɪ] adv lourdement; (drink, smoke) beaucoup; (sleep, sigh) profondément

heavy ['hɛvɪ] adj lourd(e); (work, rain, user, eater) gros(se); (drinker, smoker) grand(e); (schedule, week) chargé(e)

Hebrew ['hiːbruː] adj hébraïque ▷ n (Ling) hébreu m

Hebrides ['hɛbrɪdiːz] npl: **the ~** les Hébrides fpl

hectare ['hɛktɑː'] n (BRIT) hectare m

hectic ['hɛktɪk] adj (schedule) très chargé(e); (day) mouvementé(e); (lifestyle) trépidant(e)

he'd [hiːd] = **he would; he had**

hedge [hɛdʒ] n haie f ▷ vi se dérober ▷ vt: **to ~ one's bets** (fig) se couvrir

hedgehog ['hɛdʒhɔg] n hérisson m

heed [hiːd] vt (also: **take ~ of**) tenir compte de, prendre garde à

heel [hiːl] n talon m ▷ vt retalonner

hefty ['hɛftɪ] adj (person) costaud(e); (parcel) lourd(e); (piece, price) gros(se)

height [haɪt] n (of person) taille f, grandeur f; (of object) hauteur f; (of plane, mountain) altitude f; (high ground) hauteur, éminence f; (fig: of glory, fame, power) sommet m; (: of luxury, stupidity) comble m; **at the ~ of summer** au cœur de l'été; **heighten** vt hausser, surélever; (fig) augmenter

heir [εə^r] n héritier m; **heiress** n héritière f

held [hεld] pt, pp of **hold**

helicopter ['hεlɪkɔptə^r] n hélicoptère m

hell [hεl] n enfer m; **oh ~!** (inf) merde!

he'll [hi:l] = **he will; he shall**

hello [hə'ləu] excl bonjour!; (to attract attention) hé!; (surprise) tiens!

helmet ['hεlmɪt] n casque m

help [hεlp] n aide f; (cleaner etc) femme f de ménage ▷ vt aider; **~!** au secours!; **~ yourself** servez-vous; **can you ~ me?** pouvez-vous m'aider?; **can I ~ you?** (in shop) vous désirez?; **he can't ~ it** il n'y peut rien; **help out** vi aider ▷ vt: **to ~ sb out** aider qn; **helper** n aide m/f, assistant(e); **helpful** adj serviable, obligeant(e); (useful) utile; **helping** n portion f; **helpless** adj impuissant(e); (baby) sans défense; **helpline** n service m d'assistance téléphonique (free) = numéro vert

hem [hεm] n ourlet m ▷ vt ourler

hemisphere ['hεmɪsfɪə^r] n hémisphère m

hemorrhage ['hεmərɪdʒ] n (us) = **haemorrhage**

hemorrhoids ['hεmərɔɪdz] npl (us) = **haemorrhoids**

hen [hεn] n poule f; (female bird) femelle f

hence [hεns] adv (therefore) d'où, de là; **2 years ~** d'ici 2 ans

hen night, hen party n soirée f entre filles (avant le mariage de l'une d'elles)

hepatitis [hεpə'taɪtɪs] n hépatite f

her [hə:^r] pron (direct) la, l' + vowel or h mute; (indirect) lui; (stressed, after prep) elle ▷ adj son (sa), ses pl; see also **me; my**

herb [hə:b] n herbe f; **herbal** adj à base de plantes; **herbal tea** n tisane f

herd [hə:d] n troupeau m

here [hɪə^r] adv ici; (time) alors ▷ excl tiens!, tenez!; **~! (present)** présent!; **~ is, ~ are** voici; **~ he/she is** le (la) voici

hereditary [hɪ'rεdɪtrɪ] adj héréditaire

heritage ['hεrɪtɪdʒ] n héritage m, patrimoine m

hernia ['hə:nɪə] n hernie f

hero (pl **-es**) ['hɪərəu] n héros m; **heroic** [hɪ'rəuɪk] adj héroïque

heroin ['hεrəuɪn] n héroïne f (drogue)

heroine ['hεrəuɪn] n héroïne f (femme)

heron ['hεrən] n héron m

herring ['hεrɪŋ] n hareng m

hers [hə:z] pron le (la) sien(ne), les siens (siennes); see also **mine'**

herself [hə:'sεlf] pron (reflexive) se; (emphatic) elle-même; (after prep) elle; see also **oneself**

he's [hi:z] = **he is; he has**

hesitant ['hεzɪtənt] adj hésitant(e), indécis(e)

hesitate ['hεzɪteɪt] vi: **to ~ (about/to do)** hésiter (sur/à faire); **hesitation** [hεzɪ'teɪʃən] n hésitation f

heterosexual ['hεtərəu'sεksjuəl] adj, n hétérosexuel(le)

hexagon ['hεksəgən] n hexagone m

hey [heɪ] excl hé!

heyday ['heɪdeɪ] n: **the ~ of** l'âge m d'or de, les beaux jours de

HGV n abbr = **heavy goods vehicle**

hi [haɪ] excl salut!; (to attract attention) hé!

hibernate ['haɪbəneɪt] vi hiberner

hiccough, hiccup ['hɪkʌp] vi hoqueter ▷ n: **to have (the) ~s** avoir le hoquet

hid [hɪd] pt of **hide**

hidden ['hɪdn] pp of **hide** ▷ adj: **~ agenda** intentions non déclarées

hide [haɪd] n (skin) peau f ▷ vb (pt **hid**, pp **hidden**) ▷ vt cacher ▷ vi: **to ~ (from sb)** se cacher (de qn)

hideous ['hɪdɪəs] adj hideux(-euse), atroce

hiding ['haɪdɪŋ] n (beating) correction f, volée f de coups; **to be in ~** (concealed) se tenir caché(e)

hi-fi ['haɪfaɪ] *adj, n abbr* (= high fidelity) hi-fi *inv*

high [haɪ] *adj* haut(e); (*speed, respect, number*) grand(e); (*price*) élevé(e); (*wind*) fort(e), violent(e); (*voice*) aigu(ë) ▷ *adv* haut, en haut; **20 m ~** haut(e) de 20 m; **~ in the air** haut dans le ciel; **highchair** *n* (*child's*) chaise haute; **high-class** *adj* (*neighbourhood, hotel*) chic *inv*, de grand standing; **higher education** *n* études supérieures; **high heels** *npl* talons hauts, hauts talons; **high jump** *n* (*Sport*) saut *m* en hauteur; **highlands** ['haɪləndz] *npl* région montagneuse; **the Highlands** (*in Scotland*) les Highlands *mpl*; **highlight** *n* (*fig: of event*) point culminant ▷ *vt* (*emphasize*) faire ressortir, souligner; **highlights** *npl* (*in hair*) reflets *mpl*; **highlighter** *n* (*pen*) surligneur (lumineux); **highly** *adv* extrêmement, très; (*unlikely*) hautement; **to speak highly of** dire beaucoup de bien de; **highness** *n*: **His/Her Highness** son Altesse *f*; **high-rise** *n* (*also*: **high-rise block, high-rise building**) tour *f* (d'habitation); **high school** *n* lycée *m*; (*US*) établissement *m* d'enseignement supérieur; **high season** *n* (*BRIT*) haute saison; **high street** *n* (*BRIT*) grand-rue *f*; **high-tech** (*inf*) *adj* de pointe; **highway** *n* (*BRIT*) route *f* de pointe; (*US*) route nationale; **Highway Code** *n* (*BRIT*) code *m* de la route

hijack ['haɪdʒæk] *vt* détourner (*par la force*); **hijacker** *n* auteur *m* d'un détournement d'avion, pirate *m* de l'air

hike [haɪk] *vi* faire des excursions à pied ▷ *n* excursion *f* à pied, randonnée *f*; **hiker** *n* promeneur(-euse), excursionniste *m/f*; **hiking** *n* excursions *fpl* à pied, randonnée *f*

hilarious [hɪ'lɛərɪəs] *adj* (*behaviour, event*) désopilant(e)

hill [hɪl] *n* colline *f*; (*fairly high*) montagne *f*; (*on road*) côte *f*; **hillside** *n* (flanc *m* de) coteau *m*; **hill walking** *n*

randonnée *f* de basse montagne; **hilly** *adj* vallonné(e), montagneux(-euse)

him [hɪm] *pron* (*direct*) le, l' *+ vowel or h mute*; (*stressed, indirect, after prep*) lui; *see also* **me**; **himself** *pron* (*reflexive*) se; (*emphatic*) lui-même; (*after prep*) lui; *see also* **oneself**

hind [haɪnd] *adj* de derrière

hinder ['hɪndə'] *vt* (*hamper*) gêner; (*delay*) retarder

hindsight ['haɪndsaɪt] *n*: **with (the benefit of) ~** avec du recul, rétrospectivement

Hindu ['hɪndu:] *n* Hindou(e); **Hinduism** *n* (*Rel*) hindouisme *m*

hinge [hɪndʒ] *n* charnière *f* ▷ *vi* (*fig*): **to ~ on** dépendre de

hint [hɪnt] *n* allusion *f*; (*advice*) conseil *m*; (*clue*) indication *f* ▷ *vt*: **to ~ that** insinuer que ▷ *vi*: **to ~ at** faire une allusion à

hip [hɪp] *n* hanche *f*

hippie, hippy ['hɪpɪ] *n* hippie *m/f*

hippo ['hɪpəu] (*pl* **-s**) *n* hippopotame *m*

hippopotamus [hɪpə'pɒtəməs] (*pl* **-es** *or* **hippopotami**) *n* hippopotame *m*

hippy ['hɪpɪ] *n* = **hippie**

hire ['haɪə'] *vt* (*BRIT: car, equipment*) louer; (*worker*) embaucher, engager ▷ *n* location *f*; **for ~** à louer; (*taxi*) libre; **I'd like to ~ a car** je voudrais louer une voiture; **hire(d) car** *n* (*BRIT*) voiture *f* de location; **hire purchase** *n* (*BRIT*) achat *m* (*or* vente *f*) à tempérament *or* crédit

his [hɪz] *pron* le (la) sien(ne), les sien(ne)s (siennes) ▷ *adj* son (sa), ses *pl*; *see also* **mine**; *my*

Hispanic [hɪs'pænɪk] *adj* (*in US*) hispano-américain(e) ▷ *n* Hispano-Américain(e)

hiss [hɪs] *vi* siffler

historian [hɪ'stɔ:rɪən] *n* historien(ne)

historic(al) [hɪ'stɔrɪk(l)] *adj* historique

history ['hɪstərɪ] *n* histoire *f*

hit [hɪt] *vt* (*pt, pp* **~**) frapper; (*reach: target*) atteindre, toucher; (*collide with: car*) entrer en collision avec, heurter;

(fig: affect) toucher ▷ coup m; *(success)* succès m; *(song)* tube m; *(to website)* visite f; *(on search engine)* résultat m de recherche; **to ~ it off with sb** bien s'entendre avec qn; **hit back** vi: **to ~ back at sb** prendre sa revanche sur qn

hitch [hɪtʃ] vt *(fasten)* accrocher, attacher; *(also: ~ up)* remonter d'une saccade ▷ vi faire de l'autostop ▷ n *(difficulty)* anicroche f, contretemps m; **to ~ a lift** faire du stop; **hitch-hike** vi faire de l'auto-stop; **hitch-hiker** n auto-stoppeur(-euse); **hitch-hiking** n auto-stop m, stop m *(inf)*
hi-tech ['haɪ'tɛk] adj de pointe
hitman ['hɪtmæn] *(irreg)* n *(inf)* tueur m à gages
HIV n abbr *(= human immunodeficiency virus)* HIV m, VIH m; **~-negative/positive** séronégatif(-ive)/positif(-ive)
hive [haɪv] n ruche f
hoard [hɔːd] n *(of food)* provisions fpl, réserves fpl; *(of money)* trésor m ▷ vt amasser
hoarse [hɔːs] adj enroué(e)
hoax [həuks] n canular m
hob [hɔb] n plaque chauffante
hobble ['hɔbl] vi boitiller
hobby ['hɔbɪ] n passe-temps favori
hobo ['həubəu] n *(us)* vagabond m
hockey ['hɔkɪ] n hockey m; **hockey stick** n crosse f de hockey
hog [hɔg] n porc *(châtré)* m ▷ vt *(fig)* accaparer; **to go the whole ~** aller jusqu'au bout
Hogmanay [hɔgmə'neɪ] n réveillon m du jour de l'An, Saint-Sylvestre f; *voir encadré*

rende chez ses amis et voisins en apportant quelque chose à boire (du whisky en général) et un morceau de charbon en gage de prospérité pour la nouvelle année.

hoist [hɔɪst] n palan m ▷ vt hisser
hold [həuld] *(pt, pp held)* vt tenir; *(contain)* contenir; *(meeting)* tenir; *(keep back)* retenir; *(believe)* considérer; *(possess)* avoir ▷ vi *(withstand pressure)* tenir *(bon)*; *(be valid)* valoir; *(on telephone)* attendre ▷ n prise f; *(fig)* influence f; *(Naut)* cale f; **to catch** *or* **get (a) ~ of** saisir; **to get ~ of** *(find)* trouver; **~ the line!** *(Tel)* ne quittez pas!; **to ~ one's own** *(bien)* se défendre; **hold back** vt retenir; *(secret)* cacher; **hold on** vi tenir bon; *(wait)* attendre; **~ on!** *(Tel)* ne quittez pas!; **to ~ on to** sth *(grasp)* se cramponner à qch; *(keep)* conserver *or* garder qch; **hold out** vt offrir ▷ vi *(resist)*: **to ~ out (against)** résister *(devant)*, tenir bon *(devant)*; **hold up** vt *(raise)* lever; *(support)* soutenir; *(delay)* retarder; *(: traffic)* ralentir; *(rob)* braquer; **holdall** n *(BRIT)* fourre-tout m inv; **holder** n *(container)* support m; *(of ticket, record)* détenteur(-trice); *(of office, title, passport etc)* titulaire m/f
hole [həul] n trou m
holiday ['hɔlədɪ] n *(BRIT: vacation)* vacances fpl; *(day off)* jour m de congé; *(public)* jour m férié; **to be on ~** être en vacances; **I'm here on ~** je suis ici en vacances; **holiday camp** n *(also: holiday centre)* camp m de vacances; **holiday job** n *(BRIT)* boulot m *(inf)* de vacances; **holiday-maker** n *(BRIT)* vacancier(-ière); **holiday resort** n centre m de villégiature *or* de vacances
Holland ['hɔlənd] n Hollande f
hollow ['hɔləu] adj creux(-euse); *(fig)* faux *(fausse)* ▷ n creux m; *(in land)* dépression f *(de terrain)*, cuvette f ▷ vt: **to ~ out** creuser, évider
holly ['hɔlɪ] n houx m
Hollywood ['hɔlɪwud] n Hollywood

holocaust ['hɔləkɔːst] n holocauste m

holy ['həulɪ] adj saint(e); (bread, water) bénit(e); (ground) sacré(e)

home [həum] n foyer m, maison f; (country) pays natal m, patrie f; (institution) maison f ⊳ adj de famille; (Econ, Pol) national(e), intérieur(e); (Sport: team) qui reçoit; (: match, win) sur leur (or notre) terrain ⊳ adv chez soi, à la maison; au pays natal; (right in: nail etc) à fond; **at ~** chez soi, à la maison; **to go** (or **come**) **~** rentrer (chez soi), rentrer à la maison (or au pays); **make yourself at ~** faites comme chez vous; **home address** n domicile permanent; **homeland** n patrie f; **homeless** adj sans foyer, sans abri; **homely** adj (plain) simple, sans prétention; (welcoming) accueillant(e); **home-made** adj fait(e) à la maison; **home match** n match m à domicile; **Home Office** n (BRIT) ministère m de l'Intérieur; **home owner** n propriétaire occupant; **home page** n (Comput) page f d'accueil; **Home Secretary** n (BRIT) ministre m de l'Intérieur; **homesick** adj: **to be homesick** avoir le mal du pays; (missing one's family) s'ennuyer de sa famille; **home town** n ville natale; **homework** n devoirs mpl

homicide ['hɔmɪsaɪd] n (us) homicide m

homoeopathic (us **homeopathic**) [həumɪə'pæθɪk] adj (medicine) homéopathique; (doctor) homéopathe

homoeopathy (us **homeopathy**) [həumɪ'ɔpəθɪ] n homéopathie f

homosexual [həmə'sɛksjuəl] adj, n homosexuel(le)

honest ['ɔnɪst] adj honnête; (sincere) franc (franche); **honestly** adv honnêtement; franchement; **honesty** n honnêteté f

honey ['hʌnɪ] n miel m; **honeymoon** n lune f de miel, voyage m de noces; **we're on honeymoon** nous sommes en voyage de noces; **honeysuckle** n chèvrefeuille m

Hong Kong ['hɔŋ'kɔŋ] n Hong Kong

honorary ['ɔnərərɪ] adj honoraire; (duty, title) honorifique; **~ degree** diplôme m honoris causa

honour (us **honor**) ['ɔnər] vt honorer ⊳ n honneur m; **to graduate with ~s** obtenir sa licence avec mention; **honourable** (us **honorable**) adj honorable; **honours degree** n (Scol) ≈ licence f avec mention

hood [hud] n capuchon m; (of cooker) hotte f; (BRIT Aut) capote f; (us Aut) capot m; **hoodie** ['hudɪ] n (top) sweat m à capuche

hoof (pl **~s** or **hooves**) [huːf, huːvz] n sabot m

hook [huk] n crochet m; (on dress) agrafe f; (for fishing) hameçon m ⊳ vt accrocher; **off the ~** (Tel) décroché

hooligan ['huːlɪɡən] n voyou m

hoop [huːp] n cerceau m

hooray [huː'reɪ] excl = **hurray**

hoot [huːt] vi (BRIT: Aut) klaxonner; (siren) mugir; (owl) hululer

Hoover® ['huːvər] n (BRIT) aspirateur m ⊳ vt: **to hoover** (room) passer l'aspirateur dans; (carpet) passer l'aspirateur sur

hooves [huːvz] npl of **hoof**

hop [hɔp] vi sauter; (on one foot) sauter à cloche-pied; (bird) sautiller

hope [həup] vt, vi espérer ⊳ n espoir m; **I ~ so** je l'espère; **I ~ not** j'espère que non; **hopeful** adj (person) plein(e) d'espoir; (situation) prometteur(-euse), encourageant(e); **hopefully** adv (expectantly) avec espoir, avec optimisme; (one hopes) avec un peu de chance; **hopeless** adj désespéré(e); (useless) nul(le)

hops [hɔps] npl houblon m

horizon [hə'raɪzn] n horizon m; **horizontal** ['hɔrɪ'zɔntl] adj horizontal(e)

hormone ['hɔːməun] n hormone f

horn [hɔːn] n corne f; (Mus) cor m; (Aut) klaxon m

horoscope ['hɔrəskəup] n

horoscope *m*

horrendous [hə'rɛndəs] *adj* horrible, affreux(-euse)

horrible ['hɔrɪbl] *adj* horrible, affreux(-euse)

horrid ['hɔrɪd] *adj* (*person*) détestable; (*weather*, *place*, *smell*) épouvantable

horrific [hɔ'rɪfɪk] *adj* (*accident*) horrible; (*price*) épouvantable

horrifying ['hɔrɪfaɪɪŋ] *adj* horrifiant(e)

horror ['hɔrə'] *n* horreur *f*; **horror film** *n* film *m* d'épouvante

hors d'œuvre [ɔː'dəːvrə] *n* hors d'œuvre *m*

horse [hɔːs] *n* cheval *m*; **horseback**: **on horseback** *adj*, *adv* à cheval; **horse chestnut** *n* (*nut*) marron *m* (d'Inde); (*tree*) marronnier *m* (d'Inde); **horsepower** *n* puissance *f* (en chevaux); (*unit*) cheval-vapeur *m* (CV); **horse-racing** *n* courses *fpl* de chevaux; **horseradish** *n* raifort *m*; **horse riding** *n* (*BRIT*) équitation *f*

hose [həʊz] *n* (*also*: ~**pipe**) tuyau *m*; (*also*: **garden** ~) tuyau d'arrosage; **hosepipe** *n* tuyau *m*; (*in garden*) tuyau d'arrosage

hospital ['hɔspɪtl] *n* hôpital *m*; **in** ~ à l'hôpital; **where's the nearest** ~? où est l'hôpital le plus proche?

hospitality [hɔspɪ'tælɪtɪ] *n* hospitalité *f*

host [həʊst] *n* hôte *m*; (*TV*, *Radio*) présentateur(-trice), animateur(-trice); (*large number*): **a** ~ **of** une foule de; (*Rel*) hostie *f*

hostage ['hɔstɪdʒ] *n* otage *m*

hostel ['hɔstl] *n* foyer *m*; (*also*: **youth** ~) auberge *f* de jeunesse

hostess ['həʊstɪs] *n* hôtesse *f*; (*BRIT*: *also*: **air** ~) hôtesse de l'air; (*TV*, *Radio*) animatrice *f*

hostile ['hɔstaɪl] *adj* hostile

hostility [hɔ'stɪlɪtɪ] *n* hostilité *f*

hot [hɔt] *adj* chaud(e); (*as opposed to only warm*) très chaud(e); (*spicy*) fort(e); (*fig*: *contest*) acharné(e); (*topic*) brûlant(e); (*temper*) violent(e), passionné(e); **to be ~** (*person*) avoir chaud; (*thing*) être (très)

chaud; (*weather*) faire chaud; **hot dog** *n* hot-dog *m*

hotel [həʊ'tɛl] *n* hôtel *m*

hot-water bottle [hɔt'wɔːtə-] *n* bouillotte *f*

hound [haʊnd] *vt* poursuivre avec acharnement ▷ *n* chien courant

hour ['aʊə'] *n* heure *f*; **hourly** *adj* toutes les heures; (*rate*) horaire

house *n* [haʊs] maison *f*; (*Pol*) chambre *f*; (*Theat*) salle *f*; auditoire *m* ▷ *vt* [haʊz] (*person*) loger, héberger; **on the ~** (*fig*) aux frais de la maison; **household** *n* (*Admin etc*) ménage *m*; (*people*) famille *f*, maisonnée *f*; **householder** *n* propriétaire *m/f*; (*head of house*) chef *m* de famille; **housekeeper** *n* gouvernante *f*; **housekeeping** *n* (*work*) ménage *m*; (*money*) argent *m* du ménage; **housewife** (*irreg*) *n* ménagère *f*; femme *f* au foyer; **house wine** *n* cuvée *f* maison ou du patron; **housework** *n* (travaux *mpl* du) ménage *m*

housing ['haʊzɪŋ] *n* logement *m*; **housing development** (*BRIT* **housing estate**) *n* (*blocks of flats*) cité *f*; (*houses*) lotissement *m*

hover ['hɔvə'] *vi* planer; **hovercraft** *n* aéroglisseur *m*, hovercraft *m*

how [haʊ] *adv* comment; ~ **are you?** comment allez-vous?; ~ **do you do?** bonjour; (*on being introduced*) enchanté(e); ~ **long have you been here?** depuis combien de temps êtes-vous là?; ~ **lovely/awful!** que *or* comme c'est joli/affreux!; ~ **much time/many people?** combien de temps/gens?; ~ **much does it cost?** ça coûte combien?; ~ **old are you?** quel âge avez-vous?; ~ **tall is he?** combien mesure-t-il?; ~ **is school?** ça va à l'école?; ~ **was the film?** comment était le film?

however [haʊ'ɛvə'] *conj* pourtant, cependant ▷ *adv*: ~ **I do it** de quelque manière que je m'y prenne; ~ **cold it is** même s'il fait très froid; ~ **did you do it?** comment êtes-vous donc arrivé?

howl [haʊl] *n* hurlement *m* ▷ *vi* hurler;

(wind) mugir

H.P. n abbr (BRIT) = **hire purchase**

h.p. abbr (Aut) = **horsepower**

HQ n abbr (= headquarters) QG m

hr(s) abbr (= hour(s)) h

HTML n abbr (= hypertext markup language) HTML m

hubcap ['hʌbkæp] n (Aut) enjoliveur m

huddle ['hʌdl] vi: **to ~ together** se blottir les uns contre les autres

huff [hʌf] n: **in a ~** fâché(e)

hug [hʌg] vt serrer dans ses bras; (shore, kerb) serrer ⊳ n: **to give sb a ~** serrer qn dans ses bras

huge [hjuːdʒ] adj énorme, immense

hull [hʌl] n (of ship) coque f

hum [hʌm] vt (tune) fredonner ⊳ vi fredonner; (insect) bourdonner; (plane, tool) vrombir

human ['hjuːmən] adj humain(e) ⊳ n (also: **~ being**) être humain

humane [hjuːˈmeɪn] adj humain(e), humanitaire

humanitarian [hjuːmænɪˈtɛərɪən] adj humanitaire

humanity [hjuːˈmænɪtɪ] n humanité f

human rights npl droits mpl de l'homme

humble ['hʌmbl] adj humble, modeste

humid ['hjuːmɪd] adj humide; **humidity** [hjuːˈmɪdɪtɪ] n humidité f

humiliate [hjuːˈmɪlɪeɪt] vt humilier

humiliating [hjuːˈmɪlɪeɪtɪŋ] adj humiliant(e)

humiliation [hjuːmɪlɪˈeɪʃən] n humiliation f

hummus ['hʊməs] n houm(m)ous m

humorous ['hjuːmərəs] adj humoristique

humour (us **humor**) ['hjuːməʳ] n humour m; (mood) humeur f ⊳ vt (person) faire plaisir à; se prêter aux caprices de

hump [hʌmp] n bosse f

hunch [hʌntʃ] n (premonition) intuition f

hundred ['hʌndrəd] num cent; **~s of** des centaines de; **hundredth** [-dθ]

num centième

hung [hʌŋ] pt, pp of **hang**

Hungarian [hʌŋˈgeərɪən] adj hongrois(e) ⊳ n Hongrois(e); (Ling) hongrois m

Hungary ['hʌŋgərɪ] n Hongrie f

hunger ['hʌŋgəʳ] n faim f ⊳ vi: **to ~ for** avoir faim de, désirer ardemment

hungry ['hʌŋgrɪ] adj affamé(e); **to be ~** avoir faim; **~ for** (fig) avide de

hunt [hʌnt] vt (seek) chercher; (Sport) chasser ⊳ vi (search): **to ~ for** chercher (partout); (Sport) chasser ⊳ n (Sport) chasse f; **hunter** n chasseur m; **hunting** n chasse f

hurdle ['həːdl] n (Sport) haie f; (fig) obstacle m

hurl [həːl] vt lancer (avec violence); (abuse, insults) lancer

hurrah, hurray [hʊˈrɑː, -ˈreɪ] excl hourra!

hurricane ['hʌrɪkən] n ouragan m

hurry ['hʌrɪ] n hâte f, précipitation f ⊳ vi se presser, se dépêcher ⊳ vt (person) faire presser, faire se dépêcher; (work) presser; **to be in a ~** être pressé(e); **to do sth in a ~** faire qch en vitesse; **hurry up** vi se dépêcher

hurt [həːt] (pt, pp ~) vt (cause pain to) faire mal à; (injure, fig) blesser ⊳ vi faire mal ⊳ adj blessé(e); **my arm ~s** j'ai mal au bras; **to ~ o.s.** se faire mal

husband ['hʌzbənd] n mari m

hush [hʌʃ] n calme m, silence m ⊳ vt faire taire; **~!** chut!

husky ['hʌskɪ] adj (voice) rauque ⊳ n chien m esquimau or de traîneau

hut [hʌt] n hutte f; (shed) cabane f

hyacinth ['haɪəsɪnθ] n jacinthe f

hydrangea [haɪˈdreɪndʒə] n hortensia m

hydrofoil ['haɪdrəfɔɪl] n hydrofoil m

hydrogen ['haɪdrədʒən] n hydrogène m

hygiene ['haɪdʒiːn] n hygiène f; **hygienic** [haɪˈdʒiːnɪk] adj hygiénique

hymn [hɪm] n hymne m; cantique m

hype [haɪp] n (inf) matraquage m

publicitaire *or* médiatique

hypermarket ['haɪpəmɑːkɪt] (BRIT) n
hypermarché m

hyphen ['haɪfn] n trait m d'union

hypnotize ['hɪpnətaɪz] vt hypnotiser

hypocrite ['hɪpəkrɪt] n hypocrite m/f

hypocritical [hɪpə'krɪtɪkl] adj
hypocrite

hypothesis (pl **hypotheses**)
[haɪ'pɒθɪsɪs, -siːz] n hypothèse f

hysterical [hɪ'sterɪkl] adj hystérique;
(funny) hilarant(e)

hysterics [hɪ'sterɪks] npl: **to be in/
have ~** (anger, panic) avoir une crise de
nerfs; (laughter) attraper un fou rire

I

I [aɪ] pron je; (before vowel) j'; (stressed)
moi

ice [aɪs] n glace f; (on road) verglas m
▷ vt (cake) glacer ▷ vi (also: **~ over**)
geler; (also: **~ up**) se givrer; **iceberg**
n iceberg m; **ice cream** n glace f; **ice
cube** n glaçon m; **ice hockey** n hockey
m sur glace

Iceland ['aɪslənd] n Islande f; **Icelander**
n Islandais(e); **Icelandic** [aɪs'lændɪk]
adj islandais(e) ▷ n (Ling) islandais m

ice: **ice lolly** n (BRIT) esquimau m;
ice rink n patinoire f; **ice skating** n
patinage m (sur glace)

icing ['aɪsɪŋ] n (Culin) glaçage m; **icing
sugar** n (BRIT) sucre m glace

icon ['aɪkɒn] n icône f

ICT n abbr (BRIT: Scol: = information and
communications technology) TIC fpl

icy ['aɪsɪ] adj glacé(e); (road) verglacé(e);
(weather, temperature) glacial(e)

I'd [aɪd] = **I would**; **I had**

ID card n carte f d'identité

idea [aɪ'dɪə] n idée f

ideal [aɪ'dɪəl] n idéal m ▷ adj idéal(e).
ideally [aɪ'dɪəlɪ] adv (preferably) dans l'idéal; (perfectly): **he is ideally suited to the job** il est parfait pour ce poste
identical [aɪ'dentɪkl] adj identique
identification [aɪdentɪfɪ'keɪʃən] n identification f; **means of ~** pièce f d'identité
identify [aɪ'dentɪfaɪ] vt identifier
identity [aɪ'dentɪtɪ] n identité f;
identity card n carte f d'identité;
identity theft n usurpation f d'identité
ideology [aɪdɪ'ɔlədʒɪ] n idéologie f
idiom ['ɪdɪəm] n (phrase) expression f idiomatique; (style) style m
idiot ['ɪdɪət] n idiot(e), imbécile m/f
idle ['aɪdl] adj (doing nothing) sans occupation, désœuvré(e); (lazy) oisif(-ive), paresseux(-euse); (unemployed) au chômage; (machinery) au repos; (question, pleasures) vain(e), futile ▷ vi (engine) tourner au ralenti
idol ['aɪdl] n idole f
idyllic [ɪ'dɪlɪk] adj idyllique
i.e. abbr (= id est: that is) c. à d., c'est-à-dire
if [ɪf] conj si; **if necessary** si nécessaire, le cas échéant; **if so** si c'est le cas; **if not** sinon; **if only I could!** si seulement je pouvais!; see also **as**; **even**
ignite [ɪg'naɪt] vt mettre le feu à, enflammer ▷ vi s'enflammer
ignition [ɪg'nɪʃən] n (Aut) allumage m;
to switch on/off the ~ mettre/couper le contact
ignorance ['ɪgnərəns] n ignorance f
ignorant ['ɪgnərənt] adj ignorant(e);
to be ~ of (subject) ne rien connaître en; (events) ne pas être au courant de
ignore [ɪg'nɔː] vt ne tenir aucun compte de; (mistake) ne pas relever; (person: pretend to not see) faire semblant de ne pas reconnaître; (: pay no attention to) ignorer
ill [ɪl] adj (sick) malade; (bad) mauvais(e) ▷ n mal m ▷ adv: **to speak/think/ of sb** dire/penser du mal de qn; **to be**

taken ~ tomber malade
I'll [aɪl] = **I will**; **I shall**
illegal [ɪ'liːgl] adj illégal(e)
illegible [ɪ'ledʒɪbl] adj illisible
illegitimate [ɪlɪ'dʒɪtɪmət] adj illégitime
ill health n mauvaise santé
illiterate [ɪ'lɪtərət] adj illettré(e)
illness ['ɪlnɪs] n maladie f
illuminate [ɪ'luːmɪneɪt] vt (room, street) éclairer; (for special effect) illuminer
illusion [ɪ'luːʒən] n illusion f
illustrate ['ɪləstreɪt] vt illustrer
illustration [ɪlə'streɪʃən] n illustration f
I'm [aɪm] = **I am**
image ['ɪmɪdʒ] n image f; (public face) image de marque
imaginary [ɪ'mædʒɪnərɪ] adj imaginaire
imagination [ɪmædʒɪ'neɪʃən] n imagination f
imaginative [ɪ'mædʒɪnətɪv] adj imaginatif(-ive); (person) plein(e) d'imagination
imagine [ɪ'mædʒɪn] vt s'imaginer; (suppose) imaginer, supposer
imbalance [ɪm'bæləns] n déséquilibre m
imitate ['ɪmɪteɪt] vt imiter; **imitation** [ɪmɪ'teɪʃən] n imitation f
immaculate [ɪ'mækjulət] adj impeccable; (Rel) immaculé(e)
immature [ɪmə'tjuə] adj (fruit) qui n'est pas mûr(e); (person) qui manque de maturité
immediate [ɪ'miːdɪət] adj immédiat(e); **immediately** adv (at once) immédiatement; **immediately next to** juste à côté de
immense [ɪ'mɛns] adj immense, énorme; **immensely** adv (+adj) extrêmement; (+vb) énormément
immerse [ɪ'məːs] vt immerger, plonger; **to be ~d in** (fig) être plongé dans
immigrant ['ɪmɪgrənt] n

immigrant(e); *(already established)* immigré(e); *(immigration* [ɪmɪˈɡreɪʃən] *n* immigration *f*

imminent [ˈɪmɪnənt] *adj* imminent(e)

immoral [ɪˈmɔrl] *adj* immoral(e)

immortal [ɪˈmɔːtl] *adj, n* immortel(le)

immune [ɪˈmjuːn] *adj*: **~ (to)** immunisé(e) (contre); **immune system** *n* système *m* immunitaire

immunize [ˈɪmjunaɪz] *vt* immuniser

impact [ˈɪmpækt] *n* choc *m*, impact *m*; *(fig)* impact *m*

impair [ɪmˈpεəʳ] *vt* détériorer, diminuer

impartial [ɪmˈpɑːʃl] *adj* impartial(e)

impatience [ɪmˈpeɪʃəns] *n* impatience *f*

impatient [ɪmˈpeɪʃənt] *adj* impatient(e); **to get** *or* **grow ~** s'impatienter

impeccable [ɪmˈpεkəbl] *adj* impeccable, parfait(e)

impending [ɪmˈpεndɪŋ] *adj* imminent(e)

imperative [ɪmˈpεrətɪv] *adj (need)* urgent(e), pressant(e); *(tone)* impérieux(-euse) ⊳ *n (Ling)* impératif *m*

imperfect [ɪmˈpəːfɪkt] *adj* imparfait(e); *(goods etc)* défectueux(-euse) ⊳ *n (Ling: also:* **~ tense**) imparfait *m*

imperial [ɪmˈpɪərɪəl] *adj* impérial(e); *(BRIT: measure)* légal(e)

impersonal [ɪmˈpəːsənl] *adj* impersonnel(le)

impersonate [ɪmˈpəːsəneɪt] *vt* se faire passer pour; *(Theat)* imiter

impetus [ˈɪmpətəs] *n* impulsion *f*; *(of runner)* élan *m*

implant [ɪmˈplɑːnt] *vt (Med)* implanter; *(fig: idea, principle)* inculquer

implement *n* [ˈɪmplɪmənt] outil *m*, instrument *m*; *(for cooking)* ustensile *m* ⊳ *vt* [ˈɪmplɪmεnt] exécuter

implicate [ˈɪmplɪkeɪt] *vt* impliquer, compromettre

implication [ɪmplɪˈkeɪʃən] *n* implication *f*; **by ~** indirectement

implicit [ɪmˈplɪsɪt] *adj* implicite; *(complete)* absolu(e), sans réserve

imply [ɪmˈplaɪ] *vt (hint)* suggérer, laisser entendre; *(mean)* indiquer, supposer

impolite [ɪmpəˈlaɪt] *adj* impoli(e)

import *vt* [ɪmˈpɔːt] importer ⊳ *n* [ˈɪmpɔːt] *(Comm)* importation *f*; *(meaning)* portée *f*, signification *f*

importance [ɪmˈpɔːtns] *n* importance *f*

important [ɪmˈpɔːtnt] *adj* important(e); **it's not ~** c'est sans importance, ce n'est pas important

importer [ɪmˈpɔːtəʳ] *n* importateur(-trice)

impose [ɪmˈpəuz] *vt* imposer ⊳ *vi*: **to ~ on sb** abuser de la gentillesse de qn; **imposing** *adj* imposant(e), impressionnant(e)

impossible [ɪmˈpɔsɪbl] *adj* impossible

impotent [ˈɪmpətnt] *adj* impuissant(e)

impoverished [ɪmˈpɔvərɪʃt] *adj* pauvre, appauvri(e)

impractical [ɪmˈpræktɪkl] *adj* pas pratique; *(person)* qui manque d'esprit pratique

impress [ɪmˈprεs] *vt* impressionner, faire impression sur; *(mark)* imprimer, marquer; **to ~ sth on sb** faire bien comprendre qch à qn

impression [ɪmˈprεʃən] *n* impression *f*; *(of stamp, seal)* empreinte *f*; *(imitation)* imitation *f*; **to be under the ~ that** avoir l'impression que

impressive [ɪmˈprεsɪv] *adj* impressionnant(e)

imprison [ɪmˈprɪzn] *vt* emprisonner, mettre en prison; **imprisonment** *n* emprisonnement *m*; *(period)*: **to sentence sb to 10 years' imprisonment** condamner qn à 10 ans de prison

improbable [ɪmˈprɔbəbl] *adj* improbable; *(excuse)* peu plausible

improper [ɪmˈprɔpəʳ] *adj (unsuitable)* déplacé(e), de mauvais goût; *(indecent)* indécent(e); (*dishonest*) malhonnête

improve [ɪmˈpruːv] *vt* améliorer ▷ *vi* s'améliorer; (*pupil etc*) faire des progrès; **improvement** *n* amélioration *f*; (*of pupil etc*) progrès *m*

improvise [ˈɪmprəvaɪz] *vt, vi* improviser

impulse [ˈɪmpʌls] *n* impulsion *f*; **on ~** impulsivement, sur un coup de tête; **impulsive** [ɪmˈpʌlsɪv] *adj* impulsif(-ive)

O **KEYWORD**

in [ɪn] *prep* **1** (*indicating place, position*) dans; **in the house/the fridge** dans la maison/le frigo; **in the garden** dans le or au jardin; **in town** en ville; **in the country** à la campagne; **in school** à l'école; **in here/there** ici/là

2 (*with place names: of town, region, country*) à; **in London** à Londres; **in England** en Angleterre; **in Japan** au Japon; **in the United States** aux États-Unis

3 (*indicating time: during*): **in spring** au printemps; **in summer** en été; **in May/2005** en mai/2005; **in the afternoon** (dans) l'après-midi; **at 4 o'clock in the afternoon** à 4 heures de l'après-midi

4 (*indicating time: in the space of*) en; (: *future*) dans; **I did it in 3 hours/days** je l'ai fait en 3 heures/jours; **I'll see you in 2 weeks** or **in 2 weeks' time** je te verrai dans 2 semaines

5 (*indicating manner etc*) à; **in a loud/soft voice** à voix haute/basse; **in pencil** au crayon; **in writing** par écrit; **in French** en français; **the boy in the blue shirt** le garçon à or avec la chemise bleue

6 (*indicating circumstances*): **in the sun** au soleil; **in the shade** à l'ombre; **in the rain** sous la pluie; **a change in policy** un changement de politique

7 (*indicating mood, state*): **in tears** en larmes; **in anger** sous le coup de la

colère; **in despair** au désespoir; **in good condition** en bon état; **to live in luxury** vivre dans le luxe

8 (*with ratios, numbers*): **1 in 10 households, 1 household in 10** 1 ménage sur 10; **20 pence in the pound** 20 pence par livre sterling; **they lined up in twos** ils se mirent en rangs (deux) par deux; **in hundreds** par centaines

9 (*referring to people, works*) chez; **the disease is common in children** c'est une maladie courante chez les enfants; **in (the works of) Dickens** chez Dickens, dans (l'œuvre de) Dickens

10 (*indicating profession etc*) dans; **to be in teaching** être dans l'enseignement

11 (*after superlative*) de; **the best pupil in the class** le meilleur élève de la classe

12 (*with present participle*): **in saying this** en disant ceci

▷ *adv*: **to be in** (*person: at home, work*) être là; (*train, ship, plane*) être arrivé(e); (*in fashion*) être à la mode; **to ask sb in** inviter qn à entrer; **to run/limp** *etc* **in** entrer en courant/boitant etc

▷ *n*: **the ins and outs (of)** (*of proposal, situation etc*) les tenants et aboutissants de

inability [ɪnəˈbɪlɪtɪ] *n* incapacité *f*; **~ to pay** incapacité de payer

inaccurate [ɪnˈækjʊrət] *adj* inexact(e); (*person*) qui manque de précision

inadequate [ɪnˈædɪkwət] *adj* insuffisant(e), inadéquat(e)

inadvertently [ɪnədˈvəːtntlɪ] *adv* par mégarde

inappropriate [ɪnəˈprəuprɪət] *adj* inopportun(e), mal à propos; (*word, expression*) impropre

inaugurate [ɪˈnɔːgjʊreɪt] *vt* inaugurer; (*president, official*) investir de ses fonctions

Inc. *abbr* = **incorporated**

incapable [ɪnˈkeɪpəbl] *adj*: **~ (of)** incapable (de)

incense n ['ɪnsɛns] encens m ▷ vt [ɪn'sɛns] (anger) mettre en colère

incentive [ɪn'sɛntɪv] n encouragement m, raison f de se donner de la peine

inch [ɪntʃ] n pouce m (=2,54 cm; 12 in a foot); **within an ~ of** à deux doigts de; **he wouldn't give an ~** (fig) il n'a pas voulu céder d'un pouce

incidence ['ɪnsɪdns] n (of crime, disease) fréquence f

incident ['ɪnsɪdnt] n incident m

incidentally [ɪnsɪ'dɛntəlɪ] adv (by the way) à propos

inclination [ɪnklɪ'neɪʃən] n inclination f; (desire) envie f

incline n ['ɪnklaɪn] pente f, plan incliné ▷ vb [ɪn'klaɪn] ▷ vt incliner ▷ vi (surface) s'incliner; **to be ~d to do** (have a tendency to do) avoir tendance à faire

include [ɪn'kluːd] vt inclure, comprendre; **service is/is not ~d** le service est compris/n'est pas compris; **including** prep y compris; **inclusion** n inclusion f; **inclusive** adj inclus(e), compris(e); **inclusive of tax** taxes comprises

income ['ɪnkʌm] n revenu m; (from property etc) rentes fpl; **income support** n (BRIT) ≈ revenu m minimum d'insertion, RMI m; **income tax** n impôt m sur le revenu

incoming ['ɪnkʌmɪŋ] adj (passengers, mail) à l'arrivée; (government, tenant) nouveau (nouvelle)

incompatible [ɪnkəm'pætɪbl] adj incompatible

incompetence [ɪn'kɒmpɪtns] n incompétence f, incapacité f

incompetent [ɪn'kɒmpɪtnt] adj incompétent(e), incapable

incomplete [ɪnkəm'pliːt] adj incomplet(-ète)

inconsistent [ɪnkən'sɪstnt] adj qui manque de constance; (work) irrégulier(-ière); (statement) peu cohérent(e); **~ with** en contradiction avec

inconvenience [ɪnkən'viːnjəns] n inconvénient m; (trouble) dérangement m ▷ vt déranger

inconvenient [ɪnkən'viːnjənt] adj malcommode; (time, place) mal choisi(e), qui ne convient pas; (visitor) importun(e)

incorporate [ɪn'kɔːpəreɪt] vt incorporer; (contain) contenir

incorrect [ɪnkə'rɛkt] adj incorrect(e); (opinion, statement) inexact(e)

increase n ['ɪnkriːs] augmentation f ▷ vi, vt [ɪn'kriːs] augmenter; **increasingly** adv de plus en plus

incredible [ɪn'krɛdɪbl] adj incroyable; **incredibly** adv incroyablement

incur [ɪn'kəː'] vt (expenses) encourir; (anger, risk) s'exposer à; (debt) contracter; (loss) subir

indecent [ɪn'diːsnt] adj indécent(e), inconvenant(e)

indeed [ɪn'diːd] adv (confirming, agreeing) en effet, effectivement; (for emphasis) vraiment; (furthermore) d'ailleurs; **yes ~!** certainement!

indefinitely [ɪn'dɛfɪnɪtlɪ] adv (wait) indéfiniment

independence [ɪndɪ'pɛndns] n indépendance f; **Independence Day** n (US) fête de l'Indépendance américaine; voir encadré

  ◦ **INDEPENDENCE DAY**
  ◦
  ◦ L'**Independence Day** est la fête
  ◦ nationale aux États-Unis, le 4
  ◦ juillet. Il commémore l'adoption
  ◦ de la déclaration d'Indépendance,
  ◦ en 1776, écrite par Thomas Jefferson
  ◦ et proclamant la séparation des 13
  ◦ colonies américaines de la Grande-
  ◦ Bretagne.

independent [ɪndɪ'pɛndnt] adj indépendant(e); (radio) libre; **independent school** n (BRIT) école privée

index ['ɪndɛks] n (pl **-es**) (in book)

index m; (: in library etc) catalogue m (pl **indices**) (ratio, sign) indice m

India ['ɪndɪə] n Inde f; **Indian** adj indien(ne) ▷ n Indien(ne); **(American) Indian** Indien(ne) (d'Amérique)

indicate ['ɪndɪkeɪt] vt indiquer ▷ vi (BRIT Aut): **to ~ left/right** mettre son clignotant à gauche/à droite; **indication** [ɪndɪ'keɪʃən] n indication f, signe m; **indicative** [ɪn'dɪkətɪv] adj: **to be indicative of sth** être symptomatique de qch ▷ n (Ling) indicatif m; **indicator** n (sign) indicateur m; (Aut) clignotant m

indices ['ɪndɪsiːz] npl of **index**

indict [ɪn'daɪt] vt accuser; **indictment** n accusation f

indifference [ɪn'dɪfrəns] n indifférence f

indifferent [ɪn'dɪfrənt] adj indifférent(e); (poor) médiocre, quelconque

indigenous [ɪn'dɪdʒɪnəs] adj indigène

indigestion [ɪndɪ'dʒestʃən] n indigestion f, mauvaise digestion

indignant [ɪn'dɪgnənt] adj: **~ (at sth/ with sb)** indigné(e) (de qch/contre qn)

indirect [ɪndɪ'rekt] adj indirect(e)

indispensable [ɪndɪ'spensəbl] adj indispensable

individual [ɪndɪ'vɪdjuəl] n individu m ▷ adj individuel(le); (characteristic) particulier(-ière), original(e); **individually** adv individuellement

Indonesia [ɪndə'niːzɪə] n Indonésie f

indoor ['ɪndɔː'] adj d'intérieur; (plant) d'appartement; (swimming pool) couvert(e); (sport, games) pratiqué(e) en salle; **indoors** [ɪn'dɔːz] adv à l'intérieur

induce [ɪn'djuːs] vt (persuade) persuader; (bring about) provoquer; (labour) déclencher

indulge [ɪn'dʌldʒ] vt (whim) céder à, satisfaire; (child) gâter ▷ vi: **to ~ in** (luxury) s'offrir qch, se permettre qch; (fantasies etc) se livrer à qch; **indulgent** adj indulgent(e)

industrial [ɪn'dʌstrɪəl] adj

industriel(le); (injury) du travail; (dispute) ouvrier(-ière); **industrial estate** n (BRIT) zone industrielle; **industrialist** n industriel m; **industrial park** n (US) zone industrielle

industry ['ɪndəstrɪ] n industrie f; (diligence) zèle m, application f

inefficient [ɪnɪ'fɪʃənt] adj inefficace

inequality [ɪnɪ'kwɔlɪtɪ] n inégalité f

inevitable [ɪn'evɪtəbl] adj inévitable; **inevitably** adv inévitablement, fatalement

inexpensive [ɪnɪk'spensɪv] adj bon marché inv

inexperienced [ɪnɪk'spɪərɪənst] adj inexpérimenté(e)

inexplicable [ɪnɪk'splɪkəbl] adj inexplicable

infamous ['ɪnfəməs] adj infâme, abominable

infant ['ɪnfənt] n (baby) nourrisson m; (young child) petit(e) enfant

infantry ['ɪnfəntrɪ] n infanterie f

infant school n (BRIT) classes fpl préparatoires (entre 5 et 7 ans)

infect [ɪn'fekt] vt (wound) infecter; (person, blood) contaminer; **infection** [ɪn'fekʃən] n infection f; (contagion) contagion f; **infectious** [ɪn'fekʃəs] adj infectieux(-euse); (also fig) contagieux(-euse)

infer [ɪn'fəː'] vt: **to ~ (from)** conclure (de), déduire (de)

inferior [ɪn'fɪərɪə'] adj inférieur(e); (goods) de qualité inférieure ▷ n inférieur(e); (in rank) subalterne m/f

infertile [ɪn'fəːtaɪl] adj stérile

infertility [ɪnfəː'tɪlɪtɪ] n infertilité f, stérilité f

infested [ɪn'festɪd] adj: **~ (with)** infesté(e) (de)

infinite ['ɪnfɪnɪt] adj infini(e); (time, money) illimité(e); **infinitely** adv infiniment

infirmary [ɪn'fəːmərɪ] n hôpital m; (in school, factory) infirmerie f

inflamed [ɪn'fleɪmd] adj enflammé(e)

inflammation [ɪnflə'meɪʃən] n

inflammation f

inflatable [ɪnˈfleɪtəbl] adj gonflable

inflate [ɪnˈfleɪt] vt (tyre, balloon) gonfler; (fig: exaggerate) grossir; (: increase) gonfler; **inflation** [ɪnˈfleɪʃən] n (Econ) inflation f

inflexible [ɪnˈfleksɪbl] adj inflexible, rigide

inflict [ɪnˈflɪkt] vt: **to ~ on** infliger à

influence [ˈɪnfluəns] n influence f ▷ vt influencer; **under the ~ of alcohol** en état d'ébriété; **influential** [ɪnfluˈɛnʃl] adj influent(e)

influenza [ɪnfluˈɛnzə] n grippe f

influx [ˈɪnflʌks] n afflux m

info (inf) [ˈɪnfəu] n (= information) renseignements mpl

inform [ɪnˈfɔːm] vt: **to ~ sb (of)** informer or avertir qn (de) ▷ vi: **to ~ on sb** dénoncer qn, informer contre qn

informal [ɪnˈfɔːml] adj (person, manner, party) simple; (visit, discussion) dénué(e) de formalités; (announcement, invitation) non officiel(le); (colloquial) familier(-ère)

information [ɪnfəˈmeɪʃən] n information(s) f(pl); renseignements mpl; (knowledge) connaissances fpl; **a piece of ~** un renseignement; **information office** n bureau m de renseignements; **information technology** n informatique f

informative [ɪnˈfɔːmətɪv] adj instructif(-ive)

infra-red [ɪnfrəˈred] adj infrarouge

infrastructure [ˈɪnfrəstrʌktʃəʳ] n infrastructure f

infrequent [ɪnˈfriːkwənt] adj peu fréquent(e), rare

infuriate [ɪnˈfjuərɪeɪt] vt mettre en fureur

infuriating [ɪnˈfjuərɪeɪtɪŋ] adj exaspérant(e)

ingenious [ɪnˈdʒiːnjəs] adj ingénieux(-euse)

ingredient [ɪnˈɡriːdɪənt] n ingrédient m; (fig) élément m

inhabit [ɪnˈhæbɪt] vt habiter

inhabitant n habitant(e)

inhale [ɪnˈheɪl] vt inhaler; (perfume) respirer; (smoke) avaler ▷ vi (breathe in) aspirer; (in smoking) avaler la fumée; **inhaler** n inhalateur m

inherent [ɪnˈhɪərənt] adj: **~ (in or to)** inhérent(e) (à)

inherit [ɪnˈherɪt] vt hériter (de); **inheritance** n héritage m

inhibit [ɪnˈhɪbɪt] vt (Psych) inhiber; (growth) freiner; **inhibition** [ɪnhɪˈbɪʃən] n inhibition f

initial [ɪˈnɪʃl] adj initial(e) ▷ n initiale f ▷ vt parafer; **initials** npl initiales fpl; (as signature) parafe m; **initially** adv initialement, au début

initiate [ɪˈnɪʃɪeɪt] vt (start) entreprendre; amorcer; (enterprise) lancer; (person) initier; **to ~ proceedings against sb** (Law) intenter une action à qn, engager des poursuites contre qn

initiative [ɪˈnɪʃətɪv] n initiative f

inject [ɪnˈdʒekt] vt injecter; (person): **to ~ sb with sth** faire une piqûre de qch à qn; **injection** [ɪnˈdʒekʃən] n injection f, piqûre f

injure [ˈɪndʒəʳ] vt blesser; (damage: reputation etc) compromettre; **to ~ o.s.** se blesser; **injured** adj (person, leg etc) blessé(e); **injury** n blessure f; (wrong) tort m

injustice [ɪnˈdʒʌstɪs] n injustice f

ink [ɪŋk] n encre f; **ink-jet printer** [ˈɪŋkdʒet] n imprimante f à jet d'encre

inland adj [ˈɪnlənd] intérieur(e) ▷ adv [ɪnˈlænd] à l'intérieur, dans les terres; **Inland Revenue** n (BRIT) fisc m

in-laws [ˈɪnlɔːz] npl beaux-parents mpl; belle famille

inmate [ˈɪnmeɪt] n (in prison) détenu(e); (in asylum) interné(e)

inn [ɪn] n auberge f

inner [ˈɪnəʳ] adj intérieur(e); **inner-city** adj (schools, problems) de quartiers déshérités

inning [ˈɪnɪŋ] n (us: Baseball) tour m de batte; **innings** npl (Cricket) tour de batte

innocence ['ɪnəsns] n innocence f

innocent ['ɪnəsnt] adj innocent(e)

innovation [ɪnəʊ'veɪʃən] n innovation f

innovative ['ɪnəʊˈveɪtɪv] adj novateur(-trice); (product) innovant(e)

in-patient ['ɪnpeɪʃənt] n malade hospitalisé(e)

input ['ɪnpʊt] n (contribution) contribution f; (resources) ressources fpl; (Comput) entrée f (de données); (: data) données fpl ▷ vt (Comput) introduire, entrer

inquest ['ɪnkwest] n enquête f (criminelle); (coroner's) enquête judiciaire

inquire [ɪn'kwaɪəʳ] vi demander s'informer de, se renseigner sur; **to ~ when/where/whether** demander quand/où/si; **inquiry** n demande f de renseignements; (Law) enquête f, investigation f; **"inquiries"** "renseignements"

ins. abbr = **inches**

insane [ɪn'seɪn] adj fou (folle); (Med) aliéné(e)

insanity [ɪn'sænɪtɪ] n folie f; (Med) aliénation (mentale)

insect ['ɪnsekt] n insecte m; **insect repellent** n crème f anti-insectes

insecure [ɪnsɪ'kjuəʳ] adj (person) anxieux(-euse); (job) précaire; (building etc) peu sûr(e)

insecurity [ɪnsɪ'kjʊərɪtɪ] n insécurité f

insensitive [ɪn'sensɪtɪv] adj insensible

insert vt [ɪn'səːt] insérer ▷ n ['ɪnsəːt] insertion f

inside ['ɪn'saɪd] n intérieur m ▷ adj intérieur(e) ▷ adv à l'intérieur, dedans ▷ prep à l'intérieur de; (of time): **~ 10 minutes** en moins de 10 minutes; **to go ~** rentrer; **inside lane** n (Aut: in Britain) voie f de gauche; (: in US, Europe) voie f de droite; **inside out** adv à l'envers; (know) à fond; **to turn sth inside out** retourner qch

insight ['ɪnsaɪt] n perspicacité f; (glimpse, idea) aperçu m

insignificant [ɪnsɪg'nɪfɪkənt] adj insignifiant(e)

insincere [ɪnsɪn'sɪəʳ] adj hypocrite

insist [ɪn'sɪst] vi insister; **to ~ on doing** insister pour faire; **to ~ on sth** exiger qch; **to ~ that** insister pour que + sub; (claim) maintenir or soutenir que; **insistent** adj insistant(e), pressant(e); (noise, action) intérrompu(e)

insomnia [ɪn'sɔmnɪə] n insomnie f

inspect [ɪn'spekt] vt inspecter; (BRIT: ticket) contrôler; **inspection** [ɪn'spekʃən] n inspection f; (BRIT: of tickets) contrôle m; **inspector** n inspecteur(-trice); (BRIT: on buses, trains) contrôleur(-euse)

inspiration [ɪnspə'reɪʃən] n inspiration f; **inspire** [ɪn'spaɪəʳ] vt inspirer; **inspiring** adj inspirant(e)

instability [ɪnstə'bɪlɪtɪ] n instabilité f

install (us **instal**) [ɪn'stɔːl] vt installer; **installation** [ɪnstə'leɪʃən] n installation f

instalment (us **installment**) [ɪn'stɔːlmənt] n (payment) acompte m, versement partiel; (of TV serial etc) épisode m; **in ~s** (pay) à tempérament; (receive) en plusieurs fois

instance ['ɪnstəns] n exemple m; **for ~** par exemple; **in the first ~** tout d'abord, en premier lieu

instant ['ɪnstənt] n instant m ▷ adj immédiat(e), urgent(e); (coffee, food) instantané(e); in powder; **instantly** adv immédiatement, tout de suite; **instant messaging** n messagerie f instantanée

instead [ɪn'sted] adv au lieu de cela; **~ of** au lieu de; **~ of sb** à la place de qn

instinct ['ɪnstɪŋkt] n instinct m; **instinctive** adj instinctif(-ive)

institute ['ɪnstɪtjuːt] n institut m ▷ vt instituer, établir; (inquiry) ouvrir; (proceedings) entamer

institution [ɪnstɪ'tjuːʃən] n institution f; (school) établissement

m (scolaire); (for care) établissement
(psychiatrique etc)

instruct [ɪnˈstrʌkt] vt: **to ~ sb in sth**
enseigner qch à qn; **to ~ sb to do**
charger qn or ordonner à qn de faire;
instruction [ɪnˈstrʌkʃən] n instruction
f; **instructions** npl (orders) directives
fpl; **instructions for use** mode m
d'emploi; **instructor** n professeur m;
(for skiing, driving) moniteur m

instrument [ˈɪnstrʊmənt] n
instrument m; **instrumental**
[ɪnstrʊˈmɛntl] adj (Mus)
instrumental(e); **to be instrumental
in sth/in doing sth** contribuer à qch/à
faire qch

insufficient [ɪnsəˈfɪʃənt] adj
insuffisant(e)

insulate [ˈɪnsjʊleɪt] vt isoler; (against
sound) insonoriser; **insulation**
[ɪnsjʊˈleɪʃən] n isolation f; (against
sound) insonorisation f

insulin [ˈɪnsjʊlɪn] n insuline f

insult n [ˈɪnsʌlt] insulte f, affront
m ▷ vt [ɪnˈsʌlt] insulter, faire un
affront à; **insulting** adj insultant(e),
injurieux(-euse)

insurance [ɪnˈʃuərəns] n assurance
f; **fire/life ~** assurance-incendie/-vie;
insurance company n compagnie f
or société f d'assurances; **insurance
policy** n police f d'assurance

insure [ɪnˈʃuər] vt assurer; **to ~ (o.s.)
against** (fig) parer à

intact [ɪnˈtækt] adj intact(e)

intake [ˈɪnteɪk] n (Tech) admission
f; (consumption) consommation f;
(BRIT Scol) **an ~ of 200 a year** 200
admissions par an

integral [ˈɪntɪɡrəl] adj (whole)
intégral(e); (part) intégrant(e)

integrate [ˈɪntɪɡreɪt] vt intégrer ▷ vi
s'intégrer

integrity [ɪnˈtɛɡrɪtɪ] n intégrité f

intellect [ˈɪntəlɛkt] n intelligence f

intellectual [ɪntəˈlɛktjʊəl] adj, n
intellectuel(le)

intelligence [ɪnˈtɛlɪdʒəns] n

intelligence f; (Mil etc) informations fpl,
renseignements mpl

intelligent [ɪnˈtɛlɪdʒənt] adj
intelligent(e)

intend [ɪnˈtɛnd] vt (gift etc): **to ~ sth
for** destiner qch à; **to ~ to do** avoir
l'intention de faire

intense [ɪnˈtɛns] adj intense; (person)
véhément(e)

intensify [ɪnˈtɛnsɪfaɪ] vt intensifier

intensity [ɪnˈtɛnsɪtɪ] n intensité f

intensive [ɪnˈtɛnsɪv] adj intensif(-ive);
intensive care n: **to be in intensive
care** être en réanimation; **intensive
care unit** n service m de réanimation

intent [ɪnˈtɛnt] n intention f ▷ adj
attentif(-ive), absorbé(e); **to all ~s and
purposes** en fait, pratiquement; **to
be ~ on doing sth** être (bien) décidé à
faire qch

intention [ɪnˈtɛnʃən] n intention f;
intentional adj intentionnel(le),
délibéré(e)

interact [ɪntərˈækt] vi avoir une action
réciproque; (people) communiquer;
interaction [ɪntərˈækʃən] n
interaction f; **interactive** adj (Comput)
interactif, conversationnel(le)

intercept [ɪntəˈsɛpt] vt intercepter;
(person) arrêter au passage

interchange n [ˈɪntətʃeɪndʒ]
(exchange) échange m; (on motorway)
échangeur m

intercourse [ˈɪntəkɔːs] n: **sexual ~**
rapports sexuels

interest [ˈɪntrɪst] n intérêt m; (Comm:
stake, share) participation f, intérêts
mpl ▷ vt intéresser; **interested** adj
intéressé(e); **to be interested in sth**
s'intéresser à qch; **I'm interested
in going** ça m'intéresse d'y aller;
interesting adj intéressant(e);
interest rate n taux m d'intérêt

interface [ˈɪntəfeɪs] n (Comput)
interface f

interfere [ɪntəˈfɪər] vi: **to ~ in** (quarrel)
s'immiscer dans; (other people's business)
se mêler de; **to ~ with** (object) tripoter,

toucher à; (plans) contrecarrer; (duty) être en conflit avec; **interference** n (gen) ingérence f; (Radio, TV) parasites mpl

interim ['ɪntərɪm] adj provisoire; (post) intérimaire ▷ n: **in the ~** dans l'intérim

interior [ɪn'tɪərɪə] n intérieur m ▷ adj intérieur(e); (minister, minister) de l'intérieur; **interior design** n architecture f d'intérieur

intermediate [ɪntə'miːdɪət] adj intermédiaire; (Scol: course, level) moyen(ne)

intermission [ɪntə'mɪʃən] n pause f; (Theat, Cine) entracte m

intern vt [ɪn'təːn] interner ▷ n ['ɪntəːn] (us) interne m/f

internal [ɪn'təːnl] adj interne; (dispute, reform etc) intérieur(e); **Internal Revenue Service** n (us) fisc m

international [ɪntə'næʃənl] adj international(e) ▷ n (BRIT Sport) international m

Internet [ɪntə'nɛt] n: **the ~** l'Internet m; **Internet café** n cybercafé m; **Internet Service Provider** n fournisseur d'accès à Internet; **Internet user** n internaute m/f

interpret [ɪn'təːprɪt] vt interpréter ▷ vi servir d'interprète; **interpretation** [ɪntəːprɪ'teɪʃən] n interprétation f; **interpreter** n interprète m/f; **could you act as an interpreter for us?** pourriez-vous nous servir d'interprète?

interrogate [ɪn'tɛrəʊgeɪt] vt interroger; (suspect etc) soumettre à un interrogatoire; **interrogation** [ɪntɛrəʊ'geɪʃən] n interrogation f; (by police) interrogatoire m

interrogative [ɪntə'rɒgətɪv] adj interrogateur(-trice) ▷ n (Ling) interrogatif m

interrupt [ɪntə'rʌpt] vt, vi interrompre; **interruption** [ɪntə'rʌpʃən] n interruption f

intersection [ɪntə'sɛkʃən] n (of roads) croisement m

interstate ['ɪntəsteɪt] (us) n

autoroute f (qui relie plusieurs États)

interval ['ɪntəvl] n intervalle m; (BRIT: Theat) entracte m; (: Sport) mi-temps f; **at ~s** par intervalles

intervene [ɪntə'viːn] vi (time) s'écouler (entre-temps); (event) survenir; (person) intervenir

interview ['ɪntəvjuː] n (Radio, TV etc) interview f; (for job) entrevue f ▷ vt interviewer; avoir une entrevue avec; **interviewer** n (Radio, TV etc) interviewer m

intimate adj ['ɪntɪmət] intime; (friendship) profond(e); (knowledge) approfondi(e) ▷ vt ['ɪntɪmeɪt] suggérer, laisser entendre; (announce) faire savoir

intimidate [ɪn'tɪmɪdeɪt] vt intimider

intimidating [ɪn'tɪmɪdeɪtɪŋ] adj intimidant(e)

into ['ɪntu] prep dans; **~ pieces/French** en morceaux/français

intolerant [ɪn'tɔlərnt] adj: **~ (of)** intolérant(e) (de)

intranet [ɪn'trənɛt] n intranet m

intransitive [ɪn'trænsɪtɪv] adj intransitif(-ive)

intricate ['ɪntrɪkət] adj complexe, compliqué(e)

intrigue [ɪn'triːg] n intrigue f ▷ vt intriguer; **intriguing** adj fascinant(e)

introduce [ɪntrə'djuːs] vt introduire; (TV show etc) présenter; **to ~ sb (to sb)** présenter qn (à qn); **to ~ sb to** (pastime, technique) initier qn à; **introduction** [ɪntrə'dʌkʃən] n introduction f; (of person) présentation f; (to new experience) initiation f; **introductory** [ɪntrə'dʌktərɪ] adj préliminaire, introductif(-ive)

intrude [ɪn'truːd] vi (person) être importun(e); **to ~ on** or **into** (conversation etc) s'immiscer dans; **intruder** n intrus(e) f

intuition [ɪntjuː'ɪʃən] n intuition f

inundate ['ɪnʌndeɪt] vt: **to ~ with** inonder de

invade [ɪn'veɪd] vt envahir

invalid n ['ɪnvəlɪd] malade m/f; (with disability) invalide m/f ⊳ adj [ɪn'vælɪd] (not valid) invalide, non valide

invaluable [ɪn'væljuəbl] adj inestimable, inappréciable

invariably [ɪn'vɛərɪəblɪ] adv invariablement; **she is ~ late** elle est toujours en retard

invasion [ɪn'veɪʒən] n invasion f

invent [ɪn'vɛnt] vt inventer; **invention** [ɪn'vɛnʃən] n invention f; **inventor** n inventeur(-trice)

inventory ['ɪnvəntrɪ] n inventaire m

inverted commas [ɪn'vɜːtɪd-] npl (BRIT) guillemets mpl

invest [ɪn'vɛst] vt investir ⊳ vi: **to ~ in** placer de l'argent or investir dans; (fig: acquire) s'offrir, faire l'acquisition de

investigate [ɪn'vɛstɪgeɪt] vt étudier, examiner; (crime) faire une enquête sur; **investigation** [ɪnvɛstɪ'geɪʃən] n (of crime) enquête f; **investigator** [ɪn'vɛstɪgeɪtə'] n investigateur(-trice); **private ~** détective privé

investment [ɪn'vɛstmənt] n investissement m, placement m

investor [ɪn'vɛstə'] n épargnant(e); (shareholder) actionnaire m/f

invisible [ɪn'vɪzɪbl] adj invisible

invitation [ɪnvɪ'teɪʃən] n invitation f

invite [ɪn'vaɪt] vt inviter; (opinions etc) demander; **inviting** adj engageant(e), attrayant(e)

invoice ['ɪnvɔɪs] n facture f ⊳ vt facturer

involve [ɪn'vɔlv] vt (entail) impliquer; (concern) concerner; (require) nécessiter; **to ~ sb in** (theft etc) impliquer qn dans; (activity, meeting) faire participer qn à; **involved** adj (complicated) complexe; **to be involved in** (take part) participer à; **involvement** n (personal role) rôle m; (participation) participation f; (enthusiasm) enthousiasme m

inward ['ɪnwəd] adj (movement) vers l'intérieur; (thought, feeling) profond(e), intime ⊳ adv = **inwards**; **inwards** adv

vers l'intérieur

IQ n abbr (= intelligence quotient) Q.I. m

IRA n abbr (= Irish Republican Army) IRA f

Iran [ɪ'rɑːn] n Iran m; **Iranian** [ɪ'reɪnɪən] adj iranien(ne) ⊳ n Iranien(ne)

Iraq [ɪ'rɑːk] n Irak m; **Iraqi** adj irakien(ne) ⊳ n Irakien(ne)

Ireland ['aɪələnd] n Irlande f

iris, irises ['aɪrɪs, -ɪz] n iris m

Irish ['aɪrɪʃ] adj irlandais(e) ⊳ npl: **the ~** les Irlandais, mpl; **Irishman** (irreg) n Irlandais m; **Irishwoman** (irreg) n Irlandaise f

iron ['aɪən] n fer m; (for clothes) fer à repasser ⊳ adj de or en fer ⊳ vt (clothes) repasser

ironic(al) [aɪ'rɔnɪk(l)] adj ironique; **ironically** adv ironiquement

ironing ['aɪənɪŋ] n (activity) repassage m; (clothes: ironed) linge repassé; (: to be ironed) linge à repasser; **ironing board** n planche f à repasser

irony ['aɪrənɪ] n ironie f

irrational [ɪ'ræʃənl] adj irrationnel(le); (person) qui n'est pas rationnel

irregular [ɪ'rɛgjulə'] adj irrégulier(-ière); (surface) inégal(e); (action, event) peu orthodoxe

irrelevant [ɪ'rɛləvənt] adj sans rapport, hors de propos

irresistible [ɪrɪ'zɪstɪbl] adj irrésistible

irresponsible [ɪrɪ'spɔnsɪbl] adj (act) irréfléchi(e); (person) qui n'a pas le sens des responsabilités

irrigation [ɪrɪ'geɪʃən] n irrigation f

irritable ['ɪrɪtəbl] adj irritable

irritate ['ɪrɪteɪt] vt irriter; **irritating** adj irritant(e); **irritation** [ɪrɪ'teɪʃən] n irritation f

IRS n abbr (US) = **Internal Revenue Service**

is [ɪz] vb see **be**

ISDN n abbr (= Integrated Services Digital Network) RNIS m

Islam ['ɪzlɑːm] n Islam m; **Islamic** [ɪz'lɑːmɪk] adj islamique

island ['aɪlənd] n île f; (also: **traffic ~**) refuge m (pour piétons); **islander** n

habitant(e) d'une île, insulaire m/f
isle [aɪl] n île f
isn't ['ɪznt] = **is not**
isolated ['aɪsəleɪtɪd] adj isolé(e)
isolation [aɪsə'leɪʃən] n isolement m
ISP n abbr = **Internet Service Provider**
Israel ['ɪzreɪl] n Israël m; **Israeli** [ɪz'reɪlɪ] adj israélien(ne) ▷ n Israélien(ne)
issue ['ɪʃuː] n question f, problème m; (of banknotes) émission f; (of newspaper) numéro m; (of book) publication f, parution f ▷ vt (rations, equipment) distribuer; (orders) donner; (statement) publier, faire; (certificate, passport) délivrer; (banknotes, cheques, stamps) émettre, mettre en circulation; **at ~** en jeu, en cause; **to take ~ with sb (over sth)** exprimer son désaccord avec qn (sur qch)
IT n abbr = **information technology**

⭕ **KEYWORD**

it [ɪt] pron 1 (specific: subject) il (elle); (: direct object) le (la, l'); (: indirect object) lui; **it's on the table** c'est or il (or elle) est sur la table; **I can't find it** je n'arrive pas à le trouver; **give it to me** donne-le-moi
2 (after prep): **about/from/of it** en; **I spoke to him about it** je lui en ai parlé; **what did you learn from it?** qu'est-ce que vous en avez retiré?; **I'm proud of it** j'en suis fier; **in/to it** y; **put the book in it** mettez-y le livre; **he agreed to it** il y a consenti; **did you go to it?** (party, concert etc) est-ce que vous y êtes allé(s)?
3 (impersonal) il; ce, cela, ça; **it's raining** il pleut; **it's Friday tomorrow** demain, c'est vendredi or nous sommes, vendredi; **it's 6 o'clock** il est 6 heures; **how far is it? — it's 10 miles** c'est loin? — c'est à 10 miles; **who is it? — it's me** qui est-ce? — c'est moi

Italian [ɪ'tæljən] adj italien(ne) ▷ n Italien(ne); (Ling) italien m

italics [ɪ'tælɪks] npl italique m
Italy ['ɪtəlɪ] n Italie f
itch [ɪtʃ] n démangeaison f ▷ vi (person) éprouver des démangeaisons; (part of body) démanger; **I'm ~ing to do** l'envie me démange de faire; **itchy** adj: **my back is itchy** j'ai le dos qui me démange
it'd ['ɪtd] = **it would**; **it had**
item ['aɪtəm] n (gen) article m; (on agenda) question f, point m; (also: **news ~**) nouvelle f
itinerary [aɪ'tɪnərərɪ] n itinéraire m
it'll ['ɪtl] = **it will**; **it shall**
its [ɪts] adj son (sa), ses pl
it's [ɪts] = **it is**; **it has**
itself [ɪt'sɛlf] pron (reflexive) se; (emphatic) lui-même (elle-même)
ITV n abbr (BRIT: = Independent Television) chaîne de télévision commerciale
I've [aɪv] = **I have**
ivory ['aɪvərɪ] n ivoire m
ivy ['aɪvɪ] n lierre m

J

jab [dʒæb] vt: **to ~ sth into** enfoncer or planter qch dans ▷ n (Med: inf) piqûre f

jack [dʒæk] n (Aut) cric m; (Cards) valet m

jacket ['dʒækɪt] n veste f, veston m; (of book) couverture f, jaquette f; **jacket potato** n pomme f de terre en robe des champs

jackpot ['dʒækpɒt] n gros lot

Jacuzzi® [dʒə'kuːzɪ] n jacuzzi®

jagged ['dʒægɪd] adj dentelé(e)

jail [dʒeɪl] n prison f ▷ vt emprisonner, mettre en prison; **jail sentence** n peine f de prison

jam [dʒæm] n confiture f; (also: **traffic ~**) embouteillage m ▷ vt (passage etc) encombrer, obstruer; (mechanism, drawer etc) bloquer, coincer; (Radio) brouiller ▷ vi (mechanism, sliding part) se coincer, se bloquer; (gun) s'enrayer; **to be in a ~** (inf) être dans le pétrin; **to ~ sth into** (stuff) entasser or comprimer qch dans; (thrust) enfoncer qch dans

Jamaica [dʒə'meɪkə] n Jamaïque f

jammed [dʒæmd] adj (window etc) coincé(e)

Jan abbr (= January) janv

janitor ['dʒænɪtə'] n (caretaker) concierge m

January ['dʒænjuərɪ] n janvier m

Japan [dʒə'pæn] n Japon m; **Japanese** [dʒæpə'niːz] adj japonais(e) ▷ n (pl inv) Japonais(e); (Ling) japonais m

jar [dʒɑː'] n (stone, earthenware) pot m; (glass) bocal m ▷ vi (sound) produire un son grinçant or discordant; (colours etc) détonner, jurer

jargon ['dʒɑːgən] n jargon m

javelin ['dʒævlɪn] n javelot m

jaw [dʒɔː] n mâchoire f

jazz [dʒæz] n jazz m

jealous ['dʒeləs] adj jaloux(-ouse); **jealousy** n jalousie f

jeans [dʒiːnz] npl jean m

Jello® ['dʒeləu] (us) n gelée f

jelly ['dʒelɪ] n (dessert) gelée f; (us: jam) confiture f; **jellyfish** n méduse f

jeopardize ['dʒepədaɪz] vt mettre en danger or péril

jerk [dʒəːk] n secousse f, saccade f; (of muscle) spasme m; (inf) pauvre type m ▷ vt (shake) donner une secousse à; (pull) tirer brusquement ▷ vi (vehicles) cahoter

jersey ['dʒəːzɪ] n tricot m; (fabric) jersey m

Jesus ['dʒiːzəs] n Jésus

jet [dʒet] n (of gas, liquid) jet m; (Aviat) avion m à réaction, jet m; **jet lag** n décalage m horaire; **jet-ski** vi faire du jet-ski or scooter des mers

jetty ['dʒetɪ] n jetée f, digue f

Jew [dʒuː] n Juif m

jewel ['dʒuːəl] n bijou m, joyau m; (in watch) rubis m; **jeweler** (us **jeweler**) n bijoutier(-ière), joaillier m; **jeweler's (shop)** n bijouterie f, joaillerie f; **jewellery** (us **jewelry**) n bijoux mpl

Jewish ['dʒuːɪʃ] adj juif (juive)

jigsaw ['dʒɪgsɔː] n (also: **~ puzzle**) puzzle m

job [dʒɔb] n (chore, task) travail m, tâche

f; (employment) emploi m, poste m, place f; **it's a good ~ that ...** c'est heureux or c'est une chance que ... + subj; **just the ~!** (c'est) juste or exactement ce qu'il faut!; **job centre** (BRIT) n ≈ ANPE f, ≈ Agence nationale pour l'emploi; **jobless** adj sans travail, au chômage

jockey ['dʒɔkɪ] n jockey m ▷ vi: **to ~ for position** manœuvrer pour être bien placé

jog [dʒɔg] vt secouer ▷ vi (Sport) faire du jogging; **to ~ sb's memory** rafraîchir la mémoire de qn; **jogging** n jogging m

join [dʒɔɪn] vt (put together) unir, assembler; (become member of) s'inscrire à; (meet) rejoindre, retrouver; (queue) se joindre à ▷ vi (roads, rivers) se rejoindre, se rencontrer; (Mil) s'engager

joiner ['dʒɔɪnə*] (BRIT) n menuisier m

joint [dʒɔɪnt] n (Tech) jointure f; joint m; (Anat) articulation f, jointure; (BRIT Culin) rôti m; (inf: place) boîte f; (of cannabis) joint m ▷ adj commun(e), aequo; **joint account** n compte joint; **jointly** adv ensemble, en commun

joke [dʒəuk] n plaisanterie f; (also: **practical ~**) farce f ▷ vi plaisanter; **to play a ~ on** jouer un tour à, faire une farce à; **joker** n (Cards) joker m

jolly ['dʒɔlɪ] adj gai(e), enjoué(e); (enjoyable) agréable, plaisant(e) ▷ adv (BRIT inf) rudement, drôlement

jolt [dʒəult] n cahot m, secousse f; (shock) choc m ▷ vt cahoter, secouer

Jordan ['dʒɔːdən] n (country) Jordanie f

journal ['dʒəːnl] n journal m; **journalism** n journalisme m; **journalist** n journaliste m/f

journey ['dʒəːnɪ] n voyage m; (distance covered) trajet m; **the ~ takes two hours** le trajet dure deux heures; **how was your ~?** votre voyage s'est bien passé?

joy [dʒɔɪ] n joie f; **joyrider** n

voleur(-euse) de voiture (qui fait une virée dans le véhicule volé); **joy stick** n (Aviat) manche m à balai; (Comput) manche à balai, manette f (de jeu)

Jr abbr = **junior**

judge [dʒʌdʒ] n juge m ▷ vt juger; (estimate: weight, size etc) apprécier; (consider) estimer

judo ['dʒuːdəu] n judo m

jug [dʒʌg] n pot m, cruche f

juggle ['dʒʌgl] vi jongler; **juggler** n jongleur m

juice [dʒuːs] n jus m; **juicy** adj juteux(-euse)

Jul abbr (= July) juil

July [dʒuː'laɪ] n juillet m

jumble ['dʒʌmbl] n fouillis m ▷ vt (also: **~ up, ~ together**) mélanger, brouiller; **jumble sale** n (BRIT) vente f de charité

JUMBLE SALE

- Les **jumble sales** ont lieu dans les
- églises, salles des fêtes ou halls
- d'écoles, et l'on y vend des articles
- de toutes sortes, en général bon
- marché et surtout d'occasion, pour
- collecter des fonds pour une œuvre
- de charité, une école (par exemple,
- pour acheter un ordinateur), ou
- encore une église (pour réparer un
- toit etc).

jumbo ['dʒʌmbəu] adj (also: **~ jet**) (avion) gros porteur (à réaction)

jump [dʒʌmp] vi sauter, bondir; (with fear etc) sursauter; (increase) monter en flèche ▷ vt sauter, franchir ▷ n saut m, bond m; (with fear etc) sursaut m; (fence) obstacle m; **to ~ the queue** (BRIT) passer avant son tour

jumper ['dʒʌmpə*] n (BRIT: pullover) pull-over m; (US: pinafore dress) robe-chasuble f

jump leads (US **jumper cables**) npl câbles mpl de démarrage

Jun. abbr = **June**; **junior**

junction ['dʒʌŋkʃən] n (BRIT:

of roads) carrefour *m; (of rails)*
embranchement *m*

June [dʒuːn] *n* juin *m*

jungle ['dʒʌŋɡl] *n* jungle *f*

junior ['dʒuːnɪə*] *adj, n*: **he's ~ to me
(by 2 years), he's my ~ (by 2 years)**
il est mon cadet (de 2 ans), il est plus
jeune que moi (de 2 ans); **he's ~ to me**
(seniority) il est en dessous de moi *(dans
la hiérarchie),* j'ai plus d'ancienneté que
lui; **junior high school** *n (US)* = collège
m d'enseignement secondaire; *see also*
high school; junior school *n* (BRIT)
école *f* primaire, cours moyen

junk [dʒʌŋk] *n (rubbish)* camelote *f;
(cheap goods)* bric-à-brac *m inv;* **junk
food** *n* snacks vite prêts *(sans valeur
nutritive)*

junkie ['dʒʌŋkɪ] *n (inf)* junkie *m,*
drogué(e)

junk mail *n* prospectus *mpl; (Comput)*
messages *mpl* publicitaires

Jupiter ['dʒuːpɪtə*] *n (planet)* Jupiter *f*

jurisdiction [dʒuərɪs'dɪkʃən] *n*
juridiction *f;* **it falls or comes within/
outside our ~** cela est/n'est pas de
notre compétence or ressort

jury ['dʒuərɪ] *n* jury *m*

just [dʒʌst] *adj* juste ▷ *adv*: **he's ~ done
it/left** il vient de le faire/partir; **~
right/two o'clock** exactement or juste
ce qu'il faut/deux heures; **we were ~
going** nous partions; **I was ~ about to
phone** j'allais téléphoner; **~ as he was
leaving** au moment or à l'instant précis
où il partait; **~ before/enough/here**
juste avant/assez/là; **it's ~ me/a
mistake** ce n'est que moi/(rien) qu'une
erreur; **~ missed/caught** manqué/
attrapé de justesse; **~ listen to this!**
écoutez un peu ça!; **she's ~ as clever
as you** elle est tout aussi intelligente
que vous; **it's ~ as well that you ...**
heureusement que vous ...; **~ a
minute!, ~ one moment!** un instant
(s'il vous plaît)!

justice ['dʒʌstɪs] *n* justice *f; (US: judge)*
juge *m* de la Cour suprême

justification [dʒʌstɪfɪ'keɪʃən] *n*
justification *f*

justify ['dʒʌstɪfaɪ] *vt* justifier

jut [dʒʌt] *vi (also: ~ out)* dépasser,
faire saillie

juvenile ['dʒuːvənaɪl] *adj* juvénile;
(court, books) pour enfants ▷ *n*
adolescent(e)

K

K, k [keɪ] *abbr* (= *one thousand*) K;
(= *kilobyte*) Ko

kangaroo [kæŋgə'ruː] *n* kangourou *m*

karaoke [kɑːrə'əʊkɪ] *n* karaoké *m*

karate [kə'rɑːtɪ] *n* karaté *m*

kebab [kə'bæb] *n* kébab *m*

keel [kiːl] *n* quille *f*; **on an even ~**
(*fig*) à flot

keen [kiːn] *adj* (*eager*) plein(e)
d'enthousiasme; (*interest, desire,
competition*) vif (vive); (*eye, intelligence*)
pénétrant(e); (*edge*) effilé(e); **to be ~ to
do** *or* **on doing sth** désirer vivement
faire qch, tenir beaucoup à faire qch;
to be ~ on sth/sb aimer beaucoup
qch/qn

keep [kiːp] (*pt, pp* **kept**) *vt* (*retain,
preserve*) garder; (*hold back*) retenir;
(*shop, accounts, promise, diary*) tenir;
(*support*) entretenir; (*chickens, bees,
pigs etc*) élever ▷ *vi* (*food*) se conserver;
(*remain: in a certain state or place*)
rester ▷ *n* (*of castle*) donjon *m*; (*food
etc*): **enough for his ~** assez pour

(*assurer*) sa subsistance; **to ~ doing
sth** (*continue*) continuer à faire qch;
(*repeatedly*) ne pas arrêter de faire
qch; **to ~ sb from doing/sth from
happening** empêcher qn de faire *or* que
qn (ne) fasse/que qch (n')arrive; **to ~ sb
happy/a place tidy** faire que qn soit
content/qu'un endroit reste propre; **to
~ sth to o.s.** garder qch pour soi, tenir
qch secret; **to ~ sth from sb** cacher qch
à qn; **to ~ time** (*clock*) être à l'heure,
ne pas retarder; **for ~s** (*inf*) pour de
bon, pour toujours; **keep away** *vt*: **to
~ sth/sb away from sb** tenir qch/qn
éloigné de qn ▷ *vi*: **to ~ away (from)**
ne pas s'approcher (de); **keep back** *vt*
(*crowds, tears, money*) retenir; (*conceal:
information*): **to ~ sth back from sb**
cacher qch à qn ▷ *vi* rester en arrière;
keep off *vt* (*dog, person*) éloigner ▷ *vi*: **if
the rain ~s off** s'il ne pleut pas; **"~ your
hands off!** (*inf*): **"~ your
hands off!"** pas touche! (*inf*); **"~ off the
grass"** "pelouse interdite"; **keep on** *vi*
continuer; **to ~ on doing** continuer à
faire; **don't ~ on about it!** arrête (d'en
parler)!; **keep out** *vt* empêcher d'entrer
▷ *vi* (*stay out*) rester en dehors; **"~ out"**
"défense d'entrer"; **keep up** *vi* (*fig: in
comprehension*) suivre ▷ *vt* continuer,
maintenir; **to ~ up with sb** (*in work
etc*) se maintenir au même niveau
que qn; (*in race etc*) aller aussi vite que
qn; **keeper** *n* gardien(ne); **keep-fit** *n*
gymnastique *f* (d'entretien); **keeping**
n (*care*) garde *f*; **in keeping with** en
keeping with

kennel ['kɛnl] *n* niche *f*; **kennels** *npl*
(*for boarding*) chenil *m*

Kenya ['kɛnjə] *n* Kenya *m*

kept [kɛpt] *pt, pp* of **keep**

kerb [kəːb] *n* (*BRIT*) bordure *f* du trottoir

kerosene ['kɛrəsiːn] *n* kérosène *m*

ketchup ['kɛtʃəp] *n* ketchup *m*

kettle ['kɛtl] *n* bouilloire *f*

key [kiː] *n* (*gen, Mus*) clé *f*; (*of piano,
typewriter*) touche *f*; (*on map*) légende
f ▷ *adj* (*factor, role, area*) clé *inv* ▷ *vt*
(*also: ~ in: text*) saisir; **can I have my**

~? je peux avoir ma clé?; **a ~ issue** un problème fondamental; **keyboard** n clavier m; **keyhole** n trou m de la serrure; **keyring** n porte-clés m

kg abbr (= kilogram) K

khaki ['kɑːkɪ] adj, n kaki m

kick [kɪk] vt donner un coup de pied à ▷ vi (horse) ruer ▷ n coup m de pied; (inf: thrill): **he does it for ~s** il le fait parce que ça l'excite, il le fait pour le plaisir; **to ~ the habit** (inf) arrêter; **kick off** vi (Sport) donner le coup d'envoi; **kick-off** n (Sport) coup m d'envoi

kid [kɪd] n (inf: child) gamin(e), gosse m/f; (animal, leather) chevreau m ▷ vi (inf) plaisanter, blaguer

kidnap ['kɪdnæp] vt enlever, kidnapper; **kidnapping** n enlèvement m

kidney ['kɪdnɪ] n (Anat) rein m; (Culin) rognon m; **kidney bean** n haricot m rouge

kill [kɪl] vt tuer ▷ n mise fà mort; **to ~ time** tuer le temps; **killer** n tueur(-euse); (murderer) meurtrier(-ière); **killing** n meurtre m; (of group of people) tuerie f, massacre m; (inf): **to make a killing** se remplir les poches, réussir un beau coup

kiln [kɪln] n four m

kilo ['kiːləu] n kilo m; **kilobyte** n (Comput) kilo-octet m; **kilogram(me)** n kilogramme m; **kilometre** (us **kilometer**) ['kɪləmiːtəʳ] n kilomètre m; **kilowatt** n kilowatt m

kilt [kɪlt] n kilt m

kin [kɪn] n see **next-of-kin**

kind [kaɪnd] adj gentil(le), aimable ▷ n sorte f, espèce f; (species) genre m; **to be two of a ~** se ressembler; **in ~** (Comm) en nature; **~ of** (inf: rather) plutôt; **a ~ of** une sorte de, une espèce de; **what ~ of …?** quelle sorte de …?

kindergarten ['kɪndəgɑːtn] n jardin m d'enfants

kindly ['kaɪndlɪ] adj bienveillant(e), plein(e) de gentillesse ▷ adv avec bonté; **will you ~ …** auriez-vous la bonté ou l'obligeance de …

kindness ['kaɪndnɪs] n (quality) bonté f, gentillesse f

king [kɪŋ] n roi m; **kingdom** n royaume m; **kingfisher** n martin-pêcheur m; **king-size(d) bed** n grand lit (de 1,95 m de large)

kiosk ['kiːɔsk] n kiosque m; (BRIT: also: **telephone ~**) cabine f (téléphonique)

kipper ['kɪpəʳ] n hareng fumé et salé

kiss [kɪs] n baiser m ▷ vt embrasser; **to ~ (each other)** s'embrasser; **kiss of life** n (BRIT) bouche à bouche m

kit [kɪt] n équipement m, matériel m; (set of tools etc) trousse f; (for assembly) kit m

kitchen ['kɪtʃɪn] n cuisine f

kite [kaɪt] n (toy) cerf-volant m

kitten ['kɪtn] n petit chat, chaton m

kitty ['kɪtɪ] n (money) cagnotte f

kiwi ['kiːwiː] n (also: **~ fruit**) kiwi m

km abbr (= kilometre) km

km/h abbr (= kilometres per hour) km/h

knack [næk] n: **to have the ~ (of doing)** avoir le coup (pour faire)

knee [niː] n genou m; **kneecap** n rotule f

kneel [niːl] (pt, pp **knelt**) [niːl, nɛlt] vi (also: **~ down**) s'agenouiller

knelt [nɛlt] pt, pp of **kneel**

knew [njuː] pt of **know**

knickers ['nɪkəz] npl (BRIT) culotte f (de femme)

knife [naɪf] n (pl **knives**) couteau m ▷ vt poignarder, frapper d'un coup de couteau

knight [naɪt] n chevalier m; (Chess) cavalier m

knit [nɪt] vt tricoter ▷ vi tricoter; (broken bones) se ressouder; **to ~ one's brows** froncer les sourcils; **knitting** n tricot m; **knitting needle** n aiguille f à tricoter; **knitwear** n tricots mpl, lainages mpl

knives [naɪvz] npl of **knife**

knob [nɔb] n bouton m; (BRIT): **a ~ of butter** une noix de beurre

knock [nɔk] vt frapper; (bump into) heurter; (fig: col) dénigrer ▷ vi (at

door etc): **to ~ at/on** frapper à/sur ▷ *n*
coup *m*; **knock down** *vt* renverser;
(price) réduire; **knock off** *vi (inf: finish)*
s'arrêter (de travailler) ▷ *vt (vase,
object)* faire tomber; *(inf: steal)* piquer;
(fig: from price etc): **to ~ off £10** faire
une remise de 10 livres; **knock out**
vt assommer; *(Boxing)* mettre k.-o.;
(in competition) éliminer; **knock over**
vt (object) faire tomber; *(pedestrian)*
renverser; **knockout** *n (Boxing)* knockout *m*, K.-O. *m*; **knockout competition**
(BRIT) compétition *f* avec épreuves
éliminatoires

knot [nɔt] *n (gen)* nœud *m* ▷ *vt* nouer
know [nəu] *vt (pt* **knew**, *pp* **~n**) savoir;
(person, place) connaître; **to ~ that**
savoir que; **to ~ how to do** savoir faire;
to ~ how to swim savoir nager; **to ~
about/of sth** *(event)* être au courant
de qch; *(subject)* connaître qch; **I don't
~** je ne sais pas; **do you ~ where I
can ...?** savez-vous où je peux ...?;
know-all *n* (BRIT *pej*) je-sais-tout
m/f; **know-how** *n* savoir-faire *m*,
technique *f*, compétence *f*; **knowing**
adj (look etc) entendu(e); **knowingly**
adv (on purpose) sciemment; *(smile, look)*
d'un air entendu; **know-it-all** *n* (US)
= know-all

knowledge ['nɔlidʒ] *n* connaissance
f; *(learning)* connaissances, savoir
m; **without my ~** à mon insu;
knowledgeable *adj* bien informé(e)
known [nəun] *pp* of **know** ▷ *adj (thief,
facts)* notoire; *(expert)* célèbre
knuckle ['nʌkl] *n* articulation *f* (des
phalanges), jointure *f*
koala [kəu'ɑːlə] *n (also:* **~ bear**) koala *m*
Koran [kɔ'rɑːn] *n* Coran *m*
Korea [kɔ'riːə] *n* Corée *f*; **Korean** *adj*
coréen(ne) ▷ *n* Coréen(ne)
kosher ['kəuʃə'] *adj* kascher *inv*
Kosovar, Kosovan ['kɒsəvɑː',
'kɒsəvan] *adj* kosovar(e)
Kosovo ['kɒsəvəu] *n* Kosovo *m*
Kuwait [ku'weit] *n* Koweït *m*

L *abbr* (BRIT Aut: *= learner*) signale un
conducteur débutant
l. *abbr (= litre)* l
lab [læb] *n abbr (= laboratory)* labo *m*
label ['leibl] *n* étiquette *f*; *(brand: of
record)* marque *f* ▷ *vt* étiqueter
labor *etc* ['leibər'] *(US)* **= labour** *etc*
laboratory [lə'bɒrətəri] *n* laboratoire *m*
Labor Day *(US, CANADA)* fête *f* du
travail *(le premier lundi de septembre)*

● **LABOR DAY**
●
● La fête du Travail aux États-Unis et au
● Canada est fixée au premier lundi de
● septembre. Instituée par le Congrès
● en 1894 après avoir été réclamée par
● les mouvements ouvriers pendant
● douze ans, elle a perdu une grande
● partie de son caractère politique
● pour devenir un jour férié assez
● ordinaire et l'occasion de partir pour
● un long week-end avant la rentrée
● des classes.

labor union n (US) syndicat m

Labour ['leɪbəʳ] n (BRIT Pol: also: **the ~ Party**) le parti travailliste, les travaillistes mpl

labour (US **labor**) ['leɪbəʳ] n (work) travail m; (workforce) main-d'œuvre f ▷ vi: **to ~ (at)** travailler dur (à), peiner (sur) ▷ vt: **to ~ a point** insister sur un point; **in ~** (Med) en travail; **labourer** n manœuvre m; **farm labourer** ouvrier m agricole

lace [leɪs] n dentelle f; (of shoe etc) lacet m ▷ vt (shoe: also: **~ up**) lacer

lack [læk] n manque m ▷ vt manquer de; **through** or **for ~ of** faute de, par manque de; **to be ~ing** manquer, faire défaut; **to be ~ing in** manquer de

lacquer ['lækəʳ] n laque f

lacy ['leɪsɪ] adj (of lace) en dentelle; (like lace) comme de la dentelle

lad [læd] n garçon m, gars m

ladder ['lædəʳ] n échelle f; (BRIT: in tights) maille filée f ▷ vt, vi (BRIT: tights) filer

ladle ['leɪdl] n louche f

lady ['leɪdɪ] n dame f; **"ladies and gentlemen..."** "Mesdames (et) Messieurs..."; **young ~** jeune fille f; (married) jeune femme f; **the ladies' (room)** les toilettes fpl des dames; **ladybird** (US **ladybug**) n coccinelle f

lag [læg] n retard m ▷ vi (also: **~ behind**) rester en arrière, traîner; (fig) rester à la traîne ▷ vt (pipes) calorifuger

lager ['lɑːgəʳ] n bière f blonde

lagoon [lə'guːn] n lagune f

laid [leɪd] pt, pp of **lay**; **laid back** adj (inf) relaxe, décontracté(e)

lain [leɪn] pp of **lie**

lake [leɪk] n lac m

lamb [læm] n agneau m

lame [leɪm] adj (also fig) boiteux(-euse)

lament [lə'ment] n lamentation f ▷ vt pleurer, se lamenter sur

lamp [læmp] n lampe f; **lamppost** n (BRIT) réverbère m; **lampshade** n abat-jour m inv

land [lænd] n (as opposed to sea)

terre f (ferme); (country) pays m; (soil) terre; (piece of land) terrain m; (estate) terre(s), domaine(s) m(pl) ▷ vi (from ship) débarquer; (Aviat) atterrir; (fig: fall) (re)tomber ▷ vt (passengers, goods) débarquer; (obtain) décrocher; **to ~ sb with sth** (inf) coller qch à qn; **landing** n (from ship) débarquement m; (Aviat) atterrissage m; (of staircase) palier m; **landing card** n carte f de débarquement; **landlady** n propriétaire f, logeuse f; (of pub) patronne f; **landlord** n propriétaire m, logeur m; (of pub etc) patron m; **landmark** n (point m de) repère m; **to be a landmark** (fig) faire date ou époque; **landowner** n propriétaire foncier ou terrien; **landscape** n paysage m; **landslide** n (Geo) glissement m (de terrain); (fig: Pol) raz-de-marée (électoral)

lane [leɪn] n (in country) chemin m; (Aut: of road) voie f; (: line of traffic) file f; (in race) couloir m

language ['læŋgwɪdʒ] n langue f; (way one speaks) langage m; **what ~ do you speak?** quelles langues parlez-vous?; **bad ~** grossièretés fpl, langage grossier; **language laboratory** n laboratoire m de langues; **language school** n école f de langue

lantern ['læntn] n lanterne f

lap [læp] n (of track) tour m de piste; (of body): **in** or **on one's ~** sur les genoux ▷ vt (also: **~ up**) laper ▷ vi (waves) clapoter

lapel [lə'pel] n revers m

lapse [læps] n défaillance f; (in behaviour) écart m (de conduite) ▷ vi (Law) cesser d'être en vigueur; (contract) expirer; **to ~ into bad habits** prendre de mauvaises habitudes; **~ of time** laps m de temps, intervalle m

laptop (computer) ['læptɔp-] n portable m

lard [lɑːd] n saindoux m

larder ['lɑːdəʳ] n garde-manger m inv

large [lɑːdʒ] adj grand(e); (person,

animal) gros (grosse); **at ~** (*free*) en liberté; (*generally*) en général; pour la plupart; *see also* **by; largely** *adv* en grande partie; (*principally*) surtout; **large-scale** *adj* (*map, drawing etc*) à grande échelle; (*fig*) important(e)

lark [lɑːk] *n* (*bird*) alouette *f*; (*joke*) blague *f*, farce *f*

laryngitis [lærɪnˈdʒaɪtɪs] *n* laryngite *f*

lasagne [ləˈzænjə] *n* lasagne *f*

laser [ˈleɪzə*] *n* laser *m*; **laser printer** *n* imprimante *f* laser

lash [læʃ] *n* coup *m* de fouet; (*also:* **eye~**) cil *m* ▷ *vt* fouetter; (*tie*) attacher; **lash out** *vi:* **to ~ out** (**at** *or* **against sb/sth**) attaquer violemment (qn/qch)

lass [læs] (BRIT) *n* (*jeune*) fille *f*

last [lɑːst] *adj* dernier(-ière) ▷ *adv* en dernier; (*most recently*) la dernière fois; (*finally*) finalement ▷ *vi* durer; **~ week** la semaine dernière; **~ night** (*evening*) hier soir; (*night*) la nuit dernière; **at ~** enfin; **~ but one** avant-dernier(-ière); **lastly** *adv* en dernier lieu, pour finir; **last-minute** *adj* de dernière minute

latch [lætʃ] *n* loquet *m*; **latch onto** *vt fus* (*cling to: person, group*) s'accrocher à; (*idea*) se mettre en tête

late [leɪt] *adj* (*not on time*) en retard; (*far on in day etc*) tardif(-ive); (*: edition, delivery*) dernier(-ière); (*dead*) défunt(e) ▷ *adv* tard; (*behind time, schedule*) en retard; **to be 10 minutes ~** avoir 10 minutes de retard; **sorry I'm ~** désolé d'être en retard; **it's too ~** il est trop tard; **of ~** dernièrement; **in ~ May** vers la fin (du mois) de mai, fin mai; **the ~ Mr X** feu M. X; **latecomer** *n* retardataire *m/f*; **lately** *adv* récemment; **later** *adj* (*date etc*) ultérieur(e); (*version etc*) plus récent(e) ▷ *adv* plus tard; **latest** [ˈleɪtɪst] *adj* tout(e) dernier(-ière); **at the latest** au plus tard

lather [ˈlɑːðə*] *n* mousse *f* (de savon) ▷ *vt* savonner

Latin [ˈlætɪn] *n* latin *m* ▷ *adj* latin(e); **Latin America** *n* Amérique latine;

Latin American *adj* latino-américain(e), d'Amérique latine ▷ *n* Latino-Américain(e)

latitude [ˈlætɪtjuːd] *n* (*also fig*) latitude *f*

latter [ˈlætə*] *adj* deuxième, dernier(-ière) ▷ *n:* **the ~** ce dernier, celui-ci

laugh [lɑːf] *n* rire *m* ▷ *vi* rire; **(to do sth) for a ~** (faire qch) pour rire; **laugh at** *vt fus* se moquer de; (*joke*) rire de; **laughter** *n* rire *m*; (*of several people*) rires *mpl*

launch [lɔːntʃ] *n* lancement *m*; (*also:* **motor~**) vedette *f* ▷ *vt* (*ship, rocket, plan*) lancer; **launch into** *vt fus* se lancer dans

launder [ˈlɔːndə*] *vt* laver; (*fig: money*) blanchir

Launderette® [lɔːnˈdrɛt] (BRIT) (US **Laundromat®** [ˈlɔːndrəmæt]) *n* laverie *f* (automatique)

laundry [ˈlɔːndrɪ] *n* (*clothes*) linge *m*; (*business*) blanchisserie *f*; (*room*) buanderie *f*; **to do the ~** faire la lessive

lava [ˈlɑːvə] *n* lave *f*

lavatory [ˈlævətərɪ] *n* toilettes *fpl*

lavender [ˈlævəndə*] *n* lavande *f*

lavish [ˈlævɪʃ] *adj* copieux(-euse); (*person: giving freely*): **~ with** prodigue de ▷ *vt:* **to ~ sth on sb** prodiguer qch à qn; (*money*) dépenser qch sans compter pour qn

law [lɔː] *n* loi *f*; (*science*) droit *m*; **lawful** *adj* légal(e), permis(e); **lawless** *adj* (*action*) illégal(e); (*place*) sans loi

lawn [lɔːn] *n* pelouse *f*; **lawnmower** *n* tondeuse *f* à gazon

lawsuit [ˈlɔːsuːt] *n* procès *m*

lawyer [ˈlɔːjə*] *n* (*consultant, with company*) juriste *m*; (*for sales, wills etc*) ≈ notaire *m*; (*partner, in court*) ≈ avocat *m*

lax [læks] *adj* relâché(e)

laxative [ˈlæksətɪv] *n* laxatif *m*

lay [leɪ] *pt of* **lie** ▷ *adj* laïque; (*not expert*) profane ▷ *vt* (*pt, pp* **laid**) poser, mettre; (*eggs*) pondre; (*trap*) tendre; (*plans*) élaborer; **to ~ the table** mettre la table;

lay down vt poser; (*rules etc*) établir; **to ~ down the law** (*fig*) faire la loi; **lay off** vt (*workers*) licencier; (*provide: meal etc*) fournir; **lay out** vt (*design*) dessiner, concevoir; (*display*) disposer; (*spend*) dépenser; **lay-by** n (BRIT) aire f de stationnement (sur le bas-côté)

layer ['leɪə'] n couche f

layman ['leɪmən] (*irreg*) n (Rel) laïque m; (*non-expert*) profane m

layout ['leɪaʊt] n disposition f, plan m, agencement m; (Press) mise f en page

lazy ['leɪzɪ] adj paresseux(-euse)

lb. abbr (*weight*) = **pound**

lead[1] [liːd] n (*front position*) tête f; (*distance, time ahead*) avance f; (*clue*) piste f; (Elec) fil m; (*for dog*) laisse f; (Theat) rôle principal ▷ vb (*pt, pp* **led**) ▷ vt (*guide*) mener, conduire; (*be leader of*) être à la tête de ▷ vi (*road, pipe*) mener à, conduire à; (*result in*) conduire à; aboutir à; **to be in the ~** (Sport: *in race*) mener, être en tête; (*in match*) mener (à la marque); **to ~ sb to do sth** amener qn à faire qch; **to ~ the way** montrer le chemin; **lead up to** vt conduire à; (*in conversation*) en venir à

lead[2] [lɛd] n (*metal*) plomb m; (*in pencil*) mine f

leader ['liːdə'] n (*of team*) chef m; (*of party etc*) dirigeant(e), leader m; (Sport: *in league*) leader m; (: *in race*) coureur m de tête; **leadership** n (*position*) direction f; **under the leadership of ...** sous la direction de ...; **qualities of leadership** qualités fpl de chef or de meneur

lead-free ['lɛdfriː] adj sans plomb

leading ['liːdɪŋ] adj de premier plan; (*main*) principal(e); (*in race*) de tête

lead singer [liːd-] n (*in pop group*) (chanteur m) vedette f

leaf (*pl* **leaves**) [liːf, liːvz] n feuille f; (*of table*) rallonge f; **to turn over a new ~** (*fig*) changer de conduite or d'existence; **leaf through** vt (*book*) feuilleter

leaflet ['liːflɪt] n prospectus m, brochure f; (Pol, Rel) tract m

league [liːg] n ligue f; (Football) championnat m; **to be in ~ with** avoir partie liée avec, être de mèche avec

leak [liːk] n (*out: also: fig*) fuite f ▷ vi (*pipe, liquid etc*) fuir; (*shoes*) prendre l'eau; (*ship*) faire eau ▷ vt (*liquid*) répandre; (*information*) divulguer

lean [liːn] adj maigre ▷ vb (*pt, pp* **~ed** or **~t**) ▷ vt: **to ~ sth on** appuyer qch sur ▷ vi (*slope*) pencher; (*rest*): **to ~ against** s'appuyer contre; être appuyé(e) contre; **to ~ on** s'appuyer sur; **lean forward** vi se pencher en avant; **lean over** vi se pencher; **leaning** n: **leaning (towards)** penchant m (pour)

leant [lɛnt] pt, pp of **lean**

leap [liːp] n bond m, saut m ▷ vi (*pt, pp* **~ed** or **~t**) bondir, sauter

leapt [lɛpt] pt, pp of **leap**

leap year n année f bissextile

learn (*pt, pp* **~ed** or **~t**) [ləːn, -t] vt, vi apprendre; **to ~ (how) to do sth** apprendre à faire qch; **to ~ about sth** (Scol) étudier qch; (*hear, read*) apprendre qch; **learner** n débutant(e); (BRIT: *also:* **learner driver**) (conducteur(-trice) débutant(e)); **learning** n savoir m

learnt [ləːnt] pp of **learn**

lease [liːs] n bail m ▷ vt louer à bail

leash [liːʃ] n laisse f

least [liːst] adj: **the ~** (+ *noun*) (la) plus petit(e), le (la) moindre; (*smallest amount of*) le moins de ▷ pron: (*the*) **~ le moins** ▷ adv (+ *verb*) le moins; (+ *adj*): **the ~** (la) moins; (*the* ~ **money** le moins d'argent; **the ~ expensive** le (la) moins cher (chère); **the ~ possible effort** le moins d'effort possible; **at ~** au moins; (*or rather*) du moins; **you could at ~ have written** tu aurais au moins pu écrire; **not in the ~** pas le moins du monde

leather ['lɛðə'] n cuir m

leave [liːv] (*pt, pp* **left**) vt laisser; (*go away from*) quitter; (*forget*) oublier ▷ vi partir, s'en aller ▷ n (*time off*) congé m; (Mil, *also: consent*) permission f; **what time does the train/bus ~?** le train/le bus part à quelle heure?; **to ~ sth to sb** (money etc) laisser qch à qn; **to be left** rester; **there's some milk left over** il reste du lait; **~ it to me!** laissez-moi faire!, je m'en occupe!; **on ~** en permission; **leave behind** vt (also fig) laisser; (forget) laisser, oublier; **leave out** vt oublier, omettre

leaves [liːvz] npl of **leaf**

Lebanon ['lebənən] n Liban m

lecture ['lektʃəʳ] n conférence f; (Scol) cours (magistral) ▷ vi donner des cours; enseigner ▷ vt (scold) sermonner, réprimander; **to give a ~ (on)** faire une conférence (sur), faire un cours (sur); **lecture hall** n amphithéâtre m; **lecturer** n (speaker) conférencier(-ière); (BRIT: at university) professeur m (d'université), prof m/f de fac (inf); **lecture theatre** n = **lecture hall**

> Be careful not to translate lecture by the French word lecture.

led [led] pt, pp of **lead**

ledge [ledʒ] n (of window, on wall) rebord m; (of mountain) saillie f, corniche f

leek [liːk] n poireau m

left [left] pt, pp of **leave** ▷ adj gauche ▷ adv à gauche ▷ n gauche f; **there are two ~** il en reste deux; **on the ~, to the ~** à gauche; **the L~** (Pol) la gauche; **left-hand** adj: **the left-hand side** la gauche; **left-hand drive** n (BRIT: vehicle) véhicule m avec la conduite à gauche; **left-handed** adj gaucher(-ère); (scissors etc) pour gauchers; **left-luggage locker** n (BRIT) (casier m à) consigne f automatique; **left-luggage (office)** n (BRIT) consigne f; **left-overs** npl restes mpl; **left-wing** adj (Pol) de gauche

leg [leg] n jambe f; (of animal) patte f; (of furniture) pied m; (Culin: of chicken) cuisse f; (of journey) étape f; **1st- ~ and - 2nd ~** (Sport) match m aller/retour; **~ of lamb** (Culin) gigot m d'agneau

legacy ['legəsɪ] n (also fig) héritage m, legs m

legal ['liːgl] adj (permitted by law) légal(e); (relating to law) juridique; **legal holiday** (US) n jour férié; **legalize** vt légaliser; **legally** adv légalement

legend ['ledʒənd] n légende f; **legendary** ['ledʒəndrɪ] adj légendaire

leggings ['legɪŋz] npl caleçon m

legible ['ledʒəbl] adj lisible

legislation [ledʒɪs'leɪʃən] n législation f

legislative ['ledʒɪslətɪv] adj législatif(-ive)

legitimate [lɪ'dʒɪtɪmət] adj légitime

leisure ['leʒəʳ] n (free time) temps libre, loisirs mpl; **at ~** (tout) à loisir; **at your ~** (later) à tête reposée; **leisure centre** n (BRIT) centre m de loisirs; **leisurely** adj tranquille, fait(e) sans se presser

lemon ['lemən] n citron m; **lemonade** n (fizzy) limonade f; **lemon tea** n thé m au citron

lend (pt, pp **lent**) [lend, lent] vt: **to ~ sth (to sb)** prêter qch (à qn); **could you ~ me some money?** pourriez-vous me prêter de l'argent?

length [leŋθ] n longueur f; (section: of road, pipe etc) morceau m, bout m; **~ of time** durée f; **it is 2 metres in ~** cela fait 2 mètres de long; **at ~** (at last) enfin, à la fin; (lengthily) longuement; **lengthen** vt allonger, prolonger ▷ vi s'allonger; **lengthways** adv dans le sens de la longueur, en long; **lengthy** adj (très) long (longue)

lens [lenz] n (of spectacles) verre m; (of camera) objectif m

Lent [lent] n carême m

lent [lent] pt, pp of **lend**

lentil ['lentl] n lentille f

Leo ['liːəu] n le Lion

leopard ['lepəd] n léopard m

leotard ['liːətɑːd] n justaucorps m

leprosy ['leprəsɪ] n lèpre f

lesbian ['lezbɪən] n lesbienne f ▷ adj lesbien(ne)

less [les] adj moins de ▷ pron, adv moins ▷ prep: **~ tax/10% discount** avant impôt/moins 10% de remise; **~ than**

that/you moins que cela/vous; **~ than half** moins de la moitié; **~ than ever** moins que jamais; **~ and ~** de moins en moins; **the ~ he works ...** moins il travaille ...; **lessen** vi diminuer, s'amoindrir, s'atténuer ▷ vt diminuer, réduire, atténuer; **lesser** ['lɛsə'] adj moindre; **to a lesser extent** or **degree** à un degré moindre

lesson ['lɛsn] n leçon f; **to teach sb a ~** (fig) donner une bonne leçon à qn

let (pt, pp ~) [lɛt] vt laisser; (BRIT: lease) louer; **to ~ sb do sth** laisser qn faire qch; **to ~ sb know sth** faire savoir qch à qn, prévenir qn de qch; **to ~ go** lâcher prise; **to ~ go of sth** lâcher qch; **to ~ sth go** lâcher qch; **~'s go** allons-y; **~ him come** qu'il vienne; **"to ~"** (BRIT) "à louer"; **let down** vt (lower) baisser; (BRIT: tyre) dégonfler; (disappoint) décevoir; **let in** vt laisser entrer; (visitor etc) faire entrer; **let off** vt (allow to leave) laisser partir; (not punish) ne pas punir; (firework etc) faire partir; (bomb) faire exploser; **let out** vt laisser sortir; (scream) laisser échapper; (BRIT: rent out) louer

lethal ['li:θl] adj mortel(le), fatal(e); (weapon) meurtrier(-ère)

letter ['lɛtə'] n lettre f; **letterbox** n (BRIT) boîte f aux or à lettres

lettuce ['lɛtɪs] n laitue f, salade f

leukaemia (us **leukemia**) [lu:'ki:mɪə] n leucémie f

level ['lɛvl] adj (flat) plat(e), plan(e), uni(e); (horizontal) horizontal(e) ▷ n niveau m ▷ vt niveler, aplanir; **"A ~s** npl (BRIT) ≈ baccalauréat m; **to be ~ with** être au même niveau que; **to draw ~ with** (runner, car) arriver à la hauteur de, rattraper; **on the ~** (fig: honest) régulier(-ère); **level crossing** n (BRIT) passage m à niveau

lever ['li:və'] n levier m; **leverage** n (influence): **leverage (on** or **with)** prise f (sur)

levy ['lɛvɪ] n taxe f, impôt m ▷ vt (tax) lever; (fine) infliger

liability [laɪə'bɪlətɪ] n responsabilité f;

(handicap) handicap m

liable ['laɪəbl] adj (subject): **~ to** sujet(te) à, passible de; (responsible): **~ (for)** responsable de(); (likely): **~ to do** susceptible de faire

liaise [li:'eɪz] vi: **to ~ with** assurer la liaison avec

liar ['laɪə'] n menteur(-euse)

libel ['laɪbl] n (document) écrit m diffamatoire ▷ vt diffamer

liberal ['lɪbərl] adj libéral(e); (generous): **~ with** prodigue de, généreux(-euse) avec ▷ n: **L~** (Pol) libéral(e); **Liberal Democrat** n (BRIT) libéral-démocrate m/f

liberate ['lɪbəreɪt] vt libérer

liberation [lɪbə'reɪʃən] n libération f

liberty ['lɪbətɪ] n liberté f; **to be at ~** (criminal) être en liberté; **at ~ to do** libre de faire; **to take the ~ of** prendre la liberté de, se permettre de

Libra ['li:brə] n la Balance

librarian [laɪ'brɛərɪən] n bibliothécaire m/f

library ['laɪbrərɪ] n bibliothèque f

> ❚ Be careful not to translate **library** by the French word **librairie**.

Libya ['lɪbɪə] n Libye f

lice [laɪs] npl of **louse**

licence (us **license**) ['laɪsns] n autorisation f, permis m; (Comm) licence f; (Radio, TV) redevance f; (also: **driving ~**, us: also: **driver's license**) permis m de conduire)

license ['laɪsns] n (us) = **licence**; **licensed** adj (for alcohol) patenté(e) pour la vente des spiritueux, qui a une patente de débit de boissons; (car) muni(e) de la vignette; **license plate** n (us Aut) plaque f minéralogique; **licensing hours** (BRIT) npl heures fpl d'ouvertures (des pubs)

lick [lɪk] vt lécher; (inf: defeat) écraser, flanquer une piquette or raclée à; **to ~ one's lips** (fig) se frotter les mains

lid [lɪd] n couvercle m; (eyelid) paupière f

lie [laɪ] n mensonge m ▷ vi (pt, pp ~d) (tell lies) mentir; (pt **lay**, pp **lain**) *(rest)* être étendu(e) *or* allongé(e) *or* couché(e); *(object: be situated)* se trouver, être; **to ~ low** *(fig)* se cacher, rester caché(e); **lie about, lie around** *vi (things)* traîner; *(BRIT: person)* traînasser, flemmarder; **lie down** *vi* se coucher, s'étendre

Liechtenstein ['lɪktənstaɪn] *n* Liechtenstein *m*

lie-in ['laɪɪn] *n (BRIT)*: **to have a ~** faire la grasse matinée

lieutenant [lef'tɛnənt, *US* lu:'tɛnənt] *n* lieutenant *m*

life *(pl* **lives)** [laɪf, laɪvz] *n* vie *f*; **to come to ~** *(fig)* s'animer; **life assurance** *n (BRIT)* = **life insurance**; **lifeboat** *n* canot *m or* chaloupe *f* de sauvetage; **lifeguard** *n* surveillant *m* de baignade; **life insurance** *n* assurance-vie *f*; **life jacket** *n* gilet *m or* ceinture *f* de sauvetage; **lifelike** *adj* qui semble vrai(e) *or* vivant(e), ressemblant(e); *(painting)* réaliste; **life preserver** *n (US)* gilet *m or* ceinture *f* de sauvetage; **life sentence** *n* condamnation *f* à vie *or* à perpétuité; **lifespan** *n* (durée *f* de) vie *f*; **lifestyle** *n* style *m* de vie; **lifetime** *n*: **in his lifetime** de son vivant

lift [lɪft] *vt* soulever; lever; *(end)* supprimer, lever ▷ *vi (fog)* se lever ▷ *n (BRIT: elevator)* ascenseur *m*; **to give sb a ~** *(BRIT)* emmener *or* prendre qn en voiture; **can you give me a ~ to the station?** pouvez-vous m'emmener à la gare?; **lift up** *vt* soulever; **lift-off** *n* décollage *m*

light [laɪt] *n* lumière *f*; *(lamp)* lampe *f*; *(Aut: rear light)* feu *m*; *(: headlamp)* phare *m*; *(for cigarette etc)*: **have you got a ~?** avez-vous du feu? ▷ *vt (pt, pp* **~ed** *or* **lit)** *(candle, cigarette, fire)* allumer; *(room)* éclairer ▷ *adj (room, colour)* clair(e); *(not heavy, also fig)* léger(-ère); *(not strenuous)* peu fatigant(e); **lights** *npl (traffic lights)* feux *mpl*; **to come to ~** être dévoilé(e) *or* découvert(e); **in the ~ of** à la lumière de; étant donné; **light up** *vi* s'allumer; *(face)* s'éclairer; *(smoke)* allumer une cigarette *or* une pipe *etc* ▷ *vt (illuminate)*

éclairer, illuminer; **light bulb** *n* ampoule *f*; **lighten** *vt (light up)* éclairer; *(make lighter)* éclaircir; *(make less heavy)* alléger; **lighter** *n (also:* **cigarette lighter)** briquet *m*; **light-hearted** *adj* gai(e), joyeux(-euse), enjoué(e); **lighthouse** *n* phare *m*; **lighting** *n* éclairage *m*; *(in theatre)* éclairages; **lightly** *adv* légèrement; **to get off lightly** s'en tirer à bon compte

lightning ['laɪtnɪŋ] *n* foudre *f*; *(flash)* éclair *m*

lightweight ['laɪtweɪt] *adj (suit)* léger(-ère) ▷ *n (Boxing)* poids léger

like [laɪk] *vt* aimer (bien) ▷ *prep* comme ▷ *adj* semblable, pareil(le) ▷ *n*: **the ~** *(pej)* (d')autres du même genre *or* acabit; **his ~s and dislikes** ses goûts *mpl or* préférences *fpl*; **I would ~**, **I'd ~** je voudrais, j'aimerais; **would you ~ a coffee?** voulez-vous du café?; **to be/look ~ sb/sth** ressembler à qn/qch; **what's he ~?** comment est-il?; **what does it look ~?** de quoi est-ce que ça a l'air?; **what does it taste ~?** quel goût est-ce que ça a?; **that's just ~ him** c'est bien de lui, ça lui ressemble; **do it ~ this** fais-le comme ceci; **it's nothing ~ ...** ce n'est pas du tout comme ...; **likeable** *adj* sympathique, agréable

likelihood ['laɪklɪhud] *n* probabilité *f*

likely ['laɪklɪ] *adj (result, outcome)* probable; *(excuse)* plausible; **he's ~ to leave** il va sûrement partir, il risque fort de partir; **not ~!** *(inf)* pas de danger!

likewise ['laɪkwaɪz] *adv* de même, pareillement

liking ['laɪkɪŋ] *n (for person)* affection *f*; *(for thing)* penchant *m*, goût *m*; **to be to sb's ~** être au goût de qn, plaire à qn

lilac ['laɪlək] *n* lilas *m*

Lilo® ['laɪləu] *n* matelas *m* pneumatique

lily ['lɪlɪ] *n* lis *m*; **~ of the valley** muguet *m*

limb [lɪm] *n* membre *m*

limbo ['lɪmbəu] *n*: **to be in ~** *(fig)* être tombé(e) dans l'oubli

lime [laɪm] n (tree) tilleul m; (fruit) citron vert, lime f; (Geo) chaux f

limelight ['laɪmlaɪt] n: **in the ~** (fig) en vedette, au premier plan

limestone ['laɪmstəun] n pierre f à chaux; (Geo) calcaire m

limit ['lɪmɪt] n limite f ▷ vt limiter; **limited** adj limité(e), restreint(e); **to be limited to** se limiter à, ne concerner que

limousine ['lɪməziːn] n limousine f

limp [lɪmp] n: **to have a ~** boiter ▷ vi boiter ▷ adj mou (molle)

line [laɪn] n (gen) ligne f; (stroke) trait m; (wrinkle) ride f; (rope) corde f; (wire) fil m; (of poem) vers m; (row, series) rangée f; (of people) file f, queue f; (railway track) voie f; (Comm: series of goods) article m (pl), ligne de produits; (work) métier m ▷ vt: **to ~ (with)** (clothes) doubler (de); (box) garnir ou tapisser (de); (subj: trees, crowd) border; **to stand in ~** (us) faire la queue; **in his ~ of business** dans sa partie, dans son rayon; **to be in ~ for sth** (fig) être en lice pour qch; **in ~ with** en accord avec, en conformité avec; **in a ~** aligné(e); **line up** vi s'aligner, se mettre en rang(s); (in queue) faire la queue ▷ vt aligner; (event) prévoir; (find) trouver; **to have sb/sth ~d up** avoir qn/qch en vue ou de prévu(e)

linear ['lɪnɪəᵣ] adj linéaire

linen ['lɪnɪn] n linge m (de corps ou de maison); (cloth) lin m

liner ['laɪnəᵣ] n (ship) paquebot m de ligne; (for bin) sac-poubelle m

line-up ['laɪnʌp] n (us: queue) file f; (also: **police ~**) parade f d'identification; (Sport) composition f de l'équipe f

linger ['lɪŋgəᵣ] vi s'attarder; traîner; (smell, tradition) persister

lingerie ['lænʒəriː] n lingerie f

linguist ['lɪŋgwɪst] n linguiste m/f; **to be a good ~** être doué(e) pour les langues; **linguistic** adj linguistique

lining ['laɪnɪŋ] n doublure f; (of brakes) garniture f

link [lɪŋk] n (connection) lien m, rapport m; (Internet) lien; (of a chain) maillon m ▷ vt relier, lier, unir; **links** npl (Golf) terrain m de golf m; **link up** vt relier ▷ vi se rejoindre; (companies etc) s'associer

lion ['laɪən] n lion m; **lioness** n lionne f

lip [lɪp] n lèvre f; (of cup etc) rebord m; **lipread** vi lire sur les lèvres; **lip salve** [-sælv] n pommade f pour les lèvres, pommade rosat; **lipstick** n rouge m à lèvres

liqueur [lɪˈkjuəᵣ] n liqueur f

liquid ['lɪkwɪd] n liquide m ▷ adj liquide; **liquidizer** ['lɪkwɪdaɪzəᵣ] n (BRIT Culin) mixer m

liquor ['lɪkəᵣ] n spiritueux m, alcool m; **liquor store** (us) n magasin m de vins et spiritueux

Lisbon ['lɪzbən] n Lisbonne

lisp [lɪsp] n zézaiement m ▷ vi zézayer

list [lɪst] n liste f ▷ vt (write down) inscrire; (make list of) faire la liste de; (enumerate) énumérer

listen ['lɪsn] vi écouter; **to ~ to** écouter; **listener** n auditeur(-trice)

lit [lɪt] pt, pp of **light**

liter ['liːtəᵣ] n (us) = **litre**

literacy ['lɪtərəsɪ] n degré m d'alphabétisation, fait m de savoir lire et écrire

literal ['lɪtərl] adj littéral(e); **literally** adv littéralement; (really) réellement

literary ['lɪtərərɪ] adj littéraire

literate ['lɪtərət] adj qui sait lire et écrire; (educated) instruit(e)

literature ['lɪtrɪtʃəᵣ] n littérature f; (brochures etc) copie f publicitaire, prospectus mpl

litre (us **liter**) ['liːtəᵣ] n litre m

litter ['lɪtəᵣ] n (rubbish) détritus mpl; (dirtier) ordures fpl; (young animals) portée f; **litter bin** n (BRIT) poubelle f; **littered** adj: **littered with** (scattered) jonché(e) de

little ['lɪtl] adj (small) petit(e); (not much): **~ milk** peu de lait ▷ adv peu; **a ~** un peu (de); **a ~ milk** un peu de lait; **a ~ bit** un peu; **as ~ as possible**

le moins possible; **~ by ~** petit à petit,
peu à peu; **little finger** n auriculaire
m, petit doigt

live² [laɪv] adj (animal) vivant(e), en
vie; (wire) sous tension; (broadcast)
(transmis(e)) en direct; (unexploded)
non exposé(e)

live² [lɪv] vi vivre; (reside) vivre, habiter;
to ~ in London habiter (à) Londres;
where do you ~? où habitez-vous?; **live
together** vivre ensemble, cohabiter;
live up to vt fus se montrer à la
hauteur de

livelihood ['laɪvlihud] n moyens mpl
d'existence

lively ['laɪvlɪ] adj vif (vive), plein(e)
d'entrain; (place, book) vivant(e)

liven up ['laɪvn-] vt (room etc) égayer;
(discussion, evening) animer ▷ vi
s'animer

liver ['lɪvə²] n foie m

lives [laɪvz] npl of **life**

livestock ['laɪvstɔk] n cheptel m,
bétail m

living ['lɪvɪŋ] adj vivant(e), en vie ▷ n:
to earn or **make a ~** gagner sa vie;
living room n salle f de séjour

lizard ['lɪzəd] n lézard m

load [ləʊd] n (weight) poids m; (thing
carried) chargement m, charge f;
(Elec, Tech) charge ▷ vt (also: **~ up**):
to ~ (with) (lorry, ship) charger (de);
(gun, camera) charger (avec); (Comput)
charger; **a ~ of, ~s of** (fig) un or des
tas de, des masses de; **to talk a ~
of rubbish** (inf) dire des bêtises;
loaded adj (dice) pipé(e); (question)
insidieux(-euse); (inf: rich) bourré(e)
de fric

loaf (pl **loaves**) [ləʊf, ləʊvz] n pain m,
miche f ▷ vi (also: **~ about, ~ around**)
fainéanter, traîner

loan [ləʊn] n prêt m ▷ vt prêter; **on ~**
prêté(e), en prêt

loathe [ləʊð] vt détester, avoir en
horreur

loaves [ləʊvz] npl of **loaf**

lobby ['lɔbɪ] n hall m, entrée f; (Pol)

groupe m de pression, lobby m ▷ vt
faire pression sur

lobster ['lɔbstə²] n homard m

local ['ləʊkl] adj local(e) ▷ n (BRIT: pub)
pub m or café m du coin; **the locals** npl
les gens mpl du pays or du coin; **local
anaesthetic** n anesthésie locale;
local authority n collectivité locale,
municipalité f; **local government** n
administration locale or municipale n;
locally ['ləʊkəlɪ] adv localement; dans
les environs or la région

locate [ləʊ'keɪt] vt (find) trouver,
repérer; (situate) situer; **to be ~d in** être
situé à or en

location [ləʊ'keɪʃən] n emplacement
m; **on ~** (Cine) en extérieur

> Be careful not to translate **location**
> by the French word **location**.

loch [lɔx] n lac m, loch m

lock [lɔk] n (of door, box) serrure f; (of
canal) écluse f; (of hair) mèche f, boucle f
▷ vt (with key) fermer à clé ▷ vi (door etc)
fermer à clé; (wheels) se bloquer; **lock
in** vt enfermer; **lock out** vt enfermer
dehors; (on purpose) mettre à la porte;
lock up vt (person) enfermer; (house)
fermer à clé ▷ vi tout fermer (à clé)

locker ['lɔkə²] n casier m; (in station)
consigne f automatique; **locker-room**
(us) n (Sport) vestiaire m

locksmith ['lɔksmɪθ] n serrurier m

locomotive [ləʊkə'məʊtɪv] n
locomotive f

locum ['ləʊkəm] n (Med) suppléant(e)
de médecin etc

lodge [lɔdʒ] n pavillon m (de gardien);
(also: **hunting ~**) pavillon de chasse ▷ vi
(person): **to ~ (with)** être logé(e) chez,
être en pension chez; (bullet) se loger
▷ vt (appeal etc) présenter; déposer; **to
~ a complaint** porter plainte; **lodger**
n locataire m/f; (with room and meals)
pensionnaire m/f

lodging ['lɔdʒɪŋ] n logement m

loft [lɔft] n grenier m; (apartment)
grenier aménagé (en appartement)
(gén dans ancien entrepôt ou fabrique)

log [lɒg] *n* (*of wood*) bûche *f*; (*Naut*) livre *m* or journal *m* de bord; (*of car*) = carte grise ▷ *vt* enregistrer; **log in, log on** *vi* (*Comput*) ouvrir une session, entrer dans le système; **log off, log out** *vi* (*Comput*) clore une session, sortir du système

logic ['lɒdʒɪk] *n* logique *f*; **logical** *adj* logique

logo ['ləugəu] *n* logo *m*

Loire [lwɑː] *n*: **the (River) ~** la Loire

lollipop ['lɒlɪpɒp] *n* sucette *f*; **lollipop man/lady** (*BRIT: inf*) *n* contractuel qui fait traverser la rue aux enfants

lolly ['lɒlɪ] *n* (*inf: ice*) esquimau *m*; (: *lollipop*) sucette *f*

London ['lʌndən] *n* Londres; **Londoner** *n* Londonien(ne)

lone [ləun] *adj* solitaire

loneliness ['ləunlɪnɪs] *n* solitude *f*, isolement *m*

lonely ['ləunlɪ] *adj* seul(e); (*childhood etc*) solitaire; (*place*) solitaire, isolé(e)

long [lɒŋ] *adj* long (longue) ▷ *adv* longtemps ▷ *vi*: **to ~ for sth/to do sth** avoir très envie de qch/de faire qch, attendre avec impatience de faire qch; **how ~ is this river/course?** quelle est la longueur de ce fleuve/la durée de ce cours?; **6 metres ~** (long) de 6 mètres; **6 months ~** qui dure 6 mois, de 6 mois; **all night ~** toute la nuit; **he no ~er comes** il ne vient plus; **I can't stand it any ~er** je ne peux plus le supporter; **~ before** longtemps avant; **before ~** (+ *future*) avant peu, dans peu de temps; (+ *past*) peu de temps après; **don't be ~!** fais vite!, dépêche-toi!; **I shan't be ~** je n'en ai pas pour longtemps; **at ~ last** enfin; **so or as ~ as** à condition que *sub*; **long-distance** *adj* (*race*) de fond; (*call*) interurbain(e); **long-haul** *adj* (*flight*) long-courrier; **longing** *n* désir *m*, envie *f*; (*nostalgia*) nostalgie *f* ▷ *adj* plein(e) d'envie or de nostalgie

longitude ['lɒŋgɪtjuːd] *n* longitude *f*

long: **long jump** *n* saut *m* en longueur;

long-life *adj* (*batteries etc*) longue durée *f/inv*; (*milk*) longue conservation; **long-sighted** *adj* (*BRIT*) presbyte; (*fig*) prévoyant(e); **long-standing** *adj* de longue date; **long-term** *adj* à long terme

loo [luː] *n* (*BRIT inf*) w.-c *mpl*, petit coin

look [luk] *vi* regarder; (*seem*) sembler, paraître, avoir l'air; (*building etc*): **to ~ south/on to the sea** donner au sud/ sur la mer ▷ *n* regard *m*; (*appearance*) air *m*, allure *f*, aspect *m*; **looks** *npl* (*good looks*) physique *m*, beauté *f*; **to ~ like** ressembler à; **to have a ~** regarder; **to have a ~ at sth** jeter un coup d'œil à qch; **~ (here)!** (*annoyance*) écoutez!; **look after** *vt fus* s'occuper de; (*luggage etc: watch over*) garder, surveiller; **look around** *vi* regarder autour de soi; **look at** *vt fus* regarder; (*problem etc*) examiner; **look back** *vi*: **to ~ back at sth/sb** se retourner pour regarder qch/qn; **to ~ back on** (*event, period*) évoquer, repenser à; **look down on** *vt fus* (*fig*) regarder de haut, dédaigner; **look for** *vt fus* chercher; **we're ~ing for a hotel/restaurant** nous cherchons un hôtel/restaurant; **look forward to** *vt fus* attendre avec impatience; **~ing forward to hearing from you** (*in letter*) dans l'attente de vous lire; **look into** *vt fus* (*matter, possibility*) examiner, étudier; **look on** *vi* (*beware*): **to ~ out (for)** prendre garde (à), faire attention (à); **~ out!** attention!; **look out for** *vt fus* (*seek*) être à la recherche de; (*try to spot*) guetter; **look round** *vt fus* (*house, shop*) faire le tour de ▷ *vi* (*turn*) regarder derrière soi, se retourner; **look through** *vt fus* (*papers, book*) examiner; (: *briefly*) parcourir; **look up** *vi* lever les yeux; (*improve*) s'améliorer ▷ *vt* (*word*) chercher; **look up to** *vt fus* avoir du respect pour; **lookout** *n* (*tower etc*) poste *m* de guet; (*person*) guetteur *m*; **to be on the lookout (for)** guetter

loom [luːm] *vi* (*also: ~ up*) surgir; (*event*) paraître imminent(e); (*threaten*) menacer

loony ['lu:nɪ] adj, n (inf) timbré(e), cinglé(e) m/f

loop [lu:p] n boucle f ▷ vt: **to ~ sth round sth** passer qch autour de qch; **loophole** n (fig) porte f de sortie; échappatoire f

loose [lu:s] adj (knot, screw) desserré(e); (clothes) vague, ample, lâche; (hair) dénoué(e), épars(e); (not firmly fixed) pas solide; (morals, discipline) relâché(e); (translation) approximatif(-ive) ▷ n: **to be on the ~** être en liberté; **~ connection** (Elec) mauvais contact; **to be at a ~ end** or **(us) ~ ends** (fig) ne pas trop savoir quoi faire; **loosely** adv sans serrer; (imprecisely) approximativement; **loosen** vt desserrer, relâcher, défaire

loot [lu:t] n butin m ▷ vt piller

lop-sided ['lɔp'saɪdɪd] adj de travers, asymétrique

lord [lɔ:d] n seigneur m; **L~ Smith** lord Smith; **the L~** (Rel) le Seigneur; **my L~** (to noble) Monsieur le comte/le baron; (to judge) Monsieur le juge; (to bishop) Monseigneur; **good L~!** mon Dieu!; **Lords** npl (BRIT: Pol): **the (House of) Lords** (BRIT) la Chambre des Lords

lorry ['lɔrɪ] n (BRIT) camion m; **lorry driver** n (BRIT) camionneur m, routier m

lose (pt, pp **lost**) [lu:z, lɔst] vt perdre ▷ vi perdre; **i've lost my wallet/passport** j'ai perdu mon portefeuille/passeport; **to ~ (time)** (clock) retarder; **lose out** vi être perdant(e); **loser** n perdant(e)

loss [lɔs] n perte f; **to make a ~** enregistrer une perte; **to be at a ~** être perplexe or embarrassé(e)

lost [lɔst] pt, pp of **lose** ▷ adj perdu(e); **to get ~** vi se perdre; **I'm ~** je me suis perdu; **~ and found property** n (us) objets trouvés; **~ and found** n (us) (bureau m des) objets trouvés; **lost property** n (BRIT) objets trouvés; **lost property office** or **department** (bureau m des) objets trouvés

lot [lɔt] n (at auctions, set) lot m; (destiny) sort m, destinée f; **the ~** (everything) tout; (everyone) tous mpl, toutes fpl; **a ~ beaucoup; **a ~ of** beaucoup de; **~s of** des tas de; **to draw ~s (for sth)** tirer (qch) au sort

lotion ['ləʊʃən] n lotion f

lottery ['lɔtərɪ] n loterie f

loud [laʊd] adj bruyant(e), sonore; (voice) fort(e); (condemnation etc) vigoureux(-euse); (gaudy) voyant(e), tapageur(-euse) ▷ adv (speak etc) fort; **out ~** tout haut; **loudly** adv fort, bruyamment; **loudspeaker** n haut-parleur m

lounge [laʊndʒ] n salon m; (of airport) salle f; (BRIT: also: **~ bar**) (salle de) café m or bar m ▷ vi (also: **~ about** or **around**) se prélasser, paresser

louse (pl **lice**) [laʊs, laɪs] n pou m

lousy ['laʊzɪ] (inf) adj (bad quality) infect(e), moche; **I feel ~** je suis mal fichu(e)

love [lʌv] n amour m ▷ vt aimer; (caringly, kindly) aimer beaucoup; **I ~ chocolate** j'adore le chocolat; **to ~ to do** aimer beaucoup or adorer faire; **"15 ~"** (Tennis) "15 à rien or zéro"; **to be/fall in ~ with** être/tomber amoureux(-euse) de; **to make ~** faire l'amour; **~ from Anne, ~** Anne affectueusement, Anne; **I ~ you** je t'aime; **love affair** n liaison (amoureuse); **love life** n vie sentimentale

lovely ['lʌvlɪ] adj (pretty) ravissant(e); (friend, wife) charmant(e); (holiday, surprise) très agréable, merveilleux(-euse)

lover ['lʌvə] n amant m; (person in love) amoureux(-euse); (amateur): **a ~ of** un(e) ami(e) de, un(e) amoureux(-euse) de

loving ['lʌvɪŋ] adj affectueux(-euse), tendre, aimant(e)

low [ləʊ] adj bas (basse); (quality) mauvais(e), inférieur(e) ▷ adv bas ▷ n (Meteorology) dépression f; **to feel ~** se sentir déprimé(e); **he's very ~** (*ill*) il est bien bas or très affaibli; **to turn (down)** ~ vt baisser; **to be ~ on** (*supplies etc*) être à court de; **to reach a new ~** or an **all-time ~** tomber au niveau le plus bas; **low-alcohol** adj à faible teneur en alcool, peu alcoolisé(e); **low-calorie** adj hypocalorique

lower ['ləuə^r] adj inférieur(e) ▷ vt baisser; (*resistance*) diminuer; **to ~ o.s. to** s'abaisser à

low-fat ['ləu'fæt] adj maigre

loyal ['lɔɪəl] adj loyal(e), fidèle; **loyalty** n loyauté f, fidélité f; **loyalty card** n carte f de fidélité

L.P. n abbr = **long-playing record**

L-plates ['ɛlpleɪts] npl (BRIT) plaques f pl (obligatoires) d'apprenti conducteur

Lt abbr (= *lieutenant*) Lt.

Ltd abbr (Comm: *company*: = *limited*) = S.A.

luck [lʌk] n chance f; **bad ~** malchance f, malheur m; **good ~!** bonne chance!; **bad** or **hard** or **tough ~!** pas de chance!; **luckily** adv heureusement, par bonheur; **lucky** adj (*person*) qui a de la chance; (*coincidence*) heureux(-euse); (*number etc*) qui porte bonheur

lucrative ['lu:krətɪv] adj lucratif(-ive), rentable, qui rapporte

ludicrous ['lu:dɪkrəs] adj ridicule, absurde

luggage ['lʌgɪdʒ] n bagages mpl; **our ~ hasn't arrived** nos bagages ne sont pas arrivés; **could you send someone to collect our ~?** pourriez-vous envoyer quelqu'un chercher nos bagages?; **luggage rack** n (*in train*) porte-bagages m inv; (*on car*) galerie f

lukewarm ['lu:kwɔ:m] adj tiède

lull [lʌl] n accalmie f; (*in conversation*) pause f ▷ vt: **to ~ sb to sleep** bercer qn pour qu'il s'endorme; **to be ~ed into a false sense of security** s'endormir dans une fausse sécurité

lullaby ['lʌləbaɪ] n berceuse f

lumber ['lʌmbə^r] n (*wood*) bois m de charpente; (*junk*) bric-à-brac m inv ▷ vt (BRIT inf): **to ~ sb with sth/sb** coller or

refiler qch/qn à qn

luminous ['lu:mɪnəs] adj lumineux(-euse)

lump [lʌmp] n morceau m; (*in sauce*) grumeau m; (*swelling*) grosseur f ▷ vt (*also*: ~ **together**) réunir, mettre en tas; **lump sum** n somme globale or forfaitaire; **lumpy** adj (*sauce*) qui a des grumeaux; (*bed*) défoncé(e), peu confortable

lunatic ['lu:nətɪk] n fou (folle), dément(e) ▷ adj fou (folle), dément(e)

lunch [lʌntʃ] n déjeuner m ▷ vi déjeuner; **lunch break, lunch hour** n pause f de midi, heure f du déjeuner; **lunchtime** n: **it's lunchtime** c'est l'heure du déjeuner

lung [lʌŋ] n poumon m

lure [luə^r] n (*attraction*) attrait m, charme m; (*in hunting*) appât m, leurre m ▷ vt attirer or persuader par la ruse

lurk [lə:k] vi se tapir, se cacher

lush [lʌʃ] adj luxuriant(e)

lust [lʌst] n (*sexual*) désir m (sexuel); (*Rel*) luxure f; (*fig*): **~ for** soif f de

Luxembourg ['lʌksəmbə:g] n Luxembourg m

luxurious [lʌg'zjuəriəs] adj luxueux(-euse)

luxury ['lʌkʃəri] n luxe m ▷ cpd de luxe

Lycra® ['laɪkrə] n Lycra® m

lying ['laɪɪŋ] n mensonge(s) m(pl) ▷ adj (*statement, story*) mensonger(-ère), faux (fausse); (*person*) menteur(-euse)

Lyons ['ljɔ̃] n Lyon m

lyrics ['lɪrɪks] npl (*of song*) paroles f pl

m

m. abbr (= metre) m; (= million) M; (= mile) mi

M.A. n abbr (Scol) = **Master of Arts**

ma [mɑː] (inf) n maman f

mac [mæk] n (BRIT) imper(méable m) m

macaroni [mækəˈrəʊnɪ] n macaronis mpl

Macedonia [mæsɪˈdəʊnɪə] n Macédoine f; **Macedonian** [mæsɪˈdəʊnɪən] adj macédonien(ne) ▷ n Macédonien(ne); (Ling) macédonien m

machine [məˈʃiːn] n machine f ▷ vt (dress etc) coudre à la machine; (Tech) usiner; **machine gun** n mitrailleuse f; **machinery** n machinerie f, machines fpl; (fig) mécanisme(s) m(pl); **machine washable** adj (garment) lavable en machine

macho [ˈmætʃəʊ] adj macho inv

mackerel [ˈmækrl] n (pl inv) maquereau m

mackintosh [ˈmækɪntɔʃ] n (BRIT) imperméable m

mad [mæd] adj fou (folle); (foolish) insensé(e); (angry) furieux(-euse); **to be ~ (keen) about** or **on sth** (inf) être follement passionné de qch, être fou de qch

Madagascar [mædəˈgæskəʳ] n Madagascar m

madam [ˈmædəm] n madame f

mad cow disease n maladie f des vaches folles

made [meɪd] pt, pp of **make**; **made-to-measure** adj (BRIT) fait(e) sur mesure; **made-up** [ˈmeɪdʌp] adj (story) inventé(e), fabriqué(e)

madly [ˈmædlɪ] adv follement; **~ in love** éperdument amoureux(-euse)

madman [ˈmædmən] (irreg) n fou m, aliéné m

madness [ˈmædnɪs] n folie f

Madrid [məˈdrɪd] n Madrid

Mafia [ˈmæfɪə] n maf(f)ia f

mag [mæg] n abbr (BRIT inf: = magazine) magazine m

magazine [mægəˈziːn] n (Press) magazine m, revue f; (Radio, TV) magazine

maggot [ˈmægət] n ver m, asticot m

magic [ˈmædʒɪk] n magie f ▷ adj magique; **magical** adj magique; (experience, evening) merveilleux(-euse); **magician** [məˈdʒɪʃən] n magicien(ne)

magistrate [ˈmædʒɪstreɪt] n magistrat m; juge m

magnet [ˈmægnɪt] n aimant m; **magnetic** [mægˈnɛtɪk] adj magnétique

magnificent [mægˈnɪfɪsnt] adj superbe, magnifique; (splendid: robe, building) somptueux(-euse), magnifique

magnify [ˈmægnɪfaɪ] vt grossir; (sound) amplifier; **magnifying glass** n loupe f

magpie [ˈmægpaɪ] n pie f

mahogany [məˈhɔgənɪ] n acajou m

maid [meɪd] n bonne f; (in hotel) femme f de chambre; **old** ~ (pej) vieille fille

maiden name n nom m de jeune fille

mail [meɪl] n poste f; (letters) courrier m ▷ vt envoyer (par la poste); **by ~** par la poste; **mailbox** n (us: also Comput) boîte f aux lettres; **mailing list** n liste f d'adresses; **mailman** (irreg) n (us) facteur m; **mail-order** n vente f or achat m par correspondance

main [meɪn] adj principal(e) ▷ n (pipe) conduite principale, canalisation f; **the ~s** (Elec) le secteur; **the ~ thing** l'essentiel m; **in the ~** dans l'ensemble; **main course** n (Culin) plat m de résistance; **mainland** n continent m; **mainly** adv principalement, surtout; **main road** n grand axe, route nationale; **mainstream** n (fig) courant principal; **main street** n rue f principale

maintain [meɪnˈteɪn] vt entretenir; (continue) maintenir, préserver; (affirm) soutenir; **maintenance** [ˈmeɪntənəns] n entretien m; (Law: alimony) pension f alimentaire

maisonette [meɪzəˈnɛt] n (BRIT) appartement m en duplex

maize [meɪz] n (BRIT) maïs m

majesty [ˈmædʒɪstɪ] n majesté f; (title): **Your M~** Votre Majesté

major [ˈmeɪdʒəʳ] n (Mil) commandant m ▷ adj (important) important(e); (most important) principal(e); (Mus) majeur(e) ▷ vi (us Scol): **to ~ (in)** se spécialiser en

Majorca [məˈjɔːkə] n Majorque f

majority [məˈdʒɔrɪtɪ] n majorité f

make [meɪk] vt (pt, pp **made**) faire; (manufacture) faire, fabriquer; (earn) gagner; (decision) prendre; (friend) se faire; (speech) prononcer; (cause to be): **to ~ sb sad** etc rendre qn triste etc; (force): **to ~ sb do sth** obliger qn à faire qch, faire faire qch à qn; (equal): **2 and 2 ~ 4** 2 et 2 font 4 ▷ n (manufacture) fabrication f; (brand) marque f; **to ~ the bed** faire le lit; **to ~ a fool of sb** (ridicule) ridiculiser qn; (trick) avoir or duper qn; **to ~ a profit** faire un or des bénéfice(s); **to ~ a loss** essuyer une perte; **to ~ it** (in time etc) y arriver; (succeed) réussir;

what time do you ~ it? quelle heure avez-vous?; **I ~ it £249** d'après mes calculs ça fait 249 livres; **to be made of** être en; **to ~ do with** se contenter de; se débrouiller avec; **make off** vi filer; **make out** vt (write out: cheque) faire; (decipher) déchiffrer; (understand) comprendre; (see) distinguer; (claim, imply) prétendre, vouloir faire croire; **make up** vt (invent) inventer, imaginer; (constitute) constituer; (parcel, bed) faire ▷ vi se réconcilier; (with cosmetics) se maquiller, se farder; **to be made up of** se composer de; **make up for** vt fus compenser; (lost time) rattraper; **makeover** [ˈmeɪkəuvəʳ] n (by beautician) soins mpl de maquillage; (change of image) changement m d'image; **maker** n fabricant m; (of film, programme) réalisateur(-trice); **makeshift** adj provisoire, improvisé(e); **make-up** n maquillage m

making [ˈmeɪkɪŋ] n (fig): **in the ~** en formation or gestation; **to have the ~s of** (actor, athlete) avoir l'étoffe de

malaria [məˈlɛərɪə] n malaria f, paludisme m

Malaysia [məˈleɪzɪə] n Malaisie f

male [meɪl] n (Biol, Elec) mâle m ▷ adj (sex, attitude) masculin(e); (animal) mâle; (child etc) du sexe masculin

malicious [məˈlɪʃəs] adj méchant(e), malveillant(e)

> Be careful not to translate *malicious* by the French word *malicieux*.

malignant [məˈlɪɡnənt] adj (Med) malin(-igne)

mall [mɔːl] n (also: **shopping ~**) centre commercial

mallet [ˈmælɪt] n maillet m

malnutrition [mælnjuːˈtrɪʃən] n malnutrition f

malpractice [mælˈpræktɪs] n faute professionnelle; négligence f

malt [mɔːlt] n malt m ▷ cpd (whisky) pur malt

Malta ['mɔ:ltə] n Malte f; **Maltese**
[mɔ:l'ti:z] adj maltais(e) ▷ n (pl inv)
Maltais(e)

mammal ['mæml] n mammifère m

mammoth ['mæməθ] n mammouth m
▷ adj géant(e), monstre

man (pl **men**) [mæn, mɛn] n homme
m; (Sport) joueur m; (Chess) pièce f ▷ vt
(Naut: ship) garnir d'hommes; (machine)
assurer le fonctionnement de; (Mil: gun)
servir; (: post) être de service à; **an old ~**
un vieillard; **~ and wife** mari et femme

manage ['mænɪdʒ] vi se débrouiller;
(succeed) y arriver, réussir ▷ vt (business)
gérer; (team, operation) diriger;
(control: ship) manier, manœuvrer;
(: person) savoir s'y prendre avec; **to
~ to do** se débrouiller pour faire;
(succeed) réussir à faire; **manageable**
adj maniable; (task etc) faisable;
(number) raisonnable; **management**
n (running) administration f, direction
f; (people in charge: of business, firm)
dirigeants mpl, cadres mpl; (: of hotel,
shop, theatre) direction; **manager**
n (of business) directeur m; (of institution
etc) administrateur m; (of department,
unit) responsable m/f; (of hotel etc)
gérant m; (Sport) manager m; (of
artist) impresario m; **manageress**
n directrice f; (of hotel etc) gérante f;
managerial [mænɪ'dʒɪərɪəl] adj
directorial(e); (skills) de cadre, de
gestion; **managing director** n
directeur général

mandarin ['mændərɪn] n (also: **~
orange**) mandarine f

mandate ['mændeɪt] n mandat m

mandatory ['mændətərɪ] adj
obligatoire

mane [meɪn] n crinière f

maneuver [mə'nu:vəʳ] (US)
= **manoeuvre**

mangetout ['mɔnʒ'tu:] n mangetout m inv

mango (pl **~es**) ['mæŋgəu] n mangue f

man: manhole n trou m d'homme;
manhood n (age) âge m d'homme;

(manliness) virilité f

mania ['meɪnɪə] n manie f; **maniac**
['meɪnɪæk] n maniaque m/f; (fig)
fou(folle)

manic ['mænɪk] adj maniaque

manicure ['mænɪkjuəʳ] n manucure f

manifest ['mænɪfɛst] vt manifester
▷ adj manifeste, évident(e)

manifesto [mænɪ'fɛstəu] n (Pol)
manifeste m

manipulate [mə'nɪpjuleɪt] vt
manipuler; (system, situation) exploiter

man: mankind [mæn'kaɪnd] n
humanité f, genre humain; **manly** adj
viril(e); **man-made** adj artificiel(le);
(fibre) synthétique

manner ['mænəʳ] n manière f, façon f;
(behaviour) attitude f, comportement
m; **manners** npl: **(good) ~s** (bonnes)
manières; **bad ~s** mauvaises manières;
all - of toutes sortes de

manoeuvre (US **maneuver**)
[mə'nu:vəʳ] vt (move) manœuvrer;
(manipulate: person) manipuler;
(: situation) exploiter ▷ n manœuvre f

manpower ['mænpauəʳ] n main-
d'œuvre f

mansion ['mænʃən] n château m,
manoir m

manslaughter ['mænslɔ:təʳ] n
homicide m involontaire

mantelpiece ['mæntlpi:s] n
cheminée f

manual ['mænjuəl] adj manuel(le)
▷ n manuel m

manufacture [mænju'fæktʃəʳ]
vt fabriquer ▷ n fabrication f;
manufacturer n fabricant m

manure [mə'njuəʳ] n fumier m;
(artificial) engrais m

manuscript ['mænjuskrɪpt] n
manuscrit m

many ['mɛnɪ] adj beaucoup de, de
nombreux(-euses) ▷ pron beaucoup,
un grand nombre; **a great ~** un grand
nombre (de); **~ a ...** bien des ..., plus
d'un(e) ...

map [mæp] n carte f; (of town) plan

m; **can you show it to me on the ~?** pouvez-vous me l'indiquer sur la carte?; **map out** *vt* tracer; *(fig: task)* planifier

maple ['meɪpl] *n* érable *m*

Mar *abbr* = **March**

mar [mɑːʳ] *vt* gâcher, gâter

marathon ['mærəθən] *n* marathon *m*

marble ['mɑːbl] *n* marbre *m*; *(toy)* bille *f*

March [mɑːtʃ] *n* mars *m*

march [mɑːtʃ] *vi* marcher au pas; *(demonstrators)* défiler ▷ *n* marche *f*; *(demonstration)* manifestation *f*

mare [mɛəʳ] *n* jument *f*

margarine [mɑːdʒəˈriːn] *n* margarine *f*

margin ['mɑːdʒɪn] *n* marge *f*; **marginal** *adj* marginal(e); **marginal seat** *(Pol)* siège disputé; **marginally** *adv* très légèrement, sensiblement

marigold ['mærɪɡəʊld] *n* souci *m*

marijuana [mærɪ'wɑːnə] *n* marijuana *f*

marina [mə'riːnə] *n* marina *f*

marinade *n* [mærɪ'neɪd] marinade *f*

marinate ['mærɪneɪt] *vt* (faire) mariner

marine [mə'riːn] *adj* marin(e) ▷ *n* fusilier marin; *(us)* marine *m*

marital ['mærɪtl] *adj* matrimonial(e); **marital status** *n* situation *f* de famille

maritime ['mærɪtaɪm] *adj* maritime

marjoram ['mɑːdʒərəm] *n* marjolaine *f*

mark [mɑːk] *n* marque *f*; *(of skid etc)* trace *f*; *(BRIT Scol)* note *f*; *(oven temperature)*: **(gas) ~ 4** thermostat *m* 4 ▷ *vt* *(also Sport: player)* marquer; *(stain)* tacher; *(BRIT Scol)* corriger, noter; **to ~ time** marquer le pas; **marked** *adj* *(obvious)* marqué(e), net(te); **marker** *n* *(sign)* jalon *m*; *(bookmark)* signet *m*

market ['mɑːkɪt] *n* marché *m* ▷ *vt* *(Comm)* commercialiser; **marketing** *n* marketing *m*; **marketplace** *n* place *f* du marché; *(Comm)* marché *m*; **market research** *n* étude *f* de marché

marmalade ['mɑːməleɪd] *n* confiture *f* d'oranges

maroon [mə'ruːn] *vt*: **to be ~ed** être

abandonné(e); *(fig)* être bloqué(e) ▷ *adj (colour)* bordeaux *inv*

marquee [mɑː'kiː] *n* chapiteau *m*

marriage ['mærɪdʒ] *n* mariage *m*; **marriage certificate** *n* extrait *m* d'acte de mariage

married ['mærɪd] *adj* marié(e); *(life, love)* conjugal(e)

marrow ['mærəʊ] *n (of bone)* moelle *f*; *(vegetable)* courge *f*

marry ['mærɪ] *vt* épouser, se marier avec; *(subj: father, priest etc)* marier ▷ *vi* *(also: **get married**)* se marier

Mars [mɑːz] *n (planet)* Mars *m*

Marseilles [mɑː'seɪ] *n* Marseille

marsh [mɑːʃ] *n* marais *m*, marécage *m*

marshal ['mɑːʃl] *n* maréchal *m*; *(us: fire, police)* ≈ capitaine *m*; *(for demonstration, meeting)* ≈ membre *m* du service d'ordre ▷ *vt* rassembler

martyr ['mɑːtəʳ] *n* martyr(e)

marvel ['mɑːvl] *n* merveille *f* ▷ *vi*: **to ~ (at)** s'émerveiller (de); **marvellous** *(us* **marvelous)** *adj* merveilleux(-euse)

Marxism ['mɑːksɪzəm] *n* marxisme *m*

Marxist ['mɑːksɪst] *adj, n* marxiste *(m/f)*

marzipan ['mɑːzɪpæn] *n* pâte *f* d'amandes

mascara [mæs'kɑːrə] *n* mascara *m*

mascot ['mæskət] *n* mascotte *f*

masculine ['mæskjulɪn] *adj* masculin(e) ▷ *n* masculin *m*

mash [mæʃ] *vt (Culin)* faire une purée de; **mashed potato(es)** *n(pl)* purée *f* de pommes de terre

mask [mɑːsk] *n* masque *m* ▷ *vt* masquer

mason ['meɪsn] *n (also:* **stone~)** maçon *m*; *(also:* **free~)** franc-maçon *m*; **masonry** *n* maçonnerie *f*

mass [mæs] *n* multitude *f*, masse *f*; *(Physics)* masse *f*; *(Rel)* messe *f* ▷ *cpd (communication)* de masse; *(unemployment)* massif(-ive) ▷ *vi* se masser; **masses** *npl*: **the ~es** les masses; **~es of** *(inf)* des tas de

massacre ['mæsəkəʳ] *n* massacre *m*

massage ['mæsɑːʒ] n massage m
▷ vt masser
massive ['mæsɪv] adj énorme,
massif(-ive)
mass media npl mass-media mpl
mass-produce ['mæsprə'djuːs] vt
fabriquer en série
mast [mɑːst] n mât m; (Radio, TV)
pylône m
master ['mɑːstə*] n maître m; (in
secondary school) professeur m; (in
primary school) instituteur m; (title for
boys): **M~ X** Monsieur X ▷ vt maîtriser;
(learn) apprendre à fond; **M~ of Arts/
Science (MA/MSc)** n = titulaire m/f
d'une maîtrise (en lettres/science); **M~
of Arts/Science degree (MA/MSc)**
n = maîtrise f; **mastermind** n esprit
supérieur ▷ vt diriger, être le cerveau
de; **masterpiece** n chef-d'œuvre m
masturbate ['mæstəbeɪt] vi se
masturber
mat [mæt] n petit tapis; (also: **door~**)
paillasson m; (also: **table~**) set m de
table ▷ adj =**matt**
match [mætʃ] n allumette f; (game)
match m, partie f; (fig) égal(e) ▷ vt (also:
~ up) assortir; (go well with) aller bien
avec, s'assortir à; (equal) égaler, valoir
▷ vi être assorti(e); **to be a good ~**
être bien assorti(e); **matchbox** n boîte f
d'allumettes; **matching** adj assorti(e)
mate [meɪt] n (inf) copain (copine);
(animal) partenaire m/f, mâle (femelle);
(in merchant navy) second m ▷ vi
s'accoupler
material [mə'tɪəriəl] n (substance)
matière f, matériau m; (cloth) tissu m,
étoffe f; (information, data) données fpl
▷ adj matériel(le); (relevant) evidence)
pertinent(e); **materials** npl (equipment)
matériaux mpl
materialize [mə'tɪəriəlaɪz] vi se
matérialiser, se réaliser
maternal [mə'təːnl] adj maternel(le)
maternity [mə'təːnɪti] n maternité f;
maternity hospital n maternité f;
maternity leave n congé m de
maternité

math [mæθ] n (us: = mathematics)
maths fpl
mathematical [mæθə'mætɪkl] adj
mathématique
mathematician [mæθəmə'tɪʃən] n
mathématicien(ne)
mathematics [mæθə'mætɪks] n
mathématiques fpl
maths [mæθs] n abbr (BRIT:
' = mathematics) maths fpl
matinée ['mætɪneɪ] n matinée f
matron ['meɪtrən] n (in hospital)
infirmière-chef f; (in school) infirmière f
matt [mæt] adj mat(e)
matter ['mætə*] n question f; (Physics)
matière f, substance f; (Med: pus) pus
m ▷ vi importer; **matters** npl (affairs,
situation) la situation; **it doesn't ~** cela
n'a pas d'importance; (I don't mind) cela
ne fait rien; **what's the ~?** qu'est-ce
qu'il y a?, qu'est-ce qui ne va pas?; **no ~
what** quoi qu'il arrive; **as a ~ of course**
tout naturellement; **as a ~ of fact** en
fait; **reading ~** (BRIT) de quoi lire, de
la lecture
mattress ['mætrɪs] n matelas m
mature [mə'tjuə*] adj mûr(e); (cheese)
fait(e); (wine) arrivé(e) à maturité ▷ vi
mûrir; (cheese, wine) se faire; **mature
student** n étudiant(e) plus âgé(e) que la
moyenne; **maturity** n maturité f
maul [mɔːl] vt lacérer
mauve [məuv] adj mauve
max abbr =**maximum**
maximize ['mæksɪmaɪz] vt (profits etc,
chances) maximiser
maximum ['mæksɪməm] (pl **maxima**)
adj maximum ▷ n maximum m
May [meɪ] n mai m
may [meɪ] (conditional **might**) vi
(indicating possibility): **he ~ come** il se
peut qu'il vienne; (be allowed to): **~ I
smoke?** puis-je fumer?; (wishes): **~ God
bless you!** (que) Dieu vous bénisse!;
you ~ as well go vous feriez aussi
bien d'y aller
maybe ['meɪbiː] adv peut-être; **~**

he'll ... peut-être qu'il ...

May Day n le Premier mai

mayhem ['meɪhem] n grabuge m

mayonnaise [meɪə'neɪz] n mayonnaise f

mayor [mɛə*] n maire m; **mayoress** n (female mayor) maire m; (wife of mayor) épouse f du maire

maze [meɪz] n labyrinthe m, dédale m

MD n abbr (Comm) = **managing director**

me [miː] pron me, m' + vowel or h mute; (stressed, after prep) moi; **it's me** c'est moi; **he heard me** il m'a entendu; **give me a book** donnez-moi un livre; **it's for me** c'est pour moi

meadow ['medəʊ] n prairie f, pré m

meagre (us **meager**) ['miːgə*] adj maigre

meal [miːl] n repas m; (flour) farine f; **mealtime** n heure f du repas

mean [miːn] adj (with money) avare, radin(e); (unkind) mesquin(e), méchant(e); (shabby) misérable; (average) moyen(ne) ▷ vt (pt, pp ~t) (signify) signifier, vouloir dire; (refer to) faire allusion à, parler de; (intend): **to ~ to do** avoir l'intention de faire ▷ n moyenne f; **means** npl (way, money) moyens mpl; **by ~s of** (instrument) au moyen de; **by all ~s** je vous en prie; **to be ~t for** être destiné(e) à; **do you ~ it?** vous êtes sérieux?; **what do you ~?** que voulez-vous dire?

meaning ['miːnɪŋ] n signification f, sens m; **meaningful** adj significatif(-ive); (relationship) valable; **meaningless** adj dénué(e) de sens

meant [ment] pt, pp of **mean**

meantime ['miːntaɪm] adv (also: **in the ~**) pendant ce temps

meanwhile ['miːnwaɪl] adv = **meantime**

measles ['miːzlz] n rougeole f

measure ['meʒə*] vt, vi mesurer ▷ n mesure f; (ruler) règle f (graduée)

measurements ['meʒəmənts] n mesures fpl; **chest/hip ~** tour m de poitrine/hanches

meat [miːt] n viande f; **I don't eat ~** je ne mange pas de viande; **cold ~s** (BRIT) viandes froides; **meatball** n boulette f de viande

Mecca ['mekə] n la Mecque

mechanic [mɪ'kænɪk] n mécanicien m; **can you send a ~?** pouvez-vous nous envoyer un mécanicien?; **mechanical** adj mécanique

mechanism ['mekənɪzəm] n mécanisme m

medal ['medl] n médaille f; **medallist** (us **medalist**) n (Sport) médaillé(e)

meddle ['medl] vi: **to ~ in** se mêler de, s'occuper de; **to ~ with** toucher à

media ['miːdɪə] npl media mpl ▷ npl of **medium**

mediaeval [medɪ'iːvl] adj = **medieval**

mediate ['miːdɪeɪt] vi servir d'intermédiaire

medical ['medɪkl] adj médical(e) ▷ n (also: **~ examination**) visite médicale; (private) examen médical; **medical certificate** certificat médical

medicated ['medɪkeɪtɪd] adj traitant(e), médicamenteux(-euse)

medication [medɪ'keɪʃən] n (drugs etc) médication f

medicine ['medsɪn] n médecine f; (drug) médicament m

medieval [medɪ'iːvl] adj médiéval(e)

mediocre [miːdɪ'əʊkə*] adj médiocre

meditate ['medɪteɪt] vi: **to ~ (on)** méditer (sur)

meditation [medɪ'teɪʃən] n méditation f

Mediterranean [medɪtə'reɪnɪən] adj méditerranéen(ne); **the ~ (Sea)** la (mer) Méditerranée

medium ['miːdɪəm] adj moyen(ne) ▷ n (pl **media**: means) moyen m; (pl **~s**: person) médium m; **the happy ~** le juste milieu; **medium-sized** adj de taille moyenne; **medium wave** n (Radio) ondes moyennes, petites ondes

meek [miːk] adj doux (douce), humble

meet (pt, pp **met**) [miːt, met] vt rencontrer; (by arrangement) retrouver, rejoindre; (for the first time) faire la connaissance de; (go and fetch): **I'll ~ you at the station** j'irai te chercher à la gare; (opponent, danger, problem) faire face à; (requirements) satisfaire à, répondre à ▷ vi (friends) se rencontrer; se retrouver; (in session) se réunir; (join: lines, roads) se joindre; **nice -ing** vous ravi d'avoir fait votre connaissance; **meet up** vi: **to ~ with sb** rencontrer qn; **meet with** vt fus (difficulty) rencontrer; **to ~ with success** être couronné(e) de succès; **meeting** n (of group of people) réunion f; (between individuals) rendez-vous m; (Comm) elle est en réunion; **meeting place** n lieu de (la) réunion; (for appointment) lieu de rendez-vous

megabyte ['mɛgəbaɪt] n (Comput) méga-octet m

megaphone ['mɛgəfəʊn] n porte-voix m inv

megapixel ['mɛgəpɪksl] n mégapixel m

melancholy ['mɛlənkəlɪ] n mélancolie f ▷ adj mélancolique

melody ['mɛlədɪ] n mélodie f

melon ['mɛlən] n melon m

melt [mɛlt] vi fondre ▷ vt faire fondre

member ['mɛmbə'] n membre m; **Member of Congress** (us) n membre m du Congrès, = député m; **Member of Parliament (MP)** n (BRIT) député m; **Member of the European Parliament (MEP)** n Eurodéputé m; **Member of the House of Representatives (MHR)** n (us) membre m de la Chambre des représentants; **Member of the Scottish Parliament (MSP)** n (BRIT) député m au Parlement écossais; **membership** n (becoming a member) adhésion f; admission f; (the members) membres mpl, adhérents mpl; **membership card** n carte f de membre

memento [mə'mɛntəʊ] n souvenir m

memo ['mɛməʊ] n note f (de service)

memorable ['mɛmərəbl] adj mémorable

memorandum (pl **memoranda**) [mɛmə'rændəm, -də] n note f (de service)

memorial [mɪ'mɔːrɪəl] n mémorial m ▷ adj commémoratif(-ive)

memorize ['mɛməraɪz] vt apprendre or retenir par cœur

memory ['mɛmərɪ] n (also Comput) mémoire f; (recollection) souvenir m; **in ~ of** à la mémoire de; **memory card** n (for digital camera) carte f mémoire

men [mɛn] npl of **man**

menace ['mɛnɪs] n menace f; (inf: nuisance) peste f, plaie f ▷ vt menacer

mend [mɛnd] vt réparer; (darn) raccommoder, repriser ▷ n: **on the ~** en voie de guérison; **to ~ one's ways** s'amender

meningitis [mɛnɪn'dʒaɪtɪs] n méningite f

menopause ['mɛnəʊpɔːz] n ménopause f

men's room (us) n: **the men's room** les toilettes fpl pour hommes

menstruation [mɛnstru'eɪʃən] n menstruation f

menswear ['mɛnzwɛə'] n vêtements mpl d'hommes

mental ['mɛntl] adj mental(e); **mental hospital** n hôpital m psychiatrique; **mentality** [mɛn'tælɪtɪ] n mentalité f; **mentally** adv: **to be mentally handicapped** être handicapé(e) mental(e); **the mentally ill** les malades mentaux

menthol ['mɛnθɔl] n menthol m

mention ['mɛnʃən] n mention f ▷ vt mentionner, faire mention de; **don't ~ it!** je vous en prie, il n'y a pas de quoi!

menu ['mɛnjuː] n (set menu, Comput) menu m; (list of dishes) carte f; **could we see the ~?** est-ce qu'on peut voir la carte?

MEP n abbr = **Member of the European Parliament**

mercenary ['məːsɪnərɪ] adj (person) intéressé(e), mercenaire ▷ n mercenaire m

merchandise ['mɜːtʃəndaɪz] n
marchandises fpl
merchant ['mɜːtʃənt] n négociant
m, marchand m; **merchant bank** n
(BRIT) banque f d'affaires; **merchant
navy** (US **merchant marine**) n marine
marchande
merciless ['mɜːsɪlɪs] adj impitoyable,
sans pitié
mercury ['mɜːkjurɪ] n mercure m
mercy ['mɜːsɪ] n pitié f, merci f; (Rel)
miséricorde f; **at the ~ of** à la merci de
mere [mɪə*] adj simple; (chance) pur(e);
a ~ two hours seulement deux heures;
merely adv simplement, purement
merge [mɜːdʒ] vt unir; (Comput)
fusionner, interclasser ▷ vi (colours,
shapes, sounds) se mêler; (roads) se
joindre; (Comm) fusionner; **merger** n
(Comm) fusion f
meringue [mə'ræŋ] n meringue f
merit ['merit] n mérite m, valeur f ▷ vt
mériter
mermaid ['mɜːmeɪd] n sirène f
merry ['merɪ] adj gai(e); **M~
Christmas!** joyeux Noël!; **merry-go-
round** n manège m
mesh [meʃ] n mailles fpl
mess [mes] n désordre m, fouillis m,
pagaille f; (muddle: of life) gâchis m;
(: of economy) pagaille f; (dirt) saleté f;
(Mil) mess m, cantine f; **to be (in) a
~** être en désordre; **to be/get o.s. in a
~** (fig) être/se mettre dans le pétrin;
mess about or around (inf) vi perdre
son temps; **mess up** vt (dirty) salir;
(spoil) gâcher; **mess with** (inf) vt fus
(challenge, confront) se frotter à;
(interfere with) toucher à
message ['mesɪdʒ] n message m; **can I
leave a ~?** est-ce que je peux laisser un
message?; **are there any ~s for me?**
est-ce que j'ai des messages?
messenger ['mesɪndʒə*] n messager m
Messrs, Messrs. ['mesəz] abbr (on
letters: = messieurs) MM
messy ['mesɪ] adj (dirty) sale; (untidy)
en désordre

met [met] pt, pp of **meet**
metabolism [me'tæbəlɪzəm] n
métabolisme m
metal ['metl] n métal m ▷ cpd en métal;
metallic [me'tælɪk] adj métallique
metaphor ['metəfə*] n métaphore f
meteor ['miːtɪə*] n météore m;
meteorite ['miːtɪəraɪt] n météorite
m or f
meteorology [miːtɪə'rɒlədʒɪ] n
météorologie f
meter ['miːtə*] n (instrument) compteur
m; (also: **parking ~**) parc(o)mètre m; (us:
unit) = **metre** ▷ vt (us Post) affranchir
à la machine
method ['meθəd] n méthode f;
methodical [mɪ'θɒdɪkl] adj
méthodique
methylated spirit ['meθɪleɪtɪd-] n
(BRIT: also: **meths**) alcool m à brûler
meticulous [me'tɪkjuləs] adj
méticuleux(-euse)
metre (US **meter**) ['miːtə*] n mètre m
metric ['metrɪk] adj métrique
metro ['metrəu] n métro m
metropolitan [metrə'pɒlɪtən] adj
métropolitain(e); **the M~ Police** (BRIT)
la police londonienne
Mexican ['meksɪkən] adj mexicain(e)
▷ n Mexicain(e)
Mexico ['meksɪkəu] n Mexique m
mg abbr (= milligram) mg
mice [maɪs] npl of **mouse**
micro... ['maɪkrəu] prefix: **microchip**
n (Elec) puce f; **microphone** n
microphone m; **microscope** n
microscope m; **microwave** n (also:
microwave oven) four m à micro-
ondes
mid [mɪd] adj: **~ May** la mi-mai; **~
afternoon** le milieu de l'après-midi; **in
~ air** en plein ciel; **he's in his ~ thirties**
il a dans les trente-cinq ans; **midday**
n midi m
middle ['mɪdl] n milieu m; (waist)
ceinture f, taille f ▷ adj du milieu;
(average) moyen(ne); **in the ~ of the
night** au milieu de la nuit; **middle-**

aged adj d'un certain âge, ni vieux ni jeune; **Middle Ages** npl: **the Middle Ages** le moyen âge; **middle-class** adj bourgeois(e); **middle class(es)** n(pl): **the middle class(es)** = les classes moyennes; **Middle East** n: **the Middle East** le Proche-Orient, le Moyen-Orient; **middle name** n second prénom; **middle school** n (US) école pour les enfants de 12 à 14 ans, ≈ collège m; (BRIT) école pour les enfants de 8 à 14 ans

midge [mɪdʒ] n moucheron m
midget ['mɪdʒɪt] n nain(e)
midnight ['mɪdnaɪt] n minuit m
midst [mɪdst] n: **in the ~ of** au milieu de
midsummer [mɪd'sʌmə'] n milieu m de l'été
midway [mɪd'weɪ] adj, adv: **~ (between)** à mi-chemin (entre); **~ through** ... au milieu de ..., en plein(e) ...
midweek [mɪd'wi:k] adv au milieu de la semaine, en pleine semaine
midwife (pl **midwives**) ['mɪdwaɪf, -vz] n sage-femme f
midwinter [mɪd'wɪntə'] n milieu m de l'hiver

might [maɪt] vb see **may** ▷ n puissance f, force f; **mighty** adj puissant(e)
migraine ['mi:greɪn] n migraine f
migrant ['maɪgrənt] n (bird, animal) migrateur m; (person) migrant(e) ▷ adj migrateur(-trice); migrant(e); (worker) saisonnier(-ière)
migrate [maɪ'greɪt] vi migrer
migration [maɪ'greɪʃən] n migration f
mike [maɪk] n abbr (= microphone) micro m
mild [maɪld] adj doux (douce); (reproach, infection) léger(-ère); (illness) bénin(-igne); (interest) modéré(e); (taste) peu relevé(e); **mildly** ['maɪldlɪ] adv doucement; légèrement; **to put it mildly** (inf) c'est le moins qu'on puisse dire
mile [maɪl] n mil(l)e m (= 1609 m.); **mileage** n distance f en milles, ≈ kilométrage m; **mileometer**

[maɪ'lɔmɪtə'] n compteur m kilométrique; **milestone n borne f; (fig) jalon m
military ['mɪlɪtərɪ] adj militaire
militia [mɪ'lɪʃə] n milice f
milk [mɪlk] n lait m ▷ vt (cow) traire; (fig: person) dépouiller, plumer; (: situation) exploiter à fond; **milk chocolate** n chocolat m au lait; **milkman** (irreg) n laitier m; **milky** adj (drink) au lait; (colour) laiteux(-euse)
mill [mɪl] n moulin m; (factory) usine f, fabrique f; (spinning mill) filature f; (flour mill) minoterie f ▷ vt moudre, broyer ▷ vi (also: **~ about**) grouiller
millennium (pl **~s** or **millennia**) [mɪ'lenɪəm, -'lenɪə] n millénaire m
milli... ['mɪlɪ] prefix milli...;
milligram(me) n milligramme m;
millilitre (US **milliliter**) ['mɪlɪli:tə'] n millilitre m; **millimetre** (US **millimeter**) n millimètre m
million ['mɪljən] n million m; **a ~ pounds** un million de livres sterling; **millionaire** [mɪljə'nɛə'] n millionnaire m; **millionth** [-θ] num millionième
milometer [maɪ'lɔmɪtə'] n = **mileometer**
mime [maɪm] n mime m ▷ vt, vi mimer
mimic ['mɪmɪk] n imitateur(-trice) ▷ vt, vi imiter, contrefaire
min. abbr (= minute(s)) mn.; (= minimum) min.
mince [mɪns] vt hacher ▷ n (BRIT Culin) viande hachée, hachis m; **mincemeat** n hachis de fruits secs utilisés en pâtisserie; (US) viande hachée, hachis m; **mince pie** n sorte de tarte aux fruits secs
mind [maɪnd] n esprit m ▷ vt (attend to, look after) s'occuper de; (be careful) faire attention à; (object to): **I don't ~ the noise** je ne crains pas le bruit, le bruit ne me dérange pas; **it is on my ~** cela me préoccupe; **to change one's ~** changer d'avis; **to my ~** à mon avis, selon moi; **to bear sth in ~** tenir compte de qch; **to have sb/sth**

in → avoir qn/qch en tête; **to make up one's ~** se décider; **do you ~ if ...?** est-ce que cela vous gêne si ...?; **I don't ~** cela ne me dérange pas; *(don't care)* ça m'est égal; **~ you,** ... remarquez, ...; **never ~** peu importe, ça ne fait rien; *(don't worry)* ne vous en faites pas; **"~ the step"** "attention à la marche"

mindless adj irréfléchi(e); *(violence, crime)* insensé(e); *(boring: job)* idiot(e)

mine¹ [maɪn] *pron* le (la) mien(ne), les miens (miennes); **a friend of ~** un de mes amis, un ami à moi; **this book is ~** ce livre est à moi

mine² [maɪn] *n* mine *f* ▷ *vt (coal)* extraire; *(ship, beach)* miner; **minefield** *n* champ *m* de mines; **miner** *n* mineur *m*

mineral [ˈmɪnərəl] adj minéral(e) ▷ *n* minéral *m*; **mineral water** *n* eau minérale

mingle [ˈmɪŋgl] *vi*: **to ~ with** se mêler à

miniature [ˈmɪnətʃəʳ] adj (en) miniature ▷ *n* miniature *f*

minibar [ˈmɪnibɑ:ʳ] *n* minibar *m*

minibus [ˈmɪnibʌs] *n* minibus *m*

minicab [ˈmɪnikæb] *n (BRIT)* taxi *m* indépendant

minimal [ˈmɪnɪml] adj minimal(e)

minimize [ˈmɪnɪmaɪz] *vt (reduce)* réduire au minimum; *(play down)* minimiser

minimum [ˈmɪnɪməm] *n (pl* **minima**) minimum *m* ▷ *adj* minimum

mining [ˈmaɪnɪŋ] *n* exploitation minière

miniskirt [ˈmɪniskə:t] *n* mini-jupe *f*

minister [ˈmɪnɪstəʳ] *n (BRIT Pol)* ministre *m*; *(Rel)* pasteur *m*

ministry [ˈmɪnɪstrɪ] *n (BRIT Pol)* ministère *m*; *(Rel)*: **to go into the ~** devenir pasteur

minor [ˈmaɪnəʳ] adj petit(e), de peu d'importance; *(Mus, poet: problem)* mineur(e) ▷ *n (Law)* mineur(e)

minority [maɪˈnɒrɪtɪ] *n* minorité *f*

mint [mɪnt] *n (plant)* menthe *f*; *(sweet)* bonbon *m* à la menthe ▷ *vt (coins)*

battre; **the (Royal) M~**, **the (US) M~** = l'hôtel *m* de la Monnaie; **in ~ condition** à l'état de neuf

minus [ˈmaɪnəs] *n (also:* **~ sign**) signe moins *m* ▷ *prep* moins; **12 ~ 6 equals 6** 12 moins 6 égal 6; **~ 24 °C** moins 24 °C

minute¹ [ˈmɪnɪt] minuté *f*; **minutes** *npl (of meeting)* procès-verbal *m*, compte rendu; **wait a ~!** (attendez) un instant!; **at the last ~** à la dernière minute

minute² adj [maɪˈnju:t] minuscule; *(detailed)* minutieux(-euse); **in ~ detail** par le menu

miracle [ˈmɪrəkl] *n* miracle *m*

miraculous [mɪˈrækjuləs] adj miraculeux(-euse)

mirage [ˈmɪrɑ:ʒ] *n* mirage *m*

mirror [ˈmɪrəʳ] *n* miroir *m*, glace *f*; *(in car)* rétroviseur *m*

misbehave [mɪsbɪˈheɪv] *vi* mal se conduire

misc. *abbr* = **miscellaneous**

miscarriage [ˈmɪskærɪdʒ] *n (Med)* fausse couche; **~ of justice** erreur *f* judiciaire

miscellaneous [mɪsɪˈleɪnɪəs] adj *(items, expenses)* divers(es); *(selection)* varié(e)

mischief [ˈmɪstʃɪf] *n (naughtiness)* sottises *fpl*; *(playfulness)* espièglerie *f*; *(harm)* mal *m*, dommage *m*; *(maliciousness)* méchanceté *f*; **mischievous** [ˈmɪstʃɪvəs] adj *(playful, naughty)* coquin(e), espiègle

misconception [ˈmɪskənˈsepʃən] *n* idée fausse

misconduct [mɪsˈkɒndʌkt] *n* inconduite *f*; **professional ~** faute professionnelle

miser [ˈmaɪzəʳ] *n* avare *m/f*

miserable [ˈmɪzərəbl] adj *(person, expression)* malheureux(-euse); *(conditions)* misérable; *(weather)* maussade; *(offer, donation)* minable; *(failure)* pitoyable

misery [ˈmɪzərɪ] *n (unhappiness)* tristesse *f*; *(pain)* souffrances *fpl*;

misfortune (*wretchedness*) misère *f*; malchance *f*, malheur *m*

misgiving [mɪsˈɡɪvɪŋ] *n* (*apprehension*) craintes *fpl*; **to have ~s about sth** avoir des doutes quant à qch

misguided [mɪsˈɡaɪdɪd] *adj* malavisé(e)

mishap [ˈmɪshæp] *n* mésaventure *f*

misinterpret [mɪsɪnˈtəːprɪt] *vt* mal interpréter

misjudge [mɪsˈdʒʌdʒ] *vt* méjuger, se méprendre sur le compte de

mislay [mɪsˈleɪ] *vt* (*irreg: like* **lay**) égarer

mislead [mɪsˈliːd] *vt* (*irreg: like* **lead**) induire en erreur; **misleading** *adj* trompeur(-euse)

misplace [mɪsˈpleɪs] *vt* égarer; **to be ~d** (*trust etc*) être mal placé(e)

misprint [ˈmɪsprɪnt] *n* faute *f* d'impression

misrepresent [mɪsreprɪˈzɛnt] *vt* présenter sous un faux jour

Miss [mɪs] *n* Mademoiselle *f*

miss [mɪs] *vt* (*fail to get, attend, see*) manquer, rater; (*regret the absence of:*) **I ~ him/it** il/cela me manque ▷ *vi* manquer ▷ *n* (*shot*) coup manqué; **we ~ed our train** nous avons raté notre train; **you can't ~ it** vous ne pouvez pas vous tromper; **miss out** *vt* (*BRIT*) oublier; **miss out on** *vt fus* (*fun, party*) rater, manquer; (*chance, bargain*) laisser passer

missile [ˈmɪsaɪl] *n* (*Aviat*) missile *m*; (*object thrown*) projectile *m*

missing [ˈmɪsɪŋ] *adj* manquant(e); (*after escape, disaster: person*) disparu(e); **to go ~** disparaître; **~ in action** (*Mil*) porté(e) disparu(e)

mission [ˈmɪʃən] *n* mission *f*; **on a ~ to sb** en mission auprès de qn; **missionary** *n* missionnaire *m/f*

misspell [ˈmɪsˈspɛl] *vt* (*irreg: like* **spell**) mal orthographier

mist [mɪst] *n* brume *f* ▷ *vi* (*also:* **~ over**, **~ up**) devenir brumeux(-euse); (*BRIT: windows*) s'embuer

mistake [mɪsˈteɪk] *n* erreur *f*, faute

f ▷ *vt* (*irreg: like* **take**) (*meaning*) mal comprendre; (*intentions*) se méprendre sur; **to ~ for** prendre pour; **by ~** par erreur, par inadvertance; **to make a ~** (*in writing*) faire une faute; (*in calculating etc*) faire une erreur; **there must be some ~** il doit y avoir une erreur, se tromper; **mistaken** *pp of* **mistake** ▷ *adj* (*idea etc*) erroné(e); **to be mistaken** faire erreur, se tromper

mister [ˈmɪstə*] *n* (*inf*) Monsieur *m*; *see* **Mr**

mistletoe [ˈmɪsltəʊ] *n* gui *m*

mistook [mɪsˈtʊk] *pt of* **mistake**

mistress [ˈmɪstrɪs] *n* maîtresse *f*; (*BRIT: in primary school*) institutrice *f*; (*: in secondary school*) professeur *m*

mistrust [mɪsˈtrʌst] *vt* se méfier de

misty [ˈmɪstɪ] *adj* brumeux(-euse); (*glasses, window*) embué(e)

misunderstand [mɪsʌndəˈstænd] *vt*, *vi* (*irreg: like* **stand**) mal comprendre; **misunderstanding** *n* méprise *f*, malentendu *m*; **there's been a misunderstanding** il y a eu un malentendu

misunderstood [mɪsʌndəˈstʊd] *pt*, *pp of* **misunderstand** ▷ *adj* (*person*) incompris(e)

misuse *n* [mɪsˈjuːs] mauvais emploi; (*of power*) abus *m* ▷ *vt* [mɪsˈjuːz] mal employer; abuser de

mitt(en) [ˈmɪt(n)] *n* moufle *f*; (*fingerless*) mitaine *f*

mix [mɪks] *vt* mélanger; préparer ▷ *vi* se mélanger; (*socialize*): **he doesn't ~ well** il est peu sociable ▷ *n* mélange *m*; **to ~ sth with sth** mélanger qch à qch; **cake ~** préparation *f* pour gâteau; **mix up** *vt* mélanger; (*confuse*) confondre; **to be ~ed up in sth** être mêlé(e) à qch *ou* impliqué(e) dans qch; **mixed** *adj* (*feelings, reactions*) contradictoire; (*school, marriage*) mixte; **mixed grill** (*BRIT*) assortiment *m* de grillades; **mixed salad** *n* salade *f* de crudités; **mixed-up** *adj* (*person*) désorienté(e), embrouillé(e); **mixer**

n (for food) batteur *m*, mixeur *m*;
(drink) boisson gazeuse *(servant à
couper un alcool)*; *(person)*: **he is a good
mixer** il est très sociable; **mixture**
n assortiment *m*, mélange *m*; *(Med)*
préparation *f*; **mix-up** *n*: **there was a
mix-up** il y a eu confusion

ml *abbr (= millilitre(s))* ml

mm *abbr (= millimetre)* mm

moan [məʊn] *n* gémissement *m* ▷ *vi*
gémir; *(inf: complain)*: **to ~ (about)** se
plaindre (de)

moat [məʊt] *n* fossé *m*, douves *fpl*

mob [mɒb] *n* foule *f*; *(disorderly)* cohue
f ▷ *vt* assaillir

mobile ['məʊbaɪl] *adj* mobile ▷ *n (Art)*
mobile *m*; **mobile home** *n* caravane *f*;
mobile phone *n* téléphone portatif

mobility [məʊ'bɪlɪtɪ] *n* mobilité *f*

mobilize ['məʊbɪlaɪz] *vt, vi* mobiliser

mock [mɒk] *vt* ridiculiser; *(laugh at)*
se moquer de ▷ *adj* faux (fausse);
mocks *npl (BRIT: Scol)* examens blancs;
mockery *n* moquerie *f*, raillerie *f*

mod cons ['mɒd'kɒnz] *npl abbr
(BRIT)* = **modern conveniences**; *see*
convenience

mode [məʊd] *n* mode *m*; *(of transport)*
moyen *m*

model ['mɒdl] *n* modèle *m*; *(person:
for fashion)* mannequin *m*; *(: for artist)*
modèle ▷ *vt (with clay etc)* modeler ▷ *vi*
travailler comme mannequin ▷ *adj
(railway: toy)* modèle réduit *inv*; *(child,
factory)* modèle; **to ~ clothes** présenter
des vêtements; **to ~ o.s. on** imiter

modem ['məʊdɛm] *n* modem *m*

moderate *adj* ['mɒdərət] modéré(e);
(amount, change) peu important(e)
▷ *vb* ['mɒdəreɪt] ▷ *vi* se modérer, se
calmer ▷ *vt* modérer; **moderation**
[mɒdə'reɪʃən] *n* modération *f*, mesure
f; **in ~** à dose raisonnable, pris(e) *or*
pratiqué(e) modérément

modern ['mɒdən] *adj* moderne;
modernize *vt* moderniser; **modern
languages** *npl* langues vivantes

modest ['mɒdɪst] *adj* modeste;

modesty *n* modestie *f*; **modification** [mɒdɪfɪ'keɪʃən] *n*
modification *f*

modify ['mɒdɪfaɪ] *vt* modifier

module ['mɒdjuːl] *n* module *m*

mohair ['məʊhɛər] *n* mohair *m*

Mohammed [mə'hæmɛd] *n*
Mahomet *m*

moist [mɔɪst] *adj* humide, moite;
moisture ['mɔɪstʃər] *n* humidité
f; *(on glass)* buée *f*; **moisturizer**
['mɔɪstʃəraɪzər] *n* crème hydratante

mold *etc* [məʊld] *(us)* = **mould** *etc*

mole [məʊl] *n (animal, spy)* taupe *f*;
(spot) grain *m* de beauté

molecule ['mɒlɪkjuːl] *n* molécule *f*

molest [məʊ'lɛst] *vt (assault
sexually)* attenter à la pudeur de

molten ['məʊltən] *adj* fondu(e); *(rock)*
en fusion

mom [mɒm] *n (us)* = **mum**

moment ['məʊmənt] *n* moment *m*,
instant *m*; **at the ~** en ce moment;
momentarily ['məʊməntrɪlɪ] *adv*
momentanément; *(us: soon)* bientôt;
momentary *adj* momentané(e),
passager(-ère); **momentous**
[məʊ'mɛntəs] *adj* important(e),
capital(e)

momentum [məʊ'mɛntəm] *n* élan
m, vitesse acquise; *(fig)* dynamique *f*;
to gather ~ prendre de la vitesse; *(fig)*
gagner du terrain

mommy ['mɒmɪ] *n (us: mother)*
maman *f*

Mon *abbr (= Monday)* l.

Monaco ['mɒnəkəʊ] *n* Monaco *f*

monarch ['mɒnək] *n* monarque *m*;
monarchy *n* monarchie *f*

monastery ['mɒnəstərɪ] *n*
monastère *m*

Monday ['mʌndɪ] *n* lundi *m*

monetary ['mʌnɪtərɪ] *adj* monétaire

money ['mʌnɪ] *n* argent *m*; **to
make ~** *(person)* gagner de l'argent;
(business) rapporter; **money belt** *n*
ceinture-portefeuille *f*; **money order**
n mandat *m*

mongrel ['mʌŋɡrəl] n (dog) bâtard m

monitor ['mɒnɪtə'] n (TV, Comput) écran m, moniteur m ▷ vt contrôler; (foreign station) être à l'écoute de; (progress) suivre de près

monk [mʌŋk] n moine m

monkey ['mʌŋkɪ] n singe m

monologue ['mɒnəlɒɡ] n monologue m

monopoly [mə'nɒpəlɪ] n monopole m

monosodium glutamate [mɒnə'səʊdɪəm 'ɡluːtəmeɪt] n glutamate m de sodium

monotonous [mə'nɒtənəs] adj monotone

monsoon [mɒn'suːn] n mousson f

monster ['mɒnstə'] n monstre m

month [mʌnθ] n mois m; **monthly** adj mensuel(le) ▷ adv mensuellement

Montreal [mɒntrɪ'ɔːl] n Montréal

monument ['mɒnjumənt] n monument m

mood [muːd] n humeur f, disposition f; **to be in a good/bad ~** être de bonne/mauvaise humeur; **moody** adj (variable) d'humeur changeante, lunatique; (sullen) morose, maussade

moon [muːn] n lune f; **moonlight** n clair m de lune

moor [muə'] n lande f ▷ vt (ship) amarrer ▷ vi mouiller

moose [muːs] n (pl inv) élan m

mop [mɒp] n balai m à laver; (for dishes) lavette f à vaisselle ▷ vt éponger, essuyer; **~ of hair** tignasse f; **mop up** vt éponger

mope [məʊp] vi avoir le cafard, se morfondre

moped ['məʊped] n cyclomoteur m

moral ['mɒrl] adj moral(e) ▷ n morale f; **morals** npl moralité f

morale [mɒ'rɑːl] n moral m

morality [mə'rælɪtɪ] n moralité f

morbid ['mɔːbɪd] adj morbide

KEYWORD

more [mɔː'] adj 1 (greater in number etc) plus (de), davantage (de); **more**

people/work (than) plus de gens/de travail (que)

2 (additional) encore (de); **do you want (some) more tea?** voulez-vous encore du thé?; **is there any more wine?** reste-t-il du vin?; **I have no** or **I don't have any more money** je n'ai plus d'argent; **it'll take a few more weeks** ça prendra encore quelques semaines ▷ pron plus, davantage; **more than 10** plus de 10; **it cost more than we expected** cela a coûté plus que prévu; **I want more** je veux plus or davantage; **is there any more?** est-ce qu'il en reste?; **there's no more** il n'y en a plus; **a little more** un peu plus; **many/much more** beaucoup plus, bien davantage ▷ adv plus; **more dangerous/easily (than)** plus dangereux/facilement (que); **more and more expensive** de plus en plus cher; **more or less** plus ou moins; **more than ever** plus que jamais; **once more** encore une fois, une fois de plus

moreover [mɔː'rəʊvə'] adv de plus

morgue [mɔːɡ] n morgue f

morning ['mɔːnɪŋ] n matin m; (as duration) matinée f ▷ cpd matinal(e); (paper) du matin; **in the ~** le matin; **7 o'clock in the ~** 7 heures du matin; **morning sickness** n nausées matinales

Moroccan [mə'rɒkən] adj marocain(e) ▷ n Marocain(e)

Morocco [mə'rɒkəʊ] n Maroc m

moron ['mɔːrɒn] n idiot(e), minus m/f

morphine ['mɔːfiːn] n morphine f

morris dancing ['mɒrɪs-] n (BRIT) danses folkloriques anglaises

○ **MORRIS DANCING**

● Le **Morris dancing** est une
● danse folklorique anglaise
● traditionnellement réservée aux
● hommes. Habillés tout en blanc
● et portant des clochettes, ils

 exécutent différentes figures avec des mouchoirs et de longs bâtons.
 Cette danse est très populaire dans les fêtes de village.

Morse [mɔːs] n (also: **~ code**) morse m

mortal ['mɔːtl] adj, n mortel(le)

mortar ['mɔːtə'] n mortier m

mortgage ['mɔːgɪdʒ] n hypothèque f; (loan) prêt m (or crédit m) hypothécaire ▷ vt hypothéquer

mortician [mɔː'tɪʃən] n (US) entrepreneur m de pompes funèbres

mortified ['mɔːtɪfaɪd] adj mort(e) de honte

mortuary ['mɔːtjuəri] n morgue f

mosaic [məu'zeiɪk] n mosaïque f

Moscow ['mɔskəu] n Moscou

Moslem ['mɔzləm] adj, n = **Muslim**

mosque [mɔsk] n mosquée f

mosquito (pl **~es**) [mɔs'kiːtəu] n moustique m

moss [mɔs] n mousse f

most [məust] adj (majority of) la plupart de; (greatest amount of) le plus de ▷ pron la plupart ▷ adv le plus; (very) très, extrêmement; **the ~** le plus; **~ fish** la plupart des poissons; **the ~ beautiful woman in the world** la plus belle femme du monde; **~ of** (with plural) la plupart de; (with singular) la plus grande partie de; **~ of them** la plupart d'entre eux; **~ of the time** la plupart du temps; **I saw ~** (a lot but not all) j'en ai vu la plupart; (more than anyone else) c'est moi qui en ai vu le plus; **at the (very) ~ au plus**; **to make the ~ of** profiter au maximum de; **mostly** adv (chiefly) surtout, principalement; (usually) généralement

MOT n abbr (BRIT) = **Ministry of Transport**; **the ~ (test)** visite technique (annuelle) obligatoire des véhicules à moteur

motel [məu'tɛl] n motel m

moth [mɔθ] n papillon m de nuit; (in clothes) mite f

mother ['mʌðə'] n mère f ▷ vt (pamper, protect) dorloter; **motherhood** n maternité f; **mother-in-law** n belle-mère f; **mother-of-pearl** n nacre f; **Mother's Day** n fête f des Mères; **mother-to-be** n future maman; **mother tongue** n langue maternelle

motif [məu'tiːf] n motif m

motion ['məuʃən] n mouvement m; (gesture) geste m; (at meeting) motion f ▷ vb, vi: **to ~ (to) sb to do** faire signe à qn de faire; **motionless** adj immobile, sans mouvement; **motion picture** n film m

motivate ['məutɪveɪt] vt motiver

motivation [məutɪ'veɪʃən] n motivation f

motive ['məutɪv] n motif m, mobile m

motor ['məutə'] n moteur m; (BRIT inf: vehicle) auto f; **motorbike** n moto f; **motorboat** n bateau m à moteur; **motorcar** n (BRIT) automobile f; **motorcycle** n moto f; **motorcyclist** n motocycliste m/f; **motoring** (BRIT) n tourisme m automobile; **motorist** n automobiliste m/f; **motor racing** n (BRIT) course f automobile; **motorway** n (BRIT) autoroute f

motto (pl **~es**) ['mɔtəu] n devise f

mould (US **mold**) [məuld] n moule m; (mildew) moisissure f ▷ vt mouler, modeler; (fig) façonner; **mouldy** adj moisi(e); (smell) de moisi

mound [maund] n monticule m, tertre m

mount [maunt] n (hill) mont m, montagne f; (horse) monture f; (for picture) carton m de montage ▷ vt monter; (horse) monter à; (bike) monter sur; (picture) monter sur carton ▷ vi (inflation, tension) augmenter; **mount up** vi s'élever, monter; (bills, problems, savings) s'accumuler

mountain ['mauntɪn] n montagne f ▷ cpd de (la) montagne; **mountain bike** n VTT m, vélo m tout terrain; **mountaineer** n alpiniste m/f; **mountaineering** n alpinisme m; **mountainous** adj montagneux(-euse);

mountain range n chaîne f de montagnes

mourn [mɔːn] vt pleurer ▷ vi: **to ~ for sb** pleurer qn; **to ~ for sth** se lamenter sur qch; **mourner** n parent(e) ou ami(e) du défunt; personne f en deuil qui vient rendre hommage au défunt; **mourning** n deuil m; **in mourning** en deuil

mouse (pl **mice**) [maus, maɪs] n (also Comput) souris f; **mouse mat** n (Comput) tapis m de souris

moussaka [mu'sɑːkə] n moussaka f

mousse [muːs] n mousse f

moustache (us **mustache**) [məs'tɑːʃ] n moustache(s) f(pl)

mouth [mauθ, pl -ðz] n bouche f; (of dog, cat) gueule f; (of river) embouchure f; (of hole, cave) ouverture f; **mouthful** n bouchée f; **mouth organ** n harmonica m; **mouthpiece** n (of musical instrument) bec m, embouchure f; (spokesperson) porte-parole m inv; **mouthwash** n eau f dentifrice

move [muːv] n (movement) mouvement m; (in game) coup m; (: turn to play) tour m; (change of house) déménagement m; (change of job) changement m d'emploi ▷ vt déplacer, bouger; (emotionally) émouvoir; (Pol: resolution etc) proposer ▷ vi (gen) bouger, remuer; (traffic) circuler; (also: **~ house**) déménager; (in game) jouer; **can you ~ your car, please?** pouvez-vous déplacer votre voiture, s'il vous plaît?; **to ~ sb to do sth** pousser ou inciter qn à faire qch; **to get a ~ on** se dépêcher, se remuer; **move back** vi revenir, retourner; **move in** vi (to a house) emménager; (police, soldiers) intervenir; **move off** vi s'éloigner, s'en aller; **move on** vi se remettre en route; **move out** vi (of house) déménager; **move over** vi se pousser, se déplacer; **move up** vi avancer; (employee) avoir de l'avancement; (pupil) passer dans la classe supérieure; **movement** n mouvement m

movie ['muːvɪ] n film m; **movies** npl: **the ~s** le cinéma; **movie theater** (us) n cinéma m

moving ['muːvɪŋ] adj en mouvement; (touching) émouvant(e)

mow (pt **~ed**, pp **~ed** or **~n**) [məu, -d, -n] vt faucher; (lawn) tondre; **mower** n (also: **lawnmower**) tondeuse f à gazon

Mozambique [məuzəm'biːk] n Mozambique m

MP n abbr (BRIT) = **Member of Parliament**

MP3 n mp3 m; **MP3 player** n lecteur m mp3

mpg n abbr = miles per gallon (30 mpg = 9,4 l. aux 100 km)

m.p.h. abbr = miles per hour (60 mph = 96 km/h)

Mr (us **Mr.**) ['mɪstə'] n: **Mr X** Monsieur X, M. X

Mrs (us **Mrs.**) ['mɪsɪz] n: **~ X** Madame X, Mme X

Ms (us **Ms.**) [mɪz] n (Miss or Mrs): **Ms X** Madame X, Mme X

MSP n abbr (= Member of the Scottish Parliament) député m au Parlement écossais

Mt abbr (Geo: = mount) Mt

much [mʌtʃ] adj beaucoup de ▷ adv, n or pron beaucoup; **we don't have ~ time** nous n'avons pas beaucoup de temps; **how ~ is it?** combien est-ce que ça coûte?; **it's not ~** ce n'est pas beaucoup; **too ~** trop (de); **so ~** tant (de); **I like it very/so ~** j'aime beaucoup/tellement ça; **as ~ as** autant (que); **that's ~ better** c'est beaucoup mieux

muck [mʌk] n (mud) boue f; (dirt) ordures fpl; **muck up** vt (inf: ruin) gâcher, esquinter; (: dirty) salir; (: exam, interview) se planter à; **mucky** adj (dirty) boueux(-euse), sale

mucus ['mjuːkəs] n mucus m

mud [mʌd] n boue f

muddle ['mʌdl] n (mess) pagaille f, fouillis m; (mix-up) confusion f ▷ vt (also: **~ up**) brouiller, embrouiller; **to get in a ~** (while explaining etc) s'embrouiller

muddy ['mʌdɪ] adj boueux(-euse)

mudguard ['mʌdgɑːd] n garde-boue m inv

muesli ['mjuːzlɪ] n muesli m

muffin ['mʌfɪn] n (roll) petit pain rond et plat; (cake) petit gâteau au chocolat ou aux fruits

muffled ['mʌfld] adj étouffé(e), voilé(e)

muffler ['mʌfləʳ] n (scarf) cache-nez m inv; (us Aut) silencieux m

mug [mʌg] n (cup) tasse f (sans soucoupe); (: for beer) chope f; (inf: face) bouille f; (: fool) poire f ▷ vt (assault) agresser; **mugger** ['mʌgəʳ] n agresseur m; **mugging** n agression f

muggy ['mʌgɪ] adj lourd(e), moite

mule [mjuːl] n mule f

multicoloured (us **multicolored**) ['mʌltɪkʌləd] adj multicolore

multimedia ['mʌltɪ'miːdɪə] adj multimédia inv

multinational [mʌltɪ'næʃənl] n multinationale f ▷ adj multinational(e)

multiple ['mʌltɪpl] adj multiple ▷ n multiple m; **multiple choice (test)** n QCM m, questionnaire m à choix multiple; **multiple sclerosis** [-sklɪ'rəusɪs] n sclérose f en plaques

multiplex (cinema) ['mʌltɪpleks-] n (cinéma m) multisalles m

multiplication [mʌltɪplɪ'keɪʃən] n multiplication f

multiply ['mʌltɪplaɪ] vt multiplier ▷ vi se multiplier

multistorey ['mʌltɪ'stɔːrɪ] adj (BRIT: building) à étages; (: car park) à étages ou niveaux multiples

mum [mʌm] n (BRIT) maman f ▷ adj: **to keep ~** ne pas souffler mot

mumble ['mʌmbl] vt, vi marmotter, marmonner

mummy ['mʌmɪ] n (BRIT: mother) maman f; (embalmed) momie f

mumps [mʌmps] n oreillons mpl

munch [mʌntʃ] vt, vi mâcher

municipal [mjuː'nɪsɪpl] adj municipal(e)

mural ['mjuərl] n peinture murale

murder ['məːdəʳ] n meurtre m, assassinat m ▷ vt assassiner; **murderer** n meurtrier m, assassin m

murky ['məːkɪ] adj sombre, ténébreux(-euse); (water) trouble

murmur ['məːməʳ] n murmure m ▷ vt, vi murmurer

muscle ['mʌsl] n muscle m; (fig) force f; **muscular** ['mʌskjuləʳ] adj musculaire; (person, arm) musclé(e)

museum [mjuː'zɪəm] n musée m

mushroom ['mʌʃrum] n champignon m ▷ vi (fig) pousser comme un (or des) champignon(s)

music ['mjuːzɪk] n musique f; **musical** adj musical(e); (person) musicien(ne) ▷ n (show) comédie musicale; **musical instrument** n instrument m de musique; **musician** [mjuː'zɪʃən] n musicien(ne)

Muslim ['mʌzlɪm] adj, n musulman(e)

muslin ['mʌzlɪn] n mousseline f

mussel ['mʌsl] n moule f

must [mʌst] aux vb (obligation): **I ~ do it** je dois le faire, il faut que je le fasse; (probability): **he ~ be there by now** il doit y être maintenant, il y est probablement maintenant; (suggestion, invitation): **you ~ come and see me** il faut que vous veniez me voir ▷ n nécessité f, impératif m; **it's a must** c'est indispensable; **I ~ have made a mistake** j'ai dû me tromper

mustache ['mʌstæʃ] n (us) = **moustache**

mustard ['mʌstəd] n moutarde f

mustn't ['mʌsnt] = **must not**

mute [mjuːt] adj, n muet(te)

mutilate ['mjuːtɪleɪt] vt mutiler

mutiny ['mjuːtɪnɪ] n mutinerie f ▷ vi se mutiner

mutter ['mʌtəʳ] vt, vi marmonner, marmotter

mutton ['mʌtn] n mouton m

mutual ['mjuːtʃuəl] adj mutuel(le), réciproque; (benefit, interest) commun(e)

muzzle ['mʌzl] n museau m; (protective device) muselière f; (of gun) gueule f ▷ vt museler

my [maɪ] adj mon (ma), mes pl; **my house/car/gloves** ma maison/ma voiture/mes gants; **I've washed my hair/cut my finger** je me suis lavé les cheveux/coupé le doigt; **is this my pen or yours?** c'est mon stylo ou c'est le vôtre?

myself [maɪ'sɛlf] pron (reflexive) me; (emphatic) moi-même; (after prep) moi; see also **oneself**

mysterious [mɪs'tɪərɪəs] adj mystérieux(-euse)

mystery ['mɪstərɪ] n mystère m

mystical ['mɪstɪkl] adj mystique

mystify ['mɪstɪfaɪ] vt (deliberately) mystifier; (puzzle) ébahir

myth [mɪθ] n mythe m; **mythology** [mɪ'θɒlədʒɪ] n mythologie f

n/a abbr (= not applicable) n.a.

nag [næg] vt (scold) être toujours après, reprendre sans arrêt

nail [neɪl] n (human) ongle m; (metal) clou m ▷ vt clouer; **to ~ sth to sth** clouer qch à qch; **to ~ sb down to a date/price** contraindre qn à accepter or donner une date/un prix; **nailbrush** n brosse f à ongles; **nailfile** n lime f à ongles; **nail polish** n vernis m à ongles; **nail polish remover** n dissolvant m; **nail scissors** npl ciseaux mpl à ongles; **nail varnish** n (BRIT) = **nail polish**

naïve [naɪ'iːv] adj naïf(-ive)

naked ['neɪkɪd] adj nu(e)

name [neɪm] n nom m; (reputation) réputation f ▷ vt nommer; (identify: accomplice etc) citer; (price, date) fixer, donner; **by ~** par son nom; de nom; **in the ~ of** au nom de; **what's your ~?** comment vous appelez-vous?, quel est votre nom?; **namely** adv à savoir

nanny ['nænɪ] n bonne f d'enfants

nap [næp] n (sleep) (petit) somme

napkin ['næpkɪn] n serviette f (de table)

nappy ['næpɪ] n (BRIT) couche f

narcotics [nɑːˈkɒtɪkz] npl (illegal drugs) stupéfiants mpl

narrative ['nærətɪv] n récit m ▷ adj narratif(-ive)

narrator [nəˈreɪtəʳ] n narrateur(-trice)

narrow ['nærəʊ] adj étroit(e); (fig) restreint(e), limité(e) ▷ vi (road) devenir plus étroit, se rétrécir; (gap, difference) se réduire; **to have a ~ escape** l'échapper belle; **narrow down** vt restreindre; **narrowly** adv: **he narrowly missed injury/the tree** il a failli se blesser/rentrer dans l'arbre; **he only narrowly missed the target** il a manqué la cible de peu or de justesse; **narrow-minded** adj à l'esprit étroit, borné(e); (attitude) borné(e)

nasal ['neɪzl] adj nasal(e)

nasty ['nɑːstɪ] adj (person: malicious) méchant(e); (: rude) très désagréable; (smell) dégoûtant(e); (wound, situation) mauvais(e), vilain(e)

nation ['neɪʃən] n nation f

national ['næʃənl] adj national(e) ▷ n (abroad) ressortissant(e); (when home) national(e); **national anthem** n hymne national; **national dress** n costume national; **National Health Service** n (BRIT) service national de santé, ≈ Sécurité Sociale; **National Insurance** n (BRIT) ≈ Sécurité Sociale; **nationalist** adj, n nationaliste m/f; **nationality** [næʃəˈnælɪtɪ] n nationalité f; **nationalize** vt nationaliser; **national park** n parc national; **National Trust** n (BRIT) ≈ Caisse f nationale des monuments historiques et des sites

● **NATIONAL TRUST**
●
● Le **National Trust** est un organisme
● indépendant, à but non lucratif,
● dont la mission est de protéger et
● de mettre en valeur les monuments

● et les sites britanniques en raison
● de leur intérêt historique ou de leur
● beauté naturelle.

nationwide ['neɪʃənwaɪd] adj s'étendant à l'ensemble du pays; (problem) à l'échelle du pays entier

native ['neɪtɪv] n habitant(e) du pays, autochtone m/f ▷ adj du pays, indigène; (country) natal(e); (language) maternel(le); (ability) inné(e); **Native American** n Indien(ne) d'Amérique ▷ adj amérindien(ne); **native speaker** n locuteur natif

NATO ['neɪtəʊ] n abbr (= North Atlantic Treaty Organization) OTAN f

natural ['nætʃrəl] adj naturel(le); **natural gas** n gaz naturel; **natural history** n histoire naturelle; **naturally** adv naturellement; **natural resources** npl ressources naturelles

nature ['neɪtʃəʳ] n nature f; **by ~** par tempérament, de nature; **nature reserve** n (BRIT) réserve naturelle

naughty ['nɔːtɪ] adj (child) vilain(e), pas sage

nausea ['nɔːsɪə] n nausée f

naval ['neɪvl] adj naval(e)

navel ['neɪvl] n nombril m

navigate ['nævɪgeɪt] vt (steer) diriger, piloter ▷ vi naviguer; (Aut) indiquer la route à suivre; **navigation** [nævɪˈgeɪʃən] n navigation f

navy ['neɪvɪ] n marine f

navy-blue ['neɪvɪ'bluː] adj bleu marine inv

Nazi ['nɑːtsɪ] n Nazi(e)

NB abbr (= nota bene) NB

near [nɪəʳ] adj proche ▷ adv près ▷ prep (also: ~ **to**) près de ▷ vt approcher de; **in the ~ future** dans un proche avenir; **nearby** [nɪəˈbaɪ] adj proche ▷ adv tout près, à proximité; **nearly** adv presque; **I nearly fell** j'ai failli tomber; **it's not nearly big enough** ce n'est vraiment pas assez grand, c'est loin d'être assez grand; **near-sighted** adj myope

neat [niːt] adj (person, work) soigné(e);

(room etc) bien tenu(e) or rangé(e); (solution, plan) habile; **neatly** adv avec soin or ordre; (skilfully) habilement

necessarily ['nɛsɪsrɪlɪ] adv nécessairement; **not ~** pas nécessairement or forcément

necessary ['nɛsɪsrɪ] adj nécessaire; **if ~** si besoin est, le cas échéant

necessity [nɪ'sɛsɪtɪ] n nécessité f; chose nécessaire or essentielle

neck [nɛk] n cou m; (of horse, garment) encolure f; (of bottle) goulot m; **~ and ~** à égalité; **necklace** ['nɛklɪs] n collier m; **necktie** ['nɛktaɪ] n (esp us) cravate f

nectarine ['nɛktərɪn] n brugnon m, nectarine f

need [niːd] n besoin m ▷ vt avoir besoin de; **to ~ to do** devoir faire; avoir besoin de faire; **you don't ~ to go** vous n'avez pas besoin or vous n'êtes pas obligé de partir; **a signature is ~ed** il faut une signature; **there's no ~ to do ....** il n'y a pas lieu de faire ..., il n'est pas nécessaire de faire ...

needle ['niːdl] n aiguille f ▷ vt (inf) asticoter, tourmenter

needless ['niːdlɪs] adj inutile; **~ to say, ...** inutile de dire que ...

needlework ['niːdlwəːk] n (activity) travaux mpl d'aiguille; (object) ouvrage m

needn't ['niːdnt] = **need not**

needy ['niːdɪ] adj nécessiteux(-euse)

negative ['nɛgətɪv] n (Phot, Elec) négatif m; (Ling) terme m de négation ▷ adj négatif(-ive)

neglect [nɪ'glɛkt] vt négliger; (garden) ne pas entretenir; (duty) manquer à ▷ n (of person, duty, garden) le fait de négliger; **(state of) ~** abandon m; **to ~ to do sth** négliger or omettre de faire qch; **to ~ one's appearance** se négliger

negotiate [nɪ'gəʊʃɪeɪt] vi négocier; (obstacle) franchir, négocier; **to ~ with sb for sth** négocier avec qn en vue d'obtenir qch

negotiation [nɪgəʊʃɪ'eɪʃən] n

négociation f, pourparlers mpl

negotiator [nɪ'gəʊʃɪeɪtə^r] n négociateur(-trice)

neighbour (us **neighbor** etc) ['neɪbə^r] n voisin(e); **neighbourhood** n (place) quartier m; (people) voisinage m; **neighbouring** adj voisin(e), avoisinant(e)

neither ['naɪðə^r] adj, pron aucun(e) (des deux), ni l'un(e) ni l'autre ▷ conj: **~ do I** moi non plus ▷ adv: **~ good nor bad** ni bon ni mauvais; **~ of them** ni l'un ni l'autre

neon ['niːɔn] n néon m

Nepal [nɪ'pɔːl] n Népal m

nephew ['nɛvjuː] n neveu m

nerve [nəːv] n nerf m; (bravery) sang-froid m, courage m; (cheek) aplomb m, toupet m; **nerves** npl (nervousness) nervosité f; **he gets on my ~s** il m'énerve

nervous ['nəːvəs] adj nerveux(-euse); (anxious) inquiet(-ète), plein(e) d'appréhension; (timid) intimidé(e); **nervous breakdown** n dépression nerveuse

nest [nɛst] n nid m ▷ vi (se) nicher, faire son nid

Net [nɛt] n (Comput): **the ~** (Internet) le Net

net [nɛt] n filet m; (fabric) tulle f ▷ adj net(te) ▷ vt (fish etc) prendre au filet; **netball** n netball m

Netherlands ['nɛðələndz] npl: **the ~** les Pays-Bas mpl

nett [nɛt] adj = **net**

nettle ['nɛtl] n ortie f

network ['nɛtwəːk] n réseau m

neurotic [njuə'rɔtɪk] adj névrosé(e)

neuter ['njuːtə^r] adj neutre ▷ vt (cat etc) châtrer, couper

neutral ['njuːtrəl] adj neutre ▷ n (Aut) point mort

never ['nɛvə^r] adv (ne ...) jamais; **I ~ went** je n'y suis pas allé; **I've ~ been to Spain** je ne suis jamais allé en Espagne; **~ again** plus jamais; **~ in my life** jamais de ma vie; see also **mind**; **never-ending**

adj interminable; **nevertheless** [nevəðə'les] adv néanmoins, malgré tout

new [nju:] adj nouveau (nouvelle); (brand new) neuf (neuve); **New Age** n New Age m; **newborn** adj nouveau-né(e); **newcomer** ['nju:kʌmə*] n nouveau venu (nouvelle venue); **newly** adv nouvellement, récemment

news [nju:z] n nouvelle(s) f(pl); (Radio, TV) informations fpl, actualités fpl; **a piece of ~** une nouvelle; **news agency** n agence f de presse; **newsagent** n (BRIT) marchand m de journaux; **newscaster** n (Radio, TV) présentateur(-trice); **news dealer** n (US) marchand m de journaux; **newsletter** n bulletin m; **newspaper** n journal m; **newsreader** n = **newscaster**

newt [nju:t] n triton m

New Year n Nouvel An; **Happy ~!** Bonne Année!; **New Year's Day** n le jour de l'An; **New Year's Eve** n la Saint-Sylvestre

New York [-'jɔ:k] n New York

New Zealand [-'zi:lənd] n Nouvelle-Zélande f; **New Zealander** n Néo-Zélandais(e)

next [nekst] adj (in time) prochain(e); (seat, room) voisin(e), d'à côté; (meeting, bus stop) suivant(e) ▷ adv la fois suivante; la prochaine fois; (afterwards) ensuite; **~ to** prep à côté de; **~ to nothing** presque rien; **~ time** adv la prochaine fois; **the ~ day** le lendemain, le jour suivant or d'après; **~ year** l'année prochaine; **~ please!** (at doctor's etc) au suivant!; **the week after ~** dans deux semaines; **next door** adv à côté ▷ adj (neighbour) d'à côté; **next-of-kin** n parent m le plus proche

NHS n abbr (BRIT) = **National Health Service**

nibble ['nɪbl] vt grignoter

nice [naɪs] adj (holiday, trip, taste) agréable; (flat, picture) joli(e); (person) gentil(le); (distinction, point) subtil(e);

nicely adv agréablement; joliment; gentiment; subtilement

niche [ni:ʃ] n (Archit) niche f

nick [nɪk] n (indentation) encoche f; (wound) entaille f; (BRIT inf): **in good ~** en bon état ▷ vt (cut): **to ~** se couper; (inf: steal) faucher, piquer; **in the ~ of time** juste à temps

nickel ['nɪkl] n nickel m; (US) pièce f de 5 cents

nickname ['nɪkneɪm] n surnom m ▷ vt surnommer

nicotine ['nɪkəti:n] n nicotine f

niece [ni:s] n nièce f

Nigeria [naɪ'dʒɪərɪə] n Nigéria m or f

night [naɪt] n nuit f; (evening) soir m; **at ~** la nuit; **by ~** de nuit; **last ~** (evening) hier soir; (night-time) la nuit dernière; **night club** n boîte f de nuit; **nightdress** n chemise f de nuit; **nightie** ['naɪtɪ] n chemise f de nuit; **nightlife** n vie f nocturne; **nightly** adj (news) du soir; (by night) nocturne ▷ adv (every evening) tous les soirs; (every night) toutes les nuits; **nightmare** n cauchemar m; **night school** n cours mpl du soir; **night shift** n équipe f de nuit; **night-time** n nuit f

nil [nɪl] n (BRIT Sport) zéro m

nine [naɪn] num neuf; **nineteen** num dix-neuf; **nineteenth** [naɪn'ti:nθ] num dix-neuvième; **ninetieth** ['naɪntɪθ] num quatre-vingt-dixième; **ninety** num quatre-vingt-dix

ninth [naɪnθ] num neuvième

nip [nɪp] vt pincer ▷ vi (BRIT inf): **to ~ out/down/up** sortir/descendre/ monter en vitesse

nipple ['nɪpl] n (Anat) mamelon m, bout m du sein

nitrogen ['naɪtrədʒən] n azote m

KEYWORD

no [nəu] (pl **noes**) adv (opposite of "yes") non; **are you coming? — no (I'm not)** est-ce que vous venez? — non; **would you like some more? — no thank you**

vous en voulez encore? — non merci
▷ *adj* (*not any*) (ne ...) pas de, (ne ...)
aucun(e); **I have no money/books** je
n'ai pas d'argent/de livres; **no student
would have done it** aucun étudiant ne
l'aurait fait; **"no smoking"** "défense de
fumer"; **"no dogs"** "les chiens ne sont
pas admis"
▷ *n* non *m*

nobility [nəʊˈbɪlɪtɪ] *n* noblesse *f*
noble [ˈnəʊbl] *adj* noble
nobody [ˈnəʊbədɪ] *pron* (ne ...)
personne
nod [nɒd] *vi* faire un signe de (la) tête
(*affirmatif ou amical*); (*sleep*) somnoler
▷ *vt*: **to ~ one's head** faire un signe de
(la) tête; (*in agreement*) faire signe que
oui ▷ *n* signe *m* de (la) tête; **nod off** *vi*
s'assoupir
noise [nɔɪz] *n* bruit *m*; **I can't sleep for
the ~** je n'arrive pas à dormir à cause du
bruit; **noisy** *adj* bruyant(e)
nominal [ˈnɒmɪnl] *adj* (*rent, fee*)
symbolique; (*value*) nominal(e)
nominate [ˈnɒmɪneɪt] *vt* (*propose*)
proposer; (*appoint*) nommer;
nomination [nɒmɪˈneɪʃən] *n*
nomination *f*; **nominee** [nɒmɪˈniː] *n*
candidat agréé; personne nommée
none [nʌn] *pron* aucun(e); **~ of you**
aucun d'entre vous, personne parmi
vous; **I have ~ left** je n'en ai plus; **he's
~ the worse for it** il ne s'en porte pas
plus mal
nonetheless [ˈnʌnðəˈles] *adv*
néanmoins
non-fiction [nɒnˈfɪkʃən] *n* littérature *f*
non-romanesque
nonsense [ˈnɒnsəns] *n* absurdités *fpl*,
idioties *fpl*; **~!** ne dites pas d'idioties!
non: **non-smoker** *n* non-fumeur *m*;
non-smoking *adj* non-fumeur; **non-
stick** *adj* qui n'attache pas
noodles [ˈnuːdlz] *npl* nouilles *fpl*
noon [nuːn] *n* midi *m*
no-one [ˈnəʊwʌn] *pron* = **nobody**
nor [nɔː] *conj* = **neither** ▷ *adv* see

neither
norm [nɔːm] *n* norme *f*
normal [ˈnɔːml] *adj* normal(e);
normally *adv* normalement
Normandy [ˈnɔːməndɪ] *n* Normandie *f*
north [nɔːθ] *n* nord *m* ▷ *adj* nord *inv*;
(*wind*) du nord ▷ *adv* au or vers le nord;
North Africa *n* Afrique *f* du Nord;
North African *adj* nord-africain(e),
d'Afrique du Nord ▷ *n* Nord-Africain(e);
North America *n* Amérique *f* du Nord;
North American *adj* nord-américain(e),
d'Amérique
du Nord ▷ *n* nord-américain(e), d'Amérique
du Nord; **northbound** [ˈnɔːθbaʊnd]
adj (*traffic*) en direction du nord;
(*carriageway*) nord (du nord); **north-east** *n*
nord-est *m*; **northeastern** *adj* (du)
nord-est *inv*; **northern** [ˈnɔːðən] *adj*
du nord, septentrional(e); **Northern
Ireland** *n* Irlande *f* du Nord; **North
Korea** *n* Corée *f* du Nord; **North
Pole** *n*: **the North Pole** le pôle Nord;
North Sea *n*: **the North Sea** la mer
du Nord; **north-west** *n* nord-ouest *m*;
northwestern [ˈnɔːθˈwestən] *adj* (du)
nord-ouest *inv*
Norway [ˈnɔːweɪ] *n* Norvège *f*;
Norwegian [nɔːˈwiːdʒən] *adj*
norvégien(ne) ▷ *n* Norvégien(ne);
(*Ling*) norvégien *m*
nose [nəʊz] *n* nez *m*; (*of dog, cat*)
museau *m*; (*fig*) flair *m*; **nose about,
nose around** *vi* fouiner or fureter
(partout); **nosebleed** *n* saignement *m*
de nez; **nosey** *adj* (*inf*) curieux(-euse)
nostalgia [nɒsˈtældʒɪə] *n* nostalgie *f*
nostalgic [nɒsˈtældʒɪk] *adj*
nostalgique
nostril [ˈnɒstrɪl] *n* narine *f*; (*of horse*)
naseau *m*
nosy [ˈnəʊzɪ] (*inf*) *adj* = **nosey**
not [nɒt] *adv* (ne ...) pas; **he is ~ or isn't
here** il n'est pas ici; **you must ~ or
mustn't do that** il ne faut pas faire
ça; **I hope ~** j'espère que non; **~ at
all** pas du tout; (*after thanks*) de rien;
it's too late, isn't it? c'est trop tard,
n'est-ce pas?; **~ yet/now** pas encore/

maintenant; *see also* **only**
notable ['nəʊtəbl] *adj* notable;
notably *adv* (*particularly*) en
particulier; (*markedly*) spécialement
notch [nɒtʃ] *n* encoche *f*
note [nəʊt] *n* note *f*; (*letter*) mot *m*;
(*banknote*) billet *m* ▷ *vt* (*also*: ~ **down**)
noter; (*notice*) constater; **notebook**
n carnet *m*; (*for shorthand etc*) bloc-
notes *m*; **noted** ['nəʊtɪd] *adj* réputé(e);
notepad *n* bloc-notes *m*; **notepaper** *n*
papier *m* à lettres
nothing ['nʌθɪŋ] *n* rien *m*; **he does ~**
il ne fait rien; **~ new** rien de nouveau; **for
~** (*free*) pour rien, gratuitement; (*in vain*)
pour rien; **~ at all** rien du tout; **~ much**
pas grand-chose
notice ['nəʊtɪs] *n* (*announcement,
warning*) avis *m* ▷ *vt* remarquer,
s'apercevoir de; **advance ~** préavis *m*;
at short ~ dans un délai très court;
until further ~ jusqu'à nouvel ordre;
to give ~, hand in one's ~ (*employee*)
donner sa démission, démissionner;
to take ~ of prêter attention à; **to
bring sth to sb's ~** porter qch à la
connaissance de qn; **noticeable** *adj*
visible
notice board *n* (*BRIT*) panneau *m*
d'affichage
notify ['nəʊtɪfaɪ] *vt*: **to ~ sb of sth**
avertir qn de qch
notion ['nəʊʃən] *n* idée *f*; (*concept*)
notion *f*; **notions** *npl* (*US: haberdashery*)
mercerie *f*
notorious [nəʊ'tɔːrɪəs] *adj* notoire
(*souvent en mal*)
notwithstanding [nɒtwɪθ'stændɪŋ]
adv néanmoins ▷ *prep* en dépit de
nought [nɔːt] *n* zéro *m*
noun [naʊn] *n* nom *m*
nourish ['nʌrɪʃ] *vt* nourrir;
nourishment *n* nourriture *f*
Nov. *abbr* (= *November*) nov.
novel ['nɔvl] *n* roman *m* ▷ *adj* nouveau
(nouvelle), original(e); **novelist** *n*
romancier *m*; **novelty** *n* nouveauté *f*
November [nəʊ'vɛmbər] *n*

novembre *m*
novice ['nɔvɪs] *n* novice *m/f*
now [naʊ] *adv* maintenant ▷ *conj*: **~
(that)** maintenant (que); **right ~** tout
de suite; **by ~** à l'heure qu'il est; **just ~**:
that's the fashion just ~ c'est la mode
en ce moment or maintenant; **~ and
then, ~ and again** de temps en temps;
from ~ on dorénavant; **nowadays**
['naʊədeɪz] *adv* de nos jours
nowhere ['nəʊwɛər] *adv* (*ne ...*)
nulle part
nozzle ['nɔzl] *n* (*of hose*) jet *m*, lance *f*;
(*of vacuum cleaner*) suceur *m*
nr *abbr* (*BRIT*) **= near**
nuclear ['njuːklɪər] *adj* nucléaire
nucleus (*pl* **nuclei**) ['njuːklɪəs,
'njuːklɪaɪ] *n* noyau *m*
nude [njuːd] *adj* nu(e) ▷ *n* (*Art*) nu *m*; **in
the ~** (*tout(e)) nu(e)
nudge [nʌdʒ] *vt* donner un (petit) coup
de coude à
nudist ['njuːdɪst] *n* nudiste *m/f*
nudity ['njuːdɪtɪ] *n* nudité *f*
nuisance ['njuːsns] *n*: **it's a ~** c'est
(très) ennuyeux or gênant; **he's a ~** il est
assommant or casse-pieds; **what a ~!**
quelle barbe!
numb [nʌm] *adj* engourdi(e); (*with fear*)
paralysé(e)
number ['nʌmbər] *n* nombre *m*;
(*numeral*) chiffre *m*; (*of house, car,
telephone, newspaper*) numéro *m* ▷ *vt*
numéroter; (*amount to*) compter; **a ~
of** un certain nombre de; **they were
seven in ~** ils étaient (au nombre de)
sept; **to be ~ed among** compter parmi;
number plate *n* (*BRIT Aut*) plaque *f*
minéralogique or d'immatriculation;
Number Ten (*BRIT*: *10 Downing Street*)
résidence f du Premier ministre
numerical [njuː'mɛrɪkl] *adj*
numérique
numerous ['njuːmərəs] *adj*
nombreux(-euse)
nun [nʌn] *n* religieuse *f*, sœur *f*
nurse [nəːs] *n* infirmière *f*; (*also*: **~maid**)
bonne *f* d'enfants ▷ *vt* (*patient, cold*)

soigner

nursery [ˈnəːsərɪ] *n* (room) nursery *f*; (institution) crèche *f*, garderie *f*; (for plants) pépinière *f*; **nursery rhyme** *n* comptine *f*, chansonnette *f* pour enfants; **nursery school** *n* école maternelle; **nursery slope** *n* (BRIT Ski) piste *f* pour débutants

nursing [ˈnəːsɪŋ] *n* (profession) profession *f* d'infirmière; (care) soins *mpl*; **nursing home** *n* clinique *f*; (for convalescence) maison *f* de convalescence or de repos; (for old people) maison de retraite

nurture [ˈnəːtʃər] *vt* élever

nut [nʌt] *n* (of metal) écrou *m*; (fruit: walnut) noix *f*; (: hazelnut) noisette *f*; (: peanut) cacahuète *f* (terme générique en anglais)

nutmeg [ˈnʌtmɛg] *n* (noix *f*) muscade *f*

nutrient [ˈnjuːtrɪənt] *n* substance nutritive

nutrition [njuːˈtrɪʃən] *n* nutrition *f*, alimentation *f*

nutritious [njuːˈtrɪʃəs] *adj* nutritif(-ive), nourrissant(e)

nuts [nʌts] (*inf*) *adj* dingue

NVQ *n abbr* (BRIT) = **National Vocational Qualification**

nylon [ˈnaɪlɔn] *n* nylon *m* ▷ *adj* de or en nylon

O

oak [əuk] *n* chêne *m* ▷ *cpd* de or en (bois de) chêne

O.A.P. *n abbr* (BRIT) = **old age pensioner**

oar [ɔːr] *n* aviron *m*, rame *f*

oasis (*pl* **oases**) [əuˈeɪsɪs, əuˈeɪsiːz] *n* oasis *f*

oath [əuθ] *n* serment *m*; (swear word) juron *m*; **on** (BRIT) or **under ~** sous serment; assermenté(e)

oatmeal [ˈəutmiːl] *n* flocons *mpl* d'avoine

oats [əuts] *n* avoine *f*

obedience [əˈbiːdɪəns] *n* obéissance *f*

obedient [əˈbiːdɪənt] *adj* obéissant(e)

obese [əuˈbiːs] *adj* obèse

obesity [əuˈbiːsɪtɪ] *n* obésité *f*

obey [əˈbeɪ] *vt* obéir à; (instructions, regulations) se conformer à ▷ *vi* obéir

obituary [əˈbɪtjuərɪ] *n* nécrologie *f*

object *n* [ˈɔbdʒɪkt] objet *m*; (purpose) but *m*, objet; (Ling) complément *m* d'objet ▷ *vi* [əbˈdʒɛkt]: **to ~ to** (attitude) désapprouver; (proposal) protester contre, élever une objection contre; **I ~!** je proteste; **he ~ed that ...** il a fait valoir or a objecté que ...; **money is no ~** l'argent n'est pas un problème; **objection** [əb'dʒekʃən] n objection f; **if you have no objection** si vous n'y voyez pas d'inconvénient; **objective** a ▷ adj objectif(-ive)

obligation [ɔblɪ'geɪʃən] n obligation f, devoir m; (debt) dette f (de reconnaissance)

obligatory [ə'blɪgətərɪ] adj obligatoire

oblige [ə'blaɪdʒ] vt (force): **to ~ sb to do** obliger or forcer qn à faire; (do a favour) rendre service à, obliger; **to be ~d to sb for sth** être obligé(e) à qn de qch

oblique [ə'bliːk] adj oblique; (allusion) indirect(e)

obliterate [ə'blɪtəreɪt] vt effacer

oblivion [ə'blɪvɪən] n oubli m

oblivious [ə'blɪvɪəs] adj: **~ of** oublieux(-euse) de

oblong [ɔblɔŋ] adj oblong(ue) ▷ n rectangle m

obnoxious [əb'nɔkʃəs] adj odieux(-euse); (smell) nauséabond(e)

oboe [ˈəubəu] n hautbois m

obscene [əb'siːn] adj obscène

obscure [əb'skjuər] adj obscur(e) ▷ vt obscurcir; (hide: sun) cacher

observant [əb'zəːvnt] adj observateur(-trice)

observation [ɔbzə'veɪʃən] n observation f; (by police etc) surveillance f

observatory [əb'zəːvətrɪ] n observatoire m

observe [əb'zəːv] vt observer; (remark) faire observer or remarquer; **observer** n observateur(-trice)

obsess [əb'ses] vt obséder; **obsession** [əb'seʃən] n obsession f; **obsessive** adj obsédant(e)

obsolete [ˈɔbsəliːt] adj dépassé(e), périmé(e)

obstacle [ˈɔbstəkl] n obstacle m

obstinate [ˈɔbstɪnɪt] adj obstiné(e); (pain, cold) persistant(e)

obstruct [əb'strʌkt] vt (block) boucher, obstruer; (hinder) entraver; **obstruction** [əb'strʌkʃən] n obstruction f; (to plan, progress) obstacle m

obtain [əb'teɪn] vt obtenir

obvious [ˈɔbvɪəs] adj évident(e), manifeste; **obviously** adv manifestement; (of course): **obviously!** bien sûr!; **obviously not!** évidemment pas!, bien sûr que non!

occasion [ə'keɪʒən] n occasion f; (event) événement m; **occasional** adj pris(e) (or fait(e) etc) de temps en temps; (worker, spending) occasionnel(le); **occasionally** adv de temps en temps, quelquefois

occult [ɔ'kʌlt] adj occulte ▷ n: **the ~** le surnaturel

occupant [ˈɔkjupənt] n occupant m

occupation [ɔkju'peɪʃən] n occupation f; (job) métier m, profession f

occupy [ˈɔkjupaɪ] vt occuper; **to o.s. with** or **by doing** s'occuper à faire

occur [ə'kəːr] vi se produire; (difficulty, opportunity) se présenter; (phenomenon, error) se rencontrer; **to ~ to sb** venir à l'esprit de qn; **occurrence** [ə'kʌrəns] n (existence) présence f, existence f; (event) cas m, fait m

ocean [ˈəuʃən] n océan m

o'clock [ə'klɔk] adv: **it is 5 o'clock** il est 5 heures

Oct. abbr (= October) oct

October [ɔk'təubər] n octobre m

octopus [ˈɔktəpəs] n pieuvre f

odd [ɔd] adj (strange) bizarre, curieux(-euse); (number) impair(e); (not of a set) dépareillé(e); **60-~** 60 et quelques; **at ~ times** de temps en temps; **the ~ one out** l'exception f; **oddly** adv bizarrement, curieusement; **odds** npl (in betting) cote f; **it makes no odds** cela n'a pas d'importance; **odds and ends** de petites choses; **at odds** en désaccord

odometer [ɔ'dɔmɪtər] n (us) odomètre m

odour (US **odor**) [ˈəʊdə*] n odeur f

⭕ **KEYWORD**

of [ɔv, əv] prep 1 (gen) de; **a friend of ours** un de nos amis; **a boy of 10** un garçon de 10 ans; **that kind of you** c'était gentil de votre part
2 (expressing quantity, amount, dates etc) de; **a kilo of flour** un kilo de farine; **how much of this do you need?** combien vous en faut-il?; **there were three of them** (people) ils étaient 3; (objects) il y en avait 3; **three of us went** 3 d'entre nous y sont allé(e)s; **the 5th of July** le 5 juillet; **a quarter of 4** (US) 4 heures moins le quart
3 (from, out of) en, de; **a statue of marble** une statue de or en marbre; **made of wood** (fait) en bois

off [ɔf] adj, adv (engine) coupé(e), (light, TV) éteint(e); (tap) fermé(e); (BRIT: food) mauvais(e), avancé(e); (: milk) tourné(e); (absent) absent(e); (: cancelled) annulé(e); (removed): **the lid was ~** le couvercle était retiré or n'était pas mis; (away): **to run/drive ~** partir en courant/en voiture ▷ prep de; **to be ~** (to leave) partir, s'en aller; **to be ~ sick** être absent pour cause de maladie; **a day ~** un jour de congé; **to have an ~ day** n'être pas en forme; **he had his coat ~** il avait enlevé son manteau; **10% ~** (Comm) 10% de rabais; **5 km ~ (the road)** à 5 km (de la route); **~ the coast** au large de la côte; **it's a long way ~** c'est loin (d'ici); **I'm ~ meat** je ne mange plus de viande; je n'aime plus la viande; **on the ~ chance** à tout hasard; **~ and on, on and ~** de temps à autre

offence (US **offense**) [əˈfɛns] n (crime) délit m, infraction f; **to take ~ at** se vexer de, s'offenser de

offend [əˈfɛnd] vt (person) offenser, blesser; **offender** n délinquant(e); (against regulations) contrevenant(e)

offense [əˈfɛns] n (US) = **offence**

offensive [əˈfɛnsɪv] adj offensant(e), choquant(e); (smell etc) très déplaisant(e); (weapon) offensif(-ive) ▷ n (Mil) offensive f

offer [ˈɔfə*] n offre f, proposition f ▷ vt offrir, proposer; **"on ~"** (Comm) "en promotion"

offhand [ɔfˈhænd] adj désinvolte ▷ adv spontanément

office [ˈɔfɪs] n (place) bureau m; (position) charge f, fonction f; **doctor's ~** (US) cabinet (médical); **to take ~** entrer en fonctions; **office block** (US **office building**) n immeuble m de bureaux; **office hours** npl heures fpl de bureau; (US Med) heures de consultation

officer [ˈɔfɪsə*] n (Mil etc) officier m; (also: **police ~**) agent m (de police); (of organization) membre m du bureau directeur

office worker n employé(e) de bureau

official [əˈfɪʃl] adj (authorized) officiel(le) ▷ n officiel m; (civil servant) fonctionnaire m/f; (of railways, post office, town hall) employé(e)

off-licence n (BRIT: shop) débit m de vins et de spiritueux; **off-line** adj (Comput) (en mode) autonome; (: switched off) non connecté(e); **off-peak** adj aux heures creuses; (electricity, ticket) au tarif heures creuses; **off-putting** adj (BRIT: remark) rébarbatif(-ive); (person) rebutant(e), peu engageant(e); **off-season** adj, adv hors-saison inv

offset [ˈɔfsɛt] vt (irreg: like **set**) (counteract) contrebalancer, compenser

offshore [ɔfˈʃɔː*] adj (breeze) de terre; (island) proche du littoral; (fishing) côtier(-ière)

offside [ˈɔfsaɪd] adj (Sport) hors jeu; (Aut: in Britain) de droite; (: in US, Europe) de gauche

offspring [ˈɔfsprɪŋ] n progéniture f

often [ˈɔfn] adv souvent; **how ~ do you go?** vous y allez tous les combien?; **every so ~** de temps en temps, de temps à autre

oh [əu] *excl* ô!, oh!, ah!

oil [ɔɪl] *n* huile *f*; *(petroleum)* pétrole *m*; *(for central heating)* mazout *m* ▷ *vt* *(machine)* graisser; **oil filter** *n (Aut)* filtre *m* à huile; **oil painting** *n* peinture *f* à l'huile; **oil refinery** *n* raffinerie *f* de pétrole; **oil rig** *n* derrick *m*; *(at sea)* plate-forme *f* pétrolière; **oil slick** *n* nappe *f* de mazout; **oil tanker** *n* *(ship)* pétrolier *m*; *(truck)* camion-citerne *m*; **oil well** *n* puits *m* de pétrole; **oily** *adj* huileux(-euse); *(food)* gras(se)

ointment [ˈɔɪntmənt] *n* onguent *m*

O.K., okay [ˈəuˈkeɪ] *(inf)* *excl* d'accord! ▷ *vt* approuver, donner son accord à ▷ *adj (not bad)* pas mal; **is it O.K.?**, **are you O.K.?** ça va?

old [əuld] *adj* vieux (vieille); *(person)* vieux, âgé(e); *(former)* ancien(ne), vieux; **how ~ are you?** quel âge avez-vous?; **he's 10 years ~** il a 10 ans, il est âgé de 10 ans; **~er brother/sister** frère/sœur aîné(e); **old age** *n* vieillesse *f*; **old-age pension** *n (BRIT)* pension *f* de retraite *(de la sécurité sociale)*; **old-age pensioner** *n (BRIT)* retraité(e); **old-fashioned** *adj* démodé(e); *(person)* vieux jeu *inv*; **old people's home** *n (esp BRIT)* maison *f* de retraite

olive [ˈɔlɪv] *n (fruit)* olive *f*; *(tree)* olivier *m* ▷ *adj* *(also:* **~-green)** (vert) olive *inv*; **olive oil** *n* huile *f* d'olive

Olympic [əuˈlɪmpɪk] *adj* olympique; **the ~ Games**, **the ~s** les Jeux *mpl* olympiques

omelet(te) [ˈɔmlɪt] *n* omelette *f*

omen [ˈəumən] *n* présage *m*

ominous [ˈɔmɪnəs] *adj* menaçant(e), inquiétant(e); *(event)* de mauvais augure

omit [əuˈmɪt] *vt* omettre

KEYWORD

on [ɔn] *prep* **1** *(indicating position)* sur; **on the table** sur la table; **on the wall** sur le mur ou au mur; **on the left** à gauche
2 *(indicating means, method, condition*

etc): **on foot** à pied; **on the train/plane** *(be)* dans le train/l'avion; *(go)* en train/avion; **on the telephone/radio/television** au téléphone/à la radio/à la télévision; **to be on drugs** se droguer; **on holiday** *(BRIT)*, **on vacation** *(US)* en vacances

3 *(referring to time)*: **on Friday** vendredi; **on Fridays** le vendredi; **on June 20th** le 20 juin; **a week on Friday** vendredi en huit; **on arrival** à l'arrivée; **on seeing this** en voyant cela

4 *(about, concerning)* sur, de; **a book on Balzac/physics** un livre sur Balzac/de physique

▷ *adv* **1** *(referring to dress)*: **to have one's coat on** avoir (mis) son manteau; **to put one's coat on** mettre son manteau; **what's she got on?** qu'est-ce qu'elle porte?

2 *(referring to covering)*: **screw the lid on tightly** vissez bien le couvercle

3 *(further, continuously)*: **to walk** *etc* **on** continuer à marcher *etc*; **from that day on** depuis ce jour

▷ *adj* **1** *(in operation: machine)* en marche; *(: radio, TV, light)* allumé(e); *(: tap, gas)* ouvert(e); *(: brakes)* mis(e); **is the meeting still on?** *(not cancelled)* est-ce que la réunion a bien lieu?; *(in progress)* la réunion dure-t-elle encore?; **when is this film on?** quand passe ce film?

2 *(inf)*: **that's not on!** *(not acceptable)* cela ne se fait pas!; *(not possible)* pas question!

once [wʌns] *adv* une fois; *(formerly)* autrefois ▷ *conj* une fois que + *sub*; **he had left/it was done** une fois qu'il fut parti/que ce fut terminé; **at ~** tout de suite, immédiatement; *(simultaneously)* à la fois; **all at ~** *adv* tout d'un coup; **~ a week** une fois par semaine; **~ more** encore une fois; **~ and for all** une fois pour toutes; **~ upon a time there was ...** il y avait une fois ..., il était une fois ...

oncoming ['ɒnkʌmɪŋ] *adj* (traffic) venant en sens inverse

 KEYWORD

one [wʌn] *num* un(e); **one hundred and fifty** cent cinquante; **one by one** un(e) à or par un(e); **one day** un jour ▷ *adj* 1 (*sole*) seul(e), unique; **the one book which** l'unique or le seul livre qui; **the one man who** le seul (homme) qui 2 (*same*) même; **they came in the one car** ils sont venus dans la même voiture
▷ *pron* 1: **this one** celui-ci (celle-ci); **that one** celui-là (celle-là); **I've already got one/a red one** j'en ai déjà un(e)/un(e) rouge; **which one do you want?** lequel voulez-vous?
2: **one another** l'un(e) l'autre; **to look at one another** se regarder
3 (*impersonal*) on; **one never knows** on ne sait jamais; **to cut one's finger** se couper le doigt; **one needs to eat** il faut manger

one-off [wʌn'ɒf] (*BRIT inf*) *n* exemplaire *m* unique

oneself [wʌn'sɛlf] *pron* se; (*after prep, also emphatic*) soi-même; **to hurt ~** se faire mal; **to keep sth for ~** garder qch pour soi; **to talk to ~** se parler à soi-même; **by ~** tout seul

one: **one-shot** [wʌn'ʃɒt] (*US*) *n* = **one-off**; **one-sided** *adj* (*argument, decision*) unilatéral(e); **one-to-one** (*relationship*) univoque; **one-way** *adj* (*street, traffic*) à sens unique

ongoing ['ɒngəʊɪŋ] *adj* en cours; (*relationship*) suivi(e)

onion ['ʌnjən] *n* oignon *m*

on-line ['ɒnlaɪn] *adj* (*Comput*) en ligne; (: *switched on*) connecté(e)

onlooker ['ɒnlʊkə*] *n* spectateur(-trice)

only ['əʊnlɪ] *adv* seulement ▷ *adj* seul(e), unique ▷ *conj* seulement, mais; **an ~ child** un enfant unique; **not ~ ... but also** non seulement ... mais aussi; **I**

~ took one j'en ai seulement pris un, je n'en ai pris qu'un

on-screen [ɒn'skri:n] *adj* à l'écran

onset ['ɒnsɛt] *n* début *m*; (*of winter, old age*) approche *f*

onto ['ɒntu] *prep* = **on to**

onward(s) ['ɒnwəd(z)] *adv* (*move*) en avant; **from that time ~** à partir de ce moment

oops [ʊps] *excl* houp!

ooze [u:z] *vi* suinter

opaque [əʊ'peɪk] *adj* opaque

open ['əʊpn] *adj* ouvert(e); (*car*) découvert(e); (*road, view*) dégagé(e); (*meeting*) public(-ique); (*admiration*) manifeste ▷ *vt* ouvrir ▷ *vi* (*flower, eyes, door, debate*) s'ouvrir; (*shop, bank, museum*) ouvrir; (*book etc*: *commence*) commencer, débuter; **is it ~ to the public?** est-ce ouvert au public?; **what time do you ~?** à quelle heure ouvrez-vous?; **in the ~ (air)** en plein air; **open up** *vt* ouvrir; (*blocked road*) dégager ▷ *vi* s'ouvrir; **open-air** *adj* en plein air; **opening** *n* ouverture *f*; (*opportunity*) occasion *f*; (*work*) débouché *m*; (*job*) poste vacant; **opening hours** *npl* heures *fpl* d'ouverture; **open learning** *n* enseignement universitaire à la carte, notamment par correspondance; (*distance learning*) télé-enseignement *m*; **openly** *adv* ouvertement; **open-minded** *adj* à l'esprit ouvert; **open-necked** *adj* à col ouvert; **open-plan** *adj* sans cloisons; **Open University** *n* (*BRIT*) cours universitaires par correspondance

● **OPEN UNIVERSITY**

● L'**Open University** a été fondée en
● 1969. L'enseignement comprend
● des cours (certaines plages horaires
● sont réservées à cet effet à la
● télévision et à la radio), des devoirs
● qui sont envoyés par l'étudiant à son
● directeur ou sa directrice d'études, et
● un séjour obligatoire en université
● d'été. Il faut préparer un certain

- nombre d'unités de valeur pendant
- une période de temps déterminée
- et obtenir la moyenne à un certain
- nombre d'entre elles pour recevoir le
- diplôme visé.

opera ['ɔpərə] n opéra m; **opera house** n opéra m; **opera singer** n chanteur(-euse) d'opéra

operate ['ɔpəreɪt] vt (machine) faire marcher, faire fonctionner ▷ vi fonctionner; **to ~ on sb (for)** (Med) opérer qn (de)

operating room n (us: Med) salle f d'opération

operating theatre n (BRIT: Med) salle f d'opération

operation [ɔpə'reɪʃən] n opération f; (of machine) fonctionnement m; **to have an ~ (for)** se faire opérer (de); **to be in ~** (machine) être en service; (system) être en vigueur; **operational** adj opérationnel(le); (ready for use) en état de marche

operative ['ɔpərətɪv] adj (measure) en vigueur ▷ n (in factory) ouvrier(-ière)

operator ['ɔpəreɪtə*] n (of machine) opérateur(-trice); (Tel) téléphoniste m/f

opinion [ə'pɪnjən] n opinion f, avis m; **in my ~** à mon avis; **opinion poll** n sondage m d'opinion

opponent [ə'pəunənt] n adversaire m/f

opportunity [ɔpə'tjuːnɪtɪ] n occasion f; **to take the ~ to do or of doing** profiter de l'occasion pour faire

oppose [ə'pəuz] vt s'opposer à; **to be ~d to sth** être opposé(e) à qch; **as ~d to** par opposition à

opposite ['ɔpəzɪt] adj (house etc) d'en face ▷ adv en face ▷ prep en face de ▷ n opposé m, contraire m; (of word) contraire

opposition [ɔpə'zɪʃən] n opposition f

oppress [ə'prɛs] vt opprimer

opt [ɔpt] vi: **to ~ for** opter pour; **to ~ to do** choisir de faire; **opt out** vi: **to ~ out**

ne pas faire

optician [ɔp'tɪʃən] n opticien(ne)

optimism ['ɔptɪmɪzəm] n optimisme m

optimist ['ɔptɪmɪst] n optimiste m/f; **optimistic** [ɔptɪ'mɪstɪk] adj optimiste

optimum ['ɔptɪməm] adj optimum

option ['ɔpʃən] n choix m, option f; (Scol) matière f à option; **optional** adj facultatif(-ive)

or [ɔː*] conj ou; (with negative): **he hasn't seen or heard anything** il n'a rien vu ni entendu; **or else** sinon; ou bien

oral ['ɔːrəl] adj oral(e) ▷ n oral m

orange ['ɔrɪndʒ] n (fruit) orange f ▷ adj orange inv; **orange juice** n jus m d'orange; **orange squash** n orangeade f

orbit ['ɔːbɪt] n orbite f ▷ vt graviter autour de

orchard ['ɔːtʃəd] n verger m

orchestra ['ɔːkɪstrə] n orchestre m; (us: seating) (fauteuils mpl d')orchestre

orchid ['ɔːkɪd] n orchidée f

ordeal [ɔː'diːl] n épreuve f

order ['ɔːdə*] n ordre m; (Comm) commande f ▷ vt ordonner; (Comm) commander; **in ~** en ordre; (of document) en règle; **out of ~** (not in correct order) en désordre; (machine) hors service; (telephone) en dérangement; **a machine in working ~** une machine en état de marche; **in ~ to do/that** pour faire/que + sub; **could I ~ now, please?** je peux commander, s'il vous plaît?; **to be on ~** être en commande; **to ~ sb to do** ordonner à qn de faire; **order form** n bon m de commande; **orderly** n (Mil) ordonnance f; (Med) garçon m de salle ▷ adj (room) en ordre; (mind) méthodique; (person) qui a de l'ordre

ordinary ['ɔːdnrɪ] adj ordinaire, normal(e); (pej) ordinaire, quelconque; **out of the ~** exceptionnel(le)

ore [ɔː*] n minerai m

oregano [ɔrɪ'gɑːnəu] n origan m

organ ['ɔːgən] n organe m; (Mus) orgue m, orgues fpl; **organic** [ɔː'gænɪk] adj organique; (crops etc) biologique, naturel(le); **organism** n organisme m

organization [ˌɔːgənaɪˈzeɪʃən] n organisation f

organize [ˈɔːgənaɪz] vt organiser; **organized** [ˈɔːgənaɪzd] adj (planned) organisé(e); (efficient) bien organisé(e); **organizer** n organisateur(-trice)

orgasm [ˈɔːgæzəm] n orgasme m

orgy [ˈɔːdʒɪ] n orgie f

oriental [ɔːrɪˈɛntl] adj oriental(e)

orientation [ɔːrɪɛnˈteɪʃən] n (attitudes) tendance f; (in job) orientation f; (of building) orientation, exposition f

origin [ˈɔrɪdʒɪn] n origine f

original [əˈrɪdʒɪnl] adj original(e); (earliest) originel(le) ▷ n original m; **originally** adv (at first) à l'origine

originate [əˈrɪdʒɪneɪt] vi: **to ~ from** être originaire de; (suggestion) provenir de; **to ~ in** (custom) prendre naissance dans, avoir son origine dans

Orkney [ˈɔːknɪ] n also: **the ~s, the ~ Islands** les Orcades fpl

ornament [ˈɔːnəmənt] n ornement m; (trinket) bibelot m; **ornamental** [ɔːnəˈmɛntl] adj décoratif(-ive); (garden) d'agrément

ornate [ɔːˈneɪt] adj très orné(e)

orphan [ˈɔːfn] n orphelin(e)

orthodox [ˈɔːθədɒks] adj orthodoxe

orthopaedic (us **orthopedic**) [ɔːθəˈpiːdɪk] adj orthopédique

osteopath [ˈɔstɪəpæθ] n ostéopathe m/f

ostrich [ˈɔstrɪtʃ] n autruche f

other [ˈʌðər] adj autre ▷ pron: **the ~ (one)** l'autre; **~s** (other people) d'autres ▷ adv: **~ than** autrement que, à part; **the ~ day** l'autre jour; **otherwise** adv, conj autrement

Ottawa [ˈɔtəwə] n Ottawa

otter [ˈɔtər] n loutre f

ouch [autʃ] excl aïe!

ought (pt ~) [ɔːt] aux vb: **I ~ to do it** je devrais le faire, il faudrait que je le fasse; **this ~ to have been corrected** cela aurait dû être corrigé; **he ~ to win**

(probability) il devrait gagner

ounce [auns] n once f (28.35g; 16 in a pound)

our [ˈauər] adj notre, nos pl; see also **my**; **ours** pron le (la) nôtre, les nôtres; see also **mine**[1]; **ourselves** pron pl (reflexive, after preposition) nous; (emphatic) nous-mêmes; see also **oneself**

oust [aust] vt évincer

out [aut] adv dehors; (published, not at home etc) sorti(e); (light, fire) éteint(e); **~ there** là-bas; **he's ~** (absent) il est sorti; **to be ~ in one's calculations** s'être trompé dans ses calculs; **to run/back** etc **~** sortir en courant/en reculant etc; **~ loud** adv à haute voix; **~ of** prep (outside) en dehors de; (because of: anger etc) par; (from among): **10 ~ of 10** 10 sur 10; (without): **~ of petrol** sans essence, à court d'essence; **~ of order** (machine) en panne; (Tel: line) en dérangement; **outback** n (in Australia) intérieur m; **outbound** adj: **outbound (from/for)** en partance (de/pour); **outbreak** n (of violence) éruption f, explosion f; (of disease) de nombreux cas; **the outbreak of war south of the border** la guerre qui s'est déclarée au sud de la frontière; **outburst** n explosion f, accès m; **outcast** n exilé(e); (socially) paria m; **outcome** n issue f, résultat m; **outcry** n tollé (général); **outdated** adj démodé(e); **outdoor** adj de or en plein air; **outdoors** adv dehors; au grand air; **outer** [ˈautər] adj extérieur(e); **outer space** n espace m cosmique

outfit [ˈautfɪt] n (clothes) tenue f

out: outgoing adj (president, tenant) sortant(e); (character) ouvert(e), extraverti(e); **outgoings** npl (BRIT: expenses) dépenses fpl; **outhouse** n appentis m

outing [ˈautɪŋ] n sortie f; excursion f

out: outlaw n hors-la-loi m inv ▷ vt (person) mettre hors la loi; (practice) proscrire; **outlay** n dépenses fpl; (investment) mise f de fonds; **outlet** n (for liquid etc) issue f, sortie f; (for emotion) exutoire m; (also: **retail outlet**) point m de vente; (us: Elec) prise f de courant; **outline** n (shape) contour m; (summary) esquisse f, grandes lignes ▷ vt (fig: theory, plan) exposer à grands traits; **outlook** n perspective f; (point of view) attitude f; **outnumber** vt surpasser en nombre; **out-of-date** adj (passport, ticket) périmé(e); (theory, idea) dépassé(e); (custom) désuet(-ète); (clothes) démodé(e); **out-of-doors** adv = **outdoors**; **out-of-the-way** adj loin de tout; **out-of-town** adj (shopping centre etc) en périphérie; **outpatient** n malade m/f en consultation externe; **outpost** n avant-poste m; **output** n rendement m, production f; (Comput) sortie f ▷ vt (Comput) sortir

outrage ['aʊtreɪdʒ] n (anger) indignation f; (violent act) atrocité f, acte m de violence; (scandal) scandale m ▷ vt outrager; **outrageous** [aʊt'reɪdʒəs] adj atroce; (scandalous) scandaleux(-euse)

outright adv [aʊt'raɪt] complètement; (deny, refuse) catégoriquement; (ask) carrément; (kill) sur le coup ▷ adj ['aʊtraɪt] complet(-ète); catégorique

outset ['aʊtsɛt] n début m

outside [aʊt'saɪd] n extérieur m ▷ adj extérieur(e) ▷ adv (au) dehors, à l'extérieur ▷ prep hors de, à l'extérieur de; (in front of) devant; **at the ~** (fig) au plus or maximum; **outside lane** n (Aut: in Britain) voie f de droite; (: in US, Europe) voie f de gauche; **outside line** n (Tel) ligne extérieure; **outsider** n (stranger) étranger(-ère)

out: **outsize** adj énorme; (clothes) grande taille inv; **outskirts** npl faubourgs mpl; **outspoken** adj très franc (franche); **outstanding** adj remarquable, exceptionnel(le); (unfinished: work, business) en souffrance; (debt) impayé(e); (problem) non réglé(e)

outward ['aʊtwəd] adj (sign, appearances) extérieur(e); (journey)

(d')aller; **outwards** adv (esp BRIT) = **outward**

outweigh [aʊt'weɪ] vt l'emporter sur

oval ['əʊvl] adj, n ovale m

ovary ['əʊvərɪ] n ovaire m

oven ['ʌvn] n four m; **oven glove** n gant m de cuisine; **ovenproof** adj allant au four; **oven-ready** adj prêt(e) à cuire

over ['əʊvə'] adv (par-)dessus ▷ adj (or adv) (finished) fini(e), terminé(e); (too much) en plus ▷ prep sur; par-dessus; (above) au-dessus de; (on the other side of) de l'autre côté de; (more than) plus de; (during) pendant; (about, concerning): **they fell out ~ money/her** ils se sont brouillés pour des questions d'argent/à cause d'elle; **~ here** ici; **~ there** là-bas; **all ~** (everywhere) partout; **~ and ~ (again)** à plusieurs reprises; **~ and above** en plus de; **to ask sb ~** inviter qn (à passer); **to fall ~** tomber; **to turn sth ~** retourner qch

overall ['əʊvərɔːl] adj (length) total(e); (study, impression) d'ensemble ▷ n (BRIT) blouse f ▷ adv [əʊvər'ɔːl] dans l'ensemble, en général; **overalls** npl (boiler suit) bleus mpl de travail

overboard ['əʊvəbɔːd] adv (Naut) par-dessus bord

overcame [əʊvə'keɪm] pt of **overcome**

overcast ['əʊvəkɑːst] adj couvert(e)

overcharge [əʊvə'tʃɑːdʒ] vt: **to ~ sb for sth** faire payer qch trop cher à qn

overcoat ['əʊvəkəʊt] n pardessus m

overcome [əʊvə'kʌm] vt (irreg: like come) (defeat) triompher de; (difficulty) surmonter ▷ adj (emotionally) bouleversé(e); **~ with grief** accablé(e) de douleur

over: **overcrowded** adj bondé(e); (city, country) surpeuplé(e); **overdo** vt (irreg: like do) exagérer; (overcook) trop cuire; **to overdo it**, **to overdo things** (work too hard) en faire trop, se surmener; **overdone** [əʊvə'dʌn] adj (vegetables, steak) trop cuit(e); **overdose** n dose excessive; **overdraft** n découvert m;

overdrawn adj (account) à découvert;
overdue adj en retard; (bill) impayé(e);
(change) qui tarde; **overestimate** vt
surestimer

overflow vi [ˌəuvəˈfləu] déborder
▷ n [ˈəuvəfləu] (also: ~ **pipe**) tuyau m
d'écoulement, trop-plein m

overgrown [ˌəuvəˈgrəun] adj (garden)
envahi(e) par la végétation

overhaul vt [ˌəuvəˈhɔːl] réviser ▷ n
[ˈəuvəhɔːl] révision f

overhead adv [ˌəuvəˈhɛd] au-dessus
▷ adj, n [ˈəuvəhɛd] (road) aérien(ne);
(lighting) vertical(e) ▷ n (US)
= **overheads**; **overhead projector**
n rétroprojecteur m; **overheads** npl
(BRIT) frais généraux

overhear vt (irreg: like **hear**)
entendre (par hasard); **overheat** vi
(engine) chauffer; **overland** adj, adv par
voie de terre; **overlap** vi se chevaucher;
overleaf adv au verso; **overload** vt
surcharger; **overlook** vt (have view of)
donner sur; (miss) oublier, négliger;
(forgive) fermer les yeux sur

overnight adv [ˌəuvəˈnaɪt] (happen)
durant la nuit; (fig) soudain ▷ adj
[ˈəuvənaɪt] d'une (or de) nuit;
soudain(e); **to stay ~ (with sb)** passer
la nuit (chez qn); **overnight bag** n
nécessaire m de voyage

overpass [ˈəuvəpɑːs] n (US: for cars)
pont autoroutier; (: for pedestrians)
passerelle f, pont m

overpower [ˌəuvəˈpauə] vt vaincre;
(fig) accabler; **overpowering** adj
irrésistible; (heat, stench) suffocant(e)

over: **overreact** vi [ˌəuvərɪˈækt] vi
réagir de façon excessive; **overrule**
vt (decision) annuler; (claim) rejeter;
(person) rejeter l'avis de; **overrun** vt
(irreg: like **run**) (Mil: country etc) occuper;
(time limit etc) dépasser ▷ vi dépasser le
temps imparti

overseas [ˌəuvəˈsiːz] adv outre-mer;
(abroad) à l'étranger ▷ adj (trade)
extérieur(e); (visitor) étranger(-ère)

oversee [ˌəuvəˈsiː] vt (irreg: like **see**)

surveiller

overshadow [ˌəuvəˈʃædəu] vt (fig)
éclipser

oversight [ˈəuvəsaɪt] n omission f,
oubli m

oversleep [ˌəuvəˈsliːp] vi (irreg: like
sleep) se réveiller (trop) tard

overspend [ˌəuvəˈspɛnd] vi (irreg: like
spend) dépenser de trop

overt [əuˈvəːt] adj non dissimulé(e)

overtake [əuvəˈteɪk] vt (irreg: like **take**)
dépasser; (BRIT: Aut) dépasser, doubler

over: **overthrow** vt (irreg: like **throw**)
(government) renverser; **overtime** n
heures fpl supplémentaires

overtook [əuvəˈtuk] pt of **overtake**

over: **overturn** vt renverser; (decision,
plan) annuler ▷ vi se retourner;
overweight adj (person) trop gros(se);
overwhelm vt (subj: emotion) accabler,
submerger; (enemy, opponent) écraser;
overwhelming adj (victory, defeat)
écrasant(e); (desire) irrésistible

ow [au] excl aïe!

owe [əu] vt devoir; **to ~ sb sth, to ~ sth
to sb** devoir qch à qn; **how much do I ~
you?** combien est-ce que je vous dois?;
owing to prep à cause de, en raison de

owl [aul] n hibou m

own [əun] vt posséder ▷ adj propre;
a room of my ~ une chambre à moi,
ma propre chambre; **to get one's ~
back** prendre sa revanche; **on one's
~** tout(e) seul(e); **own up** vi avouer;
owner n propriétaire m/f; **ownership**
n possession f

ox (pl **oxen**) [ɔks, ˈɔksn] n bœuf m

Oxbridge [ˈɔksbrɪdʒ] n (BRIT) les
universités d'Oxford et de Cambridge

oxen [ˈɔksən] npl of **ox**

oxygen [ˈɔksɪdʒən] n oxygène m

oyster [ˈɔɪstə] n huître f

oz. abbr = **ounce(s)**

ozone [ˈəuzəun] n ozone m; **ozone
friendly** adj qui n'attaque pas or qui
préserve la couche d'ozone; **ozone
layer** n couche f d'ozone

p

p *abbr* (BRIT) = **penny; pence**

P.A. *n abbr* = **personal assistant; public address system**

p.a. *abbr* = **per annum**

pace [peɪs] *n* pas *m*; (*speed*) allure *f*, vitesse *f* ▷ *vi*: **to ~ up and down** faire les cent pas; **to keep ~ with** aller à la même vitesse que; (*events*) se tenir au courant de; **pacemaker** *n* (*Med*) stimulateur *m* cardiaque; (*Sport: also*: **pacesetter**) meneur(-euse) de train

Pacific [pə'sɪfɪk] *n*: **the ~ (Ocean)** le Pacifique, l'océan *m* Pacifique

pacifier ['pæsɪfaɪə'] *n* (US: *dummy*) tétine *f*

pack [pæk] *n* paquet *m*; (*of hounds*) meute *f*; (*of thieves, wolves etc*) bande *f*; (*of cards*) jeu *m*; (*us: of cigarettes*) paquet; (*back pack*) sac *m* à dos ▷ *vt* (*goods*) empaqueter, emballer; (*in suitcase etc*) emballer; (*box*) remplir; (*cram*) entasser ▷ *vi*: **to ~ (one's bags)** faire ses bagages; **pack in** (BRIT inf) ▷ *vi* (*machine*) tomber en panne

▷ *vt* (*boyfriend*) plaquer; **~ it in!** laisse tomber!; **pack off** *vt*: **to ~ sb off to** expédier qn à; **pack up** *vi* (BRIT inf: *machine*) tomber en panne; (: *person*) se tirer ▷ *vt* (*belongings*) ranger; (*goods, presents*) empaqueter, emballer

package ['pækɪdʒ] *n* paquet *m*; (*also*: **~ deal**: *agreement*) marché global; (: *purchase*) forfait *m*; (*Comput*) progiciel *m* ▷ *vt* (*goods*) conditionner; **package holiday** *n* (BRIT) vacances organisées; **package tour** *n* voyage organisé

packaging ['pækɪdʒɪŋ] *n* (*wrapping materials*) emballage *m*

packed [pækt] *adj* (*crowded*) bondé(e); **packed lunch** (BRIT) *n* repas froid

packet ['pækɪt] *n* paquet *m*

packing ['pækɪŋ] *n* emballage *m*

pact [pækt] *n* pacte *m*, traité *m*

pad [pæd] *n* bloc-notes) *m*) *m*; (*to prevent friction*) tampon *m* ▷ *vt* rembourrer; **padded** *adj* (*jacket*) matelassé(e); (*bra*) rembourré(e)

paddle ['pædl] *n* (*oar*) pagaie *f*; (*us: for table tennis*) raquette *f* de ping-pong ▷ *vi* (*with feet*) barboter, faire trempette ▷ *vt*: **to ~ a canoe** *etc* pagayer; **paddling pool** *n* petit bassin

paddock ['pædək] *n* enclos *m*; (*Racing*) paddock *m*

padlock ['pædlɔk] *n* cadenas *m*

paedophile (US **pedophile**) ['pi:dəufail] *n* pédophile *m*

page [peɪdʒ] *n* (*of book*) page *f*; (*also*: **~ boy**) groom *m*, chasseur *m*; (*at wedding*) garçon *m* d'honneur ▷ *vt* (*in hotel etc*) (faire) appeler

pager ['peɪdʒə'] *n* bip *m* (*inf*), Alphapage® *m*

paid [peɪd] *pt, pp of* **pay** ▷ *adj* (*work, official*) rémunéré(e); (*holiday*) payé(e); **to put ~ to** (BRIT) mettre fin à, mettre par terre

pain [peɪn] *n* douleur *f*; (*inf: nuisance*) plaie *f*; **to be in ~** souffrir, avoir mal; **to take ~s to do** se donner du mal pour faire; **painful** *adj* douloureux(-euse); (*difficult*) difficile, pénible; **painkiller**

n calmant *m*, analgésique *m*;
painstaking ['peɪnzteɪkɪŋ] *adj* (person) soigneux(-euse); (work) soigné(e)
paint [peɪnt] *n* peinture *f* ▷ *vt* peindre; **to ~ the door blue** peindre la porte en bleu; **paintbrush** *n* pinceau *m*; **painter** *n* peintre *m*; **painting** *n* peinture *f*; (picture) tableau *m*
pair [pɛə^r] *n* (of shoes, gloves etc) paire *f*; (of people) couple *m*; **~ of scissors** (paire de) ciseaux *mpl*; **~ of trousers** pantalon *m*
pajamas [pəˈdʒɑːməz] *npl* (US) pyjama(s) *m(pl)*
Pakistan [pɑːkɪˈstɑːn] *n* Pakistan *m*; **Pakistani** *adj* pakistanais(e) ▷ *n* Pakistanais(e)
pal [pæl] *n* (inf) copain (copine)
palace ['pæləs] *n* palais *m*
pale [peɪl] *adj* pâle; **~ blue** *adj* bleu pâle *inv*
Palestine ['pælɪstaɪn] *n* Palestine *f*; **Palestinian** [pælɪsˈtɪnɪən] *adj* palestinien(ne) ▷ *n* Palestinien(ne)
palm [pɑːm] *n* (Anat) paume *f*; (also: ~ **tree**) palmier *m* ▷ *vt*: **to ~ sth off on sb** (inf) refiler qch à qn
pamper ['pæmpə^r] *vt* gâter, dorloter
pamphlet ['pæmflət] *n* brochure *f*
pan [pæn] *n* (also: **sauce~**) casserole *f*; (also: **frying ~**) poêle *f*
pancake ['pænkeɪk] *n* crêpe *f*
panda ['pændə] *n* panda *m*
pane [peɪn] *n* carreau *m* (de fenêtre), vitre *f*
panel ['pænl] *n* (of wood, cloth etc) panneau *m*; (Radio, TV) panel *m*, invités *mpl*; (for interview, exams) jury *m*
panhandler ['pænhændlə^r] *n* (US inf) mendiant(e)
panic ['pænɪk] *n* panique *f*, affolement *m* ▷ *vi* s'affoler, paniquer
panorama [pænəˈrɑːmə] *n* panorama *m*
pansy ['pænzɪ] *n* (Bot) pensée *f*
pant [pænt] *vi* haleter
panther ['pænθə^r] *n* panthère *f*
panties ['pæntɪz] *npl* slip *m*, culotte *f*

pantomime ['pæntəmaɪm] *n* (BRIT) spectacle *m* de Noël; *voir encadré*

○ **PANTOMIME**
○
○ Une **pantomime** (à ne pas confondre
○ avec le mot tel qu'on l'utilise en
○ français), que l'on appelle également
○ de façon familière "panto", est un
○ genre de farce où le personnage
○ principal est souvent une jeune
○ garçon et où il y a toujours une
○ "dame", c'est-à-dire une vieille
○ femme jouée par un homme, et
○ un méchant. La plupart du temps,
○ l'histoire est basée sur un conte de
○ fées comme Cendrillon ou Le Chat
○ botté, et le public est encouragé
○ à participer en prévenant le héros
○ d'un danger imminent. Ce genre de
○ spectacle, qui s'adresse surtout aux
○ enfants, vise également un public
○ d'adultes au travers des nombreuses
○ plaisanteries faisant allusion à des
○ faits d'actualité.

pants [pænts] *n* (BRIT: woman's) culotte *f*, slip *m*; (: man's) slip, caleçon *m*; (US: trousers) pantalon *m*
pantyhose ['pæntɪhəuz] (US) *npl* collant *m*
paper ['peɪpə^r] *n* papier *m*; (also: **wall~**) papier peint; (also: **news~**) journal *m*; (academic essay) article *m*; (exam) épreuve écrite *f* ▷ *adj* en or de papier ▷ *vt* tapisser (de papier peint); **papers** *npl* (also: **identity ~s**) papiers *mpl* (d'identité); **paperback** *n* livre broché or non relié; (small) livre *m* de poche; **paper bag** *n* sac *m* en papier; **paper clip** *n* trombone *m*; **paper shop** *n* (BRIT) marchand *m* de journaux; **paperwork** *n* papiers *mpl*; (pej) paperasserie *f*
paprika ['pæprɪkə] *n* paprika *m*
par [pɑː^r] *n* (Golf) normale *f* du parcours; **on a ~ with** à égalité avec, au même niveau que

paracetamol [pærə'si:təmɒl] (BRIT) n
paracétamol m

parachute [pærəʃu:t] n parachute m

parade [pə'reɪd] n défilé m ▷ vt (fig)
faire étalage de ▷ vi défiler

paradise [pærədaɪs] n paradis m

paradox [pærədɒks] n paradoxe m

paraffin [pærəfɪn] (BRIT): ~ **(oil)**
pétrole (lampant)

paragraph [pærəgrɑːf] n
paragraphe m

parallel [pærəlɛl] adj: ~ **(with** or **to)**
parallèle (à); (fig) analogue (à) ▷ n (line)
parallèle f; (fig, Geo) parallèle m

paralysed [pærəlaɪzd] adj paralysé(e)

paralysis (pl **paralyses**) [pə'rælɪsɪs,
-siːz] n paralysie f

paramedic [pærə'mɛdɪk] n auxiliaire
m/f médical(e)

paranoid [pærənɔɪd] adj (Psych)
paranoïaque; (neurotic) paranoïde

parasite [pærəsaɪt] n parasite m

parcel [pɑːsl] n paquet m, colis m ▷ vt
(also: ~ **up**) empaqueter

pardon [pɑːdn] n pardon m; (Law)
grâce f ▷ vt pardonner à; (Law) gracier;
~**!** pardon!; ~ **me!** (after burping etc)
excusez-moi!; **I beg your** ~**!** (I'm sorry)
pardon, je suis désolé!; **(I beg your)** ~**?**,
(us) ~ **me?** (what did you say?) pardon?

parent [pɛərənt] n (father) père
m; (mother) mère f; **parents** npl
parents mpl; **parental** [pə'rɛntl] adj
parental(e), des parents

Paris [pærɪs] n Paris

parish [pærɪʃ] n paroisse f; (BRIT: civil)
≈ commune f

Parisian [pə'rɪzɪən] adj parisien(ne), de
Paris ▷ n Parisien(ne)

park [pɑːk] n parc m, jardin public ▷ vt
garer ▷ vi se garer; **can I** ~ **here?** est-ce
que je peux me garer ici?

parking [pɑːkɪŋ] n stationnement
m; **"no** ~**"** "stationnement interdit";
parking lot n (us) parking m, parc m
de stationnement; **parking meter**
n parc(o)mètre m; **parking ticket**
n P.-V. m

Be careful not to translate **parking**
by the French word **parking**.

parkway [pɑːkweɪ] n (us) route f
express (en site vert ou aménagé)

parliament [pɑːləmənt] n
parlement m; **parliamentary**
[pɑːlə'mɛntərɪ] adj parlementaire

Parmesan [pɑːmɪ'zæn] n (also: ~
cheese) Parmesan m

parole [pə'rəʊl] n: **on** ~ en liberté
conditionnelle

parrot [pærət] n perroquet m

parsley [pɑːslɪ] n persil m

parsnip [pɑːsnɪp] n panais m

parson [pɑːsn] n ecclésiastique m;
(Church of England) pasteur m

part [pɑːt] n partie f; (of machine) pièce
f; (Theat etc) rôle m; (of serial) épisode
m; (us: in hair) raie f ▷ vt séparer ▷ vi
séparer ▷ vi (people) se séparer; (crowd)
s'ouvrir; **to take** ~ **in** participer à,
prendre part à; **to take sb's** ~ prendre
le parti de qn, prendre parti pour qn;
for my ~ en ce qui me concerne; **for
the most** ~ en grande partie; dans la
plupart des cas; **in** ~ en partie; **to take
sth in good/bad** ~ prendre qch du
bon/mauvais côté; **part with** vt fus
(person) se séparer de; (possessions) se
défaire de

partial [pɑːʃl] adj (incomplete)
partiel(le); **to be** ~ **to** aimer, avoir un
faible pour

participant [pɑː'tɪsɪpənt] n (in
competition, campaign) participant(e)

participate [pɑː'tɪsɪpeɪt] vi: **to** ~ **(in)**
participer (à), prendre part (à)

particle [pɑːtɪkl] n particule f; (of
dust) grain m

particular [pə'tɪkjʊlə] adj (specific)
particulier(-ière); (special) particulier,
spécial(e); (fussy) difficile, exigeant(e);
(careful) méticuleux(-euse); **in** ~ en
particulier, surtout; **particularly** adv
particulièrement; (in particular) en
particulier; **particulars** npl détails mpl;
(information) renseignements mpl

parting [pɑːtɪŋ] n séparation f; (BRIT:

in hair) raie f

partition [pɑːˈtɪʃən] n (Pol) partition f,
division f; (wall) cloison f

partly [ˈpɑːtlɪ] adv en partie,
partiellement

partner [ˈpɑːtnər] n (Comm)
associé(e); (Sport) partenaire m/f;
(spouse) conjoint(e); (lover) ami(e); (at
dance) cavalier(-ière); **partnership** n
association f

part of speech n (Ling) partie f du
discours

partridge [ˈpɑːtrɪdʒ] n perdrix f

part-time [ˈpɑːtˈtaɪm] adj, adv à mi-
temps, à temps partiel

party [ˈpɑːtɪ] n (Pol) parti m; (celebration)
fête f; (: formal) réception f; (: in evening)
soirée f; (group) groupe m; (Law) partie f

pass [pɑːs] vt (time, object) passer;
(place) passer devant; (friend) croiser;
(exam) être reçu(e) à, réussir; (overtake)
dépasser; (approve) approuver, accepter
▷ vi passer; (Scol) être reçu(e) ou
admis(e), réussir ▷ n (permit) laissez-
passer m inv; (membership card) carte f
d'accès ou d'abonnement; (in mountains)
col m; (Sport) passe f; (Scol: also: ~ **mark**):
to get a ~ être reçu(e) (sans mention);
to ~ sb sth passer qch à qn; **could you
~ the salt/oil, please?** pouvez-vous
me passer le sel/l'huile, s'il vous plaît?;
to make a ~ at sb (inf) faire des avances
à qn; **pass away** vi mourir; **pass by** vi
passer ▷ vt (ignore) négliger; **pass on**
vt (hand on): **to ~ on (to)** transmettre
(à); **pass out** vi s'évanouir; **pass over**
vt (ignore) passer sous silence; **pass up**
vt (opportunity) laisser passer; **passable**
adj (road) praticable; (work) acceptable

> Be careful not to translate *to pass
> an exam* by the French expression
> *passer un examen.*

passage [ˈpæsɪdʒ] n (also: **~way**)
couloir m; (gen, in book) passage m; (by
boat) traversée f

passenger [ˈpæsɪndʒər] n
passager(-ère)

passer-by [pɑːsəˈbaɪ] n passant(e)

passing place n (Aut) aire f de
croisement

passion [ˈpæʃən] n passion f;
passionate adj passionné(e); **passion
fruit** n fruit m de la passion

passive [ˈpæsɪv] adj (also Ling)
passif(-ive)

passport [ˈpɑːspɔːt] n passeport m;
passport control n contrôle m des
passeports; **passport office** n bureau
m de délivrance des passeports

password [ˈpɑːswɜːd] n mot m de
passe

past [pɑːst] prep (in front of) devant;
(further than) au delà de, plus loin que;
après; (later than) après ▷ adv: **to run
~** passer en courant ▷ adj (president etc)
ancien(ne) ▷ n passé m;
he's ~ forty il a dépassé la quarantaine,
il a plus de or passé quarante ans;
ten/quarter ~ eight huit heures
dix/un or et quart; **for the ~ few/3 days**
depuis quelques/3 jours; ces derniers/3
derniers jours

pasta [ˈpæstə] n pâtes fpl

paste [peɪst] n pâte f; (Culin: meat)
pâté m (à tartiner); (: tomato) purée
f, concentré m; (glue) colle f (de pâte)
▷ vt coller

pastel [ˈpæstl] adj pastel inv ▷ n (Art:
pencil) (crayon m) pastel m; (: drawing)
(dessin m au) pastel; (colour) ton m
pastel inv

pasteurized [ˈpæstəraɪzd] adj
pasteurisé(e)

pastime [ˈpɑːstaɪm] n passe-temps m
inv, distraction f

pastor [ˈpɑːstər] n pasteur m

past participle [-ˈpɑːtɪsɪpl] n (Ling)
participe passé

pastry [ˈpeɪstrɪ] n pâte f; (cake)
pâtisserie f

pasture [ˈpɑːstʃər] n pâturage m

pasty¹ [ˈpæstɪ] n petit pâté (en croûte)

pasty² [ˈpeɪstɪ] adj (complexion)
terreux-euse

pat [pæt] vt donner une petite tape à;
(dog) caresser

patch [pætʃ] n (of material) pièce f; (eye patch) cache m; (spot) tache f; (of land) parcelle f; (on tyre) rustine f ▷ vt (clothes) rapiécer; **a bad ~** (BRIT) une période difficile; **patchy** adj inégal(e); (incomplete) fragmentaire

pâté ['pæteɪ] n pâté m, terrine f

patent ['peɪtnt, us'pætnt] n brevet m (d'invention) ▷ vt faire breveter ▷ adj patent(e), manifeste

paternal [pə'tə:nl] adj paternel(le)

paternity leave [pə'tə:nɪtɪ-] n congé m de paternité

path [pɑ:θ] n chemin m, sentier m; (in garden) allée f; (of missile) trajectoire f

pathetic [pə'θetɪk] adj (pitiful) pitoyable; (very bad) lamentable, minable

pathway ['pɑ:θweɪ] n chemin m, sentier m; (in garden) allée f

patience ['peɪʃns] n patience f; (BRIT: Cards) réussite f

patient ['peɪʃnt] n malade m/f; (of dentist etc) patient(e) ▷ adj patient(e)

patio ['pætɪəʊ] n patio m

patriotic [pætrɪ'ɒtɪk] adj patriotique; (person) patriote

patrol [pə'trəʊl] n patrouille f ▷ vt patrouiller dans; **patrol car** n voiture f de police

patron ['peɪtrən] n (in shop) client(e); (of charity) patron(ne); **~ of the arts** mécène m

patronizing ['pætrənaɪzɪŋ] adj condescendant(e)

pattern ['pætən] n (Sewing) patron m; (design) motif m; **patterned** adj à motifs

pause [pɔ:z] n pause f, arrêt m ▷ vi faire une pause, s'arrêter

pave [peɪv] vt paver, daller; **to ~ the way for** ouvrir la voie à

pavement ['peɪvmənt] n (BRIT) trottoir m; (US) chaussée f

pavilion [pə'vɪlɪən] n pavillon m; (Sport) stand m

paving ['peɪvɪŋ] n (material) pavé m, dalle f

paw [pɔ:] n patte f

pawn [pɔ:n] n (Chess, also fig) pion m ▷ vt mettre en gage; **pawnbroker** n prêteur m sur gages

pay [peɪ] n salaire m; (of manual worker) paie f ▷ vb (pt, pp **paid**) vt payer ▷ vi payer; (be profitable) être rentable; **can I ~ by credit card?** est-ce que je peux payer par carte de crédit?; **to ~ attention (to)** prêter attention (à); **to ~ sb a visit** rendre visite à qn; **to ~ one's respects to sb** présenter ses respects à qn; **pay back** vt rembourser; **pay for** vt fus payer; **pay in** vt verser; **pay off** vt (debts) régler, acquitter; (person) rembourser ▷ vi (scheme, decision) se révéler payant(e); **pay out** vt (money) payer, sortir de sa poche; **pay up** vt (amount) payer; **payable** adj payable; **to make a cheque payable to sb** établir un chèque à l'ordre de qn; **pay day** n jour m de paie; **pay envelope** n (US) paie f; **payment** n paiement m; (of bill) règlement m; (of deposit, cheque) versement m; **monthly payment** mensualité f; **payout** n (from insurance) dédommagement m; (in competition) prix m; **pay packet** n (BRIT) paie f; **pay phone** n cabine f téléphonique, téléphone public; **pay raise** n (US) = **pay rise**; **pay rise** n (BRIT) augmentation f (de salaire); **payroll** n registre m du personnel; **pay slip** n (BRIT) bulletin m de paie, feuille f de paie; **pay television** n chaînes fpl payantes

PC n abbr = **personal computer**; (BRIT) = **police constable** ▷ adj abbr = **politically correct**

p.c. abbr = **per cent**

PDA n abbr (= personal digital assistant) agenda m électronique

PE n abbr (= physical education) EPS f

pea [pi:] n (petit) pois

peace [pi:s] n paix f; (calm) calme m, tranquillité f; **peaceful** adj paisible, calme

peach [pi:tʃ] n pêche f

peacock ['piːkɔk] n paon m

peak [piːk] n (mountain) pic m, cime f; (of cap) visière f; (fig: highest level) maximum m; (: of career, fame) apogée m; **peak hours** npl heures fpl d'affluence or de pointe

peanut ['piːnʌt] n arachide f, cacahuète f; **peanut butter** n beurre m de cacahuète

pear [pɛə'] n poire f

pearl [pəːl] n perle f

peasant ['pɛznt] n paysan(ne)

peat [piːt] n tourbe f

pebble ['pɛbl] n galet m, caillou m

peck [pɛk] vt (also: **~ at**) donner un coup de bec à; (food) picorer ▷ n coup m de bec; (kiss) bécot m; **peckish** adj (BRIT inf): **I feel peckish** je mangerais bien quelque chose, j'ai la dent

peculiar [pɪ'kjuːlɪə'] adj (odd) étrange, bizarre, curieux(-euse); (particular) particulier(-ière); **~ to** particulier à

pedal ['pɛdl] n pédale f ▷ vi pédaler

pedalo ['pɛdələu] n pédalo m

pedestal ['pɛdəstl] n piédestal m

pedestrian [pɪ'dɛstrɪən] n piéton m; **pedestrian crossing** n (BRIT) passage clouté; **pedestrianized** adj: **a pedestrianized street** une rue piétonne; **pedestrian precinct** (US **pedestrian zone**) n (BRIT) zone piétonne

pedigree ['pɛdɪgriː] n ascendance f; (of animal) pedigree m ▷ cpd (animal) de race

pedophile ['piːdəufaɪl] (US) n = **paedophile**

pee [piː] vi (inf) faire pipi, pisser

peek [piːk] vi jeter un coup d'œil furtif

peel [piːl] n pelure f, épluchure f; (of orange, lemon) écorce f ▷ vt peler, éplucher ▷ vi (paint etc) s'écailler; (wallpaper) se décoller; (skin) peler

peep [piːp] n (BRIT: look) coup d'œil furtif; (sound) pépiement m ▷ vi (BRIT) jeter un coup d'œil (furtif)

peer [pɪə'] vi: **to ~ at** regarder attentivement, scruter ▷ n (noble) pair

m; (equal) pair, égal(e)

peg [pɛg] n (for coat etc) patère f; (BRIT: also: **clothes ~**) pince f à linge

pelican ['pɛlɪkən] n pélican m; **pelican crossing** n (BRIT Aut) feu m à commande manuelle

pelt [pɛlt] vt: **to ~ sb (with)** bombarder qn (de) ▷ vi (rain) tomber à seaux; (inf: run) courir à toutes jambes ▷ n peau f

pelvis ['pɛlvɪs] n bassin m

pen [pɛn] n (for writing) stylo m; (for sheep) parc m

penalty ['pɛnltɪ] n pénalité f; sanction f; (fine) amende f; (Sport) pénalisation f; (Football) penalty m; (Rugby) pénalité f

pence [pɛns] npl of **penny**

pencil ['pɛnsl] n crayon m; **pencil in** vt noter provisoirement; **pencil case** n trousse f (d'écolier); **pencil sharpener** n taille-crayon(s) m inv

pendant ['pɛndnt] n pendentif m

pending ['pɛndɪŋ] prep en attendant ▷ adj en suspens

penetrate ['pɛnɪtreɪt] vt pénétrer dans; (enemy territory) entrer en

penfriend ['pɛnfrɛnd] n (BRIT) correspondant(e)

penguin ['pɛŋgwɪn] n pingouin m

penicillin [pɛnɪ'sɪlɪn] n pénicilline f

peninsula [pə'nɪnsjulə] n péninsule f

penis ['piːnɪs] n pénis m, verge f

penitentiary [pɛnɪ'tɛnʃərɪ] n (US) prison f

penknife ['pɛnnaɪf] n canif m

penniless ['pɛnɪlɪs] adj sans le sou

penny (pl **pennies** or **pence**) ['pɛnɪ, 'pɛnɪz, pɛns] n (BRIT) penny m; (US) cent m

penpal ['pɛnpæl] n correspondant(e)

pension ['pɛnʃən] n (from company) retraite f; **pensioner** n (BRIT) retraité(e)

pentagon ['pɛntəgən] n: **the P~** (US Pol) le Pentagone

penthouse ['pɛnthaus] n appartement m (de luxe) en attique

penultimate [pɪ'nʌltɪmət] adj pénultième, avant-dernier(-ière)

people ['piːpl] npl gens mpl; personnes

fpl: (inhabitants) population f; (Pol)
peuple m ▷ n (nation, race) peuple m;
several ~ came plusieurs personnes
sont venues; **~ say that ...** on dit or les
gens disent que ...

pepper ['pepə'] n poivre m; (vegetable)
poivron m ▷ vt (Culin) poivrer;
peppermint n (sweet) pastille de
menthe

per [pɜ:'] prep par; **~ hour** (miles etc) à
l'heure; (fee) (de) l'heure; **~ kilo** etc le kilo
etc; **~ day/person** par jour/personne; **~
annum** par an

perceive [pə'siːv] vt percevoir; (notice)
remarquer, s'apercevoir de

per cent adv pour cent

percentage [pə'sentɪdʒ] n
pourcentage m

perception [pə'sepʃən] n perception f;
(insight) sensibilité f

perch [pɜːtʃ] n (fish) perche f; (for bird)
perchoir m ▷ vi (se) percher

percussion [pə'kʌʃən] n percussion f

perennial [pə'renɪəl] n (Bot) (plante f)
vivace f, plante pluriannuelle

perfect ['pɜːfɪkt] adj parfait(e); (also:
~ tense) parfait m ▷ vt [pə'fekt]
(technique, skill, work of art) parfaire;
(method, plan) mettre au point;
perfection [pə'fekʃən] n perfection f;
perfectly ['pɜːfɪktlɪ] adv parfaitement

perform [pə'fɔːm] vt (carry out)
exécuter; (concert etc) jouer, donner ▷ vi
(actor, musician) jouer; **performance**
n représentation f, spectacle m; (of an
artist) interprétation f; (Sport: of car,
engine) performance f; (of company,
economy) résultats mpl; **performer** n
artiste m/f

perfume ['pɜːfjuːm] n parfum m

perhaps [pə'hæps] adv peut-être

perimeter [pə'rɪmɪtə'] n périmètre m

period ['pɪərɪəd] n période f; (History)
époque f; (Scol) cours m; (full stop)
point m; (Med) règles fpl ▷ adj (costume,
furniture) d'époque; **periodical**
[pɪərɪ'ɒdɪkl] n périodique m;
periodically adv périodiquement

perish ['perɪʃ] vi périr, mourir; (decay)
se détériorer

perjury ['pɜːdʒərɪ] n (Law: in court) faux
témoignage; (breach of oath) parjure m

perk [pɜːk] n (inf) avantage m, à-côté m

perm [pɜːm] n (for hair) permanente f

permanent ['pɜːmənənt] adj
permanent(e); **permanently** adv
de façon permanente; (move abroad)
définitivement; (open, closed)
en permanence; (tired, unhappy)
constamment

permission [pə'mɪʃən] n permission f,
autorisation f

permit n ['pɜːmɪt] permis m

perplex [pə'pleks] vt (person) rendre
perplexe

persecute ['pɜːsɪkjuːt] vt persécuter

persecution [pɜːsɪ'kjuːʃən] n
persécution f

persevere [pɜːsɪ'vɪə'] vi persévérer

Persian ['pɜːʃən] adj persan(e); **the ~
Gulf** le golfe Persique

persist [pə'sɪst] vi: **to ~ (in doing)**
persister (à faire), s'obstiner (à faire);
persistent adj persistant(e), tenace

person ['pɜːsn] n personne f;
in ~ en personne; **personal** adj
personnel(le); **personal assistant** n
secrétaire personnel(le); **personal
computer** n ordinateur individuel,
PC m; **personality** [pɜːsə'nælɪtɪ]
n personnalité f; **personally** adv
personnellement; **to take sth
personally** se sentir visé(e) par
qch; **personal organizer** n agenda
(personnel) (style Filofax®); (electronic)
agenda électronique; **personal stereo**
n Walkman® m, baladeur m

personnel [pɜːsə'nel] n personnel m

perspective [pə'spektɪv] n
perspective f

perspiration [pɜːspɪ'reɪʃən] n
transpiration f

persuade [pə'sweɪd] vt: **to ~ sb to do
sth** persuader qn de faire qch, amener
or décider qn à faire qch

persuasion [pə'sweɪʒən] n persuasion f

f; (creed) conviction f

persuasive [pə'sweɪsɪv] adj persuasif(-ive)

perverse [pə'vɜːs] adj pervers(e); (contrary) entêté(e), contrariant(e)

pervert n ['pɜːvɜːt] perverti(e) ▷ vt [pə'vɜːt] pervertir; (words) déformer

pessimism ['pesɪmɪzəm] n pessimisme m

pessimist ['pesɪmɪst] n pessimiste m/f; **pessimistic** [pesɪ'mɪstɪk] adj pessimiste

pest [pest] n animal m (or insecte m) nuisible; (fig) fléau m

pester ['pestə*] vt importuner, harceler

pesticide ['pestɪsaɪd] n pesticide m

pet [pet] n animal familier ▷ cpd (favourite) favori(e) ▷ vt (stroke) caresser, câliner; **teacher's ~** chouchou m du professeur; **~ hate** bête noire

petal ['petl] n pétale m

petite [pə'tiːt] adj menu(e)

petition [pə'tɪʃən] n pétition f

petrified ['petrɪfaɪd] adj (fig) mort(e) de peur

petrol ['petrəl] n (BRIT) essence f; **I've run out of ~** je suis en panne d'essence

Be careful not to translate **petrol** by the French word **pétrole**.

petroleum [pə'trəʊlɪəm] n pétrole m

petrol: petrol pump n (BRIT: in car, at garage) pompe f à essence; **petrol station** n (BRIT) station-service f; **petrol tank** n (BRIT) réservoir m d'essence

petticoat ['petɪkəʊt] n jupon m

petty ['petɪ] adj (mean) mesquin(e); (unimportant) insignifiant(e), sans importance

pew [pjuː] n banc m (d'église)

pewter ['pjuːtə*] n étain m

phantom ['fæntəm] n fantôme m

pharmacist ['fɑːməsɪst] n pharmacien(ne)

pharmacy ['fɑːməsɪ] n pharmacie f

phase [feɪz] n phase f, période f; **phase in** vt introduire progressivement; **phase out** vt supprimer

progressivement

Ph.D. abbr = Doctor of Philosophy

pheasant ['feznt] n faisan m

phenomena [fə'nɒmɪnə] npl of **phenomenon**

phenomenal [fə'nɒmɪnl] adj phénoménal(e)

phenomenon [fə'nɒmɪnən, -nə] n phénomène m

Philippines ['fɪlɪpiːnz] npl (also: **Philippine Islands**): **the ~** les Philippines fpl

philosopher [fɪ'lɒsəfə*] n philosophe m

philosophical [fɪlə'sɒfɪkl] adj philosophique

philosophy [fɪ'lɒsəfɪ] n philosophie f

phlegm [flem] n flegme m

phobia ['fəʊbjə] n phobie f

phone [fəʊn] n téléphone m ▷ vt téléphoner à ▷ vi téléphoner; **to be on the ~** avoir le téléphone; (be calling) être au téléphone; **phone back** vt, vi rappeler; **phone up** vt téléphoner à ▷ vi téléphoner; **phone book** n annuaire m; **phone box** (US **phone booth**) n cabine f téléphonique; **phone call** n coup m de fil or de téléphone; **phonecard** n télécarte f; **phone number** n numéro m de téléphone

phonetics [fə'netɪks] n phonétique f

phoney ['fəʊnɪ] adj faux (fausse), factice; (person) pas franc (franche)

photo ['fəʊtəʊ] n photo f; **photo album** n album m de photos; **photocopier** n copieur m; **photocopy** n photocopie f ▷ vt photocopier

photograph ['fəʊtəɡræf] n photographie f ▷ vt photographier; **photographer** [fə'tɒɡrəfə*] n photographe m/f; **photography** [fə'tɒɡrəfɪ] n photographie f

phrase [freɪz] n expression f; (Ling) locution f ▷ vt exprimer; **phrase book** n recueil m d'expressions (pour touristes)

physical ['fɪzɪkl] adj physique; **physical education** n éducation f physique; **physically** adv physiquement

physician [fɪˈzɪʃən] n médecin m

physicist [ˈfɪzɪsɪst] n physicien(ne)

physics [ˈfɪzɪks] n physique f

physiotherapist [fɪzɪəʊˈθerəpɪst] n kinésithérapeute m/f

physiotherapy [fɪzɪəʊˈθerəpɪ] n kinésithérapie f

physique [fɪˈziːk] n (appearance) physique m; (health etc) constitution f

pianist [ˈpiːənɪst] n pianiste m/f

piano [pɪˈænəʊ] n piano m

pick [pɪk] n (tool: also: **~-axe**) pic m, pioche f ▷ vt choisir; (gather) cueillir; (remove) prendre; (lock) forcer; **take your ~** faites votre choix; **the ~ of** le (la) meilleur(e) de; **to ~ one's nose** se mettre les doigts dans le nez; **to ~ one's teeth** se curer les dents; **to ~ a quarrel with sb** chercher noise à qn; **pick on** vt fus (person) harceler; **pick out** vt choisir; (distinguish) distinguer; **pick up** vi (improve) remonter, s'améliorer ▷ vt ramasser; (collect) passer prendre; (Aut: give lift to) prendre; (learn) apprendre; (Radio) capter; **to ~ up speed** prendre de la vitesse; **to ~ o.s. up** se relever

pickle [ˈpɪkl] n (also: **~s**: as condiment) pickles mpl ▷ vt conserver dans du vinaigre ou dans de la saumure; **in a ~** (fig) dans le pétrin

pickpocket [ˈpɪkpɔkɪt] n pickpocket m

pick-up [ˈpɪkʌp] n (also: **~ truck**) pick-up m inv

picnic [ˈpɪknɪk] n pique-nique m ▷ vi pique-niquer; **picnic area** n aire f de pique-nique

picture [ˈpɪktʃə*] n (also TV) image f; (painting) peinture f, tableau m; (photograph) photo(graphie) f; (drawing) dessin m; (film) film m; (fig: description) description f ▷ vt (imagine) se représenter; **pictures** npl: **the ~s** (BRIT) le cinéma; **to take a ~ of sb/sth** prendre qn/qch en photo; **would you take a ~ of us, please?** pourriez-vous

nous prendre en photo, s'il vous plaît?; **picture frame** n cadre m; **picture messaging** n picture messaging m, messagerie f d'images

picturesque [pɪktʃəˈresk] adj pittoresque

pie [paɪ] n tourte f; (of fruit) tarte f; (of meat) pâté m en croûte

piece [piːs] n morceau m; (item): **a ~ of furniture/advice** un meuble/conseil ▷ vt: **to ~ together** rassembler; **to take to ~s** démonter

pie chart n graphique m à secteurs, camembert m

pier [pɪə*] n jetée f

pierce [pɪəs] vt percer, transpercer; **pierced** adj (ears) percé(e)

pig [pɪg] n cochon m, porc m; (pej: unkind person) mufle m; (: greedy person) goinfre m

pigeon [ˈpɪdʒən] n pigeon m

piggy bank [ˈpɪgɪ-] n tirelire f

pigsty [ˈpɪgstaɪ] n porcherie f

pigtail [ˈpɪgteɪl] n natte f, tresse f

pike [paɪk] n (fish) brochet m

pilchard [ˈpɪltʃəd] n pilchard m (sorte de sardine)

pile [paɪl] n (pillar, of books) pile f; (heap) tas m; (of carpet) épaisseur f; **pile up** vi (accumulate) s'entasser, s'accumuler ▷ vt (put in heap) empiler, entasser; (accumulate) accumuler; **piles** npl hémorroïdes fpl; **pile-up** n (Aut) télescopage m, collision f en série

pilgrim [ˈpɪlgrɪm] n pèlerin m

fondateurs des États-Unis, et l'on commémore chaque année, le jour de "Thanksgiving", la réussite de leur première récolte.

pilgrimage ['pɪlgrɪmɪdʒ] n pèlerinage m

pill [pɪl] n pilule f; **the ~** la pilule

pillar ['pɪlə*] n pilier m

pillow ['pɪləu] n oreiller m; **pillowcase, pillowslip** n taie f d'oreiller

pilot ['paɪlət] n pilote m ▷ cpd (scheme etc) pilote, expérimental(e) ▷ vt piloter; **pilot light** n veilleuse f

pimple ['pɪmpl] n bouton m

PIN n abbr (= personal identification number) code m confidentiel

pin [pɪn] n épingle f; (Tech) cheville f ▷ vt épingler; **~s and needles** fourmis fpl; **to ~ sb down** (fig) coincer qn; **to ~ sth on sb** (fig) mettre qch sur le dos de qn

pinafore ['pɪnəfɔ:*] n tablier m

pinch [pɪntʃ] n pincement m; (of salt etc) pincée f ▷ vt pincer; (inf: steal) piquer, chiper ▷ vi (shoe) serrer; **at a ~** à la rigueur

pine [paɪn] n (also: ~ **tree**) pin m ▷ vi: **to ~ for** aspirer à, désirer ardemment

pineapple ['paɪnæpl] n ananas m

ping [pɪŋ] n (noise) tintement m; **ping-pong®** n ping-pong m

pink [pɪŋk] adj rose m ▷ n (colour) rose m

pinpoint ['pɪnpɔɪnt] vt indiquer (avec précision)

pint [paɪnt] n pinte f (BRIT = 0.57 l; US = 0.47 l), (BRIT inf) = demi-litre, = pot m

pioneer [paɪə'nɪə*] n pionnier m

pious ['paɪəs] adj pieux(-euse)

pip [pɪp] n (seed) pépin m; **pips** npl the **~s** (BRIT: time signal on radio) le top

pipe [paɪp] n tuyau m, conduite f; (for smoking) pipe f ▷ vt amener par tuyau; **pipeline** n (for gas) gazoduc m, pipeline m; (for oil) oléoduc m, pipeline; **piper** n (flautist) joueur(-euse) de pipeau; (of bagpipes) joueur(-euse) de cornemuse

pirate ['paɪərət] n pirate m ▷ vt (CD, video, book) pirater

Pisces ['paɪsi:z] n les Poissons mpl

piss [pɪs] vi (inf!) pisser (!); **pissed** (inf!) adj (BRIT: drunk) bourré(e); (US: angry) furieux(-euse)

pistol ['pɪstl] n pistolet m

piston ['pɪstən] n piston m

pit [pɪt] n trou m, fosse f; (also: **coal ~**) puits m de mine; (also: **orchestra ~**) fosse d'orchestre; (US: fruit stone) noyau m ▷ vt: **to ~ o.s. or one's wits against** se mesurer à

pitch [pɪtʃ] n (BRIT Sport) terrain m; (Mus) ton m; (fig: degree) degré m; (tar) poix f ▷ vt (throw) lancer; (tent) dresser ▷ vi (fall): **to ~ into/off** tomber dans/de; **pitch-black** adj noir(e) comme poix

pitfall ['pɪtfɔ:l] n piège m

pith [pɪθ] n (of orange etc) intérieur m de l'écorce

pitiful ['pɪtɪful] adj (touching) pitoyable; (contemptible) lamentable

pity ['pɪtɪ] n pitié f ▷ vt plaindre; **what a ~!** quel dommage!

pizza ['pi:tsə] n pizza f

placard ['plækɑ:d] n affiche f; (in march) pancarte f

place [pleɪs] n endroit m, lieu m; (proper position, job, rank, seat) place f; (home): **at/to his ~** chez lui ▷ vt (position) placer, mettre; (identify) situer; reconnaître; **to take ~** avoir lieu; **to change ~ with sb** changer de place avec qn; **out of ~** (not suitable) déplacé(e), inopportun(e); **in the first ~** d'abord, en premier; **place mat** n set m de table; (in linen etc) napperon m; **placement** n (during studies) stage m

placid ['plæsɪd] adj placide

plague [pleɪg] n (Med) peste f ▷ vt (fig) tourmenter

plaice [pleɪs] n (pl inv) carrelet m

plain [pleɪn] adj (in one colour) uni(e); (clear) clair(e), évident(e); (simple) simple; (not handsome) quelconque, ordinaire ▷ adv franchement, carrément ▷ n plaine f; **plain chocolate** n chocolat m à croquer; **plainly** adv clairement; (frankly) carrément, sans détours

plaintiff ['pleɪntɪf] n plaignant(e)

plait [plæt] n tresse f, natte f

plan [plæn] n plan m; (scheme) projet m ▷ vt (think in advance) projeter; (prepare) organiser ▷ vi faire des projets; **to ~ to do** projeter de faire

plane [pleɪn] n (Aviat) avion m; (also: **~ tree**) platane m; (tool) rabot m; (Art, Math etc) plan m; (fig) niveau m, plan m ▷ vt (with tool) raboter

planet ['plænɪt] n planète f

plank [plæŋk] n planche f

planning ['plænɪŋ] n planification f; **family ~** planning familial

plant [plɑːnt] n plante f; (machinery) matériel m; (factory) usine f ▷ vt planter; (bomb) déposer, poser; (microphone, evidence) cacher

plantation [plæn'teɪʃən] n plantation f

plaque [plæk] n plaque f

plaster ['plɑːstə'] n plâtre m; (also: **~ of Paris**) plâtre à mouler; (BRIT: also: **sticking ~**) pansement adhésif ▷ vt plâtrer; (cover): **to ~ with** couvrir de; **plaster cast** n (Med) plâtre m; (model, statue) moule m

plastic ['plæstɪk] n plastique m ▷ adj (made of plastic) en plastique; **plastic bag** n sac m en plastique; **plastic surgery** n chirurgie f esthétique

plate [pleɪt] n (dish) assiette f; (sheet of metal, on door: Phot) plaque f; (in book) gravure f; (dental) dentier m

plateau (pl **-s** or **-x**) ['plætəu, -z] n plateau m

platform ['plætfɔːm] n (at meeting) tribune f; (stage) estrade f; (Rail) quai m; (Pol) plateforme f

platinum ['plætɪnəm] n platine m

platoon [plə'tuːn] n peloton m

platter ['plætə'] n plat m

plausible ['plɔːzɪbl] adj plausible; (person) convaincant(e)

play [pleɪ] n (Theat) pièce f (de théâtre) ▷ vt (game) jouer à; (team, opponent) jouer contre; (instrument)

jouer de; (part, piece of music, note) jouer; (CD etc) passer ▷ vi jouer; **to ~ safe** ne prendre aucun risque; **play back** vt repasser, réécouter; **play up** vi (cause trouble) faire des siennes; **player** n joueur(-euse); (Mus) musicien(ne); **playful** adj enjoué(e); **playground** n cour f de récréation; (in park) aire f de jeux; **playgroup** n garderie f; **playing card** n carte f à jouer; **playing field** n terrain m de sport; **playschool** n = **playgroup**; **playtime** n (Scol) récréation f; **playwright** n dramaturge m

plc abbr (BRIT: = public limited company) ≈ SARL f

plea [pliː] n (request) appel m; (Law) défense f

plead [pliːd] vt plaider; (give as excuse) invoquer ▷ vi (Law) plaider; (beg): **to ~ with sb (for sth)** implorer qn (d'accorder qch); **to ~ guilty/not guilty** plaider coupable/non coupable

pleasant ['pleznt] adj agréable

please [pliːz] excl s'il te (or vous) plaît ▷ vt plaire à ▷ vi (think fit): **do as you ~** faites comme il vous plaira; **~ yourself!** (inf) (faites) comme vous voulez!; **pleased** adj: **pleased (with)** content(e) (de); **pleased to meet you** enchanté (de faire votre connaissance)

pleasure ['pleʒə'] n plaisir m; **"it's a ~"** "je vous en prie"

pleat [pliːt] n pli m

pledge [pledʒ] n (promise) promesse f ▷ vt promettre

plentiful ['plentɪful] adj abondant(e), copieux(-euse)

plenty ['plentɪ] n: **~ of** beaucoup de; (sufficient) (bien) assez de

pliers ['plaɪəz] npl pinces fpl

plight [plaɪt] n situation f critique

plod [plɔd] vi avancer péniblement; (fig) peiner

plonk [plɔŋk] (inf) n (BRIT: wine) pinard m, piquette f ▷ vt: **to ~ sth down** poser brusquement qch

plot [plɔt] n complot m, conspiration f;

(of story, play) intrigue f; (of land) lot m de terrain, lopin m ▷ vt (mark out) tracer point par point; (Naut) pointer; (make graph of) faire le graphique de; (conspire) comploter ▷ vi comploter

plough (us **plow**) [plau] n charrue f ▷ vt (earth) labourer; **to ~ money into** investir dans; **ploughman's lunch** n (BRIT) assiette froide avec du pain, du fromage et des pickles

plow [plau] (US) = **plough**

ploy [plɔɪ] n stratagème m

pluck [plʌk] vt (fruit) cueillir; (musical instrument) pincer; (bird) plumer; **to ~ one's eyebrows** s'épiler les sourcils; **to ~ up courage** prendre son courage à deux mains

plug [plʌɡ] n (stopper) bouchon m, bonde f; (Elec) prise f de courant; (Aut: also: **spark(ing)~**) bougie f ▷ vt (hole) boucher; (inf: advertise) faire du battage pour, matraquer; **plug in** vt (Elec) brancher; **plughole** n (BRIT) trou m (d'écoulement)

plum [plʌm] n (fruit) prune f

plumber ['plʌmə'] n plombier m

plumbing ['plʌmɪŋ] n (trade) plomberie f; (piping) tuyauterie f

plummet ['plʌmɪt] vi (person, object) plonger; (sales, prices) dégringoler

plump [plʌmp] adj rondelet(te), dodu(e), bien en chair; **plump for** vt fus (inf: choose) se décider pour

plunge [plʌndʒ] n plongeon m; (fig) chute f ▷ vt plonger ▷ vi (fall) tomber, dégringoler; (dive) plonger; **to take the ~** se jeter à l'eau

pluperfect [plu:'pə:fɪkt] n (Ling) plus-que-parfait m

plural ['pluərl] adj pluriel(le) ▷ n pluriel m

plus [plʌs] n (also: **~ sign**) signe m plus; (advantage) atout m ▷ prep plus; **ten/twenty ~** plus de dix/vingt

ply [plaɪ] n (of wool) fil m ▷ vt (a trade) exercer ▷ vi (ship) faire la navette; **to ~ sb with drink** donner continuellement à boire à qn; **plywood**

n contreplaqué m

P.M. n abbr (BRIT) = **prime minister**

p.m. adv abbr (= post meridiem) de l'après-midi

PMS n abbr (= premenstrual syndrome) syndrome prémenstruel

PMT n abbr (= premenstrual tension) syndrome prémenstruel

pneumatic drill [nju:'mætɪk-] n marteau-piqueur m

pneumonia [nju:'məunɪə] n pneumonie f

poach [pəutʃ] vt (cook) pocher; (steal) pêcher (or chasser) sans permis ▷ vi braconner; **poached** adj (egg) poché(e)

P.O. Box n abbr = **post office box**

pocket ['pɔkɪt] n poche f ▷ vt empocher; **to be (£5) out of ~** (BRIT) en être de sa poche (pour 5 livres); **pocketbook** n (US: wallet) portefeuille m; **pocket money** n argent m de poche

pod [pɔd] n cosse f

podcast n podcast m

podiatrist [pɔ'di:ətrɪst] n (US) pédicure m/f

podium ['pəudɪəm] n podium m

poem ['pəuɪm] n poème m

poet ['pəuɪt] n poète m; **poetic** [pəu'ɛtɪk] adj poétique; **poetry** n poésie f

poignant ['pɔɪnjənt] adj poignant(e)

point [pɔɪnt] n point m; (tip) pointe f; (in time) moment m; (in space) endroit m; (subject, idea) point, sujet m; (purpose) but m; (also: **decimal ~**): **2 ~ 3 (2.3)** virgule f 3 (2.3); (BRIT Elec: also: **power ~**) prise f (de courant) ▷ vt (show) indiquer; (gun etc): **to ~ sth at** braquer or diriger qch sur ▷ vi: **to ~ at** montrer du doigt; **points** npl (Rail) aiguillage m; **to make a ~ of doing sth** ne pas manquer de faire qch; **to get/miss the ~** comprendre/ne pas comprendre; **to come to the ~** en venir au fait; **there's no ~ (in doing)** cela ne sert à rien (de faire), à quoi ça sert?; **to be on the ~ of doing sth** être sur le point de faire qch; **point out** vt (mention) faire remarquer, souligner; **point-blank** adv (fig) catégoriquement; (also: **at point-blank range**) à bout portant; **pointed** adj (shape) pointu(e); (remark) plein(e) de sous-entendus; **pointer** n (needle) aiguille f; (clue) indication f; (advice) tuyau m; **pointless** adj inutile, vain(e); **point of view** n point m de vue

poison ['pɔɪzn] n poison m ▷ vt empoisonner; **poisonous** adj (snake) venimeux(-euse); (substance, plant) vénéneux(-euse); (fumes) toxique

poke [pəʊk] vt (jab with finger, stick etc) piquer; (put or push) pousser du doigt; (put): **to ~ sth in(to)** fourrer or enfoncer qch dans; **poke about** vi fureter; **poke out** vi (stick out) sortir

poker ['pəʊkə'] n tisonnier m; (Cards) poker m

Poland ['pəʊlənd] n Pologne f

polar ['pəʊlə'] adj polaire; **polar bear** n ours blanc

Pole [pəʊl] n Polonais(e)

pole [pəʊl] n (of wood) mât m, perche f; (Elec) poteau m; (Geo) pôle m; **pole bean** n (us) haricot m (à rames); **pole vault** n saut m à la perche

police [pə'liːs] n police f ▷ vt maintenir l'ordre dans; **police car** n voiture f de police; **police constable** n (BRIT) agent m de police; **police force** n forces fpl de l'ordre; **policeman** (irreg) n agent m de police, policier m; **police officer** n agent m de police; **police station** n commissariat m de police; **policewoman** (irreg) n femme-agent f

policy ['pɒlɪsɪ] n politique f; (also: **insurance ~**) police f (d'assurance)

polio ['pəʊlɪəʊ] n polio f

Polish ['pəʊlɪʃ] adj polonais(e) ▷ n (Ling) polonais m

polish ['pɒlɪʃ] n (for shoes) cirage m; (for floor) cire f, encaustique f; (for nails) vernis m; (shine) éclat m, poli m; (fig: refinement) raffinement m ▷ vt (put polish on: shoes, wood) cirer; (make

shiny) astiquer, faire briller; **polish off** vt (food) liquider; **polished** adj (fig) raffiné(e)

polite [pə'laɪt] adj poli(e); **politeness** n politesse f

political [pə'lɪtɪkl] adj politique; **politically** adv politiquement; **politically correct** politiquement correct(e)

politician [pɒlɪ'tɪʃən] n homme/femme politique, politicien(ne)

politics ['pɒlɪtɪks] n politique f

poll [pəʊl] n scrutin m, vote m; (also: **opinion ~**) sondage m (d'opinion) ▷ vt (votes) obtenir

pollen ['pɒlən] n pollen m

polling station n (BRIT) bureau m de vote

pollute [pə'luːt] vt polluer

pollution [pə'luːʃən] n pollution f

polo ['pəʊləʊ] n polo m; **polo-neck** adj à col roulé ▷ n (sweater) pull m à col roulé; **polo shirt** n polo m

polyester [pɒlɪ'estə'] n polyester m

polystyrene [pɒlɪ'staɪriːn] n polystyrène m

polythene ['pɒlɪθiːn] n (BRIT) polyéthylène m; **polythene bag** n sac m en plastique

pomegranate ['pɒmɪɡrænɪt] n grenade f

pompous ['pɒmpəs] adj pompeux(-euse)

pond [pɒnd] n étang m; (stagnant) mare f

ponder ['pɒndə'] vt considérer, peser

pony ['pəʊnɪ] n poney m; **ponytail** n queue f de cheval; **pony trekking** n (BRIT) randonnée f équestre or à cheval

poodle ['puːdl] n caniche m

pool [puːl] n (of rain) flaque f; (pond) mare f; (artificial) bassin m; (also: **swimming ~**) piscine f; (sth shared) fonds commun; (billiards) poule f ▷ vt mettre en commun; **pools** npl (football) ≈ loto sportif

poor [pʊə'] adj pauvre; (mediocre) médiocre, faible, mauvais(e) ▷ npl: **the ~ les** pauvres mpl; **poorly** adv (badly) mal, médiocrement ▷ adj souffrant(e), malade

pop [pɔp] n (noise) bruit sec; (Mus) musique f pop; (inf: drink) soda m; (us inf: father) papa m ▷ vt (put) fourrer, mettre (rapidement) ▷ vi éclater; (cork) sauter; **pop in** vi entrer en passant; **pop out** vi sortir; **popcorn** n pop-corn m

pope [pəʊp] n pape m

poplar ['pɔplə'] n peuplier m

popper ['pɔpə'] n (BRIT) bouton-pression m

poppy ['pɔpɪ] n (wild) coquelicot m; (cultivated) pavot m

Popsicle® ['pɔpsɪkl] n (us) esquimau m (glace)

pop star n pop star f

popular ['pɔpjʊlə'] adj populaire; (fashionable) à la mode; **popularity** [pɔpjʊ'lærɪtɪ] n popularité f

population [pɔpjʊ'leɪʃən] n population f

pop-up adj (Comput: menu, window) pop up inv ▷ n pop up m inv, fenêtre f pop up

porcelain ['pɔːslɪn] n porcelaine f

porch [pɔːtʃ] n porche m; (us) véranda f

pore [pɔː'] n pore m ▷ vi: **to ~ over** s'absorber dans, être plongé(e) dans

pork [pɔːk] n porc m; **pork chop** n côte f de porc; **pork pie** n pâté m de porc en croûte

porn [pɔːn] adj (inf) porno ▷ n (inf) porno m; **pornographic** [pɔːnə'ɡræfɪk] adj pornographique; **pornography** [pɔː'nɔɡrəfɪ] n pornographie f

porridge ['pɔrɪdʒ] n porridge m

port [pɔːt] n (harbour) port m; (Naut: left side) bâbord m; (wine) porto m; (Comput) port m, accès m; **~ of call** (port d')escale f

portable ['pɔːtəbl] adj portatif(-ive)

porter ['pɔːtə'] n (for luggage) porteur m; (doorkeeper) gardien(ne); portier m

portfolio [pɔːt'fəʊlɪəʊ] n portefeuille m; (of artist) portfolio m

portion ['pɔːʃən] n portion f, part f

portrait ['pɔːtreɪt] n portrait m

portray [pɔː'treɪ] vt faire le portrait de; (in writing) dépeindre, représenter; (subj: actor) jouer

Portugal ['pɔːtjʊɡl] n Portugal m

Portuguese [pɔːtjʊ'ɡiːz] adj portugais(e) ▷ n (pl inv) Portugais(e); (Ling) portugais m

pose [pəʊz] n pose f ▷ vi poser; (pretend): **to ~ as** se faire passer pour ▷ vt poser; (problem) créer

posh [pɔʃ] adj (inf) chic inv

position [pə'zɪʃən] n position f; (job, situation) situation f ▷ vt mettre en place or en position

positive ['pɔzɪtɪv] adj positif(-ive); (certain) sûr(e), certain(e); (definite) formel(le), catégorique; **positively** adv (affirmatively, enthusiastically) de façon positive; (inf: really) impossible

possess [pə'zes] vt posséder; **possession** [pə'zeʃən] n possession f; **possessions** npl (belongings) affaires fpl; **possessive** adj possessif(-ive)

possibility [pɔsɪ'bɪlɪtɪ] n possibilité f; (event) éventualité f

possible ['pɔsɪbl] adj possible; **as big as ~** aussi gros que possible; **possibly** adv (perhaps) peut-être; **I cannot possibly come** il m'est impossible de venir

post [pəʊst] n (BRIT: mail) poste f; (: letters, delivery) courrier m; (job, situation) poste m; (pole) poteau m ▷ vt (BRIT: send by post) poster; (: appoint): **to ~ to** affecter à; **where can I post these cards?** où est-ce que je peux poster ces cartes postales?; **postage** n tarifs mpl d'affranchissement; **postal** adj postal(e); **postal order** n mandat(-poste m); **postbox** n (BRIT) boîte f aux lettres (publique); **postcard** n carte postale; **postcode** n (BRIT) code postal

poster ['pəʊstə'] n affiche f

postgraduate ['pəʊst'ɡrædjʊət] n ≈ étudiant(e) de troisième cycle

postman ['pəʊstmən] (BRIT: irreg) n

facteur m

postmark ['pəustmɑːk] n cachet m
(de la poste)

post-mortem [pəust'mɔːtəm] n
autopsie f

post office n (building) poste f;
(organization): **the Post Office** les
postes fpl

postpone [pəs'pəun] vt remettre (à
plus tard), reculer

posture ['pɒstʃə'] n posture f; (fig)
attitude f

postwoman ['pəust'wumən] (BRIT:
irreg) n factrice f

pot [pɒt] n (for cooking) marmite f,
casserole f; (teapot) théière f; (for coffee)
cafetière f; (for plants, jam) pot m; (inf:
marijuana) herbe f ▷ vt (plant) mettre en
pot; **to go to ~** (inf) aller à vau-l'eau

potato (pl **~es**) [pə'teɪtəu] n pomme
f de terre; **potato peeler** n épluche-
légumes m

potent ['pəutnt] adj puissant(e); (drink)
fort(e), très alcoolisé(e); (man) viril

potential [pə'tenʃl] adj potentiel(le)
▷ n potentiel m

pothole ['pɒthəul] n (in road) nid m
de poule; (BRIT: underground) gouffre
m, caverne f

pot plant n plante f d'appartement

potter ['pɒtə'] n potier m ▷ vi (BRIT): **to
~ around** or **about** bricoler; **pottery**
n poterie f

potty ['pɒtɪ] n (child's) pot m

pouch [pautʃ] n (Zool) poche f; (for
tobacco) blague f; (for money) bourse f

poultry ['pəultrɪ] n volaille f

pounce [pauns] vi: **to ~ (on)** bondir
(sur), fondre (sur)

pound [paund] n livre f (weight = 453g,
16 ounces; money = 100 pence); (for dogs,
cars) fourrière f ▷ vt (beat) bourrer de
coups, marteler; (crush) piler, pulvériser
▷ vi (heart) battre violemment, taper;
pound sterling n livre f sterling

pour [pɔː'] vt verser ▷ vi couler à flots;
(rain) pleuvoir à verse; **to ~ sb a drink**
verser or servir à boire à qn; **pour in**

vi (people) affluer, se précipiter; (news,
letters) arriver en masse; **pour out** vi
(people) sortir en masse ▷ vt vider; (fig)
déverser; (serve: a drink) verser; **pouring**
adj: **pouring rain** pluie torrentielle

pout [paut] vi faire la moue

poverty ['pɒvətɪ] n pauvreté f, misère f

powder ['paudə'] n poudre f ▷ vt
poudrer; **powdered milk** n lait m en
poudre

power ['pauə'] n (strength, nation)
puissance f, force f; (ability, Pol: of party,
leader) pouvoir m; (of speech, thought)
faculté f; (Elec) courant m; **to be in ~**
être au pouvoir; (Pol); **power cut** n (BRIT)
coupure f de courant; **power failure**
n panne f de courant; **powerful** adj
puissant(e); (performance etc) très
fort(e); **powerless** adj impuissant(e);
power point n (BRIT) prise f de courant;
power station n centrale f électrique

p.p. abbr (= per procurationem: by
proxy) p.p.

PR n abbr = **public relations**

practical ['præktɪkl] adj pratique;
practical joke n farce f; **practically**
adv (almost) pratiquement

practice ['præktɪs] n pratique f; (of
profession) exercice m; (at football etc)
entraînement m; (business) cabinet m
▷ vt, vi (us) = **practise**; **in ~** (in reality) en
pratique; **out of ~** rouillé(e)

practise (us **practice**) ['præktɪs]
vt (work at: piano, backhand etc)
s'exercer à, travailler; (train for: sport)
s'entraîner à; (a sport, religion, method)
pratiquer; (profession) exercer ▷ vi
s'exercer, travailler; (train) s'entraîner;
(lawyer, doctor) exercer; **practising**
(us **practicing**) adj (Christian etc)
pratiquant(e); (lawyer) en exercice

practitioner [præk'tɪʃənə'] n
praticien(ne)

pragmatic [præg'mætɪk] adj
pragmatique

prairie ['prɛərɪ] n savane f

praise [preɪz] n éloge(s) m(pl),
louange(s) f(pl) ▷ vt louer, faire

l'éloge de
pram [præm] n (BRIT) landau m, voiture f d'enfant

prank [præŋk] n farce f

prawn [prɔːn] n crevette f (rose); **prawn cocktail** n cocktail m de crevettes

pray [preɪ] vi prier; **prayer** [prɛəʳ] n prière f

preach [priːtʃ] vi prêcher; **preacher** n prédicateur m; (US: clergyman) pasteur m

precarious [prɪˈkɛərɪəs] adj précaire

precaution [prɪˈkɔːʃən] n précaution f

precede [prɪˈsiːd] vt, vi précéder; **precedent** [ˈprɛsɪdənt] n précédent m; **preceding** [prɪˈsiːdɪŋ] adj qui précède (or précédait)

precinct [ˈpriːsɪŋkt] n (US: district) circonscription f, arrondissement m; **pedestrian ~** (BRIT) zone piétonnière; **shopping ~** (BRIT) centre commercial

precious [ˈprɛʃəs] adj précieux(-euse)

precise [prɪˈsaɪs] adj précis(e); **precisely** adv précisément

precision [prɪˈsɪʒən] n précision f

predator [ˈprɛdətəʳ] n prédateur m, rapace m

predecessor [ˈpriːdɪsɛsəʳ] n prédécesseur m

predicament [prɪˈdɪkəmənt] n situation f difficile

predict [prɪˈdɪkt] vt prédire; **predictable** adj prévisible; **prediction** [prɪˈdɪkʃən] n prédiction f

predominantly [prɪˈdɔmɪnəntlɪ] adv en majeure partie; (especially) surtout

preface [ˈprɛfəs] n préface f

prefect [ˈpriːfɛkt] n (BRIT: in school) élève chargé de certaines fonctions de discipline

prefer [prɪˈfəːʳ] vt préférer; **preferable** [ˈprɛfrəbl] adj préférable; **preferably** [ˈprɛfrəblɪ] adv de préférence; **preference** [ˈprɛfrəns] n préférence f

prefix [ˈpriːfɪks] n préfixe m

pregnancy [ˈprɛgnənsɪ] n grossesse f

pregnant [ˈprɛgnənt] adj enceinte adj f; (animal) pleine

prehistoric [ˈpriːhɪsˈtɔrɪk] adj

préhistorique

prejudice [ˈprɛdʒudɪs] n préjugé m; **prejudiced** adj (person) plein(e) de préjugés; (in a matter) partial(e)

preliminary [prɪˈlɪmɪnərɪ] adj préliminaire

prelude [ˈprɛljuːd] n prélude m

premature [ˈprɛmətʃuəʳ] adj prématuré(e)

premier [ˈprɛmɪəʳ] adj premier(-ière), principal(e) ▷ n (Pol: Prime Minister) premier ministre; (Pol: President) chef m de l'État

premiere [ˈprɛmɪɛəʳ] n première f

Premier League n première division

premises [ˈprɛmɪsɪz] npl locaux mpl; **on the ~** sur les lieux; sur place

premium [ˈpriːmɪəm] n prime f; **to be at a ~** (fig: housing etc) être très demandé(e); être rarissime

premonition [prɛməˈnɪʃən] n prémonition f

preoccupied [priːˈɔkjupaɪd] adj préoccupé(e)

prepaid [priːˈpeɪd] adj payé(e) d'avance

preparation [prɛpəˈreɪʃən] n préparation f; **preparations** npl (for trip, war) préparatifs mpl

preparatory school n école primaire privée; (US) lycée privé

prepare [prɪˈpɛəʳ] vt préparer ▷ vi: **to ~ for** se préparer à

prepared [prɪˈpɛəd] adj: **~ for** préparé(e) à; **~ to** prêt(e) à

preposition [prɛpəˈzɪʃən] n préposition f

prep school n = **preparatory school**

prerequisite [priːˈrɛkwɪzɪt] n condition f préalable

preschool [ˈpriːˈskuːl] adj préscolaire; (child) d'âge préscolaire

prescribe [prɪˈskraɪb] vt prescrire

prescription [prɪˈskrɪpʃən] n (Med) ordonnance f; (: medicine) médicament m (obtenu sur ordonnance); **could you write me a ~?** pouvez-vous me faire une ordonnance?

presence [ˈprɛzns] n présence f; **in**

sb's ~ en présence de qn; ~ **of mind**
présence d'esprit
present ['preznt] *adj* présent(e);
(*current*) présent, actuel(le) ▷ *n* cadeau
m; (*actuality*) présent *m* ▷ *vt* [pri'zent]
présenter; (*prize, medal*) remettre;
(*give*): **to ~ sb with sth** offrir qch à
qn; **at ~** en ce moment; **to give sb a
~** offrir un cadeau à qn; **presentable**
[pri'zentəbl] *adj* présentable;
presentation [prezn'teɪʃən] *n*
présentation *f*; (*ceremony*) remise *f* du
cadeau (or de la médaille *etc*); **present-
day** *adj* contemporain(e), actuel(le);
presenter [pri'zentə*] *n* (*BRIT Radio,
TV*) présentateur(-trice); **presently**
adv (*soon*) tout à l'heure, bientôt; (*with
verb in past*) peu après; (*at present*) en ce
moment; **present participle**
[-'pa:tɪsɪpl] *n* participe *m* présent
preservation [prezə'veɪʃən] *n*
préservation *f*, conservation *f*
preservative [pri'zə:vətɪv] *n* agent *m*
de conservation
preserve [pri'zə:v] *vt* (*keep safe*)
préserver, protéger; (*maintain*)
conserver, garder; (*food*) mettre en
conserve ▷ *n* (*for game, fish*) réserve *f*;
(*often pl: jam*) confiture *f*
preside [pri'zaɪd] *vi* présider
president ['prezɪdənt] *n* président(e);
presidential [prezɪ'denʃl] *adj*
présidentiel(le)
press [pres] *n* (*tool, machine, newspapers*)
presse *f*; (*for wine*) pressoir *m* ▷ *vt*
appuyer sur; (*squeeze*) presser, serrer;
(*clothes: iron*) repasser; (*insist*): **to ~
sth on sb** presser qn d'accepter qch; (*urge,
entreat*): **to ~ sb to do** or **into doing sth**
pousser qn à faire qch ▷ *vi* appuyer;
we are ~ed for time le temps nous
manque; **to ~ for sth** faire pression
pour obtenir qch; **press conference**
n conférence *f* de presse; **pressing** *adj*
urgent(e), pressant(e); **press stud** *n*
(*BRIT*) bouton-pression *m*; **press-up** *n*
(*BRIT*) traction *f*
pressure ['preʃə*] *n* pression *f*; (*stress*)

tension *f*; **to put ~ on sb (to do sth)**
faire pression sur qn (pour qu'il fasse
qch); **pressure cooker** *n* cocotte-
minute *f*; **pressure group** *n* groupe *m*
de pression
prestige [pres'ti:ʒ] *n* prestige *m*
prestigious [pres'tɪdʒəs] *adj*
prestigieux(-euse)
presumably [pri'zju:məblɪ] *adv*
vraisemblablement
presume [pri'zju:m] *vt* présumer,
supposer
pretence (*US* **pretense**) [pri'tens] *n*
(*claim*) prétention *f*; **under false ~s**
sous des prétextes fallacieux
pretend [pri'tend] *vt* (*feign*) feindre,
simuler ▷ *vi* (*feign*) faire semblant
pretense [pri'tens] *n* (*US*) = **pretence**
pretentious [pri'tenʃəs] *adj*
prétentieux(-euse)
pretext ['pri:tekst] *n* prétexte *m*
pretty ['prɪtɪ] *adj* joli(e) ▷ *adv* assez
prevail [pri'veɪl] *vi* (*win*) l'emporter,
prévaloir; (*be usual*) avoir cours;
prevailing *adj* (*widespread*) courant(e),
répandu(e); (*wind*) dominant(e)
prevalent ['prevələnt] *adj* répandu(e),
courant(e)
prevent [pri'vent] *vt*: **to ~ (from doing)**
empêcher (de faire); **prevention**
[pri'venʃən] *n* prévention *f*; **preventive**
adj préventif(-ive)
preview ['pri:vju:] *n* (*of film*) avant-
première *f*
previous ['pri:vɪəs] *adj* (*last*)
précédent(e); (*earlier*) antérieur(e);
previously *adv* précédemment,
auparavant
prey [preɪ] *n* proie *f* ▷ *vi*: **to ~ on**
s'attaquer à; **it was ~ing on his mind**
ça le rongeait or minait
price [praɪs] *n* prix *m* ▷ *vt* (*goods*) fixer
le prix de; **priceless** *adj* sans prix,
inestimable; **price list** *n* liste *f* des prix
prick [prɪk] *n* (*sting*) piqûre *f* ▷ *vt*
piquer; **to ~ up one's ears** dresser or
tendre l'oreille
prickly ['prɪklɪ] *adj* piquant(e),

épineux(-euse): (fig: person) irritable
pride [praɪd] n fierté f; (pej) orgueil
m ▷ vt: **to ~ o.s. on** se flatter de;
s'enorgueillir de
priest [priːst] n prêtre m
primarily ['praɪmərɪlɪ] adv
principalement, essentiellement
primary ['praɪmərɪ] adj primaire;
(first in importance) premier(-ière),
primordial(e) ▷ n (us: election) (élection
f) primaire f; **primary school** n (BRIT)
école f primaire
prime [praɪm] adj primordial(e),
fondamental(e); (excellent) excellent(e)
▷ vt (fig) mettre au courant ▷ n: **in the
~ of life** dans la fleur de l'âge; **Prime
Minister** n Premier ministre m
primitive ['prɪmɪtɪv] adj primitif(-ive)
primrose ['prɪmrəʊz] n primevère f
prince [prɪns] n prince m
princess [prɪn'ses] n princesse f
principal ['prɪnsɪpl] adj principal(e)
▷ n (head teacher) directeur m,
principal m; **principally** adv
principalement
principle ['prɪnsɪpl] n principe m; **in ~**
en principe; **on ~** par principe
print [prɪnt] n (mark) empreinte f;
(letters) caractères mpl; (fabric) imprimé
m; (Art) gravure f, estampe f; (Phot)
épreuve f ▷ vt imprimer; (publish)
publier; (write in capitals) écrire en
majuscules; **out of ~** épuisé(e); **print
out** vt (Comput) imprimer; **printer**
n (machine) imprimante f; (person)
imprimeur m; **printout** n (Comput)
sortie f imprimante
prior ['praɪə] adj antérieur(e),
précédent(e); (more important)
prioritaire ▷ adv: **~ to doing** avant
de faire
priority [praɪ'ɒrɪtɪ] n priorité f; **to have
or take ~ over sth/sb** avoir la priorité
sur qch/qn
prison ['prɪzn] n prison f ▷ cpd
pénitentiaire; **prisoner** n
prisonnier(-ière); **prisoner of war** n
prisonnier(-ière) de guerre

pristine ['prɪstiːn] adj virginal(e)
privacy ['prɪvəsɪ] n intimité f, solitude f
private ['praɪvɪt] adj (not public)
privé(e); (personal) personnel(le);
(house, car, lesson) particulier(-ière);
(quiet: place) tranquille ▷ n soldat m
de deuxième classe; **"~"** (on envelope)
"personnelle"; (on door) "privé"; **in ~** en
privé; **privately** adv en privé; (within
oneself) intérieurement; **private
property** n propriété privée; **private
school** n école privée
privatize ['praɪvɪtaɪz] vt privatiser
privilege ['prɪvɪlɪdʒ] n privilège m
prize [praɪz] n prix m ▷ adj (example,
idiot) parfait(e); (bull, novel) primé(e)
▷ vt priser, faire grand cas de; **prize-
giving** n distribution f des prix;
prizewinner n gagnant(e)
pro [prəʊ] n (inf: Sport) professionnel(le)
▷ prep pro ...; **pros** npl: **the ~s and cons**
le pour et le contre
probability [prɒbə'bɪlɪtɪ] n probabilité
f; **in all ~** très probablement
probable ['prɒbəbl] adj probable
probably ['prɒbəblɪ] adv probablement
probation [prə'beɪʃən] n: **on ~**
(employee) à l'essai; (Law) en liberté
surveillée
probe [prəʊb] n (Med, Space) sonde f;
(enquiry) enquête f, investigation f ▷ vt
sonder, explorer
problem ['prɒbləm] n problème m
procedure [prə'siːdʒə] n (Admin, Law)
procédure f; (method) marche f à suivre,
façon f de procéder
proceed [prə'siːd] vi (go forward)
avancer; (act) procéder; (continue): **to ~
(with)** continuer, poursuivre; **to ~ to
do** se mettre à faire; **proceedings** npl
(measures) mesures fpl; (Law: against
sb) poursuites fpl; (meeting) réunion
f, séance f; (records) compte rendu;
actes mpl; **proceeds** ['prəʊsiːdz] npl
produit m, recette f
process ['prəʊses] n processus m;
(method) procédé m ▷ vt traiter
procession [prə'seʃən] n défilé m,

cortège m; **funeral ~** *(on foot)* cortège funèbre; *(in cars)* convoi m mortuaire

proclaim [prə'kleɪm] *vt* déclarer, proclamer

prod [prɒd] *vt* pousser

produce *n* ['prɒdjuːs] *(Agr)* produits *mpl* ▷ *vt* [prə'djuːs] produire; *(show)* présenter; *(cause)* provoquer, causer; *(Theat)* monter, mettre en scène; *(TV: programme)* réaliser; *(: play, film)* mettre en scène; *(Radio: programme)* réaliser; **producer** *n (Theat)* metteur *m* en scène; *(Agr, Comm, Cine)* producteur *m*; *(TV: of programme)* réalisateur *m*; *(: of play, film)* metteur *m* en scène; *(Radio: of programme)* réalisateur *m*; *(: of play)* metteur *m* en ondes

product ['prɒdʌkt] *n* produit *m*; **production** [prə'dʌkʃən] *n* production *f*; *(Theat)* mise *f* en scène; **productive** [prə'dʌktɪv] *adj* productif(-ive); **productivity** [prɒdʌk'tɪvɪtɪ] *n* productivité *f*

Prof. [prɒf] *abbr* (= *professor*) Prof

profession [prə'feʃən] *n* profession *f*; **professional** *n* professionnel(le) ▷ *adj* professionnel(le); *(work)* de professionnel

professor [prə'fesə'] *n* professeur *m* (titulaire d'une chaire); *(us: teacher)* professeur *m*

profile ['prəʊfaɪl] *n* profil *m*

profit ['prɒfɪt] *n (from trading)* bénéfice *m*; *(advantage)* profit *m* ▷ *vi*: **to ~ (by** **or from)** profiter (de); **profitable** *adj* lucratif(-ive), rentable

profound [prə'faʊnd] *adj* profond(-e)

programme (us **program**) ['prəʊgræm] *n* (Comput: also BRIT: **program**) programme *m*; *(Radio, TV)* émission *f* ▷ *vt* programmer; **programmer** *n* programmeur(-euse); **programming** (us **programing**) *n* programmation *f*

progress *n* ['prəʊgres] progrès *m(pl)* ▷ *vi* [prə'gres] progresser, avancer; **in ~** en cours; **progressive** [prə'gresɪv] *adj* progressif(-ive); *(person)* progressiste

prohibit [prə'hɪbɪt] *vt* interdire, défendre

project *n* ['prɒdʒekt] *(plan)* projet *m*, plan *m*; *(venture)* opération *f*, entreprise *f*; *(Scol: research)* étude *f*, dossier *m* ▷ *vb* [prə'dʒekt] ▷ *vt* projeter ▷ *vi (stick* *out)* faire saillie, s'avancer; **projection** [prə'dʒekʃən] *n* projection *f*; *(overhang)* saillie *f*; **projector** [prə'dʒektə'] *n* projecteur *m*

prolific [prə'lɪfɪk] *adj* prolifique

prolong [prə'lɒŋ] *vt* prolonger

prom [prɒm] *n abbr* = **promenade** (us: *ball)* bal *m* d'étudiants; **the P~s** série de concerts de musique classique; *voir encadré*

● **PROM**

En Grande-Bretagne, un **promenade** concert ou **prom** est un concert de musique classique, ainsi appelé car, à l'origine, le public restait debout et se promenait au lieu de rester assis. De nos jours, une partie du public reste debout, mais il y a également des places assises (plus chères). Les **Proms** les plus connus sont les Proms londoniens. La dernière séance (the "Last Night of the Proms") est un grand événement médiatique où se jouent des airs traditionnels et patriotiques. Aux États-Unis et au Canada, le **prom** ou **promenade** est un bal organisé par le lycée.

promenade [prɒmə'nɑːd] *n (by sea)* esplanade *f*, promenade *f*

prominent ['prɒmɪnənt] *adj (standing* *out)* proéminent(e); *(important)* important(e)

promiscuous [prə'mɪskjʊəs] *adj (sexually)* de mœurs légères

promise ['prɒmɪs] *n* promesse *f* ▷ *vt, vi* promettre; **promising** *adj* prometteur(-euse)

promote [prə'məʊt] *vt* promouvoir; *(new product)* lancer; **promotion**

[prə'məʊʃən] n promotion f

prompt [prɒmpt] adj rapide ▷ n (Comput) message m (de guidage) ▷ vt (cause) entraîner, provoquer; (Theat) souffler (son rôle ou ses répliques) à; **at 8 o'clock** ~ à 8 heures précises; **to** ~ **sb to do** inciter ou pousser qn à faire; **promptly** adv (quickly) rapidement, sans délai; (on time) ponctuellement

prone [prəʊn] adj (lying) couché(e) (face contre terre); (liable): ~ **to** enclin(e) à

prong [prɒŋ] n (of fork) dent f

pronoun ['prəʊnaʊn] n pronom m

pronounce [prə'naʊns] vt prononcer; **how do you** ~ **it?** comment est-ce que ça se prononce?

pronunciation [prənʌnsɪ'eɪʃən] n prononciation f

proof [pruːf] n preuve f ▷ adj: ~ **against** à l'épreuve de

prop [prɒp] n support m, étai m; (fig) soutien m ▷ vt (also: ~ **up**) étayer, soutenir; **props** npl accessoires mpl

propaganda [prɒpə'ɡændə] n propagande f

propeller [prə'pelər] n hélice f

proper ['prɒpər] adj (suited, right) approprié(e), bon (bonne); (seemly) correct(e), convenable; (authentic) vrai(e), véritable; (referring to place): **the village** ~ le village proprement dit; **properly** adv correctement, convenablement; **proper noun** n nom m propre

property ['prɒpətɪ] n (possessions) biens mpl; (house etc) propriété f; (land) terres fpl, domaine m

prophecy ['prɒfɪsɪ] n prophétie f

prophet ['prɒfɪt] n prophète m

proportion [prə'pɔːʃən] n proportion f; (share) part f, partie f; **proportions** npl (size) dimensions fpl; **proportional**, **proportionate** adj proportionnel(le)

proposal [prə'pəʊzl] n proposition f, offre f; (plan) projet m; (of marriage) demande f en mariage

propose [prə'pəʊz] vt proposer, suggérer ▷ vi faire sa demande en

mariage; **to** ~ **to do** avoir l'intention de faire

proposition [prɒpə'zɪʃən] n proposition f

proprietor [prə'praɪətər] n propriétaire m/f

prose [prəʊz] n prose f; (Scol: translation) thème m

prosecute ['prɒsɪkjuːt] vt poursuivre; **prosecution** [prɒsɪ'kjuːʃən] n poursuites fpl judiciaires; (accusing side: in criminal case) accusation f; (: in civil case) la partie plaignante; **prosecutor** n (lawyer) procureur m; (also: **public prosecutor**) ministère public; (us: plaintiff) plaignant(e)

prospect n ['prɒspekt] perspective f; (hope) espoir m, chances fpl ▷ vt, vi [prə'spekt] prospecter; **prospects** npl (for work etc) possibilités fpl d'avenir, débouchés mpl; **prospective** [prə'spektɪv] adj (possible) éventuel(le); (future) futur(e)

prospectus [prə'spektəs] n prospectus m

prosper ['prɒspər] vi prospérer; **prosperity** [prɒ'sperɪtɪ] n prospérité f; **prosperous** adj prospère

prostitute ['prɒstɪtjuːt] n prostituée f; **male** ~ prostitué m

protect [prə'tekt] vt protéger; **protection** [prə'tekʃən] n protection f; **protective** adj protecteur(-trice); (clothing) de protection

protein ['prəʊtiːn] n protéine f

protest n ['prəʊtest] protestation f ▷ vb [prə'test] vi: **to** ~ **against/ about** protester contre/à propos de; **to** ~ **(that)** protester que

Protestant ['prɒtɪstənt] adj, n protestant(e)

protester, protestor [prə'testər] n (in demonstration) manifestant(e)

protractor [prə'træktər] n (Geom) rapporteur m

proud [praʊd] adj fier(-ère); (pej) orgueilleux(-euse)

prove [pruːv] vt prouver, démontrer

▷ vi: **to ~ correct** etc s'avérer juste etc; **to ~ o.s.** montrer ce dont on est capable

proverb ['prɔvə:b] n proverbe m

provide [prə'vaɪd] vt fournir; **to ~ sb with sth** fournir qch à qn; **provide for** vt fus (person) subvenir aux besoins de; (future event) prévoir ▷ conj: **provided (that)** à condition que + sub; **providing** [prə'vaɪdɪŋ] conj à condition que + sub

province ['prɔvɪns] n province f; (fig) domaine m; **provincial** [prə'vɪnʃəl] adj provincial(e)

provision [prə'vɪʒən] n (supplying) fourniture f; approvisionnement m; (stipulation) disposition f; **provisions** npl (food) provisions fpl; **provisional** adj provisoire

provocative [prə'vɔkətɪv] adj provocateur(-trice), provocant(e)

provoke [prə'vəʊk] vt provoquer

prowl [praʊl] vi (also: **~ about, ~ around**) rôder

proximity [prɔk'sɪmɪtɪ] n proximité f

proxy ['prɔksɪ] n: **by ~** par procuration

prudent ['pru:dnt] adj prudent(e)

prune [pru:n] n pruneau m ▷ vt élaguer

pry [praɪ] vi: **to ~ into** fourrer son nez dans

PS n abbr (= postscript) PS m

pseudonym ['sju:dənɪm] n pseudonyme m

PSHE n abbr (BRIT: Scol: = personal, social and health education) cours d'éducation personnelle, sanitaire et sociale préparant à la vie adulte

psychiatric [saɪkɪ'ætrɪk] adj psychiatrique

psychiatrist [saɪ'kaɪətrɪst] n psychiatre m/f

psychic ['saɪkɪk] adj (also: **~al**) (méta)psychique; (person) doué(e) de télépathie or d'un sixième sens

psychoanalysis (pl **-ses**) [saɪkəʊə'nælɪsɪs, -siːz] n psychanalyse f

psychological [saɪkə'lɔdʒɪkl] adj psychologique

psychologist [saɪ'kɔlədʒɪst] n psychologue m/f

psychology [saɪ'kɔlədʒɪ] n psychologie f

psychotherapy [saɪkəʊ'θɛrəpɪ] n psychothérapie f

pt abbr = **pint(s)**; **point(s)**

PTO abbr (= please turn over) TSVP

pub [pʌb] n abbr (= public house) pub m

puberty ['pju:bətɪ] n puberté f

public ['pʌblɪk] adj public(-ique) ▷ n public m; **in ~** en public; **to make ~** rendre public

publication [pʌblɪ'keɪʃən] n publication f

public: public company n société f anonyme; **public convenience** n (BRIT) toilettes fpl; **public holiday** n (BRIT) jour férié; **public house** n (BRIT) pub m

publicity [pʌb'lɪsɪtɪ] n publicité f

publicize ['pʌblɪsaɪz] vt (make known) faire connaître, rendre public; (advertise) faire de la publicité pour

public: public limited company n = société f anonyme (SA) (cotée en Bourse); **publicly** adv publiquement, en public; **public opinion** n opinion publique; **public relations** n or npl relations publiques (RP); **public school** n (BRIT) école privée; (US) école publique; **public transport** (US **public transportation**) n transports mpl en commun

publish ['pʌblɪʃ] vt publier; **publisher** n éditeur m; **publishing** n (industry) édition f

pub lunch n repas m de bistrot

pudding ['pʊdɪŋ] n (BRIT: dessert) dessert m, entremets m; (sweet dish) pudding m, gâteau m

puddle ['pʌdl] n flaque f d'eau

puff [pʌf] n bouffée f ▷ vt: **~ out** sails, cheeks) gonfler ▷ vi (pant) haleter; **puff pastry** (US **puff paste**) n pâte feuilletée

pull [pʊl] n (tug): **to give sth a ~** tirer sur qch ▷ vt tirer; (trigger) presser;

(strain: muscle, tendon) se claquer
▷ vi tirer; **to ~ to pieces** mettre en morceaux; (fig) ménager son adversaire; **to ~ one's weight** y mettre du sien; **to ~ o.s. together** se ressaisir; **to ~ sb's leg** (fig) faire marcher qn; **pull apart** vt (break) mettre en pièces, démantibuler; **pull away** vi (vehicle: move off) partir; (draw back) s'éloigner; **pull back** vt (lever etc) tirer sur; (curtains) ouvrir ▷ vi (refrain) s'abstenir; (Mil: withdraw) se retirer; **pull down** vt baisser, abaisser; (house) démolir; **pull in** vi (Aut) se ranger; (Rail) entrer en gare; **pull off** vt enlever, ôter; (deal etc) conclure; **pull out** vi (Aut: come out of line) déboîter ▷ vi vt (from bag, pocket) sortir; (remove) arracher; **pull over** vi (Aut) se ranger; **pull up** vi (stop) s'arrêter ▷ vt remonter; (uproot) déraciner, arracher
pulley ['puli] n poulie f
pullover ['puləʊvə'] n pull-over m, tricot m
pulp [pʌlp] n (of fruit) pulpe f; (for paper) pâte f à papier
pulpit ['pʊlpɪt] n chaire f
pulse [pʌls] n (of blood) pouls m; (of heart) battement m; **pulses** npl (Culin) légumineuses fpl
puma ['pjuːmə] n puma m
pump [pʌmp] n pompe f; (shoe) escarpin m ▷ vt pomper; **pump up** vt gonfler
pumpkin ['pʌmpkɪn] n potiron m, citrouille f
pun [pʌn] n jeu m de mots, calembour m
punch [pʌntʃ] n (blow) coup m de poing; (tool) poinçon m; (drink) punch m ▷ vt (make a hole in) poinçonner, perforer; (hit): **to ~ sb/sth** donner un coup de poing à qn/sur qch; **punch-up** n (BRIT inf) bagarre f
punctual ['pʌŋktjʊəl] adj ponctuel(le)
punctuation [pʌŋktjʊ'eɪʃən] n ponctuation f
puncture ['pʌŋktʃə'] n (BRIT) crevaison f ▷ vt crever

punish ['pʌnɪʃ] vt punir; **punishment** n punition f, châtiment m
punk [pʌŋk] n (person: also: ~ rocker) punk m/f; (music: also: ~ rock) le punk; (us inf: hoodlum) voyou m
pup [pʌp] n chiot m
pupil ['pjuːpl] n élève m/f; (of eye) pupille f
puppet ['pʌpɪt] n marionnette f, pantin m
puppy ['pʌpɪ] n chiot m, petit chien
purchase ['pəːtʃɪs] n achat m ▷ vt acheter
pure [pjʊə'] adj pur(e); **purely** adv purement
purify ['pjʊərɪfaɪ] vt purifier, épurer
purity ['pjʊərɪtɪ] n pureté f
purple ['pəːpl] adj violet(te); (face) cramoisi(e)
purpose ['pəːpəs] n intention f, but m; **on ~** exprès
purr [pəː'] vi ronronner
purse [pəːs] n (BRIT: for money) porte-monnaie m inv; (us: handbag) sac m (à main) ▷ vt serrer, pincer
pursue [pə'sjuː] vt poursuivre
pursuit [pə'sjuːt] n poursuite f; (occupation) occupation f, activité f
pus [pʌs] n pus m
push [pʊʃ] n poussée f ▷ vt pousser; (button) appuyer sur; (fig: product) mettre en avant, faire de la publicité pour ▷ vi pousser; (demand): **to ~ for** (better pay, conditions) réclamer; **push in** vi s'introduire de force; **push off** vi (inf) filer, ficher le camp; **push on** vi (continue) continuer; **push over** vt renverser; **push through** vi (in crowd) se frayer un chemin; **pushchair** n (BRIT) poussette f; **pusher** n (also: **drug pusher**) revendeur(-euse) (de drogue), ravitailleur(-euse) (en drogue); **push-up** n (us) traction f
pussy(-cat) ['pusɪ-] n (inf) minet m
put (pt, pp ~) [put] vt mettre; (place) poser, placer; (say) dire, exprimer; (a question) poser; (case, view) exposer, présenter; (estimate) estimer; **put**

aside vt mettre de côté; **put away** vt (store) ranger; **put back** vt (replace) remettre, replacer; (postpone) remettre; **put by** vt (money) mettre de côté, économiser; **put down** vt (parcel etc) poser, déposer; (in writing) mettre par écrit, inscrire; (suppress: revolt etc) réprimer, écraser; (attribute) attribuer; (animal) abattre; (cat, dog) faire piquer; **put forward** vt (ideas) avancer, proposer; **put in** vt (complaint) soumettre; (time, effort) consacrer; **put off** vt (postpone) remettre à plus tard, ajourner; (discourage) dissuader; **put on** vt (clothes, lipstick, CD) mettre; (play etc) monter; (weight) prendre; (assume: accent, manner) prendre; **put out** vt (take outside) mettre dehors; (one's hand) tendre; (light etc) éteindre; (person: inconvenience) déranger, gêner; **put through** vt (Tel: caller) mettre en communication; (: call) passer; (plan) faire accepter; **put together** vt mettre ensemble; (assemble: furniture) monter, assembler; (meal) préparer; **put up** vt (raise) lever, relever, remonter; (hang) accrocher; (build) construire, ériger; (increase) augmenter; (accommodate) loger; **put up with** vt fus supporter

putt [pʌt] n putt m; **putting green** n green m

puzzle ['pʌzl] n énigme f, mystère m; (game) jeu m, casse-tête m; (jigsaw) puzzle m; (also: **crossword ~**) mots croisés ▷ vt intriguer, rendre perplexe ▷ vi: **to ~ over** chercher à comprendre; **puzzled** adj perplexe; **puzzling** adj déconcertant(e), inexplicable

pyjamas [pɪˈdʒɑːməz] npl (BRIT) pyjama m

pylon ['paɪlən] n pylône m

pyramid ['pɪrəmɪd] n pyramide f

Pyrenees [pɪrəˈniːz] npl Pyrénées fpl

q

quack [kwæk] n (of duck) coin-coin m inv; (pej: doctor) charlatan m

quadruple [kwɔˈdruːpl] vt, vi quadrupler

quail [kweɪl] n (Zool) caille f ▷ vi: **to ~ at** or **before** reculer devant

quaint [kweɪnt] adj bizarre; (old-fashioned) désuet(-ète); (picturesque) au charme vieillot, pittoresque

quake [kweɪk] vi trembler ▷ n abbr **= earthquake**

qualification [kwɔlɪfɪˈkeɪʃən] n (often pl: degree etc) diplôme m; (training) qualification(s) f(pl); (ability) compétence(s) f(pl); (limitation) réserve f, restriction f

qualified ['kwɔlɪfaɪd] adj (trained) qualifié(e); (professionally) diplômé(e); (fit, competent) compétent(e), qualifié(e); (limited) conditionnel(le)

qualify ['kwɔlɪfaɪ] vt qualifier; (modify) atténuer, nuancer ▷ vi: **to ~ (as)** obtenir son diplôme (de); **to ~ (for)** remplir les conditions requises (pour);

(Sport) se qualifier (pour)

quality ['kwɒlɪtɪ] *n* qualité *f*

qualm [kwɑːm] *n* doute *m*; scrupule *m*

quantify ['kwɒntɪfaɪ] *vt* quantifier

quantity ['kwɒntɪtɪ] *n* quantité *f*

quarantine ['kwɒrntiːn] *n* quarantaine *f*

quarrel ['kwɒrl] *n* querelle *f*, dispute *f* ▷ *vi* se disputer, se quereller

quarry ['kwɒrɪ] *n (for stone)* carrière *f*; *(animal)* proie *f*, gibier *m*

quart [kwɔːt] ≈ litre *m*

quarter ['kwɔːtəᵣ] *n* quart *m*; *(of year)* trimestre *m*; *(district)* quartier *m*; *(US, CANADA: 25 cents)* (pièce *f* de) vingt-cinq cents *mpl* ▷ *vt* partager en quartiers ou en quatre; *(Mil)* caserner, cantonner; **quarters** *npl* logement *m*; *(Mil)* quartiers *mpl*, cantonnement *m*; **a ~ of an hour** un quart d'heure; **quarter final** *n* quart *m* de finale; **quarterly** *adj* trimestriel(le) ▷ *adv* tous les trois mois

quartet(te) [kwɔːˈtɛt] *n* quatuor *m*; *(jazz players)* quartette *m*

quartz [kwɔːts] *n* quartz *m*

quash [kwɒʃ] *vt (verdict)* annuler

quay [kiː] *n (also: ~-side)* quai *m*

queasy ['kwiːzɪ] *adj*: **to feel ~** avoir mal au cœur

Quebec [kwɪˈbɛk] *n (city)* Québec; *(province)* Québec *m*

queen [kwiːn] *n (gen)* reine *f*; *(Cards etc)* dame *f*

queer [kwɪəᵣ] *adj* étrange, curieux(-euse); *(suspicious)* louche ▷ *n (inf: highly offensive)* homosexuel *m*

quench [kwɛntʃ] *vt*: **to ~ one's thirst** se désaltérer

query ['kwɪərɪ] *n* question *f* ▷ *vt (disagree with, dispute)* mettre en doute, questionner

quest [kwɛst] *n* recherche *f*, quête *f*

question ['kwɛstʃən] *n* question *f* ▷ *vt (person)* interroger; *(plan, idea)* mettre en question *ou* en doute; **beyond ~** sans aucun doute; **out of the ~** hors de question; **questionable** *adj* discutable; **question mark** *n* point *m* d'interrogation; **questionnaire**

[kwɛstʃəˈnɛəᵣ] *n* questionnaire *m*

queue [kjuː] *(BRIT) n* queue *f*, file *f* ▷ *vi (also: ~ up)* faire la queue

quiche [kiːʃ] *n* quiche *f*

quick [kwɪk] *adj* rapide; *(mind)* vif (vive); *(agile)* agile, vif (vive) ▷ *n*: **cut to the ~** *(fig)* touché(e) au vif; **be ~!** dépêche-toi!; **quickly** *adv (fast)* vite, rapidement; *(immediately)* tout de suite

quid [kwɪd] *n (pl inv: BRIT inf)* livre *f*

quiet ['kwaɪət] *adj* tranquille, calme; *(voice)* bas(se); *(ceremony, colour)* discret(-ète) ▷ *n* tranquillité *f*, calme *m*; *(silence)* silence *m*; **quietly** *adv* tranquillement; *(silently)* silencieusement; *(discreetly)* discrètement

quilt [kwɪlt] *n* édredon *m*; *(continental quilt)* couette *f*

quirky ['kwɜːkɪ] *adj* singulier(-ère)

quit [kwɪt] *(pt, pp ~ or ~ted) vt* quitter ▷ *vi (give up)* abandonner, renoncer; *(resign)* démissionner

quite [kwaɪt] *adv (rather)* assez, plutôt; *(entirely)* complètement, tout à fait; **~ a few of them** quickly un assez grand nombre d'entre eux; **that's not ~ right** ce n'est pas tout à fait juste; **~ (so)!** exactement!

quits [kwɪts] *adj*: **~ (with)** quitte (envers); **let's call it ~** restons-en là

quiver ['kwɪvəᵣ] *vi* trembler, frémir

quiz [kwɪz] *n (on TV)* jeu-concours *m* (télévisé); *(in magazine etc)* test *m* de connaissances ▷ *vt* interroger

quota ['kwəʊtə] *n* quota *m*

quotation [kwəʊˈteɪʃən] *n* citation *f*; *(estimate)* devis *m*; **quotation marks** *npl* guillemets *mpl*

quote [kwəʊt] *n* citation *f*; *(estimate)* devis *m* ▷ *vt (sentence, author)* citer; *(price)* donner, soumettre ▷ *vi*: **to ~ from** citer; **quotes** *npl (inverted commas)* guillemets *mpl*

r

Rabat [rə'bɑːt] n Rabat
rabbi ['ræbaɪ] n rabbin m
rabbit ['ræbɪt] n lapin m
rabies ['reɪbiːz] n rage f
RAC n abbr (BRIT: = Royal Automobile Club) = ACF m
rac(c)oon [rə'kuːn] n raton m laveur
race [reɪs] n (species) race f; (competition, rush) course f ▷ vt (person) faire la course avec ▷ vi (compete) battre très vite; **race car** n (US) = **racing car**; **racecourse** n champ m de courses; **racehorse** n cheval m de course; **racetrack** n piste f
racial ['reɪʃl] adj racial(e)
racing ['reɪsɪŋ] n courses fpl; **racing car** n (BRIT) voiture f de course; **racing driver** n (BRIT) pilote m de course
racism ['reɪsɪzəm] n racisme m; **racist** ['reɪsɪst] adj, n raciste m/f
rack [ræk] n (for guns, tools) râtelier m; (for clothes) portant m; (for bottles) casier m; (also: **luggage ~**) filet m à bagages; (also: **roof ~**) galerie f; (also: **dish ~**) égouttoir m ▷ vt tourmenter; **to ~ one's brains** se creuser la cervelle
racket ['rækɪt] n (for tennis) raquette f; (noise) tapage m, vacarme m; (swindle) escroquerie f
racquet ['rækɪt] n raquette f
radar ['reɪdɑː'] n radar m
radiation [reɪdɪ'eɪʃən] n rayonnement m; (radioactive) radiation f
radiator ['reɪdɪeɪtə'] n radiateur m
radical ['rædɪkl] adj radical(e)
radio ['reɪdɪəu] n radio f ▷ vt (person) appeler par radio; **on the ~** à la radio; **radioactive** adj radioactif(-ive); **radio station** n station f de radio
radish ['rædɪʃ] n radis m
RAF n abbr (BRIT) = **Royal Air Force**
raffle ['ræfl] n tombola f
raft [rɑːft] n (craft: also: **life ~**) radeau m; (logs) train m de flottage
rag [ræg] n chiffon m; (pej: newspaper) feuille f, torchon m; (for charity) attractions organisées par les étudiants au profit d'œuvres de charité; **rags** npl haillons mpl
rage [reɪdʒ] n (fury) rage f, fureur f ▷ vi (person) être fou (folle) de rage; (storm) faire rage, être déchaîné(e); **it's all the ~** cela fait fureur
ragged ['rægɪd] adj (edge) inégal(e), qui accroche; (clothes) en loques; (appearance) déguenillé(e)
raid [reɪd] n (Mil) raid m; (criminal) hold-up m inv; (by police) descente f, rafle f ▷ vt faire un raid sur or un hold-up dans or une descente dans
rail [reɪl] n (on stair) rampe f; (of ship) bastingage m; (for train) rail m; **railcard** n (BRIT) carte f de chemin de fer; **railing(s)** n(pl) grille f; **railway** (US **railroad**) n chemin m de fer; (track) voie ferrée; **railway line** n (BRIT) ligne f de chemin de fer; (track) voie ferrée; **railway station** n (BRIT) gare f
rain [reɪn] n pluie f ▷ vi pleuvoir; **in the ~** sous la pluie; **it's ~ing** il pleut;

rainbow n arc-en-ciel m; **raincoat** n imperméable m; **raindrop** n goutte f de pluie; **rainfall** n chute f de pluie; (measurement) hauteur f des précipitations; **rainforest** n forêt tropicale; **rainy** adj pluvieux(-euse)

raise [reɪz] n augmentation f ▷ vt (lift) lever; hausser; (increase) augmenter; (morale) remonter; (standards) améliorer; (a protest, doubt) provoquer, causer; (a question) soulever; (cattle, family) élever; (crop) faire pousser; (army, funds) rassembler; (loan) obtenir; **to ~ one's voice** élever la voix

raisin ['reɪzn] n raisin sec

rake [reɪk] n (tool) râteau m ▷ vt (person) débauché m ▷ vt (garden) ratisser

rally ['rælɪ] n (Pol etc) meeting m, rassemblement m; (Aut) rallye m; (Tennis) échange m ▷ vt rassembler, rallier; (support) gagner ▷ vi (sick person) aller mieux; (Stock Exchange) reprendre

RAM [ræm] n abbr (Comput: = random access memory) mémoire vive

ram [ræm] n bélier m ▷ vt (push) enfoncer; (crash into: vehicle) emboutir; (: lamppost etc) percuter

Ramadan ['ræmə'dæn] n Ramadan m

ramble ['ræmbl] n randonnée f ▷ vi (walk) se promener, faire une randonnée; (pej: also: **~ on**) discourir, pérorer; **rambler** n promeneur(-euse), randonneur(-euse); **rambling** adj (speech) décousu(e); (house) plein(e) de coins et de recoins; (Bot) grimpant(e)

ramp [ræmp] n (incline) rampe f; (Aut) dénivellation f; (in garage) pont m; **on/off ~** (US Aut) bretelle f d'accès

rampage [ræm'peɪdʒ] n: **to be on the ~** se déchaîner

ran [ræn] pt of **run**

ranch [rɑːntʃ] n ranch m

random ['rændəm] adj fait(e) or établi(e) au hasard; (Comput, Math) aléatoire ▷ n: **at ~** au hasard

rang [ræŋ] pt of **ring**

range [reɪndʒ] n (of mountains) chaîne f; (of missile, voice) portée f; (of products)

choix m, gamme f; (also: **shooting ~**) champ m de tir; (also: **kitchen ~**) fourneau m (de cuisine) ▷ vt (place) mettre en rang, placer ▷ vi: **to ~ over** couvrir; **to ~ from ... to** aller de ... à

ranger ['reɪndʒə'] n garde m forestier

rank [ræŋk] n rang m; (Mil) grade m; (BRIT: also: **taxi ~**) station f de taxis ▷ vi: **to ~ among** compter or se classer parmi ▷ adj (smell) nauséabond(e); **the ~ and file** (fig) la masse, la base

ransom ['rænsəm] n rançon f; **to hold sb to ~** (fig) exercer un chantage sur qn

rant [rænt] vi fulminer

rap [ræp] n (music) rap m ▷ vt (door) frapper sur or à; (table etc) taper sur

rape [reɪp] n viol m; (Bot) colza m ▷ vt violer

rapid ['ræpɪd] adj rapide; **rapidly** adv rapidement; **rapids** npl (Geo) rapides mpl

rapist ['reɪpɪst] n auteur m d'un viol

rapport [ræ'pɔːr] n entente f

rare [reə'] adj rare; (Culin: steak) saignant(e); **rarely** adv rarement

rash [ræʃ] adj imprudent(e), irréfléchi(e) ▷ n (Med) rougeur f, éruption f; (of events) série f (noire)

rasher ['ræʃə'] n fine tranche (de lard)

raspberry ['rɑːzbərɪ] n framboise f

rat [ræt] n rat m

rate [reɪt] n (ratio) taux m, pourcentage m; (speed) vitesse f, rythme m; (price) tarif m ▷ vt (price) évaluer, estimer; (people) classer; **rates** npl (BRIT: property tax) impôts locaux; **to ~ sb/sth as** considérer qn/qch comme

rather ['rɑːðə'] adv (somewhat) assez, plutôt; (to some extent) un peu; **it's ~ expensive** c'est assez cher; (too much) c'est un peu cher; **there's ~ a lot** il y en a beaucoup; **I would ~** or **I'd ~ go** j'aimerais mieux or je préférerais partir; **or ~** (more accurately) ou plutôt

rating ['reɪtɪŋ] n (assessment) évaluation f; (score) classement m; (Finance) cote f; **ratings** npl (Radio) indice(s) m(pl) d'écoute; (TV) Audimat®

ratio ['reɪʃɪəʊ] n proportion f; **in the ~ of 100 to 1** dans la proportion de 100 contre 1

ration ['ræʃən] n ration f ▷ vt rationner; **rations** npl (food) vivres mpl

rational ['ræʃənl] adj raisonnable, sensé(e); (solution, reasoning) logique; (Med: person) lucide

rat race n foire f d'empoigne

rattle ['rætl] n (of door, window) battement m; (of coins, chain) cliquetis m; (of train, engine) bruit m de ferraille; (for baby) hochet m ▷ vi cliqueter; (car, bus): **to ~ along** rouler en faisant un bruit de ferraille ▷ vt agiter (bruyamment); (inf: disconcert) décontenancer

rave [reɪv] vi (in anger) s'emporter; (with enthusiasm) s'extasier; (Med) délirer ▷ n (inf: party) rave f, soirée f techno

raven ['reɪvən] n grand corbeau

ravine [rə'viːn] n ravin m

raw [rɔː] adj (uncooked) cru(e); (not processed) brut(e); (sore) à vif, irrité(e); (inexperienced) inexpérimenté(e); **~ materials** matières premières

ray [reɪ] n rayon m; **~ of hope** lueur f d'espoir

razor ['reɪzər] n rasoir m; **razor blade** n lame f de rasoir

Rd abbr = **road**

RE n abbr (BRIT) = **religious education**

re [riː] prep concernant

reach [riːtʃ] n portée f, atteinte f; (of river etc) étendue f ▷ vt atteindre, arriver à; (conclusion, decision) parvenir à ▷ vi s'étendre; (stretch out hand): **to ~ out** tendre hors de/à portée; **reach out** vt tendre ▷ vi: **to ~ out (for)** allonger le bras (pour prendre)

react [riː'ækt] vi réagir; **reaction** [riː'ækʃən] n réaction f; **reactor** [riː'æktər] n réacteur m

read (pt, pp ~) [riːd, rɛd] vi lire ▷ vt lire; (understand) comprendre, interpréter; (study) étudier; (meter) relever; (subj: instrument etc) indiquer, marquer; **read out** vt lire à haute voix; **reader** n

lecteur(-trice)

readily ['rɛdɪlɪ] adv volontiers, avec empressement; (easily) facilement

reading ['riːdɪŋ] n lecture f; (understanding) interprétation f; (on instrument) indications fpl

ready ['rɛdɪ] adj prêt(e); (willing) prêt, disposé(e); (available) disponible ▷ n: **at the ~** (Mil) prêt à faire feu; **when will my photos be ~?** quand est-ce que mes photos seront prêtes?; **to get ~** (as vi) se préparer; (as vt) préparer; **ready-cooked** adj précuit(e); **ready-made** adj tout(e) fait(e)

real [rɪəl] adj (world, life) réel(le); (genuine) véritable; (proper) vrai(e) ▷ adv (US inf: very) vraiment; **real ale** n bière traditionnelle; **real estate** n biens fonciers or immobiliers; **realistic** [rɪə'lɪstɪk] adj réaliste; **reality** [riː'ælɪtɪ] n réalité f

reality TV n téléréalité f

realization [rɪəlaɪ'zeɪʃən] n (awareness) prise f de conscience; (fulfilment: also: of asset) réalisation f

realize ['rɪəlaɪz] vt (understand) se rendre compte de, prendre conscience de; (a project, Comm: asset) réaliser

really ['rɪəlɪ] adv vraiment; **~?** vraiment?, c'est vrai?

realm [rɛlm] n royaume m; (fig) domaine m

realtor ['rɪəltɔːr] n (US) agent immobilier

reappear [riːə'pɪər] vi réapparaître, reparaître

rear [rɪər] adj de derrière, arrière inv; (Aut: wheel etc) arrière ▷ n arrière m ▷ vt (cattle, family) élever ▷ vi (also: **~ up**) (animal) se cabrer

rearrange [riːə'reɪndʒ] vt réarranger

rear: rear-view mirror n (Aut) rétroviseur m; **rear-wheel drive** n (Aut) traction f arrière

reason ['riːzn] n raison f ▷ vi: **to ~ with sb** raisonner qn, faire entendre raison à qn; **it stands to ~ that** il va sans dire que; **reasonable** adj raisonnable;

(not bad) acceptable; **reasonably** adv
(behave) raisonnablement; (fairly) assez;
reasoning n raisonnement m

reassurance [riːəˈʃuərəns] n (factual)
assurance f, garantie f; (emotional)
réconfort m

reassure [riːəˈʃuəʳ] vt rassurer

rebate [ˈriːbeɪt] n (on tax etc)
dégrèvement m

rebel n [ˈrɛbl] rebelle m/f ▷ vi [rɪˈbɛl]
se rebeller, se révolter; **rebellion**
[rɪˈbɛljən] n rébellion f, révolte f;
rebellious [rɪˈbɛljəs] adj rebelle

rebuild [riːˈbɪld] vt (irreg: like build)
reconstruire

recall vt [rɪˈkɔːl] rappeler; (remember)
se rappeler, se souvenir de ▷ n [ˈriːkɔːl]
rappel m; (ability to remember) mémoire f

rec'd abbr of **received**

receipt [rɪˈsiːt] n (document) reçu m;
(for parcel etc) accusé m de réception;
(act of receiving) réception f; **receipts**
npl (Comm) recettes fpl; **can I have a
~, please?** je peux avoir un reçu, s'il
vous plaît?

receive [rɪˈsiːv] vt recevoir; (guest)
recevoir, accueillir; **receiver** n (Tel)
récepteur m, combiné m; (Radio)
récepteur m; (of stolen goods) receleur
m; (for bankruptcies) administrateur m
judiciaire

recent [ˈriːsnt] adj récent(e); **recently**
adv récemment

reception [rɪˈsɛpʃən] n réception
f; (welcome) accueil m, réception;
reception desk n réception f;
receptionist n réceptionniste m/f

recession [rɪˈsɛʃən] n (Econ) récession f

recharge [riːˈtʃɑːdʒ] vt (battery)
recharger

recipe [ˈrɛsɪpɪ] n recette f

recipient [rɪˈsɪpɪənt] n (of payment)
bénéficiaire m/f; (of letter) destinataire
m/f

recital [rɪˈsaɪtl] n récital m

recite [rɪˈsaɪt] vt (poem) réciter

reckless [ˈrɛkləs] adj (driver
etc) imprudent(e); (spender etc)

insouciant(e)

reckon [ˈrɛkən] vt (count) calculer,
compter; (consider) considérer, estimer;
(think): **I ~ (that)** ... je pense (que) ...,
j'estime (que) ...

reclaim [rɪˈkleɪm] vt (land: from sea)
assécher; (demand back) réclamer (le
remboursement ou la restitution de);
(waste materials) récupérer

recline [rɪˈklaɪn] vi être allongé(e) or
étendu(e)

recognition [rɛkəɡˈnɪʃən] n
reconnaissance f; **transformed
beyond ~** méconnaissable

recognize [ˈrɛkəɡnaɪz] vt: **to ~ (by/as)**
reconnaître (à/comme étant)

recollection [rɛkəˈlɛkʃən] n
souvenir m

recommend [rɛkəˈmɛnd] vt
recommander; **can you ~ a good
restaurant?** pouvez-vous me
conseiller un bon restaurant?;
recommendation [rɛkəmɛnˈdeɪʃən] n
recommandation f

reconcile [ˈrɛkənsaɪl] vt (two people)
réconcilier; (two facts) concilier,
accorder; **to ~ o.s. to** se résigner à

reconsider [riːkənˈsɪdəʳ] vt
reconsidérer

reconstruct [riːkənˈstrʌkt] vt
(building) reconstruire; (crime, system)
reconstituer

record n [ˈrɛkɔːd] rapport m, récit
m; (of meeting etc) procès-verbal m;
(register) registre m; (file) dossier m;
(Comput) article m; (also: **police ~**)
casier m judiciaire; (Mus: disc) disque
m; (Sport) record m ▷ adj record inv ▷ vt
[rɪˈkɔːd] (set down) noter; (Mus: song
etc) enregistrer; **public ~s** archives
fpl; **in ~ time** dans un temps record;
recorded delivery (BRIT Post): **to
send sth recorded delivery** ≈ envoyer
qch en recommandé; **recorder** n
(Mus) flûte f à bec; **recording** n (Mus)
enregistrement m; **record player** n
tourne-disque m

recount [rɪˈkaunt] vt raconter

recover [rɪˈkʌvəʳ] vt récupérer ▷ vi (from illness) se rétablir; (from shock) se remettre; **recovery** n récupération f; rétablissement m; (Econ) redressement m

recreate [riːkrɪˈeɪt] vt recréer

recreation [rɛkrɪˈeɪʃən] n (leisure) récréation f, détente f; **recreational drug** n drogue récréative; **recreational vehicle** n (US) camping-car m

recruit [rɪˈkruːt] n recrue f ▷ vt recruter; **recruitment** n recrutement m

rectangle [ˈrɛktæŋgl] n rectangle m; **rectangular** [rɛkˈtæŋgjuləʳ] adj rectangulaire

rectify [ˈrɛktɪfaɪ] vt (error) rectifier, corriger

rector [ˈrɛktəʳ] n (Rel) pasteur m

recur [rɪˈkəːʳ] vi se reproduire; (idea, opportunity) se retrouver; (symptoms) réapparaître; **recurring** adj (problem) périodique, fréquent(e); (Math) périodique

recyclable [riːˈsaɪkləbl] adj recyclable

recycle [riːˈsaɪkl] vt, vi recycler

recycling [riːˈsaɪklɪŋ] n recyclage m

red [rɛd] n rouge m; (Pol: pej) rouge m/f ▷ adj rouge; (hair) roux (rousse); **in the ~** (account) à découvert; (business) en déficit; **Red Cross** n Croix-Rouge f; **redcurrant** n groseille f (rouge)

redeem [rɪˈdiːm] vt (debt) rembourser; (sth in pawn) dégager; (fig, also Rel) racheter

red: **red-haired** adj roux (rousse); **redhead** n roux (rousse); **red-hot** adj chauffé(e) au rouge, brûlant(e); **red light** n: **to go through a red light** (Aut) brûler un feu rouge; **red-light district** n quartier mal famé

red meat n viande f rouge

reduce [rɪˈdjuːs] vt réduire; (lower) abaisser; **"~ speed now"** (Aut) "ralentir"; **to ~ sb to tears** faire pleurer qn; **reduced** adj réduit(e); **"greatly reduced prices"** "gros rabais"; **at a** **reduced price** (goods) au rabais; (ticket etc) à prix réduit; **reduction** [rɪˈdʌkʃən] n réduction f; (of price) baisse f; (discount) rabais m; **is there a reduction for children/students?** y a-t-il une réduction pour les enfants/les étudiants?

redundancy [rɪˈdʌndənsɪ] n (BRIT) licenciement m, mise f au chômage

redundant [rɪˈdʌndnt] adj (BRIT: worker) licencié(e), mis(e) au chômage; (detail, object) superflu(e); **to be made ~** (worker) être licencié, être mis au chômage

reed [riːd] n (Bot) roseau m

reef [riːf] n (at sea) récif m, écueil m

reel [riːl] n bobine f; (Fishing) moulinet m; (Cine) bande f; (dance) quadrille écossais f ▷ vi (sway) chanceler

refectory [rɪˈfɛktərɪ] n réfectoire m

refer [rɪˈfəːʳ] vt: **to ~ sb to** (inquirer, patient) adresser qn à; (reader: to text) renvoyer qn à ▷ vi: **to ~ to** (allude to) parler de, faire allusion à; (consult) se reporter à; (apply to) s'appliquer à

referee [rɛfəˈriː] n arbitre m; (BRIT: for job application) répondant(e) ▷ vt arbitrer

reference [ˈrɛfrəns] n référence f, renvoi m; (mention) allusion f, mention f; (for job application: letter) références; lettre f de recommandation; **with ~ to** en ce qui concerne; (Comm: in letter) me référant à; **reference number** n (Comm) numéro m de référence

refill vt [riːˈfɪl] remplir à nouveau; (pen, lighter etc) recharger ▷ n [ˈriːfɪl] (for pen etc) recharge f

refine [rɪˈfaɪn] vt (sugar, oil) raffiner; (taste) affiner; (idea, theory) peaufiner; **refined** adj (person, taste) raffiné(e); **refinery** n raffinerie f

reflect [rɪˈflɛkt] vt (light, image) réfléchir, refléter ▷ vi (think) réfléchir, méditer; **it ~s badly on him** c'est à son désavantage, cela lui fait du tort; **it ~s well on him** c'est tout à son honneur; **reflection** [rɪˈflɛkʃən] n réflexion f; (image) reflet m; **on reflection** réflexion faite

reflex ['ri:fleks] adj, n réflexe (m)

reform [rɪ'fɔːm] n réforme f ▷ vt réformer

refrain [rɪ'freɪn] vi: **to ~ from doing** s'abstenir de faire ▷ n refrain m

refresh [rɪ'freʃ] vt rafraîchir; (subj: food, sleep etc) redonner des forces à; **refreshing** adj (drink) rafraîchissant(e); (sleep) réparateur(-trice); **refreshments** npl rafraîchissements mpl

refrigerator [rɪ'frɪdʒəreɪtə'] n réfrigérateur m, frigidaire m

refuel [riː'fjuəl] vi se ravitailler en carburant

refuge ['refjuːdʒ] n refuge m; **to take ~ in** se réfugier dans; **refugee** [refjuˈdʒiː] n réfugié(e)

refund n ['riːfʌnd] remboursement m ▷ vt [rɪ'fʌnd] rembourser

refurbish [riː'fɜːbɪʃ] vt remettre à neuf

refusal [rɪ'fjuːzəl] n refus m; **to have first ~ on sth** avoir droit de préemption sur qch

refuse[1] ['refjuːs] n ordures fpl, détritus mpl

refuse[2] [rɪ'fjuːz] vt, vi refuser; **to ~ to do sth** refuser de faire qch

regain [rɪ'geɪn] vt (lost ground) regagner; (strength) retrouver

regard [rɪ'gɑːd] n respect m, estime f, considération f ▷ vt considérer; **to give one's ~s to** faire ses amitiés à; **"with kindest ~s"** bien amicalement; **as ~s, with ~ to** en ce qui concerne; **regarding** prep en ce qui concerne; **regardless** adv quand même; **regardless of** sans se soucier de

regenerate [rɪ'dʒenəreɪt] vt régénérer ▷ vi se régénérer

reggae ['regeɪ] n reggae m

regiment ['redʒɪmənt] n régiment m

region ['riːdʒən] n région f; **in the ~ of** (fig) aux alentours de; **regional** adj régional(e)

register ['redʒɪstə'] n registre m;

(also: **electoral ~**) liste électorale ▷ vt enregistrer, inscrire; (birth) déclarer; (vehicle) immatriculer; (letter) envoyer en recommandé; (subj: instrument) marquer ▷ vi s'inscrire; (at hotel) signer le registre; (make impression) être (bien) compris(e); **registered** adj (BRIT: letter) recommandé(e)

registered trademark n marque déposée

registrar ['redʒɪstrɑː'] n officier m de l'état civil

registration [redʒɪs'treɪʃən] n (act) enregistrement m; (of student) inscription f; (BRIT Aut: also: ~ **number**) numéro m d'immatriculation

registry office n (BRIT) bureau m de l'état civil; **to get married in a ~** se marier à la mairie

regret [rɪ'gret] n regret m ▷ vt regretter; **regrettable** adj regrettable, fâcheux(-euse)

regular ['regjulə'] adj régulier(-ière); (usual) habituel(le), normal(e); (soldier) de métier; (Comm: size) ordinaire ▷ n (client etc) habitué(e); **regularly** adv régulièrement

regulate ['regjuleɪt] vt régler; **regulation** [regjuˈleɪʃən] n (rule) règlement m; (adjustment) réglage m

rehabilitation ['riːəbɪlɪˈteɪʃən] n (of offender) réhabilitation f; (of addict) réadaptation f

rehearsal [rɪ'hɜːsəl] n répétition f

rehearse [rɪ'hɜːs] vt répéter

reign [reɪn] n règne m ▷ vi régner

reimburse [riːɪm'bɜːs] vt rembourser

rein [reɪn] n (for horse) rêne f

reincarnation [riːɪnkɑːˈneɪʃən] n réincarnation f

reindeer ['reɪndɪə'] n (pl inv) renne m

reinforce [riːɪn'fɔːs] vt renforcer; **reinforcements** npl (Mil) renfort(s) m(pl)

reinstate [riːɪn'steɪt] vt rétablir, réintégrer

reject n ['riːdʒekt] (Comm) article m de rebut ▷ vt [rɪ'dʒekt] refuser; (idea) rejeter; **rejection** [rɪ'dʒɛkʃən] n rejet m, refus m

rejoice [rɪ'dʒɔɪs] vi: **to ~ (at or over)** se réjouir (de)

relate [rɪ'leɪt] vt (tell) raconter; (connect) établir un rapport entre ▷ vi (connect) se rapporter à; **to ~ to sb** (interact) entretenir des rapports avec qn; **related** adj apparenté(e); **related to** (subject) lié(e) à; **relating to** prep concernant

relation [rɪ'leɪʃən] n (person) parent(e); (link) rapport m, lien m; **relations** npl (relatives) famille f; **relationship** n rapport m, lien m; (personal ties) relations fpl, rapports; (also: **family relationship**) lien de parenté; (affair) liaison f

relative ['rɛlətɪv] n parent(e) ▷ adj relatif(-ive); (respective) respectif(-ive); **relatively** adv relativement

relax [rɪ'læks] vi (muscle) se relâcher; (person: unwind) se détendre ▷ vt relâcher; (mind, person) détendre; **relaxation** [riːlæk'seɪʃən] n relâchement m; (of mind) détente f; (recreation) détente f, délassement m; **relaxed** adj relâché(e); détendu(e); **relaxing** adj délassant(e)

relay ['riːleɪ] n (Sport) course f de relais ▷ vt (message) retransmettre, relayer

release [rɪ'liːs] n (from prison, obligation) libération f; (of gas etc) émission f; (of film etc) sortie f; (new recording) disque m ▷ vt (prisoner) libérer; (book, film) sortir; (report, news) rendre public, publier; (gas etc) émettre, dégager; (free: from wreckage etc) dégager; (Tech: catch, spring etc) déclencher; (let go: person, animal) relâcher; (: hand, object) lâcher; (: grip, brake) desserrer

relegate ['rɛləgeɪt] vt reléguer; (BRIT Sport): **to be ~d** descendre dans une division inférieure

relent [rɪ'lɛnt] vi se laisser fléchir; **relentless** adj implacable; (non-stop) continuel(le)

relevant ['rɛləvənt] adj (question)

pertinent(e); (corresponding) approprié(e); (fact) significatif(-ive); (information) utile

reliable [rɪ'laɪəbl] adj (person, firm) sérieux(-euse), fiable; (method, machine) fiable; (news, information) sûr(e)

relic ['rɛlɪk] n (Rel) relique f; (of the past) vestige m

relief [rɪ'liːf] n (from pain, anxiety) soulagement m; (help, supplies) secours m(pl); (Art, Geo) relief m

relieve [rɪ'liːv] vt (pain, patient) soulager; (fear, worry) dissiper; (bring help) secourir; (take over from: gen) relayer; (: guard) relever; **to ~ sb of sth** débarrasser qn de qch; **to ~ o.s.** (euphemism) se soulager, faire ses besoins; **relieved** adj soulagé(e)

religion [rɪ'lɪdʒən] n religion f

religious [rɪ'lɪdʒəs] adj religieux(-euse); (book) de piété; **religious education** n instruction religieuse

relish ['rɛlɪʃ] n (Culin) condiment m; (enjoyment) délectation f ▷ vt (food etc) savourer; **to ~ doing** relever; **to ~ sth** se délecter à faire

relocate [riːləu'keɪt] vt (business) transférer ▷ vi se transférer, s'installer or s'établir ailleurs

reluctance [rɪ'lʌktəns] n répugnance f

reluctant [rɪ'lʌktənt] adj peu disposé(e), qui hésite; **reluctantly** adv à contrecœur, sans enthousiasme

rely on [rɪ'laɪ-] vt fus (be dependent on) dépendre de; (trust) compter sur

remain [rɪ'meɪn] vi rester; **remainder** n reste m; (Comm) fin f de série; **remaining** adj qui reste; **remains** npl restes mpl

remand [rɪ'mɑːnd] n: **on ~** en détention préventive ▷ vt: **to be ~ed in custody** être placé(e) en détention préventive

remark [rɪ'mɑːk] n remarque f, observation f ▷ vt (faire) remarquer, dire; **remarkable** adj remarquable

remarry [riː'mærɪ] vi se remarier

remedy ['rɛmədɪ] n: **~ (for)** remède m

(contre or à) ▷ vt remédier à

remember [rɪ'membə] vt se rappeler, se souvenir de; (send greetings): ~ **me to him** saluez-le de ma part; **Remembrance Day** [rɪ'membrəns-] n (BRIT) ≈ (le jour de) l'Armistice m, ≈ le 11 novembre

- **REMEMBRANCE DAY**
-
- **Remembrance Day** ou
- **Remembrance Sunday** est le
- dimanche le plus proche du 11
- novembre, jour où la Première
- Guerre mondiale a officiellement
- pris fin. Il rend hommage aux
- victimes des deux guerres
- mondiales. À cette occasion, on
- observe deux minutes de silence
- à 11h, heure de la signature de
- l'armistice avec l'Allemagne en
- 1918; certains membres de la
- famille royale et du gouvernement
- déposent des gerbes de coquelicots
- au cénotaphe de Whitehall, et des
- couronnes sont placées sur les
- monuments aux morts dans toute
- la Grande-Bretagne; par ailleurs,
- les gens portent des coquelicots
- artificiels fabriqués et vendus
- par des membres de la légion
- britannique blessés au combat, au
- profit des blessés de guerre et de
- leur famille.

remind [rɪ'maɪnd] vt: **to ~ sb of sth** rappeler qch à qn; **to ~ sb to do** penser à qn à faire, rappeler à qn qu'il doit faire; **reminder** n (Comm: letter) rappel m; (note etc) pense-bête m; (souvenir) souvenir m

reminiscent [remɪ'nɪsnt] adj: **~ of** qui rappelle, qui fait penser à

remnant ['remnənt] n reste m, restant m; (of cloth) coupon m

remorse [rɪ'mɔːs] n remords m

remote [rɪ'məut] adj éloigné(e), lointain(e); (person) distant(e);

(possibility) vague; **remote control** n télécommande f; **remotely** adv au loin; (slightly) très vaguement

removal [rɪ'muːvəl] n (taking away) enlèvement m; suppression f; (BRIT: from house) déménagement m; (from office: dismissal) renvoi m; (of stain) nettoyage m; (Med) ablation f; **removal man** (irreg) n (BRIT) déménageur m; **removal van** (BRIT) camion m de déménagement

remove [rɪ'muːv] vt enlever, retirer; (employee) renvoyer; (stain) faire partir; (abuse) supprimer; (doubt) chasser

Renaissance [rɪ'neɪsɑ̃s] n: **the ~** la Renaissance

rename [riː'neɪm] vt rebaptiser

render ['rendə'] vt rendre

rendezvous ['rɔndɪvuː] n rendez-vous m inv

renew [rɪ'njuː] vt renouveler; (negotiations) reprendre; (acquaintance) renouer

renovate ['renəveɪt] vt rénover; (work of art) restaurer

renowned [rɪ'naund] adj renommé(e)

rent [rent] pt, pp of **rend** ▷ n loyer m ▷ vt louer; **rental** n (for television, car) (prix m de) location f

reorganize [riː'ɔːgənaɪz] vt réorganiser

rep [rep] n abbr (Comm) = representative

repair [rɪ'pɛə'] n réparation f ▷ vt réparer; **in good/bad** ~ en bon/mauvais état; **where can I get this ~ed?** où est-ce que je peux faire réparer ceci?; **repair kit** n trousse f de réparations

repay [riː'peɪ] vt (irreg: like **pay**) (money, creditor) rembourser; (sb's efforts) récompenser; **repayment** n remboursement m

repeat [rɪ'piːt] n (Radio, TV) reprise f ▷ vt répéter; (promise, attack, also Comm: order) renouveler; (Scol: a class) redoubler ▷ vi répéter; **can you ~ that, please?** pouvez-vous répéter,

s'il vous plaît?; **repeatedly** adv
souvent, à plusieurs reprises; **repeat
prescription** n (BRIT): **I'd like a repeat
prescription** je voudrais renouveler
mon ordonnance

repellent [rɪˈpɛlənt] adj repoussant
▷ n: **insect ~** insectifuge m

repercussions [riːpəˈkʌʃənz] npl
répercussions fpl

repetition [rɛpɪˈtɪʃən] n répétition f

repetitive [rɪˈpɛtɪtɪv] adj (movement,
work) répétitif(-ive); (speech) plein(e)
de redites

replace [rɪˈpleɪs] vt (put back)
remettre, replacer; (take the place
of) remplacer; **replacement** n
(substitution) remplacement m; (person)
remplaçant(e)

replay [ˈriːpleɪ] n (of match) match
rejoué; (of tape, film) répétition f

replica [ˈrɛplɪkə] n réplique f, copie
exacte

reply [rɪˈplaɪ] n réponse f ▷ vi répondre

report [rɪˈpɔːt] n rapport m; (Press
etc) reportage m; (BRIT: also: **school
~**) bulletin m (scolaire); (of gun)
détonation f ▷ vt rapporter, faire un
compte rendu de; (Press etc) faire un
reportage sur; (notify: accident) signaler;
(: culprit) dénoncer ▷ vi (make a report)
faire un rapport; **I'd like to ~ a theft**
je voudrais signaler un vol; (present
o.s.): **to ~ (to sb)** se présenter (chez
qn); **report card** n (US, SCOTTISH)
bulletin m (scolaire); **reportedly** adv:
she is reportedly living in Spain elle
habiterait en Espagne; **he reportedly
told them to ...** il leur aurait dit de ...;
reporter n reporter m

represent [rɛprɪˈzɛnt] vt représenter;
(view, belief) expliquer; (describe):
to ~ sth as présenter or
décrire qch comme; **representation**
[rɛprɪzɛnˈteɪʃən] n représentation f;
representative n représentant(e); (US
Pol) député m ▷ adj représentatif(-ive),
caractéristique

repress [rɪˈprɛs] vt réprimer;

repression [rɪˈprɛʃən] n répression f

reprimand [ˈrɛprɪmɑːnd] n
réprimande f ▷ vt réprimander

reproduce [riːprəˈdjuːs] vt reproduire
▷ vi se reproduire; **reproduction**
[riːprəˈdʌkʃən] n reproduction f

reptile [ˈrɛptaɪl] n reptile m

republic [rɪˈpʌblɪk] n république f;
republican adj, n républicain(e)

reputable [ˈrɛpjʊtəbl] adj de bonne
réputation; (occupation) honorable

reputation [rɛpjʊˈteɪʃən] n
réputation f

request [rɪˈkwɛst] n demande f;
(formal) requête f ▷ vt: **to ~ (of or from
sb)** demander (à qn); **request stop** n
(BRIT: for bus) arrêt facultatif

require [rɪˈkwaɪər] vt (need: subj: person)
avoir besoin de; (: thing, situation)
nécessiter, demander; (want) exiger;
(order): **to ~ sb to do sth/sth of sb**
exiger que qn fasse qch/qch de qn;
requirement n (need) exigence f;
besoin m; (condition) condition f
(requise)

resat [riːˈsæt] pt, pp of **resit**

rescue [ˈrɛskjuː] n (from accident)
sauvetage m; (help) secours mpl ▷ vt
sauver

research [rɪˈsɜːtʃ] n recherche(s) f(pl)
▷ vt faire des recherches sur

resemblance [rɪˈzɛmbləns] n
ressemblance f

resemble [rɪˈzɛmbl] vt ressembler à

resent [rɪˈzɛnt] vt être contrarié(e)
par; **resentful** adj irrité(e), plein(e)
de ressentiment; **resentment** n
ressentiment m

reservation [rɛzəˈveɪʃən] n (booking)
réservation f; **to make a ~ (in a
hotel/a restaurant/on a plane)**
réserver or retenir une chambre/une
table/une place; **reservation desk** n
(US: in hotel) réception f

reserve [rɪˈzɜːv] n réserve f; (Sport)
remplaçant m ▷ vt (seats etc) réserver,
retenir; **reserved** adj réservé(e)

reservoir [ˈrɛzəvwɑː] n réservoir m

reshuffle [ˌriːˈʃʌfl] n: **Cabinet ~** (Pol) remaniement ministériel

residence [ˈrezidəns] n résidence f; **residence permit** n (BRIT) permis m de séjour

resident [ˈrezidənt] n (of country) résident(e); (of area, house) habitant(e); (in hotel) pensionnaire ⊳ adj résidant(e); **residential** [reziˈdenʃəl] adj de résidence; (area) résidentiel(le); (course) avec hébergement sur place

residue [ˈrezidjuː] n reste m; (Chem, Physics) résidu m

resign [riˈzaɪn] vt (one's post) se démettre de ⊳ vi démissionner; **to ~ o.s. to** (endure) se résigner à; **resignation** [rezigˈneɪʃən] n (from post) démission f; (state of mind) résignation f

resin [ˈrezin] n résine f

resist [rɪˈzɪst] vt résister à; **resistance** n résistance f

resit (BRIT) vt [riːˈsɪt] (pt, pp **resat**) (exam) repasser ⊳ n [ˈriːsɪt] deuxième session f (d'un examen)

resolution [rezəˈluːʃən] n résolution f

resolve [rɪˈzɔlv] n résolution f ⊳ vt (decide): **to ~ to do** résoudre or décider de faire; (problem) résoudre ⊳ vi

resort [rɪˈzɔːt] n (seaside town) station f balnéaire; (for skiing) station de ski; (recourse) recours m ⊳ vi: **to ~ to** avoir recours à; **in the last ~** en dernier ressort

resource [rɪˈsɔːs] n ressource f; **resourceful** adj ingénieux(-euse), débrouillard(e)

respect [rɪsˈpekt] n respect m ⊳ vt respecter; **respectable** adj respectable; (quite good: result etc) honorable; **respectful** adj respectueux(-euse); **respective** adj respectif(-ive); **respectively** adv respectivement

respite [ˈrespaɪt] n répit m

respond [rɪsˈpɔnd] vi répondre; (react) réagir; **response** [rɪsˈpɔns] n réponse f; (reaction) réaction f

responsibility [rɪspɔnsɪˈbɪlɪtɪ] n

responsabilité f

responsible [rɪsˈpɔnsɪbl] adj (liable): **~ (for)** responsable (de); (person) digne de confiance; (job) qui comporte des responsabilités; **responsibly** adv avec sérieux

responsive [rɪsˈpɔnsɪv] adj (student, audience) réceptif(-ive); (brakes, steering) sensible

rest [rest] n repos m; (stop) arrêt m, pause f; (Mus) silence m; (support) support m, appui m; (remainder) reste m, restant m ⊳ vi se reposer; (be supported): **to ~ on** appuyer or reposer sur ⊳ vt (lean): **to ~ sth on/against** appuyer qch sur/contre; **the ~ of them** les autres

restaurant [ˈrestərɔŋ] n restaurant m; **restaurant car** n (BRIT Rail) wagon-restaurant m

restless [ˈrestlɪs] adj agité(e)

restoration [restəˈreɪʃən] n (of building) restauration f; (of stolen goods) restitution f

restore [rɪsˈtɔː] vt (building) restaurer; (sth stolen) restituer; (peace, health) rétablir; **to ~ to** (former state) ramener à

restrain [rɪsˈtreɪn] vt (feeling) contenir; (person): **to ~ (from doing)** retenir (de faire); **restraint** n (restriction) contrainte f; (moderation) retenue f; (of style) sobriété f

restrict [rɪsˈtrɪkt] vt restreindre, limiter; **restriction** [rɪsˈtrɪkʃən] n restriction f, limitation f

rest room n (US) toilettes fpl

restructure [riːˈstrʌktʃəˠ] vt restructurer

result [rɪˈzʌlt] n résultat m ⊳ vi: **to ~ in** aboutir à, se terminer par; **as a ~ of** à la suite de

resume [rɪˈzjuːm] vt (work, journey) reprendre ⊳ vi (work etc) reprendre

résumé [ˈreɪzjuːmeɪ] n (summary) résumé m; (US: curriculum vitae) curriculum vitae m inv

resuscitate [rɪˈsʌsɪteɪt] vt (Med) réanimer

retail ['ri:teɪl] adj de or au détail ▷ adv au détail; **retailer** n détaillant(e)

retain [rɪ'teɪn] vt (keep) garder, conserver

retaliation [rɪtælɪ'eɪʃən] n représailles fpl, vengeance f

retarded [rɪ'tɑːdɪd] adj retardé(e)

retire [rɪ'taɪə*] vi (give up work) prendre sa retraite; (withdraw) se retirer, partir; (go to bed) (aller) se coucher; **retired** adj (person) retraité(e); **retirement** n retraite f

retort [rɪ'tɔːt] vi riposter

retreat [rɪ'triːt] n retraite f ▷ vi battre en retraite

retrieve [rɪ'triːv] vt (sth lost) récupérer; (situation, honour) sauver; (error, loss) réparer; (Comput) rechercher

retrospect ['retrəspekt] n: **in ~** rétrospectivement, après coup; **retrospective** [retrə'spektɪv] adj rétrospectif(-ive); (law) rétroactif(-ive) ▷ n (Art) rétrospective f

return [rɪ'tɜːn] n (going or coming back) retour m; (of sth stolen etc) restitution f; (Finance: from land, shares) rapport m ▷ cpd (journey) de retour; (BRIT: ticket) aller et retour; (match) retour ▷ vi (person etc: come back) revenir; (: go back) retourner ▷ vt rendre; (bring back) rapporter; (send back) renvoyer; (put back) remettre; (Pol: candidate) élire; **returns** npl (Comm) recettes fpl; (Finance) bénéfices mpl; **many happy ~s (of the day)!** bon anniversaire!; **by ~ (of post)** par retour (du courrier); **in ~ (for)** en échange (de); **a ~ (ticket) (for ...** un billet aller et retour pour ...; **return ticket** n (esp BRIT) billet m aller-retour

reunion [riː'juːnɪən] n réunion f

reunite [riːju'naɪt] vt réunir

revamp [riː'væmp] vt (house) retaper; (firm) réorganiser

reveal [rɪ'viːl] vt (make known) révéler; (display) laisser voir; **revealing** adj révélateur(-trice); (dress) au décolleté généreux or suggestif

revel ['revl] vi: **to ~ in sth/in doing** se

délecter de qch/à faire

revelation [revə'leɪʃən] n révélation f

revenge [rɪ'vendʒ] n vengeance f; (in game etc) revanche f; **to take ~ (on)** se venger (sur)

revenue ['revənju:] n revenu m

Reverend ['revərənd] adj (in titles): **the ~ John Smith** (Anglican) le révérend John Smith; (Catholic) l'abbé (John) Smith; (Protestant) le pasteur (John) Smith

reversal [rɪ'vɜːsl] n (of opinion) revirement m; (of order) renversement m; (of direction) changement m

reverse [rɪ'vɜːs] n contraire m, opposé m; (back) dos m, envers m; (of paper) verso m; (of coin) revers m; (Aut: also: **~ gear**) marche arrière f ▷ adj (order, direction) opposé(e), inverse f ▷ vt (order, policy) changer complètement de; (decision) annuler; (roles) renverser ▷ vi (BRIT Aut) faire marche arrière; **reverse-charge call** n (BRIT Tel) communication fpen PCV; **reversing lights** npl (BRIT Aut) feux mpl de marche arrière or de recul

revert [rɪ'vɜːt] vi: **to ~** revenir à, retourner à

review [rɪ'vju:] n revue f; (of book, film) critique f; (of situation, policy) examen m, bilan m; (US: examination) examen m ▷ vt passer en revue; faire la critique de; examiner

revise [rɪ'vaɪz] vt réviser, modifier; (manuscript) revoir, corriger ▷ vi (study) réviser; **revision** [rɪ'vɪʒən] n révision f

revival [rɪ'vaɪvl] n reprise f; (recovery) rétablissement m; (of faith) renouveau m

revive [rɪ'vaɪv] vt (person) ranimer; (custom) rétablir; (economy) relancer; (hope, courage) raviver, faire renaître; (play, fashion) reprendre ▷ vi (person) reprendre connaissance; (: from ill health) se rétablir; (hope etc) renaître; (activity) reprendre

revolt [rɪ'vəʊlt] n révolte f ▷ vi se

révolter, se rebeller ▷ vt révolter, dégoûter; **revolting** adj dégoûtant(e)

revolution [revə'luːʃən] n révolution f; (of wheel etc) tour m, révolution; **revolutionary** adj, n révolutionnaire (m/f)

revolve [rɪ'vɒlv] vi tourner

revolver [rɪ'vɒlvəʳ] n revolver m

reward [rɪ'wɔːd] n récompense f ▷ vt: **to ~ (for)** récompenser (de); **rewarding** adj (fig) qui (en) vaut la peine, gratifiant(e)

rewind [riː'waɪnd] vt (irreg: like **wind**) (tape) réembobiner

rewritable [riː'raɪtəbl] adj (CD, DVD) réinscriptible

rewrite [riː'raɪt] (pt **rewrote**, pp **rewritten**) vt récrire

rheumatism ['ruːmətɪzəm] n rhumatisme m

Rhine [raɪn] n: **the (River) ~** le Rhin

rhinoceros [raɪ'nɒsərəs] n rhinocéros m

Rhône [rəun] n: **the (River) ~** le Rhône

rhubarb ['ruːbɑːb] n rhubarbe f

rhyme [raɪm] n rime f; (verse) vers mpl

rhythm ['rɪðm] n rythme m

rib [rɪb] n (Anat) côte f

ribbon ['rɪbən] n ruban m; **in ~s** (torn) en lambeaux

rice [raɪs] n riz m; **rice pudding** n riz m au lait

rich [rɪtʃ] adj riche; (gift, clothes) somptueux(-euse); **to be ~ in sth** être riche en qch

rid [rɪd] (pt, pp ~) vt: **to ~ sb of** débarrasser qn de; **to get ~ of** se débarrasser de

riddle ['rɪdl] n (puzzle) énigme f ▷ vt: **to be ~d with** être criblé(e) de; (fig) être en proie à

ride [raɪd] n promenade f, tour m; (distance covered) trajet m ▷ vb (pt **rode**, pp **ridden**) ▷ vi (as sport) monter (à cheval), faire du cheval; (go somewhere: on horse, bicycle) aller à cheval ou à bicyclette etc); (travel: on bicycle, motor cycle, bus) rouler ▷ vt (a horse) monter;

(distance) parcourir, faire; **to ~ a horse/ bicycle** monter à cheval/à bicyclette; **to take sb for a ~** (fig) faire marcher qn; (cheat) rouler qn; **rider** n cavalier(-ière); (in race) jockey m; (on bicycle) cycliste m/f; (on motorcycle) motocycliste m/f

ridge [rɪdʒ] n (of hill) faîte m; (of roof, mountain) arête f; (on object) strie f

ridicule ['rɪdɪkjuːl] n ridicule m, dérision f ▷ vt ridiculiser, tourner en dérision; **ridiculous** [rɪ'dɪkjuləs] adj ridicule

riding ['raɪdɪŋ] n équitation f; **riding school** n manège m, école f d'équitation

rife [raɪf] adj répandu(e); **~ with** abondant(e) en

rifle ['raɪfl] n fusil m (à canon rayé) ▷ vt vider, dévaliser

rift [rɪft] n fente f, fissure f; (fig: disagreement) désaccord m

rig [rɪg] n (also: **oil ~:** on land) derrick m; (: at sea) plate-forme pétrolière f ▷ vt (election etc) truquer

right [raɪt] adj (true) juste, exact(e); (correct) bon (bonne); (suitable) approprié(e), convenable; (just) juste, équitable; (morally good) bien m; (not left) droit(e) ▷ n (moral good) bien m; (title, claim) droit m; (not left) droite f ▷ adv (answer) correctement; (treat) bien, comme il faut; (not on the left) à droite ▷ vt redresser ▷ excl bon!; **do you have the ~ time?** avez-vous l'heure juste ou exacte?; **to be ~** (person) avoir raison; (answer) être juste ou correct(e); **by ~s** en toute justice; **on the ~** à droite; **to be in the ~** avoir raison; **~ in the middle** en plein milieu; **~ away** immédiatement; **right angle** n (Math) angle droit; **rightful** adj (heir) légitime; **right-hand** adj: **the right-hand side** la droite; **right-hand drive** n (BRIT) conduite f à droite; (vehicle) véhicule m avec la conduite à droite; **right-handed** adj (person) droitier(-ière); **rightly** adv bien, correctement; (with reason) à juste titre; **right of way** n

(on path etc) droit m de passage; (Aut)
priorité f; **right-wing** adj (Pol) de droite
rigid ['rɪdʒɪd] adj rigide; (principle,
control) strict(e)
rigorous ['rɪgərəs] adj rigoureux(-euse)
rim [rɪm] n bord m; (of spectacles)
monture f; (of wheel) jante f
rind [raɪnd] n (of bacon) couenne f; (of
lemon etc) écorce f, zeste m; (of cheese)
croûte f
ring [rɪŋ] n anneau m; (on finger)
bague f; (also: **wedding ~**) alliance f;
(of people, objects) cercle m; (of spies)
réseau m; (of smoke etc) rond m; (arena)
piste f, arène f; (for boxing) ring m;
(sound of bell) sonnerie f ▷ vb (pt **rang**,
pp **rung**) ▷ vi (telephone, bell) sonner;
(ears) bourdonner; (also: **~ out**: voice,
words) retentir ▷ vt (BRIT Tel: also: **~ up**)
téléphoner à, appeler; **to ~ the bell**
sonner; **to give sb a ~** (Tel) passer un
coup de téléphone or un fil à qn; **ring
back** vt, vi (BRIT Tel) rappeler; **ring
off** vi (BRIT Tel) raccrocher; **ring up**
(BRIT) ▷ vt (Tel) téléphoner à, appeler;
ringing tone n (BRIT Tel) tonalité f
d'appel; **ringleader** n (of gang) chef m,
meneur m; **ring road** n (BRIT) rocade f
(motorway) périphérique m; **ringtone**
n (on mobile) sonnerie f (de téléphone
portable)
rink [rɪŋk] n (also: **ice ~**) patinoire f
rinse [rɪns] n rinçage m ▷ vt rincer
riot ['raɪət] n émeute f, bagarres fpl
▷ vi (demonstrators) manifester avec
violence; (population) se soulever, se
révolter; **to run ~** se déchaîner
rip [rɪp] n déchirure f ▷ vt déchirer
▷ vi se déchirer; **rip off** vt (inf: cheat)
arnaquer; **rip up** vt déchirer
ripe [raɪp] adj (fruit) mûr(e); (cheese)
fait(e)
rip-off ['rɪpɔf] n (inf): **it's a ~!** c'est du
vol manifeste!, c'est de l'arnaque!
ripple ['rɪpl] n ride f, ondulation f (of
applause, laughter) cascade f ▷ vi se
rider, onduler

rise [raɪz] n (slope) côte f, pente f; (hill)
élévation f; (increase: in wages: BRIT)
augmentation f; (: in prices, temperature)
hausse f, augmentation; (fig: to power
etc) ascension f ▷ vi (pt **rose**, pp **~n**)
s'élever, monter; (prices, numbers)
augmenter, monter; (waters, river)
monter; (sun, wind, person: from chair,
bed) se lever; (also: **~ up**: tower, building)
s'élever; (: rebel) se révolter; se rebeller;
(in rank) s'élever; **to give ~ to** donner
lieu à; **to ~ to the occasion** se montrer
à la hauteur; **risen** ['rɪzn] pp of **rise**
rising adj (increasing: number, prices) en
hausse; (tide) montant(e); (sun, moon)
levant(e)
risk [rɪsk] n risque m ▷ vt risquer; **to
take** or **run the ~ of doing** courir le
risque de faire; **at ~** en danger; **at one's
own ~** à ses risques et périls; **risky** adj
risqué(e)
rite [raɪt] n rite m; **the last ~s** les
derniers sacrements
ritual ['rɪtjuəl] adj rituel(le) ▷ n rituel m
rival ['raɪvl] n rival(e); (in business)
concurrent(e) ▷ adj rival(e); qui fait
concurrence ▷ vt (match) égaler;
rivalry n rivalité f; (in business)
concurrence f
river ['rɪvər] n rivière f; (major: also fig)
fleuve m ▷ cpd (port, traffic) fluvial(e);
up/down ~ en amont/aval; **riverbank**
n rive f, berge f
rivet ['rɪvɪt] n rivet m ▷ vt (fig) river,
fixer
Riviera [rɪvɪ'ɛərə] n: **the (French) ~** la
Côte d'Azur
road [rəud] n route f; (in town) rue f;
(fig) chemin, voie f ▷ cpd (accident) de la
route; **major/minor** ~ route principale
or à priorité/voie secondaire; **which
~ do I take for ...?** quelle route dois-je
prendre pour aller à...?; **roadblock** n
barrage routier; **road map** n carte
routière; **road rage** n comportement
très agressif de certains usagers de la
route; **road safety** n sécurité routière;
roadside n bord m de la route, bas-

côté m; **roadsign** n panneau m de signalisation; **road tax** n (BRIT Aut) taxe f sur les automobiles; **roadworks** npl travaux mpl (de réfection des routes)

roam [rəum] vi errer, vagabonder

roar [rɔːʳ] n rugissement m; (of crowd) hurlements mpl; (of vehicle, thunder, storm) grondement m ▷ vi rugir; hurler; gronder; **to ~ with laughter** rire à gorge déployée; **to do a ~ing trade** faire des affaires en or

roast [rəust] n rôti m ▷ vt (meat) (faire) rôtir; (coffee) griller, torréfier; **roast beef** n rôti de bœuf, rosbif m

rob [rɔb] vt (person) voler; (bank) dévaliser; **to ~ sb of sth** voler or dérober qch à qn; (fig: deprive) priver qn de qch; **robber** n bandit m, voleur m; **robbery** n vol m

robe [rəub] n (for ceremony etc) robe f; (also: **bath~**) peignoir m; (us: rug) couverture f ▷ vt revêtir (d'une robe)

robin ['rɔbɪn] n rouge-gorge m

robot ['rəubɔt] n robot m

robust [rəu'bʌst] adj robuste; (material, appetite) solide

rock [rɔk] n (substance) roche f, roc m; (boulder) rocher m, roche; (us: small stone) caillou m; (BRIT: sweet) = sucre m d'orge ▷ vt (swing gently: cradle) balancer; (: child) bercer; (shake) ébranler, secouer ▷ vi se balancer, être ébranlé(e) or secoué(e); **on the ~s** (drink) avec des glaçons; (marriage etc) en train de craquer; **rock and roll** n rock (and roll) m, rock'n'roll m; **rock climbing** n varappe f

rocket ['rɔkɪt] n fusée f; (Mil) fusée, roquette f; (Culin) roquette

rocking chair ['rɔkɪŋ-] n fauteuil m à bascule

rocky ['rɔkɪ] adj (hill) rocheux(-euse); (path) rocailleux(-euse)

rod [rɔd] n (metallic) tringle f; (Tech) tige f; (wooden) baguette f; (also: **fishing ~**) canne f à pêche

rode [rəud] pt of **ride**

rodent ['rəudnt] n rongeur m

rogue [rəug] n coquin m

role [rəul] n rôle m; **role-model** n modèle m à émuler

roll [rəul] n rouleau m; (of banknotes) liasse f; (also: **bread ~**) petit pain; (register) liste f; (sound: of drums etc) roulement m ▷ vt rouler; (also: **~ up:** string) enrouler; (also: **~ out:** pastry) étendre au rouleau, abaisser ▷ vi rouler; **roll over** vi se retourner; **roll up** vi (inf: arrive) s'amener ▷ vt (carpet, cloth, map) rouler; (sleeves) retrousser; **roller** n rouleau m; (wheel) roulette f; (for road) rouleau compresseur; (for hair) bigoudi m; **roller coaster** n montagnes fpl russes; **roller skates** n patins mpl à roulettes; **roller-skating** n patin m à roulettes; **to go roller-skating** faire du patin à roulettes; **rolling pin** n rouleau m à pâtisserie

ROM [rɔm] n abbr (Comput: = read-only memory) mémoire morte, ROM f

Roman ['rəumən] adj romain(e) ▷ n Romain(e); **Roman Catholic** adj, n catholique (m/f)

romance [rə'mæns] n (love affair) idylle f; (charm) poésie f; (novel) roman m à l'eau de rose

Romania etc [rəu'meɪnɪə] = **Rumania** etc

Roman numeral n chiffre romain

romantic [rə'mæntɪk] adj romantique; (novel, attachment) sentimental(e)

Rome [rəum] n Rome f

roof [ruːf] n toit m; (of tunnel, cave) plafond m ▷ vt couvrir (d'un toit); **the ~ of the mouth** la voûte du palais; **roof rack** n (Aut) galerie f

rook [ruk] n (bird) freux m; (Chess) tour f

room [ruːm] n (in house) pièce f; (also: **bed~**) chambre f (à coucher); (in school etc) salle f; (space) place f; **roommate** n camarade m/f de chambre; **room service** n service m des chambres (dans un hôtel); **roomy** adj spacieux(-euse);

(*garment*) ample

rooster [ˈruːstəʳ] n coq m

root [ruːt] n (*Bot, Math*) racine f; (*fig: of problem*) origine f, fond m ▷ vi (*plant*) s'enraciner

rope [rəup] n corde f; (*Naut*) cordage m ▷ vt (*tie up or together*) attacher; (*climbers: also:* **~ together**) encorder; (*area: also:* **~ off**) interdire l'accès de; (*: divide off*) séparer; **to know the ~s** (*fig*) être au courant, connaître les ficelles

rose [rəuz] pt of **rise** ▷ n rose f; (*also:* **~bush**) rosier m

rosé [ˈrəuzeɪ] n rosé m

rosemary [ˈrəuzmərɪ] n romarin m

rosy [ˈrəuzɪ] adj rose; **a ~ future** un bel avenir

rot [rɔt] n (*decay*) pourriture f; (*fig: pej: nonsense*) idioties fpl, balivernes fpl ▷ vt, vi pourrir

rota [ˈrəutə] n liste f, tableau m de service

rotate [rəuˈteɪt] vt (*revolve*) faire tourner; (*change round: crops*) alterner; (*: jobs*) faire à tour de rôle ▷ vi (*revolve*) tourner

rotten [ˈrɔtn] adj (*decayed*) pourri(e); (*dishonest*) corrompu(e); (*inf: bad*) mauvais(e), moche; **to feel ~** (*ill*) être mal fichu(e)

rough [rʌf] adj (*cloth, skin*) rêche, rugueux(-euse); (*terrain*) accidenté(e); (*path*) rocailleux(-euse); (*voice*) rauque, rude; (*person, manner: coarse*) rude, fruste; (*: violent*) brutal(e); (*district, weather*) mauvais(e); (*sea*) houleux(-euse); (*plan*) ébauché(e); (*guess*) approximatif(-ive) ▷ n (*Golf*) rough m ▷ vt: **to ~ it** vivre à la dure; **to sleep ~** (*BRIT*) coucher à la dure; **roughly** adv (*handle*) rudement, brutalement; (*speak*) avec brusquerie; (*make*) grossièrement; (*approximately*) à peu près, en gros

roulette [ruːˈlet] n roulette f

round [raund] adj rond(e) ▷ n rond m, cercle m; (*BRIT: of toast*) tranche f; (*duty: of policeman, milkman etc*)

tournée f; (*: of doctor*) visites fpl; (*game: of cards, in competition*) partie f; (*Boxing*) round m; (*of talks*) série f ▷ vt (*corner*) tourner ▷ prep autour de ▷ adv: **right ~, all ~** tout autour; **~ of ammunition** cartouche f; **~ of applause** applaudissements mpl; **~ of drinks** tournée f; **~ of sandwiches** (*BRIT*) sandwich m; **the long way ~** (*par*) le chemin le plus long; **all (the) year ~** toute l'année; **it's just ~ the corner** (*fig*) c'est tout près; **to go ~ to sb's (house)** aller chez qn; **go ~ the back** passez par derrière; **enough to go ~** assez pour tout le monde; **she arrived ~ (about) noon** (*BRIT*) elle est arrivée vers midi; **~ the clock** 24 heures sur 24; **round off** vt (*speech etc*) terminer; **round up** vt rassembler; (*criminals*) effectuer une rafle de; (*prices*) arrondir (au chiffre supérieur); **roundabout** n (*BRIT Aut*) rond-point m (à sens giratoire); (*at fair*) manège m (de chevaux de bois) ▷ adj (*route, means*) détourné(e); **round trip** n (*voyage m*) aller et retour m; **roundup** n rassemblement m; (*of criminals*) rafle f

rouse [rauz] vt (*wake up*) réveiller; (*stir up*) susciter, provoquer; (*interest*) éveiller; (*suspicions*) susciter, éveiller

route [ruːt] n itinéraire m; (*of bus*) parcours m; (*of trade, shipping*) route f

routine [ruːˈtiːn] adj (*work*) ordinaire, courant(e); (*procedure*) d'usage ▷ n (*habits*) habitudes fpl; (*pej*) train-train m; (*Theat*) numéro m

row¹ [rəu] n (*line*) rangée f; (*of people, seats, Knitting*) rang m; (*behind one another: of cars, people: fig*) file f ▷ vi (*in boat*) ramer; (*as sport*) faire de l'aviron ▷ vt (*boat*) faire aller à la rame or à l'aviron; **in a ~** (*fig*) d'affilée

row² [rau] n (*noise*) vacarme m; (*dispute*) dispute f, querelle f; (*scolding*) réprimande f, savon m ▷ vi (*also:* **to have a ~**) se disputer, se quereller

rowboat [ˈrəubəut] n (*us*) canot m (à rames)

rowing ['rəʊɪŋ] n canotage m; (as sport) aviron m; **rowing boat** n (BRIT) canot m (à rames)

royal ['rɔɪəl] adj royal(e); **royalty** n (royal persons) (membres mpl de la) famille royale; (payment: to author) droits mpl d'auteur; (: to inventor) royalties fpl

rpm abbr (= revolutions per minute) t/mn (= tours/minute)

R.S.V.P. abbr (= répondez s'il vous plaît) RSVP

Rt. Hon. abbr (BRIT: = Right Honourable) titre donné aux députés de la Chambre des communes

rub [rʌb] n: **to give sth a ~** donner un coup de chiffon or de torchon à qch ▷ vt frotter; (person) frictionner; (hands) se frotter; **~ sb up** (BRIT) or **to ~ sb** (US) **the wrong way** prendre qn à rebrousse-poil; **rub in** vt (ointment) faire pénétrer; **rub off** vi partir; **rub out** vt effacer

rubber ['rʌbər] n caoutchouc m; (BRIT: eraser) gomme f (à effacer); **rubber band** n élastique m; **rubber gloves** npl gants mpl en caoutchouc

rubbish ['rʌbɪʃ] n (from household) ordures fpl; (fig: pej) choses fpl sans valeur; camelote f; (nonsense) bêtises fpl, idioties fpl; **rubbish bin** n (BRIT) boîte f à ordures, poubelle f; **rubbish dump** n (BRIT: in town) décharge publique, dépotoir m

rubble ['rʌbl] n décombres mpl; (smaller) gravats mpl; (Constr) blocage m

ruby ['ruːbɪ] n rubis m

rucksack ['rʌksæk] n sac m à dos

rudder ['rʌdər] n gouvernail m

rude [ruːd] adj (impolite) impoli(e); (: word, manners) grossier(-ière); (shocking) indécent(e), inconvenant(e)

ruffle ['rʌfl] vt (hair) ébouriffer; (clothes) chiffonner; (fig: person): **to get ~d** s'énerver

rug [rʌg] n petit tapis; (BRIT: blanket) couverture f

rugby ['rʌgbɪ] n (also: **~ football**) rugby m

rugged ['rʌgɪd] adj (landscape) accidenté(e); (features, character) rude

ruin ['ruːɪn] n ruine f ▷ vt ruiner; (spoil: clothes) abîmer; (: event) gâcher; **ruins** npl (of building) ruine(s)

rule [ruːl] n règle f; (regulation) règlement m; (government) autorité f, gouvernement m ▷ vt (country) gouverner; (person) dominer; (decide) décider ▷ vi commander; (Law): **as a ~** normalement, en règle générale; **rule out** vt exclure; **ruler** n (sovereign) souverain(e); (leader) chef m d'État; (for measuring) règle f; **ruling** adj (party) au pouvoir; (class) dirigeant(e) ▷ n (Law) décision f

rum [rʌm] n rhum m

Rumania [ruːˈmeɪnɪə] n Roumanie f; **Rumanian** adj roumain(e) ▷ n Roumain(e); (Ling) roumain m

rumble ['rʌmbl] n grondement m; (of stomach, pipe) gargouillement m ▷ vi gronder; (stomach, pipe) gargouiller

rumour (US **rumor**) ['ruːmər] n rumeur f, bruit m (qui court) ▷ vt: **it is ~ed that** le bruit court que

rump steak n romsteck m

run [rʌn] n (race) course f; (outing) tour m or promenade f (en voiture); (distance travelled) parcours m, trajet m; (series) suite f, série f; (Theat) série de représentations; (Ski) piste f; (Cricket, Baseball) point m; (in pstar, stockings) maille filée, échelle f ▷ vb (pt ran, pp ~) ▷ vt (competition, course) organiser; (hotel, house) tenir; (race) participer à; (Comput: program) exécuter; (to pass: hand, finger): **to ~ sth over** promener or passer qch sur; (water, bath) faire couler; (Press: feature) publier ▷ vi courir; (pass: road etc) passer; (work: machine, factory) marcher; (bus, train) circuler; (continue: play) se jouer, être à l'affiche; (: contract) être valide or en vigueur; (flow: river, bath, nose) couler; (colours, washing) déteindre; (in election) être candidat, se présenter; **at a ~** au pas de course; **to go for a ~** aller courir or faire un peu de course à pied; (in car) faire un tour or une promenade (en voiture); **there was a ~ on** (meat, tickets) les gens se sont rués sur; **in the long ~** à la longue; **on the ~** en fuite; **I'll ~ you to the station** je vais vous emmener or conduire à la gare; **to ~ a risk** courir un risque; **run after** vt fus (to catch up) courir après; (chase) poursuivre; **run away** vi s'enfuir; **run down** vt (Aut: knock over) renverser; (BRIT: reduce: production) réduire progressivement; (: factory/shop) réduire progressivement la production/ l'activité de; (criticize) critiquer, dénigrer; **to be ~ down** (tired) être fatigué(e) or à plat; **run into** vt fus (meet: person) rencontrer par hasard; (: trouble) se heurter à; (collide with) heurter; **run off** vi s'enfuir ▷ vt (water) laisser s'écouler; (copies) tirer; **run out** vi (person) sortir en courant; (liquid) couler; (lease) expirer; (money) être épuisé(e); **run out of** vt fus se trouver à court de; **run over** vt (Aut) écraser ▷ vt fus (revise) revoir, reprendre; **run through** vt fus (recap) reprendre, revoir; (play) répéter; **run up** vi: **to ~ up against** (difficulties) se heurter à; **runaway** adj (horse) emballé(e); (truck) fou (folle); (person) fugitif(-ive); (child) fugueur(-euse)

rung [rʌŋ] pp of **ring** ▷ n (of ladder) barreau m

runner ['rʌnə*] n (in race: person) coureur(-euse); (: horse) partant m; (on sledge) patin m; (for drawer etc) coulisseau m; **runner bean** n (BRIT) haricot m (à rames); **runner-up** n second(e)

running ['rʌnɪŋ] n (in race etc) course f; (of business, organization) direction f, gestion f ▷ adj (water) courant(e); (commentary) suivi(e); **6 days ~** 6 jours de suite; **to be in/out of the ~ for sth**

être/ne pas être sur les rangs pour qch
runny ['rʌnɪ] adj qui coule
run-up ['rʌnʌp] n (BRIT): **~ to sth** période f précédant qch
runway ['rʌnweɪ] n (Aviat) piste f (d'envol or d'atterrissage)
rupture ['rʌptʃə*] n (Med) hernie f
rural ['rʊərl] adj rural(e)
rush [rʌʃ] n (of crowd, Comm: sudden demand) ruée f; (hurry) hâte f; (of anger, joy) accès m; (current) flot m; (Bot) jonc m ▷ vt (hurry) transporter or envoyer d'urgence ▷ vi se précipiter; **to ~ sth off** (do quickly) faire qch à la hâte; **rush hour** n heures fpl de pointe or d'affluence
Russia ['rʌʃə] n Russie f; **Russian** adj russe ▷ n Russe m/f; (Ling) russe m
rust [rʌst] n rouille f ▷ vi rouiller
rusty ['rʌstɪ] adj rouillé(e)
ruthless ['ruːθlɪs] adj sans pitié, impitoyable
RV n abbr (US) = **recreational vehicle**
rye [raɪ] n seigle m

S

Sabbath ['sæbəθ] n (Jewish) sabbat m; (Christian) dimanche m

sabotage ['sæbətɑːʒ] n sabotage m ▷ vt saboter

saccharin(e) ['sækərɪn] n saccharine f

sachet ['sæʃeɪ] n sachet m

sack [sæk] n (bag) sac m ▷ vt (dismiss) renvoyer, mettre à la porte; (plunder) piller, mettre à sac; **to get the ~** être renvoyé(e) or mis(e) à la porte

sacred ['seɪkrɪd] adj sacré(e)

sacrifice ['sækrɪfaɪs] n sacrifice m ▷ vt sacrifier

sad [sæd] adj (unhappy) triste; (deplorable) triste, fâcheux(-euse); (inf: pathetic: thing) triste, lamentable; (: person) minable

saddle ['sædl] n selle f ▷ vt (horse) seller; **to be ~d with sth** (inf) avoir qch sur les bras

sadistic [sə'dɪstɪk] adj sadique

sadly ['sædlɪ] adv tristement; (unfortunately) malheureusement; (seriously) fort

sadness ['sædnɪs] n tristesse f

s.a.e. n abbr (BRIT: = stamped addressed envelope) enveloppe affranchie pour la réponse

safari [sə'fɑːrɪ] n safari m

safe [seɪf] adj (out of danger) hors de danger, en sécurité; (not dangerous) sans danger; (cautious) prudent(e); (sure: bet etc) assuré(e) ▷ n coffre-fort m; **could you put this in the ~, please?** pourriez-vous mettre ceci dans le coffre-fort?; **~ and sound** sain(e) et sauf (sauve); **(just) to be on the ~ side** pour plus de sûreté, par précaution; **safely** adv (assume, say) sans risque d'erreur; (drive, arrive) sans accident; **safe sex** n rapports sexuels protégés

safety ['seɪftɪ] n sécurité f; **safety belt** n ceinture f de sécurité; **safety pin** n épingle f de sûreté or de nourrice

saffron ['sæfrən] n safran m

sag [sæg] vi s'affaisser, fléchir; (hem, breasts) pendre

sage [seɪdʒ] n (herb) sauge f; (person) sage m

Sagittarius [sædʒɪ'tɛərɪəs] n le Sagittaire

Sahara [sə'hɑːrə] n: **the ~ (Desert)** le (désert du) Sahara m

said [sɛd] pt, pp of **say**

sail [seɪl] n (on boat) voile f; (trip): **to go for a ~** faire un tour en bateau ▷ vt (boat) manœuvrer, piloter ▷ vi (travel: ship) avancer, naviguer; (set off) partir, prendre la mer; (Sport) faire de la voile; **they ~ed into Le Havre** ils sont entrés dans le port du Havre; **sailboat** n (us) bateau m à voiles, voilier m; **sailing** n (Sport) voile f; **to go sailing** faire de la voile; **sailing boat** n bateau m à voiles, voilier m; **sailor** n marin m, matelot m

saint [seɪnt] n saint(e)

sake [seɪk] n: **for the ~ of** (out of concern for) pour (l'amour de), dans l'intérêt de; (out of consideration for) par égard pour

salad ['sæləd] n salade f; **salad cream** n (BRIT) (sorte f de) mayonnaise f; **salad dressing** n vinaigrette f

salami [sə'lɑːmɪ] n salami m
salary ['sælərɪ] n salaire m,
traitement m
sale [seɪl] n vente f; (at reduced prices)
soldes mpl; **sales** npl (total amount
sold) chiffre m de ventes; **"for ~"** "à
vendre"; **on ~** en vente; **sales assistant**
(US **sales clerk**) n vendeur(-euse);
salesman (irreg) n (in shop) vendeur m;
salesperson (irreg) n (in shop)
vendeur(-euse); **sales rep** n (Comm)
représentant(e) m/f; **saleswoman**
(irreg) n (in shop) vendeuse f
saline ['seɪlaɪn] adj salin(e)
saliva [sə'laɪvə] n salive f
salmon ['sæmən] n (pl inv) saumon m
salon ['sælɔn] n salon m
saloon [sə'luːn] n (US) bar m; (BRIT Aut)
berline f; (ship's lounge) salon m
salt [sɔːlt] n sel m ▷ vt saler; **saltwater**
adj (fish etc) (d'eau) de mer; **salty** adj
salé(e)
salute [sə'luːt] n salut m; (of guns) salve
f ▷ vt saluer
salvage ['sælvɪdʒ] n (saving) sauvetage
m; (things saved) biens sauvés or
récupérés ▷ vt sauver, récupérer
Salvation Army [sæl'veɪʃən-] n
Armée f du Salut
same [seɪm] adj même ▷ pron: **the ~**
le (la) même, les mêmes; **the ~ book**
as le même livre que; **at the ~ time** en
même temps; (yet) néanmoins; **all** or
just the ~ tout de même, quand même;
to do the ~ faire de même, en faire
autant; **to do the ~ as sb** faire comme
qn; **and the ~ to you!** et à vous de
même!; (after insult) toi-même!
sample ['sɑːmpl] n échantillon m;
(Med) prélèvement m ▷ vt (food, wine)
goûter
sanction ['sæŋkʃən] n approbation
f, sanction f ▷ vt cautionner,
sanctionner; **sanctions** npl (Pol)
sanctions
sanctuary ['sæŋktjuərɪ] n (holy place)
sanctuaire m; (refuge) asile m; (for
wildlife) réserve f

sand [sænd] n sable m ▷ vt (also: ~
down: wood etc) poncer
sandal ['sændl] n sandale f
sand: **sandbox** n (US: for children) tas
m de sable; **sandcastle** n château
m de sable; **sand dune** n dune f de
sable; **sandpaper** n papier m de verre;
sandpit n (BRIT: for children) tas m de
sable; **sands** npl plage f (de sable);
sandstone ['sændstəun] n grès m
sandwich ['sændwɪtʃ] n sandwich m
▷ vt (also: ~ **in**) intercaler; **~ed**
between pris en sandwich entre; **cheese/ham ~**
sandwich au fromage/jambon
sandy ['sændɪ] adj (beach) sablonneux(-euse);
(colour) sable inv, blond roux inv
sane [seɪn] adj (person) sain(e) d'esprit;
(outlook) sensé(e), sain(e)
sang [sæŋ] pt of **sing**
sanitary towel (US **sanitary napkin**)
['sænɪtən-] n serviette f hygiénique
sanity ['sænɪtɪ] n santé mentale;
(common sense) bon sens
sank [sæŋk] pt of **sink**
Santa Claus [sæntə'klɔːz] n le Père
Noël
sap [sæp] n (of plants) sève f ▷ vt
(strength) saper, miner
sapphire ['sæfaɪə*] n saphir m
sarcasm ['sɑːkæzm] n sarcasme m,
raillerie f
sarcastic [sɑːˈkæstɪk] adj sarcastique
sardine [sɑːˈdiːn] n sardine f
SASE n abbr (US: = self-addressed stamped
envelope) enveloppe affranchie pour la
réponse
sat [sæt] pt, pp of **sit**
Sat. abbr (= Saturday) sam.
satchel ['sætʃl] n cartable m
satellite ['sætəlaɪt] n satellite m;
satellite dish n antenne f parabolique;
satellite television n télévision f par
satellite
satin ['sætɪn] n satin m ▷ adj or de
satin, satiné(e)
satire ['sætaɪə*] n satire f
satisfaction [sætɪsˈfækʃən] n
satisfaction f

satisfactory [sætɪsˈfæktərɪ] adj
satisfaisant(e)

satisfied [ˈsætɪsfaɪd] adj satisfait(e);
to be ~ with sth être satisfait(e) de qch

satisfy [ˈsætɪsfaɪ] vt satisfaire,
contenter; (convince) convaincre,
persuader

Saturday [ˈsætədeɪ] n samedi m

sauce [sɔːs] n sauce f; **saucepan** n
casserole f

saucer [ˈsɔːsəʳ] n soucoupe f

Saudi Arabia [ˈsaʊdɪ-] n Arabie f
Saoudite

sauna [ˈsɔːnə] n sauna m

sausage [ˈsɒsɪdʒ] n saucisse f; (salami
etc) saucisson m; **sausage roll** n
friand m

sautéed [ˈsəʊteɪd] adj sauté(e)

savage [ˈsævɪdʒ] adj (cruel, fierce)
brutal(e), féroce; (primitive)
primitif(-ive), sauvage ▷ n sauvage m/f
▷ vt attaquer férocement

save [seɪv] vt (person, belongings) sauver;
(money) mettre de côté, économiser;
(time) (faire) gagner; (keep) garder;
(Comput) sauvegarder; (Sport: stop)
arrêter; (avoid: trouble) éviter ▷ vi (also:
~ up) mettre de l'argent de côté ▷ n
(Sport) arrêt m (du ballon) ▷ prep sauf, à
l'exception de

savings [ˈseɪvɪŋz] npl économies fpl;
savings account n compte m
d'épargne; **savings and loan
association** (us) n ≈ société f de crédit
immobilier

savoury (us **savory**) [ˈseɪvərɪ] adj
savoureux(-euse); (dish: not sweet)
salé(e)

saw [sɔː] pt of **see** ▷ n (tool) scie f ▷ vt
(pt **~ed**, pp **~ed** or **~n**) scier; **sawdust**
n sciure f

sawn [sɔːn] pp of **saw**

saxophone [ˈsæksəfəʊn] n
saxophone m

say [seɪ] n: **to have one's ~** dire ce qu'on
a à dire ▷ vt (pt, pp **said**) dire; **to have
a ~** avoir voix au chapitre; **could you ~
that again?** pourriez-vous répéter ce

que vous venez de dire?; **to ~ yes/no**
dire oui/non; **my watch ~s 3 o'clock**
ma montre indique 3 heures, il est 3
heures à ma montre; **that is to ~** c'est-
à-dire, cela va sans dire, cela va de soi;
saying n dicton m, proverbe m

scab [skæb] n croûte f; (pej) jaune m

scaffolding [ˈskæfəldɪŋ] n
échafaudage m

scald [skɔːld] n brûlure f ▷ vt
ébouillanter

scale [skeɪl] n (of fish) écaille f; (Mus)
gamme f; (of ruler, thermometer etc)
graduation f, échelle (graduée); (of
salaries, fees etc) barème m; (of map,
also size, extent) échelle ▷ vt (mountain)
escalader; **scales** npl balance f; (larger)
bascule f; (also: **bathroom ~s**) pèse-
personne m inv; **~ of charges** tableau m
des tarifs; **on a large ~** sur une grande
échelle, en grand

scallion [ˈskæljən] n (us: salad onion)
ciboule f

scallop [ˈskɒləp] n coquille f Saint-
Jacques; (Sewing) feston m

scalp [skælp] n cuir chevelu ▷ vt
scalper

scalpel [ˈskælpl] n scalpel m

scam [skæm] n (inf) arnaque f

scampi [ˈskæmpɪ] npl langoustines
(frites), scampi mpl

scan [skæn] vt (examine) scruter,
examiner; (glance at quickly) parcourir;
(TV, Radar) balayer ▷ n (Med)
scanographie f

scandal [ˈskændl] n scandale m;
(gossip) ragots mpl

Scandinavia [skændɪˈneɪvɪə] n
Scandinavie f; **Scandinavian** adj
scandinave ▷ n Scandinave m/f

scanner [ˈskænəʳ] n (Radar, Med)
scanner m, scanographe m; (Comput)
scanner, numériseur m

scapegoat [ˈskeɪpɡəʊt] n bouc m
émissaire

scar [skɑːʳ] n cicatrice f ▷ vt laisser une
cicatrice or une marque à

scarce [skɛəs] adj rare, peu

abondant(e); **to make o.s. ~** (inf)
se sauver; **scarcely** adv à peine,
presque pas

scare [skɛə⁸] n peur f, panique f ▷ vt
effrayer, faire peur à; **to ~ sb stiff** faire
une peur bleue à qn; **bomb ~** alerte f à
la bombe; **scarecrow** n épouvantail m;
scared adj: **to be scared** avoir peur

scarf (pl **scarves**) [ska:f, ska:vz] n (long)
écharpe f; (square) foulard m

scarlet ['ska:lit] adj écarlate

scarves [ska:vz] npl of **scarf**

scary ['skɛəri] adj (inf) effrayant(e);
(film) qui fait peur

scatter ['skætə⁸] vt éparpiller,
répandre; (crowd) disperser ▷ vi se
disperser

scenario [si'nɑːriəu] n scénario m

scene [si:n] n (Theat, fig etc) scène f; (of
crime, accident) lieu(x) m(pl), endroit m;
(sight, view) spectacle m, vue f; **scenery**
n (Theat) décor(s) m(pl); (landscape)
paysage m; **scenic** adj offrant de beaux
paysages or panoramas

scent [sɛnt] n parfum m, odeur f; (fig:
track) piste f

sceptical (US **skeptical**) ['skɛptikl] adj
sceptique

schedule ['ʃɛdjuːl, US 'skɛdjuːl] n
programme m, plan m; (of trains) horaire
m; (of prices etc) barème m, tarif m ▷ vt
prévoir; **on ~** à l'heure (prévue); à la
date prévue; **to be ahead of/behind ~**
avoir de l'avance/du retard; **scheduled
flight** n vol régulier

scheme [skiːm] n plan m, projet
m; (plot) complot m, combine f;
(arrangement) arrangement m,
classification f; (pension scheme
etc) régime m ▷ vt, vi comploter,
manigancer

schizophrenic [skɪtsə'frɛnik] adj
schizophrène

scholar ['skɔlə⁸] n érudit(e); (pupil)
boursier(-ère); **scholarship** n
érudition f; (grant) bourse f (d'études)

school [skuːl] n (gen) école f; (secondary
school) collège m, lycée m; (in university)

faculté f; (US: university) université
f ▷ cpd scolaire; **schoolbook** n livre
m scolaire or de classe; **schoolboy**
n écolier m; (at secondary school)
collégien m, lycéen m; **schoolchildren**
npl écoliers mpl; (at secondary school)
collégiens mpl, lycéens mpl; **schoolgirl**
n écolière f; (at secondary school)
collégienne f, lycéenne f; **schooling** n
instruction f, études fpl; **schoolteacher**
n (primary) instituteur(-trice);
(secondary) professeur m

science ['saɪəns] n science f; **science
fiction** n science-fiction f; **scientific**
[saɪən'tɪfik] adj scientifique; **scientist**
n scientifique m/f; (eminent) savant m

sci-fi ['saɪfaɪ] n abbr (inf: = science
fiction) SF f

scissors ['sɪzəz] npl ciseaux mpl; **a pair
of ~** une paire de ciseaux

scold [skəuld] vt gronder

scone [skɔn] n sorte de petit pain rond
au lait

scoop [skuːp] n pelle f (à main); (for ice
cream) boule f à glace; (Press) reportage
exclusif or à sensation

scooter ['skuːtə⁸] n (motor cycle) scooter
m; (toy) trottinette f

scope [skəup] n (capacity: of plan,
undertaking) portée f, envergure f; (: of
person) compétence f, capacités fpl;
(opportunity) possibilités fpl

scorching ['skɔːtʃiŋ] adj torride,
brûlant(e)

score [skɔː⁸] n score m, décompte m
des points; (Mus) partition f ▷ vt (goal,
point) marquer; (success) remporter;
(cut: leather, wood, card) entailler, inciser
▷ vi marquer des points; (Football)
marquer un but; (keep score) compter
les points; **on that ~** sur ce chapitre,
à cet égard; **a ~ of** (twenty) vingt; **~s
of** (fig) des tas de; **to ~ 6 out of 10** obtenir
6 sur 10; **score out** vt rayer, barrer,
biffer; **scoreboard** n tableau m; **scorer**
n (Football) auteur m du but; buteur m;
(keeping score) marqueur m

scorn [skɔːn] n mépris m, dédain m

Scorpio ['skɔːpɪəu] n le Scorpion
scorpion ['skɔːpɪən] n scorpion m
Scot [skɔt] n Écossais(e)
Scotch [skɔtʃ] n whisky m, scotch m
Scotch tape® (us) n scotch® m,
ruban adhésif
Scotland ['skɔtlənd] n Écosse f
Scots [skɔts] adj écossais(e); **Scotsman**
(irreg) n Écossais m; **Scotswoman**
(irreg) n Écossaise f; **Scottish** ['skɔtɪʃ]
adj écossais(e); **Scottish Parliament** n
Parlement écossais
scout [skaut] n (Mil) éclaireur m; (also:
boy ~) scout m; **girl** ~ (us) guide f
scowl [skaul] vi se renfrogner, avoir l'air
maussade; **to ~ at** regarder de travers
scramble ['skræmbl] n (rush)
bousculade f, ruée f ▷ vi grimper/
descendre tant bien que mal; **to ~ for**
se bousculer or se disputer pour (avoir);
to go scrambling (Sport) faire du trial;
scrambled eggs npl œufs brouillés
scrap [skræp] n bout m, morceau
m; (fight) bagarre f; (also: ~ **iron**)
ferraille f ▷ vt jeter, mettre au rebut;
(fig) abandonner, laisser tomber
▷ vi se bagarrer; **scraps** npl (waste)
déchets mpl; **scrapbook** n album m
scrape [skreɪp] vt, vi gratter, racler ▷ n:
to get into a ~ s'attirer des ennuis;
scrape through vi (exam etc) réussir
de justesse
scrap paper n papier m brouillon
scratch [skrætʃ] n égratignure f, rayure
f; (on paint) éraflure f; (from claw) coup
m de griffe ▷ vt (rub) (se) gratter; (paint
etc) érafler; (with claw, nail) griffer ▷ vi
(se) gratter; **to start from ~** partir de
zéro; **to be up to ~** être à la hauteur;
scratch card n carte f à gratter
scream [skriːm] n cri perçant,
hurlement m ▷ vi crier, hurler
screen [skriːn] n écran m; (in room)
paravent m; (fig) écran, rideau m ▷ vt
masquer, cacher; (from the wind etc)
abriter, protéger; (film) projeter;
(candidates etc) filtrer; **screening** n
(of film) projection f; (Med) test m (or

tests) de dépistage; **screenplay** n
scénario m; **screen saver** n (Comput)
économiseur m d'écran
screw [skruː] n vis f ▷ vt (also: ~ **in**)
visser; **screw up** vt (paper etc) froisser;
to ~ up one's eyes se plisser les yeux;
screwdriver n tournevis m
scribble ['skrɪbl] n gribouillage m ▷ vt
gribouiller, griffonner
script [skrɪpt] n (Cine etc) scénario m,
texte m; (writing) (écriture f) script m
scroll [skrəul] n rouleau m ▷ vt
(Comput) faire défiler (sur l'écran)
scrub [skrʌb] n (land) broussailles fpl
▷ vt (floor) nettoyer à la brosse; (pan)
récurer; (washing) frotter
scruffy ['skrʌfɪ] adj débraillé(e)
scrum(mage) ['skrʌm(ɪdʒ)] n mêlée f
scrutiny ['skruːtɪnɪ] n examen
minutieux
scuba diving ['skuːbə-] n plongée
sous-marine (autonome)
sculptor ['skʌlptə²] n sculpteur m
sculpture ['skʌlptʃə²] n sculpture f
scum [skʌm] n écume f, mousse f; (pej:
people) rebut m, lie f
scurry ['skʌrɪ] vi filer à toute allure; **to ~**
off détaler, se sauver
sea [siː] n mer f ▷ cpd marin(e), de (la)
mer, maritime; **by or beside the ~**
(holiday, town) au bord de la mer; **by ~**
par mer, en bateau; **out to ~** au large;
(out) **at ~** en mer; **to be all at ~** (fig)
nager complètement; **seafood** n fruits
mpl de mer; **sea front** n bord m de mer;
seagull n mouette f
seal [siːl] n (animal) phoque m, (stamp)
sceau m, cachet m ▷ vt sceller;
(envelope) coller; (: with seal) cacheter;
seal off vt (forbid entry to) interdire
l'accès de
sea level n niveau m de la mer
seam [siːm] n couture f; (of coal) veine
f, filon m
search [səːtʃ] n (for person, thing,
Comput) recherche(s) f(pl); (of drawer,
pockets) fouille f; (Law: at sb's home)
perquisition f ▷ vt fouiller; (examine

examiner minutieusement; scruter
▷ vi: **to ~ for** chercher; **in ~ of** à la recherche de; **search engine** n (Comput) moteur m de recherche; **search party** n expédition f de secours

sea: **seashore** n rivage m, plage f, bord m de (la) mer; **seasick** adj: **to be seasick** avoir le mal de mer; **seaside** n bord m de mer; **seaside resort** n station f balnéaire

season ['si:zn] n saison f ▷ vt assaisonner, relever; **to be in/out of ~** être/ne pas être de saison; **seasonal** adj saisonnier(-ière); **seasoning** n assaisonnement m; **season ticket** n carte f d'abonnement

seat [si:t] n siège m; (in bus, train: place) place f; (buttocks) postérieur m; (of trousers) fond m ▷ vt faire asseoir, placer; (have room for) avoir des places assises pour, pouvoir accueillir; **I'd like to book two ~s** je voudrais réserver deux places; **to be ~ed** être assis; **seat belt** n ceinture f de sécurité; **seating** n sièges fpl, places assises

sea: **sea water** n eau f de mer; **seaweed** n algues fpl

sec. abbr (= second) sec

secluded [sɪ'klu:dɪd] adj retiré(e), à l'écart

second ['sekənd] num deuxième, second(e) ▷ adv (in race etc) en seconde position ▷ n (unit of time) seconde f; (Aut: also: **~ gear**) seconde; (Comm: imperfect) article m de second choix; (Brit Scol) ≈ licence f avec mention f (motion) appuyer; **seconds** npl (inf: food) rab m (inf); **secondary** adj secondaire; **secondary school** n collège m; lycée m; **second-class** adj de deuxième classe; (Rail) de seconde (classe); (Post) au tarif réduit; (pej) de qualité inférieure ▷ adv (Rail) en seconde; (Post) au tarif réduit; **secondhand** adj d'occasion; (information) de seconde main; **secondly** adv deuxièmement; **second-rate** adj de deuxième ordre, de qualité inférieure; **second thoughts** npl: **to**

have second thoughts changer d'avis; **on second thoughts** or **thought** (us) à la réflexion

secrecy ['si:krəsɪ] n secret m

secret ['si:krɪt] adj secret(-ète) ▷ n secret m; **in ~** adv en secret, secrètement, en cachette

secretary ['sekrətrɪ] n secrétaire m/f; **S~ of State (for)** (Brit Pol) ministre m (de)

secretive ['si:krətɪv] adj réservé(e); (pej) cachottier(-ière), dissimulé(e)

secret service n services secrets

sect [sekt] n secte f

section ['sekʃən] n section f; (Comm) rayon m; (of document) section, article m, paragraphe m; (cut) coupe f

sector ['sektə'] n secteur m

secular ['sekjulə'] adj laïque

secure [sɪ'kjuə'] adj (free from anxiety) sans inquiétude, sécurisé(e); (firmly fixed) solide, bien attaché(e) (or fermé(e) etc); (in safe place) en lieu sûr, en sûreté f ▷ vt (fix) fixer, attacher; (get) obtenir, se procurer

security [sɪ'kjuərɪtɪ] n sécurité f, mesures fpl de sécurité; (for loan) caution f, garantie f; **securities** npl (Stock Exchange) valeurs fpl, titres mpl; **security guard** n garde chargé de la sécurité; (transporting money) convoyeur m de fonds

sedan [sə'dæn] n (us Aut) berline f

sedate [sɪ'deɪt] adj calme; posé(e) ▷ vt donner des sédatifs à

sedative ['sedɪtɪv] n calmant m, sédatif m

seduce [sɪ'dju:s] vt séduire; **seductive** [sɪ'dʌktɪv] adj séduisant(e); (smile) séducteur(-trice); (fig: offer) alléchant(e)

see [si:] vb (pt **saw**, pp **~n**) ▷ vt (gen) voir; (accompany): **to ~ sb to the door** reconduire or raccompagner qn jusqu'à la porte ▷ vi voir; **to ~ that** (ensure) veiller à ce que + sub, faire en sorte que + sub, s'assurer que; **~ you soon/later/tomorrow!** à bientôt/plus tard/demain); **see off** vt accompagner (à la gare or à l'aéroport etc); **see out** vt (take to door) raccompagner à la porte; **see through** vt mener à bonne fin ▷ vt fus voir clair dans; **see to** vt fus s'occuper de, se charger de

seed [siːd] n graine f; (fig) germe m; (Tennis etc) tête f de série; **to go to ~** (plant) monter en graine; (fig) se laisser aller

seeing ['siːɪŋ] conj: **~ (that)** vu que, étant donné que

seek (pt, pp **sought**) [siːk, sɔːt] vt chercher, rechercher

seem [siːm] vi sembler, paraître; **there ~s to be ...** il semble qu'il y a ..., on dirait qu'il y a ...; **seemingly** adv apparemment

seen [siːn] pp of **see**

seesaw ['siːsɔː] n (jeu de m) bascule f

segment ['sɛɡmənt] n segment m; (of orange) quartier m

segregate ['sɛɡrɪɡeɪt] vt séparer, isoler

Seine [seɪn] n: **the (River) ~** la Seine

seize [siːz] vt (grasp) saisir, attraper; (take possession of) s'emparer de; (opportunity) saisir

seizure ['siːʒə] n (Med) crise f, attaque f; (of power) prise f

seldom ['sɛldəm] adv rarement

select [sɪˈlɛkt] adj choisi(e), d'élite; (hotel, restaurant, club) chic inv, sélect inv ▷ vt sélectionner, choisir; **selection** n sélection f, choix m; **selective** adj sélectif(-ive); (school) à recrutement sélectif

self [sɛlf] n (pl **selves**) n: **the ~** le moi inv ▷ prefix auto-; **self-assured** adj sûr(e) de soi, plein(e) d'assurance; **self-catering** adj (BRIT: flat) avec cuisine, où l'on peut faire sa cuisine; (: holiday) en appartement (or chalet etc) loué; **self-centred** (us **self-centered**) adj égocentrique; **self-confidence** n confiance f en soi; **self-confident** adj sûr(e) de soi, plein(e) d'assurance; **self-conscious** adj timide, qui manque d'assurance; **self-contained**

adj (BRIT: flat) avec entrée particulière, indépendant(e); **self-control** n maîtrise f de soi; **self-defence** (us **self-defense**) n autodéfense f; (Law) légitime défense f; **self-drive** adj (BRIT): **self-drive car** voiture f de location; **self-employed** adj qui travaille à son compte; **self-esteem** n amour-propre m; **self-indulgent** adj qui ne se refuse rien; **self-interest** n intérêt personnel; **selfish** adj égoïste; **self-pity** n apitoiement m sur soi-même; **self-raising** [sɛlfˈreɪzɪŋ] (us **self-rising** [sɛlfˈraɪzɪŋ]) adj: **self-raising flour** farine f pour gâteaux (avec levure incorporée); **self-respect** n respect m de soi, amour-propre m; **self-service** adj, n libre-service (m), self-service (m)

sell (pt, pp **sold**) [sɛl, səuld] vt vendre ▷ vi se vendre; **to ~ at** or **for 10 euros** se vendre 10 euros; **sell off** vt liquider; **sell out** vi: **to ~ out (of sth)** (use up stock) vendre tout son stock (de qch); **sell-by date** n date f limite de vente; **seller** n vendeur(-euse), marchand(e)

Sellotape® ['sɛləuteɪp] n (BRIT) scotch® m

selves [sɛlvz] npl of **self**

semester [sɪˈmɛstə] n (esp us) semestre m

semi... ['sɛmɪ] prefix semi-, demi-; à demi, à moitié; **semicircle** n demi-cercle m; **semidetached (house)** n (BRIT) maison jumelée or jumelle; **semi-final** n demi-finale f

seminar ['sɛmɪnɑː] n séminaire m

semi-skimmed ['sɛmɪˈskɪmd] adj demi-écrémé(e)

senate ['sɛnɪt] n sénat m; (us): **the S~** le Sénat; **senator** n sénateur m

send (pt, pp **sent**) [sɛnd, sɛnt] vt envoyer; **send back** vt renvoyer; **send for** vt fus (by post) se faire envoyer, commander par correspondance; **send in** vt (report, application, resignation) remettre; **send off** vt (goods) envoyer, expédier; (BRIT Sport: player) expulser or renvoyer du terrain; **send on** vt

(BRIT: letter) faire suivre; (luggage etc: in advance) (faire) expédier à l'avance; (emit: light, heat, signal) émettre; **send out** vt (invitation) envoyer (par la poste); (emit: light, heat, signal) émettre; **send up** vt (person, price) faire monter; (BRIT: parody) mettre en boîte, parodier; **sender** n expéditeur(-trice); **send-off** n: **a good send-off** des adieux chaleureux

senile ['si:naɪl] adj sénile

senior ['si:nɪə] adj (high-ranking) de haut niveau; (of higher rank): **to be ~ to sb** être le supérieur de qn; **senior citizen** n personne f du troisième âge; **senior high school** n (US) ≈ lycée m

sensation [sɛn'seɪʃən] n sensation f; **sensational** adj qui fait sensation; (marvellous) sensationnel(le)

sense [sɛns] n sens m; (feeling) sentiment m; (meaning) signification f, sens m; (wisdom) bon sens ▷ vt sentir, pressentir; **it makes ~** c'est logique; **senseless** adj insensé(e), stupide; (unconscious) sans connaissance; **sense of humour** (US **sense of humor**) n sens m de l'humour

sensible ['sɛnsɪbl] adj sensé(e), raisonnable; (shoes etc) pratique

> Be careful not to translate **sensible** by the French word **sensible**.

sensitive ['sɛnsɪtɪv] adj: **~ (to)** sensible (à)

sensual ['sɛnsjuəl] adj sensuel(le)

sensuous ['sɛnsjuəs] adj voluptueux(-euse), sensuel(le)

sent [sɛnt] pt, pp of **send**

sentence ['sɛntns] n (Ling) phrase f; (Law: judgment) condamnation f, sentence f; (: punishment) peine f ▷ vt: **to ~ sb to death/to 5 years** condamner qn à mort/à 5 ans

sentiment ['sɛntɪmənt] n sentiment m; (opinion) opinion f, avis m; **sentimental** [sɛntɪ'mɛntl] adj sentimental(e)

Sep. abbr (= September) septembre

separate adj ['sɛprɪt] séparé(e); (organization) indépendant(e); (day,

occasion, issue) différent(e) ▷ vb ['sɛpəreɪt] ▷ vt séparer; (distinguish) distinguer ▷ vi se séparer; **separately** adv séparément; **separates** npl (clothes) coordonnés mpl; **separation** [sɛpə'reɪʃən] n séparation f

September [sɛp'tɛmbə] n septembre m

septic ['sɛptɪk] adj (wound) infecté(e); **septic tank** n fosse f septique

sequel ['si:kwl] n conséquence f; séquelles fpl; (of story) suite f

sequence ['si:kwəns] n ordre m, suite f; (in film) séquence f; (dance) numéro m

sequin ['si:kwɪn] n paillette f

Serb [sə:b] adj, n = **Serbian**

Serbia ['sə:bɪə] n Serbie f

Serbian ['sə:bɪən] adj serbe ▷ n Serbe m/f; (Ling) serbe m

sergeant ['sɑ:dʒənt] n sergent m; (Police) brigadier m

serial ['sɪərɪəl] n feuilleton m; **serial killer** n meurtrier m tuant en série; **serial number** n numéro m de série

series ['sɪəriz] n série f; (Publishing) collection f

serious ['sɪərɪəs] adj sérieux(-euse); (accident etc) grave; **seriously** adv sérieusement; (hurt) gravement

sermon ['sə:mən] n sermon m

servant ['sə:vənt] n domestique m/f; (fig) serviteur/servante

serve [sə:v] vt (employer etc) servir, être au service de; (purpose) servir à; (customer, food, meal) servir; (subj: train) desservir; (apprenticeship) faire, accomplir; (prison term) faire; purger ▷ vi (Tennis) servir; (be useful): **to ~ as/for/to do** servir de/à/à faire; (Tennis) service m; **it ~s him right** c'est bien fait pour lui; **server** n (Comput) serveur m

service ['sə:vɪs] n (gen) service m; (Aut) révision f; (Rel) office m ▷ vt (car etc) réviser; **services** npl (Econ: tertiary sector) (secteur m) tertiaire m, secteur m des services; (BRIT: on motorway) station-service f; (Mil): **the**

S~s *npl* les forces armées; **to be of ~ to sb**, **to do sb a ~** rendre service à qn; **~ included/not included** service compris/non compris; **service area** *n* (*on motorway*) aire *f* de services; **service charge** *n* (BRIT) service *m*; **serviceman** (*irreg*) *n* militaire *m*; **service station** *n* station-service *f*

serviette [sɜː'viːet] *n* (BRIT) serviette *f* (de table)

session ['sɛʃən] *n* (*sitting*) séance *f*; **to be in ~** siéger, être en session or en séance

set [set] *n* série *f*, assortiment *m*; (*of tools etc*) jeu *m*; (*Radio, TV*) poste *m*; (*Tennis*) set *m*; (*group of people*) cercle *m*, milieu *m*; (*Cine*) plateau *m*; (*Theat: stage*) scène *f*; (: *scenery*) décor *m*; (*Math*) ensemble *m*; (*Hairdressing*) mise *f* en plis ▷ *adj* (*fixed*) fixe, déterminé(e); (*ready*) prêt(e) ▷ *vt* (*pt, pp* **~**) (*place*) mettre, poser, placer; (*fix, establish*) fixer; (: *record*) établir; (*assign: task, homework*) donner; (*exam*) composer; (*adjust*) régler; (*decide: rules etc*) fixer, choisir ▷ *vi* (*sun*) se coucher; (*jam, jelly, concrete*) prendre; (*bone*) se ressouder; **to be ~ on doing** être résolu(e) à faire; **to ~ to music** mettre en musique; **to ~ on fire** mettre le feu à; **to ~ free** libérer; **to ~ sth going** déclencher qch; **to ~ sail** partir, prendre la mer; **set aside** *vt* mettre de côté; (*time*) garder; **set down** *vt* (*subj: bus, train*) déposer; **set in** *vi* (*infection, bad weather*) s'installer; (*complications*) survenir, surgir; **set off** *vi* se mettre en route, partir ▷ *vt* (*bomb*) faire exploser; (*cause to start*) déclencher; (*show up well*) mettre en valeur, faire valoir; **set out** *vi*: **to ~ out (from)** partir (de) ▷ *vt* (*arrange*) disposer; (*state*) présenter, exposer; **to ~ out to do** entreprendre de faire; avoir pour but or intention de faire; **set up** *vt* (*organization*) fonder, créer; **setback** *n* (*hitch*) revers *m*, contretemps *m*; **set menu** *n* menu *m*

settee [sɛ'tiː] *n* canapé *m*

setting ['sɛtɪŋ] *n* cadre *m*; (*of jewel*) monture *f*; (*position: of controls*) réglage *m*

settle ['sɛtl] *vt* (*argument, matter, account*) régler; (*problem*) résoudre; (*Med: calm*) calmer ▷ *vi* (*bird, dust etc*) se poser; **to ~ for sth** accepter qch, se contenter de qch; **to ~ on sth** porter son choix or se décider pour qch; **settle down** *vi* (*get comfortable*) s'installer; (*become calmer*) se calmer; se ranger; (*live quietly*) se fixer; **settle in** *vi* s'installer; **settle up** *vi*: **to ~ up with sb** régler (ce que l'on doit à) qn; **settlement** *n* (*payment*) règlement *m*; (*agreement*) accord *m*; (*village etc*) village *m*, hameau *m*

setup ['sɛtʌp] *n* (*arrangement*) manière *f* dont les choses sont organisées; (*situation*) situation *f*, allure *f* des choses

seven ['sɛvn] *num* sept; **seventeen** *num* dix-sept; **seventeenth** [sɛvn'tiːnθ] *num* dix-septième; **seventh** *num* septième; **seventieth** ['sɛvntɪθ] *num* soixante-dixième; **seventy** *num* soixante-dix

sever ['sɛvə*] *vt* couper, trancher; (*relations*) rompre

several ['sɛvrəl] *adj, pron* plusieurs *pl*; **~ of us** plusieurs d'entre nous

severe [sɪ'vɪə*] *adj* (*stern*) sévère, strict(e); (*serious*) grave, sérieux(-euse); (*plain*) sévère, austère

sew (*pt* **~ed**, *pp* **~n**) [səu, səud, səun] *vt, vi* coudre

sewage ['suːɪdʒ] *n* vidange(s) *f(pl)*

sewer ['suːə*] *n* égout *m*

sewing ['səuɪŋ] *n* couture *f*; (*item(s)*) ouvrage *m*; **sewing machine** *n* machine *f* à coudre

sewn [səun] *pp* of **sew**

sex [sɛks] *n* sexe *m*; **to have ~ with** avoir des rapports (sexuels) avec; **sexism** ['sɛksɪzəm] *n* sexisme *m*; **sexist** *adj* sexiste; **sexual** ['sɛksjuəl] *adj* sexuel(le); **sexual intercourse** *n* rapports sexuels; **sexuality** [sɛksju'ælɪtɪ] *n* sexualité *f*; **sexy** *adj* sexy *inv*

shabby ['ʃæbɪ] *adj* miteux(-euse);

(behaviour) mesquin(e), méprisable

shack [ʃæk] n cabane f, hutte f

shade [ʃeɪd] n ombre f; (for lamp) abat-jour m inv; (of colour) nuance f, ton m; (us: window shade) store m; (small quantity): **a ~ of** un soupçon de ▷ vt abriter du soleil, ombrager; **shades** npl (us: sunglasses) lunettes fpl de soleil; **in the ~** à l'ombre; **a ~ smaller** un tout petit peu plus petit

shadow [ˈʃædəu] n ombre f ▷ vt (follow) filer; **shadow cabinet** n (BRIT Pol) cabinet parallèle formé par le parti qui n'est pas au pouvoir

shady [ˈʃeɪdɪ] adj ombragé(e); (fig: dishonest) louche, véreux(-euse)

shaft [ʃɑːft] n (of arrow, spear) hampe f; (Aut, Tech) arbre m; (of mine) puits m; (of lift) cage f; (of light) rayon m, trait m

shake [ʃeɪk] vb (pt **shook**, pp ~n) ▷ vt secouer; (bottle, cocktail) agiter; (house, confidence) ébranler ▷ vi trembler; **to ~ one's head** (in refusal etc) dire ou faire non de la tête; (in dismay) secouer la tête; **to ~ hands with sb** serrer la main à qn; **shake off** vt secouer; (pursuer) se débarrasser de; **shake up** vt secouer; **shaky** adj (hand, voice) tremblant(e); (building) branlant(e), peu solide

shall [ʃæl] aux vb: **I ~ go** j'irai; **~ I open the door?** j'ouvre la porte?; **I'll open the coffee, ~ I?** je vais chercher le café, d'accord?

shallow [ˈʃæləu] adj peu profond(e); (fig) superficiel(le), qui manque de profondeur

sham [ʃæm] n frime f

shambles [ˈʃæmblz] n confusion f, pagaïe f, fouillis m

shame [ʃeɪm] n honte f ▷ vt faire honte à; **it is a ~ (that/to do)** c'est dommage (que + sub/de faire); **what a ~!** quel dommage!; **shameful** adj honteux(-euse), scandaleux(-euse); **shameless** adj éhonté(e), effronté(e)

shampoo [ʃæmˈpuː] n shampooing m ▷ vt faire un shampooing à

shandy [ˈʃændɪ] n bière panachée

shan't [ʃɑːnt] = **shall not**

shape [ʃeɪp] n forme f ▷ vt façonner, modeler; (sb's ideas, character) former; (sb's life) déterminer ▷ vi (also: **~ up**: events) prendre tournure; (: person) faire des progrès, s'en sortir; **to take ~** prendre forme ou tournure

share [ʃɛə*] n part f; (Comm) action f ▷ vt partager; (have in common) avoir en commun; **to ~ out (among** or **between)** partager (entre); **shareholder** n (BRIT) actionnaire m/f

shark [ʃɑːk] n requin m

sharp [ʃɑːp] adj (razor, knife) tranchant(e), bien aiguisé(e); (point, voice) aigu(ë); (nose, chin) pointu(e); (outline, increase) net(te); (cold, pain) vif (vive); (taste) piquant(e), âcre; (Mus) dièse; (person: quick-witted) vif (vive), éveillé(e); (: unscrupulous) malhonnête ▷ n (Mus) dièse m ▷ adv: **at 2 o'clock ~** à 2 heures pile ou tapantes; **sharpen** vt aiguiser; (pencil) tailler; (fig) aviver; **sharpener** n (also: **pencil sharpener**) taille-crayon(s) m inv; **sharply** adv (turn, stop) brusquement; (stand out) nettement; (criticize, retort) sèchement, vertement

shatter [ˈʃætə*] vt briser; (fig: upset) bouleverser; (: ruin) briser, ruiner ▷ vi voler en éclats, se briser; **shattered** adj (overwhelmed, grief-stricken) bouleversé(e); (inf: exhausted) éreinté(e)

shave [ʃeɪv] vt raser ▷ vi se raser ▷ n: **to have a ~** se raser; **shaver** n (also: **electric shaver**) rasoir m électrique

shaving cream n crème f à raser

shaving foam n mousse f à raser

shavings [ˈʃeɪvɪŋz] npl (of wood etc) copeaux mpl

shawl [ʃɔːl] n châle m

she [ʃiː] pron elle

sheath [ʃiːθ] n gaine f, fourreau m, étui m; (contraceptive) préservatif m

shed [ʃed] n remise f, resserre f ▷ vt (pt, pp ~) (leaves, fur etc) perdre; (tears) verser, répandre; (workers) congédier

she'd [ʃiːd] = **she had**; **she would**

sheep [ʃiːp] n (pl inv) mouton m;
sheepdog n chien m de berger;
sheepskin n peau f de mouton

sheer [ʃɪəʳ] adj (utter) pur(e), pur et
simple; (steep) à pic, abrupt(e); (almost
transparent) extrêmement fin(e) ▷ adv à
pic, abruptement

sheet [ʃiːt] n (on bed) drap m; (of paper)
feuille f; (of glass, metal etc) feuille,
plaque f

sheik(h) [ʃeɪk] n cheik m

shelf (pl **shelves**) [ʃelf, ʃelvz] n étagère
f, rayon m

shell [ʃel] n (on beach) coquillage m; (of
egg, nut etc) coquille f; (explosive) obus
m; (of building) carcasse f ▷ vt (peas)
écosser; (Mil) bombarder (d'obus)

she'll [ʃiːl] = **she will; she shall**

shellfish [ʃelfɪʃ] n (pl inv: crab etc)
crustacé m; (: scallop etc) coquillage m
▷ npl (as food) fruits mpl de mer

shelter [ʃeltəʳ] n abri m, refuge m
▷ vt abriter, protéger; (give lodging to)
donner asile à ▷ vi s'abriter, se mettre
à l'abri; **sheltered** adj (life) retiré(e), à
l'abri des soucis; (spot) abrité(e)

shelves [ʃelvz] npl of **shelf**

shelving [ʃelvɪŋ] n (shelves)
rayonnage(s) m(pl)

shepherd [ʃepəd] n berger m ▷ vt
(guide) guider, escorter; **shepherd's pie**
n ≈ hachis m Parmentier

sheriff [ʃerɪf] (us) n shérif m

sherry [ʃerɪ] n xérès m, sherry m

she's [ʃiːz] = **she is; she has**

Shetland [ʃetlənd] n (also: **the ~s, the
~ Isles** or **Islands**) les îles fpl Shetland

shield [ʃiːld] n bouclier m; (protection)
écran m de protection ▷ vt: **to ~ (from)**
protéger (de or contre)

shift [ʃɪft] n (change) changement m;
(work period) période f de travail; (of
workers) équipe f, poste m ▷ vt déplacer,
changer de place; (remove) enlever ▷ vi
changer de place, bouger

shin [ʃɪn] n tibia m

shine [ʃaɪn] n éclat m, brillant m ▷ vb
(pt, pp **shone**) ▷ vi briller ▷ vt (torch): **to**

~ on braquer sur; (polish: pt, pp **~d**) faire
briller or reluire

shingles [ʃɪŋglz] n (Med) zona m

shiny [ʃaɪnɪ] adj brillant(e)

ship [ʃɪp] n bateau m; (large) navire
m ▷ vt transporter (par mer); (send)
expédier (par mer); **shipment** n
cargaison f; **shipping** n (ships)
navires mpl; (traffic) navigation f; (the
industry) industrie navale; (transport)
transport m; **shipwreck** n épave
f; (event) naufrage m ▷ vt: **to be
shipwrecked** faire naufrage; **shipyard**
n chantier naval

shirt [ʃəːt] n chemise f; (woman's)
chemisier m; **in ~ sleeves** en bras de
chemise

shit [ʃɪt] excl (inf!) merde (!)

shiver [ʃɪvəʳ] n frisson m ▷ vi frissonner

shock [ʃɔk] n choc m; (Elec) secousse
f, décharge f; (Med) commotion
f, choc m ▷ vt (scandalize) choquer,
scandaliser; (upset) bouleverser;
shocking adj (outrageous) choquant(e),
scandaleux(-euse); (awful)
épouvantable

shoe [ʃuː] n chaussure f, soulier m;
(also: **horse~**) fer m à cheval ▷ vt (pt,
pp **shod**) (horse) ferrer; **shoelace** n lacet
m (de soulier); **shoe polish** n cirage m;
shoeshop n magasin m de chaussures

shone [ʃɔn] pt, pp of **shine**

shook [ʃuk] pt of **shake**

shoot [ʃuːt] n (on branch, seedling)
pousse f ▷ vb (pt, pp **shot**) ▷ vt (game:
hunt) chasser; (: aim at) tirer; (: kill)
abattre; (person) blesser/tuer d'un
coup de fusil (or de revolver); (execute)
fusiller; (arrow) tirer; (gun) tirer un
coup de; (Cine) tourner ▷ vi (with gun,
bow): **to ~ (at)** tirer (sur); (Football)
shooter, tirer; **shoot down** vt (plane)
abattre; **shoot up** vi (fig: prices etc)
monter en flèche; **shooting** n (shots)
coups mpl de feu; (attack) fusillade f;
(murder) homicide m (à l'aide d'une arme
à feu); (Hunting) chasse f

shop [ʃɔp] n magasin m; (workshop)

atelier m ▷ vi (also: **go ~ping**) faire ses courses or ses achats; **shop assistant** n (BRIT) vendeur(-euse); **shopkeeper** n marchand(e), commerçant(e); **shoplifting** n vol m à l'étalage; **shopping** n (goods) achats mpl, provisions fpl; **shopping bag** n sac m (à provisions); **shopping centre** (US **shopping center**) n centre commercial; **shopping mall** n centre commercial; **shopping trolley** n (BRIT) Caddie® m; **shop window** n vitrine f

shore [ʃɔːʳ] n (of sea, lake) rivage m, rive f ▷ vt: **to ~ (up)** étayer; **on ~** à terre

short [ʃɔːt] adj (not long) court(e); (soon finished) adj court, bref (brève); (person, step) petit(e); (curt) brusque, sec (sèche); (insufficient) insuffisant(e) ▷ n (also: **~ film**) court métrage f; (Elec) court-circuit m; **to be ~ of sth** être à court de or manquer de qch; **in ~** bref; **~ of doing** à moins de faire; **everything ~ of** tout sauf; **it is ~ for** c'est l'abréviation or le diminutif de; **to cut ~** (speech, visit) abréger, écourter; **to fall ~ of** ne pas être à la hauteur de; **to run ~ of** arriver à court de, venir à manquer de; **to stop ~** s'arrêter net; **to stop ~ of** ne pas aller jusqu'à; **shortage** n manque m, pénurie f; **shortbread** n sablé m; **shortcoming** n défaut m; **short(crust) pastry** n (BRIT) pâte brisée; **shortcut** n raccourci m; **shorten** vt raccourcir; (text, visit) abréger; **shortfall** n déficit m; **shorthand** n (BRIT) sténo(graphie) f; **shortlist** n (BRIT: for job) liste f des candidats sélectionnés; **short-lived** adj de courte durée; **shortly** adv bientôt, sous peu; **shorts** npl: **(a pair of) shorts** un short; **short-sighted** adj (BRIT) myope; (fig) qui manque de clairvoyance; **short-sleeved** adj à manches courtes; **short story** n nouvelle f; **short-tempered** adj qui s'emporte facilement; **short-term** adj (effect) à court terme

shot [ʃɔt] pt, pp of **shoot** ▷ n coup m

(de feu); (try) coup, essai m; (injection) piqûre f; (Phot) photo f; **to be a good/ poor ~** (person) tirer bien/mal; **like a ~** comme une flèche; (very readily) sans hésiter; **shotgun** n fusil m de chasse

should [ʃud] aux vb: **I ~ go now** je devrais partir maintenant; **he ~ be there now** il devrait être arrivé maintenant; **I ~ go if I were you** si j'étais vous j'irais; **I ~ like to** j'aimerais bien, volontiers

shoulder [ˈʃəuldəʳ] n épaule f ▷ vt (fig) endosser, se charger de; **shoulder blade** n omoplate f

shouldn't [ˈʃudnt] = **should not**

shout [ʃaut] n cri m ▷ vt crier ▷ vi crier, pousser des cris

shove [ʃʌv] vt pousser; (inf: put): **to ~ sth in** fourrer or ficher qch dans ▷ n poussée f

shovel [ˈʃʌvl] n pelle f ▷ vt pelleter, enlever (or enfourner) à la pelle

show [ʃəu] n (of emotion) manifestation f, démonstration f; (semblance) semblant m, apparence f; (exhibition) exposition f, salon m; (Theat, Cine) spectacle m; (Cine) séance f ▷ vb (pt **~ed**, pp **~n**) ▷ vt montrer; (film) passer; (courage etc) faire preuve de, manifester; (exhibit) exposer ▷ vi se voir, être visible; **can you ~ me where it is, please?** pouvez-vous me montrer où c'est?; **to be on ~** être exposé(e); **it's just for ~** c'est juste pour l'effet; **show in** vt faire entrer; **show off** vi (pej) crâner ▷ vt (display) faire valoir; (pej) faire étalage de; **show out** vt reconduire à la porte; **show up** vi (stand out) ressortir; (inf: turn up) se montrer ▷ vt (unmask) démasquer, dénoncer; (flaw) faire ressortir; **show business** n le monde du spectacle

shower [ˈʃauəʳ] n (for washing) douche f; (rain) averse f; (of stones etc) pluie f, grêle f; (US: party) réunion organisée pour la remise de cadeaux ▷ vi prendre une douche, se doucher ▷ vt: **to ~ sb with** (gifts etc) combler qn de; **to have**

or **take a ~** prendre une douche, se
doucher; **shower cap** n bonnet m de
douche; **shower gel** n gel m douche

showing [ˈʃəʊɪŋ] n (of film) projection f

show jumping [-dʒʌmpɪŋ] n
concours m hippique

shown [ʃəʊn] pp of **show**

show: **show-off** n (inf: person)
crâneur(-euse), m'as-tu-vu(e);
showroom n magasin m or salle f
d'exposition

shrank [ʃræŋk] pt of **shrink**

shred [ʃrɛd] n (gen pl) lambeau m, petit
morceau; (fig: of truth, evidence) parcelle
f ⊳ vt mettre en lambeaux, déchirer;
(documents) détruire; (Culin: grate) râper;
(: lettuce etc) couper en lanières

shrewd [ʃruːd] adj astucieux(-euse),
perspicace; (business person) habile

shriek [ʃriːk] n cri perçant or aigu,
hurlement m ⊳ vt, vi hurler, crier

shrimp [ʃrɪmp] n crevette grise

shrine [ʃraɪn] n (place) lieu m de
pèlerinage

shrink (pt **shrank**, pp **shrunk**) [ʃrɪŋk,
ʃræŋk, ʃrʌŋk] vi rétrécir; (fig)
(also: ~ **away**) reculer ⊳ vt (wool) (faire)
rétrécir ⊳ n (inf: pej) psychanalyste m/f;
to ~ from (doing) sth reculer devant
(la perdée faire) qch

shrivel [ˈʃrɪvl] (also: ~ **up**) ratatiner,
flétrir ⊳ vi se ratatiner, se flétrir

shroud [ʃraʊd] n linceul m ⊳ vt: **~ed in
mystery** enveloppé(e) de mystère

Shrove Tuesday [ˈʃrəʊv-] n (le)
Mardi gras

shrub [ʃrʌb] n arbuste m

shrug [ʃrʌg] n haussement m d'épaules
⊳ vt, vi: **to ~ (one's shoulders)** hausser
les épaules; **shrug off** vt faire fi de

shrunk [ʃrʌŋk] pp of **shrink**

shudder [ˈʃʌdə*] n frisson m,
frémissement m ⊳ vi frissonner, frémir

shuffle [ˈʃʌfl] vt (cards) battre; **to ~
(one's feet)** traîner les pieds

shun [ʃʌn] vt éviter, fuir

shut (pt, pp ~) [ʃʌt] vt fermer ⊳ vi
(se) fermer; **shut down** vt fermer

définitivement ⊳ vi fermer
définitivement; **shut up** vi (inf: keep
quiet) se taire ⊳ vt (close) fermer;
(silence) faire taire; **shutter** n volet m;
(Phot) obturateur m

shuttle [ˈʃʌtl] n navette f; (also: ~
service) (service m de) navette f;
shuttlecock n volant m (de badminton)

shy [ʃaɪ] adj timide

siblings [ˈsɪblɪŋz] npl (formal) frères et
sœurs mpl (de mêmes parents)

Sicily [ˈsɪsɪlɪ] n Sicile f

sick [sɪk] adj (ill) malade; (BRIT:
vomiting): **to be ~** vomir; (humour)
noir(e), macabre; (team: Sport) équipe
f: (TV: channel) chaîne f ⊳ adj (door,
entrance) latéral(e) ⊳ vi: **to ~ with sb**
prendre le parti de qn, se ranger du
côté de qn; **by the ~ of** à côté de;
by ~ côte à côte; **to rock from ~ to ~**
se balancer; **to take ~s (with)** prendre
parti (pour); **sideboard** n buffet m;
sideboards (BRIT), **sideburns** npl
(whiskers) pattes fpl; **side effect** n
effet m secondaire; **sidelight** n (Aut)
veilleuse f; **sideline** n (Sport) (ligne f de)
touche f; (fig) activité f secondaire; **side
order** n garniture f; **side road** n petite
route, route transversale; **side street** n
rue transversale; **sidetrack** vt (fig) faire
dévier de son sujet; **sidewalk** n (US)
trottoir m; **sideways** adv de côté

siege [siːdʒ] n siège m

sieve [sɪv] n tamis m, passoire f ⊳ vt
tamiser, passer (au tamis)

sift [sɪft] vt passer au tamis or au crible;
(fig) passer au crible

---

sickening [ˈsɪknɪŋ] adj écœurant(e), révoltant(e),
répugnant(e); **sick leave** n congé m
de maladie; **sickly** adj maladif(-ive),
souffreteux(-euse); (causing nausea)
écœurant(e); **sickness** n maladie f;
(vomiting) vomissement(s) m(pl)

side [saɪd] n côté m; (of lake, road) bord
m; (of mountain) versant m; (fig: aspect)

sigh [saɪ] n soupir m ▷ vi soupirer, pousser un soupir

sight [saɪt] n (faculty) vue f; (spectacle) spectacle m; (on gun) mire f ▷ vt apercevoir; **in ~** visible; (fig) en vue; **out of ~** hors de vue; (fig) en vue; **~seeing** n tourisme m; **to go sightseeing** faire du tourisme

sign [saɪn] n (gen) signe m; (with hand etc) signe, geste m; (notice) panneau m, écriteau m; (also: **road ~**) panneau de signalisation ▷ vt signer; **where do I ~?** où dois-je signer?; **sign for** vt fus (item) signer le reçu pour; **sign in** vi signer le registre (en arrivant); **sign on** vi (BRIT: as unemployed) s'inscrire au chômage; (enrol) s'inscrire ▷ vt (employee) embaucher; **sign over** vt: **to ~ sth over to sb** céder qch par écrit à qn; **sign up** vi (Mil) s'engager; (for course) s'inscrire

signal ['sɪɡnl] n signal m ▷ vi (Aut) mettre son clignotant ▷ vt (person) faire signe à; (message) communiquer par signaux

signature ['sɪɡnətʃə*] n signature f

significance [sɪɡ'nɪfɪkəns] n signification f; importance f

significant [sɪɡ'nɪfɪkənt] adj significatif(-ive); (important) important(e), considérable

signify ['sɪɡnɪfaɪ] vt signifier

sign language n langage m par signes

signpost ['saɪnpəʊst] n poteau m indicateur

Sikh [siːk] adj, n Sikh m/f

silence ['saɪləns] n silence m ▷ vt faire taire, réduire au silence

silent ['saɪlənt] adj silencieux(-euse); (film) muet(te); **to keep** or **remain ~** garder le silence, ne rien dire

silhouette [sɪluːˈet] n silhouette f

silicon chip ['sɪlɪkən-] n puce f électronique

silk [sɪlk] n soie f ▷ cpd en soie

silly ['sɪlɪ] adj stupide, sot(te), bête

silver ['sɪlvə*] n argent m; (money) monnaie f (en pièces d'argent); (also: **~ware**) argenterie f ▷ adj (made of

silver) d'argent, en argent; (in colour) argenté(e); **silver-plated** adj plaqué(e) argent

similar ['sɪmɪlə*] adj: **~ (to)** semblable (à); **similarity** [sɪmɪˈlærɪtɪ] n ressemblance f, similarité f; **similarly** adv de la même façon, de même

simmer ['sɪmə*] vi cuire à feu doux, mijoter

simple ['sɪmpl] adj simple; **simplicity** [sɪm'plɪsɪtɪ] n simplicité f; **simplify** ['sɪmplɪfaɪ] vt simplifier; **simply** adv simplement; (without fuss) avec simplicité; (absolutely) absolument

simulate ['sɪmjʊleɪt] vt simuler, feindre

simultaneous [sɪməl'teɪnɪəs] adj simultané(e); **simultaneously** adv simultanément

sin [sɪn] n péché m ▷ vi pécher

since [sɪns] adv, prep depuis ▷ conj (time) depuis que; (because) puisque, étant donné que, comme; **~ then, ever ~** depuis ce moment-là

sincere [sɪn'sɪə*] adj sincère; **sincerely** adv sincèrement; **Yours sincerely** (at end of letter) veuillez agréer, Monsieur (or Madame) l'expression de mes sentiments distingués or les meilleurs

sing (pt **sang**, pp **sung**) [sɪŋ, sæŋ, sʌŋ] vt, vi chanter

Singapore [sɪŋə'pɔː*] n Singapour m

singer ['sɪŋə*] n chanteur(-euse)

singing ['sɪŋɪŋ] n (of person, bird) chant m

single ['sɪŋgl] adj seul(e), unique; (unmarried) célibataire; (not double) simple m (BRIT: also: **~ ticket**) aller m (simple); (record) 45 tours m; **singles** npl (Tennis) simple m; **every ~ day** chaque jour sans exception; **single out** vt choisir; (distinguish) distinguer; **single bed** n lit m d'une personne or à une place; **single file** n file unique, file indienne; **single-handed** adv tout(e) seul(e), sans (aucune) aide; **single-minded** adj résolu(e), tenace; **single parent** n parent unique (or célibataire); **single-parent family** famille monoparentale; **single room** n chambre f à un lit ou pour une personne

singular ['sɪŋɡjulə'] adj singulier(-ière); (odd) singulier, étrange; (outstanding) remarquable; (Ling) (au) singulier, du singulier ▷ n (Ling) singulier m

sinister ['sɪnɪstə'] adj sinistre

sink [sɪŋk] n évier m; (washbasin) lavabo m ▷ vb (pt **sank**, pp **sunk**) ▷ vt (ship) (faire) couler, faire sombrer; (foundations) creuser ▷ vi couler, sombrer; (ground etc) s'affaisser; **to ~ into sth** (chair) s'enfoncer dans qch; **sink in** vi (explanation) rentrer (inf), être compris

sinus ['saɪnəs] n (Anat) sinus m inv

sip [sɪp] n petite gorgée f ▷ vt boire à petites gorgées

sir [sə'] n monsieur m; **S~ John Smith** sir John Smith; **yes ~** oui Monsieur

siren ['saɪərn] n sirène f

sirloin ['sə:lɔɪn] n (also: ~ **steak**) aloyau m

sister ['sɪstə'] n sœur f; (nun) religieuse f, (bonne) sœur; (BRIT: nurse) infirmière f en chef; **sister-in-law** n belle-sœur f

sit (pt, pp **sat**) [sɪt, sæt] vi s'asseoir; (be sitting) être assis(e); (assembly) être en séance, siéger; (for painter) poser ▷ vt (exam) passer, se présenter à; **sit back** vi (in seat) bien s'installer, se carrer; **sit down** vi s'asseoir; **sit on** vt fus (jury, committee) faire partie de; **sit up** vi s'asseoir; (straight) se redresser; (not go to bed) rester debout, ne pas se coucher

sitcom ['sɪtkɔm] n abbr (TV: = situation comedy) sitcom f, comédie f de situation

site [saɪt] n emplacement m, site m; (also: **building ~**) chantier m ▷ vt placer

sitting ['sɪtɪŋ] n (of assembly etc) séance f; (in canteen) service m; **sitting room** n salon m

situated ['sɪtjueɪtɪd] adj situé(e)

situation ['sɪtju'eɪʃən] n situation f; **"~s vacant/wanted"** (BRIT) "offres/demandes d'emploi"

six [sɪks] num six; **sixteen** num seize; **sixteenth** [sɪks'ti:nθ] num seizième; **sixth** ['sɪksθ] num sixième; **sixth form** n (BRIT) ≈ classes f de première et de terminale; **sixth-form college** n lycée n'ayant que des classes de première et de terminale; **sixtieth** ['sɪkstɪɪθ] num soixantième; **sixty** num soixante

size [saɪz] n dimensions fpl; (of person) taille f; (of clothing) taille; (of shoes) pointure f; (of problem) ampleur f; (of glue) colle f; **sizeable** adj assez grand(e); (amount, problem, majority) assez important(e)

sizzle ['sɪzl] vi grésiller

skate [skeɪt] n patin m; (fish: pl inv) raie f ▷ vi patiner; **skateboard** n skateboard m, planche f à roulettes; **skateboarding** n skateboard m; **skater** n patineur(-euse); **skating** n patinage m; **skating rink** n patinoire f

skeleton ['skelɪtn] n squelette m; (outline) schéma m

skeptical ['skeptɪkl] (US) = **sceptical**

sketch [sketʃ] n (drawing) croquis m, esquisse f; (outline plan) aperçu m; (Theat) sketch m, saynète f ▷ vt esquisser, faire un croquis or une esquisse de; (plan etc) esquisser

skewer ['skju:ə'] n brochette f

ski [ski:] n ski m ▷ vi skier, faire du ski; **ski boot** n chaussure f de ski

skid [skɪd] n dérapage m ▷ vi déraper

ski: skier n skieur(-euse); **skiing** n ski m; **to go skiing** (aller) faire du ski

skilful (US **skillful**) ['skɪlful] adj habile, adroit(e)

ski lift n remonte-pente m inv

skill [skɪl] n (ability) habileté f, adresse f, talent m; (requiring training) compétences fpl; **skilled** adj habile, adroit(e); (worker) qualifié(e)

skim [skɪm] vt (soup) écumer; (glide over) raser, effleurer ▷ vi: **to ~ through** (fig) parcourir; **skimmed milk** (US **skim milk**) n lait écrémé

skin [skɪn] n peau f ▷ vt (fruit etc) éplucher; (animal) écorcher; **skinhead**

n skinhead *m*; **skinny** *adj* maigre, maigrichon(ne)

skip [skɪp] *n* petit bond or saut; (BRIT: *container*) benne *f* ▷ *vi* gambader, sautiller; (*with rope*) sauter à la corde ▷ *vt* (*pass over*) sauter

ski: ski pass *n* forfait-skieur(s) *m*; **ski pole** *n* bâton *m* de ski

skipper ['skɪpə'] *n* (Naut, Sport) capitaine *m*; (*in race*) skipper *m*

skipping rope ['skɪpɪŋ-] (us **skip rope**) *n* (BRIT) corde *f* à sauter

skirt [skə:t] *n* jupe *f* ▷ *vt* longer, contourner

skirting board ['skə:tɪŋ-] *n* (BRIT) plinthe *f*

ski slope *n* piste *f* de ski

ski suit *n* combinaison *f* de ski

skull [skʌl] *n* crâne *m*

skunk [skʌŋk] *n* mouffette *f*

sky [skaɪ] *n* ciel *m*; **skyscraper** *n* gratte-ciel *m inv*

slab [slæb] *n* (*of stone*) dalle *f*; (*of meat, cheese*) tranche épaisse

slack [slæk] *adj* (*loose*) lâche, desserré(e); (*slow*) stagnant(e); (*careless*) négligent(e), peu sérieux(-euse) or consciencieux(-euse); **slacks** *npl* pantalon *m*

slain [sleɪn] *pp of* **slay**

slam [slæm] *vt* (*door*) (faire) claquer; (*throw*) jeter violemment, flanquer; (*inf: criticize*) éreinter, démolir ▷ *vi* claquer

slander ['slɑ:ndə'] *n* calomnie *f*; (Law) diffamation *f*

slang [slæŋ] *n* argot *m*

slant [slɑ:nt] *n* inclinaison *f*; (*fig*) angle *m*, point *m* de vue

slap [slæp] *n* claque *f*, gifle *f*; (*on the back*) tape *f* ▷ *vt* donner une claque or une gifle (*or une tape*) à; **to ~ on** (*paint*) appliquer rapidement ▷ *adv* (*directly*) tout droit, en plein

slash [slæʃ] *vt* entailler, taillader; (*fig: prices*) casser

slate [sleɪt] *n* ardoise *f* ▷ *vt* (*fig: criticize*) éreinter, démolir

slaughter ['slɔ:tə'] *n* carnage *m*,

massacre *m*; (*of animals*) abattage *m* ▷ *vt* (*animal*) abattre; (*people*) massacrer; **slaughterhouse** *n* abattoir *m*

Slav [slɑ:v] *adj* slave

slave [sleɪv] *n* esclave *m/f* ▷ *vi* (*also*: **~ away**) trimer, travailler comme un forçat; **slavery** *n* esclavage *m*

slay (*pt* **slew**, *pp* **slain**) [sleɪ, slu:, sleɪn] *vt* (*literary*) tuer

sleazy ['sli:zɪ] *adj* miteux(-euse), minable

sled [slɛd] (US) = **sledge**

sledge [slɛdʒ] *n* luge *f*

sleek [sli:k] *adj* (*hair, fur*) brillant(e), luisant(e); (*car, boat*) aux lignes pures or élégantes

sleep [sli:p] *n* sommeil *m* ▷ *vi* (*pt, pp* **slept**) dormir; **to go to ~** s'endormir; **sleep in** *vi* (*oversleep*) se réveiller trop tard; (*on purpose*) faire la grasse matinée; **sleep together** *vi* (*have sex*) coucher ensemble; **sleeper** *n* (*person*) dormeur(-euse); (BRIT Rail: *on track*) traverse *f*; (: *train*) train-couchettes *m*; (: *berth*) couchette *f*; **sleeping bag** *n* sac *m* de couchage; **sleeping car** *n* wagon-lits *m*, voiture-lits *f*; **sleeping pill** *n* somnifère *m*; **sleepover** *n* nuit *f* chez un copain or une copine; **we're having a sleepover at Jo's** nous allons passer la nuit chez Jo; **sleepwalk** *vi* marcher en dormant; **sleepy** *adj* (*fig*) endormi(e)

sleet [sli:t] *n* neige fondue

sleeve [sli:v] *n* manche *f*; (*of record*) pochette *f*; **sleeveless** *adj* (*garment*) sans manches

sleigh [sleɪ] *n* traîneau *m*

slender ['slɛndə'] *adj* svelte, mince; (*fig*) faible, ténu(e)

slept [slɛpt] *pt, pp of* **sleep**

slew [slu:] *pt of* **slay**

slice [slaɪs] *n* (*round*) rondelle *f*; (*utensil*) spatule *f*; (*also*: **fish ~**) pelle *f* à poisson ▷ *vt* couper en tranches (*or en rondelles*)

slick [slɪk] *adj* (*skilful*) bien ficelé(e);

(*salesperson*) qui a du bagout ▷ n (*also*: **oil ~**) nappe f de pétrole, marée noire

slide [slaɪd] n (*in playground*) toboggan m; (*Phot*) diapositive f; (BRIT: *also*: **hair ~**) barrette f; (*in prices*) chute f, baisse f ▷ vb (*pt, pp* **slid**) ▷ vt (*hair*) glisser ▷ vi glisser; **sliding** (*door*) coulissant(e)

slight [slaɪt] adj (*slim*) mince, menu(e); (*frail*) frêle; (*trivial*) faible, insignifiant(e); (*small*) petit(e), léger(-ère) before n ▷ n offense f, affront m ▷ vt (*offend*) blesser, offenser; **not in the ~est** pas le moins du monde, pas du tout; **slightly** adv légèrement, un peu

slim [slɪm] adj mince ▷ vi maigrir; (*diet*) suivre un régime amaigrissant; **slimming** n amaigrissement m ▷ adj (*diet, pills*) amaigrissant(e), pour maigrir; (*food*) qui ne fait pas grossir

slimy ['slaɪmɪ] adj visqueux(-euse), gluant(e)

sling [slɪŋ] n (*Med*) écharpe f; (*for baby*) porte-bébé m; (*weapon*) fronde f, lance-pierre m ▷ vt (*pt, pp* **slung**) lancer, jeter

slip [slɪp] n faux pas; (*mistake*) erreur f, bévue f; (*underskirt*) combinaison f; (*of paper*) petite feuille, fiche f ▷ vt (*slide*) glisser ▷ vi (*slide*) glisser; (*move smoothly*) **to ~ into/out of** se glisser or se faufiler dans/hors de; (*decline*) baisser; **to ~ sth on/off** enfiler/enlever qch; **to give sb the ~** fausser compagnie à qn; **a ~ of the tongue** un lapsus; **slip up** vi faire une erreur, gaffer

slipped disc [slɪpt-] n déplacement m de vertèbre

slipper ['slɪpə'] n pantoufle f

slippery ['slɪpərɪ] adj glissant(e)

slip road n (BRIT: *to motorway*) bretelle f d'accès

slit [slɪt] n fente f; (*cut*) incision f ▷ vt (*pt, pp* **~**) fendre; couper, inciser

slog [slɒg] n (BRIT: *effort*) gros effort; (: *work*) tâche fastidieuse ▷ vi travailler très dur

slogan ['sləʊgən] n slogan m

slope [sləʊp] n pente f, côte f; (*side of mountain*) versant m; (*slant*) inclinaison f ▷ vi: **to ~ down** être or descendre en pente; **to ~ up** monter; **sloping** adj en pente, incliné(e); (*handwriting*) penché(e)

sloppy ['slɒpɪ] adj (*work*) peu soigné(e), bâclé(e); (*appearance*) négligé(e), débraillé(e)

slot [slɒt] n fente f ▷ vt: **to ~ sth into** encastrer or insérer qch dans; **slot machine** n (BRIT: *vending machine*) distributeur m (automatique), machine f à sous; (*for gambling*) appareil m or machine à sous

Slovakia [sləʊˈvækɪə] n Slovaquie f

Slovene [sləʊˈviːn] adj slovène ▷ n Slovène m/f; (*Ling*) slovène m

Slovenia [sləʊˈviːnɪə] n Slovénie f; **Slovenian** adj, n = **Slovene**

slow [sləʊ] adj lent(e); (*watch*): **to be ~** retarder ▷ adv lentement ▷ vt, vi ralentir; "**~**" (*road sign*) "ralentir"; **slow down** vi ralentir; **slowly** adv lentement; **slow motion** n: **in slow motion** au ralenti

slug [slʌg] n limace f; (*bullet*) balle f; **sluggish** adj (*person*) mou (molle), lent(e); (*stream, engine, trading*) lent(e)

slum [slʌm] n (*house*) taudis m; **slums** npl (*area*) quartiers mpl pauvres

slump [slʌmp] n baisse soudaine, effondrement m; (*Econ*) crise f ▷ vi s'effondrer, s'affaisser

slung [slʌŋ] pt, pp of **sling**

slur [slɜː'] n (*smear*): **~ (on)** atteinte f (à); insinuation f (contre) ▷ vt mal articuler

slush [slʌʃ] n neige fondue

sly [slaɪ] adj (*person*) rusé(e); (*smile, expression, remark*) sournois(e)

smack [smæk] n (*slap*) tape f; (*on face*) gifle f ▷ vt donner une tape à; (*on face*) gifler; (*on bottom*) donner la fessée à ▷ vi: **to ~ of** avoir des relents de, sentir

small [smɔːl] adj petit(e); **small ads** npl (BRIT) petites annonces; **small change** n petite or menue monnaie

smart [smɑːt] adj élégant(e), chic

inv; *(clever)* intelligent(e); *(quick)* vif (vive), prompt(e) ▷ vi faire mal, brûler; **smartcard** *n* carte f à puce

smash [smæʃ] *n (also: ~-up)* collision *f*, accident *m*; *(Mus)* succès foudroyant ▷ vt casser, briser, fracasser; *(opponent)* écraser; *(Sport: record)* pulvériser ▷ vi se briser, se fracasser; s'écraser; **smashing** *adj (inf)* formidable

smear [smɪə^r] *n (stain)* tache *f*; *(mark)* trace *f*; *(Med)* frottis *m* ▷ vt enduire; *(make dirty)* salir; **smear test** *n* (BRIT Med) frottis *m*

smell [smɛl] *n* odeur *f*; *(sense)* odorat *m* ▷ vb (pt, pp **smelt** or **~ed**) ▷ vt sentir ▷ vi *(pej)* sentir mauvais; **smelly** *adj* qui sent mauvais, malodorant(e)

smelt [smɛlt] *pt, pp* of **smell**

smile [smaɪl] *n* sourire *m* ▷ vi sourire

smirk [smə:k] *n* petit sourire suffisant or affecté

smog [smɒg] *n* brouillard mêlé de fumée

smoke [sməʊk] *n* fumée *f* ▷ vt, vi fumer; **do you mind if I ~?** ça ne vous dérange pas que je fume?; **smoke alarm** *n* détecteur *m* de fumée; **smoked** *adj (bacon, glass)* fumé(e); **smoker** *n (person)* fumeur(-euse); *(Rail)* wagon *m* fumeurs; **smoking** *n*: **"no smoking"** *(sign)* "défense de fumer"; **smoky** *adj* enfumé(e); *(taste)* fumé(e)

smooth [smu:ð] *adj* lisse; *(sauce)* onctueux(-euse); *(flavour, whisky)* moelleux(-euse); *(movement)* régulier(-ière), sans à-coups or heurts; *(flight)* sans secousses; *(pej: person)* doucereux(-euse), mielleux(-euse) ▷ vt *(also: ~ out)* lisser, défroisser; *(creases, difficulties)* faire disparaître

smother ['smʌðə^r] *vt* étouffer

SMS *n abbr (= short message service)* SMS *m*; **SMS message** *n* message *m* SMS

smudge [smʌdʒ] *n* tache *f*, bavure *f* ▷ vt salir, maculer

smug [smʌg] *adj* suffisant(e), content(e) de soi

smuggle ['smʌgl] *vt* passer en contrebande or en fraude; **smuggling** *n* contrebande *f*

snack [snæk] *n* casse-croûte *m inv*; **snack bar** *n* snack(-bar) *m*

snag [snæg] *n* inconvénient *m*, difficulté *f*

snail [sneɪl] *n* escargot *m*

snake [sneɪk] *n* serpent *m*

snap [snæp] *n (sound)* claquement *m*, bruit sec; *(photograph)* photo *f*, instantané *m* ▷ adj subit(e), fait(e) sans réfléchir ▷ vt faire claquer; *(break)* casser net ▷ vi se casser net or avec un bruit sec; *(speak sharply)* parler d'un ton brusque; **to ~ open/shut** s'ouvrir/se refermer brusquement; **snap up** *vt* sauter sur, saisir; **snapshot** *n* photo *f*, instantané *m*

snarl [snɑ:l] *vi* gronder

snatch [snætʃ] *n (small amount)* ▷ vt saisir *(d'un geste vif)*; *(steal)* voler; **to ~ some sleep** arriver à dormir un peu

sneak [sni:k] *(us: pt snuck)* *vi*: **to ~ in/out** entrer/sortir furtivement or à la dérobée ▷ n *(inf: pej: informer)* faux jeton; **to ~ up on sb** s'approcher de qn sans faire de bruit; **sneakers** *npl* tennis *mpl*, baskets *fpl*

sneer [snɪə^r] *vi* ricaner; **to ~ at sb/sth** se moquer de qn/qch avec mépris

sneeze [sni:z] *vi* éternuer

sniff [snɪf] *n* reniflement *m* ▷ vt renifler, flairer; *(glue, drug)* sniffer, respirer

snigger ['snɪgə^r] *vi* ricaner

snip [snɪp] *n (cut)* entaille *f*; *(BRIT: inf: bargain)* (bonne) occasion or affaire *f* ▷ vt couper

sniper ['snaɪpə^r] *n (marksman)* tireur embusqué

snob [snɒb] *n* snob *m/f*

snooker ['snu:kə^r] *n* sorte de jeu de billard

snoop [snu:p] *vi*: **to ~ about** fureter

snooze [snu:z] *n* petit somme ▷ vi faire un petit somme

snore [snɔ:^r] *vi* ronfler ▷ n

ronflement m

snorkel ['snɔːkl] n (of swimmer) tuba m

snort [snɔːt] n grognement m ▷ vi grogner; (horse) renâcler

snow [snəʊ] n neige f ▷ vi neiger; **snowball** n boule f de neige; **snowdrift** n congère f; **snowman** (irreg) n bonhomme m de neige; **snowplough** (US **snowplow**) n chasse-neige m inv; **snowstorm** n tempête f de neige

snub [snʌb] vt repousser, snober ▷ n rebuffade f

snug [snʌg] adj douillet(te), confortable; (person) bien au chaud

○ **KEYWORD**

so [səʊ] adv **1** (thus, likewise) ainsi, de cette façon; **if so** si oui; **so do or have I** moi aussi; **it's 5 o'clock - so it is!** il est 5 heures - en effet! or c'est vrai!; **I hope/think so** je l'espère/le crois; **so far** jusqu'ici, jusqu'à maintenant; (in past) jusque-là

2 (in comparisons etc: to such a degree) si, tellement; **so big (that)** si or tellement grand (que); **she's not so clever as her brother** elle n'est pas aussi intelligente que son frère

3: **so much** adj, adv tant (de); **I've got so much work** j'ai tant de travail; **I love you so much** je vous aime tant; **so many** tant (de)

4 (phrases): **10 or so** à peu près or environ 10; **so long!** (inf: goodbye) au revoir!, à un de ces jours!; **so (what?)** (inf) (bon) et alors?, et après?

▷ conj **1** (expressing purpose): **so as to do** pour faire, afin de faire; **so (that)** pour que or afin que + sub

2 (expressing result) donc, par conséquent; **so that** si bien que, de (telle) sorte que; **so that's the reason!** c'est donc (pour) ça!; **so you see, I could have gone** alors tu vois, j'aurais pu y aller

soak [səʊk] vt faire or laisser tremper;

(drench) tremper ▷ vi tremper; **soak up** vt absorber; **soaking** adj (also: **soaking wet**) trempé(e)

so-and-so ['səʊənsəʊ] n (somebody) un(e) tel(le)

soap [səʊp] n savon m; **soap opera** n feuilleton télévisé (quotidienneté réaliste ou embellie); **soap powder** n lessive f, détergent m

soar [sɔːʳ] vi monter (en flèche), s'élancer; (building) s'élancer

sob [sɔb] n sanglot m ▷ vi sangloter

sober ['səʊbəʳ] adj qui n'est pas (or plus) ivre; (serious) sérieux(-euse), sensé(e); (colour, style) sobre, discret(-ète); **sober up** vi se dégriser

so-called ['səʊ'kɔːld] adj soi-disant inv

soccer ['sɔkəʳ] n football m

sociable ['səʊʃəbl] adj sociable

social ['səʊʃl] adj social(e); (sociable) sociable ▷ n (party) fête; **socialism** n socialisme m; **socialist** adj, n socialiste (m/f); **socialize** vi: **to socialize with** (meet often) fréquenter; (get to know) lier connaissance or parler avec; **social life** n vie sociale; **socially** adv socialement, en société; **social security** n aide sociale; **social services** npl services sociaux; **social work** n assistance sociale; **social worker** n assistant(e) sociale(e)

society [sə'saɪətɪ] n société f; (club) société, association f; (also: **high ~**) (haute) société, grand monde

sociology [səʊsɪ'ɔlədʒɪ] n sociologie f

sock [sɔk] n chaussette f

socket ['sɔkɪt] n cavité f; (Elec: also: **wall ~**) prise f de courant

soda ['səʊdə] n (Chem) soude f; (also: **~ water**) eau f de Seltz; (us: also: **~ pop**) soda m

sodium ['səʊdɪəm] n sodium m

sofa ['səʊfə] n sofa m, canapé m; **sofa bed** n canapé-lit m

soft [sɔft] adj (not rough) doux (douce); (not hard) doux, mou (molle); (not loud) doux, léger(-ère); (kind) doux, gentil(le); **soft drink** n boisson non alcoolisée;

soft drugs npl drogues douces; **soften** ['sɔfn] vt (r)amollir; (fig) adoucir ▷ vi se ramollir; (fig) s'adoucir; **softly** adv doucement; (touch) légèrement; (kiss) tendrement; **software** n (Comput) logiciel m, software m

soggy ['sɔgɪ] adj (clothes) trempé(e); (ground) détrempé(e)

soil [sɔɪl] n (earth) sol m, terre f ▷ vt salir; (fig) souiller

solar ['səulər] adj solaire; **solar power** n énergie f solaire; **solar system** n système m solaire

sold [səuld] pt, pp of **sell**

soldier ['səuldʒər] n soldat m, militaire m

sold out adj (Comm) épuisé(e)

sole [səul] n (of foot) plante f; (of shoe) semelle f; (fish: pl inv) sole f ▷ adj seul(e), unique; **solely** adv seulement, uniquement

solemn ['sɔləm] adj solennel(le); (person) sérieux(-euse), grave

solicitor [sə'lɪsɪtər] n (BRIT: for wills etc) ≈ notaire m; (in court) ≈ avocat m

solid ['sɔlɪd] adj (not liquid) solide; (not hollow: mass) compact(e); (: metal, rock, wood) massif(-ive) ▷ n solide m

solitary ['sɔlɪtərɪ] adj solitaire

solitude ['sɔlɪtjuːd] n solitude f

solo ['səuləu] n solo m ▷ adv (fly) en solitaire; **soloist** n soliste m/f

soluble ['sɔljubl] adj soluble

solution [sə'luːʃən] n solution f

solve [sɔlv] vt résoudre

solvent ['sɔlvənt] adj (Comm) solvable ▷ n (Chem) (dis)solvant m

sombre, (us **somber**) ['sɔmbər] adj sombre, morne

○ **KEYWORD**

some [sʌm] adj **1** (a certain amount or number of): **some tea/water/ice cream** du thé/de l'eau/de la glace; **some children/apples** des enfants/ pommes; **I've got some money but not much** j'ai de l'argent mais pas

beaucoup

2 (certain: in contrasts): **some people say that …** il y a des gens qui disent que …; **some films were excellent, but most were mediocre** certains films étaient excellents, mais la plupart étaient médiocres

3 (unspecified): **some woman was asking for you** il y avait une dame qui vous demandait; **he was asking for some book (or other)** il demandait un livre quelconque; **some day** un de ces jours; **some day next week** un jour la semaine prochaine

▷ pron **1** (a certain number) quelques-un(e)s, certain(e)s; **I've got some** (books etc) j'en ai (quelques-uns); **some (of them) have been sold** certains ont été vendus

2 (a certain amount) un peu; **I've got some** (money, milk) j'en ai (un peu); **would you like some?** est-ce que vous en voulez?, en voulez-vous?; **could I have some of that cheese?** pourrais-je avoir un peu de ce fromage?; **I've read some of the book** j'ai lu une partie du livre

▷ adv: **some 10 people** quelque 10 personnes, 10 personnes environ; **somebody** ['sʌmbədɪ] pron = **someone**; **somehow** adv d'une façon ou d'une autre; (for some reason) pour une raison ou une autre; **someone** pron quelqu'un; **someplace** adv (us) = **somewhere**; **something** pron quelque chose m; **something interesting** quelque chose d'intéressant; **something to do** quelque chose à faire; **sometime** adv (in future) un de ces jours, un jour ou l'autre; (in past) **sometime last month** au cours du mois dernier; **sometimes** adv quelquefois, parfois; **somewhat** adv quelque peu, un peu; **somewhere** adv quelque part; **somewhere else** ailleurs, autre part

son [sʌn] n fils m

song [sɒŋ] n chanson f; (of bird) chant m

son-in-law ['sʌnɪnlɔː] n gendre m, beau-fils m

soon [suːn] adv bientôt; (early) tôt; **~ afterwards** peu après; see also **as**; **sooner** adv (time) plus tôt; (preference): **I would sooner do that** j'aimerais autant or je préférerais faire ça; **sooner or later** tôt ou tard

soothe [suːð] vt calmer, apaiser

sophisticated [sə'fɪstɪkeɪtɪd] adj raffiné(e), sophistiqué(e); (machinery) hautement perfectionné(e), très complexe

sophomore ['sɒfəmɔːʳ] n (us) étudiant(e) de seconde année

soprano [sə'prɑːnəu] n (singer) soprano m/f

sorbet ['sɔːbeɪ] n sorbet m

sordid ['sɔːdɪd] adj sordide

sore [sɔːʳ] adj (painful) douloureux(-euse), sensible ⊳ n plaie f

sorrow ['sɒrəu] n peine f, chagrin m

sorry ['sɒrɪ] adj (regret) triste, déplorable; **~!** pardon!, excusez-moi!; (condition, excuse, tale) triste, déplorable; **~!** pardon!, excusez-moi!; **~?** pardon?; **to feel ~ for sb** plaindre qn

sort [sɔːt] n genre m, espèce f, sorte f; (make: of coffee, car etc) marque f ⊳ vt (also: **~ out**: select which to keep) trier; (classify) classer; (tidy) ranger; **sort out** vt (problem) résoudre, régler

SOS n SOS m

so-so ['səusəu] adv comme ci comme ça

sought [sɔːt] pt, pp of **seek**

soul [səul] n âme f

sound [saund] adj (healthy) en bonne santé, sain(e); (safe, not damaged) solide, en bon état; (reliable, not superficial) sérieux(-euse), solide; (sensible) sensé(e) ⊳ adv: **~ asleep** profondément endormi(e) ⊳ n (noise, volume) son m; (louder) bruit m; (Geo) détroit m, bras m de mer ⊳ vt (alarm) sonner ⊳ vi sonner, retentir; (fig: seem) sembler (être); **to ~ like** ressembler à; **sound bite** n phrase toute faite (pour

être citée dans les médias); **soundtrack** n (of film) bande f sonore

soup [suːp] n soupe f, potage m

sour ['sauəʳ] adj aigre; **it's ~ grapes** c'est du dépit

source [sɔːs] n source f

south [sauθ] n sud m ⊳ adj sud inv; (wind) du sud ⊳ adv au sud, vers le sud; **South Africa** n Afrique f du Sud; **South African** adj sud-africain(e) ⊳ n Sud-Africain(e); **South America** n Amérique f du Sud; **South American** adj sud-américain(e) ⊳ n Sud-Américain(e); **southbound** adj en direction du sud; (carriageway) sud inv; **south-east** n sud-est m; **southeastern** [sauθ'iːstən] adj du or au sud-est; **southern** ['sʌðən] adj (du) sud; méridional(e); **South Korea** n Corée f du Sud; **South of France** n: **the South of France** le Sud de la France, le Midi; **South Pole** n: **Pôle m Sud**; **southward(s)** adv vers le sud; **south-west** n sud-ouest m; **southwestern** [sauθ'westən] adj du or au sud-ouest

souvenir [suːvə'nɪəʳ] n souvenir m (objet)

sovereign ['sɔvrɪn] adj, n souverain(e)

sow¹ [səu] (pt **-ed**, pp **-n**) vt semer

sow² n [sau] truie f

soya ['sɔɪə] (us **soy** [sɔɪ]) n: **~ bean** graine f de soja; **~ sauce** sauce f au soja

spa [spɑː] n (town) station thermale; (us: also: **health ~**) établissement m de cure de rajeunissement

space [speɪs] n (gen) espace m; (room) place f; espace; (length of time) laps m de temps ⊳ cpd spatial(e) ⊳ vt (also: **~ out**) espacer; **spacecraft** n engin or vaisseau spatial; **spaceship** n = **spacecraft**

spacious ['speɪʃəs] adj spacieux(-euse), grand(e)

spade [speɪd] n (tool) bêche f, pelle f; (child's) pelle; **spades** npl (Cards) pique m

spaghetti [spə'getɪ] n spaghetti mpl

Spain [speɪn] n Espagne f

spam [spæm] n (Comput) spam m

span [spæn] n (of bird, plane) envergure f; (of arch) portée f; (in time) espace m de temps, durée f ▷ vt enjamber, franchir; (fig) couvrir, embrasser

Spaniard ['spænjəd] n Espagnol(e)

Spanish ['spænɪʃ] adj espagnol(e), d'Espagne ▷ n (Ling) espagnol m; **the Spanish** npl les Espagnols

spank [spæŋk] vt donner une fessée à

spanner ['spænə'] n (BRIT) clé f (de mécanicien)

spare [spɛə'] adj de réserve, de rechange; (surplus) de or en trop, de reste ▷ n (part) (pièce f de rechange, pièce détachée ▷ vt (do without) se passer de; (afford to give) accorder, passer; (not hurt) épargner; **to ~** (surplus) en surplus, de trop; **spare part** n pièce f de rechange, pièce détachée; **spare room** n chambre f d'ami; **spare time** n moments mpl de loisir; **spare tyre** (us **spare tire**) n (Aut) pneu m de rechange; **spare wheel** n (Aut) roue f de secours

spark [spɑːk] n étincelle f; **spark(ing) plug** n bougie f

sparkle ['spɑːkl] n scintillement m, étincellement m, éclat m ▷ vi étinceler, scintiller

sparkling ['spɑːklɪŋ] adj (wine) mousseux(-euse), pétillant(e); (water) pétillant(e), gazeux(-euse)

sparrow ['spærəu] n moineau m

sparse [spɑːs] adj clairsemé(e)

spasm ['spæzəm] n (Med) spasme m

spat [spæt] pt, pp of **spit**

spate [speɪt] n (fig): **~ of** avalanche for torrent m de

spatula ['spætjulə] n spatule f

speak (pt **spoke**, pp **spoken**) [spiːk, spəuk, 'spəukn] vt (language) parler; (truth) dire ▷ vi parler; (make a speech) prendre la parole; **to ~ to sb/of or about sth** parler à qn/de qch; **I don't ~ French** je ne parle pas français; **do you ~ English?** parlez-vous anglais?; **can I ~ to ...?** est-ce que je peux parler

à ...?; **speaker** n (in public) orateur m; (also: **loudspeaker**) haut-parleur m; (for stereo etc) baffle m, enceinte f; (Pol): **the Speaker** (BRIT) le président de la Chambre des communes or des représentants; (US) le président de la Chambre

spear [spɪə'] n lance f ▷ vt transpercer

special ['spɛʃl] adj spécial(e); **special delivery** n (Post): **by special delivery** en express; **special effects** npl (Cine) effets spéciaux; **specialist** n spécialiste m/f; **speciality** [spɛʃɪ'ælɪtɪ] n (BRIT) spécialité f; **specialize** vi: **to specialize (in)** se spécialiser (dans); **specially** adv spécialement, particulièrement; **special needs** npl (BRIT) difficultés fpl d'apprentissage scolaire; **special offer** n (Comm) réclame f; **special school** n (BRIT) établissement m d'enseignement spécialisé; **specialty** n (US) = **speciality**

species ['spiːʃiːz] n (pl inv) espèce f

specific [spə'sɪfɪk] adj (not vague) précis(e), explicite; (particular) particulier(-ière); **specifically** adv explicitement, précisément; (intend, ask, design) expressément, spécialement

specify ['spɛsɪfaɪ] vt spécifier, préciser

specimen ['spɛsɪmən] n spécimen m, échantillon m; (Med: of blood) prélèvement m; (: of urine) échantillon m

speck [spɛk] n petite tache, petit point; (particle) grain m

spectacle ['spɛktəkl] n spectacle m; **spectacles** npl (BRIT) lunettes fpl; **spectacular** [spɛk'tækjulə'] adj spectaculaire

spectator [spɛk'teɪtə'] n spectateur(-trice)

spectrum (pl **spectra**) ['spɛktrəm, -rə] n spectre m; (fig) gamme f

speculate ['spɛkjuleɪt] vi spéculer; (try to guess): **to ~** s'interroger sur

sped [spɛd] pt, pp of **speed**

speech [spiːtʃ] n (faculty) parole f; (talk) discours m, allocution f; (manner of speaking) façon f de parler, langage m;

(enunciation) élocution f; **speechless**
adj muet(te)

speed [spiːd] n vitesse f; (promptness)
rapidité f ▷ vi (pt, pp **sped**: Aut: exceed
speed limit) faire un excès de vitesse; **at
full** or **top** ~ à toute vitesse or allure;
speed up (pt, pp **~ed up**) vi aller plus
vite, accélérer ▷ vt accélérer;
speedboat n vedette f, hors-bord m
inv; **speeding** n (Aut) excès m de
vitesse; **speed limit** n limitation f de
vitesse, vitesse maximale permise;
speedometer [spɪˈdɔmɪtəʳ] n
compteur m (de vitesse); **speedy** adj
rapide, prompt(e)

spell [spɛl] n (also: **magic ~**) sortilège
m, charme m; (period of time) (courte)
période ▷ vt (pt, pp **spelt** or **~ed**) (in
writing) écrire, orthographier; (aloud)
épeler; (fig) signifier; **to cast a ~ on
sb** jeter un sort à qn; **he can't ~** il fait
des fautes d'orthographe; **spell out** vt
(explain): **to ~ sth out for sb** expliquer
qch clairement à qn; **spellchecker**
[ˈspɛltʃɛkəʳ] n (Comput) correcteur
m or vérificateur m orthographique;
spelling n orthographe f

spelt [spɛlt] pt, pp of **spell**

spend (pt, pp **spent**) [spɛnd, spɛnt] vt
(money) dépenser; (time, life) passer;
(devote) consacrer; **spending** n:
government spending les dépenses
publiques

spent [spɛnt] pt, pp of **spend** ▷ adj
(cartridge, bullets) vide

sperm [spəːm] n spermatozoïde m;
(semen) sperme m

sphere [sfɪəʳ] n sphère f; (fig) sphère,
domaine m

spice [spaɪs] n épice f ▷ vt épicer

spicy [ˈspaɪsɪ] adj épicé(e), relevé(e);
(fig) piquant(e)

spider [ˈspaɪdəʳ] n araignée f

spike [spaɪk] n pointe f; (Bot) épi m

spill (pt, pp **spilt** or **~ed**) [spɪl, -t, -d] vt
renverser; répandre ▷ vi se répandre;
spill over vi déborder

spin [spɪn] n (revolution of wheel) tour

m; (Aviat) (chute f en) vrille f; (trip in
car) petit tour, balade f; (on ball) effet m
▷ vb (pt, pp **spun**) ▷ vt (wool etc) filer;
(wheel) faire tourner ▷ vi (turn) tourner,
tournoyer

spinach [ˈspɪnɪtʃ] n épinards mpl

spinal [ˈspaɪnl] adj vertébral(e),
spinal(e)

spinal cord n moelle épinière

spin doctor n (inf) personne employée
pour présenter un parti politique sous un
jour favorable

spin-dryer [spɪnˈdraɪəʳ] n (BRIT)
essoreuse f

spine [spaɪn] n colonne vertébrale;
(thorn) épine f, piquant m

spiral [ˈspaɪərl] n spirale f ▷ vi (fig: prices
etc) monter en flèche

spire [ˈspaɪəʳ] n flèche f, aiguille f

spirit [ˈspɪrɪt] n (soul) esprit m, âme
f; (ghost) esprit, revenant m; (mood)
esprit, état m d'esprit; (courage)
courage m, énergie f; **spirits** npl (drink)
spiritueux mpl, alcool m; **in good ~s** de
bonne humeur

spiritual [ˈspɪrɪtjuəl] adj spirituel(le);
(religious) religieux(-euse)

spit [spɪt] n (for roasting) broche f;
(spittle) crachat m; (saliva) salive f ▷ vi
(pt, pp **spat**) cracher; (sound) crépiter;
(rain) crachiner

spite [spaɪt] n rancune f, dépit m ▷ vt
contrarier, vexer; **in ~ of** en dépit de,
malgré; **spiteful** adj malveillant(e),
rancunier(-ière)

splash [splæʃ] n (sound) plouf m; (of
colour) tache f ▷ vt éclabousser ▷ vi
(also: ~ **about**) barboter, patauger;
splash out vi (BRIT) faire une folie

splendid [ˈsplendɪd] adj splendide,
superbe, magnifique

splinter [ˈsplɪntəʳ] n (wood) écharde
f; (metal) éclat m ▷ vi (wood) se fendre;
(glass) se briser

split [splɪt] n fente f, déchirure f; (fig:
Pol) scission f ▷ vb (pt, pp **~**) ▷ vt fendre,
déchirer; (party) diviser; (work, profits)
partager, répartir ▷ vi (break) se fendre,

se briser; (divide) se diviser; **split up** vi
(couple) se séparer, rompre; (meeting)
se disperser

spoil (pt, pp **~ed** or **~t**) [spɔɪl, -d, -t] vt
(damage) abîmer; (mar) gâcher; (child)
gâter

spoilt [spɔɪlt] pt, pp of **spoil** ▷ adj (child)
gâté(e); (ballot paper) nul(le)

spoke [spəʊk] pt of **speak** ▷ n rayon m

spoken ['spəʊkn] pp of **speak**

spokesman ['spəʊksmən] (irreg) n
porte-parole m inv

spokesperson ['spəʊkspɜːsn] n
porte-parole m inv

spokeswoman ['spəʊkswʊmən]
(irreg) n porte-parole m inv

sponge [spʌndʒ] n éponge f; (Culin:
also: **~ cake**) ≈ biscuit m de Savoie
▷ vt éponger ▷ vi: **to ~ off** or **on** vivre
aux crochets de qn; **sponge bag** n (BRIT)
trousse f de toilette

sponsor ['spɒnsə'] n (Radio, TV, Sport)
sponsor m; (for application) parrain m,
marraine f; (for fund-raising event)
donateur(-trice) ▷ vt sponsoriser,
parrainer, faire un don à; **sponsorship**
n sponsoring m, parrainage m; dons mpl

spontaneous [spɒn'teɪnɪəs] adj
spontané(e)

spooky ['spuːkɪ] adj (inf) qui donne la
chair de poule

spoon [spuːn] n cuiller f; **spoonful** n
cuillerée f

sport [spɔːt] n sport m; (person) chic
type m/chic fille f ▷ vt (wear) arborer;
sport jacket n (US) = **sports jacket**;
sports car n voiture f de sport;
sports centre n (BRIT) centre sportif;
sports jacket n (BRIT) veste f de sport;
sportsman (irreg) n sportif m; **sports
utility vehicle** n véhicule m de loisirs
(de type SUV); **sportswear** n vêtements
mpl de sport; **sportswoman** (irreg) n
sportive f; **sporty** adj sportif(-ive)

spot [spɒt] n tache f; (dot: on pattern)
pois m; (pimple) bouton m; (place)
endroit m, coin m; (small amount): **a ~
of** un peu de ▷ vt (notice) apercevoir,

repérer; **on the ~** sur place, sur les lieux;
(immediately) sur le champ; **spotless** adj
immaculé(e); **spotlight** n projecteur
m; (Aut) phare m auxiliaire

spouse [spaʊz] n époux (épouse)

sprain [spreɪn] n entorse f, foulure
f ▷ vt: **to ~ one's ankle** se fouler or se
tordre la cheville

sprang [spræŋ] pt of **spring**

sprawl [sprɔːl] vi s'étaler

spray [spreɪ] n jet m (en fines
gouttelettes); (from sea) embruns
mpl; (aerosol) vaporisateur m, bombe
f; (for garden) pulvérisateur m; (of
flowers) petit bouquet ▷ vt vaporiser,
pulvériser; (crops) traiter

spread [spred] n (distribution)
répartition f; (Culin) pâte f à tartiner;
(inf: meal) festin m ▷ vb (pt, pp **~**) ▷ vt
(paste, contents) étendre, étaler; (rumour,
disease) répandre, propager; (wealth)
répartir ▷ vi (disease) s'étendre; se
propager; (stain) s'étaler; **spread out**
vi (people) se disperser; **spreadsheet** n
(Comput) tableur m

spree [spriː] n: **to go on a ~** faire la fête

spring [sprɪŋ] n (season) printemps
m; (leap) bond m, saut m; (coiled metal)
ressort m; (of water) source f ▷ vb (pt
sprang, pp **sprung**) ▷ vi bondir, sauter;
spring up vi (problem) se présenter,
surgir; (plant, buildings) surgir de terre;
spring onion n (BRIT) ciboule f, cive f

sprinkle ['sprɪŋkl] vt: **to ~ water** etc
on, **~ with water** etc asperger d'eau
etc; **to ~ sugar** etc **on**, **~ with sugar** etc
saupoudrer de sucre etc

sprint [sprɪnt] n sprint m ▷ vi courir à
toute vitesse; (Sport) sprinter

sprung [sprʌŋ] pp of **spring**

spun [spʌn] pt, pp of **spin**

spur [spɜː'] n éperon m; (fig) aiguillon
m ▷ vt (also: **~ on**) éperonner,
aiguillonner; **on the ~ of the moment**
sous l'impulsion du moment

spurt [spɜːt] n jet m; (of blood)
jaillissement m; (of energy) regain m,
sursaut m ▷ vi jaillir, gicler

spy [spaɪ] n espion(ne) ▷ vi: **to ~ on**
espionner, épier ▷ vt (see) apercevoir

sq. abbr = **square**

squabble ['skwɔbl] vi se chamailler

squad [skwɔd] n (Mil, Police) escouade f,
groupe m; (Football) contingent m

squadron ['skwɔdrn] n (Mil) escadron
m; (Aviat, Naut) escadrille f

squander ['skwɔndə'] vt gaspiller,
dilapider

square [skwεə'] n carré m; (in town)
place f ▷ adj carré(e) ▷ vt (arrange)
régler; arranger; (Math) élever au carré;
(reconcile) concilier; **all ~** quitte; à
égalité; **a ~ meal** un repas convenable;
2 metres ~ (de) 2 mètres sur 2; **1 ~
metre** 1 mètre carré; **square root** n
racine carrée

squash [skwɔʃ] n (BRIT: drink): **lemon/
orange ~** citronnade f/orangeade f;
(Sport) squash m; (us: vegetable) courge
f ▷ vt écraser

squat [skwɔt] adj petit(e) et épais(se),
ramassé(e) ▷ vi (also: **~ down**)
s'accroupir; **squatter** n squatter m

squeak [skwi:k] vi (hinge, wheel)
grincer; (mouse) pousser un petit cri

squeal [skwi:l] vi pousser un or des
cri(s) aigu(s) or perçant(s); (brakes)
grincer

squeeze [skwi:z] n pression f ▷ vt
presser; (hand, arm) serrer

squid [skwɪd] n calmar m

squint [skwɪnt] vi loucher

squirm [skwə:m] vi se tortiller

squirrel ['skwɪrəl] n écureuil m

squirt [skwə:t] vi jaillir, gicler ▷ vt
faire gicler

Sr abbr = **senior**

Sri Lanka [srɪ'læŋkə] n Sri Lanka m

St abbr = **saint**; **street**

stab [stæb] n (with knife etc) coup m (de
couteau etc); (of pain) lancée f; (inf: try):
to have a ~ at (doing) sth s'essayer à
(faire) qch ▷ vt poignarder

stability [stə'bɪlɪtɪ] n stabilité f

stable ['steɪbl] n écurie f ▷ adj stable

stack [stæk] n tas m, pile f ▷ vt empiler,
entasser

stadium ['steɪdɪəm] n stade m

staff [stɑ:f] n (work force) personnel m;
(BRIT Scol: also: **teaching ~**) professeurs
mpl, enseignants mpl, personnel
enseignant ▷ vt pourvoir en personnel

stag [stæg] n cerf m

stage [steɪdʒ] n scène f; (platform)
estrade f; (point) étape f, stade m;
(profession): **the ~** le théâtre ▷ vt
(play) monter, mettre en scène;
(demonstration) organiser; **in ~s** par
étapes, par degrés

> Be careful not to translate **stage** by
> the French word **stage**.

stagger ['stægə'] vi chanceler,
tituber ▷ vt (person: amaze)
stupéfier; (hours, holidays) étaler,
échelonner; **staggering** adj (amazing)
stupéfiant(e), renversant(e)

stagnant ['stægnənt] adj stagnant(e)

stag night, stag party n
enterrement m de vie de garçon

stain [steɪn] n tache f; (colouring)
colorant m ▷ vt tacher; (wood) teindre;
stained glass n (decorative) verre
coloré; (in church) vitraux mpl; **stainless
steel** n inox m, acier m inoxydable

staircase ['stεəkeɪs] n = **stairway**

stairs [stεəz] npl escalier m

stairway ['stεəweɪ] n escalier m

stake [steɪk] n pieu m, poteau m;
(Comm: interest) intérêts mpl; (Betting)
enjeu m ▷ vt risquer, jouer; (also: **~ out:**
area) marquer, délimiter; **to be at ~**
être en jeu

stale [steɪl] adj (bread) rassis(e); (food)
pas frais (fraîche); (beer) éventé(e);
(smell) de renfermé; (air) confiné(e)

stalk [stɔ:k] n tige f ▷ vt traquer

stall [stɔ:l] n (BRIT: in street, market etc)
éventaire m, étal m; (in stable) stalle
f ▷ vt (Aut) caler; (fig: delay) retarder
▷ vi (Aut) caler; (fig) essayer de gagner
du temps; **stalls** npl (BRIT: in cinema,
theatre) orchestre m

stamina ['stæmɪnə] n vigueur f,
endurance f

stammer ['stæmə'] n bégaiement m
▷ vi bégayer

stamp [stæmp] n timbre m; (also:
rubber ~) tampon m; (mark, also fig)
empreinte f; (on document) cachet
m ▷ vi (also: **~ one's foot**) taper du
pied ▷ vt (letter) timbrer; (with rubber
stamp) tamponner; **stamp out** vt (fire)
piétiner; (crime) éradiquer; (opposition)
éliminer; **stamped addressed
envelope** n (BRIT) enveloppe f
affranchie pour la réponse

stampede [stæm'piːd] n ruée f; (of
cattle) débandade f

stance [stæns] n position f

stand [stænd] n (position) position f;
(for taxis) station f (de taxis); (Comm)
étalage m, stand m; (Sport: also: **~s**)
tribune f; (also: **music ~**) pupitre m
▷ vb (pt, pp **stood**) ▷ vi être or se tenir
(debout); (rise) se lever, se mettre
debout; (be placed) se trouver; (remain:
offer etc) rester valable ▷ vt (place)
mettre, poser; (tolerate, withstand)
supporter; (treat, invite) offrir, payer;
to make a ~ prendre position; **to ~
for parliament** (BRIT) se présenter
aux élections (comme candidat à la
députation); **I can't ~ him** je ne peux
pas le voir; **stand back** vi (move back)
reculer, s'écarter; **stand by** vi (be ready)
se tenir prêt(e) ▷ vt fus (opinion) s'en
tenir à; (person) ne pas abandonner,
soutenir; **stand down** vi (withdraw)
se retirer; **stand for** vt fus (signify)
représenter, signifier; (tolerate)
supporter, tolérer; **stand in for** vt fus
remplacer; **stand out** vi (be prominent)
ressortir; **stand up** vi (rise) se lever,
se mettre debout; **stand up for** vt fus
défendre; **stand up to** vt fus tenir tête
à, résister à

standard ['stændəd] n (norm) norme
f, étalon m; (level) niveau m (voulu);
(criterion) critère m; (flag) étendard m
▷ adj (size etc) ordinaire, normal(e);
(model, feature) standard inv; (practice)
courant(e); (text) de base; **standards**

npl (morals) morale f, principes mpl;
standard of living n niveau m de vie

stand-by ticket n (Aviat) billet m
stand-by

standing ['stændɪŋ] adj debout
inv; (permanent) permanent(e) ▷ n
réputation f, rang m, standing m; **of
many years'** ~ qui dure or existe depuis
longtemps; **standing order** n (BRIT:
at bank) virement m automatique,
prélèvement m bancaire

stand-point n point m de vue;
standstill n: **at a standstill** à l'arrêt;
(fig) au point mort; **to come to a
standstill** s'immobiliser, s'arrêter

stank [stæŋk] pt of **stink**

staple ['steɪpl] n (for papers) agrafe f
▷ adj (food, crop, industry etc) de base
principal(e) ▷ vt agrafer

star [stɑː'] n étoile f; (celebrity) vedette f
▷ vt (Cine) avoir pour vedette; **stars** npl:
the ~s (Astrology) l'horoscope m

starboard ['stɑːbəd] n tribord m

starch [stɑːtʃ] n amidon m; (in food)
fécule f

stardom ['stɑːdəm] n célébrité f

stare [steə'] n regard m fixe ▷ vi: **to ~ at**
regarder fixement

stark [stɑːk] adj (bleak) désolé(e),
morne ▷ adv: **~ naked** complètement
nu(e)

start [stɑːt] n commencement m,
début m; (of race) départ m; (sudden
movement) sursaut m; (advantage)
avance f, avantage m ▷ vt commencer;
(cause: fight) déclencher; (rumour)
donner naissance à; (fashion) lancer;
(found: business, newspaper) lancer, créer;
(engine) mettre en marche ▷ vi (begin)
commencer; (begin journey) partir, se
mettre en route; (jump) sursauter;
when does the film ~? à quelle heure
est-ce que le film commence?; **to ~
doing** or **to do sth** se mettre à faire qch;
start off vi commencer; (leave) partir;
start out vi (begin) commencer; (set
out) partir; **start up** vi commencer;
(car) démarrer ▷ vt (fight) déclencher;

(business) créer; *(car)* mettre en marche; **starter** *n (Aut)* démarreur *m*; *(Sport: official)* starter *m*; *(BRIT Culin)* entrée *f*; **starting point** *n* point *m* de départ

startle ['stɑːtl] *vt* faire sursauter; donner un choc à; **startling** *adj* surprenant(e), saisissant(e)

starvation [stɑːˈveɪʃən] *n* faim *f*, famine *f*

starve [stɑːv] *vi* mourir de faim ▷ *vt* laisser mourir de faim

state [steɪt] *n* état *m*; *(Pol)* État *m* ▷ *vt* *(declare)* déclarer, affirmer; *(specify)* indiquer, spécifier; **States** *npl*: **the S~s** les États-Unis; **to be in a ~** être dans tous ses états; **stately home** *n* manoir *m* ou château *m* *(ouvert au public)*; **statement** *n* déclaration *f*; *(Law)* déposition *f*; **state school** *n* école publique; **statesman** *(irreg)* *n* homme *m* d'État

static ['stætɪk] *n (Radio)* parasites *mpl*; *(also:* **~ electricity)** électricité *f* statique ▷ *adj* statique

station ['steɪʃən] *n* gare *f*; *(also:* **police ~)** poste *m* ou commissariat *m* (de police) ▷ *vt* placer, poster

stationary ['steɪʃnərɪ] *adj* à l'arrêt, immobile

stationer's (shop) *n (BRIT)* papeterie *f*

stationery ['steɪʃnərɪ] *n* papier *m* à lettres, petit matériel de bureau

station wagon *n (US)* break *m*

statistic [stəˈtɪstɪk] *n* statistique *f*; **statistics** *n (science)* statistique *f*

statue ['stætjuː] *n* statue *f*

stature ['stætʃə'] *n* stature *f*; *(fig)* envergure *f*

status ['steɪtəs] *n* position *f*, situation *f*; *(prestige)* prestige *m*; *(Admin: official position)* statut *m*; **status quo** *n* [-ˈkwəu] *n*: **the status quo** le statu quo

statutory ['stætjutrɪ] *adj* statutaire, prévu(e) par un article de loi

staunch [stɔːntʃ] *adj* sûr(e), loyal(e)

stay [steɪ] *n (period of time)* séjour *m* ▷ *vi* rester; *(reside)* loger; *(spend some time)*

séjourner; **to ~ put** ne pas bouger; **to ~ the night** passer la nuit; **stay away** *vi (from person, building)* ne pas s'approcher; *(from event)* ne pas venir; **stay behind** *vi* rester en arrière; **stay in** *vi (at home)* rester à la maison; **stay on** *vi* rester; **stay out** *vi (of house)* ne pas rentrer; *(strikers)* rester en grève; **stay up** *vi (at night)* ne pas se coucher

steadily ['stedɪlɪ] *adv (regularly)* progressivement; *(firmly)* fermement; *(walk)* d'un pas ferme; *(fixedly: look)* sans détourner les yeux

steady ['stedɪ] *adj* stable, solide, ferme; *(regular)* constant(e), régulier(-ière); *(person)* calme, pondéré(e) ▷ *vt* assurer, stabiliser; *(nerves)* calmer; **a ~ boyfriend** un petit ami

steak [steɪk] *n (meat)* bifteck *m*, steak *m*; *(fish, pork)* tranche *f*

steal *(pt* **stole***, pp* **stolen)** [stiːl, stəul, 'stəuln] *vt, vi* voler; *(move)* se faufiler, se déplacer furtivement; **my wallet has been stolen** on m'a volé mon portefeuille

steam [stiːm] *n* vapeur *f* ▷ *vt (Culin)* cuire à la vapeur ▷ *vi* fumer; **steam up** *vi (window)* se couvrir de buée; **to get ~ed up about sth** *(fig: inf)* s'exciter à propos de qch; **steamy** *adj* humide; *(window)* embué(e); *(sexy)* torride

steel [stiːl] *n* acier *m* ▷ *cpd* d'acier

steep [stiːp] *adj* raide, escarpé(e); *(price)* très élevé(e), excessif(-ive) ▷ *vt (faire)* tremper

steeple ['stiːpl] *n* clocher *m*

steer [stɪə'] *vt* diriger; *(boat)* gouverner; *(lead: person)* guider, conduire ▷ *vi* tenir le gouvernail; **steering** *n (Aut)* conduite *f*; **steering wheel** *n* volant *m*

stem [stem] *n (of plant)* tige *f*; *(of glass)* pied *m* ▷ *vt* contenir, endiguer; *(attack, spread of disease)* juguler

step [step] *n* pas *m*; *(stair)* marche *f*; *(action)* mesure *f*, disposition *f* ▷ *vi*: **to ~ forward/back** faire un pas en avant/arrière, avancer/reculer; **steps** *npl (BRIT)* = **stepladder**; **to be in/out of**

~ (with) (fig) aller dans le sens (de)/être déphasé(e) (par rapport à); **step down** vi (fig) se retirer, se désister; **step in** vi (fig) intervenir; **step up** vt (production, sales) augmenter; (campaign, efforts) intensifier; **stepbrother** n demi-frère m; **stepchild** (pl **-ren**) n beau-fils m, belle-fille f; **stepdaughter** n belle-fille f; **stepfather** n beau-père m; **stepladder** n (BRIT) escabeau m; **stepmother** n belle-mère f; **stepsister** n demi-sœur f; **stepson** n beau-fils m

stereo ['stɛrɪəʊ] n (sound) stéréo f; (hi-fi) chaîne f stéréo ▷ adj (also: **~phonic**) stéréo(phonique)

stereotype ['stɪərɪətaɪp] n stéréotype m ▷ vt stéréotyper

sterile ['stɛraɪl] adj stérile; **sterilize** ['stɛrɪlaɪz] vt stériliser

sterling ['stɜːlɪŋ] adj (silver) de bon aloi, fin(e) ▷ n (currency) livre f sterling inv (de Grande-Bretagne); **sterling area** n zone f sterling

stern [stɜːn] adj sévère ▷ n (Naut) arrière m, poupe f

steroid ['stɪərɔɪd] n stéroïde m

stew [stjuː] n ragoût m ▷ vt, vi cuire à la casserole

steward ['stjuːəd] n (Aviat, Naut, Rail) steward m; **stewardess** n hôtesse f

stick [stɪk] n bâton m; (for walking) canne f; (of chalk etc) morceau m ▷ vb (pt, pp **stuck**) vt (glue) coller; (thrust): **to ~ sth into** piquer ou planter ou enfoncer qch dans; (inf: put) mettre, fourrer; (: tolerate) supporter ▷ vi (adhere) tenir, coller; (remain) rester; (get jammed: door, lift) se bloquer; **stick out** vi dépasser, sortir; **stick up** vi dépasser, sortir; **stick up for** vt fus défendre; **sticker** n auto-collant m; **sticking plaster** n sparadrap m, pansement adhésif; **stick insect** n phasme m; **stick shift** n (US Aut) levier m de vitesses

sticky ['stɪkɪ] adj poisseux(-euse); (label) adhésif(-ive); (fig: situation) délicat(e)

stiff [stɪf] adj (gen) raide, rigide; (door, brush) dur(e); (difficult) difficile, ardu(e);

(cold) froid(e), distant(e); (strong, high) fort(e), élevé(e) ▷ adv: **to be bored/scared/frozen ~** s'ennuyer à mourir/être mort(e) de peur/froid

stifling ['staɪflɪŋ] adj (heat) suffocant(e)

stigma ['stɪɡmə] n stigmate m

stiletto [stɪ'lɛtəʊ] n (BRIT also: **~ heel**) talon m aiguille

still [stɪl] adj immobile ▷ adv (up to this time) encore, toujours; (even) encore; (nonetheless) quand même, tout de même

stimulate ['stɪmjʊleɪt] vt stimuler

stimulus (pl **stimuli**) ['stɪmjʊləs, 'stɪmjʊlaɪ] n stimulant m; (Biol, Psych) stimulus m

sting [stɪŋ] n piqûre f; (organ) dard m ▷ vt, vi (pt, pp **stung**) piquer

stink [stɪŋk] n puanteur f ▷ vi (pt **stank**, pp **stunk**) puer, empester

stir [stɜː] n agitation f, sensation f ▷ vt remuer ▷ vi remuer, bouger; **stir up** vt (trouble) fomenter, provoquer; **stir-fry** vt faire sauter ▷ n: **vegetable stir-fry** légumes sautés à la poêle

stitch [stɪtʃ] n (Sewing) point m; (Knitting) maille f; (Med) point de suture; (pain) point de côté ▷ vt coudre, piquer; (Med) suturer

stock [stɒk] n réserve f, provision f; (Comm) stock m; (Agr) cheptel m, bétail m; (Culin) bouillon m; (Finance) valeurs fpl, titres mpl; (descent, origin) souche f ▷ adj (fig: reply etc) classique ▷ vt (have in stock) avoir en stock, vendre; **in ~** en stock, en magasin; **out of ~** épuisé(e); **to take ~** (fig) faire le point; **~s and shares** valeurs (mobilières), titres; **stockbroker** ['stɒkbrəʊkə'] n agent m de change; **stock cube** n (BRIT Culin) bouillon-cube m; **stock exchange** n Bourse f (des valeurs); **stockholder** ['stɒkhəʊldə'] n (US) actionnaire m/f

stocking ['stɒkɪŋ] n bas m

stock market n Bourse f, marché financier

stole [stəʊl] pt of **steal** ▷ n étole f

stolen ['stəʊln] pp of **steal**

stomach ['stʌmək] n estomac m; (abdomen) ventre m ▷ vt supporter, digérer; **stomachache** n mal m à l'estomac ou au ventre

stone [stəun] n pierre f; (pebble) caillou m, galet m; (in fruit) noyau m; (Med) calcul m; (BRIT: weight) = 6.348 kg; 14 pounds ▷ cpd de or en pierre ▷ vt lancer des pierres sur, lapider; (fruit) dénoyauter

stood [stud] pt, pp of **stand**

stool [stu:l] n tabouret m

stoop [stu:p] vi (also: **have a ~**) être voûté(e); (also: **~ down**: bend) se baisser, se courber

stop [stɔp] n arrêt m; (in punctuation) point m ▷ vt arrêter; (break off) interrompre; (also: **put a ~ to**) mettre fin à; (prevent) empêcher ▷ vi s'arrêter; (rain, noise etc) cesser, s'arrêter; **to ~ doing sth** cesser or arrêter de faire qch; **to ~ sb (from) doing sth** empêcher qn de faire qch; **~ it!** arrête! **stop by** vi s'arrêter (au passage); **stop off** vi faire une courte halte; **stopover** n halte f; (Aviat) escale f; **stoppage** n (strike) arrêt m de travail; (obstruction) obstruction f

storage ['stɔ:rɪdʒ] n emmagasinage m

store [stɔ:ʳ] n (stock) provision f, réserve f; (depot) entrepôt m; (BRIT: large shop) grand magasin; (us: shop) magasin m ▷ vt emmagasiner; (information) enregistrer; **stores** npl (food) provisions; **who knows what is in ~ for us?** qui sait ce que l'avenir nous réserve or ce qui nous attend?; **storekeeper** n (us) commerçant(e)

storey (us **story**) ['stɔ:rɪ] n étage m

storm [stɔ:m] n tempête f; (thunderstorm) orage m ▷ vi (fig) fulminer ▷ vt prendre d'assaut; **stormy** adj orageux(-euse)

story ['stɔ:rɪ] n histoire f; (Press: article) article m; (us) = **storey**

stout [staut] adj (strong) solide; (fat) gros(se), corpulent(e) ▷ n bière brune

stove [stəuv] n (for cooking) fourneau m;

(: small) réchaud m; (for heating) poêle m

straight [streɪt] adj droit(e); (hair) raide; (frank) honnête, franc (franche); (simple) simple ▷ adv (drink) tout droit; (drink) sec, sans eau; **to put** or **get ~** mettre en ordre, mettre de l'ordre dans; (fig) mettre au clair; **~ away**, **~ off** (at once) tout de suite; **straighten** vt (also: **straighten out**) débrouiller; **straighten up** (stand up) se redresser; **straightforward** adj simple; (frank) honnête, direct(e)

strain [streɪn] n (Tech) tension f; pression f; (physical) effort m; (mental) tension (nerveuse); (Med) entorse f; (breed: of plants) variété f; (: of animals) race f ▷ vt (fig: resources etc) mettre à rude épreuve, grever; (hurt: back etc) se faire mal à; (vegetables) égoutter; **strains** npl (Mus) accords mpl, accents mpl; **strained** adj (muscle) froissé(e); (laugh etc) forcé(e); contraint(e); (relations) tendu(e); **strainer** n passoire f

strait [streɪt] n (Geo) détroit m; **straits** npl: **to be in dire ~s** (fig) avoir de sérieux ennuis

strand [strænd] n (of thread) fil m, brin m; (of rope) toron m; (of hair) mèche f ▷ vt (boat) échouer; **stranded** adj en rade, en plan

strange [streɪndʒ] adj (not known) inconnu(e); (odd) étrange, bizarre; **strangely** adv étrangement, bizarrement; see also **enough**; **stranger** n (unknown) inconnu(e); (from somewhere else) étranger(-ère)

strangle ['stræŋgl] vt étrangler

strap [stræp] n lanière f, courroie f, sangle f; (of slip, dress) bretelle f

strategic [strə'ti:dʒɪk] adj stratégique

strategy ['strætɪdʒɪ] n stratégie f

straw [strɔ:] n paille f; **that's the last ~!** ça c'est le comble!

strawberry ['strɔ:bərɪ] n fraise f

stray [streɪ] adj (animal) perdu(e), errant(e); (scattered) isolé(e) ▷ vi s'égarer; **~ bullet** balle perdue

streak [striːk] n bande f, filet m; (in hair) raie f ⊳ vt zébrer, strier

stream [striːm] n (brook) ruisseau m; (current) courant m, flot m; (of people) défilé m ininterrompu, flot ⊳ vt (Scol) répartir par niveau ⊳ vi ruisseler; **to ~ in/out** entrer/sortir à flots

street [striːt] n rue f; **streetcar** n (us) tramway m; **street light** n réverbère m; **street map, street plan** n plan m des rues

strength [streŋθ] n force f; (of girder, knot etc) solidité f; **strengthen** vt renforcer; (muscle) fortifier; (building, Econ) consolider

strenuous ['strenjuəs] adj vigoureux(-euse), énergique; (tiring) ardu(e), fatigant(e)

stress [stres] n (force, pressure) pression f; (mental strain) tension (nerveuse), stress m; (accent) accent m; (emphasis) insistance f ⊳ vt insister sur, souligner; (syllable) accentuer; **stressed** adj (tense) stressé(e); (syllable) accentué(e); **stressful** adj (job) stressant(e)

stretch [stretʃ] n (of sand etc) étendue f ⊳ vi s'étirer; (extend): **to ~ to or as far as** s'étendre jusqu'à ⊳ vt tendre, étirer; (fig) pousser (au maximum); **at a ~** d'affilée; **stretch out** vi s'étendre ⊳ vt (arm etc) allonger, tendre; (to spread) étendre

stretcher ['stretʃə'] n brancard m, civière f

strict [strikt] adj strict(e); **strictly** adv strictement

stride [straid] n grand pas, enjambée f ⊳ vi (pt **strode**, pp **stridden**) marcher à grands pas

strike [straik] n grève f; (of oil etc) découverte f; (attack) raid m ⊳ vb (pt, pp **struck**) ⊳ vt frapper; (oil etc) trouver, découvrir; (make: agreement, deal) conclure ⊳ vi faire grève; (attack) attaquer; (clock) sonner; **to go on or come out on ~** se mettre en grève, faire grève; **to ~ a match** frotter une allumette; **striker** n gréviste

m/f; (Sport) buteur m; **striking** adj frappant(e), saisissant(e); (attractive) éblouissant(e)

string [strɪŋ] n ficelle f, fil m; (row: of beads) rang m; (Mus) corde f ⊳ vt (pt, pp **strung**) ⊳ vt **to ~ out** échelonner; **to ~ together** enchaîner; **the strings** npl (Mus) les instruments mpl à cordes; **to pull ~s** (fig) faire jouer le piston

strip [strip] n bande f; (Sport) tenue f ⊳ vt (undress) déshabiller; (paint) décaper; (fig) dégarnir, dépouiller; (also: **~ down**: machine) démonter ⊳ vi se déshabiller; **strip off** vt (paint etc) décaper ⊳ vi (person) se déshabiller

stripe [straip] n raie f, rayure f; (Mil) galon m; **striped** adj rayé(e), à rayures

stripper ['stripə'] n strip-teaseuse f

strip-search ['stripsəːtʃ] vt: **to ~ sb** fouiller qn (en le faisant se déshabiller)

strive (pt **strove**, pp **~n**) [straiv, strəuv, strivn] vi: **to ~ to do/for sth** s'efforcer de faire/d'obtenir qch

strode [strəud] pt of **stride**

stroke [strəuk] n coup m; (Med) attaque f; (Swimming: style) (sorte f de) nage f ⊳ vt caresser; **at a ~** d'un (seul) coup

stroll [strəul] n petite promenade ⊳ vi flâner, se promener nonchalamment; **stroller** n (us: for child) poussette f

strong [strɔŋ] adj (gen) fort(e); (healthy) vigoureux(-euse); (heart, nerves) solide; **they are 50 ~** ils sont au nombre de 50; **stronghold** n forteresse f, fort m; (fig) bastion m; **strongly** adv fortement, avec force; vigoureusement; solidement

strove [strəuv] pt of **strive**

struck [strʌk] pt, pp of **strike**

structure ['strʌktʃə'] n structure f; (building) construction f

struggle ['strʌgl] n lutte f ⊳ vi lutter, se battre

strung [strʌŋ] pt, pp of **string**

stub [stʌb] n (of cigarette) bout m, mégot m; (of ticket etc) talon m ⊳ vt: **to ~ one's toe (on sth)** se heurter le doigt de pied (contre qch); **stub out** vt écraser

stubble ['stʌbl] n chaume m; (on chin) barbe f de plusieurs jours

stubborn ['stʌbən] adj têtu(e), obstiné(e), opiniâtre

stuck [stʌk] pt, pp of **stick** ▷ adj (jammed) bloqué(e), coincé(e)

stud [stʌd] n (on boots etc) clou m; (collar stud) bouton m de col; (earring) petite boucle d'oreille; (of horses: also: **~ farm**) écurie f, haras m; (also: **~ horse**) étalon m ▷ vt (fig): **~ded with** parsemé(e) or criblé(e) de

student ['stju:dənt] n étudiant(e) ▷ adj (life) estudiantin(e), étudiant(e), d'étudiant; (residence, restaurant) universitaire; (loan, movement) étudiant; **student driver** n (US) (conducteur-trice) débutant(e); **students' union** n (BRIT: association) ≈ union f des étudiants; (: building) ≈ foyer m des étudiants

studio ['stju:dɪəʊ] n studio m, atelier m; (TV etc) studio; **studio flat** (US **studio apartment**) n studio m

study ['stʌdɪ] n étude f; (room) bureau m ▷ vt étudier; (examine) examiner ▷ vi étudier, faire ses études

stuff [stʌf] n (gen) chose(s) f(pl), truc m; (belongings) affaires fpl, trucs; (substance) substance f ▷ vt rembourrer; (Culin) farcir; (inf: push) fourrer; **stuffing** n bourre f, rembourrage m; (Culin) farce f; **stuffy** adj (room) mal ventilé(e) or aéré(e); (ideas) vieux jeu inv

stumble ['stʌmbl] vi trébucher; **to ~ across** or **on** (fig) tomber sur

stump [stʌmp] n souche f; (of limb) moignon m ▷ vt: **to be ~ed** sécher, ne pas savoir que répondre

stun [stʌn] vt (blow) étourdir; (news) abasourdir, stupéfier

stung [stʌŋ] pt, pp of **sting**

stunk [stʌŋk] pp of **stink**

stunned [stʌnd] adj assommé(e); (fig) sidéré(e)

stunning ['stʌnɪŋ] adj (beautiful) étourdissant(e); (news etc)

stupéfiant(e)

stunt [stʌnt] n (in film) cascade f, acrobatie f; (publicity) truc m publicitaire ▷ vt retarder, arrêter

stupid ['stju:pɪd] adj stupide, bête; **stupidity** [stju:'pɪdɪtɪ] n stupidité f, bêtise f

sturdy ['stɜ:dɪ] adj (person, plant) robuste, vigoureux(-euse); (object) solide

stutter ['stʌtəʳ] n bégaiement m ▷ vi bégayer

style [staɪl] n style m; (distinction) allure f, cachet m, style; (design) modèle m; **stylish** adj élégant(e), chic inv; **stylist** n (hair stylist) coiffeur(-euse)

sub... [sʌb] prefix sub..., sous-; **subconscious** adj subconscient(e)

subdued [səb'dju:d] adj (light) tamisé(e); (person) qui a perdu son entrain

subject n ['sʌbdʒɪkt] sujet m; (Scol) matière f ▷ vt [səb'dʒɛkt]: **to ~ to** (law) être soumis(e) à; **subjective** [səb'dʒɛktɪv] adj subjectif(-ive); **subject matter** n (content) contenu m

subjunctive [səb'dʒʌŋktɪv] n subjonctif m

submarine [sʌbmə'ri:n] n sous-marin m

submission [səb'mɪʃən] n soumission f

submit [səb'mɪt] vt soumettre ▷ vi se soumettre

subordinate [sə'bɔ:dɪnət] adj (junior) subalterne; (Grammar) subordonné(e) ▷ n subordonné(e)

subscribe [səb'skraɪb] vi cotiser; **to ~ to** (opinion, fund) souscrire à; (newspaper) s'abonner à; être abonné(e) à

subscription [səb'skrɪpʃən] n (to magazine etc) abonnement m

subsequent ['sʌbsɪkwənt] adj ultérieur(e), suivant(e); **subsequently** adv par la suite

subside [səb'saɪd] vi (land) s'affaisser;

(flood) baisser; *(wind, feelings)* tomber

subsidiary [səb'sɪdɪərɪ] *adj* subsidiaire; accessoire; *(BRIT Scol: subject)* complémentaire ▷ *n* filiale *f*

subsidize ['sʌbsɪdaɪz] *vt* subventionner

subsidy ['sʌbsɪdɪ] *n* subvention *f*

substance ['sʌbstəns] *n* substance *f*

substantial [səb'stænʃl] *adj* substantiel(le); *(fig)* important(e)

substitute ['sʌbstɪtjuːt] *n (person)* remplaçant(e); *(thing)* succédané *m* ▷ *vt*: **to ~ sth/sb for** substituer qch/qn à, remplacer par qch/qn; **substitution** *n* substitution *f*

subtitles ['sʌbtaɪtlz] *npl (Cine)* sous-titres *mpl*

subtle ['sʌtl] *adj* subtil(e)

subtract [səb'trækt] *vt* soustraire, retrancher

suburb ['sʌbəːb] *n* faubourg *m*; **the ~s** la banlieue; **suburban** [sə'bəːbən] *adj* de banlieue, suburbain(e)

subway ['sʌbweɪ] *n (BRIT: underpass)* passage souterrain; *(US: railway)* métro *m*

succeed [sək'siːd] *vi* réussir ▷ *vt* succéder à; **to ~ in doing** réussir à faire

success [sək'ses] *n* succès *m*; réussite *f*; **successful** *adj (business)* prospère, qui réussit; *(attempt)* couronné(e) de succès; **to be successful (in doing)** réussir (à faire); **successfully** *adv* avec succès

succession [sək'seʃən] *n* succession *f*

successive [sək'sesɪv] *adj* successif(-ive)

successor [sək'sesə*] *n* successeur *m*

succumb [sə'kʌm] *vi* succomber

such [sʌtʃ] *adj* tel (telle); *(of that kind)*: **~ a book** un livre de ce genre or pareil, un tel livre; *(so much)*: **~ courage** un tel courage ▷ *adv* si; **~ a long trip** un si long voyage; **~ a lot of** tellement or tant de; **~ as** *(like)* tel (telle) que, comme; **as ~** *adv* en tant que tel (telle), à proprement parler; **such-and-such** *adj* tel ou tel (telle ou telle)

suck [sʌk] *vt* sucer; *(breast, bottle)* téter

Sudan [su'dɑːn] *n* Soudan *m*

sudden ['sʌdn] *adj* soudain(e), subit(e); **all of a ~** soudain, tout à coup; **suddenly** *adv* brusquement, tout à coup, soudain

sue [suː] *vt* poursuivre en justice, intenter un procès à

suede [sweɪd] *n* daim *m*, cuir suédé

suffer ['sʌfə*] *vt* souffrir, subir; *(bear)* tolérer, supporter, subir ▷ *vi* souffrir; **to ~ from** *(illness)* souffrir de, avoir; **suffering** *n* souffrance(s) *f(pl)*

suffice [sə'faɪs] *vi* suffire

sufficient [sə'fɪʃənt] *adj* suffisant(e)

suffocate ['sʌfəkeɪt] *vi* suffoquer, étouffer

sugar ['ʃugə*] *n* sucre *m* ▷ *vt* sucrer

suggest [sə'dʒest] *vt* suggérer, proposer; *(indicate)* sembler indiquer; **suggestion** [sə'dʒestʃən] *n* suggestion *f*

suicide ['suːɪsaɪd] *n* suicide *m*; **~ bombing** attentat *m* suicide; *see also* **commit**; **suicide bomber** *n* kamikaze *m/f*

suit [suːt] *n (man's)* costume *m*, complet *m*; *(woman's)* tailleur *m*, ensemble *m*; *(Cards)* couleur *f*; *(lawsuit)* procès *m* ▷ *vt (subj: clothes, hairstyle)* aller à; *(be convenient for)* convenir à; *(adapt)*: **to ~ sth to** adapter or approprier qch à; **well ~ed** *(couple)* faits l'un pour l'autre, très bien assortis; **suitable** *adj* qui convient; approprié(e), adéquat(e); **suitcase** *n* valise *f*

suite [swiːt] *n (of rooms, also Mus)* suite *f*; *(furniture)*: **bedroom/dining room ~** (ensemble *m* de) chambre *f* à coucher/ salle *f* à manger; **a three-piece ~** un salon (canapé et deux fauteuils)

sulfur ['sʌlfə*] *(US)* *n* = **sulphur**

sulk [sʌlk] *vi* bouder

sulphur *(US* **sulfur)** ['sʌlfə*] *n* soufre *m*

sultana [sʌl'tɑːnə] *n (fruit)* raisin (sec) de Smyrne

sum [sʌm] *n* somme *f*; *(Scol etc)* calcul *m*; **sum up** *vt* résumer ▷ *vi* résumer

summarize ['sʌməraɪz] vt résumer

summary ['sʌmərɪ] n résumé m

summer ['sʌmə'] n été m ▷ cpd d'été, estival(e); **in (the) ~** en été, pendant l'été; **summer holidays** npl grandes vacances; **summertime** n (season) été m

summit ['sʌmɪt] n sommet m; (also: **~ conference**) (conférence f au) sommet m

summon ['sʌmən] vt appeler, convoquer; **to ~ a witness** citer or assigner un témoin

Sun. abbr (= Sunday) dim

sun [sʌn] n soleil m; **sunbathe** vi prendre un bain de soleil; **sunbed** n lit pliant; (with sun lamp) lit à ultra-violets; **sunblock** n écran m total; **sunburn** n coup m de soleil; **sunburned**, **sunburnt** adj bronzé(e), hâlé(e); (painfully) brûlé(e) par le soleil

Sunday ['sʌndɪ] n dimanche m

sunflower ['sʌnflauə'] n tournesol m

sung [sʌŋ] pp of **sing**

sunglasses ['sʌnglɑːsɪz] npl lunettes fpl de soleil

sunk [sʌŋk] pp of **sink**

sun: **sunlight** n (lumière f du) soleil m; **sunlit** adj ensoleillé(e); **it is sunny** il fait (du) soleil, il y a du soleil; **sunrise** n lever m du soleil; **sun roof** n (Aut) toit ouvrant; **sunscreen** n crème f solaire; **sunset** n coucher m du soleil; **sunshade** n (over table) parasol m; **sunshine** n (lumière f du) soleil m; **sunstroke** n insolation f, coup m de soleil; **suntan** n bronzage m; **suntan lotion** n lotion f or lait m solaire; **suntan oil** n huile f solaire

super ['suːpə'] adj (inf) formidable

superb [suː'pəːb] adj superbe, magnifique

superficial [suːpə'fɪʃəl] adj superficiel(le)

superintendent [suːpərɪn'tɛndənt] n directeur(-trice); (Police) ≈ commissaire m

superior [su'pɪərɪə'] adj supérieur(e);

(smug) condescendant(e), méprisant(e) ▷ n supérieur(e)

superlative [suː'pəːlətɪv] n (Ling) superlatif m

supermarket ['suːpəmɑːkɪt] n supermarché m

supernatural [suːpə'nætʃərəl] adj surnaturel(le) ▷ n: **the ~** le surnaturel

superpower ['suːpəpauə'] n (Pol) superpuissance f

superstition [suːpə'stɪʃən] n superstition f

superstitious [suːpə'stɪʃəs] adj superstitieux(-euse)

superstore ['suːpəstɔː'] n (BRIT) hypermarché m, grande surface

supervise ['suːpəvaɪz] vt (children etc) surveiller; (organization, work) diriger; **supervision** [suːpə'vɪʒən] n surveillance f; (monitoring) contrôle m; (management) direction f; **supervisor** n surveillant(e); (in shop) chef m de rayon

supper ['sʌpə'] n dîner m; (late) souper m

supple ['sʌpl] adj souple

supplement n ['sʌplɪmənt] supplément m ▷ vt [sʌplɪ'mɛnt] ajouter à, compléter

supplier [sə'plaɪə'] n fournisseur m

supply [sə'plaɪ] vt (provide) fournir; (equip): **to ~ (with)** approvisionner or ravitailler (en); fournir (en) ▷ n provision f, réserve f; (supplying) approvisionnement m; **supplies** npl (food) vivres mpl; (Mil) subsistances fpl

support [sə'pɔːt] n (moral, financial etc) soutien m, appui m; (Tech) support m, soutien ▷ vt soutenir, supporter; (financially) subvenir aux besoins de; (uphold) être pour, être partisan de, appuyer; (Sport: team) être pour; **supporter** n (Pol etc) partisan(e); (Sport) supporter m

suppose [sə'pəuz] vt, vi supposer; imaginer; **to be ~d to do/be** être censé(e) faire/être; **supposedly** [sə'pəuzɪdlɪ] adv soi-disant; **supposing** conj si, à supposer que + sub

suppress [sə'pres] vt (revolt, feeling) réprimer; (information) faire disparaître; (scandal, yawn) étouffer

supreme [su'pri:m] adj suprême

surcharge ['sɜ:tʃɑ:dʒ] n surcharge f

sure [ʃuə'] adj (gen) sûr(e); (definite, convinced) sûr, certain(e); **~! (of course)** bien sûr!; **~ enough** effectivement; **to make ~ of sth/that** s'assurer de qch/que, vérifier qch/que; **surely** adv sûrement; certainement

surf [sɜ:f] n (waves) ressac m ▷ vt: **to ~ the Net** surfer sur Internet, surfer sur le net

surface ['sɜ:fis] n surface f ▷ vt (road) poser un revêtement sur ▷ vi remonter à la surface; (fig) faire surface ▷ cpd: **~ mail** par voie de terre; (by sea) par voie maritime

surfboard ['sɜ:fbɔ:d] n planche f de surf

surfer ['sɜ:fə'] n (in sea) surfeur(-euse); **web** or **net ~** internaute m/f

surfing ['sɜ:fɪŋ] n surf m

surge [sɜ:dʒ] n (of emotion) vague f ▷ vi déferler

surgeon ['sɜ:dʒən] n chirurgien m

surgery ['sɜ:dʒərɪ] n chirurgie f; (BRIT: room) cabinet m (de consultation); (also: **~ hours**) heures fpl de consultation

surname ['sɜ:neɪm] n nom m de famille

surpass [sɜ:'pɑ:s] vt surpasser, dépasser

surplus ['sɜ:pləs] n surplus m, excédent m ▷ adj en surplus, de trop; (Comm) excédentaire

surprise [sə'praɪz] n (gen) surprise f; (astonishment) étonnement m ▷ vt surprendre, étonner; **surprised** adj (look, smile) surpris(e), étonné(e); **to be surprised** être surpris; **surprising** adj surprenant(e), étonnant(e); **surprisingly** adv (easy, helpful) étonnamment, étrangement; **(somewhat) surprisingly, he agreed** curieusement, il a accepté

surrender [sə'rendə'] n reddition f,

capitulation f ▷ vi se rendre, capituler

surround [sə'raund] vt entourer; (Mil etc) encercler; **surrounding** adj environnant(e); **surroundings** npl environs mpl, alentours mpl

surveillance [sə'veɪləns] n surveillance f

survey n ['sɜ:veɪ] enquête f, étude f; (in house buying etc) inspection f, (rapport m d') expertise f; (of land) levé m ▷ vt [sɜ:'veɪ] (situation) passer en revue; (examine carefully) inspecter; (building) expertiser; (land) faire le levé de, (look at) embrasser du regard; **surveyor** n (of building) expert m; (of land) (arpenteur m) géomètre m

survival [sə'vaɪvl] n survie f

survive [sə'vaɪv] vi survivre; (custom etc) subsister ▷ vt (accident etc) survivre à, réchapper de; (person) survivre à; **survivor** n survivant(e)

suspect adj, n ['sʌspekt] suspect(e) ▷ vt [səs'pekt] soupçonner, suspecter

suspend [səs'pend] vt suspendre; **suspended sentence** n (Law) condamnation f avec sursis; **suspenders** npl (BRIT) jarretelles fpl; (us) bretelles fpl

suspense [səs'pens] n attente f, incertitude f; (in film etc) suspense m; **to keep sb in ~** tenir qn en suspens, laisser qn dans l'incertitude

suspension [səs'penʃən] n (gen, Aut) suspension f; (of driving licence) retrait m provisoire; **suspension bridge** n pont suspendu

suspicion [səs'pɪʃən] n soupçon(s) m(pl); **suspicious** adj (suspecting) soupçonneux(-euse), méfiant(e); (causing suspicion) suspect(e)

sustain [səs'teɪn] vt soutenir; (subj: food) nourrir, donner des forces à; (damage) subir; (injury) recevoir

SUV n abbr (esp us: = sports utility vehicle) SUV m, véhicule m de loisirs

swallow ['swɔləu] n (bird) hirondelle f ▷ vt avaler; (fig: story) gober

swam [swæm] *pt of* **swim**

swamp [swɒmp] *n* marais *m*,
marécage *m* ▷ *vt* submerger

swan [swɒn] *n* cygne *m*

swap [swɒp] *n* échange *m*, troc *m* ▷ *vt*:
to ~ (for) échanger (contre), troquer
(contre)

swarm [swɔːm] *n* essaim *m* (*of bees*)
essaimer; (*people*) grouiller; **to be ~ing
with** grouiller de

sway [sweɪ] *vi* se balancer, osciller ▷ *vt*
(*influence*) influencer

swear [sweəᵣ] (*pt* **swore**, *pp* **sworn**)
vt, vi jurer; **swear in** *vt* assermenter;
swearword *n* gros mot, juron *m*

sweat [swɛt] *n* sueur *f*, transpiration
f ▷ *vi* suer

sweater [ˈswɛtəᵣ] *n* tricot *m*, pull *m*

sweatshirt [ˈswɛtʃəːt] *n* sweat-shirt *m*

sweaty [ˈswɛtɪ] *adj* en sueur, moite or
mouillé(e) de sueur

Swede [swiːd] *n* Suédois(e)

swede [swiːd] *n* (BRIT) rutabaga *m*

Sweden [ˈswiːdn] *n* Suède *f*; **Swedish**
[ˈswiːdɪʃ] *adj* suédois(e) ▷ *n* (Ling)
suédois *m*

sweep [swiːp] *n* (*curve*) grande courbe;
(*also*: **chimney ~**) ramoneur *m* ▷ *vb* (*pt,
pp* **swept**) ▷ *vt* balayer; (*subj: current*)
emporter

sweet [swiːt] *n* (BRIT: *pudding*)
dessert *m*; (*candy*) bonbon *m* ▷ *adj*
doux (douce); (*not savoury*) sucré(e);
(*kind*) gentil(le); (*baby*) mignon(ne);
sweetcorn *n* maïs doux; **sweetener**
[ˈswiːtnəᵣ] *n* (Culin) édulcorant *m*;
sweetheart *n* amoureux(-euse);
sweetshop *n* (BRIT) confiserie *f*

swell [swɛl] *n* (*of sea*) houle *f* ▷ *adj* (US:
inf: excellent) chouette ▷ *vb* (*pt* **-ed**, *pp*
swollen or **-ed**) ▷ *vt* (*increase*) grossir,
augmenter ▷ *vi* (*increase*) grossir,
augmenter; (*sound*) s'enfler; (*Med: also*: **~
up**) enfler; **swelling** *n* (Med) enflure *f*;
(: *lump*) grosseur *f*

swept [swɛpt] *pt, pp of* **sweep**

swerve [swəːv] *vi* (*to avoid obstacle*)
faire une embardée or un écart; (*off the
road*) dévier

swift [swɪft] *n* (*bird*) martinet *m* ▷ *adj*
rapide, prompt(e)

swim [swɪm] *n*: **to go for a ~** aller nager
or se baigner ▷ *vb* (*pt* **swam**, *pp* **swum**)
▷ *vi* nager; (Sport) faire de la natation;
(*fig: head, room*) tourner ▷ *vt* traverser
(à la nage); **to ~ a length** nager une
longueur; **swimmer** *n* nageur(-euse);
swimming *n* nage *f*, natation *f*;
swimming costume *n* (BRIT) maillot *m*
(de bain); **swimming pool** *n* piscine *f*;
swimming trunks *npl* maillot *m* de
bain; **swimsuit** *n* maillot *m* (de bain)

swing [swɪŋ] *n* (*in playground*)
balançoire *f*; (*movement*) balancement
m, oscillations *fpl*; (*change in opinion etc*)
revirement *m* ▷ *vb* (*pt, pp* **swung**) ▷ *vt*
balancer, faire osciller; (*also*: **~ round**)
tourner, faire virer ▷ *vi* se balancer,
osciller; (*also*: **~ round**) virer, tourner;
to be in full ~ battre son plein

swipe card [swaɪp-] *n* carte *f*
magnétique

swirl [swəːl] *vi* tourbillonner, tournoyer

Swiss [swɪs] *adj* suisse ▷ *n* (*pl inv*)
Suisse(-esse)

switch [swɪtʃ] *n* (*for light, radio etc*)
bouton *m*; (*change*) changement *m*,
revirement *m* ▷ *vt* (*change*) changer;
switch off *vt* éteindre; (*engine,
machine*) arrêter; **could you ~ off
the light?** pouvez-vous éteindre
la lumière?; **switch on** *vt* allumer;
(*engine, machine*) mettre en marche;
switchboard *n* (Tel) standard *m*

Switzerland [ˈswɪtsələnd] *n* Suisse *f*

swivel [ˈswɪvl] *vi* (*also*: **~ round**)
pivoter, tourner

swollen [ˈswəulən] *pp of* **swell**

swoop [swuːp] *n* (*by police etc*) rafle
f, descente *f* ▷ *vi* (*also*: **~ down**)
descendre en piqué, piquer

swop [swɒp] *n, vt* = **swap**

sword [sɔːd] *n* épée *f*; **swordfish** *n*
espadon *m*

swore [swɔːᵣ] *pt of* **swear**

sworn [swɔːn] *pp of* **swear** ▷ *adj*

(*statement, evidence*) donné(e) sous
serment; (*enemy*) juré(e)
swum [swʌm] *pp* of **swim**
swung [swʌŋ] *pt, pp* of **swing**
syllable ['sɪləbl] *n* syllabe *f*
syllabus ['sɪləbəs] *n* programme *m*
symbol ['sɪmbl] *n* symbole *m*;
symbolic(al) [sɪm'bɒlɪk(l)] *adj*
symbolique
symmetrical [sɪ'metrɪkl] *adj*
symétrique
symmetry ['sɪmɪtrɪ] *n* symétrie *f*
sympathetic [sɪmpə'θetɪk] *adj*
(*showing pity*) compatissant(e);
(*understanding*) bienveillant(e),
compréhensif(-ive); **~ towards** bien
disposé(e) envers

> Be careful not to translate
> **sympathetic** by the French word
> **sympathique**.

sympathize ['sɪmpəθaɪz] *vi*: **to ~
with sb** plaindre qn; (*in grief*) s'associer
à la douleur de qn; **to ~ with sth**
comprendre qch
sympathy ['sɪmpəθɪ] *n* (*pity*)
compassion *f*
symphony ['sɪmfənɪ] *n* symphonie *f*
symptom ['sɪmptəm] *n* symptôme
m; indice *m*
synagogue ['sɪnəgɒg] *n* synagogue *f*
syndicate ['sɪndɪkɪt] *n* syndicat *m*,
coopérative *f*; (*Press*) agence *f* de presse
syndrome ['sɪndrəum] *n* syndrome *m*
synonym ['sɪnənɪm] *n* synonyme *m*
synthetic [sɪn'θetɪk] *adj* synthétique
Syria ['sɪrɪə] *n* Syrie *f*
syringe [sɪ'rɪndʒ] *n* seringue *f*
syrup ['sɪrəp] *n* sirop *m*; (*BRIT: also:*
golden ~) mélasse raffinée
system ['sɪstəm] *n* système *m*;
(*Anat*) organisme *m*; **systematic**
[sɪstə'mætɪk] *adj* systématique;
méthodique; **systems analyst** *n*
analyste-programmeur *m/f*

t

ta [tɑ:] *excl* (*BRIT inf*) merci!
tab [tæb] *n* (*label*) étiquette *f*; (*on drinks
can etc*) languette *f*; **to keep ~s on** (*fig*)
surveiller
table ['teɪbl] *n* table *f* ▷ *vt* (*BRIT: motion
etc*) présenter; **a ~ for 4, please** une
table pour 4, s'il vous plaît; **to lay** *or*
set the ~ mettre le couvert *or* la table;
tablecloth *n* nappe *f*; **table d'hôte**
[tɑ:bl'dəut] *adj* (*meal*) à prix fixe; **table
lamp** *n* lampe décorative *or* de table;
tablemat *n* (*for plate*) napperon *m*,
set *m*; (*for hot dish*) dessous-de-plat *m*
inv; **tablespoon** *n* cuiller *f* de service;
(*also:* **tablespoonful:** *as measurement*)
cuillerée *f* à soupe
tablet ['tæblɪt] *n* (*Med*) comprimé *m*; (*of
stone*) plaque *f*
table tennis *n* ping-pong *m*, tennis
m de table
tabloid ['tæblɔɪd] *n* (*newspaper*)
quotidien *m* populaire
taboo [tə'bu:] *adj, n* tabou (*m*)
tack [tæk] *n* (*nail*) petit clou *m*; (*fig*)

direction f ▷ vt (nail) clouer; (sew) bâtir ▷ vi (Naut) tirer un or des bord(s); **to ~ sth on to (the end of) sth** (of letter, book) rajouter qch à la fin de qch

tackle ['tækl] n matériel m, équipement m; (for lifting) appareil m de levage; (Football, Rugby) plaquage m ▷ vt (difficulty, animal, burglar) s'attaquer à; (person: challenge) s'expliquer avec; (Football, Rugby) plaquer

tacky ['tækɪ] adj collant(e); (paint) pas sec (sèche); (pej: poor-quality) minable; (: showing bad taste) ringard(e)

tact [tækt] n tact m; **tactful** adj plein(e) de tact

tactics ['tæktɪks] npl tactique f

tactless ['tæktlɪs] adj qui manque de tact

tadpole ['tædpəʊl] n têtard m

taffy ['tæfɪ] n (us) (bonbon m au) caramel m

tag [tæg] n étiquette f

tail [teɪl] n queue f; (of shirt) pan m ▷ vt (follow) suivre, filer; **tails** npl (suit) habit m; see also **head**

tailor ['teɪlə'] n tailleur m (artisan)

Taiwan ['taɪ'wɑːn] n Taïwan (no article); **Taiwanese** [taɪwɑː'niːz] adj taïwanais(e) ▷ n inv Taïwanais(e)

take [teɪk] vb (pt **took**, pp ~n) ▷ vt prendre; (gain: prize) remporter; (require: effort, courage) demander; (tolerate) accepter, supporter; (hold: passengers etc) contenir; (accompany) emmener, accompagner; (bring, carry) apporter, emporter; (exam) passer, se présenter à; **to ~ sth from** (drawer etc) prendre qch dans; (person) prendre qch à; **I ~ it that** je suppose que; **to ~ sb to a restaurant** emmener qn au restaurant; **take over** vt (business) reprendre ▷ vi: **to ~ over from sb** prendre la relève de qn; **take up** vt (one's story) reprendre; (dress) raccourcir; (occupy: time, space) prendre, occuper; (engage in: hobby etc) se mettre à; (accept: offer, challenge) accepter; **takeaway** (BRIT) adj (food) à emporter ▷ n (shop, restaurant) magasin m qui vend des plats à emporter; **taken** pp of **take**; **is this seat taken?** la place est prise?; **takeoff** n (Aviat) décollage m; **takeout** adj, n (us) = **takeaway**; **takeover** n (Comm) rachat m; **takings** npl (Comm) recette f

talc [tælk] n (also: **~um powder**) talc m

tale [teɪl] n (story) conte m, histoire f; (account) récit m; **to tell ~s** (fig) rapporter

talent ['tælnt] n talent m, don m; **talented** adj doué(e), plein(e) de talent

talk [tɔːk] n (a speech) causerie f, exposé m; (conversation) conversation f; (interview) entretien m; (gossip) racontars mpl (pej) ▷ vi parler; (chatter) bavarder; **talks** npl (Pol etc) entretiens mpl; **to ~ about** parler de; **to ~ sb out of/into doing** persuader qn de ne pas faire/de faire; **to ~ shop** parler métier or affaires; **talk over** vt discuter de; **talk show** n (TV, Radio) émission-débat f

(building) démolir; (letter etc) prendre, écrire; **take in** vt (deceive) tromper, rouler; (understand) comprendre, saisir; (include) couvrir, inclure; (dress, waistband) reprendre; **take off** vi (Aviat) décoller ▷ vt (remove) enlever; **take on** vt (work) accepter, se charger de; (employee) prendre, embaucher; (opponent) accepter de se battre contre; **take out** vt sortir; (remove) enlever; (invite) sortir avec; **to ~ sth out of** (out of drawer etc) prendre qch dans;

tall [tɔːl] adj (person) grand(e); (building, tree) haut(e); **to be 6 feet ~** ≈ mesurer 1 mètre 80

tambourine [tæmbə'riːn] n

tambourin m

tame [teɪm] *adj* apprivoisé(e); (fig: *story, style*) insipide

tamper ['tæmpə'] *vi*: **to ~ with** toucher à (*en cachette ou sans permission*)

tampon ['tæmpɒn] *n* tampon m hygiénique *ou* périodique

tan [tæn] *n* (*also*: **sun-**) bronzage m ▷ *vt, vi* bronzer, brunir ▷ *adj* (*colour*) marron clair *inv*

tandem ['tændəm] *n* tandem m

tangerine [tændʒə'riːn] *n* mandarine f

tangle ['tæŋgl] *n* enchevêtrement m; **to get in(to) a ~** s'emmêler

tank [tæŋk] *n* réservoir m; (*for fish*) aquarium m; (*Mil*) char m d'assaut, tank m

tanker ['tæŋkə'] *n* (*ship*) pétrolier m, tanker m; (*truck*) camion-citerne m

tanned [tænd] *adj* bronzé(e)

tantrum ['tæntrəm] *n* accès m de colère

Tanzania [tænzə'nɪə] *n* Tanzanie f

tap [tæp] *n* (*on sink etc*) robinet m; (*gentle blow*) petite tape f ▷ *vt* frapper *or* taper légèrement; (*resources*) exploiter, utiliser; (*telephone*) mettre sur écoute; **on ~** (*fig: resources*) disponible; **tap dancing** *n* claquettes *fpl*

tape [teɪp] *n* (*for tying*) ruban m; (*also*: **magnetic ~**) bande f (magnétique); (*cassette*) cassette f; (*sticky*) Scotch® m ▷ *vt* (*record*) enregistrer (au magnétoscope *ou* sur cassette); (*stick*) coller avec du Scotch®; **tape measure** *n* mètre m à ruban; **tape recorder** *n* magnétophone m

tapestry ['tæpɪstrɪ] *n* tapisserie f

tar [tɑː] *n* goudron m

target ['tɑːgɪt] *n* cible f; (*fig: objective*) objectif m

tariff ['tærɪf] *n* (*Comm*) tarif m; (*taxes*) tarif douanier

tarmac ['tɑːmæk] *n* (*BRIT: on road*) macadam m; (*Aviat*) aire f d'envol

tarpaulin [tɑː'pɔːlɪn] *n* bâche goudronnée

tarragon ['tærəgən] *n* estragon m

tart [tɑːt] *n* (*Culin*) tarte f; (*BRIT inf: pej*:

prostitute) poule f ▷ *adj* (*flavour*) âpre, aigrelet(te)

tartan ['tɑːtn] *n* tartan m ▷ *adj* écossais(e)

tartar(e) sauce *n* sauce f tartare

task [tɑːsk] *n* tâche f; **to take to ~** prendre à partie

taste [teɪst] *n* goût m; (*fig: glimpse, idea*) idée f, aperçu m ▷ *vt* goûter ▷ *vi*: **to ~ of** (*fish etc*) avoir le *ou* un goût de; **you can ~ the garlic (in it)** on sent bien l'ail; **to have a ~ of sth** goûter (à) qch; **can I have a ~?** je peux goûter?; **to be in good/bad** *or* **poor ~** être de bon/mauvais goût; **tasteful** *adj* de bon goût; **tasteless** *adj* (*food*) insipide; (*remark*) de mauvais goût; **tasty** *adj* savoureux(-euse), délicieux(-euse)

tatters ['tætəz] *npl*: **in ~** (*also*: **tattered**) en lambeaux

tattoo [tə'tuː] *n* tatouage m; (*spectacle*) parade f militaire ▷ *vt* tatouer

taught [tɔːt] *pt, pp of* **teach**

taunt [tɔːnt] *n* raillerie f ▷ *vt* railler

Taurus ['tɔːrəs] *n* le Taureau

taut [tɔːt] *adj* tendu(e)

tax [tæks] *n* (*on goods etc*) taxe f; (*on income*) impôts *mpl*, contributions *fpl* ▷ *vt* taxer; imposer; (*fig: patience etc*) mettre à l'épreuve; **tax disc** *n* (*BRIT Aut*) vignette f (automobile); **tax-free** *adj* exempt(e) d'impôts

taxi ['tæksɪ] *n* taxi m ▷ *vi* (*Aviat*) rouler (lentement) au sol; **can you call me a ~, please?** pouvez-vous m'appeler un taxi, s'il vous plaît?; **taxi driver** *n* chauffeur m de taxi; **taxi rank** (*BRIT*), **taxi stand** *n* station f de taxis

taxpayer [-peɪə'] *n* contribuable m/f

tax return *n* déclaration f d'impôts *or* de revenus

TB *n abbr* =**tuberculosis**

tea [tiː] *n* thé m; (*BRIT: snack: for children*) goûter m; **high ~** (*BRIT*) collation combinant goûter et dîner; **tea bag** *n* sachet m de thé; **tea break** *n* (*BRIT*) pause-thé f

teach (*pt, pp* **taught**) [tiːtʃ, tɔːt] *vt*: **to**

~ sb sth, to ~ sth to sb apprendre qch à qn; (in school etc) enseigner qch à qn ▷ vi enseigner; **teacher** n (in secondary school) professeur m; (in primary school) instituteur(-trice); **teaching** n enseignement m

tea: **tea cloth** n (BRIT) torchon m; **teacup** n tasse f à thé

tea leaves npl feuilles fpl de thé

team [tiːm] n équipe f; (of animals) attelage m; **team up** vi: **to ~ up (with)** faire équipe (avec)

teapot ['tiːpɔt] n théière f

tear¹ ['tɪəʳ] n larme f; **in ~s** en larmes

tear² n [tɛəʳ] déchirure f ▷ vb (pt **tore**, pp **torn**) ▷ vt déchirer ▷ vi se déchirer; **tear apart** vt (also fig) déchirer; **tear down** vt (building, statue) démolir; (poster, flag) arracher; **tear off** vt (sheet of paper etc) arracher; (one's clothes) enlever à toute vitesse; **tear up** vt (sheet of paper etc) déchirer, mettre en morceaux or pièces

tearful ['tɪəful] adj larmoyant(e)

tear gas [tɪə-] n gaz m lacrymogène

tearoom ['tiːruːm] n salon m de thé

tease [tiːz] vt taquiner; (unkindly) tourmenter

tea: **teaspoon** n petite cuiller; (also: **teaspoonful**: as measurement) ≈ cuillerée f à café; **teatime** n l'heure f du thé; **tea towel** n (BRIT) torchon m

technical ['tɛknɪkl] adj technique

technician [tɛk'nɪʃən] n technicien(ne)

technique [tɛk'niːk] n technique f

technology [tɛk'nɔlədʒɪ] n technologie f

teddy (bear) ['tɛdɪ-] n ours m (en peluche)

tedious ['tiːdɪəs] adj fastidieux(-euse)

tee [tiː] n (Golf) tee m

teen [tiːn] adj = **teenage** ▷ n (US) = **teenager**

teenage ['tiːneɪdʒ] adj (fashions etc) pour jeunes, pour adolescents; (child) qui est adolescent(e); **teenager** n

adolescent(e)

teens [tiːnz] npl: **to be in one's ~** être adolescent(e)

teeth [tiːθ] npl of **tooth**

teetotal ['tiː'təutl] adj (person) qui ne boit jamais d'alcool

telecommunications ['tɛlɪkəmjuːnɪ'keɪʃənz] n télécommunications fpl

telegram ['tɛlɪgræm] n télégramme m

telegraph pole ['tɛlɪgrɑːf-] n poteau m télégraphique

telephone ['tɛlɪfəun] n téléphone m ▷ vt (person) téléphoner à; (message) téléphoner; **to be on the ~** (be speaking) être au téléphone; **telephone book** n = **telephone directory**; **telephone booth** (BRIT), **telephone box** n cabine f téléphonique; **telephone call** n appel m téléphonique; **telephone directory** n annuaire m (du téléphone); **telephone number** n numéro m de téléphone

telesales ['tɛlɪseɪlz] npl télévente f

telescope ['tɛlɪskəup] n télescope m

televise ['tɛlɪvaɪz] vt téléviser

television ['tɛlɪvɪʒən] n télévision f; **on ~** à la télévision; **television programme** n émission f de télévision

tell (pt, pp **told**) [tɛl, təuld] vt dire; (relate: story) raconter; (distinguish): **to ~ sth from** distinguer qch de ▷ vi (talk): **to ~ of** parler de; (have effect) se faire sentir, se voir; **to ~ sb to do** dire à qn de faire; **to ~ the time** (know how to) savoir lire l'heure; **tell off** vt réprimander, gronder; **teller** n (in bank) caissier(-ière)

telly ['tɛlɪ] n abbr (BRIT inf: = television) télé f

temp [tɛmp] n (BRIT = temporary worker) intérimaire m/f ▷ vi travailler comme intérimaire

temper ['tɛmpəʳ] n (nature) caractère m; (mood) humeur f; (fit of anger) colère f ▷ vt (moderate) tempérer, adoucir; **to be in a ~** être en colère; **to lose one's ~** se mettre en colère

temperament ['tɛmprəmənt] n (nature) tempérament m; **temperamental** [tɛmprə'mɛntl] adj capricieux(-euse)

temperature ['tɛmprətʃə^r] n température f; **to have** or **run a ~** avoir de la fièvre

temple ['tɛmpl] n (building) temple m; (Anat) tempe f

temporary ['tɛmpərərɪ] adj temporaire, provisoire; (job, worker) temporaire

tempt [tɛmpt] vt tenter; **to ~ sb into doing** induire qn à faire; **temptation** n tentation f; **tempting** adj tentant(e); (food) appétissant(e)

ten [tɛn] num dix

tenant ['tɛnənt] n locataire m/f

tend [tɛnd] vt s'occuper de ▷ vi: **to ~ to do** avoir tendance à faire; **tendency** ['tɛndənsɪ] n tendance f

tender ['tɛndə^r] adj tendre; (delicate) délicat(e); (sore) sensible ▷ n (Comm: offer) soumission f; (money): **legal ~** cours légal ▷ vt offrir

tendon ['tɛndən] n tendon m

tenner ['tɛnə^r] n (BRIT inf) billet m de dix livres

tennis ['tɛnɪs] n tennis m; **tennis ball** n balle f de tennis; **tennis court** n (court m de) tennis m; **tennis match** n match m de tennis; **tennis player** n joueur(-euse) de tennis; **tennis racket** n raquette f de tennis

tenor ['tɛnə^r] n (Mus) ténor m

tenpin bowling ['tɛnpɪn-] n (BRIT) bowling m (à 10 quilles)

tense [tɛns] adj tendu(e) ▷ n (Ling) temps m

tension ['tɛnʃən] n tension f

tent [tɛnt] n tente f

tentative ['tɛntətɪv] adj timide, hésitant(e); (conclusion) provisoire

tenth [tɛnθ] num dixième

tent: tent peg n piquet m de tente; **tent pole** n montant m de tente

tepid ['tɛpɪd] adj tiède

term [tə:m] n terme m; (Scol) trimestre

m ▷ vt appeler; **terms** npl (conditions) conditions fpl; (Comm) tarif m; **in the short/long ~** à court/long terme; **to come to ~s with** (problem) faire face à; **to be on good ~s with** bien s'entendre avec, être en bons termes avec

terminal ['tə:mɪnl] adj (disease) dans sa phase terminale; (patient) incurable ▷ n (Elec) borne f; (for oil, ore etc, also Comput) terminal m; (also: **air ~**) aérogare f; (BRIT: also: **coach ~**) gare routière

terminate ['tə:mɪneɪt] vt mettre fin à; (pregnancy) interrompre

termini ['tə:mɪnaɪ] npl of **terminus**

terminology [tə:mɪ'nɔlədʒɪ] n terminologie f

terminus (pl **termini**) ['tə:mɪnəs, 'tə:mɪnaɪ] n terminus m inv

terrace ['tɛrəs] n terrasse f; (BRIT: row of houses) rangée f de maisons (attenantes les unes aux autres); **the ~s** (BRIT Sport) les gradins mpl; **terraced** adj (garden) en terrasses; (in a row: house, cottage etc) attenant(e) aux maisons voisines

terrain [tɛ'reɪn] n terrain m (sol)

terrestrial [tɪ'rɛstrɪəl] adj terrestre

terrible ['tɛrɪbl] adj terrible, atroce; (weather, work) affreux(-euse), épouvantable; **terribly** adv terriblement; (very badly) affreusement mal

terrier ['tɛrɪə^r] n terrier m (chien)

terrific [tə'rɪfɪk] adj (very great) fantastique, incroyable, terrible; (wonderful) formidable, sensationnel(le)

terrified ['tɛrɪfaɪd] adj terrifié(e); **to be ~ of sth** avoir très peur de qch

terrify ['tɛrɪfaɪ] vt terrifier; **terrifying** adj terrifiant(e)

territorial [tɛrɪ'tɔːrɪəl] adj territorial(e)

territory ['tɛrɪtərɪ] n territoire m

terror ['tɛrə^r] n terreur f; **terrorism** n terrorisme m; **terrorist** n terroriste m/f; **terrorist attack** n attentat m terroriste

test [tɛst] n (trial, check) essai m; (: of

courage etc) épreuve f; *(Med)* examen m; *(Chem)* analyse f; *(Scol)* interrogation f de contrôle; *(also: **driving ~**)* (examen du) permis m de conduire ▷ vt essayer; mettre à l'épreuve; examiner; analyser; faire subir une interrogation (de contrôle) à

testicle ['tɛstɪkl] n testicule m

testify ['tɛstɪfaɪ] vi *(Law)* témoigner, déposer; **to ~ to sth** *(Law)* attester qch

testimony ['tɛstɪmənɪ] n *(Law)* témoignage m, déposition f

test match n *(Cricket, Rugby)* match international; **test tube** n éprouvette f

tetanus ['tɛtənəs] n tétanos m

text [tɛkst] n texte m; *(on mobile phone)* texto m, SMS m inv ▷ vt *(inf)* envoyer un texto or SMS à; **textbook** n manuel m

textile ['tɛkstaɪl] n textile m

text message n texto m, SMS m inv

text messaging [-'mɛsɪdʒɪŋ] n messagerie textuelle

texture ['tɛkstʃə'] n texture f; *(of skin, paper etc)* grain m

Thai [taɪ] adj thaïlandais(e) ▷ n Thaïlandais(e)

Thailand ['taɪlænd] n Thaïlande f

Thames [tɛmz] n: **the (River) ~** la Tamise

than [ðæn, ðən] conj que; *(with numerals)*: **more ~ 10/once** plus de 10/d'une fois; **I have more/less ~ you** j'en ai plus/moins que toi; **she has more apples ~ pears** elle a plus de pommes que de poires; **it is better to phone ~ to write** il vaut mieux téléphoner (plutôt) qu'écrire; **she is older ~ you think** elle est plus âgée que tu le crois

thank [θæŋk] vt remercier, dire merci à; **thanks** npl remerciements mpl ▷ excl merci!; **~ you (very much)** merci (beaucoup); **~ God** Dieu merci!; **~s to** prep grâce à; **thankfully** adv *(fortunately)* heureusement; **Thanksgiving (Day)** n jour m d'action de grâce; *voir encadré*

THANKSGIVING (DAY)

Thanksgiving (Day) est un jour de congé aux États-Unis, le quatrième jeudi du mois de novembre, commémorant la bonne récolte que les Pèlerins venus de Grande-Bretagne ont eue en 1621; traditionnellement, c'était un jour où l'on remerciait Dieu et où l'on organisait un grand festin. Une fête semblable, mais qui n'a aucun rapport avec les Pères Pèlerins, a lieu au Canada le deuxième lundi d'octobre.

KEYWORD

that [ðæt] adj *(demonstrative: pl those)* ce, cet + vowel or h mute, cette f; **that man/woman/book** cet homme/cette femme/ce livre; *(not this)* cet homme-là/cette femme-là/ce livre-là; **that one** celui-là (celle-là)

▷ pron 1 *(demonstrative: pl those)* ce; *(not this one)* cela, ça; *(that one)* celui (celle); **who's that?** qui est-ce?; **what's that?** qu'est-ce que c'est?; **is that you?** c'est toi?; **I prefer this to that** je préfère ceci à cela or ça; **that's what he said** c'est or voilà ce qu'il a dit; **will you eat all that?** est-ce que tu vas manger tout ça?; **that is (to say)** c'est-à-dire, à savoir

2 *(relative: subject)* qui; *(: object)* que; *(: after prep)* lequel (laquelle), lesquels (lesquelles) pl; **the book that I read** le livre que j'ai lu; **the books that are in the library** les livres qui sont dans la bibliothèque; **all that I have** tout ce que j'ai; **the box that I put it in** la boîte dans laquelle je l'ai mis; **the people that I spoke to** les gens auxquels or à qui j'ai parlé

3 *(relative: of time)* où; **the day that he came** le jour où il est venu

▷ conj que; **he thought that I was ill** il pensait que j'étais malade

▷ adv (demonstrative): **I don't like it that much** ça ne me plaît pas tant que ça; **I didn't know it was that bad** je ne savais pas que c'était si or aussi mauvais; **it's about that high** c'est à peu près de cette hauteur

thatched [θætʃt] adj (roof) de chaume; **~ cottage** chaumière f

thaw [θɔː] n dégel m ▷ vi (ice) fondre; (food) dégeler ▷ vt (food) (faire) dégeler

○ **KEYWORD**

the [ðiː, ðə] def art **1** (gen) le, la f, l' + vowel or h mute, les pl (NB: à + le(s) = **au(x)**; de + le = **du**; de + les = **des**): **the boy/girl/ink** le garçon/la fille/l'encre; **the children** les enfants; **the history of the world** l'histoire du monde; **give it to the postman** donne-le au facteur; **to play the piano/flute** jouer du piano/de la flûte
2 (+ adj to form n) le, la f, l' + vowel or h mute, les pl; **the rich and the poor** les riches et les pauvres; **to attempt the impossible** tenter l'impossible
3 (in titles): **Elizabeth the First** Elisabeth première; **Peter the Great** Pierre le Grand
4 (in comparisons): **the more he works, the more he earns** plus il travaille, plus il gagne de l'argent

theatre (us **theater**) [ˈθɪətəʳ] n théâtre m; (Med: also: **operating ~**) salle f d'opération

theft [θɛft] n vol m (larcin)

their [ðɛəʳ] adj leur, leurs pl; see also **my; theirs** pron le (la) leur, les leurs; see also **mine¹**

them [ðɛm, ðəm] pron (direct) les; (indirect) leur; (stressed, after prep) eux (elles); **give me a few of ~** donnez m'en quelques uns (or quelques unes); see also **me**

theme [θiːm] n thème m; **theme park** n parc m à thème

themselves [ðəmˈsɛlvz] pl pron (reflexive) se; (emphatic, after prep) eux-mêmes (elles-mêmes); **between ~** entre eux (elles); une d' **oneself**

then [ðɛn] adv (at that time) alors, à ce moment-là; (next) puis, ensuite; (and also) et puis ▷ conj (therefore) alors, dans ce cas ▷ adj: **the ~ president** le président d'alors or de l'époque; **by ~** (past) à ce moment-là; (future) d'ici là; **from ~ on** dès lors; **until ~** jusqu'à ce moment-là, jusque-là

theology [θɪˈɒlədʒɪ] n théologie f

theory [ˈθɪərɪ] n théorie f

therapist [ˈθɛrəpɪst] n thérapeute m/f

therapy [ˈθɛrəpɪ] n thérapie f

○ **KEYWORD**

there [ðɛəʳ] adv **1**: **there is, there are** il y a; **there are 3 of them** (people, things) il y en a 3; **there is no-one here/no bread left** il n'y a personne/il n'y a plus de pain; **there has been an accident** il y a eu un accident
2 (referring to place) là, là-bas; **it's there** c'est là(-bas); **in/on/up/down there** là-dedans/là-dessus/là-haut/en bas; **he went there on Friday** il y est allé vendredi; **I want that book there** je veux ce livre-là; **there he is!** le voilà!
3: **there, there** (esp to child) allons, allons!

there: **thereabouts** adv (place) par là, près de là; (amount) environ, à peu près; **thereafter** adv par la suite; **thereby** adv ainsi; **therefore** adv donc, par conséquent

there's [ðɛəz] = **there is; there has**

thermal [ˈθəːml] adj thermique; **~ underwear** sous-vêtements mpl en Thermolactyl®

thermometer [θəˈmɒmɪtəʳ] n thermomètre m

thermostat [ˈθəːməustæt] n thermostat m

these [ðiːz] pl pron ceux-ci (celles-ci) ▷ pl adj ces; (not those): **~ books** ces

livres-ci

thesis (pl **theses**) ['θiːsɪs, 'θiːsiːz] n thèse f

they [δeɪ] pl pron ils (elles); (stressed) eux (elles); **~ say that ...** (it is said that) on dit que ...; **they'd = they had; they would; they'll = they shall; they will; they're = they are; they've = they have**

thick [θɪk] adj épais(se); (stupid) bête, borné(e) ▷ n: **in the ~ of** au beau milieu de, en plein cœur de; **it's 20 cm ~** ça a 20 cm d'épaisseur; **thicken** vi s'épaissir ▷ vt (sauce etc) épaissir; **thickness** n épaisseur f

thief (pl **thieves**) [θiːf, θiːvz] n voleur(-euse)

thigh [θaɪ] n cuisse f

thin [θɪn] adj mince; (skinny) maigre; (soup) peu épais(se); (hair, crowd) clairsemé(e) ▷ vt (also: **~ down**: sauce, paint) délayer

thing [θɪŋ] n chose f; (object) objet m; (contraption) truc m; **things** npl (belongings) affaires fpl; **the ~ is ...** c'est que ...; **the best ~ would be to** le mieux serait de; **how are ~s?** comment ça va?; **to have a ~ about** (be obsessed by) être obsédé(e) par; (hate) détester; **poor ~!** le (or la) pauvre!

think (pt, pp **thought**) [θɪŋk, θɔːt] vi penser, réfléchir ▷ vt penser, croire; (imagine) s'imaginer; **what did you ~ of them?** qu'avez-vous pensé d'eux?; **to ~ about sth/sb** penser à qch/qn; **I'll ~ about it** je vais y réfléchir; **to ~ of doing** avoir l'idée de faire; **I ~ so/not** je crois or pense que oui/non; **to ~ well of** avoir une haute opinion de; **think over** vt bien réfléchir à; **think up** vt inventer, trouver

third [θəːd] num troisième ▷ n (fraction) tiers m; (Aut) troisième (vitesse) f; (BRIT Scol: degree) ≈ licence f avec mention passable; **thirdly** adv troisièmement; **third party insurance** n (BRIT) assurance f au tiers; **Third World** n: **the Third World** le Tiers-Monde

thirst [θəːst] n soif f; **thirsty** adj qui a soif, assoiffé(e); (work) qui donne soif; **to be thirsty** avoir soif

thirteen [θəː'tiːn] num treize; **thirteenth** [-'tiːnθ] num treizième

thirtieth ['θəːtɪɪθ] num trentième

thirty ['θəːtɪ] num trente

 KEYWORD

this [δɪs] adj (demonstrative: pl **these**) ce, cet + vowel or h mute, cette f; **this man/woman/book** cet homme/cette femme/ce livre; (not that) cet homme-ci/cette femme-ci/ce livre-ci; **this one** celui-ci (celle-ci)
▷ pron (demonstrative: pl **these**) ce; (not that one) celui-ci (celle-ci), ceci; **who's this?** qui est-ce?; **what's this?** qu'est-ce que c'est?; **I prefer this to that** je préfère ceci à cela; **this is where I live** c'est ici que j'habite; **this is what he said** voici ce qu'il a dit; **this is Mr Brown** (in introductions) je vous présente Mr Brown; (on photo) c'est Mr Brown; (on telephone) c'est Mr Brown
▷ adv (demonstrative): **it was about this big** c'était à peu près de cette grandeur or grand comme ça; **I didn't know it was this bad** je ne savais pas que c'était si or aussi mauvais

thistle ['θɪsl] n chardon m

thorn [θɔːn] n épine f

thorough ['θʌrə] adj (search) minutieux(-euse); (knowledge, research) approfondi(e); (work, person) consciencieux(-euse); (cleaning) à fond; **thoroughly** adv (search) minutieusement; (study) en profondeur; (clean) à fond; (very) tout à fait

those [δəuz] pl pron ceux-là (celles-là) ▷ pl adj ces; (not these): **~ books** ces livres-là

though [δəu] conj bien que + sub, quoique + sub ▷ adv pourtant

thought [θɔːt] pt, pp of **think** ▷ n

pensée f; (idea) idée f; (opinion) avis m;
thoughtful adj (deep in thought)
pensif(-ive); (serious) réfléchi(e);
(considerate) prévenant(e); **thoughtless**
adj qui manque de considération
thousand ['θaʊzənd] num mille; **one
~** mille; **two ~** deux mille; **~s of** des
milliers de; **thousandth** num millième
thrash [θræʃ] vt rouer de coups; (as
punishment) donner une correction à;
(inf: defeat) battre à plate(s) couture(s)
thread [θrɛd] n fil m; (of screw) pas m,
filetage m ⊳ vt (needle) enfiler
threat [θrɛt] n menace f; **threaten** vi
(storm) menacer ⊳ vt: **to threaten sb
with sth/to do** menacer qn de qch/de
faire; **threatening** adj menaçant(e)
three [θriː] num trois; **three-
dimensional** adj à trois dimensions;
three-piece suite n salon m (canapé
et deux fauteuils); **three-quarters** npl
trois-quarts mpl; **three-quarters full**
aux trois-quarts plein
threshold ['θrɛʃhəʊld] n seuil m
threw [θruː] pt of **throw**
thrill [θrɪl] n (excitement) émotion f,
sensation f; (shudder) frisson m
⊳ vt (audience) électriser; **thrilled** adj:
thrilled with ravi(e) de; **thriller**
n film m (or roman m or pièce f) à
suspense; **thrilling** adj (book, play
etc) saisissant(e); (news, discovery)
excitant(e)
thriving ['θraɪvɪŋ] adj (business,
community) prospère
throat [θrəʊt] n gorge f; **to have a sore
~** avoir mal à la gorge
throb [θrɒb] vi (heart) palpiter; (engine)
vibrer; **my head is ~bing** j'ai des
élancements dans la tête
throne [θrəʊn] n trône m
through [θruː] prep à travers; (time)
pendant, durant; (by means of) par, par
l'intermédiaire de; (owing to) à cause
de ⊳ adj (ticket, train, passage) direct(e)
⊳ adv à travers; **(from) Monday ~
Friday** (US) de lundi à vendredi; **to put
sb ~ to sb** (Tel) passer qn à qn; **to be**

~ (BRIT: Tel) avoir la communication;
(esp US: have finished) avoir fini; **"no-
traffic"** (US) "passage interdit"; **"no-
road"** (BRIT) "impasse"; **throughout**
prep (place) partout dans; (time) durant
tout(e) la (le) ⊳ adv partout
throw [θrəʊ] n jet m; (Sport) lancer
m ⊳ vt (pt **threw**, pp **~n**) lancer, jeter;
(Sport) lancer; (rider) désarçonner; (fig)
déconcerter; **to ~ a party** donner
une réception; **throw away** vt jeter;
(money) gaspiller; **throw in** vt (Sport:
ball) remettre en jeu; (include) ajouter;
throw off vt se débarrasser de; **throw
out** vt jeter; (reject) rejeter; (person)
mettre à la porte; **throw up** vi vomir
thru [θruː] (US) = **through**
thrush [θrʌʃ] n (Zool) grive f
thrust [θrʌst] vt (pt, pp **~**) pousser
brusquement; (push in) enfoncer
thud [θʌd] n bruit sourd
thug [θʌɡ] n voyou m
thumb [θʌm] n (Anat) pouce m ⊳ vt: **to
~ a lift** faire de l'auto-stop, arrêter une
voiture; **thumbtack** n (US) punaise
f (clou)
thump [θʌmp] n grand coup m; (sound)
bruit sourd ⊳ vt cogner sur ⊳ vi cogner,
frapper
thunder ['θʌndə'] n tonnerre m ⊳ vi
tonner; (train etc): **to ~ past** passer dans
un grondement or un bruit de tonnerre;
thunderstorm n orage m
Thur(s) abbr (= Thursday) jeu
Thursday ['θɜːzdɪ] n jeudi m
thus [ðʌs] adv ainsi
thwart [θwɔːt] vt contrecarrer
thyme [taɪm] n thym m
Tibet [tɪ'bɛt] n Tibet m
tick [tɪk] n (sound: of clock) tic-tac m;
(mark) coche f; (Zool) tique f; (BRIT
inf): **in a ~** dans un instant ⊳ vi faire
tic-tac ⊳ vt (item on list) cocher; **tick
off** vt (item on list) cocher; (person)
réprimander, attraper
ticket ['tɪkɪt] n billet m; (for bus, tube)
ticket m; (in shop: on goods) étiquette
f; (for library) carte f; (also: **parking ~**)

contravention f. p.-v. m; **ticket barrier** n (BRIT: Rail) portillon m automatique; **ticket collector** n contrôleur(-euse); **ticket inspector** n contrôleur(-euse); **ticket machine** n billetterie f automatique; **ticket office** n guichet m, bureau m de vente des billets

tickle ['tɪkl] vi chatouiller ▷ vt chatouiller; **ticklish** adj (person) chatouilleux(-euse); (problem) épineux(-euse)

tide [taɪd] n marée f; (fig: of events) cours m

tidy ['taɪdɪ] adj (room) bien rangé(e); (dress, work) net (nette); (person) ordonné(e), qui a de l'ordre ▷ vt (also: ~ **up**) ranger

tie [taɪ] n (string etc) cordon m; (BRIT: also: **neck~**) cravate f; (fig: link) lien m; (Sport: draw) égalité f de points; match nul ▷ vt (parcel) attacher; (ribbon) nouer ▷ vi (Sport) faire match nul; finir à égalité de points; **to ~ sth in a bow** faire un nœud à or avec qch; **to ~ a knot in sth** faire un nœud à qch; **tie down** vt (fig): **to ~ sb down** contraindre qn à accepter; **to feel ~d down** (by relationship) se sentir coincé(e); **tie up** vt (parcel) ficeler; (dog, boat) attacher; (prisoner) ligoter; (arrangements) conclure; **to be ~d up** (busy) être pris(e) or occupé(e)

tier [tɪə*] n gradin m; (of cake) étage m

tiger ['taɪgə*] n tigre m

tight [taɪt] adj (rope) tendu(e), raide; (clothes) étroit(e), très juste; (budget, programme, bend) serré(e); (control) strict(e), sévère; (inf: drunk) ivre, rond(e) ▷ adv (squeeze) très fort; (shut) à bloc, hermétiquement; **hold ~!** accrochez-vous bien!; **tighten** vt (rope) tendre; (screw) resserrer; (control) renforcer ▷ vi se tendre; se resserrer; **tights** npl (BRIT) collant m

tile [taɪl] n (on roof) tuile f; (on wall or floor) carreau m

till [tɪl] n caisse (enregistreuse) ▷ prep,

conj = until

tilt [tɪlt] vt pencher, incliner ▷ vi pencher, être incliné(e)

timber ['tɪmbə*] n (material) bois m de construction

time [taɪm] n temps m; (epoch: often pl) époque f, temps; (by clock) heure f; (moment) moment m; (occasion, also Math) fois f; (Mus) mesure f ▷ vt (race) chronométrer; (programme) minuter; (visit) fixer; (remark etc) choisir le moment de; **a long ~** un long moment, longtemps; **four at a ~** quatre à la fois; **for the ~ being** pour le moment; **from ~ to ~** de temps en temps; **at ~s** parfois; **in ~** (soon enough) à temps; (after some time) avec le temps, à la longue; (Mus) en mesure; **in a week's ~** dans une semaine; **in no ~** en un rien de temps; **any ~** n'importe quand; **on ~** à l'heure; **5 ~s 5** 5 fois 5; **what ~ is it?** quelle heure est-il?; **what ~ is the museum/shop open?** à quelle heure ouvre le musée/magasin?; **to have a good ~** bien s'amuser; **time limit** n limite f de temps, délai m; **timely** adj opportun(e); **timer** n (in kitchen) compte-minutes m inv; (Tech) minuteur m; **time-share** n maison f/appartement m en multipropriété; **timetable** n (Rail) indicateur m horaire m; (Scol) emploi m du temps; **time zone** n fuseau m horaire

timid ['tɪmɪd] adj timide; (easily scared) peureux(-euse)

timing ['taɪmɪŋ] n (Sport) chronométrage m; **the ~ of his resignation** le moment choisi pour sa démission

tin [tɪn] n étain m; (also: ~ **plate**) fer-blanc m; (BRIT: can) boîte f (de conserve); (: for baking) moule m (à gâteau); (: for storage) boîte f; **tinfoil** n papier m d'étain or d'aluminium

tingle ['tɪŋgl] vi picoter; (person) avoir des picotements

tinker ['tɪŋkə*] n; **tinker with** vt fus bricoler, rafistoler

tinned [tɪnd] adj (BRIT: food) en boîte, en conserve

tin opener [-'əupnə⁣ʳ] n (BRIT) ouvre-boîte(s) m

tinsel ['tɪnsl] n guirlandes fpl de Noël (argentées)

tint [tɪnt] n teinte f; (for hair) shampooing colorant; **tinted** adj (hair) teint(e); (spectacles, glass) teinté(e)

tiny ['taɪnɪ] adj minuscule

tip [tɪp] n (end) bout m; (gratuity) pourboire m; (BRIT: for rubbish) décharge f; (advice) tuyau m ▷ vt (waiter) donner un pourboire à; (tilt) incliner; (overturn: also: ~ **over**) renverser; (empty: also: ~ **out**) déverser; **how much should I ~?** combien de pourboire est-ce qu'il faut laisser?; **tip off** vt prévenir, avertir

tiptoe ['tɪptəu] n: **on ~** sur la pointe des pieds

tire ['taɪə⁣ʳ] n (US) = **tyre** ▷ vt fatiguer ▷ vi se fatiguer; **tired** adj fatigué(e); **to be tired of** en avoir assez de, être las (lasse) de; **tire pressure** (US) = **tyre pressure**; **tiring** adj fatigant(e)

tissue ['tɪʃuː] n tissu m; (paper handkerchief) mouchoir m en papier, kleenex ® m; **tissue paper** n papier m de soie

tit [tɪt] n (bird) mésange f; **to give ~ for tat** rendre coup pour coup

title ['taɪtl] n titre m

T-junction ['tiː'dʒʌŋkʃən] n croisement m en T

TM n abbr = **trademark**

KEYWORD

to [tuː, tə] prep 1 (direction) à; (towards) vers; envers; **to go to France/Portugal/London/school** aller en France/au Portugal/à Londres/à l'école; **to go to Claude's/the doctor's** aller chez Claude/le docteur; **the road to Edinburgh** la route d'Édimbourg

2 (as far as) (jusqu')à; **to count to 10** compter jusqu'à 10; **from 40 to 50**

people de 40 à 50 personnes

3 (with expressions of time): **a quarter to 5** 5 heures moins le quart; **it's twenty to 3** il est 3 heures moins vingt

4 (for, of) de; **the key to the front door** la clé de la porte d'entrée; **a letter to his wife** une lettre (adressée) à sa femme

5 (expressing indirect object) à; **to give sth to sb** donner qch à qn; **to talk to sb** parler à qn; **to be a danger to sb** être dangereux(-euse) pour qn

6 (in relation to) à: **3 goals to 2** 3 (buts) à 2; **30 miles to the gallon** = 9,4 litres aux cent (km)

7 (purpose, result): **to come to sb's aid** venir au secours de qn, porter secours à qn; **to sentence sb to death** condamner qn à mort; **to my surprise** à ma grande surprise

▷ with vb 1 (simple infinitive): **to go/eat** aller/manger

2 (following another vb): **to want/try/start to do** vouloir/essayer de/commencer à faire

3 (with vb omitted): **I don't want to** je ne veux pas

4 (purpose, result) pour; **I did it to help you** je l'ai fait pour vous aider

5 (equivalent to relative clause): **I have things to do** j'ai des choses à faire; **the main thing is to try** l'important est d'essayer

6 (after adjective etc): **ready to go** prêt(e) à partir; **too old/young to ...** trop vieux/jeune pour ...

▷ adv: **push/pull the door to** tirez/poussez la porte

toad [təud] n crapaud m; **toadstool** n champignon m (vénéneux)

toast [təust] n (Culin) pain grillé, toast m; (drink, speech) toast m ▷ vt (Culin) faire griller; (drink to) porter un toast à; **toaster** n grille-pain m inv

tobacco [tə'bækəu] n tabac m

toboggan [tə'bɒgən] n toboggan m; (child's) luge f

today [tə'deɪ] adv, n (also fig) aujourd'hui (m)

toddler ['tɒdlə*] n enfant m/f qui commence à marcher, bambin m

toe [təʊ] n doigt m de pied, orteil m; (of shoe) bout m ▶ vt: **to ~ the line** (fig) obéir, se conformer; **toenail** n ongle m de l'orteil

toffee ['tɒfɪ] n caramel m

together [tə'gɛðə*] adv ensemble; (at same time) en même temps; **~ with** prep avec

toilet ['tɔɪlət] n (BRIT: lavatory) toilettes fpl, cabinets mpl: **to go to the ~** aller aux toilettes; **where's the ~?** où sont les toilettes?; **toilet bag** n (BRIT) nécessaire m de toilette; **toilet paper** n papier m hygiénique; **toiletries** npl articles mpl de toilette; **toilet roll** n rouleau m de papier hygiénique

token ['təʊkən] n (sign) marque f, témoignage m; (metal disc) jeton m ▶ adj (fee, strike) symbolique; **book/record** ~ (BRIT) chèque-livre/-disque m

Tokyo ['təʊkjəʊ] n Tokyo

told [təʊld] pt, pp of **tell**

tolerant ['tɒlərnt] adj: **~ (of)** tolérant(e) (à l'égard de)

tolerate ['tɒləreɪt] vt supporter

toll [təʊl] n (tax, charge) péage m ▶ vi (bell) sonner; **the accident ~ on the roads** le nombre des victimes de la route; **toll call** n (US Tel) appel m (à) longue distance; **toll-free** adj (US) gratuit(e) ▶ adv gratuitement

tomato [tə'mɑːtəʊ] (pl **~es**) n tomate f; **tomato sauce** n sauce f tomate

tomb [tuːm] n tombe f; **tombstone** n pierre tombale

tomorrow [tə'mɔrəʊ] adv, n (also fig) demain (m); **the day after ~** après-demain; **a week ~** demain en huit; **~ morning** demain matin

ton [tʌn] n tonne f (BRIT: = 1016 kg; US = 907 kg; metric = 1000 kg); **~s of** (inf) des tas de

tone [təʊn] n ton m; (of radio, BRIT Tel) tonalité f ▶ vi (also: **~ in**) s'harmoniser;

tone down vt (colour, criticism) adoucir

tongs [tɒŋz] npl pinces fpl; (for coal) pincettes fpl; (for hair) fer m à friser

tongue [tʌŋ] n langue f; **~ in cheek** adv ironiquement

tonic ['tɒnɪk] n (Med) tonique m; (also: **~ water**) Schweppes® m

tonight [tə'naɪt] adv, n cette nuit; (this evening) ce soir

tonne [tʌn] n (metric ton) tonne f

tonsil ['tɒnsl] n amygdale f; **tonsillitis** [tɒnsɪ'laɪtɪs] n: **to have tonsillitis** avoir une angine ou une amygdalite

too [tuː] adv (excessively) trop; (also) aussi; **~ much** (as adv) trop; (as adj) trop de; **~ many** trop de

took [tʊk] pt of **take**

tool [tuːl] n outil m; **tool box** n boîte f à outils; **tool kit** n trousse f à outils

tooth (pl **teeth**) [tuːθ, tiːθ] n (Anat, Tech) dent f; **to brush one's teeth** se laver les dents; **toothache** n mal m de dents; **to have toothache** avoir mal aux dents; **toothbrush** n brosse f à dents; **toothpaste** n (pâte f) dentifrice m; **toothpick** n cure-dent m

top [tɒp] n (of mountain, head) sommet m; (of page, ladder) haut m; (of box, cupboard, table) dessus m; (lid: of box, jar) couvercle m; (: of bottle) bouchon m; (toy) toupie f; (Dress: blouse etc) haut m; (: of pyjamas) veste f ▶ adj (of highest: in rank) premier(-ière); (best) meilleur(e) ▶ vt (exceed) dépasser; (be first in) être en tête de; **from ~ to bottom** de fond en comble; **on ~ of** sur; (in addition to) en plus de; **over the ~** (inf: behaviour etc) qui dépasse les limites; **top up** (US **top off**) vt (bottle) remplir; (salary) compléter; **to ~ up one's mobile (phone)** recharger son compte; **top floor** n dernier étage; **top hat** n haut-de-forme m

topic ['tɒpɪk] n sujet m, thème m; **topical** adj d'actualité

topless ['tɒplɪs] adj (bather etc) aux seins nus

topping ['tɒpɪŋ] n (Culin) couche de

crème, fromage etc qui recouvre un plat

topple ['tɒpl] vt renverser, faire tomber
▷ vi basculer; tomber

top-up ['tɒpʌp] n (for mobile phone)
recharge f, minutes fpl; **top-up card** n
(for mobile phone) recharge f

torch [tɔːtʃ] n torche f; (BRIT: electric)
lampe f de poche

tore [tɔːʳ] pt of **tear²**

torment n ['tɔːment] tourment m
▷ vt ['tɔːment] tourmenter; (fig: annoy)
agacer

torn [tɔːn] pp of **tear²**

tornado [tɔːˈneɪdəu] (pl ~es) n
tornade f

torpedo [tɔːˈpiːdəu] (pl ~es) n torpille f

torrent ['tɒrnt] n torrent m; **torrential**
[tɔˈrenʃl] adj torrentiel(le)

tortoise ['tɔːtəs] n tortue f

torture ['tɔːtʃəʳ] n torture f ▷ vt
torturer

Tory ['tɔːrɪ] adj, n (BRIT Pol) tory m/f,
conservateur(-trice)

toss [tɒs] vt lancer, jeter; (BRIT: pancake)
faire sauter; (head) rejeter en arrière
▷ vi: **to ~ up for sth** (BRIT) jouer qch à
pile ou face; **to ~ a coin** jouer à pile ou
face; **to ~ and turn** (in bed) se tourner
et se retourner

total ['təutl] adj total(e) ▷ n total m ▷ vt
(add up) faire le total de, additionner;
(amount to) s'élever à

totalitarian [təutælɪˈtɛərɪən] adj
totalitaire

totally ['təutəlɪ] adv totalement

touch [tʌtʃ] n contact m, toucher m;
(sense, skill: of pianist etc) toucher ▷ vt
(gen) toucher; (tamper with) toucher à;
a ~ of (fig) un petit peu de; une touche
de; **to get in ~ with** prendre contact
avec; **to lose ~** (friends) se perdre de
vue; **touch down** n (Aviat) atterrir;
(on sea) amerrir; **touchdown** n (Aviat)
atterrissage m; (on sea) amerrissage
m; (US Football) essai m; **touched**
adj (moved) touché(e); **touching**
adj touchant(e), attendrissant(e);
touchline n (Sport) (ligne f de) touche

f; **touch-sensitive** adj (keypad) à
effleurement; (screen) tactile

tough [tʌf] adj dur(e); (resistant)
résistant(e), solide; (meat) dur, coriace;
(firm) inflexible; (task, problem, situation)
difficile

tour [tuəʳ] n voyage m; (also: **package
~**) voyage organisé; (of town, museum)
tour m, visite f; (by band) tournée f ▷ vt
visiter; **tour guide** n (person) guide m/f

tourism ['tuərɪzm] n tourisme m

tourist ['tuərɪst] n touriste m/f ▷ cpd
touristique; **tourist office** n syndicat
m d'initiative

tournament ['tuənəmənt] n
tournoi m

tour operator n (BRIT) organisateur m
de voyages, tour-opérateur m

tow [təu] vt remorquer; (caravan,
trailer) tracter; **"on ~"**, (US) **"in ~"** (Aut)
'véhicule en remorque'; **tow away** vt
(subj: police) emmener à la fourrière;
(: breakdown service) remorquer

toward(s) [təˈwɔːd(z)] prep vers;
(of attitude) envers, à l'égard de; (of
purpose) pour

towel ['tauəl] n serviette f (de toilette);
towelling n (fabric) tissu-éponge m

tower ['tauəʳ] n tour f; **tower block** n
(BRIT) tour f (d'habitation)

town [taun] n ville f; **to go to ~** aller
en ville; (fig) y mettre le paquet; **town
centre** n (BRIT) centre m de la ville,
centre-ville m; **town hall** n ≈ mairie f

tow truck n (US) dépanneuse f

toxic ['tɒksɪk] adj toxique

toy [tɔɪ] n jouet m; **toy with** vt fus
jouer avec; (idea) caresser; **toyshop** n
magasin m de jouets

trace [treɪs] n trace f ▷ vt (draw) tracer,
dessiner; (follow) suivre la trace de;
(locate) retrouver

tracing paper ['treɪsɪŋ-] n papier-
calque m

track [træk] n (mark) trace f; (path:
gen) chemin m, piste f; (: of bullet etc)
trajectoire f; (: of suspect, animal) piste f;
(Rail) voie ferrée, rails mpl; (on tape,

Comput, Sport) piste; (on CD) piste f; (on record) plage f ▷ vt suivre la trace or la piste de; **to keep ~ of** suivre; **track down** vt (prey) trouver et capturer; (sth lost) finir par retrouver; **tracksuit** n survêtement m

tractor ['træktə'] n tracteur m

trade [treɪd] n commerce m; (skill, job) métier m ▷ vi faire du commerce ▷ vt (exchange): **to ~ sth (for sth)** échanger qch (contre qch); **to ~ with/in** faire du commerce avec/le commerce de; **trade in** vt (old car etc) faire reprendre; **trademark** n marque f de fabrique; **trader** n commerçant(e), négociant(e); **tradesman** (irreg) n (shopkeeper) commerçant m; **trade union** n syndicat m

trading ['treɪdɪŋ] n affaires fpl, commerce m

tradition [trə'dɪʃən] n tradition f; **traditional** adj traditionnel(le)

traffic ['træfɪk] n trafic m; (cars) circulation f ▷ vi: **to ~ in** (pej: liquor, drugs) faire le trafic de; **traffic circle** n (us) rond-point m; **traffic island** n refuge m (pour piétons); **traffic jam** n embouteillage m; **traffic lights** npl feux mpl (de signalisation); **traffic warden** n contractuel(le)

tragedy ['trædʒədɪ] n tragédie f

tragic ['trædʒɪk] adj tragique

trail [treɪl] n (tracks) trace f, piste f; (path) chemin m, piste f; (of smoke etc) traînée f ▷ vt (drag) traîner, tirer; (follow) suivre ▷ vi traîner; (in game, contest) être en retard; **trailer** n (Aut) remorque f; (us) caravane f; (Cine) bande-annonce f

train [treɪn] n train m; (in underground) rame f; (of dress) traîne f; (BRIT: series): **~ of events** série f d'événements ▷ vt (apprentice, doctor etc) former; (Sport) entraîner; (dog) dresser; (memory) exercer; (point: gun etc): **to ~ sth on** braquer qch sur ▷ vi recevoir sa formation; (Sport) s'entraîner; **one's ~ of thought** le fil de sa pensée; **what**

time does the **~ from Paris get in?** à quelle heure arrive le train de Paris?; **is this the ~ for ...?** c'est bien le train pour...?; **trainee** [treɪ'ni:] n stagiaire m/f; (in trade) apprenti(e); **trainer** n (Sport) entraîneur(-euse); (of dogs etc) dresseur(-euse); **trainers** npl (shoes) chaussures fpl de sport; **training** n formation f; (Sport) entraînement m; (of dog etc) dressage m; **in training** (Sport) à l'entraînement; (fit) en forme; **training course** n cours m de formation professionnelle; **training shoes** npl chaussures fpl de sport

trait [treɪt] n trait m (de caractère)

traitor ['treɪtə'] n traître m

tram [træm] n (BRIT: also: **~car**) tram(way) m

tramp [træmp] n (person) vagabond(e), clochard(e); (inf pej: woman): **to be a ~** être coureuse

trample ['træmpl] vt: **to ~ (underfoot)** piétiner

trampoline ['træmpəli:n] n trampoline m

tranquil ['træŋkwɪl] adj tranquille; **tranquillizer** (us **tranquilizer**) n (Med) tranquillisant m

transaction [træn'zækʃən] n transaction f

transatlantic ['trænzət'læntɪk] adj transatlantique

transcript ['trænskrɪpt] n transcription f (texte)

transfer n ['trænsfə'] (gen, also Sport) transfert m; (Pol: of power) passation f; (of money) virement m; (picture, design) décalcomanie f; (: stick-on) autocollant m ▷ vt ['træns'fə:'] transférer; passer; virer; **to ~ the charges** (BRIT Tel) téléphoner en P.C.V.

transform [træns'fɔ:m] vt transformer; **transformation** n transformation f

transfusion [træns'fju:ʒən] n transfusion f

transit ['trænzɪt] n: **in ~** en transit

transition [træn'zɪʃən] n transition f

transitive ['trænzɪtɪv] adj (Ling) transitif(-ive)

translate [trænz'leɪt] vt: **to ~ (from/into)** traduire (du/en); **can you ~ this for me?** pouvez-vous me traduire ceci?; **translation** [trænz'leɪʃən] n traduction f; (Scol: as opposed to prose) version f; **translator** n traducteur(-trice)

transmission [trænz'mɪʃən] n transmission f

transmit [trænz'mɪt] vt transmettre; (Radio, TV) émettre; **transmitter** n émetteur m

transparent [træns'pærənt] adj transparent(e)

transplant n ['trænspla:nt] (Med) transplantation f

transport n ['trænspɔ:t] transport m ▷ vt [træns'pɔ:t] transporter; **transportation** [trænspɔ:'teɪʃən] n (moyen m de) transport m

transvestite [trænz'vestaɪt] n travesti(e)

trap [træp] n (snare, trick) piège m; (carriage) cabriolet m ▷ vt prendre au piège; (confine) coincer

trash [træʃ] n (pej: goods) camelote f; (: nonsense) sottises fpl; (us: rubbish) ordures fpl; **trash can** n (us) poubelle f

trauma ['trɔ:mə] n traumatisme m; **traumatic** [trɔ:'mætɪk] adj traumatisant(e)

travel ['trævl] n voyage(s) m(pl) ▷ vi voyager; (news, sound) se propager ▷ vt (distance) parcourir; **travel agency** n agence f de voyages; **travel agent** n agent m de voyages; **travel insurance** n assurance-voyage f; **traveller** (us **traveler**) n voyageur(-euse); **traveller's cheque** (us **traveler's check**) n chèque m de voyage; **travelling** (us **traveling**) n voyage(s) m(pl); **travel-sick** adj: **to get travel-sick** avoir le mal de la route (or de mer or de l'air); **travel sickness** n mal m de la route (or de mer or de l'air)

tray [treɪ] n (for carrying) plateau m; (on desk) corbeille f

treacherous ['tretʃərəs] adj traître(sse); (ground, tide) dont il faut se méfier

treacle ['tri:kl] n mélasse f

tread [tred] n (step) pas m; (sound) bruit m de pas; (of tyre) chape f, bande f de roulement ▷ vi (pt trod, pp trodden) marcher; **tread on** vt fus marcher sur

treasure ['treʒə] n trésor m ▷ vt (value) tenir beaucoup à; **treasurer** n trésorier(-ière)

treasury ['treʒərɪ] n: **the T~**, (us) **the T~ Department** ≈ le ministère des Finances

treat [tri:t] n petit cadeau, petite surprise ▷ vt traiter; **to ~ sb to sth** offrir qch à qn; **treatment** n traitement m

treaty ['tri:tɪ] n traité m

treble ['trebl] adj triple ▷ vt, vi tripler

tree [tri:] n arbre m

trek [trek] n (long walk) randonnée f; (tiring walk) longue marche, trotte f

tremble ['trembl] vi trembler

tremendous [trɪ'mendəs] adj (enormous) énorme; (excellent) formidable, fantastique

trench [trentʃ] n tranchée f

trend [trend] n (tendency) tendance f; (of events) cours m; (fashion) mode f; **trendy** adj (idea, person) dans le vent; (clothes) dernier cri inv

trespass ['trespəs] vi: **to ~ on** s'introduire sans permission dans; **"no ~ing"** "propriété privée", "défense d'entrer"

trial ['traɪəl] n (Law) procès m, jugement m; (test of machine etc) essai m; **trials** npl (unpleasant experiences) épreuves fpl; **trial period** n période f d'essai

triangle ['traɪæŋgl] n (Math, Mus) triangle m

triangular [traɪ'æŋgjulə'] adj triangulaire

tribe [traɪb] n tribu f

tribunal [traɪ'bju:nl] n tribunal m

tribute ['trɪbju:t] n tribut m, hommage

m; **to pay ~ to** rendre hommage à

trick [trɪk] n (magic) tour m; (joke, prank)
tour, farce f; (skill, knack) astuce f; (Cards)
levée f ▷ vt attraper, rouler; **to play a ~
on sb** jouer un tour à qn; **that should
do the ~** (fam) ça devrait faire l'affaire

trickle ['trɪkl] n (of water etc) filet m ▷ vi
couler en un filet ou goutte à goutte

tricky ['trɪkɪ] adj difficile, délicat(e)

tricycle ['traɪsɪkl] n tricycle m

trifle ['traɪfl] n bagatelle f; (Culin)
≈ diplomate m ▷ adv: **a ~ long** un
peu long

trigger ['trɪgə'] n (of gun) gâchette f

trim [trɪm] adj (house, garden) bien
tenu(e); (figure) svelte ▷ n (haircut etc)
légère coupe; (on car) garnitures fpl
▷ vt (cut) couper légèrement;
(decorate): **to ~ (with)** décorer (de);
(Naut: a sail) gréer

trio ['triːəu] n trio m

trip [trɪp] n voyage m; (excursion)
excursion f; (stumble) faux pas ▷ vi
faire un faux pas, trébucher; **trip up** vi
trébucher ▷ vt faire un croc-en-jambe à

triple ['trɪpl] adj triple

triplets ['trɪplɪts] npl triplés(-ées)

tripod ['traɪpɒd] n trépied m

triumph ['traɪʌmf] n triomphe
m ▷ vi: **to ~ (over)** triompher (de);
triumphant [traɪ'ʌmfənt] adj
triomphant(e)

trivial ['trɪvɪəl] adj insignifiant(e);
(commonplace) banal(e)

trod [trɒd] pt of **tread**

trodden ['trɒdn] pp of **tread**

trolley ['trɒlɪ] n chariot m

trombone [trɒm'bəun] n trombone m

troop [truːp] n bande f, groupe m;
troops npl (Mil) troupes fpl; (: men)
hommes mpl, soldats mpl

trophy ['trəufɪ] n trophée m

tropical ['trɒpɪkl] adj tropical(e)

trot [trɒt] n trot m ▷ vi trotter; **on the ~**
(BRIT: fig) d'affilée

trouble ['trʌbl] n difficulté(s) f(pl),
problème(s) m(pl); (worry) ennuis mpl,
soucis mpl; (bother, effort) peine f; (Pol)

conflit(s) m(pl), troubles mpl; (Med):
stomach etc ~ troubles gastriques etc
▷ vt (disturb) déranger, gêner; (worry)
inquiéter ▷ vi: **to ~ to do** prendre la
peine de faire; **troubles** npl (Pol etc)
troubles; (personal) ennuis, soucis;
to be in ~ avoir des ennuis; (ship,
climber etc) être en difficulté; **to have
~ doing sth** avoir du mal à faire qch;
it's no ~ je vous en prie!; **the ~ is ...**
le problème, c'est que ...; **what's the
~?** qu'est-ce qui ne va pas?; **troubled**
adj (person) inquiet(-ète); (times, life)
agité(e); **troublemaker** n élément
perturbateur, fauteur m de troubles;
troublesome adj (child) fatigant(e),
difficile; (cough) gênant(e)

trough [trɒf] n (also: **drinking ~**)
abreuvoir m; (also: **feeding ~**) auge f;
(depression) creux m

trousers ['trauzəz] npl pantalon m;
short ~ (BRIT) culottes courtes

trout [traut] n (pl inv) truite f

trowel ['trauəl] n truelle f; (garden tool)
déplantoir m

truant ['truənt] n: **to play ~** (BRIT) faire
l'école buissonnière

truce [truːs] n trêve f

truck [trʌk] n camion m; (Rail) wagon
m à plate-forme; **truck driver** n
camionneur m

true [truː] adj vrai(e); (accurate) exact(e);
(genuine) vrai, véritable; (faithful) fidèle;
to come ~ se réaliser

truly ['truːlɪ] adv vraiment, réellement;
(truthfully) sans mentir; **yours ~** (in
letter) je vous prie d'agréer, Monsieur
(or Madame etc), l'expression de mes
sentiments respectueux

trumpet ['trʌmpɪt] n trompette f

trunk [trʌŋk] n (of tree, person) tronc
m; (of elephant) trompe f; (case) malle
f; (US Aut) coffre m; **trunks** npl (also:
swimming ~) maillot m or slip m
de bain

trust [trʌst] n confiance f;
(responsibility): **to place sth in sb's
~** confier la responsabilité de qch à

qn; (Law) fidéicommis m ▷ vt (rely on) avoir confiance en; (entrust): **to ~ sth to sb** confier qch à qn; (hope): **to ~ (that)** espérer (que); **to take sth on ~** accepter qch les yeux fermés; **trusted** adj en qui l'on a confiance; **trustworthy** adj digne de confiance

truth [tru:θ, (pl) tru:ðz] n vérité f; **truthful** adj (person) qui dit la vérité; (answer) sincère

try [traɪ] n essai m, tentative f; (Rugby) essai f ▷ vt (attempt) essayer, tenter; (test: sth new: also: ~ **out**) essayer, tester; (Law: person) juger; (strain) éprouver ▷ vi essayer; **to ~ to do** essayer de faire; (seek) chercher à faire; **try on** vt (clothes) essayer; **trying** adj pénible

T-shirt ['ti:ʃə:t] n tee-shirt m

tub [tʌb] n cuve f; (for washing clothes) baquet m; (bath) baignoire f

tube [tju:b] n tube m; (BRIT: underground) métro m; (for tyre) chambre f à air

tuberculosis [tjubə:kju'ləusɪs] n tuberculose f

tube station n (BRIT) station f de métro

tuck [tʌk] vt (put) mettre; **tuck away** vt cacher, ranger; (money) mettre de côté; (building): **to be ~ed away** être caché(e); **tuck in** vt rentrer; (child) border ▷ vi (eat) manger de bon appétit; attaquer le repas; **tuck shop** n (BRIT Scol) boutique f à provisions

Tue(s) abbr (= Tuesday) ma

Tuesday ['tju:zdɪ] n mardi m

tug [tʌg] n (ship) remorqueur m ▷ vt tirer (sur)

tuition [tju:'ɪʃən] n (BRIT: lessons) leçons fpl; (: private) cours particuliers; (us: fees) frais mpl de scolarité

tulip ['tju:lɪp] n tulipe f

tumble ['tʌmbl] n (fall) chute f, culbute f ▷ vi tomber, dégringoler; **to ~ to sth** (inf) réaliser qch; **tumble dryer** n (BRIT) séchoir m (à linge) à air chaud

tumbler ['tʌmblə*] n verre (droit), gobelet m

tummy ['tʌmɪ] n (inf) ventre m

tumour (us **tumor**) ['tju:mə*] n tumeur f

tuna ['tju:nə] n (pl inv: also: ~ **fish**) thon m

tune [tju:n] n (melody) air m ▷ vt (Mus) accorder; (Radio, TV, Aut) régler, mettre au point; **to be in/out of ~** (instrument) être accordé/désaccordé; (singer) chanter juste/faux; **tune in** vi (Radio, TV): **to ~ in (to)** se mettre à l'écoute (de); **tune up** vi (musician) accorder son instrument

tunic ['tju:nɪk] n tunique f

Tunis ['tju:nɪs] n Tunis

Tunisia [tju:'nɪzɪə] n Tunisie f

Tunisian [tju:'nɪzɪən] adj tunisien(ne) ▷ n Tunisien(ne)

tunnel ['tʌnl] n tunnel m; (in mine) galerie f ▷ vi creuser un tunnel (or une galerie)

turbulence ['tə:bjuləns] n (Aviat) turbulence f

turf [tə:f] n gazon m; (clod) motte f (de gazon) ▷ vt gazonner

Turk [tə:k] n Turc (Turque)

Turkey ['tə:kɪ] n Turquie f

turkey ['tə:kɪ] n dindon m, dinde f

Turkish ['tə:kɪʃ] adj turc (turque) ▷ n (Ling) turc m

turmoil ['tə:mɔɪl] n trouble m, bouleversement m

turn [tə:n] n tour m; (in road) tournant m; (tendency: of mind, events) tournure f; (performance) numéro m; (Med) crise f, attaque f ▷ vt tourner; (collar, steak) retourner; (change): **to ~ sth into** changer qch en; (age) atteindre ▷ vi (object, wind, milk) tourner; (person: look back) se (re)tourner; (reverse direction) faire demi-tour; (become) devenir; **to ~ into** se changer en, se transformer en; **a good ~** un service; **it gave me quite a ~** ça m'a fait un coup; **"no left ~"** (Aut) "défense de tourner à gauche"; **~ left/right at the next junction** tournez à gauche/droite au prochain carrefour; **it's your ~** c'est (à) votre tour; **in ~** à son tour;

à tour de rôle; **to take ~s** se relayer; **turn around** vi (person) se retourner ▷ vt (object) tourner; **turn away** vi se détourner, tourner la tête ▷ vt (reject: person) renvoyer; (: business) refuser; **turn back** vi revenir, faire demi-tour; **turn down** vt (refuse) refuser, rejeter; (reduce) baisser; (fold) rabattre; **turn in** vi (inf: go to bed) aller se coucher ▷ vt (fold) rentrer; **turn off** vi (from road) tourner ▷ vt (light, radio etc) éteindre; (tap) fermer; (engine) arrêter; **I can't ~ the heating off** je n'arrive pas à éteindre le chauffage; **turn on** vt (light, radio etc) allumer; (tap) ouvrir; (engine) mettre en marche; **I can't ~ the heating on** je n'arrive pas à allumer le chauffage; **turn out** vt (light, gas) éteindre; (produce) produire ▷ vi (voters, troops) se présenter; **to ~ out to be ...** s'avérer ...; **turn over** vi (person) se retourner ▷ vt (object) retourner; (page) tourner; **turn round** vi faire demi-tour; (rotate) tourner; **turn to** vt fus: **to ~ to sb** s'adresser à qn; **turn up** vi (person) arriver, se pointer (inf); (lost object) être retrouvé(e) ▷ vt (collar) remonter; (radio, heater) mettre plus fort; **turning** n (in road) tournant m; **turning point** n (fig) tournant m, moment décisif

turnip ['təːnɪp] n navet m

turn: turnout n (of voters) taux m de participation; **turnover** n (Comm: amount of money) chiffre m d'affaires; (: of goods) roulement m; (of staff) renouvellement m, changement m; **turnstile** n tourniquet m (d'entrée); **turn-up** n (BRIT: on trousers) revers m

turquoise ['təːkwɔɪz] n (stone) turquoise f ▷ adj turquoise inv

turtle ['təːtl] n tortue marine; **turtleneck (sweater)** n pullover m à col montant

tusk [tʌsk] n défense f (d'éléphant)

tutor ['tjuːtə*] n (BRIT Scol: in college) directeur(-trice) d'études; (private

teacher) précepteur(-trice); **tutorial** [tjuː'tɔːrɪəl] n (Scol) (séance f de) travaux mpl pratiques

tuxedo [tʌk'siːdəu] n (us) smoking m

TV [tiː'viː] n abbr (= television) télé f, TV f

tweed [twiːd] n tweed m

tweezers ['twiːzəz] npl pince f à épiler

twelfth [twelfθ] num douzième

twelve [twelv] num douze; **at ~ (o'clock)** à midi; (midnight) à minuit

twentieth ['twentɪɪθ] num vingtième

twenty ['twentɪ] num vingt

twice [twaɪs] adv deux fois; **~ as much** deux fois plus

twig [twɪg] n brindille f ▷ vt, vi (inf) piger

twilight ['twaɪlaɪt] n crépuscule m

twin [twɪn] adj, n jumeau(-elle) ▷ vt jumeler; **twin(-bedded) room** n chambre f à deux lits; **twin beds** npl lits mpl jumeaux

twinkle ['twɪŋkl] vi scintiller; (eyes) pétiller

twist [twɪst] n torsion f, tour m; (in wire, flex) tortillon m; (bend: in road) tournant m; (in story) coup m de théâtre ▷ vt tordre; (weave) entortiller; (roll around) enrouler; (fig) déformer ▷ vi (road, river) serpenter; **to ~ one's ankle/wrist** (Med) se tordre la cheville/le poignet

twit [twɪt] n (inf) crétin(e)

twitch [twɪtʃ] n (pull) coup sec, saccade f; (nervous) tic m ▷ vi se convulser; avoir un tic

two [tuː] num deux; **to put ~ and ~ together** (fig) faire le rapprochement

type [taɪp] n (category) genre m, espèce f; (model) modèle m; (example) type m; (Typ) type, caractère m ▷ vt (letter etc) taper (à la machine); **typewriter** n machine f à écrire

typhoid ['taɪfɔɪd] n typhoïde f

typhoon [taɪ'fuːn] n typhon m

typical ['tɪpɪkl] adj typique, caractéristique; **typically** adv (as usual) comme d'habitude; (characteristically) typiquement

typing ['taɪpɪŋ] n dactylo(graphie) f
typist ['taɪpɪst] n dactylo m/f
tyre (us **tire**) ['taɪə'] n pneu m; **I've got a flat ~** j'ai un pneu crevé; **tyre pressure** n (BRIT) pression f (de gonflage)

UFO ['ju:fəʊ] n abbr (= unidentified flying object) ovni m
Uganda [ju:'gændə] n Ouganda m
ugly ['ʌglɪ] adj laid(e), vilain(e); (fig) répugnant(e)
UHT adj abbr = **ultra-heat treated; ~ milk** lait m UHT or longue conservation
UK n abbr = **United Kingdom**
ulcer ['ʌlsə'] n ulcère m; **mouth ~** aphte f
ultimate ['ʌltɪmət] adj ultime, final(e); (authority) suprême; **ultimately** adv (at last) en fin de compte; (fundamentally) finalement; (eventually) par la suite
ultimatum (pl **-s** or **ultimata**) [ʌltɪ'meɪtəm, -tə] n ultimatum m
ultrasound ['ʌltrəsaʊnd] n (Med) ultrason m
ultraviolet ['ʌltrə'vaɪəlɪt] adj ultraviolet(te)
umbrella [ʌm'brelə] n parapluie m; (for sun) parasol m
umpire ['ʌmpaɪə'] n arbitre m; (Tennis) juge m de chaise

UN n abbr = United Nations

unable [ʌnˈeɪbl] adj: **to be ~ to** ne (pas) pouvoir, être dans l'impossibilité de; (not capable) être incapable de

unacceptable [ʌnəkˈsɛptəbl] adj (behaviour) inadmissible; (price, proposal) inacceptable

unanimous [juːˈnænɪməs] adj unanime

unarmed [ʌnˈɑːmd] adj (person) non armé(e); (combat) sans armes

unattended [ʌnəˈtɛndɪd] adj (car, child, luggage) sans surveillance

unattractive [ʌnəˈtræktɪv] adj peu attrayant(e); (character) peu sympathique

unavailable [ʌnəˈveɪləbl] adj (article, room, book) (qui n'est) pas disponible; (person) (qui n'est) pas libre

unavoidable [ʌnəˈvɔɪdəbl] adj inévitable

unaware [ʌnəˈwɛəᵉ] adj: **to be ~ of** ignorer, ne pas savoir, être inconscient(e) de; **unawares** adv à l'improviste, au dépourvu

unbearable [ʌnˈbɛərəbl] adj insupportable

unbeatable [ʌnˈbiːtəbl] adj imbattable

unbelievable [ʌnbɪˈliːvəbl] adj incroyable

unborn [ʌnˈbɔːn] adj à naître

unbutton [ʌnˈbʌtn] vt déboutonner

uncalled-for [ʌnˈkɔːldfɔːᵉ] adj déplacé(e), injustifié(e)

uncanny [ʌnˈkænɪ] adj étrange, troublant(e)

uncertain [ʌnˈsəːtn] adj incertain(e); (hesitant) hésitant(e); **uncertainty** n incertitude f, doutes mpl

unchanged [ʌnˈtʃeɪndʒd] adj inchangé(e)

uncle [ˈʌŋkl] n oncle m

unclear [ʌnˈklɪəᵉ] adj (qui n'est) pas clair(e) or évident(e); **I'm still ~ about what I'm supposed to do** je ne sais pas encore exactement ce que je dois faire

uncomfortable [ʌnˈkʌmfətəbl] adj inconfortable, peu confortable; (uneasy) mal à l'aise, gêné(e); (situation) désagréable

uncommon [ʌnˈkɔmən] adj rare, singulier(-ière), peu commun(e)

unconditional [ʌnkənˈdɪʃənl] adj sans conditions

unconscious [ʌnˈkɔnʃəs] adj sans connaissance, évanoui(e); (unaware): **~ (of)** inconscient(e) (de) ▷ n: **the ~** l'inconscient m

uncontrollable [ʌnkənˈtrəuləbl] adj (child, dog) indiscipliné(e); (temper, laughter) irrépressible

unconventional [ʌnkənˈvɛnʃənl] adj peu conventionnel(le)

uncover [ʌnˈkʌvəᵉ] vt découvrir

undecided [ʌndɪˈsaɪdɪd] adj indécis(e), irrésolu(e)

undeniable [ʌndɪˈnaɪəbl] adj indéniable, incontestable

under [ˈʌndəᵉ] prep sous; (less than) moins de; au-dessous de; (according to) selon, en vertu de ▷ adv au-dessous; en dessous; **~ there** là-dessous; **~ the circumstances** étant donné les circonstances; **~ repair** en (cours de) réparation; **undercover** adj secret(-ète), clandestin(e); **underdone** adj (Culin) saignant(e); (: pej) pas assez cuit(e); **underestimate** vt sous-estimer, mésestimer; **undergo** vt (irreg: like go) subir; (treatment) suivre; **undergraduate** n étudiant(e) (qui prépare la licence); **underground** adj souterrain(e); (fig) clandestin(e) ▷ n (BRIT: railway) métro m; (Pol) clandestinité f; **undergrowth** n broussailles fpl, sous-bois m; **underline** vt souligner; **undermine** vt saper, miner; **underneath** [ʌndəˈniːθ] adv (en) dessous ▷ prep sous, au-dessous de; **underpants** npl caleçon m, slip m; **underpass** n (BRIT: for pedestrians) passage souterrain; (: for cars) passage inférieur;

underprivileged adj défavorisé(e);
underscore vt souligner; **undershirt**
n (US) tricot m de corps; **underskirt** n
(BRIT) jupon m

understand [ʌndə'stænd] vt, vi (irreg:
like **stand**) comprendre; **I don't ~** je
ne comprends pas; **understandable**
adj compréhensible; **understanding**
adj compréhensif(-ive) ▷ n
compréhension f; (agreement) accord m

understatement ['ʌndəsteitmənt]
n: **that's an ~** c'est (bien) peu dire, le
terme est faible

understood [ʌndə'stud] pt, pp of
understand ▷ adj entendu(e); (implied)
sous-entendu(e)

undertake [ʌndə'teik] vt (irreg: like
take) (job, task) entreprendre; (duty)
se charger de; **to ~ to do sth** s'engager
à faire qch

undertaker ['ʌndəteikər] n (BRIT)
entrepreneur m des pompes funèbres,
croque-mort m

undertaking ['ʌndəteikiŋ] n
entreprise f; (promise) promesse f

under: underwater adv sous l'eau
▷ adj sous-marin(e); **underway**
adj: **to be underway** (meeting,
investigation) être en cours; **underwear**
n sous-vêtements mpl; (women's
only) dessous mpl; **underwent** pt of
undergo; **underworld** n (of crime)
milieu m, pègre f

undesirable [ʌndɪ'zaɪərəbl] adj peu
souhaitable; (person, effect) indésirable

undisputed ['ʌndɪs'pju:tɪd] adj
incontesté(e)

undo [ʌn'du:] vt (irreg: like **do**) défaire;
undone [ʌn'dʌn] pp of **undo** ▷ adj: **to
come ~** se défaire

undoubtedly [ʌn'dautɪdlɪ] adv sans
aucun doute

undress [ʌn'dres] vi se déshabiller

unearth [ʌn'ə:θ] vt déterrer; (fig)
dénicher

uneasy [ʌn'i:zɪ] adj mal à l'aise,
gêné(e); (worried) inquiet(-ète); (feeling)
désagréable; (peace, truce) fragile

unemployed [ʌnɪm'plɔɪd] adj sans
travail, au chômage ▷ n: **the ~** les
chômeurs mpl

unemployment [ʌnɪm'plɔɪmənt] n
chômage m; **unemployment benefit**
(US **unemployment compensation**) n
allocation f de chômage

unequal [ʌn'i:kwəl] adj inégal(e)

uneven [ʌn'i:vn] adj inégal(e); (quality,
work) irrégulier(-ière)

unexpected [ʌnɪk'spɛktɪd]
adj inattendu(e), imprévu(e);
unexpectedly adv (succeed) contre
toute attente; (arrive) à l'improviste

unfair [ʌn'fɛər] adj: ~ **(to)** injuste
(envers)

unfaithful [ʌn'feɪθful] adj infidèle

unfamiliar [ʌnfə'mɪlɪər] adj étrange,
inconnu(e); **to be ~ with sth** mal
connaître qch

unfashionable [ʌn'fæʃnəbl] adj
(clothes) démodé(e); (place) peu chic inv

unfasten [ʌn'fɑ:sn] vt défaire; (belt,
necklace) détacher; (open) ouvrir

unfavourable (US **unfavorable**)
[ʌn'feɪvrəbl] adj défavorable

unfinished [ʌn'fɪnɪʃt] adj inachevé(e)

unfit [ʌn'fɪt] adj (physically: ill) en
mauvaise santé; (: out of condition)
pas en forme; (incompetent): ~ **(for)**
impropre (à); (work, service) inapte (à)

unfold [ʌn'fəuld] vt déplier ▷ vi se
dérouler

unforgettable [ʌnfə'gɛtəbl] adj
inoubliable

unfortunate [ʌn'fɔ:tʃənət] adj
malheureux(-euse); (event, remark)
malencontreux(-euse); **unfortunately**
adv malheureusement

unfriendly [ʌn'frɛndlɪ] adj peu
aimable, froid(e)

unfurnished [ʌn'fə:nɪʃt] adj non
meublé(e)

unhappiness [ʌn'hæpɪnɪs] n tristesse
f, peine f

unhappy [ʌn'hæpɪ] adj triste,
malheureux(-euse); (unfortunate:
remark etc) malheureux(-euse); (not

pleased): ~ **with** mécontent(e) de, peu satisfait(e) de

unhealthy [ʌnˈhɛlθɪ] *adj* (gen) malsain(e); (person) maladif(-ive)

unheard-of [ʌnˈhɜːdɔv] *adj* inouï(e), sans précédent

unhelpful [ʌnˈhɛlpful] *adj* (person) peu serviable; (advice) peu utile

unhurt [ʌnˈhɜːt] *adj* indemne, sain(e) et sauf (sauve)

unidentified [ʌnaɪˈdɛntɪfaɪd] *adj* non identifié(e); see also **UFO**

uniform [ˈjuːnɪfɔːm] *n* uniforme *m*
▷ *adj* uniforme

unify [ˈjuːnɪfaɪ] *vt* unifier

unimportant [ʌnɪmˈpɔːtənt] *adj* sans importance

uninhabited [ʌnɪnˈhæbɪtɪd] *adj* inhabité(e)

unintentional [ʌnɪnˈtɛnʃənəl] *adj* involontaire

union [ˈjuːnjən] *n* union *f*; (also: **trade** ~) syndicat *m* ▷ *cpd* du syndicat, syndical(e); **Union Jack** *n* drapeau du Royaume-Uni

unique [juːˈniːk] *adj* unique

unisex [ˈjuːnɪsɛks] *adj* unisexe

unit [ˈjuːnɪt] *n* unité *f*; (section: of furniture etc) élément *m*, bloc *m*; (team, squad) groupe *m*, service *m*; **kitchen ~** élément de cuisine

unite [juːˈnaɪt] *vt* unir ▷ *vi* s'unir; **united** *adj* uni(e); (country, party) unifié(e); (efforts) conjugué(e); **United Kingdom** *n* Royaume-Uni *m* (R.U.); **United Nations (Organization)** *n* (Organisation *f* des) Nations unies (ONU); **United States (of America)** *n* États-Unis *mpl*

unity [ˈjuːnɪtɪ] *n* unité *f*

universal [juːnɪˈvɜːsl] *adj* universel(le)

universe [ˈjuːnɪvɜːs] *n* univers *m*

university [juːnɪˈvɜːsɪtɪ] *n* université *f* ▷ *cpd* (student, professor) d'université; (education, degree) universitaire

unjust [ʌnˈdʒʌst] *adj* injuste

unkind [ʌnˈkaɪnd] *adj* peu gentil(le), méchant(e)

unknown [ʌnˈnəun] *adj* inconnu(e)

unlawful [ʌnˈlɔːful] *adj* illégal(e)

unleaded [ʌnˈlɛdɪd] *n* (also: **~ petrol**) essence *f* sans plomb

unleash [ʌnˈliːʃ] *vt* (fig) déchaîner, déclencher

unless [ʌnˈlɛs] *conj*: ~ **he leaves** à moins qu'il (ne) parte; ~ **otherwise stated** sauf indication contraire

unlike [ʌnˈlaɪk] *adj* dissemblable, différent(e) ▷ *prep* à la différence de, contrairement à

unlikely [ʌnˈlaɪklɪ] *adj* (result, event) improbable; (explanation) invraisemblable

unlimited [ʌnˈlɪmɪtɪd] *adj* illimité(e)

unlisted [ʌnˈlɪstɪd] *adj* (US Tel) sur la liste rouge

unload [ʌnˈləud] *vt* décharger

unlock [ʌnˈlɔk] *vt* ouvrir

unlucky [ʌnˈlʌkɪ] *adj* (person) malchanceux(-euse); (object, number) qui porte malheur; **to be ~** (person) ne pas avoir de chance

unmarried [ʌnˈmærɪd] *adj* célibataire

unmistak(e)able [ʌnmɪsˈteɪkəbl] *adj* indubitable; qu'on ne peut pas ne pas reconnaître

unnatural [ʌnˈnætʃrəl] *adj* non naturel(le); (perversion) contre nature

unnecessary [ʌnˈnɛsəsərɪ] *adj* inutile, superflu(e)

UNO [ˈjuːnəu] *n abbr* = **United Nations Organization**

unofficial [ʌnəˈfɪʃl] *adj* (news) officieux(-euse), non officiel(le); (strike) ≈ sauvage

unpack [ʌnˈpæk] *vi* défaire sa valise ▷ *vt* (suitcase) défaire; (belongings) déballer

unpaid [ʌnˈpeɪd] *adj* (bill) impayé(e); (holiday) non-payé(e), sans salaire; (work) non rétribué(e)

unpleasant [ʌnˈplɛznt] *adj* déplaisant(e), désagréable

unplug [ʌnˈplʌg] *vt* débrancher

unpopular [ʌnˈpɔpjuləʳ] *adj* impopulaire

unprecedented [ʌn'presɪdəntl] *adj* sans précédent

unpredictable [ʌnprɪ'dɪktəbl] *adj* imprévisible

unprotected ['ʌnprə'tektɪd] *adj* (*sex*) non protégé(e)

unqualified [ʌn'kwɔlɪfaɪd] *adj* (*teacher*) non diplômé(e), sans titres; (*success*) sans réserve, total(e); (*disaster*) total(e)

unravel [ʌn'rævl] *vt* démêler

unreal [ʌn'rɪəl] *adj* irréel(le); (*extraordinary*) incroyable

unrealistic ['ʌnrɪə'lɪstɪk] *adj* (*idea*) irréaliste; (*estimate*) peu réaliste

unreasonable [ʌn'riːznəbl] *adj* qui n'est pas raisonnable

unrelated [ʌnrɪ'leɪtɪd] *adj* sans rapport; (*people*) sans lien de parenté

unreliable [ʌnrɪ'laɪəbl] *adj* sur qui (or quoi) on ne peut compter, peu fiable

unrest [ʌn'rest] *n* agitation *f*, troubles *mpl*

unroll [ʌn'rəul] *vt* dérouler

unruly [ʌn'ruːlɪ] *adj* indiscipliné(e)

unsafe [ʌn'seɪf] *adj* (*in danger*) en danger; (*journey, car*) dangereux(-euse)

unsatisfactory ['ʌnsætɪs'fæktərɪ] *adj* peu satisfaisant(e)

unscrew [ʌn'skruː] *vt* dévisser

unsettled [ʌn'setld] *adj* (*restless*) perturbé(e); (*unpredictable*) instable; incertain(e); (*not finalized*) non résolu(e)

unsettling [ʌn'setlɪŋ] *adj* qui a un effet perturbateur

unsightly [ʌn'saɪtlɪ] *adj* disgracieux(-euse), laid(e)

unskilled [ʌn'skɪld] *adj*: ~ **worker** manœuvre *m*

unspoiled [ʌn'spɔɪld], **unspoilt** ['ʌn'spɔɪlt] *adj* (*place*) non dégradé(e)

unstable [ʌn'steɪbl] *adj* instable

unsteady [ʌn'stedɪ] *adj* mal assuré(e), chancelant(e), instable

unsuccessful [ʌnsək'sesful] *adj* (*attempt*) infructueux(-euse); (*writer, proposal*) qui n'a pas de succès; **to be**

~ (*in attempting sth*) ne pas réussir; ne pas avoir de succès; (*application*) ne pas être retenu(e)

unsuitable [ʌn'suːtəbl] *adj* qui ne convient pas, peu approprié(e); (*time*) inopportun(e)

unsure [ʌn'ʃuə'] *adj* pas sûr(e); **to be ~ of o.s.** ne pas être sûr de soi, manquer de confiance en soi

untidy [ʌn'taɪdɪ] *adj* (*room*) en désordre; (*appearance, person*) débraillé(e); (*person: in character*) sans ordre, désordonné; (*work*) peu soigné(e)

untie [ʌn'taɪ] *vt* (*knot, parcel*) défaire; (*prisoner, dog*) détacher

until [ən'tɪl] *prep* jusqu'à; (*after negative*) avant ▷ *conj* jusqu'à ce que + *sub*; (*in past, after negative*) avant que + *sub*; ~ **he comes** jusqu'à ce qu'il vienne, jusqu'à son arrivée; ~ **now** jusqu'à présent, jusqu'ici; ~ **then** jusque-là

untrue [ʌn'truː] *adj* (*statement*) faux (fausse)

unused¹ [ʌn'juːzd] *adj* (*new*) neuf (neuve)

unused² [ʌn'juːst] *adj*: **to be ~ to sth/ to doing sth** ne pas avoir l'habitude de qch/de faire qch

unusual [ʌn'juːʒuəl] *adj* insolite, exceptionnel(le), rare; **unusually** *adv* exceptionnellement, particulièrement

unveil [ʌn'veɪl] *vt* dévoiler

unwanted [ʌn'wɔntɪd] *adj* (*child, pregnancy*) non désiré(e); (*clothes etc*) à donner

unwell [ʌn'wel] *adj* souffrant(e); **to feel** ~ ne pas se sentir bien

unwilling [ʌn'wɪlɪŋ] *adj*: **to be ~ to do** ne pas vouloir faire

unwind [ʌn'waɪnd] *vb* (*irreg: like* **wind**) ▷ *vt* dérouler ▷ *vi* (*relax*) se détendre

unwise [ʌn'waɪz] *adj* imprudent(e), peu judicieux(-euse)

unwittingly [ʌn'wɪtɪŋlɪ] *adv* involontairement

unwrap [ʌn'ræp] *vt* défaire; ouvrir

unzip [ʌn'zɪp] *vt* ouvrir (la fermeture

éclair de); (*Comput*) dézipper

○ KEYWORD

up [ʌp] *prep*: **he went up the stairs/the hill** il a monté l'escalier/la colline; **the cat was up a tree** le chat était dans un arbre; **they live further up the street** ils habitent plus haut dans la rue; **go up that road and turn left** remontez la rue et tournez à gauche
▷ *adv* **1** en haut; en l'air; (*upwards, higher*): **up in the sky/the mountains** (là-haut) dans le ciel/les montagnes; **put it a bit higher up** mettez-le un peu plus haut; **to stand up** (*get up*) se lever, se mettre debout; (*be standing*) être debout; **up there** là-haut; **up above** au-dessus
2: **to be up** (*out of bed*) être levé(e); (*prices*) avoir augmenté or monté; (*finished*): **when the year was up** à la fin de l'année
3: **up to** (*as far as*) jusqu'à; **up to now** jusqu'à présent
4: **to be up to** (*depending on*): **it's up to you** c'est à vous de décider; (*equal to*): **he's not up to it** (*job, task etc*) il n'en est pas capable; (*inf: be doing*): **what is he up to?** qu'est-ce qu'il peut bien faire?
▷ *n*: **ups and downs** hauts et bas *mpl*

up-and-coming [ʌpənd'kʌmɪŋ] *adj* plein(e) d'avenir or de promesses
upbringing ['ʌpbrɪŋɪŋ] *n* éducation *f*
update [ʌp'deɪt] *vt* mettre à jour
upfront [ʌp'frʌnt] *adj* (*open*) franc (franche) ▷ *adv* (*pay*) d'avance; **to be ~ about sth** ne rien cacher de qch
upgrade [ʌp'greɪd] *vt* (*person*) promouvoir; (*job*) revaloriser; (*property, equipment*) moderniser
upheaval [ʌp'hiːvl] *n* bouleversement *m*; (*in room*) branle-bas *m*; (*event*) crise *f*
uphill [ʌp'hɪl] *adj* qui monte; (*fig: task*) difficile, pénible ▷ *adv* (*face, look*) en amont, vers l'amont; **to go ~** monter
upholstery [ʌp'həʊlstərɪ] *n*

rembourrage *m*; (*cover*) tissu *m* d'ameublement; (*of car*) garniture *f*
upmarket [ʌp'mɑːkɪt] *adj* (*product*) haut de gamme *inv*; (*area*) chic *inv*
upon [ə'pɒn] *prep* sur
upper ['ʌpə*] *adj* supérieur(e); du dessus ▷ *n* (*of shoe*) empeigne *f*; **upper-class** *adj* de la haute société, aristocratique; (*district*) élégant(e), huppé(e); (*accent, attitude*) caractéristique des classes supérieures
upright ['ʌpraɪt] *adj* droit(e); (*fig*) droit, honnête
uprising ['ʌpraɪzɪŋ] *n* soulèvement *m*, insurrection *f*
uproar ['ʌprɔː*] *n* tumulte *m*, vacarme *m*; (*protests*) protestations *fpl*
upset *n* ['ʌpset] dérangement *m*
▷ *vt* (*irreg: like* **set**) [ʌp'set] (*glass etc*) renverser; (*plan*) déranger; (*person: offend*) contrarier; (: *grieve*) faire de la peine à; bouleverser ▷ *adj* [ʌp'set] contrarié(e); peiné(e); **to have a stomach ~** (*BRIT*) avoir une indigestion
upside down ['ʌpsaɪd-] *adv* à l'envers; **to turn sth ~** (*fig: place*) mettre sens dessus dessous
upstairs [ʌp'stɛəz] *adv* en haut ▷ *adj* (*room*) du dessus, d'en haut ▷ *n*: **the ~ l'étage** *m*
up-to-date ['ʌptə'deɪt] *adj* moderne; (*information*) très récent(e)
uptown ['ʌptaʊn] (*us*) *adv* (*live*) dans les quartiers chics; (*go*) vers les quartiers chics ▷ *adj* des quartiers chics
upward ['ʌpwəd] *adj* ascendant(e); vers le haut; **upward(s)** *adv* vers le haut; (*more than*): **upward(s) of** plus de
uranium [juə'reɪnɪəm] *n* uranium *m*
Uranus [juə'reɪnəs] *n* Uranus *f*
urban ['ɜːbən] *adj* urbain(e)
urge [ɜːdʒ] *n* besoin (impératif), envie (pressante) ▷ *vt* (*person*): **to ~ sb to do** exhorter qn à faire, pousser qn à faire, recommander vivement à qn de faire
urgency ['ɜːdʒənsɪ] *n* urgence *f*; (*of tone*) insistance *f*

urgent ['ə:dʒənt] adj urgent(e); (plea, tone) pressant(e)

urinal ['juərɪnl] n (BRIT: place) urinoir m

urinate ['juərɪneɪt] vi uriner

urine ['juərɪn] n urine f

URL abbr (= uniform resource locator) URL f

US n abbr = **United States**

us [ʌs] pron nous; see also **me**

USA n abbr = **United States of America**

use n [ju:s] emploi m, utilisation f; (usefulness) utilité f ▷ vt [ju:z] se servir de, utiliser, employer; **in ~** en usage; **out of ~** hors d'usage; **to be of ~** servir, être utile; **it's no ~** ça ne sert à rien; **to have the ~ of** avoir l'usage de; **she ~d to do it** elle le faisait (autrefois), elle avait coutume de le faire; **to be ~d to** avoir l'habitude de, être habitué(e) à; **use up** vt finir, épuiser; (food) consommer; **used** [ju:zd] adj (car) d'occasion; **useful** adj utile; **useless** adj inutile; (inf: person) nul(le); **user** n utilisateur(-trice), usager m; **user-friendly** adj convivial(e), facile d'emploi

usual ['ju:ʒuəl] adj habituel(le); **as ~** comme d'habitude; **usually** adv d'habitude, d'ordinaire

utensil [ju:'tɛnsl] n ustensile m; **kitchen ~s** batterie f de cuisine

utility [ju:'tɪlɪtɪ] n utilité f; (also: **public ~**) service public

utilize ['ju:tɪlaɪz] vt utiliser; (make good use of) exploiter

utmost ['ʌtməust] adj extrême, le (la) plus grand(e) ▷ n: **to do one's ~** faire tout son possible

utter ['ʌtə*] adj total(e), complet(-ète) ▷ vt prononcer, proférer; (sounds) émettre; **utterly** adv complètement, totalement

U-turn ['ju:'tə:n] n demi-tour m; (fig) volte-face f inv

v. abbr = **verse** (= vide) v.; (= versus) c.; (= volt) V

vacancy ['veɪkənsɪ] n (BRIT: job) poste vacant; (room) chambre f disponible; **"no vacancies"** complet"

vacant ['veɪkənt] adj (post) vacant(e); (seat etc) libre, disponible; (expression) distrait(e)

vacate [və'keɪt] vt quitter

vacation [və'keɪʃən] n (esp us) vacances fpl; **on ~** en vacances; **vacationer** (us **vacationist**) n vacancier(-ière)

vaccination [væksɪ'neɪʃən] n vaccination f

vaccine ['væksi:n] n vaccin m

vacuum ['vækjum] n vide m; **vacuum cleaner** n aspirateur m

vagina [və'dʒaɪnə] n vagin m

vague [veɪg] adj vague, imprécis(e); (blurred: photo, memory) flou(e)

vain [veɪn] adj (useless) vain(e); (conceited) vaniteux(-euse); **in ~** en vain

Valentine's Day ['væləntaɪnz-] n

Saint-Valentin f

valid ['vælɪd] adj (document) valide, valable; (excuse) valable

valley ['vælɪ] n vallée f

valuable ['væljuəbl] adj (jewel) de grande valeur; (time, help) précieux(-euse); **valuables** npl objets mpl de valeur

value ['vælju:] n valeur f ▷ vt (fix price) évaluer, estimer; (appreciate) apprécier; **values** npl (principles) valeurs fpl

valve [vælv] n (in machine) soupape f; (on tyre, valve f; (Med) valve, valvule f

vampire ['væmpaɪə'] n vampire m

van [væn] n (Aut) camionnette f

vandal ['vændl] n vandale m/f; **vandalism** n vandalisme m; **vandalize** vt saccager

vanilla [və'nɪlə] n vanille f

vanish ['vænɪʃ] vi disparaître

vanity ['vænɪtɪ] n vanité f

vapour (US vapor) ['veɪpə'] n vapeur f; (on window) buée f

variable ['vɛərɪəbl] adj variable; (mood) changeant(e)

variant ['vɛərɪənt] n variante f

variation [vɛərɪ'eɪʃən] n variation f; (in opinion) changement m

varied ['vɛərɪd] adj varié(e), divers(e)

variety [və'raɪətɪ] n variété f; (quantity) nombre m, quantité f

various ['vɛərɪəs] adj divers(e), différent(e); (several) divers, plusieurs

varnish ['vɑ:nɪʃ] n vernis m ▷ vt vernir

vary ['vɛərɪ] vt, vi varier, changer

vase [vɑ:z] n vase m

Vaseline® ['væsɪli:n] n vaseline f

vast [vɑ:st] adj vaste, immense; (amount, success) énorme

VAT [væt] n abbr (BRIT: = value added tax) TVA f

vault [vɔ:lt] n (of roof) voûte f; (tomb) caveau m; (in bank) salle f des coffres; chambre forte f ▷ vt (also: ~ over) sauter (d'un bond)

VCR n abbr = **video cassette recorder**

VDU n abbr = **visual display unit**

veal [vi:l] n veau m

veer [vɪə'] vi tourner; (car, ship) virer

vegan ['vi:gən] n végétalien(ne)

vegetable ['vɛdʒtəbl] n légume m ▷ adj végétal(e)

vegetarian [vɛdʒɪ'tɛərɪən] adj, n végétarien(ne); **do you have any ~ dishes?** avez-vous des plats végétariens?

vegetation [vɛdʒɪ'teɪʃən] n végétation f

vehicle ['vi:ɪkl] n véhicule m

veil [veɪl] n voile m

vein [veɪn] n veine f; (on leaf) nervure f

Velcro® ['vɛlkrəu] n velcro® m

velvet ['vɛlvɪt] n velours m

vending machine ['vɛndɪŋ-] n distributeur m automatique

vendor ['vɛndə'] n vendeur(-euse); **street ~** marchand ambulant

Venetian blind [vɪ'ni:ʃən-] n store vénitien

vengeance ['vɛndʒəns] n vengeance f; **with a ~** (fig) vraiment, pour de bon

venison ['vɛnɪsn] n venaison f

venom ['vɛnəm] n venin m

vent [vɛnt] n conduit m d'aération; (in dress, jacket) fente f ▷ vt (fig: one's feelings) donner libre cours à

ventilation [vɛntɪ'leɪʃən] n ventilation f, aération f

venture ['vɛntʃə'] n entreprise f ▷ vi s'aventurer, se risquer; **a business ~** une entreprise commerciale

venue ['vɛnju:] n lieu m

Venus ['vi:nəs] n (planet) Vénus f

verb [və:b] n verbe m; **verbal** adj verbal(e)

verdict ['və:dɪkt] n verdict m

verge [və:dʒ] n bord m; **"soft ~s"** (BRIT) "accotements non stabilisés"; **on the ~ of doing** sur le point de faire

verify ['vɛrɪfaɪ] vt vérifier

versatile ['və:sətaɪl] adj polyvalent(e)

verse [və:s] n vers mpl; (stanza) strophe f; (in Bible) verset m

version ['və:ʃən] n version f

versus ['vɜːsəs] prep contre

vertical ['vɜːtɪkl] adj vertical(e)

very ['verɪ] adv très ▷ adj: **the ~ book which** le livre même que; **the ~ last** tout dernier; **at the ~ least** au moins; **~ much** beaucoup

vessel ['vesl] n (Anat, Naut) vaisseau m; (container) récipient m; see also **blood**

vest [vest] n (BRIT: underwear) tricot m de corps; (US: waistcoat) gilet m

vet [vet] n abbr (BRIT: = veterinary surgeon) vétérinaire m/f; (US: = veteran) ancien(ne) combattant(e) ▷ vt examiner minutieusement

veteran ['vetərn] n vétéran m; (also: **war ~**) ancien combattant

veterinary surgeon ['vetrɪnərɪ−] (BRIT) (US **veterinarian** [vetrɪ'nɛərɪən]) n vétérinaire m/f

veto ['viːtəu] n (pl **−es**) veto m ▷ vt opposer son veto à

via ['vaɪə] prep par, via

viable ['vaɪəbl] adj viable

vibrate [vaɪ'breɪt] vi: **to ~ (with)** vibrer (de)

vibration [vaɪ'breɪʃən] n vibration f

vicar ['vɪkə*] n pasteur m (de l'Église anglicane)

vice [vaɪs] n (evil) vice m; (Tech) étau m; **vice-chairman** n vice-président(e)

vice versa ['vaɪsɪ'vɜːsə] adv vice versa

vicinity [vɪ'sɪnɪtɪ] n environs mpl, alentours mpl

vicious ['vɪʃəs] adj cruel(le), méchant(e); (blow) brutal(e); (dog) méchant(e), dangereux(-euse); **a ~ circle** un cercle vicieux

victim ['vɪktɪm] n victime f

victor ['vɪktə*] n vainqueur m

Victorian [vɪk'tɔːrɪən] adj victorien(ne)

victorious [vɪk'tɔːrɪəs] adj victorieux(-euse)

victory ['vɪktərɪ] n victoire f

video ['vɪdɪəu] (film) vidéo f; (also: **~ cassette**) vidéocassette f; (also: **~ cassette recorder**) magnétoscope m ▷ vt (with recorder) enregistrer;

(with camera) filmer; **video camera** n caméra f vidéo inv; **video (cassette) recorder** n magnétoscope m; **video game** n jeu m vidéo inv; **video shop** n vidéoclub m; **video tape** n bande f vidéo inv; (cassette) vidéocassette f

vie [vaɪ] vi: **to ~ with** lutter avec, rivaliser avec

Vienna [vɪ'enə] n Vienne

Vietnam, Viet Nam ['vjet'næm] n Việt-nam or Vietnam m; **Vietnamese** [vjetnə'miːz] adj vietnamien(ne) ▷ n (pl inv) Vietnamien(ne)

view [vjuː] n (opinion) avis m, vue f; (sight) vue f; **on ~** (in museum etc) exposé(e); **in full ~ of sb** sous les yeux de qn; **in my ~** à mon avis; **in ~ of the fact that** étant donné que; **viewer** n (TV) téléspectateur(-trice); **viewpoint** n point m de vue

vigilant ['vɪdʒɪlənt] adj vigilant(e)

vigorous ['vɪgərəs] adj vigoureux(-euse)

vile [vaɪl] adj (action) vil(e); (smell, food) abominable; (temper) massacrant(e)

villa ['vɪlə] n villa f

village ['vɪlɪdʒ] n village m; **villager** n villageois(e)

villain ['vɪlən] n (scoundrel) scélérat m; (BRIT: criminal) bandit m; (in novel etc) traître m

vinaigrette [vɪneɪ'gret] n vinaigrette f

vine [vaɪn] n vigne f

vinegar ['vɪnɪgə*] n vinaigre m

vineyard ['vɪnjɑːd] n vignoble m

vintage ['vɪntɪdʒ] n (year) année f, millésime m ▷ cpd (car) d'époque; (wine) de grand cru

vinyl ['vaɪnl] n vinyle m

viola [vɪ'əulə] n alto m

violate ['vaɪəleɪt] vt violer

violation [vaɪə'leɪʃən] n violation f; **in ~ of** (rule, law) en infraction à, en violation de

violence ['vaɪələns] n violence f

violent ['vaɪələnt] adj violent(e)

violet ['vaɪələt] adj (colour) violet(te)

▷ n (plant) violette f
violin [vaɪə'lɪn] n violon m
VIP n abbr (= very important person) VIP m
virgin ['vɜːdʒɪn] n vierge f
Virgo ['vɜːgəʊ] n la Vierge
virtual ['vɜːtjʊəl] adj (Comput, Physics) virtuel(le); (in effect): **it's a ~ impossibility** c'est quasiment impossible; **virtually** adv (almost) pratiquement; **virtual reality** n (Comput) réalité virtuelle
virtue ['vɜːtjuː] n vertu f; (advantage) mérite m, avantage m; **by ~ of** en vertu or raison de
virus ['vaɪərəs] n (Med, Comput) virus m
visa ['viːzə] n visa m
vise [vaɪs] n (us Tech) = **vice**
visibility [vɪzɪ'bɪlɪtɪ] n visibilité f
visible ['vɪzəbl] adj visible
vision ['vɪʒən] n (sight) vue f, vision f; (foresight, in dream) vision
visit ['vɪzɪt] n visite f; (stay) séjour m ▷ vt (person: us: also: **~ with**) rendre visite à; (place) visiter; **visiting hours** npl heures fpl de visite; **visitor** n visiteur(-euse); (to one's house) invité(e); **visitor centre** (us **visitor center**) n hall m or centre m d'accueil
visual ['vɪzjʊəl] adj visuel(le); **visualize** vt se représenter
vital ['vaɪtl] adj vital(e); **of ~ importance (to sb/sth)** d'une importance capitale (pour qn/qch)
vitality [vaɪ'tælɪtɪ] n vitalité f
vitamin ['vɪtəmɪn] n vitamine f
vivid ['vɪvɪd] adj (account) frappant(e), vivant(e); (light, imagination) vif (vive)
V-neck ['viːnɛk] n décolleté m en V
vocabulary [vəʊ'kæbjʊlərɪ] n vocabulaire m
vocal ['vəʊkl] adj vocal(e); (articulate) qui n'hésite pas à s'exprimer, qui sait faire entendre ses opinions
vocational [vəʊ'keɪʃənl] adj professionnel(le)
vodka ['vɒdkə] n vodka f
vogue [vəʊg] n: **to be in ~** être en vogue or à la mode

voice [vɔɪs] n voix f ▷ vt (opinion) exprimer, formuler; **voice mail** n (system) messagerie f vocale; (device) boîte f vocale
void [vɔɪd] n vide m ▷ adj (invalid) nul(le); (empty): **~ of** vide de, dépourvu(e) de
volatile ['vɒlətaɪl] adj volatil(e); (fig: person) versatile; (: situation) explosif(-ive)
volcano (pl **-es**) [vɒl'keɪnəʊ] n volcan m
volleyball ['vɒlɪbɔːl] n volley-(ball) m
volt [vəʊlt] n volt m; **voltage** n tension f, voltage m
volume ['vɒljuːm] n volume m; (of tank) capacité f
voluntarily ['vɒləntrɪlɪ] adv volontairement
voluntary ['vɒləntərɪ] adj volontaire; (unpaid) bénévole
volunteer [vɒlən'tɪəʳ] n volontaire m/f ▷ vt (information) donner spontanément ▷ vi (Mil) s'engager comme volontaire; **to ~ to do** se proposer pour faire
vomit ['vɒmɪt] n vomissure f ▷ vt, vi vomir
vote [vəʊt] n vote m, suffrage m; (votes cast) voix f, vote; (franchise) droit m de vote ▷ vt (chairman) élire; (propose): **to ~ that** proposer que + sub ▷ vi voter; **~ of thanks** discours m de remerciement; **voter** n électeur(-trice); **voting** n scrutin m, vote m
voucher ['vaʊtʃəʳ] n (for meal, petrol, gift) bon m
vow [vaʊ] n vœu m, serment m ▷ vi jurer
vowel ['vaʊəl] n voyelle f
voyage ['vɔɪɪdʒ] n voyage m par mer, traversée f
vulgar ['vʌlgəʳ] adj vulgaire
vulnerable ['vʌlnərəbl] adj vulnérable
vulture ['vʌltʃəʳ] n vautour m

W

waddle ['wɔdl] vi se dandiner

wade [weɪd] vi: **to ~ through** marcher dans, patauger dans; (*fig: book*) venir à bout de

wafer ['weɪfə'] n (*Culin*) gaufrette f

waffle ['wɔfl] n (*Culin*) gaufre f ▷ vi parler pour ne rien dire; faire du remplissage

wag [wæg] vt agiter, remuer ▷ vi remuer

wage [weɪdʒ] n (*also:* **~s**) salaire m, paye f ▷ vt: **to ~ war** faire la guerre

wag(g)on ['wægən] n (*horse-drawn*) chariot m; (*BRIT Rail*) wagon m (de marchandises)

wail [weɪl] n gémissement m; (*of siren*) hurlement m ▷ vi gémir; (*siren*) hurler

waist [weɪst] n taille f, ceinture f; **waistcoat** n (*BRIT*) gilet m

wait [weɪt] n attente f ▷ vi attendre; **to ~ for sb/sth** attendre qn/qch; **to keep sb ~ing** faire attendre qn; **~ for me, please** attendez-moi, s'il vous plaît; **I can't ~ to ...** (*fig*) je meurs

d'envie de ...; **to lie in ~ for** guetter; **wait on** vt fus servir; **waiter** n garçon m (de café), serveur m; **waiting list** n liste f d'attente; **waiting room** n salle f d'attente; **waitress** ['weɪtrɪs] n serveuse f

waive [weɪv] vt renoncer à, abandonner

wake [weɪk] vb (*pt* **woke** *or* **~d**, *pp* **woken** *or* **~d**) ▷ vt (*also:* **~ up**) réveiller ▷ vi (*also:* **~ up**) se réveiller ▷ n (*for dead person*) veillée f mortuaire; (*Naut*) sillage m

Wales [weɪlz] n pays m de Galles; **the Prince of ~** le prince de Galles

walk [wɔːk] n promenade f; (*short*) petit tour; (*gait*) démarche f; (*path*) chemin m; (*in park etc*) allée f ▷ vi marcher; (*for pleasure, exercise*) se promener ▷ vt (*distance*) faire à pied; (*dog*) promener; **10 minutes' ~ from** à 10 minutes de marche de; **to go for a ~** se promener; faire un tour; **from all ~s of life** de toutes conditions sociales; **walk out** vi (*go out*) sortir; (*as protest*) partir (en signe de protestation); (*strike*) se mettre en grève; **to ~ out on sb** quitter qn; **walker** n (*person*) marcheur(-euse) f; **walkie-talkie** ['wɔːkɪ'tɔːkɪ] n talkie-walkie m; **walking** n marche f à pied; **walking shoes** npl chaussures fpl de marche; **walking stick** n canne f; **Walkman®** n Walkman® m; **walkway** n promenade f, cheminement piéton

wall [wɔːl] n mur m; (*of tunnel, cave*) paroi f

wallet ['wɔlɪt] n portefeuille m; **I can't find my ~** je ne retrouve plus mon portefeuille

wallpaper ['wɔːlpeɪpə'] n papier peint ▷ vt tapisser

walnut ['wɔːlnʌt] n noix f; (*tree, wood*) noyer m

walrus (*pl* **~** *or* **~es**) ['wɔːlrəs] n morse m

waltz [wɔːlts] n valse f ▷ vi valser

wand [wɔnd] n (*also:* **magic ~**) baguette f (magique)

wander ['wɔndə'] vi (*person*) errer, aller

sans but; (*thoughts*) vagabonder ▷ *vt* errer dans

want [wɒnt] *vt* vouloir; (*need*) avoir besoin de ▷ *n*: **for ~ of** par manque de, faute de; **to ~ to do** vouloir faire; **to ~ sb to do** vouloir qn fasse; **wanted** *adj* (*criminal*) recherché(e) par la police; **"cook wanted"** "on recherche un cuisinier"

war [wɔːʳ] *n* guerre *f*; **to make ~ (on)** faire la guerre (à)

ward [wɔːd] *n* (*in hospital*) salle *f*; (*Pol*) section électorale; (*Law: child: also*: ~ **of court**) pupille *m/f*

warden [ˈwɔːdn] *n* (*BRIT: of institution*) directeur(-trice); (*of park, game reserve*) gardien(ne); (*BRIT: also*: **traffic ~**) contractuel(le)

wardrobe [ˈwɔːdrəub] *n* (*cupboard*) armoire *f*; (*clothes*) garde-robe *f*

warehouse [ˈwɛəhaus] *n* entrepôt *m*

warfare [ˈwɔːfɛəʳ] *n* guerre *f*

warhead [ˈwɔːhɛd] *n* (*Mil*) ogive *f*

warm [wɔːm] *adj* chaud(e); (*person, thanks, welcome, applause*) chaleureux(-euse); **it's ~** il fait chaud; **I'm ~** j'ai chaud; **warm up** *vi* (*person, room*) se réchauffer; (*athlete, discussion*) s'échauffer ▷ *vt* (*food*) (faire) réchauffer; (*water*) (faire) chauffer; (*engine*) faire chauffer; **warmly** *adv* (*dress*) chaudement; (*thank, welcome*) chaleureusement; **warmth** *n* chaleur *f*

warn [wɔːn] *vt* avertir, prévenir; **to ~ sb (not) to** conseiller à qn de (ne pas) faire; **warning** *n* avertissement *m*; (*notice*) avis *m*; **warning light** *n* avertisseur lumineux

warrant [ˈwɒrnt] *n* (*guarantee*) garantie *f*; (*Law: to arrest*) mandat *m* d'arrêt; (*: to search*) mandat de perquisition ▷ *vt* (*justify, merit*) justifier

warranty [ˈwɒrənti] *n* garantie *f*

warrior [ˈwɒriəʳ] *n* guerrier(-ière)

Warsaw [ˈwɔːsɔː] *n* Varsovie

warship [ˈwɔːʃip] *n* navire *m* de guerre

wart [wɔːt] *n* verrue *f*

wartime [ˈwɔːtaim] *n*: **in ~** en temps de guerre

wary [ˈwɛəri] *adj* prudent(e)

was [wɒz] *pt of* **be**

wash [wɒʃ] *vt* laver ▷ *vi* se laver; (*sea*): **to ~ over/against sth** inonder/baigner qch ▷ *n* (*clothes*) lessive *f*; (*washing programme*) lavage *m*; (*of ship*) sillage *m*; **to have a ~** se laver, faire sa toilette; **wash up** *vi* (*BRIT*) faire la vaisselle; (*US: have a wash*) se débarbouiller; **washbasin** *n* lavabo *m*; **wash cloth** *n* (*US*) gant *m* de toilette; **washer** *n* (*Tech*) rondelle *f*, joint *m*; **washing** *n* (*BRIT: linen etc: dirty*) linge *m*; (*: clean*) lessive *f*; **washing line** *n* (*BRIT*) corde *f* à linge; **washing machine** *n* machine *f* à laver; **washing powder** *n* (*BRIT*) lessive *f* (en poudre)

Washington [ˈwɔʃiŋtən] *n* Washington *m*

wash: **washing-up** *n* (*BRIT*) vaisselle *f*; **washing-up liquid** *n* (*BRIT*) produit *m* pour la vaisselle; **washroom** *n* (*US*) toilettes *fpl*

wasn't [ˈwɒznt] = **was not**

wasp [wɒsp] *n* guêpe *f*

waste [weist] *n* gaspillage *m*; (*of time*) perte *f*; (*rubbish*) déchets *mpl*; (*also*: **household ~**) ordures *fpl* ▷ *adj* (*land, ground: in city*) à l'abandon; (*leftover*): **~ material** déchets *mpl* ▷ *vt* gaspiller; (*time, opportunity*) perdre; **waste ground** *n* (*BRIT*) terrain *m* vague; **wastepaper basket** *n* corbeille *f* à papier

watch [wɒtʃ] *n* montre *f*; (*act of watching*) surveillance *f*; (*guard: Mil*) sentinelle *f*; (*: Naut*) homme *m* de quart; (*Naut: spell of duty*) quart *m* ▷ *vt* (*look at*) observer; (*: match, programme*) regarder; (*spy on, guard*) surveiller; (*be careful of*) faire attention à ▷ *vi* regarder; (*keep guard*) monter la garde; **to keep ~** faire le guet; **watch out** *vi* faire attention; **watchdog** *n* chien *m* de garde; (*fig*) gardien(ne); **watch strap** *n* bracelet *m* de montre

water [ˈwɔːtəʳ] *n* eau *f* ▷ *vt* (*plant, garden*) arroser ▷ *vi* (*eyes*) larmoyer; **in**

British ~s dans les eaux territoriales Britanniques; **to make sb's mouth ~** mettre l'eau à la bouche de qn; **water down** vt (milk etc) couper avec de l'eau; (fig: story) édulcorer; **watercolour** (us **watercolor**) n aquarelle f; **watercress** n cresson m (de fontaine); **waterfall** n chute f d'eau; **watering can** n arrosoir m; **watermelon** n pastèque f; **waterproof** adj imperméable; **water-skiing** n ski m nautique

watt [wɔt] n watt m

wave [weɪv] n vague f; (of hand) geste m, signe m; (Radio) onde f; (in hair) ondulation f; (fig: of enthusiasm, strikes etc) vague f ▷ vi faire signe de la main; (flag) flotter au vent; (grass) ondoyer ▷ vt (handkerchief) agiter; (stick) brandir; **wavelength** n longueur f d'ondes

waver ['weɪvə'] vi vaciller; (voice) trembler; (person) hésiter

wavy ['weɪvɪ] adj (hair, surface) ondulé(e); (line) onduleux(-euse)

wax [wæks] n cire f; (for skis) fart m ▷ vt cirer; (car) lustrer; (skis) farter ▷ vi (moon) croître

way [weɪ] n chemin m, voie f; (distance) distance f; (direction) chemin, direction f; (manner) façon f, manière f; (habit) habitude f, façon; **which ~? — this ~/that ~** par où or de quel côté? — par ici/par là; **to lose one's ~** perdre son chemin; **on the ~ (to)** en route (pour); **to be on one's ~** être en route; **to be in the ~** bloquer le passage; (fig) gêner; **it's a long ~ away** c'est loin d'ici; **to go out of one's ~ to do** (fig) se donner beaucoup de mal pour faire; **to be under ~** (work, project) être en cours; **in a ~** dans un sens; **by the ~** à propos; **"~ in"** (BRIT) "entrée"; **"~ out"** (BRIT) "sortie"; **the ~ back** le chemin du retour; **"give ~"** (BRIT AUT) cédez la priorité; **no ~!** (inf) pas question!

W.C. n abbr (BRIT = water closet) w.-c. mpl, waters mpl

we [wiː] pl pron nous

weak [wiːk] adj faible; (health) fragile; (beam etc) peu solide; (tea, coffee) léger(-ère); **weaken** vi faiblir ▷ vt affaiblir; **weakness** n faiblesse f; (fault) point m faible

wealth [wɛlθ] n (money, resources) richesse(s) f(pl); (of details) profusion f; **wealthy** adj riche

weapon ['wɛpən] n arme f; **~s of mass destruction** armes fpl de destruction massive

wear [wɛə'] n (use) usage m; (deterioration through use) usure f ▷ vb (pt **wore**, pp **worn**) ▷ vt (clothes) porter; (put on) mettre; (damage: through use) user ▷ vi (last) faire de l'usage; (rub etc through) s'user; **sports/baby-evening ~** tenue f de soirée; **wear off** vi disparaître; **wear out** vt (person, strength) épuiser

weary ['wɪərɪ] adj (tired) épuisé(e); (dispirited) las (lasse); abattu(e) ▷ vi: **to ~ of** se lasser de

weasel ['wiːzl] n (Zool) belette f

weather ['wɛðə'] n temps m ▷ vt (storm: lit, fig) essuyer; (crisis) survivre à; **under the ~** (fig: ill) mal fichu(e); **weather forecast** n prévisions fpl météorologiques, météo f

weave (pt **wove**, pp **woven**) [wiːv, wəʊv, 'wəʊvn] vt (cloth) tisser; (basket) tresser

web [wɛb] n (of spider) toile f; (on duck's foot) palmure f; (fig) tissu m; (Comput): **the (World-Wide) W~** le Web; **web page** n (Comput) page f Web; **website** n (Comput) site m web

wed [wɛd] (pt, pp **~ded**) vt épouser ▷ vi se marier

Wed abbr (= Wednesday) me

we'd [wiːd] = we had; we would

wedding ['wɛdɪŋ] n mariage m; **wedding anniversary** n anniversaire m de mariage; **silver/golden wedding anniversary** noces fpl d'argent/d'or; **wedding day** n jour m du mariage; **wedding dress** n robe f de mariée;

wedding ring n alliance f
wedge [wɛdʒ] n (of wood etc) coin m; (under door etc) cale f; (of cake) part f ▷ vt (fix) caler; (push) enfoncer, coincer
Wednesday ['wɛdnzdɪ] n mercredi m
wee [wiː] adj (SCOTTISH) petit(e); tout(e) petit(e)
weed [wiːd] n mauvaise herbe ▷ vt désherber; **weedkiller** n désherbant m
week [wiːk] n semaine f; **a ~ today/on Tuesday** aujourd'hui/mardi en huit; **weekday** n jour m de semaine; (Comm) jour ouvrable; **weekend** n week-end m; **weekly** adv une fois par semaine, chaque semaine ▷ adj, n hebdomadaire (m)
weep [wiːp] (pt, pp **wept**) vi (person) pleurer
weigh [weɪ] vt, vi peser; **to ~ anchor** lever l'ancre; **weigh up** vt examiner
weight [weɪt] n poids m; **to put on/ lose ~** grossir/maigrir; **weightlifting** n haltérophilie f
weir [wɪəʳ] n barrage m
weird [wɪəd] adj bizarre; (eerie) surnaturel(le)
welcome ['wɛlkəm] adj bienvenu(e) ▷ n accueil m ▷ vt accueillir; (also: **bid ~**) souhaiter la bienvenue à; (be glad of) se réjouir de; **you're ~!** (after thanks) de rien, il n'y a pas de quoi
weld [wɛld] vt souder
welfare ['wɛlfɛəʳ] n (wellbeing) bien-être m; (social aid) assistance sociale; **welfare state** n État-providence m
well [wɛl] n puits m ▷ adv bien ▷ adj: **to be ~** aller bien ▷ excl eh bien!; (relief also) bon!; (resignation) enfin!; **~ done!** bravo!; **get ~ soon!** remets-toi vite!; **to do ~** bien réussir; (business) prospérer; **as ~** (in addition) aussi, également; **as ~ as** aussi bien que or de; en plus de
we'll [wiːl] = **we will; we shall**
well: **well-behaved** adj sage, obéissant(e); **well-built** adj (person) bien bâti(e); **well-dressed** adj (person) habillé(e), bien vêtu(e)
well-groomed [-'gruːmd] adj très

soigné(e)
wellies ['wɛlɪz] (inf) npl (BRIT) = **wellingtons**
wellingtons ['wɛlɪŋtənz] npl (also: **wellington boots**) bottes fpl en caoutchouc
well: **well-known** adj (person) bien connu(e); **well-off** adj aisé(e), assez riche; **well-paid** [wɛl'peɪd] adj bien payé(e)
Welsh [wɛlʃ] adj gallois(e) ▷ n (Ling) gallois m; **the Welsh** npl (people) les Gallois; **Welshman** (irreg) n Gallois m; **Welshwoman** (irreg) n Galloise f
went [wɛnt] pt of **go**
wept [wɛpt] pt, pp of **weep**
were [wəːʳ] pt of **be**
we're [wɪəʳ] = **we are**
weren't [wəːnt] = **were not**
west [wɛst] n ouest m ▷ adj (wind) d'ouest; (side) ouest inv ▷ adv à l'or vers l'ouest; **the W~** l'Occident m, l'Ouest; **westbound** ['wɛstbaʊnd] adj (traffic) en direction de l'ouest; (carriageway) ouest inv; **western** adj occidental(e), de or à l'ouest ▷ n (Cine) western m; **West Indian** adj antillais(e) ▷ n Antillais(e)
West Indies [-'ɪndɪz] npl Antilles fpl
wet [wɛt] adj mouillé(e); (damp) humide; (soaked: also: **~ through**) trempé(e); (rainy) pluvieux(-euse); **to get ~** se mouiller; **"~ paint"** "attention peinture fraîche"; **wetsuit** n combinaison f de plongée
we've [wiːv] = **we have**
whack [wæk] vt donner un grand coup à
whale [weɪl] n (Zool) baleine f
wharf (pl **wharves**) [wɔːf, wɔːvz] n quai m

 **KEYWORD**

what [wɔt] adj 1 (in questions) quel(le); **what size is he?** quelle taille fait-il?; **what colour is it?** de quelle couleur est-ce?; **what books do you need?**

quels livres vous faut-il?
2 (in exclamations): **what a mess!** quel
désordre!; **what a fool I am!** que je
suis bête!
▷ pron 1 (interrogative) que; de/à/en
etc quoi; **what are you doing?** que
faites-vous?, qu'est-ce que vous faites?;
what is happening? qu'est-ce qui se
passe?, que se passe-t-il?; **what are
you talking about?** de quoi parlez-
vous?; **what are you thinking about?**
à quoi pensez-vous?; **what is it called?**
comment est-ce que ça s'appelle?;
what about me? et moi?; **what about
doing ...?** et si on faisait ...?
2 (relative: subject) ce qui; (: direct object)
ce que; (: indirect object) ce à quoi, ce
dont; **I saw what you did/was on the
table** j'ai vu ce que vous avez fait/ce
qui était sur la table; **tell me what
you remember** dites-moi ce dont
vous vous souvenez; **what I want is
a cup of tea** ce que je veux, c'est une
tasse de thé
▷ excl (disbelieving) quoi!, comment!

whatever [wɔtˈɛvəˀ] adj: **take ~ book
you prefer** prenez le livre que vous
préférez, peu importe lequel; **~ book
you take** quel que soit le livre que
vous preniez ▷ pron: **do ~ is
necessary** faites (tout) ce qui est
nécessaire; **~ happens** quoi qu'il
arrive; **no reason ~ or whatsoever**
pas la moindre raison; **nothing ~ or
whatsoever** rien du tout
whatsoever [wɔtsəʊˈɛvəˀ] adj see
whatever
wheat [wiːt] n blé m, froment m
wheel [wiːl] n roue f; (Aut: also:
steering ~) volant m; (Naut)
gouvernail m ▷ vt (pram etc) pousser,
rouler ▷ vi (birds) tournoyer; (also:
~ round: person) se retourner, faire
volte-face; **wheelbarrow** n brouette f;
wheelchair n fauteuil roulant;
wheel clamp n (Aut) sabot m (de
Denver)

wheeze [wiːz] vi respirer bruyamment

○ **KEYWORD**

when [wɛn] adv quand; **when did he
go?** quand est-ce qu'il est parti?
▷ conj 1 (at, during, after the time that)
quand, lorsque; **she was reading
when I came in** elle lisait quand or
lorsque je suis entré
2 (on, at which): **on the day when I met
him** le jour où je l'ai rencontré
3 (whereas) alors que; **I thought I was
wrong when in fact I was right** j'ai
cru que j'avais tort alors qu'en fait
j'avais raison

whenever [wɛnˈɛvəˀ] adv quand donc
▷ conj quand; (every time that) chaque
fois que
where [wɛəˀ] adv, conj où; **this is ~**
c'est là que; **whereabouts** adv où
donc ▷ n: **nobody knows his
whereabouts** personne ne sait où
il se trouve; **whereas** conj alors que;
whereby adv (formal) par lequel (or
laquelle etc); **wherever** adv où donc
▷ conj où que + sub; **sit wherever
you like** asseyez-vous (là) où vous
voulez
whether [ˈwɛðəˀ] conj si; **I don't know
~ to accept or not** je ne sais pas si je
dois accepter ou non; **it's doubtful ~** il
est peu probable que + sub; **~ you go or
not** que vous y alliez ou non

○ **KEYWORD**

which [wɪtʃ] adj 1 (interrogative: direct,
indirect) quel(le); **which picture do
you want?** quel tableau voulez-vous?;
which one? lequel (laquelle)?
2: **in which case** auquel cas; **we got
there at 8pm, by which time the
cinema was full** nous sommes
arrivés à 20h, le cinéma
était complet
▷ pron 1 (interrogative) lequel (laquelle).

lesquels (lesquelles) pl; **I don't mind which** peu importe lequel; **which (of these) are yours?;** lesquels sont à vous?; **tell me which you want** dites-moi lesquels or ceux que vous voulez

2 (relative: subject) qui; (: object) que; sur/vers etc lequel (laquelle) (NB: à + lequel = **auquel**; de + lequel = **duquel**); **the apple which you ate/which is on the table** la pomme que vous avez mangée/qui est sur la table; **the chair on which you are sitting** la chaise sur laquelle vous êtes assis; **the book of which you spoke** le livre dont vous avez parlé; **he said he knew, which is true/I was afraid of** il a dit qu'il le savait, ce qui est vrai/ce que je craignais; **after which** après quoi

whichever [wɪtʃˈɛvəʳ] adj: **take ~ book you prefer** prenez le livre que vous préférez, peu importe lequel; **~ book you take** quel que soit le livre que vous preniez

while [waɪl] n moment m ▷ conj pendant que; (as long as) tant que; (as, whereas) alors que; (though) bien que + sub, quoique + sub; **for a ~** pendant quelque temps; **in a ~** dans un moment

whilst [waɪlst] conj = **while**

whim [wɪm] n caprice m

whine [waɪn] n gémissement m; (of engine, siren) plainte stridente ▷ vi gémir, geindre, pleurnicher; (dog, engine, siren) gémir

whip [wɪp] n fouet m; (for riding) cravache f; (Pol: person) chef m de file (assurant la discipline dans son groupe parlementaire) ▷ vt fouetter; (snatch) enlever (or sortir) brusquement; **whipped cream** n crème fouettée

whirl [wəːl] vi tourbillonner; (dancers) tournoyer ▷ vt faire tourbillonner; faire tournoyer

whisk [wɪsk] n (Culin) fouet m ▷ vt

(eggs) fouetter, battre; **to ~ sb away** or **off** emmener qn rapidement

whiskers [ˈwɪskəz] npl (of animal) moustaches fpl; (of man) favoris mpl

whisky (IRISH, US **whiskey**) [ˈwɪskɪ] n whisky m

whisper [ˈwɪspəʳ] n chuchotement m ▷ vt, vi chuchoter

whistle [ˈwɪsl] n (sound) sifflement m; (object) sifflet m ▷ vi siffler ▷ vt siffler, siffloter

white [waɪt] adj blanc (blanche); (with fear) blême ▷ n blanc m; (person) blanc (blanche); **White House** n (us): **the White House** la Maison-Blanche; **whitewash** n (paint) lait m de chaux ▷ vt blanchir à la chaux; (fig) blanchir

whiting [ˈwaɪtɪŋ] n (pl inv: fish) merlan m

Whitsun [ˈwɪtsn] n la Pentecôte

whittle [ˈwɪtl] vt: **to ~ away, to ~ down** (costs) réduire, rogner

whizz [wɪz] vi aller (or passer) à toute vitesse

who [huː] pron qui

whoever [huːˈɛvəʳ] pron: **~ finds it** celui (celle) qui le trouve , (qui que ce soit), quiconque le trouve; **ask ~ you like** demandez à qui vous voulez; **~ he marries** qui que ce soit or quelle que soit la personne qu'il épouse; **~ told you that?** qui a bien pu vous dire ça?, qui donc vous a dit ça?

whole [həʊl] adj (complete) entier(-ière), tout(e); (not broken) intact(e), complet(-ète) ▷ n (all): **the ~ of** la totalité de, tout(e) le (la); (entire unit) tout m; **the ~ of the town** la ville tout entière; **on the ~, as a ~** dans l'ensemble; **wholefood(s)** n(pl) aliments complets; **wholeheartedly** [həʊlˈhɑːtɪdlɪ] adv sans réserve; **to agree wholeheartedly** être entièrement d'accord; **wholemeal** adj (BRIT: flour, bread) complet(-ète); **wholesale** n (vente fen) gros m ▷ adj (price) de gros; (destruction) systématique; **wholewheat**

adj = **wholemeal**; **wholly** adv
entièrement, tout à fait

O **KEYWORD**

whom [hu:m] pron 1 (interrogative) qui;
whom did you see? qui avez-vous vu?;
to whom did you give it? à qui l'avez-vous donné?
2 (relative) que; à/de etc qui; **the man whom I saw/to whom I spoke**
l'homme que j'ai vu/à qui j'ai parlé

whore [hɔ:ʳ] n (inf: pej) putain f

O **KEYWORD**

whose [hu:z] adj 1 (possessive:
interrogative): **whose book is this?**
à qui est ce livre?;
whose pencil have you taken? à qui
est le crayon que vous avez pris?, c'est
le crayon de qui que vous avez pris?;
whose daughter are you? de qui
êtes-vous la fille?
2 (possessive: relative): **the man whose
son you rescued** l'homme dont or
de qui vous avez sauvé le fils; **the girl
whose sister you were speaking to**
la fille à la sœur de qui or de laquelle
vous parliez; **the woman whose car
was stolen** la femme dont la voiture
a été volée
▷ pron à qui; **whose is this?** à qui est
ceci?; **I know whose it is** je sais à
qui c'est

O **KEYWORD**

why [waɪ] adv pourquoi?; **why not?**
pourquoi pas?
▷ conj: **I wonder why he said that** je
me demande pourquoi il a dit ça; **that's
not why I'm here** ce n'est pas pour ça
que je suis là; **the reason why** la raison
pour laquelle
▷ excl eh bien!, tiens!; **why, it's**

you! tiens, c'est vous!; **why, that's
impossible!** voyons, c'est impossible!

wicked ['wɪkɪd] adj méchant(e);
(mischievous: grin, look) espiègle,
malicieux(-euse); (crime) pervers(e);
(inf: very good) génial(e) (inf)

wicket ['wɪkɪt] n (Cricket: stumps)
guichet m; (: grass area) espace compris
entre les deux guichets

wide [waɪd] adj large; (area, knowledge)
vaste, très étendu(e); (choice) grand(e)
▷ adv: **to open ~** ouvrir tout grand;
to shoot ~ tirer à côté; **it is 3 metres
~** cela fait 3 mètres de large; **widely**
adv (different) radicalement; (spaced)
sur une grande étendue; (believed)
généralement; (travel) beaucoup;
widen vt élargir ▷ vi s'élargir;
wide open adj grand(e) ouvert(e);
widespread adj (belief etc) très
répandu(e)

widow ['wɪdəʊ] n veuve f; **widower**
n veuf m

width [wɪdθ] n largeur f

wield [wi:ld] vt (sword) manier; (power)
exercer

wife (pl **wives**) [waɪf, waɪvz] n femme
f, épouse f

wig [wɪg] n perruque f

wild [waɪld] adj sauvage; (sea)
déchaîné(e); (idea, life) fou (folle);
(behaviour) déchaîné(e), extravagant(e);
(inf: angry) hors de soi, furieux(-euse)
▷ n: **the ~** la nature; **wilderness**
['wɪldənɪs] n désert m, région f
sauvage; **wildlife** n faune f (et flore
f); **wildly** adv (behave) de manière
déchaînée; (applaud) frénétiquement;
(hit, guess) au hasard; (happy) follement

O **KEYWORD**

will [wɪl] aux vb 1 (forming future tense):
I will finish it tomorrow je le finirai
demain; **I will have finished it by
tomorrow** je l'aurai fini d'ici demain;
will you do it? - yes I will/no I won't

ferez-vous? - oui/non
2 (*in conjectures, predictions*): **he will** or **he'll be there by now** il doit être arrivé à l'heure qu'il est; **that will be the postman** ça doit être le facteur
3 (*in commands, requests, offers*): **will you be quiet!** voulez-vous bien vous taire!; **will you help me?** est-ce que vous pouvez m'aider?; **will you have a cup of tea?** voulez-vous une tasse de thé?; **I won't put up with it!** je ne le tolérerai pas!
▷ vt (*pt, pp* **willed**): **to will sb to do** souhaiter ardemment que qn fasse; **he willed himself to go on** par un suprême effort de volonté, il continua
▷ vi (*document*) testament *m*;
against one's will à contre-cœur

willing ['wɪlɪŋ] *adj* de bonne volonté, serviable; **he's ~ to do it** il est disposé à la faire, il veut bien le faire; **willingly** *adv* volontiers
willow ['wɪləʊ] *n* saule *m*
willpower ['wɪl'paʊə'] *n* volonté *f*
wilt [wɪlt] *vi* dépérir
win [wɪn] *n* (*in sports etc*) victoire *f* ▷ vb (*pt, pp* **won**) ▷ vt (*battle, money*) gagner; (*prize, contract*) remporter; (*popularity*) acquérir ▷ vi gagner; **win over** vt convaincre
wince [wɪns] *vi* tressaillir
wind[1] [wɪnd] *n* (*also Med*) vent *m*; (*breath*) souffle *m* ▷ vt (*take breath away*) couper le souffle à; **the ~(s)** (*Mus*) les instruments *mpl* à vent
wind[2] [waɪnd] (*pt, pp* **wound**) *vt* enrouler; (*wrap*) envelopper; (*clock, toy*) remonter ▷ vi (*road, river*) serpenter; **wind down** *vt* (*car window*) baisser; (*fig: production, business*) réduire progressivement; **wind up** *vt* (*clock*) remonter; (*debate*) terminer, clôturer
windfall ['wɪndfɔ:l] *n* coup *m* de chance
winding ['waɪndɪŋ] *adj* (*road*) sinueux(-euse); (*staircase*) tournant(e)
windmill ['wɪndmɪl] *n* moulin *m* à vent

window ['wɪndəʊ] *n* fenêtre *f*; (*in car, train: also:* **~-pane**) vitre *f*; (*in shop etc*) vitrine *f*; **window box** *n* jardinière *f*; **window cleaner** *n* (*person*) laveur(-euse) de vitres; **window pane** *n* vitre *f*, carreau *m*; **window seat** *n* (*in vehicle*) place *f* côté fenêtre; **windowsill** *n* (*inside*) appui *m* de la fenêtre; (*outside*) rebord *m* de la fenêtre
windscreen ['wɪndskriːn] *n* pare-brise *m inv*; **windscreen wiper** *n* essuie-glace *m inv*
windshield ['wɪndʃiːld] (*us*) *n* = **windscreen**
windsurfing ['wɪndsɜːfɪŋ] *n* planche *f* à voile
windy ['wɪndɪ] *adj* (*day*) de vent, venteux(-euse); (*place, weather*) venteux; **it's ~** il y a du vent
wine [waɪn] *n* vin *m*; **wine bar** *n* bar *m* à vin; **wine glass** *n* verre *m* à vin; **wine list** *n* carte *f* des vins; **wine tasting** *n* dégustation *f* (de vins)
wing [wɪŋ] *n* aile *f*; **wings** *npl* (*Theat*) coulisses *fpl*; **wing mirror** *n* (*BRIT*) rétroviseur latéral
wink [wɪŋk] *n* clin *m* d'œil ▷ *vi* faire un clin d'œil; (*blink*) cligner des yeux
winner ['wɪnə'] *n* gagnant(e)
winning ['wɪnɪŋ] *adj* (*team*) gagnant(e); (*goal*) décisif(-ive); (*charming*) charmeur(-euse)
winter ['wɪntə'] *n* hiver *m* ▷ *vi* hiverner; **in ~** en hiver; **winter sports** *npl* sports *mpl* d'hiver; **wintertime** *n* hiver *m*
wipe [waɪp] *n*: **to give sth a ~** donner un coup de torchon/de chiffon/d'éponge à qch ▷ *vt* essuyer; (*erase: tape*) effacer; **to ~ one's nose** se moucher; **wipe out** *vt* (*debt*) éteindre, amortir; (*memory*) effacer; (*destroy*) anéantir; **wipe up** *vt* essuyer
wire ['waɪə'] *n* fil *m* (de fer); (*Elec*) fil électrique; (*Tel*) télégramme *m* ▷ *vt* (*house*) faire l'installation électrique de; (*also:* **~ up**) brancher; (*person: send telegram to*) télégraphier à

wiring ['waɪərɪŋ] n (Elec) installation f électrique

wisdom ['wɪzdəm] n sagesse f; (of action) prudence f; **wisdom tooth** n dent f de sagesse

wise [waɪz] adj sage, prudent(e); (remark) judicieux(-euse)

wish [wɪʃ] n (desire) désir m; (specific desire) souhait m, vœu m ▷ vt souhaiter, désirer, vouloir; **best ~es** (on birthday etc) meilleurs vœux; **with best ~es** (in letter) bien amicalement; **to ~ sb goodbye** dire au revoir à qn; **he ~ed me well** il m'a souhaité bonne chance; **to ~ to do/sb to do** désirer or vouloir faire/que qn fasse; **to ~ for** souhaiter

wistful ['wɪstful] adj mélancolique

wit [wɪt] n (also: **~s**: intelligence) intelligence f, esprit m; (presence of mind) présence f d'esprit; (wittiness) esprit; (person) homme/femme d'esprit

witch [wɪtʃ] n sorcière f

O **KEYWORD**

with [wɪð, wɪθ] prep 1 (in the company of) avec; (at the home of) chez; **we stayed with friends** nous avons logé chez des amis; **I'll be with you in a minute** je suis à vous dans un instant

2 (descriptive): **a room with a view** une chambre avec vue; **the man with the grey hat/blue eyes** l'homme au chapeau gris/aux yeux bleus

3 (indicating manner, means, cause): **with tears in his eyes** les larmes aux yeux; **to walk with a stick** marcher avec une canne; **red with anger** rouge de colère; **to shake with fear** trembler de peur; **to fill sth with water** remplir qch d'eau

4 (in phrases): **I'm with you** (I understand) je vous suis; **to be with it** (inf: up-to-date) être dans le vent

withdraw [wɪð'drɔː] vt (irreg: like draw) retirer ▷ vi se retirer; **withdrawal** n retrait m; (Med) état m de manque;

withdrawn pp of **withdraw** ▷ adj (person) renfermé(e)

withdrew [wɪð'druː] pt of **withdraw**

wither ['wɪðə] vi se faner

withhold [wɪθ'həʊld] vt (irreg: like **hold**) (money) retenir; (decision) remettre; (permission): **to ~ (from)** (permission) refuser (à); (information): **to ~ (from)** cacher (à)

within [wɪð'ɪn] prep à l'intérieur de ▷ adv à l'intérieur; **~ his reach** à sa portée; **~ sight of** en vue de; **~ a mile of** à moins d'un mille de; **~ the week** avant la fin de la semaine

without [wɪð'aʊt] prep sans; **~ a coat** sans manteau; **~ speaking** sans parler; **to go** or **do ~ sth** se passer de qch

withstand [wɪð'stænd] vt (irreg: like **stand**) résister à

witness ['wɪtnɪs] n (person) témoin m ▷ vt (event) être témoin de; (document) attester l'authenticité de; **to bear ~ to sth** témoigner de qch

witty ['wɪtɪ] adj spirituel(le), plein(e) d'esprit

wives [waɪvz] npl of **wife**

wizard ['wɪzəd] n magicien m

wk abbr = **week**

wobble ['wɒbl] vi trembler; (chair) branler

woe [wəʊ] n malheur m

woke [wəʊk] pt of **wake**

woken ['wəʊkn] pp of **wake**

wolf (pl **wolves**) [wʊlf, wʊlvz] n loup m

woman (pl **women**) ['wʊmən, 'wɪmɪn] n femme f ▷ cpd: **~ doctor** femme f médecin; **~ teacher** professeur m femme

womb [wuːm] n (Anat) utérus m

women ['wɪmɪn] npl of **woman**

won [wʌn] pt, pp of **win**

wonder ['wʌndə] n merveille f, miracle m; (feeling) émerveillement m ▷ vi: **to ~ whether/why** se demander si/pourquoi; **to ~ at** (surprise) s'étonner de; (admiration) s'émerveiller de; **to ~ about** songer à; **it's no ~ that** il n'est pas étonnant que + sub; **wonderful** adj merveilleux(-euse)

won't [wəʊnt] = **will not**

wood [wʊd] n (timber, forest) bois m; **wooden** adj en bois; (fig: actor) raide; (: performance) qui manque de naturel; **woodwind** n: **the woodwind** (Mus) les bois mpl; **woodwork** n menuiserie f

wool [wʊl] n laine f; **to pull the ~ over sb's eyes** (fig) en faire accroire à qn; **woollen** (us **woolen**) adj de or en laine; **woolly** (us **wooly**) adj laineux(-euse); (fig: ideas) confus(e)

word [wɜːd] n mot m; (spoken) mot, parole f; (promise) parole f; (news) nouvelles fpl ▷ vt rédiger, formuler; **in other ~s** en d'autres termes; **to have a ~ with sb** toucher un mot à qn; **to break/keep one's ~** manquer à sa parole/tenir (la) parole; **wording** n termes mpl, langage m; (of document) libellé m; **word processing** n traitement m de texte; **word processor** n machine f de traitement de texte

wore [wɔːʳ] pt of **wear**

work [wɜːk] n travail m; (Art, Literature) œuvre f ▷ vi travailler; (mechanism) marcher, fonctionner; (plan etc) marcher; (medicine) agir ▷ vt (clay, wood etc) travailler; (mine etc) exploiter; (machine) faire marcher or fonctionner; (miracles etc) faire; **works** n (BRIT: factory) usine f; **how does this ~?** comment est-ce que ça marche?; **the TV isn't ~ing** la télévision est en panne or ne marche pas; **to be out of ~** être au chômage or sans emploi; **to ~ loose** se défaire, se desserrer; **work out** vi (plans etc) marcher; (Sport) s'entraîner ▷ vt (problem) résoudre; (plan) élaborer; **it ~s out at £100** ça fait 100 livres; **worker** n travailleur(-euse), ouvrier(-ière); **work experience** n stage m; **workforce** n main-d'œuvre f; **working class** n classe ouvrière ▷ adj; **working-class** ouvrier(-ière), de la classe ouvrière; **working week** n semaine f de travail; **workman** (irreg) n ouvrier m; **work of art** n œuvre

f d'art; **workout** n (Sport) séance f d'entraînement; **work permit** n permis m de travail; **workplace** n lieu m de travail; **worksheet** n (Scol) feuille f d'exercices; **workshop** n atelier m; **work station** n poste m de travail; **work surface** n plan m de travail; **worktop** n plan m de travail

world [wɜːld] n monde m ▷ cpd (champion) du monde; (power, war) mondial(e); **to think the ~ of sb** (fig) ne jurer que par qn; **World Cup** n: **the World Cup** (Football) la Coupe du monde; **world-wide** adj universel(le); **World-Wide Web** n: **the World-Wide Web** le Web

worm [wɜːm] n (also: **earth~**) ver m

worn [wɔːn] pp of **wear** ▷ adj usé(e); **worn-out** adj (object) complètement usé(e); (person) épuisé(e)

worried [ˈwʌrɪd] adj inquiet(-ète); **to be ~ about sth** être inquiet au sujet de qch

worry [ˈwʌrɪ] n souci m ▷ vt inquiéter ▷ vi s'inquiéter, se faire du souci; **worrying** adj inquiétant(e)

worse [wɜːs] adj pire, plus mauvais(e) ▷ adv plus mal ▷ n pire m; **to get ~** (condition, situation) empirer, se dégrader; **a change for the ~** une détérioration; **worsen** vt, vi empirer; **worse off** adj moins à l'aise financièrement; (fig): **you'll be worse off this way** ça ira moins bien de cette façon

worship [ˈwɜːʃɪp] n culte m ▷ vt (God) rendre un culte à; (person) adorer

worst [wɜːst] adj le (la) pire, le (la) plus mauvais(e) ▷ adv le plus mal ▷ n pire m; **at ~** au pis aller

worth [wɜːθ] n valeur f ▷ adj: **to be ~** valoir; **it's ~ it** cela en vaut la peine, ça vaut la peine; **it is ~ one's while (to do)** ça vaut le coup (inf) (de faire); **worthless** adj qui ne vaut rien; **worthwhile** adj (activity) qui vaut la peine; (cause) louable

worthy [ˈwɜːðɪ] adj (person) digne

(motive) louable; **~ of** digne de

KEYWORD

would [wʊd] *aux vb* 1 *(conditional tense)*: **if you asked him he would do it** si vous le lui demandiez, il le ferait; **if you had asked him he would have done it** si vous le lui aviez demandé, il l'aurait fait

2 *(in offers, invitations, requests)*: **would you like a biscuit?** voulez-vous un biscuit?; **would you close the door please?** voulez-vous fermer la porte, s'il vous plaît?

3 *(in indirect speech)*: **I said I would do it** j'ai dit que je le ferais

4 *(emphatic)*: **it WOULD have to snow today!** naturellement il neige aujourd'hui or il fallait qu'il neige aujourd'hui!

5 *(insistence)*: **she wouldn't do it** elle n'a pas voulu or elle a refusé de le faire

6 *(conjecture)*: **it would have been midnight** il devait être minuit; **it would seem so** on dirait bien

7 *(indicating habit)*: **he would go there on Mondays** il y allait le lundi

wouldn't ['wʊdnt] = **would not**

wound¹ [wuːnd] *n* blessure *f* ▷ *vt* blesser

wound² [waʊnd] *pt, pp of* **wind**

wove [wəʊv] *pt of* **weave**

woven ['wəʊvn] *pp of* **weave**

wrap [ræp] *vt* (*also:* **~ up**) envelopper; (*parcel*) emballer; (*wind*) enrouler; **wrapper** *n* (*on chocolate etc*) papier *m*; (*BRIT: of book*) couverture *f*; **wrapping** *n* (*of sweet, chocolate*) papier *m*; (*of parcel*) emballage *m*; **wrapping paper** *n* papier d'emballage; (*for gift*) papier cadeau

wreath [riːθ, *pl* riːðz] *n* couronne *f*

wreck [rɛk] *n* (*sea disaster*) naufrage *m*; (*ship*) épave *f*; (*vehicle*) véhicule accidenté *m*; (*pej: person*) loque (*humaine*) ▷ *vt* démolir; (*fig*) briser,

ruiner; **wreckage** *n* débris *mpl*; (*of building*) décombres *mpl*; (*of ship*) naufrage *m*

wren [rɛn] *n* (*Zool*) troglodyte *m*

wrench [rɛntʃ] *n* (*Tech*) clé *f* (à écrous); (*tug*) violent mouvement de torsion; (*fig*) déchirement *m* ▷ *vt* tirer violemment sur, tordre; **to ~ sth from** arracher qch (violemment) *à or de*

wrestle ['rɛsl] *vi*: **to ~ (with sb)** lutter (avec qn); **wrestler** *n* lutteur(-euse); **wrestling** *n* lutte *f*; (*also:* **all-in wrestling**: BRIT) catch *m*

wretched ['rɛtʃɪd] *adj* misérable

wriggle ['rɪgl] *vi* (*also:* **~ about**) se tortiller

wring (*pt, pp* **wrung**) [rɪŋ, rʌŋ] *vt* tordre; (*wet clothes*) essorer; (*fig*): **to ~ sth out of** arracher qch à

wrinkle ['rɪŋkl] *n* (*on skin*) ride *f*; (*on paper etc*) pli *m* ▷ *vt* rider, plisser ▷ *vi* se plisser

wrist [rɪst] *n* poignet *m*

write (*pt* **wrote**, *pp* **written**) [raɪt, rəʊt, 'rɪtn] *vt, vi* écrire; (*prescription*) rédiger; **write down** *vt* noter; (*put in writing*) mettre par écrit; **write off** *vt* (*debt*) passer aux profits et pertes; (*project*) mettre une croix sur; (*smash up: car etc*) démolir complètement; **write out** *vt* écrire; (*copy*) recopier; **write-off** *n* perte totale; **the car is a write-off** la voiture est bonne pour la casse; **writer** *n* auteur *m*, écrivain *m*

writing ['raɪtɪŋ] *n* écriture *f*; (*of author*) œuvres *fpl*; **in ~** par écrit; **writing paper** *n* papier à lettres

written ['rɪtn] *pp of* **write**

wrong [rɒŋ] *adj* (*incorrect*) faux (fausse); (*incorrectly chosen: number, road etc*) mauvais(e); (*not suitable*) qui ne convient pas; (*wicked*) mal; (*unfair*) injuste ▷ *adv* mal ▷ *n* tort *m*; **to be ~** (*answer*) être faux (fausse); (*in doing, saying*) avoir tort; (*cause harm to*) faire du tort à, léser; **you are ~ to do it** tu as tort de le faire; **you are ~ about that, you've got it ~** tu te trompes; **what's ~?** qu'est-ce qui ne va pas?; **what's ~ with the car?** qu'est-ce qu'elle a, la

y

yacht [jɔt] n voilier m; (motor, luxury yacht) yacht m; **yachting** n yachting m, navigation f de plaisance

yard [jɑːd] n (of house etc) cour f; (us: garden) jardin m; (measure) yard m (= 914 mm; 3 feet); **yard sale** n (us) brocante f (dans son propre jardin)

yarn [jɑːn] n fil m; (tale) longue histoire

yawn [jɔːn] n bâillement m ▷ vi bâiller

yd. abbr = **yard(s)**

yeah [jɛə] adv (inf) ouais

year [jɪə] n an m, année f; (Scol etc) année; **to be 8 ~s old** avoir 8 ans; **an eight-~-old child** un enfant de huit ans; **yearly** adj annuel(le) ▷ adv annuellement; **twice yearly** deux fois par an

yearn [jəːn] vi: **to ~ for sth/to do** aspirer à qch/à faire

yeast [jiːst] n levure f

yell [jɛl] n hurlement m, cri m ▷ vi hurler

yellow [ˈjɛləu] adj, n jaune (m); **Yellow Pages**® npl (Tel) pages fpl jaunes

yes [jɛs] adv oui; (answering negative question) si ▷ n oui m; **to say ~ (to)** dire oui (à)

yesterday [ˈjɛstədɪ] adv, n hier (m); **~ morning/evening** hier matin/soir; **all day** toute la journée d'hier

yet [jɛt] adv encore; (in questions) déjà ▷ conj pourtant, néanmoins; **it is not finished** ~ ce n'est pas encore fini or toujours pas fini; **have you eaten ~?** vous avez déjà mangé?; **the best** ~ le meilleur jusqu'ici or jusque-là; **as** ~ jusqu'ici, encore

yew [juː] n if m

Yiddish [ˈjɪdɪʃ] n yiddish m

yield [jiːld] n production f, rendement m; (Finance) rapport m ▷ vt produire, rendre, rapporter; (surrender) céder ▷ vi céder; (us Aut) céder la priorité

yob(bo) [ˈjɔb(əu)] n (BRIT inf) loubar(d) m

yoga [ˈjəugə] n yoga m

yog(h)ourt [ˈjɔgət] n = **yog(h)urt**

yog(h)urt [ˈjɔgət] n yaourt m

yolk [jəuk] n jaune m (d'œuf)

 KEYWORD

you [juː] pron 1 (subject) tu; (polite form) vous; (plural) vous; **you are very kind** vous êtes très gentil; **you French enjoy your food** vous autres Français, vous aimez bien manger; **you and I will go** toi et moi or vous et moi, nous irons; **there you are!** vous voilà!

2 (object: direct, indirect) te, t' + vowel; vous; **I know you** je te or vous connais; **I gave it to you** je te l'ai donné, je vous l'ai donné

3 (stressed) toi; vous; **I told YOU to do it** c'est à toi or vous que j'ai dit de le faire

4 (after prep, in comparisons) toi; vous; **it's for you** c'est pour toi or vous; **she's younger than you** elle est plus jeune que toi or vous

5 (impersonal: one) on; **fresh air does you good** l'air frais fait du bien; **you**

never know on ne sait jamais; **you can't do that!** ça ne se fait pas!

you'd [ju:d] = **you had; you would**

you'll [ju:l] = **you will; you shall**

young [jʌŋ] adj jeune ▷ npl (of animal) petits mpl; (people): **the ~** les jeunes, la jeunesse; **my ~er brother** mon frère cadet; **youngster** n jeune m/f; (child) enfant m/f

your [jɔ:ʳ] adj ton (ta), tes pl; (polite form, pl) votre, vos pl; see also **my**

you're [juəʳ] = **you are**

yours [jɔ:z] pron le (la) tien(ne), les tiens (tiennes); (polite form, pl) le (la) vôtre, les vôtres; **is it ~?** c'est à toi (or à vous)?; **a friend of ~** un(e) de tes (or de vos) amis; see also **faithfully; mine¹; sincerely**

yourself [jɔ:'sɛlf] pron (reflexive) te; (: polite form) vous; (after prep) toi; vous; (emphatic) toi-même; vous-même; see also **oneself; yourselves** pl pron vous; (emphatic) vous-mêmes; see also **oneself**

youth [ju:θ] n jeunesse f; (young man) (pl **~s**) jeune homme m; **youth club** n centre m de jeunes; **youthful** adj jeune; (enthusiasm etc) juvénile; **youth hostel** n auberge f de jeunesse

you've [ju:v] = **you have**

Yugoslav ['ju:gəʊslɑːv] adj yougoslave ▷ n Yougoslave m/f

Yugoslavia [ju:gəʊ'slɑːvɪə] n (Hist) Yougoslavie f

Z

zeal [zi:l] n (revolutionary etc) ferveur f; (keenness) ardeur f, zèle m

zebra ['zi:brə] n zèbre m; **zebra crossing** n (BRIT) passage clouté or pour piétons

zero ['zɪərəʊ] n zéro m

zest [zɛst] n entrain m, élan m; (of lemon etc) zeste m

zigzag ['zɪgzæg] n zigzag m ▷ vi zigzaguer, faire des zigzags

Zimbabwe [zɪm'bɑːbwɪ] n Zimbabwe m

zinc [zɪŋk] n zinc m

zip [zɪp] n (also: **~ fastener**) fermeture f éclair® or à glissière ▷ vt (file) zipper; (also: **~ up**) fermer (avec une fermeture éclair®); **zip code** n (US) code postal; **zip file** n (Comput) fichier m zip inv; **zipper** n (US) = **zip**

zit [zɪt] (inf) n bouton m

zodiac ['zəʊdɪæk] n zodiaque m

zone [zəʊn] n zone f

zoo [zu:] n zoo m

zoology [zu:'ɔlədʒɪ] n zoologie f

zoom [zuːm] *vi*: **to ~ past** passer en
trombe; **zoom lens** *n* zoom *m*
zucchini [zuːˈkiːnɪ] *n(pl)* (*US*)
courgette(s) *f(pl)*

TOPICS | THEMES

TOPICS | THEMES

Good evening!	Bonsoir!
Good night!	Bonne nuit!
Goodbye!	Au revoir!
What's your name?	Comment vous appelez-vous?
My name is ...	Je m'appelle ...
This is ...	Je vous présente ...
my wife.	*ma femme.*
my husband.	*mon mari.*
my partner.	*mon compagnon/ma compagne.*
Where are you from?	D'où venez-vous?
I come from ...	Je suis de ...
How are you?	Comment allez-vous?
Fine, thanks.	Bien, merci.
And you?	Et vous?
Do you speak English?	Parlez-vous anglais?
I don't understand French.	Je ne comprends pas le français.
Thanks very much!	Merci beaucoup!

Asking the Way	**Demander son chemin**
Where is the nearest …?	Où est le/la … le/la plus proche?
How do I get to …?	Comment est-ce qu'on va à/au/à la …?
Is it far?	Est-ce que c'est loin?
How far is it from here?	C'est à combien d'ici?
Is this the right way to …?	C'est la bonne direction pour aller à/au/à la …?
I'm lost.	Je suis perdu.
Can you show me on the map?	Pouvez-vous me le montrer sur la carte?
You have to turn round.	Vous devez faire demi-tour.
Go straight on.	Allez tout droit.
Turn left/right.	Tournez à gauche/à droite.
Take the second street on the left/right.	Prenez la deuxième rue à gauche/à droite.
Car Hire	**Location de voitures**
I want to hire …	Je voudrais louer …
a car.	*une voiture.*
a moped.	*une mobylette.*
a motorbike.	*une moto.*
How much is it for …?	C'est combien pour …?
one day	*une journée*
a week	*une semaine*
What is included in the price?	Qu'est-ce qui est inclus dans le prix?
I'd like a child seat for a …-year-old child.	Je voudrais un siège-auto pour un enfant de … ans.
What do I do if I have an accident/if I break down?	Que dois-je faire en cas d'accident/de panne?

Breakdowns — Pannes

My car has broken down.	Je suis en panne.
Where is the next garage?	Où est le garage le plus proche?
The exhaust	*Le pot d'échappement*
The gearbox	*La boîte de vitesse*
The windscreen	*Le pare-brise*
... is broken.	*... est cassé(e).*
The brakes	*Les freins*
The headlights	*Les phares*
The windscreen wipers	*Les essuie-glace*
... are not working.	*... ne fonctionnent pas.*
The battery is flat.	La batterie est à plat .
The car won't start.	Le moteur ne démarre pas.
The engine is overheating.	Le moteur surchauffe.
I have a flat tyre.	J'ai un pneu à plat.
Can you repair it?	Pouvez-vous le réparer?
When will the car be ready?	Quand est-ce que la voiture sera prête?

Parking — Stationnement

Can I park here?	Je peux me garer ici?
Do I need to buy a (car-parking) ticket?	Est-ce qu'il faut acheter un ticket de stationnement?
Where is the ticket machine?	Où est l'horodateur?
The ticket machine isn't working.	L'horodateur ne fonctionne pas.

Petrol Station — Station service

Where is the nearest petrol station?	Où est la station service la plus proche?
Fill it up, please.	Le plein, s'il vous plaît.

30 euros' worth of...	30 euros de ...
diesel.	*diesel.*
(unleaded) economy petrol.	*sans plomb.*
premium unleaded.	*super.*
Pump number ... please.	Pompe numéro ..., s'il vous plaît.
Please check ...	Pouvez-vous vérifier ...
the tyre pressure.	*la pression des pneus?*
the oil.	*le niveau de l'huile?*
the water.	*le niveau de l'eau?*

Accident — Accidents

Please call ...	Appelez ..., s'il vous plaît.
the police.	*la police.*
an ambulance.	*une ambulance*
Here are my insurance details.	Voici les références de mon assurance.
Give me your insurance details, please.	Donnez-moi les références de votre assurance , s'il vous plaît.
Can you be a witness for me?	Pouvez-vous me servir de témoin?
You were driving too fast.	Vous conduisiez trop vite.
It wasn't your right of way.	Vous n'aviez pas la priorité.

Travelling by Car — Voyager en voiture

What's the best route to ...?	Quel est le meilleur chemin pour aller à ...?
I'd like a motorway tax sticker ...	Je voudrais une vignette de péage ...
for a week.	*pour une semaine.*
for a year.	*pour un an.*
Do you have a road map of this area?	Avez-vous une carte de la région?

Cycling | À vélo

Where is the cycle path to ...?	Où est la piste cyclable pour aller à ...?
Can I keep my bike here?	Est-ce que je peux laisser mon vélo ici?
My bike has been stolen.	On m'a volé mon vélo.
Where is the nearest bike repair shop?	Où se trouve le réparateur de vélos le plus proche?
The brakes	*Les freins*
The gears	*Les vitesses*
... aren't working.	*... ne marchent pas.*
The chain is broken.	La chaîne est cassée.
I've got a flat tyre.	J'ai une crevaison.
I need a puncture repair kit.	J'ai besoin d'un kit de réparation.

Train | En train

How much is ...?	Combien coûte ...?
a single	*un aller simple*
a return	*un aller-retour*
A single to ..., please.	Un aller simple pour ..., s'il vous plaît.
I would like to travel first/second class.	Je voudrais voyager en première/seconde classe.
Two returns to ..., please.	Deux allers-retours pour ..., s'il vous plaît.
Is there a reduction ...?	Il y a un tarif réduit ...?
for students	*pour les étudiants*
for pensioners	*pour les seniors*
for children	*pour les enfants*
with this pass	*avec cette carte*

I'd like to reserve a seat on the train to … please.	Je voudrais faire une réservation pour le train qui va à … , s'il vous plaît.
Non smoking/smoking, please.	Non-fumeurs/Fumeurs, s'il vous plaît.
I want to book a sleeper to …	Je voudrais réserver une couchette pour …
When is the next train to …?	À quelle heure part le prochain train pour …?
Is there a supplement to pay?	Est-ce qu'il faut payer un supplément?
Do I need to change?	Est-ce qu'il y a un changement?
Where do I change?	Où est-ce qu'il faut changer?
Which platform does the train for … leave from?	De quel quai part le train pour …?
Is this the train for …?	C'est bien le train pour …?
Excuse me, that's my seat.	Excusez-moi, c'est ma place.
I have a reservation.	J'ai réservé.
Is this seat free?	La place est libre?
Please let me know when we get to …	Pourriez-vous me prévenir lorsqu'on arrivera à …?
Where is the buffet car?	Où est la voiture-bar?
Where is coach number …?	Où est la voiture numéro …?

Ferry | En ferry

Is there a ferry to …?	Est-ce qu'il y a un ferry pour …?
When is the next/first/last ferry to …?	Quand part le prochain/ premier/dernier ferry pour …?
How much is it for a camper/car with … people?	Combien coûte la traversée pour un camping-car/une voiture avec … personnes?

How long does the crossing take?	Combien de temps dure la traversée?
Where is …?	Où est …?
the restaurant	*le restaurant*
the bar	*le bar*
the duty-free shop	*le magasin hors-taxe*
Where is cabin number …?	Où est la cabine numéro …?
Do you have anything for seasickness?	Avez-vous quelque chose pour le mal de mer?

Plane | En avion

Where is …?	Où est …?
the taxi rank	*la station de taxis*
the bus stop	*l'arrêt de bus*
the information office	*le bureau de renseignements*
Where do I check in for the flight to …?	Où dois-je enregistrer pour le vol pour …?
Which gate for the flight to …?	À quelle porte faut-il embarquer pour le vol pour …?
When is the latest I can check in?	Quelle est l'heure limite d'enregistrement?
When does boarding begin?	À quelle heure commence l'embarquement?
Window/aisle, please.	Fenêtre/couloir, s'il vous plaît.
I've lost my boarding pass/ my ticket.	J'ai perdu mon ticket d'embarquement/mon billet.
Where is the luggage for the flight from …?	Où sont les bagages du vol provenant de…?
My luggage hasn't arrived.	Mes bagages ne sont pas arrivés.

Local Public Transport | Transports en commun

How do I get to …?	Comment est-ce qu'on va à …?
Where is the bus station?	Où est la gare routière?

Where is the nearest ...?	Où est ... le/la plus proche?
bus stop	*l'arrêt de bus*
underground station	*la station de métro*
A ticket to..., please.	Un ticket pour..., s'il vous plaît.
Is there a reduction ...?	Il y a un tarif réduit ...?
for students	*pour les étudiants*
for pensioners	*pour les seniors*
for children	*pour les enfants*
for the unemployed	*pour les chômeurs*
with this pass	*avec cette carte*
How does the (ticket) machine work?	Comment fonctionne le distributeur de tickets?
Do you have a map of the underground?	Avez-vous un plan du métro?
Please tell me when to get off.	Pourriez-vous me prévenir quand je dois descendre?
What is the next stop?	Quel est le prochain arrêt?

Taxi | En taxi

Where can I get a taxi?	Où puis-je trouver un taxi?
Call me a taxi, please.	Pouvez-vous m'appeler un taxi, s'il vous plaît?
To the airport/station, please.	À l'aéroport/À la gare, s'il vous plaît.
To this address, please.	À cette adresse, s'il vous plaît.
I'm in a hurry.	Je suis pressé.
How much is it?	Combien est-ce?
I need a receipt.	Il me faut un reçu.
Keep the change.	Gardez la monnaie.
Stop here, please.	Arrêtez-moi ici, s'il vous plaît.

Camping | Camping

Is there a campsite here?	Est-ce qu'il y a un camping ici?
We'd like a site for …	Nous voudrions un emplacement pour …
a tent.	*une tente.*
a camper van.	*un camping-car.*
a caravan.	*une caravane.*
We'd like to stay one night/ … nights.	Nous voudrions rester une nuit/… nuits.
How much is it per night?	Combien est-ce par nuit?
Where are …?	Où sont …?
the toilets	*les toilettes*
the showers	*les douches*
Where is …?	Où est …?
the shop	*le magasin*
the site office	*le bureau*
the restaurant	*le restaurant*
Can we camp here overnight?	Est-ce qu'on peut camper ici pour la nuit?
Can we park here overnight?	Est-ce qu'on peut stationner ici pour la nuit?

Self-Catering | Location de vacances

Where do we get the key for the apartment/house?	Où est-ce qu'il faut aller chercher la clé de l'appartement/la maison?
Do we have to pay extra for electricity/gas?	Est-ce que l'électricité/l'eau est à payer en plus?
How does … work?	Comment fonctionne …?
the washing maching	*la machine à laver*
the heating	*le chauffage*
the water heater	*le chauffe-eau*

Who do I contact if there are any problems?	Qui dois-je contacter en cas de problème?
We need ...	Il nous faut ...
a second key.	*un double de la clé.*
more sheets.	*des draps supplémentaires.*
more crockery.	*de la vaisselle en plus.*
The gas has run out.	Il n'y a plus de gaz.
There is no electricity.	Il n'y a pas d'électricité.
Do we have to clean the apartment/the house before we leave?	Est-ce qu'on doit nettoyer l'appartement/la maison avant de partir?

Hotel | Hotel

Do you have a ... for tonight?	Avez-vous une ... pour ce soir?
single room	*chambre pour une personne*
double room	*chambre pour deux personnes*
room for ... people	*chambre pour ... personnes*
Do you have a room ...?	Avez-vous une chambre ...?
with bath	*avec baignoire*
with shower	*avec douche*
I want to stay for one night/ ... nights.	Je voudrais rester une nuit/ ... nuits.
I booked a room in the name of ...	J'ai réservé une chambre au nom de ...
I'd like another room.	Je voudrais une autre chambre.
What time is breakfast?	On sert le petit déjeuner à quelle heure?
Can I have breakfast in my room?	Pouvez-vous me servir le petit déjeuner dans ma chambre?
Where is ...?	Où est ...?
the restaurant	*le restaurant*

the bar	*le bar*
the gym	*la salle de sport*
the swimming pool	*la piscine*
I'd like an alarm call for tomorrow morning at ...	Je voudrais qu'on me réveille demain matin à ...
I'd like to get these things washed/cleaned.	Pourriez-vous laver/faire nettoyer ceci?
Please bring me ...	S'il vous plaît, apportez-moi ...
The... doesn't work.	Le/la ... ne marche pas.
Room number ...	Chambre numéro ...
Are there any messages for me?	Est-ce que j'ai reçu des messages?

I'd like ...	Je voudrais ...
Do you have ...?	Avez-vous ...?
Do you have this ...?	Avez-vous ceci ...?
in another size	*dans une autre taille*
in another colour	*dans une autre couleur*
I take size ...	Je fais du ...
My feet are a size 5½.	Je fais du trente-neuf.
I'll take it.	Je le prends.
Do you have anything else?	Avez-vous autre chose?
That's too expensive.	C'est trop cher.
I'm just looking.	Je regarde juste.
Do you take credit cards?	Acceptez-vous la carte bleue?

Food shopping | Alimentation

Where is the nearest ...?	Où est ... le/la plus proche?
supermarket	*le supermarché*
baker's	*la boulangerie*
butcher's	*la boucherie*
Where is the market?	Où est le marché?
When is the market on?	Quand est-ce qu'est le marché?
a kilo/pound of ...	un kilo/demi-kilo de ...
200 grams of ...	deux cents grammes de ...
... slices of ...	... tranches de ...
a litre of ...	un litre de ...
a bottle/packet of ...	une bouteille/un paquet de ...

Post Office | Poste

Where is the nearest post office?	Où est la poste la plus proche?
When does the post office open?	La poste ouvre à quelle heure?
Where can I buy stamps?	Où peut-on acheter des timbres?

I'd like ... stamps for postcards/letters to Britain/the United States.	Je voudrais ... timbres pour cartes postales/lettres pour la Grande-Bretagne/ les États-Unis.
I'd like to send ...	Je voudrais envoyer ...
this letter.	*cette lettre.*
this parcel.	*ce colis.*
by airmail/express mail/ registered mail	par avion/en courrier urgent/en recommandé
Is there any mail for me?	Est-ce que j'ai du courrier?
Where is the nearest postbox?	Où est la boîte aux lettres la plus proche?

Photos and Videos | Photographie et vidéo

A colour/black and white film, please.	Une pellicule couleur/noir et blanc, s'il vous plaît.
With twenty-four/thirty-six exposures.	De vingt-quatre/trente-six poses.
Can I have batteries for this camera, please?	Je voudrais des piles pour ce caméscope, s'il vous plaît.
The camera is sticking.	Le caméscope se bloque.
Can you develop this film, please?	Pourriez-vous développer cette pellicule, s'il vous plaît?
I'd like the photos ...	Je voudrais les photos ...
matt.	*en mat.*
glossy.	*en brillant.*
ten by fifteen centimetres.	*en format dix sur quinze.*
When will the photos be ready?	Quand est-ce que les photos seront prêtes?
How much do the photos cost?	Combien coûtent les photos?
Could you take a photo of us, please?	Pourriez-vous nous prendre en photo, s'il vous plaît?

Sightseeing | Visites touristiques

Where is the tourist office?	Où se trouve l'office de tourisme?
Do you have any leaflets about ...?	Avez-vous des dépliants sur ...?
Are there any sightseeing tours of the town?	Est-ce qu'il existe des visites guidées de la ville?
When is ... open?	À quelle heure ouvre ...?
the museum	*le musée*
the church	*l'église*
the castle	*le château*
How much does it cost to get in?	Combien coûte l'entrée?
Are there any reductions ...?	Il y a un tarif réduit ...?
for students	*pour les étudiants*
for children	*pour les enfants*
for pensioners	*pour les seniors*
for the unemployed	*pour les chômeurs*
Is there a guided tour in English?	Est-ce qu'il y a une visite guidée en anglais?
Can I take photos here?	Je peux prendre des photos ici?
Can I film here?	Je peux filmer ici?

Entertainment | Loisirs

What is there to do here?	Qu'est-ce qu'il y a à faire ici?
Where can we ...?	Où est-ce qu'on peut ...?
go dancing	*danser*
hear live music	*écouter de la musique live*
Where is there ...?	Où est-ce qu'il y a ... ?
a nice bar	*un bon bar*
a good club	*une bonne discothèque*
What's on tonight ...?	Qu'est-ce qu'il y a ce soir ...?

LEISURE | LOISIRS

at the cinema	*au cinéma*
at the theatre	*au théâtre*
at the opera	*à l'opéra*
at the concert hall	*à la salle de concert*
Where can I buy tickets for ...?	Où est-ce que je peux acheter des places ...?
the theatre	*de théâtre*
the concert	*de concert*
the opera	*d'opéra*
the ballet	*pour le ballet*
How much is it to get in?	Combien coûte l'entrée?
I'd like a ticket/... tickets for ...	Je voudrais un billet/... billets pour ...
Are there any reductions ...?	Il y a un tarif réduit ...?
for children	*pour les enfants*
for pensioners	*pour les seniors*
for students	*pour les étudiants*
for the unemployed	*pour les chômeurs*

At the Beach | À la plage

Where is the nearest beach?	Où se trouve la plage la plus proche?
Is it safe to swim here?	Est-ce qu'on peut nager ici sans danger?
How deep is the water?	La profondeur de l'eau est de combien?
Is there a lifeguard?	Est-ce qu'il y a un maître nageur?
Where can you ...?	Où peut-on ...?
go surfing	*faire du surf*
go waterskiing	*faire du ski nautique*
go diving	*faire de la plongée*
go paragliding	*faire du parapente*

I'd like to hire ...	Je voudrais louer ...
a deckchair.	una chaise longue.
a sunshade.	un parasol.
a surfboard.	une planche de surf.
a jet-ski.	un scooter des mers.
a rowing boat.	une barque.
a pedal boat.	un pédalo.

Sport | Sport

Where can we ...?	Où peut-on ...?
play tennis/golf	jouer au tennis/golf
go swimming	aller nager
go riding	faire de l'équitation
go fishing	aller pêcher
How much is it per hour?	Combien est-ce que ça coûte de l'heure?
Where can I book a court?	Où peut-on réserver un court?
Where can I hire rackets?	Où peut-on louer des raquettes de tennis?
Where can I hire a rowing boat/a pedal boat?	Où peut-on louer une barque/ un pédalo?
Do you need a fishing permit?	Est-ce qu'il faut un permis de pêche?

Skiing | Ski

Where can I hire skiing equipment?	Où peut-on louer un équipement de ski?
I'd like to hire ...	Je voudrais louer ...
downhill skis.	des skis de piste.
cross-country skis.	des skis de fond.
ski boots.	des chaussures de ski.
ski poles.	des bâtons de ski.
Can you tighten my bindings, please?	Pourriez-vous resserrer mes fixations, s'il vous plaît?

Where can I buy a ski pass?	Où est-ce qu'on peut acheter un forfait?
I'd like a ski pass ...	Je voudrais un forfait ...
for a day.	*pour une journée.*
for five days.	*pour cinq jours.*
for a week.	*pour une semaine.*
How much is a ski pass?	Combien coûte le forfait?
When does the first/last chair-lift leave?	À quelle heure part le premier/ dernier télésiège?
Do you have a map of the ski runs?	Avez-vous une carte des pistes?
Where are the beginners' slopes?	Où sont les pistes pour débutants?
How difficult is this slope?	Quelle est la difficulté de cette piste?
Is there a ski school?	Y a-t-il une école de ski?
What's the weather forecast for today?	Quel est le temps prévu pour aujourd'hui?
What is the snow like?	Comment est la neige?
Is there a danger of avalanches?	Est-ce qu'il y a un risque d'avalanches?

A table for ... people, please.	Une table pour ... personnes, s'il vous plaît.
The ... please.	La ..., s'il vous plaît.
menu	*carte*
wine list	*carte des vins*
What do you recommend?	Qu'est-ce que vous me conseillez?
Do you have ...?	Servez-vous ...?
any vegetarian dishes	*des plats végétariens*
children's portions	*des portions pour enfants*
Does that contain ...?	Est-ce que cela contient...?
peanuts	*des cacahuètes*
alcohol	*de l'alcool*
Can you bring (more) ... please?	Vous pourriez m'apporter (plus de) ..., s'il vous plaît?
I'll have ...	Je vais prendre ...
The bill, please.	L'addition, s'il vous plaît.
All together, please.	Sur une seule note, s'il vous plaît.
Separate bills, please.	Sur des notes séparées, s'il vous plaît.
Keep the change.	Gardez la monnaie.
This isn't what I ordered.	Ce n'est pas ce que j'ai commandé.
The bill is wrong.	Il y a une erreur dans l'addition.
The food is cold/too salty.	C'est froid/trop salé.

TELEPHONE | TELEPHONE

Where can I make a phone call?	Où est-ce que je peux téléphoner?
Where is the nearest card phone?	Où est la cabine à cartes la plus proche?
Where is the nearest coin box?	Où est le téléphone à pièces le plus proche?
I'd like a twenty-five euro phone card.	Je voudrais une carte téléphonique de vingt-cinq euros.
I'd like some coins for the phone, please.	Je voudrais de la monnaie pour téléphoner.
I'd like to make a reverse charge call.	Je voudrais téléphoner en PCV.
Hello.	Allô.
This is ...	C'est ...
Who's speaking, please?	Qui est à l'appareil?
Can I speak to Mr/Ms ..., please?	Puis-je parler à Monsieur/ Madame ... s'il vous plaît?
Extension ..., please.	Poste numéro ..., s'il vous plaît.
I'll phone back later.	Je rappellerai plus tard.
Can you text me your answer?	Pouvez-vous me répondre par (minimessage) SMS?
Where can I charge my mobile phone?	Où est-ce que je peux recharger mon portable?
I need a new battery.	Il me faut une pile neuve.
Where can I buy a top-up card?	Où est-ce que je peux acheter une carte prépayée?
I can't get a network.	Je n'ai pas de réception.

Passport/Customs | Passeport/Douane

Here is …	Voici …
my passport.	*mon passeport.*
my identity card.	*ma carte d'identité.*
my driving licence.	*mon permis de conduire.*
Here are my vehicle documents.	Voici les documents de mon véhicule.
This is a present.	C'est un cadeau.
This is for my own personal use.	C'est pour mon usage personnel.

At the Bank | À la banque

Where can I change money?	Où puis-je changer de l'argent?
Is there a bank/bureau de change here?	Est-ce qu'il y a une banque/un bureau de change par ici?
When is the bank open?	La banque ouvre à quelle heure?
I'd like … euros.	Je voudrais … euros.
I'd like to cash these traveller's cheques.	Je voudrais encaisser ces chèques de voyage.
What's the commission?	Combien prenez-vous de commission?
Can I use my card to get cash?	Je peux me servir de ma carte pour retirer de l'argent?
Is there a cash machine here?	Il y a un distributeur par ici?
The cash machine swallowed my card.	Le distributeur m'a pris ma carte.

Repairs	Réparations
Where can I get this repaired?	Où puis-je faire réparer ceci?
Can you repair ...?	Pouvez-vous réparer ...?
these shoes	*ces chaussures*
this watch	*cette montre*
How much will the repairs cost?	Combien coûte la réparation?

Emergency Services	Urgences
Help!	Au secours!
Fire!	Au feu!
Please call ...	Pouvez-vous appeler ...
the emergency doctor.	*le médecin d'urgence.*
the fire brigade.	*les pompiers.*
the police.	*la police.*
I need to make an urgent phone call.	Je dois téléphoner d'urgence.
I need an interpreter.	J'ai besoin d'un interprète.
Where is the police station?	Où est le commissariat?
Where is the hospital?	Où est l'hopital?
I want to report a theft.	Je voudrais signaler un vol.
.... has been stolen.	On m'a volé ....
There's been an accident.	Il y a eu un accident.
There are ... people injured.	Il y a ... blessés.
I've been ...	On m'a ...
robbed.	*volé.*
attacked.	*attaqué.*
raped.	*violé.*
I'd like to phone my embassy.	Je voudrais appeler mon ambassade.

Pharmacy | Pharmacie

Where is the nearest pharmacy?	Où est la pharmacie la plus proche?
Which pharmacy provides emergency service?	Quelle est la pharmacie de garde?
I'd like something …	Je voudrais quelque chose …
for diarrhoea.	*contre la diarrhée.*
for a temperature.	*contre la fièvre.*
for travel sickness.	*contre le mal des transports.*
for a headache.	*contre le mal de tête.*
for a cold.	*contre le rhume.*
I'd like …	Je voudrais …
plasters.	*des pansements.*
a bandage.	*un bandage .*
some paracetamol.	*du paracétamol.*
I can't take …	Je suis allergique à …
aspirin.	*l'aspirine.*
penicillin.	*la pénicilline.*
Is it safe to give to children?	C'est sans danger pour les enfants?

At the Doctor's | Chez le médecin

I need a doctor.	J'ai besoin de voir un médecin.
Where is casualty?	Où sont les urgences?
I have a pain here.	J'ai mal ici.
I feel …	J'ai …
hot.	*chaud.*
cold.	*froid.*
I feel sick.	je me sens mal.
I feel dizzy.	J'ai la tête qui tourne.
I'm allergic to …	Je suis allergique à …

HEALTH │ SANTÉ

I am ...	Je suis ...
pregnant.	*enceinte.*
diabetic.	*diabétique.*
HIV-positive.	*séropositif(-ive).*
I'm on this medication.	Je prends ces médicaments.
My blood group is ...	Mon groupe sanguin est ...

At the Hospital │ À l'hôpital

Which ward is ... in?	Dans quelle salle se trouve ...?
When are visiting hours?	Quelles sont les heures de visite?
I'd like to speak to ...	Je voudrais parler à ...
a doctor.	*un médecin.*
a nurse.	*une infirmière.*
When will I be discharged?	Quand vais-je pouvoir sortir?

At the Dentist's │ Chez le dentiste

I need a dentist.	J'ai besoin de voir un dentiste.
This tooth hurts.	J'ai mal à cette dent.
One of my fillings has fallen out.	J'ai perdu un de mes plombages.
I have an abscess.	J'ai un abscès.
Can you repair my dentures?	Pouvez-vous réparer mon dentier?
I need a receipt for the insurance.	J'ai besoin d'un reçu pour mon assurance.

Business Travel | Voyages d'affaires

I'd like to arrange a meeting with …	Je voudrais organiser une réunion avec …
I have an appointment with Mr/Ms …	J'ai rendez-vous avec Monsieur/Madame …
Here is my card.	Voici ma carte de visite.
I work for …	Je travaille pour …
How do I get to …?	Où se trouve …?
your office	*votre bureau*
Mr/Ms …'s office	*le bureau de Monsieur/ Madame …*
I need an interpreter.	J'ai besoin d'un interprète.
May I use …?	Je peux me servir …?
your phone	*de votre téléphone*
your computer	*de votre ordinateur*
your desk	*de votre bureau*

Disabled Travellers | Voyageurs handicappés

Is it possible to visit … with a wheelchair?	Est-ce qu'on peut visiter … en chaise roulante?
Where is the wheelchair-accessible entrance?	Où est l'entrée pour les chaises roulantes?
Is your hotel accessible to wheelchairs?	Votre hôtel est-il accessible aux chaises roulantes?
I need a room …	Je voudrais une chambre …
on the ground floor.	*au rez-de-chaussée.*
with wheelchair access.	*accessible aux chaises roulantes.*
Do you have a lift for wheelchairs?	Y a-t-il un ascenseur pour chaises roulantes?
Where is the disabled toilet?	Où sont les toilettes pour handicappés?
Can you help me get on/off please?	Pouvez-vous m'aider à monter /descendre, s'il vous plaît?

The tyre has burst.	Le pneu est crevé.
The battery is flat.	La batterie est à plat.

Travelling with children | Voyager avec des enfants

Is it OK to bring children here?	Est-ce que les enfants sont admis?
Is there a reduction for children?	Il y a un tarif réduit pour les enfants?
Do you have children's portions?	Vous servez des portions pour enfants?
Do you have ...?	Avez-vous ...?
a high chair	*une chaise pour bébé*
a cot	*un berceau*
a child's seat	*un siège pour enfant*
Where can I change the baby?	Où est-ce que je peux changer mon bébé?
Where can I breast-feed the baby?	Où est-ce que je peux allaiter mon bébé?
Can you warm this up, please?	Vous pouvez me réchauffer ceci, s'il vous plaît?
What is there for children to do?	Qu'est-ce qu'il y a à faire pour les enfants ?
Where is the nearest playground?	Où est l'aire de jeux la plus proche?
Is there a child-minding service?	Est-ce qu'il y a un service de garderie?

I'd like to make a complaint.	Je voudrais faire une réclamation.
To whom can I complain?	À qui dois-je m'adresser pour faire un réclamation?
I'd like to speak to the manager, please.	Je voudrais parler au responsable, s'il vous plaît.
The light	*La lumière*
The heating	*Le chauffage*
The shower	*La douche*
... doesn't work.	... ne marche pas.
The room is ...	La chambre est ...
dirty.	*sale.*
too small.	*trop petite.*
The room is too cold.	Il fait trop froid dans la chambre.
Can you clean the room, please?	Pourriez-vous nettoyer ma chambre, s'il vous plaît?
Can you turn down the TV/the radio, please?	Pourriez-vous baisser le son de votre télé/radio, s'il vous plaît?
The food is ...	C'est ...
cold.	*froid.*
too salty.	*trop salé.*
This isn't what I ordered.	Ce n'est pas ce que j'ai commandé.
We've been waiting for a very long time.	Ça fait longtemps que nous attendons.
The bill is wrong.	Vous vous êtes trompé dans l'addition.
I want my money back.	Je veux qu'on me rembourse.
I'd like to exchange this.	Je voudrais échanger ceci.
I'm not satisfied with this.	Je ne suis pas satisfait(e).